Encyclopedia of

SPECIAL EDUCATION

Second Edition

A Reference for the Education of the Handicapped and Other Exceptional Children and Adults

VOLUME 3

Edited by

Cecil R. Reynolds
Texas A & M University

Elaine Fletcher-Janzen
University of Northern Colorado

JOHN WILEY & SONS

NEW YORK · CHICHESTER · WEINHEIM · BRISBANE · SINGAPORE · TORONTO

This publication is designed to provide accurate and authoritative
information in regard to the subject matter covered. It is sold with
the understanding that the publisher is not engaged in rendering
professional services. If legal, accounting, medical, psychological or
any other expert assistance is required, the services of a competent
professional person should be sought.

ISBN 0-471-25323-5 (Volume 1)
ISBN 0-471-25324-3 (Volume 2)
ISBN 0-471-25325-1 (Volume 3)
ISBN 0-471-25309-X (three-volume set)

Printed in the United States of America.

10 9 8 7 6 5 4 3 2 1

P

PALMAR CREASE

Human palms are covered by creases of different depths, lengths, and directions. The flexion creases are formed during early intrauterine life and are thought to be influenced by factors causing anomalies in the embryo. Variations in appearance of the palmar creases have been linked to certain medical disorders. Therefore, alterations have medical diagnostic value and usually are included in dermatoglyphic analysis. The three main creases have been the primary focus of most investigations. They are the radial longitudinal or thenar crease, the proximal transverse, and the distal transverse. Alter (1970) measured differences in the space between palmar creases, noted abnormalities, and described variations in a normal population.

A single crease across the palm of the hand frequently is described as characteristic of Down's syndrome (Robinson & Robinson, 1965; Telford & Sawery, 1977). The proximal and distal transverse creases are replaced or joined into a single crease that transverses the entire palm. This has been referred to as a single palmar crease, single transverse fold, four finger line, or simian crease. The term simian crease, although frequently used, is not appropriate. The frequency of the single palmar crease ranges between 1 and 15% in controlled populations and possibly higher in groups with developmental defects (Schaumann & Alter, 1976). Researchers noted that the variability in appearance makes determination difficult and may partially account for the wide range in reported frequency.

REFERENCES

Alter, M. (1970). Variation in palmar creases. *American Journal of Diseases of Children, 20,* 424.

Robinson, H. B., & Robinson, N. M. (1965). *The mentally retarded child: A psychological approach.* New York: McGraw-Hill.

Schaumann, B., & Alter, M. (1976). *Dermatoglyphics in medical disorders.* Heidelberg, Germany: Springer-Verlag.

Telford, C. W., & Sawery, J. M. (1977). *The exceptional individual.* Englewood Cliffs, NJ: Prentice-Hall.

SALLY E. PISARCHICK
*Cuyahoga Special Education
Service Center*

DOWN'S SYNDROME
PHYSICAL ANOMALIES

PARAPLEGIA

Paraplegia is a term used to describe a physical condition in which the individual is unable to functionally use the lower extremities of the body. The term describes the topography of the impairment and does not suggest the etiology of the physical limitations, which may be of varied origin (Best, 1978).

Paraplegia results from many disorders that interfere with the brain or spinal cord's ability to transmit stimuli to the motor effectors (muscles) of the legs, or from the inability of the larger muscles of the legs themselves to act in a functional manner. It may result from cerebral palsy, which is a nonprogressive disorder of the central nervous system where the brain is involved, or from orthopedic disorders that involve the musculoskeletal system such as muscular dystrophy. In the former condition, the neurological input to the muscles may be impeded at the level of the brain. The latter involves an asymmetrical deterioration of muscle fibers, depriving the legs of the necessary activity for gross muscular action. Conditions such as spina bifida, in which there is often a physical interruption in the continuity of the spinal cord, may also cause impairment of the body's function below the level of the lesion (injury). The origin of the paraplegia can be congenital (either the disorder or predisposition is present from birth) or adventitiously (accidentally) acquired. The former may include genetically transmitted disorders such as Werdnig-Hofmann disease, where the anterior horn cells (those cells of the spinal cord having motor function) deteriorate and lose function early in the child's development, or traumatic injury, which can occur at anytime in life.

While the disease underlying the paraplegia often suggests additional concerns for management, many of these diseases are more of a concern for medical intervention than for educational. Educational management and teaching, however, must take into consideration the limitations imposed on the individual with paraplegia, as well as safety and health considerations. When paraplegia results from neurological impairment, sensory deficits to the lower segments of the body may also be sustained as well as functional deficits (Capildeo & Maxwell, 1984). These deficits, which may include bowel and bladder incontinence (Staas & LaMantina, 1984a), also require assistance from both a psychological and hygienic perspective. The paraplegic who manifests sensory deficits and maintains a sitting posture for most of the day should avoid remaining in one position in school, at home, or in other settings for a prolonged period of time. Since sensitivity to pain may be impaired, prolonged placement in one position may increase skin irritation that goes unrecognized by the individual until sores or descubiti develop (Kottke et al., 1982; Kosiak, 1982).

In the nonsensorily impaired individual, discomfort usually accompanying skin erosion allows for the independent shift in positioning that facilitates, avoiding injury. If the primary means of movement is accomplished by use of a wheelchair, a firm seat or wheelchair insert providing a firm seat and lateral support should be used. Reliance on the webbed or sling seat often found in portable folding chairs does not allow for adequate uniform support. The paraplegic may begin to favor one side of the supportive webbed seat, asymmetrically tipping the body. To regain a vertical perspective to the environment, compensation of the spine in the opposite direction is likely to be forced, resulting in a scoliosis (lateral curvature of the spine) over time. Aside from orthopedic implications, infringement on the diaphragm may reduce vital capacities by reducing pulmonary (lung) function. This can result in shallow, rapid cycles of breathing that increase tendencies toward respiratory problems. These shallow, rapid cycles further impede reducing body noise, making localization of low-amplitude sounds more difficult and interfering with the controlled expiration necessary to speech production.

Management must also include an understanding of the nutritional needs of the individual with paraplegia. Since activities may be circumscribed, caloric intake for the active nonparaplegic is not an accurate gauge for determining diet. Such a diet would provide excess nutritive support resulting in weight gain. Diet should, therefore, be provided on an individual basis, taking into consideration the specific activity level of the individual.

The environmental experience, is regarded as part of the educational process, will be impaired if provision for available alternatives to independent ambulation are not provided. The younger child with paraplegia who is deprived of free exploration of the environment may be impeded in concept development (Connor et al., 1978). For the toddler, a device such as a scooter board or crawl-a-gator may assist in active environmental exploration. This device consists of a board on which casters are mounted. The child lies prone on the device and propels himself or herself around the floor by pushing the ground with the up-

per extremities. The older child may begin to use a wheelchair or a parapodium. The latter device allows the child and preadolescent with paraplegia to ambulate in an upright position to more freely explore and learn. Training in donning (putting on) and duffing (removing) the parapodium is essential to increasing the independent functioning of the individual. With developed upper extremities, the parapodium can also be used to climb stairs.

Within the classroom, a standing table may be used to support the child in an upright position, freeing the upper extremities for manual exploration of learning materials, and concomitantly avoiding static positioning. This table is ideal for use in the classroom where academics may require writing and other skills requiring hand use and lower body support. Thus for the special educator to accommodate the needs for education and management of the individual with paraplegia, a comprehensive understanding of methods and materials necessary to circumvent the functional impairedness becomes essential. This management includes positioning, locomotion, and the ability to attend in a learning situation, free from the distraction imposed by the disability. This also must occur on a case-by-case method to be successful (Mulcahey, 1992), and prevent further health complications (Herrick, Elliot & Crow, 1994).

REFERENCES

Best, G. A. (1978). *Individuals with physical disabilities: An introduction for educators.* Saint Louis: Mosby.

Capildeo, R., & Maxwell, A. (Eds.). (1984). *Progress in rehabilitation: Paraplegia.* London: Macmillan.

Connor, F. P., Williamson, G. G., & Siepp, J. M. (1978). *Program guide for infants and toddlers with neuromotor and other developmental disabilities.* New York: Teacher's College Press.

Herrick, S. M., Elliott, T. R., & Crow, F. (1994). Social support and the prediction of health complications among persons with spinal cord injuries. *Rehabilitation Psychology, 39*(4), 231–250.

Kosiak, M. (1982). Prevention and rehabilitation of ischemic ulcers. In F. J. Kottke, G. K. Stillwell, & J. F. Lehman (Eds.), *Krusen's handbook of physical medicine and rehabilitation.* Philadelphia: Saunders.

Kottke, F. J., Stillwell, G. K., & Lehman, J. F. (Eds.) (1982). *Krusen's handbook of physical medicine and rehabilitation.* Philadelphia: Saunders.

Mulcahey, M. J. (1992). Returning to school after a spinal cord injury: Perspectives from four adolescents, *American Journal of Occupational Therapy, 46*(4), 305–312.

Rushkin, A. P. (Ed.). (1984). *Current therapy in physiatry.* Philadelphia: Saunders.

Staas, W. E., & La Mantina, J. (1984a). The neurogenic bladder: Physiologic mechanisms and clinical problems of bladder control. In A. P. Ruskin (Ed.), *Current therapy in physiatry* (pp. 396–410). Philadelphia: Saunders.

Staas, W. E., & La Mantina, J. (1984b). Descubitus ulcers. In A P.

Ruskin (Ed.), *Current therapy in physiatry* (pp. 410–419). Philadelphia: Saunders.

ELLIS I. BAROWSKY
Hunter College

CEREBRAL PALSY
MUSCULAR DYSTROPHY
SPINA BIFIDA

PARAPROFESSIONALS

Various descriptors have been used to identify the paraprofessional in special education. MacMillan (1973) has identified as potential paraprofessionals, nonprofessional adults, older children in the role of tutor, and parents. Tucker and Horner (1977) identify a paraprofessional as any person other than the teacher who is engaged in providing educational opportunities for handicapped children. While not considered a fully trained professional, the paraprofessional is one who is expected to possess certain competencies that will promote a higher quality and more effective educational program for the handicapped.

Interest in the use of paraprofessionals in special education programs has largely been based on three issues: relieving the special education teacher from nonprofessional duties; increasing the quality of the instructional program; and meeting the needs of a burgeoning number of special education programs.

The use of paraprofessionals in the special education classroom was first reported in the 1950s (Cruickshank & Haring, 1957). The conclusions drawn from this investigation were that the teachers who had paraprofessionals assigned to their classrooms felt that they were able to do a better job of teaching. The administrators of these programs concurred with this opinion, as did the parents of the children, who felt their children had profited from the presence of a paraprofessional in the classroom. In the 1960s, as a result of professional and legislative efforts, there emerged an increased interest in the establishment of a number and variety of educational services for the handicapped. As a result of this, there was an immediate critical shortage of professional personnel to meet the rapid expansion of special education programs (President's Panel on Mental Retardation, 1962). The paraprofessional was viewed as a potential solution to this problem (Blessing, 1967).

In the ensuing years, the concept of paraprofessionals as an answer to manpower problems and improved quality of classroom instruction gained considerable acceptance. Roos (1970) recognized the need for less sophisticated trained personnel as an answer to the shortage of trained special educators. MacMillan (1973) also felt that the use of paraprofessionals in special education programs was an appropriate means for closing the manpower gap. In addition, various authors (Hanson, 1969; Karnes, Teska, & Hodgins, 1970) concluded that the instructional program in the special classroom was enhanced by the presence of paraprofessionals. Karnes and Teska (1975) determined that the use of paraprofessionals was not only effective, but that in some instances, paraprofessionals were as capable as professional teachers in carrying out instructional programs. The available evidence supported the concept that paraprofessionals can and do serve a meaningful and significant role in special education programs. However, there emerged a further concern relative to the type of training that is necessary to produce effective paraprofessionals, and their role in the classroom remains an issue for discussion.

Competency to function as an effective paraprofessional is, in many ways, directly related to the perceived role of the paraprofessional in the program. Competencies have been identified at various levels of sophistication. Tucker and Horner (1977) feel that training should be directly related to skills that would assist the paraprofessional in changing student behavior. They feel that this should include training in areas such as curriculum, task analysis, and even parent counseling. Greer and Simpson (1977) take a somewhat more generic approach by defining the paraprofessional as a tutor. In training for this role, they enumerate a number of competencies that are indigenous to a variety of teaching functions (e.g., assessment, programming, scheduling and teaching). Other authors (Fimian, Fafard, & Howell, 1984; Gartner, 1972) have been more specific in the identification of areas or topics that they feel are necessary to produce a competent paraprofessional. These topics entail many of the traditional child development and curriculum/method sequences, as well as characteristics, behavior management techniques, and routine clerical skills. In summary, the training program for paraprofessionals may vary depending on the individual's qualifications and experience as well as the perceived role of the paraprofessional in the assigned special education program.

The position of the paraprofessional in special education programs has usually been one of a subordinate. The paraprofessional is expected to carry out his or her assigned duties in tandem with the fully trained professional. The assumption is that while paraprofessionals may be a valuable addition to the overall program, the teacher must be regarded as the one ultimately responsible for the teaching function. However, paraprofessionals have been used in a variety of ways in the educational setting. Their duties have usually encompassed activities such as clerical work, supervision of nonacademic activities, housekeeping, acting as parent surrogates, and sometimes even as active teachers engaged in the instructional process under the supervision of the trained teacher

(Blessing, 1967; French & Pickett, 1997; Greer & Simpson, 1977; MacMillan, 1973).

Concerns for the extension of educational programs to a population of handicapped that has been unserved in an educational setting (e.g., the severely and profoundly handicapped) has created a potential new role for the less than baccalaureate trained (paraprofessional) teacher. Although Sontag, Burke, and York (1976) feel that teachers working with the severely handicapped should be rigorously trained and possess a number of specific and precise competencies, Burton and Hirshoren (1979) view the use of well-trained paraprofessionals as teachers as a resolution of problems that are indigenous to this level of programming (e.g., available manpower, individualization of instruction, and teacher burnout). Tucker and Horner (1977) have acknowledged the need for well-trained paraprofessionals in programs for the severely handicapped and agree that it is impractical to rely on fully trained teachers to provide the individualized instruction that is necessary in these programs.

While enjoying considerable discussion, the paraprofessional role in special education has not been clearly defined. However, the role continues to be evaluated, especially in light of inclusive practices (Doyle, 1997).

REFERENCES

Blessing, K. R. (1967). Use of teacher aides in special education: A review and possible application. *Exceptional Children, 34,* 107–113.

Burton, T. A., & Hirshoren, A. (1979). The education of the severely and profoundly retarded: Are we sacrificing the child to the concept? *Exceptional Children, 45,* 598–602.

Cruickshank, W., & Haring, N. (1957). *A demonstration: Assistants for teachers of exceptional children.* Syracuse, NY: Syracuse University Press.

Doyle, M. B. (1997). *The paraprofessional's guide to the inclusive classroom: Working as a team.* Baltimore, MD: Brookes.

Fimian, M. J., Fafard, M., & Howell, K. W. (1984). *A teacher's guide to human resources in special education.* Boston: Allyn & Bacon.

French, N. K., & Pickett, A. L. (1997). Paraprofessionals in special education: Issues for teacher educators. *Teacher Education and Special Education, 20*(1), 61–73.

Gartner, A. (1972). The curriculum: Issues in combining theory and practice in training teacher aids. *Journal of Research & Development in Education, 5,* 57–68.

Greer, B. B., & Simpson, G. A. (1977). A demonstration model for training noncertified personnel in special education. *Education & Training of the Mentally Retarded, 12,* 266–271.

Hanson, F. M. (1969). Aides for the trainable mentally retarded. *Journal of the California Teachers Association, 65,* 23–26.

Karnes, M. B., & Teska, J. (1975). Children's response to intervention programs. In J. J. Gallagher (Ed.), *The application of child development research to exceptional children.* Reston, VA: Council for Exceptional Children.

Karnes, M. B., Teska, J. A., & Hodgins, A. S. (1970). The successful implementation of a highly specific preschool instructional program by paraprofessional teachers. *Journal of Special Education, 4,* 69–80.

MacMillan, D. L. (1973). Issues and trends in special education. *Mental Retardation, 11,* 3–8.

President's Panel on Mental Retardation. (1962). *A proposed program for national action to combat mental retardation.* Washington, DC: U.S. Government Printing Office.

Roos, P. (1970). Trends and issues in special education for the mentally retarded. *Education & Training of the Mentally Retarded, 5,* 51–61.

Sontag, E., Burke, P. J., & York, R. (1976). Considerations for serving the severely handicapped in the public schools. In R. M. Anderson & J. G. Greer (Eds.), *Educating the severely and profoundly retarded.* Baltimore, MD: University Park Press.

Tucker, P. J., & Horner, R. D. (1977). Competency based training of paraprofessionals training associates for education of the severely and profoundly handicapped. In E. Sontag, J. Smith, & N. Certo (Eds.), *Educational programming for the severely and profoundly handicapped.* Reston, VA: Council for Exceptional Children.

THOMAS A. BURTON
University of Georgia

TEACHER BURNOUT
TEACHER EFFECTIVENESS

PARENTAL COUNSELING

Counseling parents of handicapped children has taken a number of different forms. Variations in counseling strategies reflect diverse professional orientations as well as differing family dynamics and needs. Because new challenges often arise as the child's disability interacts with increased demands at different developmental stages, counseling is frequently a recurrent need in families with handicapped children.

Parental counselors include teachers, guidance counselors, educational evaluators, social workers, psychologists, physicians, and other parents. Counseling can range from informal and infrequent teacher/parent exchanges to long-term programs that involve all family members. Counseling approaches can be grouped into three broad categories: those providing information about the nature of the child's disability, those offering psychotherapeutic insight into the often conflicting emotions that accompany recognition of the disability, and those providing training to improve parent/child interactions and to manage the child's behavior.

Counseling aimed at educating parents about the nature of their child's disability is probably the most common. In order for parents confronted with a handicapped child to make appropriate and realistic adjustments, they need various sources of accurate and pragmatic information. The information-focused counseling provided by physician, psychologist, and/or evaluator when the child's handicap is first identified is clearly crucial for parents. Information-centered counseling is also provided when teachers share their insights, goals, and expectations and when parent organizations (e.g., ACLD, ARC, Closer Look) offer pamphlets, telephone hotlines, and parent support groups.

Psychotherapeutic approaches to parent counseling focus on helping parents to work through and resolve emotional stresses and conflicts often precipitated by the presence of a disabled child in the family. Such counseling can occur with parents and counselor alone, jointly with the handicapped child, or with all active family members, including siblings and even caretaking grandparents. With advances in the understanding of the complex interrelations within families, the trend has been in the direction of including more family members in psychotherapeutic counseling (Foster & Berger, 1979). Sibling relationships represent one of those significant complexities that recently has spawned nationwide sibling support groups as well as greater consideration of siblings within the context of counseling (Grossman, 1972).

A third category of counseling is parent training programs. Through such programs, parents learn more effective means of communicating with their children and methods for better managing their children's problem behaviors. Parent training programs teach techniques such as active listening and problem solving (Gordon, 1975), ways to function as filial therapists (Guerney, 1969), methods for becoming behavioral change agents (McDowell, 1974). Numerous research studies demonstrate that parents can be effective in working with and modifying their children's behavior and that such parent involvement is generally positive (McDowell, 1976).

Increasingly, two theoretical notions, or frameworks, have informed many of the counseling approaches available to parents of handicapped children: stages of grief theory and family systems theory. Regardless of the particular approach (educational, psychotherapeutic, or parent training), many of those who counsel parents have been guided by, or at least sensitized by, one or both of these frameworks. The first reflects the prevalent view that many, if not all, parents of handicapped children undergo some version of a mourning process in reaction to their child's disability. To varying degrees, this represents a loss of the hoped for intact, healthy child. Variations on Kubler-Ross's (1969) stages of grief theory have been proposed to explain parents' emotional journey toward productive adjustment to their child's handicapping condition (Seligman, 1979). These mourning stages include denial of the existence, the degree, or the implications of the disability; bargaining, often evident in the pursuit of magical cures or highly questionable treatments; anger, often projected outward onto the spouse or the helping professional or projected inward, causing feelings of guilt and shame; depression, manifest in withdrawal and expressions of helplessness and inadequacy; and acceptance, the stage in which productive actions can be taken and positive family balances maintained. It is commonly believed that any of the earlier stages can be reactivated by crises or in response to the child's or the family's transitions from one developmental stage to another.

Family systems theory, particularly Minuchin's structural analysis (Minuchin, Rosman, & Baker, 1978) and Haley's (1973, 1976, 1980) strategic approach provides another highly valued conceptual framework for counseling. Within this framework, families are seen as interdependent systems whose problems are relational. This view offers concepts and techniques for considering the effects on all parts of the family of intervention with one member or with one subsystem. By focusing on the dynamics of a family's structure, hierarchy, and stage in the family life cycle, family systems theory offers a more complex, and therefore more accurate, understanding of the functioning, development, and needs of a particular family with a handicapped child (Foster, Berger, & McLean, 1981).

Both family systems theory and stages of grief theory are widely applicable conceptual influences within family counseling. Neither of these frameworks mitigates against using any of a wide variety of other educational, psychotherapeutic, or parent training methods to promote growth in families with handicapped children.

REFERENCES

Foster, M., & Berger, M. (1979). Structural family therapy: Applications in programs for preschool handicapped children. *Journal of the Division for Early Childhood, 1,* 52–58.

Foster, M., Berger, M., & McLean, M. (1981). Rethinking a good idea: A reassessment of parent involvement. *Topics in Early Childhood Special Education, 1*(3), 55–65.

Gordon, T. (1975). *Parent effectiveness training.* New York: Plume.

Grossman, P. (1972). *Brothers and sisters of retarded children.* Syracuse, NY: Syracuse University Press.

Guerney, B. G. (1969). Filial therapy: Description and rationale. *Journal of Consulting Psychology, 28,* 304–310.

Haley, J. (1973). *Uncommon therapy.* New York: Norton.

Haley, J. (1976). *Problem-solving therapy.* San Francisco: Jossey-Bass.

Haley, J. (1980). *Leaving home.* New York: McGraw-Hill.

Kubler-Ross, E. (1969). *On death and dying.* New York: Macmillan.

McDowell, R. L. (1974). *Managing behavior: A program for parent involvement.* Torrance, CA: Winch.

McDowell, R. L. (1976). Parent counseling: The state of the art. *Journal of Learning Disabilities, 9*(10), 48–53.

Minuchin, S., Rosman, B., & Baker, L. (1978). *Psychosomatic families.* Cambridge, MA: Harvard University Press.

Seligman, M. (1979). *Strategies for helping parents of exceptional children*. New York: Free Press.

KATHERINE GARNETT
Hunter College

FAMILY COUNSELING
PARENT EFFECTIVENESS TRAINING
PSYCHOTHERAPY

PARENT EDUCATION

Parents rarely receive direct instruction in how to parent. For many, such knowledge comes from their own personal experience of being parented, and from the advice of grandparents, friends, and neighbors. Parents of abused and neglected children are often reported to lack both effective parenting skills (Wolfe, 1985) and a social network of friends and neighbors who could be helpful with child rearing (Polansky, Gaudin, Ammons, & Davis, 1985).

The purposes of parent education programs are to help parents develop greater self-awareness, use effective discipline methods, assist in early intervention training programs (Peterson & Cooper, 1989) improve parent-child communication, make family life more enjoyable, and provide general information on child development (Fine, 1980). Parent education is distinguished from parent therapy in that parent education is time-limited and has behavior change as a goal rather than personality change (Dembo, Sweitzer, & Lauritzen, 1985). Approaches have been developed from a wide variety of theoretical orientations, including behavioral (Becker, 1971; Patterson & Gullison, 1971), Adlerian (Dreikurs & Soltz, 1964), systematic training for effective parenting (Dinkmeyer & McKay, 1976), transactional analysis (James, 1974), humanistic (Ginott, 1965, 1968) and parent effectiveness training (Gordon, 1975). Each of these programs is delivered in a group format; all include reading materials for parents, demonstrations of techniques, and discussions of technique applications.

Given the variety of education programs available, program evaluation is essential. Dembo, Sweitzer, and Lauritzen (1985) published an extensive review of 48 evaluation studies. In each of these studies, children with severe developmental or behavioral problems were excluded. Behavioral approaches were evaluated in 15 studies, Adlerian in 10 studies, and parent effectiveness training (PET) in 18. Only five studies compared one training program with another (Adlerian with behavioral and PET with behavioral).

Behavioral training programs are less homologous than Adlerian or PET programs, and therefore more difficult to evaluate. Most programs attempt to teach an overview of behavioral concepts, use of social and nonsocial reinforcers, techniques for strengthening and weakening behavior chains, observation and recording procedures, and parent awareness of the ways in which their behavior is shaped by their children. Behavioral approaches were evaluated in 15 studies. "The typical program included middle class parents trained by a PhD or Master's level psychologist for a period of 18 to 20 hours to deal with their male acting-out children ranging in age from 3 to 10 years" (Dembo, et al., 1985, p. 174). About three-quarters of the studies reporting follow-up data reported significantly improved child behavior compared with controls. Follow-up periods for those studies using random assignment of subjects ranged from 1 to 4 months. Studies without random assignment to training groups reported improved child behavior at 12 months' follow-up.

The goals of Adlerian approaches are to help parents understand what motivates their children's behavior and how family dynamics affect child behavior; to improve family communication through the use of the family council; and to help children develop responsibility through the use of logical consequences and democratic problem-solving (Dreikurs & Soltz, 1964). Ten studies provided evaluation data regarding the effectiveness of Adlerian approaches relative to no training. Most of the subject in these studies were mothers only; little data were provided in these studies regarding the trainers. Sessions varied from 6 to 10 weekly 1- to 1½-hour sessions. One study used random assignment with a child management discussion group as a placebo (Freeman, 1975); this study found no significant difference between the treatment group that studied the Dreikurs & Soltz (1963) test and the unstructured discussion group. Studies reporting data on parents' child-rearing attitudes generally reported positive changes, although no changes in child behavior were reported. No study included generalization or follow-up data.

Parent effectiveness training emphasizes learning human relations strategies that include the use of active listening, I-messages (e.g., "I want you to clean up your room now"), and democratic problem solving. The PET groups were evaluated in 18 studies. The training program consists of 8 weekly 3-hour sessions led by a trainer certified by Effectiveness Training Associates. Only five studies used random assignment to treatment groups. None of these studies indicated significant changes in child behavior. Only one out of four studies found significant differences in parent attitudes at follow-up; this change was in increased empathy.

Only five studies comparing different educational approaches were identified in the Dembo et al. review, one comparing Adlerian and behavioral approaches, the other four comparing behavioral and PET approaches. These studies failed to find any significant differences between approaches. Each of these approaches focuses on changing parent behaviors and attitudes toward their children. They were developed prior to the current child-effects Zeitgeist in child development research (Bell, 1979); their effectiveness could possibly be improved by consideration of children's effects on their parents and by treating the family as a unit. Other concerns raised by Dembo et al. in their review involve the effectiveness of these programs with differing cultural groups including teenage mothers (Kissman, 1992), the lack of attention by researchers and program developers to differing needs of parents, the assessment of aptitude-treatment interactions, and the lack of methodological rigor in the majority of studies.

REFERENCES

Becker, W. C. (1971). *Parents are teachers.* Champaign, IL: Research Press.

Bell, R. Q. (1979). Parent, child, and reciprocal influences. *American Psychologist, 34,* 821–826.

Dembo, M. H., Sweitzer, M., & Lauritzen, P. (1985). An evaluation of group parent education: Behavioral, PET, and Adlerian programs. *Review of Educational Research, 55,* 155–200.

Dinkmeyer, D., & McKay, G. (1976). *Systematic training for effective parenting.* Circle Pines, MN: American Guidance Service.

Dreikurs, R., & Soltz, V. (1964). *Children: The challenge.* New York: Hawthorn.

Fine, M. J. (1980). The parent education movement: An introduction. In M. J. Fine (Ed.), *Handbook on parent education.* New York: Academic.

Freeman, C. W. (1975). Adlerian mother study groups: Effects on attitudes and behavior. *Journal of Individual Psychology, 31,* 37–50.

Ginott, H. G. (1965). *Between parent and child.* New York: Macmillan.

Ginott, H. G. (1968). *Between parent and teenagers.* New York: Macmillan.

Gordon, T. (1975). *P.E.T.: Parent effectiveness training.* New York: American Library.

James, M. (1974). *Transactional analysis for moms and dads.* Reading, MA: Addison-Wesley.

Kissman, K. (1992). Parenting skills training: Expanding school-based services for adolescent mothers. *Research on Social Work Practice, 2*(2), 161–171.

Patterson, G. R., & Gullison, M. E. (1971). *Living with children.* Champaign, IL: Research Press.

Peterson, N L., & Cooper, C. S. (1989). Parent education and involvement in early intervention programs for handicapped children. *Educational Psychology, 17,* 197–234.

Polansky, N. A., Gaudin, J. M., Ammons, P. W., & Davis, K. B. (1985). The psychological ecology of the neglectful mother. *Child Abuse & Neglect, 9,* 265–275.

Wolfe, D. A. (1985). Child-abusive parents: An empirical review and analysis. *Psychological Bulletin, 97,* 462–482.

JOHN MACDONALD
Eastern Kentucky University

FAMILY RESPONSE TO A HANDICAPPED CHILD
FAMILY THERAPY
PARENT COUNSELING
PARENT EFFECTIVENESS TRAINING

PARENTING SKILLS

Parents of students with disabilities are faced with needs not apparent to parents of students without identifiable disabilities. They are no longer passive recipients of services but assume a strong advocacy role on behalf of their children. Specifically, skills to be developed include learning to reduce stress, being involved in the individualized education plan (IEP), following through on home programming, helping the child to interact with friends and siblings, and managing behavior.

According to Wikler (1983), the "various stresses experienced by families of mentally retarded children are exacerbated over time by unexpected discrepancies between what might have been and what is." Reactions to normal life experiences from birth through adulthood occur with varying intensities and resolutions. The term chronic sorrow refers to the experiences of parents when they compare their child with peers without handicaps at developmental milestones, including when peers begin walking, talking, and entering public schools, begin puberty, graduate from school, and leave home. Available support comes through local associations for retarded citizens, family therapists, and other groups that provide outlets for sharing information and receiving nonjudgmental feedback concerning the unique experiences of family members.

Active participation by parents is an encouraged and mandated aspect of the IEP. This participation occurs through systematic contact with school personnel regarding rights and responsibilities of home and school representatives. At the basic level, identification, evaluation, and placement decisions involve a due process component to ensure that decision outcomes are acceptable to all involved parties. Increasingly, teachers are assuming the role of consultant to parents and viewing the parents as the real experts in their child's life. With this perspective, teachers are initiating extensive questionnaires for parents to complete prior to the IEP conference. Included in these questionnaires are activities that are pinpointed as having the highest value to the parents for their child's development. Thus communication skills between home and school environments are essential for optimum development of the IEP.

A common characteristic of students with handicapping conditions is the lack of generalization from school to community-based settings without active planning. Accordingly, parents are increasingly solicited to continue teaching their child in the skills being addressed at school.

Principles of applied behavior analysis common to many school-based programs can be acquired by parents to ensure continuity of instruction. These instructional strategies may include prompting hierarchies, reinforcement schedules, and task modifications. Increasingly, parents are provided training in these areas when the child is very young (Hanson, 1977).

Parents express concern about the impact of a child with handicaps on siblings and peers in the neighborhood (Powell & Ogle, 1985). Developing friendships, participating in community activities, and interacting with family members are activities that contribute to a quality of life for individuals with disabilities. Parents are obtaining information and support to foster these relationships through peer support groups, journals such as *Exceptional Parent,* peer tutors, community integration specialists, and parent training seminars.

Understanding the relationships among antecedents, consequences, and a targeted child behavior is of prime concern when attempting to decrease undesirable behaviors. Antecedents involve events that immediately precede a behavior of concern to the parent and that may have a precipitating effect on the behavior. Consequences are events following the behavior of concern that may serve to reinforce and maintain an undesirable activity by the child. Finally, the undesirable behavior itself needs to be precisely defined for determining the exact parameters of attention. Numerous strategies are employed, including positive and negative reinforcement, shaping, token economy, time out, punishment, and overcorrection.

REFERENCES

Ehly, S. W., Conoley, J. C., & Rosenthal, D. (1985). *Working with parents of exceptional children.* St. Louis: Time Mirror/Mosby.

Gallagher, J. J., & Vietze, P. M. (Eds.). (1986). *Families of handicapped persons: Research, programs, and policy issues.* Baltimore, MD: Brookes.

Hanson, M. J. (1977). *Teaching your Down's syndrome infant: A guide for parents.* Baltimore, MD: University Park Press.

Powell, T. H., & Ogle, P. A. (1985). *Brothers and sisters: A special part of exceptional families.* Baltimore, MD: Brookes.

Turnbull, H. R., & Turnbull, A. P. (Eds.). (1985). *Parents speak out: Then and now* (2nd ed.) Columbus, OH: Merrill.

Wikler, L. (1983). Chronic stresses of families of mentally retarded children. In L. Wikler & M. P. Keenan (Eds.), *Developmental disabilities: No longer a private tragedy* (pp. 102–110). Washington, DC: American Association on Mental Deficiency.

ERNEST L. PANCSOFAR
University of Connecticut

FAMILY RESPONSE TO A HANDICAPPED CHILD
INDIVIDUAL EDUCATION PLAN (IEP)
SIBLINGS OF THE HANDICAPPED

PARENTS OF THE HANDICAPPED

Parents of handicapped children and youths have been one of the most influential factors in the education of and the delivery of services to handicapped youngsters throughout the history of special education. Over the past decade, groups organized by parents have been described as trailblazers in the crusade to win full acceptance of children with handicaps as human beings. These organizations have gained strength through painstaking and often self-sacrificing efforts. Parents have helped other parents, started schools, collected funds, collected facts and figures for unmet needs, lobbied for reforms, and initiated community services (Closer Look, 1978).

As early as 1930, parents began to unite efforts and band together to share problems and to seek answers regarding the education and care of exceptional children (Sarason & Doris, 1969). The first parent group to organize on behalf of handicapped children were the parents of children with cerebral palsy. A mother of a cerebral palsied child in New York ran an advertisement in *The New York Times* soliciting other parents who had children with cerebral palsy. Through this effort, the National Society of Crippled Children was formed. Subsequently, the United Cerebral Palsy Association was organized in 1948. Shortly thereafter, the National Association of Retarded Citizens was organized in 1950. This trend toward unity among parents with similar interests continued. Organizations of parents of the learning disabled and parents of the gifted and talented have formed (Barsh, 1961; Fortier, 1968; Gallagher, 1983; Orlansky, 1984).

The crippling effects of World War II among prewar professionals, businesspeople, or otherwise respected citizens, along with an increasing number of handicapped children born into middle- and upper-income families, provided new directions for the parent movement. Parents rejected the concept of institutionalization and insisted that schools provide an education for their children in their respective communities. At the same time, parents persistently encouraged educators to recognize their rights as parents to seek relief for their children and to pass laws that would meet the needs of handicapped children (Webster, 1976). PL 94-142 and subsequent amendments and legislation such as IDEA mandate parental rights and involvement in the education of handicapped children and youths. Martin (1979) summarized these rights, as follows.

Children with disabilities are entitled to an independent educational evaluation that will be considered when placement and program decisions are made. Parents have the right to be told where an independent evaluation may be obtained at no expense or low expense, to have the agency pay for the independent evaluation if the agency's evaluation is not appropriate, and to be informed of the procedures for obtaining an independent evaluation at public expense and the conditions under which such an evaluation may be obtained.

Parents have the right to notice before the agency initiates, or changes (or refuses to initiate or change), the identification, evaluation, or placement of the child; to have that notice in writing, in their native language, or other principal mode of communication, at a level understandable to the general public; to have the notice describe the proposed action and explain why those other options were rejected; and to be notified of each evaluation procedure, test, record, or report the agency will use as a basis for any proposed action. Parents also have the right to give or withhold consent before an evaluation is conducted and before initial placement is made in special education; to revoke consent at any time; and to forfeit to the agency to proceed in the absence of consent to a hearing to determine if the child should be initially placed.

Parents are entitled to request an impartial due process hearing to question the agency's identification, evaluation, or placement of the child, or to question the agency's provision of a free appropriate public education; to be told of any free or low-cost legal or other relevant services available (e.g., experts on handicapping conditions who may be a witness at the hearing); to have the hearing chaired by a person not employed by a public agency involved in the education of the child or otherwise having any personal or professional interest in the hearing; to see a statement of the qualifications of the hearing officer; to be advised and accompanied at the hearing by counsel and to be accompanied by individuals with special knowledge or training in problems of the handicapped; to have the child present; to have the hearing open to the public; to present evidence and confront, cross-examine, and compel the attendance of witnesses; to prohibit the introduction of any evidence at the hearing that has not been disclosed at least five days before the hearing; to have a record of the hearing; to obtain written findings of fact and a written decision within 45 days after the initial request for the hearing; to appeal to the State Board of Education and receive a decision within 30 days of filing of an appeal; to have a hearing and an appeal set at a time reasonably convenient to the parent; to appeal a decision from the State Board of Education in court; and to have the child remain in his or her present educational placement during the pending of the administrative proceeding, unless parent and agency agree otherwise.

Parents also have the right to have a full and individual evaluation of the child's educational needs; have more than one criterion used in determining an appropriate educational program; have the evaluation performed by a multidisciplinary team; have child assessed in all areas related to the suspected disability; have a reevaluation every 3 years or more often if conditions warrant or if the parent or the child's teacher requests it.

Parents of handicapped children are entitled to have their child educated with nonhandicapped children to the maximum extent possible; have their child removed from the regular educational environment only after supplementary aids and services are tried and found unsatisfactory; have a continuum of alternate placements so that removal from the regular educational environment can be the least necessary deviation; have available supplementary services such as a resource room or itinerant instruction to make it possible for their child to remain in regular class placement; have their child placed within the school that he or she would attend if nonhandicapped unless the individual education plan requires some other arrangement; have their child participate with nonhandicapped children in nonacademic and extracurricular services and activities such as meals, recess, counseling, clubs, athletics, and special interest groups.

It is important that parents restrict access to their child's records by withholding consent to disclose records; be informed before information in their child's file is to be destroyed; and be told to whom information has been disclosed. In addition, the law stipulates that parents or guardians must be involved in developing the individualized education program (Turnbull & Schulz, 1979).

The roles of parents of handicapped children have been outlined as advocates, resources, teachers, and counselors by Knoblock (1983), Heyward & Orlansky (1984), Brown and Moersch (1982), Nowland (1971) and Volenski (1995). Parents may obtain information and listings of state and local agencies serving handicapped individuals from the U.S. Department of Education and the Office of Civil Rights.

REFERENCES

Barsh, R. (1976). *The parents of the handicapped child.* Springfield, IL: Thomas.

Berdine, W., & Blackhurst, A. (1985). *An introduction to special education* (2nd ed.). Boston: Little, Brown.

Brown, S., & Moersch, M. (1982). *Parents on the team.* Ann Arbor: University of Michigan Press.

Bubolz, M., & Whiren, A. (1984). The family of the handicapped: An ecological model for policy and practice. *Family Relations, 33,* 5–12.

Department of Health, Education and Welfare Office of Education. (1977, August 23). Education of handicapped children. *Federal Register, 42*(163).

Farber, B. (1968). *Mental retardation: Its social context and social consequences.* Boston: Houghton Mifflin.

Fortier, L., & Wanless, R. (1984). Family crisis following the diagnosis of a handicapped child. *Family Relation, 33,* 13–24.

Hallahan, D., & Kauffman, J. *Exceptional children: Introduction to special education.* Englewood Cliffs, NJ: Prentice-Hall.

Heyward, W., & Orlansky, M. (1984). *Exceptional children: An in-*

troductory survey of special education (2nd ed.). Columbus, OH: Merrill.

Kazak, A., & Marvin, R. (1984). Differences, difficulties and adaptation: Stress and social networks in families with a handicapped child. *Family Relations, 33,* 66–77.

Kirk, S., & Gallagher, J. (1983). *Educating exceptional children* (4th ed.). Boston: Houghton Mifflin.

Knoblock, P. (1983). *Teaching emotionally disturbed children.* Boston: Houghton Mifflin.

Martin, R. (1979). *Educating handicapped children: The legal mandate.* Champaign, IL: Research Press.

National Information Center for Handicapped Children and Youth. (1978). *Closer look.* Rosslyn, VA: Interstate Research.

National Information Center for Handicapped Children and Youth. (1985). *News digest.* Rosslyn, VA: Interstate Research.

Nowland, R. (1971). *Counseling parents of the ill and handicapped.* Springfield, IL: Thomas.

Sarason, S. A., & Doris, J. (1969). *Psychological problems in mental deficiency* (4th ed.). New York: Harper & Row.

Turnbull, A., & Dixon, J. (1980). Preschool mainstreaming: Impact on parents. In J. J. Gallagher (Ed.), *New directions for exceptional children: Ecology of exceptional children* (Vol. 1). San Francisco: Jossey-Bass.

Turnbull, A., & Schulz, J. (1979). *Mainstreaming handicapped students: A guide for the classroom teacher.* Boston: Allyn & Bacon.

Turnbull, A., & Turnbull, H. (1978). *Parents speak out.* Columbus, OH: Merrill.

Volenski, L. T. (1995). Building school support systems for parents of handicapped children. *Psychology in the Schools, 32*(2), 124–129.

Webster, E. (1976). *Professional approaches with parents of handicapped children.* Springfield, IL: Thomas.

FRANCES T. HARRINGTON
Radford University

BUCKLEY AMENDMENT
FAMILY COUNSELING
FAMILY RESPONSE TO A HANDICAPPED CHILD
INDIVIDUALS WITH DISABILITIES EDUCATION ACT (IDEA)
SPECIAL EDUCATION, LEGAL REGULATION OF

PARKHURST, HELEN (1887–1973)

Helen Parkhurst devised the Dalton Plan and founded the Dalton School in New York City. The essence of the Dalton Plan, based on Parkhurst's concept of the school as a laboratory where students are experimenters and not just participants, was individualization of instruction through student contracts, with each student working individually at his or her own pace to carry out contracted assignments.

Early in her career, Parkhurst studied with Maria Montessori in Italy; from 1915 to 1918 she supervised the development of Montessori programs in the United States. She left the Montessori movement to put her own educational plan into practice at schools in Pittsfield and Dalton, Massachusetts. She founded the Dalton School in 1920 and served as its director until her retirement in 1942. Parkhurst lectured throughout the world and established Dalton schools in England, Japan, and China. Her book, *Education on the Dalton Plan,* was published in 58 languages. After retiring from the Dalton School, Parkhurst produced radio and television programs for children and conducted a discussion program in which she gave advice on family life.

REFERENCES

Parkhurst, H. (1922). *Education on the Dalton Plan.* New York: Dutton.

Parkhurst, H. (1951). *Exploring the child's world.* New York: Appleton-Century-Crofts.

PAUL IRVINE
Katonah, New York

PARTIALLY SIGHTED

The term partially sighted was used to classify and place students in special classes whose distance visual acuity was between 20/70 and 20/200 in the better eye after correction (Hatfield, 1975). In 1977 the classifications of levels of vision adopted by the World Health Organization omitted the use of partially sighted in its system (Colenbrander, 1977). As a result, this term has virtually disappeared from the recent literature (Barraga, 1983).

REFERENCES

Barraga, N. C. (1983). *Visual handicaps and learning.* Austin, TX: Exceptional Resources.

Colenbrander, A. (1977). Dimensions of visual performance. *Archives of Ophthalmology, 83,* 332–337.

Hatfield, E. M. (1975). Why are they blind? *Sight Saving Review, 45,* 3–22.

ROSEANNE K. SILBERMAN
Hunter College

BLIND
LOW VISION
VISUALLY IMPAIRED
VISUAL TRAINING

PARTIAL PARTICIPATION

The principle of partial participation entails the position that all students with severe handicaps (including the profoundly mentally retarded and the severely physically disabled) can acquire a number of skills that will enable them to function at least partially in a variety of least restrictive school and nonschool environments or activities (Baumgart et al., 1980). Because of the severity of their sensory or motor impairments as well as deficits in attentional and learning processes, some severely handicapped students have difficulty in learning skills needed to function independently in current and subsequent least restrictive environments. Rather than denying access to these environments, proponents of the principle of partial participation believe adaptations can be implemented that will allow students to participate in a wide range of activities (Demchack, 1994) as well as experience inclusive programming. The latter, however, may not always be the least restrictive environment for students with severe disabilities.

Adaptations via modes of partial participation can take on a variety of dimensions in the activities of severely handicapped learners (Baumgart et al., 1982; Wehman, Schleien, & Kiernan, 1980). Materials and devices can be used or created in an effort to adapt tasks (e.g., using an enlarged adaptive switch to operate kitchen appliances, using picture communication cards to communicate needs in a restaurant, using a bus pass instead of coins when a student is unable to count coins for bus fare, using frozen waffles rather than a waffle iron and batter when preparing breakfast). The sequence of steps in skills being taught can be modified (e.g., dress in a bathing suit before going to community pool if extra time is needed to manipulate clothing; sit on the toilet first, then pull pants down if unsteady on feet in the bathroom). Personal assistance can be provided for part or all of a task (e.g., peers push wheelchair to help deliver attendance records to office, teacher takes bread out of bag and places it in toaster prior to having student press lever on toaster). Rules can be changed or adapted to meet the needs of individual students (e.g., allow student to eat lunch in two lunch periods in cafeteria if he or she is a slow eater owing to physical disabilities). Societal or attitudinal as well as physical environments can be adapted (e.g., installing wheelchair ramps in public places, installing electronic doors in public buildings to make them more accessible for wheelchair users).

The classroom teacher will need to follow a number of steps to implement partial participation strategies successfully. These include: (1) taking a nonhandicapped person's inventory of steps/skills used in a particular task; (2) taking a severely handicapped student's inventory of steps used or skills exhibited for the same task; (3) determining the skills that the student with disabilities probably can acquire; (4) determining the skills the handicapped student probably cannot acquire; (5) generating an adaptation hypothesis; (6) conducting an inventory of adaptations currently available for use; (7) determining individualized adaptations to be used; and (8) determining skills that can probably be acquired using individualized adaptations (Baumgart, et al., 1982).

Several considerations are recommended when using individualized adaptations for severely handicapped students. These include: (1) empirically verifying the appropriateness and effectiveness of adaptations in the criterion or natural environment; (2) avoiding allowing students to become overly dependent on adaptations; and (3) carefully selecting adaptations to meet needs of individual students in critically functional environments (Baumgart et al., 1980). Appropriate applications of the principle of partial participation will enhance the access of severely handicapped individuals to integrated environments available to the nonhandicapped population at large (Brown et al., 1979; Ferguson & Baumgart, 1991).

REFERENCES

Baumgart, D., Brown, L., Pumpian, I., Nisbet, J., Ford, A., Sweet, M., Messina, R., & Schroeder, J. (1982). Principle of partial participation and individualized adaptations in education programs for severely handicapped students. *Journal of the Association for Persons with Severe Handicaps, 7*(2), 17–27.

Baumgart, D., Brown, L., Pumpian, I., Nisbet, J., Ford, A., Sweet, M., Ranieri, L., Hansen, L., & Schroeder, J. (1980). The principle of partial participation and individualized adaptations in education programs for severely handicapped students. In L. Brown, M. Falvey, I. Pumpian, D. Baumgart, J. Nisbet, A. Ford, J. Schroeder, & R. Loomis (Eds.), *Curricular strategies for teaching severely handicapped students functional skills in school and nonschool environments* (Vol. 10). Madison, WI: Madison Public Schools and the University of Wisconsin.

Brown, L., Branston-McClean, M. B., Baumgart, D., Vincent, L., Falvey, M., & Schroeder, J. (1979). Using the characteristics of current and subsequent least restrictive environments in the development of curricular content for severely handicapped students. *Journal of the Association for Persons with Severe Handicaps, 4,* 407–424.

Demchak, M. A. (1994). Helping individuals with severe disabilities find leisure activities. *Teaching Exceptional Children, 27*(1), 48–52.

Ferguson, D L., & Baumgart, D. (1991). Partial participation revisited. *Journal of the Association for Persons with Severe Handicaps, 16*(4), 218–227.

Wehman, P., Schleien, S., & Kiernan, J. (1980). Age appropriate recreation programs for severely handicapped youth and adults. *Journal of the Association for Persons with Severe Handicaps, 5,* 395–407.

CORNELIA LIVELY
University of Illinois

HUMANISTIC SPECIAL EDUCATION
LEAST RESTRICTIVE ENVIRONMENT

PASAMANICK, BENJAMIN (1914–1996)

Benjamin Pasamanick began his professional studies at Cornell University, where he received his BA in 1936. Dur-

Benjamin Pasamanick

ing this period, he began studying physiology and biochemistry, and was accepted as the sole undergraduate advisee of Nobel Laureate James Sumner. In 1937, he attended the University of Maryland School of Medicine, earning his MD in 1941. His internship psychiatry was completed at Brooklyn State Hospital and Harlem Hospital, both in New York City. Following his psychiatric residency at the New York State Psychiatric Institute in 1943, Pasamanick became an assistant at the Yale Clinic of Child Development, where he was accepted to study under Arnold Gesell.

He subsequently held numerous faculty, research, and clinical positions at medical schools and clinics throughout the northeastern United States. He was the Sir Aubrey and Lady Hilda Lewis professor of social psychiatry at the New York School of Psychiatry, professor of psychiatry at the New York University College of Medicine, and research professor of psychiatry at the State University of New York, Stony Brook. At the time of this death in 1996, he was research professor emeritus of pediatrics at Albany Medical College.

Throughout his illustrious career as a mentor, scholar, and clinician in child psychiatry, Pasamanick maintained an interest in exceptional children, particularly those with mental retardation. He challenged conventional practices, frequently promoting change and innovation, and sought a melding of basic research in child development with the practice and promotion of a clear conceptual framework for treatment.

Pasamanick is perhaps best known for his research on the multidimensional, multifactorial influences on children's development (Kawi & Pasamanick, 1979), particularly his longitudinal studies of the development of black infants (Granich, 1970). He was the first to demonstrate that the behavioral development of black infants, as an indicator of intellectual maturity, was indistinguishable from that of white infants. He ultimately came to believe

that, early in life, intelligence and related cognitive skills are primarily biologically determined but become increasingly chronologically and socially influenced with age, eventually being driven by socioeconomic factors.

Pasamanick extensively studied mental disorders and the continuum of reproductive casualty and epidemiology (Davis, Dinitz, & Pasamanick, 1974). His research in the 1950s and 1960s focused on prenatal factors involved in mental illness and treatment of mental disorders, with his work in this area finding that at least 80% of serious cases of mental illness were treatable at home using drug therapy. His investigation into the state of mental health in large cities, conducted on behalf of the American Public Health Association, indicated that at least one in ten of those living in American cities, while appearing normal, had mental problems.

In the 1960s and 1970s Pasamanick served as associate state commissioner for research in the Department of Mental Hygiene, and later became associate commissioner for research and evaluation in the Division of Mental Retardation and Child Development. His work substantially influenced service delivery to handicapped children in a variety of settings.

Among his numerous contributions, he served as president of the American Orthopsychiatric Association (1970–1971), president of the American Psychopathological Association (1967), and president of the Theobald Smith Society (1984). Pasamanick was a familiar figure at professional gatherings where he presented scientific papers, and he authored or edited numerous books and articles in scholarly journals, with more than 300 publications to his credit. His service on editorial boards included *Child Development*, the *American Journal of Mental Deficiency*, the *Merrill-Palmer Quarterly*, and the *Journal of Biological Psychiatry*.

REFERENCES

Davis, A., Dinitz, S., & Pasamanick, B. (1974). *Schizophrenics in the new custodial community: Five years after the experiment.* Columbus, OH: Ohio State University.

Granich, B. (1970). Benjamin Pasamanick. *American Journal of Orthopsychiatry, 40,* 368–372.

Kawi, A., & Pasamanick, B. (1979). *Prenatal and paranatal factors in the development of childhood reading disorders.* Millwood, NY: Kraus.

CECIL R. REYNOLDS
Texas A & M University
First edition

TAMARA J. MARTIN
The University of Texas of the Permian Basin
Second edition

AMERICAN ORTHOPSYCHIATRIC ASSOCIATION

PASE v. HANNON

PASE (Parents in Action on Special Education) v. *Hannon* (Joseph P. Hannon, superintendent of the Chicago public schools at the time this case was filed) was a class-action suit on behalf of black students who were or who might be classified as educable mentally retarded (EMR) and placed in self-contained special classes. PASE was established by a parent advocacy group assisted by the Northwestern School of Law Legal Assistance Clinic and the Legal Assistance Foundation in Chicago. The U.S. Department of Justice filed a friend of court brief on behalf of the plaintiffs. Defendants in the case were various officials employed by the Chicago Board of Education as well as the Board of Education of the State of Illinois. *PASE* resulted in a 3-week trial conducted by Judge Grady, who issued an opinion deciding the case on July 7, 1980.

The issues and expert witness testimony in *PASE* were virtually identical to the testimony in *Larry P.* v. *Riles,* heard by Federal District Court Judge Peckham in California in a trial concluded in May 1978. The fundamental allegations were that overrepresentation of black students in EMR special class programs constituted discrimination, and that overrepresentation was caused by the defendants' use of biased IQ tests. The plaintiffs claimed the overrepresentation from biased IQ tests violated constitutional and statutory protections, particularly the Equal Protection Clause of the Fourteenth Amendment and the non-discrimination protections in the Education for All Handicapped Children Act of 1975 and Section 504 of the Rehabilitation Act of 1973. The plaintiffs and defendants agreed that black students constituted about 62% of the total school population in Chicago, but 82% of the EMR population. The actual percentage of black students classified as EMR was 3.7%; in contrast, 1.3% of white students were classified as EMR.

In a 3-week trial in 1979, the plaintiffs relied heavily on several of the witnesses who appeared just under 2 years earlier in the *Larry P.* trial in California. In particular, the plaintiffs relied on Leon Kamin's analysis of the historical pattern of racist attitudes and beliefs among early developers of intelligence tests in the United States (Kamin, 1974). Robert Williams, a prominent black psychologist, provided testimony concerning the differences in the cultures of white and black students and identified a few examples of biased items. Although other witnesses appeared for the plaintiffs, the testimony of Kamin and Williams was noted prominently in Grady's decision.

Witnesses for the defendants contended overrepresentation reflected the genuine needs of black students, who were claimed to have a higher EMR incidence owing to the effects of poverty. This emphasis on socioeconomic status as an explanation for overrepresentation was also relied on by *Larry P.* defendants, though unsuccessfully. The association of EMR with poverty has been reported for many decades throughout the western world for diverse racial and ethnic groups. The defendants also contended that any biases that might exist in IQ tests were neutralized in the placement process through the use of procedural protections such as parental informed consent, the development of a multifactored assessment that focused on educational needs, and decision making by a multidisciplinary team.

Judge Grady clearly was dissatisfied with the evidence presented by both the plaintiffs and the defendants. He noted, somewhat testily, that only cursory information on the testing question was presented in the evidence. He questioned attorneys for both sides and learned that no one relied heavily on careful analysis of each of the test items in preparing for the case. He then concluded that an analysis of each of the items on the three tests in question, the Wechsler Intelligence Scale for Children, the Wechsler Intelligence Scale for Children-Revised, and the Stanford Binet, was required for him to decide on claims of bias. Judge Grady then undertook an item-by-item analysis of the questions on the three tests.

Approximately two thirds of the space in Judge Grady's lengthy opinion was devoted to his analyses of the intelligence test items. Judge Grady provided the exact wording of the item, the correct answer, and the scoring criterion, where appropriate, for determining whether a response was awarded one or two points. This unprecedented breach of test security was initially shocking to many professionals, but no known harm or serious threat to normative standards has been reported.

Judge Grady concluded from his personal analysis of the IQ test items that only eight of several hundred items were biased. He noted that four of those eight items were not on current versions of the tests, and that those that were generally appeared at the upper limits of the test. Items that appeared at the upper limits of the test typically would not be given to students who might be considered for classification as EMR. Grady concluded that any biases that existed on the test exerted a very small influence on classification and placement decisions, and agreed with the defendants that other safeguards, mentioned earlier, compensated for these negligible biases.

The sharply different opinions in *PASE* and *Larry P.* did not go unnoticed in the professional literature (Bersoff, 1982; Sattler 1980). The trial opinions were markedly different despite virtually identical issues and similar evidence. The reason different conclusions were reached can best be understood from an analysis of the different approaches taken by the federal court judges. Judge Grady required that a direct connection be established between biased items and misclassification of black students as EMR. He found no such connection in Kamin's testimony about historical patterns of racism, in Robert Williams' descriptions of differences in cultural backgrounds of white and black students, and in his own analyses of items.

Grady then ruled that the absence of a clear connection between biased items and misclassification prevented the plaintiffs from prevailing. In contrast, Judge Peckham in *Larry P.* accepted allegations of item bias and concluded that the other protections in the referral, classification, and placement process were insufficient to overcome these biases. Both decisions have been criticized; *PASE* because of the method used by Judge Grady (Bersoff, 1982) and *Larry P.* because of conclusions concerning item biases that did not reflect available evidence (Reschly, 1980; Sandoval, 1979).

The plaintiffs appealed the *PASE* trial decision. However, before the appellate court ruled, the issues in the case were rendered moot by the decision of the Board of Education in Chicago to ban the use of traditional IQ tests with black students being considered for classification and placement as EMR. This ban was part of a negotiated settlement in still another court case concerning the desegregation of the Chicago public schools. The appeal was then withdrawn by the plaintiffs. The *PASE* decision is an interesting contrast to that in *Larry P.,* but it does not have the impact of *Larry P.* for a variety of reasons.

REFERENCES

Bersoff, D. (1982). Larry P., and PASE; Judicial report cards of the validity of individual intelligence tests. In T. Kratochwill (Ed.), *Advances in school psychology* (Vol. 11), (pp. 61–95). Hillsdale, NJ: Erlbaum.

Kamin, L. J. (1974). *The science and politics of IQ.* New York: Halsted.

Reschly, D. (1980). Psychological evidence in the *Larry P.* opinion: A case of right problem-wrong solution. *School Psychology Review, 9,* 123–135.

Sandoval, J. (1979). The WISC-R and internal evidence of test bias with minority groups. *Journal of Consulting & Clinical Psychology, 47,* 919–927.

Sattler, J. (1980, November). In the opinion of.. . . .*Monitor,* pp. 7–8.

DANIEL J. RESCHLY
Iowa State University

DIANA *v.* STATE BOARD OF EDUCATION
LARRY P.
MARSHALL *v.* GEORGIA
NONDISCRIMINATORY ASSESSMENT

PATH ANALYSIS

Path analysis is a technique developed in the 1930s by Sewell Wright (1934) for the purpose of studying causal relationships among variables. Path analysis provides mathematical models expressing the direct and indirect effects of variables assumed to have causal status on variables assumed to be affected by the causal variables. A direct effect occurs when one variable influences another in the absence of mediation by a third variable. For example, one might assume that a particular educational intervention had a direct effect on student achievement. An indirect effect exists when a causal variable affects a dependent variable by influencing a third variable, which in turn affects the dependent variable directly. For example, teacher training might be assumed to affect teaching behavior, which would influence student achievement. Under these conditions, teacher training would have an indirect effect on student achievement. Its influence on achievement would occur through its effect on teaching behavior.

The mathematical models used to express causation in path analysis have their origins in regression analysis. The simplest path model is one involving the regression of a dependent variable on one or more variables assumed to explain variation in the dependent variable. For instance, student achievement might be regressed on an educational intervention assumed to affect achievement. Under this model, the intervention would have a direct effect on achievement. The residual term in the regression equation would also be included in the model. It is assumed to be uncorrelated with other variables in the equation. The residual would be treated as a causal variable indicating the effects of variables not explicitly included in the model on achievement. For instance, intelligence is a variable not explicitly identified in the model that might account for part of the variation in achievement. Many other variables that might affect achievement could be identified.

Models involving indirect effects require more than one regression equation. For instance, the example given involving the indirect effect of teacher training on achievement would require two regression equations. The first would include the regression of achievement on teacher training and teacher behavior; the second would include the regression of teacher behavior on teacher training. The general rule governing the number of equations is that one equation is needed for each dependent variable.

The two models discussed to this point assume unidirectional causation. For instance, in the indirect effects model, teacher behavior is assumed to affect achievement, but achievement is not assumed to affect teacher behavior. Models assuming unidirectional causation are called recursive. Ordinary least squares (OLS) regression can be used with recursive models. Nonrecursive models assuming bidirectional causation between one or more pairs of variables require procedures that go beyond OLS regression. Duncan (1975) provides an excellent discussion of nonrecursive models.

Causal relations may be expressed in path analysis not only through mathematical models, but also through path diagrams such as the one shown in the following Figure. Variables A and B in the diagram are called exogenous variables. An exogenous variable is a variable whose variation is explained by factors outside of the causal model. The curved double-headed arrow indicates that variables A and B are related and that no assumption is made regarding the direction of the relationship. Variables C and D are endogenous variables. Endogenous variables are affected by exogenous variables and/or other endogenous variables.

The Ps in the model represent path coefficients. In a recursive model, these are standardized regression weights. Each path coefficient is interpreted as that fraction of the standard deviation in the dependent variable for which the causal variable is directly responsible. For instance, P_{da} indicates that fraction of the standard deviation in variable D for which variable A is directly responsible. The standardized regression weights functioning as path coefficients in path models are no longer widely used in causal modeling. The assumption that all variables in a causal model should be placed on the same scale has been challenged. Unstandardized weights are now typically used. See Duncan (1975) for a discussion of the problems associated with standardized weights.

Path analysis may be regarded as a special case of a more general technique called structural equation modeling (Bentler, 1980; Joreskog & Sorbom, 1979). The major difference between path analysis as it was developed by Wright and structural equation models is that structural equation models may include latent as well as manifest variables. A latent variable is a variable that is not observed directly, but rather is inferred from two or more manifest indicators. For example, student achievement could be treated as a latent variable to be inferred from scores on two or more achievement tests. A structural equation model expresses the effects of one set of variables on another set of variables. The variables in the model may include both latent variables and manifest variables. For instance, a model might include the effects of sex on student achievement in mathematics. Sex would be a manifest variable in this model and mathematics achievement could be a latent variable inferred from two or more test scores. Structural equation modeling represents a powerful extension of Wright's pioneering work in path analysis. With structural equation techniques, it is possible not only to represent a broad range of causal relations among variables, but also to represent a wide variety of latent variables that may be of concern in educational and psychological research.

REFERENCES

Bentler, P. M. (1980). Multivariate analysis with latent variables. In M. R. Rozenweig & L. W. Porter (Eds.), *Annual review of psychology* (Vol. 31). Palo Alto, CA: Annual Review.

Duncan, O. D. (1975). *Introduction to structural equation models.* New York: Academic.

Joreskog, K. G., & Sorbom, D. (1979). *Advances in factor analysis and structural equation models.* Cambridge, MA: Abt.

Wright, S. (1934). The method of path coefficients. *Annals of Mathematical Statistics, 5,* 161–215.

JOHN BERGAN
University of Arizona

MULTIPLE REGRESSION
REGRESSION (STATISTICAL)

PATH-REFERENCED ASSESSMENT

Path-referenced assessment (Bergan, 1981, 1986, Bergan, Stone, & Feld, 1985) is a new approach that references ability to position in a developmental sequence. The path-referenced approach has been applied in the Head Start Measures Battery (Bergan & Smith, 1984; Stone & Lane, 1991), a set of six cognitive scales designed to assist in planning learning experiences to promote the development of Head Start children. Within the path-referenced framework, ability is defined as a latent (unobserved) variable estimated from overt performance on test items. The ordering of skills in a developmental sequence is indicated by variations in item difficulty. Items of low difficulty reflect tasks related to lower levels of development, whereas items of high difficulty are associated with higher levels of development. The examinee taking a path-referenced test obtains a latent ability score referred to position in a developmental sequence and used to indicate the probability of performing the various tasks in the sequence correctly. For example, a child taking the math scale of the Head Start Measure Battery might receive a latent ability score indicating high probabilities of performing simple counting tasks correctly and low probabilities of performing more complex addition tasks correctly.

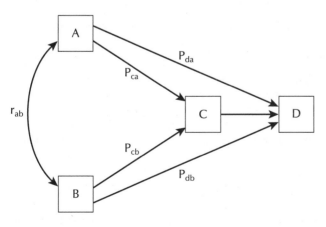

Path diagram.

The path-referenced approach applies latent trait models (Bock & Aitkin, 1981; Lord, 1980) to the problem of referencing ability to position in a developmental sequence. The general latent trait model asserts that the probability of performing a test item correctly is a function of latent ability and certain item parameters. Item parameters that may be reflected in a latent trait model include item difficulty, item discrimination (which gives the strength of the relationship of the item to the underlying latent ability), and a guessing parameter. Latent ability and item difficulty are placed on the same scale in the latent trait model. The path-referenced approach uses the latent ability parameter to estimate an individual's ability, described as his or her developmental level. Item difficulty parameters are used to quantify developmental sequences. The fact that latent ability and item difficulty are on the same scale is used to reference developmental level to position in a developmental sequence. For example, suppose that a child taking a math test including a set of counting items receives a developmental level score of 50. Assume that the difficulty of counting to 5 was 48 and the difficulty of counting to 10 was 52. The child's position in the counting sequence would lie between counting to 5 and counting to 10.

The construction of path-referenced tests requires the testing of hypotheses about the developmental sequencing of skills constituting an ability. The hypothesis testing orientation links path-referenced assessment to cognitive research and theory. Embretson (1985) has pointed out that psychometric practice generally is far removed from the hypothesis testing tradition of cognitive psychology. Hypothesis testing is typically restricted to studies of test validity and does not include the testing of hypotheses about items based on assumptions about underlying cognitive processes. The construction of developmental sequences in path-referenced tests requires that hypotheses be advanced related to the cognitive processes associated with tasks in a sequence. In particular, the demands associated with the processes involved in task performance must be identified so that the hypothesized ordering of skills in a sequence can be established. The sequence must then be empirically validated. Cognitive theory and research provide the basis for forming hypotheses about sequencing.

Path-referenced assessment differs in significant ways from both norm-referenced assessment and criterion-referenced assessment. Norm-referenced assessment references test performance to position in a norm group. An ability score is given indicating where the individual stands in the group. Ability is defined in terms of group position. In the path-referenced approach, ability is estimated from test performance using a latent trait model. Latent ability is then referenced to position in a developmental sequence. Path referencing indicates where the individual is in a sequence and in so doing specifies the competencies that have been mastered in the past and those that lie ahead as development progresses.

Criterion-referenced assessment references test performance to the mastery of objectives (Glaser, 1963; Nitko, 1980). The objectives may or may not reflect tasks that are sequenced (Nitko, 1980). Although latent trait models have been used in criterion-referenced assessment (Nitko, 1980), they have not been integrated into the theory underlying criterion-referenced tests. The criterion-referenced approach ignores the ability construct altogether. Overt test performance is linked directly to the mastery of objectives. In path-referenced assessment, overt performance is used to estimate ability. Ability is then related to position in a developmental sequence and used to establish the probability of correct performance of tasks in the sequence. Use of the ability construct requires that individual skills be part of an empirically validated system of knowledge. Each skill in the system contributes to ability. When one teaches a set of skills that are part of a knowledge system, ability is affected. The educator operating from a path-referenced perspective is concerned with teaching ability. The mastery of specific objectives is related to ability. The educator operating from a criterion-referenced framework is concerned with the mastery of objectives. No assumptions are made about the relationship of objectives to ability.

Path-referenced tests may be used in a number of ways. One major use has to do with the management of instruction. Information on path position can be used in establishing individualized learning experiences in educational settings. For example, the Head Start Measures Battery is used by teachers in the Head Start program to provide individualized learning experiences for children. Teachers use planning guides reflecting skills measured by the battery to plan learning experiences appropriate to each child's developmental level in each of the content areas measured by the battery.

A second use of path-referenced assessment involves placement in a special program. Norm-referenced instruments are typically used in making placement decisions. However, path-referenced instruments also may make a useful contribution in determining placement. The major goal of placement is typically to provide a program that is appropriate to the learning needs of the student. To assist the decision-making process, information associated with path position can be related to information about the kinds of learning opportunities available in a special program. A decision to place would imply that learning opportunities congruent with path position can be provided better in the special program than in other available alternatives.

A third use of path-referenced instruments involves evaluating learner progress. Path-referenced instruments provide quantitative ability scores reflecting a continuous ability scale. Gains can be described in terms of the difference between pretest and posttest ability. Path-referenced instruments are better suited to measuring gains than frequently used norm-referenced technology because path-referenced scores do not depend on group position (Bergan, in press). Moreover, since path-referenced ability scores are linked to path position, it is possible to determine changes in the performance of specific skills that accompany progress.

A fourth important use of path-referenced instruments has to do with curriculum design. Path-referenced instruments can provide information about the structure of knowledge in specific content areas. For example, a path-referenced math scale may provide information on the developmental sequencing of math skills. Information on the sequencing of skills can be used in formulating curriculum sequences in math. It should be noted that this does not imply that the sequence of instruction should be the same as the sequence of development.

Because the path-referenced approach is new, it is too early to specify the full variety of applications that it may find in assessment. However, it is worth noting that the need for assessment providing information related to skill sequences has been recognized for many years. This need was thoroughly articulated in Gagne's (1962, 1970, 1977) work. Latent trait technology affords a practical approach to the construction of assessment instruments that are developmental in character. Latent trait technology has been widely used in assessment (Hambleton, 1983), and it is reasonable to expect that it will find increasing application in the assessment of development.

REFERENCES

Bergan, J. R. (1980). The structural analysis of behavior: An alternative to the learning hierarchy model. *Review of Educational Research, 50,* 225–246.

Bergan, J. R. (1981). Path-referenced assessment in school psychology. In T. R. Kratochwill (Ed.), *Advances in school psychology* (Vol. 1). Hillsdale, NJ: Erlbaum.

Bergan, J. R. (1986). Path-referenced assessment: A guide for instructional management. In C. A. Maher (Ed.), *Special services in the schools.* New York: Haworth.

Bergan, J. R., & Smith, A. N. (Eds.). (1984). *Head Start Measures Battery.* Washington, DC: Department of Health and Human Services.

Bergan, J. R., Stone, C. A., & Feld, J. K. (1985). Path-referenced evaluation of individual differences. In C. R. Reynolds & V. L. Willson (Eds.), *Methodological and statistical advances in the study of individual differences.* New York: Plenum.

Bock, R. D., & Aitkin, M. (1981). Marginal maximum likelihood estimation of item parameters: Application of an algorithm. *Psychometrika, 46,* 443–459.

Embretson, S. E. (Ed.). (1985). *Test-design: Developments in psychology and psychometrics.* Orlando, FL: Academic.

Gagne, R. M. (1962). The acquisition of knowledge. *Psychological Review, 69,* 355–365.

Gagne, R. M. (1970). *The conditions of learning* (2nd ed.). New York: Holt, Rinehart, & Winston.

Gagne, R. M. (1977). *The conditions of learning* (3rd ed.). New York: Holt, Rinehart, & Winston.

Glaser, R. (1963). Instructional technology and the measurement of learning outcomes: Some questions. *American Psychologist, 18,* 519–521.

Hambleton, R. K. (Ed.). (1983). *Applications of item response theory.* Vancouver, British Columbia: Educational Research Institute of British Columbia.

Hambleton, R. K., & Eignor, D. R. (1979). *A practitioner's guide to criterion referenced test development, validation, and test score usage.* Washington, DC: National Institute of Education and Department of Health, Education, and Welfare.

Lord, F. M. (1980). *Applications of item response theory to practical testing problems.* Hillsdale, NJ: Erlbaum.

Nitko, A. J. (1980). Distinguishing the many varieties of criterion-referenced tests. *Review of Educational Research, 50,* 461–485.

Stone, C. A., & Lane, S. (1991). Use of restricted item response theory models for examining the stability of item parameter estimates over time. *Applied Measurements in Education, 4*(2), 125–141.

JOHN R. BERGAN
University of Arizona

ASSESSMENT
DEVELOPMENTAL DELAYS
HEAD START

PATTERNING

Patterning is also known as the Doman-Delacato treatment method for children with neurological disabilities. The center for the treatment program is located in Philadelphia under the name Institutes for the Achievement of Human Potential. The central theory of the Doman-Delacato treatment method is the neurological organization of the individual. The theory posits that the individual progresses through four neurological developmental stages: medulla and spinal cord, pons, midbrain, and cortex. The stages finalize in hemispheric dominance. The theory further proposes that mankind develops in an orderly manner. The rationale stresses that an individual's development in mobility, vision, audition, and language follows specific neurological stages that are correlated with anatomical progress. In this treatment method, a specific program of patterning is developed for each client. The patterning features definite time sequences for selective exercises that can be imposed either actively or passively on the nervous system. It is claimed that these exercises lead to improvement in the sensory motor functions of the individual.

The Doman-Delacato treatment was popular during the 1960s. Advocates of the treatment program have reported success with a wide range of disabilities, including mental retardation, brain damage, learning disabilities, physical handicaps, aphasia, language disorders, and dyslexia. Numerous reports from professionals, paraprofessionals, and parents have confirmed the success of the treatment program. The widespread acceptance of neurological exercises was enhanced through articles published in popular magazines such as *Good Housekeeping* and *Reader's Digest.*

Medical terms, educators, and persons serving in the human services field have studied, evaluated, and researched the claims of the advocates of neurological organization theories. The numerous studies and carefully controlled research reviews do not support the purported achievements of the patterning approach.

REFERENCES

Bower, G. (1966). *Neurophysiology of learning* (3rd ed.). New York: Appleton-Century-Crofts.

Doman, G. (1966). *Neurological organization and reading.* Springfield, IL: Thomas.

Glass, G., & Robbins, M. (1967). A critique of experiments on the role of neurological organizations in reading performance. *Reading Research Quarterly, 3,* 5–51.

Money, J. (Ed.). (1962). *Reading disabilities: Progress and research needs in dyslexia.* Baltimore, MD: Johns Hopkins Press.

Robbins, M. (1966). A study of the validity of Delacato's theory of neurological organization. *Exceptional Children, 32*(8), 517–523.

PAUL C. RICHARDSON
Elwyn Institutes

NEURODEVELOPMENTAL THERAPY
NEUROLOGICAL ORGANIZATION
NEUROPSYCHOLOGY

PDR

See PHYSICIANS' DESK REFERENCE.

PEABODY DEVELOPMENTAL MOTOR SCALES (PDMS)

The Peabody Developmental Scales (PDMS; 1983) is an early childhood motor development test for children birth through 7 years 11 months. The instrument includes a Gross-Motor Scale, which tests reflexes, balance, nonlocomotor, locomotor, and receipt and propulsion of objects; and a Fine-Motor Scale, which tests grasping, hand use, eye-hand coordination, and finger dexterity. The Gross-Motor Scale contains 170 items divided into 17 age levels, with 10 items at each level. The Fine-Motor Scale contains 112 items divided into 16 age levels, with 6 or 8 items at

each level. Items are scored on a three-point system that distinguishes among mastered skills, emerging skills, and skills clearly beyond the child's reach.

The PDMS was normed on 617 children that were representative of the nation as a whole with regard to gender, race, ethnicity, geographic region, and urban/rural residence. Raw scores are converted into scaled scores (z-scores, T-scores, developmental motor quotients) and age scores.

Reviewers (Compton, 1996; Reed, 1985; Venn, 1986) have been generally complimentary of the PDMS, finding the instrument a comprehensive measure of a fundamental aspect of child development. Weaknesses noted include the cumbersome nature of test administration.

REFERENCES

Compton, C. (1996). *A guide to 100 tests for special education.* Upper Saddle River, NJ: Globe Fearon.

Folio, M. R., & Fewell, R. R. (1983). *Peabody developmental motor scales and activity cards.* Austin, TX: Pro-Ed.

Reed, H. B. C. (1985). Review of the Peabody Developmental Motor Scales. In J. V. Mitchell, Jr. (Ed.). *The ninth mental measurements yearbook* (p. 1119). Lincoln: Buros Institute of Mental Measurements, University of Nebraska Press.

Venn, J. J. (1986). Review of the Peabody Developmental Motor Scales. In D. J. Keyser & R. C. Sweetland (Eds.), *Test critiques: Volume V* (pp. 310–313). Austin, TX: Pro-Ed.

TADDY MADDOX
Pro-Ed

PEABODY INDIVIDUAL ACHIEVEMENT TEST–REVISED/NORMATIVE UPDATE

The Peabody Individual Achievement Test–Revised (PIAT–R; Markwardt, 1989) is an individually-administered measure of academic achievement designed for children and adults, ages 5 to 22. The PIAT–R assesses six academic content areas with the following subtests: General Information, Reading Recognition, Reading Comprehension, Mathematics, Spelling, and Written Expression. The subtests are combined to yield a Total Reading score, Total Test score, and a Written Language Composite score. Administration time is approximately 60 minutes.

All subtests except for Written Expression are dichotomously scored. Detailed scoring criteria are provided for both levels of the Written Expression subtest. All subtests except Written Expression yield standard scores, percentile ranks, age equivalents, and grade equivalents. Computerized scoring software is also available for the PIAT–R.

The PIAT–R was recently renormed, and is referred to

as the PIAT–R Normative Update (PIAT–R/NU; Markwardt, 1997). A sample of 3,429 children stratified according to 1994 U.S. Census data comprised the standardization sample. Reliability of the PIAT–R/NU was demonstrated with split-half reliability coefficients of the subtests ranging from the low to mid 0.90s. The PIAT–R/NU was shown to be stable with test-retest values in the low to mid 0.90s. Validity was established by demonstrating strong correlations to other achievement measures such as the K-TEA (Kaufman & Kaufman, 1985), KeyMath–R (Connolly, 1988), and PPVT–R (Dunn & Dunn, 1981).

Reviews of the PIAT–R are generally quite favorable. Rogers (1992) comments that the test appears to be a useful instrument to both practitioners in the schools and to researchers. The subtest that continues to be the most difficult to score is the Written Expression subtest. The PIAT–R manual provides specific categories with many examples for scoring, but many examiners may find it difficult to categorize an individual child's writing nonetheless. This particular subtest is one that could utilize further research.

REFERENCES

Connolly, A. J. (1988). *KeyMath Revised: A Diagnostic Inventory of Essential Mathematics*. Circle Pines, MN: American Guidance Service.

Dunn, L. M., & Dunn, L. M. (1981). *Examiner's manual for the Peabody Picture Vocabulary Test—Revised edition*. Circle Pines, MN: American Guidance Service.

Kaufman, A. S., & Kaufman, N. L. (1985). *Kaufman Test of Educational Achievement*. Circle Pines, MN: American Guidance Service.

Markwardt, F. C. (1989). *Peabody Individual Achievement Test—Revised*. Circle Pines, MN: American Guidance Service.

Markwardt, F. C. (1997). *Peabody Individual Achievement Test-Revised/Normative Update*. Circle Pines, MN: American Guidance Service.

Rogers, B. G. (1992). Review of the Peabody Individual Achievement Test-Revised. In J. J. Kramer & J. C. Conoley (Eds.), *The eleventh mental measurements yearbook*. Lincoln, NE: Buros Institute of Mental Measurements.

ELIZABETH O. LICHTENBERGER
The Salk Institute

ACHIEVEMENT TESTS
ASSESSMENT

PEABODY LANGUAGE DEVELOPMENT KITS—REVISED

The Peabody language Development Kits—Revised (PLDK–R; Dunn et al., 1981) are multilevel programs designed to facilitate development of oral language in young children. The areas targeted by the program are receptive, associative, and expressive language, and cognitive skills. The goals of the PLDK–R are to stimulate overall language skills in standard English and to advance children's cognitive skills about one year per level. Rather than training children in selected psycholinguistic processes, the PLDK–R focuses on overall language development.

The PLDK–R contains four levels of various activities emphasizing the skills of reception through sight, hearing, and touch. Conceptualization is emphasized through divergent, convergent, and associative thinking, and expression is stressed through vocal and motor behavior. The program may target language development in the following populations: children with limited proficiency in standard English; children in preschool through third grade; children from non-English speaking backgrounds; and children with a variety of cognitive and linguistic disabilities, including mild to moderate mental retardation, hearing impairments, learning disabilities, and central nervous system disorders (Dunn et al., 1981).

Level P of the PLDK–R provides practice in syntactical and grammatical structure, logical thinking, and the labeling of language. The activities are designed primarily for 4- and 5-year-olds. There are two manuals that contain 360 lessons with two activities each. Two puppet characters are used to encourage participation and to focus attention on the activities. One puppet, P. Mooney, appears regularly in lessons that involve describing, naming, talking, and following directions, while the second puppet, Zoey, is used in lessons that involve thinking, imagining, and problem-solving activities.

Level 1 of the PDLK–R is designed for use with 6-year-olds. Oral language and cognitive development (brainstorming and problem solving) activities center around a puppet character, Peabella, a world-famous bloodhound detective. Peabella teaches problem-solving skills and is assisted by Shiner, a black-eyed puppy who is frequently confused but capable of learning. The children are able both to teach him and learn from his mistakes.

Level 2 of the PLDK–R is designed primarily for 7-year-olds. It emphasizes further stimulation of cognitive processes through various problem-solving and brainstorming activities. Two space-age puppets, Pippa and Ariel, encourage creative thinking and reasoning.

The third level of the PLDK–R is designed for 8-year-olds. All aspects of thinking and reasoning are stimulated in the Level 3 activities. Formulation of ideas and concepts are fostered through opportunities for creativity. Jayoh and Debya are central characters who, by means of a magical microphone, travel forward and backward in time.

The PLDK–R is a self-contained, comprehensive program designed to stimulate oral language and cognitive development for a diverse group of children. Speech-language pathologists, special education teachers, teachers of English as a second language, and regular-education teachers, will find the program beneficial.

REFERENCE

Dunn, L., Smith, J., Dunn, L., Horton, K., & Smith, D. (1981). *Peabody Language Development Kits—Revised Manuals Level P, 1, 2, and 3*. Circle Pines, MN: American Guidance Service.

SUSAN MAHANNA-BODEN
TRACY CALPIN CASTLE
Eastern Kentucky University
First edition

ELIZABETH O. LICHTENBERGER
The Salk Institute
Second edition

ORAL LANGUAGE OF THE HANDICAPPED
ORAL VERSUS MANUAL COMMUNICATION

PEABODY PICTURE VOCABULARY TEST— THIRD EDITION

The third edition of the Peabody Picture Vocabulary Test (PPVT–III; Dunn & Dunn, 1997) is similar to the original and revised editions published in 1959 and 1981. The PPVT–III is an individually-administered test of receptive vocabulary (of standard English) for children and adults ages 2.5 to 90. This untimed test requires examinees to examine four black and white pictures and choose which one best represents the meaning of a stimulus word that is presented orally by the examiner. Only nonverbal responses are required. The test begins with four training items and then test items are presented in order of increasing difficulty. Testing time is typically between 11 and 12 minutes, as individuals are administered only the item sets that are of appropriate difficulty for them. Items that are far too easy or too difficult are not administered. The test provides standard scores (with a mean of 100 and standard deviation of 15), percentile ranks, age equivalents, and descriptive categories.

Although there are many similarities between the 1981 Peabody and the PPVT–III, there are also some notable differences. For example, the amount of test items for each form increased to 204, test items were grouped into 17 sets of 12 in each form (leading to a change in basal and ceiling rules), new illustrations were included to modernize the content, and the kit was packaged in a way that facilitates transporting test materials.

The PPVT–III is available in two parallel forms. The test was standardized on a stratified sample of 2,725 persons, including 2,000 children and adolescents and 725 adults over age 19. The alternate forms, reliabilities for the PPVT–III standard scores ranged from .88 to .96, with a median value of .94. The internal consistency values ranged from .86 to .97, with a median reliability of .94. Scores were also very stable, with all values in the .90s. The validity of the PPVT–III was examined by correlating its scores with other measures of intelligence and verbal ability. For example, the correlation between the PPVT–III and the Verbal Scale of the Wechsler Intelligence Scale for Children-Third Edition (WISC–III; Wechsler, 1991) was .91; between the PPVT–III and the Vocabulary Scale of the Kaufman Brief Intelligence Test (K-BIT; Kaufman & Kaufman, 1993), the correlation was .82; and between the PPVT–III and the Oral and Written Language Scales (OWLS: Carrow-Woolfolk, 1995), the correlation was .75.

The PPVT–III is a solid measure of receptive vocabulary. The revisions made from the last version have made scoring easier because of the new basal and ceiling rules. This test is an easy-to-administer task that is a good part of a comprehensive battery. However, it is not a measure of intelligence and should not be used alone as a criterion for placement or diagnosis of a language disorder.

REFERENCES

Carrow-Woolfolk, E. (1995). *Oral and Written Language Scales: Listening Comprehension and Oral Expression*. Circle Pines, MN: American Guidance Service.

Dunn, L. M., & Dunn, L. M. (1997). *Examiner's manual for the Peabody Picture Vocabulary Test—Third Edition*. Circle Pines, MN: American Guidance Service.

A training item from the Peabody Picture Vocabulary Test III. The examiner says a word corresponding to one of the four pictures, and the child points to the appropriate picture of successful.

Kaufman, A. S., & Kaufman, N. L. (1990). *Kaufman Brief Intelligence Test*. Circle Pines, MN: American Guidance Service.

Wechsler, D. (1991). *Wechsler Intelligence Scale for Children-Third Edition*. San Antonio, TX: The Psychological Corporation.

ELIZABETH O. LICHTENBERGER
The Salk Institute

REFERENCE

Woodcock, R. W., Clark, C. R., & Davies, C. O. (1969). *The Peabody Rebus Reading Program*. Circle Pines, MN: American Guidance Service.

SUSAN MAHANNA-BODEN
TRACY CALPIN CASTLE
Eastern Kentucky University

PEABODY REBUS READING PROGRAM

The Peabody Rebus Reading Program is a representational symbol system designed to teach early reading skills to children. A basic vocabulary of pictographic symbols known as rebuses represent entire words or parts of words; they provide a foundation for developing reading and comprehension skills. Rebus symbols may be classified into four basic categories: combination symbols, which primarily depict objects or actions (e.g., ball = ⊘); relational symbols, which depict locations or directions (e.g., in = ⊡ , on = ⊡); and abstract symbols, which are primarily arbitrary symbols representing ideas such as "at" = ⟍ and "too" = ⟍). The fourth category combines symbols with alphabet letters, affixes (e.g., doing = ⟍ ing), and other rebuses (e.g., into = ⊡ ⟍).

The Peabody Rebus Reading Program includes two levels. The reading level is designed as an alternative, complementary, or supplementary program for traditional readiness programs (Woodcock, Clark, & Davies, 1969). Two workbooks each containing 384 exercise frames are introduced to children. As a student marks an answer using a moistened pencil eraser, a special "invisible ink" indicates the accuracy of the selection. On completion of this level, a child will have developed several prereading skills such as matching spoken words to printed words, reading in a left-to right direction, and comprehending rebus words and sentences. At the second level, the transition level, students progress from reading rebuses to reading spelled words. Teaching materials include one workbook and two rebus readers, emphasizing systematic substitution of spelled words for rebuses. Initially, the spelled words are paired with their corresponding rebus symbols. The symbols are gradually faded to effect transition to standard orthography. On completion of the transition level, a student will be able to read 122 spelled words, sound out words, recognize punctuation, and read stories.

The Peabody Rebus Reading Program is designed to introduce children to reading by first having them learn a vocabulary of rebuses in the place of spelled words. The program has additional application for facilitating the development of language skills.

PEACE CORPS, SPECIAL EDUCATION IN

The Peace Corps is a volunteer program that was established in 1961 by President John Kennedy. Its goal is to help the people of interested countries and areas of the world in meeting their needs for trained manpower through the help of American volunteers. The promotion of a better understanding of Americans on the part of the people served, and a better understanding of other people on the part of Americans, are also basic goals of the program (Shute, 1986). During the 1960s, goodwill among nations was advocated by early Peace Corps participants. During the 1970s, individuals in both the host countries and the United States recognized the need for technically skilled individuals familiar with local needs in food, job, health, and schooling areas. Thus in recent years, programs for volunteers cover such diverse assignments as work in agriculture, industrial arts/skilled trades, and health and education (Peace Corps, 1986). Over 5200 volunteers in 63 countries now offer their services in three major world regions: Africa (Sub-Saharan Africa), Inter-America (Central and South America), and NANEAP (North Africa, Near East, Asia, and the Pacific). Training is provided to the volunteers in the language, history, customs and social-political systems of the host country.

The Peace Corps offers a program for individuals interested in special education. Volunteers can be assigned specific placements working with children displaying mental retardation, learning disabilities, emotional disturbances, blindness or visual impairments, deafness or hearing impairments, multihandicaps, or speech problems. Assignments in special education cover teacher training and direct classroom teaching. Volunteers in the teacher-training program conduct needs assessments, organize and implement workshops and seminars, develop teaching aids using locally available materials, give demonstration lessons, establish criteria for evaluation, observe teachers, and monitor teachers' progress. Those participating in the direct-teaching program help to screen and assess the special child's abilities and progress; teach classes in academics, extracurricula areas, and self-help skills; and structure activities to facilitate interactions of the special child with the family and community.

To qualify as a special education volunteer, an individual must be a U.S. citizen and be at least 18 years of age. There are also medical and legal criteria. Finally, the special education volunteer should possess a four-year degree with some preservice teaching in special education (actual teaching experience is preferred but not obligatory). All volunteers receive a monthly allowance to cover housing, food, and spending money. On completion of the two-year service commitment required of all volunteers, an allotment for every month served is provided as a readjustment allowance on return to the United States (Shute, 1986).

REFERENCES

Peace Corps. (1986). *The toughest job you'll ever love.* Washington, DC: ACTION.

Shute, N. (1986). *After a turbulent youth, the Peace Corps comes of age.* Washington, DC: ACTION.

LAWRENCE O'SHEA
University of Florida

COMMUNITY BASED SERVICES
VOLUNTARY AGENCIES

PEDIATRICIAN

A pediatrician is a medical doctor or osteopathic physician who has completed a residency in pediatrics. In addition to the medical care of the newborn, infant, child, and adolescent, the pediatrician is trained in many areas important to the overall growth and development of the child: motor development and coordination, sensory development, psychosocial maturation, and moral and cognitive development.

A wide variety of medical conditions may handicap a child's ability to learn. Some may be due to hereditary factors. Others may be prenatal and relate to the health of the mother or to direct dangers to the fetus such as infections or drugs. Some may be perinatal, occurring during or immediately following the birth process. This group includes complications resulting from the mechanics of labor and delivery. Some conditions may occur or be diagnosed only after the infant has gone home. Thus it is clear that the pediatrician has an important role in special education.

First, the pediatrician may be able to diagnose a condition that could have an adverse effect on the child's ability to learn and estimate the approximate extent of the handicap. Based on this and other relevant information, a plan for intervention and education can be developed. Second, school performance may be the first valid indication that a child is not developing normally. A comprehensive pediatric examination is a vital part of the overall assessment of such developmental problems so as to identify or rule out contributing medical factors, such as visual problems. If needed, detailed remedial measures may then be implemented (Berlin, 1976).

When necessary, the pediatrician can help by referral of the child to other specialists whose expertise may be needed to identify or treat the precise problems in question. Examples of medical specialists to whom such referral may be made include ophthalmologists for disorders of the eyes, neurologists for conditions related to the brain or other parts of the central nervous system, and ear, nose, and throat specialists for children with hearing impairments. Children's health problems may manifest themselves at school. If there is a medication or other treatment program in force, teachers can both monitor and encourage compliance with this program. Over 50% of all American parents have sought help from a pediatrician for school-related problems (American Academy of Pediatrics, 1978). For this reason, it is important that pediatricians and teachers maintain open lines of communication so that they may assist one another in helping children with both school-related and health problems.

REFERENCES

American Academy of Pediatrics. (1978). *The future of pediatric education.* Washington, DC: Author.

Berlin, C. M. (1975). Medical bases of exceptional conditions. In R. M. Smith & J. T. Neisworth (Eds.), *The exceptional child: A functional approach.* New York: McGraw-Hill.

WILLIAM J. SHAW
LOGAN WRIGHT
University of Oklahoma

PEDIATRIC ACQUIRED IMMUNE DEFICIENCY SYNDROME (AIDS)

Since the first cases of Acquired Immune Deficiency Syndrome (AIDS) were reported in 1981, the human immunodeficiency virus (HIV) that causes AIDS has presented an epidemic unknown in modern history. It has been estimated that there are 1,500,000 children with AIDS worldwide. Between 32,000 and 38,000 HIV-infected children will have been born in the US by the year 2000. In the United States, 6,309 cases of pediatric AIDS have been reported to the Centers for Disease Control to date. There were an estimated 12,000 children living with HIV in the US as of January, 1994 (Children's Hope Foundation, 1998).

It is predicted that by the year 2000 in the US, between 80,000 and 100,000 uninfected children will be born to mothers who will die from HIV. Approximately 25% of infants born to HIV-infected mothers each year in the US are born HIV-infected. Approximately 89% of all children with

AIDS are perinatal cases—children who contracted the virus from their mother during pregnancy or birth. Other causes of pediatric AIDS include transmission through breast-feeding, tainted blood transfusions before 1985, and sexual abuse.

The average age for diagnosis of perinatal cases is 4.1. Only 54% of all perinatal cases are diagnosed by the age of 7.

Children with AIDS have special needs and concerns, as the variety of manifestations that occur with pediatric AIDS is larger than with adult AIDS. Children with HIV and AIDS often suffer from central nervous system complications, the inability to combat childhood diseases, and failure of growth and development (Children's Hope Foundation, 1998).

Newborns infected with HIV live an average of less than 18 months. Presently, hemophiliacs represent the largest HIV-positive school age group, but this number is declining due to an increasing safe blood supply (Adams, Marcontel, & Price, 1989). The school environment has one of the lowest exposure rates of HIV in terms of normal contact among children. This also applies for school personnel (Adams, Marcontel, & Price, 1989). However, 25 states have mandated health education prior to graduation, and specifically education on HIV transmission and prevention (Kerr, 1989). The CDC and American Academy of Pediatrics have developed guidelines for school and day care attendance. The guidelines call for consideration of exclusion of the HIV-infected child from regular classrooms or group day care only if the child lacks control of body secretion; practices frequent hand- and object-mouthing behavior; is known to be a frequent biter; or has oozing skin lesions (Black & Jones, 1988).

Curricula on HIV/AIDS education for special education populations have being focusing on defining health and prevention strategies (New Mexico State Department of Education, 1991). Unfortunately, it appears that very few school districts alter the HIV/AIDS curriculum to meet the needs of students with learning issues (Strosnider & Henke, 1992).

To date, nearly every court decision regarding the status of HIV-infected students and personnel attending school, has allowed the individual to stay in school in the absence of evidence that HIV can be spread by casual contact (Helm, 1989). Therefore, it is essential that school boards, administrators, and general personnel are thoroughly educated and repeatedly updated with information about AIDS (Rogers, 1989). CDC guidelines recommend a team approach to decisions regarding type of educational setting for HIV-infected children. The team should be composed of the child's physician, public health personnel, parents, and personnel from the educational settings (Kirkland & Ginther, 1988). One other factor that should be addressed within the team approach is the involvement of the school's administration, counselor, psychologist, and

social worker in providing emotional and social support to the HIV-infected child and children who make up his or her peer or support group, or classmates (Walker, 1991). It is crucial that at this stage of development of the AIDS disease, health policies and disease control concerns do not violate the individual's rights to privacy (Bruder, 1995) and an appropriate and humane education. Although to date, there have been no court decisions at the federal level on the application of the Education for All Handicapped Children Act or the Rehabilitation Act to children suffering from AIDS (Kirkland & Ginther, 1988), such decisions are most surely in the future of our educational institutions.

REFERENCES

Adams, R. M., Marcontel, M., & Price, A. L. (1989). The impact of AIDS on school health services. *Journal of School Health, 58,* (8), pp. 341–343.

Bruder, M. B. (1995). The challenge of pediatric AIDS: A framework for early childhood special education. *Topics in Early Childhood Special Education, 15*(1), 83–99.

Children's Hope Foundation. (1998). *Children and Aids.* http://www.childrenshope.org.

Kerr, D. L. (1989). Forum addresses HIV education for children and youth with special needs. *Journal of School Health, 59*(3), p. 139.

Kirkland, M., & Ginther, D. (1988). Acquired immune deficiency syndrome in children: Medical, legal and school related issues. *School Psychology Review, 17*(12), pp. 304–310.

New Mexico State Department of Education. (1991). *HIV/AIDS guidelines for special education populations.* Sante Fe; NM: Author.

Strosnider, R., & Henke, J. (1992). *Delivery of AIDS prevention education to students with disabilities: Implications for preservice education.* (ERIC Clearinghouse No. EC303726)

Walker, G. E. (1991). Pediatric AIDS: Toward an ecosystemic treatment model. *Family Systems Medicine, 9*(3), 211–227.

ELAINE FLETCHER-JANZEN
University of Northern Colorado

PEDIATRIC PSYCHOLOGIST

The past two decades have been a period of significant professional growth for pediatric psychology. In general, the number of psychologists in medical settings has increased rapidly and the scope of their activities has widened enormously. Wright (1967) first used the term pediatric psychologist to refer to "any psychologist who finds himself dealing with children in a medical setting which is nonpsychiatric in nature" (p. 323). A year later, in 1968, the Society of Pediatric Psychology was founded; it eventually became a section of the Division of Clinical Psychology of the American Psychological Association. The *Journal of Pedi-*

atric Psychology was established by the society in 1976; it has since become a major source of clinical and research publication for the field (Wright, 1993).

There are three major types of pediatric settings in which pediatric psychologists work: (1) the pediatric hospital or multispecialty general hospital inpatient unit, (2) the ambulatory care facility (outpatient clinic or private pediatric office), and (3) the comprehensive care center (e.g., kidney dialysis center, burn hospital) for chronic illnesses or chronic medical conditions, which may provide outpatient and/or inpatient services. The primary clinical responsibilities of the pediatric psychologist in these settings are basically twofold: to provide direct psychological services to patients and to consult to a variety of pediatric medical subspecialties including nephrology, cardiology, hematology-oncology, endocrinology, neurology, genetics, and surgery.

The longest history of association between psychology and primary health care is that between psychologists and pediatricians. This association has been strengthened recently by several groups involved in the training and certification of pediatricians. First, the educational role of pediatric psychologists has been highlighted by recommendations of the Task Force on Pediatric Education (American Academy of Pediatrics, 1978), which placed an increasing emphasis on training in the area of behavioral pediatrics. Second, the Committee on Psychosocial Aspects of Child and Family Health of the American Academy of Pediatrics (1982) noted the important role of the pediatrician in the evaluation and treatment of common behavioral and developmental disorders as well as somatic disorders with psychosocial etiology. This committee also stressed the value of a collaborative relationship between pediatricians and clinical psychologists in the treatment of these problems. Therefore, an increasing recognition of the role of health-related behaviors in the prevention, development, and maintenance or exacerbation of illness has helped to foster the expansion of pediatric psychology as a subspecialty within clinical psychology.

Pediatric psychologists work with a wide range of health-related and developmental problems in children and adolescents (Magrab, 1978; Varni, 1983). They are called on to deal with many common childhood problems and issues of child-rearing that are presented frequently to the pediatrician. Among these common problem areas are eating and sleeping difficulties, toilet training and bed wetting, learning and developmental disorders, and problems in child management.

Over the past 20 years, pediatricians have increasingly focused on the prevention of disease and the management of chronic childhood illnesses for which there are no known cures, such as cystic fibrosis, sickle cell disease, and juvenile diabetes. This shift in the practice of pediatrics has placed a new emphasis on patients' problems of daily living, issues of quality of life, and problems related to compliance with therapeutic regimens. It has further supported the active involvement of pediatric psychologists in the comprehensive delivery of health care to children.

Many children present in medical settings with physical symptoms of unclear origin or with symptoms having significant psychosocial components, including headaches, chronic abdominal pain, and failure to thrive. The psychosocial concomitants of physical illness in children represent a major source of referrals to pediatric psychologists.

Behavioral treatment procedures have shown considerable promise as an approach to alleviating or reducing the symptomatic behaviors associated with a number of somatic disorders in children (Siegel, 1983). Pediatric psychologists have used a variety of behavioral techniques such as biofeedback, relaxation training, and various operant conditioning procedures to successfully modify the symptoms associated with such disorders as asthma, ruminative vomiting, and enuresis.

Pediatric psychologists have also been concerned with the prevention of health-related problems. Among the problems that have received considerable attention in this area are the reduction of stress associated with hospitalization and painful medical procedures and the management of behaviors (e.g., overeating) that are associated with the development of physical disorders such as high blood pressure.

Finally, pediatric psychologists who work in hospital settings are often called upon to provide emotional support to health-care personnel who deal with children having life-threatening conditions. Professional burnout is a significant problem with staff who provide medical care to terminally ill children. The pediatric psychologist may consult with the staff to help them cope with the emotionally draining experiences that they encounter in these settings.

REFERENCES

American Academy of Pediatrics, Committee on Psychosocial Aspects of Child and Family Health. (1982). Pediatrics and the psychosocial aspects of child and family health. *Pediatrics, 79*, 126–127.

American Academy of Pediatrics, Task Force on Pediatric Education. (1978). *The future of pediatric education.* Evanston, IL: American Academy of Pediatrics.

Magrab, P. R. (1978). *Psychological management of pediatric problems.* Baltimore, MD: University Park Press.

Siegel, L. J. (1983). Psychosomatic and psychophysiological disorders. In R. J. Morris & T. R. Kratochwill (Eds.). *The practice of child therapy.* New York: Pergamon.

Varni, J. W. (1983). *Clinical behavioral pediatrics: An interdisciplinary biobehavioral approach.* New York: Pergamon.

Wright, L. (1967). The pediatric psychologist: A role model. *American Psychologist, 22*, 323–325.

Wright, L. (1993). The pediatric psychologist: A role model. In M. C. Roberts and G. Koocher (Eds.), *Readings in pediatric psychology*. New York: Plenum.

LAWRENCE J. SIEGEL
*University of Texas Medical
Branch at Galveston*

**PARENT EDUCATION
PEDIATRICIAN
PSYCHOSOCIAL ADJUSTMENT
PSYCHOSOMATIC DISORDERS**

PEDRO DE PONCE

See PONCE DE LEON, PEDRO DE.

PEER RELATIONSHIPS

When the topic of peer relationships is discussed in the literature, it is usually characterized as the interaction of handicapped students with their nonhandicapped classmates. This is an important and relevant topic in light of the impact IDEA has had in ensuring that students with disabilities be educated in the regular classroom whenever appropriate.

Current research suggests that students with disabilities are often not included in many activities in the regular classroom. It has been shown that the classroom teacher sometimes fails to include the handicapped child into many typical academic activities. For example, one study (Brophy & Good, 1974) found that regular classroom teachers tended to initiate more negative interactions with low-status, learning-disabled students than with high-status, nonlearning-disabled students. Other researchers have demonstrated that this type of nonproductive negative interchange between the classroom teacher and the handicapped student will have a significant impact on the relationship between the handicapped child and his or her regular class peers (Weinstein, Marshall, Brattesani, & Middlestadt, 1982). The negative interaction between the handicapped student and the teacher seems to solidify the low status of the low-performing student.

The relationship between handicapped students and their peers is a complex phenomenon that is molded by many factors. Several of the more noteworthy factors are age of the child with disabilities, attitudes and behavior of the classroom teacher, type of handicapping condition affecting the student, self-concept and skill level of the handicapped student, and whether or not the regular class students have been prepared to understand the specific needs of some mainstreamed students. For example, it has been suggested that beginning in the early elementary grades (Rubin & Coplan, 1992), the influence of the peer group increases as the handicapped child gets older. In other words, during the early years of a handicapped child's school experience, parent and teacher acceptance are more important than peer approval or acceptance.

Methods to improve the peer relationships of the handicapped child can be found in the literature. As an example of one such approach, Schwartz (1984) provides a checklist for regular class teachers to follow when preparing for the arrival of a mainstreamed handicapped child. Among other activities, teachers are asked to give regular class peers information about handicapping conditions and allow for any questions students might have. Such procedures help increase the frequency of positive interaction between the handicapped child and his or her peers. This approach is particularly important with physically handicapped students. Some research suggests that the physically handicapped child is the least likely to be accepted by his or her nonhandicapped peers.

REFERENCES

Brophy, J., & Good, T. (1974). *Teacher-student relationships: Causes and consequences*. New York: Holt, Rinehart, & Winston.

Rubin, K. H., & Coplan, R. L. (1992). Peer relationships in childhood. In M. H. Bernstein and M. Lamb (Eds.). *Developmental psychology: An advance textbook* (3rd ed., pp. 519–528). Hillsdale, NJ: Erlbaum.

Schwartz, L. L. (1984). *Exceptional students in the mainstream*. Belmont, CA: Wadsworth.

Weinstein, R. S., Marshall, H. H., Brattaseni, K., & Middlestedt, S. E. (1982). Student perceptions of differential treatment in open and traditional classrooms. *Journal of Educational Psychology, 74,* 679–692.

CRAIG DARCH
Auburn University

**MAINSTREAMING
PEER TUTORING**

PEER TUTORING

Peer and cross-age tutoring procedures have been identified in the literature as having success in the instruction of children with disabilities. Tutoring programs have been successful in improving a wide variety of academic skills. Peer tutors have been effective in teaching math (Bentz & Fuchs, 1996; Johnson & Bailey, 1974) and spelling (Harris, 1973), but have most often been applied for reading skills

(Chaing, Thorpe, & Darch, 1980). Many authors identify the need to carefully prepare children before they perform as tutors (Martella, Marchand-Martella, Young & Macfarlane, 1995; Schloss & Sedlak, 1986). Procedures for preparing children to function as tutors have not been extensively discussed in the literature. There are few sources readily available for a comprehensive description of tutor preparation techniques that have been successfully implemented.

Although there is little research that has been conducted on particular training procedures, anecdotal information leads to the conclusion that carefully designed interactions and tutor preparation are important for the success of a tutoring program. If peer tutoring programs are to be beneficial to everyone involved, the teacher must invest time in the development, implementation, and evaluation of these instructional sessions.

One issue that designers of tutoring programs should consider is the identification of potential peer tutors. This is difficult because research has not given teachers definitive answers as to the characteristics of good peer tutors.

Some studies in special education that have shown tutoring to be effective have older students tutoring younger students (Parson & Heward, 1979). Other reports indicate that large age differences are not critical to an effective peer tutoring program (Dineen, Clark, & Risley, 1977). In fact, one peer tutoring study demonstrated that learning-disabled (LD) elementary-age students were effective in teaching other elementary LD students placed in the same resource room (Chiang, Thorpe, & Darch, 1981). Therefore, based on information currently available, it is safe to conclude that tutor-tutee age difference is not in itself critical to the success of a peer tutorial program.

It appears that tutors can be selected from most special education programs. Research has demonstrated that effective peer tutors can come from either able or less able students. While studies within regular classrooms are common, low-achieving and special classroom students have also been effective tutors (Paine et al., 1983). Several studies have shown higher functioning LD students to be effective tutors for lower functioning LD classmates.

For several reasons, student assignments as tutors can be justified. Tutoring can improve self-concept, be used as a means of practicing previously learned skills, and reinforce academic or social performance. The peer tutoring program can be instrumental in helping special education students develop a more positive attitude and self-image. The success that tutees achieve in these carefully designed programs can contribute to important changes in previously unmotivated students.

REFERENCES

Bentz, J. L., & Fuchs, L. S. (1996). Improving peers' helping behavior to students with learning disabilities mathematics peer tutoring. *Learning Disability Quarterly, 19*(4), 202–215.

Chaing, B., Thorpe, H., & Darch, C. (1980). Effects of cross age tutoring on word recognition performance of learning disabled students. *Learning Disability Quarterly, 3,* 11–19.

Dineen, J. P., Clark, H. B., & Risley, T. R. (1977). Peer tutoring among elementary students: Educational benefits to the tutor. *Journal of Applied Behavior Analysis, 10,* 231–238.

Harris, V. W. (1973). Effects of peer tutoring, homework, and consequences upon the academic performance of elementary school children (Doctoral dissertation, University of Kansas, 1972). *Dissertation Abstracts International, 33,* 11-A, 6175.

Johnson, M., & Bailey, J. S. (1974). Cross-age tutoring: Fifth graders as arithmetic tutors for kindergarten children. *Journal of Applied Behavior Analysis, 7,* 223–232.

Maher, C. A. (1984). Handicapped adolescents as cross age tutors: Program description and evaluation. *Exceptional Children, 51,* 56–63.

Martella, R. C., Marchand-Martella, W. E., Young, K. R., & Macfarlane, C. A. (1995). Determining the collateral effects of peer tutoring training on a student with severe disabilities. *Behavior Modification, 19*(2), 170–191.

Paine, S., Radicchi, J., Rosellini, L., Deutchman, L., & Darch, C. (1983). *Structuring your classroom for academic success.* Champaign, IL: Research.

Parson, L. R., & Heward, W. L. (1979). Training peers to tutor: Evaluation of a tutor training package for primary learning disabled students. *Journal of Applied Behavior Analysis, 12,* 309–310.

Schloss, P., & Sedlak, R. (1986). *Instructional methods for students with learning and behavior problems.* Boston: Allyn & Bacon.

CRAIG DARCH
Auburn University

DIRECT INSTRUCTION
PEER RELATIONSHIPS
SOCIAL SKILLS TRAINING
TEACHER EFFECTIVENESS

PENNSYLVANIA ASSOCIATION FOR RETARDED CITIZENS *v.* PENNSYLVANIA (1972)

Commonly known as the *PARC* decision, the case of the *Pennsylvania Association for Retarded Citizens* v. *Pennsylvania* is one of two landmark court decisions granting educational rights to the handicapped (the other is *Mills* v. *Board of Education of Washington, DC.*) PARC and *Mills* were instrumental in the passage of state and federal laws guaranteeing equal access for the handicapped to all educational programs.

The *PARC* case was a class-action suit (the suit was certified by the court as representing all similarly situated individuals in Pennsylvania) brought by the Pennsylvania Association for Retarded Citizens and 13 mentally retarded students. The suit was brought because three students had been denied attendance in the public schools of Pennsylvania. The case was brought under the equal protection and due process clauses of the Fourteenth Amendment to the U.S. Constitution. In *PARC,* the plaintiffs argued that allowing the state to provide a free public education to some of its citizens while denying other of its citizens the right to attend the same schools or to receive an appropriate education at state expense was unfair and denied equal protection of the law. They also argued that handicapped children were excluded from public education without access to due process. (The Fourteenth Amendment does not deny the ability of a state to deprive a citizen of any fundamental right; however, before a right can be violated, the state must demonstrate a compelling interest and must grant the citizen a hearing and other such protection as may be deemed necessary under the due process clause.)

In deciding for the plaintiffs, the court clearly acknowledged that admitting seriously disturbing, profoundly retarded, physically handicapped children would be difficult and expensive at all levels; however, the court ruled that the interests of the handicapped were protected by the Fourteenth Amendment and that this protection outweighed the difficulties created by providing an education to the handicapped. The decision was extensive in its requirements and many of its provisions are routinely included in present statutes. The *PARC* decision required the state to provide a free, appropriate education to all handicapped children regardless of the nature or extent of their handicaps; to educate handicapped children alongside nonhandicapped children to the extent possible; to conduct an annual census to locate and serve handicapped children; to cease and desist from applying school exclusion laws, including prohibition of serial suspension practices; to notify parents before assessing a child to determine the presence of a handicap and prior to placement in a special education program; to establish procedures to meet the due process requirements of the Fourteenth Amendment should disagreements arise regarding the school's decision about a handicapped child's educational placement or program; to reevaluate handicapped children on a systematic basis; and to pay private school tuition if the school refers a child to a private school or cannot reasonably meet the needs of a handicapped child in a public setting. Later interpretations of the *PARC* decision by other courts have concluded that the schools must also use proven, state-of-the-art teaching methods with the handicapped (under the requirement of providing an appropriate education).

Following the *PARC* decision and the subsequent ruling in *Mills,* a flood of suits came forth arguing for the rights of the handicapped to equal educational opportunities. Few of these cases were even litigated, however, as most states during the period 1972 to 1974 passed and funded legisla-

tion requiring local school districts to provide special education programs for the handicapped.

The *PARC* decision and related cases had a profound effect on special education as currently practiced. *PARC* fostered a rapid change in American schools, bringing into local schools, for the first time in many cases, children with severe disabilities, including profound levels of mental retardation, deafness, blindness, multiple handicaps, and the severe orthopedic impairment.

CECIL R. REYNOLDS
Texas A & M University

CONSENT DECREE
EQUAL EDUCATIONAL OPPORTUNITY
EQUAL PROTECTION
LEAST RESTRICTIVE ENVIRONMENT
MAINSTREAMING
MILLS *v.* BOARD OF EDUCATION OF DISTRICT OF COLUMBIA

PEOPLE FIRST

People First is a self-advocacy organization run by and for people with mental retardation. It has the dual purpose of assuring the availability of the services, training, and support needed to maintain and increase the capabilities of people with developmental disabilities for leading independent and normal lives; and of demonstrating to society that the disabled are people first and handicapped second (People First, 1984). Groups of mentally retarded people are taught to organize their affairs, run meetings, and make decisions and carry them through. All of this is accomplished with minimal help from nonhandicapped advisers. To a large extent, these groups are not only concerned with the needs and problems of mentally retarded people, but also the needs and problems of all handicapped people. Statewide and national conventions of self-advocacy groups have been held and an international self-advocacy movement of People First groups is emerging.

One of the first self-advocacy groups was Project Two, which operated in Nebraska. In 1968 many institutionalized mentally retarded individuals were moved to community-based facilities; hence Project One was deinstitutionalization. Deinstitutionalized people felt they needed a sounding board—a self-help group; hence Project Two. Similar developments occurred in Oregon, where there were self-help groups. Three mentally retarded members and two nonhandicapped advisers attended a conference for mentally handicapped people in British Columbia, Canada. They returned inspired with the idea of starting an organization of people with mental retardation who would put together such conferences. This was the beginning of the People First movement in America. What is interesting is that the movement started up 2 years after Project Two but was unaware of the other group's existence.

Self-advocacy groups have sprung up in America and Britain. Such groups are challenging traditional views of mental handicaps, handicapped people, and mentally retarded persons who can speak for themselves. Self-advocacy groups stretch nonhandicapped people's expectations and attitudes, thereby helping to create a new independence for mentally handicapped persons. In California, People First was contracted by the State Council of Developmental Disabilities to critique the current service system for the developmentally disabled. The unique aspect of this project is that it was entirely conducted by the consumers of the services and was not the work of professionals.

REFERENCES

People First of California. (1984). *Surviving the system: Mental retardation and the retarding environment.* Sacramento, CA: State Council on Developmental Disabilities.

Williams, P., & Shoultz, B. (1982). *We can speak for ourselves.* Bloomington, IN: Indiana University Press.

MILTON BUDOFF
Research Institute for
Educational Problems

ADVOCACY FOR HANDICAPPED CHILDREN
ADVOCACY ORGANIZATIONS

PERCENTILE SCORES

A percentile score is a score derived from the relative position of a raw score in the entire distribution of raw scores. The raw score must possess at least rank information; i.e., raw scores must be able to be ranked. Usually we assume at least intervals for the raw scores, so that a one-point difference has the same meaning for all possible scores. Percentile scores lose this interval quality.

The calculation of a percentile score is based on the number of scores lower than the raw score being changed or transformed. A percentile score of 50 means that half (50%) of the scores in the raw score distribution fall below the score under consideration. This percentile score is also called the median. A percentile score of 10 means 10% of the scores are lower, and a percentile score of 90 means 90% of the scores are lower.

Percentile scores are not equal intervals. That is, a 10 percentile point difference has a different meaning when examined for a score of 10 or 50. The difference between percentile scores of 10 and 20 may represent many raw score points, while the difference between 50 and 60 may

represent only a few. This is because raw score distributions typically have most scores clustered around the average score, perhaps two thirds of the scores within one standard deviation, so that 10% of the scores will occur within a few points of each other. At the extremes of the score distribution there are few people, and 10% may represent a large raw score range. Percentile scores should not be treated as interval scores. They cannot be routinely added, subtracted, divided, or multiplied to obtain anything sensible. Their primary use is to inform the user of the relative position of a raw score with respect to all other raw scores. In standardized testing, in which a norm sample has been carefully sampled, the percentile score tells us how an observed raw score compares with the norm group distribution of raw scores.

VICTOR L. WILLSON
Texas A & M University

GRADE EQUIVALENTS
MEASUREMENT

PERCEPTUAL AND MOTOR SKILLS

Perceptual and Motor Skills (titled *Perceptual and Motor Skills Research Exchange* in 1949) is published bimonthly. Two volumes a year total between 2000 and 3000 pages. About 30% of the articles are submitted from outside the United States. The purpose of this journal is to encourage scientific originality and creativity from an interdisciplinary perspective including such fields as anthropology, physical education, physical therapy, orthopedics, anesthesiology, and time and motion study. Articles are experimental, theoretical, and speculative. Special reviews and lists of new books received are carried. Controversial material of scientific merit is welcome. Submissions are examined by multiple referees, and critical editing is balanced by specific suggestions as to changes required to meet standards.

A survey made in the 35th year of publication showed that *Perceptual and Motor Skills* was listed for the preceding decade in the top 5% of psychology journals for numbers of citations elsewhere of its articles and total numbers published of refereed, selected archival articles. For more than 30 years this journal has consistently maintained a policy of being highly experimental, open to all defensible points of view, encouraging of new and often unpopular ways of approaching problems, and protective of authors by careful but open-minded refereeing and editing.

REFERENCES

Ammons, C. H., & Ammons, R. B. (1962). Permanent or temporary journals: PR and PMS become stable. *Psychological Reports, 10,* 537.

Ammons, R. B., & Ammons, C. H. (1962). Permanent or temporary journals: Are PR and PMS stable? *Perceptual & Motor Skills, 14,* 281.

C. H. AMMONS
*Psychological Reports /
Perceptual and Motor Skills*

PERCEPTUAL CONSTANCY

Perceptual constancy refers to the ability to perceive objects possessing invariant properties such as size, shape, and position in spite of changes in the impression on the sensory surface. Essentially, this means that one recognizes a chair as not only a chair but as the same chair regardless of the viewing angle. Even though an object may have been seen only from a single point of view, we are often able to recognize that object from different distances and from nearly any angle of view.

Perceptual constancy seems to be largely an innate skill (Martindale, 1981). For example, when we observe from a great distance a man who is 6 feet in height, he may appear to be only an inch tall; however, he will be perceived as roughly his correct height nevertheless. Normal individuals can easily perform such tasks with objects not previously seen whenever any other environmental cues are present.

Perceptual constancy is an integral part of overall visual perception and is involved heavily in the early reading process. Disorders of perceptual constancy are relatively rare, but they do occur and can wreak havoc with early learning. Children learn to recognize letters and words even though they see them printed in a variety of orthographic representations. Much variability of printing by children and their teachers occurs during the early learning stages as well, yet children master these various representations with relative ease. The generalization necessary to performing such tasks of visual pattern recognition requires perceptual constancy. Children with mild disturbances of perceptual constancy or higher order visual pattern recognition will have great difficulty with many school tasks, but especially with reading. The disorder is low enough in incidence, however, that accurate estimates of its prevalence are unavailable.

REFERENCE

Martindale, C. (1981). *Cognition and consciousness.* Homewood, IL: Dorsey.

CECIL R. REYNOLDS
Texas A & M University

**DEVELOPMENTAL TEST OF VISUAL PERCEPTION
PERCEPTUAL DEVELOPMENT (LAG IN)
PERCEPTUAL TRAINING**

PERCEPTUAL DEFICIT HYPOTHESIS

The perceptual deficit hypothesis, a once widely accepted view of learning disabilities, exerted a dominant influence on special education teaching and evaluation practices from the early 1960s to the mid-1970s. While the perceptual deficit hypothesis encompasses a number of variants, its central notion is that learning disabilities arise from perceptual-motor dysfunction of neurological origin (Cruickshank, 1972). Learning-disabled children are viewed as having deficient form perception and/or visual analysis, and these deficiencies are believed to be the central feature of their difficulties in learning to read.

This view of learning disabilities widely influenced special education practice through the writings and programs of Kephart (1960), Getman (1962), Barsch (1965), and Frostig (1961). Remedial programs reflected this orientation by emphasizing gross and fine-motor training, ocular exercises, spatial orientation, balance board training, visual discrimination, sequencing, closure exercises, etc., as necessary prerequisites to more direct teaching of academics. It was believed that such foundation training in sensory-motor functions would remediate underlying processing deficits and was a required prerequisite to higher order, conceptual, or symbolic learning.

Proponents of the perceptual deficit hypothesis were influenced by Piaget's theories concerning the role of maturation and motor functioning in perception, by gestalt psychology's emphasis on perceptual development, and by Strauss and Lehtinen's (1947) work with brain-injured children. In their programs for learning-disabled children, these pioneers of special education translated stage theories of learning literally into hierarchies of preacademic remediation activities that sought to develop motor, visual, and visual-motor skills prior to focusing on academic learning. In theory, the development of academic skills required mastery of these lower-level functions.

By the mid 1970s, the perceptual deficit hypothesis and its concomitant remedial programs began to receive severe and substantial criticism. Aspects of the underlying theory were questioned and fault was found with the early foundation research. The overly simplified and literal translation of theory into practice was decried as an essential misinterpretation of the concept of perception. New research indicated that learning disabilities, and reading disabilities in particular, were attributable more to problems in the verbal realm than to perceptual deficits (Vellutino et al., 1977).

Tests used to diagnose specific aspects of perceptual deficit came under particularly heavy fire. The most commonly used, the Frostig Developmental Test of Visual Perception (DTVP; Frostig, 1961), was criticized for its weak theoretical foundation. In addition, the DTVP was found to have insufficient factorial validity, meaning that its subtests do not actually tap distinct and separate perceptual functions and therefore cannot be validly used to specify different remedial activities. Thus the widespread use of this test for diagnostic/prescriptive purposes was resoundingly invalidated. Additionally, perceptual training based on the Frostig test was found to have no relation to academic progress and only a negligible effect on DTVP performance itself (Hammill, Goodman, & Wiederhold, 1974). There arose the ethical issue of spending children's limited classroom time on pseudo prerequisite exercises with no validated relationship to academic achievement.

Remediation based on the perceptual deficit hypothesis, along with remediation based on the Illinois Test of Psycholinguistic Abilities (ITPA), continues to be debated under the broader rubric of underlying process training. Underlying process training has come to represent a genre of emphasis within special education in general, and within the study of learning disabilities in particular. Proponents of one or another of the process orientations seek to psychologically parse special students into a variety of processing strength/weakness categories in order to pinpoint areas of underlying need. While this effort has had appeal to many special educators because of the puzzling performance discrepancies of learning-disabled students, its basic assumptions have been seriously questioned.

The assumptions of a process orientation are that human performance can, in fact, be parsed into psychologically distinct categories, that any given parsing categories are valid compartments, that valid tests exist with which to parse, and that remediation based on underlying processing profiles will transfer to functional and academic learning. Currently, the state of the art in psychology and special education does not support any of these assumptions.

REFERENCES

Barsch, R. H. (1965). *A movigenic curriculum* (Publication No. 25). Madison: Wisconsin State Department of Instruction.

Cruickshank, W. M. (1972). Some issues facing the field of learning disability. *Journal of Learning Disabilities, 5,* 380–383.

Frostig, M. (1961). *The Marianne Frostig Developmental Test of Visual Perception.* Palo Alto, CA: Consulting Psychologists.

Getman, G. (1962). *How to develop your child's intelligence.* Luverne, MN: Announcer.

Hammill, D., Goodman, L., & Wiederholt, J. L. (1974). Visual-motor processes: Can we train them? *Reading Teacher, 27,* 469–480.

Kephart, N. (1960). *The slow learner in the classroom.* Columbus, OH: Merrill.

Strauss, A. A., & Lehtinen, L. E. (1947). *Psychopathology and ed-*

ucation of the brain-injured child. New York: Grune & Stratton.

Vellutino, F. R., Steger, B. M., Moyer, S. C., Harding, C. J., & Niles, J. A. (1977). Has the perceptual deficit hypothesis led us astray? *Journal of Learning Disabilities, 10,* 54–64.

KATHERINE GARNETT
Hunter College

PERCEPTUAL DEVELOPMENT

PERCEPTUAL DEVELOPMENT, LAG IN

Lag in perceptual development has been hypothesized as a major cause of learning difficulties in children by Kephart, Delacato, and Getman, among others. In general, these theorists believe there is a sequential series of strategies children use to process information from the environment; if learned incompletely at any stage, these strategies will cause learning difficulties at higher levels. These theorists maintain that proficiency in perceptual functioning provides an essential foundation for academic learning. Furthermore, they presume children experience academic failure because of developmental lags in these perceptual systems, lags that can and must be ameliorated before academic learning can occur. Although varying somewhat in theoretical orientation, these researchers, as well as Frostig, Barsch, Ayres, Doman, S. Kirk, and W. Kirk, advocate perceptual training to both establish the necessary foundation for and enhance the acquisition of academic learning. Their research provides much of the foundation for current work in the field of learning disabilities (Smith, 1984).

An early proponent of perceptual-motor training, Kephart (1971) believed that motor learning underlies all learning. Basing his theory on works of Hebb, Strauss, Werner, Piaget, and Montessori, Kephart hypothesizes that perceptual development occurs through motor activity and corresponding sensory feedback. Once developed, the perceptual system functions without sole reliance on motor response. It is only through completion of this developmental sequence that the child can readily acquire concepts necessary for academic learning. To ameliorate the underlying developmental limitations and distortions that Kephart believed result in academic failure, he developed a training program based on gross motor activities such as posturing and balancing, locomotion, and throwing and catching balls.

Delacato believes training specific locomotor tasks will influence various centers in the brain and other perceptual and cognitive functions controlled by these centers. One critical aspect of his theory is the establishment of hemispheric dominance to improve speech and other sensory functions. He advocates training the child in unilateral hand use and monocular activities and removing music from the child's environment (Cratty, 1979). Maintaining that unmastered stages of neurological development result in reading and other academic difficulties, Doman and Delacato (Ayres, 1975) emphasize remedial activities designed to recapitulate their hypothesized sequence of neurological developmental. In an effort to establish the unilateral cerebral dominance believed critical in treating reading difficulties, they prescribe training to attain sleep posturing, crawling, and activities that foster unilateral hand, eye, and foot dominance.

Getman holds a position similar to Kephart. Like Kephart he proposes movement as a prerequisite to learning. Unlike Kephart, he emphasizes the importance of vision in the learning process and uses vision in a global sense. He hypothesizes that deficiencies in some visual components will lead to learning difficulties (Cratty, 1979). Designed to enhance academic success, particularly reading, Getman's training program includes locomotor and balancing activities as well as eye-hand coordination and other tasks to enhance ocular function.

Frostig (1964) maintains that poor perceptual development precludes conceptual learning, resulting in academic difficulties. Focusing on visual-perceptual learning, training in gross motor activities and paper and pencil tasks follows assessments using Frostig's Developmental Test of Visual Perception (DTVP). According to Frostig, when integrated with regular academic tasks, these activities promote sensorimotor development, ameliorating dysfunctional perceptual processes and enhancing academic performance.

Barsch's (1967) movigenics curriculum emphasizes the academic value of efficient cognitive and physical movement. Like previous theorists, Barsch views the child as a perceptual-motor being whose successful development depends on proper spatial orientation. Movigenics emphasizes activities that enhance visual-perceptual and motor development.

Ayres' (1975) sensorimotor integration theory posits that the foundations to learning are established through the integration of sensory feedback to the brain. Maintaining that perception and movement are dependent on proper sensory integration, Ayres postulates numerous deficits resulting in poor perceptual-motor functioning. To increase integration and facilitate academic learning, Ayres advocates sensory stimulation through activities such as rolling, spinning, and swinging exercises.

Kirk and Kirk (1971) advocate a different approach to the diagnosis and remediation of learning difficulties. Focusing on the communication abilities of the child, Kirk and Kirk provide psycholinguistic evaluation and training to facilitate academic learning. Although training focuses on auditory and visual perception, Kirk and Kirk advocate training focusing on the individual's weak areas.

Although numerous perceptual-motor theories and training programs exist, research findings to support the theories on which they are based or validate their efficacy have not been found. Hammill, Goodman, and Wiederholt (1974) reviewed studies investigating the effects of the perceptual training programs of Frostig, Kephart, and Getman on readiness skills, intelligence, and academic achievement. Of the studies reviewed, positive effects of training on intelligence and academic achievement were not demonstrated and readiness skills improved in only a few cases. In a study of the effects of Delacato's training method on reading ability and visual-motor integration, O'Donnell and Eisenson (1969) found no improvements in either visual-motor integration or reading ability. Further, a number of researchers, professional groups, and parent groups have severely criticized Delacato's theory and program (Aaron & Poostay, 1982).

Finally, in an evaluation of 38 studies employing Kirk and Kirk's psycholinguistic training model, Hammill and Larsen (1978) found only six demonstrating positive results and concluded that the efficacy of psycholinguistic training remains nonvalidated. Although perceptual and psycholinguistic training theorists maintain the efficacy of their treatment programs, others question the large amounts of time and money expended on these unsubstantiated perceptual-training programs (Hammill et al., 1974). Research may validate their value in certain cases, but general use appears unwarranted.

REFERENCES

Aaron, I. E., & Poostay, E. J. (1982). Strategies for reading disorders. In C. R. Reynolds & T. B. Gutkin (Eds.). *The handbook of school psychology* (pp. 410–435). New York: Wiley.

Ayres, A. J. (1975). Sensorimotor foundations of academic ability. In W. M. Cruickshank & D. P. Hallahan (Eds.). *Perceptual and learning disabilities in children* (Vol. 2, pp. 301–360). Syracuse, NY: Syracuse University Press.

Barsch, R. H. (1967). *Achieving perceptual motor efficiency.* Seattle, WA: Special Child.

Cratty, B. J. (1979). *Perceptual and motor development in infants and children.* New York: Macmillan.

Frostig, M., & Horne, D. (1964). *The Frostig program for the development of visual perception: a teacher's guide.* Chicago: Follett.

Hammill, D., Goodman, L., & Wiederholt, J. L. (1974). Visual-motor processes: Can we train them? *Reading Teacher, 27,* 469–478.

Hammill, D., & Larsen, S. (1978). The effectiveness of psycholinguistic training: A reaffirmation of position. *Exceptional Children, 44,* 402–414.

Kephart, N. C. (1971). *The slow learner in the classroom* (2nd ed.). Columbus, OH: Merrill.

Kirk, S. A., & Kirk, W. D. (1971). *Psycholinguistic learning disabilities: Diagnosis and remediation.* Chicago: University of Illinois Press.

O'Donnell, P. A., & Eisenson, J. (1969). Delacato training for reading achievement and visual-motor integration. *Journal of Learning Disabilities, 2*, 441–447.

Smith, C. R. (1984). *Learning disabilities: The interaction of learner, task, and setting.* Boston: Little, Brown.

SHIRLEY PARKER WELLS
ELEANOR BOYD WRIGHT
University of North Carolina at Wilmington

NEUROLOGICAL ORGANIZATION REMEDIATION, DEFICIT-CENTERED MODEL OF

PERCEPTUAL DISTORTIONS

Perceptual distortion is a clinical term referring to aberrant reception and interpretation of stimuli by one or more of the five basic senses: vision, hearing, smell, taste, and touch. Perceptual distortion typically occurs in conjunction with schizophrenia, severe depression, and psychomotor and ideopathic epilepsies. Schizophrenics are particularly susceptible to perceptual distortion and often process incoming sensory information abnormally via attenuation or reduction. Schizophrenics traditionally have been thought to underestimate tactile, auditory, and visual stimuli in particular. Related to perceptual distortion is evidence that schizophrenics have a defective sensory-filtering mechanism that does not allow them to focus on the most relevant of stimuli at any given time (Pincus & Tucker, 1978). Perceptual distortions that mimic the schizophrenic's perceptual distortions also may be induced by various psychoactive drugs. Prolonged sensory deprivation can also produce perceptual distortions and full-blown hallucinations.

In contrast to schizophrenics, depressed and epileptic individuals exaggerate the intensity of incoming stimuli. Psychomotor seizures produce the most specific of the perceptual distortions but they tend to be ideopathic. Perceptual distortions may also be considered a soft sign of neurological impairment and may occur with learning disabilities, though the latter is far less frequent than commonly believed.

REFERENCE

Pincus, J. H., & Tucker, G. J. (1978). *Behavioral neurology* (2nd ed.). New York: Oxford University Press.

CECIL R. REYNOLDS
Texas A & M University

CHILDHOOD SCHIZOPHRENIA PERCEPTUAL DEVELOPMENT, LAG IN SEIZURE DISORDERS

PERCEPTUAL-MOTOR DIFFICULTIES

Perceptual-motor development is recognized as a basic foundation for later learning. The perceptual deficit hypothesis holds that academic difficulties underlie perceptual deficits (Daves, 1980) and that improving the perceptual processes will bring about improvement in academic achievement. Frequently, children with serious learning disorders have difficulty with spatial orientation, eye-hand coordination, and body image. The early work of Strauss and Lehtinen (1947) described such disorders using the term brain-injured, but later such disorders were labeled the Strauss syndrome by Stevens and Birch (1957). They described the child with perceptual-motor difficulties as one who showed disturbances (separately or in combination) in perception, thinking, and emotional behavior.

Kinsbourne (1968) drew an analogy between the developmental syndrome of cognitive deficits and the acquired Gerstmann syndrome in some adults with parietal lesions in the dominant hemisphere. In both syndromes, he noted selective delay in the ability to recall and use information regarding relative position of items in spatial or temporal sequence; selective difficulty in learning to read and write; spelling errors characterized by errors of letter order and script malorientation; delayed acquisition of finger order sense; inability to discriminate between right and left; and difficulty in arithmetic. He concluded that the developmental syndrome probably represented a developmental lag rather than an indication of localized or lateralized cerebral damage.

There is little question regarding the importance of the development of perceptual-motor skills. Cratty (1975) notes that a child with perceptual-motor difficulties cannot translate thoughts into written and printed form with the same precision as a normally developing child. Such a child also may possess various perceptual deficits within one or more modalities (touch, kinesthesia, vision, audition) that may combine as evidence of a defective nervous system and lead to learning problems. Cruickshank (1979) also emphasized that perceptual processing deficits or neurological dysfunction underlie learning problems. Such problems are related to receiving, processing, and responding to information from outside the environment and from inside the child's own body. The ability to understand, remember, think, and perform perceptual-motor skills all precede the ability to read, write, or master arithmetic. Strategies to assist children in the overall learning process were developed (Kephart, 1963) based on the notion that perceptual-motor deficits are primarily organic in nature, and further, that they can be remediated by the development of specific skills such as form perception, eye-hand coordination, and temporal-spatial relationships.

Both Frostig (1975) and Kephart (1975) emphasized the need to develop skills in their natural order. They stressed the effect of motor processes on perception and the effects of perception on cognitive processes (i.e., the use of vision and motor skills or activities in the formation of a concept). In a similar manner Barsh (1963) developed a curriculum, movigenics, involving a progressively more complex sequence of activities in which children explore and orient themselves in space. Barsh's emphasis was on the development of muscular strength, dynamics, balance, space, body awareness, and rhythmics.

Controversy exists regarding the efficacy of such programs. Much of the research to replicate beneficial results linking perceptual motor training to academic achievement (Balow, 1971; Goodman & Hammill, 1973; Zigler & Seitz, 1975) suggests that the claims are unwarranted. Little evidence has been found to support the use of perceptual-motor activities in the treatment or prevention of disabilities in reading or other specific school subjects. However, other research tends to confirm earlier claims (Ayres, 1972; Gregory, 1978; Masland, 1976; Neman, 1974). There is continued interest in and support for determining the benefits of specific sensory-motor training.

REFERENCES

Ayres, A. (1972). *Sensory integration and learning disorders,* Los Angeles, CA: Western Psychological Services.

Balow, B. (1971). Perceptual-motor activities in the treatment of severe reading disabilities. *Reading Teacher, 24,* 513–525.

Barsh, R. H. (1963). *Enriching perception and cognition: Techniques for teachers* (Vol. 2). Seattle, WA: Special Child.

Cratty, B. J. (1975). *Remedial motor activities for children.* Philadelphia: Febiger.

Cruickshank, W. M. (1979). Learning disabilities: Perceptual or other? *Association for Children with Learning Disabilities Newsbriefs, 125,* 7–10.

Daves, W. E. (1980). *Educator's resource guide to special education: Terms-laws-tests-organizations.* Boston: Allyn & Bacon.

Frostig, M. (1975). The role of perception in the integration of psychological functions. In W. Cruickshank & D. Hallahan (Eds.), *Perceptual and learning disabilities in children* (Vol. 1) (pp. 115–146). Syracuse: Syracuse University Press.

Goodman, L., & Hammill, D. (1973). The effectiveness of the Kephart-Getman activities in developing perceptual-motor and cognitive skills. *Focus on Exceptional Children, 4*(9), 19.

Gregory, R. L. (1978). Illusions and hallucinations. In E. C. Carterette & M. P. Friedman (Eds.), *Handbook of Perception: Vol. 9. Perceptual Processing* (pp. 337–358). New York: Academic.

Kephart, N. C. (1963). *The brain injured child in the classroom.* Chicago: National Society for Crippled Children and Adults.

Kephart, N. C. (1975). The perceptual-motor match. In W. Cruickshank & D. Hallahan (Eds.), *Perceptual and learning disabilities in children* (Vol. 1, pp. 63–70). Syracuse: Syracuse University Press.

Kinsbourne, M. (1968). Developmental Gerstmann syndrome. *Pediatric Clinics in North America, 15*(3), 771–778.

Masland, R. (1976). The advantages of being dyslexic. *Bulletin of the Orton Society, 26,* 10–18.

Neman, R. (1974). A reply to Zigler & Seitz. *American Journal of Mental Deficiency, 79,* 493–505.

Stevens, G. D., & Birch, J. W. (1957). A proposal of clarification of the terminology and a description of brain-injured children. *Exceptional Children, 23,* 346–349.

Strauss, A. A., & Lehtinen, L. E. (1947). *Psychopathology and education of the brain-injured child* (Vol. I). New York: Grune & Stratton.

Zigler, E., & Seitz, V. (1975). On an experimental evaluation of sensory motor patterning: A critique. *American Journal of Mental Deficiency, 79,* 483–492.

SALLY E. PISARCHICK
*Cuyahoga Special Education
Service Center*

MOVIGENICS
VISUAL-MOTOR AND VISUAL-PERCEPTUAL PROBLEMS
VISUAL PERCEPTION AND DISCRIMINATION

PERCEPTUAL SPAN

Perceptual span is a term encountered in the study of reading. It refers principally to the amount of visual information useful to a reader during a single fixation. Readers are able to apprehend only a limited amount of information during the fixation of the eye's journey across a line of print; however, it has been long noted that skilled readers are also able to recognize words that are a short distance to the right and to the left of the fixation (Woodworth, 1938). This perceptual span (or span of apprehension) is useful to the skilled reader, increasing speed and comprehension of reading. Specifying the nature and extent of this span and its relationship to disorders of reading has been a controversial process (Pirrozzolo, 1979). Pirrozzolo (1979) has described the four major methods of measuring perceptual span, another controversial topic.

The first primary method described by Pirrozzolo is the technique of dividing the number of eye movement fixations into the number of characters appearing on a line or in a passage of text. A second technique for assessing perceptual span requires the tachistoscopic exposure of letters and words and a verbal report on the material seen during these brief exposures. A third method involves visual fixation at a measured point, identification of visible stimuli that are then displaced, and gathering of new data. The fourth method of measurement requires the provision of a fixed span (or window) of information that can be manipulated by the experimenter to determine the reader's perceptual span. Sophisticated computer presentations have been devised for the last method.

Over the last century, researchers and clinicians have hypothesized that disabled readers have a less efficient or possibly a dysfunctional application of their perceptual span. Frank and Levinson (1976) have recently suggested, as one example, that disabled readers have a lower blurring speed than nondisabled readers. This is believed to be due to a cerebellar-vestibular dysfunction that adversely affects the reading process by reducing clear vision and making correct orientation more difficult.

There is sizable evidence (overwhelming in Pirrozzolo's view) from studies of visual function in reading disabilities to indicate that visual-perceptual defects are unrelated to reading disabilities. Problems in occulomotor scanning, sensory and perceptual skills, and perceptual span are clearly not causative in the vast majority of cases of reading disorders, but these areas may appear abnormal as a result of the reading disability.

REFERENCES

Frank, J., & Levinson, F. (1976). C-V dysfunction in dysmetric dyslexia. *Academic Therapy, 12,* 251–283.

Pirrozzolo, F. J. (1979). *The neuropsychology of developmental reading disorders.* New York: Praeger.

Woodworth, R. S. (1938). *Experimental psychology.* New York: Holt.

CECIL R. REYNOLDS
Texas A & M University

PERCEPTUAL DEVELOPMENTS, LAG IN
PERCEPTUAL TRAINING
READING DISORDERS
SENSORY-INTEGRATIVE THERAPY
VISUAL PERCEPTION AND DISCRIMINATION
VISUAL TRAINING

PERCEPTUAL TRAINING

Many theorists believe that perception is a learned skill; therefore, it is assumed that teaching or training can have an effect on a child's perceptual skills (Lerner, 1971). Once perceptual abilities have been assessed, there are various teaching procedures and programs that can be used to improve perceptual skills.

Some of the most frequently used educational programs for children with learning disabilities have focused on perceptual training activities. While many of these perceptual training programs have emphasized visual or visual-motor training, there are also perceptual training activities in the areas of auditory perception, haptic and kinesthetic perception, and social perception. In spite of all the available material on these perceptual training programs, many researchers have questioned their effectiveness as a way to improve school learning (Hallahan & Cruickshank, 1973; Hammill & Larsen, 1974).

Since similar perceptual training activities have been used in many different programs, it is often unclear who first used them (Hallahan & Kauffman, 1976). However, most of these training activities are based on theories that began with the work of Werner and Strauss (1939). The following descriptions of some of these perceptual training programs provide an overview of these theories and activities.

Newell Kephart worked closely with Werner and Strauss and derived many of his educational techniques from them. This perceptual-motor theory of learning disabilities stresses that perceptual-motor development helps the child establish a solid concept of his or her environment and that perceptual data only become meaningful when they are connected with previously learned motor information (in Kephart's terms, when a perceptual motor match occurs). Children with learning problems are viewed as having inadequate perceptual-motor development, manifested by motor, perceptual, and cognitive disorganization. Kephart argues that these children are unable to benefit from standard school curricula (Lerner, 1971).

The book *The Slow Learner in the Classroom* (Kephart, 1971) presented Kephart's perceptual-motor training program, which included activities involving chalkboard training, sensory-motor training, ocular-motor training, and form-perception training. The chalkboard training activities were recommended for promoting directionality, crossing the midline, orientation, tracing, copying, and eye-hand coordination. The activities presented in the sensory-motor training portion of the program were designed to help the child coordinate the movements of his or her body. Balance beams, balance boards, "angels in the snow" exercises, and trampolines are used to develop total body coordination in the gross motor systems. Ocular-motor training was proposed to help children gain control over their eye movements; it includes activities for ocular pursuit in which the child follows objects visually. Because of Kephart's belief that motor activities influence visual development, the activities in the form-perception training include assembling puzzles, constructing designs from matchsticks, and putting pegs in pegboards (Hallahan & Kauffman, 1976).

Getman (1965) also proposed a model that attempts to illustrate the sequences of children's development of motor- and visual-perceptual skills. This model, called the visuomotor complex, is applied in a manual of training activities, *The Physiology of Readiness: An Action Program for the Development of Perception in Children* (Getman, Kane, Halgren & McKee, 1964). The program described in this model has activities in the following six areas: general coordination, balance, eye-hand coordination, eye movements, form perception, and visual memory. The exercises in the general coordination section deal mainly with movements of the head, arms, and legs; they are designed to provide children with practice in total body movement. A balance beam is used for most of the activities in the balance section; the activities emphasize the use of visual perception for the acquisition of better balance.

The eye-hand coordination program involves the children in chalkboard exercises that are designed to increase their ability to coordinate eyes and hands. Activities in the eye-movement program are aimed at increasing children's ability to move their eyes rapidly and accurately from one object to another, while the form-perception program has children using templates to trace shapes on the chalkboard and on paper, eventually leading to the drawing of the figures without templates. The final part of the program, the visual-memory activities, uses a tachistoscope or slide projector to flash slides of figures for children to name, trace in the air, circle, trace on worksheets, or draw. The purpose is to develop children's visual imagery skill by showing more complex figures for shorter periods of time as the children become more proficient.

Frostig and Horne (1964) have a visual-perception training program designed for remediation or readiness training. The Frostig Program for the Development of Visual Perception has activities in the areas of eye-motor coordination, figure ground, perceptual constancy, position in space, and spatial relations. Each of these areas has worksheets for the teacher to use with the children. The eye-hand exercises focus on coordinating eye and hand movements by having the children draw lines between boundaries. The figure-ground exercises have the children find and trace figures embedded within other lines and figures. Perceptual generalization is emphasized in the perceptual constancy exercises; the children are trained to recognize that objects remain the same even if presented in different forms, colors, sizes, or contexts. The position in space exercises have the children place themselves in various positions (e.g., over or under) in relation to objects in the room; worksheets are also provided that require the children to discriminate objects in various positions. Finally, the spatial-relations exercises have the children do worksheets to observe spatial relationships.

Barsch's movigenic theory proposes that difficulties in learning are related to the learner's inefficient interaction with space. The training program that evolved from this theory has a series of activities that are a planned developmental motor program (Barsch, 1965). There are three main components to this curriculum: postural-transport orientations, which include muscular strength, dynamic balance, body awareness, spatial awareness, and temporal awareness; percepto-cognitive modes of gustatory, olfactory, tactual, kinesthetic, auditory, and visual activities; and degrees of freedom of bilaterality, rhythm, flexibility, and motor planning. Chapters on each of these aspects of

the program are included in the curriculum along with exercises to use with learning-disabled children.

Several books and training manuals that focused on training motor skills were written and developed by Cratty (1973). These materials present exercises similar to those found in physical education programs for the purpose of enhancing motor skills and improving a child's cognitive abilities.

REFERENCES

Barsch, R. (1965). *A movigenic curriculum* (Bulletin No. 25). Madison, WI: Department of Instruction, Bureau for the Handicapped.

Cratty, B. (1973). *Teaching motor skills.* Englewood Cliffs, NJ: Prentice-Hall.

Frostig, M., & Horne, D. (1964). *The Frostig program for the development of visual perception.* Chicago: Follett.

Getman, G. (1985). The visuomotor complex in the acquisition of learning skills. In J. Hellmuth (Ed.), *Learning disorders,* (Vol. 1). Seattle, WA: Special Child.

Getman, G., Kane, E., Halgren, M., & McKee, G. (1964). The physiology of readiness: An action program for the development of perception in children. Minneapolis: Programs to Accelerate School Success.

Hallahan, D., & Cruickshank, W. (1973). *Psychoeducational foundations of learning disabilities.* Englewood Cliffs, NJ: Prentice-Hall.

Hallahan, D., & Kauffman, J. (1976). *Introduction to learning disabilities.* Englewood Cliffs, NJ: Prentice-Hall.

Hammill, D., & Larsen, S. (1974). The relationship of selected auditory perceptual skills and reading ability. *Journal of Learning Disabilities, 7,* 429–436.

Kephart, N. (1971). *The slow learner in the classroom* (2nd ed.). Columbus, OH: Merrill.

Lerner, J. (1971). *Children with learning disabilities.* Boston: Houghton Mifflin.

Werner, H., & Strauss, A. (1939). Types of visuo-motor activity and their relation to low and high performance ages. *Proceedings of the American Association of Mental Deficiency, 44,* 163–168.

DEBORAH C. MAY
*State University of New York
at Albany*

MOVIGENICS

PEREIRE, JACOB R. (1715–1780)

Jacob R. Pereire, an early educator of the deaf, was the originator of lip reading and the creator of the first manual alphabet for the deaf that required the use of only one hand. Pereire also demonstrated that speech can be understood by using the tactile sense to perceive the vibrations and muscular movements produced by the voice mechanism.

Pereire conducted schools for the deaf in Paris and Bordeaux, and his methods were further developed by de l'Epée and Sicard at the National Institution for Deaf-Mutes in Paris. In recognition of his work, Pereire received an official commendation of the Parisian Academy of Science, was made a member of the Royal Society of London, and was awarded a pension by King Louis XV.

REFERENCE

Lane, H. (1984). *When the mind hears.* New York: Random House.

PAUL IRVINE
Katonah, New York

PERFORMANCE INSTABILITY

Performance instability refers to inconsistent functioning on a given task across time. As a characteristic of handicapped children, performance instability often is confused with a second type of variability referred to by O'Donnell (1980) as intraindividual discrepancy. Whereas performance instability denotes changeability within a single domain across time, intraindividual discrepancy refers to variability across different performance areas within a similar time frame.

Historically, performance instability has been viewed as a distinctive characteristic of learning-disabled children. Strauss and Lehtinen (1947) reported dramatically unstable performance among their pupils. Similarly, Ebersole, Kephart, and Ebersole (1968) indicated that learning-disabled children inconsistently retained previously learned materials. More recently, Swanson (1982) typified the learning-disabled population as performing in a fragmented, inconsistent manner. In addition, performance instability is included explicitly and implicitly in well-known classification schemes for identifying learing-disabled students, such as the Strauss syndrome (Stevens & Birch, 1957), Clements' symptoms of minimal brain dysfunction (Clements, 1966) and attention-deficit/hyperactivity disorders (American Psychiatric Association, 1994). Moreover, learning disabilities teachers appear to agree on the importance of performance instability as a descriptor of their students (Aviezer & Simpson, 1980).

Nevertheless, the validity and usefulness of performance instability as a salient learning disabilities characteristic is weakened by at least two facts. First, work in two areas that are conceptually related to performance instability—attention disorders and impulsivity—demonstrates that learning-disabled children do not behave distinctively when compared with pupils with different labels of exceptionality. Second, research exploring performance instability among normal and mildly handicapped learning-disabled and behavior-disordered students indicates that the three groups are essentially comparable in the extent to which they manifest performance instability on academic tasks (Fuchs, Fuchs, & Deno, 1985; Fuchs, Fuchs, Tindal, & Deno, 1986).

REFERENCES

American Psychiatric Association. (1994). *Diagnostic and statistical manual of mental disorders* (4th ed.). Washington, DC: Author.

Aviezer, Y., & Simpson, S. (1980). Variability and instability in perceptual and reading functions of brain injured children. *Journal of Learning Disabilities, 13,* 41–47.

Clements, S. D. (1966). *Minimal brain dysfunction in children: Terminology and identification* (NINDS Monograph No. 3, U.S. Public Health Service Publication No. 1415). Washington, DC: U.S. Government Printing Office.

Ebersole, M., Kephart, N. C., & Ebersole, J. B. (1968). *Steps to achievement for the slow learner.* Columbus, OH: Merrill.

Fuchs, D., Fuchs, L. S., & Deno, S. L. (1985). Performance instability: An identifying characteristic of learning disabled children? *Learning Disability Quarterly, 8,* 19–26.

Fuchs, D., Fuchs, L. S., Tindal, G., & Deno, S. L. (1986). Performance instability of learning disabled, emotionally handicapped, and nonhandicapped children. *Learning Disability Quarterly, 9,* 84–88.

O'Donnell, L. G. (1980). Intra-individual discrepancy in diagnosing specific learning disabilities. *Learning Disability Quarterly, 3,* 10–18.

Stevens, G. D., & Birch, J. W. (1957). A proposal for clarification of the terminology used to describe brain-injured children. *Exceptional Children, 23,* 346–349.

Strauss, A., & Lehtinen, L. (1947). *Psychopathology and education of the brain-injured child.* New York: Grune & Stratton.

Swanson, H. S. (1982). In the beginning was a strategy: Or was it a constraint? *Topics in Learning & Learning Disabilities, 2,* x–xiv.

DOUGLAS FUCHS
LYNN S. FUCHS
Vanderbilt University

ATTENTION-DEFICIT/HYPERACTIVITY DISORDER
IMPULSE CONTROL

PERINATAL FACTORS IN HANDICAPPING CONDITIONS

A number of perinatal factors increase the risk of handicapping conditions in the newborn. Social factors include lack of prenatal care; maternal age; inadequate maternal nutrition; use of alcohol, tobacco, or drugs (Alcohol, Drug Abuse, and Mental Health Administration, 1992); stress; work; handicapping condition (Lord, 1991); and fatigue.

Maternal disease factors such as hypertension, diabetes, and heart disease may also affect fetal condition at birth. However, alterations in the birth process itself may contribute to the development of fetal handicapping conditions. Preterm labor, postterm labor, premature rupture of membranes, multiple births, antepartum hemorrhage, breech presentations, Caesarean sections, and forceps deliveries all add to the risk of unfavorable fetal outcomes and handicapping conditions (Avery & Taeusch, 1984).

The purpose of prenatal care is to provide ongoing education and evaluation during pregnancy. Serial evaluations permit the physician or midwife to uncover actual or potential morbid states and institute timely interventions with the potential for improved fetal outcome. Early detection of urinary tract infections, hypertension, heart murmurs, protein or sugar in the urine, too little or too rapid uterine growth, or swelling of extremities provides the health-care team with the opportunity to arrest the development of the more serious maternal cardiac or renal disease, hypertension, premature labor, or complications of unexpected multiple births. Therefore, lack of good prenatal care can and often is associated with poor fetal and/or maternal outcome (Harrison, Golbus, & Filly, 1984).

Maternal age represents a nonspecific influence on fetal outcome at birth. Adolescent women 15 years and younger have increased incidences of newborns with neurologic disorders and low birth weights. Women 40 years and older are at increased risk for stillborns or infants with chromosomal abnormalities (Avery & Taeusch, 1984).

Inadequate maternal nutrition and insufficient maternal weight gain of less than 14 pounds have been associated with low infant birth weight. The heavy use of alcohol during pregnancy increases the newborn's risk for growth retardation, microencephaly, cardiac anomalies, and renal anomalies. Tobacco use during pregnancy increases the newborn's risk for low birth weight, prematurity, and even stillbirth. Prescribed, over-the-counter, or recreational drugs may have an adverse effect on the neonate. The probability of a drug causing harm is dependent on the drug itself, the dose, route of administration, stage of gestation, and the genetic makeup of the mother and fetus. Drugs increase the risk of low birth weight, chromosomal abnormalities, organ anomalies, and even fetal death. Further, drugs can create problems with resuscitation and potential withdrawal phenomenon in the newborn (Hobel, 1985).

Stress, work, and fatigue have been associated with an increased risk for poor fetal outcome. The association between stress, work, fatigue, and pregnancy complications is not clear, but it is related to growth retardation and/or low birth weight of the neonate (Creasy, 1984).

Maternal disease factors associated with poor fetal outcome and handicapping conditions include hypertension, diabetes, and heart disease. Hypertension is the most frequently identified maternal problem associated with growth retardation. Hypertension is also associated with preterm labor, low birth weight, cerebral palsy, mental retardation, and fetal death (Avery & Taeusch, 1984).

Poorly controlled maternal diabetes with associated high blood sugars is related to poor fetal outcome. The risk for growth retardation, congenital defects, and brain damage is increased by the complications of diabetes. Maternal heart disease with associated reduced cardiac output is also associated with the increased risk of prematurity and low birth weight. (Hobel, 1985).

Prematurity with its complications is associated with many handicapping conditions. Postterm pregnancy refers to pregnancy lasting longer than 42 weeks. Postterm pregnancy is associated with an increased risk for growth retardation, distress, and even death of the neonate (Hobel, 1985).

The premature rupture of membranes is associated with an increased risk of premature birth and an increased risk for neonatal infection (Oxorn, 1986). Multiple births, antepartum hemorrhage, breech presentation, Caesarean section, and forcep deliveries also increase the risk of handicapping conditions to the newborn. These alterations in the birth process increase the risk for neonatal mortality, central nervous system hemorrhage, asphyxia, and long-term neurologic disability (Avery & Taeusch, 1984).

REFERENCES

Alcohol, Drug Abuse, and Mental Health Administration. (1992). *Identifying the needs of drug-affected children: Public policy issues.* OSAP Prevention Monograph II. Rockville, MD: Office of Substance Abuse Prevention.

Avery, M. E., & Taeusch, H. W. (Eds.). (1984). *Schaffer's diseases of the newborn* (5th ed.). Philadelphia: Saunders.

Creasy, R. K. (1984). Preterm labor and delivery. In R. K. Creasy, & R. Resnik (Eds.), *Maternal-fetal medicine, principles and practice* (pp. 415–443). Philadelphia: Saunders.

Harrison, M. R., Golbus, M. S., & Filly, R. A. (1984). *The unborn patient, prenatal diagnosis and treatment.* Orlando, FL: Grune & Stratton.

Hobel, C. J. (1985). Factors during pregnancy that influence brain development. In J. M. Freeman (Ed.), *Prenatal and perinatal factors associated with brain disorders* (NIH Publication No. 85–1149, pp. 197–236). Bethesda, MD: U.S. Department of Health and Human Services.

Lord, C. (1991). Pre and perinatal factors in high-functioning females and males with autism. *Journal of Autism and Developmental Disorders, 21*(2), 197–209.

Oxorn, H. (1986). *Human labor and birth* (5th ed.). Norwalk, CT: Appleton-Century-Crofts.

ELIZABETH R. BAUERSCHMIDT
University of North Carolina at Wilmington

MICHAEL BAUERSCHMIDT
Brunswick Hospital

ETIOLOGY
INTERVENTION
LOW BIRTH WEIGH INFANTS
MARCH OF DIMES
NEONATAL BEHAVIOR ASSESSMENT SCALES
PREMATURITY/PRETERM

PERKINS-BINET TESTS OF INTELLIGENCE FOR THE BLIND

The Perkins-Binet Tests of Intelligence for the Blind (Davis, 1980) were designed to assess the intellectual functioning (verbal and performance) of visually handicapped children. Shortly after their appearance it became evident that there were a number of significant flaws in the tests. Reviewers (e.g., Genshaft & Ward, 1982) found the test manual lacking in technical information. Instructions for administering were vague, and in some instances, incomplete. The tests were lengthy and difficult to administer, and scoring criteria were unclear. There were also concerns about psychometric adequacy and the lack of reliability and validity data (Gutterman, Ward, & Genshaft, 1985). The tests have since been withdrawn from the market.

REFERENCES

Davis, C. J. (1980). *The Perkins-Binet Tests of Intelligence for the Blind.* Watertown, MA: Perkins School for the Blind.

Genshaft, J., & Ward, M. (1982). A review of the Perkins-Binet Tests for the Blind with suggestions for administration. *School Psychology Review, 11*(3), 338–341.

Gutterman, J. E., Ward, M., & Genshaft, J. (1985). Correlations of scores of low vision children on the Perkins-Binet Tests of Intelligence for the Blind, the WISCR-R and the WRAT. *Journal of Visual Impairment & Blindness, 79*, 55–58.

ROBERT G. BRUBAKER
Eastern Kentucky University

BLIND
VISUALLY IMPAIRED

PERKINS SCHOOL FOR THE BLIND

The Perkins School for the Blind was the first private residential school for the blind chartered in the United States. It was founded by Samuel Gridley Howe in 1832 to serve two blind students and was originally called the New England Asylum for the Blind. At that time asylum was all that even the most fortunate blind person could expect out of life. However, Howe, a strong believer in education, changed the name to the New England Institution for the Education of the Blind. Today, it is known as the Perkins School for the Blind, after Thomas Perkins, a prominent Boston merchant and one of the school's early benefactors. Probably one of its most well-known students was Helen Keller, who attended Perkins from 1887–1892.

The Perkins programs are comprehensive and serve a wide variety of blind, visually impaired, deaf-blind, and multiimpaired children, teenagers, and adults. The programs include preschool services, ages 0–5; primary and intermediate services, ages 6–15; secondary services, ages 15–22; deaf-blind program, ages 5–22; severely impaired program, ages 16–22; adult services, ages 18 and up; and community residence and independent living services, ages 18 and up. The philosophy is to prepare students and clients to meet everyday life to the best of their abilities emotionally, socially, physically, vocationally, and avocationally (Annual Report, 1998).

Perkins also provides other services besides direct care, including the Samuel P. Hayes Research Library, which collects print material about the nonmedical aspects of blindness and deaf-blindness. In addition, it houses a museum on the history of blind and deaf-blind and a historic collection of embossed books for the blind. The Howe Press is located at Perkins. It is the developer and manufacturer of the Perkins Brailler, used throughout the world. The Howe Press also distributes children's books, brailling accessories, and other aids and materials for blind and low-vision students.

REFERENCE

Perkins School for the Blind Annual Report. (1998). Watertown, MA: Author.

ROSANNE K. SILBERMAN
Hunter College

BLIND
VISUALLY IMPAIRED

PERSEVERATION

Perseveration is used in special education to describe behavior that is continued by a child beyond the normal (Cuneo & Welsch, 1992) end point of the behavior and that is accompanied by difficulty in changing tasks. Perseveration is considered to be a soft neurologically sign and is believed to be most common among learning-disabled and brain-injured children. Lerner (1971) discusses perseverative behavior as one of the four major behavioral characteristics of learning-disabled children.

In formal assessment, perseveration is often noted on

such tasks as the Bender-Gestalt, in which the child is required to reproduce a series of nine drawings. Figures one, two, and six of this series require lines or rows of circles, dots, and repeating curves. Once started on the task of making dots, circles, or repeating curves, some children have great difficulty in stopping and subsequently distort their drawings greatly. Such children seem to get carried away by a specific activity, repeating it over and over, unable to stop. Perseveration is most commonly seen in motor tasks, but it can also be present in verbal behavior and even in thought patterns.

On intelligence tests such as the Wechsler Intelligence Scale for Children-Revised, children may display verbal or ideational perseveration. Although not formally scored as perseveration, this behavior lowers children's intelligence test scores significantly. On tasks such as telling how two everyday, common objects are alike (the similarities subtest of the WISC-R), some children will give the same fundamental answer to each pair of items; they seem unable to alter their mental set once established. Anxiety may also promote perseverative behavior.

Levine, Brooks, and Shonkoff (1980) have presented an interesting, useful view of perseveration and have provided some excellent clinical examples. They note that transitional events, or even minor changes in routine, constitute common impediments to many children with learning disorders, many of whom are perseverative. At the same time, some of these children are impersistent at academic or other tasks, a finding that seems paradoxical on the surface. However, as Levine, Brooks, and Shonkoff (1980) note, there may be a fine line between impersistence and perseveration, and the two traits coexist in some children.

Difficulties with adaptability may be a component of a general biological predisposition to inefficient attentional strategies. Children who cannot shift tasks, activities, or mental sets may be reflecting anxiety linked to issues of loss or fear of failure, or may be demonstrating neurological abnormalities associated with frontal lobe or possibly reticular function. Koppitz (1963, 1975) has reviewed a number of studies in which children with brain damage demonstrate higher levels of perseverative behavior than do normal children of the same age. Perseveration is one of the best indicators of neurological impairment on the Bender-Gestalt Test (Koppitz, 1963, 1975) and is one of the least subjective scoring categories.

The following clinical illustrations from Levine, Brooks, and Shonkoff (1979) are useful in understanding the different features of perseveration as well as its relationship to impersistence.

1. A child may find the daily progression of routines difficult to manage. Getting up in the morning, dressing, eating breakfast, and preparing for school may present problems. The youngster may linger over each activity. The same pattern may appear when the youngster returns from school; there may be problems initiating routines, coming in from play, disengaging from the television set, and preparing for sleep. Parental efforts to induce a shift of activities may result in severe temper tantrums and unbridled anger.

2. A child may persist at an activity, wishing to sustain it beyond a reasonable period. Such a youngster has difficulty in suspending a project for continuation. Sometimes the behavior reflects a child's wish to pursue some enterprise that is likely to yield success rather than to move on to a riskier endeavor that might culminate in failure; such tenacity may be an avoidance response. At other times perseveration may be a consequence of cognitive inertia with regard to shifting sets. For example, some children with memory deficits or difficulties in establishing object constancy may experience change as overwhelming.

3. A child may resist any changes in daily routine. His or her behavior may deteriorate at the prospect of an unexpected visit to a relative. The youngster may be upset by the arrival of cousins for an overnight visit or by having to give up his or her own bed for the night. Some children crave consistency, or a sameness that helps provide order in a world that seems chaotic. They do not appreciate surprises and instead insist on knowing exactly what is going to happen each day (pp. 240–241).

Painting (1979) has commented, appropriately, that perseveration may occur because a particular response is so gratifying to a child that it is repeated primarily for the pleasure involved. A child with learning problems who gets a test item correct or who has mastered a particular activity may perseverate in the behavior because it promotes feelings of success and aids the child's self-esteem.

Perseveration may occur for a variety of reasons. Good diagnosis must go beyond designation of the presence of perseveration to explaining why the child perseverates. Treatment choices are likely to be impacted significantly by etiology in the case of perseverative behavior.

REFERENCES

Cuneo, K., & Welsch, C. (1992). Perseveration in young children: Developmental and Neuropsychological perspectives. *Child Study Journal, 22*(2), 73–92.

Lerner, J. (1971). *Children with learning disabilities.* Boston: Houghton Mifflin.

Levine, M. D., Brooks, R., & Shonkoff, J. P. (1980). *A pediatric approach to learning disorders.* New York: Wiley.

Koppitz, E. M. (1963). *The Bender Gestalt Test for Young Children.* New York: Grune & Stratton.

Koppitz, E. M. (1975). *The Bender Gestalt Test for Young Children. Vol. II. Research and application, 1963–1973.* New York: Grune & Stratton.

Painting, D. H. (1979). Cognitive assessment of children with SLD. In W. Adamson & K. Adamson (Eds.), *A handbook for specific learning disabilities.* New York: Halsted.

CECIL R. REYNOLDS
Texas A & M University

BENDER-GESTALT TEST

PERSONALITY ASSESSMENT

Personality assessment, defined as the description and measurement of individual characteristics, has traditionally been divided into four distinct types: interview, objective, projective, and behavioral. Clinicians frequently use one or more of these assessment methods as an integral component of psychological evaluations.

The interview, which has historical precedence over other methods, was formerly seen as unreliable and subjective. Interviewees are often unwilling to reveal negative things about themselves, and may present different information depending on the style and personal characteristics of the interviewer. On the positive side, an interview can be one of the most direct methods of obtaining information. Structured instruments such as the Schedule for Affective Disorders and Schizophrenia (SADS; Endicott & Spitzer, 1978) and the Diagnostic Interview Schedule (DIS; Robins, Helzer, Craughan & Ratcliff, 1981) have demonstrated empirical validity and adequate reliability and thus reflect a resurgence of the interview method.

Objective personality assessment, which includes questionnaires such as self-report measures and inventories, is typically the most standardized and structured method of assessing personality. Questionnaires can be scored quickly and used for group administrations; however, they are prone to poor validity when people do not give truthful answers. The most common objective instrument is the Minnesota Multiphasic Personality Inventory (MMPI; Hathaway and McKinley, 1943), which contains 10 clinical scales used in identifying specific psychological disorders. Other frequently used instruments include Gough's California Psychological Inventory (Gough, 1957), the Sixteen Personality Factor Questionnaire (16PF; Cattell & Stice, 1957), and the Guilford-Zimmerman Temperament Survey (Guilford & Zimmerman, 1949).

Projective techniques, which are less standardized, require good clinical judgment in interpretation. They include the Rorschach Test (Rorschach, 1942), the Thematic Apperception Test (TAT; McClelland, Atkinson, Clark, & Lowell, 1953), figure drawings, word association, and sentence completion tests. The Rorschach has enjoyed the most widespread use in clinical settings. The rationale behind the test is that unconscious desires, coping styles, and other personality features are projected through interpretation of the inkblots. As there are no right or wrong answers, it is believed that projective techniques are better able to assess an individual's actual personality characteristics. Critics of these techniques argue that interpretation is subjective and highly dependent on the skills of the interpreter. Exner (1974) has developed a structured, comprehensive scoring system for the Rorschach in an attempt to increase the scientific validity of this measure.

Behavioral assessment examines present behavior, with the expectation that such observation aids in the prediction of future actions. Methods include naturalistic observation, analogue observation, self-monitoring, and participant observation.

Although personality assessment has been a widely used and valuable clinical tool, the validity has been problematic. Objective criteria for diagnosis has been provided by the DSM-IV (the *Diagnostic and Statistical Manual of Mental Disorders*), but prediction of DSM-IV diagnosis via personality assessment is still a controversial issue. Ongoing research is therefore aimed at increasing predictive validity and reliability and the DSM-IV diagnostic compatibility with personality assessment (American Psychiatric Association, 1994).

REFERENCES

American Psychiatric Association (1994). *Diagnostic and Statistical Manual of Mental Disorders.* Washington, DC: Author.

Cattell, R. B., & Stice, G. F. (1957). *Handbook for the Sixteen Personality Factor Questionnaire.* Champaign, IL: Institute for Personality and Ability Testing.

Edwards, A. L. (1959). *Edwards personal preference schedule.* New York: Psychological Corporation.

Endicott, J., & Spitzer, R. L. (1978). A diagnostic interview: The schedule for affective disorders and schizophrenia. *Archives of General Psychiatry, 35,* 837–844.

Exner, J. E. (1974). *The Rorschach: A comprehensive system* (Vol. I). New York: Wiley.

Gough, H. G. (1957). *California Psychological Inventory: Manual.* Palo Alto, CA: Consulting Psychologists Press.

Guilford, J. P., & Zimmerman, W. S. (1949). *The Guilford Zimmerman Temperament Survey: Manual of instructions and interpretations.* Beverly Hills, CA: Sheridan Supply.

Hathaway, S. R., & McKinley, J. C. (1943). *MMPI manual.* New York: Psychological Corporation.

McClelland, D. C., Atkinson, J. W., Clark, R. A., & Lowell, E. I. (1953). *The achievement motive.* New York: Appleton-Century-Crofts.

Robins, L. N., Helzer, J. E., Croughan, J., & Ratcliff, K. S. (1981). The NIMH diagnostic interview schedule: Its history, characteristics, and validity. *Archives of General Psychiatry, 38,* 381–389.

Rorschach, H. (1942). *Psychodiagnostics*. Berne, Switzerland: Huber.

Constance Y. Celaya
Frances F. Worchel
Texas A & M University

DIAGNOSTIC AND STATISTICAL MANUAL OF MENTAL DISORDERS (DSM IV)
MENTAL ILLNESS
MENTAL STATUS

PERSONALITY INVENTORY FOR CHILDREN (PIC)

The Personality Inventory for Children (PIC) was developed over approximately a 20-year period, primarily by Robert Wirt and William Broen. With its 600 items, 33 subscales (3 validity scales, 1 general screening scale, 12 primary clinical scales, and 17 supplemental scales), point of origin, and emphasis on profiling of scores for interpretation, it is similar in many ways to the Minnesota Multiphasic Personality Inventory (MMPI). At least one reviewer has characterized the PIC as a junior MMPI (Achenbach, 1981).

The PIC originated with the efforts of Wirt and Broen to create an objective personality scale for children that could serve many of the same purposes with this population as the MMPI serves with adults and older adolescents. Primarily from an atheoretical, purely rational basis (though previous empirical work has apparently been consulted), Wirt and Broen initially wrote 550 test items, 50 for each of 11 content scales. The original scales included withdrawal, excitement, reality, distortion, aggression, somatic concern, anxiety, social skills, family relations, physical development, intellectual development, and asocial behavior. As with the items, the various scales of the PIC were developed largely from a logical, rational basis and retained on a purely empirical basis with no attention to theories of personality (though some individual scales have an implicit theoretical basis, many of a Freudian or psychoanalytic nature).

As opposed to virtually all other objective personality scales, the PIC is not a self-report inventory. Rather, it is completed by an informant, recommended strongly by the authors to be the child's mother, although the father or any significant other knowledgeable of the child's behavior and preferences is acceptable. Instructions to the respondent on the administration booklet are simple, straightforward, and easy to understand. No other instructions are provided. The respondent indicates true or false in response to each of the 600 declarative test items. The scale is unquestionably too lengthy for practical application in the school,

but this should not affect its use in clinics or private practice setting. School personnel may see information based on the PIC from outside referral sources, particularly when clinical child psychologists are used to evaluate emotionally disturbed children.

The PIC is normed on 2390 children ages 5½ to 16½ years, with about 100 boys and 100 girls at each year interval. The PIC was normed between 1958 and 1962; 81.5% of the children included were from a single school district and the majority of the remainder from a single medical clinic. Current practice dictates large, nationally stratified random samples of children for major assessment devices. At a minimum, the sample should be carefully stratified according to traditional demographic characteristics, even for a local sampling. Sampling essentially only from the Minneapolis area seems inexcusable for a scale published in the late 1970s. The sample is also outdated, being more than 25 years old. How parents perceive and respond to their children may well have changed over this lengthy period and a complete renorming is in order. At present, normative data for the PIC are best described as inadequate despite its positive attributes (i.e., using a large sample and normal children). The PIC provides traditional T-scores (mean = 50, standard deviation = 10) for interpretive purposes. This is a typical approach to personality inventory scores and perfectly acceptable.

The PIC is a lengthy personality scale for children that is hard to understand. It has serious psychometric deficiencies with standardization, norming, and reliability and serious problems with the construct validity of the scale. As a research tool, however, it is ready for widespread but careful use in a variety of areas. As a clinical tool, it holds promise, but its widespread use in diagnosis and decision making is premature and must await, at a minimum, a complete renorming of the scale. Better interpretive scoring systems are also needed as an aid to clinicians. The present computerized scoring and interpretive system does little more than group statements checked by the respondent into coherent paragraphs, giving little new information. Though its use is growing in clinical settings, it has not been widely adopted in schools. An extensive critique of PIC can be found in Reynolds (1985).

REFERENCES

Achenbach, T. M. (1981). A junior MMPI? *Journal of Personality, 45*, 332–330.

Reynolds, C. R. (1985). Review of Personality Inventory for Children. In J. V. Mitchell (Eds.), *Ninth mental measurements yearbook*, Lincoln: Buros Institute.

Cecil R. Reynolds
Texas A & M University

PERSONALITY ASSESSMENT

PERSONALITY TESTS, OBJECTIVE

An objective test of personality is one in which the subject is required to make forced choices in response to questions or statements. The scale is objectively scored using templates to organize responses according to the factors measured by the scale. In objective tests of personality, the test items are likely to be interpreted as asking or stating the same thing by most respondents. In most instances, those items are constructed in a manner that avoids ambiguity. The possible alternatives are "yes" or "no" or "true" or "false." In other instances, they may be in a multiple choice format with up to five options.

The validity of the test is established by analyzing the responses and response patterns of persons who have been clinically identified as deviant and comparing the responses to those selected by nondeviant (control) groups. The Minnesota Multiphasic Personality Inventory (MMPI-2) is probably the best known and most widely regarded personality inventory of this kind. In contrast to a projective test of personality such as the Rorschach Test an objective personality test allows for psychometric manipulation and profile analysis.

Another widely used objective personality test is the California Psychological Inventory (CPI). It is a pencil and paper inventory that contains 18 scales and 480 items. These scales were developed using an empirical model in much the same way as the MMPI-2 and MMPI-A. Other approaches used to construct objective personality tests are through factor analysis, intuitive-theoretical or intuitive-rational models. Studies of the different methods used for establishing the validity of objective personality tests found the methods to be comparable.

The Eysenck Personality Inventory (EPI) is a two-scale test that measures introversion-extroversion and neuroticism-stability. The scale contains 57 items and takes less time to administer than many scales. It contains a lie scale as a part of its organization; however, this aspect of the scale is not viewed as being reliable.

Objective personality assessment procedures are used by clinicians and researchers interested in identifying psychological problems. The results are used to help them better understand the individual and to help them resolve problems. There is some concern that the use of the scales for excluding persons from employment or educational opportunities is inappropriate and may carry some legal liabilities. In the future, their use in clinical settings may be more applicable than for purposes of employment screening.

ROBERT A. SEDLAK
University of Wisconsin at Stout

MMPI-2
PERSONALITY ASSESSMENT

REVISED CHILDREN'S MANIFEST ANXIETY SCALE
RORSCHACH

PERSONNEL PREPARATION FOR WORKING WITH DIVERSE INDIVIDUALS

In contrast to the increasing number of students from diverse cultural and linguistic backgrounds, the teaching force is predominantly white, monolingual, female and suburban (Zeichner, 1993). The culture clash resulting from this disparity between the characteristics of students and those of teachers is a contributing factor to the underachievement of culturally and linguistically diverse (CLD) students in both general and special education, with Hispanic/Latino, African American, and American Indian children and youth experiencing the most significant achievement difficulties. As a group, these students are disproportionately overrepresented in special education, underrepresented in gifted education, and have higher dropout rates when compared to their white counterparts (García & Dominguez, 1997).

Essential Knowledge and Skills Related to Diversity

Institutions of higher education must adopt training models that prepare special educators to be culturally and linguistically competent service providers. To effectively address the diverse backgrounds of the students in their classrooms, teachers must have both culture-general and culture-specific knowledge and skills. Culture-general knowledge emphasizes cultural phenomena that occur across cultures and that are widely applicable in a variety of settings (Brislin & Yoshida, 1994). This information provides the initial foundation for understanding cultural/linguistic factors in schooling and education. Culture-specific knowledge, on the other hand, provides an understanding of the customs, norms, traditions, and values of a specific racial/ethnic community and helps prepare teachers to better serve the communities in which they teach. In addition, there are several other essential components of culturally-responsive personnel preparation programs.

Cultural self-awareness. Cultural self-awareness serves as the foundation on which individuals build their knowledge and skills related to diversity (Brislin & Yoshida, 1994). Teachers of CLD students should have the opportunity to examine their own beliefs, attitudes, and assumptions related to individuals from culturally and linguistically diverse backgrounds. They must consider how current practices associated with labeling students (e.g., at-risk, disabled, low-performing) impact their own perceptions of, and expectations for, CLD students, and develop educationally valid perspectives that promote effective teaching practices (Cloud, 1993).

Cultural/linguistic knowledge. Educators must understand cultural/linguistic variables influencing the teaching-learning process at two levels. First, they must possess a foundation of culture-general knowledge such as cultural variations in childrearing practices, culturally-based learning and communication styles, acculturation, bilingualism, second language acquisition, and dialectal differences, as well as the influences of these on the teaching-learning process. Second, variations in these dimensions of human development and learning must be understood in relation to the specific ethnolinguistic communities of their CLD students and families (Gay, 1993). Moreover, it is important for educators to know how to gather these culture-specific data in their school communities (Hollins, 1996), and to be able to incorporate what they have learned into their professional practice; i.e., design culturally/linguistically responsive curricula and instruction, conduct non-biased assessments, and communicate effectively with diverse families.

Culturally/linguistically responsive practice. When students' background experiences are different from those expected by the school, it is important that educators design instructional programs that foster academic success as well as a positive, bicultural/bilingual identity (Cummins, 1986). Effective educational practices for CLD students include high expectations for all students, accepting and culturally pluralistic classroom and school environments, a culturally- and linguistically-inclusive curriculum, use of varied teaching and classroom management styles, teaching aimed at preventing academic failure, culturally-appropriate assessment procedures and materials, and support systems for teachers (Banks, 1990; Ortiz & Wilkinson, 1991). Special educators who serve CLD students with disabilities must also be able to design and implement individualized educational plans that are culturally and linguistically responsive (e.g., Franklin, 1992; García & Malkin, 1993). This includes the ability to provide special education services in the student's native language and/or English-as-a-second-language (ESL) instruction for students with disabilities who are also still in the process of acquiring English (Yates & Ortiz, 1998). Similarly, students who are nonstandard speakers of English need services that are responsive to their dialectal differences as well as which provide opportunities to acquire standard English. To do this effectively, professionals must be able to modify assessment, instruction, and related services to accommodate the intrapersonal interactions between culture, language, and disability (Cloud, 1993).

Collaboration. An integral aspect of a multicultural, pluralistic school is the development of collaborative partner-ships between schools and families. Recognizing that schools and professionals have often interacted with families in ways that effectively discourage their participation (Harry, Allen, & McLaughlin, 1995), teacher education programs should foster pluralistic models of family involvement. Professionals must understand cultural variations in family structures and in views about disability, and the impact of these different perspectives on how families and individuals with disabilities interact with the educational system. They must be able to work with family members to build on their strengths and available resources (Ford, 1995; Harry, 1992).

Special educators must also be able to work collaboratively with bilingual education teachers, ESL teachers, general education teachers, paraprofessionals, assessment and related services personnel, and others involved in implementing the student's intervention plan. It is likely that CLD students with disabilities will be served simultaneously by special education and a variety of other programs, resulting in the need to coordinate selection and implementation of goals and objectives, including responsibility for meeting these goals, language(s) of instruction, as well as instructional materials and procedures used across programs.

Reflection and problem-solving. The process of designing culturally- and linguistically-responsive programs and services implies that teachers can evaluate available materials and resources, adapt them to be sensitive to individual students' educational needs, and determine when and whether modifications are required (Kennedy, as cited in Burstein, Cabello, & Hamann, 1993). This is achieved by developing teachers' self-reflection and problem-solving skills through field experiences, reflective logs, structured and guided discussions, and activities designed to apply classroom-based theoretical knowledge in field-based settings (Burstein, Cabello, & Hamann, 1993). Without such guided reflection, the educational value of practica and other field-based assignments may be minimal or detrimental (Zeichner, 1993).

Cultural brokers and change agents. Finally, teachers must also be capable of functioning as change agents and as cultural brokers (Gay, 1993). They must take a leadership role in helping educational systems shift from a traditional deficit view of CLD students and communities to one which reflects acceptance of cultural and linguistic differences as assets (Obiakor & Utley, 1997). That is, they must have developed a sociopolitical or critical consciousness (Ladson-Billings, 1995) which promotes and supports changes at the institutional level (Gay, 1993). According to Gay, teachers must thus be reflective practitioners, adept at critically examining the nature of schooling, the culture of the dominant society, cultural similarities and differences, and potential sources of conflict or dissonance. They must understand the organizational culture of schooling and be able to employ effective strategies to foster student success, and to initiate and support change. Finally, they must have the requisite cross-cultural communication and counseling skills to be effective cultural brokers and change agents.

To achieve institutional change in practices affecting CLD learners, general and special educators must additionally (a) understand the historical and contemporary factors which have led to disproportionate representation of CLD students in special and gifted education; (b) develop problem solving processes to systematically eliminate school-related factors which have contributed to the underachievement of CLD students (García & Ortiz, 1988); and (c) critically examine assessment and identification procedures (Cummins, 1986) as well as programs and services to ensure that they are effectively meeting the educational needs of CLD students.

Related Issues

Many special education programs which serve CLD students are staffed by professionals who are not adequately trained and who are acquiring their expertise on the job. While efforts are underway to increase the number of CLD teachers who enter and remain in the profession, experience suggests that these efforts will not be sufficient to meet the needs of a growing CLD student population (Hill, Carjuzza, Aramburo, & Baca, 1993). Competencies must be identified and programs developed at the preservice and inservice levels to prepare all teachers to better serve the needs of culturally and linguistically diverse learners to reduce or eliminate the continuing cultural clashes resulting from the discontinuities between teachers' and students' backgrounds. In addition, institutions of higher education as well as school systems must continue to explore alternative approaches for recruitment and retention of professionals committed to working with CLD populations.

Contributing to the shortage of special education teachers with skills and competencies to serve CLD students is the serious shortage of university faculty who themselves have expertise related to CLD students with disabilities. This is a critical issue in that higher education faculty play a central role in the creation of new knowledge relative to the education of language minority students. Of particular concern, then, is the serious shortage of researchers from CLD backgrounds. Attention must be given to the retooling of university faculty to participate in the preparation of teachers for an increasingly pluralistic society. The special education literature on the preparation of teachers and other professionals to serve CLD populations is quite limited (Tulbert, Sindelar, Correa, & LaPorte, 1996), and studies of effective practices or program designs for diversity training in special education are even more scarce (Artiles & Trent, 1997). Several issues surround the question

of how best to prepare professionals in general and special education to meet the needs of an increasingly diverse student population. Questions which must be addressed by future research in teacher education include:

What competencies are needed by all educators who serve CLD exceptional learners?

What is the role of bilingual/multicultural special education specialists in services for CLD exceptional children and youth?

What are essential professional competencies related to diversity that produced high student outcomes for CLD exceptional learners?

What is the most effective program design for multicultural/bilingual special education?

How does program philosophy and design (e.g., inclusion vs. specialized courses) influence the quality of the teachers' learning?

Professional Standards

There are several efforts underway aimed at identifying essential knowledge and skills of novice and exemplary teachers. For example, the Council for Exceptional Children has developed professional standards for the preparation of special educators (Council for Exceptional Children, 1996) and is currently collaborating with its Division for Culturally and Linguistically Diverse Exceptional Learners to identify entry-level knowledge and skills associated with teaching CLD students. Similarly, the National Board for Professional Teaching Standards is preparing standards for what accomplished special education teachers should know and be able to do, and has designed a system for recognizing exemplary teachers of special needs students. All Board certificates include equity, fairness, and diversity standards which underscore the importance of respecting and responding to individual and group differences and of ensuring that all students have access to academically challenging curricula and opportunities to learn.

REFERENCES

Artiles, A., & Trent, S. (1997). Forging a research program on multicultural preservice teacher education in special education: A proposed analytic scheme. In J. W. Lloyd, E. J. Kameenui, & D. Chard (Eds.), *Issues in educating students with disabilities* (pp. 275–304). Hillsdale, NJ: Erlbaum.

Banks, J. A. (1990). *Preparing teachers and administrators in a multicultural society.* Austin, TX: Southwest Educational Development Laboratory.

Brislin, R., & Yoshida, T. (1994). *Intercultural communication training: An introduction.* Thousand Oaks, CA: Sage.

Burstein, N., Cabello, B., & Hamann, J. (1993). Teacher preparation for culturally diverse urban students: Infusing competencies across the curriculum. *Teacher Education and Special Education, 16*(1), 1–13.

Cloud, N. (1993). Language, culture and disability: Implications for instruction and teacher preparation. *Teacher Education and Special Education, 16*, 60–72.

Council for Exceptional Children (1996). *What every special educator must know: The international standards for the preparation and certification of special education teachers* (2nd ed.). Reston, VA: Author.

Cummins, J. (1986). Empowering language minority students. *Harvard Educational Review, 56*, 18–36.

Ford, B. A. (1995). African American community involvement processes and special education: Essential networks for effective education. In B. A. Ford, F. E. Obiakor, & J. M. Patton (Eds.), *Effective education for African American exceptional learners* (pp. 235–272). Austin, TX: Pro-Ed.

Franklin, M. (1992). Culturally sensitive instructional practices for African-American learners with disabilities. *Exceptional Children, 59*, 115–122.

García, S. B., & Dominguez, L. (1997). Cultural contexts that influence learning and academic performance. *Child and Adolescent Psychiatric Clinics of North America, 6*, 621–655.

García, S. B., & Malkin, D. H. (1993). Toward defining programs and services for culturally and linguistically diverse learners in special education. *Teaching Exceptional Children, 26*(1), 52–58.

García, S. B., & Ortiz, A. A. (1988). *Preventing inappropriate referrals of Hispanic students to special education.* New Focus Series No. 3. Washington, DC: National Clearinghouse for Bilingual Education.

Gay, G. (1993). Building cultural bridges: A bold proposal for teacher education. *Education and Urban Society, 25*(3), 285–299.

Harry, B. (1992). Making sense of disability: Low-income, Puerto Rican parents' theories of the problem. *Exceptional Children, 59*, 27–40.

Harry, B., Allen, N., & McLaughlin, M. (1995). Communication versus compliance: African-American parents' involvement in special education. *Exceptional Children, 61*, 354–377.

Hill, R., Carjuzza, J., Aramburo, D., & Baca, L. (1993). Culturally and linguistically diverse teachers in special education: Repairing or redesigning the leaky pipeline. *Teacher Education and Special Education, 16*, 258–269.

Hollins, E. (1996). *Culture in school learning: Revealing the deep meaning.* Mahwah, NJ: Erlbaum.

Ladson-Billings, G. (1995). Toward a theory of culturally relevant pedagogy. *American Educational Research Journal, 32*, 465–491.

Obiakor, F. E., & Utley, C. A. (1997). Rethinking preservice preparation for teachers in the learning disabilities field: Workable multicultural strategies. *Learning Disabilities Research and Practice, 12*, 110–106.

Ortiz, A. A., & Wilkinson, C. Y. (1991). Assessment and Intervention Model for the Bilingual Exceptional Student (AIM for the BEST). *Teacher Education and Special Education, 14*, 37–42.

Tulbert, B., Sindelar, P. T., Correa, V. I., & La Porte, M. A. (1996). Looking in the rear view mirror: A content analysis of *Teacher Education and Special Education. Teacher Education and Special Education, 19*, 248–261.

Yates, J R., & Ortiz, A A. (1998). Developing individualized education programs for exceptional language minority students. In L. M. Baca & H. T. Cervantes (Eds.), *The bilingual special education interface* (3rd ed.; pp. 188–210). Upper Saddle River, NJ: Merrill/Prentice-Hall.

Zeichner, K. M. (1993). *Educating teachers for cultural diversity.* NCRTL Special Report. East Lansing, MI: Michigan State University, National Center for Research on Teacher Learning.

Shernaz B. García
Alba A. Ortiz
University of Texas

PERSONNEL TRAINING IN SPECIAL EDUCATION

See SPECIAL EDUCATION, TEACHER TRAINING IN.

PERÚ, SPECIAL EDUCATION IN

Overview and Demographics

Perú has an estimated population of 24,400,000. Using international estimation guidelines, there should be approximately 2,440,000 or 10% of the general population with disabilities. The last official census reported in 1993 indicated only a total of 289,526 disabled people, which must be assumed to be an incorrect count because it represents only 1% of the actual population. Assuming that 7% of the estimated number of people with disabilities are under 18, the number of children needing service would be 170,800. The Ministry of Education, however, remains responsible for students until they are 26, so that percentage would probably grow by another 5%, or 14,476 people, for a total of 185,276 people with disabilities eligible for special educational services (Census, 1993).

As of 1997, 20,373 people eligible for special education were enrolled in 356 state schools and 3,515 were enrolled in 88 private schools of special education. Regular schools integrated another 221 pupils. The total of 24,109 being educated represents only 13% of the eligible estimated population. The actual total population that is disabled is probably much larger than the world estimation of 10% because Perú has the second highest rate of malnutrition in South America. Thus, those served are likely less than 13% of the actual number of children and youths below 26 years of age (Demographic Statistics, 1997).

The quality of special education that is provided is generally considered inadequate because of poor teacher salaries, poor school conditions, difficult travel, lack of professional education for the majority of the teachers, and lack of government priority. The people who receive no education generally are those who have severe to profound disabilities or multiple handicaps, those in the severest levels of poverty, and those who live in the Andes and the Amazon jungle.

Most schools, state or private, do not accept students with severe to profound retardation, autism, behavior problems, or those with multiple handicaps. The one state psychiatric institution to which they can go is severely limited for funds and space. Thus, there are many adults and children with various types of disabilities living in the streets. The majority live at home with their families. There are two group homes, one in Lima and one in Trujillo, each serving about 20 students. There are many people with retardation who are abandoned and who live in the streets. Adults and children with disabilities have only one state psychiatric institution, located in Lima, to turn to if they have no family, and even then, they can only be admitted if there is space.

Model Programs

There are 30 state early intervention programs for children from birth to five years of age and their caregivers. This program is similar to the Portage Project operated by U.S. researchers in Perú in 1977, which did not flourish due to lack of government support. These programs are unable to serve large numbers of children, however, because they work with one family at a time, for two or three times a week. In 1995, the Ministry began a program of integration in four districts. Although a commendable program, most of the children are very mildly handicapped and many are placed into the program because of behavioral problems. Similar behavioral placements occur in special education classes (The Portage Project, 1995).

Perú does have one private internationally-known model center, Centro Ann Sullivan del Perú, founded in 1979, which is recognized for its excellent functional/natural curriculum, its required family participation program, its individualized life plans and integration into life for its student/workers, and its national and international professional and parent training. It serves 250 people with severe retardation, autism, and behavior problems who live with their families. The center has over 15 different programs ranging from early stimulation to supported employment. Students and professionals from Perú and many other countries come to study and the staff travels around the world to teach the procedures and programs of the center, which is recognized by the University of Kansas as a model center for international cooperation and multiplicative education. The dedicated staff, with help from consultants, has developed the various training programs around the theme of "Treat me like a person and educate me to succeed in life." Currently recognized best practices

are used in this low-budget, small-staff, diversified program that serves large numbers of student/workers, ranging in age from birth through adulthood and their families.

History of Special Education in Perú

In 1911, the first special education school in Perú was founded in Lima to educate blind children. Even with no governmental office of special education, in 1969, a UNESCO study reported 12 government-supported state special education schools, 9 in Lima and 3 in other cities. This report also revealed 6 private schools located in Lima and one for abandoned children located in the Andes. Only 9 of the 12 state schools were exclusively dedicated to educating exceptional children as they are known today. The others served populations of young, poor mothers, and children with malnutrition, incipient TB, or other medical complications (UNESCO, 1969).

In 1971, when the first department of special education was created in the Ministry of Education in the area of primary education, there were only 10 state and 6 private special education schools. Subsequently courses were developed by 5 universities, the first at San Marcos University, the oldest university in the western hemisphere. By 1979, the number of special education schools had grown to 78—49 state schools and 29 private schools.

In 1983, the first law giving the right to free education to children with all types of disabilities was passed in the Peruvian Congress. The objectives of special education were to teach special people to be integrated into the normal social and occupational life, and to educate families and communities to participate in the identification, treatment, and recognition of the rights of special people. Special education would be supervised by the Ministry of Education and coordinated with the Ministries of Health, Justice, Work, and Social Promotion. Included were the rights to be accepted in special education without discrimination; to receive education that permits students to be effectively incorporated into society, especially in workplaces; and to be treated with dignity and respect for differences. Although the law was quite forward-looking, it contained no guidelines for implementation and/or enforcement. Thus, few of the stated objectives have been accomplished (Special Education Law, 1983).

In 1991, the Department of Special Education was abolished and special schools were generally subsumed into the area of primary education. Subsequently little innovative activity, other than the integration program, has occurred.

Professional Education

In 1979, 143 teachers had received education in mental retardation. Education of teachers occurred through special summer and short postgraduate courses taught in San

Marcos University and the Catholic University in Lima. In 1974, The Womans' University opened a course in special education, and in 1976, through an agreement between the Ministry of Education, the Hope Program of the US, and Trujillo, two courses in special education were started outside Lima. Currently, there are 6 to 8 universities offering special education courses.

Challenges to Special Education in Perú

The Peruvian government does not make special education a priority because of greater problems of street children, malnutrition, unemployment, and abject poverty which affect much larger numbers of the total population. Because of travel, communication, financial, and professional/parent education problems, creative approaches are needed if education of children with special needs is going to improve. The Ministry of Education continually seeks ways to upgrade the education of all of its teachers, but few resources go directly to special education. The Centro Ann Sullivan del Perú is currently developing a long-distance parent/professional education program, with donations and foundation projects aimed at alleviating problems of substandard professional education and communication in the next few years.

REFERENCES

Central Government of Perú. (1993). *Official census.* Perú: Author.
Centro Ann Sullivan. (1997). *Program description.* Perú: Author.
Ministry of Education of the Central Government of Perú. (1983). *Special Education Law.* Perú: Author.
Ministry of Education of the Central Government of Perú. (1995). *The Portage project.* Perú: Author.
Ministry of Education of the Central Government of Perú. (1997). *Demographic statistics of education and services.* Perú: Author.
UNESCO. (1969). *Services for the handicapped in Perú.* Author.

LILIANA MAYO
Centro Ann Sullivan Perú

PESTALOZZI, JOHANN HEINRICH (1746–1827)

Johann Heinrich Pestalozzi, a Swiss educator, greatly influenced education in Europe and the United States. Believing that ideas have meaning only as related to concrete things and that learning must therefore proceed from the concrete to the abstract, he developed a system of education through object lessons that were designed to help the child develop abstract concepts from concrete experience.

Pestalozzi operated a number of orphanages and schools, the most notable being his boarding school at Yver-

don, founded in 1805. His school demonstrated concepts such as readiness, individual differences, ability grouping, and group instruction, and contributed to the inclusion in the curriculum of the practical subjects of geography, nature, art, music, and manual training. Large numbers of educators visited Yverdon and hundreds of Pestalozzian schools were established in Europe. Pestalozzi's object method was first used in the United States in the schools of Oswego, New York; the Oswego Normal School trained teachers in Pestalozzi's methods. Of his numerous publications, Pestalozzi's *How Gertrude Teaches Her Children* best sets forth his educational principles.

REFERENCES

Pestalozzi, J. H. (1978). *How Gertrude teaches her children.* New York: Gordon.
Silber, K. (1973). *Pestalozzi: The man and his work.* New York: Schocken.

PAUL IRVINE
Katonah, New York

PETS IN SPECIAL EDUCATION

Animals have long been used in classrooms throughout the world (Hulme, 1995). The classic goldfish and gerbils have been used to teach basic animal facts. Teachers have also used pets to foster responsibility in their students. Animals can provide valuable classroom or instructional assistance far beyond the traditional expectations. Sustenance instruction, responsible behavior training, and abstract concepts development can be enhanced by involving special education students with animals. These animals may be provided in the classroom or they may be pets from home.

Any pet (fish, dog, cat, bird, etc.) may be used for sustenance instruction. Special education students can better learn the basic needs of animals through active participation in the pet's care. The students identify the need for food, water, shelter, and love. Instruction may include concepts such as appropriate food for different species, appropriate quantities of food and water, how climate affects the need for shelter, and how animals exhibit and respond to affection.

Teaching responsibility is a multifaceted, often difficult task. Whenever special education students have the responsibility for pets in the classroom or at home, the teacher should be attempting to develop various components of responsible behavior. Students should learn to create feeding, watering, bathing, walking, etc., schedules. In creating schedules for their pets, students may learn to develop schedules for their own lives. Caring for pets also aids in developing task commitment, as well as relationship commitment. Another facet of responsibility, self-initiation, is readily taught when students must care, without reminders from the teacher, for classroom animals.

Students may also develop observation skills through involvement with pets. Because pets are basically nonverbal, students must watch for changes, in the animals' appearance or mannerisms to detect illness or injury.

Many special education students have difficulty in understanding abstract concepts such as life, death, and love. The birth or death of a classroom pet may be used to teach the rudiments and sentiments of such abstract concepts. The emotions of love, caring, and affection may be developed or more objectively understood by special education students when pets are used.

REFERENCE

Hulme, P. (1995). *Historical overview of nonstandard treatments.* (ERIC Clearinghouse No. EC303986)

JONI J. GLEASON
University of West Florida

EQUINE THERAPY
RECREATION

PEVZNER, MARIA SEMENOVNA (1901–1986)

As a physician-psychiatrist and doctor of pedagogical sciences, Maria Pevzner is known for her work on oligophrenia (mental deficiency). Her research has been concentrated in the areas of child psychopathology and clinical assessment of atypical children. She suggested classification of oligophrenics into five groups: (1) with diffuse maldevelopment of the cortical hemispheres without serious neurological implications; (2) with cortical deficits and impaired perceptual abilities; (3) with various sensory, perceptual, and motor deficits; (4) with psychopathological behavior; and (5) with maldevelopment of the frontal lobes (Pevzner, 1970). Pevzner has extensively studied the criteria and clinical aspects necessary for a diagnosis of oligophrenia in school-age children (Mastyukova, Pevzner, & Peresleni, 1986), and she and her colleagues have also investigated the intellectual development of children with cerebral palsy, finding considerable variation in intellectual disorders, thus suggesting the benefit of comprehensive examination for these children (Mastyukova, Pevzner, & Peresleni, 1987, 1988). Well-known publications of Pevzner are *Children Psychopaths* (1941), *Developmental Assessment and Education of Oligophrenic Children* (1963), and *Children with Atypical Development* (1966).

REFERENCES

Mastyukova, E. M., Peresleni, L. I., & Pevzner, M. S. (1988). A study of intellectual structure impairment in children with cerebral, palsy. *Defektologiya, 4,* 12–17.

Mastyukova, E. M., Pevzner, M. S., & Peresleni, L. I. (1986). The diagnosis and clinical picture of oligophrenia in school children with cerebral palsy. *Zhurnal Nevropatologii I Psikhiatrii Imeni S-S-Korsakova, 86*(3), 386–389.

Mastyukova, E. M., Pevzner, M. S., & Peresleni, L. I. (1987). Diagnostic and clinical aspects of congenital mental retardation in pupils with cerebral palsy. *Soviet Neurology and Psychiatry, 20*(3), 36–43.

Pevzner, M. S. (1970). Etiopathogenesis and classification of oligophrenia (translated by G. Malashko). *Szkola Specjalna* (4), 289–293.

IVAN HOLOWINSKY
Rutgers University
First edition

TAMARA J. MARTIN
*The University of Texas of the
Permian Basin*
Second edition

PHENOBARBITAL

Of the many available anticonvulsant medications, phenobarbital is the least expensive, most effective, best known, and most widely used barbiturate. It is the drug of choice for tonic-clonic (grand mal) epilepsy, neonatal fits, and febrile convulsions (Maheshwari, 1981), and may be viewed as the drug of choice for childhood epilepsy except in cases of absence (petit mal) attacks (Swanson, 1979). It even may be used as an effective agent in pure petit mal epilepsy as a measure against the development of grand mal epilepsy (Livingston, Pruce, & Pauli, 1979).

All anticonvulsant medications have side effects and the extent and severity of such side effects often influence medication choice. Unlike many anticonvulsant drugs, phenobarbital has few somatic side effects; however, it appears to have more pronounced effects on mental or cognitive functions in children (National Institutes of Health, 1980). Sedation or drowsiness is the chief side effect of phenobarbital in children. This initial effect of mental slowing is most pronounced when the drug is first administered. The effect generally declines within several weeks (Livingston, Pauli, Pruce, & Kramer, 1980; Schain, 1979) and appears to be dose related (Livingston, et al., 1980; Livingston, Pruce, Pauli, & Livingston, 1979; Swanson, 1979; Wolf, 1979). Common behavioral side effects include hyperactivity, extreme irritability, and aggression (Fishman, 1979; Livingston, et al., 1980; Nelson, 1983; Wilensky, Ojemann, Temkin, Troupin, & Dodrill, 1981). Other side effects involving cognitive or higher cortical functions include impaired attention, short-term memory deficits, defects in general comprehension, dysarthria, ataxia, and, in some cases, poor language development (Levenstein, 1984; Shinnar & Kang, 1994).

Fortunately, the side effects do not appear to be permanent, and withdrawal or replacement with other medications often produces significant amelioration of these deficits. For example, withdrawal may lead to dramatic improvements in personality patterns and learning skills (Schain, 1979). Continuous monitoring of possible side effects and appropriate adjustment of anticonvulsant medication is therefore of the utmost importance in effective management of seizure disorders.

REFERENCES

Fishman, M. A. (1979). Febrile seizures: One treatment controversy. *Journal of Pediatrics, 94,* 177–184.

Levenstein, D. (1984). Phenobarbital side effects: Hyperactivity with speech delay. *Pediatrics, 74,* 1133.

Livingston, S., Pauli, L. L., Pruce, I., & Kramer, I. I., (1980). Phenobarbital vs. phenytoin for grand mal epilepsy. *American Family Physician, 22,* 123–127.

Livingston, S., Pruce, I., & Pauli, L. L. (1979). The medical treatment of epilepsy: Initiation of drug therapy. *Pediatrics Annals, 8,* 213–231.

Livingston, S., Pruce, I., Pauli, L. L., & Livingston, H. L. (1979). The medical treatment of epilepsy: Managing side effects of antiepileptic drugs. *Pediatrics Annals, 8,* 261–266.

Maheshwari, M. C. (1981). Choice of anticonvulsants in epilepsy. *Indian Pediatrics, 18,* 331–346.

National Institutes of Health. (1980). Febrile seizures: Long-term management of children with fever-associated seizures. *British Medical Journal, 281,* 277–279.

Nelson, K. B. (1983). The natural history of febrile seizures. *Annual Review of Medicine, 34,* 453–471.

Schain, R. J. (1979). Problems with the use of conventional anticonvulsant drugs in mentally retarded individuals. *Brain & Development, 1,* 77–82.

Shinner, S., & Kang, H. (1994). Idiosyncratic phenobarbital toxicity mimicking a neurogenerative disorder. *Journal of Epilepsy, 7*(1), 34–37.

Swanson, P. D. (1979). Anticonvulsant therapy: Approaches to some common clinical problems. *Postgraduate Medicine, 65,* 147–154.

Wilensky, A. J., Ojemann, L. M., Temkin, N. R., Troupin, A. S., & Dodrill, C. B. (1981). Clorazepate and phenobarbital as antiepileptic drugs: A double-blind study. *Neurology, 31,* 1271–1276.

Wolf, H. S. (1979). Controversies in the treatment for febrile convulsion. *Neurology, 29,* 287–290.

CHARLES J. LONG
University of Tennessee
Memphis State University

ABSENCE SEIZURES
ANTICONVULSANTS
GRAND MAL SEIZURES
MEDICAL MANAGEMENT
SEIZURE DISORDERS

PHENOTHIAZINES

Phenothiazine is the class of drugs that historically has been most often prescribed in the treatment of psychotic disorders. This class of medications, which provides symptomatic relief from many of the disturbing symptoms of disorders like schizophrenia and borderline personality disorder in males (Andrulonis, 1991); has replaced the more radical methods of symptom control (e.g., psychosurgery). In addition, the significant behavioral changes that occur when medication regimens are optimally effective allow patients to be treated in outpatient clinics rather than be chronically hospitalized. There are three major classes of phenothiazines that are relatively similar in their overall actions but different in their dose/response ratios and the overall amount of sedation produced (Bassuk & Schoonover, 1977). The subgroups include

Aliphatic	
Chlorpromazine	(Thorazine)
Promazine	(Sparine)

Piperidine	
Thioridazine	(Mellaril)
Piperacetazine	(Quide)
Mesoridazine	(Serentil)

Piperazine	
Trifluoperazine	(Stelazine)
Perphenazine	(Trilafon)
Fluphenazine	(Prolixin)

The major criticisms of phenothiazines revolve around the exclusive, long-term use of these drugs to control observable symptoms without an attempt to deal with etiology or overall adaptiveness (Marholin & Phillips, 1976). Crane (1973) provides an additional criticism indicating that phenothiazines also have been used within long-term treatment centers to control reactions to institutionalization and enforced restrictions: i.e., punitively.

Phenothiazines produce side effects that may be grouped into four classes: involuntary muscular contractions, especially in the area of the face; motor restlessness; parkinsonlike symptoms such as rigidity, motor slowing, excess salivation, slurred speech, flat facial expression, and gait disturbance; and tardive dyskinesia, a syndrome that consists of stereotyped, repetitive involuntary movements and persists even after medication is discontinued

(Bassuk & Schoonover, 1977). Side effects in children are similar to those of adults; however, parents additionally should be aware of sun sensitivity, when children are outside for extended periods of time, and learning/concentration difficulties, especially during onset of treatment (Bassuk & Schoonover, 1977).

REFERENCES

Andrulonis, P. A. (1991). Disruptive behavior disorders in boys and borderline personality disorder in men. *Annals of Clinical Psychiatry, 3*(1), 23–26.

Bassuk, E. L., & Schoonover, S. C. (1977). *The practitioner's guide to psychoactive drugs.* New York: Plenum Medical.

Crane, G. (1973). Clinical pharmacology in its 20th year. *Science, 181,* 124–128.

Marholin, D., & Phillips, D. (1976). Methodological issues in psychopharmacological research: Chlorpromazine—a case in point. *American Journal of Orthopsychiatry, 46,* 477–495.

ROBERT F. SAWICKI
*Lake Erie Institute of
Rehabilitation*

MELLARIL
STELAZINE
THORAZINE
TRANQUILIZERS

PHENYLKETONURIA (PKU)

Phenylketonuria (PKU) was one of the earliest biochemical irregularities associated with mental retardation. Folling noted in 1934 that a few institutionalized retardates had urine with a peculiar "mousy" odor, which was found to arise from the excretion of phenylacetic acid. Classic PKU results from the absence of the enzyme phenylalanine hydroxylase, which normally converts phenylalanine, an essential amino acid common to most proteins and many other foods, into tyrosine and its constituent components. The resulting high levels of phenylalanine damage developing brain tissue. Since brain damage is irreversible, permanent and severe retardation is a predictable outcome, as are seizures, tremors, and hypopigmentation of skin (Smith, 1985).

An autosomal recessive inborn error of amino-acid metabolism, PKU is expressed only in those homozygotic for the defective gene. Incidence is about 1 in 10,000 births in Whites and Asians, but much lower in Blacks. Heterozygotes typically produce enough enzymes for normal metabolism. Affected homozygotes are usually normal at birth since prenatally they received already metabolized nutrients through the umbilical cord. If the disorder is undiagnosed and untreated, progressive brain damage begins. Until the 1950s, prognosis was poor; most affected individuals had IQs of about 30 and were institutionalized.

Neonatal screening is now universal. Although a urine test was originally used, diagnosis is now through the Guthrie test, which reveals excess phenylalanine through a blood test 24 to 48 hours after birth. If PKU is diagnosed, the infant is placed on a low phenylalanine diet, which is synthetic because of the ubiquitous presence of phenylalanine in protein. Dietary treatment must begin within a few days of birth for maximal effectiveness. Adult IQ of early treated PKU individuals is about 90; IQ becomes lower with delay of treatment so that by about 3 years of age, maximal damage has occurred. The diet is the sole nutrient fed in infancy. Some (e.g., Berkow, 1977) suggest that thereafter low-protein foods such as fruits and vegetables may be tolerated, whereas others (e.g., Smith, 1985) recommend strict adherence to the diet. The taste of the diet is aversive, and maintaining the child on it while the rest of the family eats regular food can be an increasingly serious problem as the child grows.

Since phenylalanine is toxic only to developing brain tissue, treatment can cease or be relaxed when brain development is complete. Authorities disagree on when the diet can be terminated, but common practice has been to return the child to normal food at about age eight. However, research suggests that longer dietary treatment may be advisable. Dietary treatment for PKU is a classic example of genetic-environmental interaction. On a normal diet, individuals with PKU genotype will develop phenotypic IQ of about 30; dietary intervention alters the predicted developmental pathway, resulting in nearly normal phenotypic IQ (Brown, 1986).

However, treated PKU children may show specific deficits in perceptual motor functioning and arithmetic achievements that are more serious than would be expected on the basis of their slightly below average IQs. They appear to have neuropsychological deficits similar to those of brain-damaged children (Brunner, Jordon, & Berry, 1983; Pennington, von Doorninck, McCabe, & McCabe, 1985), and have particular deficits in visuospatial and conceptual skills, which may partially account for their problems with mathematics. Pennington et al. (1985) suggest that the deficits may occur because the children are taken off of the diet before the completion of relevant brain development. Although the number of subjects in these studies was small and the findings need confirmation, those working with treated PKU children should be aware that such children may have some specific learning deficits.

The effectiveness of the diet has had one tragic and unexpected effect. In the late 1960s, it became clear that children born to PKU women who had eaten normal food during pregnancy suffered prenatal growth retardation,

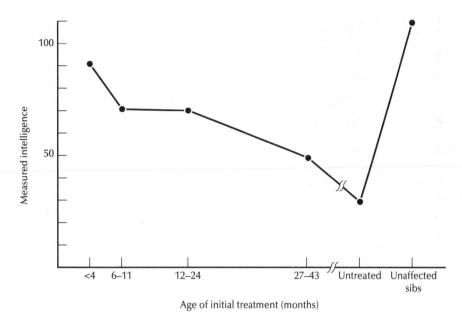

Mean IQ of PKU children as a function of the age at which dietary treatment began.

microcephaly, and brain damage, even though the children did not have the PKU genotype. Although the effects were variable, many of the children died early or became severely retarded. The problems may have been more serious than in untreated PKU itself (Lenke & Levy, 1980). The pregnant women had transmitted unmetabolized phenylalanine to their embryos and fetuses at the prenatal critical period for adverse influences on brain development. A common recommendation now is for PKU women to return to the diet throughout the time they may become pregnant. But regulation of optimal phenylalanine levels is difficult, and no dietary program is completely effective. The safest recommendation is for PKU women not to have children. Thus treated women have an additional responsibility during childbearing years, and some who are at a marginal level of functioning may need some social service assistance (Brown, 1986).

Recent research has changed previous recommendations that children with PKU could discontinue the special diet at about 8 years. Early-treated children who stop the diet actually show deterioration in functioning (IQ, reading and spelling, social behavior). Further, children on the diet show deficits in short-term memory and "executive functioning" relative to normal children. Some studies suggest that children with PKU who are on the diet still have higher levels of phenylalanine relative to tyrosine in their brains than do normal children. Tyrosine is a precursor to dopamine, a main neurotransmitter in frontal lobe functioning, and some of the problems shown by children with PKU who are on the diet resemble those associated with frontal-lobe syndrome. Thus, life-long dietary treatment is now recommended, and even then, some specific

deficits in functioning are likely. Some of this information can be found in Batshaw (1997).

REFERENCES

Batshaw, M. L. (1997). PKU and other inborn errors of metabolism. In M. L. Batshaw (Ed.), *Children with disabilities* (4th ed.) (pp. 389–404). Baltimore: Brookes.

Berkow, R. (Ed.). (1977). *The Merck manual* (13th ed.). Rahway, NJ: Merck, Sharpe, & Dohme.

Brown, R. T. (1986). Etiology and development of exceptionality. In R. T. Brown & C. R. Reynolds (Eds.), *Psychological perspectives on childhood exceptionality* (pp. 181–229). New York: Wiley.

Brunner, R. L., Jordon, M. K., & Berry, H. K. (1983). Early treated PKU: Neuropsychologic consequences. *Journal of Pediatrics, 102,* 381–385.

Lenke, R. R., & Levy, H. (1980). Maternal phenylketonuria and hyperphenylalaninia: An international survey of untreated and treated pregnancies. *New England Journal of Medicine, 303,* 1202–1208.

Pennington, B. F., von Doorninck, W. J., McCabe, L. L., & McCabe, E. R. B. (1985). Neuropsychological deficits in early treated phenylketonuric children. *American Journal of Mental Deficiency, 89,* 467–474.

Smith, L. H., Jr. (1985). The hyperphenylalaninemias. In J. B. Wyngaarden & L. H. Smith, Jr. (Eds.), *Cecil textbook of medicine* (17th ed., pp. 1126–1128). Philadelphia: Saunders.

ROBERT T. BROWN
University of North Carolina at Wilmington

BIOCHEMICAL IRREGULARITIES
INBORN ERRORS OF METABOLISM

Beeman N. Phillips

PHILLIPS, BEEMAN N. (1927–   )

A mathematics and physics major, Beeman N. Phillips completed his BA degree at Evansville College in 1949. He pursued graduate training at Indiana University, earning both his MS (1950) and EdD (1954) in educational psychology. Immediately following the completion of his doctoral degree, Phillips served as director of the Division of Research of the Indiana State Department of Public Instruction. In 1956 Phillips joined the faculty of the Department of Educational Psychology at the University of Texas, Austin, where he has remained.

At the University of Texas, Austin, Phillips founded one of the first doctoral training programs in school psychology, a program considered by many in the field to be the leading program in the country. Though its focus has changed in recent years, the program was particularly successful in pioneering and promoting consultation models for indirect service delivery in the provision of school psychological services. As the director and only continuous faculty member of the program, Phillips has been a key element in the development of the profession of school psychology. Among other professional leadership roles, Phillips has served as president of the Division of School Psychology of the American Psychological Association and was the editor of the *Journal of School Psychology* from 1972 to 1980. In 1978 Phillips was given the Division of School Psychology Distinguished Service Award. He was also the recipient of the 1991 Outstanding Education Alumnus Award from the School of Education, Indiana University (Bloomington), and in 1992 received the first annual Dean's Distinguished Faculty Award in the College of Education from the University of Texas at Austin. In June, 1998 he became professor emeritus.

Applied educational and psychological research has been the consistent focus of Phillips' research program. He has also been concerned with developing conceptual and methodological rigor in school psychological research, the latter perhaps best exemplified in his chapters in the *Handbook of School Psychology*. As a major research interest, Phillips has studied school stress and its relationship to school adjustment and learning. His work as a whole reflects a strong educational orientation to psychological research coupled with a concern for theoretical relevance and practical applications of research. He has emphasized the need for a better interface between psychology and schooling as well as the means for achieving it. Phillips's books include *School Psychology at a Turning Point: Ensuring a Bright Future for the Profession* (1990) and *Educational and Psychological Perspectives on Stress in Students, Teachers, and Parents* (1993).

REFERENCES

Phillips, B. N. (1978). *School stress and anxiety: Theory, research, and intervention.* New York: Human Sciences.

Phillips, B. N. (1982). Reading and evaluating research in school psychology. In C. R. Reynolds & T. B. Gutkin (Eds.), *The handbook of school psychology.* New York: Wiley.

Phillips, B. N. (1990). Reading, evaluating, and applying research in school psychology. In T. B. Gutkin & C. R. Reynolds (Eds.), *The handbook of school psychology* (2nd ed.). New York: Wiley.

Phillips, B. N. (1990). *School Psychology at a turning point: Ensuring a bright future for the Profession.* San Francisco: Jossey-Bass.

Phillips, B. N. (1993). *Educational and psychological perspectives on stress in students, teachers, and parents.* Brandon, VT: Clinical Psychology.

Phillips, B. N. (in press). Strengthening the links between science and practice: Reading, evaluating, and applying research in school psychology. In C. R. Reynolds & T. B. Gutkin (Eds.), *The handbook of school psychology* (3rd ed.). New York: Wiley.

CECIL R. REYNOLDS
Texas A & M University
First edition

TAMARA J. MARTIN
The University of Texas of the Permian Basin
Second edition

JOURNAL OF SCHOOL PSYCHOLOGY

PHILOSOPHY OF EDUCATION FOR THE HANDICAPPED

The philosophical beliefs and values that underlie special education are diverse, dynamic, and interrelated. They reflect broad social issues such as attitudes toward individuals with handicaps as well as specific educational concerns. Three key issues are access to education, placement, and instruction.

Issues of access to education involve questions relating to which children have a right to education and whether all children can benefit from instruction. Questions of access and educability were first raised with respect to individuals with severe and obvious handicaps—the blind, deaf, mentally retarded, and seriously emotionally disturbed. Concern for these individuals prompted the earliest intervention efforts, beginning in the United States as early as 1817. The achievements of educators such as Edouard Seguin gave rise to optimism that education could cure or ameliorate severe handicapping conditions and resulted in an expansion in the number of available treatment programs for these populations (Kauffman, 1981).

The enactment of compulsory school attendance laws in the early twentieth century brought a wider range of students to the public schools. As a result, the special educational needs of moderately handicapped students became apparent. Special classes were instituted, providing these students with some measure of access to education, but few programs were designed to deliver the type of instructional program necessary to ensure that these students could profit from their schooling. (See Kauffman, 1981, Reynolds & Birch, 1982 for a detailed chronology of major historical influences in special education.)

The beginnings of the civil rights movement in the 1950s set the stage for further changes in philosophies of educational access. Equal educational opportunity became a focus for the efforts of increasingly active parent groups and professionals in special education. A body of case law, beginning with the *Brown v. Board of Education* decision, eventually developed and affirmed the principle of handicapped children's right to education.

The question of what organizational setting, or placement, is most appropriate for students with disabilities has been answered differently through the history of special education. Beginning with residential institutions, the range of placement options has gradually increased to include special schools, special classes within public schools, and, finally, integration into regular public school classes (mainstreaming) and inclusion. IDEA requires that handicapped students be placed, to the maximum extent appropriate, in regular educational environments with their nonhandicapped peers. This mandate is known as placement in the least restrictive environment. Inclusion and least restrictive placement are outgrowths of the broader philosophical concept of normalization—the belief that handicapped persons should, to the greatest extent possible, be integrated into society.

Without appropriate instructional strategies, any inclusive or least restrictive placement efforts are unlikely to succeed. Individualized instruction, first advocated by nineteenth-century educators such as Itard and Seguin,

has been formalized through IDEA's requirement that an individualized education program be developed and its execution monitored for each child placed in special education.

The philosophical issues that have shaped special education have evolved and changed significantly over the past two centuries. A contemporary philosophy of education for the handicapped incorporates a diversity of complex issues that include those related to access to education, educability, placement, and instruction.

REFERENCES

Hallahan, D. P., & Kauffman, J. M. (1982). *Exceptional children: Introduction to special education.* Englewood Cliffs, NJ: Prentice-Hall.

Kauffman, J. M. (1981). Historical trends and contemporary issues in special education in the United States. In J. M. Kauffman & D. P. Hallahan (Eds.), *Handbook of special education* (pp. 3–24). Englewood Cliffs, NJ: Prentice-Hall.

Paul, J. L. (1981). Service delivery models for special education. In J. M. Kauffman & D. P. Hallahan (Eds.), *Handbook of special education* (pp. 291–310). Englewood Cliffs, NJ: Prentice-Hall.

Reynolds, M. C., & Birch, J. W. (1982). *Teaching exceptional children in all America's schools.* Reston, VA: Council for Exceptional Children.

MARY LOUISE LENNON
RANDY ELLIOT BENNETT
Educational Testing Service

INDIVIDUALS WITH DISABILITIES EDUCATION ACT (IDEA)

PHOBIAS AND FEARS

Fear in children and youths is a very strong emotion and is associated with behavioral, cognitive, and physiological indicators of anxiety. When a handicapped child or youth experiences fear that is not age-related in a setting where there is no obvious external danger, the fear is irrational, and the person is said to have a phobia. When the person begins to avoid the nondangerous feared situation, even while maintaining that such action is foolish, the phobia is commonly referred to as a phobic reaction (Morris & Kratochwill, 1983). Fear, on the other hand, is an integral part of normal child development. Many children's fears are transitory, appear in children of similar age, and generally do not interfere with everyday functioning. In fact, some fears that occur during development provide children with a means of adapting to various life stressors.

Those fears observed in infancy typically occur as a reaction to something taking place in the child's environment (e.g., the presence of strangers or loud noises). As the child grows into the toddler and preschool years, the fears broaden and involve the dark, ghosts and other supernatural figures, parent separation, and fears of particular events, objects, or persons. With growth in to the early to middle school years, developmental fears continue to broaden and include such stimuli as animals, thunder and lightning, the dark, parent separation, bodily injury, and sleeping alone. As the child enters preadolescence and adolescence, the normative fears turn more toward school performance, physical appearance, bodily injury, peer acceptance, death, and imaginary figures (Morris & Kratochwill, 1983).

Separating the meaning of fear from the meaning of phobia has been discussed by Marks (1969). He suggests that phobia is a subcategory of fear that "(1) is out of proportion to the demands of the situation, (2) cannot be explained or reasoned away, (3) is beyond voluntary control, and (4) leads to avoidance of the feared situations" (p. 3). In addition, Miller, Barrett, and Hampe (1974) have stated that a phobia "persists over an extended period of time . . . is unadaptive . . . [and] is not age or stage specific" (p. 90).

Although a fair amount of research has been conducted on the incidence and prevalence of children's fears, less research has been published on children's phobias. Miller et al. (1974), for example, report that the incidence of intense fears (phobias) was about 5% of their sample of 7- to 12-year-old children. Similarly, Marks (1969) reported that the percentage of children having phobias who were referred to a British clinic was only 4%. Other studies estimated the prevalence of phobias among children to be less than 8% of the number of child referrals to a clinic or in the general child population.

With respect to developmental or normative fears, studies have shown that young children, 24 to 71 months of age, experience on the average 4.6 fears (Jersild & Holmes, 1935). Forty-three percent of children who are 6 to 12 years of age experience at least seven or more fears (Lapouse & Monk, 1959). In preadolescent and adolescent youths, 66% of those sampled reported fears of violence (Orton, 1982). Although girls tend to be more fearful than boys in the early years, this difference does not seem to appear on a regular basis in pre- and early adolescence. No literature exists on the incidence or prevalence of phobias and fears in handicapped children and youths.

Numerous studies have been published over the past several years on intervention approaches for reducing fears and phobias. The assumptions underlying these approaches have generally followed a behavioral orientation. There are five major behavior therapy approaches for fear or phobia reduction in children and youths: systematic desensitization (including variations of this procedure); flooding-related therapies; contingency management procedures; modeling; and self-control procedures. Of these methods, the one that has been used primarily in research is systematic desensitization or variations of this method.

Although there are many studies on fears and phobias available for study, with regard to handicapped children and youths, few research studies have been published on the treatment of fears and phobias; however, of those studies that have been published, the majority have used a procedure that is based on systematic desensitization.

REFERENCES

Jersild, A. T., & Holmes, F. B. (1935). Methods of overcoming children's fears. *Journal of Psychology, 1,* 75–104.

Lapouse, R., & Monk, M. A. (1959). Fears and worries in a representative sample of children. *American Journal of Orthopsychiatry, 29,* 803–818.

Marks, I. M. (1969). *Fears and phobias.* New York: Academic.

Miller, L. C., Barrett, C. L., & Hampe, E. (1974). Phobias in childhood in a prescientific era. In A. Davids (Ed.), *Child personality and psychopathology: Current topics* (pp. 84–120). New York: Wiley.

Morris, R. J., & Kratochwill, T. R. (1983). *Treating children's fears and phobias: A behavioral approach.* New York: Pergamon.

Orton, G. L. (1982). A comparative study of children's worries. *Journal of Psychology, 110,* 153–162.

RICHARD J. MORRIS
University of Arizona

THOMAS R. KRATOCHWILL
University of Wisconsin at Madison

ANXIETY DISORDERS
EMOTIONAL DISORDERS

PHONOLOGY

Phonology is a study of the rule-based system underlying phoneme development and speech production. The focus is not on the emergence of specific phonemes but rather on sound classes such as stridency and nasality. The organizational schemata for the formation and use of the phoneme system is the focus of attention.

The need to convey meaning drives this system. At first, children may have only gross classifications like consonant versus vowel as tools to communicate. To get their needs met, they learn that words need beginnings and ends and that there are classes of sounds like stops and front sounds. They acquire the global classes and gradually refine within those classes to ultimately differentiate between a /t/ and a /k/. Children's productions, at any point in time, may be transcribed, analyzed and the rules written to describe the strategies they are using to articulate.

Phonological maturation information exists, but it relates to phonological process usage, the rule-bound simplification and (at times) complication strategies children use to produce speech. In contrast to articulation, the developmental data for phonological maturation is not when sound classes emerge but rather when the processes cease to operate. As children's oral motor, sensory, and discrimination skills develop and their knowledge about combining phonemes into words and larger units of speech increases, process usage decreases. Eighteen-month-old children are likely to know that words need a beginning sound but they are unlikely to use word final consonants. Thus, they exhibit the process *final consonant deletion*. This process typically drops out by the time a child is three. Higher level processes such as stopping and stridency deletion drop out much later in normal developing children (Grunwell, 1987).

Children with phonological disorders have difficulty abstracting the rules for articulation from the input they hear from others. Their speech is generally unintelligible. The number of phonemes in error will be in excess of 10, and the errors will have a rule-based pattern. Children with phonological disorders generally use the same processes that younger, normal-developing children use, but they have more processes functioning and tend to maintain them longer (Ingram, 1976). In evaluating the severity of the disorder, two considerations are the age of the child and the number of processes being used. In addition, if there are vowel errors, a more complex disorder is signaled because vowels emerge very early in speech production. Similarly, if a child has truly been taught to self-evaluate and does not do so after a reasonable amount of time, it may be the first indicator of an accompanying auditory processing difficulty. Most children with phonological process disorders are normal developing children with intact systems who for no known reason are having trouble with the organizational structure of speech production. The prognosis for this latter group is very good. Children with auditory processing deficits and those with motor/neurological involvement also benefit from phonological process treatment but progress more slowly.

Prior to treatment, an extensive speech analysis is needed to determine the rules being applied and the extent of process usage. Treatment focuses on providing children with information that assists them in revising the rules they are using for speech production. For example, they are taught that most words must have endings and that any consonantal ending is acceptable. They are reinforced for putting on any end. Once endings emerge, refinement of the process may begin. They may be then told that for these particular words, a ending is still needed but it has to be a stop. As the child progresses, finer and finer distinctions are made. Treatment moves from global to specific. Geirut, Elbert, and Dinnsen (1987) report that the more children are taught what they do not know, the quicker generalization will occur throughout the sound system. Gierut advocates the use of maximal oppositions in treatment; contrasting two phonemes representing processes the child does not know (Gierut, 1989). Sound classes are taught on a cognitive level by modeling and labeling, having the youngster produce exemplars representative of the class, and then having them self-evaluate whether they produced, for example, a strident.

Phonological processes are most frequently discussed relative to developing rule systems, typically that of children. Older individuals with mental retardation or neurological involvement which presents as apraxia and/or dysarthria also benefit from process-based treatment. The person with retardation may not have mastered the rule-based system for speech. Focus on low level processes like ends-on-words, syllableness, front and back sounds, and others produces gains in intelligibility. Adults with dysarthria and apraxia have previously learned the rules for speech production but due to neurological insult, now have difficulty executing or planning movements. Broader-based treatment which organizes speech by category, assists these persons in improving their speech. For example, if a patient is substituting one sound for another, in-class substitutions will produce greater intelligibility than those which are out-of-class. Thus, the applicability of phonological process treatment is broad and not limited solely to young children.

REFERENCES

Gierut, J. (1989). Maximal opposition approach to phonological treatment. *Journal of Speech and Hearing Disorders, 54,* 9–19.

Geirut, J., Elbert, M., & Dinnsen, D. (1987). A functional analysis of phonological knowledge and generalization learning in misarticulating children. *Journal of Speech and Hearing Research, 30,* 462–479.

Grunwell, P. (1987). *Clinical phonology* (2nd ed.). Baltimore: Williams and Wilkins.

Ingram, D. (1976). *Phonological disability in children.* New York: Elsevier.

SUSANN DOWLING
University of Houston

LINGUISTIC READERS
READING DISORDERS
READING REMEDIATION

PHOTO ARTICULATION TEST-THIRD EDITION (PAT–3)

The Photo Articulation Test-Third Edition (PAT–3; Lippke, Dickey, Selmar, & Soder, 1997) is a completely revised edition of the Photo Articulation Test. It a standardized way to document the presence of articulation errors. The PAT–3 enables the clinician to rapidly and accurately assess and interpret articulation errors. The test consists of 72 color photographs (9 photos on each of eight sheets). The first 69 photos test consonants and all but one vowel and one diphthong. The remaining 3 pictures measure connected speech and the remaining vowel and diphthong. Consonant sounds are differentiated into the initial, medial, and final positions within the stimulus words. A deck of the same 72 color photographs, each on a separate card, is provided for further diagnosis and may be used in speech-language remediation.

The PAT–3 was standardized in a 23-state sample of more than 800 public and private school students in prekindergarten through grade 4. The students have the same characteristics as those reported in the 1990 Statistical Abstract of the United States. Percentiles, standard scores (mean = 100, SD = 15), and age equivalents are provided. Internal consistency, test-retest, and interscorer reliability coefficients approximate .80 at most ages, and many are in the .90s. Information is provided for content, criterion-related, and construct validity.

Earlier editions of the PAT were reviewed; references for the newest edition of the instrument are unavailable because of its recent publication date. Shriberg (1978) reviewed the PAT (Pendergast, Dickey, Selmar, & Soder, 1969) and reported that the one feature that distinguished the PAT from other commercially available three-position tests is that children do respond readily to the photographs.

REFERENCES

Lippke, B. A., Dickey, S. E., Selmar, J. W., & Soder, A. L. (1997). *Photo Articulation Test–Third Edition.* Austin, TX: Pro-Ed.

Shriberg, L. D. (1978). Review of the Photo Articulation Test. In O. K. Buros (Ed.), *The eighth mental measurements yearbook* (pp. 1506–1508). Lincoln: Buros Institute of Mental Measurements.

TADDY MADDOX
Pro-Ed

PHYSICAL ANOMALIES

A physical anomaly is any bodily attribute that deviates significantly from normal variation. Technically, physical anomalies need not be disabling or handicapping though, as will be noted, they often occur concomitant to a variety of handicapping conditions. For instance, prematurely gray-haired individuals exhibit a physical anomaly, yet,

the anomaly is unlikely to be viewed as an impairment (i.e., a disability). It is also unlikely to serve as a disadvantage that makes achievement in particular circumstances exceptionally difficult (i.e., a handicap).

Special educators are most directly concerned with physical anomalies that limit an individual's success in typical life activities (e.g., occupational, familial, and social activities). Such physical anomalies may be found in virtually all of the traditional exceptionalities. However, they are most clearly apparent in the following categories: visual, hearing, and physical handicaps, health problems, and mental retardation.

Physical anomalies can impose handicaps in one or many important domains (e.g., cognition, affect, and motor). Functionally, the individual may have difficulty in academic achievement (e.g., reading, mathematics), in social/emotional adjustment (e.g., making and sustaining friendships, attaining a positive self-concept), and in physical activities (e.g., locomotion, orientation).

Visual anomalies, depending on the age at onset, may be classified as congenital (present at birth) or adventitious acquired sometime after birth). Generally, the impairment concerns visual acuity, field of vision, ocular motility, accommodation, color vision, or corneal opacity.

Like visual anomalies, hearing problems may be classified in different ways. For instance, classification may depend on age of onset (congenital vs. adventitious). Distinctions are also based on the degree of hearing loss (i.e., deaf or hard of hearing). Finally, hearing problems may be conductive or sensorineural in nature. A conductive hearing loss results from interference with the physical transmission of sound waves from the outer ear to the inner ear. On the other hand, a sensorineural hearing loss, as suggested by the name, is caused by neurological damage to nerve tissue in the inner ear. Sound may be grossly distorted to the listener or may not be transmitted at all. In general, sensorineural hearing losses have the more pessimistic prognosis.

Physical handicaps are varied but are commonly categorized as neurological or orthopedic in origin. The former results from injuries, congenital defects, or the progressive deterioration of portions of the central nervous system (CNS). Because most human functions are heavily dependent on an intact CNS, neurological disorders may present particular difficulty for the child and the educator. For instance, it is often difficult to determine a child's true intellectual ability because a motoric handicap may prevent the child from exhibiting it. Cerebral palsy, spina bifida, convulsive disorders, and poliomyelitis are common neurological disorders.

Orthopedic, or musculoskeletal, disorders may be congenital or adventitious. They affect the bones (including joints) and muscles. Accidents, diseases, and hereditary anomalies cause most of the orthopedic disorders. Some of the more common of these conditions are muscular dystrophy, amputations, osteogenesis imperfecta, scoliosis, arthritis, and Legg-Perthes disease.

Other children have conditions in which physical health is poor either permanently of intermittently. Although their conditions are frequently less visually apparent than neurological or orthopedic disorders, they may well face handicapping circumstances in many functional areas (e.g., academic performance, social acceptance). Among the most common of these conditions are epilepsy, cystic fibrosis, juvenile diabetes mellitus, sickle cell anemia, and hemophilia.

The physical anomalies that exist among the mentally retarded population are extensive. Over 250 have been classified so far. Even so, these represent no more than about 25% of the diagnosed cases of mental retardation in the United States. The American Association on Mental Deficiency (Grossman, 1973) has classified the known causal agents of mental retardation as follows: (1) infections and intoxication; (2) trauma and physical agents; (3) metabolism and nutrition; (4) gross brain disease; (5) prenatal influence; (6) chromosomal abnormality; (7) gestational disorders; (8) psychiatric disorders. As with other physical anomalies, individuals with mental retardation suffer from a wide array of affective and motor problems. However, it is their difficulty in cognition and adaptive behavior that best characterizes these children.

Physical anomaly is a term also used to describe a variety of physical aberrations that accompany a host of medical syndromes that typically require special education. Many of these syndromes are genetic disorders that are diagnosed by the specific constellation of physical anomalies apparent to the trained eye. In cases where only one or two minor physical anomalies are present (e.g., hair whorls and a palmar crease), they are often considered to be "soft signs" indicative of neurological problems. Observable minor physical anomalies are often related to neurological problems through coincidental development. The same initial tissue that develops during the embryonic stage into the central nervous system (the neural tube) also forms the epidermis, the outer covering of the body. Also, human chromosomes control more than one aspect of physical development and where one abnormality occurs, others are likely to be present.

Minor physical anomalies occur in many forms and in conjunction with a host of disorders. In Down's syndrome (trisomy 21) one finds a broad flat face, pronounced epicanthal folds, a small palate, and malformed ears. Trisomy 13 will result in microcephaly, physical cardiac defects, polydactyly, cleft lip and palate, and malformation of the eyes and ears. Both of these syndromes frequently result in mental retardation ranging from mild to profound. Marfan's syndrome, most often associated with learning disabilities, though occasionally resulting in mild retarda-

tion, occurs with elongated arms and legs, arachnodactyly (long, spiderlike fingers), and malformations of the eyes and heart.

REFERENCES

Abuelo, D. N. (1983). Genetic disorders. In J. L. Matson & J. A. Mulick (Eds.), *Handbook of mental retardation*. New York: Pergamon.

Brown, R. T. (1986). Etiology and development of exceptionality. In R. T. Brown & C. R. Reynolds (Eds.), *Psychological perspectives on childhood exceptionality: A handbook*. New York: Wiley-Interscience.

Grossman, H. J. (Ed.). (1973). *Manual on terminology and classification in mental retardation*. Washington, DC: American Association on Mental Deficiency.

RONALD C. EAVES
Auburn University

CECIL R. REYNOLDS
Texas A & M University

DOWN'S SYNDROME
GENETIC FACTORS AND BEHAVIOR
MENTAL RETARDATION
MINOR PHYSICAL ANOMALIES

PHYSICAL EDUCATION FOR STUDENTS WITH DISABILITIES

Physical education is a means of developing motor and sports skills and physical fitness with handicapped populations. Physical education programs for the handicapped have been ongoing throughout the United States in residential, private, and public educational institutions (American Association of Health, Physical Education and Recreation, 1981).

The federal government's concern for disabled veterans during and after World War II and its provisions to mainstream and rehabilitate them played a seminal role in the development of adapted physical education. Adapted physical education is the commonly accepted term to designate physical education instruction to handicapped persons in a public or private school setting. Veterans Administration hospitals use corrective, occupational, and physical therapists to help the veterans get back into the mainstream of society and to lead productive lives. Also, innovations developed through federally supported research have found their way in adapted physical education programs across the country (Sherrill, 1985).

From 1950, owing to a variety of political and legal means used by advocacy groups, programs for other handicapped populations began to grow as the rights of handicapped persons with congenital disorders advanced across a broad front. Evidence from numerous research studies began to indicate the positive value of sports participation for all handicapped populations. Programs such as wheelchair sports and the Special Olympics focused on promoting athletic participation among handicapped populations. From 1952 to 1979 the American Association for Health, Physical Education and Recreation (AAHPER) published a series of monographs on curriculum training of staff and guidelines for adapted physical education for schools (Adams, 1981).

It was not until the late 1960s and early 1970s that the federal government began to play a vital role in spurring the growth of adapted physical education programs in the public schools. Large sums of money were allocated for staff training of adapted physical education teachers, and for research and demonstration projects (Adams, 1981). The focus of these federally supported projects was to place more adapted physical education teachers in the field and to use special demonstration centers as models for others looking to upgrade their programs.

During the mid-1970s the federal government enacted the Rehabilitation Act of 1973 (PL 93-112) and the Education for All Handicapped Children Act of 1975 (PL 94-142). The most far-reaching part of PL 93-112 was section 504. It stated that "no qualified person . . . shall be excluded from participation or denied the benefits . . . under any program receiving federal assistance" (Sherrill, 1985). This nondiscriminatory clause indicated physical education was an important concern.

Until the enactment of PL 94-142, there were very few physical education programs in the public schools for handicapped children. The new law, however, stated that education for the handicapped shall include instruction in physical education. Also, the regulations called for equal opportunities for the handicapped to intramural and interscholastic sports competition. As a result, all handicapped children were accorded rights to physical education instruction to the same extent as the nonhandicapped (Auxter & Pyer, 1985).

Since 1975 more and more handicapped persons are being identified and placed in adapted physical education programs. About 12% of the school-age population is handicapped and receiving appropriate instruction. According to IDEA, children with disabilities must be placed in the least restricted school environment with an individualized educational program prepared by the appropriate personnel. This law provided the impetus for the use of individualized education plans (IEP) in physical education and the opportunity for the handicapped to participate with nonhandicapped children in actual physical activity.

Because of the need to collaborate with other professionals regarding each handicapped student's activity needs and educational goals, adapted physical educators may serve as part of a multidisciplinary team with occupational and physical therapists and the special education teacher.

Many terms have been applied to programs of physical activity for the handicapped. Each of these terms represents a specific approach to improving motor and physical performance. Terms such as corrective, developmental, modified, therapeutic, or special physical education are representative of aspects of adapted physical education.

Corrective physical education is a means of remediating structural and functional dysfunctions through physical exercise or motor activities. The dysfunctions, although impairing, are generally correctable. Developmental physical education focuses on improving delayed motor and physical development through exercise and motor skill activities. Modified physical education has activities that are adapted to the learning levels of the handicapped regardless of individual differences. Therapeutic physical education denotes the use of physical education activities under the prescription of a medical doctor. Special physical education is a selected program of developmental activities designed to meet the limitations of those who cannot participate in unrestricted and regular physical education. This term has not gained nationwide acceptance owing to its controversial connotation.

Adapted physical education is a "diversified program of developmental activities, games, sports, and rhythms suited to the interests, capacities, and limitations of students with disabilities who may not safely and successfully engage in unrestricted participation in vigorous activities of the general physical education program" (AAHPER, 1952).

By definition, adapted physical education includes activities:

Planned for persons with learning problems owed to motor, mental, or emotional impairment, disability, or dysfunction.

Planned for the purpose of rehabilitation, remediation, prevention, or physical development.

Modified so the impaired, disabled, or handicapped can participate.

Designed for modifying movement capabilities.

Planned to promote optimum motor development.

Occurring in a school setting or within a clinic, hospital, residence facility, daycare center or other locale where the primary intent is to influence learning and movement potential through motor activity.

Adapted physical education differs from regular physical education in that it has a federally mandated base and a multidisciplinary approach to individual program planning, covers an age spectrum from early childhood to adulthood, has educational accountability through the individualized education plan (IEP), and emphasizes cooperative service among the school, community, and home to enhance a handicapped person's capabilities (Sherrill, 1985).

The aim of physical education for the handicapped is to aid in achieving physical, social, and emotional growth commensurate with their potential. Objectives of adapted physical education programs vary from program to program depending on population characteristics, instructional expertise, facilities, and equipment. Some of the commonly accepted objectives of most programs are

To help students correct physical conditions that can be improved.

To help students protect themselves from any conditions that would be aggravated through physical activity.

To provide students with opportunities to learn about and participate in a number of appropriate recreational leisure time sports and activities.

To help students to become self-sufficient in the community.

To help students to understand their physical and mental limitations.

To help students to understand and appreciate a variety of sports that they can enjoy as spectators.

Prior to participation in a physical education program conducted by a public school, the student with disabilities must have a thorough physical examination. Abnormalities are identified by the physician and suggestions for management are made to school personnel. The physician's suggestions usually include follow-through procedures to ensure proper class placement and appropriate educational placement based on the extent of physical activity needs and limitations. The adapted physical education teacher must be aware of the physician's guidelines and interpret them into an appropriate physical activity program.

Often, identification of the student needing special help is made by teacher observation in the regular physical education class or in the student's regular classroom. Sometimes the student is not making adequate progress or is frustrated by his or her present involvement in games and sports. The student may not be classified as needing special help because he or she passed the medical examination by the physician. In this case, the physical education program is adapted to suit the capabilities of the student.

Students with disabilities are required to take a battery of motor, physical fitness, and perceptual-motor tests for the making of the yearly IEP (AAHPER, 1981). Short- and long-term goals for the academic year are developed from the test results along with the specific activities recommended for each goal.

After being identified as needing special help, a handicapped student, depending on the size of the school, may be assigned to different types of programming classes. The first is a segregated program in which all of the students are in need of adapted physical education. The student receives individual attention, is accepted, and is protected from unlimited competition. The disadvantage of a segregated program is that the class fosters isolation and non-acceptance from peers. In the second type, a student may be placed in an integrated class participating with able-bodied students in the least restricted environment in terms of physical activity. Studies indicate that inclusive practices in physical education do not necessarily lead to peer acceptance for students with physical disabilities (Toon & Gench, 1990; Tripp, French & Sherrill, 1995).

A third type of physical education program for the handicapped is the dual class, in which the student is placed one day in the segregated class and one day in the integrated class. With this approach, individual attention may be given for special needs. At the same time, the student is able to interact with peers in the regular physical education class. Again, there is no guarantee that inclusion will work; therefore, consistent evaluations must be made and kept ongoing.

Once a pupil with disabilities is given an appropriate physical education class placement, it is the role of the physical education instructor to provide a program of physical activity throughout the school year. In addition to planning and implementing the IEP, the physical education instructor acts as a counselor to aid the student in:

Setting reasonable physical activity goals

Transferring class skills and habits to other environments

Promoting healthful practices

Coordinating program goals with the student's family and related services within the school and community

Providing a framework that fosters socialization skills in the least restrictive environment

Recording progress and continually evaluating needs and interests through physical activity

The aim of a physical education curriculum for the handicapped is to develop physical fitness and motor skills through exercise and sports. For effective learning to take place, it is necessary to know the different levels of functioning in motor learning that affect a student's performance in class. There are three levels of functioning in motor skill acquisition: (1) input functions, (2) abilities, and (3) motor skill.

Basic input functions include the equilibrium reflexes, the vestibular system, vision, audition, and tactile and the kinesthetic senses. Their role is to provide sensory information to the central nervous system. If all systems are intact, the person will have a coordinated sense of movement and motion. If one or more are not intact, as is the case in many handicaps, it is important for the instructor to adapt activities that either develop or compensate for that input function.

The second level of functioning includes abilities that are perceptual-motor and physical in nature. Perceptual-motor abilities include balance, laterality, directionality, body image, spatial awareness and cross-lateral integration. Physical fitness parameters consist of strength, muscle and cardiovascular endurance, and flexibility. Motor fitness includes speed, power, agility, and motor coordination. If the sensory input functions are intact, the abilities develop through developmental motor and fitness experiences. If all of the abilities are intact, their use and development provide the groundwork for learning motor and sports skills.

The highest level of functioning is motor and sport skill acquisition. Motor skills are fundamental movement patterns of daily activity such as walking, running, hopping, etc. Sports skills are motor in nature but are specific to learning a particular sport. Examples of sports skills are throwing a ball, doing the crawl stroke, and riding a bike. If the input systems and the abilities are intact, then skill acquisition occurs through movement and sports experiences. This means instruction, practice, and instructional feedback in sport and movement activities.

Activities to develop motor, sports, and physical fitness are classified according to the number of participants and the level of skill acquisition. Individual activities include swimming, self-defense, tennis, bowling, dancing, weight training, and karate. Team sports include such activities as wheelchair basketball, soccer, frisbee, and softball. The third type are activities that enhance physical and motor development such as aerobics, dance, and weight training. In many schools, classes may be subdivided according to skill levels within the particular activity. In swimming, for instance, there may be classes or subdivisions within a class for beginners, intermediates, and advanced swimmers.

For the handicapped student to meaningfully participate in a sport, it is often necessary to modify some aspect of the sport to suit the capabilities of the student. For instance, wheelchair basketball is an adaptation of regular basketball in which the participants wheel around and pass the ball as opposed to dribbling and running. General guidelines followed by most instructors who teach adapted physical education state that the activity must be adaptable for effective learning to occur. This means that equipment, rules, or the manner of play may need to be modified for the participants. For instance, to accommodate the limited motor capabilities of a developmentally delayed group, the soccer field could be smaller and the ball could be lighter for it to be kicked farther and more accurately. In addition, activities could be designed to suit the students'

abilities and not their disabilities. For example, a student with spina bifida is capable of learning how to swim because of intact upper body coordination. Finally, the instructor should be able to sequence and time learning experiences according to the students' capabilities.

REFERENCES

Adams, R. C. (1981). Adapted physical education. In J. Kauffman & D. Hallahan (Eds.), *Handbook of special education* (pp. 1–27). Englewood Cliffs, NJ: Prentice-Hall.

American Association of Health, Physical Education and Recreation. (1981). Resource guide in adapted physical education. Reston, VA: Author.

Auxter, D., & Pyer, J. (1985). *Adapted physical education.* St. Louis: Mosby.

Guiding principles for adapted physical education. (1952). *Journal of Health, Physical Education & Recreation, 35,* 15–16.

Sherrill, C. (1985). *Adapted physical education and recreation* (3rd ed.). Dubuque, IA: Brown.

Toon, C. J., & Gench, B. E. (1990). Attitudes of handicapped and nonhandicapped high school students towards physical education. *Perceptual and Motor Skills, 70*(3), 1328–1330.

Tripp, A., French, R., & Sherrill, C. (1995). Contact theory and attitudes of children in physical education programs towards peers with disabilities. *Adapted Physical Activity Quarterly, 12*(4), 323–332.

THOMAS R. BURKE
Hunter College

ADAPTED PHYSICAL EDUCATION
ADAPTIVE BEHAVIOR
OLYMPICS, SPECIAL
RECREATION FOR THE HANDICAPPED

PHYSICALLY HANDICAPPED

A variety of interchangeable terms have been used to describe persons with physical handicaps. For example, these individuals will often be categorized as physically disabled, physically impaired, crippled, orthopedically impaired, other health impaired, or multiply handicapped. The legal definition for orthopedically impaired is a severe orthopedic impairment that adversely affects a child's education performance (IDEA). The term includes impairments caused by a congenital anomaly (e.g., clubfoot, absence of some member, etc.), impairments caused by disease (e.g., poliomyelitis, bone tuberculosis, etc.), and impairments from other causes (e.g., cerebral palsy, amputations, and fractures or burns that cause contractures). The legal definition for other health impaired is having a condition that is manifested by severe communication and other developmental and educational problems; or having limited strength, vitality, or alertness because of chronic or acute health problems (e.g., a heart condition, tuberculosis, rheumatic fever, nephritis, asthma, sickle cell anemia, hemophilia, epilepsy, lead poisoning, leukemia, or diabetes) that adversely affect a child's educational performance (IDEA).

The range of disability varies from mild to profound physical impairment. Nonetheless, it is current practice to categorize students with physical handicaps as having average to above average intelligence, and physically handicapped/multiply handicapped students as having additional impairments such as mental retardation, blindness, or deafness. Additionally, mild to moderate learning disabilities often are found with students whose only handicapping condition is physical.

It is estimated that the incidence of physical handicaps is 2% (Smith, 1984). In the school year 1984–1985, 73,292 multihandicapped, 58,924 orthopedically impaired, and 69,688 other health-impaired students received special education services (Office of Special Education and Rehabilitation, 1985). The most common physical impairments found in schools are cerebral palsy, myelomeningocele (spina bifida), and muscular dystrophy. Although children with communicable diseases such as cytomeglavirous, herpes, hepatitis, and acquired immune deficiency syndrome (AIDS) are being denied entry into some schools (Dykes, 1984–1985), the incidence of these diseases is on the rise and will have to be addressed within the public school system.

Most physically handicapped and health-impaired students are served in a combination of regular and special programs (Walker & Jacobs, 1984). Nevertheless, Dykes (1984–1985) suggests that 85% of health-impaired and 35% of orthopedically impaired children should be served solely in regular classrooms. Physically and multiply handicapped students are usually served in special education classrooms, separate facilities, or hospital/home-bound programs if their conditions do not permit inclusive programming.

The educational needs of physically handicapped students vary as widely as the definitions, etiologies, and educational placements. For most physically handicapped students, the regular academic curriculum is most appropriate. In addition, an emphasis is placed on helping the students to gain independent living skills such as grooming, dressing, and food preparation. Perhaps the greatest needs of these students are in the areas of adaptive equipment (Campbell, 1983) and technology (Vanderheiden & Walstead, 1982). Often physically handicapped students require wheelchairs, crutches, head pointers, arm and leg braces, etc. It is common for the physically handicapped child to use a nonverbal/augmentative communication system (e.g., Zygo 100, Tetra-Scan II, Omni) or use microcomputers for a variety of instructional purposes (Rushakoff & Lombardino, 1983). Technological advances have narrowed the gap in providing adequate educational instruction to students who cannot speak, move, or use their hands.

Another major area for intervention with physically handicapped students is in social and self-concept development. Often the physically impaired student is characterized as passive, less persistent, having a shorter attention span, engaging in less exploration, and displaying less motivation (Jennings et al., 1985) and less self-esteem (Lawrence, 1991). Additionally, physically handicapped students are found to be more dependent on adults and to interact less with their peers. Programs serving these students must consider socialization and independence. Parents as well as teachers need to find ways to facilitate independence and build self-esteem.

The education of physically handicapped students requires a transdisciplinary team effort. Because the students have a variety of medical needs, educational program planning often will include pediatricians, neurologists, physical therapists, occupational therapists, speech clinicians, nurses, orthopedic surgeons, vision specialists, and most important, the families of these students. Often, families of physically handicapped children must be the central focus of the educational process. It is with their support that programs in daily living and social skills training can actually work. Likewise, it is team support that enables families to more easily adjust to the demands of raising a child with physical or other health impairments.

REFERENCES

Campbell, P. (1983). Basic considerations in programming for students with movement difficulties. In M. Snell (Ed.), *Systematic instruction of the moderately and severely handicapped* (2nd ed.) (pp. 168–102). Columbus, OH: Merrill.

Dykes, M. K. (1984–1985). Assessment of students who are physically or health impaired. *Diagnostique, 10,* 128–143.

Jennings, K., Connors, R., Stegman, C., Sankaranarayan, P., & Mendelson, S. (1985). Mastery motivation in young preschoolers: Effect of a physical handicap and implications for educational programming. *Journal of the Division for Early Childhood, 9,* 162–169.

Lawrence, B. (1991). Self-concept formation and physical handicap: Some educational implications for integration. *Disability, Handicap & Society, 6*(2), 139–146.

Office of Special Education and Rehabilitation. (1985). *School year 1984–85 report of services by category.* Washington, DC: U.S. Department of Education.

Rushakoff, G., & Lombardino, L. (1983). Comprehensive microcomputer applications for severely physically handicapped children. *Teaching Exceptional Children, 16,* 18–22.

Smith, O. S. (1984). Severely and profoundly physically handicapped students. In P. Valletutti & B. Sims-Tucker (Eds.), *Severely and profoundly handicapped students: Their nature and needs* (pp. 85–152). Baltimore, MD: Brookes.

Vanderheiden, G., & Walstead, L. (1982). *Trace Center interna-*

tionally software / hardware registry. Madison: University of Wisconsin, Trace Center.

Walker, D. K., & Jacobs, F. H. (1984). Chronically ill children in school. *Peabody Journal of Education, 61*(2), 28–74.

VIVIAN I. CORREA
University of Florida

ACCESSIBILITY OF BUILDINGS
AUGMENTATIVE COMMUNICATION DEVICES
MULTIPLY HANDICAPPED
OTHER HEALTH IMPAIRED

PHYSICAL RESTRAINT

A punishment procedure that involves the immobilization of limbs or the entire body is referred to as physical restraint. The intent of physical restraint is to decrease or eliminate the unacceptable behavior immediately preceding the onset of the physical restraint procedure. Physical restraint should be employed only after ample documentation is obtained that lesser intrusive interventions were ineffective.

Immobilization methods vary and may range from holding a student's hands by the side of the body to applying a mechanical arm restraint at the elbows to prevent self-injurious blows to the face. Several recommendations have been offered for implementing physical restraint procedures. Bitgood, Peters, Jones, and Hathorn (1982) recommend that the teacher be positioned behind the student and firmly grasp the student's shoulders to hold them against the back of the seat. A second method of physical restraint involves holding the shoulders while the student is in a bent-over position in a chair (Reid, Tombaugh, & Heuvel, 1981). A third method is holding both of the student's hands behind the back of a chair (Rapoff, Altman, & Christopherson, 1980). The exact method of restraint will vary along several lines, including the size of the student; the size of the teacher; the alternative activity to be taught to the student to replace previously observed unacceptable behaviors; and the position of the student relative to the activity being taught.

In addition to actively immobilizing parts of a student's body, mechanical restraints can be employed. These restraints can restrict the student's movements to strike parts of the body, or materials (e.g., elbow pads, helmets, face masks) can be worn over injured areas to prevent future injuries.

The duration of time during which each instance of physical restraint is employed has varied from 3 seconds to 15 minutes, with most reported studies containing recommendations of 10 seconds to 1 minute. That is, following the occurrence of an unacceptable behavior, the teacher would employ a restraint procedure for a pre-established time interval. If the student is calm, nonagressive and willing to verbally process the incident (Rich, 1997) at the end of the time interval, the restraint is removed. However, if the student continues to struggle as the time expires, an additional duration of time must elapse during which the student is calm prior to removing the physical restraint.

Applying physical restraint as a behavioral intervention should not automatically be associated with punishment. Researchers have observed that physical restraint may act as a reinforcer for continued maladaptive behaviors. Favell, McGimsey, and Jones (1978) evaluated situations in which physical restraint actually resulted in increased frequencies of aggressive behaviors. Similarly, Singh, Winton, and Ball (1984) documented an increase in out-of-seat behavior when followed by contingent physical restraint. Finally, Foxx and Dufrense (1984) evaluated the reinforcing effects of hinged metal splints on the self-injurious behavior of a mentally retarded resident within a large residential facility. Interestingly, the authors were able to fade a self-restraint of a preferred object (large plastic glass) to a socially accepted form of self-restraint in the form of a wristwatch and eyeglasses.

Reasons cited for the reinforcing properties of physical restraint include a relaxing feeling of being immobile and resultant drowsiness; physical contact from a reinforcing adult i.e. attachment (Bath, 1994); reduction in demands placed on the student who escapes from disliked activities by engaging in unacceptable behaviors resulting in physical restraint procedures.

When physical restraint results in a decrease or elimination of unacceptable behavior, several potential advantages may occur: undue physical strength or endurance by the teacher may not be required; little staff training is required; no verbal instruction is necessary, although some teachers include a verbalization of the unacceptable behavior prior to the physical restraint; minimum level of discomfort is afforded the student; the student cannot engage in unacceptable behaviors while being restrained; long-lasting effects are observed; and few side effects are noted.

Potential disadvantages that need to be considered prior to the implementation of a physical restraint procedure include an inability of small-frame teachers to restrain physically stronger students; the association of restraint with close physical contact and attention from the teacher; time lost from educational activities while the student is restrained; restraint itself may be reinforcing for the student; procedures have the potential to be highly aversive and intrusive; the student's physical strength may be increased through isometric type of exercising while resisting the restraint; an inexperienced teacher may use physical restraint in an arbitrary, capricious manner; physical restraint has the potential for injury.

Guidelines have been offered for the judicious application of physical restraint procedures, and teachers need to safeguard the rights of each student by adhering to at least the following:

1. Obtain informed consent from the student's guardian

2. Closely monitor the procedure to prevent intentional or unintentional abuse

3. Positively reinforce appropriate behaviors

4. Consider less restrictive alternatives prior to physical restraint

5. Use minimum physical force

6. Document length of time and frequency of instances of physical restraint

7. Administer physical restraint only in a contingent manner

8. Train all individuals in all environments frequented by the student

9. Maintain a resource file of successful documentations of the use of physical restraint to guide the development of the parameters for a targeted student

10. Fade the intensity of restraint materials to socially acceptable, nondebilitating materials (Foxx & Dufrense, 1984)

11. Identify functional, life skill activities to replace self-injurious or stereotypic behaviors when decreasing unacceptable behaviors via physical restraint

REFERENCES

Bath, H. (1994). The physical restraint of children: Is it therapeutic? *American Journal of Orthopsychiatry, 64*(1), 40–49.

Bitgood, S. C., Peters, R. D., Jones, M. L., & Hathorn, N. (1982). Reducing out-of-seat behaviors in developmentally disabled children through brief immobilization. *Education & Treatment of Children, 5,* 249–260.

Favell, J. E., McGimsey, J. F., & Jones, M. L. (1978). The use of physical restraint in the treatment of self-injury and as positive reinforcement. *Journal of Applied Behavior Analysis, 11,* 225–241.

Foxx, R. M. (1982). *Decreasing behaviors of severely retarded and autistic persons* (pp. 51–60). Champaign, IL: Research Press.

Foxx, R. M., & Dufrense, D. (1984). "Harry": The use of physical restraint as a reinforcer, timeout from restraint, and fading restraint in treating a self-injurious man. *Analysis & Intervention in Developmental Disabilities, 4,* 1–13.

LaGraw, S. J., & Repp, A. C. (1984). Stereotypic responding: A review of intervention research. *American Journal of Mental Deficiency, 88,* 595–609.

Rapoff, M. A., Altman, K., & Christophersen, R. (1980). Elimination of a retarded blind child's self-hitting by response-contingent brief restraint. *Education & Treatment of Children, 3,* 231–237.

Reid, J. G., Tombaugh, T. N., & Heuvel, K. V. (1981). Application of contingent physical restraint to suppress stereotyped body rocking of profoundly mentally retarded persons. *American Journal of Mental Deficiency, 86,* 78–85.

Rich, C. R. (1997). The use of physical restraint in residential treatment. *Residential Treatment for Children Youth, 14*(3), 1–12.

Shapiro, E. S., Barrett, R. P., & Ollendick, T. H. (1980). A comparison of physical restraint and positive practice overcorrection in treating stereotypic behaviors. *Behavior Therapy, 11,* 227–233.

Singh, N. N., Winton, A. S. W., & Ball, P. M. (1984). Effects of physical restraint on the behavior of hyperactive mentally retarded persons. *American Journal of Mental Deficiency, 89,* 16–22.

Waddell, P. A., Singh, N. N., & Beale, I. L. (1984). Conditioned punishment of self-injurious behavior. In S. E. Breuning, J. L. Matson, & R. P. Barrett (Eds.), *Advances in mental retardation and developmental disabilities* (pp. 85–134). Greenwich, CT: JAI.

ERNEST L. PANCSOFAR
University of Connecticut

PHYSICAL THERAPY

Physical therapists are responsible for physical restoration. Employing a variety of equipment, they use massage and regulated exercise to improve coordination and balance, reeducate muscles, restore joint motion, and increase the patient's tolerance for activity.

A physical therapist employs mechanical and muscle strengthening exercises to assist students who will benefit from these activities to improve their quality of life. Physical therapists are frequently members of interdisciplinary teams, where they contribute to the overall management of the patient. The goal of most client service is to obtain entry into independent living and competitive employment. An example of services might include deep heat, paraffin baths, hydrotherapy, mild stretching, or strengthening exercises for a person with a crippling arthritis; strengthening and coordinating exercises for a person with a cerebral palsy; development, frequently in concert with an occupational therapist, of exercises for mobility through walking, leg braces, a wheelchair, or some combination; and the appropriate use of any prosthetic devices. Braces, wheelchairs, and other appliances require instruction in their use and care. Physical therapists generally teach these skills. They also join with occupational, speech, hearing, or other therapists in assisting the patient in the use of the prosthetic device to accomplish independent living or vocational skills.

Physical therapy, then, is the act of teaching motor strengthening, motor control, balance, and other skills to handicapped persons. It combines these motoric trainings with prosthetic devices to help the patient to accomplish needed goals by reducing the effects of disability. Physical therapy is one aspect of the total training needed to reduce the effects of disability to enable the handicapped person to profit from residual (normal) bodily functions. Frequently, both the general public and the handicapped person, particularly the newly handicapped person, become overwhelmed at the presence of a handicapping condition. What frequently is not seen is the amount of usable function that remains. The principle involved is to provide the handicapped person with training of muscle groups, motor control, balance, etc., to promote the use of the residual, nonhandicapped functions.

A few of the categories and types of skills taught in physical therapy as they apply to special education are listed.

1. Health (severity of problem health behaviors)

2. Attendance and promptness (degree of presence in school and time-telling behaviors)

3. Feeding/eating (degree of competency in eating skills)

4. Drinking (degree of competency in drinking skills)

5. Toileting (degree of competency in toilet skills)

6. Grooming (degree of competency in washing, showering, and personal hygiene skills)

7. Dressing (degree of competency in independent dressing skills)

8. Undressing (degree of competency in independent undressing skills)

9. Nasal hygiene (degree of competency in maintaining hygienic and socially acceptable conditions of the nose)

10. Oral hygiene (degree of competency in toothbrushing behavior)

11. Self-identification (degree of competency in pointing to body parts, knowing family members, and information about self)

12. Sensory perception (degree of competency in discriminating among stimuli on the basis of touch, taste, smell)

13. Auditory perception (degree of competency in discriminating among stimuli on the basis of auditory cues)

14. Visual Motor I (degree of competency in interpreting simple fine-visual motor skills)

15. Visual Motor II (degree of competency in integrating complex visual motor skills)

16. Gross Motor I (degree of competency in demonstrating simple mobility, eye-hand coordination, and gross motor skills)

17. Gross Motor II (degree of competency in demonstrating complex gross motor skills, motor sports)

18. Prearticulation (degree of competency in controlling mouth parts)

19. Articulation (degree of competency in making vowel and consonant sounds)

20. Language comprehension (degree of competency in understanding communication)

21. Language development (degree of competency in using gestures, sounds, and words to communicate)

22. Listening (degree of competency in attending and reacting to verbal communication)

23. Adaptive behaviors (degree of competency involving exploratory play and problem-solving skills)

24. Impulse control (degree of competency in controlling disruptive behaviors and accepting criticism)

25. Interpersonal relations (degree of competency in cooperating and interacting with others in social situations)

26. Responsible behaviors (degree of competency in accepting rules, obeying authorities, and demonstrating socially approved behaviors)

27. Personal welfare (degree of competency in demonstrating safe behaviors in hazardous conditions)

DAVID A. SABATINO
*West Virginia College of
Graduate Studies*

**OCCUPATIONAL THERAPY
PHYSICAL DISABILITY**

PHYSICIANS' DESK REFERENCE (PDR)

The *Physicians' Desk Reference,* known popularly as the PDR, is an annual publication of Medical Economics Company. It reports information on more than 2500 drugs. The information is supplied entirely by the drug's manufacturer but is edited and approved by medical personnel employed by the publisher. The PDR contains descriptions of drugs (with pictures in many cases of the most common form), indications for use, recommendations regarding dosage levels, and antidotes for some drugs. Management information for overdosage developed by the Institute for Clinical Toxicology is also presented. The *PDR* is intended primarily for use by physicians and was developed to make readily available essential information on major pharmaceutical products. The *PDR* is useful to allied health professionals and to special educational personnel. It is particularly useful to the latter because of the high incidence of medication usage by handicapped children. The *PDR* is likely to be available in the reference library of any special education program.

Cecil R. Reynolds
Texas A & M University

PHYSIOTHERAPY

Physiotherapy or physiatry is the treatment of disease with the aid of physical agents such as light, heat, cold, water, and electricity, or with mechanical apparatus. The person responsible for physiotherapy is a physiatrist: a physician who specializes in physiotherapeutics or physiotherapy. Physical therapy, or the application of physiotherapy as practiced by physical therapists or occupational therapists, is supervised by the physiatrist responsible for the physical therapy unit.

The primary purpose of physiotherapy is to provide for the controlled movement of the extremities and for the other muscle and joint articulation necessary for the activities of daily living or competitive employment. Muscles are strengthened, coordination exercises are offered, and mechanical (nonchemical) applications to increase the range of motion and strength for each joint are provided.

The range of patients includes those suffering from damage to either the central or peripheral nervous systems; those suffering from any disease or mechanical injury; and those afflicted with a birth defect affecting muscle and bone. Two primary systems treated are the skeletal and nervous systems. Some of the more common conditions treated are strokes (cerebral vascular accidents), cerebral palsy, head trauma, spinal cord injuries, arthritis, polio, and a number of inherited and acquired bone, joint, or muscle problems.

Educators have traditionally used the term physically handicapped to categorize those children and youths who, because of bodily disability, require specialized education. Under such a rubric, physical handicap equates with bodily disability; therefore, practically all handicapping conditions are physical (e.g., vision and hearing impairments, forms of mental retardation, and brain injury).

Generally, a physical handicap can contain four characteristics: (1) a neuromuscular disability resulting from damage to the central nervous system; (2) a disability related to a lower common neural pathway (nerves and muscles outside of the central nervous system); (3) a disability resulting from an injury or disease that destroys nerves, muscles, or bone peripheral to the central nervous system; or (4) a health impairment that reduces vitality and thereby results in a weakened physical condition.

Diagnostically the two major groups are orthopedically handicapped and other health impaired. The orthopedically handicapped constitute the group that is neuromus-

cularly handicapped as a result of insult or trauma to the central nervous system or as a result of lower common neural-muscular-orthopedic (skeleton system) damage peripheral to the central nervous system. Other health-impaired conditions have numerous etiologies but have in common a condition that so weakens the individual that he or she must limit or modify the activities and therefore participate in physiotherapy to obtain relief.

David A. Sabatino
*West Virginia College of
Graduate Studies*

**ORTHOPEDICALLY IMPAIRED
OTHER HEALTH IMPAIRED**

PIAGETIAN APPROACH TO SPECIAL EDUCATION

Jean Piaget (1950, 1952, 1977), Switzerland's noted genetic epistemologist, proposed a developmental and constructivist model of human cognition from birth to adolescence based on biological processes. Although his theory has been applied to regular education for several decades, fewer efforts have been made to apply his work to exceptional populations (Gallagher & Reid, 1981; Reid, 1981; Wachs & Furth, 1980). One reason for this apparent lack of interest is Piaget's derivation of theoretical principles from observations of essentially normal children, with the consequent assumption of lack of applicability to handicapped individuals. A second obstacle has been an assumed lack of fit between more holistic and social/linguistic (Beilin, 1996) instructional goals and strategies compatible with Piagetian theory and the specific, step-by-step goals and methods typically prescribed for handicapped learners. Nevertheless, Piaget's cognitive-development theory provides a useful means of understanding and teaching children with exceptional needs.

Concepts integral to Piaget's theory include structures, adaptation, stages of development, conservation, equilibration, and egocentrism. According to his theory, cognitive development consists of progression through an invariant sequence of stages, with the child incorporating the structures (organized patterns for dealing with the environment) acquired at each stage into qualitatively different, higher order structures at each succeeding stage. The child's progression from stage to stage results from adaptation, which describes the process of interaction between the child's current maturational level and environmental stimuli. Two complementary processes constitute adaptation: assimilation and accommodation. Assimilation refers to the child's incorporation of features of the environment into his or her existing structures. Accommodation is the modifying of one's structures in response to environmental demands. To illustrate, when an infant desires to touch a new mobile dangling from the crib, the infant must accommodate his or her vision and movements to the distance. Simultaneously, the infant assimilates the mobile into already existing patterns of behavior: structures for reaching and grasping.

As a result of adaptation, the developing child continually creates new structures out of previously acquired structures to better interact with the environment. Piaget describes the development of these structures in terms of a series of stages: sensorimotor, preoperational, concrete operational, and formal operational. The sensorimotor stage (birth to 1_ years) describes the infant and prelinguistic child. The infant manifests cognition through actions on objects, such as jiggling the crib to set a mobile in motion. The preoperational stage (1_ to 7 years) is characterized by use of language, symbolic behavior, and lack of conversational logic. The 2-year-old child demonstrates symbolic behavior by pretending that a broom is a horse and "riding" it. The preoperational child has not yet acquired the structures necessary for conservation: the ability to recognize that matter is conserved despite superficial changes in shape or form. For example, when a 3 year old is presented with two identical balls of clay, one of which is subsequently rolled into a cigar shape, the child perceives the remaining ball and the cigar as being unequal in size. When asked which is larger (or "has more"), the child may attend only to length and select the cigar, or only to width, and choose the ball. The child does not consider the two dimensions simultaneously.

Children in the stage of concrete operations (7 to 12 years) have acquired the rules of conservation as well as an understanding of relational concepts. The fourth state, formal operations (12 and above) describes children who can use abstract rules in problem solving and conceptualize in hypothetical terms.

Piaget's theory postulates that although children vary in the age at which they reach a given stage, all follow the same sequence. Progression from stage to stage occurs through equilibration, or the reorganization of structures through assimilation and accommodation, resulting in higher order structures. Disequilibrium, or a state of conflict, occurs when the child's current structures are applied (assimilation) and found insufficient to the task. According to Piaget, the child is inherently motivated toward equilibrium and therefore toward resolving the conflict. For example, the child entering the stage of concrete operations recognizes that the cigar-shaped clay is longer than the ball and yet was an equivalent ball in its original form. To resolve the conflict, the child reorganizes (accommodates) his or her structures; new structures for the simultaneous consideration of the two dimensions of length and width and for conservation result. The child thus reaches a new state of equilibrium.

Piaget's constructivist model has been used to explain social cognition, or children's logical understanding of themselves and other individuals in interaction. Children's development of social cognition parallels their intellectual development, progressing through a sequence of stages from egocentric to sociocentric thought. The infant is egocentric, or centered around the self. As children mature and gain experience with the environment, they become decentered; they learn that the self is separate from other people, that other people have thoughts and feelings, and that other people's thoughts and feelings may differ from their own. Development of social cognition in several areas parallels stages of cognitive development. These areas include referential communication, role taking, moral judgment, and rule implementation.

Referential communication refers to one's ability to describe a stimulus such that the listener can correctly locate the same stimulus out of an array of similar items, and is examined using speaker-listener pairs or dyads. Young children's referential communication is often termed egocentric in that they usually fail to consider the listener's perspective. For example, a 2 year old requesting a favorite cup may ask a listener to bring the "cup Grandpa gave me," not recognizing that the listener is not privy to Grandpa's gift. Role or perspective taking refers to the ability to consider other people's point of view: their thoughts, feelings, or, literally, what is in their range of vision. Children progress from a lack of separation between self and environment (early infancy) to simultaneous consideration of multiple perspectives.

Three stages characterize children's development of moral judgment: objective morality, subjective morality, and interpretation of the act (Piaget, 1932). Children in the stage of objective morality base their judgments of good and bad behavior on objective criteria such as the amount of damage incurred, for example, when someone breaks a lamp while trying to clean the table. In subjective morality, good or bad intentions become a prime criterion for judging behavior. At the highest level, children simultaneously consider intent and outcome and develop a sense of moral responsibility for the own actions.

Children's play and use of rules in play follow a similar developmental pattern. In parallel play, young children share materials and physical proximity but act independently, without a common set of rules. At a later stage (incipient cooperation), they know the rules and attempt to win at games. Finally, children together develop and elaborate rules appropriate for the situation (genuine cooperation).

Much of the research on Piaget's theory has addressed the invariance of the sequence of stages: the impact of specific training on development, especially on acquisition of conservation; the relationship of social cognition to cognitive development; and the relationship between social cognition and social behavior. For a more comprehensive discussion of the research, the reader is referred to Flavell (1971, 1972) on invariant sequence, Klein and Safford (1977) on training, and Shantz (1975) on social cognition.

In general, the research in all four areas has produced somewhat inconsistent results interpretable in a variety of ways depending on the researcher's theoretical orientation. Moreover, attempts to measure level of cognitive development have been criticized as producing merely another assessment of general intelligence. Studies of cognitive development in young children have questioned preschoolers' apparent egocentricity and inability to conserve as artifacts of task difficulty (Gelman, 1979). On the other hand, inconsistent findings regarding stage invariance, training of conservation concepts, and correlation between stages of cognitive and social cognitive development may be interpreted within a Piagetian framework as reflective of the fact that a given child may simultaneously be at different stages of development for different concepts (e.g., conservation of quantity, conservation of mass, role taking, moral judgment). Inconsistencies may result from investigators' use of different measures to assess levels of cognitive development. In addition, procedures may fail to discriminate between children who have already attained a given stage and children who are in transition between stages.

Because cognitive development results from an interaction between child structures and environmental stimuli, differences in quantity and quality of experience may affect acquisition of concepts. For example, a mentally handicapped child with a chronological age of 10 and a mental age of 7 might be expected to perform at approximately the same level as an intellectually average child with a chronological and mental age of 7 and a gifted child with a chronological age of 5 and a mental age of 7. However, differences among these children in years of experience would impact on acquisition of cognitive concepts. In short, although more definitive research is needed, Piaget's theory of cognitive development has contributed significantly to thinking about the learning process.

Piaget himself made little reference to the application of his theory to educational practice. However, psychologists and educators have derived from Piaget's work several principles for instruction appropriate for both academic and social learning. Piaget's theory, applied to special populations, assumes that all children, handicapped and nonhandicapped, proceed through the same invariant sequence of stages using the same processes of assimilation, accommodation, and equilibration. Thus, while the rate of development may differ for exceptional learners, the instructional principles continue to be applicable. Experimental attempts to propel children (exceptional and nonexceptional) to a higher level of development through training generally have been unsuccessful (Gallagher & Reid, 1981), theoretically because children's stage progression depends on maturation as well as environment. The instructional principles that follow are directed at the teaching of concepts, generalizations, and thinking processes rather than at increasing the level of cognitive development.

1. Because children's thinking is qualitatively different at the various stages of development, teaching objectives should be matched to children's level of development.

2. Learning is the acquisition of higher order structures transformed from and built on previous structures. Thus, learning involves the acquisition of broad, general rules or frameworks rather than particular, isolated facts. As such, learning proceeds through understanding rather than through incorporation of rote responses.

3. Children are internally motivated by a desire for achieving equilibrium. Thus, learning is facilitated by the presentation of optimally challenging tasks and discrepant events that predispose the child to disequilibrium.

4. Children learn best through interacting with and manipulating environmental stimuli.

5. Group interactions may present children with ideas that challenge their own, leading to disequilibrium, reorganization, and new structures.

These principles have been translated into more specific guidelines for teaching learning-disabled students (Moses, 1981). These guidelines are appropriate for other special needs children:

1. Begin with an encountering stage that permits children to interact with the materials before a problem is posed. Present concrete materials that permit children to experience and impose many kinds of change.

2. Allow children to set goals before they deal with transformations.

3. Present problems that involve puzzling transformations. Create situations that stimulate children to infer and reason spontaneously.

4. Permit children's creation and use of alternative methods of problem solving.

5. Accept children's methods of problem solving, even if they lead to failure.

6. Create a nonthreatening, nonexternally evaluating atmosphere. Avoid praise, criticism, or other announcements that label children's responses, since external evaluation reinforces dependence on the environment.

7. Require children to anticipate or predict the results of their actions, observe outcomes, and compare their hypothesized outcomes with results.

8. Be responsive to the children: listen, accept all responses, and respond with appropriate feedback.

Teaching methods consistent with these principles and guidelines include cooperative learning, hypothesis testing, discovery learning, inquiry, and other approaches that encourage inductive thinking. Cooperative learning is an instructional strategy whereby students work together in small groups to complete academic tasks. Potential benefits include gains in academic content, basic skill development, problem solving, and socialization. More research is needed on the efficacy of cooperative learning with exceptional students (Pullis & Smith, 1981). Gallagher and Reid (1981) describe hypothesis testing approaches for teaching exceptional students as another method consonant with Piagetian theory.

The inductive approaches developed by Taba and her colleagues (Taba et al., 1971), and Suchman's problem-solving methods (Kitano & Kirby, 1986), provide step-by-step information for developing teaching activities consistent with Piagetian theory and applicable to mildly handicapped and gifted students. Taba's inductive approaches include methods for developing concepts, attaining concepts, applying generalizations, exploring feelings, and solving interpersonal problems. For example, a concept attainment strategy for the concept "square" requires teacher presentation of examples and nonexamples of squares and children's induction of a definition for square. Teachers may use the developing concepts strategy for assessing children's current ideas about a subject and for encouraging classification of concepts related to the subject. Suchman's problem-solving approach provides a concrete method for children's attainment of such objectives as letter, numeral, color, and shape names, vocabulary, sight words, and arithmetic facts.

A federally funded research project (Kitano et al., 1982) provides preliminary data supporting the use of inductive methods based on Suchman's problem-solving approach with mildly mentally retarded and learning-disabled elementary-age students. Results indicated that learning-disabled children who received instruction in language arts using inductive methods showed gains similar to those achieved by learning-disabled controls who received instruction with traditional didactic and behavioral approaches. As a group, the educable mentally handicapped children demonstrated greater achievement in language arts objectives with inductive approaches than matched peers in the control condition. These results suggest that inductive methods may constitute a viable addition to traditional approaches to instruction with mildly handicapped learners. While more research is needed to validate the efficacy of such approaches for special populations, the approaches have theoretical merit and provide alternatives to traditional deductive methods.

Piaget's theory of cognitive development has had specific application to mild and severe/profound mental retardation, learning disabilities, gifted, and other categories.

Mental Retardation

Although Piaget's writings reflect little interest in individual differences, his ideas have been used to interpret the cognitive behavior of exceptional individuals. For example, Inhelder (1968) noted that the level of cognitive development ultimately achieved by mentally retarded individuals depended on their degree of impairment, with the severe-profound fixated at the sensorimotor level, the moderately retarded at the preoperational stage, and the mildly retarded rarely advancing beyond the level of concrete operations.

During the 1960s and 1970s, Piaget's theory sparked a new view on the field of mental retardation. The developmental approach to mild, familial mental retardation provided a positive alternative to deficit approaches, which assume that mentally handicapped individuals by definition possess deficits (e.g., in processes such as attention, memory, organization, or in neurological structures) that require remediation. The developmental view, articulated by Zigler (1967; Zigler & Balla, 1982) and Iano (1971), suggests instead that the familial educable mentally retarded constitute the lower end of the normal curve and differ from the intellectually average only in terms of rate of development and final level achieved. Mental age serves as an indicator of current developmental level.

In general, proponents of developmental theory as applied to the mildly mentally retarded suggest that this approach enables teachers to view retarded children in terms of normal stages achieved at a slower rate. Klein and Safford (1977) concluded from their review of research literature that stages of development in the mentally retarded population parallel those described by Piaget for nonhandicapped children, but appear at later chronological periods. Hence, the mildly retarded can be expected to perform according to their mental ages. The implication for educators is that methods applied to normal children can be used effectively with mildly retarded students of similar mental age. Thus, these individuals can profit from many regular instructional techniques and a broader curriculum appropriate to normally achieving children. Iano (1971) noted that educators too often assume that the mentally retarded have deficiencies in learning rate, retention, and the ability to generalize and abstract. As a result, teachers emphasize great amounts of repetition, structure, concrete presentation, and slow, step-by-step introduction of new material. He asks whether the retarded child's failure to reason and problem solve is due to an inability to understand or to an emphasis in teaching on the rote and mechanical.

Although the developmental approach as applied to

mental retardation has received serious criticism (e.g., Spitz, 1983), research has neither disproved the developmental approach nor proved the deficit position, and probably never will (Spitz, 1983). In the meantime, the application of Piagetian instructional methods with the mildly retarded merits serious investigation and offers an exciting alternative to teachers wishing to broaden their instructional repertoire. Most important, application of Piagetian approaches to instruction may provide variety and challenge to the children themselves.

Piaget's descriptions of the sensorimotor stage, normally covering birth to 18 months, have served as a basis for interpreting the behavior of the severely/profoundly handicapped, assessing their level of cognitive development, and developing appropriate curricula. The six substages of the sensorimotor period can be summarized as follows (Stephens, 1977), together with sample instructional tasks appropriate to each.

Reflexive (birth–1 month). This phase is initially characterized by reflex actions (e.g., hand waving, kicking, crying, sucking, grasping) and visual tracking of objects. These actions become more coordinated and generalized. Sample task: To encourage visual tracking, hold a bright moving object 10 inches from the subject's eyes and move the object slowly across the subject's field of vision. If visual tracking fails to occur spontaneously, physically turn the subject's head to follow the object.

Primary Circular Reactions (1–4.5 months). Reflexive behavior becomes elaborated and coordinated. The infant becomes interested in movement itself, as in observing his or her own hand waving. Repeated as ends in themselves, these actions are "circular" responses. Sample task: Move a colorful, sound-producing object from side to side and up and down to encourage coordination of visual tracking and touching of the object with the hand. If visual tracking coordinated with touching the object does not occur spontaneously, physically guide the behavior.

Secondary Circular Reactions (4.5–9 months). The infant intentionally repeats chance movements that produce a desirable effect (e.g., shaking a rattle to produce a sound). Sample task: Demonstrate a squeeze toy and hand it to the subject. Guide the squeezing behavior to elicit the sound if the behavior does not occur spontaneously.

Coordination of Secondary Schema (9–12 months). The infant begins to discriminate between self and environment, to imitate speech sounds and movements of others, and to differentiate means and ends. Sample task: Demonstrate and guide a means-ends activity such as dropping an object into water to create a splash.

Tertiary Circular Reactions (12–18 months). The infant actively experiments and discovers new means to ends, such as pulling a blanket to reach a toy that is resting on it. Sample task: Provide opportunities for (and guidance as necessary) discovering a means-ends activity such as obtaining an unreachable object using a stick.

Invention of New Means Through Mental Combinations (18–24 months). The infant considers alternatives, solves problems, and completes development of object permanence. Sample task: Demonstrate and permit experimentation with fitting objects of different sizes and shapes into slots of various size and shape.

Based on her earlier work with severely retarded individuals, Woodward (1963) concluded that many of the seemingly inappropriate behaviors of this population are explainable within a Piagetian framework. Given that profoundly handicapped individuals operate at a sensorimotor level, mannerisms such as hand flapping in front of the eyes can be interpreted as sensorimotor patterns developed in the course of coordinating vision and grasping, as in the subphase of primary circular reactions.

Uzgiris and Hunt (1975) developed an assessment procedure for charting infant development founded on major areas of cognitive functioning during the sensorimotor period. Such an assessment procedure can be adapted for use with severely/profoundly handicapped individuals of various chronological ages. Areas of functioning assessed by Uzgiris and Hunt include visual pursuit and object permanence; means for achieving desired environmental events; gestural and vocal imitation; operational causality; object relations in space; and development of schemas in relation to objects.

Because severely/profoundly handicapped individuals generally do not proceed beyond the preoperational stage, curricula can be derived for this population based on the sensorimotor subphases and adapted according to chronological age. Development of appropriate curricula of a Piagetian nature for the severely/profoundly handicapped requires matching objectives to the individual's present level of development; active involvement of the individual; opportunity for the individual to proceed at his or her own pace; opportunities for exploration and manipulation; opportunities for repetition and practice; and adaptation for any associated sensory or motor impairments.

Learning Disabilities

By most definitions, learning-disabled students possess average to superior intellectual potential but manifest academic and social achievement at levels significantly lower than this potential would predict. Delays in cognitive and social-cognitive development have been explored through research as possible factors in explaining the discrepancy between potential and achievement in academic and social areas. Suggestions for teaching interventions based on Piagetian theory have also been offered in the literature.

Research. In general, the research suggests that learning-disabled (LD) children demonstrate performance inferior to that of nondisabled (NLD) children on tasks designed to measure cognitive development and social cognition. Speece, McKinney, and Appelbaum (1986) found a developmental delay in LD children's attainment of concrete operations compared with nondisabled (NLD) controls over a 3-year-period. However, their results also suggested that when the LD children attained the concrete operational stage, they acquired specific concepts in the same sequence and at the same rate as did NLD children. Moreover, for the LD but not the NLD group, Piagetian measures of cognitive development (conservation scores) and age better predicted academic achievement than did verbal intelligence. Most important was the finding that while the LD children as a group improved over the 3-year period, they failed to catch up with their NLD peers. Speece et al. (1986) concluded that delayed cognitive development may constitute an important explanatory factor for continued academic underachievement experienced by LD children despite intervention.

Dickstein and Warren (1980) reported similar delays in LD children's role-taking ability compared with NLD children in cognitive, affective, and perceptual tasks. Their analysis of the performance of children from 5 to 10 years of age suggested that larger differences in scores occurred in the younger age groups and that performance among LD children improved little between ages 8 and 10. Horowitz (1981) also found lower performance for LD children on an interpersonal role-taking task, but no significant differences between the two groups on a perceptual role-taking measure. However, as indicated by Horowitz, results were confounded by differences between the two groups in intelligence. Wong and Wong (1980) found significant differences between LD and NLD children in role taking, with LD girls demonstrating much poorer skills than LD boys.

Finally, investigations of LD children's referential communication skills corroborate the findings on role taking that LD children possess deficits in social cognition relative to their NLD peers. Noel (1980) found LD students less effective in providing descriptive information about objects than NLD controls because of the LD children's tendency to describe objects by shape rather than by label or name. Spekman (1981) further reported that LD speakers tended to give more unproductive, irrelevant, or repetitious messages than did NLD children on communication tasks. These findings suggest that LD children communicate less effectively than do NLD children.

As a whole, results of investigations on role taking and communication suggest that deficits in these skills may be one source of social problems evidenced by some LD children. Having difficulty in anticipating other people's views and accommodating their messages to others' needs reduces LD children's chances for successful social interactions.

Teaching. The literature has suggested Piagetian-derived instructional strategies for LD students both as tools for presenting academic content and for remediating deficits in social-cognitive skills. Gallagher and Quandt (1981) presented questioning strategies consistent with Piagetian theory for improving reading comprehension of LD students. They suggest, for example, the use of inference questions that require students go beyond the information given. Such questioning strategies present puzzling problems that stimulate equilibration. Moses (1981) offers examples of arithmetic instruction to illustrate the use of Piagetian guidelines for teaching LD students. Role-taking training through each child's sequential adoption of the various roles in a story also has been suggested (Chandler, 1971) as a vehicle for improving role-taking skills and social behavior.

Gifted

As with other areas of exceptionality, Piaget's theory as applied to the gifted has implications for research and practice.

Research. Piaget's theory would predict that the intellectually gifted, like the intellectually handicapped, follow the same sequence of stages as average children but differ in rate of progression. Carter and Ormrod (1982) found through their review of research that mentally retarded, average, and gifted children follow the same sequence of stages, supporting Piaget's view of sequence invariance. However, studies investigating differences between gifted and nongifted learners in rate of progression have yielded conflicting results. Carter and Ormrod suggest that discrepant findings might be due in part to differences in age groups studied. For example, young gifted children may not show superiority over average children in rate of cognitive development because such development, according to Piaget, is limited by maturity and experience, which may not differ significantly in quantity or quality in the early years.

There is some evidence to suggest that gifted children progress more rapidly than average children within a stage but achieve transitions to concrete and formal operations at approximately the same age as their peers. However, research by Carter (1985) and Carter and Ormrod (1982) indicates that gifted children both progress more rapidly than average children within a stage and demonstrate earlier transition to succeeding stages. In a study of 125 gifted and 98 average children aged 10 through 15, Carter and Ormrod (1982) found that the gifted outperformed controls at each age level and achieved formal operations at earlier ages. Specifically, the gifted students appeared to enter formal operations by age 12 or 13, while the average students, including 15 year olds, had not yet attained formal operations. Carter (1985) compared the cognitive development of 180 intellectually gifted, 325 bright average, and 168 average children ages 10 to 16. Major findings were that the gifted children outperformed intellectually average children at all age levels and outperformed bright average children at the lower age levels (10 to 14). Data were interpreted as indicating that gifted children establish their cognitive advantage as early as age 10. These studies suggest that intellectually gifted children may achieve higher stages of cognitive development at earlier ages than their average peers.

Despite common observations that gifted children express earlier concerns about morals and values, research on gifted children's social-cognitive development does not provide clear evidence that gifted children are advanced in this area relative to their average peers. Moral reasoning has some relationship to verbal intelligence. However, while some intellectually gifted students demonstrate advanced levels of moral judgment development, this is not true of all gifted students.

Teaching. Gifted children who are advanced in cognitive development compared with their intellectually average peers may require special interventions to prevent boredom and accompanying frustration. However, educators should not assume that all gifted children function at an advanced stage of cognitive development relative to their chronological age. Rather, every child should be assessed to determine level of cognitive development.

The process of concept acquisition through equilibration described by Piaget has relevance to instruction for the gifted. Guidelines for instruction consistent with Piaget's theory, described earlier, appear highly appropriate for gifted students because of their consistency with goals for the gifted, including optimum use of intellectual abilities, development of self-direction, and practice in higher level thinking skills (e.g., analysis, synthesis, evaluation). Kitano and Kirby (1986) describe specific methods for teaching the gifted consistent with Piagetian guidelines.

Other Categories

A few investigators have examined the application of Piagetian principles to children with other types of exceptionalities: cerebral palsy, hearing handicaps, visual impairments, and emotional disturbance. A review of these studies by Gallagher and Reid (1981) suggests that (1) intellectually normal children who have cerebral palsy progress at approximately the same rate as nonhandicapped children, although the former are slower to perform on tasks requiring manipulation, need more trials and encouragement, and have a lower frustration toler-

ance; (2) deaf children and blind children display minor or no delays in attainment of conservation compared with normal peers when accommodations are made for language and sensory differences and subjects are carefully matched; and (3) seriously emotionally disturbed children show deviations from normal developmental patterns.

In conclusion, the available research on cognitive development of exceptional learners suggests, for the most part, that exceptional individuals progress through the same sequence of stages described by Piaget for normal children, although they vary in rate of development and level ultimately attained. Application of Piagetian theory to practice suggests use of strategies that engage children in active problem solving appropriate to their current level of development. Additional research is required to demonstrate the efficacy of Piagetian-derived instructional strategies for handicapped and gifted learners. Such strategies have potential as additions to the instructional repertoire of special education teachers.

REFERENCES

Beilin, H. (1996). Mind and meaning: Piaget and Vygotsky on causal explanation. *Human Development, 39*(5), 277–286.

Carter, K. R. (1985). Cognitive development of intellectually gifted: A Piagetian perspective. *Roeper Review, 7*(3), 180–184.

Carter, K. R., & Ormrod, J. E. (1982). Acquisition of formal operations by intellectually gifted children. *Gifted Child Quarterly, 26*(3), 110–115.

Chandler, M. J. (1973). Egocentrism and antisocial behavior: The assessment and training of social perspective-taking skills. *Developmental Psychology, 9*(3), 326–332.

Dickstein, E. B., & Warren, D. R. (1980). Role-taking deficits in learning disabled children. *Journal of Learning Disabilities, 13*(7), 378–382.

Flavell, J. (1971). Stage-related properties of cognitive development. *Cognitive Psychology, 2,* 421–453.

Flavell, J. (1972). An analysis of cognitive developmental sequences. *Genetic Psychology Monographs, 86,* 279–350.

Gallagher, J. M., & Quandt, I. J. (1981). Piaget's theory of cognitive development and reading comprehension: A new look at questioning. *Topics in Learning & Learning Disabilities, 1*(1), 21–30.

Gallagher, J. M. & Reid, D. K. (1981). *The learning theory of Piaget and Inhelder.* Austin, TX: Pro-Ed.

Gelman, R. (1979). Preschool thought. *American Psychologist, 34*(10), 900–905.

Horowitz, E. C. (1981). Popularity, decentering ability, and role-taking skills in learning disabled and normal children. *Learning Disability Quarterly, 4*(1), 23–30.

Iano, R. P. (1971). Learning deficiency versus developmental conceptions of mental retardation. *Exceptional Children, 58,* 301–311.

Inhelder, B. (1968). *The diagnosis of reasoning in the mentally retarded.* New York: John Day.

Kitano, M. K., Julian, N., Shoji, C., Trujillo, R., & Padilla, E.

(1982). *Heuristic methods for the mildly handicapped: Research report and manual for teaching language arts and reading.* Las Cruces, NM: New Mexico State University.

Kitano, M. K., & Kirby, D. F. (1986). *Gifted education: A comprehensive view.* Boston: Little, Brown.

Klein, N. K., & Safford, P. L. (1977). Application of Piaget's theory to the study of thinking of the mentally retarded: A review of research. *Journal of Special Education, 11*(2), 201–216.

Moses, N. (1981). Using Piaget principles to guide instruction of the learning disabled. *Topics in Learning and Learning Disabilities, 1*(1), 11–19.

Noel, M. M. (1980). Referential communication abilities of learning disabled children. *Learning Disability Quarterly, 3*(3), 70–75.

Piaget, J. (1932). *The moral judgment of the child* (M. Gabain, Trans.). New York: Harcourt, Brace & World.

Piaget, J. (1950). *The psychology of intelligence* (M. Percy & D. E. Berlyne, Trans.). London: Routledge & Kegan Paul.

Piaget, J. (1952). *The origins of intelligence in children.* (M. Cook, Trans.). New York: International University.

Piaget, J. (1977). *The development of thoughts: Equilibration of cognitive structures.* New York: Viking.

Pullis, M., & Smith, D. C. (1981). Social cognitive development of learning disabled children: Implications of Piaget's theory for research and intervention. *Topics in Learning & Learning Disabilities, 1*(1), 43–55.

Reid, D. K. (Ed.). (1981). Piaget learning and learning disabilities. *Topics in Learning & Learning Disabilities, 1*(1).

Shantz, C. U. (1975). The development of social cognition. In E. M. Heatherington (Ed.), *Review of child development research* (Vol. 5, pp. 257–323). Chicago: University of Chicago Press.

Speece, D. L., McKinney, J. D., & Appelbaum, M. I. (1986). Longitudinal development of conservation skills in learning disabled children. *Journal of Learning Disabilities, 19*(5), 302–307.

Spekman, N. J. (1981). Dyadic verbal communication abilities of learning disabled and normally achieving fourth- and fifth-grade boys. *Learning Disability Quarterly, 4*(2), 139–151.

Spitz, H. H. (1983). Critique of the developmental position in mental-retardation research. *Journal of Special Education, 17*(3), 261–294.

Stephens, B. (1977). A Piagetian approach to curriculum development for the severely, profoundly, and multiply handicapped. In E. Sontag (Ed.), *Educational programming for the severely and profoundly handicapped* (pp. 237–249). Reston, VA: Council for Exceptional Children, Division on Mental Retardation.

Taba, H., Durkin, M. C., Fraenkel, J. R., & McNaughton, A. H. (1971). *A teacher's handbook to elementary social studies. An inductive approach* (2nd ed.). Menlo Park, CA: Addison-Wesley.

Uzgiris, I. C., & Hunt, J. M. (1975). *Assessment in infancy ordinal scales of psychological development.* Urbana, IL: University of Illinois Press.

Wachs, H., & Furth, H. (1980). Piaget's theory and special education. In B. K. Keogh (Ed.), *Advances in special education* (Vol. 2, pp. 51–78). Greenwich, CT: JAI.

Wong, B. Y. L., & Wong, R. (1980). Role-taking skills in normal achieving and learning disabled children. *Learning Disability Quarterly, 3*(2), 11–18.

Woodward, M. (1963). The application of Piaget's theory to research in mental deficiency. In N. Ellis (Ed.), *Handbook of mental deficiency: Psychological theory and research.* New York: McGraw-Hill.

Zigler, E. (1967). Familial mental retardation: A continuing dilemma. *Science, 155,* 292–298.

Zigler, E., & Balla, D. (Eds.). (1982). *Mental retardation: The developmental-difference controversy.* Hillsdale, NJ: Erlbaum.

MARGIE K. KITANO
New Mexico State University

COGNITIVE DEVELOPMENT
DIRECT INSTRUCTION
INDIVIDUALIZATION OF INSTRUCTION
INTELLIGENCE
PIAGET, JEAN

PIAGET, JEAN (1896–1980)

Jean Piaget was a Swiss psychologist whose explorations of the cognitive development of children helped to revolutionize education in the twentieth century. He described the sequence of mental development in three phases: (1) the sensory-motor phase, from birth to about age 2, during which children obtain a basic knowledge of objects; (2) the phase of concrete operations, from about 2 to 11, characterized by concrete thinking and the development of simple concepts; and (3) the formal operations phase, from about age 11, emphasizing abstract thinking, reasoning, and logical thought. Piaget's theories and descriptions of developmental sequences have encouraged teaching methods that emphasize the child's discovery of knowledge through the presentation of developmentally appropriate problems to be solved.

Born in Neuchatel, Switzerland, Piaget was educated at the university there, was director of the Jean Jacques Rousseau Institute in Geneva, and professor at the University of Geneva. In 1955 he established in Geneva the International Center of Genetic Epistomology, where he and his associates published voluminously on child development.

REFERENCES

Furth, H. G. (1969). *Piaget and knowledge.* Englewood Cliffs, Prentice-Hall.

Piaget, J. (1926). *The language and thought of the child.* New York: Humanities.

PAUL IRVINE
Katonah, New York

PIC

See PERSONALITY INVENTORY FOR CHILDREN.

PICA

The word "pica" originates from the Latin word for magpie, a bird known for ingesting a wide variety of food and non-food items (Danford & Huber, 1982). Pica is seen in various species, including birds, fish, apes, and humans (Diamond & Stermer, 1998). Pica as a disorder is characterized by habitual ingestion of inedible substances (Kerwin & Berkowitz, 1996). It is frequently associated with mental retardation (Danford & Huber, 1982), but also occurs in normal young children (less than age 3) and pregnant women within certain cultural groups. As many as 90% of children with elevated levels of blood-lead may show pica behavior. Pica sometimes continues into adolescence and adulthood (Diamond & Stermer, 1998). In infancy and early childhood, children often chew on their cribs, wood, sand, and grass as a method of early exploration (Erickson, 1998).

According to DSM-IV, pica is defined as "persistent eating of nonnutritive substances for a period of at least 1 month" that is "inappropriate to the developmental level" or "not part of a culturally sanctioned practice." DSM-IV also states that if pica behavior occurs in conjunction with another mental disorder (e.g., mental retardation, pervasive developmental disorder, or schizophrenia), it should be sufficiently severe to warrant independent clinical attention for a separate diagnosis to be given (APA, 1994, p. 96). Pica may be both underdiagnosed and undertreated (Katsiyannis, Torrey, & Bond, 1998).

Paint chips, dirt and sand, paper, fabric, feces, cigarette stubs, and bugs are among the substances commonly consumed by those with pica. Pica is a prevalent cause of lead poisoning, especially in children, due to lead-based paint that is common in cribs, other wooden objects, and some dirt. Dirt near houses may particularly contain lead in paint that has flaked off outside walls. Pica can also lead to severe nutritional deficits, intestinal obstruction or perforation, parasitic infections such as toxoplasmosis (through eating of cat feces), and even death (Katsiyannis et al., 1998; Kerwin & Berkowitz, 1996; Wiley, Henretig, & Selbst, 1992). Intestinal blockage may necessitate surgery to remove the obstruction.

Although pica is generally associated with adverse consequences, eating dirt or clay under some conditions may have benefits. The practice of eating soil is termed "geophagy." Geophagy may relieve hunger, provide grit for grinding food, provide nutritional value, cure diarrhea, buffer stomach contents, or protect against toxins (Diamond & Stermer, 1998). In the southeastern United States, pregnant women may eat clay and/or laundry starch owing to a superstitious belief that the practice prevents fetal curses and reduces the side effects of pregnancy (Nelson-Wicks & Israel, 1997). In one area of China, where geophagy is common, some people consume soil in a belief that it provides valuable nutrients. Indeed, a soil sample from the area contained iron, calcium, and manganese. In Zimbabwe, where people eat soil to soothe upset stomachs, one sample contained kaolinire, an ingredient that pharmaceutical companies use to treat diarrhea (Current Science, 1998). South American Indians reportedly regularly eat toxic potatoes mixed with an alkaloid-containing clay. The clay neutralizes the potatoes' toxicity (Diamond & Stermer, 1998).

Pica is a learned behavior, but its maintenance may owe to a number of factors. Since one of those factors may relate to a nutritional inadequacy, medical and nutritional analyses should precede any treatment program (Katsiyannis et al., 1998). If it is associated with some nutritional inadequacy, pica may be successfully treated with some dietary changes or mineral supplements targeted at the particular deficiency. In cases where no nutritional problem is found, a functional analysis of behavior should be conducted. Several types of behavioral interventions have been used successfully, ranging from less intrusive (e.g., differential reinforcement for non-pica behavior) to more aversive (e.g., overcorrection or brief physical restraint contingent upon pica). Obviously, any treatment program should begin with the least restrictive interventions unless the child's behavior presents an immediate risk. One interesting treatment uses a "pica box." A pica box is a small box containing edible items for a child. When a child attempts to eat a nonedible item, he or she is stopped, and after a brief time-out, is reinforced by being allowed to get a treat out of the pica box. This method has been especially useful in working with mildly retarded and autistic children (Hirsch & Myles, 1996). A particular source for those in special education is Katsiyannis et al. (1998), who not only describe several programs in detail but provide useful case studies.

REFERENCES

American Psychiatric Association. (1994). *Diagnostic and statistical manual of mental disorders* (4th ed.). Washington, DC: American Psychiatric Association.

Danford, D., & Huber, A. (1982). Pica among mentally retarded adults. *American Journal of Mental Deficiency, 87,* 141–146.

Diamond, J., & Stermer, D. (1998). Eat dirt. *Discover, 19*(2), 70–76.

Erickson, M. T. (1998). *Behavior disorders of children and adolescents.* Upper Saddle River, NJ: Prentice Hall.

Hirsch, N., & Myles, B. (1996). The use of a pica box in reducing pica behavior in a student with autism. *Focus on Autism and Other Developmental Disabilities, 11,* 222.

How would you like a dirt sandwich? (1998). *Current Science, 16,* 12–15.

Katsiyannis, A., Torrey, G., & Bond, V. (1998). Current considerations in treating pica. *Teaching Exceptional Children, 30*(4), 50–53.

Kerwin, M. E., & Berkowitz, R. I. (1996). Feeding and eating disorders: Ingestive problems of infancy, childhood, and adolescence. *School Psychology Review, 25,* 316–329.

Wicks-Nelson, R., Israel, A. C. (1997). *Behavior disorders of childhood.* Upper Saddle River, NJ: Prentice Hall.

Lauren M. Webster
Robert T. Brown
University of North Carolina at Wilmington

ANOREXIA NERVOSA
EATING DISORDERS
LEAD POISONING
OBESITY

PIERRE-ROBIN SYNDROME

Hypoplasia of the mandible, prior to 9 weeks of intrauterine development, results in a posteriorly located tongue which, in turn, impairs closure of the posterior or soft palate. Children born with the syndrome of micrognathia (small lower jaw) are at risk for airway obstruction which may be present at birth or develop over the first month of life, requiring endotracheal tube or tracheostomy. Lack of oxygen can lead to damage to the heart and brain during this critical period. Most infants are otherwise normal and mandibular growth catches up, the long-term prognosis is good both for appearance and function. This anomaly is, however, also seen as part of other multiple malformation syndromes that may include mental retardation.

REFERENCES

Dennison, W. M. (1965). The Pierre-Robin syndrome. *Pediatrics, 36,* 336–341.

Jones, K. J., (1997). *Robin sequence: Smith's recognizable patterns of human malformation* (5th ed., pp. 234–235). Philadelphia: W. B. Saunders.

Patricia L. Hartlage
Medical College of Georgia

PIERS-HARRIS CHILDREN'S SELF-CONCEPT SCALE

The Piers-Harris Children's Self-Concept Scale (Piers, 1969) is a self-report inventory designed to measure self-concept in children ages 9 through 16. The 80-item scale consists of short statements reflecting concerns children have about themselves. There are 36 positive statements and 44 negative statements written at a third-grade reading level. Responses indicative of a favorable self-concept are worth one point and total scores can range from 0 through 80. Scores are also obtained on six subscales: behavior, intellectual and school status, physical appearance and attributes, anxiety, popularity, and happiness and satisfaction. The test takes 15 to 20 minutes to complete and may be administered to an individual or a group. Test-retest reliability has ranged from .62 to .75 (over a 2 to 7 month period) and from .80 to .96 (over a 3 to 9 week period; Hughes, 1984). Evidence of construct validity was reviewed by Piers (1977). Moderate relationships were reported with other measures of self-concept, and relationships with personality and behavioral measures were generally in the direction expected.

Although the norms for the Piers-Harris are several decades old, more recent research has provided general continuing support for the use of the instrument (Epstein, 1985). When integrated with other data on a child, the Piers-Harris may prove to be quite clinically useful. Therapists or counselors may find it to be a helpful screening tool or a useful introductory activity for therapy (Epstein, 1985).

REFERENCES

Epstein, J. H. (1985). Review of The Piers-Harris Children's Self-Concept Scale. In J. V. Mitchell (Ed.), *The ninth mental measurements yearbook.* Lincoln, NE: Buros Institute of Mental Measurements.

Hughes, H. M. (1984). Measures of self-concept and self-esteem of children ages 3–12 years: Review and recommendations. *Clinical Psychology Review, 4,* 657–692.

Piers, E. V. (1969). *The Piers-Harris Children's Self-Concept Scale.* Nashville, TN: Western Psychological Services.

Piers, E. V. (1977). *The Piers-Harris Children's Self-Concept Scale, research monograph No. 1.* Nashville, TN: Western Psychological Services.

Robert G. Brubaker
Eastern Kentucky University
First edition

Elizabeth O. Lichtenberger
The Salk Institute
Second edition

CHILDREN'S MANIFEST ANXIETY SCALE
SELF-CONCEPT

PINEL, PHILIPPE (1745–1826)

Phillipe Pinel, French physician and pioneer in the humane treatment of the mentally ill, served as chief physician at two famous mental hospitals in France, the Bicêtre and the Salpêtrière. Convinced that mental illness was not a result of demoniacal possession, as was commonly believed, but of brain dysfunction, Pinel released his patients from the chains that were used to restrain them and replaced deleterious remedies such as bleeding and purging with psychological treatment by physicians.

Through publications in which he set forth his methods for the care and treatment of the mentally ill, Pinel's ideas gained wide acceptance throughout the western world. France, through Pinel's efforts, became the first country to attempt the provision of adequate care for the mentally ill.

REFERENCE

Pinel, P. (1801). *Traité médico-philosophique sur l'aliénation mentale*. Paris: Richard, Caille & Revier.

PAUL IRVINE
Katonah, New York

PITUITARY GLAND

The pituitary is a small gland located at the base of the brain immediately beneath the hypothalamus, above the roof of the mouth, and behind the optic chiasma. The pituitary lies in a bony depression called the sella turcia. The pituitary is also sometimes referred to as the hypothysis.

The pituitary regulates the secretions of a number of other endocrine glands and often is referred to as the master gland. However, its function is closely linked to the hypothalamus, and the pituitary and hypothalamus must be thought of as a system rather than independent entities. The hypothalamus and the pituitary are connected by a rich supply of nerves called the infundibulum.

Morphologically, the pituitary is a small gland. It weighs less than a gram and is only about a centimeter in diameter. It consists of two major lobes, the anterior pituitary (adenohypophysis) and the posterior pituitary (neurohypophysis). These two lobes are connected by a much smaller pars intermedia. The anterior pituitary manufactures a number of hormones that serve to trigger the release of still others. The hormones directly secreted by the anterior pituitary include growth hormone, thyroid-stimulating hormone (TSH), adrenocorticotrophic hormone (ACTH), and gonadotrophic hormones such as follicle-stimulating hormone (FSH), luteinizing hormone (LH), and lactogenic hormone (prolactin).

Adrenocorticotrophic hormone (ACTH) is intimately involved in stress reactions. Release of this hormone by the pituitary causes the adrenal cortex to produce cortisol and other steroid hormones that help prepare the body for fight or flight. Gonadotrophic hormones (e.g., follicle-stimulating hormone and luteinizing hormone) activate the ovaries and testes so that estrogen and testosterone, respectively, are produced.

Prolactin is a hormone that affects the mammary glands and that appears to be involved in the regulation of maternal behavior in vertebrates. Somatotropin (STH or growth hormone) is a hormone necessary for normal growth. Excesses of somatotropin result in the clinical condition of acromegaly.

It is useful to view the pituitary as a link in a complex chain of events that tie the hypothalamus to other glands. However, the hypothalamus lacks direct neural connection with the anterior pituitary, and instead influence is exerted by release factors transported through a complex system of blood vessels called the hypothalamic-hypophyseal portal system.

The posterior pituitary (neurohypophysis) secretes antidiuretic hormone (ADH) and oxytocin. Release of these hormones is triggered by complex connections with other parts of the nervous system. The cells of the posterior pituitary do not produce hormones themselves but instead serve as storage sites for hormones produced by the anterior hypothalamus. When blood pressure falls, the secretion of ADH stimulates the kidneys to reduce their excretion of water into the urine. Lack of ADH can produce diabetes insipidus. Oxytocin plays an important role in inducing contractions during labor, and it is necessary for the contraction of the smooth muscles of the mammary glands, which are needed to produce milk in response to sucking.

It has been found that individuals with anorexia and bulimia have same pituitary atrophy due to nutritional and/or endocrine alterations (Doraiswamy, Krishnan, Figiel, & Husain, 1990).

REFERENCES

Asterita, M. F. (1985). *The physiology of stress*. New York: Human Sciences.

Doraiswamy, P., Krishnan, K., Figiel, G. S., & Husain, M. (1990). A brain magnetic resonance imaging study of pituitary gland morphology in anorexia nervosa and bulimia. *Biological Psychiatry, 28*(2), 110–116.

Groves, P., & Schlesinger, K. (1979). *Biological psychology*. Dubuque, IA: Brown.

DANNY WEDDING
Marshall University

DIABETES

PKU

See PHENYLKETONURIA.

PLACEBOS

Placebos are substances or therapeutic interventions that produce their effects as a result of the expectations of the recipient and the therapist. As originally applied in medicine, placebo therapies improved patients' conditions despite the fact that the placebos had no direct physiological action. Placebos, therefore, became an aid to physicians who lacked a specific therapy and a nuisance variable to researchers studying therapeutic effectiveness.

The placebo effect is most powerful in social situations where an experimental approach produces high hopes for success (Orne, 1969). To differentiate between placebo and direct therapeutic physiological effects, it has become commonplace in drug research to use a double-blind procedure. In such a design, both the person administering the therapy and the subject are unaware (blind) as to whether a given dose contains the experimental substance or a physiologically inert placebo. If the placebo and treatment interventions result in similar effects, the value of the new therapy is called into question. Practical or ethical considerations often limit the applicability of double-blind studies, and the existence of potential placebo effects remains a problem in a variety of areas of research.

Although placebos may be physiologically inert, recent research has indicated that they may have a biological effect. For example, Levine, Gordon, and Fields (1978) have provided some evidence that placebos that were supposedly analgesics activated the endorphins that are the body's internal painkillers.

There has been great controversy concerning the use of the placebo concept in understanding behavioral change interventions. Simeon & Willins (1993) suggest that there has not been enough research done in the use of placebos with children. Critelli and Neumann (1984) have argued that the placebo effect is more than a nuisance variable and the display of empathy, nonpossessive warmth, etc., that may occur in a placebo intervention may be an important part of the therapy. In the classroom, the expectations of teachers and students about the probabilities of high student performance during an educational intervention may play a significant role in its effectiveness (Zanna, Sheras, Cooper & Shaw, 1975).

Thus both the special education researcher and classroom teacher may need to take placebos into account. The researcher may wish to provide a placebo control group where subjects receive a treatment that is irrelevant to the planned intervention. Such a treatment allows control subjects to experience the attention that goes to those undergoing the treatment of interest (Cook & Campbell, 1979). The classroom teacher should be aware of the combination of placebo and direct effect of interventions and, therefore, foster expectations of success.

REFERENCES

Cook, T., & Campbell, D. (1979). *Quasi-experimentation: Design and analysis issues in field settings.* Boston: Houghton Mifflin.

Critelli, J., & Neumann, K. N. (1984). The placebo: Conceptual analysis of a construct in transition. *American Psychologist, 39,* 32–39.

Levine, J., Gordon, N., & Fields, H. (1978). The mechanism of placebo analgesia, *Lancet, 2,* 654–657.

Orne, M. (1969). Demand characteristics and the concept of quasi-controls. In R. Rosenthal & R. Rosnow (Eds.), *Artifact in behavioral research* (pp. 147–181). New York: Academic.

Simeon, J. G. & Wiggins, D. M. (1993). The placebo problem in children and adolescent psychiatry. *International Journal of Child and Adolescent Psychiatry, 56*(2), 119–122.

Zanna, M., Sheras, P., Cooper, J., & Shaw, C. (1975). Pygmalion and Galatea: The interactive effect of teacher and student expectancies. *Journal of Experimental Social Psychology, 11,* 279–287.

LEE ANDERSON JACKSON, JR.
University of North Carolina at Wilmington

DOUBLE-BLIND DESIGN
TEACHER EXPECTANCIES

PLACENTA

The placenta (Latin for "cake") transfers life-sustaining supplies from the mother to the prenate, disposes of the prenate's wastes, and protects the prenate from some harmful substances. It begins to form during the germinal period and becomes differentiated as a separate disk-shaped organ during the embryonic phase (Annis, 1978). The umbilical cord extends from the center of the smooth fetal surface. The maternal surface is composed of many convoluted branches, creating a surface area of about 13 m², which provides maximum exposure to blood vessels in the uterine lining. At term the placenta is about 18 cm in diameter and weighs about 570 g.

The placenta includes two completely separate sets of blood vessels—one fetal and one maternal. Only small, light molecules may pass through the placental barrier; maternal and fetal blood never mix. Although the exact mechanisms of transfer of nutrients and wastes between the two systems are not completely understood, transfer of gases and water is accomplished by simple diffusion (Hytten & Leitch, 1964). The placenta protects the prenate from overexposure to elements in the mother's blood (e.g., hormones and cholesterol) by reducing their concentration in the fetal blood; it also prevents some teratogens from reaching the fetus.

In a small percentage of pregnancies, impairments involving the placenta create serious consequences. In about 10% of pregnancies the placenta fails to produce progesterone in the early weeks, resulting in spontaneous abortion. Infrequently, the placenta is small or malformed, causing retarded fetal growth or possibly stillbirth. When the placenta partially or entirely covers the cervical opening (placenta previa), the membranes usually rupture early in the third trimester, leading to a premature delivery.

Even during normal functioning, the placenta is an imperfect filter. As the fetus matures, placental blood vessels enlarge and stretch the placental barrier more thinly, thus decreasing its ability to filter larger molecules. Many harmful agents (e.g., bacteria) are kept out during the early prenatal stages, when teratogens are potentially most dangerous. For example, syphilis cannot cross until after the twentieth week. Viruses (including rubella), because they are so small, are able to pass through during this critical period. Many chemicals that the mother ingests that are potentially harmful (e.g., alcohol, caffeine, and carbon monoxide) pass through in ever-increasing dose levels as the placental barrier thins.

REFERENCES

Annis, L. F. (1978). *The child before birth.* Ithaca, NY: Cornell University Press.

Assali, N. S., Ditts, P. V., Jr., Plentl, A. A., Kirschbaum, T. H., & Gross, S. J. (1968). Physiology of the placenta. In N. S. Assali (Ed.), *Biology of gestation.* New York: Academic.

Hytten, F. E., & Leitch, I. (1964). *The physiology of human pregnancy.* Oxford, England: Blackwell.

PAULINE F. APPLEFIELD
University of North Carolina at Wilmington

CONGENITAL DISORDERS
PREMATURITY/PRETERM

PLANTAR REFLEX

The word plantar means "of, pertaining to, or occurring on the sole of the foot" (Rothenberg & Chapman, 1994). The plantar reflex is observed when the sole of the foot is scratched or stroked with a dull object and the toes bunch or curl downwards. The plantar response is a reflex that involves all the muscles that shorten the leg and the toes and is present in normal children (after the age of one year), adolescents, and adults.

Abnormal response to the plantar stimulation is usually in the form of the big toe extending upwards towards the head, the toes fanning out, and withdrawal of the leg. This response is known as the Babinski reflex or sign and is indicative of neurological damage.

REFERENCES

Bassetti, C. (1995). Babinski and Babinski sign. *Spine, 20*(23), 2591–4.

Rothenberg, M. A., & Chapman, C. F. (1994). *Dictionary of medical terms* (3rd ed.). Hauppauge, NY: Barron's.

van Gijn, J. (1995). The Babinski reflex. *Postgraduate Medical Journal, 71*(841), 645–8.

ELAINE FLETCHER-JANZEN
University of North Colorado

APGAR RATING SCALE
BABINSKI REFLEX
DEVELOPMENTAL MILESTONES

PLASTICITY

Plasticity in the human sciences is the absence in an individual of predetermined developmental characteristics and a concomitant modifiability by organismic or environmental influences. The concept is not limited to the capacity to change in accord with outside pressure. It includes the power to learn from experience and modify behavior while retaining predisposing genetic inheritance (Kolb & Whishaw, 1998). Educator John Dewey (1916) emphasized the characteristic plasticity of the immature child as a specific adaptability for growth. Basic to this concept is a person's power to modify actions on the basis of the results of prior experiences. In addition, plasticity implies the development of definite dispositions or habits. Habits, Dewey wrote, give control over the environment and power to use it for human purposes.

As a feature of the young child, plasticity is often most evident in exceptional children where deviation from the norm is significant. It has been seen frequently in gifted children, in schizophrenic children, and in some children with organic brain disorders (Bender, 1952). Many such children show prodigious accomplishments or become late bloomers and manage to make up for what they might have missed in earlier years both in educational and social development.

A study by Chess, Korn, and Fernandez (1971) of 235 victims of a 1964 worldwide rubella epidemic began when the youngsters were 2 years old. Development showed an overall delay during the first years of life, with characteristic impairment in language and motor sensorimotor functions. One-third of the children were diagnosed as showing varying degrees of mental retardation during the preschool period, while only one-fourth showed evidence of mental retardation at ages eight and nine. The IQs of the nonretarded children also showed progressive increases as they entered the school-age period. Detailed case studies of a number of the children who showed such improvement demonstrated that they came through a diverse and roundabout pattern to normal school functioning. Often they pioneered new territory in the acquisition of language, social development, and learning—thereby affirming the inherent plasticity of human brain function in the young child.

Similar individual-specific roads to cognitive language and social functioning have been demonstrated for children with congenital heart disease who had corrective surgery, children who contracted polio before the days of the Salk vaccine, children with rheumatic fever, and children with chronic kidney disease. Studies of blind children have demonstrated similar plasticity (Fraiberg, 1977) and attention-deficit/hyperactivity disorder (Jensen et al., 1997).

Plasticity takes on a negative connotation as applied by Bender (1953) to the concept of childhood schizophrenia. According to Bender, a physiological crisis may interfere with the maturation of the child in every area of functioning. The disturbance has a plastic quality that gives a primitive pattern to all behavior and renders the child incapable of satisfactorily dealing with autonomic responses, motility, perceptions, symbol formation, language, ideation, and interpersonal relationships. This causes anxiety and elicits defense mechanisms. Because of the plastic quality of the disorder, any function or area of behavior can be retarded, regressed, fixated, or accelerated. In *Principles of Education*, Bolton (1910) stated, "Where there is evolution, there is plasticity" (p. 8). Biological plasticity underlies the adaptive physiological process primary to organic evolution. Psychological plasticity underlies the adaptive behavior process primary to education and social evolution.

REFERENCES

Bender, L. (1952). *Child psychiatric techniques.* Springfield, IL: Thomas.

Bender, L. (1953). *Aggression, hostility and anxiety in children.* Springfield, IL: Thomas.

Bolton, F. E. (1910). *Principles of education.* New York: Scribner.

Chess, S., Korn, S., & Fernandez, P. (1971). *Psychiatric disorders of children with congenital rubella.* New York: Brunner/Mazel.

Dewey, J. (1916). *Democracy and education.* New York: Macmillan.

Fraiberg, S. (1977). *Insights from the blind.* New York: International Universities Press.

Jensen, P. S., Mrazek, D., Knapp, P. K., Steinberg, L., Pfeffer, C., Schowalter, J., & Shapiro, T. (1997). Evolution and revolution in child psychiatry: ADHD as a disorder of adoption. *Journal of*

American Academy of Child & Adolescent Psychiatry, 36(12), 1672–1681.

Kolb, B., & Whishaw, I. Q. (1998). Brain plasticity and behavior. *Annual Review of Psychology, 49,* 43–64.

WARNER H. BRITTON
Auburn University

INTELLIGENCE
ZONE OF PROXIMAL DEVELOPMENT

PLATO AND THE GIFTED

Plato was among the earliest philosophers to formulate a classification of students within three levels of public education. Plato wanted to separate "men with hearts and intellects of gold" to train and educate them for the highest functions of the state as kings, rulers, or executives. Without proper nurture, the brightest student would not be likely to be willing to serve the state's citizens (Burt, 1975).

Plato's three levels of public education included common elementary school, secondary school with selective admission, and a state university with admission still more selective. On the elementary level, the curriculum covered literature, music, and civics. On the secondary level, students were prepared for future military and civil service posts by studying in the curriculum areas of mathematics, arithmetic, plane and solid geometry, astronomy, and harmonics. In higher education there were 5 years of "dialectic" learning followed by 15 years of practical experience for those chosen to be the leaders of the ideal state (Brumbaugh, 1962).

These rulers or guardians were trained and later employed for external warfare and internal police work. The 15 years of rigorous intellectual training prepared the select few for lives as philosophers. Plato's ideal state depended on its kings being philosophers or its philosophers being kings (Plato, 1973/393BC).

The republic of Plato required education for both men and women. This was thought to be revolutionary at the time. Women received the same educational opportunities and training for the mind and body; they were also instructed in the art of war. If a woman possessed the right natural gifts, she shared the highest of public duties equally with men. Every occupation was open to her, but it understood that she was physically weaker. A man's nature was thought to be suited for majesty and valor and a woman's for orderliness and temperance (Morrow, 1960).

The idea of gifted students within the educational system was especially evident in the republic during the open discussions on mathematics. Plato believed that all students should be introduced to mathematics and discussed how this subject had an effect on the mental powers of a student; he believed it sharpened a student's wits and helped to fix attention. The skills of higher mathematics were seen as needed by the chosen few future rulers. These gifted students would study with systematic thoroughness and exactness (Morrow, 1960). Students were chosen for this advanced curriculum if they demonstrated that they understood the general connection of the various curriculum areas. If a student successfully grasped both a practical and theoretical connection, at the age of 30 the student would be admitted to the highest and most complete of all possible studies—philosophy.

REFERENCES

Bosanquet, B. (1908). *The education of the young in the republic of Plato.* Cambridge, England: Cambridge University Press.

Brumbaugh, R. S. (1962). *Plato for the modern age.* New York: Crowell-Collier.

Burt, C. (1975). *The gifted child.* New York: Wiley.

Morrow, G. R. (1960). *Plato's Cretan city: A historical interpretation of the laws.* Princeton, NJ: Princeton University Press.

Plato. (1972). *The republic of Plato* (F. M. Cornford, Trans.). New York: Oxford University Press. (Original work published 370 BC)

Plato. (1973). *Plato: Laches and charmides* (R. E. Sprague, Trans.). Indianapolis: Bobbs-Merrill. (Original work published 393 BC)

DEBORAH A. SHANLEY
Medgar Evers College

GIFTED CHILDREN
HISTORY OF SPECIAL EDUCATION

PLAY

Play among humans can be described as an attitude rather than a category of behaviors (Damon, 1983). Play is often regarded as the opposite of work in so far as attitude is concerned. A child who is having fun with an activity (as evidenced by laughing and smiling) is playing. Conversely, a child who is practicing his game skills to perfection is working. In fact, it has been suggested that the word play is most effectively used as an adverb, as in "the child stacked the blocks playfully" (Miller, 1968).

Regardless of its seemingly nonserious origins, play is a critical developmental activity. Many aspects of our social, motor, and cognitive lives have their origins in childhood play. The famous Russian psychologist Lev Vygotsky argued throughout his short, albeit brilliant career, that play creates the conditions for the child's acquisition of new competence in imaginative, social, and intellectual skills. Recently, computers and the internet have provided a new

form of play for many children and adolescents (Griffiths & Hunt, 1995).

One method of classifying children's play is based on interactions with other children. Five categories of play can be distinguished (Parten, 1932). The first type, solitary play, involves no interaction at all with other children. In onlooker play, the second type, the child simply observes other children at play. This is thought to be the first phase of a preschooler's interaction with other children.

When children begin to engage in the same activity side by side without taking much notice of each other, parallel play is said to occur. Associative play, the fourth type, occurs in older preschoolers; in this type, play becomes much more interactive. During this phase, two or more children partake in the same activity doing basically the same thing; however, there is no attempt to organize the activity or take turns.

Cooperative play, an organized activity in which individual children cooperate to achieve some sort of group goal, usually does not appear until age 3. At this stage children become more able and eager to participate in social forms of play. Solitary play does not ever disappear. Most children are capable of playing alone if a companion is not available. Onlooker behavior persists even into adulthood.

The symbolic nature of play is vital to the development of the child; it performs several functions in that development. First, children can use their symbolic skills, like language, in new and different ways, in a sense testing the limits of those skills. Second, children can, through play, do and say things that are normally difficult to express or taboo. Third, as children exit infancy they can use play in a cooperative, social fashion. "Make believe" allows children to explore social roles, work in cooperation with others, and experiment with social roles and rules (Damon, 1983).

Children who are handicapped may be less able to use play effectively and therefore may lose out on some of the important outcomes of play. For example, a physically handicapped child may not be able to engage in normal social play with other children. Hence, that child needs special arrangements or interventions to make sure that he or she has access to normal opportunities for play (Cattanach, 1995).

REFERENCES

Cattanach, A. (1995). Drama and play therapy with young children. *Arts in Psychotherapy, 22*(3), 223–228.

Damon, W. (1983). *Social and personality development: Infancy through adolescence.* New York: Norton.

Griffiths, M. D., & Hunt, N. Computer game playing in adolescence: Prevalence and demographic indicators. *Journal of Community & Applied Social Psychology, 5*(3), 189–193.

Miller, S. (1968). *The psychology of play.* Middlesex, England: Penguin.

Parten, M. B. (1932). Social participation among preschool children. *Journal of Abnormal & Social Psychology, 27,* 243–269.

MICHAEL J. ASH
JOSE LUIS TORRES
Texas A & M University

CONCEPT OF ACTIVITY
VYGOTSKY, L. S.
ZONE OF PROXIMAL DEVELOPMENT

PLAYTEST

The PLAYTEST procedure is recognized as one possible approach to screening and direct assessment of an infant's auditory functioning (Butterfield, 1982). The PLAYTEST system was originally developed by B. Z. Friedlander as a research tool for measuring infants' selective listening and receptive voice discrimination abilities within the home environment (Friedlander, 1968).

The system consists of a simple, portable, automated toy apparatus that attaches to the infant's crib or playpen. An audio or video-audio recorder and response recorder complete the equipment. The apparatii are attached at different locations on the crib or playpen. When the infant attends to either device, the responses activate the accompanying stereophonic tape recorder. The tape recorder is fitted with an endless loop audio tape. Certain systems are equipped to provide video-audio feedback instead of just audio feedback. Separate channels on the device carry different prerecorded sound samples.

The infant's frequency and duration of response to the various sources of auditory stimuli are used to infer the current level of auditory discrimination and selective listening abilities. Both the audio and the video-audio PLAYTEST systems use a response recorder to register the infant's differential response to the various auditory stimuli.

The PLAYTEST system has proven a valuable research tool in the investigation of auditory functioning in infants (Friedlander, 1968, 1970, 1971, 1975). One interesting finding is that very young infants show a clear preference for the mother's voice as opposed to a simple musical score.

It appears that the PLAYTEST system also provides an invaluable means of identifying infants at high risk for developing significant language disorders later in life (Butterfield, 1982; Friedlander, 1975). Butterfield (1982) envisions the PLAYTEST procedure as an instrumental screening and assessment procedure in the very early detection of auditory processing and/or discrimination problems in infants. He has described modifications of the existing system that would enable professionals to assess infants less than 6 months of age for possible auditory dysfunctions (Butterfield, 1982).

REFERENCES

Butterfield, E. C. (1982). Behavioral assessment of infants' hearing. In M. Lewis & L. T. Taft (Eds.), *Developmental disabilities: Theory, assessment, and intervention.* New York: SP Medical & Scientific.

Friedlander, B. Z. (1968). The effect of speaker identity, voice inflection, vocabulary, and message redundancy on infants' selection of vocal reinforcement. *Journal of Experimental Child Psychology, 6,* 443–459.

Freidlander, B. Z. (1970). Receptive language development in infancy: Issues and problems. *Merrill Quarterly of Behavior & Development, 16,* 7–51.

Friedlander, B. Z. (1971). Listening, language, and the auditory environment: Automated evaluation and intervention. In J. Hellmuth (Ed.), *The exceptional infant* (Vol. 2). New York: Brunner/Mazel.

Friedlander, B. Z. (1975). Automated evaluation of selective listening in language impaired and normal infants and young children. In B. Z. Friedlander, G. M. Sterritt, & G. E. Kirk (Eds.), *The exceptional infant* (Vol. 3). New York: Brunner/Mazel.

JULIA A. HICKMAN
University of Texas

AUDITORY DISCRIMINATION
DEAF
LANGUAGE DISORDERS

PLAY THERAPY

Play therapy is a therapeutic technique used with children that emphasizes the medium of play as a substitute for the traditional verbal interchange between therapists and adult clients. The roots of play therapy can be traced back to the psychoanalytic work of Sigmund Freud (1909), and the classic case of Little Hans, in which Freud directed the child's father in techniques used to treat the child's severe phobia. Direct work with a child was first initiated by Hug-Hellmuth (Gumaer, 1984), who applied Freudian analysis to children under age 7. It soon became apparent that children lacked the verbal ability, interest, and patience to talk with a therapist for an extended period of time. Thus in the late 1920s, both Melanie Klein and Anna Freud developed therapeutic methods that used play as the child's primary mode of expression (see Figure). Anna Freud stressed the importance of play in building the therapeutic relationship, deemphasizing the need for interpretation. Klein, however, approached play therapy much like traditional adult psychoanalytic work, with free play becoming a direct substitution for free associations, and insights and interpretation retaining primary importance.

In the following decade, Otto Rank was an important

Small furniture, a pleasant atmosphere, and a caring therapist, all prerequisite to successful play therapy.

contributor with his notion of relationship therapy. Rank stressed the importance of the emotional attachment between the child and the therapist, focusing mainly on present feelings and actions of the child. In the 1940s and 1950s, Carl Rogers client-centered therapy was modified by Virginia Axline (1947) into a nondirective play therapy. Axline's work, which has remained one of the cornerstones of current play therapy, is predicated on the belief that the child has within himself or herself the ability to solve emotional conflicts. According to Axline, it is the job of the play therapist to provide the optimal conditions under which the child's natural growth and development will occur. The basic rules of Axline's approach have become the standard for nondirective play therapy. They include the development of a warm relationship, acceptance, permissiveness with a minimum of limits, reflection of feelings, and giving the child responsibility for directing the sessions, making choices, and implementing change.

The effectiveness of play therapy has been attributed to its direct relevance to the child's developmental level and abilities. Woltmann (1964) stresses that play allows the child to act out situations that are disturbing, conflicting, and confusing and, in so doing, to clarify his or her own position in relation to the world around. Inherent to the success of play therapy is the make-believe element. Through fantasy and play, children are able to master tasks (drive a car, fly a spaceship), reverse roles (become parent or teacher), or express overt hostility without being punished. Woltmann believes that play therapy allows the child to "eliminate guilt and become victorious over forces otherwise above his reach and capabilities." Caplan and Caplan (1974) provide a further rationale for the effectiveness of play therapy. They contend that the voluntary nature of play makes it intrinsically interesting to the child and reduces the occurrence of resistance. The child is free to express himself or herself without fear of evaluation or retaliation. Through fantasy, the child can gain a sense of control over the environment without direct competition from others. Finally, play therapy is seen as developing both the child's physical and mental abilities.

The selection of the play media is an important part of the therapy. Gumaer (1984) notes that toys should be durable, inexpensive, and safe. They should be versatile (e.g., clay, paints) so that children may use them in a number of ways. Toys should encourage communication between the child and therapist (e.g., telephones, puppets). Some toys should be selected for their ability to elicit aggression such as a toy gun or a soldier doll. Finally, toys should be relatively unstructured; items such as board games or books leave little room for creativity. In addition to the toys already mentioned, Axline (1947) commonly employs a set of family dolls, a nursing bottle, trucks and cars, and, if possible, a sandbox and water.

In recent years, play therapy has expanded to include a number of settings, participants, and techniques (Phillips & Landreth, 1995). Ginott (1961) has developed a method that provides a specific rationale for toy selection and that emphasizes the importance of limit setting. Dreikurs and Soltz (1964) use play therapy that emphasizes the natural and logical consequences of a child's behavior. Myrick and Haldin (1971) describe a play process that is therapist directed and shorter in duration than Axlinian therapy, thus making it more practical for use in school settings. For further study, the reader is directed to *The Handbook of Play Therapy* (Schaefer & O'Conner, 1983), which describes specific techniques such as family play and art therapy, as well as play therapy directly tailored to such childhood disturbances as abuse and neglect, divorced parents, aggression, learning disability, and mental retardation.

REFERENCES

Axline, Virginia (1947). *Play therapy*. Boston: Houghton Mifflin.

Caplan, F., & Caplan, T. (1974). *The power of play*. New York: Anchor.

Dreikurs, R., & Soltz, V. (1964). *Children: The challenge*. New York: Hawthorne.

Freud, S. (1909). Analysis of a phobia in a five-year-old boy. In *Standard Edition* (Vol. 10). London: Hogarth.

Ginott, H. (1961). *Group psychotherapy with children*. New York: McGraw-Hill.

Gumaer, J. (1984). *Counseling and therapy for children*. New York: Free Press.

Myrick, R., & Haldin, W. (1971). A study of play process in counseling. *Elementary School Guidance and Counseling, 5*(4), 256–263.

Phillips, R. D., & Landreth, G. L. (1995). Play therapists on play therapy: A report of methods, demographics and professional practices. *International Journal of Play Therapy, 4*(1), 1–26.

Schaefer, C., & O'Conner, K. (1983). *The handbook of play therapy*. New York: Wiley.

Woltmann, A. (1964). Concepts of play therapy techniques. In M. Haworth (Ed.), *Child psychotherapy* (pp. 20–31). New York: Basic Books.

FRANCES F. WORCHEL
Texas A & M University

FAMILY THERAPY
PLAY
PSYCHOTHERAPY

PLURALISM, CULTURAL

Cultural pluralism is a sociological concept that refers to the dual enterprise of acceptance and mobility within the mainstream, majority culture while preserving the minority cultural heritage. Cultural pluralism is seen by many as the most desirable cultural milieu and has been promoted in a variety of settings, including education and employment.

The term is recognized in special education in relation to the work of Mercer et al. (Mercer & Lewis, 1979) in the assessment of mental retardation. Mercer has argued that past efforts in assessment and placement in special education programs for mildly mentally retarded children have failed to recognize the pluralistic nature of American society. In addition to the mainstream Anglo cultural, Mercer has proposed that black, Hispanic, and other cultures need to be recognized and their norms and mores accepted as equivalent to Anglo norms and mores. Mercer attempts to equate these groups' performance on intelligence tests by developing pluralistic norms. According to Mercer (Mercer & Lewis, 1979), traditional intelligence tests developed and normed on the white majority only measure the degree of Anglocentrism (i.e., relative adherence to white middle-class values) in the home when used with minorities. To accommodate other cultures, principally black and Hispanic, Mercer developed a set of regression equations to equate the IQ distributions of each ethnic group. Mercer hopes to promote cultural pluralism in special education by equating the relative proportions of each ethnic group in special education programs. Mercer believes that by equating these distributions, the stigma associated with special education placement will be evenly distributed, leading to greater tolerance and acceptance of alternative cultures.

The cultural competence movement in teacher education has grown considerably in recent years in terms of legislative support (IDEA, Part H in particular) and with the development of instruments such as the Pluralism and Diversity Attitude Assessment (PADAA) instrument, which assesses preservice attitudes of educators (Stanley, 1997). Cultural competence is becoming a good for special and regular education.

REFERENCES

Mercer, J. R., & Lewis, J. (1979). *System of multicultural pluralistic assessment.* New York: Psychological Association.

Stanley, L. S. (1997). Preservice educator's attitudes toward cultural pluralism: A preliminary analysis. *Journal of Teaching in Physical Education, 16*(2), 241–249.

CULTURAL BIAS IN TESTING
CULTURAL/LINGUISTICALLY DIVERSE STUDENTS
DISPROPORTIONALITY
SYSTEM OF MULTICULTURAL PLURALISTIC ASSESSMENT

POLAND, SPECIAL EDUCATION IN

Special education in Poland has a long history. In 1817, the Institute of Deaf-Mute and Blind was established in Warsaw. In 1922 Maria Grzegorzewska (1888–1967) established the Institute of Special Education, which conducted research and trained teachers. In 1924 a special education section of the Polish Teachers Association was established (Kirejczyk, 1975). In 1976 the National Institute of Special Education was reorganized into the Graduate School of Special Education.

In the 1950s programs for the mentally retarded were segregated into 120 self-contained schools. In the 1960s there were 331 special classes within elementary schools with an enrollment of over 5000 youngsters. By the 1970s the number of such classes increased to 698, with an enrollment of nearly 11,000. Currently, there are over 250 special schools in Poland, in addition to a considerable number of special classes within public schools.

Handicapped pupils in Poland are educated in special preschool facilities, special elementary schools, special vocational schools, residential boarding schools, and rehabilitation and therapeutic facilities; they also receive home instruction (Belcerek, 1977). Various levels of interaction of exceptional children within the mainstream of education are also provided (Hulek, 1979), e.g., regular programs with some supplemental instruction, special classes within regular schools (there are presently over 1100 such classes for the mildly handicapped within the Polish public schools and 57 within the vocational schools), selected activities within regular schools, and special schools in the vicinity of regular schools, with cooperative programs.

The intellectually subnormal population in Poland has been estimated to range from 1.3 to 1.87% of the general population. Polish psychologists are using IQs in their classification of the mentally retarded. The ranges of the levels of classification are similar to the AAMD classification system. In addition to health examinations, psychological and social-developmental examinations are also given. An evaluation for the purpose of special class placement consists of a detailed classroom observation, educational evaluation, and psychological and medical evaluation. Structural classroom observation usually lasts 1 school year. Additionally, a detailed anecdotal record of the child's activities is maintained. The record includes a description of the role of the parents and the extent of their cooperation with the school. Detailed records with samples of the child's performance are sent to the child study team as additional information. Slow learners and children who do not show good educational progress are directed to prevocational classes at 14 or 15 years of age. Curriculum in Polish special schools consists of the study of the Polish language, geography, music, history, and nature.

Special educators in Poland prefer the term therapeutic pedagogy, or special pedagogy, rather than defectology, a term widely used in the Soviet Union. The mildly retarded attend 8 years of basic special school, followed by 3 years of specialized vocational training. A new 10-year curriculum for the mentally retarded recommends the following areas of training and education: adaptation and social living, language stimulation, arithmetic, visual-motor tasks, music, physical exercise, technical-practical activities, and prevocational training. Training goals and objectives for the severely handicapped include physical development and acquisition of manual skills, development of self-help and everyday activity skills, development of basic information, appropriate interpersonal relationships, and prevocational training.

Elska (1985) reported that vocational curriculum for the mildly handicapped consists of two periods per week in grades 1 through 4, four periods in grade 4, and six periods in grades 5 through 8.

Within the system of special education exist numerous vocational schools, e.g., 248 schools with a 3-year curriculum, 5 with a 4-year, and 6 with a 5-year.

Special education teachers in Poland are prepared at 4-year teacher's training institutions which they enter after graduation from high school. Some experienced teachers of subjects enter universities that have a special education teachers' training program. Since 1973, in addition to the National Institute of Special Education, special education teachers are also prepared at 11 universities (Belcerek, 1977). In 1977 the Polish Ministry of Education opened postgraduate studies in special education at the Graduate School of Special Education in Warsaw. The areas of study at the school include diagnosis and assessment of exceptionalities and the study of deaf, hard-of-hearing, chronically ill, and socially maladaptive children. Special educators are also trained at the Graduate School of Education in Krakow.

Guidelines for the training of special educators have been developed by the special education team of the Pedagogical Science Committee of the Polish Academy of Sciences (Hulek, 1978). Guidelines recommend that a student in special education become familiar with teaching non-handicapped and subsequently handicapped children; teachers should cooperate with various agencies and institutions outside the school; and teachers should continuously be upgrading their education after graduation by attending in-service classes.

Special education studies in Poland are published in *Informator Szkolnictwa Specjalnego* (Bulletin of Special Education), *Nowa Szkola* (New School), *Szkola Specjalna* (Special School), and *Educacja* (Education; formerly *Badania Os'wiatowe,* Educational Research).

REFERENCES

Belcerek, M. (1977). Organization of special education in Poland. In A. Hulek (Ed.), *Therapeutic pedogogy.* Warsaw: State Scientific Publication.

Elska, V. (1985). Organization of vocational training of abnormal children in special schools in Polish Peoples Republic. *Defectologia* (Defectology), *1,* 62.

Holowinsky, I. Z. (1980). Special education in Poland and the Soviet Union: Current developments. In L. Mann & D. Sabatino (Eds.), *The fourth review of special education.* New York: Grune & Stratton.

Hulek, A. (1978, June). *Personnel preparation: International comparison.* Paper presented at the First World Congress on Future Special Education, Sterling, Scotland.

Hulek, A. (1979). Basic assumptions of mainstreaming exceptional children and youth. *Badania Oswiatowe* (Educational Research), *3*(15), 99–112.

Kirejczyk, K. (1975). Half-century of activity of the Special Education Section of the Polish Teacher's Association. *Szkola Specjalna* (Special School), *1,* 7–18.

IVAN Z. HOLOWINSKY
Rutgers University

POLITICS AND SPECIAL EDUCATION

Through the middle of the twentieth century, the politics surrounding special education can be characterized as the politics of exclusion. The primary decision makers were school officials who excluded from the public schools students with special needs requiring services not provided to the majority of students (Copeland, 1983). The grounds for exclusion tended to be observably inappropriate or disruptive behavior, rather than rigorous identification of the nature of students' needs or impediments to learning. Parents typically acquiesced in such decisions without questioning the denial of public school resources to their children.

A minority of the excluded students were kept at home, while the majority were referred to publicly or charitably supported residential institutions, often at some distance from their homes. There is little evidence to suggest that either local government authorities or school officials sought to establish locally situated residential institutions. Presumably, they sought to avoid the tax burden that might be incurred owing to the high costs of providing for severely impaired students.

By the beginning of the twentieth century, state-supported systems of residential institutions had emerged, with annual budgets and bureaucracies to administer them and ensure implementation of state regulations (Lynn, 1983). The institutions tended to specialize in one particular type of handicap. Funding formulas varied according to labeled disabilities. Children and youths with special needs were often improperly classified and placed because of inadequate evaluation and subjective if not prejudicial stereotypes (Kirp & Yudof, 1974). Few handicapped students transferred from one institution to another, and few permanently exited the institutions of initial placement to enter public schools. There was little coordination among different institutions. Many were, in fact, in competition with each other for scarce state resources.

Organized advocacy groups tended to lobby state legislatures individually on behalf of their particular clients (Lynn, 1983). Public policies were differentiated by type of handicap and servicing institution, advocates and clients, and implementing bureaucracies. They also varied from state to state. The overall pattern, however, was for the major portion of special needs students, funds, and service delivery systems to be located outside the public school systems.

Around the turn of the century, forces began to emerge that would contribute toward the inclusion rather than the exclusion of special needs students from public school systems (Sarason & Doris, 1979). Refinements in evaluation technology facilitated the identification of the special needs of handicapped students and suggested management and instructional methods appropriate to them. As a result, there was a widespread increase in the number of special classes within public schools (though outside the mainstream of regular students). State and federal legislative bodies enacted programs and provided funds for such classes. Parent advocacy groups and associations of special educators pressed for increased outlays to meet the needs of specific categories of handicapped children and youths.

Since services for different disabilities incurred different costs, there are indications that various funding formulas may have had a significant effect on local school policies and practices (Lynn, 1983). The proportion of students labeled as having particular disabilities varied from district to district and among states, often in relation to variations in the amounts of funds that could be obtained for specific handicaps. It also varied in relation to the type of diagnostic instruments used, the type of specialists in

the school, and the type of specialized services already provided. The politics of inclusion were thus influenced by local practices and political configurations and maneuverings of special education interest groups, legislators, and bureaucracies.

Although emerging special education policies, funds, programs, and practices may not have always matched the needs of special education students, their legitimacy was increasingly accepted, and they provided the leverage for progressively including special needs students within the public schools. By 1975 mandatory legislation that provided for the education of special needs students had been passed in all but two states. By that time, the states' financial contribution had risen to more than half the total revenues allocated to special education. By 1979 approximately 140 different federal programs serving the handicapped had been enacted. By the early 1980s, localities and special districts were contributing a total of $5.8 billion; states $3.4 billion; and the federal government a total of $804 million (Lynn, 1983).

However, it became clear as support for special education advanced, that two separate systems had developed: one outside the public schools, the other inside. Parent advocates now moved to expand the one that had been established within the public schools by pressing for geographic, social, and educational inclusion of special needs students within the system. These efforts contributed to the exodus of the majority of special education students from state-run residential institutions into the public schools, and to considerable cost shifting from the former to the latter.

The legal basis for this shift came from landmark court decisions establishing the rights of special education students to free and appropriate public schooling (*Watt* v. *Stickney,* 1970; *Diana* v. *State Board of Education,* 1970 and 1973; *PARC* v. *Pennsylvania,* 1972.) The Fourteenth Amendment guarantees of due process and equal protection were invoked to affirm the rights of special needs children to the free public schooling offered to other children. The U.S. Constitution was applied to protect these students from discriminatory public school practices in the same manner in which it had been applied to protect minority group students in such decisions as *Brown* v. *Board of Education* in 1954.

While court action gave significant impetus to recognition of the rights of access of students with special needs to public schools, it did so by declaring prior school policies and practices unconstitutional. Yet such determinations tended not to specify what was or would be judged constitutional. Rather, the courts began to act as umpires, ordering plaintiffs and defendants to negotiate compromises that would be acceptable to both and not unconstitutional (Kirp, 1981). Their role was to set up a structured, adversarial process within state and local school systems in which the courts would act as mediators rather than law-givers. The process would thus be open-ended in terms of its duration, given the lengthiness of legal proceedings, and unpredictable in terms of its possible outcomes.

The debates and conflicts as to placement of handicapped students, as well as services to be provided them, spread to the federal arena as well, where advocates sought to apply the inclusionary principles of court decisions to congressional enactments. These advocates rode on the coattails of the civil rights movement and the Civil Rights Act of 1964. They encountered countervailing forces similar to those that hampered civil rights activists in their efforts to obtain federal enactments and implement them through the federal system. The movement and the act and its numerous amendments sought to eliminate discriminatory practices by public schools that had denied students geographic, social, and educational inclusion because of their ethnicity, national origin, sex, or impoverishment (Bordier, 1983).

They provided the U.S. Congress with a model for a major legislative enactment designed to protect the rights of special needs students. Passed in 1975, the Education for All Handicapped Children Act, PL 94-142, affirmed their right to a free, appropriate public education in the least restrictive environment; required the identification, evaluation, and placement of students with special needs according to an individual educational plan (IEP); and guaranteed parental rights of participation in educational decisions concerning their children.

Under PL 94-142, the federal government was to pay a graduated percentage of average per pupil expenditures by public elementary and secondary schools, starting with 5% in 1979 and culminating in 40% by 1982. Implementation of the legislature was nominally nonmandatory. However, most school districts followed suit, presumably because they would have been hard pressed by the parents of special needs students if they did not seek to obtain available federal funds. Furthermore, an earlier law, Section 504 of the Vocational Rehabilitation Act of 1973; forbade discrimination against handicapped students in programs receiving federal financial assistance. Under 504, school districts were routinely required to sign compliance statements affirming that they did not discriminate against students on the basis of race, national origin, sex, or handicap. Since the law was initially interpreted to mean that failure to sign compliance statements could jeopardize receipt of federal financial assistance, compliance (at least on paper) via these statements became the norm.

Program guidelines and regulations of federal implementing agencies such as the Department of Health, Education, and Welfare reflected court decisions and congressional enactments and established compliance machinery within the department (later the Department of Education) and the Justice Department. The Office of Civil Rights was established to coordinate the compliance activities of the federal agencies involved. While this machinery has not been shown to have had a significant impact on ed-

ucational practices, it provided an institutional and legal context for the politics of inclusion at state and local levels.

By the middle 1980s, at the end of the first Reagan presidency and at the beginning of the second term, funding for implementation of PL 94-142 was curtailed. The law and its regulations were weakened by congressional interventions and Department of Education actions designed to lessen the federal role in education and to devolve social sector responsibilities (including education in general and special education in particular) to the states.

However, because PL 94-142 had assigned significant responsibilities and funds for implementation to state authorities, by the early 1980s, the latter had already adopted laws and regulations reflective of the principles and the delivery system the federal government had mandated earlier. Such legal frameworks, created at state levels, remained in force even after the federal law itself was weakened in the 1980s. Furthermore, state and local authorities had voted to increase expenditures in order to comply with PL 94-142.

When cutbacks in funding occurred at the federal level, and signs of backlash against rapidly increasing expenditures for previously underserved groups appeared at local and state levels, advocates seeking to protect the rights of special needs students used these policies and funding allocations as precedents to justify continuing aid to special education. The role and responsibilities of state and local authorities became established independent of federal laws and regulations. Local school systems followed suit, and the progressive inclusion of special education students proceeded, geographically, socially, and educationally, in more depth than ever anticipated (Brantlinger, 1997).

The enrollment of special needs students increased significantly. Schools formalized their identification, evaluation, and referral procedures, and included new participants in the process. These included committees on the handicapped, appointed by local school boards; parents and their counsels; new categories of special educators and clinicians; "regular" teachers, administrators, and ancillary personnel who had not previously had responsibility for special needs students; and multidisciplinary evaluation teams. The earlier politics of inclusion that affected the federal court system and the federal government had thus significantly increased the number of participants in the politics of inclusion at the local level. Their participation was focused on the legally specified, formalized procedures that court decisions and legislative enactments had established to improve educational services provided to students with special needs.

In the meantime, the signs of a new movement in the field of special education appeared; this would engender new policy approaches designed to integrate a whole spectrum of institutions providing services to handicapped students, including but not limited to school systems (Copeland, 1983). The needs of special education students for services beyond those provided by public schools had became increasingly apparent, and new service providers outside the schools had emerged. The institutions that provided these services, and the funding sources on which they drew, were separate from the public schools.

Interinstitutional cooperation and coordination was needed, but it would require the development of policies, regulations, and funding formulas that were complementary. For example, agencies dealing with public welfare (e.g., social services, aid for dependent children, foster care, Medicaid), health (e.g., maternal and child health), mental health/retardation/developmental disabilities, vocational rehabilitation, and corrections needed to work more closely. As the public schools incorporated the major portion of the children and youths who had previously been assigned to residential institutions, it became clear that the schools could not provide all the collateral services that these students would require.

Linking these services required interagency cooperation (as mandated by IDEA) and the development of coalitions of advocacy groups to formulate legislation and programs to link their budgets, staffs, and services into an integrated delivery system of which the public schools would be a part. It also required intricate planning that would continue to promote the inclusion of special needs students within the educational mainstream while at the same time requiring the differentiation of these students according to their needs for external services. This blueprint for the 1990s and beyond would require interagency policy making, programming, and budgeting. It would provide an ambitious and complex political agenda for the advocates of special and general education, as well as external social services for children and youths.

REFERENCES

Bordier, J. (1983). Governance and management of special education. *The Forum, 4*(3), 4–13.

Brantlinger, E. (1997). Using ideology: Cases of non recognition of the politics of research and practice in education. *Review of Educational Research, 67*(4), 425–459.

Copeland, W. C. (1983, January). Strategies for special education in the 1980s. *Policy Studies Review, 2* (Special Issue 1), 242–260.

Kirp, D. (1981). The bounded politics of school desegregation litigation. *Harvard Educational Review, 51*(3), 395–414.

Kirp, D., & Yudof, M. (1974). *Education and the law.* Berkeley, CA: McCutchan.

Lynn, L., Jr. (1983). The emerging system for educating handicapped children [Special issue]. *Policy Studies Review, 2,* 21–58.

Sarason, S., & Doris, J. (1979). *Educational handicap, public policy, and social history.* New York: Free Press.

NANCY BORDIER
Hunter College

HISTORY OF SPECIAL EDUCATION
INCLUSION
INDIVIDUALS WITH DISABILITIES EDUCATION ACT
MAINSTREAMING

POLYDIPSIA

Polydipsia is excessive drinking of water. It is often associated with water intoxication and polyuria (excessive urination). It is essential to distinguish polydipsia that is biologically based from psychogenic polydipsia (Singh, Padi, Bullard, & Freeman, 1985). Most cases of polydipsia are not due to psychogenic factors (Wright, Schaefer, & Solomons, 1979). Psychogenic polydipsia involves the consumption of excessive quantities of water over a brief time period that is often associated with water intoxication. Water intoxication symptoms include headache, excessive perspiration, and vomiting, as well as more severe symptoms such as convulsions and even death (Blum, Tempey, & Lynch, 1983). Psychogenic polydipsia in children is reported to be rare and there is a lack of epidemiological studies available reporting reliable incidence. Among psychiatric patients, the incident is reported to range from 6.6 to 17.5% (Singh et al., 1985).

Biological determinants of abnormal thirst and polydipsia include diabetes, hypercalcemia, congestive heart failure, intracranial disease, potassium deficiency associated with renal disease, and meningitis (Chevalier, 1984). Another physical form of polydipsia during infancy occurs when infants are fed on demand with an overly diluted formula (Horev & Cohen, 1994; Wright et al., 1979).

Psychogenic polydipsia is associated with a wide spectrum of psychopathology ranging from mild personality disorders to severe psychosis (Singh et al., 1985). Various explanations for psychogenic polydipsia have been provided including the psychodynamic concept of an oral personality (Singh et al., 1985) or an obsessive-compulsive personality (Wright et al., 1979). It may also result from a behavioral condition such as a conditioned response (Linshaw, Hipp, & Gruskin, 1974).

There is presently no single treatment recommended in the literature for psychogenic polydipsia. The treatment would depend on the aspects of the aspects of the condition relative to a particular case. Polydipsic children with central nervous system (CNS) involvement would be at risk for learning disorders and possibly special education services. Those with more severe psychological disorders may be in need of special programs for behavioral handicaps.

REFERENCES

Blum, A., Tempey, F. W., & Lynch, W. J. (1983). Somatic findings in patients with psychogenic polydipsia. *Journal of Clinical Psychiatry, 44,* 55–56.

Chevalier, R. L. (1984). Polydipsia and enuresis in childhood renin-dependent hypertension. *Journal of Pediatrics, 104,* 591–593.

Horev, Z., & Cohen, H. H. (1994). Compulsive water drinking in infants and young children. *Clinical Pediatrics, 33*(4), 209–213.

Linshaw, M. A., Hipp, T., & Gruskin, A. (1974). Infantile psychogenic water drinking. *Journal of Pediatrics, 85,* 520–522.

Singh, S., Padi, M. H., Bullard, H., & Freeman, H. (1985). Water intoxication in psychiatric patients. *British Journal of Psychiatry, 146,* 127–131.

Wright, L., Schaefer, A. B., Solomons, G. (1979). *Encyclopedia of pediatric psychology.* Baltimore, MD: University Park Press.

JOSEPH D. PERRY
Kent State University

MEDICAL HISTORY
MEDICAL MANAGEMENT

POMPE'S DISEASE

See RARE DISEASES.

PONCE DE LEON, PEDRO DE (1520–1584)

Pedro de Ponce de Leon, a Spanish Benedictine monk, is credited with creating the art of teaching the deaf. His method, as described by early historians, consisted of teaching the student to write the names of objects and then drilling the student in the production of the corresponding sounds. Whether lip reading was taught is not known, nor from the surviving accounts of his work can it be ascertained whether Ponce de Leon used any signs in teaching his students. It is known that his methods were successful with a number of children.

After Ponce de Leon's death in 1584, no one continued his work, but it is probable that his success, which received much publicity, influenced the development of methods to educate the deaf in Spain in the early seventeenth century.

REFERENCE

Bender, R. E. (1970). *The conquest of deafness.* Cleveland, OH: Case Western Reserve University Press.

PAUL IRVINE
Katonah, New York

POPLITEAL PTERYGIUM SYNDROME

See RARE DISEASES.

PORCH INDEX OF COMMUNICATIVE ABILITIES (PICA)

The Porch Index of Communicative Ability (PICA) is designed to assess and quantify gestural, verbal, and graphic abilities of aphasic patients. As a reliable standardized instrument, the PICA provides quantitative information about a patient's change in communicative function and enables the examiner to make predictive judgments relative to amount of recovery (Porch, 1971).

The PICA is a battery of 18 subtests; 4 verbal subtests ranging from object naming to sentence completion; 8 gestural ranging from demonstrating object function to matching identical objects; and 6 graphic on a continuum from writing complete sentences to copying geometric forms. For consistency, 10 common objects are used within each subtest (e.g., toothbrush, cigarette, fork, pencil). A multidimensional binary choice 16-point scoring system is used to determine the degrees of correctness of a patient's response. The scoring system judges responses according to their accuracy, responsiveness, completeness, promptness, and efficiency. Administration time is variable, usually averaging approximately 60 minutes.

Prior to administering the PICA, participation in a 40-hour workshop for test administration, scoring, and interpretation is required. Examiners must complete a rigid testing protocol to insure a high degree of reliability. The PICA is a valuable clinical tool for providing valid and accountable descriptions of an aphasic patient's current and future level of communicative performance.

REFERENCE

Porch, B. (1971). Porch Index of Communicative Ability. Vol. 2. Administration, scoring, and interpretation (Rev. ed.). Palo Alto, CA: Consulting Psychologists.

SUSAN MAHANNA-BODEN
TRACY CALPIN CASTLE
Eastern Kentucky University

APHASIA
DEVELOPMENTAL APHASIA

PORTAGE PROJECT

The Portage project was first funded in 1969 as a model home-based program by the Bureau of Education for the Handicapped under the Handicapped Children's Early Education Program (HCEEP). In rural Portage, Wisconsin, the project's staff traveled to the homes of children to help parents learn how to work with children in a home setting (Lerner, 1985). The experimental edition of the Portage project was developed during the first 3 years of the project and was published by McGraw-Hill in 1972. The revised edition (1976) was developed by Susan Bluma, Marsha Shearer, Alma Froham, and Jean Hillard (Bailey & Worley, 1984; Bluma, et al., 1976; Thurman & Widerstrom, 1985). The project was a developmental, criterion-referenced, behavioral model that employs precision teaching to evaluate a child's developmental level and to plan an educational program for children from birth to 6 years of age. The complete guide came in three parts: a checklist of behaviors on which to record an individual child's developmental progress; a file card listing possible methods of teaching these behaviors; and a manual of directions for use of the checklists, card files, and various methods of remediation. The assessment procedure was administered in 20 to 40 minutes. The behavioral checklist consisted of a 25-page color coded booklet that contains 580 developmentally sequenced behaviors.

Ages were listed at one-year intervals. The first 45 items were grouped under infant stimulation. Many of the items in this development area were activities that a parent or teacher performed with a child. These behaviors served as a guide for teaching infants up to 4 months. The area of socialization evaluated the young child's interactions with other people. A systematic pattern of language development that focuses on content and the form that was used to express that content was outlined in the checklist. The self-help-category defined those behaviors that enabled the child to care for himself or herself in feeding, dressing, and toileting. The motor area was primarily concerned with the coordinated movements of the large muscles of the body. For each of the 580 items, there were curriculum cards that provide teaching suggestions. These cards were in a card file and were color coded to match corresponding sections in the checklist.

For a home-based program, children were assigned to a home teacher who spent about an hour and a half a week with each child assigned. Instruction during the remainder of the week was the responsibility of the parent. Prescriptions were modified according to each child's individual progress from week to week. Three new behavior targets were identified each week, and it became the parents' responsibility to provide instruction on these behaviors between the home teacher's visits. The home teacher collected data before and after instruction and helped parents with their teaching skills by modeling techniques and allowing parents to try the skills each week.

The success of the Portage model was seen in its wide dissemination and replication. Over 30 replications across the United States have been reported as well as international recognition (Mittler, 1990). The project staff provided training and technical assistance to the replicated sites while the sites provided input regarding changes and additions. (Thurman & Widerstrom, 1981; Southworth, Burr, & Cox, 1980; Bluma et al., 1976).

REFERENCES

Bailey, D., & Worley, M., (1984). *Teaching infants and preschoolers with handicaps.* Columbus, OH: Merrill.

Bluma, S., Shearer, M., Froham, A., & Hilliard, J. (1976). *The Portage project: Portage guide to early education manual* (Rev. ed.). Portage, WI: Cooperative Educational Services Agency.

Lerner, J. (1985). *Learning disabilities: Theories, diagnosis, and educational strategies* (4th ed.). Boston: Houghton Mifflin.

Mittler, P. (1990). Prospects for disabled children and their families: An international perspective. *Disability, Handicap, & Society, 5*(1), 53–64.

Southworth, L., Burr, R., & Cox, A. (1980). *Screening and evaluating the young child: A handbook of instruments to use from infancy to six years.* Springfield, IL: Thomas.

Thurman, K. S., & Widerstrom, H. A. (1985). *Young children with special needs: A developmental and ecological approach.* Boston: Allyn & Bacon.

FRANCES T. HARRINGTON
Radford University

HOMEBOUND INSTRUCTION
PARENT EFFECTIVENESS TRAINING
PARENTS OF THE HANDICAPPED

POSITIVE PRACTICE

Positive practice is a behavior change technique whereby a misbehaving individual is required to practice correct or appropriate behaviors repeatedly. The term positive practice is frequently used as a synonym for overcorrection, a punishment technique (MacKenzie-Keating & McDonald, 1990). In fact, positive practice is actually a subcomponent of overcorrection. With overcorrection, a misbehaving individual is required to overcorrect the environmental effects of his or her inappropriate act and/or repeatedly practice correct forms of relevant behavior in situations where the misbehavior commonly occurs (Foxx & Bechtel, 1982a). The first part of the overcorrection procedure outlined is commonly referred to as restitution and the latter portion of the procedure is often labeled positive practice. Foxx and Bechtel (1982a) have recommended the terms restitution and positive practice be dropped and replaced by overcorrection for purposes of conceptual clarity and communication.

The concept of positive practice has been the central feature of numerous intervention techniques such as theft reversal (Azrin & Wesolowski, 1974), cleanliness training (Azrin & Foxx, 1971), and social apology training (Carey & Bucher, 1981). Two common misconceptions about positive practice, however, exist. The first is that positive reinforcement is part of positive practice. This is probably owed to the fact that many people associate the performance of appropriate behaviors solely with the delivery of positive reinforcers. In overcorrection, the performance of appropriate behaviors is elicited by graduated guidance (verbal and physical) from a therapist, not positive reinforcement (Carr, 1997). The second misconception is that positive practice is similar to negative practice (Dunlap, 1930), a procedure whereby an individual repeatedly practices an inappropriate behavior. Clearly, positive practice is conceptually and pragmatically antithetical to negative practice.

By design, positive practice is a consequence to be used as an aversive stimuli following the occurrence of an inappropriate behavior. Therefore, when the presentation of positive practice results in the reduction of a response in the future, it functions as a punishment procedure. The research literature documents that positive practice, or more accurately overcorrection, can produce large, fairly enduring reductions in inappropriate behavior. Overcorrection procedures have been used with several response classes of behaviors (e.g., aggressive-disruptive behaviors, self-stimulating behaviors, self-injurious behaviors, personal hygiene, social interactions), populations (e.g., mentally handicapped, behaviorally disordered, undersocialized children and adults), and settings (e.g., schools, homes, and institutions). Foxx and Bechtel (1982b) provide an extensive review of the outcomes and side effects of overcorrection, and detailed guidelines for the use of overcorrection.

REFERENCES

Azrin, N. H., & Foxx, R. M. (1971). A rapid method of toilet training the institutionalized retarded. *Journal of Applied Behavior Analysis, 4*, 89–99.

Azrin, N. H., & Wesolowski, M. D. (1974). Theft reversal: An overcorrection procedure for eliminating stealing by retarded persons. *Journal of Applied Behavior Analysis, 7*, 577–581.

Carey, R. G., & Bucher, B. (1981). Identifying the educative and suppressive effects of positive practice and restitutional overcorrection. *Journal of Applied Behavior Analysis, 14*, 71–80.

Carr, A. (1997). Positive practice in family therapy. *Journal of Marital & Family Therapy, 23*(3), 271–293.

Dunlap, K. (1930). Repetition in the breaking of habits. *Scientific Monthly, 30*, 66–70.

Foxx, R. M., & Bechtel, D. R. (1982a). Overcorrection. In M. Hersen, R. M. Eisler, & P. M. Miller (Eds.), *Progress in behavior modification* (pp. 227–288). New York: Academic.

Foxx, R. M., & Bechtel, D. R. (1982b). Overcorrection: A review and analysis. In S. Axelrod & J. Apsche (Eds.), *The effects of punishment on human behavior* (pp. 133–220). New York: Academic.

MacKenzie-Keating, S. E., & McDonald, L. (1990). Overcorrection reviewed, revisited, and revised. *Behavior Analyst, 13*(1), 39–48.

STEPHEN N. ELLIOTT
Louisiana State University

APPLIED BEHAVIOR ANALYSIS
BEHAVIOR MODIFICATION
NEGATIVE PUNISHMENT
OVERCORRECTION
POSITIVE PUNISHMENT

POSITIVE REINFORCEMENT

Behavioral psychology, in particular operant conditioning theory, is based on the supposition that behavior is maintained by its consequences. A consequence that leads to an increase in the frequency of a behavior is called a reinforcer. Conversely, a consequence that results in a decrease in the frequency of a behavior is called punishment.

The principle of positive reinforcement has two parts: (1) if in a given situation a person's behavior is followed close in time by a consequence, then (2) that person is more likely to exhibit the same behavior when he or she is in a similar situation at a later time. This consequence is referred to as a positive reinforcer and is roughly synonomous with the concept of reward.

The person credited with first experimentally investigating the effects of rewards on learning is E. L. Thorndike. In 1898 he began seminal work with hungry cats who learned to escape from a cage to acquire food. After many investigations, Thorndike (1911) conceptualized the law of effect, which in part stated that if a stimulus was followed by a response and then a satisfier, the stimulus-response connection would be strengthened. Skinner (1938, 1953) followed up on Thorndike's work and chose the term positive reinforcer in place of satisfier because he felt satisfier was clumsy and not appropriate for a scientific system of behavior. With the work of Skinner and others such as Premack (1959), the principle of positive reinforcement has become the cornerstone of behavior theory and technology.

The application of positive reinforcement is deceptively simple. Two important components in the successful application of positive reinforcement are the selection of a reinforcer and the schedule for delivering the reinforcer. Some stimuli are positive reinforcers for virtually everyone. For example, food is a reinforcer for almost anyone who has not eaten in several hours; money also is generally reinforcing. It is very important, however, to understand that one can actually determine if a stimulus is reinforcing only after it has been administered contingent on the appearance of a desired behavior. In other words, a stimulus is defined as a reinforcer only by its effect on behavior. Failure to select a stimulus that is reinforcing is one of the most common errors in implementing a behavior change program.

The relationship between a behavior and its consequence is called a contingency. Contingencies can operate continuously (i.e., the consequence follows every occurrence of the target behavior) or intermittently (i.e., the consequence follows only a portion of the occurrences of the target behavior). Most contingencies operate on intermittent schedules (e.g., variable ratio, variable interval, fixed ratio, fixed interval). Each reinforcement schedule has been demonstrated to have a different effect on behavior. In general, continuous schedules are used effectively to develop a new behavior, whereas intermittent schedules are used effectively to increase and maintain a behavior already in a person's repertoire. Ratio schedules generally produce high rates of response, and interval schedules produce lower rates of response. In summary, the selection of a stimulus that is reinforcing and the schedule by which it is administered will determine the strength of the positive reinforcement.

REFERENCES

Premack, D. (1959). Toward empirical behavioral laws. I. Positive reinforcement. *Psychological Review, 66,* 219–233.

Skinner, B. F. (1938). *The behavior of organisms.* New York: Appleton-Century-Crofts.

Skinner, B. F. (1953). *Science and human behavior.* New York: Macmillan.

Thorndike, E. L. (1898). Animal intelligence: An experimental study of associative processes in animals. *Psychological Review, Monograph Supplement, 2,* 8–7, 28–31.

Thorndike, E. L. (1911). *Animal intelligence.* New York: Macmillan.

STEPHEN N. ELLIOTT
Louisiana State University

APPLIED BEHAVIOR ANALYSIS
BEHAVIOR MODIFICATION

POST-INSTITUTIONALIZED CHILD PROJECT

One of the most devastating examples of early childhood neglect and deprivation can be seen in the experiences of children living in some foreign orphanages. It is known that maternal deprivation, neglect, and severe malnutrition in the early lives of children put them at greater risk for growth failure and developmental delays in the early years. Little is known, however, about long-term growth and development of these children. More and more of these children are being adopted by families within the United States. Individual reports suggest that these children may experience long-term growth failure, continued developmental delays and abnormalities related to the onset of puberty. Definitive data are not yet available.

Physicians from Emory University School of Medicine, The Marcus Institute for Development and Learning, and The Hughes Spalding International Adoption Evaluation Center are researching the potential problems that children adopted from international orphanages who are exposed to severe deprivation and/or neglect may struggle with as they grow. Currently, the research is focusing on children adopted from Romania. Efforts to expand this research may be taken.

Families who have experience with a child adopted from an orphanage or institution from any country and who are interested in assisting with the development of knowledge in the field are encouraged to contact the project.

Further information can be obtained on the Internet at http://www.emory.edu/PEDS/ENDO/orphan/ or http://www.adopt@oz.ped.emory.edu.

PATRICK MASON
KRISTA BIERNATH
The Hughes Spalding
International Adoption
Evaluation Center

POST-INSTITUTIONALIZED CHILDREN

A wide variation of scenarios are envisioned when a child is described as neglected. Tangible resources that are considered primary needs of a child such as food, shelter, and clothing may not be provided by caretakers. Services such as appropriate medical care or education may be withheld. In addition, less tangible neglect may occur in the form of lack of emotional interaction with caregivers and/or lack of developmental or intellectual stimulation.

This emotional neglect, which is a product of social, developmental, and intellectual understimulation, may result from a variety of early environmental situations. The parent who is too busy or too overwhelmed by his or her own issues may not take the time to provide stimulation and attention that the child needs. Likewise, a child who has been moved from one overcrowded foster care home to another may also be exposed to such neglect. One of the most devastating examples of neglect and deprivation can be seen in the experiences of children living in some foreign orphanages.

After the fall of the Romanian communist regime in 1989, a disturbing system of state-run child care was discovered. The government was housing up to 300,000 children in an orphanage system. These orphanages became a dumping ground for either the country's most severely diseased and damaged children or for those that were without a home or family. Children were often placed into orphanages that provided minimal amounts of clothing and food, and little medical attention. The orphanages were also generally devoid of personal contact, with ratios of children to caregivers often as high as 60 to 1. Children were left unattended, with contact only for adding food to the bottle suspended above the crib and occasional diaper changes.

Children raised in such understimulating, neglectful, and even abusive environments may suffer a host of adverse consequences. The following discussion will focus on the severely neglected and sometimes abused children; in particular, children with a history of institutionalization. The discussion will address the neurobiological and physiological effects of such neglect, the stress on family systems, and recommendations for educational modifications.

In the 1940s, scientists such as Rene Spitz, William Goldfarb, and John Bowlby described the effects of deprivation, severe neglect, and institutionalization on the well-being of children. At this early time, emotional attachment between the caregiver and infant or young child was already described as important for the child's future development. In the 1960s and early 1970s, definitive work was done to show that the effects of institutionalization on a child was linked to social impairment in the development of that child. This work was carried out by Drs. Sally Province and Rose Lipton. In addition, animal studies at this time demonstrated the effects of sensory deprivation on the animal's well-being. The famous experiments with monkeys performed by Dr. Harry Harlow are an example of such important work.

As these research findings became more widely credited, the orphanage system in the United States became less accepted in favor of the currently-used foster care system. Other countries, however, continued to place unwanted children in institutions. Many families in the United States are now adopting these post-institutionalized children from countries within Eastern Europe, China, Korea, and elsewhere. Many of these children are suffering from numerous psychological and developmental disorders.

Studies suggest that approximately 80% of children adopted from foreign institutions show some developmental delay at the time of entry into the United States (Johnson et al., 1992). Long-term studies of these children are few due to the relatively short time that the majority of these children have been in the United States. One study demonstrated that after approximately 3 years in the United States, 30% of the children continued to demonstrate language delays, 28% demonstrated delayed fine motor skills, and 25% demonstrated delayed social skills (Groze & Ileana, 1996).

The exact mechanism in the brain for the cause or etiology of these developmental problems is usually unknown. Children in an orphanage system are at risk for factors before birth, at the time of birth, and after birth which may contribute to the injury of the brain causing developmental difficulties.

Alcohol use is prominent in many of the countries, especially in Eastern European countries. This substance can have a profound negative impact on the developing neurologic system of the developing fetus.

Fetal alcohol syndrome is a combination of clinical characteristics including growth retardation, abnormal facial features, and neurocognitive or neurobehavioral effects. But alcohol may also have a partial effect on the fetus. The child may then have only one or two of the above characteristics in a pattern that has been labeled partial fetal alcohol effects (PFAE).

Stress may also have a negative effect on the developing brain. The exact mechanism for this is unknown. Some postulated theories suggest negative effects are due to excess cortisol on the developing brain (Carlson, 1997). The brain's limbic system may also be involved. It is thought that even young infants, when exposed to severe environmental deprivation, neglect, or abuse can manifest negative developmental and psychological consequences (Frank, 1996).

Whatever the cause may be, some of the diagnoses these children may have include symptoms of include post traumatic stress disorder (PTSD), attachment disorders, functional mental retardation, learning disabilities, sensory integration abnormalities, depression, anxiety, behavioral disturbances, personality disorders, fetal alcohol syndrome (FAS), partial fetal alcohol effects (PFAE), attention-deficit hyperactivity disorder (ADHD) and others. Children may also be diagnosed with pervasive developmental disorder (PDD) and/or autism. Dr. Ronald Federici, a developmental neuropsychologist who specializes in the care of post-institutionalized children, proposes a unique type of autism sometimes seen in these children. He terms this autism: an acquired syndrome.

Unique medical problems can also be seen in these children. These may include infectious diseases, gastrointestinal problems, and heart conditions. A common medical problem that may be related to the negative effects on the brain is growth retardation. Some research has also pointed to an increased risk of early puberty onset (Proos et al., 1991).

It is very important that a child adopted from such an institution be followed by medical specialists who have experience and expertise in some of the medical, developmental, and psychiatric issues that these children and their families face. A primary pediatrician who is willing to work with subspecialists, educators and service providers is valuable. Other specialists who may be needed include a pediatric infectious disease specialist, a developmental pediatrician, a pediatric gastroenterologist (stomach doctor), a pediatric endocrinologist (hormone doctor), and a pediatric psychiatrist, among many others. The primary pediatrician, however, can coordinate appropriate referrals as needed.

The adoptive parents and siblings may have difficulty integrating the child into the family. Unfortunately, some agencies organizing such adoptions may promise a perfect child who just needs a little TLC. Families may become very frustrated if the child continues to demonstrate delays or behavioral difficulties.

Likewise, the child may have great difficulty adapting to his or her new environment. Culture shock is common. A modestly decorated home in the United States may be as stimulating as a crowded, colorful amusement park to a post-institutionalized child. Some things that we take for granted may be threatening or scary to the child who has been deprived. These things may include new foods; the introduction to warm and hot water at bath time; car rides; being outside; hugs, kisses, and other forms of physical affection. Professional assistance from individuals such as pediatric psychologists and/or pediatric and family counselors who are familiar with foreign adoption issues may be of great benefit to such families and children.

As for educational recommendations, Debra Schell-Frank, special education consultant for the Parent Network for the Post-Institutionalized Child, strongly recommends that initially these children be considered as special needs children. Parents, educators, and physicians must work together to evaluate the child's strengths and weaknesses and to offer appropriate intervention services early with close monitoring in order to help the child develop to his or her maximum potential.

Resources

The Parent Network for the Post-Institutionalized Child (PNPIC)
Tel: (724) 222-1766
Fax: (770) 979-3140
E-mail: PNPIC@aol.com

The Hughes Spalding International Adoption Evaluation Center
Tel: (404) 616-0650
Fax: (404) 616-1982
E-mail: adopt@oz.ped.emory.edu

Help for the Hopeless Child: A Guide for Families by Dr. Ronald S. Federici.

Children with Backgrounds of Deprivation: Educational Issues for Children Adopted from Institutions by Dr. Debra Schell-Frank.

The above two books may be obtained through the PNPIC.

REFERENCES

Carlson, M., & Earls, F. (1997). Psychological and neuroendocrinological sequelae of early social deprivation in institutionalized children in Romania. *Annals of New York Academy of Sciences, 807,* 419–28.

Federici, R. (1998). *Help for the hopeless child: A guide for families.* Alexandria, Virginia: Dr. Ronald S. Federici and Associates.

Fischer, K., & Lazerson, A. (1984). *Human development: From conception through adolescence.* New York, Oxford: W.H. Freeman.

Frank, D., Klass, P., Earls, F., & Elsenberg, L. (1996). Infants and young children in orphanages: One view from pediatrics and child psychiatry. *Pediatrics, 97,* 569–78.

Groze, V., & Ileana, D. (1996). A follow-up study of adopted children from Romania. *Child and Adolescent Social Work Journal, 13,* 541–565.

Johnson, D., Miller, L., Iverson, S., Thomas, W., Franchino, B., Dole, K., Kieman, M., Georgieff, M., & Hostetter, M. (1992). The health of children adopted from Romania. *JAMA, 268,* 3446–51.

Proos, L., Hofvander, Y., & Tuveno, T. Menarcheal age and growth pattern of Indian girls adopted in Sweden. *Acta Paediatrica Scandanavia, 80,* 852–8.

Schell-Frank, D. (1996). *Children with backgrounds of deprivation: Educational issues for children adopted from institutions.* (ERIC Clearinghouse No: EC 302143)

Spitz, R. (1945). Hospitalism: An inquiry into the genesis of psychiatric conditions in early childhood. *Psychoanalytic Study of the Child, 1,* 53–74.

KRISTA R. BIERNATH
*The Hughes Spalding
International Adoption
Evaluation Center*

POSTLINGUAL DEAFNESS

Postlingual deafness is a general term for profound hearing loss that occurs after the normal acquisition of language and speech. It is also called acquired or adventitious deafness. Those who sustain this type of hearing loss are referred to as deafened rather than deaf.

Postlingual deafness is differentiated from prelingual deafness. The latter interferes with the normal acquisition of language and speech, and frequently affects educational achievement to such an extent that deaf students leaving special schools at the age of 18 are often 7 or 8 years behind their hearing peers (Thomas, 1984). A postlingually deafened child has learned to speak before losing his or her hearing. The child has the memory of the sound and rhythm of speech and has acquired vocabulary and grammar normally. If the child had normal hearing, even for a short time, the outlook is improved (Webster & Elwood, 1985) however not necessarily predictive of cerebral symmetry (Szelag, 1996). The education of postlingually deaf children should encourage creative thinking and verbal expression, and include vocabulary enrichment, aural rehabilitation, and the opportunity for speech refinement and maintenance (Northcott, 1984).

The etiology of acquired or adventitious hearing loss may be familial, noise-induced, by accident or illness, or, in the case of adults, the result of old age (presbycusis). The onset of a hearing loss is sometimes so gradual that it may go unnoticed for a long time. However, any hearing loss, whether acquired gradually or suddenly, that is extensive enough to interfere with the normal communication process creates a myriad of problems so complex that coping with the hearing world becomes difficult (Giolas, 1982). Formal speech-reading lessons are required in most instances. Sometimes individual hearing aids and cochlear implants (Langereis, Bosman, van Olphen, & Smoorenburg, (1997) can supplement residual hearing to facilitate communication.

Children who lose their hearing between the ages of 3 and 12 sometimes complete their education in programs for the deaf and later become the leaders and spokespeople of the deaf community. Children who lose their hearing at ages older than 12 are more likely to remain with their former hearing friends and not join the community of deaf adults (Jacobs, 1980). Modern technological devices such as hearing aids, auditory trainers, TDDs (telecommunication devices), and television decoders that display captions, are of great assistance in the education of deaf and deafened children.

REFERENCES

Giolas, T. (1982). *Hearing-handicapped adults*. Englewood Cliffs, NJ: Prentice-Hall.

Jacobs, L. (1980). *A deaf adult speaks out*. Washington, DC: Gallaudet College Press.

Langereis, M. C., Bosman, A. J., van Olphen, A. F., & Smoorenburg, G. F. (1997). Changes in vowel quality in post-lingually deafened cochlear implant users. *Audiology, 36*(5), 279–297.

Northcott, W. (1984). *Oral interpreting: Principles and practices*. Baltimore, MD: University Park Press.

Szelag, E. The effect of auditory experience on hemispheric asymmetry in a post-lingually deaf child. *Cortex, 32*(4), 647–661.

Thomas, A. (1984). *Acquired hearing loss: Psychological and psychosocial implications*. Orlando, FL: Academic.

Webster, A., & Ellwood, J. (1985). *The hearing-impaired child in the ordinary school*. Dover, NH: Croom Helm.

ROSEMARY GAFFNEY
Hunter College

DEAF
DEAF EDUCATION

POVERTY, RELATIONSHIP TO SPECIAL EDUCATION

Poverty alone does not cause learning and behavior problems. However, poverty is associated with a variety of environmental variables that could result in the manifestation of learning and behavior problems in children. Mental retardation, learning disabilities, and emotional disturbances have all been linked to environmental circumstances associated with poverty. The vast majority of retarded individuals fall into the mild category, and the majority of mildly retarded children come from lower socioeconomic status families (MacMillan, 1982). Although difficult to confirm, poverty has also been linked to learning disabilities (Reid & Hresko, 1981). There is evidence that supports the lower socioeconomic environment's contribution to learning problems. Furthermore, many of these same environmental circumstances have also been linked with emotional disturbance and social maladjustment (Smith, Price, & Marsh, 1985).

Although the connection between poverty and special education is easy to establish, it is difficult to separate the many variables and determine which is the most critical to the child. This is because many of the variables are interwoven at points in the child's development. Malnutrition, poor maternal health, inadequate prenatal care, a child's poor health, homelessness (Masten, 1992) and general environmental deprivation demonstrate complex interrelationships that make it difficult to isolate a single and specific causal agent. Nevertheless, all of these factors associated with poverty have been shown to have an influence on an individual's cognitive and behavioral development.

A lower socioeconomic environment harbors many potential hazards for a developing child (Robinson & Robinson, 1976). For instance, children from these environments are exposed to greater health risks, and their health care is generally inferior to that of children from higher socioeconomic families; nutritional deficiencies are more common in poor families owing to a lack of food or adequate nutritional intake; and the use of standard English in this environment is generally poorer than it is in more affluent families.

Child rearing also takes a somewhat different form in many poor families than in middle-class families. Low-income families tend to have more children and fewer adults. Discipline in lower-income families tends to rely on punishment, especially physical punishment; middle-class families tend to rely more on reasoning, isolation, and appeals to guilt. Poor families also tend to delay training their children for independence until they are able to learn rapidly, which provides few opportunities for learning how to make mistakes without disgrace.

Another negative aspect of this environment is a restricted range of sensory stimulation. Low-income families are usually associated with restricted developmental stimulation because there are fewer objects for the child to react to (Smith, Neisworth, & Hunt, 1983). This restricted range of sensory stimulation will hinder a child's interaction with physical and social environments by providing fewer behavioral cues.

An inadequate home environment that fails to interest children and promote learning is still another environmental factor associated with poverty. It is common to find less value placed on education in lower income homes. Parents existing at the poverty level may have experienced poor academic progress themselves and dropped out of school early. They may not see education as a vehicle for their child's escape from a similar situation. After all, education did not help them escape poverty. In addition, the parents may be more concerned with day-to-day survival than the perceived value of education. Consequently, when their children ask questions, they may fail to respond or regard that behavior as an interruption.

The environmental factors mentioned are not meant to be inclusive. There are many other factors associated with poverty that also influence learning and behavior. But these factors do point out that poverty is an underlying cause for many of the negative environmental variables associated with handicapping conditions. In some cases (e.g., poor maternal nutrition and health care), these factors can affect the child's development prenatally, resulting in an organic origin for the disability (e.g., damage to brain cells). In other cases, poor environmental circumstances cause children to be ill-prepared to start school. These children lack the experiences that are common to children of higher income families and can be overcome by preservice intervention programs (Barnett, 1998; Evans, Okifuji, Engler & Bromley, 1993).

Even though these poverty factors underlie many of the negative variables associated with handicapping conditions, it must be remembered that these learning and behavior problems apply to only a small number of children. The large majority of children living in poor environments will show normal development. While these factors can cause cognitive and behavioral problems in some children, they produce no ill effects in others.

REFERENCES

Barnett, S. W. (1998). Long-term cognitive and academic effects of early childhood education of children in poverty. *Preventative Medicine, 27*(2), 204–207.

Evans, I. M., Okifuji, A., Engler, L., & Bromley, K. (1993). Home-school communication in the treatment of childhood behavior problems. *Child & Family Behavior Therapy, 15*(2), 37–60.

MacMillan, D. L. (1982). *Mental retardation in school and society* (2nd ed.). Boston: Little, Brown.

Masten, A. S. (1992). Homeless children in the United States:

Math of a nation. *Current Directions in Psychological Science, 1*(12), 41–44.

Reid, D. K., & Hresko, W. P. (1981). *A cognitive approach to learning disabilities.* New York: McGraw-Hill.

Robinson, N. M., & Robinson, H. B. (1976). *The mentally retarded child* (2nd ed.). New York: McGraw-Hill.

Smith, R. M., Neisworth, J. T., & Hunt, F. M. (1983). *The exceptional child: A functional approach* (2nd ed.). New York: McGraw-Hill.

Smith, T. E. C., Price, B. J., & Marsh, G. E. (1985). *Mildly handicapped children and adults.* St. Paul, MN: West.

LARRY J. WHEELER
Southwest Texas State University

CULTURAL DEPRIVATION
CULTURAL FAMILIAL RETARDATION
SOCIOECONOMIC IMPACT OF DISABILITIES
SOCIOECONOMIC STATUS

POWER AND RESEARCH IN SPECIAL EDUCATION

The scientific method has evolved in such a way as to allow researchers to observe phenomena, question, formulate hypotheses, conduct experiments, and develop theories. In hypotheses testing, one compares scientific theories in the form of a statistical hypothesis (H^1) versus a null hypothesis (H^0). According to Kirk (1984), the "statistical hypothesis is a statement about one or more parameters of a population distribution that requires verification" (p. 236). An example is

$$H^1 : m > 80,$$

where the mean score of a population of children is hypothesized to be greater than 80 after participating in a remedial reading program. The statistical hypothesis is thus based on the researcher's deductions from the appropriate theory and on prior research. The null hypothesis involves formulating a hypothesis that is mutually exclusive of the statistical hypothesis. In other words, if the researcher believes that children's mean reading scores will be greater than 80 after participating in a reading program, a mutually exclusive hypothesis by which to test the researcher's premise is given by

$$H^0 : < 80.$$

If the null hypothesis is rejected, by default the statistical or alternative hypothesis is assumed to be true but not proven; it is retained as the most likely truth.

Decision Outcomes for Hypothesis Testing

Decision		True State	
		H_0 True	H_0 False
	Fail to reject H_0	Correct acceptance	Incorrect acceptance (Type II error)
	Reject H_0	Incorrect rejection (Type I error)	Correct rejection

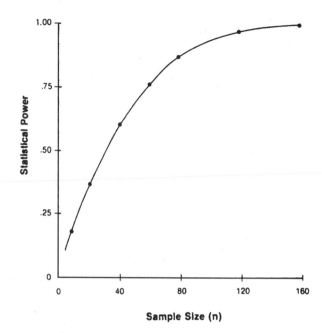

Figure 2. The relationship between sample size and statistical power for detecting a correlation of approximately .30 when p < .05.

In hypothesis testing, rejection or nonrejection of the null hypothesis is based on probability. Incorrect decisions can occur in two ways. If the null hypothesis is rejected when it is in reality true, this is defined as a Type I error. Should the null hypothesis fail to be rejected when it is in fact false, a Type II error is said to have occurred. The following Table displays the possible decision outcomes.

Power is a basic statistical concept that should be taken into consideration in the design of any research study that samples data for inferential purposes. Rejecting the null hypothesis is dependent on whether the test statistic falls within a specified critical region at a particular level of significance, or alpha level (a). The probability of committing a Type I error depends on the alpha level specified. The alpha level also determines the probability of correctly accepting the true null hypothesis (1 − a). The probability of committing a Type II error is labeled b; the probability of a correct rejection is based on 1 − b, or the power level. Figure 1 illustrates the relationship among the four outcomes a, 1 − a, b, and 1 − b, or power. b and power are affected by (1) the size of the sample; (2) the level of significance (a); (3) the size of the difference between m1 and m0; (4) the size of the population; and (5) whether a one-

or two-tailed test is used. One method of increasing the power of a statistical test is to increase the sample size. Figure 2 demonstrates this relationship in a correlational study.

Using power in an a priori fashion enables the researcher to compute the sample size necessary for testing the null hypothesis, given a level of power and alpha. Often, a researcher is faced with a restricted or small sample size on which he or she wishes to determine the power level. Furthermore, in many research situations, as in evaluating special education programs, assessing the impact of a new teaching technique, or exploring the effectiveness of new medication compared with existing therapies, power allows the experimenter to consider, while in the planning stages, what effect size is needed to detect a significant difference. Similarly, the use of two-tailed tests, greater alpha levels, and small population standard deviations contribute to studies with more powerful results. However, it is worthy to note that the cost of committing a Type I error can be as damaging as committing a Type II error. Adopting a new diet program for the treatment of attention deficit children by falsely deciding that the diet is more effective than behavior therapies and medications is as serious as denying the new diet plan any effectiveness as a springboard for future research. Although power is of central consideration in research design and planning, its contribution must be weighted with other important statistical, methodological, and practical facets of the study.

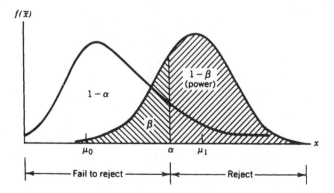

Figure 1. Relationship among power, alpha, one minus alpha, and beta.

REFERENCE

Kirk, R. E. (1984). *Elementary statistics* (2nd ed.). Monterey, CA: Brooks/Cole.

MARY LEON PEERY
Texas A & M University

RESEARCH

PRACTICAL INTELLIGENCE

While most people in society are aware of the existence of both "book smarts" and "street smarts," psychology, in general, has chosen to focus on "book smarts" when it examines intelligence. Intelligence tests sometimes measure topics that have real-world implications (e.g., auditory comprehension on the Kaufman Adolescent and Adult Intelligence Test assesses understanding of a mock news broadcast; Kaufman & Kaufman, 1993), but psychometric testing of intelligence has been more focused on academic intelligence (Sternberg & Kaufman, 1996, 1998).

The history of scientific research on practical intelligence is a short one (Sternberg, 1996; Torff & Sternberg, 1998). Neisser (1976) provided a theoretical distinction between academic and everyday intelligence, and Sternberg, Conway, Ketron, and Bernstein (1981) demonstrated that both laypeople and intelligence researchers had implicit beliefs that academic and practical intelligence were separate things. Ceci and Liker (1986) and Scribner (1984) did early research on how adult subjects performed much better on tasks of mathematical reasoning when these tasks were presented in the context of a more familiar domain (e.g., filling orders in a factory), showing subjects who may not do well on traditional intelligence tests may be able to solve similar problems if they are presented in the guise of their day-to-day work.

Robert Sternberg (1984, 1988), in his triarchic theory of intelligence, proposed that there are three kinds of intelligences: Analytical intelligence, Practical intelligence, and Creative intelligence (see entry for triarchic theory of intelligence). He defines practical intelligence as being similar to street smarts—the ability to apply one's knowledge in a hands-on, real-world manner. One key element required for practical intelligence is tacit knowledge (Wagner & Sternberg, 1985, 1986; Sternberg, Williams, Wagner, & Horvath, 1995), i.e., knowledge that is acquired without being explicitly taught. There are three features of tacit knowledge that are considered characteristic: (1) it is procedural; (2) it is related to the pursuit and achievement of valued outcomes; and (3) it is learned without assistance from other people. The third condition is one of the key distinctions between tacit and academic knowledge. Several tacit knowledge tests have been developed and researched. The Tacit Knowledge Inventory for Managers (TKIM: Wagner & Sternberg, 1991) is the only published instrument as of this writing, but many more have been used for research purposes (Sternberg, 1997; Sternberg et al., 1995). These tests examine a subject's tacit knowledge by presenting scenarios specific to a particular job (e.g., business manager or military officer) and then asking questions about what actions should be taken in this situation. One typical question might be to ask subjects what they would do if a colleague asked for their advice on a project that looked terrible. Would the correct response be to give an honest assessment of the project's worth, or to give complimentary but inaccurate feedback? The subject rates each potential answer on a 1 to 7 scale, with 1 meaning that the solution is "extremely bad" and 7 meaning the solution is "extremely good."

Empirical research by Sternberg, Wagner, and others (Sternberg, 1997; Sternberg, Okagaki, & Jackson, 1990; Sternberg, Wagner, & Okagaki, 1993; Wagner & Sternberg, 1986) has found several consistent results. Tacit knowledge increases with hands-on experience; measures of tacit knowledge have repeatedly correlated at significant levels with job performance, yet show only small correlations with traditional measures of intelligence; and early results show that if one wants to teach tacit knowledge, such training should improve results on tests of practical intelligence and tacit knowledge.

Practical intelligence has many important implications for education. Sternberg, Gardner, and other colleagues have combined to form a collaborative project called "Practical Intelligence for Schools" (PIFS; see Gardner, Krechevsky, Sternberg, & Okagaki, 1994). The authors defined the practically intelligent student as one who is aware of his or her individual learning styles; knows how to draw on individual strengths; understands the requirements for the variety of problems encountered across many different school subjects; and can function well interpersonally as well as academically. The authors propose a curriculum for enhancing PIFS that has three units: one that focuses on self-awareness and self-management, another that focuses on task management, and a final unit that shows students how to interact beneficially with others (Gardner et al., 1994; Sternberg, Okagaki, & Jackson, 1990). This curriculum resulted in improvement on a variety of measures of practical intelligence.

REFERENCES

Ceci, S., & Liker, J. (1986). Academic and nonacademic intelligence: An experimental separation. In R. J. Sternberg & R. K. Wagner (Eds.), *Practical intelligence: Nature and origins of competence in the everyday world* (pp. 119–142). New York: Cambridge University Press.

Gardner, H., Krechevsky, M., Sternberg, R. J., Okagaki, L. (1994).

Intelligence in context: Enhancing students' practical intelligence for school. In K. McGilly (Ed.), *Classroom lessons: Integrating cognitive theory and classroom practice* (pp. 105–127). Cambridge, MA: Bradford Books.

Kaufman, A. S., & Kaufman, N. L. (1993). *Kaufman Adult and Adolescent Intelligence Test.* Circle Pines, MN: American Guidance Service.

Neisser, U. (1976). General, academic and artificial intelligence. In L. Resnick (Ed.), *Human Intelligence: Perspectives on its theory and measurement* (pp. 135–146). Norwood, NJ: Ablex.

Scribner, S. (1984). Studying working intelligence. In B. Rogoff & J. Lave (Eds.), *Everyday cognition* (pp. 9–40). Cambridge, MA: Harvard University Press.

Sternberg, R. J. (1984). Toward a triarchic theory of human intelligence. *Behavioral and Brain Sciences, 7,* 269–287.

Sternberg, R. J. (1988). *The triarchic mind: A new theory of human intelligence.* New York: Viking.

Sternberg, R. J. (1996). What should we ask about intelligence? *American Scholar, 65*(2), 205–217.

Sternberg, R. J. (1997). Tacit knowledge and job success. In N. Anderson & P. Herriot (Eds), *International handbook of selection and assessment* (pp. 201–213). New York: Wiley.

Sternberg, R. J., & Kaufman, J. C. (1996). Innovation and intelligence testing: The curious case of the dog that didn't bark. *European Journal of Psychological Assessment, 12,* 175–182.

Sternberg, R. J., & Kaufman, J. C. (1998). Human abilities. *Annual Review of Psychology, 49,* 479–502.

Sternberg, R. J., Okagaki, L., & Jackson, A. (1990). Practical intelligence for success in school. *Educational Leadership, 48,* 35–39.

Sternberg, R. J., Wagner, R. K., & Okagaki, L. (1993). Practical intelligence: The nature and role of tacit knowledge in work and at school. In H. Reese & J. Puckett (Eds.), *Advances in lifespan development* (pp. 205–227). Hillsdale, NJ: Erlbaum.

Sternberg, R. J., Wagner, R. K., Williams, W. M., & Horvath, J. A. (1995). Testing common sense. *American Psychologist, 50*(11), 912–927.

Torff, B., & Sternberg, R. J. (1998). Changing mind, changing world: Practical intelligence and tacit knowledge in adult learning. In R. Sternberg (Series Ed.), & C. M. Smith & T. Pourchot (Vol. Eds.), *Adult learning and development: Perspectives from educational psychology* (pp. 109–126). Mahweh, NJ: Lawrence Erlbaum Associates.

Wagner, R. K., & Sternberg, R. J. (1985). Practical intelligence in real-world pursuits: The role of tacit knowledge. *Journal of Personality and Social Psychology, 49,* 436–458.

Wagner, R. K., & Sternberg, R. J. (1986). Tacit knowledge and intelligence in the everyday world. In R. J. Sternberg & R. K. Wagner (Eds.), *Practical intelligence: Nature and origins of competence in the everyday world* (pp. 51–83). New York: Cambridge University Press.

Wagner, R. K., & Sternberg, R. J. (1991). *Tacit Knowledge Inventory for Managers (TKIM).* New York: Psychological Corporation.

JAMES C. KAUFMAN
Yale University

PRADER-WILLI SYNDROME (PWS)

First described in 1956 by Swiss physicians A. Prader, A. Labhart, and H. Willi, Prader-Willi syndrome (PWS) is a complex disorder and a rare birth defect. Common characteristics include hypotonia in early infancy, hypogonadism, short stature, and, after age 2, excessive weight gain and obesity (Cassidy, 1984). Perhaps the most outstanding characteristic of PWS is the individual's constant preoccupation with food and the compulsion to be eating all the time (Otto, Sulzbacher, & Worthington-Roberts, 1982; Pipes, 1978). This voracious craving for food finds PWS victims often exhibiting unselective and bizarre food behaviors such as eating spoiled meat, rotten vegetables, and/or cat food as well as foraging, stealing, or gorging food (Bottel, 1977; Clarren & Smith, 1977; Dykens & Cassidy, 1996; Otto et al., 1982).

The excessive appetite of PWS victims is not the only factor contributing to their obesity. They seem to require fewer calories than the average person of comparable age to maintain weight (Nardella, Sulzbacher, & Worthington-Roberts, 1983; Neason, 1978). In order to lose weight, further reduction in caloric intake is necessary, sometimes restricting the person to a 1000-calorie or less daily diet plan (Cassidy, 1984; Nardella et al., 1983).

Characteristics of PWS individuals usually include erratic and unpredictable behavior such as stubbornness, outbursts of temper, depression (Watanabe & Ohmori, 1997), and even rage (Otto et al., 1982). Personality problems, behavioral disorders, and emotional problems are frequent though not consistent findings in people with PWS (Cassidy, 1984). Many of the more aggressive behaviors escalate out of anger or desire for food.

Current research indicates that an aberration in a portion of chromosome 15 may be the cause of PWS (Nardella et al., 1983). However, PWS is not a high-risk condition and is most likely a noninherited chromosome defect (Neason, 1978). Another prevailing theory is that PWS is due to a defect within the hypothalamus and thus PWS victims never reach a sense of satiety (Clarren & Smith, 1977).

Mental retardation, particularly in the borderline to moderate range, has been considered to be an integral part of the syndrome (Cassidy, 1984; Neason, 1978). However, recent reports by Holm (1981) indicate that for many of these people, cognitive functioning is more typical of learning disabilities. That is, the child has strengths in several areas and weaknesses in others, unlike a retarded child, who tends to be developmentally delayed across skill areas. Academic weaknesses are commonly found in arithmetic, particularly in the understanding of time and the handling of money, and in writing. Reading and language commonly are mentioned as academic strengths. Holm (1981) sees the intellectual functioning of the PWS individual as a central nervous system disorder.

Because of its rarity, insufficient evidence exists on the

social and emotional consequences of having PWS. However, there is no question that those afflicted with the disorder have sufficient intelligence to recognize the social stigma obesity has in our society (Cassidy, 1984). At the present time there is no known cure or treatment for PWS. The critical component of any program, however, is the constant monitoring of caloric intake. If the weight of the individual with PWS is not kept under control, death may occur at an early age from complications associated with extreme obesity.

Educational intervention for individuals with Prader-Willi syndrome should begin in early childhood with a program that assists and supports parents and children in managing eating behaviors. Food and nutrition management must be the first and foremost objective of any school program. Deliberate and calculated attempts by the teacher must be made to rid the classroom of any and all food, including pet food. Alternate reward and reinforcement systems other than food reinforcers such as candy must also be instituted. All school personnel who come in contact with the child (particularly lunchroom aides) must be made aware of the child's condition and the consequences of additional caloric intake. The child should be encouraged to stay away from food at all cost.

Physical activity designed to enhance body awareness and activities that encourage social interaction should be stressed and deliberately planned in any class with a PWS child. Academic weaknesses should be addressed as well, and particular attention should be paid to eliminating or modifying temper tantrums or extreme stubbornness by using a behavior-modification approach (Cassidy, 1984). Secondary-level students should be prepared in independent living skills such as math in daily living and vocational/occupational skills, with an emphasis on increasing the child's responsibility for weight control. Competitive employment is rare and most adults are employed in noncompetitive structured workshops and centers. At all times, in any school or workshop program, students with PWS must be watched to prevent their consuming other people's leftovers and food items.

REFERENCES

Bottel, H. (1977, May). The eating disease. *Good Housekeeping,* 176–177.

Cassidy, S. B. (1984). Prader-Willi syndrome. *Current Problems in Pediatrics, 14*(1), 18.

Clarren, S. K., & Smith, D. W. (1977). Prader-Willi syndrome: Variable severity and recurrence risk. *American Journal of Diseases in Children, 131,* 798–800.

Dykens, E. M., & Cassidy, S. B. (1996). Prader-Willi syndrome: Genetic, behavioral, and treatment issues. *Child & Adolescent Psychiatric Clinics of North America, 5*(4), 913–927.

Hom, V. A. (1981). The diagnosis of Prader-Willi syndrome. In V. A. Holm, S. Sulzbacher, & P. L. Pipes (Eds.), *Prader-Willi syndrome.* Baltimore, MD: University Park Press.

Nardella, M. T., Sulzbacher, S. I., Worthington-Roberts, B. S. (1983). Activity levels of persons with Prader-Willi syndrome. *American Journal of Mental Deficiency, 89,* 498–505.

Neason, S. (1978). *Prader-Willi syndrome: A handbook for parents.* Longlake, MN: Prader-Willi Syndrome Association.

Otto, P. L., Sulzbacher, S. I., Worthington-Roberts, B. S. (1982). Sucrose-induced behavior changes of persons with Prader-Willi syndrome. *American Journal of Mental Deficiency, 86,* 335–341.

Pipes, P. L. (1978). Weight control. In S. Neason (Ed.), *Prader-Willi syndrome: A handbook for parents.* Longlake, MN: Prader-Willi Syndrome Association.

Watanabe, H., & Ohmori, A. K. (1997). Recurrent brief depression in Prader-Willi syndrome: A case report. *Psychiatric Genetics, 7*(1), 41–44.

MARSHA H. LUPI
Hunter College

CHROMOSOME ABNORMALITIES
GENETIC DISORDERS

PRAGMATICS AND PRAGMATIC COMMUNICATION DISORDERS

Pragmatics is the study of language use independent of language structure, rules, and principles which relate the structure of language to its use (Duchan, 1995; Duchan, Hewitt, & Sonnenmeier, 1994). The rules and principles of pragmatics define who can communicate (talking, writing, signing) what, to whom, how, when, where, and why. Pragmatics includes verbal and nonverbal dimensions of communication and the rules are often implicit and dynamic. Competence in pragmatics includes the development of scripts (the stereotypical knowledge structures that people have for common routines) and schemas (hierarchical cognitive categories of synthesized scripts) (Hedberg & Westby, 1993; Nelson, 1998). Social, academic, and employment schemas and scripts are important in development. The social scripts of eating at different fast-food restaurants and eating at a full-service restaurant contribute to the schema of "eating out." The academic scripts of studying for a multiple choice test, studying for an essay exam, and making a diorama contribute to the schema "doing homework." The employment scripts of knowing and following the "rules" of a job setting and knowing and using the "politics" of a job setting contribute to the schema of "employment success."

Communication registers, or codes, occur as people adapt to the social and communication demands of situations (Lane & Molyneaux, 1992). Registers are differences observable within speakers, across situations. The different registers allow speakers to convey their social position relative to that of their listeners while simultaneously communicating a message. Registers range from "frozen," which is the most distant, noninteractive form of communication code, to "intimate," a form that excludes public information. Restricted codes are the context-dependent modes of communication used with close friends and coworkers when details are unnecessary. Precise, detailed, context-independent statements that anyone can understand are elaborated codes.

Pragmatic theory suggests that every communication act has three aspects: (1) the illocutionary intent of the sender to accomplish some goal, such as to inform, request, persuade, or promise; (b) the locutionary dimension, i.e., the actual words and sentence structure of the communication act; (c) the perlocutionary effect that the act has on the receiver (e.g., did the receiver comply with the request, understand the information?; Haynes & Shulman, 1998; Hulit & Howard, 1997; Lane & Molyneaux, 1992; McLaughlin, 1998; Nelson, 1998; Owens, 1996; Paul, 1995; Wallach & Butler, 1994).

Communication style is a type of language variation that distinguishes individual speakers in different contexts. A formal, grammatically correct style, acrolect, would be appropriate for academic or some employment situations; a conversational, everyday style, mesolect, would be appropriate for conversations and some types of employment; and basolect (vulgarity) may be used by some individuals in certain situations (Muma, 1978).

Pragmatic communication disorders include violating the verbal, nonverbal, oral, and written rules of communication styles, codes, or scripts. They can interfere with social and academic aspects of the communication-learning process. Pragmatic communication disorders are seen frequently in persons with developmental or acquired disorders such as autism, blindness, deafness, language-learning disorders, mental retardation, and emotional-behavioral disorders (Duchan, 1995; Duchan et al., 1994). Individuals who are gifted and talented may also manifest pragmatic communication problems. Pragmatics of communication varies from culture to culture and should not be confused with a pragmatic language disorder.

REFERENCES

Duchan, J. F. (1995). *Supporting language learning in everyday life.* San Diego: Singular.

Duchan, J. F., Hewitt, L. E., & Sonnenmeier, R. M. (Eds.). (1994). *Pragmatics: From theory to practice.* Englewood Cliffs, NJ: Prentice Hall.

Haynes, W. O., & Shulman, B. B. (1998). *Communication development: Foundations, processes, and clinical applications.* Baltimore: Williams & Wilkins.

Hedberg, N. L., & Westby, C. E. (1993). *Analyzing storytelling skills: Theory to practice.* Tucson, AZ: Communication Skill Builders.

Hulit, L. M., & Howard, M. R. (1997). *Born to talk: An introduction to speech and language development.* Boston: Allyn & Bacon.

Lane, V. W., & Molyneaux, D. (1992). *The dynamics of communicative development.* Englewood Cliffs, NJ: Prentice Hall.

McLaughlin, S. (1998). *Introduction to language development.* San Diego: Singular Publishing Group.

Muma, J. R. (1978). *Language handbook: Concepts, assessment, intervention.* Englewood Cliffs, NJ: Prentice Hall.

Nelson, N. W. (1998). *Childhood language disorders in context: Infancy through adolescence* (2nd ed.). Boston: Allyn & Bacon.

Owens, R. E. (1996). *Language development: An introduction* (4th ed.). Boston: Allyn & Bacon.

Paul, R. (1995). *Language disorders from infancy through adolescence: Assessment and intervention.* St. Louis: Mosby.

Wallach, G. P., & Butler, K. G. (1994). *Language learning disabilities in school-age children and adolescents: Some principles and applications* (2nd ed.). New York: Merrill/Macmillan College Publishing.

STEPHEN S. FARMER
New Mexico State University

PRECISION TEACHING

Precision teaching, a measurement system developed by Ogden R. Lindsley at the University of Kansas in the mid-1960s (McGreevy, 1984; Potts, Eshleman, & Cooper, 1993), involves daily measurement and graphing of student performance for the purpose of formative evaluation. Frequency of behavior (the number of occurrences divided by minutes of observation) is charted on the Standard Behavior Chart, a graph designed to highlight changes in frequency. Data are evaluated daily to determine if changes in curriculum are necessary to promote learning and progress toward performance goals (or, in the language of precision teaching, aims).

There are four steps in precision teaching. First, a precisely stated behavior or pinpoint is selected. An example of a pinpoint statement is "see word/say word." Next, frequencies of correct and incorrect responses are obtained and charted on the Standard Behavior Chart. Third, curricular events are modified to change performance in the desired direction. Finally, the graph is evaluated and instructional decisions are made according to trends in the data. Of course, these final two steps are repeated as necessary until progress allows for the attainment of aims.

The Standard Behavior Chart is a semilogarthmic or equal-ratio graph. Frequency is represented along its vertical axis as Movements/minute (M/m). Equal changes in

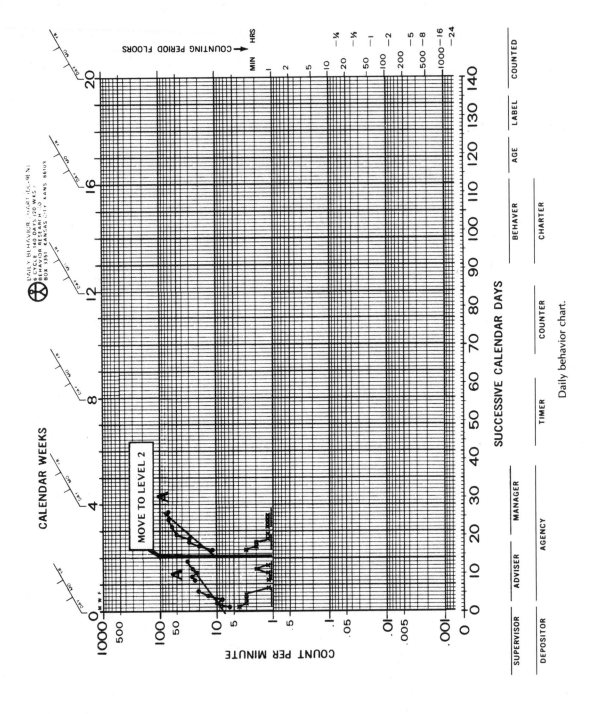

Daily behavior chart.

the frequency of behavior are represented by equal distances along this Y-axis. Thus, the distance between 10 and 20 M/m is identical to the distance between 50 and 100 M/m since both represent a 2 × (times 2) change. In fact, any 2 × change, regardless of where along the Y-axis it occurs, will appear as the same distance on the Standard Behavior Chart. Behaviors ranging in frequency from 1 to 1000 minutes (.001 M/m) to 1000 in 1 minute (1000 M/m) can be represented on the Standard Behavior Chart. The unit along the X or horizontal axis is actual calendar days.

Data are obtained directly through observations of student behavior. For example, word recognition could be measured each day by counting the number of words said correctly and incorrectly per minute of reading. Also, in precision teaching, data are recorded continuously. Once recording starts, behavior is monitored without interruption until the recording period stops.

One of the principal measures used in precision teaching is celeration (Pennypacker, Koenig, & Lindsley, 1972). Celerations are standard straight line measures describing the trend of graphed data. For example, an upward trend or acceleration in correct responses and a downward trend or deceleration in incorrect responses, describe a desirable pattern. Precision teaching suggests that certain teaching decisions be based on a minimum acceptable celeration toward a performance aim. In practice, if the teacher sees the student's performance drop below acceptable minimums, then decisions are made to change some aspect of the curriculum (White & Haring, 1980). The changes are evaluated to see if restoration of student progress is obtained. Various adjustments are tried until acceptable celerations and progress toward aims are achieved.

The Figure shows examples of correct (•) and incorrect (x) data points on a standard behavior chart. The lines drawn through the data represent celerations. Various changes in the teaching procedures are indicated by notations on the chart. The correct data are accelerating to the previously chosen performance aim, the symbol "A" on the chart. Incorrect responses are decelerating. This pattern is a desirable one showing learning and growth in both accuracy and fluency (Binder, 1996) of performance. If the data change in an undesirable manner—e.g., if frequency correct decelerates and frequency wrong accelerates—then teachers must select a program adjustment and try again (Lindsley, 1971).

Thus the process of precision teaching is an optimistic one. Once responses are precisely defined, observed, and recorded, the elements of a self-correcting instructional system are in place. Teachers may not interpret failure to maintain adequate progress toward an aim as a limitation of the student. Rather, such failure signals a limitation of the existing instructional program. Their ability to solve even the most difficult instructional problems of handi-capped learners is limited only by their creativity in developing program adjustments.

The *Journal of Precision Teaching* is dedicated to dissemination of data-based information about human performance and is an excellent resource. The journal is available through Louisiana State University, Special Education, 201 Peabody Hall, Baton Rouge, Louisiana 70803.

REFERENCES

Binder, C. (1996). Behavioral fluency: Evaluation of a new paradigm. *Behavior Analyst, 19*(2), 163–197.

Lindsley, O. R. (1971). From Skinner to precision teaching: The child knows best. In J. B. Jordan & L. S. Robbins (Eds.), *Let's try doing something else kind of thing* (pp. 1–11). Arlington, VA: Council for Exceptional Children.

McGreevy, P. (1984). Frequency and the standard celeration chart: Necessary components of precision teaching. *Journal of Precision Teaching, 5*(2), 28–36.

Pennypacker, H. S., Koenig, C. H., & Lindsley, O. R. (1972). *Handbook of the standard behavior chart.* Kansas City, KS: Precision Media.

Potts, L., & Eshleman, J. W., & Cooper, J. O. (1993). Ogden R. Lindsley and the historical development of precision teaching. *Behavior Analyst, 16*(2), 177–189.

White, O. R., & Haring, N. G. (1980). *Exceptional children* (2nd ed.). Columbus, OH: Merrill.

MARK A. KOORLAND
PAUL T. SINDELAR
Florida State University

DIRECT INSTRUCTION
DATA-BASED INSTRUCTION
TEST-TEACH-TEST

PREHM, HERBERT J. (1937–1986)

A native of Aurora, Illinois, Herbert J. Prehm obtained his BS (1959) in elementary education and psychology from Concordia Teacher's College, River Forest, Illinois, later earning both his MS (1962) and PhD (1964) in education and psychology from the University of Wisconsin, Madison.

Trained as an elementary school teacher and experienced as a reading consultant for children with dyslexia, Prehm maintained an interest in the learning problems of children throughout his distinguished career. As a professor of education at various universities for some 20 years, his work primarily concerned the effective teaching of mentally retarded children (Hersh & Prehm, 1977; Prehm, 1967; Prehm & Stinnett, 1970). Prehm's publications regarding the elements necessary for preparation of stu-

Herbert J. Prehm

dents in the special education field at the doctoral level was a result of this experience as a teacher and advisor of those entering the profession (Prehm, 1980).

Prehm's later work included instructional strategies for individuals with severe handicaps, with this research resulting in the development of a model allowing for controlled formal investigation of relevant variables, including handicapping condition, race, and age (Zucker & Prehm, 1984). This model was an important tool utilized in studying teaching methods via the use of results of previous investigations.

Among his numerous contributions, Prehm served as assistant executive director of the Department of Professional Development of the Council for Exceptional Children and president of the Teacher Education Division of the Council for Exceptional Children. Additionally, he was a fellow of the American Association on Mental Deficiency and recipient of the TED-Merril Award for Excellence in Teacher Education. The book he coauthored with Kathleen McCoy, *Teaching Mainstreamed Students* (1987), was published only a short time after his death in 1986.

REFERENCES

Hersh, R., & Prehm, H. J. (Eds.). (1977). Issues in teacher preparation. *Teacher Education & Special Education, 1*(1), 320–349.

McCoy, K. M., & Prehm, H. J. (1987). *Teaching mainstreamed students: Methods and techniques.* Denver, CO: Love.

Prehm, H. J. (1967). Rote learning and memory in the retarded: Some implications for the teacher-learning process. *Journal of Special Education, 1,* 397–399.

Prehm, H. J. (1980). Research training and experience in special education doctoral programs. *Teacher Education and Special Education, 3*(4), 3–9.

Prehm, H. J., & Stinnett, R. D. (1970). Effects of learning method on learning stage in retarded and normal adolescents. *American Journal of Mental Deficiency, 75,* 319–322.

Zucker, S. H., & Prehm, H. J. (1984). *Parameters of cumulative programming with severely/profoundly handicapped pupils.* Tempe, AZ: Arizona State University.

E. VALERIE HEWITT
Texas A & M University
First edition

TAMARA J. MARTIN
*The University of Texas of the
Permian Basin*
Second edition

PRELINGUAL DEAFNESS

Prelingual deafness refers to profound hearing loss sustained before language has been acquired. Age at onset of profound hearing loss is a major factor because of its implications for language development. The critical age at onset of profound hearing loss is about 2 years (Quigley & Kretschmer, 1982). Children born deaf, or deafened before the age of 2 years, are prelingually deaf. Deafness is a profound degree of hearing impairment, a bilateral loss of 90 dB or greater on the audiometric scale of –10 to 110 dB (Quigley & Paul, 1984).

Prelingually deaf children rely on vision as their primary channel of communication and language acquisition. Since language plays such a important role in thinking and in conceptual growth (Webster & Ellwood, 1985), prelingually deaf children require special educational programs with emphasis on all the skills related to language and communication.

Prelingual deafness is more than the inability to hear sound. It is a pervasive handicap that, because of its effects on language and communication, has an impact on almost all aspects of child development.

REFERENCES

Forecki, M. C. (1985). *Speak to me,* Washington, DC: Gallaudet College Press.

Quigley, S., & Kretschmer, R. (1982). *The education of deaf children: Issues, theory and practice.* Baltimore, MD: University Park Press.

Quigley, S., & Paul, P. (1984). *Language and deafness,* San Diego, CA: College-Hill.

Webster, A., & Ellwood, J. (1985). *The hearing-impaired child in the ordinary school.* Dover, NH: Croom Helm.

ROSEMARY GAFFNEY
Hunter College

DEAF
DEAF EDUCATION
SPEECH, ABSENCE OF

PREMACK PRINCIPLE

The original definition of reinforcement (Skinner, 1938; Spence, 1956) was circular. A stimulus could not be identified as a reinforcer until it had been tested and shown to increase the probability of a response. This left behavior modifiers with no a priori method of choosing effective reinforcers. However, Premack (1965) solved this problem of circularity by devising an independent means of determining the reinforcing power of different consequences. Premack found that under certain circumstances, an organism's own behavior can function as a reinforcer. More specifically, a less probable behavior within a person's repertoire can be strengthened by making the occurrence of a more probable behavior contingent on it.

This principle was first demonstrated in an intensive set of experiments in which Premack shifted the probability of animals drinking or running by alternately depriving them of water or activity. When drinking was made a high-probability behavior by depriving the animals of water, drinking reinforced the low-probability behavior of running. Similarly, when running was made a high-probability behavior by depriving the animals of activity, running served as a reinforcer for drinking. In both situations, low-probability behavior was increased by following it with high-probability behavior.

Moving from the animal laboratory to the applied setting is always a difficult transition. Identifying reinforcers by the Premack principle requires assessing the relative probabilities of the reinforcing behavior and the behavior to be changed by counting their rate of occurrence in a free environment. This arduous task seriously limits the usefulness of the Premack principle in applied settings. Fortunately, behavior modifiers have found it adequate to identify high-probability behaviors by asking a person about preferred activities or by casually observing the person to determine the activities from which he or she derives overt pleasure (Danaher, 1974). Once the preferred behavior is identified, the behavior modifier will allow the person to engage in that behavior only after performing the targeted low-probability or less preferred behavior. Because of this formulation, the Premack principle is sometimes referred to as "Grandma's rule" (Becker, 1971; Homme, 1971) or "you do what I want you to do before you get to do what you want to do."

Preferred activities have been frequently used in special education to reinforce or increase the rate of less pre-

ferred activities as demonstrated in the following three examples. First, in a deaf education class, Osborne (1969) allowed students to earn 5 minutes of free time, the preferred activity, for every 15 minutes they remained in their seats, the less preferred activity. Second, Hart and Risley (1968) gave economically disadvantaged children access to recreational materials contingent on the appropriate use of adjectives in spontaneous speech. Third, Kane and Gantzer (1977) showed that in a special class, academically preferred activities could be used to increase the amount of time spent in less desirable academic activities. The Premack principle has been particularly successful in the treatment of feeding disorders and diet maintenance (Amari, Grace & Fisher, 1995; O'Brien, Repp, Williams & Christophersen, 1991).

REFERENCES

Amari, A., Grace, N. C., & Fisher, W. W. (1995). Achieving and maintaining compliance with the ketogenic diet. *Journal of Applied Behavior Analysis, 28*(3), 341–342.

Becker, W. C. (1971). *Parents are teachers*. Champaign, IL: Research.

Danaher, B. G. (1974). Theoretical foundations and clinical applications of the Premack principle: Review and critique. *Behavior Therapy, 5,* 307–324.

Hart, B. M., & Risley, T. R. (1968). Establishing use of descriptive adjectives in the spontaneous speech of disadvantaged preschool children. *Journal of Applied Behavior Analysis, 1,* 109–120.

Homme, L. (1971). *How to use contingency contracting in the classroom*. Champaign, IL: Research.

Kane, G., & Gantzer, S. (1977). Preferred lessons as reinforcers in a special class: An investigation of the Premack principle. *Zeitschrift fur Entwicklungspsychologie and Padagogische Psychologie, 9,* 79–89.

O'Brien, S., Repp, A. C., Williams, G. E., & Christophersen, E. R. (1991). Pediatric Feeding disorders. *Behavior Modification, 15*(3), 394–418.

Osborne, J. G. (1969). Free time as a reinforcer in the management of classroom behavior. *Journal of Applied Behavior Analysis, 2,* 113–118.

Premack, D. (1965). Reinforcement theory. In D. Levine (Ed.), *Nebraska symposium on motivation*. Lincoln: University of Nebraska Press.

Skinner, B. F. (1938). *The Behavior of organisms*. New York: Appleton-Century-Crofts.

Spence, K. (1956). *Behavior theory and conditioning*. New Haven, CT: Yale University Press.

JOHN O'NEILL
Hunter College

BEHAVIOR MODIFICATION
OPERANT CONDITIONING
POSITIVE REINFORCEMENT

PREMATURITY

Prematurity or preterm refers to infants born prior to completion of 37 weeks gestation. Although the overall survival rate of premature infants has steadily increased with advances in perinatal and neonatal care, the incidence of prematurity has not significantly changed in the past 20 years and remains at about 10% of all live births (Spitzer, 1996).

The exact cause of the majority of premature births remains unknown. The cause is hypothesized to be a combination of maternal, paternal, fetal, and environmental factors. Maternal risk factors for prematurity include pregnancy-induced hypertension, antepartum hemorrhage, infection, and premature rupture of membranes. Maternal social factors often contributing to prematurity are low socioeconomic status, age less than 16 or greater than 40 years, history of premature births, history of repeated abortions, non-white race, maternal substance abuse (including cigarettes and alcohol), lack of prenatal care, and poor nutritional status (Spitzer, 1996). Paternal factors include genetic makeup and older age. Fetal factors related to prematurity include presence of congenital anomalies, fetal disease, and multiple gestation. Environmental factors include stress, injury, and exposure to teratogens (Johnson, 1986). The cause of prematurity continues to be elusive, making prediction of premature births difficult.

Gestational maturity is determined by both neurological and physical characteristics (Dubowitz and Dubowitz, 1977). The premature infant's head generally appears large for its small body and the skin is bright pink, wrinkled, and translucent. The eyes remain fused until about 22–25 weeks gestation and after opening appear large for the face. The abdomen looks distended, and genitalia are not fully developed (Merenstein and Gardner, 1998). The fingernails are thin and the body is covered with fine downy hair and a layer of sebaceous skin covering. The preterm infant's arms and legs are thin and muscle tone is poor, causing it to lie in an extended position unless supported against gravity. Reflex movements are only partially developed, and breathing and crying are often spasmodic and weak (Schuster & Ashburn, 1986).

Preterm infants have physiologically immature organ systems that cause many clinical problems. These problems include immature lungs, apnea, hemorrhaging into the brain, infections of the gastrointestinal tract, poor weight gain, inability to maintain body temperature, and infection (Merenstein and Gardner, 1998).

The clinical problems often require intensive management involving a team of healthcare professionals providing multisystem support. This support may include the use of incubators, ventilators, intravenous fluids, and physiologic monitoring. Survival rates are improving, with reports of 61% survival of infants born between 23–26 weeks gestation. Of those infants, 6% to 36% survived intact without long-term handicapping conditions. The more immature the infant, the greater the incidence and severity of long-term complications. Survival rates improve and incidence of complications diminish rapidly after 26 weeks gestation (Goldsen, 1996).

The long-range sequelae of prematurity are closely associated with both prenatal and postnatal complications and the disruption of the parent-infant attachment process. Long-term sequelae include breathing disorders, retinopathy of prematurity, increased incidence of SIDS, and neurologic impairment leading to sensorimotor and developmental delays (Merenstein & Gardner, 1998).

Preterm infants may develop breathing disorders such as apnea, in which breathing is not regular and rhythmical, or bronchopulmonary dysplasia (BPD), in which the lungs are damaged and infants require supplemental oxygen and breathing support. Another potential complication is impaired vision or blindness associated with retinopathy of prematurity (ROP). Once believed to be caused solely by excess oxygen, ROP is now known to owe to many contributing factors, including the degree of prematurity, nutritional status, and exposure to light (Spitzer, 1996). Serious and sometimes devastating complications arise from intracranial hemorrhage and other forms of hypoxic brain damage. Intracranial bleeding into the ventricular system in the brain is graded in severity from I–IV (one the least damaging, four meaning bleeding has progressed into the brain tissue itself).

Other potential long-range effects of preterm birth include lack of parent-infant attachment and delays in growth and development. Lack of attachment can be caused by separation, guilt, fear, and poor parenting skills. Attachment can be strengthened by encouraging and supporting early parent-infant interaction and involving parents in the care of their hospitalized child. Teaching parents developmentally appropriate interactions, helping them to understand their infant's cues, and encouraging skin to skin contact all help in the attachment process (Merenstein & Gardner, 1998).

Preterm infants often experience a lag in growth and development. Improved infant formulas and the increased support of breastfeeding greatly contribute to improved nutrition and growth. Environmental control of light and noise, positioning that provides containment and support, and intervention strategies that avoid overstimulation encourage normal growth and development. Early and regular developmental assessment to detect delays is important to allow for early intervention and improved outcomes for these infants.

REFERENCES

Dubowitz, L. M. S., & Dubowitz, V. (1977). *Gestational age of the newborn.* Menlo Park, CA: Addison-Wesley.

Goldsen, E. (1996). The micropremie: Infants with birthweights less than 800 grams. *Infants and Young Children, 8*(3), 1–10.

Johnson, S. H. (1986). *Nursing assessment and strategies for the family at risk: High risk parenting* (2nd ed.). Philadelphia: Lippincott.

Merenstein, G. B., & Gardner, S. L. (1998). *Handbook of Neonatal Care* (4th ed.). St. Louis: Mosby.

Shuster, C. S., & Ashburn, S. S. (1986). *The process of human development. A holistic lifespan approach* (2nd ed.). Boston: Little, Brown.

Spitzer, A. R. (Ed.). (1996). *Intensive care of the fetus and neonate.* St. Louis: Mosby.

Elizabeth R. Bauerschmidt
University of North Carolina at Wilmington
First edition

Brenda Melvin
New Hanover Regional Medical Center
Second edition

AMNIOCENTESIS
APGAR SCALE
BABY JANE DOE
BIRTH INJURIES
LOW BIRTH WEIGHT INFANTS

PREREFERRAL INTERVENTION

Graden, Casey, and Christenson (1985) state that the goal of a prereferral intervention model "is to implement systematically intervention strategies in the regular classroom and to evaluate the effectiveness of these strategies before a student is formally referred for consideration for special education placement" (p. 378). The prereferral intervention model is intended to prevent unnecessary referrals for psychoeducational testing for purposes of determining eligibility for special education programs. The prereferral intervention model is an indirect, consultative service, and has several advantages as an alternative to the traditional process of teacher referral, psychoeducational testing, determination of eligibility, and special education placement. It has also paralleled the movement towards inclusion (Wilson, Gutkin, Hugen, & Oats, 1998).

First, while traditional psychoeducational testing assumes the child's problem resides in the child (e.g., a learning disability, low intelligence, or a personality disorder), the prereferral intervention model assumes that the child's problems are a result of the interaction of the child's characteristics with setting and task variables. When those setting and task variables that result in improved child performance are identified through careful observa-tion and problem-solving efforts, modifications can be implemented in the classroom without removing the child from the regular class. Second, in the traditional testing approach, if the child is found ineligible for special education services, a great deal of resources are allocated to the child, but the child does not necessarily benefit from these resources. Third, because some testing does not use instructional data, the recommendations may not have instructional ramifications. Contributing to the problem of the relevance of recommendations is the fact that the problem for which the child is referred often does not show up in the testing situation. For example, a child who is fidgety and has trouble concentrating in the classroom may demonstrate excellent concentration in the one-on-one testing relationship. In this example, the testing results and recommendations would not address the referral problem. Fourth, when special education services are the only assistance available to children with problems, teachers will refer children whose needs could be met in the less restrictive environment of the regular classroom. If consultative help were available to the teacher, the child's needs could be served through an indirect model. Fifth, indirect services serve preventive goals. If teachers can request consultation from a school psychologist or special education teacher-consultant soon after a child's problem becomes evident, more severe problems can be avoided. In the traditional testing model, children who do not qualify tend to get referred again and again by teachers until the problems are severe enough to qualify these children for special education programs. Finally, the teacher develops new knowledge and skills in consultation that will assist in providing for the needs of other children.

Because 73% of referred children are placed in special education (Algozzine, Christenson, & Ysseldyke, 1982), referral for testing is a critical point in the referral-testing-determination-placement process. The preferral interventions model is aimed at increasing the probability that a child referred for testing has needs that cannot be met by modifications in the regular classroom. Graden et al. (1985a) delineate four steps in the preferral intervention model. These steps occur prior to a formal referral for special education testing. First, the teacher requests consultation from the school psychologist or special education teacher-consultant. This step may be a requirement or an option for the teacher. Second, the consultant and teacher engage in a problem-solving process that involves specifying the problem, generating alternative interventions, and evaluating the intervention. This step may be repeated. Third, if the interventions tried out during the first consultation are unsuccessful, the consultant and teacher collect additional observational data. The data include an analysis of antecedents and consequences of the child's behavior. These more detailed observations are used to plan interventions that are then implemented and evaluated. If these interventions are unsuccessful, the teacher and consultant refer the child to a child review team that reviews the problem and the data collected. This team may recommend additional data to collect or additional interventions, or it may formally refer the child for psychoeducational testing for purposes of determining eligibility for special education. If the child is referred for testing, the data collected in the prereferral phases are used to select an assessment strategy and to plan for the child's instructional needs.

The prereferral model is a consultative model. The consultant must possess the consultation skills necessary to engage the teacher in a collaborative, problem-solving process to create an open and trusting relationship with the consultee and to guide the teacher in a problem-solving sequence.

Although there have been many studies evaluating the effectiveness of consultation, few of these have evaluated consultation as a systematic strategy for reducing inappropriate referrals for special education testing. An exception is the case study by Graden, Casey, and Bonstrom (1985), they found that four out of six schools that implemented the prereferral model experienced a decrease in referrals for testing and special education placements. The authors suggest that the model was not successful in the other two schools because there was a lack of system support and the model was not fully implemented.

REFERENCES

Algozzine, B., Christenson, S., & Ysseldyke, J. E. (1982). Probabilities associated with the referral to placement process. *Teacher Education and Special Education, 5*, 19–23.

Graden, J., Casey, A., & Bonstrom. (1985). Implementing a prereferral intervention system: Part II. The Data. *Exceptional Children, 51*, 487–496. (a)

Graden, J., Casey, A., & Christenson, S. (1985). Implementing a prereferral intervention system: Part I. The Model. *Exceptional Children, 51*, 377–384. (b)

Wilson, C. P., Gutkin, T. B., Hagen, K. M., & Oats, R. G. (1998). General education teacher's knowledge and self-reported use of classroom interventions: Implications for consultation prereferral intervention and inclusive services. *School Psychology Quarterly, 13*(1), 45–62.

JAN N. HUGHES
Texas A & M University

PRESCHOOL SCREENING CONSULTATION
PREVENTION, PRIMARY

PRESCHOOL-AGE GIFTED CHILDREN

Services for gifted children below kindergarten age have received increased attention as a means of encouraging development of the child's potential, stimulating interest in learning, and providing support for parents. Several authors (Fox, 1971; Isaacs, 1963; Whitmore, 1979, 1980) have pointed to lack of support and intellectual challenge in the early years as one source of later underachievement among the gifted. Programs for young gifted children facilitate early interaction between parents and educators that can promote supportive parenting practices and parent advocacy (Karnes, Shwedel, & Linnemeyer, 1982). Early identification and parent training are particularly critical for gifted children from economically disadvantaged backgrounds.

Despite the need, few programs exist that are specifically designed for preschool 3- to 4-year-old children (Roedell, Jackson, & Robinson, 1980). Several factors account for the sparsity of such programs. First, lacking state and federal incentives for providing appropriate education to preschool-age gifted and talented children, few systematic procedures have been implemented for early identification and service delivery. Second, critics have questioned the reliability and validity of currently available measures for identifying giftedness in 3- and 4-year-old children. Third, parents of young gifted children frequently have little access to information about referral characteristics, available services, and need for advocacy in initiating services.

A review of current literature on gifted education, however, reveals growing recognition of the special needs of gifted and talented children in the early years (Karnes, 1983; Whitmore, in press). Significant topics include identification procedures, characteristics, programs, and cultural issues (Sandel, McCallister, & Nash, 1993).

As indicated, one of the major obstacles to large-scale development of preschool programs for the gifted has been the concern that current measures lack reliability and validity in discriminating among children who are truly precocious, children of average ability who are early developers, and children of average ability whose high performance stems from an enriched environment. Another concern has been the efficacy of such measures in identifying gifted children who are "late bloomers." However, it has recently been argued that standardized intelligence measures truly differentiate between advanced and normal development at the preschool level (Silverman, 1986), and that giftedness should be conceptualized as significantly advanced development at the time of testing rather than as potential for adult achievement. Moreover, the imperfection of currently available measures should not preclude the delivery of services to children.

Because of concerns about reliability and validity of standardized measures when employed with young children, there is general consensus that multiple sources of data, formal and informal, should be used to identify gifted preschool-age children.

Karnes and Johnson (1986) list a number of formal instruments that have been used to assess the potential and current functioning of young gifted and talented children in intellectual, perceptual-motor, social, creative, self-concept, and musical areas. Commonly used formal measures for identifying gifted preschool-age children are the Stanford-Binet and Draw-a-Man for intelligence; the Peabody Individual Achievement Test and Woodcock-Johnson Psychoeducational Battery, Part II, for achievement; and Thinking Creatively in Action and Movement (Torrance, 1981) and the Structure of Intellect Learning Ability Tests, Primary Form (Meeker, 1984) for creativity and divergent thinking.

Informal data sources include parent and community nominations, teacher checklists, and child products (Karnes & Johnson, 1986). The Seattle Child Development Preschool Comprehensive Parent Questionnaire (Roedell, Jackson, & Robinson, 1980) provides an excellent source of data based on both parent perception and parent assessment of child performance. Pediatricians, artists, religious instructors, and other community members who are familiar with the child constitute valuable referral sources. Teacher checklists (Karnes et al., 1978a, 1978b) have been developed to assess young children's performance in a variety of talent areas. Finally, collections developed by the child as well as artistic, scientific, and other creative products provide useful assessment data.

Formal and informal data collected for each child being assessed may be reviewed by an identification/selection committee composed of professionals in gifted education, diagnostic specialists, parents, and community members. While not always possible or desirable, use of identification criteria consistent with criteria used by local school districts can facilitate children's transition to programs after preschool age.

Characteristics of young gifted children are most readily observable in comparison with other children of the same age, sex, and cultural group. Cognitively, young gifted children often display advanced vocabulary and general information, early interest in books and numbers, long attention spans, persistence and creativity in solving problems, vivid imaginations, broad or intense interests, metacognition (Moss & Strayer, 1990) unusual memory for detail, and an intense desire to know "why."

Many young gifted children also possess social-emotional characteristics such as preference for associating with older children, capacity for intense emotions, and a high level of empathy, traits that render them vulnerable to stress. Additionally, young gifted children may become frustrated by their uneven development, e.g., when their advanced thinking but average fine-motor coordination results in products that fail to meet their goals. Kitano (1985a) found characteristics of competitiveness and perfectionism in some children attending a preschool for the gifted. These socio-emotional vulnerabilities (Roedell, 1986) may become manifested in withdrawn, shy, aggressive, or attention-getting behaviors.

Program goals for gifted children in preschool settings derive from these children's cognitive, socio-emotional, and developmental characteristics and from the rationale underlying early identification: the need to provide challenge and stimulation. Goals include (1) developing a positive attitude toward oneself and toward learning; (2) developing positive social values and interaction skills, including prosocial attitudes, independence, responsibility, task commitment, and risk taking; (3) developing and using creative and higher level thinking skills; and (4) developing competency in basic skills (language, readiness, motor) and in general knowledge.

Many of the models employed in programs for elementary-age gifted children have been successfully applied to preschool-level programs. For example, programs at the University of Illinois, Champaign-Urbana (Karnes & Bertschi, 1978; Karnes, Shwedel, & Linnemeyer, 1982) have incorporated Structure-of-Intellect and open classroom models. The Hunter College (Camp, 1963) and New Mexico State University (Kitano & Kirby, 1986a, 1986b) programs involve children in unit-based curricula and independent projects. The Astor program (Ehrlich, 1980) focuses on the higher level skills of Bloom's (1956) taxonomy as well as on academic skills and creative investigation. Taylor's (1968) multiple talent approach and Renzulli's (1977) enrichment triad model have also been applied to programs for preschool-level gifted children.

Experience with gifted preschool-age children over the last several years raises a number of issues that must be considered in serving this population (Kitano, 1985b). Evaluation studies of individual preschool programs for the gifted (Karnes, Shwedel, & Lewis, 1983a, 1983b; Vantassel-Baska, Schuler, & Lipschutz, 1982) indicate that young gifted children make academic, social, and affective gains if given services designed to meet their needs. However, several questions pertinent to preschool programs for the gifted have yet to be answered: Should gifted children acquire skills at an early age just because they are able to? What are the long-term effects of early identification and early education for the gifted? Does early identification as gifted alter parent expectations for the child as well as the child's self-expectations? Does enriched preschool programming render later regular education experiences redundant?

Many gifted children enter preschool programs with academic skills and knowledge well above their chronological age expectancy levels. A major focus for these children might well be the encouragement of humanistic values and prosocial motivation. Some gifted children lose their previously acquired status as top achievers when they enter homogeneously grouped preschools for the gifted. Further research might explore the effects of early identification and early education on self-concept. Finally, it is clear that many gifted preschool-age children acquire new knowledge and skills at a rapid rate. Without stimulation and challenge, some will find their first school experiences to be alienating. It is critical that preschools for the gifted facilitate the continuation of enrichment programs beyond the preschool level.

REFERENCES

Bloom, B. S. (1956). *Taxonomy of educational objectives, the classification of educational goals—Handbook I: Cognitive domain.* New York: McKay.

Camp, L. T. (1963). Purposeful preschool education. *Gifted Child Quarterly, 7,* 106–107.

Ehrlich, V. Z. (1980). The Astor program for gifted children. In *Educating the preschool/primary gifted and talented* (pp. 248–250). Ventura, CA: Office of the Ventura County Superintendent of Schools.

Fox, A. E. (1971). Kindergarten: Forgotten year for the gifted? *Gifted Child Quarterly, 15,* 42–48.

Isaacs, A. F. (1963). Should the gifted preschool child be taught to read? *Gifted Child Quarterly, 7,* 72–77.

Karnes, M. B. (Ed.). (1983). *The underserved: Our young gifted children.* Reston, VA: Council for Exceptional Children.

Karnes, M. B. et al. (1978a). *Preschool talent checklists manual.* Urbana, IL: Institute for Child Development and Behavior, University of Illinois.

Karnes, M. B. et al. (1978b). *Preschool talent checklists record booklet.* Urbana, IL: Institute for Child Behavior and Development, University of Illinois.

Karnes, M. B., & Bertschi, J. D. (1978). Teaching the young gifted handicapped child. *Teaching Exceptional Children, 10*(4), 114–119.

Karnes, M. B., & Johnson, L. J. (1986). Identification and assessment of the gifted/talented handicapped and nonhandicapped children in early childhood. In J. R. Whitmore (Ed.), *Intellectual giftedness in young children: Recognition and development.* New York: Haworth.

Karnes, M. B., Shwedel, A. M., & Lewis, G. F. (1983a). Long-term effects of early programming for the gifted/talented handicapped. *Journal for the Education of the Gifted, 6*(4), 266–278.

Karnes, M. B., Shwedel, A. M., & Lewis, G. F. (1983b). Short-term effects of early programming for the young gifted handicapped child. *Exceptional Children, 50*(2), 103–109.

Karnes, M. B., Shwedel, A. M., & Linnemeyer, S. A. (1982). The young gifted/talented child: Programs at the University of Illinois. *Elementary School Journal, 82*(3), 195–213.

Kitano, M. K. (1985a). Ethnography of a preschool for the gifted: What gifted young children actually do. *Gifted Child Quarterly, 29*(2), 67–71.

Kitano, M. K. (1985b). Issues and problems in establishing preschool programs for the gifted. *Roeper Review, 7*(4), 212–213.

Kitano, M. K., & Kirby, D. F. (1986a). *Gifted education: A comprehensive view.* Boston: Little, Brown.

Kitano, M. K., & Kirby, D. F. (1986b). The unit approach to curriculum planning for the gifted. *G/C/T, 9*(2), 27–31.

Meeker, M. (1984). *The structure of intellect: Its interpretation and uses.* Los Angeles: Western Psychological Services.

Moss, E., & Strayer, F. F. (1990). Interactive problem-solving of gifted and non-gifted preschoolers with their mothers. *International Journal of Behavioral Development, 13*(2), 177–197.

Renzulli, J. S. (1977). *The enrichment triad model: A guide for developing defensible programs for the gifted and talented.* Wethersfield, CT: Creative Learning.

Roedell, W. C. (1986). Socioemotional vulnerabilities of young gifted children. In J. R. Whitmore (Ed.), *Intellectual giftedness in young children: Recognition and development.* New York: Haworth.

Roedell, W. C., Jackson, N. E., & Robinson, H. B. (1980). *Gifted young children.* New York: Teachers College Press.

Sandel, A., McCallister, C., & Nash, W. R. (1993). Child search and screening activities for preschool gifted children. *Roeper Review, 16*(2), 98–102.

Silverman, L. K. (in press). What happens to the gifted girl? In C. J. Maker (Ed.), *Critical issues in gifted education.* Rockville, MD: Aspen.

Taylor, C. W. (1968). Multiple talent approach. *The Instructor, 77*(8), 27, 142, 144, 146.

Torrance, E. P. (1981). *Thinking creatively in action and movement.* Bensenville, IL: Scholastic Testing Service.

Vantassel-Baska, J., Schuler, A., & Lipschutz, J. (1982). An experimental program for gifted four year olds. *Journal for the Education of the Gifted, 5*(1), 45–55.

Whitmore, J. R., (1979). The etiology of underachievement in highly gifted young children. *Journal for the Education of the Gifted, 3*(1), 38–51.

Whitmore, J. R. (1980). *Giftedness, conflict, and underachievement.* Boston: Allyn & Bacon.

Whitmore, J. R. (Ed.). (in press). *Intellectual giftedness in young children: Recognition and development.* New York: Haworth.

Margie K. Kitano
New Mexico State University

GIFTED CHILDREN
GIFTED CHILDREN, MINORITIES
GIFTED CHILDREN, UNDERACHIEVEMENT

PRESCHOOL ASSESSMENT

Preschool assessment has been conceptualized as a "continuous, general-to-specific process of defining functional capabilities and establishing treatment goals" (Bagnato & Neisworth, 1981, p. 7) for children between the ages of 3 and 6 years. Broadly conceived, the process is carried out for the purpose of determining eligibility for services, obtaining information for individual program development, and evaluating program effectiveness (Neisworth et al., 1980). With these as broadly based goals, preschool assessment encompasses screening procedures, but it also involves in-depth and comprehensive analyses of developmental strengths and weaknesses, the setting of instructional goals, and the evaluation of progress made by a child within a particular intervention plan.

To accomplish these purposes effectively, preschool assessment is comprised of multidimensional processes. It involves the synthesis of developmental information from multiple measures and sources and across multiple domains that include cognitive, social, language, motor, and adaptive behavior areas. The emphasis on multidimensionality is essential at the preschool level because of the lack of reliability of global scores and assessment devices for children undergoing rapid behavioral and developmental change.

Related to the concept of multidimensionality is the ecological validity of preschool assessment procedures. To be ecologically valid, the procedures must sample behavior and developmental skills as they are exhibited in a number of different environments at multiple points in time (Paget & Nagle, 1986). This emphasis implies that (1) a preschool child's functioning is assessed in an individual examining situation, as well as in the home, and when appropriate, in the classroom environment; (2) professionals who assess preschool-age children must be knowledgeable about a variety of assessment devices and be able to apply them adaptively in various situations to answer specific referral problems; (3) a multidisciplinary perspective on referral problems is necessary, both from legal and ethical vantage points; (4) such a perspective may produce incongruence among the results, which is important to correct interpretation; and (5) a longer time frame is needed than for assessment of older children to tap variations in performance at multiple points in time (Lidz, 1983; Paget, 1985). Moreover, ecologically valid assessment at the preschool level depends as much on nontest-based assessment as on test-based assessment (Barnett, 1984). Thus the results from norm-referenced and criterion-referenced instruments are important but must be supplemented by behavioral observation and interview procedures.

Norm-referenced preschool measures typically yield developmental age and standard scores that represent the child's most stable level of skill development (Bagnato & Neisworth, 1981). A profile of strengths and weaknesses across developmental domain areas is also provided by these instruments. The standard scores are sometimes termed IQ scores (e.g., from the Wechsler Preschool and Primary Scale of Intelligence and the Stanford-Binet), but they have also been given alternative designations (e.g., the Mental Processing Index from the Kaufman Assessment Battery for Children and the General Cognitive In-

dex from the McCarthy Scales of Children's Abilities). Regardless of the label used, the global standard scores are considered to represent a construct that is similar, yet different from, later IQ scores (McCarthy, 1972). Thus, the power of these instruments to predict later IQ and school achievement is an important practical and research issue that has encountered much debate (Bracken, 1994). Given this issue, all normative comparisons made at the preschool level must be made with an understanding of the influence of behavioral variation on the scores.

Criterion-referenced measures provide the opportunity for task analysis, or the specific breakdown of skills that precede or follow the skills from norm-referenced tests. Thus criterion-referenced tests are important to the identification of partially developed and emerging skills that characterize young, rapidly developing children (Barnett, 1984). This process of task analysis also lends itself to the identification of processes and strategies used by a child to solve problems and master skills. This procedure assists in the translation of assessment results to instructional strategies. Practical guidelines for the translation of results from criterion-referenced measures to intervention strategies are provided by Bagnato & Neisworth (1981).

Balancing formal testing procedures with informal "testing the limits" procedures and "test-teach-test" approaches is also essential at the preschool level. Advocates of this approach, termed dynamic assessment (Lidz, 1983) or adaptive-process assessment (Bagnato & Neisworth, 1982), suggest a flexible yet systematic method of evaluating upper and lower limits of the child's ability to complete tasks. In particular, they stress the need to modify activities in a structured manner to compensate for a particular impairment and to allow for alternative response modes. Thus, this less formal approach combines testing and teaching as part of a single diagnostic process. Applying these procedures after the administration of tests in a standardized format provides a basis for comparing a preschool child's performance under standardized and adapted conditions.

Naturalistic observations and interview procedures comprise the cornerstone of nontest-based preschool assessment and provide information on the environmental influences that impact a preschool-age child. The Social Assessment Manual for Preschool Level (SAMPLE) (Greenwood, Todd, Walker, & Hops, 1979) is an example of a structured observation instrument that guides observation in a preschool classroom setting. The Home Observation for Measurement of the Environment (HOME) (Caldwell & Bradley, 1978) is an instrument for home observation. Additionally, there are numerous developmental checklists that structure analyses of developmental concerns from teachers and parents (Linder, 1983). Such procedures are essential in revealing adults' perceptions of a child's development, their teaching and coping strategies, belief systems, goals, and caregiving skills (Barnett, 1984).

Given the complexity of the preschool assessment process, it is clear that determining eligibility and establishing instructional objectives involve much more than the administration of a standard battery with one measure as the prime integral component. Similarly, the limitations of traditional test scores in evaluating program effectiveness have been enumerated (Bracken, 1994; Keogh & Sheehan, 1981) and should be noted.

REFERENCES

Bagnato, S. J., & Neisworth, J. T. (1980). The Intervention Efficiency Index: An approach to preschool program accountability. *Exceptional Children, 46,* 264–271.

Bagnato, S. J., & Neisworth, J. T. (1981). *Linking developmental assessment and curricula.* Rockville, MD: Aspen Systems.

Barnett, D. W. (1984). An organizational approach to preschool services: Psychological screening, assessment, and intervention. In C. Maher, R. Illback, & J. Zins (Eds.), *Organizational psychology in the schools: A handbook for practitioners* (53–82). Springfield, IL: Thomas.

Bracken, B. A. (1994). Advocating for effective preschool assessment practices: A comment on Bagnato and Neisworth. *School Psychology Quarterly, 9*(2), 103–108.

Caldwell, B. W., & Bradley, R. H. (1978). *Home Observation for Measurement of the Environment.* Little Rock, AR: University of Arkansas.

Greenwood, C. R., Walker, H. M., Todd, N. M., & Hops, H. (1979). Selecting a cost-effective screening device for the assessment of preschool social withdrawal. *Journal of Applied Behavioral Analysis, 12,* 639–652.

Keogh, B., & Sheehan, R. (1981). The use of developmental test data for documenting handicapped children's progress: Problems and recommendations. *Journal of the Division for Early Childhood, 3,* 42–47.

Lidz, C. S. (1983). Dynamic assessment and the preschool child. *Journal of Psychoeducational Assessment, 1,* 59–72.

Linder, T. W. (1983). *Early childhood special education: Program developmental administration.* Baltimore, MD: Brookes.

McCarthy, D. (1972). *Manual for the McCarthy Scales of Children's Abilities.* New York: Psychological Corporation.

Neisworth, J. T., Willoughby-Herb, S., Bagnato, S. J., Cartwright, C. A., & Laub, K. W. (1980). *Individualized education for preschool exceptional children.* Germantown, MD: Aspen Systems.

Page, K. D. (1985). Preschool services in the schools: Issues and implications. *Special Services in the Schools, 2,* 3–25.

Paget, K. D., & Nagle, R. J. (1986). A conceptual model of preschool assessment. *School Psychology Review, 15,* 154–165 (See additional references on).

KATHLEEN D. PAGET
University of South Carolina

PRESCHOOL SCREENING
PRESCHOOL SPECIAL EDUCATION

PRESCHOOL SCREENING

Preschool screening is the evaluation of large groups of children 3 to 5 years of age with brief, low-cost procedures to identify those who may be at risk for later problems. It is based on the assumptions that early intervention should produce a significant positive effect on development, that children with developmental problems must be identified accurately as their problems are developing, and that early identification and intervention programs should be implemented without prohibitively high costs (Holland & Merrell, 1998; Lichtenstein & Ireton, 1984). While also used frequently in the field of medicine, screening in special education and related fields refers to the early identification of risk factors associated with later school achievement and social adjustment. Because of the complexity of outcomes from many early childhood health problems such as otitis media (Mandell & Johnson, 1984), screening approaches that draw from several disciplines are considered the most comprehensive (Elder & Magrab, 1980).

Historically, several movements and philosophies from various disciplines have been associated with preschool screening and have defined its methods and purposes. These movements include the early enrichment and compensatory education programs (e.g., Head Start); the Early and Periodic Screening, Diagnosis, and Treatment (EPSDT) program designed to focus on medically oriented services for children with developmental handicaps or neurological impairment; and the Education for All Handicapped Children Act (PL 94-142), which included "child find" provisions and mandated a broad range of special educational and related services for handicapped children in schools.

Preschool screening can be seen as a continuum of opportunities available any time in a child's early development. Within this larger conceptual context, procedures can be initiated before the child's birth, with the identification of mothers who possess characteristics linked with developmental or learning problems (e.g., genetic defects, maternal illness, high maternal age, exposure to drugs, toxins, and radiation, and poor maternal health or nutrition during pregnancy). Factors occurring at birth or shortly thereafter can also impact a child's later development. These include anoxia, birth injury, low birth weight, and physical or sensory defects. Because some infants with known risk factors show no early signs of disability, have mild impairments, or exhibit developmental delay falling within the boundaries of normal functioning, the establishment of registries for periodic rescreening has been suggested as a strategy for identifying and monitoring the progress of these hard-to-detect children (Lloyd, 1976).

Screening activities constitute the first stage of a longer assessment process. Other stages include readiness, diagnosis, instructional-related assessment, evaluation of the results of instruction, and program evaluation (Boehm & Sandberg, 1982). Screening is sometimes confused with readiness, which focuses on a child's preparedness to benefit from a specific academic program (Meisels, 1980). All stages of the assessment process comprise a sequence proceeding from general to specific, culminating with individualized programming and ongoing monitoring of the child's progress within the intervention program (Bagnato & Neisworth, 1981). As the first stage of this process, screening does not comprise diagnostic procedures leading to recommendations about instructional programming. Rather, it involves general decision making that differentiates children in need of further assessment. This must be done with the knowledge that most screening instruments do not meet the requirements of PL 94-142 for educational placement. When done with proper understanding of its major purpose and the limitations of screening instruments, screening can enhance a school's or district's ability to identify and serve handicapped preschoolers. If used to substitute for comprehensive individual examinations, it can lead to major errors in identification and educational programming (Reynolds & Clark, 1983).

Screening can be conceptualized as a process consisting of two components (Lichtenstein & Ireton, 1984). The first component, outreach, involves initial contact with parents, professionals, preschool centers, and community agencies to inform them about the services offered and to arrange for children to participate in the screening program. Other terms used to refer to this initial location of children are "child find" (Harbin, Danaher, & Derrick, 1994; Meisels, 1980), from the provisions of IDEA Part H, and "case finding" (Barnes, 1982; Harrington, 1984). The major goals are to locate a target population and to maximize attendance at the actual screenings. To these ends, it has been recommended (Zehrback, 1975) that outreach procedures emphasize the growth-related needs of all children instead of developmental impairments. Thus strong case finding and publicity efforts are essential so that services will be rendered to all families rather than only those families who have the sophistication to find out about them. (Crocker & Cushna, 1976).

An approach designed to maximize correct identification within the target population is mass screening. This refers to a program that has the goal of screening every child in the target population. Such a program serves an entire preschool population; hence, there is little stigma associated with parents' positive response to the offer of screening services. Selective screening, a variation of mass screening, provides services to particular demographic subgroups or geographic areas that have a large number of unidentified children with special needs.

The second component of the screening process consists of the assessment of those children found eligible, the synthesis of information, and the determination of need for further assessment. Generally, the structure of this component is based on: (1) the kinds of questions that need to be answered; (2) the types and severity of handicapping conditions to be assessed; (3) the ages of the children; and (4) the psychometric properties of available instruments (Harrington, 1984; Scott & Hogan, 1982). Specifically, screening activities should answer whether the child is delayed enough in one or more domains (cognitive, sensory, motor, social/emotional, speech, language) to be considered at risk and in need of further diagnosis. If so, the screening should provide direction regarding what types of diagnostic assessments are needed to confirm or refute the screening impressions (Horowitz, 1982). The handicapping conditions should have a prevalence rate high enough to justify screening large numbers of children but not so high that every child must receive a diagnostic evaluation. Also, instruments should be chosen that have been normed on the ages of children represented in the target population and that have good reliability and validity. The precision of screening instruments is not as crucial as that of diagnostic instruments because of the general nature of the decisions made from them. A review of various screening systems and instruments, their psychometric properties, and their usefulness is provided by Buros (1985), Harrington (1984), and Lichtenstein and Ireton (1984). Although group and individually administered instruments are reviewed in these sources, it should be realized that individual administration maximizes the validity of test results with preschool-age children (Reynolds & Clark, 1983).

With respect to the psychometric properties of screening instruments, reliability and validity are often reported in correlational terms. These correlations provide only an approximation of a measure's accuracy in assigning individuals for further assessment (Lichtenstein, 1981). Thus a more strongly recommended method of determining a screening instrument's psychometric adequacy is in terms of classificational outcomes. In this way, validity is measured by comparing the screening decision (whether or not to refer a child for further evaluation) with the child's actual status as determined by a criterion measure. This is called the hit rate method (Lichtenstein & Ireton, 1984) and provides a direct indication of the suitability of decisions from screening. The validity of an entire screening system rests on correct understanding of the problem to be identified (the base rate), the rate of referrals for further assessment (the referral rate), and the hit rate (the percentage of children identified as needing services).

Generally, screening outcomes can be organized into

screening positives (children regarded as high risk and referred for further assessment) and screening negatives (children regarded as low risk and not referred). For each child screened, four results are possible, based on the accuracy of the screening decision and the child's actual performance on criterion measures during a diagnostic evaluation. A child may be found to be in need of special services and referred by the screening procedures, or a child may be found to not need additional help. Given the possibility of error in screening decisions, however, a child may be referred by the screening procedure but not need special services (a false positive or overreferral error), or not referred but be in need of services (a false negative or underreferral error). To evaluate the consequences of using a given screening system, then, it must be determined whether children are referred at the rate intended, whether the right children are referred, and whether alternative procedures might accomplish the task more successfully. Other relevant issues are the appropriateness of the criterion measures used, the possibility of bias in the screening process (Reynolds & Clark, 1983), and strategies for maximizing parent involvement.

Given the long-held recognition that parents are vitally important in meeting the educational needs of their children, they should be involved in every phase of screening (Lichtenstein & Ireton, 1984). Not only is parent involvement mandated by IDEA, Part H but parents also constitute a rich source of information about specific aspects of their child's development that may be unavailable elsewhere. Parents can also make sure that the assessment of their child is culturally competent. The screening of environmental influences from home and classroom settings is a rapidly growing area of research and clinical attention (Adelman, 1982).

REFERENCES

Adelman, H. S. (1982). Identifying learning problems at an early age: A critical appraisal. *Journal of Clinical Child Psychology, 11,* 255–261.

Bagnato, S. J., & Neisworth, J. T. (1981). *Linking developmental assessment and curricula.* Rockville, MD: Aspen Systems.

Barnes, K. E. (1982). *Preschool screening: The measurement and prediction of children at-risk.* Springfield, IL: Thomas.

Boehm, A., & Sandberg, B. (1982). Assessment of the preschool child. In C. R. Reynolds & T. B. Gutkin (Eds.), *Handbook of school psychology* (82–120). New York: Wiley.

Buros, O. K. (Ed.). (1985). *The ninth mental measurements yearbook.* Highland Park, NJ: Gryphon.

Coons, C. E., Gay, E. C., Fandal, A. W., Ker, C., & Frankenburg, W. K. (1981). *The Home Screening Questionnaire.* Denver, CO: Ladoca.

Crocker, H. C., & Cushna, B. (1976). Ethical considerations and attitudes in the field of developmental disorders. In R. B. John-son & P. R. Magrab (Eds.), *Developmental disorders.* Baltimore, MD: University Park Press.

Elder, J. O., & Magrab, P. R. (1980). *Coordinating services to handicapped children.* Baltimore, MD: Brookes.

Frankenburg, W. K., van Doornick, W. J., Liddell, R. N., & Dick, N. P. (1976). The Denver Prescreening Developmental Questionnaire. *Pediatrics, 57,* 744–753.

Harbin, G., Danaher, J., & Derrick, T. (1994). Comparison of eligibility policies for infant/toddler programs and preschool special education programs. *Topics in Early Childhood Special Education, 14*(4), 455–471.

Harrington, R. (1984). Preschool screening: The school psychologist's perspective. *School Psychology Review, 13,* 363–374.

Holland, M. L., & Merrell, K. W. (1998). Social emotional characteristics of preschool-aged children referred for child find screening and assessment: A comparative study. *Research in Developmental Disabilities, 19*(2), 167–179.

Horowitz, F. D. (1982). Methods of assessment for high risk and handicapped infants. In C. T. Ramey & P. L. Trohanis (Eds.), *Finding and educating high risk and handicapped infants.* Baltimore, MD: University Park Press.

Lichtenstein, R. (1981). Comparative validity of two preschool screening tests: Correlational and classificational approaches. *Journal of Learning Disabilities, 14,* 68–73.

Lichtenstein, R., & Ireton, H. (1984). *Preschool screening.* Orlando, FL: Grune & Stratton.

Lloyd, L. L. (1976). Discussant's comments: Language and communication aspects. In T. D. Tjossem (Ed.), *Intervention strategies for high risk infants and children* (199–212). Baltimore, MD: University Park Press.

Mandell, C. J., & Johnson, R. A. (1984). Screening for otitis media: Issues and procedural recommendations. *Journal of the Division of Early Childhood, 8,* 86–93.

Meisels, S. J. (1980). *Developmental screening in early childhood: A guide.* Washington, DC: National Association for the Education of Young Children.

Reynolds, C. R., & Clark, J. (1983). Assessment of cognitive abilities. In K. D. Paget & B. A. Bracken (Eds.), *The psychoeducational assessment of preschool children* (163–189). New York: Grune & Stratton.

Scott, G., & Hogan, A. E. (1982). Methods for the identification of high-risk and handicapped infants. In C. T. Ramey & P. L. Trohanis (Eds.), *Finding and educating high-risk and handicapped infants.* Baltimore, MD: University Park Press.

Zehrback, R. R. (1975). Determining a preschool handicapped population. *Exceptional Children, 42,* 76–83.

KATHLEEN D. PAGET
J. MICHAEL COXE
University of South Carolina

HEAD START
HEAD START FOR THE HANDICAPPED
PRESCHOOL ASSESSMENT
PRESCHOOL SPECIAL EDUCATION

PRESCHOOL SPECIAL EDUCATION

Preschool special education is the delivery of therapeutic and educational services to handicapped infants and children from birth to age 6. These services are designed to provide optimum learning experiences during the crucial early childhood developmental period for children with a wide variety of handicapping conditions. The importance of the preschool years to future success has been documented by many child development authorities, who emphasize that the first 5 or 6 years of a child's life are the periods of highest potential growth in physical, perceptual, linguistic, cognitive, and affective areas (Lerner, Mardell-Czudnowski, & Goldenberg, 1981). These early periods of development are particularly important to the handicapped child, since the earlier that these children are identified and education begun, the greater the chances of lessening the impact of the handicapping condition on the child and society. A recent report by the House Select Committee on Children, Youth, and Families (1985) stated that for every dollar invested in preschool special education programs, there is a $3 reduction in special education cost later.

In 1968 Congress recognized the need for services and models of effective preschool special education programs, and the Handicapped Children's Early Education Assistance Programs (HCEEP; PL 90-583) was enacted. This act, sometimes known as the First Chance program, provided monies for the development and implementation of experimental projects for young handicapped children and their families. These projects developed effective programs for children, but they also were required to include parents in the activities, operate in-service training, evaluate the progress of both the children and the programs, coordinate their activities with the public schools and other agencies, and disseminate information on the projects (DeWeerd, 1977). Legislative support continues with IDEA Part H and Part B.

The Head Start movement, which began in 1964 as part of the War on Poverty and was funded by the Office of Economic Opportunity, was another reason for the growth of preschool special education programs. The goal of the Head Start program was to offer preschool children from economically deprived homes a comprehensive program to compensate for their deprivation. These programs involved medical care, nutrition, parent involvement, socialization, and educational intervention.

A further influence on preschool special education was the passage and implementation of PL 94-142, the Education for All Handicapped Children Act of 1975, which mandated services for all handicapped children from 3 to 5 years of age unless such a mandate conflicted with state law. This legislation provided the following two sources of funds for handicapped preschool children: state entitlement money, which depends on the number of handicapped children counted by the state in its child-find activities; and incentive grants, available to states with approved state plans that offer services for 3- to 5-year-old handicapped children (Lerner et al., 1981). Current issues of service provision under IDEA focus on eligibility continuity for children moving from early intervention programs under Part H to preschool special education programs under Part B of IDEA (Harbin, Danaher, & Derrick, 1994).

One of the important areas in preschool special education is the early identification of children with handicapping conditions. Attempts are being made to locate children who will need additional or special assistance in order to succeed in school because of physical, social, intellectual, emotional, or communications problems. The federal child-find program, which mandates states to actively seek out handicapped children, is one way to locate children who can benefit from early intervention services. Identifying children who should receive special services is a complex task because of the wide variety of needs and characteristics of the children (Lerner et al., 1981). Children with severe handicapping conditions are often identified at birth or shortly thereafter; however, many children with milder or less obvious handicaps are not so easily identified. Tjossem (1976) has presented three categories of high-risk infants. First, there are those at established risk; they have diagnosed medical disorders that are known to result in developmental delays. The early medical, social, and educational interventions used with these children are designed to help them function at the higher end of potential for those with their disorders. Second, children at biological risk have a history that suggests biological insults to their developing central nervous system. While early diagnosis is often inconclusive for these children, close monitoring and modified care are important during the developmental years. Third, children at environmental risk are those who are biologically sound, but who have early life experiences, that, without intervention, have high probability for resulting in delayed development. These early experiences could include problems with maternal and family care, health care, and opportunities for expression and stimulation. These three categories are not mutually exclusive, and when they interact, they increase the probability of abnormal development.

Being identified and placed into preschool intervention programs is a difficult process for many handicapped young children. However, for early intervention to be effective, provisions must be made for early identification and rapid entrance into community preschool special education programs (Tjossem, 1976). This identification process begins with both medical and educational screening to locate children at high risk for developmental and learning problems. Three comprehensive screening tests used in this process are the Denver Developmental Screening Test,

Developmental Indicators for the Assessment of Learning, and the Developmental Screening Inventory. Once these children have been identified, the next step, a comprehensive diagnostic assessment, can be done to pinpoint a child's particular skills and deficits. The purpose of this assessment should be to prepare appropriate intervention programs. It is critical to match the assessment techniques to the needs of the individual child (Hayden & Edgar, 1977). Two criterion referenced tests that can be used for diagnosis and program planning for many children with handicaps, in many curriculum areas, are the Brigance Diagnostic Inventory of Early Development and the Learning Accomplishment Profile Diagnostic Assessment Kit. Detailed descriptions of screening instruments and diagnostic tests can be found in Lerner et al. (1981), Fallen and McGovern (1978), Safford (1978), and Salvia and Ysseldyke (1985). This assessment of handicapped children requires the expertise of many professionals and needs to be a team effort.

Identifying, screening, and assessing handicapped preschool children are meaningless tasks unless appropriate services are then provided to them (Hobbs, 1975). Once the child has been identified and diagnostic information is complete, then an appropriate program plan and curriculum must be developed. There are many different program delivery models that can be used, as well as a wide variety of philosophical bases for the programs.

Preschool special education programs have evolved from many varied theoretical positions, ranging from a child development model to precision teaching and systematic instruction. These approaches may be used with different populations, or in different environments, but they have all been shown to be beneficial. The child development model is mainly an enrichment model that provides multiple activity centers such as often found in many regular preschool programs. This is the model that many Head Start programs follow, and it is most successful with children with mild handicapping conditions. The sensory-cognitive model is based on the work of Maria Montessori. It emphasizes materials designed for the child's developmental level; these materials are presented in a carefully constructed environment. Other programs are based on the verbal-cognitive model, which draws heavily from the developmental theory of Piaget and stresses structured teacher-child interactions. A more formal approach was proposed by Bereiter and Englemann in their verbal-didactic model; this approach attempts to raise each child to the essential level for success in first grade by frequent repetition of teacher-child responses accompanied by the principles of reinforcement (Ackerman & Moore, 1976). Severely handicapped children often benefit from highly structured systematic instruction programs that rely on detailed task analysis and behavioral theory.

Other factors to be considered include the type of handicapping condition, the age of the child, and the geograph-

ical area to be served. Some programs are noncategorical and serve children from a wide variety of handicapping conditions; the Portage Project and the Rutland Center are examples. Other programs specialize in serving children from limited categories or even subcategories of handicapping conditions. One of the best known programs of this type is the Seattle Model Preschool Center for children with Down's syndrome.

The age of the child often affects where the educational services are delivered; since it is difficult to transport infants for long distances, many of the programs for younger children are home-based, with the teacher traveling to the students. As the child becomes older, programs may be center-based, with the child attending a school program or a combination of home and school program. Another factor that affects where programs are delivered is the geographic region. Sparsely populated rural regions may not have sufficient numbers of children within a reasonable distance of a school; therefore, they may rely on more home-based services than might be found in large urban areas. Examples of home-based projects are the Portage project, the Marshalltown project, and Project SKI*HI; the Precise Early Education of Children with Handicaps (PEECH) project, the Chapel Hill project, and the Magnolia Preschool are all combined home- and center-based programs. Center-based programs include the Rutland Center, the Seattle Model Preschool Center, and the UNISTAPS project. These programs were all originally supported by HCEEP funding and are representative of many programs across the United States (Karnes & Zehrbach, 1977).

The actual curriculum content in preschool special education programs varies depending on the needs of the children; however, in most cases, the programs are based on one or more of the following approaches. Some preschool special education curricula are organized around an amelioration of deficits approach, which builds the curriculum based on an assessment of a child's problems; the content areas are directed toward correcting identified deficits. Other programs use a basic skills area approach. In this, curricula are organized around skills or processes such as attention, language, sensory motor processes, social skills, perception, auditory processes, gross and fine motor skills, self-help skills, and memory. The developmental tasks approach uses sequences of normal development to derive the curricula. The content areas in this approach are broad categories of child development that are task analyzed and sequenced. Finally, the educational content approach begins with areas of academic content; it defines areas of learning on the basis of preacademic or academic content. The most often included areas are prereading, numbers, music, art, dance, play, storytelling, social studies, and nature. In many cases these various approaches are combined to develop appropriate educational programs (Wood & Hurley, 1977).

A crucial component to any preschool special education program is parent involvement. As stated by Shearer & Shearer (1977), there are several reasons to involve parents in their child's education. The parents are the consumers and often want to participate in the education of their children. When parents are taught how to teach their children, they can help transfer what is being learned in school to the home environment. These teaching skills can also be used in new situations, and with the handicapped child's siblings, making the parents better teachers of all their children. Research has shown that significant gains made by children are often lost when the school programs end. A key factor in preventing this is the effective involvement of parents. In addition, if parents are knowledgeable about their child's program, they can be advocates for the services that the child needs; this skill can be used all through the child's life.

Recent research studies have demonstrated the effectiveness of preschool special education programs for handicapped young children. Karnes et al. (1981) presented a review of many studies that examined the efficacy of preschool special education. While there are some methodological questions about early studies by Skeels and Dye, the research, in general, has shown that early stimulation and preschool attendance make a significant difference in the rate of growth of children, and that these gains are maintained over time. It has been shown that diverse curriculum models can be equally effective in promoting school success if high standards of quality are maintained (Schweinhart & Weikart, 1981). In addition, inclusive programming for there children is being heavily supported (Cavallaro, Ballard-Rosa, & Lynch, 1998; Holland, Guitierrez, Morgan, Brennan, & Zercher, 1997).

A longitudinal study of the Perry Preschool Program (Schweinhart & Weikart, 1981) has provided a strong argument for preschool special education programs. This study followed 123 children from age three through the school years. It found that those children who attended preschool had consistently higher school achievement, higher motivation, fewer placements in special education programs, and less delinquent behavior. An economic benefit-cost effectiveness analysis of the Perry Preschool Program was conducted; it found that there was a 248% return on the original investment when savings from lowered costs for education, benefits from increases in projected earnings, and value of mothers' time released when the child attended preschool were considered.

There are many reports of successful preschool special education programs. While many of these programs differ greatly in the populations they serve, their theoretical bases, and their curriculum content, their effectiveness has been demonstrated. It is essential that these benefits be recognized, and that programs for all handicapped preschool children be supported.

REFERENCES

Ackerman, P., & Moore, M. (1976). Delivery of educational services to preschool handicapped children. In T. Tjossem (Ed.), *Intervention strategies for high risk infants and young children* (pp. 669–689). Baltimore, MD: University Park Press.

Cavallaro, C. C., Ballard-Rosa, & Lynch, E. W. (1998). A preliminary study of inclusive special education services for infants, toddlers, and pre-school children in California. *Topics in Early Childhood Special Education, 18*(3), 169–182.

DeWeerd, J. (1977). Introduction. In J. Jordan, A. Hayden, M. Karnes, & M. Wood (Eds.), *Early childhood education for exceptional children* (pp. 2–7). Reston, VA: Council for Exceptional Children.

Fallen, N., & McGovern, J. (1978). *Young children with special needs.* Columbus, OH: Merrill.

Hanson, M. J., Guitierrez, S., Morgan, M., Brennan, E. L., & Zercher, C. (1997). Language, culture, & disability: Preschool inclusion. *Topics in Early Childhood Special Education, 17*(3), 307–336.

Hayden, A. (1979). Handicapped children, birth to age three. *Exceptional Children, 45,* 510–517.

Hayden, A., & Edgar, E. (1977). Identification, screening, and assessment. In J. Jordan, A. Hayden, M. Karnes, & M. Wood (Eds.), *Early childhood education for exceptional children* (pp. 66–93). Reston, VA: Council for Exceptional Children.

Hayden, A., & Gotts, E. (1977). Multiple staffing patterns. In J. Jordan, A. Hayden, M. Karnes, & M. Wood (Eds.), *Early childhood education for exceptional children* (pp. 236–253). Reston, VA: Council for Exceptional Children.

Harbin, G., Danaher, J., & Derrick, T. (1994). Comparison of eligibility policies for infant/toddler programs and preschool special education programs. *Topics in Early Childhood Special Education, 14*(4), 455–471.

Hobbs, N. (1975). *The futures of children.* San Francisco: Jossey-Bass.

Karnes, M., Schwedel, A., Lewis, G., & Esry, D. (1981). Impact of early programming for the handicapped: A follow-up study into the elementary school. *Journal of the Division for Early Childhood, 4,* 62–79.

Karnes, M., & Zehrbach, R. (1977). Alternative models for delivering services to young handicapped children. In J. Jordan, A. Hayden, M. Karnes, & M. Wood (Eds.), *Early childhood education for exceptional children* (pp. 20–65). Reston, VA: Council for Exceptional Children.

Lerner, J., Mardell-Czudnowski, C., & Goldenberg, D. (1981). *Special education for the early childhood years.* Englewood Cliffs, NJ: Prentice-Hall.

Safford, P. (1978). *Teaching young children with special needs.* St. Louis: Mosby.

Salvia, J., & Ysseldyke, J. (1985). *Assessment in special and remedial education* (3rd ed.). Boston: Houghton Mifflin.

Schweinhart, L., & Weikart, D. (1981). Effects of the Perry Preschool Program on youths through age 15. *Journal of the Division for Early Childhood, 4,* 29–39.

Select Committee on Children, Youth, and Families. (1985). *Op-*

portunities for success: Cost effective programs for children. Washington, DC: U.S. Government Printing Office.

Shearer, M., & Shearer, D. (1977). Parent involvement. In J. Jordan, A. Hayden, M. Karnes, & M. Wood (Eds.), *Early childhood education for exceptional children* (pp. 208–235). Reston, VA: Council for Exceptional Children.

Swan, W. (1981). Efficacy studies in early childhood special education: An overview. *Journal of the Division for Early Childhood, 4,* 1–4.

Tjossem, T. (1976). Early intervention: Issues and approaches. In T. Tjossem (Ed.), *Intervention strategies for high risk infants and young children* (pp. 3–33). Baltimore, MD: University Park Press.

Wood, M., & Hurley, O. (1977). Curriculum and instruction. In J. Jordan, A. Hayden, M. Karnes, & M. Wood (Eds.), *Early childhood education for exceptional children* (pp. 132–157). Reston: VA: Council for Exceptional Children.

DEBORAH C. MAY
State University of New York at Albany

PRESCHOOL ASSESSMENT
PRESCHOOL SCREENING

PRESIDENT'S COMMITTEE ON MENTAL RETARDATION (PCMR)

The President's Committee on Mental Retardation (PCMR) was formally established in 1966 to focus on mental retardation. The mission of the PCMR is to act in an advisory capacity to the President and the Secretary of Health and Human Services on matters relating to policy and programs affecting services and supports for people with mental retardation.

Since 1974, the committee has organized national planning; stimulated the development of plans, policies, and programs; and advanced the concept of community inclusion and participation for individuals with mental retardation. Several national goals have been adopted by the committee. These goals recognize and uphold the right of all people with mental retardation to create for themselves a life that reflects independence, self-determination, and participation as productive members of society. They include the assurance of full citizenship rights of people with mental retardation, the provision of all necessary supports to individuals and their families, the reduction of the occurrence and severity of mental retardation, and the promotion of the widest possible dissemination of information on policies, programs, and service models that foster independence, self-determination, and social and economic participation.

The PCMR is comprised of 21 citizen members appointed by the President, and six public members including the Secretaries of Health and Human Services, Housing and Urban Development, Labor, and Education; the Attorney General; and the President and CEO of the Corporation for National and Community Service. The committee meets quarterly and has established the following five subcommittees to support its mission: Federal Policy, Federal Research and Demonstration, State Policy Collaboration, Minority and Cultural Diversity Issues, and Mission and Public Awareness.

PCMR recognizes the key role of frontline workers in successful community inclusion for people with mental retardation as well as the critical need to empower and enhance direct support workers. *Opportunities for Excellence: Supporting the Frontline Workforce,* a major resource publication for state and agency policymakers, was produced by the committee as a result of this focus.

PCMR conducts forums and publishes numerous materials addressing the field of mental retardation and the needs, interests, concerns, and quality of life experienced by citizens with mental retardation. These publications include *Collaborating for Inclusion: 1995 Report to the President,* addressing the need for collaborative efforts among policymakers on all government levels, people with mental retardation, families, service providers, and advocacy organizations; and *Putting People First* (1994), presenting a new vision for people with mental retardation in the areas of healthcare, welfare, long-term care, housing, education, and employment. Additional information and single copies of publications may be obtained at no cost by contacting the U.S. Department of Health and Human Services at (202) 619-0634, (202) 205-9519 (fax), or *tlion@acf.dhhs.gov* (e-mail).

REFERENCE

President's Committee On Mental Retardation. (1997). *Voices and visions: Building leadership for the 21st century.* (DHHS Publication No. 520-562/90153). Washington, DC: U.S. Government Printing Office.

TAMARA J. MARTIN
The University of Texas of the Permian Basin

MENTAL RETARDATION

PREVENTION, PRIMARY

This term refers to efforts made to reduce the incidence or prevalence of handicapping conditions through the establishment of medical and social programs that attempt to change those conditions responsible for their development.

During the past 30 years, several approaches have been emphasized that have resulted in significant progress in the prevention of handicapping conditions.

A number of programs have been developed to provide neonatal care for those children delivered at risk. Some of these programs have been effective in reducing various postnatal factors that result in retardation. For example, infant stimulation programs have been established in hospitals to facilitate the development of low-birth-weight or high-risk infants (Brown & Hepler, 1976). These programs use such measures as involving mothers in infant stimulation techniques, making infants in incubators more attractive to staff who interact with them by placing ribbons on them, and providing intensive follow-up services to both mothers and infants. These programs have been brief and the results somewhat time-limited, but they have resulted in increased attention to opportunities for preventive intervention models.

It is widely recognized that a small proportion of children are mentally retarded because of organic causes; the majority are retarded because of environmental and cultural deficiencies, poverty, and inadequate child-rearing approaches (Grossman, 1983). Massive social changes that address these causes must occur to achieve comprehensive prevention of mental retardation and other handicapping conditions.

The President's Committee on Mental Retardation set a goal of preventing the occurrence of 50% of all cases of mental retardation by the year 2000 (President's Committee on Mental Retardation, 1976). As a result, research has been done on virtually all known causes of mental retardation. Patton, Payne, and Beirne-Smith (1986) indicate that for each cause, a specific preventive measure has been found. The most fruitful approaches to prevention include carrier detection, prenatal monitoring, and newborn screening. Combinations of these approaches appear to be more successful in preventing various handicapping conditions than the use of individual techniques (Sells & Bennett, 1977). Prevention is often approached within the framework of determining cause. The major causes appear to result from infections and intoxications, trauma or physical agents, disorders of metabolism and nutrition, gross brain disease, unknown prenatal influence, and chromosomal abnormalities (Grossman, 1983).

Preventive measures implemented during the preconception period can significantly reduce hereditary, innate, congenital, and other constitutional disorders. Adequate prenatal care and analysis for possible genetic disorders are two general approaches to prevention usually associated with the gestational period. Yet one out of every four women who gives birth in a hospital has never received prenatal care from a physician during her pregnancy (Koch & Koch, 1976). Anticipating potential problems that may occur at delivery can avert problems during the perinatal period. For example, anoxia (lack of oxygen to the brain that may cause mental retardation and other learning problems) is a condition that can be prevented (Kirk & Gallagher, 1979).

Environmental intervention, adequate nutrition, and avoidance of hazards constitute the bulk of preventive measures during the childhood period. For example, a high correlation between ingestion of lead in drinking water and mental retardation has been reported (Gearheart, 1980; Needleman, 1994).

Blood-screening techniques can be used to identify some conditions (e.g., Tay-Sachs disease) transmitted through autosomal recessive genes or x-linked genes. Using several screening procedures, Thoene et al. (1981) identified seven metabolic disorders caused by an enzyme deficiency. Because of the low incidence rate of most conditions, carriers are so rare that general screening procedures would have to involve massive numbers of people to be effective (Westling, 1986). Thus genetic screening is most often used by those who have already had one child with a disorder or who are aware that the condition exists in their family.

Monitoring the fetus prior to birth has resulted in the identification of over 100 inherited disorders (Sells & Bennett, 1977). Amniocentesis (drawing some of the amniotic fluid surrounding the fetus for cellular examination) is used to detect three types of problems: those identified through the chromosomal structure, those identified through enzyme deficiencies, and neural tube defects. Milunsky (1976) indicated that women who are over 35, couples in which one parent is a balanced carrier of translocation, and couples who have already had one Down's syndrome child are the three groups that most frequently seek chromosomal analysis through amniocentesis. The use of fetoscopy permits the physician to insert a small tube through the mother's abdominal wall to examine parts of the fetus. This permits the determination of physical characteristics that may be useful in determining whether a disorder exists. Senography consists of the use of ultrasound waves to outline the fetus and identify structures indicative of handicapping conditions (e.g., spina bifada, microcephaly) through different densities. Rh incompatibility may be prevented through Rh gamma gloubulin injections for the Rh-negative mother after the birth of her first Rh-positive child or after a miscarriage.

Newborn screening tests permit the identification of many infants with inborn errors of metabolism (e.g., galactosemia, phenylketonuria). In some cases, mental retardation may be prevented by altering the diet (Carpenter, 1975). Hypothyroidism can also be detected through birth screening using the same blood samples used with phenylketonuria (Dussualt et al., 1975). Since some diagnostic indicators develop slowly during the first 6 months, the newborn screening should be followed with additional testing during later infant examinations.

Avoidance of certain substances (e.g., drugs, alcohol, X-rays) is the only current source of prevention for some disorders. Avoidance behavior can sometimes be the only method of prevention, as in the case of HIV/AIDS (Kelly, Murphy, Sikkema, & Kalichman, 1993). Preconceptual vaccinations can fight some bacterial infections (e.g., rubella, syphilis). Yet it has been estimated that 25% of children, older girls, and young women in the United States are not protected against rubella (Gearheart, 1980). A Caesarean-section birth may be used with women who have a herpes virus at the time of delivery. Postnatal causes that can often be prevented include direct trauma to the head, cerebral hemorrhage, lesions on the brain, infections that cause conditions such as encephalitis and meningitis, and electric shock. Although controversy still surrounds the role that chronic malnutrition plays in mental development, there is evidence that it can result in a greater risk of infection and increased likelihood of disease from other agents (Westling, 1986).

REFERENCES

Brown, J., & Hepler, R. (1976). Care of the critically ill newborn. *American Journal of Nursing, 76*, 578–581.

Carpenter, D. G. (1975). Metabolic and transport anomalies. In C. H. Carter (Ed.), *Handbook of mental retardation syndromes* (3rd ed.). Springfield, IL: Thomas.

Dussault, H. H., Coulombe, P., Laberge, C., Letarte, J., Guyda, H., Khoury, K. (1975). Preliminary report on a mass screening program for neonatal hypothyroidism. *Journal of Pediatrics, 86,* 670–674.

Gearheart, B. R. (1980). *Special education for the 80s.* St. Louis: Mosby.

Grossman, H. J. (1983). *Classification in mental retardation.* Washington, DC: American Association on Mental Deficiency.

Kelly, J. A., Murphy, D. A., Sikkema, K. J., & Kalichman, S. C., (1993). Psychological interventions to prevent HIV infection: New priorities for behavioral research in the second decade of AIDS. *American Psychologist, 48*(10), 1023–1034.

Kirk, S. A., & Gallagher, J. J. (1979). *Educating exceptional children* (3rd ed.). Dallas: Houghton Mifflin.

Koch, R., & Koch, J. H. (1976). We can do more to prevent the tragedy of retarded children. *Psychology Today, 107*, 88–93.

Milunsky, A. (1976). A prenatal diagnosis of genetic disorders. *New England Journal of Medicine, 295*, 377–380.

Needleman, H. L. (1994). Preventing childhood lead poisoning. *Preventative Medicine, 23*(5), 634–637.

Patton, J. R., Payne, J. S., & Beirne-Smith, M. (1986). *Mental retardation* (2nd ed.). London: Merrill.

President's Committee on Mental Retardation. (1976). *Mental retardation: The known and the unknown.* Washington, DC: U.S. Government Printing Office.

Sells, C. J., & Bennett, F. C. (1977). Prevention of mental retardation: The role of medicine. *American Journal of Mental Deficiency, 82*, 117–129.

Thoene, J., Higgins, J., Krieger, I., Schmickel, R., & Weiss, L. (1981). Genetic screening for mental retardation in Michigan. *American Journal of Mental Deficiency, 85,* 335–340.

Westling, D. L. (1986). *Introduction to mental retardation.* Englewood Cliffs, NJ: Prentice-Hall.

LONNY W. MORROW
*Northeast Missouri State
University*

SUE ANN MORROW
EDGE, Inc.

**GENETIC COUNSELING
INBORN ERRORS OF METABOLISM
PHENYLKETONURIA
PREMATURITY/PRETERM**

PREVOCATIONAL SKILLS

Secondary handicapped students may have difficulty in learning vocational concepts because they have not mastered prerequisite basic skills that serve as the foundation for many vocational activities. Three areas closely related to vocational skills are reading skills such as vocabulary, comprehension, and the use of a glossary; mathematic skills such as time, measurement, and application of algorithms; communication skills, including listening, speaking, and writing.

Essential to learning vocational skills is a set of hands-on exploratory experiences that will help each individual to answer self-awareness questions and develop work values. Examples of hands-on experiences include setting up a printing press, practicing laboratory safety, and following directions. These prevocational hands-on activities help students to identify materials, tools, and processes, discover physical properties of materials, measure sizes and quantities, compute costs, and develop social skills (Phelps & Lutz, 1977).

A student's success in a vocational program is influenced by his or her readiness to participate. Readiness skills are often identified as prevocational knowledge and attitudes. Brolin and Kokaska (1979) identified three curriculum areas with 22 major competencies. The areas and skills are (1) daily living (i.e., managing family finances, caring for personal needs, and engaging in civic activities); (2) personal-social abilities (i.e., interpersonal relationships, problem solving, independence); (3) occupational guidance and preparation (i.e., knowing and exploring occupational possibilities, work habits, and behaviors; being able to seek, secure, and maintain satisfactory employment).

Several factors can be considered predictors of vocational development for handicapped individuals. These include achievement of basic academic skills, adaptive behavior, verbal manners and communication skills, performance on vocational checklists, and actual samples of work behavior (Forness, 1982). A closer look at these predictors indicates that assessing a handicapped individual's vocational potential be evaluating his or her academic and social skills within the context of a work-related situation is valuable. Skills learned in a classroom setting may not generalize when applied to work settings. One step toward achieving generalization of academic skills is to develop a technique to assess applied academic and social skills. Neff (1966) suggested four approaches to the evaluation of the work potential of handicapped individuals. They are the mental testing approach, the job analysis approach, the work sample approach, and the situational assessment approach.

REFERENCES

Brolin, D. E., & Kokaska, C. J. (1979). *Career education for handicapped children and youth*. Columbus, OH: Merrill.

Forness, S. R. (1982). Prevocational academic assessment of children and youth with learning and behavior problems. In K. P. Lynch, W. E. Kiernan, & J. A. Stark (Eds.), *Prevocational and vocational education for special needs youth*. Baltimore, MD: Brooks.

Neff, W. S. (1966). Problems of work evaluation. *Personnel and Guidance Journal of Mental Deficiency, 44*, 682–688.

Phelps, A. L., & Lutz, R. J. (1977). *Career exploration and preparation for the special needs learner*. Boston: Allyn & Bacon.

KAREN L. HARRELL
University of Georgia

VOCATIONAL EVALUATION
VOCATIONAL REHABILITATION
VOCATIONAL TRAINING OF THE HANDICAPPED

PRIMARY IMMUNODEFICIENCY DISORDERS

This classification of health-related disorders encompasses over fifty distinct, genetically determined illnesses and does not include HIV, AIDS, or secondary causes such as chemotherapy. The incidence of these disorders range from 1 in 500 to 1 in 1,000,000, with approximately 25,000 patients identified in the U.S. at the time of this submission. As the title suggests, these disorders affect the immune system, and though most are congenital (patients are born with them), symptoms may not become apparent until adulthood.

Perhaps the most famous case of primary immunodeficiency disorders involved David, "the bubble boy" in Houston, Texas. His particular type of disorder involved several different parts of his immune system, causing severe susceptibility to infections from all viruses and bacteria. David lived 12 courageous years inside a sterile environment. Though the immune system disorders were first recognized in the mid 1950s, David's ordeal advanced our understanding of immune deficiencies, autoimmune disorders, cancer, and infection process in general.

As with David, children and adults with primary immunodeficiency disorders are susceptible to infectious diseases. Some experience chronic, recurrent, unusual, invasive, or severe infections, and have multiple concurrent conditions before the immune system is evaluated. Some of these disorders are treatable by replacing the portions of the immune system that is missing. An example would be intravenous gamma globulin (IVIG; a product containing antibodies from pooled human plasma donations) for patients with X-linked aggamaglobulinanemia or Common Variable Immunodeficiency. Patients with one particular disorder were the first to undergo "gene therapy," in which affected cells were removed and DNA containing the normal genes was inserted. When these cells were reintroduced to the patient, the symptoms of their disorder were relieved, allowing a decrease in reliance on costly, complicated medical therapies. Similar to David's story, these patients have contributed to a very promising new field of study that may help most genetically determined illnesses (i.e. cystic fibrosis, sickle cell anemia, and so on).

Due to the chronic nature of these disorders and their sequelae, many of those affected alter their lifestyle to preserve their health. Most patients and family members quickly become experts in their particular disease and must be accepted as such in order to create the most "normal" lifestyle possible. The most common obstacles to overcome are those associated with absences from work or school. Absences may frequently occur due to illnesses or the need for doctor visits and therapy. Anticipation of this need allows for unique, innovative solutions. Homebound programs and dual enrollment options provide the flexibility needed to adapt to this unusual situation. As always, open communication between school officials, families, physicians, and students is required. Often, the school setting provides the opportunity for affected children to become more responsible for their own health care. Public education, though it results in increased infection exposure, is usually well tolerated by patients whose immune systems are being reconstituted. Outbreak of any infectious diseases (such as measles, chicken pox, hepatitis A, or influenza) should result in immediate notification of patients so that physicians can decide on the appropriate course of action.

Other special needs may be required on an individual basis, not as a direct result of the immune disorders but due to the sequelae of repeated infections. Some examples include special diets, frequent meals or special restroom privileges due to intestinal malabsorption, hall passes or scheduled nursing visits for medication administration, or assignment of classes to minimize absences.

Physicians, patients, and families should be flexible to work within the school system when possible, scheduling routine care around important times and dates; however, they must also rely on the patience, compassion, and understanding of others in their lives to reach the goals set by the patients themselves. Further information and support can be obtained from the Immune Deficiency Foundation at 25 West Chesapeake Avenue, Suite 206, Towson, MD, 21204.

REFERENCE

Immune Deficiency Foundation. (1998). *Informational brochure.* Towson, MD: Author.

STEPHEN E. MILES
Immune Deficiency Foundation

SUSIE WHITMAN
Immune Deficiency Foundation

CHRONIC ILLNESS
NATIONAL ORGANIZATION OF RARE DISORDERS (NORD)
OFFICE OF RARE DISEASES
OTHER HEALTH IMPAIRED

PRIMARY MENTAL ABILITIES TEST (PMA)

The Primary Mental Abilities Test (PMA; Thurstone & Thurstone, 1965) is a group-administered measure of both general intelligence and specific intellectual factors that the authors call primary mental abilities. In earlier versions of the PMA, six to eight primary mental abilities were identified. Subsequently, this number was reduced to the current five factors. There are six levels of the test (K–1, 2–4, 4–6, 6–9, 9–12, and adult). The adult test is identical to that for grades 9–12. No attempt was made to prepare adult norms, and no additional psychometric characteristics at the adult level are included in the documentation.

A description of the behaviors sampled by the five subtests of the PMA is provided by Salvia and Ysseldyke (1978). Verbal meaning assesses one's ability to derive meaning from words. Number facility assesses one's ability to work with numbers, to handle simple quantitative problems rapidly and accurately, and to understand and recognize quantitative differences. Reasoning requires a person to solve problems logically. Perceptual speed assesses quick and accurate recognition of similarities and differences in pictured objects or symbols. Spatial rela-

tionships assesses ability to visualize how parts of objects or figures fit together, what their relationships are, and what they look like when rotated in space. The presence of and emphasis given to each of the specific intellectual factors within the various levels reflect the judgment of the authors as to their relative importance within each grade level. Only one level (grades 4–6) includes all five factors; perceptual speed is omitted from levels 6–9 and 9–12 and reasoning is omitted from K–1 and 2–4.

The test has several technical limitations. Standardization of the scale was based only on geographic, age, and grade stratification; reliabilities of the subtests are not included for K–1 and are relatively low for the other levels (Salvia & Ysseldyke, 1978). The test-retest reliability estimates for total scores range between .83 and .95 and may be deemed satisfactory, while the reliability estimates for the levels vary considerably from one grade to another and frequently are too low to be used with confidence (Quereshi, 1972). As expected, the total score is superior to any of the subtest/factor scores in predicting grades in separate school subject areas (Milholland, 1965). The PMA was developed using techniques to demonstrate that there are several factors involved in intelligence and learning. Yet, the total score is superior to single factors in predicting achievement in any one subject area. This contradicts the theoretical underpinnings of the test itself.

Historically, the PMA occupied a prominent position in the development of cognitive tests. The original series, published between 1938 and 1941, was based on extensive factor analytic work and represented a major contribution to test construction. The high aspirations held for the PMA battery reflected in early reviews were never realized (Schutz, 1972). While the Thurstones continued to contribute to both multifactor science and technology after the PMA was commercially available, very little of this new knowledge and technology found its way back into subsequent PMA revisions. Thus the PMA soon became outstripped by competing tests in terms of technical quality and functional utility. Because of the technical superiority of other instruments assessing similar abilities, reviewers have questioned the continued use of the PMA (Quereshi, 1972; Schutz, 1972).

REFERENCES

Milholland, J. E. (1965). SRA Primary Mental Abilities, Revised. In O. K. Buros (Ed.), *The sixth mental measurements yearbook* (pp. 1048–1050). Highland Park, NJ: Gryphon.

Quereshi, M. Y. (1972). SRA Primary Mental Abilities (1962 ed.). In O. K. Buros (Ed.), *The seventh mental measurements yearbook* (pp. 1064–1066). Highland Park, NJ: Gryphon.

Salvia, J., & Ysseldyke, J. E. (1978). *Assessment in special and remedial education* (pp. 293–295). Boston: Houghton Mifflin.

Schutz, R. E. (1972). SRA Primary Mental Abilities (1962 ed.). In O. K. Buros (Ed.), *The seventh mental measurements yearbook* (pp. 1066–1068). Highland Park, NJ: Gryphon.

Thurstone, L., & Thurstone, T. (1965). *Primary Mental Abilities Test*. Chicago: Science Research.

JEFF LAURENT
THOMAS OAKLAND
University of Texas

PRIVATE SCHOOLS AND SPECIAL EDUCATION

Prior to the passage of the Education for All Handicapped Children Act of 1975 (PL 94-142), private schools that existed to provide services to handicapped children were mainly tuition-based, profit-making institutions that held the parents responsible for costs. With the passage of PL 94-142, it became the local education agency's responsibility to provide a free, appropriate, public education to all children regardless of severity of handicap.

Until 1977, handicapped children, especially those with severe handicapping conditions, had fewer, consistent options for receiving educational services. Although many school districts had developed programs, especially for the less severely handicapped, there were still areas of the United States where children remained at home without an education, were institutionalized without an education, or received private education at the parents' expense (Bajan & Susser, 1982).

After 1977, local education agencies began to quickly develop or expand their own programs to meet this new responsibility. There still remained those few students for whom appropriate services could not be provided, either because of the severity of their handicap or because of a lack of appropriate numbers of a specific handicapping condition within the local education agency. These are the students who were typically enrolled in private schools as of 1985. Public Law 94-142 and subsequent amendments also mandated that it was the local education agency's (LEA) responsibility to provide the tuition for those students that the LEA placed in private schools (McQuain, 1982). Although it is clear that the LEA must be responsible for paying the tuition for students who are in private placement as a result of LEA placement, it is unclear as to the responsibility for payment for those students who are in church-related or other private schools at the request of the parent or a social agency (Wylie, 1981). For example, if a child's handicapping condition necessitates placement in a residential school to provide education, the placement, including nonmedical care and room and board, becomes the responsibility of the LEA. If placement is for noneducational concerns, home or community problems, then the LEA is responsible only for the educational costs. It sometimes becomes extremely difficult to separate education from other needs (McQuain, 1982).

Some decisions have been made by the courts related to placement issues. A program must be state approved to receive tuition payments from the LEA (Grumet & Inkpen, 1982). If an appropriate program exists within the LEA for a child, the LEA will not be responsible for private tuition (McQuain, 1982). Parents are not entitled to reimbursement for tuition as a result of voluntary placement in non-approved schools (Grumet & Inkpen, 1982), unless a clear case can be made that the program was appropriate and the LEA failed to take timely and appropriate action in evaluation or placement. The decision as to whether a child should attend a private school should involve the availability of an appropriate program in the LEA, the proximity of the program to home, the severity of the handicapping condition, and the provision of related services (Guarino, 1982). The LEA must ensure that all children in private placement receive the same rights and procedures that they would receive if in public placement (Grumet & Inkpen, 1982). Therefore, the LEA, in conjunction with the state education agency, has the responsibility to monitor the programs in the private sector.

Within the continuum of services concept, a private placement is seen as most restrictive because of the inability to mainstream. Therefore, being placed in a residential setting, a child must first receive the full benefit of opportunities provided within the LEA (Grumet & Inkpen, 1982).

A recent Supreme Court decision has lifted restrictions on on-site instruction, and the 1997 IDEA amendments have helped to clarify an LEA's obligation to provide services to parochial school students (Osborne, DiMattia, & Russo, 1998).

Audette (1982) described additional areas in which concerns must be addressed in the future. These include transportation, coordination of individual education plans, artificiality of environment of private placement, rising costs of placement, unanticipated placements, and due process issues. The questions about whether parochial school students with disabilities must have the same level of service as their peers, and on-site services remain and need to be satisfied (Osborne, DiMattia, & Russo, 1998).

REFERENCES

Audette, D. (1982). Private school placement: A local director's perspective. *Exceptional Children, 49*(3), 214–219.

Bajan, J. W., & Susser, P. L. (1982). Getting on with the education of handicapped children: A policy of partnership. *Exceptional Children, 49*(3), 208–212.

Grumet, L., & Inkpen, T. (1982). The education of children in private schools: A state agency's perspective. *Exceptional Children, 49*(3), 100–106.

Guarino, R. L. (1982). The education of handicapped children in private schools. *Exceptional Children, 49*(3), 198–199.

McQuain, S. (1982). Special education private placements: Financial responsibility under the law. *Journal of Educational Finance, 7*(4), 425–435.

Osborne, A. G., DiMattia, P., & Russo, C. J. (1998). Legal considerations improving special education services in parochial schools. *Exceptional Children, 64*(3), 385–394.

Wylie, R. J. (1981). The handicapped child and private education. *Journal of Adventist Education, 8*(9), 35–36.

SUSANNE BLOUGH ABBOTT
Stamford, Connecticut

INDIVIDUALS WITH DISABILITIES EDUCATION ACT (IDEA)
MAGNET SCHOOLS
MAINSTREAMING

PRIVILEGED COMMUNICATION

Privileged communication is a legal concept which protects the communications within certain professional relationships from disclosure in a court of law without the client's consent. Privileged relationships have historically included the attorney-client and spousal privileges, which are based in common law traditions, and clergy-communicant and physician-patient relationships, which have been established by statute in all fifty states and U.S. territories. All fifty states have also enacted privileged communication laws covering licensed psychiatrists and psychologists and their patients. Only a few states, however, have included other counselors and psychotherapists, licensed or unlicensed, under their privilege statutes.

Privileged communication laws are an exception to most rules of evidence for court proceedings, which generally work to promote the discovery of any relevant information. Privilege exists in response to society's acknowledgement that the effectiveness of certain relationships depends upon allowing clients to speak freely within the professional relationship, with the assurance that what is said within that relationship will remain private and will not later be used against the person's interests. All groups that have received privileged status have done so because they made the successful argument that their ability to help their clients would be seriously impaired or even destroyed if they were forced to reveal confidential information against the client's wishes.

Legal privilege must be distinguished from confidentiality; though they are related in the sense that both address conditions in which professional communications may or may not be disclosed, they originate from different sources and provide different levels of protection from unwanted disclosure. Confidentiality is a professional duty to refrain from disclosing client information gained during the course of the professional interaction with a client, and

is based upon the ethical standards and rules of the various professions. In addition, confidentiality requirements have been incorporated into legislation and the licensure laws of every state, prohibiting certain professionals from revealing client information without client consent, and specifying the conditions under which confidentiality may or must be broken (Knapp & Vandecreek, 1996). Confidentiality is not, however, protected when the professional is required to testify in court.

In contrast, privilege "is an exception to the general rule that the public has a right to relevant evidence in a court proceeding..." (Smith-Bell & Winslade, 1994, p. 184), and is based in privileged communication laws enacted by state legislatures and Congress. Thus, privilege is strictly a legal principle, applies only in legal situations, and is the only legally permissible basis for a professional's refusal to disclose client information in a legal court. The distinction between confidentiality and privilege is, most simply, that confidentiality *restricts* what the professional can reveal without the client's consent, whereas privilege *relieves* the professional from revealing client information in court.

However, there are a number of statutory limitations to both confidential and privileged communications. The most common exceptions to privilege require the professional to disclose privileged information when (a) there is reason to believe the client may be a danger to him or herself or others (b) child abuse is suspected, (c) the client puts his or her own mental state at issue, and (d) various other conditions are present, as specified by individual state statutes, such as elder abuse, sexual abuse by a psychotherapist, in malpractice suits against one's therapist, among others.

A recent Supreme Court case has established new and important precedent regarding the psychotherapist-patient privilege. In the case of *Jaffe* v. *Redmond* (1996), the Court held "the confidential communications between a licensed psychotherapist and the psychotherapist's patient in the course of diagnosis or treatment are protected from compelled disclosure under Rule 501 of the Federal Rules of Evidence" (p. 338). This finding addressed two major problems in the privileged communication arena: it effectively established a federal psychotherapist-patient privilege for the first time, and it extended the privilege to licensed "psychotherapists," thus acknowledging the many professionals, other than physicians and psychologists, who provide mental health services that warrant privileged status. Although the Court's finding is binding only in federal courts, it delivers clear guidance to state courts and legislatures through its message about the importance the nation's highest Court gives to therapeutic relationships.

Privileged communication laws are not, however, applicable to most educational settings, including special education contexts. Educators have not been included in the groups whose communications with clients have been afforded privileged status, with the possible exception of doctoral-level, licensed school psychologists. The *Jaffe* v. *Redmond* case discussed above did extend privilege to a master's level therapist, but did not address whether privilege would apply to any educational setting. It is possible that school counselors, if they are licensed, could make a case for the need for privileged communication in certain circumstances, but this has not happened to date. Thus, communications with school counselors and other education professionals must be disclosed in court when required.

In summary, privileged communication is a legal concept that protects the communications between certain groups of professionals and their clients from disclosure in court. Most education professionals are not currently covered under these statutes, however, and thus their communications with students and parents are not protected from disclosure in legal proceedings. Legal views of privilege are continuing to evolve on both state and federal levels, and new statutes and interpretations are most likely to appear in the future.

REFERENCES

Jaffe v. *Redmond,* 135 L.Ed.2d 337 (S. Ct. 1996).

Knapp, S. & VandeCreek, L. (1997). *Jaffe* v. *Redmond*: The Supreme Court recognizes a psychotherapist-patient privilege in federal courts. *Professional Psychology: Research and Practice, 28,* 567–572.

Smith-Bell, M. & Winslade, W. J. (1994). Privacy, confidentiality, and privilege in psychotherapeutic relationships. *American Journal of Orthopsychiatry, 64,* 180–193.

KAY E. KETZENBERGER
*The University of Texas of the
Permian Basin*

CONFIDENTIALITY OF INFORMATION
PARENTS OF THE HANDICAPPED

PROBLEM SOLVING, CREATIVE

See CREATIVE PROBLEM SOLVING.

PROCEDURAL SAFEGUARDS

See DUE PROCESS.

PROCESS TRAINING

See ABILITY TRAINING.

PRODUCTION DEFICIENCY

Production deficiency is closely tied to mediation theory (Flavell, 1970). Mediation refers to the intervention of some process between the initial stimulating event and the final response (Reese & Lipsitt, 1970). Special education students are often unable to "mediate" or use other task-appropriate strategies as intermediate steps in the learning process (Torgersen, 1977). Such inability may be due to special education students being inactive learners lacking goal-directed motivation (Torgerson, 1977). Or the learning environment not stimulating mediational interventions with the learner (Kozulin, & Falik, 1995).

Additional research in this area has resulted in an alternative explanation to those previously mentioned; special education students' poor academic performance may reflect a production deficiency (Naron, 1978; Wong, 1980). A production deficiency suggests that a student may have the ability to use the mediation strategy or another strategy but fails to spontaneously and appropriately produce it (Wong, 1980). For these children, prompting and training in metacognition and related processes might prove helpful.

REFERENCES

Flavell, J. H. (1970). Developmental studies in mediated memory. In H. W. Reese & L. P. Lipsitt (Eds.), *Advances in child development and behavior.* New York: Academic.

Kozulin, A., & Falik, L. (1995). Dynamic cognitive assessment of the child. *Current Directions in Psychological Science, 4*(6), 192–196.

Naron, N. K. (1978). Developmental changes in word attribute utilization for organization and retrieval in free recall. *Journal of Experimental Child Psychology, 25,* 279–297.

Reese, H. W., & Lipsitt, L. P. (1970). *Experimental child psychology.* New York: Academic.

Torgersen, J. K. (1977). The role of nonspecific factors in the task performance of learning disabled children: A theoretical assessment. *Journal of Learning Disabilities, 10,* 27–34.

Wong, B. Y. L. (1980). Activating the inactive learner: Use of questions/prompts to enhance comprehension and retention of implied information in learning disabled children. *Learning Disability Quarterly, 3,* 29–37.

JOHN R. BEATTIE
*University of North Carolina at
Charlotte*

MEDIATIONAL DEFICIENCY

PRO-ED, INCORPORATED

Pro-Ed is a publishing company that deals exclusively in the disability area (i.e., special education, counseling, rehabilitation, psychology, and speech/language pathology). The product line focuses on assessment measures, remedial and therapy materials, professional books, and periodicals. Among the latter are the following journals: *Journal of Learning Disabilities, Journal of Special Education, Remedial and Special Education, Intervention in School and Clinic, Reclaiming Children and Youth, Focus on Autism and other Developmental Disabilities, Topics in Early Childhood Special Education, Journal of Emotional and Behavioral Disorders*. Pro-Ed is a privately held corporation founded in 1977. Its current address is 8700 Shoal Creek Blvd, Austin, Texas, 78757-6897. In 1999, the company had approximately 1400 active titles.

DONALD D. HAMMILL
Pro-Ed

RASE
TECSE

PROFESSIONAL SCHOOL PSYCHOLOGY

Professional School Psychology is the official journal of Division 16 of the American Psychological Association. *Professional School Psychology* in intended as a forum to promote and maintain high standards of preparation for professional school psychologists and effective delivery of school psychological services. The journal publishes empirically and theoretically based papers intended to reflect a cross-section of school psychology and suitable for a broad readership. Papers that analyze, synthesize, reformulate, or offer an empirical or conceptual perspective to issues involving the underpinnings of the profession, the delivery and evaluation of services, ethical and legal aspects, and approaches to education and training are encouraged. Of special interest are articles that outline innovative professional procedures with rigorous, theoretical, and empirical support.

The type of manuscripts published in *Professional School Psychology* include theoretical pieces, literature reviews, models of professional practice, policy examinations, ethical/legal manuscripts, major addresses, interviews, proceedings from national or international conferences or symposiums, miniseries devoted to special topics in the field of school psychology, and reviews of books and materials. *Professional School Psychology* is published quarterly by Lawrence Erlbaum Associates.

THOMAS R. KRATOCHWILL
University of Wisconsin at Madison

PROFESSIONAL COMPETENCIES FOR WORKING WITH CULTURALLY AND LINGUISTICALLY DIVERSE STUDENTS

Students in public schools today look, sound, learn, and live in ways that differ from past populations. Of the 45 million students enrolled in public and private elementary and secondary schools, over 30% are from groups designated as racial/ethnic minorities (Gonzalez, Brusca-Vega & Yawkey, 1997). In addition, many students are at risk for school failure because they live in poverty, live in a single-parent family, or have a poorly educated mother (Pallas, Natriello, & McDill, 1989). Therefore, culture, as used in this article, refers to differences in race and ethnicity as well as socioeconomic status, beliefs, values, modes of expression, ways of thinking, and ways of resolving problems. The competencies listed below represent minimal competencies that teachers working with culturally and linguistically diverse students with exceptionalities (CLDE) should have.

Culture

All educators working with CLDE students should (1) understand culture in relation to child-rearing practices, socialization systems, and differences in attitudes toward education and motivation; (2) understand cross-cultural patterns, practices, and attitudes and their effect on learning and behavior; (3) understand diversity in behavior and learning styles; and (4) understand the historical origins of local communities (Baca & Almanza, 1991).

Language

As there is considerable research to suggest that inclusion of minority students' language and culture into the school program is a significant predictor of academic success, all educators working with CLDE students should (1) understand the basic concepts regarding the nature of language; (2) understand the theories of first and second language acquisition; (3) identify and understand regional, social, and developmental varieties in language use; and (4) encourage parents to provide appropriate language models for their children, whether that be English or another language (Baca & Almanza, 1991). Educators should be able to use functional language and purposeful conversational interactions (Tharp, 1994). If educators are not fluent in the student's native language, they will need to work in collaboration with their bilingual and ESL colleagues.

Consultation and Collaboration

The basic collaboration abilities needed by educators working with CLDE students have been identified by Harris (1991, 1996). The first is "to understand one's own perspective." Educators should be able to understand their own cultures and their relationship to other cultures. Educators also need to understand their own beliefs and expectations, especially regarding the abilities of students from various cultures.

The second collaborative ability is "the effective use of interpersonal, communication, and problem-solving skills." Educators must be caring, respectful, empathetic, congruent, and open in collaborative interactions. They must be able to communicate clearly and effectively in oral and written form. For effective cross-cultural communication, educators must be aware of cultural differences in communication and relationships and, when necessary, use interpreters appropriately. Educators should be familiar with the kinds of information that can be easily interpreted and conduct pre- and post-sessions with interpreters so that the language and intent of communications are clearly expressed. Educators must be able to grasp and validate overt as well as covert meanings and affects in communication. They also must be able to interview effectively to elicit information, explore problems, and set goals and objectives for the collaboration (Harris, 1991, 1996).

The third ability is "to understand the roles of collaborators." In a multicultural society, educators should be able to facilitate problem-solving sessions with individuals with different values and problem-solving styles and collaborate with culturally diverse personnel (Harris, 1996). Therefore, educators working with CLDE students need to be familiar with familial and institutional objectives relevant to CLDE students, and understand the resources that can be provided by other personnel such as bilingual educators, ESL educators, parents, and paraprofessionals (Harris, 1991).

Working with Families and Communities

According to Baca and Almanza (1991), educators who work with CLDE students should be able to plan and provide for the direct participation of parents and families of CLDE students in the instructional program and related activities. They should also know local community resources for CLDE students.

Assessment

Alternative assessment models have been present over the last two decades in response to inconsistencies found with students from culturally and linguistically diverse backgrounds (Mercer & Rueda, 1991). Therefore, it is of critical importance for educators to be able to use a wide variety of alternative assessments with CLDE students. Because language assessment is key to documenting the difference between language difference and language disability, educators working with CLDE students should know existing assessment procedures and instruments in language

proficiency, language dominance, and language development, as well as cognitive/intellectual development, social-emotional behavior, adaptive behavior, and achievement. They should also be able to adapt evaluation procedures to compensate for potential cultural and linguistic biases of the assessment process (Baca & Almanza, 1991).

Curriculum

Educators working with CLDE students should know and understand the philosophies and content of general education, bilingual education, special education, bilingual special education, multicultural education, and ESL (Baca & Almanza, 1991), because these programs may represent the least restrictive environment for CLDE students.

Instructional Planning

Educators working with CLDE students should be able to use data from language and achievement assessment to plan instructional programs and determine appropriate instructional goals and objectives. They should be able to monitor the effectiveness of instructional programs and modify them when needed to meet the unique needs of CLDE students (Baca & Almanza, 1991). Educators also need to plan for the instructional roles of other adults, e.g., paraprofessionals, bilingual educators, and ESL educators.

Instruction

All educators should be able to adapt instruction, use ESL strategies, and use appropriate behavior management strategies. Educators should have, as a primary objective, the establishment of a classroom climate that fosters successful experiences for *all* students (Baca & Almanza, 1991).

Materials

Educators working with CLDE students should know sources for materials appropriate for students from various cultural and linguistic backgrounds and should be able to evaluate materials in terms of their quality, availability, and appropriateness. The materials educators use should stimulate active, meaningful, and purposeful involvement of students (Baca & Almanza, 1991).

REFERENCES

Baca, L. M., & Almanza, E. (1991). *Language minority students with disabilities.* Reston, VA: The Council for Exceptional Children.

Gonzalez, V., Brusca-Vega, R., & Yawkey, R. (1997). *Assessment and instruction of culturally and linguistically diverse stu-*

dents with or at-risk of learning problems: From research to practice. Boston: Allyn & Bacon.

Harris, K. C. (1991). An expanded view on consultation competencies for educators serving culturally and linguistically diverse exceptional students. *Teacher Education and Special Education, 14*(1), 25–29.

Harris, K. C. (1996). Collaboration within a multicultural society: Issues for consideration. *Remedial and Special Education, 17*(6), 355–362, 376.

Mercer, J. R., & Rueda, R. (1991, November). *The impact of changing paradigms of disabilities on assessment for special education.* Paper presented at The Council for Exceptional Children Topical Conference on At-Risk Children and Youth, New Orleans, LA.

Pallas, A. M., Natriello, G., & McDill, E. L. (1989). The changing nature of the disadvantaged population: Current dimensions and future trends. *Educational Researcher, 18,* 16–22.

Tharp, R. G. (1994, June). *Cultural compatibility and the multicultural classroom: Oxymoron or opportunity.* Paper presented at the Training and Development Improvement Quarterly Meeting, Albuquerque, NM.

KATHLEEN C. HARRIS
Arizona State University West

PROFESSIONAL STANDARDS FOR SPECIAL EDUCATORS

Professional standards for special educators are rules and guidelines governing the conduct of persons who work in special education. The development of competency standards is an attempt to increase the overall quality of service in the field and to strive for excellence in the profession. In 1966 the Council for Exceptional Children developed Professional Standards for Personnel in the Education of Exceptional Children. In 1979 the council approved Guidelines for Personnel in the Education of Exceptional Children. These standards did not include formal definable criteria for determining whether a teacher had acquired the necessary competencies. The most recent set of standards published by the council (*Exceptional Children,* 1983), consists of three policy statements focusing on common requirements for the practice of special education: Code of Ethics, Professional Practice, and Standards for the Preparation of Special Education Personnel. These statements describe the philosophical position of special education professionals, the skills the specialists should exhibit in their jobs, and how training organizations should best prepare future special educators.

The development of competency standards for special educators is important for a variety of reasons. One is to increase the consistency and quality of service across the special education field. Another is to require excellence so

that it may translate into greater academic and social achievements for the handicapped students being served. Standards also serve as a way to measure the quality of performance of special educators. They help protect the profession from embracing techniques or skills that are based more on subjectivity than on empirical data. Heller (1983) suggested that if professionals in special education do not oversee themselves, someone else will.

Standards of professional competence for special educators describe expectations in two general categories of duties: those that are necessary for successful and ethical treatment of persons labeled with special needs, and those that are necessary for the growth and stature of the field of special education. The specific details can be found in *Exceptional Children* (1983). Professionals have several obligations, including the use of their training to help those with special needs. Their methods must be appropriate and effective. Special educators must also use techniques to manage behavior that are ethical, humane, and consistent with existing rules and regulations. Aversive techniques may not be used except as a last resort. Professionals also serve the parents of exceptional children by communicating clearly and by soliciting and using their advice and information. Parents should be informed of all matters related to their particular situations and of the rights afforded them by law. Special educators should serve as advocates for the exceptional person in a variety of ways—changing government policy, monitoring adequacy of available resources, and protecting the individual rights of the special needs person. Special educators also have the responsibility of keeping abreast of new developments and findings in special education.

Professional standards exist to guide the conduct of special education professionals. One way to ensure that special educators are influenced by these standards is for all institutions that prepare special education teachers and professionals to provide for their students the most current standards and to incorporate those standards into the educational process (Standards for the Preparation of Special Education Personnel, 1983). At the state and national levels, any licensing or accreditation requirements in existence could be compared with the profession's standards and adjusted accordingly.

Once the development and implementation of the standards are completed, professionals in the field need to concentrate their efforts in three areas. First, the development of continuing or in-service education must address the competencies needed by professionals already in the field (Stedman, Smith, & Baucom, 1981). Second, as mentioned by Gersten (1985), efforts should focus on which teacher competencies actually make a difference to people with special needs (Englert, 1983). Interviewing experts to develop professional competencies (Zane, Sulzer-Azaroff, Handen, & Fox, 1982) is useful in developing a large number of skills and standards that seem logical, but such a strategy is insufficient in that it does not provide for a determination of whether such skills are functionally related to student improvement. Third, updating and changing of the standards must continue (Standards for the Preparation of Special Education Personnel, 1983). The validation process is one way that new skills and competencies will become known and incorporated into the standards as the nature of the field changes and the needs of the developmentally disabled shift over time. By validating them, updating as needed, and incorporating them into institutions that train special educators, the standards will become an integral part of the training of special educators and will achieve the original purpose for their development—producing qualified professionals and providing maximum improvement of persons with special needs.

REFERENCES

Englert, C. S. (1983). Measuring special education teacher effectiveness. *Exceptional Children, 50,* 247–254.

Gersten, R. (1985). Direct instruction with special education students: A review of evaluation research. *Journal of Special Education, 19,* 41–58.

Heller, H. H. (1983). Special education professional standards: Need, value, and use. *Exceptional Children, 50,* 199–204.

Standards for the preparation of special education personnel. (1983). *Exceptional Children, 50,* 210–218.

Stedman, D. J., Smith, R. R., & Baucom, L. D. (1981). Toward quality in special education programs. In D. Stedman & J. Paul (Eds.), *New directions for exceptional children: Professional preparation for teachers of exceptional children* (No. 8). San Francisco: Jossey-Bass.

Zane, T., Sulzer-Azaroff, B., Handen, B. L., & Fox, C. J. (1982). Validation of a competency-based training program in developmental disabilities. *Journal of the Severely Handicapped, 7,* 21–31.

THOMAS ZANE
Johns Hopkins University

ETHICS
TEACHER EFFECTIVENESS

PROFILE ANALYSIS

Profile analysis is the evaluation of scatter, or irregular performance, on the subtests and scales of a test. Whenever a profile of performance across specific areas is generated from a test, analysis of the profile is possible on a formal or informal basis. Thus, the patterns of scores from numerous intelligence, achievement, personality, aptitude, and vocational interest measures can be interpreted through the analysis of the relative positions of subtests and scales to each other (Goldstein & Hersen, 1984).

For a growing number of instruments, this process is facilitated through the availability of computerized programs for automated scoring and interpretation. Controversy surrounds this movement toward computer-assisted analysis, however, because of the wide-ranging quality of the available programs. Regardless of whether profile analysis is done with the assistance of these programs, the intent should be to evaluate areas of intraindividual strength and weakness (Sattler, 1982) and to use this information as hypotheses that merit further evaluation and that offer clues to instructional programming.

Empirical support exists for the use of profile analysis with various instruments. Among personality measures, the Minnesota Multiphasic Personality Inventory (MMPI) has been the focus of numerous research efforts (Lewandowski & Graham, 1972), while the Wechsler scales have been the most closely scrutinized intelligence measures. Among the latter, the strongest support exists for the use of profile analysis with the Wechsler Intelligence Scale for Children–Revised (WISC–R), but only when careful consideration is given to three important caveats enumerated in Kaufman (1979), Sattler (1982), and Salvia and Ysseldyke (1981).

Of prime importance is that profile analysis is dependent on the presence of statistically significant differences among the subscales or among the subtests. Thus, before statements can be made about whether the examinee obtained higher or lower IQs, scaled scores, or subtest scores, significant differences among the subscales or the subtests must be present. Statistically significant differences among subtests or scales suggest that the differences are attributed to the abilities tapped by the respective subtests or scales rather than to measurement error.

Even with statistical differences, ideas generated must be viewed simply as hypotheses to be checked against other information about the examinee. Thus, a second caution is that profile analysis should be done with an understanding that uneven scores can be caused by many factors, including unreliability of the subtests, examiner/situational variability, background factors, physical disability, and minority group status (Sattler, 1982). In other words, experts agree that profile analysis is done only when the examinee's entire performance is evaluated to exclude the influence of other factors before specific strengths and weaknesses in cognitive ability are inferred. Moreover, when taken alone, uneven skill development does not allow one to make decisions about pathological conditions or the possible causes and cures of the uneven development. Thus, an understanding of the range of scores that exists among normal functioning children is necessary (Kaufman, 1976). Even when scatter is outside normal limits, however, it does not necessarily indicate the presence of pathology (Kaufman, 1979; Sattler, 1982).

Not only do the caveats apply to the Wechsler Scales and other intelligence tests, they also provide a context for understanding the potential for misuse of profile analysis on tests that do not have a strong research base. Nevertheless, when done with careful consideration to statistically significant differences, other information about a child's functioning, and the extent of uneven skill development among normal functioning children, the analysis of profiles from intelligence tests and other instruments can assist in the process of uncovering clues to effective treatment, educational programming, or vocational placement.

REFERENCES

Goldstein, G., & Hersen, M. (1984). *Handbook of psychological assessment.* New York: Pergamon.

Kaufman, A. S. (1976). A new approach to the interpretation of test scatter on the WISC–R. *Journal of Learning Disabilities, 9,* 166–168.

Kaufman, A. S. (1979). *Intelligent testing with the WISC–R.* New York: Wiley.

Lewandowski, D., & Graham, J. R. (1972). Empirical correlates of frequently occurring two-point MMPI code types: A replicated study. *Journal of Consulting and Clinical Psychology, 39,* 467–472.

Salvia, J., & Ysseldyke, J. E. (1981). *Assessment in special and remedial education* (special ed.). New York: Houghton Mifflin.

Sattler, J. M. (1982). *Assessment of children's intelligence and special abilities.* Boston: Allyn & Bacon.

KATHLEEN D. PAGET
University of South Carolina

INTELLIGENCE TESTING

PROFILE VARIABILITY

Profile variability is an index of test scatter (individual variation in test scores between or within various psychological and educational tests) first defined by Plake, Reynolds, and Gutkin (1981). It is used as a diagnostic aid in determining the degree of intratest variability in an individual's performance on the subtests of any multiscale assessment device. A large degree of within test scatter has long been held to be an indicator of the presence of a learning disability (Chalfant & Scheffelin, 1969).

Test scatter has typically been determined by range (the highest minus the lowest score for an individual on a common family of tests), or by the number of test scores deviating at a statistically significant level from the individual's mean score on all tests administered (the latter sometimes is referred to as the number of deviant signs, or NDS). Profile variability is similar in some respects to range, but it is more accurate, more stable, and more powerful than older indexes of scatter. Profile variability encompasses data from all tests or subtests administered to an individual. It is not limited to the two most extreme scores as is the range.

Calculation of the index of profile variability is straightforward because it is the variance of a set of scores for one person on more than one measure, hence, the name profile variability. Profile variability for each member of a group or population can be estimated to be (Plake, Reynolds, & Gutkin, 1981):

$$S^2 = \sum_{j=1}^{k} \frac{\left(x_{ij-\bar{x}_i}\right)}{k-1}$$

where S^2 = the index of profile variability

x_{ij} = the score of person i on test or subtest j

$\bar{x}_j$ = the mean score for person i on all tests (k) administered

k = the number of tests administered

The resulting value can then be compared with data taken from the standardization sample of a test or some other group to determine whether the variance of the individual's profile is an unusual or a common occurrence. In a research setting, it may also be of interest to know if the mean S^2 for one group differs at a statistically significant level from the mean S^2 for another group. A statistical test of the significance of the difference has been developed and is detailed in Plake, Reynolds, and Gutkin (1981).

Relatively little research on the clinical utility of S^2 has been completed as yet. However, of the various scatter indexes, profile variability is the most stable and the most mathematically sound.

REFERENCES

Chalfant, J. C., & Scheffelin, M. A. (1969). *Central processing dysfunctions in children.* (NINDS Monograph No. 9). Bethesda MD: U.S. Department of Health, Education, and Welfare.

Plake, B., Reynolds, C. R., & Gutkin, T. B. (1981). A technique for the comparison of profile variability between independent groups. *Journal of Clinical Psychology, 37,* 142–146.

CECIL R. REYNOLDS
Texas A & M University

PROFILE ANALYSIS
TEST SCATTER

PROFOUNDLY HANDICAPPED, COMPETENCIES OF TEACHERS OF

Students considered to be profoundly handicapped (PH) may include individuals who have been diagnosed and labeled as either profoundly mentally retarded, autistic, deaf-blind, severely multiply handicapped, or severely emotionally disturbed. In recent years, increased emphasis has been placed on determining the competencies or skills needed by teachers of these students (Burke & Cohen, 1977; Horner, 1977; Southeastern Regional Coalition, 1982).

The competencies that have been suggested in the professional literature, as necessary for teachers of PH students, can be divided into nine general areas (Whitten & Westling, 1985). These include (1) curriculum development or selection; (2) behavioral programming and behavior management; (3) working with parents; (4) assessment; (5) methods of instructional delivery; (6) medical aspects; (7) child development; (8) use of other professionals and paraprofessionals; and (9) characteristics of mental, emotional, and physical disabilities.

In addition to knowing how to teach, teachers must also know what to teach profoundly handicapped students. Teachers must be able to select or develop curriculum in a variety of content areas including self-help skills, sensory-motor development, social, and recreational skills.

Among the specific competency areas considered to be most important in the area of behavioral programming and management are development of task analyses, understanding of behavior modification techniques, and the ability to arrange and manage reinforcement contingencies and principles. In addition, within this area, the ability to develop strategies for appropriate acquisition, maintenance, and generalization of behaviors, and the ability to measure behavior and competencies (Gresham, MacMillan, & Siperstein, 1995) precisely, are considered to be important competencies.

The ability to involve parents in educational planning and to function as an effective parent trainer are often suggested as important competencies for teachers of profoundly handicapped students.

The ability to maintain an ongoing assessment of learning is important. Knowledge of instrumentation and procedures appropriate for screening, diagnosis, and educational assessment, and the ability to comprehend and interpret diagnostic reports, are necessary skills.

Instructional delivery is an additional competency area that includes the ability to develop or select instructional materials, the use of a high percentage of minutes per day for instruction, and the ability to facilitate skill acquisition.

Knowledge of medical aspects has been determined to be an important area of needed competence. The skills of using modified equipment, administering medication, and providing assistance to a student having a seizure are often necessary competencies.

An understanding of the normative developmental sequence and early academic learning processes is paramount in the education of profoundly handicapped students.

A frequently stated competency is the ability to communicate and work effectively with other professionals. Other skills include the ability to supervise paraprofessional personnel and the understanding and use of support services in the school and community.

The final area includes the specific competencies of understanding cognitive, language, social, motor, and behavioral development and knowledge of clinical syndromes. Although an abundance of competencies have been suggested for teachers of PH students, the majority of these statements are based on the opinions of the author(s), groups of professionals, or citations from the professional literature. Only five suggested competencies have been validated as a result of an established empirical link between the demonstration of a specific competency and gain in student achievement.

Four of the competency statements based on student gains involved the use of behavioral principles, while a fifth statement focused on instructional delivery. Statements based on empirically validated behavioral techniques include the ability to conduct task analyses (Fredericks, Anderson, & Baldwin, 1979), the ability to use behavior management techniques (Koegel, Russo, & Rincover, 1977), the use of successive approximation procedures (Katz, Goldberg, & Shurka, 1977), and the delivery of primary reinforcement (Whitten & Westling, 1985). In addition, according to research conducted by Fredericks et al. (1979), students of teachers who used a higher percentage of time each day for instruction achieved more than students of teachers who provided a lower percentage of instructional time.

While it appears that a considerable amount of attention has been focused on the delineation of competencies needed by teachers of profoundly handicapped students, as previously noted, the majority of the suggested competencies have been based on opinions (Thurman & Hare, 1979; Whitten & Westling, 1985). It is, therefore, important to determine empirically the skills that teachers of profoundly handicapped students should demonstrate so that the optimal functioning levels of these students may be achieved. According to Turner (1971), the highest criterion to judge effectiveness of teacher practices is to determine the effect to these practices on student learning over an extended period of time. Rather than basing the practices teachers use on opinion, it appears to be essential that the validity of the suggested teacher competencies be determined as a result of empirical research.

In reviewing the competency statements, it appears that many of those suggested may be applicable to all teachers and especially all special educators. However, teachers of profoundly handicapped students need to be much more proficient in their use. Sontag, Burke, and York (1973) noted an inverse relationship between the level of competence needed by the teacher and the functioning level of the student. Therefore, if profoundly handicapped students are to reach their optimal functioning levels, it is essential that their teachers demonstrate a higher level of competence than teachers of regular or other special students.

REFERENCES

Burke, P., & Cohen, M. (1977). The quest for competencies in serving the severely/profoundly handicapped: A critical analysis of personnel preparation programs. In E. Sontag, J. Smith, & N. Certo (Eds.), *Educational programming for the severely and profoundly handicapped* (pp. 445–465). Reston, VA: Council for Exceptional Children.

Fredericks, H. D., Anderson, R., & Baldwin, V. (1979). The identification of competency indicators of teachers of the severely handicapped. *American Association for the Education of the Severely/Profoundly Handicapped Review, 4,* 81–95.

Gresham, F. M., MacMillan, D. L., & Siperstein, G. N. (1995). Critical analysis of the 1992 AAMR definition: Implications for school psychology. *School Psychology Quarterly, 10*(1), 1–19.

Horner, R. D. (1977). A competency based approach to preparing teachers of the severely and profoundly handicapped: Perspective II. In E. Sontag, J. Smith, & N. Certo (Eds.), *Educational programming for the severely and profoundly handicapped* (pp. 430–444). Reston, VA: Council for Exceptional Children.

Katz, S., Goldberg, J., & Shurka, E. (1977). The use of operant techniques in teaching severely retarded clients work habits. *Education & Training of the Mentally Retarded, 12,* 14–20.

Koegel, R. L., Russo, D. C., & Rincover, A. (1977). Assessing and training teachers in the generalized use of behavior modification with autistic children. *Journal of Applied Behavior Analysis, 10,* 197–205.

Sontag, E., Burke, P. J., & York, R. (1973). Considerations for serving the severely handicapped in public schools. *Education & Training of the Mentally Retarded, 8,* 20–26.

Southeastern Regional Coalition for Personnel Preparation to Work with Severely/Profoundly Handicapped. (1982). Developing personnel preparation programs to train personnel to teach severely handicapped individuals. *Teacher Education & Special Education, 5*(1), 46–51.

Thurman, S. K., & Hare, B. A. (1979). Training teachers in special education: Some perspectives circa 1980. *Education & Training of the Mentally Retarded, 14,* 292–295.

Turner, R. L. (1971). Levels of criteria. In B. Rosner (Eds.), *The power of competency-based teacher education.* Washington, DC: U. S. Office of Education, National Center for Educational Research and Development.

Whitten, T. M., & Westling, D. L. (1985). Competencies for teachers of severely and profoundly handicapped: A review. *Teacher Education & Special Education, 8*(2), 104–111.

THOMAS M. WHITTEN
Florida State University

COMPETENCY TEST
MILDLY HANDICAPPED, TEACHER COMPETENCIES FOR MENTAL RETARDATION
TEACHER TRAINING

PROFOUNDLY RETARDED

See MENTAL RETARDATION.

PROGRAM EVALUATION

Program evaluation in elementary school and secondary school education has been an area of considerable activity during the past 20 years. Program evaluation has been such an active area largely because of public concern about program accountability as well as a desire by school professionals to provide quality programs, and outcomes services, (Cronbach, 1982). Although no universal definition exists, program evaluation can be characterized by two essential activities: systematic, purposeful data collection relative to one or more important evaluation questions; and the use of evaluation information to judge whether a program is worthwhile (Rossi, Freeman, & Wright, 1985).

Numerous educational program evaluations have been conducted in school settings, with many of the evaluations focused on federally funded programs and projects such as Head Start, Follow-Through, and Chapter I programs. Essentially, these program evaluations have been summative in nature, whereby large numbers of students who received the program were compared with large groups of students with similar characteristics who did not receive the program or who received another program. The primary intent of these evaluations has been to determine program effectiveness and to decide whether the outcome justifies disseminating the program to other sites and students as part of public policy initiatives.

Large-scale educational program evaluation has been proven beneficial to federal and state policy makers in terms of aggregate data for decision-making purposes. Additionally, issues and methods have been clarified in important ways for those interested in evaluation design and measurement. Despite these gains in understanding, what does not seem to have been readily established is the direct and practical relevance of program evaluation to local level programs, especially small-size school districts. More specifically, local school professionals have voiced concern over how they can use program evaluation to help them develop and improve local offerings (Dunst, 1979; Kennedy, 1982).

In special education, program evaluation has become an area of avid interest and increasing activity at local school district levels nationwide, with collaborative efforts being undertaken among administrators, staff, and outside consultants. An important impetus to this avid interest and increasing activity at the local level was a two-day national conference on special education program evaluation held in St. Louis during December 1983 (Council of Administrators of Special Education, 1984). At that conference, which was jointly sponsored by the Council of Administrators of Special Education and the Office of Special Education and Rehabilitation Services, four proven models of local-level special education program evaluation were presented by their proponents. The invited audience of over 100 special education directors and supervisors from throughout the nation took part in workshops to learn about these practical approaches. Subsequent to the conference, local school district applicants were reviewed and the various models were field tested during 1984 at about 20 local sites (Associate Consultants, 1985).

Case study results of these field tests, along with empirical results from additional evaluations of local special education programs that occurred during 1985 and 1986 through state department initiatives, coupled with professional publications on special education program evaluation, have all coalesced to delineate and propose several important features and characteristics of this rapidly developing area. These features and characteristics are reflected in terms of the process of special education program evaluation, the foci of evaluation efforts, the methods, procedures, and instruments for conducting evaluations of special programs, and the enhancement of the use of evaluation information for program planning.

The process of special education program evaluation is best considered in the generic sense, i.e., as the systematic gathering of data about a program or service to answer one or more clearly articulated evaluation questions. For special education programs, the following evaluation questions usually have been raised by local level practitioners when planning an evaluation: (1) What were the characteristics of the students who were provided the program? (2) How was the program actually implemented? (3) Were program goals attained? (4) How did various individuals—teachers, parents, students—react to the program and its outcomes? (5) Was the program responsible for the outcome results? (6) Was the program worth the investment? Although it is not possible for all of these questions to be addressed in a particular evaluation, the questions are im-

portant in that the evaluation information gathered in response to them can lead to particular program planning actions.

The foci of special education program evaluation can be numerous, since a special education services delivery system includes a range of programs and services (Maher & Bennett, 1984). For instance, various instructional programs serving special needs learners can be the foci of evaluation efforts including programs such as resources rooms, self-contained classrooms, supplemental instructional programs, regular class mainstreaming programs and, of course, individualized education programs (IEPs). In the area of related services, a district's student counseling program, for example, can be the object of an evaluation as can other programs such as parent education programs or physical therapy services. Similarly, a special education program evaluation can focus on a staff development course or on an important, yet often neglected type of program, e.g., an assessment program such as preplacement evaluation. In deciding the evaluation questions to be addressed in relation to special education programs and services, a local-level team or committee approach has been found to be useful in selecting the most appropriate questions and in facilitating the involvement of staff in the evaluation endeavor (Maher & Illback, 1984).

Since diverse evaluation questions can be addressed in relation to various special programs and services, it is not surprising that a plan for special education program evaluation lists many kinds of methods, procedures, and instruments. At the local level, special education program evaluation plans seem to reflect not comparative group evaluation designs, as has been typical in regular education special evaluation, but special education evaluation plans characterized by a single case approach, where the program (e.g., resource room) is compared with itself over time (e.g., over a 2- to 3-year period) to determine whether it is effective (Tawney & Gast, 1984). Usually, evaluations include use of instruments and procedures that rely on teacher or staff retrospective judgment, especially through use of behavioral checklists and rating scales and parent and teacher interviews. Additionally, criterion-referenced testing and review of IEP goal attainment data have been commonly employed to answer important evaluation questions. Hence, both qualitative and quantitative data gathering approaches appear to be necessary to the conduct of practical and meaningful special education program evaluation.

An emphasis on the use of special education program evaluation information seems to have been a positive outgrowth of practitioners' desires to act on the information for program planning purposes. In this regard, it has been found important that written evaluation reports be kept brief, that they be written in the nontechnical language of the school audience for which it is intended, and that the narrative be augmented with clearly developed tables, graphs, figures, and other illustrations to emphasize important points. Most important, recommendations for program planning should be specific as to how to take the next steps and clear as to how the steps were derived. To facilitate use of the information, it has been found useful to hold group meetings or forums between evaluation personnel and target audiences.

REFERENCES

Associate Consultants. (1985). *Results of the field tests of the special education program evaluation models.* Washington, DC: Author.

Council of Administrators of Special Education. (1984). *Proceedings of the national conference on special education program evaluation.* Indianapolis, IN: Author.

Cronbach, L. J. (1982). *Designing evaluations of educational and social programs.* San Francisco: Jossey-Bass.

Dunst, C. J. (1979). Program evaluation and the Education for All Handicapped Children Act. *Exceptional Children, 46,* 26–31.

Kennedy, M. M. (1982). *Recommendations of the Division H Task Force on Special Education Program Evaluation.* Washington, DC: American Educational Research Association.

Maher, C. A., & Bennett, R. E. (1984). *Planning and evaluating special education services.* Englewood Cliffs, NJ: Prentice-Hall.

Maher, C. A., & Illback, R. J. (1984). A team approach to evaluating special services. In C. A. Maher, R. J. Illback, & J. E. Zins (Eds.), *Organizational psychology in the schools.* Springfield, IL: Thomas.

Rossi, P., Freeman, H., & Wright, L. (1985). *Evaluation: A systematic approach.* Beverly Hills, CA: Sage.

Tawney, J. W., & Gast, D. L. (1984). *Single subject research in special education.* Columbus, OH: Merrill.

CHARLES A. MAHER
Rutgers University

LOUIS J. KRUGER
Tufts University

NATIONAL CENTER FOR EDUCATIONAL OUTCOMES
SCHOOL EFFECTIVENESS
SUPERVISION IN SPECIAL EDUCATION

PROGRAMMED INSTRUCTION

Programmed instruction is a unique educational method based on principles emphasized by B. F. Skinner (1954, 1958). First, the use of positive reinforcement is preferable to punishment or lack of feedback. Second, positive reinforcement is more effective in producing behavioral changes if given frequently and immediately after each response. Last, there is value in presenting students with small chunks of information to learn that will eventually result in desired behaviors. Skinner sought to apply these principles through programmed learning and the use of teaching machines.

The development of an automated teaching machine by Pressley in the 1920s anticipated Skinner's work. Pressley's machine required students to read questions and then press buttons to answer (in multiple-choice format). The machine presented the next question in a sequence only after the student made the correct choice. Pressley's concept and technology were not readily accepted or widely used. Skinner (1958) attributed the limited use of Pressley's teaching machine to "cultural inertia" and the incomplete or inappropriate application of learning principles. Skinner developed another teaching machine that not only provided frequent and immediate feedback, but also presented the information to be learned in small, easily acquired segments that the student had to master before moving on to new material. The small steps increased the chances of a student's making a correct response, provided positive reinforcement and student motivation, and ensured student success at each step as well as at the final goal.

Programmed learning has been hailed as allowing truly individualized instruction permitting students to progress at their own pace. In many cases, it seems to be highly motivating to the student because of the immediacy of results, high density of reinforcement, and enjoyment from manipulating the machine (when a teaching machine is used). It has also been instrumental in showing how to teach complex tasks by breaking them down into small, teachable segments. In addition, when using teaching machines, teachers are freer to use their time in more productive ways than presenting information to students.

While the early application of programmed instruction used machines to present learning programs, programmed texts and workbooks soon followed. The increasing use of computers in special education has been revitalizing interest in variations of programmed instruction. An impressive characteristic of modern computers is the great degree of individualized instruction now possible for each student because of the development of branching programs (Rubin & Weisgerber, 1985; Schackenberg & Sullivan, 1997). Students diagnosed as learning disabled and mentally retarded (mild to profound) have learned a variety of skills on computers, such as addition, subtraction, word recognition, matching to sample (Richmond, 1983).

However, it is the application of learning principles and not the use of a computer that is the important issue. A computer does not automatically incorporate programmed instruction principles; in fact, much of the educational software in use today is to a large extent based on the traditional trial-and-error procedures that may result in academic failure in many children (LeBlanc, Hoko, Aangeenbrug, & Etzel, 1985). Integrating instructional principles of programmed learning into the development of educational methodologies, whether in software, textbooks, or other forms, is a way to maximize the chances for learning in special education students.

REFERENCES

LeBlanc, J. M., Hoko, J. A., Aangeenbrug, M. H., & Etzel, B. C. (1985). Microcomputers and stimulus control: From the laboratory to the classroom. *Journal of Special Education Technology, 7,* 23–30.

Richmond, G. (1983). Comparison of automated and human instruction for developmentally retarded preschool children. *Journal of the Association for the Severely Handicapped, 8,* 78–84.

Rubin, D. P., & Weisgerber, R. A. (1985). The center for research and evaluation in the application of technology to education. *Technological Horizons in Education, 12,* 83–87.

Schackenberg, H. L., & Sullivan, H. J. (1997). *Learner ability and learner control in computer assisted instructional programs.* Paper presented at the National Convention of the Association for Educational Communications and Technology, February 14–18, Albuquerque, New Mexico.

Skinner, B. F. (1954). The science of learning and the art of teaching. *Harvard Educational Review, 24,* 86–97.

Skinner, B. F. (1958). Teaching machines. *Science, 128,* 969–977.

THOMAS ZANE
Johns Hopkins University

**COMPUTER MANAGED INSTRUCTION
COMPUTER USE WITH HANDICAPPED
DIRECT INSTRUCTION
OPERANT CONDITIONING**

PROJECTIVE TECHNIQUES

See PERSONALITY ASSESSMENT.

PROJECT ON CLASSIFICATION OF EXCEPTIONAL CHILDREN

In the early 1970s, Nicholas Hobbs was asked to direct a systematic review of the classification and labeling practices for exceptional children. Sponsored by 10 federal agencies and organized by Elliot Richardson, then secretary of health, education, and welfare, this review had several objectives.

The first objective was to increase public understanding of the issues associated with labeling and classifying handicapped individuals. The second objective was to formulate a statement of rationale for public policy, including suggestions for regulatory guidelines. The third objective was to educate professionals who were ultimately responsible for the provision of services to the population of exceptional children (Hobbs, 1975a).

The results of this review, known as the Project on Classification of Exceptional Children, were reported in the publication *The Futures of Children* (Hobbs, 1975b). Included in this report was a list of recommendations that detail actions to be taken as well as who should be responsible for the implementation, the cost of service, and the length of time required to accomplish the project objectives.

Hobbs, a distinguished psychologist and educator, was generally opposed to the practice of labeling individuals. His major argument against labeling was that it is very limited in value. Hobbs pointed out that while the original intent of classification was to provide equal access and opportunity for the handicapped population, the process usually resulted in the transfer of the label or classification to a negative condition or description of the child. For example, a child who was classified within the category of mental retardation became known as a mental retardate.

Hobbs (1975b), citing the current practices of the time, warned:

> categories and labels are powerful instruments for social regulation and control, and they are often employed for obscure, covert, or hurtful purposes: to degrade people, to deny them access to opportunity, to exclude "undesirables" whose presence in some way offends, disturbs familiar custom, or demands extraordinary effort. (p. 11)

One of the seven major recommendations to emerge from the project was the call to improve the classification system. Specifically, the project report suggested five ways to improve the existing process. The suggestions included (1) revision of the classification process; (2) constraints in the use of psychological testing; (3) improvements in early identification procedures; (4) safeguards in the handling of confidential records; and (5) provision of due process in identification and placement.

One finding of the project was that the current classification systems were inadequate. Citing arbitrary and outmoded conceptual guidelines, the members called for a comprehensive classification system that would be based on the needs of exceptional children. According to the general recommendations, the classification system should reflect the full range of conditions of children who need special services. Under this model, classification would emphasize the services required rather than the types of children served.

The specific recommendations of the project members included the formation of a national advisory committee for the purpose of establishing a comprehensive classification system. As a result of such a system, there would be increased understanding of the complexities of the characteristics and etiology of handicapping conditions. The changes proposed in the classification system were not regarded as an end product but rather as a vehicle for improving service and programming for handicapped individuals and their families.

Historically, there has been a great deal of controversy associated with the classification systems for handicapped populations. Since the introduction of the first special education textbook in the early 1920s, there has been a demand for more accurate classification systems Kaufman & Hallahan, 1981).

Currently, there is little evidence in relevant literature that the recommendations resulting from the Project on Classification of Exceptional Children have been implemented on a national level. Individual agencies have made progress in several areas identified by the project report (e.g., improvement of diagnostic procedures, increases in services for the families of handicapped individuals, reclassification of mental retardation based on structural support needed [Gresham, MacMillan, & Siperstein, 1995] and protection of individual's right to due process). However, the major recommendation calling for a national advisory panel that would help to establish policy and direct relevant research has yet to be realized.

REFERENCES

Gresham, F. M., MacMillan, D. L., Siperstein, G. N. (1995). Critical analysis of the 1992 AAMR definition: Implication for school psychology. *School Psychology Quarterly, 10*(1), 1–19.

Hobbs, N. (Ed.). (1975a). *Issues in the classification of children* (Vols. 1, 2). San Francisco: Jossey-Bass.

Hobbs, N. (1975b). *The futures of children.* San Francisco: Jossey Bass.

Kaufman, J. M., & Hallahan, D. P. (Eds.). (1981). *Handbook of special education.* Englewood Cliffs, NJ: Prentice-Hall.

FRANCINE TOMPKINS
University of Cincinnati

AAMD CLASSIFICATION SYSTEM
CLASSIFICATION SYSTEMS
LABELING

PROJECT RE-ED

The project on the Re-Education of Emotionally Disturbed Children (Project Re-ED) evolved after a 1953 study of mental health needs by the Southern Regional Education Board. The study indicated that there was great need for child mental health programs with demonstrated effectiveness, reasonable cost, access to a large talent pool of trained personnel, and potential for transfer of techniques to public schools. In 1956 the federal government sponsored a study of mental health programs in France and Scotland, where mental health services were provided by French *educateurs* and Scottish "educational psychologists" to children with desperate needs because of the effects of evacuation and other traumas resulting from World War II. The National Institute for Mental Health (NIMH) study group recommended a pilot project using trained personnel in the United States (Hobbs, 1983).

In 1961 a NIMH grant of $2 million was awarded to George Peabody College for Teachers (now part of Vanderbilt University) and the states of Tennessee and North Carolina. Nicholas Hobbs was the primary developer of the 8-year pilot project for moderately to severely disturbed children (ages 6 to 12) in residential centers in Nashville, Tennessee, and Durham, North Carolina. Centers were in residential areas and provided services to groups of 24 and 40, subdivided into groups of eight. Program planning emphasis was on health rather than illness, teaching rather than therapy, the present rather than the past, and the operation of a total social system of which the child is a part rather than intrapsychic processes alone. Initial planning was pragmatic rather than theoretical; the theory developed with project research and experience. Hobbs (1978) later commented that one of the important ideas in the planning and development of Project Re-ED was that there should be no orthodoxy or dogma, but a "colleagueship" of discovery guiding the activities of professional individuals working together closely.

Basic ideas underlying program development included (1) insight is a possible consequence but not a cause of behavioral change; (2) health and happiness must grow out of life as it is lived, not as talked about in the context of personality theory; and (3) emotional disturbance in children is not something within the child, but a symptom of a malfunctioning ecosystem. Teacher-counselors and liaison teachers were carefully selected and provided with condensed, highly functional training (master's level) and a dependable system of day-to-day consultation by highly trained and skilled professional personnel. Teachers were not expected to solve complex problems intuitively, but were trained in understanding psychodynamics of individual development and families. Training also included child development, remedial instruction, management of behavior, recreational skills, and use of consultants.

Hobbs believed that trust between children and adults is basic to reeducation and that training of the children should be designed to encourage development of self-confidence by ensuring success. Symptoms were treated directly (controlled) without emphasis on causality. Family and school contacts were maintained while children were in residence. By 1970 the age range was expanded to include adolescents and preschool children.

Follow-up studies of Project Re-ED children (Weinstein, 1974) indicated that although the reeducation program did not change the students into "normal" children, they were better adjusted than disturbed children who were not in the project. Since the average length of stay in centers was about 7 months (contrasted to several years in some other types of residential centers), it appears that the project met its goal, which was not to cure children, but to restore to effective operation the small social system of which the child is an integral part. Hobbs thought that Project Re-ED would be most likely to pay off when its concepts were applied in public schools. By 1983 about two dozen reeducation centers were established in nine states and several others were being planned. Professional consensus now is the Project Re-ED is a viable means of providing effective services to disturbed children.

REFERENCES

Hobbs, N. (1975). *The future of children.* San Francisco: Jossey-Bass.

Hobbs, N. (1978). Perspectives on re-education. *Behavior Disorders, 3*(2), 65–66.

Hobbs, N. (1983). Project Re-Education: From demonstration project to nationwide program. *Peabody Journal of Education, 60*(3), 8–24.

Weinstein, L. (1974). *Evaluation of a program for re-educating disturbed children: A follow-up comparison with untreated children* (ERIC Document Reproduction Service No. ED-141-966). Washington, DC: U.S. Department of Health Education, and Welfare.

SUE ALLEN WARREN
Boston University

LIFE SPACE INTERVIEWING
RESIDENTIAL FACILITIES

PROJECT SUCCESS (PS)

Project Success (PS) is an academic and social remediation program for the college-bound specific language-handicapped or dyslexic student. The intent of the program is for the language-handicapped student to become language-independent as well as socially and psychologically adjusted to the new environment.

Becoming language-independent means that the dyslexic individual learns how to read and spell any word by relying on his or her own integrated knowledge of the phonemic structure of the American-English language. Students in PS acquire this knowledge initially by memorizing how the 50 phonemes and 26 letters can be employed to identify 271 sound symbol assignments for reading and 245 sound symbols assignments for spelling.

This total number of assignments for both reading and spelling are taught using a multisensory approach. The in-

structional methodology used is Nash's (1984) adaptation of the original Orton Gillingham, Tri-Modal, Simultaneous Multi-Sensory Instructional Procedure (OG, TM, SMSIP). This procedure trains the learner to use the senses simultaneously to memorize and to integrate up to 84% of all American-English words. In addition to reading and spelling remediation, the program remediates math and writing deficits. There is also a social habilitation program.

The written expression program concentrates on teaching the writing of sentences as outlined by Langan (1983). The social habilitation/remediation component of PS was developed to give students an opportunity to give back to fellow students what they have received in a therapeutic, personal, and productive way. As students go through the PS social component, they learn about the secondary characteristics associated with dyslexia. In addition, students have the opportunity to enhance their sense of self-awareness and to be more sensitive to the psychosocial implications of being dyslexic.

The project's arithmetic remediation component assumes that the carrying out of math functions is an exercise in decoding. Thus students who are deficient in math skills are taught to analyze a math problem into a sequence of sentences; each sentence is representative of a particular step or procedure associated with the solving of a particular math problem.

REFERENCES

Langan, J. (1983). *Sentence skills* (3rd ed.). New York: Holt, Rinehart, & Winston.

Nash, R. (1984). *Manual for remediating the reading and spelling deficits of elementary, secondary, and postsecondary students.* Oshkosh, WI: Robert T. Nash Language Training School.

ROBERT T. NASH
University of Wisconsin

READING DISORDERS

PROJECT TALENT

Project Talent was conceived in the late 1950s as an ambitious survey of American youth. A two-day battery of specially designed tests and inventories was administered to a 5% sample of high-school students from across the United States. The intention was to follow-up those tested at regular intervals, and through this process develop an information base about the processes by which men and women develop and use their abilities. The goals of Project Talent were to develop a national inventory of human resources; to achieve a better understanding of how young people choose and develop their careers; and to identify the educational and life experiences that are most important in preparing individuals for their life work (Flanagan et al., 1962).

The group tested included over 400,000 students, constituting a 5% probability sample of all students in grades 9, 10, 11, and 12 in public and nonpublic secondary schools in the United States in the spring of 1960. In addition, several supplemental samples were tested in 1960 to address special questions. These included a probability sample of all 15 year olds, whether or not they happened to be in the grade 9 to 12 range or, for that matter, in school. Also included were all high-school students in Knox County (Knoxville), Tennessee. Finally, over 10,000 students from 100 schools originally tested as ninth graders in 1960 were retested for two days as twelfth graders in 1963.

The Project Talent battery included a wide variety of aptitude and achievement tests, sample information in academic and nonacademic areas, and a questionnaire on vocational interests. There was also a personality inventory and a biographical questionnaire containing nearly 400 questions about school life, out-of-school activities, general health, plans, aspirations, home, and family. In addition, each of the more than 1000 participating junior and senior high schools provided information on its instructional and guidance programs, facilities, staffing, and student/community characteristics.

The original plan for Project Talent called for follow-up of those tested 1, 5, 10, and 20 years following the expected graduation of each class. There were subsequent modifications with follow-up surveys 1, 5, and 11 years following the year of class graduation. For example, the original twelfth-, eleventh-, tenth-, and ninth-grade students were surveyed in 1961 through 1963, respectively, when students in each sample were at the model age of 19 years. Surveys were by mail, with a random sample of nonrespondents intensively pursued (by questionnaire or, if necessary, interview) to allow the development of accurate population statistics.

Each of the follow-up surveys sought information on postsecondary education, career choices, work experiences, and family plans, and were timed to occur at key points in individuals' personal and career development. The first- and fifth-year follow-ups focused on the years in which the participants began to put their career choices into action, either through education, training, or direct job experience. Most individuals had completed their formal education had entered the labor force, and had started their families at the time of the 11-year follow-up. The most recent survey focused on each individual's satisfaction with educational preparation, careers, and general quality of life.

Another more limited line of research involved the follow-back design. This approach was based on the fact that approximately 5% of those entering medical school in the mid 1960s, for example, were part of the Project Talent sample. It is possible to check names of those enrolling in medical school against the Project Talent files, and as a result have valuable precollege data on a random sample of those entering medical school.

The results of Project Talent are far more extensive than can be covered in this report. The body of knowledge includes technical reports and published articles by the Project Talent staff between 1962 and the present, as well as articles by researchers accessing the information through the Project Talent Data Bank. Many of these reports are in university libraries; others can be obtained through Publications Service, American Institutes for Research, P.O. Box 1113, Palo Alto, California 94302.

The initial report of results from the Project Talent staff was in 1964; it described the inventory of talent in the United States (Flanagan et al., 1964). One highlight from the one-year, follow-up surveys was the tremendous amount of change in career plans. For example, those tested in 1960 were asked to indicate career plans. One year after high school graduation, more than half of those electing each of the career alternatives as high school seniors had changed their plans (Flanagan et al., 1966). Percentages were even lower for those graduating in 1961 to 1963. Of interest was the fact that changes were toward career choices more in line with abilities and interests.

Results of the fifth- (Flanagan et al., 1971) and the eleventh-year (Wilson & Wise, 1975; Wise, McLaughlin, & Gilmartin, 1977) follow-up studies have also been reported. An important finding from the eleventh-year follow-up was that nearly 25% of the men and women at age 29 still planned to obtain further education toward various degrees (Wise, et al., 1977).

The data collected in conjunction with Project Talent are available to scientists, stripped of identifying information and on a cost-recovery basis. The most comprehensive study done by an outside investigator using this data was that published by Christopher Jencks and his colleagues in the book *Inequality: A Reassessment of the Effect of Family and Schooling in America* (1972).

REFERENCES

Flanagan, J. C., Cooley, W. W., Lohnes, P. R., Schoenfeldt, L. F., Holdeman, R. W., Combs, J., & Becker, S. (1966). *Project Talent one-year follow-up studies*. Pittsburgh: Project Talent.

Flanagan, J. C., Dailey, J. T., Shaycoft, M. F., Gorham, W. A., Orr, D. B., & Goldberg, I. (1962). *Design for a study of American youth*. Boston: Houghton Mifflin.

Flanagan, J. C., Davis, F. B., Dailey, J. T., Shaycoft, M. F., Orr, D. B., Goldberg, I., & Neyman, C. A., Jr. (1964). *The American high school student*. Pittsburgh: American Institutes for Research.

Flanagan, J. C., Shaycoft, M. F., Richards, J. M., Jr., & Claudy, J. G. (1971). *Five years after high school*. Palo Alto, CA: American Institutes for Research.

Jencks, C., Smith, M., Acland, H., Bane, M. J., Cohen, D., Gintis, H., Heyns, B., & Michelson, S. (1972). *Inequality: A reassessment of the effect of family and schooling in America.* New York: Basic Books.

Wilson, S. R., & Wise, L. L. (1975). *The American citizen: 11 years after high school* (Vol. 1). Palo Alto, CA: American Institutes for Research.

Wise, L. L., McLaughlin, D. H., & Gilmartin, K. J. (1977). *The American citizen: 11 years after high school* (Vol. 2). Palo Alto, CA: American Institutes for Research.

LYLE F. SCHOENFELDT
Texas A & M University

PROSOPAGNOSIA

Prosopagnosia is a rare acquired defect in facial recognition that is a consequence of focal brain damage. Visual acuity remains intact. Individuals that develop prosopagnosia are unable to recognize faces as familiar and so do not know whose specific face they are seeing. This is true despite adequate ability to recognize the generic face. For example, a young patient who developed prosopagnosia was puzzled as to why all the actors on a favorite television program had been changed. The faces no longer looked familiar to her, nor could she recognize particular characters by sight. Similarly, she was unable to recognize pictures of members of her own family. This deficit in visual recognition of familiar faces occurs independently of any defect in language or cognition.

Prosopagnosia is often accompanied by other specific kinds of visual disturbances. Individuals with prosopagnosia usually have either a unilateral or bilateral visual field defect. That is, they are unable to see one portion of what ordinarily can be seen when the eyes are held fixed at mid position. This defect is secondary to brain damage or damage to the optic nerve radiations, not to eye damage. In addition, prosopagnosia frequently is accompanied by central achromatopsia, the acquired inability to perceive color as a consequence of central nervous system disease despite adequate retinal function. Visual agnosia also is often present. Visual agnosia is normal ability to see and perceive without the ability to give meaning to what one sees. Normal visual acuity, visual scanning, and visual perception must be demonstrable in an individual diagnosed with visual agnosia. Despite the adequacy of visual skills, the individual is unable to recognize what is seen. Difficulty in identification is not a consequence of deficits in language or cognition. Indeed, many of these patients can recognize objects once they touch them, or once their function is described to them.

Historically, there has been substantial contention about the localization of the brain lesion producing prosopagnosia. Initially, most authors identified the necessary lesion as restricted to the right hemisphere (Hecaen & Albert, 1978), as many of the individuals who had prosopagnosia had left-sided visual field defects indicative of right hemisphere pathology. Recent studies using both radiologic and autopsy findings suggest that prosopagnosia requires bilateral damage to the mesial and inferior visual association cortex (Damasio & Damasio, 1983; Damasio, Damasio, & Van Hoesen, 1982).

REFERENCES

Damasio, A. R., & Damasio, H. (1983). Localization of lesions in achromotopsia and prosopagnosia. In A. Kertesz (Ed.), *Localization in neuropsychology* (pp. 331–341). New York: Academic.

Damasio, A. R., Damasio, H., & VanHoesen, G. W. (1982). Prosopagnosia: Anatomic basis and behavioral mechanisms. *Neurology, 32,* 331–341.

Hecaen, H., & Albert, N. L. (1978). *Human neuropsychology.* New York: Wiley.

GRETA N. WILKENING
Children's Hospital

VISUALLY IMPAIRED
VISUAL PERCEPTION AND DISCRIMINATION
VISUAL TRAINING

PROSTHETIC DEVICES

A prosthesis is any additional device, or artificial appliance, to support or replace a missing part of the body. Prosthetics are the dental and surgical specialties concerned with the artificial replacement of missing parts of the body. Examples of prosthetic devices are artificial legs, dental bridges, wheelchairs, and long leg braces. Devices supporting hand or arm control for eating or drinking such as specialized drinking cups, a molded lower arm supports, or upper arm frames, are also examples of prosthetic devices.

Physical therapists and occupational therapists under the supervision of physiatrists are two of the professional groups that train persons in the use, care, and applications of a prosthetic device. A prosthetic device makes the world reachable for the handicapped by bringing the disabling condition to that point where it places the least restriction on the handicapped person.

Modern technology has not only added to the number of prosthetic devices, it has elevated their functional involvement to a considerable degree. The expanded use of microchips, lasers, and microcomputer technology has greatly expanded readers, laser canes, and opticons for the visually impaired. Technology capable of changing auditory signals into appropriate letters and reflecting them in eyeglasses, or capable of generally improving hearing aid quality, has been miraculous for the hearing impaired. Other important changes in signal systems that permit guided mobility for artificial limbs, stimulated by either movement or voice, now provide auto-regulating movement for the orthopedically handicapped and amputees.

Technology continues to push back the restrictions placed on the handicapped by disabilities. Rehabilitation engineering and rehabilitation technology are fields that, when connected to biomedical, electronic, and other areas of engineering, may well restore usable vision, hearing, ambulation, or upper arm control. The horizons of tomorrow are boundless in terms of the possibilities that technology offers in prosthetic development.

DAVID A. SABATINO
West Virginia College of
Graduate Studies

OCCUPATIONAL THERAPY
PHYSICAL THERAPY

PROTECTION AND ADVOCACY SYSTEM— DEVELOPMENTALLY DISABLED (P&A)

The protection and advocacy system (P&A) was established under federal legislation for the developmentally disabled (Section 113, PL 94-103). Each state or territory receiving funding from the Administration on Developmental Disabilities is required to have a P&A agency. The P&A agencies must be independent of any other state agency or governmental unit to ensure their ability to freely protect and advocate the rights of developmentally disabled (DD) individuals.

Activities of P&A staff may involve negotiation, administrative or legal remedies on behalf of clients seeking programs, services, or protection of clients' rights as DD citizens. The agency's staff is also responsible for information dissemination concerning the rights of DD clients. Activities include presentations and workshops for lay and professional groups on the rights of the disabled. Areas such as education, employment, transportation, housing, architectural barriers, and legal aid are concerns of a P&A agency. The P&A office for each state or territory may be located through the Office of the Governor or by contacting Commissioner, Administration on Developmental Disabilities, OHDS/HHS, Washington, DC 20201.

PHILIP R. JONES
Virginia Polytechnic Institute
and State University

PRUNE BELLY SYNDROME

See RARE DISEASES.

PSYCHOANALYSIS AND SPECIAL EDUCATION

Until the beginning of the twentieth century, mental illness was believed to be the result of biological and organic factors residing within the individual. Sigmund Freud, who was a practicing physician and neurologist at the turn of the century, began to doubt that the hysterical reactions he was treating in his patients had solely an organic basis. Freud formulated an alternative theory to the development of personality that has subsequently had a profound effect on the way the behavior of an individual is explained. From Freud's psychoanalytic point of view, the psychological processes are the primary determinants of emotionally disturbed behavior. Psychological processes include all mental operations, thoughts, emotions, desires, needs, and perceptions.

Psychoanalysis is a specialized technique in which the individual verbalizes all of his or her thoughts and feelings without censorship (Finch, 1960). Freud's theory holds that individuals are only minimally aware of the causes of their behavior. Behavior is propelled by unconscious forces that are too threatening to be part of the conscious. In treatment, patients are taught to free associate to understand the meaning of their behavior and become better acquainted with the unconscious. Eventually, basic conflicts emerge and are understood and dealt with by the individual. Psychoanalysis is a long, tedious, and complex process that has had limited use in the schools (Finch, 1960). It is based on a medical or disability model where the pathology is believed to reside within the individual. To educators who do not have extensive training in psychology or, more specifically, psychoanalysis, the process seems complex and mysterious. Teachers prefer to refer students with emotional problems to outside agencies or self-contained special education classes rather than to risk making a serious mistake that would do further damage to the student.

Newcomer (1980) discusses both the positive and negative contributions of psychoanalysis to special education. There is the notion in psychoanalytic theory that personality characteristics are determined by childhood events; thus, pathology would develop before a child arrives in school. The problems in school are caused by disorders that are within the child. Therefore the strategies for remediation focus on the child and the family rather than the school. This may result in the school having a passive role in resolution of the conflict.

In addition, because of the psychoanalytic belief that

abnormal behaviors are symptoms of unconscious conflicts and that resolution lies in open expression, educators are encouraged to treat disturbed children carefully to avoid repressing their behavior. A nonrepressive environment often provides little structure, and the expectations for normal behavior are reduced. Teachers are encouraged to stop teaching content material until the child's behavior is stable (Newcomer, 1980). It is not clear that this is the most effective way to deal with abnormal behavior. However, there has been a longstanding close association between special education and psychoanalysis in terms of understanding and providing for the needs of students (Pajak, 1981). Psychoanalytic theory has promoted the idea that children do not always consciously plan and cannot always control their disruptive behaviors, but they do respond to internal conflicts (Newcomer, 1980). These beliefs have resulted in more understanding and less primitive treatment of children with emotional disturbance.

Significant contributions to psychoanalysis and special education have been made by Bruno Bettleheim and Fritz Redl (Haring & Phillips, 1962). Their approaches have been primarily permissive in nature, and school work is often used as a vehicle to assist the child in bringing the unconscious conflict to a conscious level of awareness. In general, special education programs have moved from child-directed, psychoanalytic models to more teacher-directed behavioral models where emphasis is primarily on academics and behavior control. IDEA mandates teaching students in the least restrictive environment. Therefore, the emphasis in special education is on teaching children appropriate and acceptable behavior in school, which is in conflict with the free and open expression advocated by Freud and his followers.

REFERENCES

Finch, S. M. (1960). *Fundamentals of child psychiatry*. New York: Norton.

Haring, N. G., & Phillips, E. L. (1962). *Educating emotionally disturbed children*. New York: McGraw-Hill.

Mendelsohn, S. R., Jennings, K. D., Kerr, M. M., Marsh, J., May, K., & Strain, P. S. (1985). Psychiatric input as part of a comprehensive evaluation program for socially and emotionally disturbed children. *Behavioral Disorders, 10*(4), 257–267.

Newcomer, P. L. (1980). *Understanding and teaching emotionally disturbed children*. Boston: Allyn & Bacon.

Pajak, E. F. (1981, Nov.). Teaching and the psychology of the self. *American Journal of Education*, 1–13.

Rezmierski, V., & Kotre, J. (1977). A limited literature review of theory of the psychodynamic model. In W. C. Rhodes & M. L. Tracy (Eds.), *A study of child variance: Vol. 1. Conceptual models* (pp. 181–258). Ann Arbor, MI: University Press.

NANCY J. KAUFMAN
University of Wisconsin at Stevens Point

CHILD PSYCHIATRY
PSYCHODRAMA
PSYCHOTHERAPY

PSYCHODRAMA

Psychodrama is a method of group psychotherapy devised and developed by Moreno (1946). Psychodrama requires a well-trained therapist, preferably one with special certification as a psychodramatist. Psychodrama consists of using dramatic techniques with clients who act out real-life situations, past, present, or projected, in an attempt to gain insight into their behavior and emotions. Psychodrama also provides the opportunity to practice specific behaviors in a supportive group atmosphere. The method of psychodrama integrates insight and cognitions with experiential, participatory involvement, taking advantage of the group therapy setting and using physical movement to bring nonverbal cues to the client's attention. This component of psychodrama can be crucial in therapy with individuals who have limited verbal skills, particularly children and delinquent adolescents (Blatner, 1973). Another significant advantage of psychodrama is its ability to convert the child or adolescent's urge to act out into a more constructive form of "acting in," with guided role playing.

Many production techniques have been devised since psychodrama was introduced, including the auxiliary ego, the double, and the soliloquy. Important to the success of psychodrama is a time for warm-up at the beginning of each session. Participants must also know that the dramatic qualities of the production are not being evaluated, nor are they crucial to the success of therapy. Trust and support of the group are far more important. The role of the director (the psychodramatist) is primarily one of keeping the action moving and helping to lead the participants toward a resolution of the problem situation presented. Keeping the audience (the remainder of the group) involved is also an important role for the director. Three phases will typically constitute a psychodrama, the warm-up phase, the action phase, and the discussion phase.

Psychodrama can be a particularly useful form of psychotherapy with children and adolescents with a variety of behavior disorders. It offers an opportunity for understanding and gaining insight, but it also offers a setting for the development of alternative behaviors and an opportunity for rehearsal in a realistic and supportive setting.

REFERENCES

Blatner, H. A. (1973). *Acting-in: Practical application of psychodramatic methods*. New York: Springer.

Moreno, J. L. (1946). *Psychodrama* (Vol. 1). New York: Beacon House.

CECIL R. REYNOLDS
Texas A & M University

SOCIODRAMA

PSYCHOEDUCATIONAL METHODS

Psychoeducational methods generally refer to the processes of psychological assessment and the subsequent design of remedial programs. Historically, special educators have attempted to develop a variety of psychoeducational methods, all with the goal of facilitating the learning of the exceptional child. This effort has been intensified in the years following the passage of federal and state special education laws mandating the link between psychoeducational assessment data and the development of instructional strategies in the form of the individualized educational plan (IEP).

Hundreds of different types of psychoeducational methods are currently in use. However, the choice of a particular psychoeducational method is often tied to the educator's assumptions or beliefs regarding the nature and etiology of a child's exceptionality (Quay, 1983; Ysseldyke & Mirkin, 1982).

One view of exceptionality is what Quay (1973) refers to as process dysfunction, which is based on the assumption that the child suffers from dysfunctions or impairments in processes that are necessary for learning. The viewpoint holds that the problem resides within the child and the cause of the child's learning problems is the particular dysfunction or deficit. These dysfunctions, according to Ysseldyke and Mirkin (1982), can be in any number of areas, including sensory processes (visual acuity), response processes (motor coordination), specific hypothetical internal processes (attention, visual-perception, and memory) or global hypothesized internal processes (intelligence, personality, and motivation).

Guided by the process dysfunction view of exceptionality, the psychoeducational assessment is geared toward identifying the specific nature of the dysfunction or deficit responsible for the learning problem and then the development of psychoeducational methods to "cure" the dysfunction. This particular view of exceptionality has been popular in special education and has led to the development of numerous types of psychoeducational methods.

Historically, psycholinguistic training programs (Kirk & Kirk, 1971; Minskoff, Wiseman, & Minskoff, 1972) tied to the Illinois Test of Psycholinguistic Abilities have represented some of the more popular psychoeducational meth-

ods. However, research investigating the effectiveness of these psycholinguistic training programs in facilitating the learning and increasing the academic achievement of exceptional children has been equivocal (Hammill & Larsen, 1974, 1978; Kavale, 1981; Lund, Foster, & McCall-Perez, 1978). Many of the criticisms have centered around the methodological flaws of the research investigating the effectiveness of the programs. The level of empirical support of these psycholinguistic training programs suggests they should be implemented only for research purposes.

Another popular psychoeducational method based on the process dysfunction view of exceptionality is the perceptual-motor training program. This program includes training in visual discrimination, spatial relations, visual memory, auditory-visual integration, and auditory-perceptual skills (Ysseldyke & Mirkin, 1982). Typical training activities include walking a balance beam, jumping and hopping, chalkboard drawing, copying geometric shapes, and moving arms and legs, as in "angels in the snow." Programs developed by Barsch (1967, 1968), Frostig and Horne (1964), Johnson and Myklebust (1967), and Kephart (1964) represent the better known psychoeducational methods in this area. Little empirical support exists for any relationship between perceptual-motor processes and academic achievement (Larsen & Hammill, 1975) or for the effectiveness of these types of psychoeducational methods in improving academic performance (Ysseldyke & Mirkin, 1982).

Psychoeducational methods based on modality training (Johnson & Myklebust, 1967; Lerner, 1981; Wepman, 1967) have also received little empirical support (Arter & Jenkins, 1977). Modality training rests on the assumption that a child may learn better through one modality than through another. In modality training, children are taught using their stronger modality, strengthening the modality of deficit, or a combination approach. An example of the combination approach would include a child who has a strong auditory but weak visual modality being taught reading using a phonetic as opposed to a whole word approach while strengthening the child's weaker visual skills with separate lessons.

Optometric vision training has been another commonly prescribed psychoeducational method, but there exists little empirical support for the training's improving academic achievement (Keogh, 1974). This was formally acknowledged when the American Academies of Pediatrics and Ophthalmology together with the American Association for Pediatric Ophthalmology and Strabismus (1984) issued a policy statement. The policy pertaining to children and adults with dyslexia or a related learning disability stressed the need for early medical, educational, and/or psychological evaluation and diagnosis, and for remediation with valid educational procedures. The groups explicitly included the statement that "no known scientific evidence supports claims for improving the academic abilities of dyslexic or learning disabled children with treatment based on visual training, including muscle exercises, or glasses (with or without bifocals or prisms)" (p. 2).

Psychoeducational methods have also been developed based on process dysfunctions in intellectual skills (Cutrona, 1975; Jacobson & Kovalinsky, 1969). As an example, expressive language skills are tapped on the vocabulary subtest of the Wechsler Intelligence Scale for Children-III. Psychoeducational methods developed to remediate this deficit include activities such as making extensive use of show-and-tell games at the younger age levels, playing crossword puzzles and Scrabble games, and making up stories after arranging pictures, at the older age levels. Other psychoeducational methods to remediate intellectual process dysfunctions draw from psychodynamic, perceptual, behavioral, and motivational theories in developing remedial programs. However, tasks on tests like the Wechsler represent only samples of behavior and inadequate performance on some of these samples should not automatically suggest the need to remediate those behaviors. Low scores should be viewed only as symptoms of problems that need to be corroborated to determine whether they represent global or pervasive deficits (Kaufman, 1979). Further, there is little empirical support that in isolation the psychoeducational methods designed to remediate deficits in cognitive skills are effective in facilitating academic learning (Ysseldyke & Mirkin, 1982).

Sensory integration (Ayres, 1972) and training in rhythm and balance (Rice, 1962) represent two additional psychoeducational methods designed to alleviate underlying dysfunctions. As is true for the other methods discussed, little evidence exists to support their use to improve academic achievement (Ysseldyke & Mirkin, 1982).

The opposite end of the continuum, in relation to views of the etiology of exceptionality, is represented by Quay's (1973) experience deficit notion. This viewpoint suggests that a student's learning problems are due not to deficits within the child but to the student's limited behavioral repertoire. The student's learning apparatus is intact and underlying process deficits are not assumed. The goal of the psychoeducational assessment guided by this notion of exceptionality is to identify experiential deficits and develop remedial or compensatory interventions or psychoeducational methods to eliminate them.

The task-analytic or skills-training approach represents a class of psychoeducational methods that is based on this experience deficit notion. Example methods include direct instruction (Carnine & Silbert, 1979) and precision teaching (Lindsley, 1971). Both of these methods focus on the academic and social skill requirements of the school program. They also share the characteristics of being sequential, systematic, and intensive, and are typically implemented in individualized or small group settings. Further, complex learning tasks are broken up into simpler component subskills so they can be taught more easily, us-

ing behavioral principles such as reinforcement and modeling. These various psychoeducational methods differ in the frequency and directness of their measurements. Precision teaching involves the continuous measurement of a student's performance in the mastery of academic or social skill objectives. The method also includes the direct assessment of skills that have been taught rather than the assessment of effectiveness through sampling from a larger domain. All of the task-analytic or skills-training psychoeducational methods are based on the assumption that the teacher cannot predict consistently the particular interventions that will be most effective with a particular child; therefore, the methods are used as tentative hypotheses that are always being tested and modified if necessary.

Compared with the other psychoeducational methods discussed, the task-analytic or skill-development approaches that use direct and continuous measurement tend to be the most effective in increasing academic achievement (Ysseldyke & Mirkin, 1982; Ysseldyke & Salvia, 1974). However, future research may indeed demonstrate that those who assess, develop, and implement psychoeducational methods for exceptional children should hold the belief that exceptionality is explained by an interaction view. Learning problems may well result from deficits resulting from process deficits and/or experiential deficits. However, most special educators exclusively use psychoeducational methods that are based on one or the other viewpoint (Ysseldyke & Mirkin, 1982). Special education needs more psychoeducational methods that rely on an interactive approach.

REFERENCES

American Academy of Pediatrics, American Academy of Ophthalmology. (1984). *Policy statement on learning disabilities, dyslexia, & vision.* San Francisco: Authors.

Arter, J. A., & Jenkins, J. R. (1977). Explaining the benefits and prevalence of modality consideration in special education. *Journal of Special Education, 11,* 281–298.

Ayres, A. J. (1972). *Sensory integration and learning disorders.* Los Angeles: Western Psychological Services.

Barsch, R. H. (1967). *Achieving perceptual-motor efficiency.* Seattle, WA: Special Child.

Barsch, R. H. (1968). *Enriching perception and cognition.* Seattle, WA: Special Child.

Carnine, D., & Silbert, J. (1979). *Direct instruction reading.* Columbus, OH: Merrill.

Cutrona, M. P. (1975). A psychoeducational interpretation of the Wechsler Intelligence Scale for Children-Revised (2nd ed.). Belleville, NJ: Cutronics.

Frostig, M., & Horne, D. (1964). *The Frostig program for the development of visual perception.* Chicago: Follett.

Hammill, D. D., & Larsen, S. C. (1974). The effectiveness of psycholinguistic training. *Exceptional Children, 41,* 5–14.

Hammill, D. D., & Larsen, S. C. (1978). The effectiveness of psycholinguistic training: A reaffirmation of position. *Exceptional Children, 44,* 402–412.

Jacobson, S., & Kovalinsky, T. (1969). *Educational interpretation of the Wechsler Intelligence Scale for Children-Revised (WISC–R).* Linden, NJ: Remediation Associates.

Johnson, D., & Myklebust, H. R. (1967). *Learning disabilities: Educational principles and practices.* New York: Grune & Stratton.

Kaufman, A. S. (1979). *Intelligent testing with the WISC-R.* New York: Wiley.

Kavale, K. (1981). Functions of the Illinois Test of Psycholinguists Abilities (IPTA): Are they trainable? *Exceptional Children, 47,* 496–513.

Keogh, B. K. (1974). Optometric vision training programs for children with learning disabilities: Review of issues and research. *Journal of Learning Disabilities, 7,* 36–48.

Kephart, N. C. (1964). Perceptual motor aspects of learning disabilities. *Exceptional Children, 31,* 201–206.

Kephart, N. C. (1971). *The slow learner in the classroom* (2nd ed.). Columbus, OH: Merrill.

Kirk, S. A., & Kirk, W. D. (1971). *Psycholinguistic learning disabilities: Diagnosis and remediation.* Urbana, IL: University of Illinois Press.

Larsen, S. C., & Hammill, D. D. (1975). The relationship between selected visual perceptual abilities to school learning. *Journal of Special Education, 9,* 281–291.

Lerner, J. S. (1981). *Children with learning disabilities* (3rd ed.). Boston: Houghton Mifflin.

Lindsley, O. R. (1971). Precision teaching in perspective: An interview with Ogden R. Lindsley. *Teaching Exceptional Children, 3,* 114–119.

Lund, K., Foster, G., & McCall-Perez, F. (1978). The effectiveness of psycholinguistic training. A re-evaluation. *Exceptional Children, 44,* 310–321.

Minskoff, E., Wiseman, D. E., & Minskoff, J. G. (1972). *The MWM program for developing language abilities.* Ridgewood, NJ: Educational Performance Associates.

Quay, H. C. (1973). Special education: Assumptions, techniques, and evaluative criteria. *Exceptional Children, 40,* 165–170.

Rice, A. (1962). Rhythmic training and board balancing prepares a child for learning. *Nation's Schools, 6,* 72.

Wepman, J. (1967). The perceptual bases for learning. In E. C. Friersen & W. B. Barbe (Eds.), *Educating children with learning disabilities: Selected readings.* New York: Appleton-Century-Crofts.

Ysseldyke, J. E., & Mirkin, P. K. (1982). The use of assessment information to plan instructional interventions: A review of the research. In C. R. Reynolds & T. B. Gutkin (Eds.), *The handbook of school psychology.* New York: Wiley.

Ysseldyke, J., & Salvia, J. (1974). Diagnostic prescriptive teaching: Two models. *Exceptional Children, 4,* 181–186.

MARK E. SWERDLIK
Illinois State University

ASSESSMENT
ETIOLOGY
MEASUREMENT
TASK ANALYSIS
TEACHING STRATEGIES

PSYCHOGENIC MODELS

Psychogenic models present causes of human behavior in terms of the psychological functioning of the individual. The cognitive and emotional aspects of personality are central to explaining behavior. The psychogenic approach emphasizes emotional distress as the root of deviant behavior (Bootzin, 1984). The model stands in contrast to the biogenic approach in placing little emphasis on the physiological factors underlying behavior.

Psychogenic models, however, emphasize factors internal to the individual as mechanisms of behavior. For example, personality integration is the central construct of psychological definitions of mental health (Freeman & Giovannoni, 1969). The effects of the ecology of the family or school are mediated by psychological factors, and changes in behavior result from improvements in psychological functioning. The psychogenic model may share with the biogenic model a tendency to blame the victim.

Balow (1979) noted that psychological models are compatible with special education practice because most educational interventions are based on psychological principles. The models, techniques, and measurements of special education used to be expressed typically in terms of psychological function of individual students. The current focus in special education has moved away from the psychogenic model and is much more based in outcome assessments and are more focused on outcome.

REFERENCES

Balow, B. (1979). Biological defects and special education: An empiricist's view. *Journal of Special Education, 13,* 35–40.

Bootzin, R. (1984). *Abnormal psychology: Current perspectives* (4th ed.). New York: Random House.

Freeman, H., & Giovannoni, J. (1969). Social psychology and mental health. In G. Lindzey & E. Aronson (Eds.), *The handbook of social psychology.* (Vol. 5, 2nd ed. pp. 660–719). Reading, MA: Addison-Wesley.

LEE ANDERSON JACKSON, JR.
University of North Carolina at Wilmington

BIOGENIC MODEL OF BEHAVIOR
ETIOLOGY

PSYCHOLINGUISTICS

In the late 1950s, with the aid of workers in philosophy and anthropology and the earlier insights of distinguished scholars such as von Humboldt and Wundt, psychologists and linguists joined forces to study the content and organization of mature linguistic (i.e., phonological, syntactic, morphological, and semantic) knowledge. In addition, they studied the content and organization of mature communicative (e.g., conversational) competence, linguistic and communicative development, speech production and comprehension processes, memory for linguistic input, and the relationship between language and thought (Blumenthal, 1970; Foss & Hakes, 1978). Thus was born the science of psycholinguistics, which soon attracted the attention of workers in fields such as special education, speech-hearing-language disorders, reading, and second-language learning.

One of the factors responsible for this attraction in special education and related fields was the recognition of the need to describe and explain normal language acquisition when attempting to assess the language problems of, for example, mentally retarded or autistic children (Rosenberg, 1992) or dyslexic children (Greene, 1996). At the same time, however, basic researchers in psycholinguistics began to recognize that their theories of normal language acquisition and functioning could be illuminated by observations of language disorders in children and adults. The fact, for example, that there are rarely any qualitative differences between normal and language-disordered children in the course of language acquisition or in the structure of the language acquired suggests "that there are strong specifically linguistic biological constraints on first-language acquisition that limit significantly the manner in which a wide variety of insults can affect language competence and its development" (Rosenberg, 1984, p. 228).

As indicated, psycholinguistics has been influential in the field of special education, with its longstanding commitment to children with language and communicative disorders associated with mental retardation, hearing impairment, visual impairment, learning disabilities, and other handicaps. This influence has been apparent in work with handicapped children on the assessment and remediation of disorders of linguistic competence (Bloom & Lahey, 1978), on linguistic coding and reading ability (Vellutino & Scanlon, 1982), and on the development of communicative competence (Donahue & Bryan, 1983). The work on communicative competence is the result of an increased emphasis in special education on preparing handicapped students for community living and mainstreaming.

Thus, progress has been made in the education of handicapped children in the areas of language and communication, although much remains to be done, particularly concerning the role of first-language competence in learning to read and mathematics (Osherson, 1995).

Recent applied psycholinguistic research that has particular implications for special education includes Abbeduto and Rosenberg (1980) who have shown that the conversational communicative competence of mildly retarded adults (and possibly moderately retarded adults as well) is mostly indistinguishable from that of normal adults. Therefore, although mentally retarded children tend to get off to a slow start in the area of conversational communicative competence, many of them may be able to catch up to their nonretarded peers. Such findings could inspire special educators to expand their efforts to facilitate communicative development in mentally retarded children.

An appreciable number of psycholinguists believe that a major factor in a child's ability to "crack the code" of the language he or she hears is the meanings inferred from the sensory input provided by nonlinguistic context. Therefore, blind children should be unable to master word meanings that require sight, and should be considerably delayed in other aspects of language development. However, as Landau and Gleitman (1985) have shown, blind children can learn a good deal about the meanings of such words, and their language development is only minimally delayed. Like sighted children, blind children bring to the task of language acquisition native resources or expectations that facilitate language acquisition independent, to a significant extent, of sensory experience. Clearly, blind children should be encouraged by teachers and others to use their vocabulary of sight to whatever extent is possible, and to engage in age-appropriate language and communicative activities generally.

REFERENCES

Abbeduto, L., & Rosenberg, S. (1980). The communicative competence of mildly retarded adults. *Applied Psycholinguistics, 1,* 405–426.

Bloom, L., & Lahey, M. (1978). *Language development and language disorders.* New York: Wiley.

Blumenthal, A. L. (1970). *Language and psychology.* New York: Wiley.

Donahue, M., & Bryan, T. (1983). Conversational skills and modeling in learning disabled boys. *Applied Psycholinguistics, 4,* 251–278.

Foss, D. J., & Hakes, D. T. (1978). *Psycholinguistics.* Englewood Cliffs, NJ: Prentice-Hall.

Greene, J. F. (1996). Psycholinguistic assessment: The clinical base for identification of dyslexia. *Topics in Language Disorders, 16*(2), 45–72.

Landau, B., & Gleitman, L. R. (1985). *Language and experience.* Cambridge, MA: Harvard University Press.

Osherson, D., & Weinstein, S. (1995). On the study of first language acquisition. *Journal of Mathematical Psychology, 39*(2), 129–145.

Rosenberg, S. (Ed.). (1982). *Handbook of applied psycholinguistics; Major thrusts of research and theory.* Hillsdale, NJ: Erlbaum.

Rosenberg, S. (1984). Disorders of first-language development: Trends in research and theory. In E. S. Gollin (Ed.), *Malformations of development: Biological and psychological sources and consequences.* NY: Academic.

Vellutino, F. R., & Scanlon, D. M. (1982). Verbal processing in poor and normal readers. In C. J. Brainerd & M. Pressley (Eds.), *Verbal processes in children.* NY: Springer-Verlag.

SHELDON ROSENBERG
University of Illinois

LANGUAGE DISORDERS
LANGUAGE THERAPY

PSYCHOLOGICAL ABSTRACTS (PA)

Psychological Abstracts (PA) provides nonevaluative summaries of the world's literature in psychology and related disciplines. Over 950 journals, technical reports, monographs, and other scientific documents provide material for coverage in PA. *Psychological Abstracts* includes bibliographic citations or annotations that are used to cover books, secondary sources, articles peripherally relevant to psychology, or articles that can be represented adequately in approximately 30 to 50 words. Since 1967 the abstracts have been entered into machine-readable tapes that now provide the basis for the automated search and retrieval service known as Psychological Abstracts Information Service (PsychINFO).

As psychology has multiple roots in the older disciplines of philosophy, medicine, education, and physics, the vocabulary of psychological literature is characterized by considerable diversity. Each new generation of psychologists added to the vocabulary in attempting to describe their research and perceptions of behavioral processes. As a result, the American Psychological Association standardized the vocabulary by designing a Thesaurus of Psychological Index Terms in 1974, a few years after establishing the computerized version of PA. By 1967 there were over 800 terms that indexed psychological research and writing. In 1974, when the first *Thesaurus* was published, the index and terms were based on the frequency of the occurrence of single words in titles or abstracts in PA over the preceding years. The *Thesaurus* was revised in 1977 and 1982. Each entry in the *Abstracts* and the PsychINFO system is indexed for retrieval by one or more *Thesaurus* index terms, which reflect broader, narrower, and related terms that may describe content in the article. In addition, each article is identified as belonging to one of 16 major content categories and 64 subcategories.

Using these index and content classification terms en-

ables the user to locate articles of interest for hand searchers of *PA* issues or for computerized retrieval from the PsychINFO system.

Further information about PA or the PsychINFO system can be obtained from the American Psychological Association, 750 First St., N. E., Washington, DC 20002-4242, or by telephone at (202)336-5568.

NADINE M. LAMBERT
University of California
First edition

MARIE ALMOND
The University of Texas of the Permian Basin
Second edition

PSYCHOLOGICAL CLINICS

University psychological clinics are generally student training facilities that have a cooperative relationship with the surrounding community. The clinics provide undergraduate and graduate students in disciplines such as education, counseling, and psychology with an opportunity to apply their theoretical and technical knowledge in working with a variety of clients in a closely supervised practicum. Individuals from the communities surrounding the university psychological clinics are able to receive innovative, state-of-the-art evaluations and treatments at reasonable fees from professionals in training. Each clinic usually has a director who is responsible for the coordination and overall functioning of the clinic and each student's activities are generally scrutinized by one or more qualified supervisors (i.e., licensed psychologists, speech pathologists, or special educators). A number of types of services are usually offered in the psychological clinics, including: child assessment and treatment; parent training; family counseling; teacher consultation; program evaluation; and organizational consultation. Therefore, the clinic provides clients with a wide array of psychological services and the students in training with exposure to a number of different approaches to a particular problem.

TIMOTHY L. TURCO
STEPHEN N. ELLIOTT
Louisiana State University

CHILD GUIDANCE CLINIC
COLLEGE PROGRAMS FOR DISABLED COLLEGE STUDENTS

PSYCHOLOGICAL CORPORATION

The Psychological Corporation is the world's oldest and largest commercial test publisher. It was founded in New York City in 1921 by three noted professors from Teachers College of Columbia University; James M. Cattell, Edward L. Thorndike, and Robert S. Woodworth. Over its 65-year history, the corporation's primary mission has been the application of principles of psychology and measurement to the solution of educational, clinical, industrial, and social problems. On the eve of its fiftieth anniversary, the Psychological Corporation merged with the test department of Harcourt, Brace, & World, and in 1975 it became a subsidiary of Harcourt Brace Jovanovich. Growth in development programs, services, and professional staff required the corporation to move from New York to Cleveland, Ohio, in 1983. The corporation continued to expand rapidly, employing over 200 people, including 50 psychologists specializing in measurement, child development, and education, by 1985. In 1986 the corporation relocated to permanent headquarters at 555 Academic Court, San Antonio, Texas 78204, with field offices in New York, Chicago, Atlanta, San Diego, Orlando, and Toronto.

The corporation is well known for high-quality educational and psychological tests. Names such as the Wechsler Intelligence Scales for Children-Revised, Children's Memory Scales, McCarthy Scales of Children's Abilities, Baley Scales of Infant Development, and Stanford Diagnostic Reading and Mathematics Tests are familiar to scholars throughout the world. The corporation also provides tests and services to many of the nation's largest companies, government agencies, and health care institutions, and holds contracts for large-scale assessment programs in English- and non-English-speaking countries worldwide. The corporation now publishes over 200 tests and has a computer software development program.

PAUL A. MCDERMOTT
University of Pennsylvania

PSYCHOLOGICAL REPORTS

Psychological Reports is published bimonthly, two volumes a year, the first with issues in February, April, and June and the second with issues in August, October, and December. Between 2000 and 3000 pages are published annually. Approximately one-third of the articles come from outside the United States. The purpose of this journal is to encourage scientific originality and creativity in the field of general psychology for the person who is first a psychologist and then a specialist. It carries experimental, theoretical, and speculative articles; comments; special reviews; and a listing of new books and other materials received. Controversial material of scientific merit is welcomed. Multiple referees examine submissions. Critical editing is balanced by specific suggestions as to changes required to meet standards (Ammons & Ammons, 1962a).

The complete publication process requires as little as 8 to 12 weeks. Distribution of the journal is international. Abstracts appear in standard outlets (e.g., *Psychological Abstracts*), in numerous on-line services for special interest areas, and in journals with particular emphases. A survey made in 1985 (the thirty-first year of publication) showed that *Psychological Reports* appeared in the top 5% of psychology journals for number of citations of articles and number of refereed, selected archival articles published, and that it had held that position for the preceding decade. The journal has consistently maintained for 30 years a policy of being highly experimental, open to all defensible points of view, encouraging of new and often unpopular ways of looking at problems, and protective of authors by careful but open-minded refereeing and editing (Ammons & Ammons, 1962b).

REFERENCES

Ammons, R. B., & Ammons, C. H. (1962a). Permanent or temporary journals: Are PR and PMS stable? *Perceptual & Motor Skills, 14,* 281.

Ammons, C. H., & Ammons, R. B. (1962b). Permanent or temporary journals: PR and PMS become stable. *Psychological Reports, 10,* 537.

C. H. AMMONS
*Psychological
Reports / Perceptual and
Motor Skills*

PSYCHOLOGY IN THE SCHOOLS

Psychology in the Schools began in 1964 with William Hunt serving as editor. He was followed briefly by B. Claude Mathis and then in 1970 by Gerald B. Fuller of Central Michigan University, who remains as editor. In an attempt to meet the practical needs of professionals in the field, this journal emphasizes an applied orientation. It addresses practicing school and clinical psychologists, guidance personnel, teachers, educators, and university faculty. Articles of preference clearly describe the relevancy of the research for these practitioners. However, occasionally important experimental and theoretical papers may be included.

The major areas of focus include (1) theoretical papers and interpretive reviews of literature when these relate to some aspect of school psychology; (2) opinions that are well formulated and presented; (3) treatment and remediation approaches; (4) evaluation of treatment and remediation or other program evaluations; (5) deviant or atypical features of the behavior of school children; (6) social or group effects on adjustment and development; (7) educational, intellectual, and personality assessments; (8) etiology and diagnosis; and (9) case studies. These areas are grouped into four categories within the journal: evaluation and assessment; educational practices and problems; strategies for intervention; and general topics.

GERALD B. FULLER
Central Michigan University

PSYCHOMETRICS

See MEASUREMENT.

PSYCHOMOTOR SEIZURES

The term psychomotor was introduced in 1938 by Gibbs and Lennox (Lennox & Lennox, 1960) to describe epileptic manifestations composed of various multiple psychic or motor activities. These manifestations are associated with spikes, sharp or slow waves on the electroencephalogram over the anterior area of the temporal lobe; therefore, the manifestations are also called temporal lobe seizures. According to the classification of the International League Against Epilepsy (1981), the seizures are partial, as they begin locally, and also complex, as they are associated with "a clouding of consciousness and complete or partial amnesia for the event" (Livingston, 1972). They may be followed by generalized tonic-clonic seizures.

Psychomotor seizures are more frequent in older children, adolescents, and young adults (Currie et al., 1971; Gastaut, 1953; Livingston, 1972). However, Holowach et al. (1961) and Chao et al. (1962) reported this kind of seizure in 11 and 15.7% of children with all types of epilepsy up to 15 years of age. The onset occurred before the age of 6 years in more than 50% and before the age of 3 years in almost 30%.

As in every partial seizure, the temporal lobe epilepsy may start with an aura that is the first subjective and remembered symptom of the seizure. This aura is indicative of the starting point of the fit, and sometimes of its spreading. In psychomotor epilepsy, the wide variety of symptoms, sensory, motor, or mental, are due to the structures encountered in the temporal lobe area, such as the tempo-

ral convolutions, the cortex in the fissure of Sylvius, the insula, the amygdaloid nucleus, the uncus, and the hippocampal zone. The International League Against Epilepsy (1985) proposes to classify the multiple clinical pictures into four subtypes: hippocampal (mesiobasal limbic or primary rhinencephalic psychomotor), amygdalar (anterior polaramygdalar), lateral posterior temporal, and opercular (insular) epilepsies. The symptoms may be motor, sensory, or psychic, appearing simultaneously or consecutively, but they present some clinical patterns (Chao et al. 1962; Gastaut, 1953; Holowach et al., 1961; Livingston, 1972).

Young children may, as an aura, run to their mother with fear or complain of gastric discomfort or unpleasant smell or taste before the loss of consciousness. The symptoms often start with an arrest of motion, with eye staring eventually followed by simple and/or complex automatisms such as repetitive oral movements (e.g., lip smacking, chewing, and swallowing) (Ebner, Noachter, Dinner, & Lueders, 1996; Serafetinides, 1996). The motor activities, like rubbing the face, fumbling with buttons of clothing, or wandering around the room, appear purposive but inappropriate at the time. Speech may become incoherent or mumbled. Autonomic disturbances such as urination, vomiting, salivation, or flushing of the face may be present. Awareness is impaired and amnesia of the attack is a fairly constant finding. The episodes are not very frequent (from one to five per day to one to five per month) and usually brief, 2 to 3 minutes, but the return to consciousness is often gradual. Mental or psychic seizures are variable, but visual or auditory hallucinations are frequent and owed to connections with the vicinity. Affective manifestations such as fear or aggressiveness are frequently present. The attack may terminate in a grand mal seizure. The symptomatology is often associated with mental retardation, cerebral palsy, and hyperkinetic syndrome (as with any organic brain disorder of childhood).

In children the etiology is most often the result of a chronic, nonprogressive neurologic disease. The seizures may be due to previous insult to the brain in the neonatal period as in hypoxia, infection, trauma, or congenital malformations, but also to severe or prolonged seizures in early life or to febrile convulsions. Tumors are rare. Often, no definite cause can be established (Gomez & Klass, 1983). The most common abnormality is mesial temporal sclerosis (incisural sclerosis). The prognosis is better than previously thought (Lindsay et al., 1979; Staff, 1980), and treatment is mainly medical through drug therapy.

REFERENCES

Chao, D., Sexton, J. A., & Santos Pardo, L. S. (1962). Temporal lobe epilepsy in children. *Journal of Pediatrics, 60,* 686–693.

Currie, S., Heathfield, K. W. G., Henson, R. A., & Scott, D. F.

(1971). Clinical course and prognosis of temporal lobe epilepsy: A survey of 666 patients. *Brain, 94,* 173–190.

Ebner, A., Noachter, S., Dinner, D., & Lueders, H. (1996). Automatisms with preserved responsiveness: A lateralizing sign in psychomotor seizures: Commentary Reply. *Neurology, 46*(4), 1189.

Gastaut, H. (1953). So called "psychomotor" and "temporal" epilepsy—A critical review. *Epilepsia, 2,* 59–99.

Gomez, M. R., & Klass, D. W. (1983). Epilepsies of infancy and childhood. *Annals of Neurology, 13,* 113–124.

Holowach, J., Renda, Y. A., & Wapner, J. (1961). Psychomotor seizures in childhood. A clinical study of 120 cases. *Journal of Pediatrics, 59,* 339–346.

International League Against Epilepsy. (1981). Proposal for revised clinical and electroencephalographic classification of epileptic seizures. *Epilepsia, 22,* 489–501.

International League Against Epilepsy. (1985). Proposal for classification of epilepsies and epileptic syndromes. *Epilepsia, 26,* 268–278.

Lennox, W. G., & Lennox, M. A. (1960). *Epilepsy and related disorders.* Boston: Little, Brown.

Lindsay, J., Ounsted, C., & Richards, P. (1979). Long-term outcome in children with temporal lobe, seizures. *Developmental Medicine and Child Neurology, 21,* 285–636.

Livingston, S. (1972). *Comprehensive management of epilepsy in infancy, childhood and adolescence.* Springfield, IL: Thomas.

Serafetinides, E. A. (1996). Automatisms with preserved responsiveness: A lateralizing sign in pscyhomotor seizures: Comment. *Neurology, 46*(4), 1189.

Staff. (1980). Prognosis of temporal lobe epilepsy in childhood. *British Medical Journal, 280,* 812–813.

HENRI B. SZLIWOWSKI
Hôpital Erasme

ABSENCE SEIZURES
DRUG THERAPY
EPILEPSY
SEIZURE DISORDERS

PSYCHOMOTRICITY

An independent science firmly established in France, psychomotricity is based on the interdependence of physical, affective, and intellectual functions and thus covers a wide field that encompasses neurology, pedagogy, and psychoanalysis.

Numerous scientific ideas from various disciplines have contributed for more than a century to the elaboration of the concept of psychomotricity. Near the end of the nineteenth century, scientific achievements made it necessary to abandon Cartesian dualism, which separated body and mind and led to a mechanistic approach to the body. Instead, the integrative action of the nervous system and its role in the regulation of the organism interacting with its environment were stressed. Neurophysiologists started to examine the bases of tonus and movement (gamma loop and Renshaw recurrent circuit, cerebellum, subcortical nuclei, neocortex, etc.). Penfield's center-encephalic theory of motor adjustment (counter to traditional associationism) underscored the importance of the basal centers and their integrating role, and of the vertical cortical-subcortical relationships.

Dupré, a neuropsychiatrist, described the syndrome of motor deficiency in relation to mental deficiency and compared it with the immature state of newborn babies (limb hypertonicity, enuresis, etc.). For the first time, motricity and intelligence were linked.

In *La naissance de l'intelligence chez l'enfant* (1936), Piaget stated that the first stage in the development of intelligence is the coordination of sensorimotor schemas (i.e., feeling and movement systems such as suction, sight, prehension, etc.) leading to adaptations and assimilations that enable the individual to reach a higher (preoperative) type of intelligence. Piaget's ideas were developed further. De Ajuriaguerra showed that the tonic state is used by the newborn baby as a mode of relation (e.g., crying hypertonicity, contentment hypotonicity). A structuring dialogue actually takes place between mother and child. Wallon studied the relationship between motricity and character (*L'enfant turbulent,* 1925). He described the body image as a progressive construction involving all our perceptive, motor, and affective experiences. Phenomenology, too, played a role in the coming about of psychomotricity. It gave birth to the gestalt theory, in which every physical or psychological phenomenon is seen as an indivisible whole known as the form. This theory helped shape the notions of body schema, behavior, and movement. According to Merleau-Ponty and Buytendijk, the different types of behavior are modalities of the *in-der-Welt-sein,* i.e., of mind and body as they interact continuously in the flow of life. Thus, in the phenomenal world body and mind were no longer separated and psychomotricity could enter the field.

Psychoanalysis also contributed to the elaboration of the concept. The body was defined as a scene of pleasure, and psychic development was divided into organic stages: oral, anal, phallic, and genital. Moreover, it was contended that an organic or perceptual-motor function could be used effectively only if it had been effectively invested. An emotional disorder can easily bring about physical dysfunctions such as conversion hysteria or organic neurosis. Reich stated that the social-emotional state of a person influences his or her tonic state (tension rings). The ethology of the child also played a role. Montagner gave a minute description of the child's behavior in the nursery and highlighted socio-affective correlations.

In France, psychomotricity was recognized as a discipline in the early 1960s. The first French Psychomotricity Charter (de Ajuriaguerra-Soubiran) was promulgated and a curriculum was created. A trade union and various publications came about.

As far as practice is concerned, a distinction is usually made between education, remedial work, and therapy. Education aims at stimulating the healthy child's psychomotor functions. This concept is slowly spreading in nursery schools. Remedial exercises aim at improving psychomotor symptomatology through a reprogramming of the neuromotor sphere. Model lessons by the well-known team of the Henri-Rousselle Hospital in Paris are available. Therapy aims at deblocking and developing the disturbed child's psychic structures through bodily and relational interaction with the therapist and mediatory objects. According to Aucouturier, technicity consists of working out sensorimotor pleasure and treatment of aggressive and fantasmatic productions. These various approaches are used primarily with children up to 7 years of age when symbolizing processes enable them to dissociate themselves from their bodily experiences. However, the concept of psychomotricity applies in theory to every stage of life.

REFERENCES

Piaget, J. (1936). *Le naissance de l'intelligence chez l'enfant.* Neuchatel: Delachaux et Niestlé

Wallon, H. (1925). *L'enfant turbulent.* Paris: Alcan.

DANIELLE MICHAUX
Vrije Universiteit Brussel

PSYCHONEUROTIC DISORDERS

The term psychoneurotic as a description of childhood emotional disorders is associated with the psychoanalytic tradition of Sigmund Freud. It is a general term that has been applied to specific clinical syndromes, including phobias, anxiety reactions, obsessive-compulsive behavioral patterns, and hysterical or conversion disorders. Anxiety is postulated by all authorities as being the prime causal process in these clinical syndromes. Some authorities also include childhood and adolescent depressive reactions under the conceptual rubric of psychoneurotic disorders.

Obsessive-compulsive neurosis is characterized by recurrent thoughts or actions that the child feels he or she must think about or perform. To the objective outside observer, these appear to be irrational ideas and unnecessary or ridiculous behaviors. The obsessive child is seen as a highly anxious child whose obsessional thoughts and compulsive behaviors are a way to defend against intense anxiety. Unfortunately for the child, this cognitive and behavioral style never totally alleviates the anxiety and often leads to new problems in adapting to the social environment.

Virtually all people have occasional obsessive thoughts. A highly valued activity may lead to recurrent thoughts and excitement, or a catchy tune may roll over and over in one's head. Clinicians also observe a degree of compulsiveness in anxious children that, while of a significant proportion, does not occur with enough frequency or intensity to warrant the diagnosis of an obsessive-compulsive syndrome. For example, a 9-year-old boy was seen for an evaluation. Psychological tests revealed a clear compulsive style in executing a variety of cognitive and educational tasks. He was a slow worker with perfectionistic tendencies who functioned at a fairly high level academically and socially. His role in the family was that of a "pleaser." His sister had recently been discharged from a psychiatric hospital after a suicide attempt, and there was an inordinate amount of external stress on the family. It was clear that this child was developing a compulsive behavioral style in defense against the insecurity he felt as a member of this family system.

When the obsessive compulsiveness reaches a high degree, the child can become extremely dysfunctional. Obsessive compulsive children are haunted by extreme irrational thinking and ritualistic behavioral patterns. Kesler (1972) classifies obsessional fears experienced by such children into two types. The first is precautionary fear, which includes worries about one's health, safety, or cleanliness. The second is repugnant fears such as concern that one might engage in sexual abnormalities or some type of conspicuously taboo behavior. Kesler also suggests that compulsive acts can be dichotomized into those that are precautionary such as washing one's hands repeatedly to rid oneself of germs, and those that act as self-punishment such as compulsive counting or bed making.

It should be stressed that the diagnosis of this disorder is made only when the pattern leads to dysfunctional behavior and that a certain degree of compulsive traits are functional. Attention to cleanliness and detail can be very helpful in participation in the family and performing well in school. A bedtime ritual such as reading stories before bed is a beneficial quieting behavior at the end of the day. Few teachers complain about elementary school children who have their desks neatly organized each school day. Most authorities agree that the incidence of obsessive-compulsive disorders is extremely rare (Achenbach, 1974). It appears to be roughly equally distributed among both sexes (Templer, 1972).

Conversion reaction also is described as hysteria. It is most closely associated with the psychoanalytic tradition. Anxiety is presumed to be converted into physical complaints and illnesses. A hysterical syndrome can be contrasted with a psychosomatic disorder in that the former has no medical basis and may be totally contradicted by medical findings. The types of physical symptoms that may represent conversion reactions are almost limitless. Sometimes they mimic known physical diseases and specific organic dysfunctions such as blindness.

A clinical case demonstrates the unique form that conversion reactions can take. A 14-year-old girl was seen for the presenting complaint of a sudden onset of the inability to read normally. She was, in fact, reading backward in mirror-image form. Examinations by a neurologist and an ophthalmologist suggested there was no organic basis for the problem. The case was treated as a conversion reaction. Individual psychotherapy revealed a highly stressful family environment. The father suffered from a terminal illness. Emerging adolescent sexuality also was an issue. The girl was very afraid of growing up and was treated like a young child by the family. The inability to read was treated as a manipulation to avoid these developmental issues. Both the patient and her family denied that this was a psychologically caused symptom. Denial is common among hysterical syndromes. An unorthodox paradoxical treatment approach was employed whereby the girl was not allowed to read and was given the message by the parents that she needed to be more independent and grown up. After much hostility and acting out behavior by the patient, she did begin to read again. It is noteworthy that when stress again peaked several months later, the same symptoms resurfaced. They again remitted with treatment.

Most approaches to the study of psychoneurotic abnormalities follow either a psychoanalytic theory or a learning-behavioral approach. Each theoretical orientation has a substantial following and, at this point, there is no basis for rejecting or accepting the superiority of one approach over the other for the treatment of psychoneurotic dysfunction. Each of these two general theoretical frameworks also have application to the explanation and treatment of a wide range of abnormal behaviors.

The psychoanalytic approach is primarily based on Freud's theory of neurosis. According to this approach, psychoneurotic manifestations result from the individual's response to unconscious conflicts involving sexual and aggressive impulses. At the center of Freud's theory is his emphasis on defense mechanisms, particularly repression. In hysterical behavior, the affective arousal (presumed to be sexual in origin) is pushed out of consciousness and converted into somatic complaints. According to Freud, the obsessive-compulsive child, in contrast, is unable to convert anxiety into physical symptoms so repression is used to destroy the emotional link between an unacceptable idea and the feelings about it. The obsessive can be aware of the unacceptable idea, but manages to keep from thinking about it.

The sexual conflict that leads to neurotic symptoms was postulated by Freud to involve a conflict between the ego, or the child's emerging personality structure, and the libido, the unconscious psychological energy. Symptoms reflect this conflict between the ego and unacceptable ideas. Freud's theory, often labeled the libido theory, proposes that the effect of excitation can be displaced, discharged, or converted into other forms such as bodily or compulsive behaviors. For more complete descriptions of the psychoanalytic theory of neurosis, including Freud's revision of his theory in 1923, see Kesler (1972) or Achenbach (1974).

A learning theory approach discounts the importance of internal unconscious impulses or a personality structure. The learning theorist traces the cause of anxiety to specific environmental circumstances. The operant conditioning paradigm focuses on environmental or behavioral contingencies that reinforce symptomatic behavior (e.g., make it more likely to be repeated). Psychoneurotic symptoms emerge as a way of reducing the aversive effects of feeling anxious; in this way they reinforce the hysterical or obsessive-compulsive behaviors. The reinforced behavior can be generalized to different but similar situations. Thus the learning theory approach discusses complex associations that are learned as the child attempts to cope with anxiety.

Conversion reactions and obsessive-compulsive disorders have traditionally been treated with individual psychotherapy from a psychoanalytic approach. Behavioral approaches have been more frequently applied to the anxiety disorders such as phobias where their efficacy is well established. Noticeably fewer applications of behavioral therapy to obsessive-compulsive and conversion reactions have been reported. Psychodynamic individual therapy with children with these disorders is based on the intensity of the relationship between the child and the therapist. This approach attempts to examine the intrapsychic conflicts that produce the anxiety and then the psychoneurotic disorder. Play therapy is often used for younger children as part of the therapeutic process so that the child can express his or her conflicts through play. The Freudian approach emphasizes that the symptom must be removed by resolving the basic conflict. Otherwise, it is postulated that symptom substitution will occur where the intrapsychic conflict that is left unresolved will resurface in the form of a different pattern of abnormal behavior.

In contrast, behavior therapists reject the notion of symptom substitution and directly attack the symptom or problem behavior. Reinforcement contingencies may be set up by the therapist and implemented by the significant adults in the child's life. The problem behaviors would no longer be positively reinforced and may be negatively reinforced; more appropriate ways of responding would be positively reinforced with the goal that the child would learn new ways of coping with anxiety. For example, in the classroom setting, the teacher, after consultation with the therapist, would implement responses to compulsive behavior by the child that would encourage the child to be less perfectionistic and work at a greater rate of speed. The case of the 14-year-old with conversion reaction discussed at the beginning of the chapter illustrates a behavioral intervention following a psychodynamic formulation. The secondary gain from the conversion reaction behavior (i.e., failing to read) was eliminated. The child was not allowed to read and did not receive special tutoring at school. Emphasis was placed on normal social behavior involved with growing up and focus was shifted away from the symptom.

Family therapy is usually a valuable, if not necessary, adjunct to individual therapy for psychoneurotic children. Recent trends are highlighting short-term dynamic psychotherapy, probably as a response to managed care as well as progression in theory (Davanloo, 1995). The traditional psychoanalytic point of view would assign a separate therapist to work with the parents while the individual psychotherapist worked with the child. More often today, the same therapist works individually with the child and consults with the parents. Family therapy sessions may also be held. The behavior therapist often consults with the parents on specific behavioral interventions that they could make at home. In this way, the parents become collateral therapists. School consultation is frequently a valuable adjunct to effective intervention. The therapist can educate the teacher on the nature of the problem and give suggestions for appropriate responses. These teacher behaviors might include being more patient, as in the case of a conversion reaction or excessive compulsivity; specific behavioral interventions by the teacher can play an important role in changing behavior. Drug therapy is generally inappropriate for these disorders, as there is little evidence of biological causes. An exception would be if a parallel disorder, such as depression in an older adolescent, called for antidepressant medication.

REFERENCES

Achenbach, T. M. (1974). *Developmental psychopathology.* New York: Ronald.

Davanloo, H. (1995). Intensive short-term dynamic psychotherapy: Spectrum of psychoneurotic disorders. *International Journal of Short-Term Psychotherapy, 10*(3), 121–155.

Kesler, J. W. (1972). Neurosis in childhood. In B. B. Wolman (Ed.), *Manual of child psychopathology* (pp. 387–435). New York: McGraw-Hill.

Templer, D. (1972). The obsessive-compulsive neurosis: Review of research findings. *Comprehensive Psychiatry, 13,* 375–398.

WILLIAM G. AUSTIN
Cape Fear Psychological
Services

ANXIETY DISORDERS
CHILDHOOD PSYCHOSIS
DEPRESSION
EMOTIONAL DISORDERS
SERIOUSLY EMOTIONALLY DISTURBED

PSYCHOPATHY

See SOCIOPATHY.

PSYCHOSIS, AMPHETAMINE

See AMPHETAMINE PSYCHOSIS.

PSYCHOSOCIAL ADJUSTMENT

Psychosocial adjustment refers to social and emotional functioning: the way a person relates to and interacts with other people in his or her environment. It is one noticeable area of difference between special needs students and those labeled normal. While problems in psychosocial development and intrafamily relations may contribute to later psychosocial difficulties (Erickson, 1963), a behavioral analysis position (Bryant & Budd, 1984) emphasizes the importance of environmental stimuli in reinforcing and maintaining appropriate social skills.

A number of remedial techniques have been used when an exceptional child exhibits psychosocial problems. Often parents can be taught to provide a more positive family environment and to more effectively communicate with their child. In school and during play, specific appropriate social behaviors, such as approaching other children, sharing, and playing social games, can be targeted for training and shaping using reinforcement techniques (Davies & Rogers, 1985). A high density of positive reinforcement for correct approximations of social contact may also be used to strengthen appropriate social relationships.

REFERENCES

Bryant, L. E., & Budd, K. S. (1984). Teaching behaviorally handicapped preschool children to share. *Journal of Applied Behavior Analysis, 17,* 45–56.

Davies, R. R., & Rogers, E. S. (1985). Social skills with persons who are mentally retarded. *Mental Retardation, 23,* 186–196.

Erickson, E. H. (1963). *Childhood and society* (2nd ed.). New York: Norton.

THOMAS ZANE
Johns Hopkins University

EMOTIONAL DISORDERS
FAMILY COUNSELING
FUNCTIONAL ASSESSMENT
SOCIAL SKILLS

PSYCHOSOMATIC DISORDERS

The somatic expression of anguish is a frequent phenomenon in childhood and adolescence. More than 90% of children between the ages of 3 and 18 years have established a psychological relationship with the surrounding world and expressed a confusion in a psychosomatic form at some time during their development. Somatic expression in childhood is always bound with anxiety either in reaction to a situation objectively traumatic or in relation to the perceptive distortion of an objectively nontraumatic situation. Somatic expression in the child in regard to the adult is specific and evolutionary in relation to the maturational stage of the child (affective and neurological). It is associated with a quantitative or qualitative deficiency in the parent/child relationship, most often with the mother.

Somatizations are frequent in the everyday life of a family, and are expressed through abdominal pain, headaches, fatigue, syncopal tendencies, and breathing difficulties without any objective clinical manifestation. The causes are multiple and often related to situational stress, e.g., divorce of the parents, death, academic examinations, personal crises, and approaching adolescence. Through somatic symptoms, the child frequently aims to provoke a modification in the family system by focusing the tension on himself or herself. Sometimes the child preserves the equilibrium of parents who are ready to break down. There is always a message in somatization; it is chosen consciously or unconsciously by the child in families where only this type of expression is tolerated. The underlying personality is not specific but is generally strong. The somatization is a means of expression limited in time and related to a difficult situation experienced by the child that could regress through verbal exchanges and dramatization. At times, somatization presents itself in a family context called psychosomatic and is characterized through a systematic avoidance of conflicts, enmeshment of roles, pseudomutuality, and functional rigidity. The treatment will then be systemic (familial). The somatization cannot be underestimated even if physical examination is normal; the symptoms are real. It is not a simulation, and the symptoms must be seriously taken into account and the context carefully analyzed.

Psychosomatic diseases of children differ from those of adults and result from the conjunction of various factors. A calendar of psychosomatic diseases exists: colic at 3 months, vomiting at 6 months, eczema between 8 and 12 months, breath-holding spells at 2 years, abdominal pain at 3 years, asthma at 5 years, headaches at 6 years, and Crohn's disease at adolescence. The development of a psychosomatic syndrome is associated with (1) a genetically fragile somatic background (repetitive infections); (2) a precocious inappropriate parent–child relationship (rejection, overprotection, aggression, anxiety); (3) physical stress (allergene) or psychological reactivation of a previous problem of anguish until compensated; and (4) a familial functioning of the psychosomatic type. According to age, the prevalent etiology, and the therapeutic possibilities, the treatment will be made along an organistic or psychological point of view, individually or familial, and symptomatic or global.

Every serious somatic disease is stressful for the child, the family, and those surrounding the child (teachers, grandparents, etc.). The factors of adaptation are related to the nature of the disease itself, to the child (age and personality), and to the possibilities of modification in the functioning of the family facing a distressing situation, e.g., new context of life, hospital, family doctor. Frequently the child uses the physical symptoms to express feelings of discomfort. The diabetic child cheats with treatment, the hemophiliac tempts the danger of bleeding, and the child with cystic fibrosis refuses treatment. The use of an organic symptom that does not have objective reality (e.g., pain in the appendicular region after appendectomy) is frequent and testifies to the nonrecognition of an underlying message by the family of the child: the organ is removed but the psychic suffering persists.

The psychosomatic symptomatology of the child is the borderline of the physical and the psychical, of the inborn and the acquired, of the personal and the relational, and of the conscious and the unconscious. The approach to such a symptomatology needs a great deal of empathy, tact, and comprehension of the global context of the child, the family, and the society surrounding the child. Special educators are in an optimal situation to assist in the diagnosis of these disorders because of the consistent daily observations made by all teachers. School clinicians can refer to the Diagnostic and Statistical Manual of Mental Disorders (DSM-IV) for diagnostic criteria (APA, 1994). If physical complaints over a period of time alert the teacher to suspect a somatic disorder, the school psychologist and parents should be made aware of the situation. Referrals to support professionals in the community should be on hand to assist the family in diagnosis and treatment.

REFERENCES

American Psychiatric Association. (1994). *Diagnostic and statistical manual of mental disorders* (4th ed.). Washington, DC: Author.

Ajuriaguerra, J de. (1984). *Psychopathologie de l'enfant* (2nd ed.). Paris: Masson.

Kreisler, L. (1981). *L'enfant du désordre psychosomatique*. Toulouse: Privat Editeur.

Kreisler, L., Fain, M., & Soule, M. (1974). *L'enfant et son corps*. Paris: Presses Universitaires de France.

J. Appelboom-Fondu
Henri B. Szliwowski
Université Libre de Bruxelles

EMOTIONAL DISORDERS
FAMILY COUNSELING
PHYSICAL HANDICAPS
SCHOOL PHOBIA

PSYCHOSURGERY

Psychosurgery is not an intervention that responds to a specific mental disorder. Instead, it is a neurosurgical procedure that was derived from observations made in animal aggression research (Fulton, 1949; Jacobsen, 1935) and applied to humans to control more violent psychiatric and neurological symptoms. Psychosurgical techniques were employed in the United States starting in the 1940s (Freeman & Watts, 1950). A variety of techniques that proceeded from gross frontal destruction by means of injections of alcohol into the frontal white matter (Kalinowsky, 1975) to sophisticated stereotaxic, electrically produced, ablative procedures (Kelly, Richardson, & Mitchell-Heggs, 1973) have been used. The location of lesions also has become more sophisticated. Initially, the goal of practitioners appeared to be to destroy enough anterior brain matter to create the desired effect, which was pacification of the patient. Contemporary techniques focus on greater localization of a lesion, hence avoiding large-scale brain destruction. Sites include parts of the limbic system, the anterior cingulum, and the posteromedial hypothalamus (Sano, Sekino, & Mayanagi, 1972).

The effectiveness of psychosurgery is straightforward. The issue is not one of vitiating the disorder but of limiting an individual's responsiveness to frightening and disturbing mental symptoms (Kalinowsky, 1975). Thus an individual is still likely to perceive threatening voices, but not react to them. Much like patients suffering the residuals of an accidental traumatic brain injury, leucotomized patients often were perceived by others as generally less spontaneous, more socially withdrawn, and more interpersonally distant. Psychosurgery has been used for schizophrenic conditions, obsessive compulsive neuroses, and affective disorders. As may be expected, given the more general effects of the lesions, psychosurgery with affective disorders produces the least favorable outcome. With the prevalence of psychotropic medications, the use of psychosurgery for behavioral management has diminished significantly.

Recent applications of neurosurgical procedures have noted success in dealing with pain (Culliton, 1976), obsessive-compulsive disorder (Rappaport, 1992) and uncontrolled seizures (Spiers, Schomer, Blume, & Mesulam, 1985). The latter approach is the best example of what psychosurgery was intended to do; that is, to remove a brain area that is intimately involved in producing a disorder. The goal of surgical intervention with an uncontrolled epileptic disorder is to remove the brain tissue that is producing a seizure focus. Thus, the techniques used to identify that focus are as important as the surgical procedure itself. This last point draws the most clear distinction between earlier psychosurgical procedures and current methods. When performed to alleviate behavioral dysfunction, psychosurgery was essentially an approach to limit reactivity without affecting the underlying disorder; in contrast, when surgery is performed to alleviate uncontrolled seizures, the underlying cause is removed with changes in behavior following.

REFERENCES

Culliton, B. J. (1976). In R. N. De Jong, & O. Sugar (Eds.), *The year book of neurology and neurosurgery*: 1978 Chicago: Year Book Medical.

Freeman, W., & Watts, J. W., (1950). *Psychosurgery*. Springfield, IL: Thomas.

Fulton, J. F. (1949). *Functional localization in the frontal lobes and cerebellum*. Oxford, England: Oxford University Press.

Jacobsen, C. F. (1935). Functions of frontal association areas in primates. *Archives of Neurology and Psychiatry, 33,* 558.

Kalinowsky, L. (1975). Psychosurgery. In A. M. Freedman, H. I. Kaplan, & B. J. Sadock (Eds.), *Comprehensive textbook of psychiatry–II* (pp. 1979–1982). Baltimore, MD: Williams & Wilkins.

Kelly, D., Richardson, A., & Mitchell-Heggs, N. (1973). Techniques and assessment of limbic leucotomy. In L. V. Laitinen & K. E. Livingston (Eds.), *Surgical approaches in psychiatry* (p. 201). Lancaster, England: Medical & Technical.

Rappaport, Z. H. (1992). Psychosurgery in the modern era: Therapeutic and ethical aspects. *Medicine & Law, 11*(5), 449–453.

Sano, K., Sekino, H., & Mayanagi, Y. (1972). Results of stimulation and destruction of the posterior hypothalmus in cases with violent, aggressive, or restless behavior. In E. Hitchcock, L. Laitinen, & K. Vaernet (Eds.), *Psychosurgery* (p. 203). Springfield, IL: Thomas.

Spiers, P. A., Schomer, D. L., Blume, H. W., & Mesulam, M. (1985). Temperolimbic epilepsy and behavior. In M. Mesulam (Ed.),

Principles of behavioral neurology (pp. 289–326). Philadelphia: Davis.

ROBERT F. SAWICKI
Lake Erie Institute of
Rehabilitation

ELECTROCONVULSIVE THERAPY
NEUROPSYCHOLOGY

PSYCHOTHERAPY WITH INDIVIDUALS WITH DISABILITIES

Psychotherapy is defined as the application of psychological theories and principles to the treatment of problems of abnormal behavior, emotions, and thinking. The three major schools of psychotherapy are psychodynamic therapies, behavior therapies, and humanistic therapies.

The goal of psychodynamic, or insight, therapies is to help the client gain a sound understanding of his or her problems. Psychodynamic therapies are rooted in Freud's personality theory. Current behavioral and emotional problems are assumed to be the result of unconscious, intrapsychic conflicts and the unconscious mechanisms (i.e., defense mechanisms) employed to deal with them. It is a major goal of insight therapies to help bring this unconscious material into consciousness and thereby allow the client to exercise conscious, rationale control over his or her actions. Hostile and sexual impulses as well as other motives or needs not acceptable to the individual's conscious sense of morality exert an influence on behavior through the unconscious. Techniques used in classical psychoanalysis to accomplish the goal of insight include free association, interpretation, and transference. Through free association, the client is encouraged to say whatever comes into his or her mind, no matter how trivial, embarrassing, or illogical. The analyst minimizes his or her influence on the client's verbal associations by responding minimally and nondirectively. At critical times during the free association, the analyst provides interpretations of the verbalizations in an attempt to help the client gain insight.

Transference refers to the expected tendency on the part of the client to experience the therapist-client relationship as similar to the parent-child relationship. Because the origin of the client's problems is assumed to reside in early parent-child interactions, transference permits the client to resolve problems from the past in the context of a new relationship. It is hoped that in the process, the client will discover insight into his or her behavior. When the patient sees a replaying of the old role of helpless child, he or she realizes the possibility of assuming adult roles in relationships with significant others rather than being driven by old, unresolved feelings experienced in the original parent-child relationship. Psychoanalysis is a complex and time-consuming process (50 minutes per day for months or years). Scientific evidence of its effectiveness is inadequate compared with that on more recent behavior therapies. Contemporary psychodynamic therapists retain an appreciation for unconscious influences on behavior but use more direct and focused techniques to help the client gain insight and exercise more rational control. The goal is to help clients find more realistic and effective ways to cope with their emotional needs. The client is helped to accept emotional needs and to find ways to meet them within the demands of external reality.

Behavior therapies differ from psychodynamic therapies in several ways. First, the presenting problem is viewed as the appropriate focus for the treatment rather than assumed underlying causes in the client's intrapsychic life. Second, principles of learning derived from experimental psychology studies are applied to modifying maladaptive behaviors and cognitions. Maladaptive behaviors and cognitions are assumed to be learned, and they can be modified through the application of learning principles. Behavior therapists focus on the here and now rather than on the historical causes of a problem. Behavior therapy is a broad term encompassing a wide variety of therapeutic techniques. A basic tenet of behavior therapy is that different problems require different treatments. Furthermore, the selection of treatment procedures are based on empirical studies of the effectiveness of different procedures with similar problems.

Humanistic therapies also incorporate a wide range of techniques. Therapies with a humanistic orientation share a belief that each client is a unique individual striving for personal growth, or self-actualization. Carl Rogers' (1951) client-centered therapy is the best known example of the humanistic therapies. Key therapy techniques include the therapist's positive regard for the client and empathic, or reflective, listening. In reflective listening, the therapist is nondirective, serving as a mirror for the client, helping the client to sort out thoughts, attitudes, and feelings. It is assumed that the patient has the personal resources for solving his or her problem but needs the support of the therapist and an opportunity to see the problems more clearly.

The rationale for providing psychotherapy to handicapped pupils is that handicapped persons have the same or greater need for improved psychological functioning as nonhandicapped persons. Some pupils may not be able to focus their mental energies on learning because they are experiencing psychological stress and emotional confusion. When a child's emotional and behavioral problems interfere with his or her learning and social behavior, educational interventions need to be supplemented by interventions that focus on the interfering emotional and behavioral problems.

REFERENCE

Rogers, C. (1951). *Client-centered therapy: Its current practice, implications, and theory.* Boston: Houghton-Mifflin.

JAN N. HUGHES
Texas A & M University

**ADJUSTMENT OF THE HANDICAPPED
FAMILY COUNSELING
FAMILY THERAPY**

PSYCHOTROPIC DRUGS

The majority of drugs classified as psychotropic affect brain processes and thus indirectly produce behavioral changes. Their chemicals work by either increasing or decreasing the availability of specific neurotransmitters. The major classifications include hypnotics, major tranquilizers (antipsychotic agents), minor tranquilizers (antianxiety agents), stimulants, opiates, and psychedelics (hallucinogens). In most cases, these drugs increase or decrease activity level by producing effects on an individual's level of arousal. Potent psychedelic drugs add perceptual distortions to the more general effects.

Hypnotics are intended to produce drowsiness, enhance the onset of sleep, and maintain the sleep state (Katzung, 1982). These drugs produce a more profound depression on the central nervous system. They typically are referred to as barbiturates. Examples of this class of drugs are pentobarbital (Nembutal); secobarbital (Seconal); amobarbital (Amytal); and glutethimide (Doriden, Tuinal).

Barbiturates often are called "downers" because of their soporific action. Intoxication from barbiturates produces effects similar to those noted with alcohol. (For a complete review of barbiturate effects, see Blum, 1984, pp. 165–210). Of particular concern in the use of barbiturates is the tendency to produce physical dependence over time. Additionally, unless withdrawal is performed in graded steps under medical supervision, there is the possibility of mortality during sudden withdrawal.

Barbiturates are the drugs most involved in suicides, including accidental suicides (automatisms). The latter refers to a state of confusion during which an individual who habitually uses sedatives is unsure whether a pill has been ingested and proceeds to take additional pills (Ray, 1972).

Tranquilizers are intended to diminish the discomfort associated with anxiety states. Stimulants are intended to combat fatigue and have been used with children to limit hyperactivity. Moderate doses of stimulants (amphetamines) have been prescribed as adjuncts to weight reduction programs. Examples of these drugs are amphetamines (Benzedrine), caffeine (coffee, cola), cocaine, dextroamphetamine (Dexedrine), methamphetamine (Methedrine), methylphenidate (Ritalin), and nicotine (tobacco).

Stimulants may be drunk (coffee), smoked (tobacco), inhaled (cocaine), ingested (amphetamines of various types), or injected (amphetamines). Though the following effects are seen most often in amphetamine abuse, they also are evident in relative degrees with the abuse of any of the stimulants. After use, the individual experiences a mild flush, which in the case of injectable amphetamines is compared to sexual orgasm. Feelings of euphoria, invulnerability, absence of boredom, and unlimited energy follow. Since abusers are likely to build up a tolerance for a specific drug, increased dosages or drug mixtures are used to create the "high." Continued abuse of a stimulant appears related both to the wish to recreate the high and to the desire to avoid the fatigue and depression that occur during withdrawal.

Negative side effects of chronic abuse include malnutrition, insomnia, impulsiveness, defective reasoning, delusional thinking, hallucinations, and paranoia (Blum, 1984). Owing to the affective lability of abusers, the associated hyperactivity, and the significant paranoia, abuse of amphetamines tends to set up conditions in which violence may occur.

Opiates are intended to provide relief from pain and appear to mimic natural analgesics (endorphins). Historically, morphine was used not only to provide relief from extreme pain, but also for diarrhea, cough, anxiety, and insomnia (Katzung, 1982). Examples of drugs in this class include opium, morphine, codeine, heroin, dihydromorphine (Dilaudid), and meperidine (Demerol).

Of particular concern with this class of drug is that, along with tolerance for a specific drug, physical dependence also occurs. Though central nervous system depressants, opiates produce feelings of euphoria in persons who are experiencing either physical or emotional pain (Leavitt, 1982). Persons appear to start abusing opiates secondary to situational stress, unenlightened treatment for severe pain, and comradeship (Blum, 1984). Chronic abuse produces periods of nausea, vomiting, constipation, respiratory inefficiency, and limited pain awareness. The latter produces additional effects since abusers are unaware of physical distress (Leavitt, 1982). Mortality rates among heroine addicts under 30 are approximately 8 times that of nonaddicts (Leavitt, 1982).

Psychedelics have been used in various research programs, from perceptual research to brainwashing techniques (Leavitt, 1982). They have no consistent, specified therapeutic value. Some, like peyote, have been used in religious ceremonies because they bring on visions (hallucinations). It is this hallucinogenic property that makes these drugs attractive to abusers.

REFERENCES

Blum, K. B. (1984). *Handbook of abusable drugs.* New York: Gardner.

Katzung, B. G. (1982). *Basic & clinical pharmacology.* Los Altos, CA: Lange Medical.

Leavitt, F. (1982). *Drugs and behavior.* New York: Wiley.

Ray, O. S. (1972). *Drugs, society and human behavior.* St. Louis: Mosby.

ROBERT F. SAWICKI
*Lake Erie Institute of
Rehabilitation*

**DRUG ABUSE
DRUG THERAPY
HALLUCINOGENS
TRANQUILIZERS**

PSYC SCAN

During the past decade, a vast amount of information, traditionally available only in print, has been placed into computer-readable and retrievable form. Consequently, psychologists, special educators, and researchers have at their disposal a wealth of knowledge that has been classified, summarized, and stored for easy, quick, inexpensive retrieval by computer. Psyc SCAN is a service of Psyc INFO, which is part of the Psychological Abstract Information Services Department of the American Psychological Association.

Psyc SCAN provides computer-readable information and publications in various areas that are important to professionals involved in special education: applied, clinical, and developmental psychology, learning/communication disorders (LD) and mental retardation (MR). On a quarterly basis, Psyc SCAN offers subscribers an effective and efficient way of keeping up to date on practice and research in their fields by providing citations and abstracts from recently published journal articles.

Abstracts in the applied, clinical, and developmental psychology sections of Psyc SCAN are derived from a set of core journals. When a publication is selected for one of these three areas, all relevant articles are summarized and listed by journal title along with complete citation, abstract, and index terms.

Abstracts in the LD/MR section of Psyc SCAN likewise are published quarterly and offer a practical way of keeping abreast of clinical and educational literature in the field. For this section, however, material is taken from all of the approximately 13,000 serial publications covered by the Psyc INFO Data Base. As such, each issue is arranged by three broad areas: learning disorders, communication disorders, and mental retardation; they are further subdivided into theories, research, and assessment and educational issues. All entries in this section contain full bibliographic citations, index terms, and abstracts.

Additional information about Psyc SCAN and related services can be obtained from Psych INFO Services, American Psychological Association, 750 First St., N.E., Washington, DC 20002-4242.

CHARLES A. MAHER
Rutgers University

LOUIS J. KRUGER
Tufts University
First edition

MARIE ALMOND
*The University of Texas of the
Permian Basin*
Second edition

**COMPUTER ASSISTED INSTRUCTION
SPECIAL NET**

PUBLIC LAW 94-142

See INDIVIDUALS WITH DISABILITIES EDUCATION ACT (IDEA).

PUBLIC LAW 95-561

The Gifted and Talented Children's Education Act of 1978 was added, by PL 95-561, as Part A of Title IX of the Elementary and Secondary Education Act. The statute and its companion regulations describe gifted and talented children as individuals from birth through 18 years of age who require special educational services or activities because they possess demonstrated or potential abilities that give evidence of high performance capability in areas such as intellectual, creative, specific academic, or leadership ability, or in the performing and visual arts.

Financial assistance was provided under the Gifted and Talented Children's Education Program through two types of awards. Each state educational agency was eligible for a grant to plan, develop, operate, and improve programs for gifted and talented children. Eligible public or private organizations, agencies, or institutions also could compete for awards to conduct personnel training, model projects, information dissemination, or research.

On August 13, 1981, this funding program was consolidated into a block grant under Chapter 2 of the Education and Consolidation Improvement Act of 1981. States and localities may use the block grant funds, as appropriate, for continued services to gifted and talented children.

SHIRLEY A. JONES
*Virginia Polytechnic Institute
and State University*

PUBLIC SCHOOLS AND SPECIAL EDUCATION

Interest in both special education and public schools in the mid 1990s is providing an unprecedented opportunity for educators to analyze and develop programs sharply contrasting from those of the past 50 years. Such evaluation and interest in developing effective schools has arisen from several major forces. First, concern is growing for the implementation of programs that truly enhance the academic and social skills of the nation's youth. Second, popular and accepted conceptions about handicapping conditions have changed, as have those toward the responsibilities of special and regular education. The result of this has been a drastic change in the procedures used in classifying students, in part as a function of the research providing an empirical critique of current practice, but also as a function of the consequences of such practice. Third, the relationship between special and regular education has been questioned both in terms of the content and the outcomes and reformed. These three forces have provided a major impetus behind the current efforts at designing our educational system.

As Ysseldyke and Algozzine (1983) have noted, the general goals and objectives of American education include instruction in basic skills, inculcation of social principles in a democratic society, and provision of the opportunity to develop to the greatest potential possible. While there is little disagreement about the value of these goals, considerable controversy abounds regarding the procedures for attainment of such goals. Ysseldyke and Algozzine (1983) cite data from the Children's Defense Fund that indicate problems in the lack of attendance for a significant number of students, and refer to *The Literacy Hoax* (Cooperman, 1978), which provides data on the decline in achievement scores through the 1960s and 1970s.

Recently, criticism has been generated with the report from the National Commission on Excellence in Education, *A Nation at Risk: The Imperative for Educational Reform* (1983). Following its publication, a series of task forces and commissions were assembled to review and/or evaluate the educational process in America's schools (Gross & Gross, 1985). Despite differing focuses, methods, and proposals, the consistent message in all of the reports is that reform of our schools is both necessary and imperative if the social benefits conferred through education are to be maintained. Critical areas addressed in all reports include: (1) curriculum and course content, (2) students' attitudes toward and needs in learning, and (3) teachers and teaching, including expectations and demands.

In part, the disagreement in procedures for educating the nation's youth is a function of the failure of schools to adequately address the great diversity present in the classrooms. While education is meant to be appropriate and applicable to all students regardless of background, race, sex, or creed, it is clear that success or failure in the schools is not uniform for all students. As reported nearly 20 years ago in the Equality of Educational Opportunity (Coleman, 1966) public education is not equal in most regions of the country. This concern for equality has expanded beyond a concern for race and has also addressed the inclusion of the handicapped.

The ideal that an appropriate education should be available to all children has profoundly influenced the direction of education in our country, especially the education of handicapped students. Special education services in public schools emerged in response to this ideal. However, the commitment to providing "education for all" is a recent development (Ysseldyke & Algozzine, 1983). In fact, the right of any citizen to a free and appropriate education began in the mid-1970s as a consequence of PL 94-142, the Education for All Handicapped Act. Up to the late nineteenth century, only a very small percentage of the population enjoyed the benefits of a formal education (Lilly, 1979).

The early nineteenth century marked the beginning of special education in the United States. Special education in the 1800s was characterized by residential programs that were narrowly categorical in their orientation. The programs served students with visual or hearing impairments, who were severely emotionally disturbed, or who were moderately to severely mentally retarded. Residential schools comprised the primary mode of service delivery in special education and those whose problems were less severe in nature and not as obvious in appearance often were overlooked.

Initially, the goals of many residential programs, especially for the mentally retarded, were highly optimistic. However, it was apparent by the early 1900s that earlier hopes of curing mental retardation were not realistic. Consequently, the residential institutions became more custodial than educational and it was assumed that residents would spend the rest of their lives in the sheltered environments of the institutions.

The development of intelligence tests in France, and their subsequent translation into English, were two of the most significant events of the early twentieth century with respect to special education in the United States. As a result, mildly retarded students were identified and special education services expanded. Perhaps more important, the emphasis on intelligence testing created the assumption that learning problems were centered in the individual, rather than due to an interaction between the individual and the school environment. Unfortunately, this assumption still is held by some to this day.

The period between 1920 and 1960 can be viewed as one of rapid expansion for special education. Public school education programs for those with behavior disorders emerged in the 1920s. Previously, programs for children with severe emotional disturbance had been primarily residential. The 1930s witnessed the development of special classes within public schools for children who were judged too disruptive for the regular classroom, but who did not score low enough on tests of intelligence to qualify as mildly mentally retarded. This period saw a dramatic increase in special classes for the mildly retarded, who eventually came to be called educable mentally retarded. The result was a virtual explosion during the decade between 1950 and 1960 in regard to the number of classes available and the number of children served.

Many university programs were founded in the area of special education in the 1950s. Such programs were responsible for training personnel for special education teaching positions and were especially important because of the emphasis on research. To some extent, the research of this period questioned ineffective or inefficient practices and prevented these practices from becoming a permanent part of the special education service delivery system.

Although few states adopted mandatory special education legislation in the 1950s, state involvement in special education finance and planning grew rapidly during the decade. In the 1960s, the federal government emerged as a major influence in the financing and policymaking of special education. The federal government provided grants to state agencies, universities, and colleges for the training of special education teachers. Federal support also consisted of grants for demonstration projects and research into the education of the handicapped. An additional type of federal support was direct aid to states for the initiation, improvement, and expansion of special education services. This type of federal support exhibited the greatest rate of growth in the 1970s.

In the late 1960s, the category of learning disabilities was added to a few states lists of disabilities eligible to receive special education services. This new category was established because a number of children were in need of special services, but neither exhibited the behavioral aberrance necessary to be considered emotionally disturbed nor scored low enough on intelligence tests to qualify as mentally retarded. This new category permitted the extension of special education services to children who previously had been neglected. The brief history of the field of learning disabilities has been characterized by a series of controversies regarding its definition, labeling practices, and the provision of services.

The 1960s saw an increase in the number of states mandating special education services for handicapped children. An extensive search for the most effective, comprehensive, and cost efficient system of special education was initiated by the establishment of special education as a right of all children.

The tools used as the primary determiner of mental retardation, intelligence tests, were the subject of heated controversy during the 1960s and 1970s. The tests were criticized as racially and socioeconomically biased. Indeed, it was obvious that special classes for the educable mentally retarded contained disproportionate numbers of minority and economically disadvantaged children. Controversy also raged about the efficacy of various types of special education services that were being provided to children. Much of the discussion centered on the advisability of special class placement for children labeled educable mentally retarded or behavior disordered (Lilly, 1979).

In the late 1970s, Congress funded five research centers throughout the country to investigate the practices and procedures in use with learning disabled students. At one of these centers, the Institute for Research on Learning Disabilities at the University of Minnesota, a 6-year investigation was initiated to document the state of the art in assessment practices. In summarizing the results from the university's research program, Ysseldyke and Thurlow (1983) state that

1. Considerable variability exists in the assessment practices and classification criteria used by schools.
2. The instruments used in the assessment process are, for the most part, technically inadequate.
3. Generally, students are placed in special education programs because of a deficit between ability and achievement.
4. Current criteria for identifying learning disabled students are inadequate and inaccurate.
5. Classification decisions often are unrelated to the data generated during the assessment process.
6. Decision makers do not use assessment data reliably to identify students as learning disabled.
7. The focus of most teams is on reporting of data, with

little time spent on integrating the data or attending to instructional interventions.

8. Professional opinions about the definition and prevalence of learning disabilities are discordant.

9. The most important determinant in placement in special education is the referral itself. Once a student is referred, the probability of assessment is 92%; once assessed, the probability of placement is 73%.

10. Placement in special education often does not result in substantive changes in educational programs that are different from those programs implemented in regular education.

Litigation pertaining to education began on a small scale during the 1960s, and evolved to a major area of concern among the special education community during the 1970s. In the 1960s, advocates for and parents of handicapped children first used the legal system to ensure the protection of the children's rights in the special education placement process. The area of special education litigation expanded greatly during the 1970s, and the courts became a primary arena for change in the field of special education.

An extremely significant legislative mandate emerged in response to the educational litigation of the 1960s and early 1970s. The adoption of PL 94-142, the Education for All Handicapped Children Act of 1975, which became fully effective October 1, 1977, had a profound effect on assessment procedures and the delivery of psychological and educational services for minority group children. Two of the most important changes mandated by the law were the establishment of due process procedures in each state to safeguard the rights of handicapped children and their parents or guardians in the provision of special education services, and the requirement of an individualized educational program (IEP). The IEP must include statements documenting the child's current level of performance, short term objectives, annual goals, educational services to be provided, the child's participation in regular education programs, anticipated length of the services, date of service initiation, and progress evaluation procedures (Lilly, 1979).

Legal action has been effective in drawing attention to a number of relevant issues such as nondiscriminatory testing and the use of multiple measures on the evaluation and placement of children. Furthermore, litigation can be recognized for encouraging our society to expect free appropriate public education for all children. This expectation has become well established and is widely pursued by the field of special education and our society as a whole.

The emphasis on litigation, and the still present inequities in the way students are identified and served in special education, has resulted in a renewed effort to more precisely determine the procedures for assessing and placing students in special education. The problem with current assessment and placement practices has had great impact on the provision of equal opportunity to all students. The most dramatic effect has been in the over-identification of minority children and males. The Office for Civil Rights (OCR) of the U.S. Department of Education has revealed that these two groups of students have been overrepresented in special education. This issue has continued for two decades and will most likely be monitored for two more.

Current practice in the delivery of special education programs is being reformulated. In part, this modification is based upon the lack of empirical support for the present procedures. As noted by Tindal (1985), the effectiveness of special education has been consistently questioned over the past 20 years by a number of reviewers. Most of these reviewers have found little evidence clearly indicating superior achievement gains as a result of special education. However, the methodology of the research in these efficacy studies has been sufficiently poor to question the validity of the findings.

In a related review by Epps and Tindal (1985), the analysis of special education programs was expanded to include not only the achievement outcomes, but also the definition of program components. In particular, this review investigated the differences between special and regular education programs in the content and context of instruction. Several studies were reviewed utilizing the process-product research paradigm, in which classrooms are observed in terms of organization and teacher behaviors and students' performance is monitored for gains in achievement. The major conclusion was that few, if any, differences exist between the two environments. Instruction has been defined in substantially the same manner in both special and regular education. Students receive approximately the same amounts of time and are required to engage in many of the same behaviors in receiving instruction. The only clear difference to emerge in the manner in which instruction is defined in special education is that students are instructed in one to one setting rather than the small or large group settings.

In response to both of these issues, the lack of markedly different or superior instruction in special education, evolved in to the reformulating of delivery of special education. The major model was the cascade of services originally proposed by Deno (1970) and revamped by Reynolds and Birch (1982). However, the regular education initiative and inclusion movements have changed the entire concept of the cascade of services, and research and outcome assessment will determine how delivery of services progresses.

Implementation of this system generally has acknowledged the importance of consultants and coteaches to regular classroom teachers. The consultation's content includes assessment procedures, development of individualized instructional procedures, direct instruction and evaluation of program outcomes.

In summary, current practice in the assessment and placement of students in special education generally has been judged inappropriate in the past. One new direction being proposed, in response to both empirical practices as well as legal mandates, is the implementation of inclusion. In this system, specialized staff serve as consultants and collaborators in the development of IEPs. By implementing such an approach, special education would indeed become a part of, rather than be apart from, the public schools.

REFERENCES

Coleman, J. (1966). *Equality of educational opportunity.* Washington, DC: U.S. Government Printing Office.

Cooperman, P. (1978). *The literacy hoax: The decline of reading, writing, and learning in the public schools and what we can do about it.* New York: Morrow.

Deno, E. (1970). Special education as developmental capital. *Exceptional Children, 37,* 229–337.

Epps, S., & Tindal, D. (1985). The effectiveness of differentiated programming in severely mildly handicapped students: Placement options and instruction programming, In M. Wong, M. Reynolds, & H. Walberg (Eds.), Oxford England: Pergamon Press.

Gross, R., & Gross, B. (1985). *The great school debate: Which way for American education.* New York: Simon & Schuster.

Idol-Maestas, L. (1983). *Special educator's consultation handbook.* Rockville, MD: Aspen.

Knight, M., Meyers, H., Paolucci-Whitcomb, P., Hasazi, S., & Nevin, A. (1981). A four year evaluation of consulting teacher service. *Behavior Disorders, 6,* 92–100.

Lilly, M. S. (1979). *Children with exceptional needs.* Chicago: Holt, Rinehart, & Winston.

National Commission on Excellence in Education. (1983). *A nation at risk: The imperative for educational reform.* Washington, DC: Government Printing Office.

Reynolds, M., & Birch, J. (1982). *Teaching exceptional children in all America's schools* (Rev. ed.). Reston, VA: Council for Exceptional Children.

Tindal, G. (1985). Investigation the effectiveness of special education: Analysis of methodology. *Journal of Learning Disabilities, 18,* 101–112.

U.S. Department of Education. *To assure the free appropriate public education of all handicapped children: Seventh annual report to Congress on the implementation of Public Law 94-142: The Education for All Handicapped Children Act.* Washington, DC: Department of Education.

U.S. Department of Education. (1986). *Annual Report Congress on Implications of PL 94-142.* Washington, DC: Author.

Ysseldyke, J., & Algozzine, B. (1983). *Critical issues in special and remedial education.* Boston: Houghton-Mifflin.

Ysseldyke, J., & Thurlow, M. (1983). *Identification/classification research: An integrative summary of findings.* (Research Report No. 142). Minneapolis: University of Minnesota Institute for Research on Learning Disabilities.

GERALD TINDAL
KATHLEEN RODDEN-NORD
University of Oregon

ASSESSMENT
CASCADE MODELS OF SPECIAL EDUCATION
INCLUSION
INDIVIDUAL EDUCATION PLAN
INDIVIDUALS WITH DISABILITIES EDUCATION ACT
  (IDEA)
LEAST RESTRICTIVE ENVIRONMENT

PUERTO RICO, SPECIAL EDUCATION IN

Special education services in Puerto Rico are administered under the legislative provisions of IDEA which are reflected in territorial law concerning the handicapped. Before IDEA and PL 94-142, there were few services. Since the legislation there has been greater consistency and continuity of services, improvement and expansion of personnel preparation, reduction of negative attitudes, and increasing movement of children toward the mainstream (Smith-Davis, Burke, & Noel, 1984).

Until a few years ago, the handicapped population in Puerto Rico was generally served in self-contained classes at the elementary level. Since 1979 programming has shifted to the mild and moderately handicapped, to mainstreaming, and to programs at intermediate and secondary levels. Prevocational and vocational centers for the handicapped have also been established (Smith-Davis, Burke, & Noel, 1984).

Teacher certification policies in Puerto Rico are primarily noncategorical, with categorical certification reserved for those serving low-incidence populations. Smith-Davis et al. (1984) report that the University of Puerto Rico, which has had a special education program since 1965, and the Inter-American University, both offer undergraduate and graduate programs in special education. The University of the Sacred Heart and the Catholic University of Puerto Rico offer primarily undergraduate programs. In addition, two American universities, Fordham University–Puerto Rico Campus, and New York University's extension program offer graduate training at campuses on the island. All of these institutions offer adequate programs learning disabilities, mental retardation, emotional disorders, and behavioral disorders. However, formal programs on the severely retarded and multiply handicapped are inadequate although some course work is available. The Department of Education carries on a vigorous in-service program at both local and regional levels and employs tuition assistance and other means to retrain and recertify practitioners.

Special education practices in Puerto Rico must be interpreted in light of the school system, which is highly centralized. It is organized into a central office responsible for all administrative and policy decisions, and six educational regions, each under a director appointed by the secretary of education (who is appointed by the governor at cabinet level). Each region is subdivided into districts run by superintendents. Within this structure, special education is largely centralized. It is directed by a special education director and is divided into four units: administrative, curricular, academic, and vocational. Regional special education supervisors are appointed to each region. Thus there are six plus two supervisors, one each for prevocational and vocational programs (Brown, 1977).

Unlike the United States, where Puerto Ricans are a linguistic minority, in Puerto Rico they are the majority. Consequently, all services and instructional aids and materials for special education are in Spanish. It is important that U.S. special educators be aware that Puerto Rico, through the governor's office and other agencies, is ready to offer technical assistance in these areas to anyone who requests it (Cruz, 1979).

REFERENCES

Brown, F. M. (1977, August). *Southeast Area Learning Resource Center: Final technical report, Sept. 1, 1974 through May 31, 1977.* Washington, DC: Bureau of Education for the Handicapped.

Cruz, D. (1979, June). Outreach problems in Puerto Rico. In G. Dixon & D. Bridges (Eds.), *On being Hispanic and disabled: The special challenge of an underserved population.* Chicago: Illinois State Board of Vocational Education and Rehabilitation.

Olizares, G. (1979, June). Hispanic and disabled. In G. Dixon & D. Bridges (Eds.), *On being Hispanic and disabled: The special challenge of an underserved population.* Chicago: Illinois State Board of Vocational Education and Rehabilitation.

Smith-Davis, J., Burke, P. J., & Noel, M. M. (1984). *Personnel to educate the handicapped in America: Supply and demand from a programmatic viewpoint.* College Park, MD: Maryland University College of Education.

H. Roberta Arrigo
Hunter College

MEXICO, SPECIAL EDUCATION IN

PUNISHMENT

Punishment, defined functionally, occurs when the presentation of an aversive consequence contingent on the emission of a behavior reduces the subsequent rate of that behavior. It is a commonly employed operant conditioning procedure. As Alberto and Troutman (1986) state, "Any stimulus can be labeled a punisher if its contingent application results in a reduction of the target behavior. A punisher, like a reinforcer, can be identified only by its effect on behavior—not on the nature of the consequent stimulus" (p. 245). Thus the mere application of an aversive stimulus (such as a spanking) or removal of a positive stimulus (such as a token or money) cannot be termed a punishment procedure unless a reductive effect on the target behavior occurs. Unfortunately, this reductive effect on behavior by a consequent stimulus is seldom evaluated in everyday use, thus resulting in inappropriate and ineffective use of the punishment procedure.

Although punishment may involve the removal of a positive stimulus, it is most commonly applied by parents and teachers as the application of an aversive stimulus contingent on a behavior in order to reduce that behavior (Walker & Shea, 1984). A common example of this form would be physical or corporal punishment. Although the application of aversive stimuli has been documented as an effective procedure in reducing self-injurious behaviors (Dorsey et al., 1980; Sajwaj, Libet, & Agras, 1974) and severe aggressive behaviors toward others (Ludwig et al., 1969), its use in the form of physical punishment is not generally advocated by most professionals in the field of behavior management as the preferred means of reducing inappropriate behaviors. Besides legal, humane, and ethical concerns, there are a multitude of other disadvantages associated with the use of punishment:

> In the long run, it could cause people to punish more often and to harm themselves and their victims by injuring them, if the punishment is physical, or by impairing social relationships and promoting aggression or escape, self-blame, imitative aggression, and other harmful side-effects. (Sulzer-Azaroff, & Mayer, 1986, p. 146)

REFERENCES

Alberto, P. A., & Troutman, A. C. (1986). *Applied behavior analysis for teachers* (2nd. ed.). Columbus, OH: Merrill.

Dorsey, M. F., Iwata, B. A., Ong, P., & McSween, T. E. (1980). Treatment of self-injurious behavior using a water mist: Initial response suppression and generalization. *Journal of Applied Behavior Analysis, 13,* 324–333.

Kerr, M. M., & Nelson, M. N. (1983). *Strategies for managing behavior problems in the classroom.* Columbus, OH: Merrill.

Ludwig, A. M., Marx, A. J., Hill, P. A., & Browning, R. M. (1969). The control of violent behavior through faradic shock. *Journal of Nervous & Mental Disease, 148,* 624–637.

Sajwaj, T., Libet, J., & Agras, S. (1974). Lemon juice therapy: The control of life-threatening rumination in a six-month old infant. *Journal of Applied Behavior Analysis, 7*, 557–563.

Sulzer-Azaroff, B., & Mayer, G. R. (1986). *Achieving educational excellence using behavioral strategies.* New York: Holt, Rinehart, & Winston.

Walker, J. E., & Shea, T. M. (1984). *Behavior management: A practical approach for educators* (3rd ed.). St. Louis: Mosby.

Louis J. LaNunziata
University of North Carolina at Wilmington

APPLIED BEHAVIOR ANALYSIS
AVERSIVE STIMULUS
NEGATIVE PUNISHMENT
PUNISHMENT, POSITIVE

PUNISHMENT, POSITIVE

Punishment is a procedure in which the presentation of a stimulus contingent on a behavior reduces the rate of emission of the behavior (Azrin & Holz, 1966). Punishment, like reinforcement, is defined by its effect on behavior. Numerous behavior change techniques used by psychologists and educators can be classified as punishment techniques (e.g., timeout, response cost, overcorrection, verbal reprimands, and electric shock; Axelrod & Apsche, 1983).

The use of adjectives such as "positive" and "negative" are most frequently associated with reinforcement techniques, but occasionally have been employed to further define punishment techniques. Behaviorists use these adjectives to describe the contingent presentation of a stimulus (positive) or the contingent removal of a stimulus (negative). These terms should *not* be interpreted as value judgments synonymous with "good" and "bad." Therefore, *positive punishment* is the contingent presentation of an aversive stimuli for a misbehavior or rule violation. Spanking a child for fighting with a peer is a classic example of positive punishment. Socially more acceptable examples of positive punishment include undertaking a noxious task such as cleaning a restroom (i.e., the aversive stimulus) contingent on messing it up. *Negative punishment* is the contingent removal of a positive stimulus. Common examples of negative punishment techniques include response cost or timeout.

REFERENCES

Axelrod, S., & Apsche, J. (1983). *The effects of punishment on human behavior.* New York: Academic.

Azrin, N. H., & Holz, W. C. (1966). Punishment. In W. A. Honig (Ed.), *Operant Behavior: Areas of research and application* (pp. 380–447). New York: Appleton.

Stephen N. Elliott
Louisiana State University

PUNISHMENT

PURDUE PERCEPTUAL-MOTOR SURVEY (PPMS)

The Purdue Perceptual-Motor Survey (PPMS) (Roach & Kephart, 1966) was developed to enable qualitative observations of problem areas of perceptual-motor development. Subtests include walking board, jumping, identification of body parts, imitation of movements (following the examiner's arm movements), obstacle course, Kraus Weber (requiring the child to raise first the upper and then the lower torso while prone), angels in the snow (differentiation of arms and legs in various patterns), chalkboard (e.g., drawing simple to complex patterns), ocular pursuits (visual tracking), and visual achievement forms (a paper and pencil copying task).

The theoretical and practical implications of the scale were described in Kephart (1971). The major assumptions that were controversial (Hammill, 1982) were that higher levels of learning are dependent on a motor base of achievement, and that perceptual-motor interventions are important for the remediation of academic deficits.

The norms were based on data from 200 children in grades one through four. Means and standard deviations were provided by grade. Test-retest reliability was .95 ($n = 30$, one-week interval). A validation study compared the performance of a sample of 97 nonachieving children with the normative sample (mentally retarded children were excluded). With one exception, items differentiated between groups.

REFERENCES

Hammill, D. D. (1982). Assessing and training perceptual-motor skills. In D. D. Hammill & N. R. Bartel, *Teaching children with learning and behavior problems* (3rd ed., pp. 379–408). Boston: Allyn & Bacon.

Kephart, N. C. (1971). *The slow learner in the classroom* (2nd ed.). Columbus, OH: Merrill.

Roach, E. G., & Kephart, N. C. (1966). *The Purdue Perceptual-Motor Survey.* Columbus, OH: Merrill.

David W. Barnett
University of Cincinnati

PERCEPTUAL AND MOTOR SKILLS

PUTAMEN

The putamen is the largest nucleus of the basal ganglia (caudate nucleus, putamen, globus pallidus, claustrum and amygdala) that function in background motor control via the extrapyramidal motor system (Carpenter & Sutin, 1983). The putamen also houses receptor sites for the dopamine containing neurons projecting from the substantia nigra. (The nigrastriatal system with the striatum is the putamen and candate nucleus.) The putamen is located lateral to the thalamus and internal capsule but medial to the external capsule and inner aspect of the Sylvian fissure (see Figure 1 under CAT scan of the brain for depictions of its location). Since dopamine is an essential neurotransmitter for both normal motor and mental functioning, damage to the putamen may result in a wide spectrum of neurobehavioral changes. The prototype disorder of the basal ganglia that best exemplifies these motor and mental changes is Huntington's chorea. In Huntington's chorea there are specific motor deficits characterised by uncontrolled choreic movements as well as progressive dementia (Heilman & Valenstein, 1985). The disruption of any part of the nigrastriatal system will affect dopamine production and will have significant neurobehavioral effects. These are discussed in the section on the substantia nigra. Recent research has also implicated a greater role of the basal ganglia in language function than had been suspected (Segalowitz, 1983).

REFERENCES

Carpenter, M. B., & Sutin, J. (1983). *Human neuroanatomy* (8th ed.). Baltimore, MD: Williams & Wilkins.

Heilman, K. M., & Valenstein, E. (1985). *Clinical neuropsychology*. New York: Oxford University Press.

Segalowitz, S. J. (1983). *Language functions and brain organization*. New York: Academic.

ERIN D. BIGLER
Austin Neurological Clinic,
University of Texas

HUNTINGTON'S CHOREA
SUBSTANTIA, NIGRA

PYGMALION EFFECT

According to Rosenthal and Jacobson (1966, 1968), one of the possible relationships between prophecies and events can be described as the pygmalion effect. The central concept behind the pygmalion effect is that of the self-fulfilling prophecy. That is, people behave in ways that increase the likelihood that their predictions and expectations will be realized. One person's expectation of another person's behavior becomes an accurate prediction as a result of its having been made.

Rosenthal and Jacobson (1966, 1968) applied this concept to children who performed poorly in school. "If school children who perform poorly are those expected by their teachers to perform poorly, one cannot say in the normal school situation whether the teacher's expectation was the cause of the performance or whether she simply made an accurate prognosis based on her knowledge of past performance by the particular children involved" (1968, p. 19). To test this, Rosenthal and Jacobson (1966, 1968) designed an experiment that rested on the premise that some deficiencies (and therefore some remedies) may lie in the attitudes of teachers toward children labeled disadvantaged. They established an expectation that some five pupils in each classroom in a school might demonstrate superior academic performance. The names of these children were chosen randomly. The treatment was simply to give their names to their new teachers. The only real difference between the children pointed out as gifted and the undesignated control group was in the minds of the teachers. The children in the treatment group (for whom the teachers expected superior academic gains) demonstrated superior academic achievement.

Early researchers (Gottlieb & Budoff, 1972; Jones, 1972; Lilly, 1970) in the area of attitudes toward children labeled mildly retarded looked at what is expected of those who carry the label and how this expectation affects performance. Labels may engender specific behavioral expectations, particularly on the part of teachers. These expectations, in turn, may be reflected in the teacher's behavior toward the labeled child, and eventually in the child's level of performance.

Much concern about the pygmalion effect in special education was stimulated by minority groups who pointed out the disproportionate numbers of their children in special classes (*Larry P.* v. *Riles*; *Diana* v. *California Board of Education; Lora* v. *Board of Education of the City of New York*). The concern was focused on the consequences of special class placement as seen in the child's rejection by teachers, parents, and peers, poor self-image, and poor prospects for post school adjustment and employment.

REFERENCES

Gottlieb, J., & Budoff, M. (1972). Attitudes toward school by segregated and integrated retarded children. *Studies in Learning Potential, 2,* 1–10.

Jones, R. L., (1972). Labels and stigma in special education. *Exceptional Children, 38,* 553–564.

Lilly, M. S. (1970). Special education: A teapot in a tempest. *Exceptional Children, 36,* 43–48.

Rosenthal, R., & Jacobson, L. (1966). Teacher expectancies: Determinants of pupils IQ gains. *Psychological Reports, 19,* 115–118.

Rosenthal, R., & Jacobson, L. (1968). *Pygmalion in the classroom.* New York: Holt, Rinehart, & Winston.

CAROLE REITER GOTHELF
Hunter College

LABELING
TEACHER EXPECTANCIES

Q

Q-SORT

The Q-sort is a technique used to implement Q-methodology, a set of philosophical, psychological, statistical, and psychometric ideas propounded by William Stephenson (1953). The Q-sort was developed as a research tool, in particular a tool for exploring and testing theoretical formulations (e.g., about the existence of different educational philosophies). However, its use has been extended to both clinical assessment and to program evaluation.

The Q-sort is a way of rank-ordering objects. The objects ranked usually take the form of statements written on cards (though real objects, such as works of art, have been subjected to the Q-sort also). The sorter is given a set of cards—usually between 60 and 120—and instructed to distribute them into a fixed number of piles arranged along some continuum (e.g., approval to disapproval). The sorter is required to put a specified number of cards in each pile, resulting in a normal or quasi-normal distribution. This distribution permits the use of conventional statistical techniques, including correlation, analysis of variance, and factor analysis, in analyzing the results.

The results of the Q-sort typically are used to draw inferences about people (not the objects they are ranking) for theoretical, clinical, or program evaluation purposes. For example, a preliminary theory about the existence of two opposing educational philosophies can be tested by creating a set of statements reflecting each philosophy, having the combined set sorted on an "approval-disapproval" continuum, and analyzing the results to determine if there are groups of people who rank-order the statements in the same way. In the clinical setting, the patient's sort can be compared with those associated with known pathological syndromes. Finally, in program evaluation, sorts made before and after a program can be compared with one another or with a criterion sort meant to represent the desired outcome of the program.

Q-methodology is not universally accepted in the research community (Kerlinger, 1973). Criticisms of Q are based primarily on the fact that it cannot be used easily with large samples and on its violation of the statistical assumption of independence (i.e., the response to one item should not be affected by the response to any other). However, even with these liabilities, Q is regarded by many as a useful tool for particular research and applied purposes.

REFERENCES

Kerlinger, F. N. (1973). *Foundations of behavioral research* (2nd ed.). New York: Holt, Rinehart, & Winston.

Stephenson, W. (1953). *The study of behavior.* Chicago: University of Chicago Press.

RANDY ELLIOT BENNETT
MARY LOUISE LENNON
Educational Testing Service

FACTOR ANALYSIS
MEASUREMENT
PHILOSOPHIES OF SPECIAL EDUCATION
RESEARCH IN SPECIAL EDUCATION

QUADRIPLEGIA

Quadriplegia is often referred to as paralysis from the neck down. Although this definition may be accurate for certain conditions, it is also misleading. A more accurate description of quadriplegia is a nonspecific paralysis or loss of normal function in all four limbs of the body. The condition most often affects motor skills but also may affect sensory awareness. Quadriplegia may result from damage to or dysfunction of the brain (e.g., cerebral palsy, stroke, traumatic head injury), spinal cord (e.g., spinal cord injury, amyotrophic lateral sclerosis), or peripheral structures (e.g., muscular dystrophy, multiple sclerosis). The condition also may occur as a result of tumor, toxic chemicals, congenital abnormalities, or infection. The term sometimes includes quadriparesis, which is considered a weakness or incomplete paralysis of the four extremities. Quadriplegia is not generally associated with the head or neck, but it may involve these structures in some conditions (e.g., cerebral palsy).

The specific skills or functions that are lost or impaired for persons with quadriplegia may vary considerably and depend largely on the individual's primary impairment. For example, a person who experiences quadriplegia as a result of a spinal cord injury experiences a loss of sensation and movement below the level of the injury. When the injury occurs at the level of the third cervical vertebra (C3), the person has essentially no sensation or functional use of the body below the neck. On the other hand, a person with a C5 injury has some active movement available at the elbow (flexion and supination) and shoulder (abduction and external rotation), but most other movements are lost. In the latter stages of the Duchenne's form of muscular dystrophy, a person may be able to use the fingers to write, type, or manipulate other small objects. Because of progressive weakness in the large muscles of the body, people with this type of quadriplegia are unable to move their arms at the shoulder or wrist. Unlike quadriplegia from spinal cord injury, sensation in this type of impairment remains intact. Children with quadriplegia owed to cerebral palsy are almost always able to move the joints in their upper extremities. They usually experience normal tactile sensation, but they may have abnormal kinesthetic sensation. Because of abnormal changes in muscle tone in various groups of muscles, movements are either very rigid and stiff, uncoordinated, or limp and flaccid. Children with quadriplegic cerebral palsy also may experience abnormal muscle tone and movement patterns in their neck or facial muscles in addition to involvement in all four extremities.

The specific treatment, education, or other intervention for persons with quadriplegia also is dependent on the impairment that causes this condition. A team approach using multidisciplinary, transdisciplinary, or interdisciplinary models is essential in the care and management of an individual with quadriplegia. Team members may include physicians, nurses, teachers, physical therapists, occupational therapists, speech pathologists, rehabilitation engineers, family members, attendants, and, as often as possible, the affected individual. Sometimes individuals with quadriplegia need considerable assistance for even the most routine activities (e.g., eating a meal), while others are able to live independently, pursue a career, and raise a family.

Although quadriplegia usually results in extensive disability, a variety of electronic and nonelectronic devices may be used to facilitate more normal experiences or abilities. Electrically powered wheelchairs, specially designed passenger vans, adapted eating utensils, augmentative communication systems, and personal hygiene and grooming devices are only a few examples that may be used to compensate for impaired skills. These technologic advances have fostered a more independent lifestyle for many people with quadriplegia, but some advocates for people with disabilities would argue that social changes also are needed to permit the greatest level of independence. Elimination of environmental and attitudinal barriers and affirmative action for employment often are identified as essential components of a productive and satisfying life. References illuminating etiology, definition and management are cited below for further reading.

REFERENCES

Bobath, B. (1985). *Abnormal postural reflex activity caused by brain lesions* (3rd ed.). Rockville, MD: Aspen Systems.

Bobath, B., & Bobath, K. (1975). *Motor development in the different types of cerebral palsy.* London: Heinemann Medical Books.

Ford, J., & Duckworth, B. (1974). *Physical management for the quadriplegic patient.* Philadelphia: Davis.

Miller, B., & Keane, C. (1983). *Encyclopedia and dictionary of medical nursing and allied health* (3rd ed.). Philadelphia: Saunders.

Nagel, D. A. (1975). Traumatic paraplegia and quadriplegia. In E. E. Bleck & D. A. Nagel (Eds.), *Physically handicapped children—A medical atlas for teachers* (pp. 209–214). New York: Grune & Stratton.

Trombly, C. A. (1983). Spinal cord injury. In C. A. Trombly (Ed.), *Occupational therapy for physical dysfunction* (2nd ed., pp. 385–398). Baltimore, MD: Williams & Wilkins.

DANIEL D. LIPKA
*Lincoln Way Special Education
Regional Resource Center*

ACCESSIBILITY OF BUILDINGS

QUAY, HERBERT C. (1927–   )

Born in Portland, Maine, Herbert C. Quay received his BS (1951) and MS (1952) in psychology from Florida State University. He later earned his PhD (1958) in clinical psychology from the University of Illinois. During his distinguished career as a teacher and researcher, Quay was chairman of the department of psychology, director of the program in applied sciences, and professor of psychology and pediatrics at the University of Miami. He is currently retired.

Quay questioned the traditional classification system of special education categories, and in 1971 he discovered that the number, rather than type, of behavior symptoms was more effective in identifying psychopathology in a child. This finding acknowledges that most children exhibit most behaviors labeled pathologic at some point in their development without becoming pathological themselves (Werry & Quay, 1971). He also found that an assessor's theory of development and pathology was a factor in how that assessor diagnosed a child (Quay, 1973). That is, if an assessor believed in a theory of process dysfunctions, there would be a different diagnosis than from an assessor who believed in experiential deficits.

His work in the area of psychopathology in children includes the development of the Behavior Problem Checklist, a three-point scale devised using factor analysis to rate traits of problem behaviors in children and adolescents. Quay advocated the checklist to differentiate dimensions of deviance, select treatment programs, and determine systematic differences among children with divergent patterns of deviance (Quay, 1977). Revised procedures for assessment using this tool are delineated in the *Manual for the Revised Behavior Problem Checklist* (1987).

Since the early 1980s, the vast majority of Quay's work has been in the field of child clinical psychology, including *Handbook of Juvenile Delinquency* (1987), part of a Wiley series on personality processes, and *Disruptive Behavior Disorders in Childhood* (1994), a compilation of papers prepared in honor of his retirement (H. C. Quay, pers. comm., May 21, 1998). Quay has been recognized in *Who's Who in the World, Who's Who in America, American Men of Science, and Leaders in Education*.

REFERENCES

Quay, H. C. (1973). Special education: Assumptions, techniques, and evaluative criteria. *Exceptional Children, 40,* 165–170.

Quay, H. C. (1977). Measuring dimensions of deviant behavior: The Problem Behavior Checklist. *Journal of Abnormal Child Psychology, 5,* 277–287.

Quay, H. C. (1987). *Handbook of juvenile delinquency.* New York: Wiley.

Quay, H. C., & Peterson, D. R. (1987). *Manual for the Revised Behavior Problem Checklist.* Coral Gables, FL: University of Miami.

Quay, H. C., & Routh, D. K. (1994). *Disruptive behavior disorders in childhood.* New York: Plenum.

Werry, J. S., & Quay, H. C. (1971). The prevalence of behavior symptoms in younger elementary children. *American Journal of Orthopsychiatry, 41,* 136–143.

E. Valerie Hewitt
Texas A & M University
First edition

Tamara J. Martin
The University of Texas of the Permian Basin
Second edition

QUESTIONNAIRES IN SPECIAL EDUCATION

Questionnaires are often used for gathering research data in special education. They are relatively inexpensive, can assure anonymity, and can be used with relative ease by novice researchers as well as seasoned professionals.

Pride (1979) has observed that the mail questionnaire in particular is useful in obtaining data from distant populations. It reaches subjects too busy to be interviewed, en-

ables targeting subgroups of respondents, and is conducive in format to framing responses in a manner suitable for statistical analysis. The mail questionnaire can also "eliminate interviewer bias to questions that are sensitive or embarrassing when posed by an interviewer" (Pride, 1979, p. 59).

As popular survey research tools questionnaires (whether mailed, completed by telephone, or administered in person) require careful design. The design process includes separate decisions about (1) the kind of information sought (e.g., attitudinal, behavioral), (2) the question structure (e.g., open-ended, close-ended with ordered categories), and (3) the actual choice of words (Dillman, 1978, pp. 79–80). Every investigation presents special requirements and different problems. Oppenheim (1966), Dillman (1978), and Sudman and Bradburn (1982) provide thorough discussions about the many factors to be considered when designing questionnaires and detailed recommendations for writing and presenting questions.

Despite the fact that the mail survey is, in many cases, the most feasible approach for retrieving data from large, widely dispersed samples, many researchers have expressed concern about its methodological rigor and adequacy. This concern is based largely on the grounds of seriously deficient response rates. "The most common flaw is nonresponse of a size or nature which makes the answers nonrepresentative of the total sample and thus the total universe" (Erdos, 1970, p. 142). Returns of less than 40 or 50% are common. Additionally, there are limitations on the nature of data that may be obtained and the quality of responses to many mail questionnaires.

Kanuk and Berenson (1975) confirmed that, despite the proliferation of research studies (well over 200) reporting techniques to reduce nonresponse bias, "there is no strong empirical evidence favoring any techniques other than follow-up and the use of monetary incentives" (p. 451). Research on the topic generally has been narrowly focused, poorly integrated, and contradictory. Erdos (1970) and Dillman (1978) represent the few attempts to improve response rates to mail questionnaires from the perspective of addressing the entire mail survey process.

Dillman's recommendations offer a fully integrated, planned sequence of procedures and techniques that are designed to increase response rates and that are fully adaptable to research problems in special education. His total design method (TDM) attempts to present mail surveys in such a way that respondents develop proprietary attitudes toward the research project in which they are being asked to participate. Based on the tenets of motivational psychology, Dillman has postulated that the process of designing and sending a questionnaire, and getting respondents to complete it in an honest manner and return it, is a special kind of social exchange. His highly prescribed method and related strategies are designed to minimize the costs for responding, maximize the rewards for doing so, and establish trust that those rewards will be delivered. Readily adaptable in its present form, the TDM also provides a useful frame of reference against which the design aspects of each mail survey research problem may be considered.

REFERENCES

Dillman, D. (1978). *Mail and telephone surveys: The total design method.* New York: Wiley.

Erdos, P. L. (1970). *Professional mail surveys.* New York: McGraw-Hill.

Kanuk, L., & Berenson, C. (1975). Mail survey and response rates: A literature review. *Journal of Marketing Research, 12,* 440–453.

Oppenheim, A. N. (1966). *Questionnaire design and attitudes measurement.* New York: Basic Books.

Pride, C. (1979). Building response to a mail survey. *New Directions for Institutional Advancement, 6,* 59–69.

Sudman, S., & Bradburn, N. M. (1982). *Asking questions.* San Francisco: Jossey-Bass.

LAWRENCE S. COTE
Pennsylvania State University

RESEARCH IN SPECIAL EDUCATION

QUIGLEY, STEPHEN P. (1927–   )

Born in Belfast, Northern Ireland, Stephen P. Quigley obtained his BA (1953) in psychology from the University of Denver. He went on to earn both his MA (1954) in speech and hearing disorders and PhD (1957) in speech science and psychology at the University of Illinois. Prior to his retirement, Quigley was professor of education, speech, and hearing at the University of Illinois, Urbana-Champaign.

Quigley is best known for his work in the area of communication, language, and the improvement of education for children with hearing impairments (McAnally, Rose, & Quigley, 1999; Paul & Quigley, 1994; Quigley, 1992). His investigations of Noam Chomsky's theory that careful manipulation of stimulus-response could produce more effective insights into language acquisition led to his development of the Test of Syntactical Abilities (1978), a standardized test for the diagnosis and assessment of the syntactical abilities of deaf children.

Quigley has noted the absence of a well-developed first language for deaf children entering school and the manner in which this deficit prevents the examination of language development. He has thus conducted important research on the instructional use of American Sign Language and English (Quigley & Paul, 1984a, 1984b). Findings of these investigations suggest the benefits of teaching children with deafness American Sign Language and, as a second language, providing instruction in English.

In addition to his work involving language development, Quigley advocates reading materials for deaf children that recognize their needs while avoiding overspecialization (Quigley, 1982). Among his numerous publications, he has written several books on the topic of reading, including *Reading Practices With Deaf Learners* (1999) and *Reading Milestones* (1992).

REFERENCES

MacAnally, P. L., Rose, S., & Quigley, S. P. (1999). *Reading practices with deaf learners.* Austin, TX: Pro-Ed.

Paul, P. V., & Quigley, S. P. (1994). *Language and deafness.* San Diego, CA: Singular.

Quigley, S. P. (1982). Reading achievement and special reading materials. *Volta Review, 84*(5), 95–106.

Quigley, S. P. (1992). *Reading milestones. Level 6. The orange books.* England: Dormac.

Quigley, S. P., & Paul, P. V. (1984a). ASL and ESL? *Topics in Early Childhood Education, 3*(4), 17–26.

Quigley, S. P., & Paul, P. V. (1984b). *Language and deafness.* San Diego, CA: College Hill.

Quigley, S. P., Steinkamp, M., Power, D., & Jones, B. (1978). *Test of syntactical abilities.* Beaverton, OR: Dormac.

E. VALERIE HEWITT
Texas A & M University
First edition

TAMARA J. MARTIN
The University of Texas of the Permian Basin
Second edition

R

RACIAL BIAS IN TESTING

See CULTURAL BIAS IN TESTING.

RACIAL DISCRIMINATION IN SPECIAL EDUCATION

The right to education, nondiscriminatory treatment, equal protection, and due process protection for all handicapped children was first established by Congress with the Education Amendments of 1974 and the Education For All Handicapped Children Act of 1975. Prior to this national policy, more than 36 court cases throughout the country brought convincing documentation that racially and culturally discriminatory practices existed in special education. Racially and culturally diverse school children continue to be disproportionately represented in special education programs while local and state education officials attempt to improve testing and classification procedures.

Racially and culturally biased identification and placement procedures in special education were initially disputed in *Hobson v. Hansen* (1967). Judge J. Skelly Wright found that the ability grouping track system in the public schools of the District of Columbia deprived black disadvantaged and handicapped students of "their right to equal educational opportunity with white and more affluent public school children" (401). Relying on factual findings of discrimination, the Court ordered the track system abolished in 1969. Subsequently, seven black exceptional children labeled as either behavior problems, mentally retarded, emotionally disturbed, or hyperactive, sued the District of Columbia Public Schools for failing to provide them with special education while providing such education to other children (*Mills v. Board of Education, District of Columbia,* (1972). Holding "that Constitutional rights must be afforded citizens despite the greater expense involved" (p. 876), the court's decree established (1) standards and procedures for an "appropriate educational program," (2) a required "comprehensive plan" for identification and notification of exceptional students and their parents, and (3)

"alternative program of education, placement in a regular public school class with appropriate ancillary services is preferable to placement in a special class" (p. 880).

In California, nine Mexican-American students in *Diana v. State Board of Education* (1970) and six black students in *Larry P. v. Riles* (1972) alleged that they were being misplaced in special classes for the educable mentally retarded on the basis of inappropriate tests and testing procedures that ignored their cultural and racial learning experiences. Both cases were brought to the Northern California Federal District Court and documented statewide, the statistically significant overrepresentation of minorities in special education. *Diana's* stipulated settlement agreement (1973) established testing procedures in the student's primary language, retesting of Mexican-American and Chinese-American students currently in classes for the retarded, and a mandate for a state developed and appropriate standardized intelligence test.

Judge Peckham in *Larry P.* cited California's historical racial discriminatory use of Intelligence Quotient (I.Q.) tests against blacks and issued a preliminary injunction in 1972 against the San Francisco Unified School District. The injunction prevented the use of intelligence tests for placement purposes and ordered the elimination of the disproportionate placement of black children in special classes for the educable retarded. Similarly, a statewide order on December 13, 1974, by the court and a state imposed moratorium in January, 1975, stopped all IQ testing of the educable mentally retarded for the purposes of placement (1979, p. 931, n.4). The decision was affirmed in 1984.

Matti T. v. Holladay was a class action suit filed on April 25, 1975 on behalf of 26 handicapped students from seven local school districts in Mississippi against state and local school officials. The suit challenged the policies and practices in special education. The plaintiffs in *Matti T.* claimed that the schools used racially and culturally discriminatory procedures in the identification, evaluation, and education placement of handicapped children. Evidence showed that three times as many black children than white children were placed in educable retarded classes and conversely, twice as many white children than black children were placed in higher costs and more integrated specific learning disability classes. The court ordered an agreement decree on January 26, 1979, requiring the state to substantially reduce the racial disparity by 1982 by establishing new identification practices and monitoring and enforcement procedures.

Isaac *Lora v. Board of Education of the City of New York,* in June 1975, represented all black and hispanic students assigned to special day schools for emotionally disturbed in New York City. Citing statistically significant disparities between minorities and white students with the same problems, the class of plaintiffs alleged discriminatory testing and that "the special day schools are intentionally segregated dumping grounds for minorities forced into inadequate facilities without due process" (1978, p. 1214). Following lengthy proceedings, appeals, and recommendations of a national "Lora Advisory Panel," a conciliatory agreement produced nondiscriminatory standards and procedures in 1984.

REFERENCES

Diana v. Board of Education, No. C-70-37 RFP (N.D. Cal. Jan. 7, 1970, June 18, 1973, and Order of May 27, 1974).

Hobson v. Hansen, 269 F. Supp. 401 (D.D.C. 1967), *Smuck v. Hobson,* 408 F.2d. 175 (D.C. Cir. 1969).

Larry P. v. Riles, 343 F. Supp. 1306 (N.D. Cal. 1972), 502 F.2d. 963 (9th Cir. 1974), 495 F. Supp. 926 (N.D. Cal. 1979), aff'd. 9th Cir., Jan. 23, 1984 (EHLR 555:304, Feb. 3, 1984).

Lora v. Board of Educ. of City of New York, 456 F. Supp. 1211 (E.D.N.Y. 1978), 623 F.2d. 248 (2d Cir. 1980), 587 F. Supp. 1572 (E.D.N.Y. 1984).

Mattie T. v. Holladay, No. DC-75-31 (N.D. Miss. Jan. 26, 1979), EHLR 551:109, Apr. 1, 1979.

Mills v. Board of Education of District of Columbia, 348 F. Supp. 866 (D.D.C. 1972).

Louis Schwartz
Florida State University

DIANA *v.* BOARD OF EDUCATION
EDUCATION FOR ALL HANDICAPPED CHILDREN ACT OF 1975
HOBSON *v.* HANSEN
INDIVIDUALS WITH DISABILITIES EDUCATION ACT
LARRY P.
SPECIAL EDUCATION, LEGAL REGULATIONS OF
MATTIE T. *v.* HOLLADAY
MILLS *v.* BOARD OF EDUCATION
PASE

RARE DISEASES

Popliteal Pterygium Syndrome

Popliteal pterygium syndrome is also known as popliteal web syndrome and Febre-Languepin syndrome. It is a congenital syndrome consisting chiefly of popliteal webs, cleft palate, lower lip pits, and dysplasia of the toenails. A wide variety of other abnormalities may be associated with popliteal pterygium syndrome.

There is a web in the popliteal fossa that may present in several forms—from a dense, fibrous cord containing the tibial nerve to a large fold through the entire limb. There may be toenail dysplasia, the cleft palate can occur with or without a cleft lip, and the lower lip may display salivary pits. The syndrome is hereditary in acquisition and does not affect intelligence.

Prune Belly Syndrome

Prune belly syndrome, also known as Eagle-Barrett syndrome, presents with the congenital absence of the lower portion of the rectus abdominis muscle and the inferior and midportions of the oblique muscles. These patients also have marked dilation of the bladder and ureters, with small, dysplastic kidneys that are hydronephrotic. The testis are usually undescended. Because the anterior wall of the abdomen is muscularly unstructured, the wrinkled skin contains the intra-abdominal organs which bulge out, giving the appearance of a prune.

Leopard Syndrome

Leopard syndrome is an acronym for Lentigines, ECG abnormalities, Ocular hypertelorism, Pulmonary stenosis, Abnormalities of genitalia, Retardation of growth, and Deafness. It is a hereditary syndrome, inherited as an autosomal dominant trait. The syndrome is manifested as multiple lentigines (tan, dark brown, or black pigmented lesions, measuring between one and two millimeters in diameter, oval, circular, or irregular in shape, located in any mucocutaneous surface). The heart defects do not usually produce any symptoms in spite of appearing on an ECG. Ocular hypertelorism refers to an increased distance between the eyes which may impair the patient's ability to focus on an object. Pulmonary valvular stenosis makes it difficult for these patients to engage in physical activities. Since the pulmonary valve connecting the heart to the lungs is narrowed, it does not allow for the adequate circulation of venous blood to be oxygenated in the lungs. With time, pulmonary stenosis produces many serious consequences. Also associated are retardation of growth and sensory-neural deafness. A profound impact on the patient's learning process occurs, especially when the input of information is verbal. It is necessary that diagnosis be made early.

Macroglossia

Macroglossia is defined by excessive tongue size. This can physically interfere with effective verbal communication and contribute to dysphagia. It should be considered when speech difficulties are encountered. It is readily diagnosed on physical examination by a medical health care provider.

Lenz Microphthalmia Syndrome

Lenz's syndrome is an inherited syndrome, linked to the X chromosome. The patients have microphthalmia or anophthalmia (very small eyes or absence of eyes). It can affect one or both eyes. There may be many skeletal deformities, including finger anomalies, double thumbs, and narrow shoulders. Patients may have other defects affecting the cardiovascular, genital, or urinary systems. Dental defects are also found. It is present from birth and is detected due to the general physical appearance of the child. Special education programs directed at visual perception and dexterity enhancement are necessary in this group of patients.

McCune-Albright Syndrome

The hallmark manifestation of this syndrome is found in children displaying hyperpigmented macules (very dark skin lesions), precocious sexual development, and thinning and hardening of bones with fractures. There are multiple endocrine alterations with increased glandular function. These can include goiter with thyroid disease, increased growth hormone secretion, Cushing's syndrome, increased prolactin production, hyperparathyroidism, rickets, and precocious puberty.

Precocious sexual development is the most common presentation and vaginal bleeding is the presenting feature in young girls. The ovaries are asymmetrically enlarged because of cysts and hormonal stimulation. Bone lesions may not be seen for years. The skin lesions are an inconsistent feature.

Each individual child will have some special needs to be addressed due to the varying presentations which directly depend on the endocrine organs involved.

Mannosidosis

Mannosidosis is a lysosomal storage disease due to a defective α–mannosidase with resultant oligosaccharide accumulation. Clinically there are coarse facies, upper respiratory congestion and infections, profound mental retardation, hepatosplenomegaly, cataracts, radiographic signs of dyostosis multiplex, and gibbus deformity.

Mannosidosis is divided into type I for infantile and type II for juvenile-onset, respectively. Mannosidosis type I will appear between three and 12 months of age; type II manifests itself between one and four years of age. The clinical presentation is very similar for both diseases. Patients have gargoyle-like facies, frequent and recurrent respiratory infections, mental retardation, hearing loss and impaired speech, cataract formation, corneal clouding,

and abnormal bone structure (especially of the calvaria, long bones, and vertebral bodies). The liver and spleen are enlarged and there is a gibbus formation; the gingiva may be hyperplastic.

The diagnosis for this disease is based on finding a specific acid α-mannosidase deficiency in leucocytes, serum, or cultured cells.

Medium Chain Acyl-Coenzyme A Dehydrogenase Deficiency (MCAD)

MCAD is a defect in mitochondrial beta oxidation due to deficiency of the acyl-Coenzyme A dehydrogenase acting on medium-chain-length fatty acids. It is characterized by recurring episodes of hypoglycemia, vomiting, and lethargy with urinary excretion of medium-chain decarboxylic acids, minimal ketogenesis, and low plasma and tissue levels of carnitine. MCAD occurs in 1 of every 10,000 births, and the patients may have severe hypoglycemia without hyperinsulinism, encephalopathies, floppines, and an enlarged liver. The level of free fatty acids is elevated, as well as ammonia, creatine kinase (liver enzyme), and lactic dehydrogenase (muscle enzyme). Reye syndrome and SIDS are differential diagnoses considered with this condition. Fatty acid oxidation may be impaired at any of the steps.

The diagnosis is made when finding hypoglycemia in the absence of ketonuria. Treatment consists of increasing the frequency of oral feeding and oral carnitine replacement. Intravenous glucose may be essential during treatment periods of increased catabolism. The frequency of attacks diminishes with age, as the child grows into a larger body mass and develops fasting tolerance. In the absence of an attack, the illness may go undetected; about 50% of patients never have an attack and hence do not know they are medium chain acyl-coenzyme A dehydrogenase deficient. Such problems interfere with the education process of the individual, particularly due to episodes of hypoglycemia.

Pompe's Disease

Pompe's disease, also known as acid maltase deficiency or α–1,4 glucosidase deficiency, is a type II glycogen storage disease due to a defective lysosomal enzyme. This disease stands in contrast with most other glycogenoses where the enzyme abnormality is cytoplasmic rather than lysosomal. The glycogenosis observed is due to the lack of hydroxylation of glycogen particles by the lysosomes. Symptomatology is then a result of accumulation of glycogen inside the lysosomes. Patients with this disease display marked hypotonia, cardiomegaly, cardiac failure, cyanosis, and death during the first twelve months of life. The pathological process is stored glycogen that is degraded, due to deficiency of the acid maltase enzyme, causing cellular swelling, dysfunction, and death.

There are other forms of the disease that present later in life, such as the skeletal muscle form. Demonstrating the deficiency of acid maltase in the patient's lymphocytes or tissue biopsy makes the diagnosis of this autosomal recessive genetic disease. There is no treatment available for this disease, and it ultimately results in the patient's death.

Mixed Connective Tissue Disease

This disease is a variant of systemic lupus erythematosus. It displays evident symptoms and signs of various connective tissue diseases. Mixed connective tissue disease commonly presents as a diffuse interstitial disease, and occurs more frequently in females than in males. The patient may present with features of there rheumatic diseases including juvenile arthritis, juvenile dermatomyosytis, and scleroderma. Because of the varied features that can be present, the management is geared to the specific problems of the individual patient.

This disease occurs only rarely in children. The prognosis is usually correlated to the degree of pulmonary involvement, with a five year survival rate similar to idiopathic pulmonary fibrosis. Young patients with minimal fibrosis and active alveolitis (inflammation of the alveoli) have a 90% survival rate, and those with minimum cellularity and severe pulmonary fibrosis have less than 25% survival rate. The educational approaches for these patients should be tailored to the specific needs and sequelae that require management.

Occulocerebral-Hypopigmentation Syndrome

This is an autosomal recessive syndrome that is also known as Cross syndrome and Cross-McKusic-Breen syndrome. Children with this problem present with microphthalmus (small eyes), small opaque corneas, and marked oculocutaneous (skin and eyes) albinism. These serious problems call for special educational efforts concentrating on the visual perception disadvantages manifested by these patients. Apart from the eyes, the skeletal structure is affected with scoliosis that may impact on the ability to participate in physical activities, gingival hyperplasia, and a high-arched palate.

Robinow's Syndrome

Robinow's syndrome is also known as Robinow's dwarfism and fetal face syndrome. Patients display dwarfism and ocular hypertelorism (an increased distance between the eyes), which may impair the patient's ability to focus on an object. The name "fetal face" is supported by the patient's bulging forehead, flattened nasal bridge, unaligned teeth, and short extremities.

Rothmund-Thompson Syndrome

This syndrome is also known as poikiloderma congenitale because poikiloderma (a condition characterized by pigmentary and atrophic changes in the skin, giving a mottled appearance) is one of the predominant features. The skin is usually normal at birth, and begins to express the changes between the third and twenty-fourth month. The lesions begin as erythema (redness), followed by poikiloderma with atrophy, telangiectasia (dilation of blood vessels), and hyperpigmented and hypopigmented patchy areas. These lesions are seen in the face, extremities, and buttocks. During late childhood, some patients develop verrucous lesions (wart-like lesions) to the back and sides of the hands. These warts may also be found on palms and soles, as well as the other extremities. The verrucous lesions and the atrophic patches may predispose to squamous cell carcinoma.

Severe photosensitivity occurs in some 30% of the patients. Some patients will suffer alopecia of the scalp and secondary sexual hair (pubic and axillary), and the finger and toenails may be dystrophic. There is short stature and impaired sexual development. More than half the patients will develop juvenile cataracts (opacifications of the lens of the eye). There may be some skeletal deformities. Mental development and life expectancy are generally not affected. Special education targeting the visual disturbance of juvenile cataracts should be stressed.

Rubenstein-Taybi Syndrome

This is a congenital disease. It is characterized by skeletal derangements that lead to motor development retardation. Mental retardation is also present. Special education needs should address both problems on patients with this syndrome.

The thumbs and toes are broad, and abnormalities of the vertebral bodies and the sternum (breast bone) are present. Patients display a characteristic facie due to a beaked or straight nose and a high, arched palate. Patients can develop pulmonary valvular stenosis and diverse eye abnormalities. Their skin undergoes keloid formation upon scarring, producing thick, white scars.

Russell-Silver Syndrome

This syndrome is found in small babies who have grown slowly during most of the pregnancy. Babies experiencing slow growth before the 35th gestational week have increased potential for complications. They usually feed very poorly and will show asymmetry between the two sides of the body, clinodactyly, elfin faces and short stature. They will have an increased secretion of gonadotropins that will lead to precocious puberty.

Schwartz-Jampel Syndrome

Patients affected by this autosomal recessive disorder will display a variety of features including dwarfism blepharophimosis (abnormal narrowness of the eyelid fissures) and myotonic myopathy. Their joints also develop contractures, and they have flat faces. These patients have posture problems which need to be considered when developing a care strategy.

Smith-Lemli-Opitz Syndrome

This syndrome is characterized by a variety of congenital abnormalities. These may comprise incomplete development of the male genital organs, microcephaly, hypotonia, anterior inversion of nostrils on a short nose, syndactyly of toes, and mental retardation. This condition is hereditary and is transmitted as an autosomal recessive trait. Special education efforts should be geared toward the mental retardation status and the added complications caused by diverse physical impairments present.

Treacher-Collins Syndrome

This is also known as Franceschetti-Klein syndrome and mandibulofacial dystosis. Patients present with characteristic facies with the mandible and malar bones markedly hypoplastic, a cleft or high-arched palate, and dental malocclusion. The eyes show lids with an antimongoloid inclination and a coloboma (absence or defect of ocular tissue) is often found in the outer lower lid. The ears are affected with the absence of external auditory canal. All children with Treacher-Collins are assumed to be deaf until proven differently. There may be other malformations including congenital heart disease, mental retardation, and skeletal structural malformations. There may be milder variants of the syndrome. Patients with Treacher-Collins present a major challenge for special education.

REFERENCES

Cacciari, E., Frejauille, E., Cicognani, A, et al. (1983). How many cases of true precocious puberty in girls are idiophatic? *Journal of Pediatrics, 102,* 357–360.

Crouch, E. (1990). Pathobiology of pulmonary fibrosis. *American Journal of Physiology, 259,* 159.

Finberg, L. (1998). *Saunders manual of pediatric practice.* Philadelphia: Saunders.

Foster, C. M., Ross, J. L., Shawker, T. H., et al. (1984). Absence of pubertal gonadotropin secretion in girls with McCune-Albright syndrome. *Journal of Clinical Endocrinology and Metabolism, 58,* 1161–1165.

Gorlin, R. J., Sedano, H. O., and Cervenka, J. (1968). Popliteal pterygium syndrome. *Pediatrics, 41,* 503–509.

Hill, D. J., and Milner, R. D. G. (1989). Mechanisms of fetal growth. In C. G. D. Brook (Ed.), *Clinical pediatric endocrinology* (2nd ed.). Oxford: Blackwell Scientific Publications.

Kennedy, J. I., and Fulmer, J. D. (1991). Collagen vascular diseases. In J. P. Kkassirer (Ed.), *Current therapy in internal medicine.* Philadelphia.

Roth, J. C., and Williams, H. E. (1967). The muscular variant of Pompe's disease. *Journal of Pediatrics, 71*(4), 567.

Ruttenberg, H. D., Steidl, R. M., Carey, L. S., and Edwards, J. E. (1964). Glycogen storage disease of the heart. *American Heart Journal, 67*(4), 469.

SERGIO R. CRISALLE
SAUL B. WILEN
Medical Horizons Unlimited

RASE

See REMEDIAL AND SPECIAL EDUCATION.

RATIO IQ

A ratio intelligence quotient or ratio IQ is a score from a test of intelligence (or cognitive or mental ability). Now obsolete as a statistical term, it is still a useful concept for interpreting current levels of mental functioning and, to a limited extent, for predicting future mental development. The ratio IQ has been replaced by most authors of mental ability tests with a standard score such as a deviation IQ.

At the turn of the century, and for the next several decades, tests of mental ability were administered to children of several different chronological ages. The average number of items answered correctly at each age level was recorded. Then the number of items answered correctly by a given child could be compared with the average performance of children of various ages. Such scores were known as a mental age (MA) or age equivalent (AE). Such scores made it possible to say that a particular child of a given age performed on the test as a typical 4 year old, or another as a typical 6 year old, or another as an 8 year old, etc., but MAs describe only present status.

The concept of a mental quotient to indicate the rate of cognitive development was introduced by William Stern in a paper to the German Congress of Psychology in Berlin in April 1912. With the Stanford Revision and Extension of the Binet-Simon Intelligence Scale in 1916, Lewis Terman introduced the term intelligence quotient and its abbreviation, IQ, as a prediction of the rate of future mental development (based on the rate of previous accomplishment). Early IQs were simply the ratio of the mental age to the chronological age, multiplied by 100 to eliminate the decimals (i.e., IQ = MA/CAx 100). However, mental ages represent ordinal not interval data and therefore the distance between two ages, e.g., 4 and 6, is not necessarily the same as between two other ages, e.g., 12 and 14. Also, test authors have not been able to construct tests with equal variability at each age level. As a result, the standard deviation of scores is not the same at each age and, therefore, the same ratio IQ obtained at different age levels may not be equal to the same percentile rank. (A ratio IQ that equals or exceeds 3% of the population might be 75 at one age, 68 at another, and 60 at another.) Whereas the statistical properties of a ratio IQ present too many difficulties for its use to be continued except as a concept for interpretation, the simplicity of the concept is still helpful in explaining performance to many consumers. With an IQ of 65, one can say that a 10-year-old child is functioning mentally much like most 6 to 7 year olds and is exhibiting about two-thirds of a year of mental growth each year. The concept of ratio IQ and mental age seem almost nonsensical when applied to adults. Since ratio IQs represent only ordinal scaling, they can neither be multiplied, divided, added, or subtracted across ages and are obsolete for most needs in diagnostic settings.

JOSEPH L. FRENCH
Pennsylvania State University

DEVIATION IQ
INTELLIGENCE QUOTIENT

RAVEN'S MATRICES

The Standard Progressive Matrices and the Colored Progressive Matrices (Raven, 1938–1983) are a collection of figures that resemble swatches removed from a wallpaper pattern. The test requires the examinee to locate the swatch that best fits the removed pattern. The test is purportedly an excellent measure of *g* factor intelligence (general intellectual ability; Marshalek, Lohman, & Snow, 1983). The matrices have received wide use around the world because of their easy administration, nonverbal format, and high correlations with traditional measures of intelligence and achievement. The progressive matrices have been used in hundreds of psychological studies internationally.

Since the progressive matrices (developed in the United Kingdom) originated in a psychometric era known for providing examiners with minimal information on standardized sample characteristics, technical adequacy, item construction and use, rationale and theory, and potential uses and misuses of instruments, the progressive matrices manuals provide little information in these areas. Additionally, Levy and Goldstein (1984), editors of *Tests in Ed-*

ucation, the British equivalent of the *Buros Mental Measurements Yearbook,* note that the British have lagged behind the Americans in the care that psychologists have used in the development of psychoeducational assessment measures. However, the large number of studies compiled on the progressive matrices attest to the instruments' use and value.

The matrices are appropriate for individuals ages 5 through adult and are printed both in color (ages 5 to 11) and standard black and white versions (ages 6 and over). The test provides only percentile ranks as an individual's reported score, but even these are not complete; the manual reports performance level only at the 5, 10, 25, 50, 75, 90, and 95th percentiles. Thus, the test only approximates levels of performance. As such, the matrices are useful for the rough assessment of the nonverbal reasoning abilities of individuals 5 years and above. Because of the many deficiencies in the tests' manuals and standardized samples, it is best used as an assessment tool for research purposes and those occasional clinical instances in which an estimate of an individual's intellectual abilities are needed.

REFERENCES

Levy, P., & Goldstein, H. (1984). *Tests in education: A book of critical reviews.* London: Academic.

Marshalek, B., Lohman, D. F., & Snow, R. (1983). The complexity continuum in the radex and hierarchical models of intelligence. *Intelligence, 7,* 107–127.

BRUCE A. BRACKEN
LINDSAY S. GROSS
University of Wisconsin

"*g*" FACTOR THEORY
INTELLIGENCE
INTELLIGENCE TESTING

RAY ADAPTATION OF THE RAY WECHSLER INTELLIGENCE SCALE FOR CHILDREN-REVISED

Ray (1979) adapted the Wechsler Intelligence Scale for Children-Revised (WISC-R) performance scales for an intelligence tests designed especially for the hearing impaired. He introduced a set of simplified verbal instructions and added more practice items in an attempt to provide standardized test administration techniques to increase a deaf child's comprehension and performance. Therapists who are unskilled in American Sign Language are able to administer the test. In addition to Ray's version of instructions, several different techniques exist for nonverbal administration (Sullivan, 1982). Seven scores are yielded in the adaptation: Picture Completion, Picture Arrangement, Block Design, Object Assembly, Coding,

Mazes, and Total. Administration time averages about 45 minutes.

The adaptation was normed on 127 hearing-impaired children from 6 to 16 years old. The sample used was not representative of the deaf school-age population, including no low-verbal deaf children and no multiply handicapped children (Sullivan, 1985). Norms provided in Ray's test should be regarded with caution, and thought should be given to other deaf norms developed. The WISC–R performance scales can be a suitable alternative to the Hiskey-Nebraska if the Anderson and Sisco norms are used with a total communication approach for administration (Phelps & Enson, 1986). Genshaft (1985) thinks that the most useful improvement in the adaptation would be separate, representative norms for deaf children.

REFERENCES

Genshaft, J. L. (1985). Review of the WISC-R: For the deaf. In J. V. Mitchell, Jr. (Ed.), *The ninth mental measurements yearbook* (Vol. 2). Lincoln, NE: University of Nebraska.

Phelps, L., & Enson, A. (1986). Concurrent validity of the WISC-R using deaf norms and the Hiskey-Nebraska. *Psychology in the schools, 23,* 138–141.

Ray, S. (1979). *An adaptation of the Wechsler Intelligence Scale for Children-Revised for the deaf.* Natchitoches: Northwestern State University of Louisiana.

Sullivan, R. M. (1982). Modified instructions for administering the WISC-R performance scale subtests to deaf children (Appendix B). In J. M. Sattler (Ed.), *Assessment of children's intelligence and special abilities* (2nd ed.). Boston: Allyn & Bacon.

Sullivan, P. M. (1985). Review of the WISC-R: For the deaf. In J. V. Mitchell, Jr. (Ed.), *The ninth mental measurements yearbook* (Vol. 2). Lincoln, NE: University of Nebraska.

LISA J. SAMPSON
Eastern Kentucky University

DEAF WECHSLER INTELLIGENCE SCALE FOR CHILDREN—REVISED

REACTION TIME

The time required for a person to respond to a stimulus was one of the most frequent measures of human behavior by early psychologists. Indeed, E. G. Boring, a historian of psychology, characterized the late nineteenth century as the period of "mental chronometry." During this period Galton first used reaction time to an auditory stimulus as a measure of intelligence; similar reaction-time items were incorporated into several early intelligence tests. When reaction time was found to have negligible correlation with seemingly more valid measures of intelligence, however, interest in it waned. In retrospect, it appears that the failure of reaction time may have been due to unreliable measurement and other methodological difficulties. It is now recognized that a large number of trials are required to obtain a reliable average reaction time for an individual person.

As the computer analogy has come to dominate cognitive psychology in recent years, there has been a resurgence of interest in reaction time. The goal of current reaction time research is to measure the time required for the brain to perform a variety of elementary cognitive tasks. From such information it may be possible to infer how the mind is functioning.

Basically, the procedure is to measure reaction time in a task that requires a simple mental operation. The complexity of the mental operation is then increased, and the increase in reaction time is used as a measure of the time required for the brain to process the increased complexity. The following three basic paradigms have been frequently used.

Hick (1952) measured the increase in time required to choose among several visual or auditory stimuli as the number of stimuli increased. The time required is a log function of the number of stimuli, which can be interpreted as the amount of information involved in the choice. Thus the brain appears to be making a block-wise comparison among the various stimuli.

Sternberg (1966) presented subjects with a set of digits followed by a probe digit; the subjects then indicated whether the probe digit was included in the set. This task appears to measure speed of scanning short-term memory. Reaction time increases linearly with the number of items in the set, suggesting a sequential scanning mechanism.

Posner (1969) asked subjects to indicate whether two letters were the same or different, with similarity being first defined as physical similarity, in which A and a are different, and then as semantic similarity, in which A and a are the same. The latter task requires considerably more time than the first, since the letters must be identified, evidently by a search of long-term memory.

Jensen (1980) has studied the relationship of individual differences in time required to perform these elementary cognitive tasks to scores on traditional psychometric tests of intelligence. The surprising finding is that, with careful measurement and allowing for certain sources of error, about half of the variance in psychometric intelligence test scores is predictable from the several measures of speed of mental processing.

REFERENCES

Hick, W. (1952). On the rate of gain of information. *Quarterly Journal of Experimental Psychology, 4,* 11–26.

Jensen, A. R. (1980). Chronometric analysis of intelligence. *Journal of Social & Biological Structures, 3,* 103–122.

Posner, M. I. (1969). Abstraction and the process of recognition. In G. H. Bower & J. T. Spense (Eds.), *The psychology of learning and motivation* (Vol. 3, pp. 43–100). New York: Academic.

Sternberg, S. (1966). High speed scanning in human memory. *Science, 153,* 652–654.

Robert C. Nichols
Diane Jarvis
State University of New York at Buffalo

CULTURE FAIR TESTS
"*g*" FACTOR THEORY
INTELLIGENCE TESTING
SPEARMAN'S HYPOTHESIS OF BLACK/WHITE
  DIFFERENCES

READABILITY AND READABILITY FORMULAS

Readability refers to the difficulty level of a passage of text, and is often presented as a grade level number. Typically, reading curricula are designed to match the readability level of stories to the grade level in which the materials are to be used. Textbooks often are described in terms of their readability level. Various readability formulas are used to determine these readability levels.

Klare (1982) provides a general definition of a readability formula: "a predictive device that uses counts of word and sentence variables in a piece of writing to provide a quantitative, objective index of style difficulty" (p. 1522). More than 200 formulas have been published since the first one was developed in the 1920s.

To predict the readability level of a complete text, formulas typically are applied to 100-word samples drawn randomly from throughout the text. Formulas generally are based on regression equations, using weighted scores for word and sentence counts to predict a comprehension score that roughly corresponds to a tested reading grade level. Formulas either rely on word lists or counts of syllables that estimate semantic difficulty (Klare, 1982).

The analogy of a thermometer is often used to explain readability and its limitations (Klare, 1982, 1984). Just as a thermometer is an index of the warmth of a room, particular characteristics of words and sentences index reading difficulty, but do not necessarily cause it. Altering words and sentences in a text may change the readability level, but may not make the text any more comprehensible, just as holding a lighted match under a thermometer will change the temperature reading but will not substantially warm the room.

As Duffelmeyer (1985) notes, a formula's reliance on word length as an index of difficulty can be misleading. Although there is a high correlation between average word length and prose difficulty, long words (more than six letters) in very easy reading materials are often plurals or variations of simple roots (e.g., schools, ru*nning*) and should not be weighted as much as words of equal length that involve more complex concepts.

Formulas also do not necessarily adequately capture aspects of text familiarity and complexity. Familiar words make reading easier because they are easier to recall from memory; yet, the familiarity or processing difficulty of a word for a particular reader is not defined by the statistical frequency of that word. For example, an unfamiliar word is easier to process if it appears in a familiar story. And more familiar words may be less precise in communicating the author's meaning.

Similarly, measures that rely on sentence length as an index of difficulty assume that the demand on working memory increases as the length of clauses or sentences increases. The number of words does not accurately reflect the amount of effort expended by readers, however, since readers chunk together text segments. Dividing long sentences in a passage into shorter ones will reduce the readability level of the passage, but may make the text more difficult to understand. The elimination of words connecting ideas—such as *because, since,* and *then*—places greater demands on the reader to draw inferences about the relationships between those ideas.

Beck and her colleagues (Beck, McKeown, Omanson, & Pople, 1984) argue that "readability formulas are at best, useless, and at worst, misleading, for assisting in the development of readable texts" (p. 263). They found that traditional readability formulas do not adequately describe what makes a text more or less comprehensible. When two stories from basal readers were revised to improve their coherence (story events were organized and clarified, and connections in the text were made more apparent), readability levels increased by one grade level even though the revised stories were more easily comprehended and recalled than the original ones with lower readability levels.

Davison (1984) notes that making changes in text to conform to readability formulas may

> seriously distort the logical relations between the parts of the text, sentences, or paragraphs; and may disrupt the presentation of ideas. . . . The less information is expressed explicitly in the words and syntactic structures of the text, the more load is placed on the ability to make inferences and to use background information. (p. 124)

Davison (1984) also notes that "it is possible—and in some cases *probable*—that a text may be simplified to the point of being readable at a particular level as measured by readability formulas without being *comprehensible*" (p. 128).

Similarly, the Commission on Reading (Anderson Hiebert, Scott, & Wilkinson, 1985) suggests that "it is quite possible to write a disorganized text, full of incomprehensible sentences, and still achieve a desired readability score" (p. 64).

Variability in readability levels of different sections within the same basal reader also has been noted (Fuchs, Fuchs, & Deno, 1982). Fuchs et al. examined how many simple passages from basal texts were required to obtain a consistent readability level for those texts. From 5 to 14 passages had to be sampled at every reading level before the readability scores for any two passages agreed with the mean readability levels established for each text. More than half of the 19 textbooks included in the study required sampling of 10 or more passages before two or more representative passages could be identified.

A related study (Fuchs, Fuchs, & Deno, 1984) examined the usefulness of six readability formulas in predicting the relative difficulty of three passages, with difficulty measured as students' reading scores (number of words read aloud correctly in 1 minute). Rank orderings of passage difficulty based on the formulas did not agree with the students' reading scores on the passages.

Many common readability measures are available in microcomputer format. A program may consist of a single procedure or as many as eight procedures. Kennedy (1985) provides information on nearly a dozen such programs. Duffelmeyer (1985) contends that although computer programs compute formulas quickly and easily, teacher judgment still is required to assess the conceptual difficulty of the material.

REFERENCES

Anderson, R. C., Hiebert, E. H., Scott, J. A., & Wilkinson, I. A. G. (1985). *Becoming a nation of readers: The report of the Commission on Reading.* Champaign, IL: Center for the Study of Reading.

Beck, I. L., McKeown, M. G., Omanson, R. C., & Pople, M. T. (1984). Improving the comprehensibility of stories: The effects of revisions that improve coherence. *Reading Research Quarterly, 19*(3), 263–277.

Davison, A. (1984). Readability—Appraising text difficulty. In R. C. Anderson, J. Osborn, & R. J. Tierney (Eds.), *Learning to read in American schools: Basal readers and content texts* (pp. 121–139). Hillsdale, NJ: Erlbaum.

Duffelmeyer, F. A. (1985). Estimating readability with a computer. Beware the aura of precision. *Reading Teacher, 38*(4), 392–394.

Fuchs, L. S., Fuchs, D., & Deno, S. L. (1982). Reliability and validity of curriculum-based Informal Reading Inventories. *Reading Research Quarterly, 18*(1), 6–26.

Fuchs, L. S., Fuchs, D., & Deno, S. L. (1984). Inaccuracy among readability formulas: Implications for the management of reading proficiency and selection of instructional materials. *Diagnostique, 9*(2), 86–95.

Kennedy, K. (1985). Determining readability with a microcomputer. *Curriculum Review, 25*(2), 40–43.

Klare, G. R. (1982). Readability. In H. E. Mitzel (Ed.), *Encyclopedia of educational research* (5th ed., pp. 1520–1531). New York: Free Press.

Klare, G. R. (1984). Readability. In P. D. Pearson (Ed.), *Handbook of reading research* (pp. 681–744). New York: Longman.

LINDA J. STEVENS
University of Minnesota

READING
READING DISORDERS
READING IN THE CONTENT AREAS

READABILITY FORMULAS

Readability formulas are employed to predict the readability level of text. To develop these formulas, researchers select a criterion index of text difficulty and a set of predictor variables or indicators of text structure and relate the criterion index and set of predictor variables through application of multiple regression. This statistical procedure identifies formulas that best predict the criterion index. With the selection of easily calculated predictor variables, estimating text difficulty is relatively simple.

Perhaps because of the comparative simplicity of this approach, the use of formulas has proliferated. Nevertheless, research demonstrates the often dramatic inaccuracy of readability formulas in predicting passage difficulty (Britton & Lumpkin, 1977; Fuchs, Fuchs, & Deno, 1982; Fuchs, Fuchs, & Deno, 1984). This imprecision may be explained in the following ways. First, formulas have been derived and refined to predict difficulty estimates of criterion passages for which there is little evidence to support the correctness of text readability designations (Fitzgerald, 1980). Second, formulas rely on surface characteristics of text rather than on passage content and student characteristics, despite evidence that pupils' familiarity with the content of text influences passage difficulty (Kemper, 1983; Pearson, 1974–1975). Recently, some progress has been made in developing formulas that move beyond the surface structure of text and that predict more valid criterion indices of text difficulty (Kemper, 1983).

However, until more appropriate procedures for predicting readability are developed to account for text content and student characteristics, special education diagnosticians and practitioners should interpret cautiously reading assessments based on basal texts or tests that have been developed with readability formulas. This caveat may be especially relevant for work with handicapped pupils whose background information may be influenced by their handicapped experience and may be different from that of the norm (Fuchs et al., 1984).

REFERENCES

Britton, G. E., & Lumpkin, M. C. (1977). Computerized readability verification of textbook reading levels. *Reading Improvement, 14,* 193–199.

Fitzgerald, G. G. (1980). Reliability of the Fry sampling procedures. *Reading Research Quarterly, 15,* 489–503.

Fuchs, L. S., Fuchs, D., & Deno, S. L. (1982). The reliability and validity of curriculum-based informal reading inventories. *Reading Research Quarterly, 18,* 6–26.

Fuchs, L. S., Fuchs, D., & Deno, S. L. (1984). Inaccuracy among readability formulas: Implications for the measurement of reading proficiency and selection of instructional material. *Diagnostique, 9,* 86–97.

Kemper, S. (1983). Measuring the inference load of a text. *Journal of Educational Psychology, 75,* 391–401.

Pearon, P. D. (1974–1975). The effects of grammatical complexity on children's comprehension, recall, and conception of certain semantic relations. *Reading Research Quarterly, 10,* 155–192.

Lynn S. Fuchs
Douglas Fuchs
Vanderbilt University

BASAL READERS
MULTIPLE REGRESSION

READING

Reading is the process of deriving meaning from print. While people have been reading as long as language has been written down, at no other time in recorded history has interest in reading, both from a research and practical standpoint, been greater (Anderson, R., Hiebert, Scott, & Wilkerson, 1984). In the past 15 years, there has been a concerted effort to understand how the reading process occurs and to translate that knowledge into materials and strategies that more effectively teach reading. Reading educators, long concerned with reading research and its implementation, have recently been joined by cognitive, educational, and developmental psychologists, linguists, and sociolinguists in the attempt to unravel the mysteries of reading.

Although the word reading characterizes any meaningful interaction between an individual and print, we can subdivide reading into four basic types. Each of these types is differentiated by the purpose for which the reading act is undertaken. The four types of reading to be discussed are developmental reading, studying, functional reading, and recreational reading.

Developmental reading can be described as the activity undertaken for the purpose of learning how to read. During the colonial period, the *Bible,* the *Psalter,* and other religious materials were used to teach children to read. A century later, the McGuffey readers were published. These readers were the forerunners of the graded readers in use today, and their appearance paralleled the development of graded schools. Several decades ago, children learned to read with the assistance of the "Dick and Jane" books. With such familiar phrases as, "See Dick. See Jane," school-aged children across the United States entered the world of formal reading instruction. Today, much of the formal reading instruction in the early elementary grades is still devoted to developmental reading, although the commercially produced reading materials far outdistance their predecessors both in their extensiveness and their sophistication. However, the effectiveness of the current basal series and current instructional methodologies to produce better readers remains the source of great controversy (Anderson, et al., 1984).

As students progress through elementary school, developmental reading remains an integral part of their schooling, with the goal of increasing reading proficiency. Although developmental reading was confined to elementary grades in years past, it is now common to find developmental reading courses being offered at the college level. The rationale for this upward trend in developmental reading is the presence of larger numbers of college students who have not reached proficiency in reading, and who still require some instruction in learning how to read.

In the upper elementary grades, and throughout formal schooling, developmental reading is joined by another type of reading: studying. According to Anderson (1979), studying is a special form of reading that is concerned with the accomplishment of some instructional goal. The type of reading engaged in during studying is special for various reasons.

While the material used for developmental reading is mainly narrative text (i.e., storylike text), the kind of text students most often study is expository in nature. In terms of its demands on comprehension and recall, expository text appears to possess certain disadvantages over narrative text in that it has no identifiable elements such as plot, character, and setting. In addition, expository text is frequently less colorful, and filled with more technical language. Therefore, the task of studying may be more difficult than other forms of reading because expository text may be more difficult and less motivational to read. Not only is the text used in studying potentially more difficult to process, but when students study expository text it is often with the realization that they will be tested on the content; that fact is likely to make the studying experience less enjoyable.

Because of its nature, studying requires individuals to employ specialized learning and study skills. In addition to the well known SQ3R method (Robinson, 1970), there are such cognitive strategies as note-taking, outlining, paraphrasing, imaging, and rereading that might enhance student performance. Some of the other study strategies that have been looked at by researchers in recent years are look-backs (Alexander, Hare, & Garner, 1984; Garner, et al., 1984), elaborative or generative processes (Wittrock, 1983), and cooperative learning strategies (Dansereau, et al., 1979).

While developmental reading and studying are the forms of reading most directly associated with school, there is another form of reading that arises from real-world needs. This form of reading is called functional or survival reading. When we read road signs or find our way on a map, follow a recipe, or order from a menu, we are employing functional reading. Simply stated, functional reading is the reading that is required to accomplish some personal as opposed to instructional goal.

It is disheartening to note that there are many individuals in the United States who cannot even read well enough to make sense of the critical print around them. They cannot read the road signs along the road, or follow a recipe, fill out a job application, or read the dosage on a medicine bottle. Individuals who lack even this limited reading proficiency are called functionally illiterate. According to government estimates, they number in the tens of millions in the United States.

The final form of reading, recreational, is internally motivated. This form of reading is sometimes described as reading for enjoyment. Recreational reading serves no other goal than the reader's entertainment. When you read the comics, a novel, or poetry for pleasure, then you are engaging in recreational reading. There appears to be a strong relationship between the amount of recreational reading individuals engage in and their performance on other types of reading tasks such as studying. Because of this relationship, programs such as Sustained Silent Reading (SSR; McCracken, 1971) were developed to encourage schoolchildren to read more often. The hope of such programs is that students will begin to read more often and, ultimately, more effectively.

Whether developmental, for study, functional, or recreational, reading remains a complex and much investigated cognitive process. Although most reading researchers and educators would agree that reading is an extremely complex activity involving written language, there is much debate as to how the reading process takes place. Of course, how individuals view the reading process will directly affect the aspects of reading that they emphasize, as well as the instructional materials or strategies they select. Because of its overall importance, therefore, it seems worthwhile to consider the predominant perspectives of the reading process.

According to Smith (1979), reading as a communications task is basically concerned with two types of information. The first of these is visual information. Visual information is linguistic in nature, that aspect of reading that we can see on the printed page. It is comprised of words, spaces, sentences, paragraphs, and so on. In Smith's words, visual information is that part of reading that disappears when the lights are turned off. The second type of information critical in the reading process is nonvisual or metalinguistic information, that knowledge about language and about the world that makes print meaningful. The views of reading that we will discuss place differential importance on visual and nonvisual information.

The top-down view of reading, for example, weighs the nonvisual information most heavily. Advocates of this perspective (e.g., Goodman & Goodman, 1979) believe that it is the reader's prior knowledge that makes print comprehensible. Without appropriate knowledge, the individual is helpless to convert written language into meaning.

To illustrate, consider how impossible a task it would be to read in a foreign language that you did not know. From this example it can be argued that you need to know a language before you can learn to read it, just as young children learn to speak long before they learn to read. Similarly, consider how difficult it would be to read a technical report on a subject, such as hydronuclear reactors, unless you already possessed some knowledge of that subject.

Those who hold to a top-down view approach the instruction of reading with the assumption that the acquisition of reading is a natural by-product of development. Given the right environment and the right stimulation, the child will easily and quickly move from oral to written language. Within that framework, it is the teacher's function to surround children with print by reading to them, letting them manipulate books, and engaging them in related language activities such as writing or speaking. As a consequence, one would expect that in a "top-down classroom," there would be much creative writing, storytelling, and listening activities planned.

In the early elementary grades the Language Experience Approach (Hall, 1981), a method of using students' dictated stories as the basis of reading instruction, would be the primary basis for teaching reading. Another characteristic of a top-down classroom would be that it would be devoid of skills instruction; that is, teachers would not focus on any unit of language smaller than the whole word. In this view it is assumed that students participating in holistic language activities, like reading and writing, would acquire such basic reading skills such as knowing letter names or vowel sounds.

A very different, if not opposite, view is taken by those advocating a bottom-up approach to the reading process. Those holding a bottom-up view of reading believe that most everything that an individual needs to be able to read can be found on a page of text. To these individuals, the visual or linguistic information is significantly more important in the reading process than anything the reader brings to the task.

In other words, it is believed that if reading is carefully broken down into teachable skills, ordered from simpler to more complex, and if individuals master those skills, then reading will result. The impact of this approach can be seen each day in reading classrooms across the country. Look at any scope and sequence chart for a commercial basal reading series and you will find evidence of the bottom-up perspective. These basals, which are the primary tools of reading instruction, are systematically organized according to a hierarchy of reading skills. Much of the instructional time in reading classes is devoted to the presentation of these specified reading skills.

In sharp contrast to the top-down view previously described, those advocating a bottom-up model of reading do not assume that the acquisition of reading is natural. To the contrary, it would appear that it is predominantly through consistent, ordered skill instruction that an individual learns to read effectively. In the bottom-up model, the teacher's role is instructive rather than facilitative. As noted previously, the basal series provides the structure and the content for teachers taking primarily a skills-acquisition approach to reading instruction.

What the previous two views represent in many ways are the two extreme positions on a continuum that describes the reading process. At one end is the top-down position, which stresses nonvisual information almost to the exclusion of visual information. In the other position we find the bottom-up view, which focuses almost exclusively on visual or linguistic information. In actuality, most existing interpretations of the reading process fall somewhere between these two extremes.

According to the interactive model, the successful accomplishment of any reading task requires some interaction between both visual and nonvisual information (Smith, 1979). The degree to which the reading act is more or less dependent on either source of information is a consequence of many factors, including the reader's existing knowledge of the subject being read, the reason for reading, interest in the subject, and the system of evaluation.

For example, if you were reading a familiar nursery rhyme such as "Hey, Diddle-Diddle" for pleasure, you would require very little visual or linguistic information. If, however, you were reading a manual for preparing your income taxes, or studying a difficult chapter in your statistics textbook for an exam, then it is likely that you would focus much more heavily on the text. In each case, the reader is the same individual, but what is read and why it is read differ. Consequently, the reading process engaged in differs as well.

An individual's purpose for reading is directly linked to the type of reading (i.e., developmental, for study, functional, or recreational) engaged in. Likewise, an individual's purpose for reading impacts the nature of the process that occurs. Regardless of the type or view of reading, one fact remains clear: in an information-processing age, the ability to read well is an essential life skill. Further, reading and the investigation of the reading process will continue as long as there is written language.

REFERENCES

Alexander, P. A., Hare, V. C., & Garner, R. (1984). Effects of time, access, and question type on the response accuracy and frequency of lookbacks in older, proficient readers. *Journal of Reading Behavior, 16,* 119–130.

Anderson, R. C., Hiebert, E. H., Scott, J. A., & Wilkerson, I. A. G. (1984). *Becoming a nation of readers.* Champaign, IL: University of Illinois, Center for the Study of Reading.

Anderson, T. H. (1979). Study skills and learning strategies. In H. F. O'Neil & C. D. Spielberger (Eds.), *Cognitive and affective learning strategies* (pp. 77–98). New York: Academic.

Dansereau, D. F., McDonald, B. A., Collins, K. W., Garland, J. C., Holley, C. D., Diekhoff, G. M., & Evans, S. H. (1979). Evaluation of a learning strategy system. In H. F. O'Neil & C. D. Spielberger (Eds.), *Cognitive and affective learning strategies* (pp. 3–44). New York: Academic.

Garner, R., Hare, V. C., Alexander, P. A., Haynes, J., & Winograd, P. (1984). Inducing use of a text lookback strategy among unsuccessful readers. *American Educational Research Journal, 21,* 780–798.

Goodman, K. S., & Goodman, Y. M. (1979). Learning to read is natural. In L. B. Resnick & P. A. Weaver (Eds.), *Theory and practice of early reading* (Vol. 1, pp. 137–154). Hillsdale, NJ: Erlbaum.

Hall, M. (1981). *Teaching reading as a language experience* (3rd ed.). Columbus, OH: Merrill.

McCracken, R. A. (1971). Initiating sustained silent reading. *Journal of Reading, 14,* 582–583.

Robinson, E. P. (1970). *Effective study* (2nd ed.). New York: Harper & Row.

Smith, F. (1978). *Understanding reading* (2nd ed.). New York: Holt, Rinehart & Winston.

Smith, F. (1979). Conflicting approaches to reading research and instruction. In L. B. Resnick & P. A. Weaver (Eds.), *Theory and practice of early reading.* (Vol. 2, pp. 31–42). Hillsdale, NJ: Erlbaum.

Wittrock, M. C. (1983, April). *Generative reading comprehension.* Address presented at the annual meeting of the American Educational Research Association, Montreal.

PATRICIA A. ALEXANDER
University of Maryland

READING DISORDERS
READING REMEDIATION

READING AND EYE MOVEMENTS

Cognitive processes may be inferred from observation of a reader's eye movements (Pavlidis, 1985; Rayner, 1985).

The reading process requires that readers focus their eyes on a relatively small region of the visual field. The eyes do not make a continuous sweep across the visual field. Instead, they make a series of jumps and pauses from left to right, across the line of print. Each pause is called a fixation. When the eye is fixated, the print is processed. A jump is called a visual saccade (interfixation movement). During the saccade, vision is blurred and detailed processing of the print is not possible. A backward movement and pause is made when a reader fails to process the print during the fixation. The good reader is assumed to have more regular, fewer, and shorter fixations than the poor reader, as well as fewer regressions.

It has been asserted that poor reading can be improved by training eye movement patterns (Getman, 1985). The nature of the relationship between eye movement behavior and reading has been fraught with controversy. Empirical evidence supporting the efficacy of this training with the reading disabled is sparse. Tinker (1958) reviewed studies in which the performance of poor readers was compared before and after such training. The studies that he reviewed suggest that poor readers could be taught to make more efficient eye movements, but that reading ability remained unchanged.

Evidence that eye movements cause reading disabilities is meager. Rayner (1985) reviewed the characteristics of eye movements during reading and concluded that eye movements are not a cause of reading problems. Rather, eye movement characteristics appear to reflect the difficulty that readers have in reading; they are caused by the reading disturbance and not vice versa.

REFERENCES

Getman, G. N. (1985). A commentary on vision training. *Journal of Learning Disabilities, 18,* 505–512.

Pavlidis, G. T. (1985). Eye movements in dyslexia: Their diagnostic significance. *Journal of Learning Disabilities, 18,* 42–50.

Rayner, K. (1985). The role of eye movements in learning to read and reading disability. *Remedial & Special Education, 6,* 53–59.

Tinker, M. A. (1958). Recent studies of eye movements in reading. *Psychological Bulletin, 55,* 215–231.

HARRISON C. STANTON
Texas A & M University

READING DISORDERS

READING DISORDERS

It is an understatement to say that the process of reading is complex. Those who have sought to model the reading process serve as evidence of this complexity (LaBerge & Samuels, 1974). However, it is also true that most individuals will master the demanding skill of reading without much difficulty, and in spite of the instructional methods by which they are taught. For many, it would seem, the acquisition of reading appears to be more or less second nature; i.e., an easy and relatively unmemorable feat (Smith, 1978). Yet there are those for whom the task of reading is anything but second nature. For these individuals, attempts to acquire even rudimentary reading skills seem destined to fail. Rather than being "reading-able," these are the reading disabled. It is the purpose of this discussion to look more closely at this reading disabled population and to consider potential sources of their reading failures.

Before we deal specifically with sources of reading failure, it is important that this examination of reading disorders be placed into a historical framework. By dealing briefly with the historical perspective, the reader may come to understand some of the controversy that underlies present thinking in the area of reading disorders.

References to reading failures can be traced as far back as the early seventeenth century. The earliest published studies of reading disorders, appearing around the turn of the twentieth century, were undertaken by people in the medical profession. In 1896, W. Pringle Morgan, a British ophthalmologist, published what is credited as the first report of a reading disorder. In this report, Morgan presented a detailed account of a young man who could not read despite seemingly adequate intelligence. Morgan speculated that the youth suffered from "congenital word blindness." The explanation of reading failure articulated by Morgan was followed by a series of clinical studies published by Hinshelwood (1917). In his internationally recognized book, Hinshelwood, a Scottish eye surgeon, investigated the role of the brain in congenital word blindness.

The research of British medical professionals like Morgan and Hinshelwood, although generally stimulating little interest among most educators and psychologists at home and abroad, did influence the work of others. Notable among this work was Orton's (1925) studies of hemispheric imbalance. Orton, a neurologist, felt that the principal symptom of reading disorders was strephomymbolia, or severe reversals of language symbols. He felt that this condition was attributable to the lack of cerebral dominance. This pattern of letter reversal, which is often associated with the condition of dyslexia, remains a popular but poor indicator of reading problems.

Two important outcomes of the early medical writings on reading disabilities were evident. First, a medical perspective of reading disorders became firmly established. As a consequence of this perspective, which is still evident in certain circles today, the causes of reading problems were primarily sought among neurological factors. In other words, the focus of reading disorders was seen as within the reader (Lipson & Wixson, 1986): a neurological deficit that prevented the reader from successfully completing the reading act.

Even today, those who do not embrace the strongly neurological or psychoneurological view of reading problems, as projected in the early medical writings, cannot dismiss the lasting impression made by early medical research on the identification and treatment of reading disorders. To illustrate, we need only look at the language of reading assessment. In a clinical setting, in order to provide remediation (improvement) of reading difficulties, the client (reader) is diagnosed (tested), and an instructional treatment (program) is prescribed (developed).

The second outcome of the early medical influence in reading disorders was that it led to the development of scientific instruments that would be useful in isolating the source of reading problems. For example, in 1914 Thorndike developed a group test of reading ability, and in 1915 Gray followed with an oral reading test. As the number of such assessment tools grew, so did the concern for the improvement of the identified disorder or remediation. Diagnostic instruments became components of early clinical programs, established most often in conjunction with medical schools, and for the purpose of determining the cause of reading problems (etiology).

Initially, the diagnosis of reading disorders consisted of an extensive battery of physical, neurological, and language assessments that often entailed the individual's admission into a hospital. Today, while these more extensive diagnostic screenings are still administered, particularly in medically related clinics, briefer, more educationally related screenings have become far more prevalent. These school-based assessments focus heavily on reading achievement and aptitude measures, and only slightly on the physical characteristics of the reader such as visual discrimination and visual acuity and even less on the neurological factors.

Further, at the school level, most initial decisions about students' reading abilities or disabilities are made on the basis of group testings administered by classroom teachers, not by individual tests administered by trained specialists as in the case of clinical programs. These variations in tests and testing procedures between school-based and medically based reading programs are indicative of fundamental differences between such programs with regard to reading disorders. As noted, the neurological view of reading disorders focuses on deficits within the reader. Alternative perspectives in reading disorders center attention elsewhere.

Even from the beginning, with the work of Morgan and others, there have been those who have preferred to look outside the reader for factors contributing to reading failure. Some have sought to place the blame for reading problems squarely on the shoulders of the instruction these readers received (Judd, 1918; Uhl, 1916). For example, Judd (1918) contended that the emphasis on phonics instruction in education led to confusion in the reader's eye fixations, thus producing reading disability. Gray (1922) also put the burden for reading failure outside the reader and inside the educational system. As with those holding strongly to neurological views of reading disorders, those, like Judd and Gray, holding as strongly to instructional explanations for reading failures found only limited support.

In contrast to either view, the predominant approach to reading disorders is an interaction of the two positions, reflecting a position somewhere between the two extremes. Within this more moderate perspective, failure to read can be not only a consequence of neurological deficits or of misguided instruction, but reading failure can be attributed to multiple factors that include physical, emotional, and social conditions. For the remainder of this discussion, we will examine each of these potential contributors to reading failure.

Reading is a complex mental activity that involves the acquisition, manipulation, and retrieval of language symbols by the reader. As discussed, when a failure to read exists, there is the tendency to examine that failure in terms of its etiology or cause. Familiar terms such as brain injury, damage, dysfunction, and neuropsychological disorder reflect a neurological etiology. Harris and Sipay (1980) summarize the symptoms of neurological problems as encompassing (1) a history of a difficult birth, perhaps involving prolonged labor, an instrumental delivery, or deformity of the head; (2) prenatal conditions or premature birth; (3) poor balance or general awkwardness; (4) marked language delay; (5) attention deficit, or (6) a history of seizures or brief lapses in consciousness.

According to Spache (1976), there has been a resurgence in emphasis on neurological factors over the past two decades. This resurgence may be accounted for, in part, by the increased awareness of the brain and brain functioning provided by expanding technology. However, Spache cautions that even though brain damage can result in such evident conditions as aphasias, cerebral palsy, or mental retardation, "it appears that almost any failure to learn to read is now being interpreted, by some medical and/or reading specialists, as proof of the presence of brain damage or dysfunction" (p. 177).

Among the most common neurologically related reading disorders are alexia, partial or total loss of reading ability, dyslexia, deficit language production, and learning disability, reading underachievement. Because of the widespread application of the labels of dyslexia and learning disability, we will consider these conditions in more depth.

Dyslexia is certainly one of the most widely applied and perhaps one of the most misused labels for reading problems. References to dyslexic conditions, which can be linked all the way back to Morgan's writings on congenital word blindness and Orton's research on strephomymbolia, have continued to appear with regularity in the literature. Although a multitude of definitions of dyslexia do exist, the root of the word relates to word distortion, and it is frequently associated with letter or word reversals. Critchley (1970) identified two types of dyslexia: developmental and symptomatic. Developmental dyslexia, in his opinion, has an organic source, while symptomatic dyslexia may be influenced by a variety of factors, both organic and psychiatric.

Despite the popularity of the term, many, principally in the educational community, prefer to believe that such a condition as dyslexia does not exist (Cartwright, Cartwright, & Ward, 1995). While it seems likely that the word dyslexia is too easy and invalidly applied by the general populace, it is equally difficult to discount the number of individuals who display an inability to encode, or to manipulate, written language, and problems in decoding language in written form is central to most current definitions of dyslexia (e.g., Reid, 1998).

Some of the same characteristics that apply to the condition of dyslexia apply as well to the condition of learning disability (LD). According to IDEA a specific learning disability is "a disorder in one or more of the basic psychological processes" required to understand language. "The term includes such conditions as perceptual handicaps, brain injury, minimal brain dysfunction, dyslexia, and developmental aphasia" (p. 65083, 1977).

Beyond this legal definition, however, there is ample disagreement about the nature, identification, and treatment procedures for learning disabilities. What is most interesting about LD is that in many ways the condition is primarily an educational problem. What frequently unites the vast numbers of students labeled LD is that there is a significant gap between perceived potential and demonstrated performance. In addition, there is no apparent cause for the significant gap between potential and performance. This gap may be related to a combination of affective and cognitive factors, and may be reflected both in learning and behavioral problems within the learner. Often, teachers and specialists struggle to bring the LD student's performance up to potential through the application of medical and educational treatments.

While important, neurological factors such as those discussed here account for relatively few of the reading problems encountered in classrooms (Harris & Sipay, 1980; Reid, 1998). Other factors such as physical ones, may also contribute to reading difficulties.

Reading, as we have observed, is a mental undertaking. Beyond its purely neurological aspects, however, the act of reading is very much a sensory activity, relying heavily on visual and auditory stimuli. There are several sensory deficits that can have an immediate and significant effect on an individual's acquisition and maintenance of reading proficiency. Several of those deficits will be examined in this section.

Although the terms sight and vision are frequently used interchangeably, there are semantic differences in these terms that become important in a discussion of reading disorders. Basically, the word sight refers to the eye's response to light. By comparison, the word vision implies that there is some interpretation of the information transmitted by the eye to the brain. In reading disability research, the term visual acuity is employed to represent the state of having good sight. Visual discrimination refers to the individual's ability to interpret minute differences between and among visual stimuli. During reading, the learner's eyes must not only see and discriminate among single stimuli but most also make saccadic movements or smooth left-to-right progressions and sweeps from line to line of text. The eyes are also required to pause and focus periodically in the reading process. These periodic pauses are called fixations.

Without a doubt, clear and appropriate visual access to the printed page facilitates the individual's ability to process written language. When visual acuity is impaired, the process of reading is diminished, at best, or made extremely difficult, at worst. What precisely is the effect of various visual defects on reading performance? Reviews of the research present inconclusive evidence on the relationship of visual defects of reading performance (Harris & Sipay, 1980; Spache, 1976). Several factors that can account for the inconsistent findings of this research include (1) variations in what supposedly similar tests are actually measuring; (2) the brief and unreliable nature of visual tests; (3) the lack of comparability in the ages and visual development of subjects; and (4) the adaptability of learners.

There are many visual problems that can impede the reading process. Among the most common visual deficiencies are nearsightedness (myopia), farsightedness (hyperopia), and astigmatism; all are refractive errors or abnormalities in eye shape. In one longitudinal study of the role of vision defects (Kelley, 1957), it was found that myopia increased with age and was correlated with high achievement, whereas hyperopia was correlated with poor reading performance. These findings have been supported in other studies of the relationship of visual defects to reading performance (Grosvenor, 1970; Terman, 1925).

When functioning during the reading process, the eyes must make several critical adjustments, and difficulties in performing these adjustments can interfere with the reading process. For example, the muscles of the eyes must operate together in a coordinated fashion, focusing and centering on the visual target in such a way as to produce a single, clear image. When functioning effectively, the eyes allow us to perceive the depth or thickness of a visual target (stereopsis). This muscular balance of the eyes is referred to as binocular coordination, and the process of centering the visual stimuli is labeled fusion.

At times, there can be a muscular imbalance preventing the eyes from operating in a coordinated way. In certain cases, one eye may assume dominance over the other eye (amblyopia), a condition commonly referred to as lazy eye. If binocular coordination is impaired, there may be occurrences of heterophoria, or a muscular resistance to fusion. When this condition is mild, the reader sees a blurred image, but when severe, two images may actually be seen. In the milder cases of heterophoria, one eye may turn inward (esophoria), or outward (exophoria), or may focus higher than the other (hyperphoria). In more severe cases, the eyes appear crossed or "walleyed." This extreme form of binocular imbalance is known as strabismus. In general, partial fusion with its blurring effect is more problematic to readers than complete lack of fusion. For the most part, readers with milder cases of muscular imbalance can accommodate well, except when they experience fatigue, tension, or headaches; when extreme, the individual tends to ignore one eye.

While reading, particularly oral reading, depends on auditory skills, few severe reading problems can be directly linked to auditory factors. However, in our discussion of reading disorders, several auditory classifications should be considered. Those categories are auditory acuity, auditory discrimination, and auditory memory. Auditory acuity refers the state of having good hearing. Auditory discrimination involves the recognition of minute differences in speech sounds. Students' appropriate production of speech sounds is dependent on their ability to hear such differences. Many early reading programs stress phonic analysis, which relies on students' ability to recognize and reproduce the common sound-symbol patterns in language. Consequently, deficits in auditory acuity or discrimination would place the child at a disadvantage.

Also of importance in the reception of auditory stimuli is the individual's ability to mask or eliminate extraneous noises in the environment. As most of us know, the classroom, where so much information is transmitted auditorily, is anything but noise-proof. Focusing on important information in the classroom demands that the learner mask out sounds that would otherwise interfere with the acquisition of salient information. Overall, however, auditory deficits play a much less critical role in reading disorders than the visual or neurological conditions already discussed.

Beyond the visual or auditory factors presented, there are other physical conditions that may contribute to reading problems. Among those conditions are illnesses, general awkwardness, glandular problems, poor nutrition, and allergies. It must be noted, however, that there is little direct evidence that such conditions significantly affect reading performance. For example, illnesses tend to come into play in reading problems when students suffer from prolonged or chronic ailments. Yet, in most instances, prolonged illnesses prevent the learner from attending school, and it is this lack of school attendance that contributes most to reading failures. General awkwardness is not, itself, a factor in reading problems, but it is of importance in that it is frequently a symptom of minimal brain dysfunc-

tion. Further, while glandular abnormalities can result in such physical abnormalities as dwarfism and obesity, there is limited understanding of the effects of endocrine treatment on reading disorders. The effect of malnutrition on reading disorders is also difficult to pinpoint since this condition is also closely tied to low socioeconomic status.

To this point we have been discussing neurological and physical factors that impact reading performance. There are also less easily measured factors within the individual that may influence the reading process. Among these less measurable factors are psychosocial characteristics of the reader. Even from the beginning of work in the area of reading disorders, writers such as Orton (1925) and Gray (1922) have contended that good readers are socially and emotionally different from poor readers. Good readers have been seen as not only good at reading skills, but good at psychosocial adjustment. By comparison, disabled readers have been categorized by such descriptors as restless, withdrawn, or introverted (Robinson, 1953).

That certain psychosocial behaviors have been frequently related to poor reading performance is widely accepted. However, the significance of emotional and social factors in causing reading disorders is unclear. Do certain psychosocial behaviors result in reading failure? Does the presence of reading problems have certain emotional or social effects on the learner? Do certain emotional or social behaviors and reading problems develop simultaneously? These questions remain unanswered by the existing literature.

In part, we know little about the relationship of psychosocial conditions and reading disorders because the techniques for gathering data in these areas are somewhat unreliable. For example, teacher observation, which may be employed to gather information on a learner's emotional or social behavior, can be biased. Further, teachers generally conduct observations without the benefit of training. Interviews may also be used to collect data on these factors. Yet, even when these interviews are performed by training specialists, there is little assurance that what the learner says is an accurate reflection of the internal state. Personality measures are another tool for assessing an individual's emotional and social condition. While such measures may provide a better understanding of the condition of the learner than observations and interviews, the reliability of these measures is still a point of contention.

Although failing to produce consistent differences between disabled and able readers, research (Harris, 1971; Harris & Sipay, 1980) has generated various aspects of psychosocial behavior that may contribute to reading problems. For example, Harris and Sipay (1980) delineate the following characteristics as related to reading problems:

Conscious refusal to learn
Overt hostility

Negative conditioning to reading

Displacement of hostility

Resistance to pressure

Clinging to dependency

Quick discouragement

Success seen as dangerous

Extreme distractibility or restlessness

Absorption in a private world

Harris and Sipay's characteristic of extreme distractibility and restlessness as indicative of reading problems relates to the work on attention deficit disorders in the literature on learning disabilities. Since the research of Bandura (1969) and Gibson (1969), the importance of attention to learning has been widely accepted. It would appear that LD students, for whom there is a gap between potential and academic performance, suffer from a developmental lag with regard to attention (Reid, 1998; Ross, 1976). Often, LD students are unable to sustain attention to task, and the effect is decreased learning. To assist LD students in improving reading performance, Bateman (1979) has suggested that instructional programs (1) attend to relevant phoneme features; (2) increase the number of repetitions to mastery; and (3) use reinforcement.

Several of the psychosocial characteristics listed by Harris and Sipay (e.g., quick discouragement and negative conditioning) are more closely examined in the literature on achievement motivation (Dweck & Bempechat, 1983; Nicholls, 1983; Weiner, 1983). Achievement motivation can be distinguished from other forms of motivation by its purpose, which involves an increase in learner competence. Dweck and Bempechat (1983) describe the importance of achievement motivation to learning as follows:

> Motivational factors can have pronounced and far-reaching effects on children's learning and performance. They determine such critical things as whether children see or avoid challenges and whether they persist in the face of obstacles—in short, whether children actually pursue and master the skills they value and are capable of mastering. (p. 239)

In his research on achievement motivation, Nicholls (1983) has identified two types of motivation, labeled ego-involvement and task-involvement. In ego-involvement motivation, it is the individual who is the focus of attention. For the ego-involved, learning is of little value in and of itself, except as a personal reflection of worth. In the task-involvement form of achievement motivation, the task becomes the focal point and the individual exerts effort on the task primarily for the sake of learning. The task-involved student will view success as the result of effort applied to learning tasks, and failure as the need to increase that effort. By comparison, the ego-involved student will view academic success or failure in a personal light, as something removed from the task. Because of this attitude, ego-involved students seem less likely to seek help when confronted with a difficult task because they would be admitting that they lack the necessary ability (Ames, 1981).

There are also those in reading classes who have given up any chance of increased competence, for whom learning represents little more than an unbroken chain of failure and frustration. These individuals suffer from a condition called learned helplessness. Because the learned helpless expect failure to occur, they seem unwilling to exert the effort that may be required to achieve in the reading classroom. Indeed, they are so conditioned to failure that they that may be uncomfortable with successful learning experiences. Observations in remedial reading classrooms reveal many who attribute their reading problems to personal failure, and who have chosen to abandon any attempts to gain competence in reading. Such motivational conditions are apt to make improvements in reading performance unlikely.

Two important points need to be made with regard to psychosocial behaviors and reading disorders. First, reading, as it occurs in the context of schooling, remains a social activity. The reader must not only process text to meet personal ends, but must interpret and verify understanding of text for teachers and peers in a way that is seen as appropriate. Therefore, whether or not social and emotional factors are significant in a causal way, they will continue to be related to reading performance. Second, schools tend to see themselves in the business of teaching reading skills, not of treating emotional and social problems. Consequently, in few classrooms or clinics are the emotional and social needs of the problem reader given serious attention. It would seem that those working with problem readers often feel that the emotional and social conditions of these individuals will be taken care of when the specific reading problems are dealt with. Others, however, would argue that to treat only the reading problem without treating the concomitant emotional and social concerns would result in only partial and temporary gains in learner performance. Continued research in the area of psychosocial factors is necessary if we are to understand how best to improve the performance of disabled readers.

REFERENCES

Ames, C. (1981). Competitive versus cooperative reward structures: The influence of individual and group performance factors on achievement attributions and affect. *American Educational Research Journal, 18,* 273–287.

Bandura, A. (1969). *Principles of behavior modification.* New York: Holt, Rinehart, & Winston.

Bateman, B. (1979). Teaching reading to learning disabled and other hard-to-teach children. In L. B. Resnick & P. A. Weaver (Eds.), *Theory and practice in early reading* (Vol. 1, pp. 227–259). Hillsdale, NJ: Erlbaum.

Cartwright, P., Cartwright, C., & Ward, M. (1995). *Educating special learners* (4th ed.). Boston: Wadsworth.

Critchley, M. (1970). *The dyslexic child.* Springfield, IL: Thomas.

Dweck, C. S., & Bempechat, J. (1983). Children's theories of intelligence: Consequences for learning. In S. G. Paris, G. M. Olson, & H. W. Stevenson (Eds.), *Learning and motivation in the classroom* (pp. 239–256). Hillsdale, NJ: Erlbaum.

Gibson, E. J. (1969). *Principles of perceptual learning and development.* Englewood Cliffs, NJ: Prentice-Hall.

Gray, C. T. (1922). *Deficiencies in reading ability: Their diagnosis and remedies.* Boston: Heath.

Gray, W. S. (1915). *Oral reading paragraph test.* Bloomington, IN: Public School.

Grosvenor, T. (1970). Refractive state, intelligence test scores and academic ability. *American Journal of Optometry & Archives of American Academy of Optometry, 47,* 355–360.

Harris, A. J. (1971). Psychological and motivational problems. In D. K. Bracken & E. Malmquist (Eds.), *Improving reading ability around the world* (pp. 97–103). Neward, DE: International Reading Association.

Harris, A. J., & Sipay, E. R. (1980). *How to increase reading ability* (7th ed.). New York: Longman.

Hinshelwood, J. (1917). *Congenital word-blindness.* London: Lewis.

Judd, C. H. (1918). *Reading: Its nature and development* [Educational Monograph No. 10]. Chicago: University of Chicago.

Kelley, C. R. (1957). *Visual screenings and child development: The North Carolina Study.* Raleigh, NC: Department of Psychology, North Carolina State College.

LaBerge, D., & Samuels, S. J. (1974). Toward a theory of automatic information processing in reading. *Cognitive Psychology, 6,* 292–323.

Lipson, M. Y., & Wixson, K. K. (1986). Reading disability research: An interactionist perspective. *Review of Educational Research, 56,* 111–136.

Morgan, W. P. (1896). A case of congenital word-blindness. *British Medical Journal, 2,* 1612–1614.

Nicholls, J. G. (1983). Conceptions of ability and achievement motivation: A theory and its implications for education. In S. G. Paris, G. M. Olson, & H. W. Stevenson (Eds.), *Learning and motivation in the classroom* (pp. 211–237). Hillsdale, NJ: Erlbaum.

Orton, S. T. (1925). Word-blindness in school children. *Archives of Neurology & Psychiatry, 14,* 582–615.

Reid, G. (1998). *Dyslexia: A practitioner: handbook. 2nd Ed.* New York: Wiley.

Robinson, H. M. (1953). Personality and reading. In A. E. Traxler (Ed.), *Modern educational problems* (pp. 87–99). Washington, DC: American Council on Education.

Ross, A. O. (1976). *Psychological aspects of learning disabilities and reading disorders.* New York: McGraw-Hill.

Smith, F. (1978). *Reading without nonsense.* New York: Teachers College Press.

Spache, G. D. (1976). *Investigating the issues of reading disabilities.* Boston: Allyn & Bacon.

Terman, L. M. (1925). Genetic studies of genius. *Mental and physical traits of 1000 gifted children.* Stanford, CA: Stanford University Press.

Thorndike, E. L. (1914). The measurement of ability in reading. *Teachers College Record, 15,* 207–227.

Uhl, W. L. (1916). The use of the results of reading tests as bases for planning remedial work. *Elementary School Journal, 17,* 266–275.

Weiner, B. (1983). Some thoughts about feelings: In S. G. Paris, G. M. Olson, & H. W. Stevenson (Eds.), *Learning and motivation in the classroom* (pp. 165–178). Hillsdale, NJ: Erlbaum.

Patricia A. Alexander
University of Maryland

AMBLOYOPIA
DEVELOPMENTAL DELAY
DYSLEXIA
DYSPEDAGOGIA
LEARNED HELPLESSNESS
READING REMEDIATION

READING IN THE CONTENT AREAS

For over at least half a century, reading and curriculum specialists have claimed that every teacher is a teacher of reading. Many books, articles, and research reports have been published during this period and courses in teaching reading in the content areas are offered in many colleges of education. Despite these efforts, content teachers have typically maintained that they are teachers of subject matter and not teachers of reading. In a comprehensive and critical review of the research in reading in the content areas, Dupois (1984) concludes that content teachers know too little about reading in general and reading in their subjects in particular. She further reports that teachers feel "helplessness and frustration in the face of students who cannot read classroom materials" (p. 1).

This frustration is further amplified when students are labeled as special or disabled. Teachers feel especially helpless in their attempts to deal with the reading needs of the special student, assuming they lack some vital prerequisite training or technique. Yet what has been repeatedly revealed in research studies is the need for good holistic language teaching for students of all ability levels, rather than separate programs for special populations.

Specialists have a vital role to play in the field of special education, but it is not in the creation of separate programs focused on subskills of language; these programs often are less of a solution than a perpetuation of a problem with a child's reading. One major role of the special education specialist is that of collaborator and consultant to the content teacher in mainstream classrooms. The purpose of this relationship is to strengthen the regular classroom teacher as he or she plans to more fully involve special children in the intellectual and social life of the classroom.

Recently, 27 national organizations of teachers, supervisors, administrators, and lay groups endorsed a statement called "The Essentials Approach: Rethinking the Curriculum for the 80's" (1981), which proclaims the interdependence of skills and content as well as interdependence of knowledge in the several content areas. Interdependence of skills and content refers to the learner's use of reading, writing, talking, and thinking in learning literature, social studies, science, and math. The "Essentials" consortium argued that teachers will teach their subjects more effectively if they teach students the special reading, writing, and study strategies for acquiring and critically responding to knowledge in their disciplines. Ultimately, such a concerted effort will prepare students for a lifetime of learning but helping to make them independent learners. Clearly, the direction proposed is not limited to the relationship between reading and learning but rather extends to writing, studying, talking, and thinking.

The "Essentials" consortium warned against two related practices in many schools that stand in the way of fostering the interdependence principle. The first faulty practice defines basic skills by what can be measured at a time when tests are severely limited in what they can measure. Related to this is the practice of teaching the skills identified by such tests in isolation from significant content, i.e., from texts that look like the tests rather than real content texts. In short, reading skill has been fragmented away from the content areas and further fragmented into discrete subskills. Goodlad (1983) documented this state of the schools, which he characterized as being preoccupied with lower intellectual processes and boredom of epidemic proportions. The problem is exacerbated in special and mainstream classrooms for special educational populations, where it has been erroneously believed that there needs to be more emphasis on isolated subskills to remediate the poor reading skills of these students.

In 1985, the Commission on Reading of the National Academy of Education published *Becoming A Nation of Readers* (Anderson et al., 1985), which synthesized current sociopsycholinguistic theory and research on learning to read and reading to learn. This document provides a theoretical rationale for teachers who would implement the "Essentials" approach.

Reading is not defined as a product or as a set of subskills to be tested but rather as "a process for constructing meaning from written texts ... a complex skill requiring the coordination of a number of interrelated sources of information" (p. 7). Those sources lie in the reader, in the text, in fellow students, and in the teacher. Readers bring to the reading task knowledge of the world, of language, of strategies for reading various texts, and of their teachers'

purposes and expectations. They also bring their own interests and purposes. Texts present world knowledge in special ways; for example, literary texts have different conventions and structures from informational texts. They vary in purpose, content, and style. Fellow students constitute a community of comprehenders. Through interaction they can share relevant prior knowledge, text knowledge, and reading strategies.

The role of teachers is to orchestrate these interrelated sources, developing productive transactions among readers and texts that lead to more efficient strategies for information processing by students. Information processing involves such active mental searches as drawing on prior knowledge, predicting, questioning, elaborating, transforming, structuring, restating, summarizing, synthesizing, reflecting, and critically evaluating. In practical terms, content teachers can teach reading and study by modeling strategies that incorporate one or more of these searches by having students practice strategies in pairs and in small groups as well as on their own and by having students reflect on and share their experiences with each other in using the strategies.

Two lists of such strategies follow. They were developed by Botel (1984) at the University of Pennsylvania for preparing teachers and reading specialists. The first list includes strategies for reading and comprehending literary texts; the second includes strategies for reading and comprehending expository texts. These strategies are no less vital for the special education student than the regular student. It will be noted that these strategies enable students to experience reading at their own levels.

Strategies for Reading, Writing, and Studying Library Texts

Before Reading

Brainstorming

What questions, ideas or experiences were suggested by the title and opening paragraph(s) or verse?

Write or Talk and Write

Write nonstop about what comes to mind as you think about the title.

Write whatever questions come to mind as you think about the title.

Recall a related remembered experience; share it; write it.

Take notes on the way of life of a character from another culture (categories: family relationships, sources of food, beliefs about nature, housing, community, recreation, education).

While Reading

If you do not understand something, put a mark in the margin and go on.

Picture in your mind's eye what happens in the story

After Reading

Personal Responding

What stands out for you in the selection?

Retelling

Retell history from the point of view of different characters.

Tell the story to someone in the family, to a friend, to a younger person, etc.

Vocabulary Development

Write key words or expressions and define them in context.

Write words the writer uses to describe a character; then write a brief paragraph about the character using these words.

Write synonyms for key words.

Writing

Prepare questions you would ask if you could interview a character.

Write a journal entry about an important event as if you were the character who experienced it.

Write notes as if you were one of the characters.

Write an eyewitness or reporter's account of a scene as it might appear in a newspaper.

Making Tests

Prepare tests on content studied using the same form found in standardized and other tests.

Illustrating

Draw a floor plan of a major setting.

Illustrate a scene.

Make a map or graphic diagram of a key concept or relationship.

Illustrate key words and expressions.

Show the story or episode in a four-frame cartoon.

Dramatizing

Plan a "Reader's Theater."

Plan a panel discussion as if you were characters in the story.

Plan an informal dramatization.

Plan a debate.

Compare similarities and differences between your culture and that of a character.

Strategies for Reading, Writing, and Studying Expository Texts

Before Reading

Brainstorming

List words and phrases you associate with the title; see if your items can be grouped or chunked.

What questions are suggested by the title or opening paragraphs?

What questions would you hope would be answered by the selection?

Previewing

Read the headings and first and last paragraphs; then say or recite briefly what they suggest about the text.

Based on your review, what are the main questions that the author probably set out to answer in the selection?

Making Tests

Prepare tests on content studied using the same form found in standardized and criterion-referenced tests.

While and After Reading

Personal Responding

What stands out for you in the selection?

Taking Notes

Turn headings into questions and answer them.

Underline one or two key words in each paragraph.

Write a question for each paragraph or section.

Make marginal notes.

Make a map or graphic diagram of a key concept or relationship.

Develop Vocabulary

Write key words and expressions and define them in context.

Reread and Recite

Reread only the key words and write them from memory.

Reread only the key words and write a summary.

As noted earlier, Dupois reported that content teachers know little about teaching reading of their subject. Adaptation of the two lists of strategies in teaching subject matter should correct that problem. That leaves the problem of students who cannot read texts on their own. These students would benefit greatly from having the material read to them while others in the class read silently. But they can also benefit from involvement with classmates in the learning of the strategies, in particular when they are practiced and reflected on collaboratively.

Beyond the learning of strategies for comprehending texts, students in the content areas should be reading a variety of periodicals and library books independently to broaden their perspectives, deepen their knowledge, and excite their interest in the content. Self-selected independent reading provides another way of accommodating the varying reading levels in a classroom (Anderson, et al., 1985; Botel, 1981). Librarians and professional associations of content teachers are excellent sources for such reading. In social studies, the Children's Book Council (1984) produces an excellent list. Earle (1976) prepared a list of high-interest materials for the math classroom.

It is clear that reading in the content areas today deals with how teachers can organize and plan for instruction so as to relate the basic academic competencies (language processes of not only reading, but also writing, listening, and speaking) to learning the basic academic subjects. That is true for all students, including special education students in mainstream classrooms as well as in learning centers.

In summary, from the point of view of special education, the proposed ways of teaching content reading would have the effect of providing for more learning and less isolation and fragmentation, less stigmatization and separation from peers, less isolation of teachers, and less fragmentation of language.

REFERENCES

Anderson, R. C., Hiebert, E. H., Scott, J. A., Wilkinson, I. A. G., (1985). *Becoming a nation of readers: The report of the Commission on Reading.* Washington, DC: National Institute of Education.

Botel, M. (1981). *A Pennsylvania comprehensive reading/communication arts plan.* Harrisburg: Pennsylvania Department of Education.

Botel, M. (1984). *Comprehending texts: Subskills or strategies.* Philadelphia: Graduate School of Education, University of Pennsylvania.

Children's Book Council. *Notable children's trade books in the field of social studies.* New York: Author.

Dupois, M. M. (Ed.). (1984). *Reading in the content areas: Research for teachers.* Newark, DE: International Reading Association.

Earle, R. A. (1976). *Teaching reading and math.* Newark, DE: International Reading Association.

Goodlad, J. I. (1983). What some schools and classrooms teach. *Educational Leadership, 40*(7), 8–19.

Mercier, L. Y. (Ed.). (1981). *The essentials approach: Rethinking the curriculum for the 80's.* Washington, DC: U.S. Department of Education, Basic Skills Improvement Program.

MORTON BOTEL
University of Pennsylvania

READING DISORDERS
READING REMEDIATION

READING MILESTONES (SECOND EDITION)

Reading Milestones, a basal reading series developed by Stephen P. Quigley, Cynthia M. King, Patricia L. McAnally, and Susan Rose, was designed specifically for individuals with hearing impairment and originally published in the early 1980s by Dormac, Inc. The series was then acquired by Pro-Ed, Inc. in 1995.

Reading Milestones is the most popular reading program of its kind. This successful alternative, language-controlled program is designed to take readers to approximately a fifth-grade reading level. It is especially effective for students with hearing impairments and language delays and is also widely used with others who have special language and reading needs, including individuals with learning disabilities and students learning English as a second language (ESL).

The *Reading Milestones* program includes student readers, teacher's guides, placement tests, and student workbooks at each of six levels. The *Reading Bridge* series includes extension materials for students reading at grade levels 4–5. Additional resources that adhere to the structured approach presented in *Reading Milestones* include the *Simple Language Fairy Tales, Simple English Classics,* and *Most Loved Classics* series.

Extensive revisions were made in the second edition of the program based on recent research, new practices in reading, and feedback from users of the series. Because most students with hearing impairments and/or other special needs lack a basic knowledge base in oral/aural aspects of language, there can be a resulting gap in their language experience and the assumptions inherent in the materials they are given to read. *Reading Milestones* was designed to minimize this gap by beginning with the simplest possible language to ensure initial success in reading and by increasing language acquisition. Students are guided to progress in small increments, accompanied by constant reinforcement and review of concepts, vocabulary, and language constructions, to ensure continuing success and motivation.

REFERENCES

Brockmiller, P., & Coley, J. (1981). A survey of methods, materials, and teacher preparation among teachers of reading to the hearing-impaired. *The Reading Teacher, 34,* 526–529.

King, C., & Quigley, S. (1985). *Reading and deafness.* Austin, TX: Pro-Ed.

Lasso, C. J., & Mobley, R. T. (1997). National survey of reading instruction for deaf or hard-of-hearing students in the U.S. *The Volta Review, 99,* 31–58.

Lasso, C. (1987). Survey of reading instruction for hearing-impaired students in the United States. *The Volta Review, 89,* 85–98.

McAnally, P., Rose, S., & Quigley, S. (in press). *Reading practices with deaf learners.* Austin, TX: Pro-Ed.

Quigley, S., & King, C. (Eds.). (1991). *Reading milestones* (2nd ed.). Austin, TX: Pro-Ed.

PEGGY KIPPING
Pro-Ed, Inc.

READING REMEDIATION

Reading can be described as an essential and highly complex cognitive activity. As a cognitive task, the outcomes of the reading act require the successful completion of many simple and complex linguistic skills (Perfetti, 1983). To illustrate, consider the task of reading aloud the word *dog.* To accomplish this seemingly simple task, a reader must know the letters of the alphabet, must have internalized the sound/symbol patterns common to the English language, and must be able to decode or sound out the word accurately. Decoding alone can be a troublesome venture in the English language, where exceptions appear to outnumber phonetic rules. Further, if an understanding of dog is also required, then the reader must relate the abstract symbols and sounds to the concept of dog stored in long-term memory.

If many skills are required to read and understand a single word, then the skills necessary to make sense of the previous paragraph are far more extensive. It is therefore not surprising that some individuals never acquire reading proficiency. Those individuals who consistently experience difficulties in processing print are part of a population of learners who require special instruction. This special instruction is referred to as reading remediation.

Reading remediation is a branch of language instruction that is concerned with the identification and treatment of reading problems. The following text will examine factors that contribute to reading difficulties, consider how the cycle of remediation occurs, discuss levels of reading diagnosis, survey principles that should guide effective diagnosis, and review profiles of problem readers.

Even before an individual is asked to read, there are factors that are likely to enhance or inhibit reading performance. Rupley and Blair (1983) identify two broad categories of variables that relate to reading performance: functional and facilitative factors. Functional factors are those variables that actually pertain to reading. Sight vocabulary, reading rate, and oral language development are examples of functional factors. In many ways, these functional variables are the outcome of other variables that are not directly part of the reading performance but contribute to it. These variables are called facilitative factors, and they are of particular importance in reading remediation. Facilitative factors fall under such broad headings as physical, cognitive, and emotional characteristics. Within each of these broad areas there are conditions that can significantly influence reading performance.

For example, among physical characteristics, we know that gender, visual and auditory ability, and general health influence reading performance. Whether owed to genetic or environmental factors, or a combination of both, females tend to have an advantage over males in language acquisition and early language proficiency. Males' linguistic disadvantage may be a partial explanation for the disproportionate number of boys enrolled in remedial reading classes.

It is also clear that individuals who suffer from visual or auditory impairments will have more difficulty in acquiring proficiency in written language. The ability to see and hear adequately are basic to reading. Among young children, many suspected reading problems can be traced to visual or auditory impairments, many of which are correctable. Once the vision or hearing problem has been corrected, many young children go on to acquire reading proficiency. Consequently, analysis of reading problems frequently begins with vision and hearing screening. In these screenings, visual and auditory acuity and discrimination are tested.

Cognitive factors also contribute significantly to the reading process. As we will see in the discussion of reader profiles, the cognitive ability an individual brings to the reading act is a major determinant of the level of proficiency expected. While there is no one-to-one correspondence between intelligence and reading ability, the relationship between the two is strong indeed. Cognitive factors may be assessed by means of achievement or intelligence test data, or school performance records.

Similarly, an individual's emotional well-being can positively or negatively affect the ability to read. The significant influence of affective factors on learning should not be ignored in the evaluation of reading problems (Cartwright, Cartwright, & Ward, 1995; Reid, 1998). Learners who have the cognitive potential may lack the desire or commitment that is required to do well in reading. Parent/student interviews and self-concept and personality tests may be used to gather information on the emotional condition of a reader.

When a reading problem is suspected, it is prudent first to determine whether existing physical, cognitive, and emotional as well as socioeconomic, cultural, or educational factors are potential sources of the problem. The systematic assessment of functional and facilitative factors is part of reading diagnosis, which, in turn, is a major component in the remediation cycle.

Much of the language of reading remediation is borrowed from medical science. The medical influence is particularly apparent in the cycle of reading remediation. This cycle is comprised of three phases: diagnosis, prescription, and treatment.

The diagnosis or data-collection phase of the remediation cycle refers to the systematic assessment of existing conditions: a search for evidence that might indicate the source of a reader's problems. It is in this phase that information about the reader and reading performance is gathered and analyzed. Knowledge about the reader may be collected in a spontaneous fashion within the classroom, or it may be amassed through a formal and extensive procedure.

On the basis of careful diagnosis, the second phase of the cycle, the prescription or program-specification phase, is put into place. Prescription is the delineation of the appropriate instructional treatment to be administered. It is expected that a carefully prescribed instructional program will ameliorate the reader's problems. As with the diagnostic procedure, the instructional plan may be informal or formal in nature. An informal prescription might entail little more than the teacher's specification of instructional objectives that seem appropriate for a reader. A formal prescription, by comparison, may be an elaborate instructional program to be administered by a specialist within a clinic or resource room.

Finally, there is the treatment or program-implementation phase of the cycle. In this phase, the prescribed instructional treatment is carried out and its effectiveness evaluated. From the knowledge gained during instruction and evaluation, additional information about the reader and reading performance is gathered. Based on these new data, a revised diagnosis may be rendered and the remediation cycle begins anew. This remediation cycle forms the basis of reading instruction, whether it occurs in the regular classroom or in the resource room (Cheek & Cheek, 1980).

Diagnosis can take place at several levels of complexity. Those levels, in order of increasing formality, are informal, classroom, and clinical diagnosis (Wilson & Cleland, 1985). In the previous section, the data gathering was apt to be part of the more extensive form of clinical reading diagnosis. Meeting the needs of most readers does not often require that diagnosis reach such a formal level, however. Rather, clinical diagnosis should be the last stage is the diagnostic procedure. For the most part, serving the needs of the reader entails only the first two levels in the sequence of diagnosis, informal, and classroom diagnosis.

Informal diagnosis is an ongoing process that takes place continuously in the regular reading classroom. This stage of diagnosis encompasses the teacher's monitoring of reading instruction to determine whether that instruction is appropriate for the learner. If found inappropriate or ineffective, the instruction should be adjusted in some fashion to suit more adequately the learner's needs and capabilities.

For example, let us say that a teacher asks a child to read aloud from a basal reader. The teacher finds that the child's oral reading is poor, containing many errors and little expression. Based on this informal assessment, the teacher adjusts instruction by telling the child to read the basal passage silently first before reading it aloud. After an opportunity to practice the basal passage, the teacher finds that the reading is smooth and expressive. In this instance, the teacher engaged in informal diagnosis and altered the instruction accordingly. The results in this case were successful.

What if the minor adjustments in reading instruction were not successful in improving the situation? What would the teacher do next? In the second stage of diagnosis, the teacher would conduct some testing within the classroom in an attempt to identify the nature of the reading problem. Classroom diagnosis may involve the use of teacher-made or commercial tests that can be administered and interpreted by teachers who have no specialized knowledge of reading or assessment. Perhaps, as in the preceding case, the teacher constructs a cloze test (Tierney, Readence, & Dishner, 1980) from the basal text. From this cloze test, the teacher determines that the reading book that the child has been assigned is too difficult. The teacher then moves the child to a more appropriate read-ing group and the problem with oral reading seems to disappear.

Should the classroom teacher's attempts to identify or remediate the reading problem fail, then it is time to call in a specialist. It is at this point in the diagnostic sequence that a clinical assessment of the reading problem should be conducted. Following the assessment of facilitative factors, a battery of reading tests are given. Among the reading skills frequently tested in a clinical diagnosis are sight vocabulary, oral reading, silent reading, listening comprehension, and word analysis skills. The information amassed in diagnosis permits the clinical specialist to ascribe a remediation program for the learner that is likely to improve reading performance.

Because of the major role that diagnosis plays in the remediation cycle, it is imperative that the assessment provides valid and reliable information. Bond and Tinker (1973) have outlined some guiding principles for clinical diagnosis that should result in the more effective remediation of reading problems. Many of these principles can also be applied to informal and classroom diagnosis.

1. Diagnosis should be directed toward formulating methods of improvement.
2. Diagnosis should involve more than an appraisal of reading skills and abilities.
3. Diagnosis should be efficient and effective.
4. Diagnosis should be continuous.
5. Diagnosis should seek to identify patterns of behavior.

According to the first of these principles, it is important to remember that diagnosis is not an end in itself. It is conducted to provide accurate information from which effective remediation can be developed. Without the other components of prescription and treatment, diagnosis would be an isolated and meaningless undertaking. Further, for diagnosis to be effective it must be beyond the assessment of reading alone and examine the learner in a more holistic fashion. That is, the physical, cognitive, emotional, socioeconomic, and educational characteristics of the learner must also be part of the decision-making process.

Another pragmatic concern in the diagnostic procedure is that the amount of testing and the instrumentation be appropriate for the individual case under examination. For example, if a physical condition is suspected as the primary cause for existing reading problems, and if visual/auditory screening confirms that situation, then further testing may prove costly and unwarranted. Likewise, it would be essential to employ valid and reliable measures to determine physical factors and to have those measures administered and evaluated by qualified individuals.

Diagnosis should generally be an ongoing process. Once information has been gathered and an instructional program prescribed, the effects of the prescribed program should be assessed. Even as it pertains to clinical diagnosis, no diagnosis is final and the treatment prescribed on the basis of formal assessment should be periodically reviewed and revised. It is important to remember that converging evidence is essential for an effective diagnosis. One piece of information is, under most circumstances, insufficient for building a remediation program that will lead to improvement for the learner. Patterns of scores are more likely to convey a more accurate view of the reader's strengths and needs.

Not only do scores produce certain patterns, but the diagnostic data across readers also tend to fall into certain patterns. It is on the basis of these diagnostic patterns that several commonly encountered reader profiles have been generated (Bond & Tinker, 1973; Harris & Sipay, 1980). Gifted readers are individuals who manifest normal or above normal intelligence and who possess reading skills that are markedly above grade level. Although the definition of markedly above grade level may vary somewhat, a rule of thumb for determining a significant difference is two years above grade level. It is important to note that the gifted reader may or may not be gifted in other domains. That is, the learner may be advanced in reading skills but average in math or science. Therefore, a gifted reader with reading skills that are significantly above grade level may have an intelligence only slightly above average. For example, Ruth is a fourth grader with a measured intelligence of 125. According to diagnosis, Ruth's sight vocabulary was 6–8 (grade equivalent of sixth grade, eighth month), oral reading 6–3, silent reading 7–1, and listening comprehension 7–5. As these scores indicate, Ruth's overall reading performance is well above the fourth-grade level. We would say that Ruth appears to be a gifted reader.

The needs of the gifted reader may be served within the context of the regular reading class or within a specific gifted program. However, if mainstreamed in the regular reading classroom, it is expected that these proficient readers will be provided with reading materials and instruction that is commensurate with their demonstrated abilities. In many schools, these advanced readers are grouped for reading instruction so that the teacher can more effectively provide them with appropriate instruction.

Underachievers are similar to gifted learners in that they demonstrate exceptional cognitive potential. However, they may fail to demonstrate reading skills that approach their potential. Dave, for example, is Ruth's fourth-grade classmate. Dave's IQ is estimated to be 140, yet he is performing just barely at grade level in reading class. His sight vocabulary is 4-6, silent reading and listening comprehension 4-1, and oral reading 3-8. While Dave's reading scores are not significantly below his grade level, they are significantly below his potential. Although further diagno-

sis is appropriate in this case, Dave would be classified as a reading underachiever at this level.

The underachieving reader is often the most difficult case to identify. Primarily because reading performance is near grade level, many classroom teachers do not recognize or attend to the gap between the underachiever's potential and performance. Further, prescribing and treating the underachiever is a complex undertaking; reading problems may be tied to any number of emotional, physical, neurological, social, or cultural factors that cannot be easily detected or treated.

Sometimes there are those learners who do fairly well in reading but who have a problem in one or two skills areas. This type of reader possesses a specific skills deficiency, the most common problem-reader profile. For the most part, these skill-deficient readers remain in the regular classroom with help provided by the reading teacher.

When reading assistance is given in the context of the classroom and is administered by the classroom teacher, it is labeled a corrective reading program. Jake is a case in point. Jake is also in Ruth's fourth grade class. Although he usually does well in reading, Jake has problems with his listening comprehension. As part of his corrective reading program, Jake's teacher works with him on a weekly basis to improve his listening skills. In this way, it is hoped that Jake's listening skills can be brought in line with his other reading skills.

Some readers' problems are not as limited or as easily treated as Jake's. There are those cases in which a learner with normal intelligence performs well below grade level on the majority of reading skills. For example, another fourth grader, Betsy, has an IQ of 101, but her reading grade equivalency scores are as follows: sight vocabulary, 1-5; oral reading, preprimer; silent reading 1-3; listening comprehension 2-0. The remediation program required to meet the needs of this type of problem reader is referred to as a remedial reading program. Because of the serious nature of the reading problems being treated, remedial reading programs become the responsibility of a reading specialist or resource teacher. Regular classroom teachers rarely have the training to deal effectively with remedial readers, nor can they provide these individuals the highly individualized attention they need to remediate their reading problems.

The determination to place a learner in a remedial reading program is often the result of a group decision-making process similar to that followed for other categories of special learners. While the primary responsibility for reading remediation falls to the reading specialist, the remediation program can and should involve parents, outside specialists, content-area teachers, and school administrators. Both long- and short-term goals are established for the reader, focusing on cognitive, metacognitive, and affective needs. Progress toward these goals are carefully documented, so that accurate evaluation of the program and the learner is possible.

The last reader profile is that of the slow learner. Like the remedial reader, the slow learner demonstrates reading skills that are far below grade level. However, unlike the remedial reader, the slow learner's reading performance is commensurate with cognitive ability. In other words, the slow learner is basically performing up to his or her potential. Victor, who is also in Ruth's classroom, has reading scores similar to Betsy's. However, when he was tested by the school psychologist, it was found that Victor's IQ is 85. Victor's reading scores appear to correspond to his cognitive ability. Because of the specialized treatment they require, slow learners may be assigned to a reading specialist or resource teacher for remediation.

As long as there is the complex process of reading there will be learners who encounter difficulties and who will require special reading instruction. It is the purpose of effective reading remediation programs to provide appropriate instruction to those learners for whom proficient reading is a goal yet to be achieved.

REFERENCES

Bond, G. L., & Tinker, M. A. (1973). *Reading difficulties: Their diagnosis and correction* (3rd ed.). Englewood Cliffs, NJ: Prentice-Hall.

Cartwright, P., Cartwright, C., & Ward, M. (1995) *Educating special learners. 4th ed.* Boston: Wadsworth.

Cheek, M. C., & Cheek, E. H. (1980). *Diagnostic-prescriptive reading instruction.* Dubuque, IA: Brown.

Harris, A. J., & Sipay, E. R. (1980). *How to increase reading ability* (7th ed.). New York: Longman.

Perfetti, C. A. (1983). Individual differences in verbal processes. In R. F. Dillon & R. R. Schmeck (Eds.), *Individual differences in cognition* (Vol. I, pp. 65–104). New York: Academic.

Reid, G. (1998). *Dyslexia: A practitioner: handbook* (2nd ed.). New York: Wiley.

Rupley, W. H., & Blair, T. R. (1983). *Reading diagnosis and remediation: Classroom and clinic* (2nd ed.). Boston: Houghton Mifflin.

Tierney, R. J., Readence, J. E., & Dishner, E. K. (1980). *Reading strategies and practices: A guide for improving instruction.* Boston: Allyn & Bacon.

Wilson, R. M., & Cleland, C. S. (1985). *Diagnostic and remedial reading for classroom and clinic* (5th ed.). Columbus, OH: Merrill.

PATRICIA A. ALEXANDER
Texas A & M University

DIAGNOSTIC-PRESCRIPTIVE TEACHING
DIAGNOSTIC REMEDIAL APPROACH
READING DISORDERS
READING IN THE CONTENT AREAS
REMEDIATION, DEFICIT CENTERED MODELS OF

REALITY THERAPY

Reality therapy is a recently developed method of psychotherapy that stresses the importance of clients learning more useful behaviors to deal with their current situations. Reality therapy stresses internal motivation, behavior change, and development of the "success identity." In terms of philosophical or theoretical stance, reality therapy can be described as strongly cognitive or rational in its approach, appealing to the client's reason and emphasizing the possibility of meaningful change, not just in feelings, but in behavior. The therapist takes an active, directive role as teacher, but remains supportive and nonpunitive.

William Glasser, a physician, developed the theory of reality therapy over a period of years beginning with his psychiatric training. Both Glasser's reaction against traditional psychoanalytic psychotherapy and his experiences in working with delinquent youths at a California school for girls probably played major roles in the development of reality therapy (Belkin, 1975).

Glasser (1965) sees the individual as motivated internally by need to belong, to be loved, and to be a successful, worthwhile person. Control is seen as a major element in the human system: the individual works to control the environment so that internal, personal needs can be met. The individual's interface with the reality of his or her current life situation is the arena of action. Therefore, reality therapy stresses personal commitment, change in behavior, responsibility and the here and now. The individual's past history is not seen as particularly significant, and the medical model or orthodox concept of mental illness has no place in this approach (Corey, 1986).

The therapist is viewed as a coach or instructor who provides clients with assistance and encouragement in evaluating the usefulness of their current behavior in satisfying their needs. Where the appropriateness of change is recognized, the therapist assists in the development and execution of plans for remediation. Development of the client's strengths and feelings of self-worth leading to a success identity is a key responsibility of the therapist.

Reality therapy is basically a didactic activity, by which the client develops an understanding of reality and learns to act responsibly and effectively in accordance with that reality. A summary of the techniques and procedures of reality therapy is provided by Corey (1986), based on his adaptation and integration of material from several sources. Corey discusses eight steps in therapy: create a relationship, focus on current behavior, invite clients to evaluate their behavior, help clients develop an action plan, get commitment, refuse to accept excuses, refuse to use punishment, and refuse to give up.

Glasser has promoted the acceptance of his approach by numerous presentations and publications. In *Reality Ther-*

apy: A New Approach to Psychiatry (1965), *Stations of the Mind* (1981), and *Take Effective Control of Your Life* (1984), Glasser develops his theoretical approach to psychotherapy and demonstrates its application to clinical cases. Glasser's *Schools Without Failure* (1969) applies the concepts of reality therapy to the school setting. *Positive Addiction* (1976) treats a different, but related, theme; it also has met with wide public acceptance.

Reality therapy has grown in popularity and influence. It is particularly well received in schools and the criminal justice system, and with counselors who work to rehabilitate handicapped individuals. This psychotherapeutic approach lends itself to short-term, direct, and active therapy.

REFERENCES

Belkin, G. S. (1975). *Practical counseling in the schools.* Dubuque, IA: Brown.

Corey, G. (1986). *Theory and practice of counseling and psychotherapy* (3rd ed.). Monterey, CA: Brooks/Cole.

Glasser, W. (1965). *Reality therapy: A new approach to psychiatry.* New York: Harper & Row.

Glasser, W. (1969). *Schools without failure.* New York: Harper & Row.

Glasser, W. (1976). *Positive addiction.* New York: Harper & Row.

Glasser, W. (1981). *Stations of the mind.* New York: Harper & Row.

Glasser, W. (1984). *Take effective control of your life.* New York: Harper & Row.

ROBERT R. REILLEY
Texas A & M University

PSYCHOSOCIAL ADJUSTMENT
PSYCHOTHERAPY

RECEPTIVE–EXPRESSIVE EMERGENT LANGUAGE TEST—SECOND EDITION (REEL-2)

The *Receptive–Expressive Emergent Language Test—Second Edition* (REEL-2; Bzoch & League, 1991) is a multidimensional analysis of emergent language. The REEL-2 is specifically designed for use with a broad range of infants and toddlers up to age 3 who are at risk. The instrument is a system of measurement and intervention planning based on neurolinguistic development to identify young children who have specific language problems based on specific language behaviors. Results are obtained from a parent interview and are given in terms of an Expressive Language Age, a Receptive Language Age, and a Combined Language Age.

Bachman (1995) reviewed the instrument and summarized that the REEL-2 covers a wide range of behaviors and could be used with direct observation to elicit infor-mation for developing a qualitative description of a child's early language development. Bliss (1995) reported that the advantages of the REEL-2 are in its easy administration and scoring.

REFERENCES

Bachman, L. F. (1995). Review of the Receptive–Expressive Emergent Language Test, Second Edition. In J. C. Conoley & J. C. Impara (Eds.), *The twelfth mental measurements yearbook* (pp. 843–845). Lincoln: Buros Institute of Mental Measurements, University of Nebraska Press.

Bliss, L. S. (1995). Review of the Receptive–Expressive Emergent Language Test, Second Edition. In J. C. Conoley & J. C. Impara (Eds.), *The twelfth mental measurements yearbook* (pp. 845–846). Lincoln: Buros Institute of Mental Measurements, University of Nebraska Press.

Bzoch, K. R., & League, R. (1991). *Receptive–Expressive Emergent Language Scale—Second Edition.* Austin, TX: Pro-Ed.

TADDY MADDOX
Pro-Ed, Inc.

RECEPTIVE LANGUAGE DISORDERS

A language disorder in which there is a severe loss or impairment in the understanding or use of language owing to brain injury or dysfunction is known as aphasia. This disorder may be dichotomized into expressive or motor aphasia, in which the ability to form speech is impaired, and receptive or sensory aphasia, in which the ability to comprehend the spoken word is affected. In adults, aphasia is acquired through brain damage and results in cessation or regression from a prior ability to use language. In children, language disorders may be acquired as a result of brain injury, or they may be developmental in nature. That is, because of abnormal development or injury to the language centers of the central nervous system prenatally, perinatally, or postnatally during the first year, the child has difficulty in developing normal understanding and use of language (Gaddes, 1980). This condition is also known as a primary or congenital language disorder (Deuel, 1983). When the dysfunction in the language centers of the brain is mild, it may be referred to as a learning disability.

Although many parts of the brain are active and interrelated in language and speech, certain areas are of greater importance to specific language functions (Benson, 1983). In 1874, Carl Wernicke, a German neurologist, identified the superior lateral surface of the left temporal lobe as the cortical area for decoding oral speech. Geschwind (1972) stressed the importance of subcortical bundles of neural fibers that connect distant cortical areas. However, the precise boundaries of important cortical areas remain vague owing to considerable interindividual variation and the fact that most brain lesions are not highly localized (Benson, 1983; Gaddes, 1980). Although the left hemisphere is dominant for language in most right-handed individuals, those who are left-handed or ambidextrous may have right hemisphere or bilateral language functions (Lezak, 1983). Some experts believe that comprehension of spoken language is more likely to have bilateral representation than other language functions (Benson, et al., 1973).

Receptive language disorders may be classified in several ways. Johnson and Myklebust (1967) discuss a generalized deficit in auditory learning in which a child hears but does not interpret. Other children, less affected, can interpret nonverbal, social sounds, but cannot relate the spoken word to an appropriate unit of experience. In cases of less severe receptive language deficits, the inability to comprehend may be limited to abstract language or to specific parts of speech. Benson (1983) cites four clinically distinguishable comprehension disturbances and suggests a neuroanatomical locus of pathology for each. These are (1) receptive disturbances, involving comprehension and repetition of spoken language; (2) perceptive disturbances (also known as Wernicke's aphasia), in which comprehension of written and spoken language is involved; (3) semantic disturbances, characterized by an inability to understand the meaning of spoken and written language despite relatively normal ability to repeat spoken language; and (4) syntactic disturbances, involving difficulties with syntactical structures and sequencing. Benson emphasizes that there is much overlap among these comprehension problems, and they are rarely found in isolation.

Receptive language disorders frequently are observed in conjunction with other disabilities. In the developmental hierarchy of language outlined by Myklebust (1954), expressive language follows and is dependent on inner and receptive language. In a similar way, reading and written language are dependent on the acquisition of earlier levels of language. Therefore, it is not surprising that reading, writing, and the problem-solving areas of arithmetic may be affected by receptive language disorders. Johnson and Myklebust (1967) suggest that auditory cognitive skills, including discrimination, rhyming, and blending, often are correlates of receptive language disorders. Such skills are prerequisite to the success of an auditory-phonetic reading program and indicate the need for a global language approach to instruction.

To remediate receptive language disorders, it is necessary to create a match between the auditory symbol and a meaningful unit of experience. Although Myklebust (1971) stresses the importance of comprehensive diagnostic testing to determine a profile of strengths and weaknesses on which highly individualized remediation may be based, he acknowledges certain similarities common to all instructional programs. Johnson and Myklebust (1967) list several of these principles to be incorporated into successful remediation. The first is that training should begin early. Benson (1983) suggests the presence of residual language competency in the nondominant hemisphere that slowly decreases with age. The plasticity of a young brain may allow language function to be taken over by the nondominant hemisphere or be shared bilaterally. Other principles of remediation suggested by Johnson and Myklebust include (1) input precedes output (comprehension precedes expression); (2) auditory symbol and unit of experience are simultaneous; (3) repetition is used; and (4) vocabulary is carefully selected. Myklebust (1971) cautions against the indiscriminate use of a multisensory motor approach. In some cases, such a remedial approach may result in overloading and have a negative effect on attention, orientation, and motivation. McGinnis (1963) gives a detailed description of additional remedial procedures.

REFERENCES

Benson, D. F. (1983). The neural basis of spoken and written language. In H. R. Myklebust (Ed.), *Progress in learning disabilities* (Vol. 5, pp. 3–25). New York: Grune & Stratton.

Benson, D. F., Sheremata, W. A., Buchard, R., Segarra, J., Price, D., & Geschwind, N. (1973). Conduction aphasia. *Archives of Neurology, 28,* 339–346.

Deuel, R. K. (1983). Aphasia in childhood. In H. R. Myklebust (Ed.), *Progress in learning disabilities* (Vol. 5, pp. 29–43). New York: Grune & Stratton.

Gaddes, W. H. (1980). *Learning disabilities and brain function: A neuropsychological approach* (2nd ed.). New York: Springer-Verlag.

Geschwind, N. (1972). Language and the brain. *Scientific American, 226*(4), 76–83.

Johnson, D. J., & Myklebust, H. R. (1967). *Learning disabilities: Educational principles and practices.* New York: Grune & Stratton.

Lezak, M. D. (1983). *Neuropsychological assessment* (2nd ed.). New York: Oxford University Press.

McGinnis, M. A. (1963). *Aphasic children: Identification and education by the association method.* Washington, DC: Alexander Graham Bell Association for the Deaf.

Myklebust, H. R. (1954). *Auditory disorders in children: A manual for differential diagnosis.* New York: Grune & Stratton.

Myklebust, H. R. (1971). Childhood aphasia: Identification, diagnosis, remediation. In L. E. Travis (Ed.), *Handbook of speech pathology and audiology* (pp. 1203–1217). New York: Appleton-Century-Crofts.

BARBARA S. SPEER
Shaker Heights City School
District Shaker Heights, Ohio

APHASIA
AUDITORY DISCRIMINATION
AUDITORY PERCEPTION
DEVELOPMENTAL APHASIA

RECIPROCAL DETERMINISM

Throughout the history of the behavioral sciences and human service professions, there have been a number of theoretical models proposed to provide insights for understanding, predicting, and manipulating human behavior. The most traditional perspective is commonly referred to as the medical model. Within this framework, human behavior is viewed as emanating primarily from forces that are internal to the individual (e.g., personality, IQ, neurological characteristics, hormonal activity). This orientation evolved from psychodynamic views of psychopathology and advances in the field of medicine. The work of Sigmund Freud (1943) provides a classic example of this perspective. A behavioral model developed in reaction to the medical model and as a result of the research and theory generated by leading behaviorists such as Skinner (1938, 1953). In contrast to the medical model, the behavioral model places primary emphasis on the influence of the immediate external environment (e.g., reinforcement, punishment) as a means for understanding human behavior. In the late 1970s and early 1980s, an ecological model of human behavior has emerged. Prompted largely by the work of Barker (1965), this set of principles focuses on the impact of the broad external environment (e.g., behavior settings, organizational policies, social norms) on the behavior of persons who function within that environment.

Reciprocal determinism is a model of human behavior that effectively synthesizes the medical, behavioral, and ecological models into a single integrated perspective. Proposed by Bandura (1978) as a result of his extensive theoretical and empirical work on social learning theory, reciprocal determinism postulates that human activity is a function of the mutual and reciprocal interactions that occur between a person's behavior (B), cognitive and other internal events related to the person (P), and the external environment (E). The model hypothesizes that human behavior results from an ongoing interaction among the B, P, and E factors in each person's life. According to this point of view, meaningful insight into a person's behavior is best attained if one can discern (1) the salient B, P, and E factors operating on and within that individual and (2) how those factors interact and influence each other.

The reciprocal determinism model holds important theoretical and practical insights for special educators. Consider, for example, the hypothetical case of a fourth-grade boy who has developed reading difficulties. Approaching this child's problem from a medical model perspective would lead special educators to examine the IQ, neurological status, health, etc. Those who subscribe to a behavioral model would focus primarily on information such as the nature of classroom interactions with teachers, peers, and academic materials during reading lessons. If special educators were to use the ecological model, it would lead them to consider the nature of the school's reading pro-gram, the district's resources in the area of reading, the home environment, etc. From the perspective of reciprocal determinism, however, special educators can see that each of these pieces of information may be important and that none should be overlooked.

Even more significant, the reciprocal determinism model highlights that one cannot really understand the causal factors behind children's educational and psychological difficulties without understanding how the B, P, and E factors affect each other. For example, the behavior of this hypothetical child in reading class (B) is continuously affected by his intellectual abilities (P), which are in turn either heightened or diminished as a function of the school's academic programs and his home environment (E), which are themselves influenced by how the child behaves both in and out of school (B). By sensitizing special educators to this dynamic interaction among B, P, and E forces, reciprocal determinism provides a comprehensive framework within which children's problems can be conceptualized, assessed, diagnosed, and treated (Reynolds, Gutkin, Elliott, & Witt, 1984).

REFERENCES

Bandura, A. (1978). The self-system in reciprocal determinism. *American Psychologist, 33,* 344–358.

Barker, R. G. (1965). Explorations in ecological psychology. *American Psychologist, 20,* 1–14.

Freud, S. (1943). *A general introduction to psychoanalysis.* Garden City, NY: Garden City.

Reynolds, C. R., Gutkin, T. B., Elliott, S. N., & Witt, J. C. (1984). *School psychology: Essentials of theory and practice.* New York: Wiley.

Skinner, B. F. (1938). *The behavior of organisms.* New York: Appleton-Century-Crofts.

Skinner, B. F. (1953). *Science and human behavior.* New York: Macmillan.

TERRY B. GUTKIN
University of Nebraska

BANDURA A.
BEHAVIORAL MODIFICATION
ECOLOGICAL ASSESSMENT
ECOLOGICAL EDUCATION OF THE HANDICAPPED
HUMANISTIC SPECIAL EDUCATION

RECLAIMING CHILDREN AND YOUTH: JOURNAL OF EMOTIONAL AND BEHAVIORAL PROBLEMS

Reclaiming Children and Youth: Journal of Emotional and Behavioral Problems is a quarterly journal publishing practical, research-validated strategies for professionals and policy leaders concerned with young people in conflict within school, family, or community. Each issue is topical. The journal was first published in 1992 under the title of *Journal of Emotional and Behavioral Problems*. In 1995, the title was changed to the present title to better reflect the journal's emphasis on a positive, reclaiming environment in which changes are made to meet the needs of both youth and society. The journal is owned by Journal of Emotional and Behavioral Problems, Inc. and is published by Pro-Ed, Inc.

JUDITH K. VORESS
Pro-Ed, Inc.

RECORDING FOR THE BLIND (RFB)

Recording for the Blind (RFB) is an organization that was founded in 1951 for the purpose of recording textbooks at no charge for persons unable to use ordinary print, whether because of visual, perceptual, or physical conditions. Kirchner and Simon (1984), in a study conducted in 1982–1983, stated that RFB serves over 7300 students in higher education; 57% of the students served are visually impaired.

Recording programs such as RFB are invaluable to the education of visually impaired learners. Other service organizations provide audio-formatted materials for this population (Ferrell, 1985). The Talking Book Program, sponsored by the American Printing House for the Blind, is a source of materials for parents and teachers serving visually impaired students. American Printing House also distributes the variable speech control cassette recorder to be used with their audio cassettes. The National Library Service for the Blind and Physically Handicapped, of the Library of Congress, offers free library services to visually impaired persons. The Library of Congress also lends special talking book record and cassette players to applicants. Many of the materials available from these organizations are popular leisure books, magazines, religious materials, and newspapers.

Addresses for these organizations are:

American Printing House for the Blind
1839 Frankfort Avenue
Louisville, KY 40206

National Library Service for the Blind and Physically
  Handicapped
Library of Congress
Washington, DC 20542

Recording for the Blind, Inc.
215 E. 58th Street
New York, NY 10022

REFERENCES

Ferrell, K. (1985). *Reach out and teach: Meeting the training needs of parents of visually and multiply handicapped young children*. New York: American Foundation for the Blind.

Kirchner, C., & Simon, Z. (1984). Blind and visually handicapped college students—Part I: Estimated numbers. *Journal of Visual Impairment & Blindness, 78,* 78–81.

VIVIAN I. CORREA
University of Florida

BLIND
VERSABRAILLE

RECREATION, THERAPEUTIC

Therapeutic recreation is a form of play or physical activity that is used to improve a variety of behaviors that may occur in the cognitive, emotional, social, and physical domains. These activities include games, dancing, horseback riding, and a wide range of other individual and group games and sports.

The intellectual domain may be influenced through gross and fine motor movement activities. There are many theories of cognitive development occurring in sequential order in which motor abilities are the basis for higher thought processes (Kephart, 1960; Piaget, 1950). Theoretically, motor skills help to develop higher skill levels in handicapped persons by increasing memory, language, and problem solving (Major & Walsh, 1977). Forms of recreation may be used as an alternate to more traditional teaching methods. Humphrey (1976) used games and dancing to aid in reversal difficulties, sequencing difficulties, left and right directionality, and improvement in following direction skills. Physical movement helped to present concepts and skills in a more concrete form. Through imitation and role playing, children were able to use intellectual concepts they had already learned and developed (Yawkey, 1979).

Other forms of learning may be influenced by physical activities and games that have the objective of increasing motivation and attention span. Naville and Blom (1968) stressed educational achievements of concentration, willpower, and self-control through movement.

Emotions can be influenced through recreational activities, which may help individuals improve self-concepts and self-confidence. Being aware of one's body and feeling good about one's self can be associated with the pleasure of recreation. Socially, organized group activities may offer social skills learning through structured interpersonal play. Individuals have opportunities to work together, follow leaders, engage in appropriate behaviors, and develop various forms of self-expression. Recreation can be used not only as a medium for communication but also to help integrate the handicapped with the nonhandicapped and teach activities to decrease isolation.

Physically, recreational activities have endless limits. Movement may help individuals increase coordination and range of motion of body movement. For example, water sports, swimming, or water therapy can be extremely valuable to a variety of handicapped children and youths, as can free motion activities such as creative dance. These activities can increase physical strength and flexibility; having a strong, attractive body correlates with a positive self-image.

Specific programs such as bowling, folk dancing, and even competitive sports have incorporated recreational activities as therapy for different populations; a good example of one of these programs is the Special Olympics for various groups of handicapped students. Jacques-Dalcroze (1930) first developed eurhythmics for the blind to increase self-confidence and expression through music and rhythm. Gollnitz (1970) developed a rhythmic-psychomotor therapy that combined movement, music, and rhythm for individuals with psychic and developmental disorders. Lefco (1974) followed the idea of the integration of the body and mind when she used dance therapy to promote mental and physical well being. The Cove Schools in Racine, Wisconsin, and Evanston, Illinois, were designed for brain-injured students to provide play experiences that may have been missed because of slow rates of development. The Halliwick method deals with the swimming ability of the physically handicapped. Norway has a horseback riding school for the disabled. Mann, Berger, and Proger (1974) offer a comprehensive review of the research on the influence of physical education on the cognitive, physical, affective, and social domains in which movement was significant in helping the handicapped with different variables in these areas.

In summary, therapeutic recreation includes structured physical and social activities that are designed to have as objectives the enjoyment of leisure time, improved movement, and development of physical strength and social skills. Recreation, adaptive physical education, and physical activities increase or improve social, physical, and mental abilities.

REFERENCES

Gollnitz, G. (1970). Fundamentals of rhythmic-psychomotor music therapy: An objective-oriented therapy for children and adolescents with developmental disturbances. *Acta Paedopsychiatrica. The International Journal of Child Psychiatry, 37,* 130–134.

Humphrey, J. H. (1976). *Improving learning ability through compensatory physical education.* Springfield: IL: Thomas.

Jacques-Dalcroze, E. (1930). *Eurhythmics: Art and education.* London: Chatto & Windum.

Kephart, N. (1960). *The slower learner in the classroom.* Columbus, OH: Merrill.

Lefco, H. (1974). *Dance therapy.* Chicago, IL: Nelson-Hall.

Major, S., & Walsh, M. (1977). *Learning activities for the learning disabled.* Belmont, CA: Fearon-Pitman.

Mann, L., Berger, R., & Proger, B. (1974). Physical education intervention with the exceptional child. In L. Mann & D. A. Sabatino (Eds.), *The second review of special education.* NY: Grune & Stratton.

Naville, S., & Blom, G. E. (1968). *Psychomotor education: Theory and practice.* Denver, CO: University of Colorado Medical Center.

Piaget, J. (1950). *Psychology of intelligence.* New York: Harcourt & Brace.

Yawkey, T. D. (1979). More in play as intelligence in children. *Journal of Creative Behavior, 13,* 247–256.

DONNA FILIPS
Steger, Illinois

EQUINE THERAPY
RECREATIONAL THERAPY
RECREATION FOR THE HANDICAPPED

RECREATIONAL READING FOR THE HANDICAPPED

According to most dictionaries, recreation is an agreeable art, a pastime, or a diversion that affords relaxation and enjoyment. However, most handicapped students would not link recreation with reading because books symbolize failure and emotional distress (Schanzer, 1973). Therefore, the goal of education should be to encourage students to be independent readers who regularly choose to read. For this to occur, it is necessary for teachers, librarians, and parents to become involved.

Teachers are likely to be the only reading models for many students (Smith, Smith, & Mikulecky, 1978). Therefore, they should be active reading models, talking about what they have been reading and allowing students to see them carrying personal books or magazines. In the classroom, free reading time, when everyone reads without the threat of book reports or lengthy comprehension checks, should be scheduled (Smith, Smith, & Mikulecky, 1978). Teachers should be sure to have large classroom libraries of recreational reading materials. However, standard, off-the-shelf novels or biographies present frustrating hurdles such as reading level, subject matter, and length (Hallenbeck, 1983). Therefore, such books should be didactic, with important words repeated several times. The themes should relate closely to the lives of the students and the sentences should be short with simple verb tenses. In addition, pronouns should be placed near the nouns that they modify and characters should be human beings, not abstract things or ideas. Finally, the style of writing should be conversational (Slick, 1969). This will help to eliminate the selection of reading material that is too difficult.

To halt deterioration of positive reading attitudes, teachers should talk to students about their reading habits and interests, observe what they read, and get to know their interests so appropriate suggestions can be made (Smith, et al., 1978). In addition, reading-attitude measures and interest inventories are desirable since there is much intrinsic motivation in reading about something relevant and familiar. When vocabulary and concepts are known, rate may increase with excitement, and the likelihood of a successful, pleasurable experience is high (Smith et al., 1978). When reading material is matched to interests, students tend to comprehend from one to two grade levels above tested reading levels (Estes & Vaughn, 1973, cited in Smith et al., 1978). Matching students with reading materials dealing with life interests helps to initiate lifelong reading habits (Smith et al., 1978). To encourage students to read past the school experience, reading must be motivated outside the classroom by curiosity; pleasure and excitement at the new; practicality; prestige and social status with peers; escape and vicarious experiences; expansion and reinforcement of present attitudes and interests; and reflection of personal situations and dilemmas (Smith et al., 1978). Teachers can create this desire to read by conferencing with students about what they have read; by allowing students to conference with one another, and by engaging in motivational activities such as brief oral readings to students and games and gimmicks such as book auctions. (Smith et al., 1978).

Librarians can also be helpful in encouraging recreational reading among handicapped students because they come in contact with all students in an average school week. The librarian should remove all stumbling blocks so that special education students feel free to use the library. For example, the borrowing period may have to be adjusted because these students may need more time to complete a book. In addition, it is important to eliminate the frustration of book selection by establishing a one-to-one relationship with the student and having enough high-interest low-reading-level books available. As special education students begin to frequent the library, praise and commendation should be given. In addition, individual guidance and personal service are needed. It would also be helpful for the librarian to supply the special education class with a list of the new books in the library so that students can request a particular book when visiting the library. Finally, it is helpful to have students act as library aides to assure them that they are needed, are helpful, and are appreciated (Slick, 1969).

For many students, reading takes place at school or not at all. If reading is to become an enjoyable and lifelong experience, it is necessary for reading to occur at home. However, pressure from the parents to read is not the answer since pressure violates the spirit of free reading (Haimowitz, 1977). As early as the 1940s in Japan, there were two home reading programs. One was a 20-minute mother-child reading process in which parents and children sat for 20 minutes a day and the children read to the mothers. The second was scheduled reading hours once a week in which everyone in the family read (Smith et al., 1978). Programs such as these and others initiated by PTA groups and community groups can be helpful in encouraging recreational reading among handicapped students.

REFERENCES

Haimowitz, B. (1977, December). Motivating reluctant readers in inner-city classes. *Journal of Reading, 21,* 227–230.

Hallenbeck, M. J. (1983, March). A free reading journal for secondary LD students. *Academic Therapy, 18,* 479–485.

Schanzer, S. S. (1973, Fall). Independent reading for children with learning disabilities. *Academic Therapy, 9,* 109–114.

Slick, M. H. (1969, April 10). *Recreational reading materials for special education students.* Pittsburgh: University of Pittsburgh, School of Library Science. (ERIC Document Reproduction Service No. ED 046 173)

Smith, C. B., Smith, S. L., & Mikulecky, L. (1978). *Teaching reading in secondary school content subjects: A book-thinking process.* New York: Holt, Rinehart, & Winston.

CAROLINE D'IPPOLITO
*Eastern Pennsylvania Special
Education Resources Center*

HIGH INTEREST-LOW VOCABULARY READING

LIBRARY SERVICES FOR THE HANDICAPPED
READING

RECREATIONAL THERAPY

Recreational activities are necessary for the total wellbeing of any individual. They provide an important source of pleasure and relaxation. Most individuals learn how to use recreational activities from a lifetime of learning how to play. But as with other skill areas, the handicapped often experience difficulties in using free time appropriately. They may have been sheltered during much of their developmental period, or their disability may have prohibited them from acquiring the skills necessary for participation in recreational activities. Consequently, many handicapped individuals will require intentional and systematic instruction if they are to acquire those skills. In that regard, recreational therapy is a planned intervention process developed to promote the growth and development of recreational skills and leisure-time activities.

Recreational therapy attempts to eliminate or minimize an individual's disability. It uses recreation to assist the handicapped in changing certain physical, emotional, or social characteristics so they may pursue leisure activities and live as independently as possible (National Recreation and Park Association, 1978). Recreational therapy is also concerned with helping the handicapped participate in activities with the nonhandicapped as much as possible. This integration allows the handicapped to move into the recreational mainstream and become more involved in community recreational activities. In addition to helping the handicapped to engage in recreational activities, recreational therapy also provides other benefits. A second advantage of the program is that appropriate recreational and leisure-time skills can lead to increased physical development, socialization skills, and even cognitive and language development (Schulz & Turnbull, 1984). Therefore, recreational therapy may be recommended to help the handicapped to maintain their physical skills, interact socially, and increase academic progress.

REFERENCES

National Recreation and Park Association. (1978). *The therapeutic recreator.* In W. L. Heward & M. D. Orlansky (1980). *Exceptional children.* Columbus: Charles E. Merrill.

Schulz, J. B., & Turnbull, A. P. (1984). *Mainstreaming handicapped students. A guide for classroom teachers* (2nd ed.). Boston: Allyn & Bacon.

LARRY J. WHEELER
*Southwest Texas State
University*

EQUINE THERAPY
OCCUPATIONAL THERAPY

RECREATION FOR THE HANDICAPPED

Recreation for the handicapped includes individual and group programs of outdoor, social, sports, or educational activities conducted during leisure time. Such programs conducted in medically supervised institutions are identified as therapeutic recreation while those conducted in schools and the community are called community programs (Pomeroy, 1983). The overall goal of recreation programs is to enable each handicapped person the right to participate at the lowest effective care level as independently as abilities and disabilities permit (Stein, 1985).

Recreation services for the handicapped should be distinguished from therapeutic recreation. The latter is a means of intervention to bring about desired changes. In schools, therapeutic recreation is medically prescribed and programmed by recreational therapists. In contrast, the purpose of recreation programs for the handicapped is to provide these students with opportunities to realize their leisure and recreational needs whether on an individual or group basis. Recreation programs in schools or communities for handicapped students are voluntary in nature and programmed by recreational leaders.

Prior to 1960, most recreation programs for the handicapped were segregated or held in institutions (Robinson & Skinner, 1985). Since 1960 legislative forces and concerned professional organizations have sought to deinstitutionalize and desegregate such programs. With the enactment of PL 94-142, recreation came to be considered as a related service in the schools. During the late 1970s the federal government provided grants to colleges and universities to set up training programs for recreation therapists and adapted physical education teachers and for the development of regional information and resource centers (Robinson & Skinner, 1985). Private organizations such as Wheelchair Sports and the Association for the Help of Retarded Children have also been active in promoting recreational programs in schools and communities.

Although only 5 to 10% of all handicapped persons are being reached by existing park and recreation service providers, the prognosis for the future appears to be positive. Statutes to promote barrier design, and the changing attitudes of service providers and participants, seem to indicate a trend toward more handicapped people availing themselves of school or community recreation programs.

Delineated on the basis of the degree of supervision required, there are four types of recreation programs for the handicapped. First, there are special programs limited to persons with specific disabilities, e.g. blind, deaf, or physically disabled persons. These programs often revolve around a single activity for the purposes of fun, socialization, and skill development. Second, there are semiintegregated services that allow the handicapped to mix with the nonhandicapped in activities that lend themselves to integration. Third, some communities have a buddy system where handicapped persons participate with nonhandicapped persons in the same activities and programs; scouting and Camp Fire Girls have used the buddy system extensively in their programs. The fourth type of program is one that provides opportunities for total integration in all activities, as is the case in many national parks and recreation areas.

The major categories of recreational activities for the handicapped listed by Russell (1983) are sports and games, hobbies, music, outdoor recreation, mental and literary recreation, arts and crafts, dance, and drama.

Handicapped programs at the national and international levels are usually of a competitive nature. Examples of these include the Para-olympics, which meets every 4 years in a different part of the world and has four disability groups: deaf, amputee, cerebral palsy, and paraplegic competition. Wheelchair Sports, sponsored by the National Wheelchair Athletic Association, provides competition in track, basketball, and weightlifting. The National Handicapped Sports and Recreation Association promotes sports and recreational activities through 29 regional offices across the United States.

Most state and regional programs are part of national structures such as the Special Olympics program. Some state programs are resident or day camps or outdoor activity centers. There are very few recreation centers that exclusively serve the handicapped. The majority are in large urban areas e.g., the Anchor Program in New York City and the Recreation Center for the Handicapped in San Francisco.

Many schools, colleges, and communities sponsor local recreational programs for the handicapped. Community swim programs seem to be the most popular and widespread. Hunter College in New York City conducts a recreation program for mentally retarded and physically disabled teenagers from the city, most of whom are minorities.

REFERENCES

Pomeroy, J. (1983). Community recreation for persons with disabilities. In E. Pan, T. Backer, & C. Vosh (Eds.), *Annual review of rehabilitation* (pp. 241–291). St. Louis: Mosby.

Robinson, F., & Skinner, S. (1985). *Community recreation for the handicapped.* Springfield, IL: Thomas.

Russell, R. (1983). *Planning programs in recreation.* St. Louis: Mosby.

Stein, J. (1985). Mainstreaming in recreational settings. *Journal of Physical Education, Recreation & Dance, 5*(56), 25–27.

THOMAS BURKE
Hunter College

EQUINE THERAPY
GAMES FOR THE HANDICAPPED
MUSIC THERAPY
OLYMPICS

REDL, FRITZ (1902–1988)

Fritz Redl was born and educated in Austria, and obtained PhD in philosophy and psychology in 1925 from the University of Vienna. From 1925 to 1936, he trained as an analyst at the Wiener Psychoanalysis Institute, and was strongly influenced by the founders of child analytic work, particularly Anna Freud and August Aichhorn.

Redl maintained an interest in group psychology throughout his career. After coming to the United States in 1936, he accepted a teaching position at the University of Michigan and helped establish a guidance program at the

Fritz Redl

Cranbook School, later moving to a position as professor of group work at Wayne State University, where he remained for 12 years. Redl's service to children and the field of mental health included his positions as clinical director of the University of Michigan Fresh Air Camp, chief of the Child Research Branch of the National Institute of Mental Health (1953–1959), and president of the American Orthopsychiatric Association.

Redl's work focused on the exploration of children's behavioral controls, their defenses, and how to prevent or treat the disorganization that results when the behavioral control system is maladaptive (Redl, 1966, 1975). His development of the "life space interview," providing strategies and techniques for immediately dealing with crises in the lives of children, showed his keen awareness of the effects of temporal and spatial arrangements (e.g., the stress of transition) on children's behaviors. Redl also saw how studying the behavior of severely disturbed children helped to illuminate techniques used by the normal child. As an outgrowth of his studies, group work, camp experience, and involvement with social agencies, he established Pioneer House, a residential program for the study and treatment of delinquent children, and the Detroit Group Project, providing clinical group work with children and a summer camp for children from low-income families. Redl's Pioneer House work is summarized in his book, *The Aggressive Child* (1957).

A renowned lecturer and consultant worldwide, Redl was a Pinkerton guest professor in the School of Criminal Justice of New York State University, and a visiting professor in the Department of Child Psychiatry of University of Utrecht in Holland. He died in 1988 in North Adams, Massachusetts, where he had retired in 1973.

REFERENCES

Redl, F., & Wineman, D. (1957). *The aggressive child.* New York: Free Press.

Redl, F. (1966). *When we deal with children: Selected writings.* New York: Free Press.

Redl, F. (1975). Disruptive behavior in the classroom. *School Review, 83*(4), 569–594.

E. Valerie Hewitt
Texas A & M University
First edition

Tamara J. Martin
*The University of Texas of the
Permian Basin*
Second edition

LIFE-SPACE INTERVIEWING

REFERRAL PROCESS

Referral is the process by which potentially handicapped or gifted students are identified for comprehensive individual evaluation by school officials. The identification of students for evaluation is a federally mandated activity for which all school districts and state education departments must have specific policies and procedures (U.S. Office of Education, 1977, sections 121a.128 and 121a.220). The law holds districts and state departments responsible for identifying all handicapped children within their jurisdictions who require special education or related services, including those in the care of other public and private agencies.

It is reported that some 3 to 5% of the school-age population are referred each year (Algozzine, Christenson, & Ysseldyke, 1982). Of those referred, about three-fourths are placed in special education. While these averages may characterize the nation as a whole, individual districts may vary widely in the percentage of students referred, evaluated, and placed.

Students can be referred in one of two major ways (Heller, Holtzman, & Messick, 1982). The first is through the systematic efforts of school districts, community agencies, or government institutions. For example, districts may use very low or very high performance on annually administered achievement tests to refer students. Similarly, hospitals may screen newborns for referral to early intervention programs. Finally, state education departments may conduct print and electronic media campaigns and establish toll-free hotlines aimed at encouraging the referral of handicapped or gifted students currently not receiving services.

The second major referral mechanism involves the efforts of individuals who know the child. Such individuals include the child's teachers, parents, and physician. Of these individuals, the large majority of referrals appear to emanate from teachers (Heller, Holtzman, & Messick, 1982). The advent of PL 94-142, increased the involvement of others both in and outside the school (Bickel, 1982).

Referrals made by teachers (and other individuals) are generally personal decisions based on subjective criteria. As such, these decisions are open to a variety of influences. The specific factors that influence teacher referrals are difficult to identify with any certainty (Bickel, 1982). However, research suggests that teachers are influenced by several considerations. One consideration is program availability; if no program exists to meet the student's needs, or if no room is available in an existing program, referral is unlikely. Second, teachers seem hesitant to refer if there is a large backlog in assessment. Such backlogs cause teachers to consider referral a meaningless action. Third, parents may influence the process. Teachers may hesitate to refer children whose parents would be likely to react in a hostile manner, or be quick to refer those whose parents exert positive pressure. Finally, eligibility criteria affect the decision. For example, some states and districts require that teachers refer students for placement in a specific program such as one for educable mentally retarded pupils. Hence, teachers may be encouraged to refer only children with particular characteristics.

In addition to these factors, other influences on referral undoubtedly exist (Ysseldyke & Algozzine, 1984). Teachers' decisions likely are affected by their own beliefs about what constitutes normal child development and proper behavior, and by the extent to which a given child violates those assumptions. The referral decision is also governed by the teacher's skills in dealing with deviations; those who are less adept in handling learning or behavioral differences may be more likely to refer.

It should be clear, then, that a great amount of personal discretion exists in the referral process (Bickel, 1982). Such discretion allows substantial variation in referral practice within and across districts, suggesting that referral often depends as much on what class or school a child attends as on actual learning capabilities and performance. Because of this personal discretion, there is a tendency to refer children who disrupt school routines and those with more severe, easily verifiable problems.

The subjectivity inherent in the referral process has social and ethical implications. First, there is the possibility that substantial numbers of children are being referred inappropriately. Inappropriate referral is problematic because it wastes valuable resources; creates backlogs in assessment, thereby denying services to those truly in need; and subjects children to the potential stigma of special education placement and to education in an environment that may not meet their needs.

Second, inappropriate referral may disproportionately affect particular social groups. For many years, disproportionate placements of minority children and of males in programs for educable mentally retarded (EMR) students have been documented (Heller, Holtzman, & Messick, 1982). The reasons for these disproportionate placements are many and complex. While these placements are not necessarily inappropriate, their existence raises the question of whether teacher referrals, too, are disproportionate.

Relatively little research has been conducted on the topic of disproportionate referral. Those studies that do exist have used two basic methodologies. Some investigators have analyzed existing referral data to determine whether disproportionate numbers of students from particular groups are referred. Other researchers have presented different groups of teachers with simulated data describing a student and have asked them to make referral decisions. The data received by the groups differed only in the social group membership assigned to the student. While no definitive conclusions can be drawn, the studies have shown a tendency toward higher rates of referral for minorities even though these students presented problems that appeared little different from those of their majority peers (Bickel, 1982).

Concern regarding both the possibility that children are being inappropriately referred and disproportionate placement of minority students in special education has led many school districts to refine their referral processes. These refinements have primarily occurred with respect to teacher referrals. Such referrals were originally passed directly through to the pupil evaluation team. Most refinements have focused on inserting checks and balances into this teacher-to-evaluation team pathway.

The most immediately useful refinement probably has been the introduction of consultation (Zins & Curtis, 1984). Consultation may be provided by a resource teacher, school psychologist, or other specialist. The aim of consultation is to help the teacher deal with the student in the regular classroom. The consultant may work with the teacher to develop, apply, and evaluate the effects of alternative instructional or behavior management strategies (Bennett, 1981).

A second type of referral refinement requires the provision of extensive evidence to support the need for referral. The aim of this evidence is to rule out deficiencies in the learning environment as explanations for failure. Failures of the educational system should be discounted first, lest they be interpreted erroneously as failures of the child (Messick, 1984).

Reporting the findings of the National Research Council Panel on Selection and Placement of Students in Programs for the Mentally Retarded, Messick, (1984) suggests the provision of four kinds of evidence. First, evidence should be offered that the school is using effective programs and curricula. This evidence should support the effectiveness of those programs and curricula not just for students in general, but for the ethnic, linguistic, or socioeconomic group from which the referred students actually come. Second, evidence should be presented that the student in question has been adequately exposed to the curriculum. It should be documented that the student was not absent regularly from school and that the teacher implemented the curriculum effectively. Third, objective evidence should be offered that the child has not learned what was taught (e.g., through criterion-referenced tests, systematic behavioral recordings, student work samples). Finally, documentation should be provided to show that systematic efforts were made to correct the problem such as introducing remedial approaches, changing the curriculum materials, or trying a new teacher.

A third refinement is the review of referral requests. Review seems to be conducted most often at the building level. In this system, teacher referrals are reviewed by the principal—or by a committee consisting of the principal, guidance counselor, or other building staff—before being forwarded to the pupil evaluation team. The review is designed to encourage teachers and principals to make greater attempts to deal with problem situations within the regular classroom and local school, and, as a result, to limit the occurrence of inappropriate referrals.

The three refinements described—consultation, evidence, and review—are the major elements of a prereferral intervention model. While many variations on this model exist, prereferral intervention has become an important component in the referral process, helping to ensure that those students referred are truly the ones most in need of special education services.

REFERENCES

Algozzine, B., Christenson, S., & Ysseldyke, J. (1982). Probabilities associated with the referral to placement process. *Teacher Education & Special Education, 5,* 19–23.

Bennett, R. E. (1981). Assessment of exceptional children: Guidelines for practice. *Diagnostique, 7,* 5–13.

Bickel, W. E. (1982). Classifying mentally retarded students: A review of placement practices in special education. In K. A. Heller, W. H. Holtzman, & S. Messick, *Placing children in special education: A strategy for equity.* Washington, DC: National Academy.

Heller, K. A., Holtzman, W. H., & Messick, S. (1982). *Placing children in special education: A strategy for equity.* Washington, DC: National Academy.

Messick, S. (1984). Placing children in special education: Findings of the National Academy of Sciences Panel. *Educational Researcher, 13*(3), 3–8.

U.S. Office of Education. (1977). Education of handicapped children: Implementation of Part B of the Education of the Handicapped Act. *Federal Register, 42*(163), 42474–42518.

Ysseldyke, J. E., & Algozzine, B. (1984). *Introduction to special education.* Boston: Houghton Mifflin.

Zins, J. E., & Curtis, M. (1984). Building consultation into the educational service delivery system. In C. A. Maher, R. J. Illback, & J. E. Zins (Eds.), *Organizational psychology in the schools: A handbook for professionals.* Springfield, IL: Thomas.

RANDY ELLIOT BENNETT
MARY LOUISE LENNON
Educational Testing Service

EDUCATION FOR ALL HANDICAPPED CHILDREN ACT OF 1975

INDIVIDUALS WITH DISABILITIES EDUCATION ACT

PREREFERRAL INTERVENTIONS

REFLEX

A reflex is an automatic connection between a stimulus and a response. One example is the knee-jerk reflex. Another is the reflexive constriction of the pupil in response to light.

Historically, the concept of the reflex has captured the imagination of many theorists who wished to emphasize the mechanical nature of behavior. René Descartes proposed a hydraulic model to account for the behavior of non-human animals. The Russian physiologist Ivan Sechenov (1863/1965) argued that all behavior, including that of humans, is reflexive (meaning that it is determined). Ivan Pavlov and other theorists of learning have used such terms as conditioned reflex to imply that even learned behaviors are mechanically determined and that they can be described as stimulus-response connections.

Certain human reflexes can be observed only in infancy (Peiper, 1963). For example, infants reflexively grasp any object placed firmly in the palm of the hand. Newborns grasp an elevated bar tightly enough to support their own weight, at least briefly. If someone strokes the sole of an infant's foot, the infant extends the big toe and fans the others (this is known as the Babinski reflex). If someone touches an infant's cheek, an infant who is awake will often, but not always, turn toward the stroked cheek and begin to suck.

Infant reflexes are suppressed in older children and adults, but the connections responsible for the reflexes are not destroyed. The infant reflexes may return as a result of brain damage, especially damage to the frontal lobes of the cerebral cortex. Neurologists often test for the presence of the Babinski reflex or the grasp reflex as a means of detecting possible dysfunction of the frontal lobes. The infant reflexes may also return temporarily as a result of interference with cerebral activity, such as that caused by an epileptic seizure, excessive levels of carbon dioxide, or certain drugs (Paterson & Richter, 1933).

REFERENCES

Paterson, A. S., & Richter, C. P. (1933). Action of scopolamine and carbon dioxide on catalepsy produced by bulbocapnine. *Archives of Neurology & Psychiatry, 29,* 231–240.

Peiper, A. (1963). *Cerebral function in infancy and childhood.* New York: Consultants Bureau.

Sechenov, I. (1863/1965). *Reflexes of the brain.* Cambridge, MA: MIT.

JAMES W. KALAT
North Carolina State University

BEHAVIORISM
BEHAVIOR MODIFICATION
DEVELOPMENTAL MILESTONES

REGIONAL MEDIA CENTERS FOR THE DEAF

In 1959 the U.S. Office of Education implemented a program, under PL 85-905, to provide captioned films and related media to assist in bringing deaf persons into the mainstream of American life. The program featured the development and dissemination of highly specialized media services and products through four regional media centers. In the 1960s, 13 special education instructional media centers were established in addition to the four regional centers for the deaf. By the end of that decade, those 17 centers had been consolidated into four area learning resource centers (ALRCs). The ALRCs conducted activities related to educational media and technology for all handicapped persons, but specialized centers within the ALRC structure provided educational media and technology services for deaf persons. In 1972 the National Center on Education Media and Materials for the Handicapped replaced the ALRCs.

SHIRLEY A. JONES
*Virginia Polytechnic Institute
and State University*

REGIONAL RESOURCE CENTERS (RRCs)

The Regional Resource Centers (RRCs) were created by the Elementary and Secondary Education Act, Title 6, of 1965. They were intended to assist state educational agencies (SEAs) in the implementation of special education services at a time when special education was just beginning to be recognized as a national concern. The RRCs were intended to help SEAs and local educational agencies (LEAs) in the development of special education services and resources by serving as agents in planning, programming, service delivery, training, and the creation of instructional materials.

The actual operations of the RRCs proceeded through a variety of agencies, including state educational departments, universities, and LEAs. The funding was not as generous as originally intended because the federal government envisioned RRCs as a nationwide enterprise. In the first funding cycle (1970–1974), Pennsylvania established an RRC whose services were directed statewide. Other RRCs, however, had multistate service areas; e.g., the Southwest Regional Resource Center served Arizona, Colorado, Nevada, New Mexico, and the Bureau of Indian Affairs. In multistate agencies, the major modes of service were information, consultation, and in-service training. In state-limited programs such as that of Pennsylvania, it was easier to focus services on specified state needs. For example, Pennsylvania used its funds to create diagnostic-prescriptive programs and to help fund classes to validate them (National Association of State Directors of Special Education, 1976).

A later round of funding of RRCs (1974–1977) resulted in some states being refunded and others funded for the first time. While some states such as New York and Pennsylvania, maintained statewide services, efforts were being made to move to multistate and regional operations. Thus, the Southeastern Regional Resource Center at Auburn University, in Montgomery, Alabama, was given the responsibility for Alabama, Florida, Georgia, Louisiana, Mississippi, Puerto Rico, South Carolina, and the U.S. Virgin Islands. Separate agencies were split off from the RRCs to assist in the provision of instructional resources to special educators. These were the Area Learning Resource Centers. By 1983, with legislative amendments to the Education of the Handicapped Act, the RRCs became a matter of discretionary support and funding on the part of states. They were adopted in various forms by state educational agencies or subsumed by the SEAs into other entities.

REFERENCE

National Association of State Directors of Special Education. (1976). *A survey of opinions of state directors of special education on Regional Resource Centers: Report.* Washington, DC: Bureau of Education for the Handicapped.

DON BRASWELL
*Research Foundation, City
University of New York*

SPECIAL EDUCATION, FEDERAL IMPACT ON SPECIAL EDUCATION PROGRAMS

REGRESSION (STATISTICAL)

Regression is a term widely used in behavioral research (multiple regression). It has come to mean both a statistical technique and a statistical phenomenon. The phenomenon or artifact of statistical regression is addressed here. Simply, regression is a way to say that two behaviors or variables are not perfectly related to each other. For example, high school performance and freshman year grade point average (GPA) typically correlate about .5. Regression refers to the fact that when a researcher uses one variable to predict the other (high school performance to predict freshman GPA), the predicted score will be less extreme than the predictor score. In the example just given, a predicted freshman GPA will be .5 times the high school rank in standard deviation units. A student one standard deviation above average on high school performance will be predicted to be one-half standard deviation

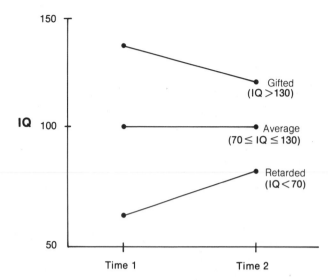

Examples of hypothetical regression effects between two testings for groups of children with IQs at three levels.

above average for his or her class in GPA at the end of the freshman year.

The phenomenon was noted by Galton (and others before him) in his studies of human characteristics in the nineteenth century. He termed it regression to the mean, since the expected or predicted performance is always closer to the mean in standard deviations than is the predictor. Galton showed that sons of tall fathers were less extreme in their tallness than their fathers. Note that regression does not describe the actual performance, only its relative extremity. Thus the sons, through better nutrition, were generally taller than their fathers. They were generally, however, less extreme. Also, the regression phenomenon is a statistical condition applied to groups of scores. While we can use the prediction for an individual, we cannot specify that every individual will be less extreme, only that on average, the cases to which the prediction applies will be less extreme. Thus sons of 6-ft fathers who, let us say, are one standard deviation above average, may average 6 ft, 1 in. (which is .7 standard deviations above average height of the sons), but they are not uniformly the same height. Some may be under 6 ft in height, others well over 6 ft. Their average is 6 ft, 1 in.

The significance of regression for special education is that the clients tend to be extreme in some way. Special education students by definition score differently, often extremely, on tests or observation scales with respect to the entire population of students. Thus when a second measure is made on the students, they will be observed, through regression, to be less extreme (see Figure, for example). Sometimes this artifact is confused with instructional or program improvement. Hopkins (1968), in a classic paper on the topic, detailed the problem for special educators. He pointed out that in attempting to test the effects of treatments for special education students, the students are sometimes matched with nonspecial education students. Matching is a keyword that should always force the researcher or reader to consider regression effect. In such studies, the special education students, having been selected as extreme on one test, will exhibit regression on another test, perhaps the posttest in a research study. Their matched control group, also extreme owing to matching, will also show regression on the posttest. Unless the two groups have identical population means (a highly unlikely condition), they will show different amounts of regression, so that the difference between the groups found on the posttest may be due entirely to differential regression. Thus matching is a poor substitute for techniques such as randomization in comparative research. Similarly, single group designs, in which one treatment group is measured before and after treatment, is at risk to show regression effects. While the regression effect can be estimated in some situations, such designs are poor substitutes for carefully planned experimental designs.

REFERENCE

Hopkins, K. D. (1968). Regression and the matching fallacy in quasi-experimental research. *Journal of Special Education, 3,* 329–336.

VICTOR L. WILLSON
Texas A & M University

REGULAR CLASS PLACEMENT

See MAINSTREAMING AND INCLUSION.

REHABILITATION

The term rehabilitation refers to any process, procedure, or program that enables a disabled individual to function at a more independent and personally satisfying level. This functioning should include all aspects—physical, mental, emotional, social, educational, and vocational—of the individual's life. A disabled person may be defined as one who has any chronic mental or physical incapacity caused by injury, disease, or congenital defect that interferes with his or her independence, productivity, or goal attainment. The range of disabilities is wide and varied, including such conditions as autism, mental retardation, muscular dystrophy, and a variety of neurological and orthopedic disorders. These disparate conditions may appear singly or in concert. Clearly, the process that is designed to

assist persons in obtaining an optimal level of functioning is a complex one.

The complexity of the rehabilitation process necessitates a team approach that involves a range of professionals almost as broad and varied as the types of conditions addressed. Goldenson, Dunham, and Dunham (1978) discuss no fewer than 39 rehabilitation specialists in their handbook. Their list includes such diverse professions as orientation and mobility training, genetic counseling, biomedical engineering, and orthotics and prosthetics, in addition to numerous medical, mental health, therapeutic, and special education fields. In view of the potential involvement of such an array of professionals, it becomes particularly important to remember that the rehabilitation process is not one that is done to or for disabled persons, but rather one that is done with disabled persons and often their families as well. If a person is to become as fully functional as his or her abilities will allow, a process that fosters dependence is a self-defeating one.

It is necessary for the professionals involved in the rehabilitation process to function as a team rather than as separate individuals. McInerney and Karan (1981) have pointed out that without information sharing and cooperative integration, the rehabilitation process will not fit the needs of the client. The client should not be expected to fit the needs of the service delivery system. As rehabilitation is a process, not an isolated treatment, a continuum of services must be provided to give the disabled person assistance in all aspects of life. A program that is cohesive in approach, regardless of the number of professionals involved, is essential. In addition, these services must alter to meet the client's changing needs.

REFERENCES

Goldenson, R. M., Dunham, J. R., & Dunham, C. S. (Eds.). (1978). *Disability and rehabilitation handbook.* New York: McGraw-Hill.

McInerney, M., & Karan, O. C. (1981). Federal legislation and the integration of special education and vocational rehabilitation. *Mental Retardation, 19,* 21–24.

LAURA KINZIE BRUTTING
*University of Wisconsin at
Madison*

**REHABILITATION COUNSELING
VOCATIONAL TRAINING OF THE HANDICAPPED**

REHABILITATION ACT OF 1973

The Rehabilitation Act of 1973 authorizes comprehensive vocational rehabilitation services designed to help physically and mentally handicapped persons become employable. The act also authorizes service projects for persons with special rehabilitation needs. For severely handicapped persons without apparent employment potential, the act authorizes services to promote independent living. Training programs are provided to help ensure a supply of skilled persons to rehabilitate handicapped persons. The act also authorizes a research program, a national council to review federal policy regarding handicapped persons, and a compliance board to help enforce accessibility standards for the handicapped.

The act authorizes state grants for comprehensive services designed to enable handicapped individuals to become employable. Each state receives an allotment of federal funding that must be matched on a 20% state to 80% federal ratio. Federal funds are allotted on the basis of population and per capita income, with the lower per capita income states receiving a relatively higher allotment on a per capita basis.

Funds are authorized for various service projects for handicapped persons. These projects include funds for programs to serve the severely handicapped, migrant workers, American Indians, and other groups with special needs. Support is provided for training of rehabilitation personnel. State grants and discretionary funds are authorized for independent living services. A client assistance program is required in each state to help clients and applicants obtain services funded under the act.

The National Council on the Handicapped is composed of 15 members appointed by the president. The council establishes general policies for the National Institute on Handicapped Research, advises the president and Congress on the development of programs carried out under the Rehabilitation Act, and reviews and evaluates federal policy regarding programs for the handicapped.

The Architectural and Transportation Barriers Compliance Board was authorized to ensure compliance with the Architectural Barriers Act of 1968 and to promote accessibility for handicapped individuals. The board is composed of 11 members from the general public (five of whom must be handicapped individuals) and 11 representatives of federal agencies.

The National Institute on Handicapped Research administers funds for the rehabilitation research programs. The institute, through a federal interagency committee, is responsible for the coordination of all major federal research related to handicapped persons.

JAMES BUTTON
United States Department of Education

REHABILITATION ACT OF 1973, SECTION 504 OF

REHABILITATION ACT OF 1973, SECTION 504 OF

Section 504 of what is commonly called the Rehabilitation Act is frequently cited as an important precursor to the passage of *PL 94-142* two years later (Bersoff, 1982). Section 504, among other things, protects the rights of handicapped children and precludes discrimination in employment and education. The stipulations of the Rehabilitation Act apply to the programs receiving federal financial assistance.

The Rehabilitation Act was cited in the noted *Larry P.* vs. *Riles* decision by Judge Peckham in 1979. This decision cited the state as being in noncompliance with Section 504 in its use of intelligence tests for making placement decisions in special education. Certainly, the Rehabilitation Act of 1973 has had an important impact on special education practice by encouraging more sophisticated and humane treatment of handicapped children.

REFERENCE

Bersoff, D. N. (1982). The legal regulation of school psychology. In C. R. Reynolds & T. B. Gutkin (Eds.), *The handbook of school psychology*. New York: Wiley.

RANDY W. KAMPHAUS
Eastern Kentucky University

LARRY P.

REHABILITATION LITERATURE

Rehabilitation Literature is a bimonthly journal published by the National Easter Seal Society. It is principally an educational service journal that abstracts articles published elsewhere and reviews books, journals, films, treatment programs, etc. dealing with the rehabilitation of all types of human disabilities. At least one original feature article appears in each issue. It is written at a level for professional personnel and students training to become professional service providers in all disciplines concerned with the rehabilitation of persons with handicapping conditions.

This abstracting and review journal receives wide circulation among rehabilitation workers and is well regarded in the field. It has been in continuous publication since January 1940; it was taken over by the National Easter Seal Society in 1959. *Rehabilitation Literature* has taken the position that, as an educational service of a large charitable organization, up to 100 reproductions of articles may be made without permission provided they are for free distribution within an organization or classroom. Other rights of reproduction have been reserved. Frequent topics of interest to special educators appear in nearly every issue, bridging such broad areas as stuttering, learning disabilities, aphasias, spina bifida, reading, and general techniques in special education.

CECIL R. REYNOLDS
Texas A & M University

Fredricka Kauffman Reisman

REISMAN, FREDRICKA KAUFFMAN (1930–   )

Fredricka Kauffman Reisman obtained her BA (1952) in psychology, her MS (1963) in education, and her PhD (1968) in math education from Syracuse University. Formerly a professor of mathematics education and special education at the University of Georgia in Athens (1979–1983), Reisman began teaching at Drexel University in Philadelphia in 1985 where she became director of the Division of Instruction and Programs and head of teacher preparation (1991). She currently holds the position of Director of the School of Education at Drexel. Her primary fields of interest include mathematics education, the integration of computing into the assessment and instruction of mathematics, teacher preparation, and diagnostic teaching. Her work has emphasized the prevention of learning difficulties rather than prescription or remediation. Reisman advocates teacher awareness of learner and content characteristics as well as the design of instructional environments that use modern technology.

Reisman has been recognized in *Who's Who in the East* and *Who's Who in America* (1997). Her major publications include *A Guide to the Diagnostic Teaching of Arithmetic*

(1982), *Sequential Assessment in Mathematics Inventories* (1986), and *Becoming a Teacher: Grades K–8* (1987).

REFERENCES

Reisman, F. K. (1982). *A guide to the diagnostic teaching of arithmetic* (3rd ed.). Columbus, OH: Merrill.

Reisman, F. K. (1986). *Sequential assessment in mathematics inventories: K–8.* San Antonio, TX: Psychological Corporation.

Reisman, F. K. (1987). *Becoming a teacher: Grades K–8.* Columbus, OH: Merrill.

E. VALERIE HEWITT
Texas A & M University
First edition

TAMARA J. MARTIN
The University of Texas of the
Permian Basin
Second edition

REITAN-INDIANA NEUROPSYCHOLOGICAL TEST BATTERY FOR CHILDREN (RINTBC)

The Reitan-Indiana Neuropsychological Test Battery for Children (RINTBC; ages 5 through 8), along with the Halstead Neuropsychological Test Battery for Children (ages 9 through 14) and the Halstead Neuropsychological Test Battery for Adults (ages 15 and older), constitute a global battery commonly referred to as the Halstead-Reitan Neuropsychological Test Battery. Each of these three batteries was devised as a tool for the assessment of brain-behavior relationships. The RINTBC was developed after it became apparent that many of the items on the battery for older children were too difficult for children below the age of 9 (Reitan, 1979).

The developmental research for the RINTBC, conducted at the Neuropsychology Laboratory of the Indiana University Medical Center, began in the mid-1950s. R. M. Reitan, a student of W. C. Halstead, modified several of the tests from Halstead's original adult battery (Halstead, 1947), and also created six new tests to complete this battery for young children. The modified tests include children's versions of the Category Test, Tactual Performance Test, Sensory-Perceptual Disturbances Tests, Finger Oscillation Test, and Aphasia Screening Test. New tests include the Color Form Test, Progressive Figures Test, and Matching Picture Tests; these were designed to measure cognitive flexibility and concept formation. The Target Test and the Individual Performance Test assess reception and expression of visuo-spatial relationships, while the Marching Test measures gross motor coordination (Reitan, 1979). The RINTBC customarily is supplemented by the Reitan-Klove Lateral Dominance Examination, the Reitan-Klove

Sensory-Perceptual Examination, Strength of Grip, the Wechsler Preschool and Primary Scale of Intelligence, and the Wide Range Achievement Test (Reitan, 1974).

Reitan and Davison (1974) present a review of research that has demonstrated that the RINTBC effectively differentiates brain-damaged from normal functioning children, provided the test is administered and interpreted properly by trained professionals. An interpretive guide is available from Reitan (1987).

REFERENCES

Halstead, W. C. (1947). *Brain and intelligence.* Chicago: University of Chicago Press.

Reitan, R. M. (1974). Psychological effects of cerebral lesions in children of early school age. In R. M. Reitan & L. A. Davison (Eds.), *Clinical neuropsychology: Current status and applications* (pp. 53–89). New York: Hemisphere.

Reitan, R. M. (1979). *Manual for the administration of neuropsychological test batteries for adults and children.* Tucson, AZ: Reitan Neuropsychology Laboratories.

Reitan, R. M. (1987). *Neuropsychological evaluation of children.* Tucson, AZ: Reitan Neuropsychology Laboratories.

Reitan, R. M., & Davison, L. A. (1974). *Clinical neuropsychology,* New York: Hemisphere.

GALE A. HARR
Maple Heights City Schools
Maple Heights, Ohio

HALSTEAD-REITAN NEUROPSYCHOLOGICAL TEST BATTERY
NEUROPSYCHOLOGY

RELATED SERVICES

The Education for All Handicapped Children Act of 1975 (PL 94-142) was the first Federal law to hold education agencies responsible not only for the provision of special education services, but for the delivery of related services as well. Related services are defined as "transportation, and such developmental, corrective, and other supportive services…as may be required to assist a handicapped child to benefit from special education." (Section 4a). IDEA advances nearly identical language.

Among the services specifically included within the related services definition are speech pathology and audiology, psychological services, medical services (for diagnostic and evaluation purposes only), physical and occupational therapy, recreation, and counseling. However, because the phrase "other supportive services…as may be required" is included in the law, the precise definition of related services remains the subject of debate.

Disputes regarding the type and extent of related services required under PL 94-142 have been the focus of a series of court cases, including the first Supreme Court decision on federal special education law. Litigation has involved questions of eligibility, definition, and financial responsibility. All three issues were addressed in *Hendrick Hudson Board of Education* v. *Rowley.* In this case, the Supreme Court ruled that a high-achieving deaf student need not be provided a sign language interpreter at the school district's expense, given her demonstrated ability to benefit from the educational program already provided. While the Court's decision focused on the narrow issue of one student's right to a particular related service, it suggested that the term "related services" need not be interpreted broadly to mean any service that would improve the quality of a handicapped child's education.

In the subsequent case of *Irving Independent School District* v. *Tatro,* definition was again at issue, with the focus on medical services required by the law. Medical services are defined in the law as those services provided by a physician for diagnostic and evaluation purposes. The school district argued that catheterizing a student (inserting a tube to drain the bladder) several times daily constituted a nondiagnostic medical service and therefore was not a related service for which the district was responsible. However, the Supreme Court ruled that catheterization is included within the related services definition because it is a simple nonmedical procedure that can be administered by a school nurse. As such, the Court felt that catheterization was representative of the other supportive services needed to provide "the meaningful access to education that Congress envisioned" ("Court Backs Catheterization," 1984).

A major issue underlying both Supreme Court cases is financial responsibility. Related services are expensive to provide and school districts are struggling to define the limits of their fiscal responsibility. Interpreting the *Rowley* decision, U.S. District Judge John A. Nordberg said, "the Court recognized the unfairness of imposing large financial burdens on states on the basis of broad interpretation of ambiguous language in funding statutes" ("Students Have," 1983). Even with a conservative interpretation of what constitutes related services, state and local education agencies often find themselves in a difficult financial position.

Dealing with the financial ramifications of providing related services is a continuing challenge. In its *Seventh Annual Report to Congress* (1985), the United States Department of Education described effective policies developed to provide related services in cost-efficient ways. One strategy has been to pool resources among local education agencies to make a range of related service specialists available to students. Another has been to seek third-party funding from public and private insurance providers. A third approach involves establishing joint funding and cooperative programming arrangements among education and human service agencies. For example, a school district and local mental health agency agree that the mental health agency will provide and assume the related services costs for the district's seriously emotionally disturbed children (Maher & Bennett, 1984). Each of these arrangements exemplifies efforts to share financial responsibility and work cooperatively to improve the quality of related services available to handicapped children.

REFERENCES

Court backs catheterization; limits fees in handicap cases. (1984). *Education of the Handicapped, 10*(14), 1–3.

Maher, C. A., & Bennett, R. E. (1984). *Planning and evaluating special education services.* Englewood Cliffs, NJ: Prentice-Hall.

Students have no right to free psychiatric care, court rules. (1983, Aug. 24). *Education of the Handicapped, 9*(17), 7–8.

U.S. Department of Education. (1984). *Seventh annual report to Congress on the implementation of the Education of the Handicapped Act.* Washington, DC: U.S. Government Printing Office.

MARY LOUISE LENNON
RANDY ELLIOT BENNETT
Educational Testing Service

DIAGNOSIS IN SPECIAL EDUCATION
EDUCATION FOR ALL HANDICAPPED CHILDREN ACT
    OF 1975
INDIVIDUALS WITH DISABILITIES EDUCATION ACT
INTERPRETERS FOR THE DEAF
SPEECH-LANGUAGE SERVICES

RELIABILITY

Test reliability refers to the precision of a test as a measuring device. What is the likelihood of obtaining similar results on a second administration of a test? If test results are to be meaningful and useful, precision of measurement is a highly desirable characteristic for the test or measurement procedure used. Test users must evaluate carefully information about test reliability provided in a test manual to determine the reliability of a test for its stated purpose.

Two types of statistical evidence of reliability are usually reported in test manuals: the reliability coefficient and the standard error of measurement. The reliability coefficient is a general indicator of test precision and is useful when making comparisons among tests. The standard error of measurement, on the other hand, is useful when interpreting the test score of an individual because it permits a statement of confidence to be placed in the particular score (Anastasi, 1982). Both aspects of test reliability will be discussed, along with certain principles that merit careful consideration in the interpretation of reliability data.

Gulliksen (1950) notes that a basic definition underlying reliability states that an obtained test score (X_0) is composed of two parts: a true score (X_t) portion and error (X_e) (Formula 1):

$$X_0 = X_t + X_e.$$

Formula 1 can be rewritten in terms of the variation among individuals, or variance (s^2), attributable to these sources (Formula 2):

$$s_0^2 = s_t^2 + s_e^2.$$

Formula 2 states that the variance that occurs among observed, or obtained, scores (s_0^2) equals the true score variance (s_t^2) plus the error variance (s_e^2). Reliability (r_{xx}) is defined as the ratio of total variance attributable to true scores to the total variance of observed scores (Formula 3):

$$r_{xx} = \frac{s_t^2}{s_0^2}.$$

The r_{xx} in Formula 3 indicates that the reliability coefficient is actually a type of correlation coefficient. In practice, the reliability coefficients for most published tests cluster in the .80s and .90s (Anastasi, 1982). If, for example, a standardized reading test for grade six reported a reliability coefficient of .90, this would mean that 90% of the variance among individuals was true variance, with 10% attributable to error. Obviously, the smaller the error, the greater the confidence in the accuracy of the test scores.

There are several procedures for estimating reliability. Readers of test manuals will encounter several types of reliability coefficients: test-retest, alternate forms, split-half, and internal consistency are the most common. Each of these permits different sources of error to be reflected in the test scores. Each type of reliability coefficient is estimated from either a single test administration or from two test administrations separated by a brief time interval (Thorndike & Hagen, 1977).

Test-retest reliability is determined by administering the same test twice, with an intervening time interval, and then correlating the scores. Differences in individual scores on the two testings would be attributed to the differential effects of factors specific to each test session. Alternate-forms reliability is estimated by administering two parallel test forms on separate occasions, with an intervening time interval, and then correlating the scores. Differences in individual scores on the two testings would be attributed both to differential factors affecting performance on each test occasion, and to different samples of content used in each test form. Alternate-forms reliability provides the most rigorous estimate of reliability (Thorndike & Hagen, 1977). Both test-retest and alternate-forms reliability require two separate test administrations; however, it is possible to estimate reliability from a single administration of a test. Split-half reliability estimates are obtained by dividing a test into two equivalent half-tests and correlating the results. Actually, the results are based on tests half as long as the total test and must be corrected to full-length estimates by use of the Spearman-Brown formula to adjust for test length. Individual score differences would be attributed to differences in the two content samples. Internal consistency reliability is estimated from item performance. Sources of error variance reflected include content and heterogeneity of the construct or trait measured by the test (Anastasi, 1982).

Reliability coefficients must be interpreted cautiously because a number of factors may affect their magnitude. Among these influences are the range of ability present in the group used to estimate reliability, the ability level of the group, and the extent to which test scores are dependent on speed or rate of work (Anastasi, 1982).

The size of a reliability coefficient is directly related to the range or extent of individual differences present in the group used to obtain reliability estimates. If, for example, an easy mathematics test were administered to a group of mathematicians, the reliability coefficient would be low owing to the fact that all the mathematicians would probably achieve perfect scores. There is little or no variability in a group such as this; hence, the reliability coefficient would be near zero. In a related sense, reliability coefficients may differ for groups different in overall ability or other demographic characteristics. The composition of a particular group must always be described clearly to sharpen the meaning of a particular reliability coefficient (Anastasi, 1982).

One additional consideration needing careful attention is the extent to which test scores are influenced by speed or rate of work. To the extent that a test is a speed test, the reliability coefficient will be spuriously high if reliability is estimated from a single test administration, such as that used to estimate split-half or internal-consistency reliability. Alternate-forms reliability or some variant of this procedure is recommended for tests dependent on speed (Anastasi, 1982). Most educational tests are power tests that do not depend on speed but allow ample time for most examinees to answer items appropriate to their ability.

The standard error of measurement (SEM), which is obtained from a reliability coefficient, is useful in the interpretation of individual test scores. If it were possible to test an individual many times with the same test and ignore any practice effects, the scores could he expected to vary owing to measurement error. The SEM indicates the extent to which an individual's test score could be expected to deviate from his or her unknown "true" test score. If it is assumed that the various observed test scores are distributed normally around the person's "true" score, then it becomes possible to specify that the observed score is expected to be within the range ±1 SEM about two times out of three, or ±2 SEMs 95 times out of 100. The SEM is computed from Formula 4:

$$SEM = S_x\sqrt{1 - r_{xx}},$$

where S_x = the standard deviation of scores on measure X, and

r_{xx} = the obtained reliability coefficient

Once the SEM is obtained, it becomes possible to construct confidence bands that portray realistically the amount of error associated with a particular test score (Anastasi, 1982). For example, if the corrected split-half reliability coefficient for a 50-item reading comprehension test given in grade six were found to be .91, and the standard deviation of raw scores was observed to be 10, then the SEM (using Formula 4) is 3.0. If a particular pupil obtains a raw score of 35, it becomes possible to state with 68% certainty that the pupil's "true" reading score occurs within the range 35 ± 3, or 32–38; the obtained score ±1 SEM is used for most types of test score interpretation (Mehrens & Lehmann, 1984). If the test user wants a greater degree of certainty, it is possible to use ±2 SEM. Thus, in the same example it is possible to state with 95% certainty that the pupil's "true" score occurred within the range 35 ± 6, or 29–41. Establishing confidence bands such as these is highly recommended because it represents a sound way to take account of measurement error in the interpretation of test results.

REFERENCES

Anastasi, A. (1982). *Psychological testing* (5th ed.). New York: Macmillan.

Gulliksen, H. (1950). *Theory of mental tests.* New York: Wiley.

Mehrens, W. A., & Lehmann, I. J. (1984). *Measurement and evaluation in education and psychology.* New York: CBS College.

Thorndike, R. L., & Hagen, E. P. (1977). *Measurement and evaluation in psychology and education.* New York: Wiley.

GARY J. ROBERTSON
American Guidance Service

ASSESSMENT
MEASUREMENT

RELIGIOUS EDUCATION FOR THE HANDICAPPED

Religious education for the handicapped refers to the moral and spiritual education of children with disabilities. It can be traced to l'Abbé de l' Epée and other ordained ministers who established schools for handicapped children with the specific purpose of bringing their students to the knowledge of God. Parents have also been instrumental in procuring religious education for their handicapped children by demanding that these children be given religious instruction and taught to participate in religious activities. Both priests and parents have insisted that handicapped children have the same need for spiritual development as other children and that they have the right to an equal place in the church or synagogue (Ellis, Ellis, & Warren, 1984).

The 1980s saw a growing focus on the religious needs of handicapped individuals, as evidenced by the designation of the year 1983 as the International Religious Year of Persons with Disabilities (Ellis, Ellis, & Warren, 1984). There have been a number of church groups throughout the country that have adopted resolutions, or issued pastoral or policy statements, related to ministering to persons with handicapping conditions. In addition, a questionnaire concerning religion and handicapped persons was sent by the President's Committee on Employment of the Handicapped to 24 religious groups having a million or more members.

Issues in the religious education of handicapped persons include the integration of individuals with disabilities into the church/synagogue community; the sparseness of literature on special religious education; church/synagogue accessibility (architecture, attitudes, communication, awareness); formation programs for the religious educators of children with special needs; organizational considerations; and effective teaching techniques. There is also the issue of the unique position of the church or synagogue in informing, educating, and motivating people to become involved in facilitating the transition of the severely disabled from social isolation to full participation in the community (Hawkins-Shepard, 1984).

Curriculum materials for the religious education of children with special needs are available (Hall, 1982), as well as suggestions for the adaptation of regular religious education curricula (Paul, 1983) and advice about religious education for parents and teachers of handicapped children (Hall, 1982; Paul, 1983).

Common difficulties concerning religious education for handicapped learners include complaints that religious development is a neglected area in the lives of handicapped children; that too few churches and synagogues provide programs on a national, regional, or local level for the religious involvement of handicapped individuals; and that many churches separate handicapped worshippers into special groups in special parts of the church or only provide opportunities for participation in part of the total worship experience (Denton, 1972).

REFERENCES

Denton, D. (1972). Religious services for deaf people. *Journal of Rehabilitation of the Deaf, 6,* 42–46.

Ellis, H., Ellis E., & Warren, G. T. (Feb. 1984). An open letter to pastors and parents. *The Exceptional Parent, 14*(1), 39.

Hall, S. (1982). Into the Christian community: Religious education with disabled persons. Washington, DC: National Catholic Educational Association.

Hawkins-Shepard, C. (1984). Bridging the gap between religious education and special education. *Proceedings of the 1984 National Convention of the Council for Exceptional Children,* Washington, DC.

Paul, J. (1983). *The exceptional child: A guidebook for churches and community agencies.* Syracuse, NY: Syracuse University Press.

ROSEMARY GAFFNEY
Hunter College

PRIVATE SCHOOLS AND SPECIAL EDUCATION
PRIVILEGED COMMUNICATION

REMEDIAL AND SPECIAL EDUCATION (RASE)

In 1982, Pro-Ed, Inc., purchased the journal *Exceptional Education Quarterly* from Aspen Systems Corporation. In 1984, the name of the journal was changed to *Remedial and Special Education* (RASE), and the journal became a bimonthly. That same year, Pro-Ed acquired two additional journals, *Topics in Learning and Learning Disabilities* (from Aspen Press) and *The Journal for Special Educators* (from the American Association of Special Educators); these were also merged into RASE. This journal is devoted to topics involving the education of persons for whom typical instruction is not effective. Emphasis is on the interpretation of research literature and recommendations for the practice of remedial and special education. RASE thus is alternative to practitioner-oriented teacher journals and pure research journals within the field. All published articles have been peer reviewed.

JUDITH K. VORESS
Pro-Ed, Inc.

REMEDIAL INSTRUCTION

The term remediation is derived from the word *remedy,* meaning a correction, repair, or cure of something that is awry. Medicines are medical remedies. Remedies in education are called remediations (Ysseldyke, & Algozzine, 1984).

Remedial teaching has been distinguished from developmental teaching and from corrective teaching. As usually construed, developmental teaching is the type of instruction given to the majority of students attending regular classes (Otto & McMenemy, 1966; Rupley & Blair, 1983).

Developmental instruction in the modern classroom is likely to be guided by clearly defined instructional objectives. Thus developmental reading instruction has been described as "a systematic guided series of steps, procedures or actions intended to result in learning or in the reaching of a desired goal" (Harris & Hodges, 1981, p. 157).

Corrective and remedial instruction both are forms of academic assistance provided to students who need special help in various areas of instruction. When that assistance is offered by the classroom teacher within a regular classroom setting to students who are deficient in some particular skills or not achieving up to expectations in particular subject matters, help is identified as corrective instruction. Corrective instruction is given when the type of learning problem, or its degree, is not judged as severe enough to require specific types of remediation. Remedial instruction is usually given to students with more severe or persistent academic difficulties. Usually it is provided by a specialist in a particular skill or content area and in circumstances apart from the child's regular classroom. Remedial instruction often suggests a learning disability; indeed, remedial instructors often act as learning disability specialists.

Arbitrary standards often are set for eligibility for corrective or remedial services: within 2 years of grade expectation the child may be given corrective instruction, but beyond 2 years the child will receive remedial instruction. Such criteria are often insensitive to growth curves and normal developmental changes and make little sense.

While developmental and corrective as well as remedial instruction attempt to individualize according to students' needs, remedial instruction is most likely to address a student and his or her problems diagnostically and to offer intensive interventions (Reisman, 1982). Thus remedial instruction is likely to be provided to students whose academic deficiencies or disabilities appear so severe or specialized as to require more precise, intense, or individualized assistance.

In remedial instruction the distinction may be made between skill remediation and ability or process remediation. The first attempts to correct or strengthen particular academic skills such as decoding in reading, carrying in two column addition, and not writing out silent sounds in spelling. In the second, efforts are made to correct presumed deficits in cognitive processes such as perception, memory, and attention. A popular current process approach is that of teaching learning-handicapped children to more effectively use cognitive strategies in learning and school performance.

Since special education is based on individualized intensive interventions addressed to students who, because of their handicapping conditions, may not be able to keep up with their nonhandicapped peers, the notion of remediation, from a special educator's point of view, may be redundant. Indeed, the special education resource room, whether in regular or special education, is likely to be a place where remedial education is offered. Cawley (1984) believes that carefully controlled curricular approaches to the problems of learning-disabled students are likely to be more effective than traditional diagnostic-prescriptive remedial methods so often emphasized in remediation.

Remedial reading is the most frequently offered form of remedial or corrective help provided in grade school, both elementary and secondary. Remedial mathematics, writing, etc., also go on in regular education settings, but they are less likely to be carried out by remedial specialists. Remedial instruction is often provided at the college level as well as during the earlier grades. It is most often required by students who, either because of poor earlier preparation, problems in managing English, or specific cognitive deficits, require specialized help to succeed in higher education. Many colleges and other institutions of higher learning provide remedial writing.

REFERENCES

Cawley, J. F. (1984). Preface. In J. F. Cawley (Ed.), *Developmental teaching of mathematics for the learning disabled*. Rockville, MD: Aspen.

Harris, T. L., & Hodges, R. E. (Eds.). (1981). *A dictionary of reading and related terms Newark,* DE: International Reading Association.

Otto, W., & McMenemy, R. A. (1966). *Corrective and remedial reading*. Boston: Houghton Mifflin.

Reisman, F. (1982). *A guide to the diagnostic teaching of arithmetic*. Columbus, OH: Merrill.

Rupley, W. H., & Blair, T. R. (1983). *Reading diagnosis and remediation: Class & clinic*. Boston: Houghton Mifflin.

Ysseldyke, J. E., & Algozzine, B. (1984). *Introduction to special education*. Boston: Houghton Mifflin.

LESTER MANN
Hunter College

DIAGNOSTIC PRESCRIPTIVE TEACHING
DIRECT INSTRUCTION
REMEDIAL READING

REMEDIAL READING

According to Smith (1965), the term remedial reading first appeared in the professional literature in a 1916 journal article by W. H. Uhl; however, like so many of the terms in the field of reading, the term remedial reading has no universally agreed on operational definition. The amount of confusion that exists with respect to the term was expressed well some years ago by Goldberg and Schiffman (1972), who noted:

> Some educators refer to the problem category as remedial, strephosymbolia, associative learning disability, specific reading or language disability, congenital word blindness, primary reading retardation, or developmental dyslexia. One school district may refer to all retarded readers as remedial; another agency, in the same community, may use the term remedial for a small group of children with specific learning disabilities. (pp. 156–157)

Goldberg and Schiffman go on to point out that, because of the widely varying definitions, estimates of the percent of students requiring remedial reading instruction vary from as low as 1% to as high as 20%.

A Dictionary of Reading and Related Terms (Harris & Hodges, 1981) provides a realistic, though somewhat vague, definition of the term remedial reading:

> Any specialized reading instruction adjusted to the needs of a student who does not perform satisfactorily with regular reading instruction.

> Intensive specialized reading instruction for students reading considerably below expectancy.

Before examining this definition, it might be helpful to quickly introduce two reading terms that are frequently contrasted with the term remedial reading; they are developmental reading, and corrective reading. Developmental reading refers to instruction that is designed for and offered to the average child who is acquiring reading skills at an average rate. Group instruction, centering around the use of basal readers, is the typical approach to developmental reading instruction.

Corrective reading is a term usually applied to instruction that is offered to children who are essentially average intellectually, but who are slower than average in the rate at which they are acquiring reading skills; however, the disparity between where they are expected to be reading, usually based on age, grade placement, and intelligence, is not large. The difficulties that they are encountering are mild enough so that with some adjustments, the responsibility for their reading instruction can be assumed by a regular classroom teacher.

While it seems fairly easy to separate developmental reading from remedial reading, the distinction between corrective and remedial reading is not so clear. The first definition offered by Harris and Hodges would make the two indistinguishable; however, even the second definition offers no clear criteria for separating the two. Harris and Sipay (1985) list four characteristics that distinguish corrective from remedial programs. The first characteristic relates to where the treatment takes place. Remedial reading usually takes place in a special classroom or even in a special clinic. The second characteristic relates to who provides the treatment. Corrective instruction is usually offered by a classroom teacher while remedial instruction is within the province of a reading or learning disabilities specialist. Third is the number of children treated in a session. Group size is smaller for remedial instruction or is on a one-to-one basis. The final characteristic is the severity of the problem. Otto and McMenemey (1966) sum up this definitional problem when they write:

> In terms of diagnostic and instructional techniques, the distinction between actual corrective and remedial instruction is often one of degree rather than kind. Strictly remedial techniques tend to be more intensive and more highly individualized but usually not intrinsically different from corrective techniques. (pp. 38–39)

Some authors have tried to bring objectivity to the definition of remedial reading by defining it as referring to children who are reading 2 or more years below grade level. Unfortunately, this simple approach is fraught with problems. To begin with, years with regard to reading skill development are not equal interval units. Reading skills tend to develop rapidly during grades 1 through 3 and to develop at a negatively accelerating rate thereafter. A child who at the end of grade 2 has acquired no reading skills (hence is 2 years behind) is very different from an grade 8 student who has acquired grade 6 skills. Even Otto and McMenemy (1966), who are among the few professionals who attempt to justify the adoption of a 2-year criterion for defining a remedial reader, are quick to point out that it is "clearly unrealistic" in the early grades and that "slavish application of such an arbitrary criterion would be unfortunate" (p. 37).

A second major problems in adopting a 2-year disparity between where a child is expected to be in reading skill acquisition and where that child actually is relates to the method for calculating that disparity. In most cases, the disparity is based on a difference between actual, measured reading achievement of a student and the level he or she should have attained based on some measure of capacity to learn, usually an intelligence test. Unfortunately, there is no agreed on method for calculating the amount of disparity between expectancy and achievement. Stauffer, Abrams, and Pikulski (1978) have shown how widely different results will be achieved depending on the formula used to calculate the expected level of reading achievement. In addition, tests of intelligence and of reading can yield widely differing results depending on the tests used.

Yet another problem in defining remedial reading lies in the enormous overlap between the concepts of learning disabilities and remedial reading. Given our present level of diagnostic sophistication, distinguishing between these two classifications appears to depend almost totally on arbitrary local definitions or regulations or on funding considerations. Lewis (1983) presents an excellent summary of some of the major considerations that need to be taken into account in providing instruction for the student who is severely disabled in reading, regardless of whether that student is labeled as a remedial reader or as a child with a learning disability. The article is also excellent in providing evidence that challenges some widely held misconceptions about students who have severe reading problems.

The confused situation relative to the use of the term remedial reading and related terms, described by Goldberg and Schiffman earlier, continues to exist today; in fact, the confusion may be exacerbated by the introduction of even more terms.

While there are apparently no clear-cut ways to diagnostically differentiate among remedial readers, the learning disabled, corrective readers, dyslexics, etc., one might wonder if there are any instructional methods or materials that are unique to remedial reading. Textbooks dealing with this topic imply that there are. For example, Bond, et al. (1984) indicate that there are four important elements of remedial instruction: it is individualized; it encourages the reader; it uses effective teaching procedures; and it enlists cooperative efforts. While these elements are important to remedial reading, they are also important to all reading instruction. These authors go on to suggest that basal readers, the hallmark of developmental reading instruction, are a primary source of materials for remedial reading.

A careful reading of discussions of remedial reading suggests that the principles of teaching reading are the same regardless of whether we are concerned with remedial or developmental readers. The basic consideration is that remedial reading to based on a careful assessment of what the reader knows and needs to learn in terms of reading skills and that instruction then be at an appropriate level of challenge. Many of the techniques are similar to those used for teaching reading to achieving readers. For example, Rude and Oehlkers (1984) describe how a language experience approach to teaching reading, which centers around the use of reading materials that are dictated by the reader and written by the teacher, can be used for remedial reading; the language experience approach is also a major developmental technique for teaching reading. Nevertheless, there are three approaches that might be considered specifically designed for use in remedial reading.

The first approach is the use of high interest-low vocabulary materials. These materials are books, usually designed as a series, that are specifically written to appeal to the interests of older children, but that use a limited vocabulary. Harris and Sipay (1985) include a list of over 90 such series.

In the Fernald V-A-K-T approach, the letters V-A-K-T stand for visual, auditory, kinesthetic, and tactile. The approach was devised by Grace Fernald (1943) to treat children with learning problems. In this approach, children learn to read by using all four senses; they see words written by a teacher, they pronounce and hear those same words; they trace the written copy of the words so as to receive tactile and kinesthetic stimulation. The technique, which is highly prescribed, forces the learner to pay full attention to the word learning process. See Johnson (1966) and Stauffer, Abrams, and Pikulski (1978) for descriptions of this approach.

The Orton-Gillingham approach stresses the importance of learning phonics as the major reading skill. Students learn sounds for letters and are taught to blend the sounds to make words. This, too, is a highly structured and prescribed approach. It also uses multiple sensory stimuli. It is based on the work of an influential neurologist, Samuel T. Orton. The technique is fully described by Orton (1966) and Gillingham and Stillman (1966).

REFERENCES

Bond, G. L., Tinker, M. A., Wasson, B. B., & Wasson, J. B. (1984). *Reading difficulties: Their diagnosis and correction* (5th ed.). Englewood Cliffs, NJ: Prentice-Hall.

Fernald, G. M. (1943). *Remedial techniques in basic school subjects.* New York: McGraw-Hill.

Gillingham, A., & Stillman, B. W. (1966). *Remedial training for children with specific difficulty in reading, spelling, and penmanship* (7th ed.). Cambridge, MA: Educators Publishing Service.

Goldberg, H. K., & Schiffman, G. B. (1972). *Dyslexia: Problems of reading disabilities.* New York: Grune & Stratton.

Harris, A. J., & Sipay, E. R. (1985). *How to increase reading ability* (5th ed.). White Plains, NY: Longman.

Harris, T. L., & Hodges, R. E. (Eds.). (1981). *A dictionary of reading and related terms.* Newark, DE: International Reading Association.

Johnson, M. S. (1966). Tracing and kinesthetic techniques. In J. Money (Ed.), *The disabled reader.* Baltimore, MD: Johns Hopkins University Press.

Lewis, R. B. (1983). Learning disabilities and reading: Instructional recommendations from current research. *Exceptional Children, 50*(3), 230–240.

Orton, J. L. (1966). The Orton-Gillingham approach. In J. Money (Ed.), *The disabled reader.* Baltimore, MD: Johns Hopkins University Press.

Otto, W., & McMenemy, R. A. (1966). *Corrective and remedial reading: Principles and practices.* Boston: Houghton Mifflin.

Rude, R. T., & Oehlkers, W. J. (1984). *Helping students with reading problems.* Englewood Cliffs, NJ: Prentice-Hall.

Smith, N. B. (1965). *American reading instruction.* Newark, DE: International Reading Association.

Stauffer, R. G., Abrams, J. C., & Pikulski, J. J. (1978). *Diagnosis, correction and prevention of reading disabilities.* New York: Harper & Row.

JOHN J. PIKULSKI
University of Delaware

BASAL READERS
FERNALD METHOD
HIGH INTEREST-LOW VOCABULARY MATERIALS
ORTON-GILLINGHAM METHOD
READING
READING DISORDERS

REMEDIATION, DEFICIT-CENTERED MODELS OF

Deficit-centered models for the remediation of children's learning problems have been the predominant model, though certainly not the only model, of special education worldwide throughout the twentieth century. Deficit-centered remediation focuses on the identification of underlying process deficiencies on the part of the child; it then directs any subsequent intervention at the remediation of these process deficiencies. The assumption of such programs is that once the underlying deficit has been remediated (fixed, removed, or cured), academic learning will occur at a more or less normal pace. Deficit-centered remediation has undergone numerous facelifts since the 1930s, although the strong influence of Samuel T. Orton, is felt in most of these programs even today.

One of the most notable examples of deficit-centered remediation is the Illinois Test of Psycholinguistic Abilities (ITPA; Kirk, McCarthy, & Kirk, 1971) and its accompanying curriculum, interventions, and training materials. (Perhaps a more popularly known deficit-centered program, and also one of the most heavily refuted and ineffective, is the Doman and Delacato program at the Institute for the Achievement of Human Potential. This is the approach that calls on the concept of neurological organization and treatment through patterning among other activities.) The ITPA focuses on the identification and assessment of basic psycholinguistic processes such as auditory reception, auditory sequential memory, visual sequential memory, auditory association, etc. If a deficit appears in one or more of these areas, a remedial program is then prescribed (Kirk & Kirk, 1971). For example, if a child is referred for a reading program and found to have an auditory reception deficit (determined on the ITPA by the child's inability to respond correctly at an age-appropriate level to such questions as, Do bananas fly? Do barometers congratulate? Do chairs sit?), exercises might be prescribed for the child aimed at practicing the hearing and discrimination of similar sounds (e.g., noting the differences between pin and pen, pet and let, then and tin, dot and spot). The child also might be given practice in the following of instructions. Once these activities are mastered, the deficit-centered model argues, learning to read would proceed more or less normally since the cognitive process-ing (or central process) dysfunction that was the stumbling block to reading has been removed.

Many other assessment techniques and programs exist to identify weaknesses or deficits in cognitive processes for subsequent intervention. Some of the approaches that emphasize treating the child's greatest area of weakness in cognitive processing include those of Ayres (1974), Bannatyne (1980), Ferinden and Jacobson (1969). Frostig and Horne (1964), Kephart (1963), and Vallett (1967). The efficacy of deficit-centered models has been the subject of considerable scrutiny by researchers in psychology and special education for some time. Unfortunately, support for the effectiveness of deficit-centered remediation programs for the remediation of academic deficits is nil, particularly when reading and math are the academic problem areas (Glass & Robbins, 1967; Mann, 1979; Reynolds, 1981a, 1981b; and Ysseldyke & Mirkins, 1982). Perceptual and visual-motor functioning can be improved by deficit-centered remediation programs (Myers & Hammill, 1976), but there is, as yet, no documentable generalization for the remediation of the learning problems that trigger the referral.

Other, related areas of research have repeatedly noted potentially major limiting factors in the application of deficit-centered models. Findings from the fields of neurology, genetics, and related areas demonstrate neurological (Adams & Victor, 1977; Hartlage, 1975; Hartlage & Givens, 1982; Kolb & Whishaw, 1980; Levine, Brooks, & Shonkoff, 1980) or genetic bases (Adams & Victor, 1977; Hartlage & Hartlage 1973a, 1973b) for many learning problems in which deficit-centered models or remediation had been thought to be appropriate as the primary method of intervention. From the point of view of many contemporary neuropsychological models, the deficit-centered process approach to remediation is doomed to failure because it takes damaged, dysfunctional, or undeveloped areas of the brain and focuses training specifically on those areas. Not only does our existing knowledge of neurology predict failure for such efforts, but the efforts will not withstand empirical scrutiny.

Hartlage and Reynolds (1981) have criticized deficit-centered models of remediation as potentially harmful to children. The emotional trauma that may accompany the treatment approach of Doman and Delacato has been widely discussed and the method has been condemned (Levine, Brooks, & Shankoff, 1980). While it is unlikely that other deficit-centered models are as emotionally damaging, it is likely (though unproven) that making children work and practice for lengthy periods process skills in which they are deficient (in some cases, years) without noticeable academic gains is emotionally damaging, particularly to the child's self-esteem, motivation, and the likelihood of continuing in school. Glass (1981), in a meta-analysis of the effectiveness of what were deficit-centered models of remediation, reported that a significant number had net negative effects on academic skills—that is, many deficit-centered remediation programs resulted in less academic gains than no special education program at all. In some instances, then, doing nothing is superior to a deficit-centered approach to remediation, when only academic skills are considered.

Recently, cognitive psychologists have become interested in children's information-processing strategies and have made great strides in understanding how children organize, store, and manipulate stimuli. Concomitant with the revival of interest in cognitivism have been attempts to assess "new" cognitive deficits and provide remedial strategies. Haywood and Switzky (1986), among others, propose that through such techniques as Feuerstein's (1979) Learning Potential Assessment Device (known popularly as the LPAD), deficiencies in children's cognitive processes can be identified and targeted for remediation. Conceptually, this new "cognitive science" approach is no different from the approaches of the past—only the names of the processes thought to be deficient are new. The new deficit-centered models have been the subject of debate (Gresham, 1986; Haywood & Switzky, 1986; Reynolds, 1986), and there is evidence that, through the use of a like set of materials, children's scores on tests such as Raven's Matrices (a nonverbal test of intelligence) improve.

However, many of the specific abilities included in the cognitive science models of deficit-centered remediation are covered overtly in prior models and implicitly in many training programs. The cognitive science models do give us some new abilities to train, notably thinking skills and strategies such as metacognition, regrouping, rehearsal, and various methods of classification, but merely leave us with new labels for others. The intelligence test score improvement reported by Feuerstein, Haywood, and others (Haywood & Switzky, 1986) likely is due to teaching the test, and generalizability to other tests or to academic skills is not in evidence. As with deficit-centered remediation programs throughout the twentieth century, the new cognitive science model is narrow and highly task-specific in its effects. While improvements in these characteristics of children's thinking are desirable, they are not desirable at the neglect of the academic deficiencies that trigger the referral.

There is no evidence that deficit-centered remediation programs aid in such real-world tasks as learning to read, write, or cipher. They remain popular largely on the basis of rational, intuitive appeal and personal testimony or anecdotal data. However, occasional children do improve without treatment and the same percentage or less improve under deficit-centered remediation. As Mann (e.g., 1979) periodically reminds us, we are better off training or teaching for the task at hand, not for the latest process. In assessing the new cognitive science approach to remediation, we are forced to conclude, as has Mann (1979) in his review of process training, "The new scientific pedagogy

was going to revitalize education, provide individual prescriptive correctives for learning problems, reclaim the cognitively impaired. Down with models of general intellectual incompetency! Down with medical models of noneducational etiology!" (pp. 529, 538). "The promised land was at hand. Alas, neither Moses nor we ever crossed to the other side" (Mann, 1979, p. 539). Process is not a useless variable, however. It is crucial to consider in the diagnosis of learning disabilities as well as certain other disorders; efforts to use process approaches to remediate academic problems seem better built on strength models of remediation than on deficit-centered models.

Strength Models of Remediation

Strength models of remediation also invoke the concept of cognitive or intellectual processes and often measure them in the same way. The resulting approach and techniques differ greatly, however. Strength models argue that the best remedial approach for a child who cannot read is to teach the child reading, not metacognition, rehearsal strategies, auditory reception, or grouping and classification.

In strength models of remediation, direct instruction is encouraged in the area(s) of academic or behavioral difficulty. However, instruction is formatted around the child's best developed processes, taking advantage of the child's best intellectual abilities and avoiding those processes that are poorly developed, dysfunctional, or inept in this function. As Reynolds (1981b) describes this method, "The strength model is based on processes that are sufficiently intact so as to subserve the successful accomplishment of the steps in the educational program, so that the interface between cognitive strengths [determined from the assessment process]...and the intervention is the cornerstone of meaningfulness for the entire diagnostic-intervention process" (p. 344). In Lurian terminology, this would denote the need for locating a complex functional system within the brain that operates well enough to be capable of taking control and moderating the learning process necessary to acquire the academic skills in question.

This view is hardly new, though it remains largely untested. Woodrow (1919) suggested teaching to cognitive strengths on the basis of scientific psychology and the interpretation of "laws" of factor analysis, while attempting to reconcile the views of Spearman and of Thurstone (Mann, 1979). Woodrow (1919) observed that "sometimes a high order of intelligence is accompanied by defects which make it imperative to use ... the stronger faculties" (p. 293). More directly and in reference to the mildly mentally retarded, Woodrow (1919) argued that since "Their most valuable asset is rote memory.... Its training should, therefore, form a conspicuous part in their education" (pp. 285–286). Today we hope to use the stronger faculties in developing instructional strategies, as Woodrow also proposed, rather than in training the stronger processes to become even stronger; the latter is not an unlikely side effect of strength models of remediation, however.

Strength models do not tell us specifically what to teach children, as do deficit-centered models. The latter tells us to teach the specific process that has been found to be deficient. In strength models, the specifics of what to teach come from a detailed task analysis or a diagnostic achievement test that delineates precisely what academic skills are problematic for the child. The strength model of remediation tells us how to teach: how the material best can be organized and presented so that learning has the best opportunity to occur (Reynolds, 1985). The specific techniques of strength models of remediation have been elaborated in a variety of sources, as has validity evidence for the approach (Gunnison & Kaufman, 1982; Hartlage & Reynolds, 1981; Reynolds, 1981a, 1981b, 1985). Building on strengths has intuitive appeal as well. Deficit models focus on the child's weakest, least developed areas of cognitive processing, the areas in which failures have been experienced most frequently. The stress, anxiety, and self-denigration that may be fostered can be intolerable for many children. Using the child's strengths as building blocks for the acquisition of academic skills or even the remediation of behavioral disorders increases the probability of more positive and successful experiences, reducing stress and alleviating anxiety. Strength models of remediation may have other emotional benefits for children as well.

A strength model of remediation also can serve as a meeting ground for a variety of divergent theoretical models in use in the remediation of a child's problems. One can easily blend cognitive, behavioral, neuropsychological, and psychoeducational models in a strength approach. Behavioral and psychoeducational models that focus on academic skill delineation through task analysis or diagnostic achievement testing are needed to tell us specifically what to teach; cognitive and neuropsychological models that focus on how the child best thinks and processes information tell us how to organize, present, and teach the content and behaviors; behavioral models, particularly positive reinforcement programs using operant techniques, are best at giving the child reason, purpose, and motivation, the why of learning. Of the various processing theories from which to build the how, to implement strength models of remediation, the neuropsychological model seems the most promising (Reynolds, 1981b, 1985), and a blending of this model with others has been proposed on several occasions.

An Illustrative Example

Some authors have advocated the use of behavioral principles in conjunction with neuropsychological techniques for the remediation of academic problems (Horton, 1981;

Reynolds, 1981a, 1985). Others have presented exemplary case studies that recommend inclusion of behavior management techniques based on the unique patterns of cognitive strengths within a given child (Hartlage, 1981; Hartlage & Telzrow, 1983). The focus in all cases is on assessing as accurately as possible the various dysfunctional or intact neuropsychological processing systems for the child using a variety of assessment devices integrated with data from numerous other sources (e.g., teachers, parents, physicians). The goal is then to design a behavior management program (usually in conjunction with an academic remediation program) that emphasizes the child's particular strengths.

Although this approach seems almost matter of fact in terms of face validity, what actually occurs in schools is usually quite contrary to this model. The following hypothetical case can illustrate how a remediation program might be designed for a given child, based first on a deficit-centered model and second on a strength model.

Tina is an eight-year-old female who is experiencing problems learning to read. The teacher describes her as immature, distractible, and unable to follow classroom instruction. Results of a complete evaluation reveal that Tina possesses average to above average intellectual abilities with significant weakness in her auditory and visual sequencing abilities. She seems to exhibit above average visuo-spatial skills. A classroom observation reveals that she appears to be daydreaming when the teacher gives the morning's assignments and she is frequently reprimanded for talking while she attempts to get information from her peers. Achievement data indicate that she is functioning significantly below her ability in reading, exhibiting almost no knowledge of grapheme-phoneme relationships. Auditory comprehension of material is excellent.

The resultant educational plan based on a traditional deficit-centered model might proceed as follows: Tina would go to a resource room for 45 minutes, 3 days a week, for drill in phonics. This is in addition to the 30 minutes she spends each day in her regular reading program where phonics is also heavily emphasized. In addition, once a week Tina is provided with training in auditory sequencing skills. A behavior management system is designed whereby she stays in from recess when she has not completed assignments as instructed by the teacher. If this fails, she also stays after school to complete assignments.

On adoption of a strength model perspective, a radically different plan would be designed for Tina. Based on the identical assessment information, the emphasis would shift to capitalizing on Tina's strong visuo-spatial skills while bypassing her weaknesses in auditory sequencing to the maximum extent possible. Therefore, Tina may still benefit from additional reading instruction with a resource teacher but the emphasis of the techniques would be quite different. It is probable that for a child with deficient auditory sequencing abilities, a strong phonics program to teach reading would prove futile and subsequently frustrating to the child and the teacher. Under the strength model, one would incorporate techniques into the reading program that would allow Tina to use her stronger visuospatial abilities. Look-say, rebus, and language experience stories with pictures are all reading programs that have techniques to emphasize visuo-spatial skills and deemphasize sequencing skills. Context would be emphasized. That is not to say that strength models demand an emphasis on one system to the exclusion of the other, but rather in preference to it.

Another obvious recommendation would be to have Tina sit as close to the teacher as possible and for the teacher to provide additional visual cues whenever giving oral directions to the class. Writing the directions on the board, having Tina copy them and then illustrate them, might be helpful in maintaining her attention. Tina also might benefit from direct instruction in the use of visual imagery for remembering sight words, following direction, etc.

As for the appropriate behavior management technique, it is possible that simply changing the classroom environment and the demands of the activities would result in an increase in work completed and a reduction in the time spend off task. Strategies that emphasize verbal understanding or memory of specific rules should be avoided. Techniques that provide Tina with visual representation of her behavioral progress (e.g., charting amount of tasks completed) might be the most effective for her. These recommendations may be more difficult to implement only in that they require more creative teachers and support staff. There are, as yet, no purely canned programs or specific techniques for strength models of remediation, since the approach is relatively new and requires great individualization of instruction. It does appear to be worth the effort. Student characteristics should affect the choice of an instructional method. As obvious as this seems, given the tremendous differences observed among children in the depth and breadth of their learning when exposed to a common method, this is clearly not the case in regular or special education at present (Hayes & Jenkins, 1986). Convenience and the needs of administrators all too often dictate the choice of curriculum and methods in special education instruction. Allowing students' characteristics to drive this process under a strength approach to implementing differential instruction offers far greater promise than current practice.

REFERENCES

Adams, R. D., & Victor, M. (1977). *Principles of neurology.* New York: McGraw-Hill.

Ayres, A. J. (1974). *Sensory integration and learning disorders.* Los Angeles: Western Psychological Services.

Bannatyne, A. (1980, September). *Neuropsychological remediation of learning disorders.* Paper presented at the NATO/ASI International Conference on Neuropsychology and Cognition, Augusta, GA.

Ferinden, W. E., & Jacobson, S. (1969). *Educational interpretation of the Wechsler Intelligence Scale for Children (WISC).* Linden, NJ: Remediation Associates.

Feuerstein, R. (1979). *The dynamic assessment of retarded performers. The learning potential assessment device, theory, instruments and techniques.* Baltimore, MD: University Park Press.

Frostig, M., & Horne, D. (1964). *The Frosting program for the development of visual perception.* Chicago: Follett.

Glass, G. V., & Robbins, M. P. (1967). A critique of experiments on the role of neurological organization in reading performance. *Reading Research Quarterly, 3,* 5–52.

Glass, G. V. (1981, September). *Effectiveness of special education.* Paper presented at the Working Conference of Social Policy and Educational Leaders to Develop Strategies for Special Education in the 1980s, Wingspread, Racine, WI.

Gresham, F. (1986). On the malleability of intelligence: Unnecessary assumptions, reifications, and occlusion. *School Psychology Review, 15,* 261–262.

Gunnison, J., & Kaufman, N. L. (1982, August). Cognitive processing styles: Assessment and intervention. In *Assessment and diagnostic—prescriptive intervention: Diversity and perspective.* Symposium conducted at the annual meeting of the American Psychological Association, Washington, DC.

Hartlage, L. C. (1975). Neuropsychological approaches to predicting outcome of remedial educational strategies for learning disabled children. *Pediatric Psychology, 3,* 23–28.

Hartlage, L. C. (1981). Clinical application of neuropsychological test data: A case study. *School Psychology Review, 10,* 362–366.

Hartlage, L. C., & Reynolds, C. R. (1981). Neuropsychological assessment and the individualization of instruction. In G. W. Hynd & J. E. Obrzut (Eds.), *Neuropsychological assessment of the school-aged child: Issues and procedures.* New York: Grune & Stratton.

Hartlage, L. C., & Telzrow, C. F. (1983). Neuropsychological assessment. In K. D. Paget & B. A. Bracken (Eds.), *The psychoeducational assessment of preschool children.* New York: Grune & Stratton.

Hartlage, P. L., & Givens, T. S. (1982). Common neurological problems of school age children. In C. R. Reynolds & T. B. Gutkin (Eds.), *The handbook of school psychology,* New York: Wiley.

Hartlage, P. L., & Hartlage, L. C. (1973a). Comparison of hyperlexic and dyslexic children. *Neurology, 23,* 436–437.

Hartlage, P. L., & Hartlage, L. C. (1973b). *Dermatoglyphic markers in dyslexia.* Paper presented at the annual meeting of the Child Neurology Society, Atlanta, GA.

Hayes, M. C., & Jenkins, J. R. (1986). Reading instruction in special education resource rooms. *American Educational Research Journal, 23,* 161–190.

Haywood, H. C., & Switzky, H. N. (1986). The malleability of intelligence: Cognitive processes as a function of polygenic experiential interaction. *School Psychology Review, 15*(2), 245–255.

Horton, A. M. (1981). Behavioral neuropsychology in the schools. *School Psychology Review, 10,* 367–373.

Kephart, N. C. (1963). *The brain injured child in the classroom.* Chicago: National Society for Crippled Children and Adults.

Kirk, S. A., & Kirk, W. D. (1971). *Psycholinguistic learning disabilities: Diagnosis and remediation.* Urbana: University of Illinois Press.

Kirk, S. A., McCarthy, J., & Kirk, W. D. (1971). *Illinois Test of Psycholinguistic Abilities.* Urbana: University of Illinois Press.

Kolb, B., & Whishaw, I. Q. (1980). *Fundamentals of human neuropsychology.* San Francisco: Freeman.

Levine, M. D., Brooks, R., & Shonkoff, J. P. (1980). *A pediatric approach to learning disorders.* New York: Wiley.

Mann, L. (1979). *On the trail of process.* New York: Grune & Stratton.

Myers, P., & Hammill, D. (1976). *Methods of learning disorders* (2nd ed.). New York: Wiley.

Reynolds, C. R. (1981a). The neuropsychological basis of intelligence. In G. Hynd & J. Obrzut (Eds.), *Neuropsychological assessment of the school aged child: Issues and procedure.* New York: Grune & Stratton.

Reynolds, C. R. (1981b). Neuropsychological assessment and the habilitation of learning: Considerations in the search for the aptitude x treatment interaction. *School Psychology Review, 10,* 343–349.

Reynolds, C. R. (1985, August). *Putting the individual into the ATI.* Paper presented at the annual meeting of the American Psychological Association, Los Angeles.

Reynolds, C. R. (1986). Transactional models of intellectual development, yes. Deficit models of process remediation, no. *School Psychology Review, 15,* 256–260.

Vallett, R. E. (1967). *The remediation of learning disabilities: A handbook of psychoeducational resource programs.* Palo Alto, CA: Fearon.

Woodrow, H. (1919). *Brightness and dullness in children.* Philadelphia: Lippincott.

Ysseldyke, J., & Mirkin, P. K. (1982). The use of assessment information to plan instructional intervention: A review of research. In C. R. Reynolds & T. B. Gutkin (Eds.), *The handbook of school psychology.* New York: Wiley.

CECIL R. REYNOLDS
Texas A & M University

JULIA A. HICKMAN
Bastrop Mental Health Associates

FROSTIG, MARIANNE
ILLINOIS TEST OF PSYCHOLINGUISTIC ABILITIES
INFORMATION PROCESSING
KAUFMAN ASSESSMENT BATTERY FOR CHILDREN
LEARNING POTENTIAL ASSESSMENT DEVICE
NEUROLOGICAL ORGANIZATION
ORTON, SAMUEL T.
PERCEPTUAL TRAINING
SEQUENTIAL AND SIMULTANEOUS COGNITIVE PROCESSING

REMEDIATION, STRENGTH MODELS OF

See REMEDIATION, DEFICIT-CENTERED MODELS.

RENZULLI, JOSEPH S. (1936–   )

Joseph S. Renzulli received his BS (1958) from Glassboro State College, his MEd (1962) from Rutgers University, and his EdD (1966) in educational psychology from the University of Virginia. He is currently the Neag Professor of Gifted Education and Talent Development at the University of Connecticut, where he also serves as the director of the National Research Center on the Gifted and Talented.

Joseph S. Renzulli

Renzulli's research has focused on identification and programming models for both gifted education and general school improvement. In this area, he has developed means of identifying high potential in individuals and creating educational models to maximize giftedness. Developed in the early 1970s, his Three Ring Conception of Giftedness (1978) is considered by many to be the foundation of a more flexible approach to identifying and developing high levels of potential in young people. The Enrichment Triad Model (Renzulli, 1984), a widely used approach for special programs for the gifted and talented, includes general exploratory activities, group training activities, and individual and small-group investigators of real problems. Renzulli is also credited with devising the Revolving Door Identification Model (1981), a flexible approach to identifying high potential in young people, and the Schoolwide Enrichment Model (1985), a plan for general schoolwide enrichment which applies practices developed for the gifted and talented to a system that serves the highly able as well as providing all students a general upgrade of the curriculum.

Renzulli has contributed numerous books and articles to professional literature. His two most recent books are *Schools for Talent Development: A Practical Plan for Total School Improvement* (1994) and *The Schoolwide Enrichment Model: A How-To Guide for Educational Excellence* (Renzulli & Reis, 1997).

REFERENCES

Renzulli, J. S. (1978). What makes giftedness? Re-examining a definition. *Phi Delta Kappan, 60*, 180–184.

Renzulli, J. S. (1984). The triad/revolving door system: A research based approach to identification and programming for the gifted and talented. *Gifted Child Quarterly, 28*, 163–171.

Renzulli, J. S. (1994). *Schools for talent development: A practical plan for total school improvement.* Mansfield Center, CT: Creative Learning.

Renzulli, J. S., & Reis, S. M. (1997). *The schoolwide enrichment model: A how-to guide for educational excellence.* Mansfield Center, CT: Creative Learning.

Renzulli, J. S., Reis, S. M., & Smith, L. H. (1981). *The revolving door identification model.* Mansfield Center, CT: Creative Learning.

TAMARA J. MARTIN
The University of Texas of the Permian Basin

REPEATED READING

Repeated reading is a remedial reading technique designed to improve fluency and indirectly increase comprehension. The method is based largely on the teaching implications of automatic information processing theory in reading (LaBerge & Samuels, 1974). In automaticity theory, fluent readers are assumed to decode text automatically; attention is therefore free for comprehension. Nonfluent, word-by-word readers, on the other hand, must focus excessive amounts of attention on decoding, making comprehension difficult. The purpose of repeated reading is to make decoding of connected discourse automatic, thus fluency is increased and the reader is able to concentrate on comprehension.

The method involves multiple oral rereadings of connected discourse until a prescribed level of fluency is attained. Samuels' (1979) method, intended as a supplement to developmental reading programs, consists of multiple rereadings of a short passage of from 50 to 200 words, depending on the skill of the student. Reading speed and number of word recognition errors are recorded for each repetition. When the fluency criterion is reached, the student moves on to a new passage.

Chomsky (1976) proposes a similar method. In this variation, students listen to a tape recording of a storybook while following the text. Students read and listen repeatedly to the text until oral reading fluency is achieved. In addition to reported gains in fluency and comprehension, the method of repeated reading is said to promote more positive attitudes toward reading in that it virtually ensures a successful reading experience (Kann, 1983).

Moyer (1982) offers a theoretical rationale for the potential effectiveness of the method with disabled readers. She suggests that for some poor readers, the amount of repetition/redundancy offered by traditional reading programs is insufficient to permit the acquisition of reading. Repeated reading of entire passages, however, maximizes redundancy at all levels of written expression. Thus readers are given much practice in using syntactic and semantic cues, as well as in acquiring knowledge of graphophonemic word structure.

REFERENCES

Chomsky, C. (1976). After decoding: What? *Language Arts, 53*, 288–296.

Kann, R. (1983). The method of repeated readings: Expanding the neurological impress method for use with disabled readers. *Journal of Learning Disabilities, 16*, 90–92.

LaBerge, D., & Samuels, S. J. (1974). Toward a theory of automatic information processing in reading. *Cognitive Psychology, 6*, 293–323.

Moyer, S. B. (1982). Repeated reading. *Journal of Learning Disabilities, 15*, 619–623.

Samuels, S. J. (1979). The method of repeated readings. *Reading Teacher, 32*, 403–408.

TIMOTHY D. LACKAYE
Hunter College

READING
READING REMEDIATION

RESEARCH IN SPECIAL EDUCATION

Research in special education is the means through which knowledge and methods of treatment are acquired and verified for application to persons exhibiting special needs. Such research encompasses a wide range of methodologies, data collection and analysis techniques, subjects, and issues. Although all special education research contributes to the ever increasing knowledge base of the field, all are different to some extent. Research ranges from case studies to single subject and group designs. Each method differs from the others in terms of ease of use, confidence and validity of results obtained, and generality of findings.

Through the process of research, advances are made in what is known about disabilities and how to prevent and treat them through education and training. The importance of research methodology in validating the findings of research must be emphasized. Many hypotheses related to developmental disabilities are advanced in the form of anecdotal reporting and logical analyses. But these hypotheses are speculative and before being applied to the special education field, they must be subjected to verification through research. Only by careful study through controlled research designs can research findings be considered useful and applied to persons other than those involved in the research study.

Special education research is usually applied research; in other words, it is conducted primarily in the places where handicapped persons live, work, and attend school. For example, research has been conducted in group homes, sheltered workshops, resource rooms, and the community. Although less rigorous than research in the experimental laboratory, special education research has the advantage of being relevant to and practical for the subjects involved; that is, the issues studied are usually of high priority for the well-being of the people involved because of their functional relevance. Through rigorously applied research programs, professionals in special education can confirm observations by testing hypotheses on persons with special needs and verifying known effects with different populations. In the long view, research provides a solid foundation of knowledge from which to progress and maintain the intellectual vitality of special education (Drew, Preator, & Buchanan, 1982).

Observation of phenomena is inherent in all research and particularly in special education research Naturalistic observation is one way to collect information about subjects. With this technique, the researcher observes a person (or group of people) and makes extensive records of the subject's behaviors. The purpose is to be as descriptive as possible to provide a post-hoc analysis of possible mediating factors. For example, Currin and Rowland (1985) assessed the communication ability of persons who were labeled profoundly handicapped. These researchers videotaped interactions among adult teachers and 15 nonverbal youths and then divided the communications behaviors exhibited by the subjects into eight categories. The researchers provided no training or other intervention. Such a naturalistic account is important because it can provide an accurate description of specific skills in a certain population. This description can, in turn, later be used as a base from which to provide more precise analyses or from which to guide subsequent interventions. Authors of the majority of articles published from 1983 to 1985 in four major special education research journals used naturalistic observation for collecting and reporting their respective information.

Another important characteristic of research is that of systematically manipulating variables and observing the effects of such manipulations on other variables. Typically, a researcher wants to measure accurately how the de-

pendent variable (e.g., subject behaviors targeted for change) is affected when the subject is exposed to the independent variable (one or more factors manipulated by the researcher). Some examples of dependent variables in special education research are number of words read, frequency of correct expressive signs made, number of problems solved, percentage of inappropriate social behaviors exhibited, and frequency of interruptions. Some examples of independent variables in research are teacher praise, repetition of task, removal of child from activity, use of a particular prompting strategy, and administration of drugs.

A third characteristic of most research is use of an experimental method to determine the extent to which independent variables are functionally related to changes in dependent variables. Researchers carefully design how and when their subjects are exposed to independent variables. Experimental designs minimize the possibility that uncontrolled, extraneous factors play a part in changing dependent variables. Research that is not adequately designed to decrease the impact of extraneous factors must be viewed with caution (Sidman, 1960).

A final characteristic of research concerns analysis of findings. Typically, researchers have used statistical methods to determine whether their results demonstrate a strong (significant) change. Whether the research compares a pre- and postintervention difference, or whether the results obtained from one subject exposed to an independent variable is compared with those of another subject who is not exposed, the intent of the analysis is to assess the degree of difference and make a statement as to whether such a difference could be expected by chance. Statistical methods used in special education research include t-tests, analysis of variance, analysis of covariance; and regression analysis. Numerous authors have addressed the role of statistics and research (e.g., Edwards, 1985; Galfo, 1983). In addition, researchers can determine whether their work has caused an observable practical change in their subjects. This determination is termed functional or clinical significance. For example, assume that a researcher is testing a new method for teaching handicapped students to tell time. For those subjects who learn to use a clock during their daily routine, a definite functional skill has been learned regardless of whether or not a statistical test indicates statistical significance.

A research design describes the manner in which subjects are exposed to independent variables. Researchers must structure their designs to meet basic criteria that permit confidence in results obtained by the research. All researchers must control for extraneous variables entering into and possibly affecting the research outcome. In other words, the dependent variables measured by the researcher must be affected only by variables manipulated by the researcher. Campbell and Stanley (1963) proposed eight factors that may cause changes in dependent measures regardless of the effect of the independent variables studied. These eight threats to the validity of research follow:

1. *History*. Experiences (in addition to the independent variable) of the subjects. For example, assume that a student is a subject in a research project focusing on peer tutoring to increase appropriate social skills. If the peer tutor becomes ill and misses 3 days of the study, causing the subject to be in training for a fewer number of sessions than the other subjects, this will threaten the validity of the results.

2. *Maturation*. Uncontrolled changes in subjects. For example, handicapped infants may become fatigued and lose attentiveness over a few hours or late in the day. Behavior changes owed to weariness, hunger, or aging illustrate a maturation threat.

3. *Testing*. The effect of taking a first test on subsequent tests. For example, students who repeatedly take a test improve their test scores over time.

4. *Instrumentation*. Changes in the devices measuring behavior of subjects. For example, mechanical items such as a video camera or cumulative recorder may fail to operate properly. Human observers may become bored or fatigued and as a result unknowingly alter their scoring.

5. *Statistical Regression*. Subjects selected for inclusion in a study because of extreme scores on some test or measure. For example, assume some learning-disabled students are selected for a research study on improving reading. These particular students are selected because of their low scores on a reading achievement test given as a pretest measure. The experimental treatment is applied and then a posttest is given (the same reading achievement assessment). Any increases in posttest scores cannot be assumed to be related to the experimental manipulation because there is a tendency for low scores on a test to increase on subsequent testing.

6. *Selection*. Subjects for experimental and control groups. If a project involves the comparison of two subject groups, the research results may be a function of the subjects being different initially rather than a function of the experimental manipulation. For example, assume that a school district receives financial support to hire extra vocational counselors and trainers to work with handicapped students for a year in vocational training. At the end of the year, the superintendent of the district decides to assess whether the extra staff made a positive impact on the vocational success of the students. The administrator arranges for a standard vocational assessment to be given to all of the vocational students who received the assistance, and to students in another district who did not. Differences in the assessment scores may be due to a basic difference between the students of the two districts.

7. *Experimental Mortality*. Losing subjects from a research study. For example, researchers frequently group subjects along relevant variables such as age, sex, and handicapping condition. If several subjects in one group drop out of the study for any reason, any results of the research showing a difference between the two groups may be due to the loss of the subjects rather than an effect of the independent variable.

8. *Selection-Maturation Interaction, Etc.* A combination of any of the previous factors.

According to Campbell and Stanley, if a researcher arranges the experimental design to minimize the possibility of the mentioned potential alternative explanations, then any changes in the dependent measures can be confidently assumed to be due to the experimental intervention.

A second criterion for all research designs concerns the extent to which results can generalize (be applied directly) to other subjects or conditions. In special education particularly, the results of research need to be relevant to persons similar to those involved in the particular research project. Campbell and Stanley recognized four factors that reduce confidence in generalizing the results of a research study to special needs persons not participating in that study or in settings other than the experimental one:

1. *Effect of Testing*. Subjects who are tested may be affected by testing and thus react differently than an untested population. For example, assume that handicapped students are enlisted as subjects in a research project testing the impact of an innovative procedure for increasing spelling accuracy. The subjects are given a preintervention spelling test followed by treatment. Finally, the subjects complete a posttest. The subjects may do better than other students simply because they were given a spelling test before the intervention.

2. *Effect of Selection of Subjects and Experimental Variable*. Subjects may be more or less sensitive to the experimental intervention than other students. For instance, a special education classroom may be used extensively by special education researchers for research purposes. If the students in such a classroom are frequently involved as research subjects, and if there are constant visitors and observers in the classroom, then these students may be more or less sensitive to any experimental manipulations than students in other special education classes.

3. *Effect of Experimental Arrangements*. Conditions of the research itself may affect subjects in a special way. For example, this threat exists when students

from several classes are randomly selected to be in an experimental group and are taken to a new classroom for the study. Subjects who are in an unfamiliar environment with unfamiliar people may react differently to experimental procedures than those in their familiar surroundings.

4. *Multiple-Treatment/Interference of Previous Treatments*. Previous treatments may have effects on subjects that are unknown and when working with humans as subjects, locating experimentally naive individuals can be extremely difficult. For example, some researchers study the effect of different variations of a prompting strategy known as stimulus-delay on academic skills. If they were to use the same subjects repeatedly in different experiments, over time these subjects might become familiar with the stimulus-delay method and do better or worse than subjects not initially exposed.

It is important to note that to the greatest extent possible, research in special education must meet these concerns of generalization. The importance of educational research lies both with the improvement of the particular subjects in a research project and the belief that the results and knowledge gained from the research can be applied to other persons with special needs.

All research projects involve either one or more subjects. Single-subject and group designs are labels that describe the primary categories used in special education. The majority of published articles between 1983 and 1985 in four journals devoted exclusively to research on special needs incorporated a group experimental design, either random or matched. A variety of single-subject designs were used as well.

Typically, a single-subject design involves one subject being exposed to all of the experimental conditions involved in the research. One unique characteristic of such designs is that an individual is compared with his or her own performance only. The measurement of behavior takes place before and repeatedly during the intervention. This permits a comparison of an individual's performance at regular points in time. Such within-subject analyses (Sulzer-Azaroff & Mayer, 1977) potentially yield richer information on the performance of individuals than the traditional experimental and control group designs that stress comparing average scores of large groups of subjects. Single-subject designs are particularly useful with both mildly and severely handicapped persons.

The single-subject designs are withdrawal of treatment, alternating treatment, and multiple baseline. Each is relatively easy to use in a classroom, has strong validity, and has been proven useful in many classroom situations. These designs are adaptable for use when targeting academic and social behavior, when attempting to increase or decrease a response, or when working with a single student or groups.

The withdrawal of treatment evaluation technique typically involves four distinct phases. First, the researcher measures the subject's performance on the target skill prior to a formal attempt at changing the instructional method (baseline). In some cases, the baseline consists of a previous intervention or teaching method other than the intervention of interest. Once this phase is completed, the experimenter intervenes with the independent variable(s) selected. There is frequent measurement of subject performance, usually either per lesson or daily. After the period of time during which the subject's performance stabilizes, the experimenter terminates the intervention and continues to measure the subject's behavior during this second baseline phase. Finally, the researcher reinstates the instruction and continues to measure performance.

Correa, Poulson, and Salzberg (1984) used this design to test the effects of a graduated prompting procedure on the behavior of toy grasping in a two-year-old visually impaired and mentally retarded youngster. The general procedure involved the presentation of a noise-making toy in front of the child and the opportunity for the child to grasp it with no assistance. If the child did so within 10 seconds, he was given praise and the opportunity to manipulate the toy. The experimenters first conducted a series of baseline trials and found that the child touched the toy only when assisted. During the first treatment condition, unassisted touching of the toy increased to a mean of 7% of the trials. Although the following return-to-baseline phase resulted in no unassisted touching of the toy, the subsequent treatment condition increased touching once again to a mean of approximately 18%.

The rationale and strength of this design are apparent. If there is improvement in performance during the times in which the intervention is in effect, and deterioration in performance during the baseline conditions, then the researcher can have confidence that the teaching is the factor resulting in the learning. Such a research design demonstrates experimental control of behavior (Hersen & Barlow, 1976) and minimizes the possibility that uncontrolled factors are responsible for the changes in the subject's performance. On the other hand, there are times when a withdrawal of treatment design is not used (Tawney & Gast, 1984). Ethical concerns may contraindicate withdrawing an intervention if the target behavior is very important (e.g., aggression toward peers), or if a clear, clinically significant change in behavior occurs in the first intervention phase. Methodological concerns may also argue against the use of this design when the target behavior is one that, once learned, is not likely to return to preintervention levels (e.g., learning addition).

The alternating treatments design involves the exposure of the subject to two or more different treatment strategies for the same behaviors. The treatments are alternated over time. Although obtaining a baseline measure of the behavior is desirable, the researcher need not do this because the primary variable of interest is observed changes in the behavior with respect to the different treatments.

An important characteristic of this design is the use of teacher instructions or cues to signal the student as to which intervention is in effect. Typically, the design is used as follows. The researcher first develops the different strategies and selects a means for notifying the subject of each. The researcher also determines a schedule of when each treatment is to be used. The schedule must allow for each treatment to be used an equal number of times in random order. Once the research begins, the experimenter alternates the conditions, measures the subject's behavior, and records it separately for each treatment.

Barrera and Sulzer-Azaroff (1983) used such a design to compare two different language training programs (oral and total communication) in an attempt to improve expressive labeling of three autistic children. Each day, subjects were exposed to both training programs, but the sequence in which they were used alternated randomly. The experimenter signaled which treatment was in use by providing either vocal cues only (oral communication training) or vocal and gestural cues (total communication).

With this design, a teacher can immediately start to remediate a behavior rather than waiting for the rate of behavior to stabilize during a baseline period. In addition, this design can be used with behaviors irreversible once learned. However, this design is unusual in that it does not reflect the "natural" form of classroom instruction whereby one treatment strategy is used consistently over a period of time. There is also the possibility that the subject might be affected by the sequence of the various treatments. Last, a behavior that changes slowly will not be discovered with this design owing to the frequent switching of independent variables.

The multiple baseline design involves measurement of multiple target behaviors, subjects, or situations. The targeted responses, for example, may be from one subject, different behaviors of several subjects, or one behavior exhibited by a subject in different situations. After obtaining baseline measures, the researcher applies the intervention to just one behavior while continuing to collect baseline data on the others. The intervention is subsequently applied to the remaining targets in a successive fashion. This design objectively demonstrates the success of intervention if a target response changes only when the intervention is applied to it.

The multiple baseline design can be used in a variety of different situations. First, it is excellent for use when teaching a student similar behaviors. For example, Haring (1985) used such a design when teaching students labeled

moderately/severely handicapped to play with different toys. Haring first noted that the children exhibited no appropriate play with any of four different toys. He then trained the children to play correctly with one toy while noting whether spontaneous play occurred with any of the other three toys. Although the child learned to play correctly with the trained toy, there was no generalized play to the other three toys. The children played correctly only after receiving direct training with the other toys.

Such a design is used across individuals and situations in the same manner as with behaviors. Foxx, McMorrow, and Mennemeier (1984) trained two groups of three adults labeled mildly and moderately retarded to exhibit appropriate social skills such as being polite and responding to criticism. After obtaining a preintervention assessment on all subjects, they taught one group while assessing the other. After several sessions, the subjects in the second group received the training. A multiple baseline across settings is used in a similar fashion. Instead of targeting different behaviors or students, the teacher assesses one behavior of a single student in different situations (e.g., at recess, lunch, in reading class, etc.) and applies the intervention in one setting at a time.

There are limitations associated with the multiple baseline design (Tawney & Gast, 1984). One concerns repeated testing during the baseline conditions; this could potentially continue for many sessions, especially for the third or fourth behavior (or setting or person). Such a lengthy assessment period precludes training and increases the potential for student frustration. However, this problem is minimized by either providing some type of treatment during baseline—so that the student receives some intervention, albeit not the one of interest—or by collecting baseline assessment infrequently. For example, although a minimum of three assessments is recommended, they could be done at random points throughout the baseline phase. Another disadvantage concerns measuring several behaviors or the behaviors of several different subjects, possibly even in different settings. Such a demanding requirement could be time-consuming and impractical in some situations.

There are several research methodologies incorporating a group design approach such as random group, matched group, counterbalanced, and norm-referenced.

In the random group design, subjects are randomly selected from a defined population and assigned to two groups. Both groups are given the same pretest. One group is then given the experimental treatment while the other group is given either no treatment or a treatment that will be compared with the experimental treatment. Finally, both groups are given the same posttest. Wang and Birch (1984) used the random group design when comparing the instructional effectiveness of two different remedial programs for handicapped students. A total of 179 children were randomly assigned to either a part-day resource room or a full-day class representing an adaptive learning environments model (ALEM). Dependent measures consisted of scores from standardized achievement tests, student attitude surveys, and classroom processes. The results indicated that on the average, students in the ALEM class progressed more than students in the part-day resource room.

Another design, matched group, involves subjects in both groups being matched as closely as possible with each other. The matching can occur on variables such as age, sex, learning histories, or intelligence. The variables along which the matching will occur depend on the purposes of the research. For example, Jago, Jago, and Hart (1984) matched subjects in the experimental and control groups along the dimensions of age and etiology of disability. Pretesting, experimental manipulation, and post-testing are done in a manner similar to that in the random group design.

Counter-balanced design involves subjects being exposed to identical experimental interventions but in a different sequence. For example, Carr and Durand (1985) assessed the rate of disruptive behavior exhibited by four developmentally disabled children in four conditions: (1) an easy task with constant teacher attention, (2) a difficult task with constant teacher attention, (3) an easy task with limited teacher attention, and (4) a difficult task with limited teacher attention. Each child was observed in each of these four situations, but in a varying sequential order. For example, one child was exposed to easy task/limited attention, easy task/constant attention, and difficult task/constant attention. A second child was observed in the order of difficult task/constant attention, easy task/constant attention, and easy task/limited attention.

With the norm-referenced design, only one group of subjects is exposed to the experimental intervention and standardized tests are used for pretest and posttest assessments. The results are then compared with results obtained by the standardization for that particular test; in other words, the standardization sample serves as the control group. For example, Gersten and Maggs (1982) assessed cognitive and academic changes in a group of moderately retarded children and adolescents over a 5-year period. The dependent measure was the score of the Stanford-Binet Intelligence Test. The independent measure was the DISTAR Language Program. After almost 5 years of language training, the subjects were given the Stanford-Binet and postexperimental scores were compared with preexperimental scores on the same test. The researchers found that the subjects were gaining points on their IQ scores faster than the population of children used to standardize the test. The norm-referenced design has serious problems since seldom will the research sample match a test's standardization sample or all key variables. Standardization samples of tests are just not good control groups.

Group designs are particularly useful when testing the effectiveness of a treatment package or when addressing questions concerning the magnitude of an effect in terms of the number of people positively or negatively affected. They are the design of choice when testing for a general effect. However, giving treatment to one group of subjects and withholding treatment from another group can be ethically questionable. This is a particular concern in the context of educational treatment, but it can be minimized by offering the control group a treatment different from the experimental intervention, or perhaps the treatment in use prior to the experimental intervention. Another limitation concerns the practical difficulty of finding a sufficient number of matched subjects. Special needs people have unique strengths and disabilities, and finding truly matched subjects may be difficult to achieve.

One other disadvantage with some group designs concerns the portrayal of results in statistical means (averages). One can determine a general outcome when experimental and control group averages are compared, but any analysis of the effect the experimental intervention has on individuals is difficult. Reporting averages ignores the number of subjects positively affected, negatively affected, or not affected at all.

A unique problem with a norm-referenced design is that virtually all of the standardized tests developed to date have used nonhandicapped persons for standardization. Using the results of such a group to assess handicapped subjects is questionable. However, tests (e.g., the American Association of Mental Deficiency Adaptive Behavior Scales) are being developed using a developmentally disabled population for standardization purposes. This could make the use of norm-referenced designs more valid.

Meta-analysis is a research approach providing a quantitative analysis of multiple studies, allowing one to address specific research questions across many studies. Kavale and Furness (1999) provide multiple examples of how meta-analysis can be useful in special education, especially in the evaluation of intervention programs.

Research conducted in special education has increased knowledge in the field and at the same time raised new questions. One important concern is the ethical conduct of the special educator while doing research. Experimenters who use humans as subjects have the responsibility of providing stringent safeguards to protect the health and well-being of their subjects. Professionals in special education must be particularly sensitive to these concerns in that developmentally disabled subjects may not be capable of understanding the issues involved in the research and thus may not be able to give truly informed consent.

Research safeguards to protect subject rights do exist and professionals must abide by them. Kelty (1981) summarized several key guidelines for researchers to consider when planning studies using humans. Generally, these involve informed consent on the part of the subject so that the subject truly understands the purpose of the study, any risks benefits to the subject, and the option to volunteer or to withdraw so that there is maximum possibility for benefit with minimum possibility of harm.

A standard component of research studies is a description of reliability procedures to verify that the primary data collector is accurate in recording the responses of the subjects. Unfortunately, few researchers present a similar case verifying that an experimental treatment is actually applied as proposed. This issue has been termed integrity of treatment (Salend, 1984) and is crucial for confidence in research results. For example, if an experimenter inadvertently implements a different intervention than the one planned, relating the proposed experimental method to the results would be erroneous. Integrity of treatment may be verified with little extra effort on the part of the research designers. As reported in Zane, Handen, Mason, and Geffin (1984), the integrity check can be made part of the traditional reliability check. The reliability scorer notes whether the person implementing the experimental program uses the correct intervention and scores the subject response correctly. By presenting both sets of data, readers can judge to what extent the proposed intervention is actually implemented.

What are some recognized areas of special education in which more research could profitably be done? One area is diagnosis. Techniques that accurately assess the etiology of a person's deficits and discovery of the youngest age at which a true diagnosis can be achieved for various handicapping conditions would have a significant impact. Another area concerns the success of mainstreaming. Ideally, a solid research base should exist to support mainstreaming as well as to delineate ways of making it more successful. Several important questions can be addressed. What is the optimal class ratio of children labeled normal and developmentally disabled? How does mainstreaming affect the individual student in terms of academic and social success? What affect is there, if any, on the students labeled normal? Answers to these questions obtained from systematic research will shed light on the future direction of mainstreaming and lead to even further improvements for disabled people.

One final research area to pursue concerns the extent to which practitioners in the field actually apply the findings from special education research (Englert, 1983). The purpose of research is to provide information that can be used to improve the lives of special needs persons. To what extent do the techniques and knowledge of special education professionals reflect the most recent research findings? If research findings are not being used by teachers and other special education professionals, the reasons must be sought and corrected. Such a discrepancy may be due to limited access to sources of research findings, a possible lack of skills training, or research that is not useful to practitioners. Whatever the reason(s), research findings must make their way to the people who can use them to enhance the lives of special needs people.

REFERENCES

Barrera, R. D., & Sulzer-Azaroff, B. (1983). An alternating treatment comparison of oral and total communication training programs with echolalic autistic children. *Journal of Applied Behavior Analysis, 16*, 379–394.

Campbell, D. T., & Stanley, J. C. (1963). *Experimental and quasi-experimental designs for research*. Chicago: Rand McNally College.

Carr, E. G., & Durand, V. M. (1985). Reducing behavior problems through functional communication training. *Journal of Applied Behavior Analysis, 18*, 111–126.

Correa, V. I., Poulson, C. L., & Salzberg, C. L. (1984). Training and generalization of reach-grasp behavior in blind, retarded young children. *Journal of Applied Behavior Analysis, 17*, 57–69.

Currin, F. M., & Rowland, C. M. (1985). Communicative assessment of nonverbal youths with severe/profound mental retardation. *Mental Retardation, 2*, 52–62.

Drew, C. J., Preator, K., & Buchanan, M. L. (1982). Research and researchers in special education. *Exceptional Education Quarterly, 2*, 47–56.

Edwards, A. L. (1985). *Multiple regression and the analysis of variance and covariance*. New York: Freeman.

Englert, C. S. (1983). Measuring special education teacher effectiveness. *Exceptional Children, 50*, 247–254.

Foxx, R. M., McMorrow, M. J., & Mennemeier, M. (1984). Teaching social/vocational skills to retarded adults with a modified table game: An analysis of generalization. *Journal of Applied Behavior Analysis, 17*, 343–352.

Galfo, A. J. (1983). *Educational research design and data analysis*. New York: University Press of America.

Gersten, R. M., & Maggs, A. (1982). Teaching the general case to moderately retarded children: Evaluation of a five-year project. *Analysis & Intervention in Developmental Disabilities, 2*, 329–334.

Haring, T. G. (1985). Teaching between class generalization of toy play behavior to handicapped children. *Journal of Applied Behavior Analysis, 18*, 127–139.

Hersen, M., & Barlow, D. H. (1976). *Single-case experimental designs: Strategies for studying behavior change*. New York: Pergamon.

Jago, J. L., Jago, A. G., & Hart, M. (1984). An evaluation of the total communication approach for teaching language skills to developmentally delayed preschool children. *Education & Training of the Mentally Retarded, 19*, 175–182.

Kavale, K., & Furness, S. (1999). Effectiveness of special education. In C. R. Reynolds & T. B. Gutkin (Eds.), *The Handbook of School Psychology* (3rd Ed.) New York: Wiley.

Kelty, M. F. (1981). Protection of persons who participate in applied research. In G. T. Hannah, W. P. Christian, & H. B. Clark (Eds.), *Preservation of client rights: A handbook for practitioners providing therapeutic, educational, and rehabilitative services*. New York: Free Press.

Salend, S. J. (1984). Integrity of treatment in special education research. *Mental Retardation, 6*, 309–315.

Sidman, M. (1960). *Tactics of scientific research*. New York: Basic Books.

Sulzer-Azaroff, B., & Mayer, G. R. (1977). *Applying behavior-analysis procedures with children and youth*. New York: Holt, Rinehart, & Winston.

Tawney, J. W., & Gast, D. L. (1984). *Single subject research in special education*. Columbus, OH: Merrill.

Wang, M. C., & Birch, J. W. (1984). Comparison of a full-time mainstreaming program and a resource room approach. *Exceptional Children, 51*, 33–40.

Zane, T., Handen, B. L., Mason, S. A., & Geffin, C. (1984). Teaching symbol identification: A comparison between standard prompting and intervening response procedures. *Analysis & Intervention in Developmental Disabilities, 4*, 367–377.

THOMAS ZANE
Johns Hopkins University

MEASUREMENT
MULTIPLE BASELINE DESIGN
MULTIPLE REGRESSION
REGRESSION (STATISTICAL)

RESIDENTIAL FACILITIES

Residential facilities in America have been provided a variety of labels, including school, hospital, colony, prison, and asylum. Both the role and the labels that institutions for the handicapped have taken on have been reflective of the social and cultural climate of the time (Wolfensberger, 1975). The periods that had major influence on residential institutions have been characterized as follows: early optimism, 1800–1860; disillusionment, 1860–1900; reconsideration, 1920–1920; ebb and flow, 1930–1950; new reconsideration, 1950–1960; and enthusiasm, 1960–1970 (Cegelka & Prehm, 1982).

In the United States no public provisions were made for residential placement and care for the handicapped until the 1800s. Prior to that time handicapped individuals were placed in a variety of settings. These ranged from poorhouses to charitable centers. Such institutions provided no systematic attempts at rehabilitation or training of the handicapped. Rather, they served as facilities that stored and maintained handicapped and other persons. It has been estimated that as late as 1850, 60% of the inhabitants of all institutions in the United States were deaf, blind, insane, or mentally retarded (National Advisory Committee for the Handicapped, 1976).

The first residential institution designed for handicapped individuals was established in 1817. That year the American Asylum for the Education and Institution of the Deaf was established in Hartford, Connecticut. In 1819 a second school, for the blind, was established in Watertown, Massachusetts; it was named the New England Asylum for the Blind. During this period and continuing until the Civil War, a number of eastern states established residential schools for the deaf, blind, orphaned, and mentally retarded (National Advisory Committee for the Handicapped, 1976).

The development of residential institutions for the mentally retarded in the United States began in the 1840s. The growth of such institutions was strongly influenced by the work of Johann Guggenbuhl in Switzerland. In 1848 Samuel Howe convinced the Massachusetts Legislature to allocate funds for the establishment of the first public setting for individuals with retardation. That same year Harvey Wilbur founded the first private institution for treating retarded persons. These institutions were designed to provide education and training to mildly, and occasionally to moderately, handicapped children and adolescents. After the Civil War, residential institutions fell into disfavor. However, the latter portion of the century was marked by continued growth, both in numbers of facilities and numbers of individuals within those facilities. As the nineteenth century came to a close, it became clear that institutions were not accomplishing training that would lead to the reintegration of handicapped individuals into the community. By 1900, 7000 handicapped individuals were housed in institutions. During this time, the role of residential institutions changed significantly. Their emphasis shifted from training to prevention of retardation through systematic segregation of the mentally retarded from society (Wolfensberger, 1975).

The view of institutions held by state legislatures and the general public fluctuated until after World War II. By this time institutions were overcrowded and understaffed. The effects of the baby boom in the late 1940s and the early 1950s placed further pressures on these settings. After World War II, a growing acknowledgment of the existence and needs of the exceptional person was experienced by the nation. This awareness was fostered by parental pressures, returning servicemen's needs, professional enthusiasm, and the availability of public and private funding. These factors led to a reevaluation of procedures, research, and a new understanding of the handicapped and the role of institutions in their treatment, care, and training. By 1969, 190,000 handicapped individuals were housed in institutions (Cegelka & Prehm, 1982).

By the 1970s a new view of the dangers and inadequacies of institutions was recognized. The courts played a major role in bringing this realization to the fore. *Watt* v. *Stickney* (1972) affirmed mentally retarded persons' right to treatment. *Lessard* v. *Schmidt* (1972) ensured due process for institutionalized individuals. *Souder* v. *Brennan* (1973) outlawed involuntary servitude of institutionalized persons. The federal government also caused major reforms with the passage of Title XIX (Medicaid) provisions in 1971. These provisions brought institutions under the same controls and review processes as other service providers for the handicapped. A nationwide push to return handicapped individuals to the community was experienced. Deinstitutionalization became a social, fiscal, and moral goal within each of the states. Between the late 1960s and the early 1980s, the number of handicapped persons being served by public residential institutions declined by over 50,000. At the same time, staff-to-client ratios improved along with the physical quality of many institutions. During the 1980s and 1990s, nearly half of state-operated residential facilities for persons with mental retardation were closed in favor of movement to group homes and other less restrictive environments.

To facilitate the deinstitutionalization process, community-based alternatives were developed and expanded during the 1970s and 1980s. During the same period, a number of small institutions (less than 100 residents) were built. Small group homes, foster placements, semiindependent residences, and nursing homes were heavily relied on to handle individuals leaving institutional placements and as alternatives to initial placement in large residential institutions. Although anticipated, few of the older large institutions were closed and many of the handicapped stayed within those larger institutions. Changes in the nation's economic stability during the late 1970s and early 1980s also led to many difficulties in realizing the successful integration of the majority of handicapped persons into the community (Cegelka & Prehmn, 1982).

Current data concerning residential institutions for individuals with mental retardation reveal a clear picture of institutions in general throughout the United States. In summary, facilities with 15 or fewer residents increased over 500% from 1977 to 1982; they are continuing to increase. Each year in the recent past, 17% of residential facilities have closed or moved, displacing approximately 2.7% of all retarded individuals. The large institutions are far more stable. Within these institutions (generally exceeding 300 clients), the profoundly retarded make up the largest portion of residents. In public institutions, staff-to-client ratio is approximately 1.6 to 1. In these facilities, the direct-care staff ratio is .82 to 1 and the clinical staff ratio is .32 to 1. On the other hand, in community-based residential facilities, the functioning level of the individuals served is notably higher while at the same time staff ratios are notably lower (Hill et al., 1985; Eplle, Jacobson, & Janicki, 1985).

From this data, general conclusions may be drawn concerning the future of residential institutions. First, large residential facilities will continue to provide services for the handicapped. These institutions will serve increasingly involved persons. This will be done at an increased actual dollar cost per resident. Community-based residential programs will grow as alternative residential settings for handicapped individuals. These community-based programs will provide services to the majority of previously unserved handicapped individuals. Such settings will provide financially and morally appropriate residential services to a large percent of all handicapped individuals, thus reducing, but not eliminating, the need for the large residential institutions.

REFERENCES

Cegelka, P. T., & Prehm, H. J. (1982). *Mental retardation*. Columbus, OH: Merrill.

Eplle, W. A., Jacobson, J. W., & Janicki, M. R. (1985). Staffing ratios in public institutions for persons with mental retardation. *Mental Retardation, 23*, 115–124.

Giffth, R. G. (1985). Symposium: Residential institutions. *Mental Retardation, 23*, 105–106.

Hill, B. K, Bruininks, R. H., Lakin, K. C., Hauber, F. A., & McGuire, S. P. (1985). Stability of residential facilities for people who are mentally retarded 1977–82. *Mental Retardation, 23*, 108–114.

National Advisory Committee for the Handicapped. (1976). *The unfinished revolution: Education for the handicapped, 1976 annual report*. Washington, DC: U.S. Government Printing Office.

Wolfensberger, W. (1975). *The origin and nature of our institutional models*. Syracuse, NY: Human Policy.

ALAN HILTON
Seattle University

HISTORY OF SPECIAL EDUCATION
PHILOSOPHY OF EDUCATION FOR THE HANDICAPPED

RESOURCE ROOM

The resource room concept gained popularity following the *Hobsen* v. *Hansen* litigation, which declared tracking systems illegal and required reevaluation on a regular basis. This litigation was a forerunner for mainstreaming and the concept of least restrictive alternative (environment). This model of service delivery allows the handicapped child to remain in the educational mainstream as much as possible. With the passage of PL 94-142, and further emphasis on the least restrictive alternative, the resource room gained even further popularity. There are over 100,000 resource room teachers in the United States today. Professional special educators have consistently cited the importance of the resource room concept and have noted its viability as a promising alternative to placement in self-contained classes or regular classes without support services (Cartwright, Cartwright, & Ward, 1995; Fimian, Zaback, & D'Alonzo, 1983; Kasik, 1983; Learner,

1985; Marsh, Price, & Smith, 1983; Meyen, 1982; Reger, 1973; Sabatino, 1972; Sindelar & Deno, 1978; Wiederholdt, 1974).

Usually, students attending resource rooms are identified as mildly handicapped (4 to 6% of the total school population). Resource rooms are a widespread means of service delivery for the mildly handicapped, and are gaining acceptance for use with gifted exceptional children.

There are voluminous data available on the definition of resource rooms (Chaffin, 1974; Deno; 1973; Fox, et al. 1973; Hammil & Wiederholdt, 1972; Kasik, 1983; Lilly, 1971; Reger, 1972, 1973; Sabatino, 1972; Wiederholdt, 1974). According to Kasik (1983), a resource room is a place where special education students attend for less than 50% of their school day for support services. The student remains in the regular classroom for the majority of the academic instruction. The resource room is staffed by a resource room teacher. Attendance in the resource room is determined by a multidisciplinary staff according to the student's individual needs. Students are scheduled into specific time slots to attend the resource room, where they receive remedial instruction from a trained specialist in their deficit areas. A resource room should be well equipped with a wide variety of instructional materials. Individualized instruction may include perceptual training, language development, motor training, social and emotional development, and academic skills development. Resource room class size should be small. A recommended caseload per teacher would be no more than 20 students at any one time. Class sessions are either individual or in small groups of up to five students per session. They are a minimum of 20 minutes and a maximum of 45 minutes in length. The resource room should have the same comfortable characteristics of a regular classroom such as at least 150 square feet, adequate lighting, ventilation, and temperature control. The resource room should be easily accessible to teachers and students and possess adequate storage space for folders and materials. In general, the resource room should provide a positive learning environment.

Placement in the resource room is intended to be of short duration (Kasik, 1983). As students progress toward specified goals, they are returned to full-time placement in the regular classroom. Return to the regular classroom should progress through a gradual phasing out of support services. The resource room is to be considered as one type of service delivery within the continuum of services available.

REFERENCES

Cartwright, P., Cartwright, C., & Ward, M. (1995). *Educating special learners* (4th ed.). Boston: Wadsworth.

Chaffin, J. D. (1974). Will the real mainstreaming program please stand up! *Focus on Exceptional Children, 5*(6), 1–18.

D'Alonzo, B. (1983). *Educating adolescents with learning and behavior problems*. Rockville, MD: Aspen Systems.

Deno, E. (1973). *Instructional alternatives for exceptional children*. Reston, VA: Council For Exceptional Children.

Fox, W. L., Egnar, A. N., Polucci, P. E., Perelman, P. F., & McKenzie, H. S. (1972). An introduction to regular classroom approaches to special education. In E. Deno (Ed.), *Instructional alternatives for exceptional children*. Reston, VA: Council For Exceptional Children.

Hammill, D. D., & Wiederholdt, L. (1972). *The resource room: Rationale and implementation*. Ft. Washington, PA: Journal of Special Education Press.

Kasik, M. M. (1983). Analysis of the professional preparation of the resource room teacher. *Dissertation Abstracts International*. (University Microfilms International No. DAO 56766)

Learner, J. (1985). *Learning disabilities: Theories, diagnosis, and teaching strategies* (4th ed.). Boston: Houghton Mifflin.

Lilly, M. S. (1971). A training based model for special education. *Exceptional Children, 37*, 747–749.

Marsh, G. E., Price, B. J., & Smith, T. E. C. (1983). *Teaching mildly handicapped children: Methods and materials: A generic approach to comprehensive teaching*. St. Louis: Mosby.

McLaughlin, J. A., & Kelly, D. (1982). Issues facing the resource teacher. *Learning Disability Quarterly, 5*, 58–64.

Meyen, E. L. (1982). *Exceptional children and youth* (2nd ed.). Chicago: Love.

Reger, R. (1972). Resource rooms: Change agents or guardians of the status quo? *Journal of Special Education, 6*, 355–360.

Reger, R. (1973). What is a resource room program? *Journal of Learning Disabilities, 6*, 609–614.

Sabatino, D. A. (1972). Resource rooms: The renaissance in special education. *Journal of Special Education, 6*, 235–348.

Sindelar, P. T., & Deno, E. (1978). The effectiveness of resource room programming. *Journal of Special Education, 12*, 17–28.

Wiederholdt, J. L. (1974). Planning resource rooms for the mildly handicapped. *Focus on Exceptional Children, 5*(8), 1–10.

MARIBETH MONTGOMERY KASIK
Governors State University

CASCADE OF SERVICES
HOBSEN *v.* HANSEN
INCLUSION
LEAST RESTRICTIVE ENVIRONMENT
RESOURCE TEACHER
SELF-CONTAINED CLASSROOM

RESOURCE TEACHER

Much of the research literature calls for resource rooms to be staffed by highly trained special educators who are personable, demonstrate good human interactional skills, and are prepared professionally in the diagnosis and remediation of single or multiple groups of handicapped children.

Wallace and McLoughlin (1979) identify the resource teacher's main role as including assessment, instructional planning, teacher evaluation, and liaison-consultant duties. Learner (1985) describes the resource teacher as a highly trained professional who is capable of diagnosing the child, planning and implementing the teaching program, assisting the classroom teacher, providing continuous evaluation of the student, and conducting in-service sessions with other educators and the community. Sabatino (1981) states that the role of the resource teacher includes direct service to individuals and small groups of children, consultant services to classroom teachers, and responsibility for assessment and delivery of individualized programs. Kasik (1983) states that the resource teacher needs to be well organized, flexible, self-directed, and effective in time management. Paroz, Siegenthaler, and Tatum (1977) suggest that the resource teacher be actively involved with the total school community, including students and staff members. They add that the "teacher's role is open ended and limited only by time, talent, and acceptance of the teacher by the school administration and staff" (p. 15). The resource teacher is a trained specialist who works with, and acts as a consultant to, other teachers, providing materials and methods to help children who are having difficulties within the regular classroom. Usually, the resource teacher works with the mildly handicapped population in a centralized resource room where appropriate materials are housed.

Some of the most common responsibilities a resource teacher will probably be asked to undertake have been identified by Sabatino (1982). The resource teacher will conduct and participate in screening for children with learning disabilities, determine the nature of their learning, and prepare final reports for each referral. Instruction will be provided individually or in small groups. The resource teacher will prepare lessons for use when a child cannot function within the framework of the regular lesson. Students will participate in the resource room until they are integrated full time or until successful transition is complete. Schedules should include six or seven sessions daily, except on Fridays, which should be half a day. This allows the teacher to complete reports, observations, parent meetings, consultations, etc. Consultation with classroom teachers and other pupil services personnel should be consistent. The resource teacher should serve as a resource person and provide supportive assistance for all classroom teachers. Observation in the regular classroom and conferences with regular class teachers and parents about pupil progress should be continuous. In addition to meeting with teachers, the resource teacher may be required to prepare in-service materials and supervise the work of paraprofessionals and volunteers. Despite these suggestions, there is no consistency within the field regarding actual practice.

There are four different types of resource room teachers: (1) categorical, (2) noncategorical, (3) itinerant (or mobile), and (4) teacher-consultant. Categorical programs serve one specific population; noncategorical programs may serve one or more populations. The itinerant resource room teacher travels from one building to another and usually does not have an assigned room from which to work. The teacher-consultant resource room teacher provides consultation to regular class teachers, parents, and other service delivery personnel. Cartwright, Cartwright, and Ward (1995) provide a description of a typical day in the life of a resource teacher in today's schools.

REFERENCES

Cartwright, P., Cartwright, C., & Ward, M. (1995). *Educating special learners* (4th ed.). Boston: Wadsworth.

Kasik, M. M. (1983). Analysis of the professional preparation of the special education resource room teacher. *Dissertation Abstracts International*. (University Microfilms International No. DAO 56766)

Learner, J. (1985). *Learning disabilities: Theories, diagnosis, and teaching strategies* (4th ed.). Boston: Houghton Mifflin.

Paroz, J., Siegenthaler, L., & Tatum, V. (1977). A model for a middle school resource room. *Journal of Learning Disabilities, 8*, 7–15.

Sabatino, D. A. (1981). Overview for the practitioner in learning disabilities. In D. A. Sabatino, T. L. Miller, & C. R. Schmidt (Eds.), *Learning disabilities: Systemizing teaching and service delivery*. Rockville, MD: Aspen.

Sabatino, D. A. (1982). An educational program guide for secondary schools. In D. A. Sabatino & L. Mann (Eds.), *A handbook of diagnostic and prescriptive teaching*. Rockville, MD: Aspen Systems.

Wallace, G., & McLoughlin, J. A. (1979). *Learning disabilities: Concepts and characteristics* (2nd ed.). Columbus, OH: Merrill.

MARIBETH MONTGOMERY KASIK
Governors State University

**DIAGNOSTIC PRESCRIPTIVE TEACHING
RESOURCE ROOM**

RESPITE CARE

Respite care complements special education in providing support to families of handicapped children. Respite care may be defined as temporary care given to a disabled or otherwise dependent individual for the purpose of providing relief to the primary caregiver (Cohen & Warren, 1985). The concept of respite care is generally associated with intermittent services, although this term is also sometimes used to refer to regularly scheduled services occurring once or twice a week.

Respite care programs first appeared in the mid 1970s

in response to the deinstitutionalization movement. Deinstitutionalization meant that many families who would probably have placed their disabled children in institutions, either out of choice or as a result of professional advice, no longer had the option to do so. In addition, some children who had been placed in institutions in earlier years were being returned to their families. Thus a substantial number of parents now had to cope with the care needs of their severely handicapped children each day. The natural breaks that parents of nonhandicapped children experience when their children sleep at a friend's home, or visit with relatives, or go to camp were usually not available. It was virtually impossible to obtain paid babysitters and even relatives were reluctant to assume this responsibility. The primary caregiver, usually the mother, found it impossible to engage in normal activities such as shopping, caring for medical and dental needs, or seeing friends. Parents rarely had time for each other or for their other children. Families experienced severe problems in coping.

The cries of parents for help were heard by some professionals. Other parents, receiving no help from the service field, organized themselves and initiated respite care programs while continuing to bring their plight to the attention of service agencies. It was not until the late 1970s that professionals recognized the importance of respite care services. Parents were the primary advocates for these services prior to that time.

Respite care is a family-support service, designed to improve family functioning and help normalize families of the disabled. This service is of particular importance to families with weak natural support systems, poor coping skills, or strenuous care demands. Difficulty in care provision may reflect the severity of the behavioral problems or the extensiveness of the physical and health care needs of the disabled person. Primary caregivers use the relief provided through respite care services to rest, meet their own medical needs, improve relationships with other family members, and engage in some of the common personal or social activities that other adults are able to enjoy (e.g., visiting with a friend, taking a vacation, going shopping).

Models of respite care may vary along several dimensions such as where the service is provided, what the content/nature of the care is, who provides the care, how the service is administered, and how much time is allotted. The most important variation in models is whether services are provided in the home or in some other setting. In-home services are preferred by a majority of families. In-home services are economical and minimize the adjustments that must be made by the disabled individual and the family. These services may be of short duration, as when the parents go to a movie, or for a period of a week or two when parents take a vacation. In-home services may be provided by a sitter with only a few hours of training or by a homemaker/home health aide with substantial training.

About 40% of families experience a strong need to have their disabled members temporarily out of the home (Cohen & Warren, 1985). Out-of-home services may be provided on evenings, weekends, and holidays, or for continuous periods up to 30 days. These services may be provided in a respite care facility, in a residential facility that reserves some beds for temporary care, or in the home of the respite care provider. Services based in the home of the provider are personalized and economical. They can help expand the social/community experiences of the disabled child, and they allow for the development of an ongoing relationship between the provider family and the disabled child.

Babysitting and companionship are the major ingredients of respite care services that are of brief duration. Personal care and nursing care may be required when the client has severe physical or health problems. Social/recreational programming is usually a major component of longer respite care episodes.

Respite care services are often funded through state mental retardation/developmental disabilities agencies, with families obtaining services either directly through local offices of these agencies or through community programs supported by funds from these state sources. The provision of respite care services is uneven from state to state and from region to region within states. States that have made strong efforts to provide sufficient respite care services of good quality include Massachusetts, California, Washington, and most recently, Ohio. Funding problems remain the greatest impediment to the provision of adequate respite care services. In light of funding limitations, parent co-ops and volunteer models of respite care have become popular. Such programs are low in cost and are congruent with the zeitgeist of the 1980s that emphasizes self-help and alternatives to government provision.

REFERENCE

Cohen, S., & Warren, R. D. (1985). *Respite care: Principles, programs, and policies.* Austin, TX: Pro-Ed.

SHIRLEY COHEN
Hunter College

DEINSTITUTIONALIZATION

RESPONSE GENERALIZATION

Response generalization occurs when the effects of reinforcement or punishment of one response increase or decrease, respectively, functionally similar behaviors. Such generalization is an implicit goal of teaching because learning would be of little value if it affected only a specific response. Unfortunately, as Baer (1981) has emphasized, such generalization is not automatic and may be restricted in some handicapped children and adults, particularly retardates (Robinson & Robinson, 1976).

For generalization to occur, it may need to be trained explicitly. Techniques for training generalization may be found in Baer (1981) and Sulzer-Azeroff and Mayer (1977).

REFERENCES

Baer, D. M. (1981). *How to plan for generalization*. Lawrence, KA: H & H Enterprises.

Robinson, N. M., & Robinson, H. B. (1976). *The mentally retarded child* (2nd ed.). New York: McGraw-Hill.

Sulzer-Azeroff, B., & Mayer, G. R. (1977). *Applied behavior analysis procedures with children and youth*. New York: Holt, Rinehart, & Winston.

ROBERT T. BROWN
LISSEN SIMONSEN
University of North Carolina at Wilmington

GENERALIZATION
TRANSFER OF LEARNING

RESTRAINT

See PHYSICAL RESTRAINT.

RETARDATION

See CULTURAL-FAMILIAL RETARDATION; See MENTAL RETARDATION.

RETENTION IN GRADE

Retention in grade or nonpromotion has been an issue of interest to educators since the turn of the century. The first comprehensive study of pupil progress was done by Ayres (1909) in his book *Laggards in Our Schools*. Literally hundreds of articles and studies have argued the pros and cons of nonpromotion. Since 1975 the number of students retained in grade has been on the increase. A great deal of this increase appears to be related to the establishment of performance standards in skill subjects. In 1979 and 1980 about half of the first, second, and third graders in Washington, DC, were retained in a grade because they failed to meet the new reading and math standards.

The results of studies conducted over the years on retention have generally borne mixed results. The quality of those studies has also been suspect (Jackson, 1975). Jackson concluded that studies that compared promoted students with nonpromoted students were biased in favor of promotion because promoted students did better than those retained. Using a technique called meta-analysis, Holmes and Matthews (1984) analyzed 44 studies that compared retained students with those promoted. In 18 of the studies they found matched subject designs that used control factors such as IQ, achievement, socioeconomic status, sex, and grades. The studies they analyzed used a variety of dependent means to evaluate the effects of nonpromotion. Included were academic achievement, personal adjustment, self-concept, and attitude toward school. On all variables, nonpromotion resulted in negative effects. The average size of effect for all variables was −.38. This means that students who were promoted performed about one-third of a standard deviation better than those who were retained.

The results from variable to variable were surprisingly consistent. For academic achievement, the size of effect was .44, for personal adjustment it was .27, for self-concept .19, and for attitude toward school .16. All differences showed a more positive performance for students who were promoted than for those who were retained. The outcomes seem to demonstrate that the potential for negative effects far outweighs the benefits for nonpromotion. Based on the preceding evidence, there would need to be compelling evidence to warrant a retention decision. Simple retention in the absence of other planned supportive services produces negative consequences.

REFERENCES

Ayres, L. P. (1909). *Laggards in our schools*. New York: Russell Sage Foundation.

Holmes, C. T., & Matthews, K. M. (1984). The effects of nonpromotion in elementary and junior high school pupils: A meta-analysis. *Review of Educational Research, 54*(2), 225–236.

Jackson, G. B. (1975). The research evidence in the effect of grade retention. *Review of Educational Research, 45*, 438–460.

ROBERT A. SEDLAK
University of Wisconsin at Stout

DEVELOPMENTAL DELAYS
PREREFERRAL INTERVENTIONS
RESEARCH IN SPECIAL EDUCATION

RETICULAR ACTIVATING SYSTEM

The reticular activating system is the mass of cells in the brain stem associated with arousal, wakefulness, attention, and habituation. Its dysfunction may be associated with the hyperactivity and attention deficits often observed in brain-damaged children.

The major function of the reticular system is to provide for cortical activation via its connections through the diffuse thalamic projection system. If the reticular system is significantly impaired, as in severe head trauma, coma results. However, even with less severe impairment, wakefulness, perception (Livingston, 1967), or cognitive functions are attenuated. The second major function is through the posterior hypothalamus, an area that provides a similar activating influence on the limbic system (Feldman & Waller, 1962; Iwamura & Kawamura, 1962; Routtenberg, 1968).

Specific investigations of the dual arousal systems have revealed different functions of each. Damage to the reticular system attenuates its cortical activation effects but does not impair behavioral arousal. In contrast, damage to the posterior hypothalamus impairs arousal but cortical activation remains (Feldman & Waller, 1962; Kawamura, Nakamura, & Tokizane, 1961; Kawamura & Oshima, 1962). Because of their anatomical proximity and the neuronal interconnections between the posterior hypothalamus and the reticular system, it is likely that both systems will become impaired by injury or disease, although one system may be affected to a greater extent. This may account for some of the variability observed in brain-impaired children.

REFERENCES

Feldman, S., & Waller, H. (1962). Dissociation of electrocortical activation and behavioral arousal. *Nature, 196*, 1320.

Iwamura, G., & Kawamura, H. (1962). Activation pattern in lower level in the neo-, paleo-, archicortices. *Japanese Journal of Physiology, 11*, 494–505.

Kawamura, H., Nakamura, Y., & Tokizane, T. (1961). Effect of acute brain stem lesions on the electrical activities of the limbic system and neocortex. *Japanese Journal of Physiology, 11*, 564–575.

Kawamura, H., & Oshima, K. (1962). Effect of adrenaline on the hypothalamic activating system. *Japanese Journal of Physiology, 12*, 225–233.

Livingston, R. (1967). Brain in circuitry relating to complex behavior. In G. Quarton, T. Melnechuk, & Schmitt, F. (Eds.), *The neurosciences: A study program.* New York: Rockefeller University Press.

Routtenberg, A. (1968). The two arousal hypothesis: Reticular formation and limbic system. *Psychological Review, 75*, 51–80.

CHARLES J. LONG
GERI R. ALVIS
University of Tennessee
Memphis State University

ATTENTION DEFICIT DISORDER
BRAIN DAMAGE
HYPERKINESIS

RETINITIS PIGMENTOSA (RP)

Retinitis pigmentosa (RP) was first described in the mid 1800s. The term pigmentary retinal dystrophy is more accurate, as retinitis suggests an inflammation of the retina although none is present. The condition is often hereditary and characterized by a progressive deterioration of retinal photoreceptor cells and associated layers of pigment epithelium and choroid (Krill, 1972). Clinical features include spiculated clumping of pigment in association with retinal vessels, pallor (atrophy) of the optic disk and thinning of the retinal vessels. The condition is always bilateral in familial cases, but sporadic unilateral cases have been reported. Pigmentary changes typically become noticeable during the first decade of life, and begin as fine dots that gradually assume the spidery bone corpuscle appearance. Unusual pigmentary distributions may be noted, including central and sector defect patterns. The pigment flecks may be sparse or absent (i.e., RP *sine pigmenti*) (Tasman, 1971).

Three basic modes of inheritance are recognized: autosomal recessive, autosomal dominant, and sex linked. The recessive form is the most common, the sex linked form often the most disabling. Approximately 40% of patients reveal no hereditary pattern. Ocular associations include posterior polar cataract, glaucoma, myopia, and keratoconus. Extraocular associations include deafness and neurologic and endrocrine abnormalities such as oligophrenia, ophthalmoplegia, sphingolipidoses, Friedreich's ataxia, amyotrophic lateral sclerosis (Lou Gehrig's disease), and progressive muscular atrophy. Perhaps the best known syndrome in the differential diagnosis of RP is that of Laurence-Moon-Biedl, encompassing mental retardation, hypogenitalism, polydactyly, shoulder and hip girdle obesity, retinal changes, and a recessive inheritance pattern. Less common RP syndromes include Refsum's (polyneuritis, cerebellar ataxia, atypical pigmentary degeneration, cardiac anomalies, paresis of the lower extremities, and autosomal recessive pattern) and Bassen and Kornzweig's (spinocerebella degeneration, low blood cholesterol, celiac disease, and beta-lipoprotein deficiency). Hallgren's and Cockayne's syndromes are autosomal recessive disorders associated with RP and deafness; Hallgren's with cerebellar ataxia and Cockayne's a progeria-like dwarfism (Walsh & Hoyt, 1969).

Attempts at treatment have been disappointing. Current theory suggests the disease represents an abnormal sensitivity to light, with light being the agent leading to retinal photoreceptor degeneration. Occlusion of one eye, in an attempt to slow the progress of the disease, has been attempted with equivocal results. Injections of extracts from placental tissues have been tried in the past with no effect.

This disease tends not to affect school performance until late in its course. Clues for educators may include walking into objects (constricted or "gun-barrel" visual field defects), night blindness, and other defects such as hearing loss and degenerative central nervous system disease. Constriction of the visual field may make location of material on a chalkboard difficult. Braille instruction is typically ineffective unless no useful vision is present.

REFERENCES

Krill, A. E. (1972). *Hereditary retinal and choroidal diseases.* Hagerstown, MD: Harper & Row.

Tasman, W. (1971). *Retinal diseases in children.* New York: Harper & Row.

Walsh, F. B., & Hoyt, W. F. (1969). *Clinical neuro-ophthalmology.* Baltimore: MD: Williams & Wilkins.

GEORGE R. BEAUCHAMP
Cleveland Clinic Foundation

RETROLENTAL FIBROPLASIA (RLF)

Retrolental fibroplasia (RLF) was first recognized in the early 1940s, with the first literature description published in 1942. Over the ensuing decade, many unrelated and sometimes conflicting etiologies for the disease were considered. Among these were water miscible vitamins, iron, oxygen, cow's milk, and abnormal electrolytes, all of which have been shown in positive association to the incidence of RLF. Experimental evidence implicated vitamin E deficiency as a possible cause. Other factors that have been associated with RLF are viral infections, hormonal imbalances, premature exposure of infant eyes to light, and vitamin A deficiency in the mother. The observation that the incidence of the disease increases in direct relation to the duration and exposure of premature infants to oxygen was reported first in 1952. A controlled study was completed in 1954; it established oxygen as the most likely etiologic agent for the condition. The rise of this disease, called by some an epidemic, closely parallels the development of the ability to effectively concentrate oxygen administration to infants in incubators (Silverman, 1980).

The importance of oxygen concentration monitoring became apparent as experimental evidence of the early 1950s accumulated. Ambient oxygen levels were limited whenever possible to 40%, and measurements of oxygen concentration in the blood were made. This did not entirely resolve the issue for several reasons: the disease occurred in the absence of supplemental oxygen therapy; it occurred when 40% oxygen was administered "appropriately"; and this level of supplemental oxygen often was not sufficient to relieve the respiratory distress syndrome that often accompanies prematurity. The important relationship between arterial blood oxygen (PO^2), the respiratory distress syndrome, and retrolental fibroplasia is now well established. However, numerous attempts to monitor and control arterial blood oxygen (PO^2) have been fraught with great difficulties, both technical and physiologic.

Approximately 10% of infants under 2500 g birth weight are afflicted with the respiratory distress syndrome, accounting for approximately 40,000 infants per year in the United States; the incidence of RLF blindness following oxygen administration is a small percentage of the group, perhaps 2%. Recognizing this, many authors now designate this disease retinopathy of prematurity (ROP).

An appreciation of the clinical stages of the disease accompanied experimental evidence concerning its pathophysiology. Evidence suggests that high arterial oxygen levels cause vasospastic constriction of developing peripheral retinal vasculature, inciting the elaboration of vasoproliferative factors. New vessels grow in a mound-like elevation, typically in the temporal peripheral retina (Tasman, 1971). Such neovascularization either may proceed or spontaneously regress. With resolution of the active process, cicatrization (scarring) occurs, which on contraction may drag the retina temporally. If traction is sufficient, peripheral retinal detachment occurs. When the entire retina becomes detached and drawn into a fibrous cicatrix (scar) behind the lens, the disease has reached its most advanced stage, representing the clinical picture for which the disease was named. Additional ocular sequelae include myopia; vitreous opacification; and a variety of retinal changes, including chorioretinal atrophy, pigmentary retinopathy, and retinal folds. Based on these observations, clinical characterization of the disease recently has been reviewed and a proposed international classification published.

The relationship of oxygen therapy to neurological outcome also was studied. In general, neurologic outcome is inversely related to ocular outcome; that is, spastic diplegia incidence falls and retrolental fibroplasia rises with increased duration of oxygen treatment. Thus, there is a desire to prevent neurologic events following cyanotic attacks (secondary to cardiorespiratory insufficiency) by extending treatment with oxygen; this then increases the risk of RLF.

The full spectrum of consequences of RLF blindness to the child, family, social agencies, school, and community is beginning to be fully considered. Affected individuals tend not to see loss of sight as a major burden. Preconceptions, paternalism, and insensitivity of authorities in the visually oriented world often constrict the lives of those who wish to see this same world nonvisually. A number of factors—medical, legal, and societal—tend to perpetuate the stereotype that the blind wish to shed in their desire to move toward independence. Thus the complexity of this disease at several levels—visual, neurological, personal, and social—is only now being appreciated.

The visually disabling forms of RLF may impact on school performance by limiting sensory input, the degree of disability reflecting the severity of disease. Teachers may observe "blindness" where disability is severe. When bilateral retinal blindness is present, braille instruction is required. The educator should be aware of the complexity of problems for individuals with this condition.

REFERENCES

Silverman, W. A. (1980). *Retrolental fibroplasia: A modern parable*. New York: Grune & Stratton.

Tasman, W. (Ed.). (1971). *Retinal diseases in children*. New York: Harper & Row.

GEORGE R. BEAUCHAMP
Cleveland Clinic Foundation

RETT SYNDROME

Rett Syndrome (RS) is a disorder that initially appears as a deterioration from apparently normal development in infancy or early childhood. It involves a slowdown in normal development, deceleration of head growth, disinterest in the environment, deterioration of motor functioning, loss of hand use and subsequently locomotion, hand stereotypies (typically hand wringing or clapping), loss of expressive language, autistic and self-abusive behavior, and eventual severe/profound mental retardation. Prevalence estimates vary. Hagberg (1995b) recently has revised the estimate of prevalence of classic RS from 1:10,000 females to closer to 1:15,000. Cases have been reported in all parts of the world and in all ethnic groups (e.g., Moser & Naidu, 1991; Naidu, 1997). First described by Andreas Rett (1965), it initially came to the world's attention largely through the work of Hagberg and his associates (Hagberg, Aicardi, Dias, & Ramos, 1983).

Unique to RS is apparently normal initial development followed by rapid mental and physical deterioration followed by stabilization or even reduction in some symptoms (e.g., Budden, 1997; Hagberg, 1995b). Unusual in other ways, RS (a) apparently affects only women, whereas most gender-specific disorders affect only men; (b) is manifested in part through loss of acquired function, but is apparently neurodevelopmental and not neurogenerative (e.g., Glaze, 1995); (c) presents in a fairly striking set of behavioral symptoms that have consistent developmental trends; and (d) is almost undoubtedly genetically-based, but no marker has been identified. Although the subject of hundreds of articles, it is still relatively unknown in comparison to many other developmental disorders of comparable prevalence. As would be expected, research on the genetic basis focuses on an X-chromosome abnormality. RS is associated with numerous neuroanatomical and neurochemical distur-

bances, summaries of which can be found in Brown and Hoadley (in press), Budden (1997), Hagberg, (1996), or Percy (1996).

Diagnostic Symptoms: Classic RS and RS Variant

Necessary for diagnosis of Classic RS is apparently normal pre-, peri, and early postnatal development followed in infancy or early childhood by sudden deceleration of head growth and loss of acquired skills, including hand use and language (Rett Syndrome Diagnostic Criteria Work Group, 1988). Also required is evidence of mental retardation and the appearance of intense and persistent hand stereotypies: "The almost continuous repetitive wringing, twisting or clapping hand automatisms during wakefulness constitute the hallmark of the condition" (Hagberg, 1995b, p. 973). Girls who had developed walking must show gait abnormalities; some never develop walking. EEG abnormalities, seizure disorder, spasticity, marked scoliosis, and overall growth retardation are also typical. A number of other behaviors may also be shown, including episodic hyperventilation and breath-holding, bloating owing to air swallowing, bruxism, hypoplastic cold red-blue feet, scoliosis, and night laughing (Hagberg, 1995a).

The RS variant model was developed owing to the realization that females with RS are much more heterogeneous than originally thought (Hagberg, 1995a, b). Diagnosis of RS variant should be made only in girls of 10 years or older age when a subset of the symptoms for Classic RS have been met. These behaviors may appear throughout childhood. Typically, girls who meet the criteria for RS variant show less severe symptoms than those associated with classic RS. Both gross and fine motor control may be spared and mental retardation is less severe. RS variant girls may retain some language, although it tends to be abnormal and telegraphic. Those with language tend to have had a later and milder regression period.

For both parents and therapists, diagnosis should be made as early as possible. Some physicians may be reluctant to diagnose RS early owing to the eventual severity of the disorder, but many parents are frustrated by the lack of a diagnosis that fits their children's behaviors or has implications for treatment and care (Brown & Hoadley, in press). For that reason, the term "potential RS" (Hagberg, 1995b) has been suggested for use with young cases. RS may be confused with a number of other disorders, particularly autism, so careful diagnosis is necessary.

Developmental Trend

Most girls with classic RS develop through a fairly reliable four-stage sequence of behavioral and physical changes first described by Hagberg and Witt-Engerström (1986). Age of onset, duration of transition from one stage to another, and duration of each is highly variable, however. Except as specifically referenced, information in this section comes from Budden (1997), Hagberg (1995b), Hagberg and Witt-Engerström (1986), and Naidu (1997).

Pre-Stage 1: Early Development

Much pre-Stage 1 development appears normal until at least 5–6 months of age. Early motor skills appear, including reaching for objects. Self-feeding commonly develops, with infants weaning onto solid foods. Many children develop walking, but often with an unusual gait. However, appearance of many infant developmental milestones is delayed or absent. Some slowing of brain growth may be seen in unusually low occipito-frontal circumference as early as two months of age. Many girls develop single-word communication and a few use short phrases.

Stage 1: Early Onset Stagnation

The first stage begins from six to 18 months of age and may last from weeks to months. In many ways the infant appears to hit a developmental wall. Many aspects of cognitive development cease. A deceleration of head growth leads to head circumference generally below average by the end of the second year of life. Hypotonia, disinterest in play and the environment, and loss of acquired hand functions and random hand movements are typical. No obvious pattern of abnormalities is apparent, however.

Stage 2: Rapid Developmental Regression

Between one and three or four years of age, functioning begins to deteriorate so generally and rapidly that the onset may be taken for a toxic or encephalitic state (Hagberg & Witt-Engerström, 1986). Further, Budden (1997, p. 2) reports that the onset "may be so acute that parents can sometimes give a specific date after which their child was no longer 'normal.'" General cognitive functioning, purposeful hand use, and expressive language deteriorate. The classic hand stereotypies, including hand wringing, washing, and mouthing, typically appear and may be continuous during waking hours. Walking may deteriorate or not develop. Gait abnormalities, particularly a spread-legged stance, are generally evident in girls who can walk. Hyperventilation and breath-holding are common, as are behaviors characteristic of autism. Seizures and vacant spells resembling seizures may occur, and virtually all RS girls have abnormal EEGs.

Stage 3: Pseudostationary

Stage 3 has a highly variable age of onset, occurring at the end of the rapid deterioration, and lasts until about 10 years of age. Hand stereotypies continue, and mobility may further deteriorate. Mental retardation in the se-

vere/profound range is characteristic. On the other hand, autistic symptoms may diminish, and social interactions, hand use, communication, alertness, and self-initiated behavior may increase. Tremulousness, ataxia, teeth grinding (bruxism), hyperventilation or breath-holding, and seizures are common. Overall rigidity is likely to increase and scoliosis to appear. Nonverbal communication through eye pointing may improve.

Stage 4: Late Motor Deterioration

After about age 10 years, motor function decreases further with increased rigidity, scoliosis, and muscle wasting. Mobility continues to decrease; many girls will be wheelchair-bound. Hands may be held in mouth for long periods. Expressive language, if previously present, generally disappears, and receptive language is decreased. Eye pointing as communication may continue. Chewing and swallowing may be lost, necessitating artificial feeding. However, the final phenotypic characteristics of classic RS cases vary widely. Life span varies, but overall longevity is shorter than normal (Naidu, 1997).

Overall Intellectual Characteristics

Formal assessments indicate that RS girls function at a severe/profound level of mental retardation, but their actual cognitive functioning may be difficult to assess owing to motor and language impairments. For a group of RS girls with a mean age of 9.4 years, Perry, Sarlo-McGarvey, and Haddad (1991) reported Vineland Adaptive Behavior Scale (VABS) scores, based on potentially-biased interviews with parents, of: Communication, mean 17.4 months; Daily living skills, mean 16.9; and Socialization, mean 25.9 months. Mean mental age on the Cattell Infant Intelligence was 3.0 months. Most girls attended to visual and auditory stimuli, were interested in toys, and anticipated being fed. Only one appeared to have object permanence, and none succeeded on items requiring language or fine motor skills. The girls attended when spoken to and showed some understanding, but most did not speak or have any other communication system. Most could feed themselves, some with their fingers, and some could use a cup. Most were in diapers, and did not perform other self-care tasks. They showed some interest in other people and could discriminate among them, but showed virtually no play behaviors.

Overall Emotional Characteristics

RS girls show a variety of emotional and behavioral problems. The following information is from a survey of parents by Sansom, Krishnan, Corbett, and Kerr (1993) when the girls' mean age was 10.6 years. Over 75% showed anxiety, particularly in response to external situations. Most episodes were brief, and consisted of screaming, hyperventilation, self-injury, frightened expression, and general distress. Precipitating events included novel situations and people, sudden noises, some music, change of routine, and high activity by others close to the child. Low mood, reflected partly in crying, occurred in 70%, but for extended periods in only a few. Almost 50% showed self-injurious behaviors (SIBs). Most were relatively mild, such as biting fingers or hands, but more serious chewing of fingers, head banging, and hair-pulling also occurred. Epilepsy was reported in 63%. Although most slept well, early wakening and nighttime laughing, crying, and screaming were common.

Treatment and Management

No completely effective treatment regime is available, and the symptoms appear to follow an inexorable course. However, active intervention may delay the appearance of some symptoms and alleviate others (Glaze, 1995). RS girls typically have very long latencies to respond to directions, an important consideration in all aspects of therapy. Delay to respond may be as long as a minute. Accurate diagnosis is important both to ensure appropriate treatment and to avoid ineffective treatment. For example, three RS girls who had initially been diagnosed with autism have inadvertently been participants in Lovaas's intensive behavior modification program which has been demonstrably effective with autistic children (Smith, Klevstrand, & Lovaas, 1995.). Overall, the girls showed few if any changes that might not have occurred without treatment. Individual differences in the degree of various impairments and responsiveness to, as well as tolerance of, various interventions necessitate individualized treatment programs (e.g., Van Acker, 1991). Owing to the multiplicity and diversity of problems associated with RS, a team approach is indicated.

Specialized behavior modification programs have been successful on a variety of behaviors in RS girls of different ages. Techniques such as shaping, graduated guidance, and hand regulation have increased self-feeding and ambulation in RS girls (e.g., Bat-Haee, 1994). Use of mechanical and computer-based adaptive devices may also modify RS girls' behavior, enabling them to communicate and discriminate between such things as favored and nonfavored foods (e.g., Van Acker & Grant, 1995). One caution must be expressed, however, about the routine implementation of some of these programs, particularly by parents. Much effort, persistence, and tolerance for frustration are required, since improvement can be slow and even difficult to see. Indeed, Piazza et al. (1993) suggest that parents be warned about the effort involved and the need to keep careful response records in order to see progress.

As apraxia is one of the main effects of RS, physical therapy is critical. It helps RS girls to maintain or reac-

quire ambulation and to develop or maintain transitional behaviors needed to stand up from sitting or lying positions. The stereotypic hand movements are involuntary, so behavior modification techniques designed to reduce them will likely not only be ineffective, but may actually increase the movements by increasing anxiety. Several techniques, including restraints that prevent hand-to-mouth movements or simply holding the girl's hand may be effective. Generally, whirlpool baths may be helpful. Some of the stereotyped hand clasping and other movements may be reduced by allowing the girl to hold a favored toy (Hanks, 1990).

Most RS girls begin to develop scoliosis before age eight, and many also show kyphosis (hunchback) (Huang, Lubicky, & Hammerberg, 1994). The disorders are basically neurogenic, but exacerbated by other factors such as loss of transitional motor skills and spatial perceptual orientation, postural misalignment, and rigidity (Budden, 1997). Physical therapy and careful positioning in seated positions may help slow the development of scoliosis, but corrective surgery is often required.

Although showing strong appetites, most RS girls show serious growth retardation to the point of meeting criteria for moderate to severe malnutrition. Chewing and swallowing problems, as well as gastroesophageal reflux and digestive problems, contribute to the retardation. Speech therapy may be helpful not so much for retaining language as for facilitating chewing and swallowing. Supplementary tube feedings may be necessary to help increase growth (Glaze & Schultz, 1997). Further complicating feeding issues, constipation is common in RS. Although generally controllable through diet, laxatives or enemas may be necessary in some cases.

Seizures occur in most RS girls, and their control "is perhaps the most common problem facing the primary care provider or the treating neurologist" (Budden, 1997, p. 7). Seizures occur most commonly in Stage III (Glaze & Schultz, 1997). Most seizures can be controlled with antiseizure medication, most frequently carbamazepine and/or valproic acid. Occasionally, in otherwise intractable cases, the ketogenic diet may be used (Budden, 1997), although it presents its own management problems.

Agitation, screaming, and tantrums are frequently reported. The rapid neurologic and physical changes associated with the onset of the disease may understandably provoke emotional outbursts. RS girls frequently respond negatively to stimulus or routine change, so transitions from one setting or pattern to another should be gradual and accompanied by a parent if possible. Agitation or screaming may also reflect pain or irritation from a physical condition that in the absence of language or gestures RS individuals may have no other way to signal. Since the girls go through puberty, caretakers need to be sensitive to their menstrual cycles. Some agitation in older individuals may reflect premenstrual discomfort or some other gynecologic disorder which may be easily treatable (Budden, 1997). A variety of treatment approaches have been used; behavior modification may be helpful.

Owing to the lifelong impact of the disorder on parents and other family members, ranging from home care issues to decisions about educational and other placement, counseling for the family will be particularly important (Lieb-Lundell, 1988). Training of the parents in behavior modification may be helpful in managing some aspects of their RS daughter's behavior, including tantrums. Of importance, given the degree of care that RS adults may require and their relative longevity, parents will eventually need to face the issue of lifelong care and make financial arrangements for care of the woman after their death.

REFERENCES

Bat-Haee, M. A. (1994). Behavioral training of a young woman with Rett syndrome. *Perceptual and Motor Skills, 78,* 314.

Brown, R. T., & Hoadley, S. L. (in press). Rett syndrome. In S. Goldstein & C. R. Reynolds (Eds.). *Handbook of Neurodevelopmental and Genetic Disorders of Children,* (pp. 459–477). New York: Guilford Press.

Budden, S. S. (1997). Understanding, recognizing, and treating Rett syndrome. *Medscape Women's Health, 2*(3), 1–11. http://www.medscape.com/Medscape/WomensHealth/journal/1997/v2.n03/w3185.budden.html

Glaze, D. G., & Schultz, R. J. (1997). Rett syndrome: Meeting the challenge of this gender-specific neurodevelopmental disorder. *Medscape Women's Health, 2*(1), 1–9. http://www.medscape.com/Medscape/WomensHealth/journal/1997/v2.n01/w223.glaze.html

Hagberg, B. (1995a). Clinical delineation of Rett syndrome variants. *Neuropediatrics, 26,* 62.

Hagberg, B. (1995b). Rett syndrome: Clinical peculiarities and biological mysteries. *Acta Paediatrica, 84,* 971–976.

Hagberg, B. (1996). Rett syndrome: Recent clinical and biological aspects. In A. Arzimanoglou & F. Goutières (Eds.), *Trends in child neurology,* (pp. 143–146). Paris: John Libby Eurotext.

Hagberg, B., Aicardi, J., Dias, K., & Ramos, O. (1983). A progressive syndrome of autism, dementia, ataxia, and loss of purposeful hand use in girls: Rett's syndrome: report of 35 cases. *Annals of Neurology, 14,* 471–479.

Hagberg, B., & Witt-Engerström, I. (1986). Rett syndrome: A suggested staging system for describing impairment profile with increasing age toward adolescence. *American Journal of Medical Genetics, 24*(Suppl. 1), 47–59.

Hanks, S. (1990). Motor disabilities in the Rett syndrome and physical therapy strategies. *Brain and Development, 12,* 157–161.

Huang, T-J., Lubicky, J. P., & Hammerberg, K. W. (1994). Scoliosis in Rett syndrome. *Orthopaedic Review, 23,* 931–937.

Lieb-Lundell, C. (1988). The therapist's role in the management of girls with Rett syndrome. *Journal of Child Neurology* (3 supplement), S31–S34.

Moser, H. W., & Naidu, S. (1991). The discovery and study of Rett syndrome. In A. J. Capute & P. J. Accardo (Eds.), *Developmental disabilities in infancy childhood* (pp. 325–333). Baltimore: Brookes.

Naidu, S. (1997). Rett syndrome: A disorder affecting early brain growth. *Annals of Neurology, 42,* 3–10.

Percy, A. K. (1996). Rett syndrome: The evolving picture of a disorder of brain development. *Developmental Brain Dysfunction, 9,* 180–196.

Perry, A., Sarlo-McGarvey, & Haddad, C. (1991). Brief reports: Cognitive and adaptive functioning in 28 girls with Rett syndrome. *Journal of Autism and Developmental Disabilities, 21,* 551–556.

Piazza, C. C., Anderson, C., & Fisher, W. (1993). Teaching self-feeding skills to patients with Rett syndrome. *Developmental Medicine and Child Neurology, 35,* 991–996.

Rett, A. (1966). Uber ein eigenartiges Hirnatrophisches Syndrom bei Hyperammonamie im Kindes alter. [On an unusual brain atropic syndrome with hyperammonia in childhood] *Wiener Medizinische Wochenschrift, 116,* 425–428. (As cited in Moser & Naidu, 1991, and Rett Syndrome Diagnostic Criteria Work Group, 1988.)

Rett Syndrome Diagnostic Criteria Work Group. (1988). Diagnostic criteria for Rett syndrome. *Annals of Neurology, 23,* 425–428.

Sansom, D., Krishnan, V. H. R., Corbett, J., & Kerr, A. (1993). Emotional and behavioural aspects of Rett syndrome. *Developmental Medicine and Child Neurology, 35,* 340–345.

Smith, T., Klevstrand, M., & Lovaas, O. I. (1995). Behavioral treatment of Rett's disorder: ineffectiveness in three cases. *American Journal of Mental Retardation, 100,* 317–322.

Van Acker, R. (1991). Rett syndrome: A review of current knowledge. *Journal of Autism and Developmental Disabilities, 21,* 381–406.

Van Acker, R., & Grant, S. H. (1995). An effective-computer-based requesting system for persons with Rett syndrome. *Journal of Childhood Communication Disorders, 16,* 31–38.

ROBERT T. BROWN
University of North Carolina at Wilmington

REVERSALS IN READING AND WRITING

The term reversals is usually associated with reading or writing disabilities. Reversals are difficulties characterized in either reading or writing by reversing letters, numbers, words, or phrases (e.g., *saw for was, p* for *q*), or what some have referred to as mirror reading or writing.

In Orton's first theoretical papers on reading disabilities (1925, 1928), he suggested that such reversal problems were due to poorly established hemispheric dominance. Orton (1928) cited the following examples of strephosymbolia (literally, twisted symbols): (1) difficulty discriminating *b* and *d*; (2) confusion with words like *ton* and *not*; (3) ability to read from mirror images; and (4) facility at writing mirrorlike images. Orton further stipulated that these reversal problems were not caused by mental retardation. Other investigators have since promoted the concept of developmental lag in perceptual abilities as causally related to reading disorders (Bender, 1957; Fernald, 1943).

As a result of this initial work, a variety of programs were developed that attempted to remediate reading disabilities by treating perceptual problems (Forness, 1981). For example, Kephart (1960) focused on the use of motor activities for developing perceptual skills. Additionally, programs such as Barsch's (1965) movigenic curriculum and Delacato's (1966) patterning techniques promoted the evolutionary progression that was seen as a necessary prerequisite for complete perceptual development. Frostig and Horne (1964) developed a visual perceptual program to remediate these difficulties, while Gillingham and Stillman (1960) prescribed the language triangle approach of combining the visual, auditory, and kinesthetic modes for teaching reading and writing.

Empirical support that reversals are due to perceptual deficits has been equivocal. It has been seen that many beginning readers reverse letters and words (Gibson & Levin, 1980). In fact, more than one half of all kindergarten students typically reverse letters (Gibson & Levin, 1980). This is considered a part of the normal component of discrimination learning when children first acquire reading skills. Gibson and Levin (1980) cite research that indicates that normal children continue to make reversal errors until the age of eight or nine. It was also found that single letter reversals account for only a small percent of total reading errors exhibited by poor readers. In addition, it has been questioned whether such reversals in learning-disabled students indicate underlying perceptual problems rather than, for example, linguistic problems (Gupta, Ceci, & Slater, 1978).

Remedial programs based on visual motor perceptual training generally have not resulted in reading improvement (Keogh, 1974). Later research efforts have suggested that reversal problems can be remediated with the use of behavioral techniques. Hasazi and Hasazi (1972) reported an instance in which digit reversals (e.g., 12 for 21) of an 8-year-old boy were remediated by means of contingent teacher attention. With respect to letter reversals, Carnine (1981) provided evidence that discriminations that reflect differences in spatial orientation only (e.g., *b, d*) are best taught singly. In other words, a student should be taught to discriminate *b* from nonreversible letters first, followed by the separate introduction of the letter *d*. Some specific instructional techniques are provided by Hallahan, Kauffman, and Lloyd (1985).

REFERENCES

Barsch, R. H. (1965). *A movigenic curriculum* (Publication No. 25). Madison, WI: Wisconsin State Department of Instruction.

Bender, L. A. (1957). Specific reading disability as a maturational lag. *Bulletin of the Orton Society, 7,* 9–18.

Carnine, D. W. (1981). Reducing training problems associated with visually and auditorily similar correspondences. *Journal of Learning Disabilities, 14,* 276–279.

Delacato, C. H. (1966). *Neurological organization and reading.* Springfield, IL: Thomas.

Fernald, G. (1943). *Remedial techniques in basic school subjects.* New York: McGraw-Hill.

Forness, S. R. (1981). *Recent concepts in dyslexia: Implications for diagnosis and remediation.* Reston, VA: Council for Exceptional Children.

Frostig, M., & Horne, D. (1964). *The Frostig program for the development of visual perception: Teacher's guide.* Chicago: Follett.

Gibson, E. J., & Levin, H. (1980). *The psychology of reading.* Cambridge, MA: MIT Press.

Gillingham, A., & Stillman, B. W. (1960). *Remedial training for children with specific disability in reading, spelling, and penmanship.* Cambridge, MA: Educator's.

Gupta, R., Ceci, S. J., & Slater, A. M. (1978). Visual discrimination in good and poor readers. *Journal of Special Education, 12,* 409–416.

Hallahan, D. P., Kauffman, J. M., & Lloyd, J. W. (1985). *Introduction to learning disabilities* (2nd ed.). Englewood Cliffs, NJ: Prentice-Hall.

Hasazi, J. E., & Hasazi, S. E. (1972). Effects of teacher attention on digit-reversal behavior in an elementary school child. *Journal of Applied Behavior Analysis, 5,* 157–162.

Keogh, B. K. (1974). Optometric vision training programs for children with learning disabilities: Review of issues and research. *Journal of Learning Disabilities, 7,* 219–231.

Kephart, N. C. (1960). The slow learner in the classroom. Columbus, OH: Merrill.

Orton, S. T. (1925). Word-blindness in school children. *Archives of Neurology and Psychiatry, 14,* 581–615.

Orton, S. T. (1928). Specific reading disability-strephosymbolia. *Journal of the American Medical Association, 90,* 1095–1099.

THOMAS E. SCRUGGS
MARGO A. MASTROPIERI
Purdue University

AGRAPHIA
DYSGRAPHIA
HANDWRITING
REMEDIATION, DEFICIT-CENTERED MODELS OF

REVERSE MAINSTREAMING

Reverse mainstreaming is a procedure that involves introducing nonhandicapped students into special classrooms to work with severely handicapped students. The purpose is to maximize integration of severely handicapped and nonhandicapped students. Mainstreaming, a more familiar concept, refers to the integration of the handicapped into the nonhandicapped classroom to enable each individual to participate in patterns of everyday life that are close to the mainstream. Reverse mainstreaming is, as the name suggests, a procedure carried out in reverse of mainstreaming but striving for the same goals. Reverse mainstreaming can be used with all severe handicaps.

The primary use of reverse mainstreaming has been with the severely and profoundly mentally handicapped and the autistic. Until the early 1970s these severely handicapped students were educated in segregated environments that had only handicapped individuals. These environments included institutions and special education schools. Mildly mentally handicapped students, on the other hand, were more likely to be educated in closer proximity to nonhandicapped peers.

There has been widespread acceptance in the past 15 years of the philosophy of normalization. This philosophy implies that the handicapped should be able to live as similarly as possible to the nonhandicapped. Public Law 94-142, adopted in 1978, required that the handicapped be educated as similarly as possible to the nonhandicapped. For the mildly mentally handicapped, this has resulted in considerable integration into nonhandicapped classrooms. For the severely mentally handicapped, this has meant placement in buildings occupied by the nonhandicapped. It is frequently unrealistic to expect the severely mentally handicapped to participate in regular classrooms because of their low functioning levels and special needs. In these cases, in order to maximize interactions, special educators arrange for nonhandicapped students to participate in the classrooms of the handicapped as volunteers, or "peers"; hence, mainstreaming in reverse.

The implementation of reverse mainstreaming requires cooperation and communication between teachers of the handicapped and the nonhandicapped. They must work together to prepare the nonhandicapped "peers" who will participate. Poorman (1980), who started Project Special Friend in a central Pennsylvania community, recommends using slides of the handicapped children followed by discussions about their characteristics and behaviors and about the role of the peers. Topics include communication skills, handicaps, realistic expectations, and dealing with inappropriate behaviors. Opportunities should be provided for the nonhandicapped students to interact in a social way with their special friends.

Poorman (1980) outlines a sequential program, moving from introductions through free play activities to instructional activities in the reverse mainstreaming setting. Almond, Rodgers, and Krug (1979) provide a detailed presentation of techniques for training peer volunteers to work with severely handicapped autistic students. The volunteers initiate individualized educational programs on a one-to-one basis under the supervision of special educators. They participate in the classroom of the severely handicapped on a weekly schedule. Donder and Nietupski (1981) describe how reverse mainstreaming can be implemented to maximize social integration on the playground.

In all these instances, nonhandicapped students are introduced into the classroom and playground environment of the severely handicapped in order to maximize interactions between the handicapped and the nonhandicapped. This procedure has been shown to lead to increased learning of preacademic skills and socially appropriate behavior by the handicapped. It also contributes to greater acceptance of the handicapped by their nonhandicapped peers. While sharing goals and accomplishments with mainstreaming, the procedure is still mainstreaming in reverse—bringing the mainstream into the classrooms and the lives of the severely handicapped.

REFERENCES

Almond, P., Rodgers, S., & Krug, D. (1979). A model for including elementary students in the severely handicapped classroom. *Teaching Exceptional Children, 11*, 135–139.

Donder, D., & Nietupski, J. (1981). Nonhandicapped adolescents teaching playground skills to their mentally retarded peers: Toward a less restrictive middle school environment. *Education & Training of the Mentally Retarded, 16*, 270–276.

Poorman, C. (1980). Mainstreaming in reverse with a special friend. *Teaching Exceptional Children, 12*, 136–142.

NANCY L. HUTCHINSON
BERNICE Y. L. WONG
Simon Fraser University

INCLUSION
LEAST RESTRICTIVE ENVIRONMENT
MAINSTREAMING
PEER RELATIONSHIPS

REVISED CHILDREN'S MANIFEST ANXIETY SCALE (RCMAS)

See CHILDREN'S MANIFEST ANXIETY SCALE.

REVISUALIZATION

Revisualization has been defined as the active recall of the visual image of words, letters, and numbers (Johnson &

Myklebust, 1967). Deficiencies in revisualization prevent students from picturing the visual form of printed material, and are related to difficulty in spelling and writing. By contrast, good spellers are able to compare their productions against an auditory or visual image when checking their spelling.

In terms of memory functioning, recall tends to be the area most substantially impaired for children with revisualization deficits, while recognition is somewhat less affected. Therefore, activities such as dictated spelling tests, number sequencing, and drawing from memory are often extremely difficult for students with revisualization deficits. Such deficits will be less apparent when matching and multiple choice activities are employed.

Johnson and Myklebust (1967) have listed closure and visual sequential memory as two component subprocesses that are deficient in children who cannot revisualize printed material. Closure is the extrapolation of a whole from an incomplete gestalt. Children who have problems with closure are unable to supply missing details and, as such, are less able to code visual information for later retrieval. Deficiencies in visual sequential memory, the recall of images in order, impairs children's ability to remember the order and position of letters within words and words within sentences.

Instructional materials and techniques have been designed to help children compensate for deficits in closure and sequencing by capitalizing on their intact perceptual processes (Johnnson & Myklebust, 1967). Thus, training materials that use well-formed, heavily outlined letters have been recommended for circumventing closure problems. Sequencing deficits have been remediated by using different print sizes or colors. Multisensory techniques have also been suggested for remediating revisualization deficits. Other methods specify the use of initial consonant cues, verbal labels, verbal mediators, and categorization strategies (Peters & Cripps, 1980).

McIntyre (1982), reporting on research with learning-disabled children, criticizes the reliance on visual memory in Myklebust and Johnson's approach, and contends that reading is a verbal skill. On the other hand, Dodd (1980) has reported that deaf children, relying strictly on visual coding, are able to recognize regular spelling patterns. Peters and Cripps (1980), consolidating the two positions, state that words that have regular sound-letter associations can be coded verbally, but that irregular words must be revisualized.

REFERENCES

Dodd, B. (1980). The spelling abilities of profoundly prelingually deaf children. In U. Firth (Ed.), *Cognitive processes in spelling*. London: Academic.

Johnson, D. J., & Myklebust, H. R. (1967). *Learning disabilities*. New York: Grune & Stratton.

McIntyre, T. C. (1982). *Dyslexia: The effects of visual memory and serial recall*. (ERIC Document Reproduction Service No. ED 227 603)

Peters, M. L., & Cripps, C. (1980). *Catchwords: Ideas for teaching spelling*. New South Wales, Australia: Harcourt Brace Jovanovich Group (Australia) PTY., Limited.

GARY BERKOWITZ
Temple University

IMAGERY
VISUAL TRAINING

REYE'S SYNDROME

Reye's syndrome is an acute, frequently fatal disease of childhood. It is given the name of the Australian pathologist, R. D. K. Reye, who described the characteristics of this syndrome in the early 1960s. It is a rare condition with a reported risk of 1 to 2 per 100,000 children per year (Kolata, 1985). The onset of Reye's syndrome frequently follows an upper respiratory or gastrointestinal viral infection, such as may be associated with influenza B or chicken pox (*Mosby's*, 1983; Silberberg, 1979). Recovery from these relatively mild symptoms may appear to be under way when the life-threatening symptoms of Reye's syndrome ensue. These symptoms include persistent vomiting, fever, disturbances of consciousness progressing to coma, and convulsions. A characteristic posture (flexed elbows, clenched hands, extended legs) may be identified in some patients (Magalini, 1971). Deep, irregular respiration may occur, sometimes leading to respiratory arrest. The pathology associated with Reye's syndrome includes massive edema (swelling) of the brain and fatty infiltration of the liver and kidneys (Magalini, 1971; Silberberg, 1979).

The etiology of Reye's syndrome is unknown. A number of findings, including increased incidence following influenza B outbreaks and the localization of a virus in some Reye's patients, suggest a viral infection as the precipitating factor (Silberberg, 1979). Some studies have reported a link between aspirin given as a therapeutic agent during influenza or chicken pox and the subsequent development of Reye's syndrome. A study of 29 children with Reye's syndrome and 143 controls reported "children with chicken pox or flu who take aspirin may be 25 times more likely to get Reye's syndrome than those who do not" (Kolata, 1985, p. 391). In January 1985, Margaret Heckler, secretary of the Department of Health and Human Services, requested that manufacturers of aspirin include warning labels on aspirin products (Kolata, 1985). Further studies of the link between aspirin and Reye's syndrome are being conducted.

The course of Reye's syndrome is variable (Gillberg, 1995). A high percentage of afflicted children die. Estimates of mortality range from 25 to 50%, although more recent figures are consistent with the lower figure, probably as a result of enhanced medical management (Kolata, 1985; Silberberg, 1979). Survivors of Reye's syndrome frequently display significant neurologic sequelae, including mental retardation, seizures, hemiplegia, or behavior problems including hyperactivity and distractibility (Culbertson et al., 1985; Silberberg, 1979). There is evidence of an age effect on outcome for survivors of Reye's syndrome, with younger children exhibiting more severe impairment (Culbertson et al., 1985; Hartlage, Stovall, & Hartlage, 1980).

Although Reye's syndrome is an extremely rare condition, it is of relevance for educators since it afflicts children exclusively and is associated with sometimes devastating impairment. Because of the suspicion of an association between aspirin and Reye's syndrome, school officials should exercise caution in the use of aspirin with children. Survivors of Reye's syndrome may require special education or related services, which should be determined following a multifactored evaluation.

REFERENCES

Culbertson, J. L., Elbert, J. C., Gerrity, K., & Rennert, O. M. (1985, February). *Neuropsychologic and academic sequelae of Reye's syndrome*. Paper presented to the International Neuropsychological Society, San Diego.

Gillberg, C. (1995). *Clinical child neuropsychiatry*. Cambridge: Cambridge University Press.

Hartlage, L. C., Stovall, K. W., & Hartlage, P. L. (1980). Age related neuropsychological sequelae of Reye's syndrome. *Clinical Neuropsychology, 21*, 83–86.

Kolata, G. (1985). Study of Reye's-aspirin link raises concerns. *Science, 227*, 391–392.

Magalini, S. (1971). *Dictionary of medical syndromes*. Philadelphia: Lippincott.

Mosby's medical and nursing dictionary. (1983). St. Louis: Mosby.

Silberberg, D. (1979). Encephalitic complications of viral infections and vaccines. In P. B. Beeson, W. McDermott, & J. B. Wyngaarden (Eds.), *Cecil textbook of medicine* (pp. 836–839). Philadelphia: Saunders.

CATHY F. TELZROW
*Cuyahoga Special Education
Service Center*

ENCEPHALITIS

REYNOLDS, CECIL R. (1952–   )

Before receiving his BA in psychology in 1975 from the University of North Carolina at Wilmington, Cecil Reynolds was a professional baseball player with the New

Cecil R. Reynolds

York Mets organization for five years. He received his MEd in psychometrics in 1976, his EdS in school psychology in 1977, and his PhD in educational psychology in 1978, all from the University of Georgia. There his mentors were Alan S. Kaufman and E. Paul Torrance, both of whom have continued to strongly influence Reynolds.

Reynolds became assistant professor at the University of Nebraska in 1978, and remained there until 1981. During that time, he was acting director and subsequently associate director of the Buros Institute of Mental Measurement, and was responsible for moving the Buros Institute to Nebraska. Reynolds was the first director to succeed the institute's founder, Oscar K. Buros, who served as director from 1928 until his death in 1978. In 1981, Reynolds went to Texas A & M University as an associate professor, and later became director of the Doctoral School Psychology Training Program, which he led to American Psychological Association accreditation in 1985. He achieved the rank of professor in that year. He is currently a professor of educational psychology, professor of neuroscience, and a Distinguished Research Scholar at Texas A & M University.

Reynolds's primary interests are in the subject of measurement, particularly as related to the practical problems of individual assessment and diagnosis. He has also worked in the area of childhood emotional disturbance, and is the author of the Revised Children's Manifest Anxiety Scale (Reynolds & Richmond, 1985), the Behavior Assessment System for Children (Reynolds & Kamphaus, 1992), and the Test of Memory and Learning (Reynolds & Bigler, 1994), along with six other tests of affect and intelligence. He is best known in school psychology for his work in the area of the cultural test bias hypothesis (Reynolds, 1983) and as progenitor of *The Handbook of School Psychology*.

He is a member of the editorial board of more than 13 journals, including *Learning Disabilities Quarterly, Journal of School Psychology, Journal of Learning Disabilities*, and the *Journal of Forensic Neuropsychology*. With more than 300 scholarly and professional papers to his credit, he is the author or editor of 27 books. In addition, he is senior editor (with Terry Gutkin) of *The Handbook of School Psychology* (3rd ed.), and is editor of the Plenum book series *Perspectives on Individual Differences* and Plenum's *Critical Issues in Neuropsychology*. He is currently in his second term as editor-in-chief of the *Archives of Clinical Neuropsychology*, the official journal of the National Academy of Neuropsychology.

In 1983, Reynolds chaired the Special Education Programs Work Group on Critical Measurement Issues in Learning Disabilities of the U.S. Department of Education. The report of this task force and several related works (Reynolds, 1981, 1984) have been instrumental in developing practical, psychometrically sound models of severe discrepancy analysis in learning disabilities diagnosis.

He is the youngest recipient of the American Psychological Association (APA) Division of School Psychology's (16) Lightner Witmer Award, and has also received early career awards from the Division of Educational Psychology (15) and the Division of Evaluation, Measurement, and Statistics (5) of the APA. In 1995, he received the Robert Chin Award from the Society for the Psychological Study of Social Issues for his contributions to the scientific study of social issues. In 1997, he received the President's Medal for service to the National Academy of Neuropsychology and, in 1998, the Razor Walker Award for service to the youth of America from the University of North Carolina at Wilmington. In November of 1998, he received the American Board of Professional Neuropsychology's Distinguished Contributions Award in the areas of both science and service. He is the 1999 recipient of the American Psychological Association, Division of School Psychology Senior Scientist Award. In 2000, he will receive the National Academy of Neuropsychology Distinguished Clinical Neuropsychologist Award.

Reynolds has also been politically active, serving a three-year term on the executive board of the National Association of School Psychologists and as vice-president of the Division of School Psychology of the APA. In 1986, he was elected to a two-year term as president of the National Academy of Neuropsychology, and served as president of the American Psychological Association Division (5) of Evaluation, Measurement, and Statistics (1997–1998) and the Division (40) of Clinical Neuropsychology (1998–1999). He is a diplomate and past-president of the American Board of Professional Neuropsychology, a diplomate in school psychology of the American Board of Professional Psychology, a Fellow of the American Psychological Association (Divisions 1,5,15,16, and 40), and a Fellow of the National Academy of Neuropsychology and the American Psychological Society.

REFERENCES

Reynolds, C. R. (1981). The fallacy of "two years below grade level for age" as a diagnostic criterion for reading disorders. *Journal of School Psychology, 19*, 250–258.

Reynolds, C. R. (1983). Test bias: In God we trust, all others must have data. *Journal of Special Education, 17*, 214–268.

Reynolds, C. R. (1984). Critical measurement issues in learning disabilities. *Journal of Special Education, 18*, 451–476.

Reynolds, C. R., & Bigler, E. D. (1994). *Test of memory and learning*. Austin, TX.: Pro-Ed.

Reynolds, C. R., & Kamphaus, R. W. (1992). *Behavior assessment system for children*. Circle Pines, MN: American Guidance Service.

Reynolds, C. R., & Richmond, B. O. (1985). *Revised-children's manifest anxiety scale*. Los Angeles: Western Psychological Services.

Rand B. Evans
Texas A & M University
First edition

Tamara J. Martin
The University of Texas of the Permian Basin
Second edition

**BUROS INSTITUTE OF MENTAL MEASUREMENT
KAUFMAN, ALAN S.
REVISED CHILDREN'S MANIFEST ANXIETY SCALE
SEVERE DISCREPANCY ANALYSIS
TEST OF MEMORY AND LEARNING
TORRANCE, E. PAUL**

REYNOLDS, MAYNARD C. (1922–   )

A native of Doyan, North Dakota, Maynard Reynolds received his BS in education from Moorhead State University in 1942. He obtained his graduate degrees in educational psychology at the University of Minnesota after World War II, receiving his MA in 1947 and his PhD in 1950. After brief teaching assignments at the University of Northern Iowa and Long Beach State University, he returned to the University of Minnesota first as the director of the Psychoeducational Clinic, then as the chairman of the Department of Special Education, and, more recently, as professor of educational psychology and special education.

In the 1950s Reynolds became involved in the development of programs for exceptional students and issues con-

Maynard C. Reynolds

cerning the diagnosis of such children. In the 1960s Reynolds became the international president of the Council of Exceptional Children (CEC). Later, as the first chair of CEC's Policy Commission, he was increasingly active in advancing the concept that every child has a right to an education. Since the passage of PL 94-142, the Education for All the Handicapped Children Act, Reynolds has led national programs in technical assistance systems relating to changes in special education programs. From 1978 to 1984, with James Ysseldyke and Richard Weinberg, Reynolds also helped in Network, a technical assistance effort in the field of school psychology. He has also worked closely with organizations concerned with general and special education teacher preparation, editing a volume entitled *Knowledge Base for the Beginning Teacher* (1989) for the American Association of Colleges for Teacher Education.

Since his retirement from the University of Minnesota in 1989, Reynolds served in endowed professorships at California State University, Los Angeles and the University of San Diego. He also worked part-time, over a period of seven years, at the Research and Development Center on Inner City Education headed by Margaret Wang at Temple University. With Wang and Herbert Walberg, he edited a five-volume compendium on research and practice in special education.

Reynolds has been included in *Who's Who in America* and *American Men and Women of Science*. He has been given the J. E. Wallace Wallin Award by the CEC for service to handicapped children and the Mildred Thomson Award by the American Association on Mental Deficiencies.

Some of his principal publications include a text, *Teaching Exceptional Children in All America's Schools*, and several articles, including "Categories and Variables in

Special Education" (1972), "A Framework for Considering Some Issues in Special Education" (1962), and "A Strategy for Research" (1963).

REFERENCES

Reynolds, M. C. (1962). A framework for considering some issues in special education. *Exceptional Children, 28*, 367–370.

Reynolds, M. C. (1963). A strategy for research. *Exceptional Children, 29*(5), 213–219.

Reynolds, M. C., & Balow, B. (1972). Categories and variables in special education. *Exceptional Children, 38*(5), 357–366.

Reynolds, M. C., & Birch, J. W. (1982). *Teaching exceptional children in all America's schools* (2nd ed.). Reston, VA: Council for Exceptional Children.

Wang, M. C., Reynolds, M. C., & Walberg, H. J. (Eds.). (1987–92). *Handbook of special education: Research and practice*. Oxford: Pergamon Press. (5 volumes).

E. Valerie Hewitt
Texas A & M University
First edition

Tamara J. Martin
*The University of Texas of the
Permian Basin*
Second edition

Rh FACTOR INCOMPATIBILITY

Rh factor incompatilibility (erythroblastosis fetalis) results from an antigen-antibody reaction with destruction of the fetal red blood cells (Sherwen, Scoloveno, & Weingarten, 1999). The most lethal form of Rh factor incompatibility is erythroblastosis fetalis. Generally defined, erythroblastosis fetalis is a type of hemolytic disorder found in newborns which results from maternal-fetal blood group incompatibility of the Rh factor and blood group (Anderson, 1998). When an Rh-positive fetus begins to grow inside an Rh-negative mother, it is as though the mother's body is being invaded by a foreign agent or antigen (Pillitteri, 1995). The mother's body reacts to this invasion by forming antibodies that cross the placenta and cause hemolysis of fetal red blood cells. The fetus becomes deficient in red blood cells that transport oxygen and develops anemia; enlarged heart, spleen, and liver; and a cardiovascular system which easily decompensates (Lowdermilk, Perry, & Boback, 1997). Without prompt treatment, hypoxia, cardiac failure, respiratory distress, and death may result (Anderson, 1998).

Prenatal diagnosis of erythroblastosis fetalis is confirmed through amniocentesis and analysis of bilirubin levels within the amniotic fluid (Anderson, 1998). The treatment regime may include intrauterine transfusions to combat red blood cell destruction or immediate transfusions after birth (Pillitteri, 1995). Preterm labor may also be induced to remove the fetus from the destructive maternal environment.

In Rh factor incompatibility, the hemolytic reactions take place only when the mother is Rh-negative and the infant is Rh-positive (Sherwen et al., 1999). This isoimmunization process rarely occurs in the first pregnancy, but risk is great in subsequent pregnancies. A simple injection of a high-titer Rho(D) immune-globulin preparation after delivery or abortion of the Rh-positive fetus can prevent maternal sensitization to the Rh factor (Anderson, 1998).

Hemolytic diseases of the fetus or newborn are on the decline and occur in only 1.5% of all pregnancies (Sherwen et al., 1999). Since the availability of Rho(D) immune globulin (RhoGAM), the incidence of Rh factor incompatibilities has drastically decreased (Sherwen et al., 1999). Caucasian newborns remain most at risk (15%) for erythroblastosis fetalis; African American newborns have a 6% occurrence rate (Medical College of Wisconsin Physicians & Clinics, 1999).

REFERENCES

Anderson, K. N. (1998). *Mosby's medical, nursing, & allied health dictionary* (5th ed.). St. Louis: Mosby-Year Book.

Lowdermilk, D., Perry, S., & Bobak, I. (1997). *Maternity & women's health care* (6th ed.). St. Louis: Mosby-Year Book.

Medical College of Wisconsin Physicians & Clinics. (1999). *Erthroblastosis fetalis.* http://chorus.rad.mcw.edu/doc/00889.html.

Pillitteri, A. (1995). *Maternal & child health nursing: Care of the childbearing and childrearing family* (2nd ed.). Philadelphia: J. B. Lippincott Company.

Sherwen, L., Scoloveno, M., & Weingarten, C. (1999). *Maternity nursing: Care of the childbearing family* (3rd ed.). Stamford, CT: Appleton & Lange.

KARI ANDERSON
University of North Carolina at Wilmington

RIGHT-HANDEDNESS

Right-handedness is a species-specific characteristic of humans (Hicks & Kinsbourne; 1978). Additionally, right-handedness, also called dextrality, can be considered universal in that 90% of the human population is right-handed (Corballis & Beale, 1983). Since the majority of individuals prefer using their right hands, and are also more skilled with their right hands, more positive properties and values have come to be associated with the right than with the left. For example, throughout history the right has represented the side of the gods, strength, life, good-

ness, light, the state of rest, the limited, the odd, the square, and the singular. The left has been signified by the polar opposites of these characteristics. Maleness also has been traditionally associated with the right, providing symbolic expression of the universality of male dominance (Needham, 1974).

Although people classify themselves as right-handed or left-handed, handedness more accurately spans a continuous range from extreme right-handedness through mixed-handedness or ambidexterity to extreme left-handedness (Corballis & Beale, 1976). Investigators always have been curious about the abundance of right-handedness and the rarity of the various degrees of nonright-handedness. However, studies of historical records and artifacts have revealed enough inconsistencies in incidence to preclude any simple choice between culture or biology to explain the origin of handedness. Consequently, combinations of these various nature and nurture explanations have been invoked. Harris (1980) provides an interesting and detailed account of these various theories.

Corballis and Beale (1983), in an extensive study of the neuropsychology of right and left, have argued that right-handedness is biologically rather than culturally determined. They cite the fact that right-handedness always has been universal across diverse and seemingly unrelated cultures; moreover, although right-handedness itself is not manifest until late in the first year of life, it is correlated with other asymmetries that are evident at or before birth. They acknowledge that there are environmental pressures to be right-handed and that some naturally left-handed individuals may be compelled to use their right hands for certain tasks, but suggest that these very pressures have their origins in the fundamental right-handedness of most human beings.

Today the relationship between right-handedness and the unilateral representation of language in the left cerebral hemisphere is well documented. Case studies linking the side of brain damage and the incidence of aphasia, or language impairment, have revealed that approximately 98% of right-handers use the left hemisphere of their brain for language. A similar conclusion has been drawn from studies in which linguistic functioning has been impaired in 95% of the right-handers whose left cerebral hemispheres were injected with sodium amobarbitol, a momentarily incapacitating drug.

The hemisphere of the brain used for language in left-handers is more variable. Two-thirds of left-handers have demonstrated the use of their left hemisphere. Almost half of the remaining left-handers use their right hemispheres for speech, while the remainder have some capacity for speech in both hemispheres (Rasmussen & Milner, 1975). In view of these data, many investigators suggest that both right-handedness and left cerebral dominance for language are genetically controlled expressions of some underlying biological gradient. This relationship further reveals the significance of right-handedness in the unique cognitive functioning of the human species.

REFERENCES

Corballis, M. C., & Beale, I. L. (1976). *The psychology of left and right*. Hillsdale, NJ: Erlbaum.

Corballis, M. C., & Beale, I. L. (1983). *The ambivalent mind*. Chicago: Nelson-Hall.

Harris, L. J. (1980). Left-handedness: Early theories, facts, and fancies. In J. Herron (Ed.), *Neuropsychology of left-handedness* (pp. 3–78). New York: Academic.

Hicks, R. E., & Kinsbourne, M. (1978). Human handedness. In M. Kinsbourne (Ed.), *Asymmetrical function of the brain* (pp. 267–273). New York: Cambridge University Press.

Needham, R. (Ed.). (1974). *Right and left: Essays on dual symbolic classification*. Chicago: University of Chicago Press.

Rasmussen, T., & Milner, B. (1975). Clinical and surgical studies of the cerebral speech areas in man. In K. J. Zulch, O. Creutzfeldt, & G. Galbraith (Eds.), *Otfried Foerster symposium on cerebral localization*. Heidelberg: Springer-Verlag.

GALE A. HARR
Maple Heights City Schools
Maple Heights, Ohio

CEREBRAL DOMINANCE
HANDEDNESS
LEFT BRAIN, RIGHT BRAIN

RIGHT HEMISPHERE SYNDROME, (LINGUISTIC, EXTRALINGUISTIC, AND NON-LINGUISTIC)

The role of the right hemisphere in communication was largely unknown 20 years ago (Meyers, 1997). Since then an extensive body of research has determined that the right hemisphere handles holistic, gestalt-like stimuli and visual-spatial information, and has identified a wide range of communication impairments that can occur subsequent to right hemisphere damage. Three types of right hemisphere syndrome (RHS) deficits are *extralinguistic* (discourse), *nonlinguistic* (perceptual and attentional), and, to a lesser degree, *linguistic* deficits (phonological, semantic, syntactical, and morphological; (Hegde, 1998; Myers, 1997; Payne, 1997).

Extralinguistic deficits

Discourse is the aspect of communication that transcends individual phonemes, words, or sentences. It links "the bits and pieces of language to create representations of events, objects, beliefs, personalities, and experiences" (Brownell and Joanette, 1993, p. vii). Discourse competence is context-driven, and context includes a variety of cues—not only words and sentences, but tone of voice, gestures, body positions, facial expressions of the speaker, and the overall purpose and relative formality of the communicative event. Discourse also involves organization, sequencing, and the generation of projections, predictions, and inferences so that sentences are not taken as independent units, but as part of a larger whole (macrostructure) in which central ideas are emphasized and supported. Four major areas make up extralinguistic deficits associated with RHS (Hegde, 1998; Myers, 1997; Payne, 1997).

Macrostructure—reduced number and accuracy of core concepts and inferences, reduced specificity or explicitness of information, and reduced efficiency of listening, speaking, reading, writing, and thinking.

Impaired non-literal language—reduced sensitivity and use of figurative language (similes, metaphors, idioms, proverbs), humor (cartoons, jokes, riddles, puns), teasing, advertisements, slang, verbal aggression, ambiguity, multiple meanings, deception (irony, sarcasm), and capacity to revise original interpretations.

Rhetorical sensitivity/affective components—reduced sensitivity to communicative purposes, shared knowledge, emotional tone, partner's communicative state, turn-taking, topic maintenance, gaze; increased impulsivity, excessive talking, shallow responses, and monotonal speech.

Impaired prosody—reduced sensitivity to affective prosody (comprehension of others' emotions as reflected in the voice) and use of prosodic features (production of personal emotional states).

Nonlinguistic deficits

Nonlinguistic deficits associated with RHS include visual perceptual problems, left-side neglect, attentional deficits, and denial of deficits.

Visual perceptual deficits—reduced ability to recognize faces (prosopagnosia) and to construct or reproduce block designs, two-dimensional stick figures, or geometric designs.

Left-side neglect—reduced sensitivity to respond to information on the left, despite the motor and sensory capacity to do so. The definition of "left" may vary according to the type of neglect and the environment. In body-centered neglect, "left" may refer to the left of the body midline. In environment-centered neglect, "left" may refer to the left side of a group of stimuli, regardless of their spatial location, or to the left side of fixed environmental coordinates, such as the left side of a room or book. In other cases, neglect may occur on the left side of a given object, even if that object is located in the right visual field. Thus, neglect may occur in the left or right visual field, depending on the stimulus environment; left may, therefore, be considered relative. Left-side neglect can occur in all modalities (auditory, visual, tactile, smell, taste), but is most often noted and tested in the visual modality. In addition to ignoring the left, individuals with neglect also may demonstrate an orienting bias toward the right, i.e., right-sided stimuli "capture" the person's attention.

Attentional deficits—reduced arousal (alertness), vigilance (focusing on relevant pieces of information), and maintained attention to stimuli; selective attention.

Linguistic deficits

Unlike the communication deficits that occur with left-hemisphere impairment, linguistic deficits are less problematic in RHS. Word retrieval deficits (semantics) occur frequently. Defining categories (e.g., apple, peach, cherry are *fruit*) or identifying collective and single nouns through confrontation naming are characteristic linguistic impairments. Phonological, syntactic, and morphological errors do not characterize the communication patterns of RHS (Hegde, 1998).

Right hemisphere syndrome is associated with strokes, tumors, head trauma, and various neurological diseases in all ethnic groups (Payne, 1997). The syndrome can have significant effects on social and academic aspects of communication-learning.

REFERENCES

Brownell, H. H., & Joanette, Y. (Eds.). (1993). *Narrative discourse in neurologically impaired and normal aging adults*. San Diego: Singular.

Hegde, M. N. (1998). *A coursebook on aphasia and other neurogenic language disorders* (2nd ed.). San Diego: Singular.

Myers, P. E. (1997). Right hemisphere syndrome. In L. L. LaPointe (Ed.), *Aphasia and related neurogenic language disorders* (2nd ed.). New York: Thieme.

Payne, J. C. (1997). *Adult neurogenic language disorders: Assessment and treatment—A comprehensive ethnobiological approach*. San Diego: Singular.

STEPHEN S. FARMER
New Mexico State University

NONVERBAL LANGUAGE
PRAGMATICS

RIGHT TO EDUCATION

The right to education refers to the legal concept that justifies a school-aged person's freedom to receive educational services. The conceptual and legal development of this right has occurred in conjunction with an increasing societal concern for individuals who exhibit exceptional educational needs. These changing social attitudes have been reflected in judicial decisions and legislative efforts that have substantiated the right of all school-aged children and youths to receive educational services.

The U.S. Constitution, although not explicit in its guarantee of the right to education, has been cited as the fundamental justification for the provision of educational services. Specifically, the right to education has been implied from the Fourteenth Amendment, which states in its equal protection clause, "a state may not pass laws, nor act in any official way, so as to establish for a group of citizens benefits or penalties which other citizens do not receive." Thus, this amendment requires that, where educational services are available, such services must be available to all on an equivalent basis.

Early court cases that addressed the right of the exceptional needs learner to receive educational services did not reflect this interpretation. Generally, litigation in this area prior to the 1950s resulted in exclusionary educational policies (e.g., *Watson* v. *Cambridge*, 1883; *Beattie* v. *Board of Education*, 1919). However, with the onset of the increasing civil rights awareness apparent in the early 1950s, right to education court cases evidenced a more positive trend. Some of the more influential court cases that have related to the development of the right to education concept for the exceptional needs learner include *Brown* v. *Board of Education of Topeka* (1954), *Pennsylvania Association for Retarded Citizens* v. *the Commonwealth of Pennsylvania* (1971), and *Mills* v. *Board of Education of the District of Columbia* (1972).

The *Brown* case dealt with the rights of a class of citizens (blacks in the South) to attend public schools in their community on a nonsegregated basis. The major issues in this case were suspect classification (i.e., classification by race) and equal protection. In a unanimous decision for the plaintiff, the Supreme Court emphasized the social importance of education and also ruled that education must be made available on equal terms to all.

The *Pennsylvania Association for Retarded Citizens (PARC)* case dealt more specifically with the educational rights of exceptional needs learners. Citing the Fourteenth Amendment right to due process and equal protection, the judge in this case ruled that Pennsylvania statutes permitting denial or postponement of entry to public schools by mentally retarded children were unconstitutional. The terms of the settlement reached in this case included provision of due process rights to the plaintiffs and identification and placement in public school programs of all previously excluded children.

More general in its plaintiff class, the *Mills* case challenged the exclusion of mentally retarded, epileptic, brain-damaged, hyperactive, and behavior-disordered children from public schools. Finding for the plaintiffs, the court required the defendants to provide full public education or "adequate alternatives." These alternatives could only be provided after notice and a reasonable opportunity to challenge the services that had been given. The progression from *Brown* (1954) to *PARC* (1971) to *Mills* (1972) reflects an increasing sophistication in the awareness of the educational needs of individuals with exceptional learning characteristics. This more complete view of the educational needs and rights of exceptional individuals is also apparent in recent legislation.

Two major legislative efforts that have addressed the educational rights of exceptional needs learners are the Rehabilitation Act of 1973, Section 504, and PL 94-142 (and its successor, IDEA). Section 504 of the Rehabilitation Act of 1973 is particularly important because it deals with all programs that receive federal funds. This legislation mandates nondiscrimination on the basis of handicapping conditions if these funds are to continue.

Public Law 94-142 and the IDEA embody the intent of all legislation that it follows in its highly specific delineation of the educational rights of exceptional needs learners. This law requires that all individuals, regardless of handicapping condition or its degree, be offered a free appropriate education at public expense. Public Law 94-142 further specifies that these services must be delivered in the least restrictive environment appropriate for the individual child.

The right to education for children and youths with exceptional learning characteristics has resulted from changing societal views of the needs and rights of these individuals. These attitudes have been reflected in increased litigation questioning the adequacy, availability, and appropriateness of the educational services offered this group. The outcome of these cases has established a legal basis for a right to education. This litigation has in turn led to legislation developed to ensure that right. For a comprehensive discussion of the right to education for the exceptional needs learner see Wortis (1978) and Sales, Krauss, Sacken, & Overcast (1999).

REFERENCES

Beattie v. *State Board of Education of Wisconsin*. (1978). In J. Wortis (Ed.), *Mental retardation and developmental disabilities*. New York: Brunner/Mazel.

Sales, B. D., Krauss, D., Sacken, D., & Overcast, B. (1999). The legal rights of students. In. C. R. Reynolds & T. B. Gutkin (Eds.), *The Handbook of School Psychology* (3rd ed.). New York: Wiley.

Watson v. *Cambridge, Mass.* (1978). In J. Wortis (Ed.), *Mental retardation and developmental disabilities*. New York: Brunner/Mazel.

Wortis, J. (Ed.). (1978). *Mental retardation and developmental disabilities*. New York: Brunner/Mazel.

J. TODD STEPHENS
University of Wisconsin at Madison

BROWN v. BOARD OF EDUCATION
EDUCATION FOR ALL HANDICAPPED CHILDREN ACT OF 1975

INDIVIDUALS WITH DISABILITIES EDUCATION ACT
MILLS v. BOARD OF EDUCATION
PAR v. COMMONWEALTH OF PENNSYLVANIA

RIGHT TO TREATMENT

The term right to treatment refers to the legal concept that justifies an individual's freedom to receive therapeutic and/or curative services. Initially developed as an extension of litigation that targeted the availability of medically oriented services for institutionalized individuals, recent legal interpretations of this right have been broadened to include the right to habilitation and the right to education.

The development of the right to treatment reflects a trend of change in societal attitudes about providing services for individuals with exceptional learning or behavioral characteristics. As attitudes have changed, concerned individuals have organized systematic efforts to ensure the availability of these services. These changes have resulted in litigative and legislative efforts that have addressed both the availability and adequacy of treatment for institutionalized people.

The three major court cases that shaped the legal interpretation of the right to treatment are *Rouse* v. *Cameron* (1968), *Wyatt* v. *Stickney* (1970), a class-action suit, and *New York Association for Retarded Citizens* v. *Rockefeller* (1972). In these cases constitutional amendments and state laws were interpreted as requiring treatment services for institutionalized persons. The first court case that dealt with the right of an institutionalized person to receive treatment was *Rouse* v. *Cameron* (1968). In this case, a man was institutionalized for 4 years after having been found not guilty, by reason of insanity, of a misdemeanor. While institutionalized, Rouse did not receive treatment. Citing constitutional rights (due process, equal protection, freedom from cruel and unusual punishment) and basing the decision on state law, the court ruled that confinement for treatment purposes when treatment was not made available was equivalent to imprisonment. Rouse was subsequently freed.

The *Wyatt* v. *Stickney* case (1970) was a class-action suit filed on behalf of the residents of three residential facilities in Alabama. The case was exhaustive in its pursuit of information and remedies. In the final ruling, standards were delineated with regard to treatment, habilitation, freedom from restraint, and a host of other treatment considerations. The court-ordered remedies included development of appropriate staff ratios, individual habilitation plans, and the delineation of specific procedures for treatment. Thus according to the rulings of *Wyatt* (1970), not only must treatment be available, but such treatment must also be supported by sufficient staff and planning.

Following the initial hearing of Wyatt, the *New York Association for Retarded Citizens* (*NYARC*) filed a petition against the then governor of the state, Nelson Rockefeller (*NYARC* v. *Rockefeller*, 1972) requesting relief from the overcrowded and inhumane conditions at the Willowbrook state institution. Citing the constitutional right to due process, the judge in this case ruled for immediate reduction of the resident population and appropriate development of community-based programs. Thus the *NYARC* case indicated that in addition to the right to receive adequate services in humane conditions, residents must also be considered as members of a society to which they should be allowed reasonable access.

Each of these cases represents a litigative response to either a complete lack of treatment availability, ineffective delivery of treatment, or use of inappropriate treatment. The decisions in these cases reflect an expanding awareness of the legal right of institutionalized individuals not only to receive treatment, but to be allowed access to systematically planned programming that meets the varied needs of the resident.

J. TODD STEPHENS
*University of Wisconsin at
Madison*

**RIGHT TO EDUCATION
WYATT *v.* STICKNEY**

RILEY-DAY SYNDROME

Riley-Day syndrome, also referred to as Familial Dysautonomia (FD), is a rare, autosomal (non-sex-related chromosome) recessive, genetic disease primarily afflicting Jewish children of Ashkenazi or Eastern European heritage. First described in 1949 by Drs. Riley, Day, Greeley, and Langford, Riley-Day syndrome/FD is a malfunction of the autonomic nervous system and poses severe physical, emotional, and social problems for the afflicted patients.

Individuals affected with FD are incapable of producing overflow tears with emotional crying. Frequent manifestations of FD include inappropriate perception of heat, pain, and taste, as well as labile blood pressures and gastrointestinal difficulties. Other problems experienced by individuals with FD include dysphagia (difficulty in swallowing), vomiting, aspiration and frequent pneumonia, speech and motor incoordination, poor growth, and scoliosis. Other frequent signs are delayed developmental milestones; unsteady gait; corneal anesthesia; marked sweating with excitement, eating, or the first stage of sleep; breath-holding episodes; spinal curvature (in 90% by age 13); red puffy hands; and an absence of fungiform papillae (taste buds) on the tongue (NYU, 1999).

FD is transmitted by a recessive gene provided by both the mother and the father. Although the gene has been lo-

calized to the long arm of chromosome 9 (9q31) with flanking markers, FD carrier detection can only be offered to a family that already has an affected child (McKusick, 1999). Both males and females are equally affected. As yet, there is no screening test for the general population. It is estimated that one in 30 Jews of Eastern European (Ashkenazi) extraction are carriers of the FD gene, with an estimated prevalence of 1 out of every 10,000–20,000 of Ashkenazi heritage. The prognosis of FD is poor, with most patients dying in childhood of chronic pulmonary failure or aspiration (Gandy, 1999), although FD individuals can survive into their 20s and 30s.

There is no cure for FD, but many of the symptoms can be treated through a variety of interventions and medication. Affected individuals usually are of normal intelligence, and FD patients can be expected to function independently if treatment is begun early and major disabilities avoided. Special education services may be provided under the category of Noncategorical Early Childhood or Other Health Impaired. Early identification and intervention is extremely important for FD children to address developmental delays, gross motor and walking delays, and failure to thrive due to feeding difficulties and excessive vomiting. Upon entering school, speech, physical, and occupational therapies may be beneficial. Specialized feeding techniques may need to be taught. Adapted physical education may be needed to prevent injuries due to insensitivity to pain, and to monitor difficulties with the inability to control body temperature. Individuals affected with FD are prone to depression, anxieties, and even phobias. Families of FD affected children may need psychological support to assist with the emotional demands of caring for a child with a debilitating disease. For additional information contact the Dysautonomia Foundation Inc., 20 East 46th Street, New York, N.Y., 10017 or call (212) 949-6644.

REFERENCES

Gandy, A. (1999). *Pediatric Database* (PEDBASE). http://www.icondata.com/health/pedbase/files/LAURENCE.HTM.

McKusick, V. A. (1999). *OMIM™ Online Mendelian Inheritance in Man*. National Center for Biotechnology Information (NCBI). http://www3.ncbi.nlm.nih.gov:80/Omim/.

New York University Health System. (1999). http://www.med.nyu.edu/fd/fdcenter. html.

KIM RYAN ARREDONDO
Texas A & M University

RIMLAND, BERNARD (1928–   )

Bernard Rimland earned his BA (1950) and MA (1951) at San Diego State University and his PhD in experimental

Bernard Rimland

In addition to being an honorary board member and founder of the Autism Society of America, Rimland also serves on 32 advisory boards for publications, research organizations, and schools for children with severe behavior disorders. He has also been vice president of the Academy of Orthomolecular Psychiatry and the Orthomolecular Medical Society, and served as the chief technical advisor on autism for the popular film *Rain Man*.

MARY LEON PEERY
Texas A & M University
First edition

TAMARA J. MARTIN
The University of Texas of the Permian Basin
Second edition

psychology in 1954 from Pennsylvania State University. Upon the diagnosis of his eldest son as autistic, Rimland began extensive research that led to his neural theory of infantile autism. He later founded the National Society for Autistic Children, which later became the Autism Society of America, and established the Autism Research Institute in San Diego in 1967. He currently serves as director of the Autism Research Institute, a nonprofit organization providing parents and professionals worldwide with information on the etiology and treatment of severe behavior disorders in children.

Rimland was an early advocate of the use of behavior modification and a pioneering researcher on the effects of nutrition on behavior and mental health. In his massive review of the literature on autism in the early 1960s, Rimland found no scientific support for the widely held psychoanalytic theories that blamed supposedly unloving families for the child's severe disorder. Discarding the psychoanalytic explanation, Rimland advocated a neurophysiological cause of autism involving, in part, a possible dysfunction of the brain stem reticular formation. The reticular formation is known to play an important role in perception, and children with autism appear to have a perceptual malfunction that results in difficulty distinguishing boundaries between themselves and their surrounding world. Rimland's treatments of choice for the disorder are behavior modification and megavitamin therapy. His research and that of others have shown promising results for megavitamin therapy for treatment of autism and other childhood disorders.

Rimland's major publication is *Infantile Autism: The Syndrome and Its Implications for a Neural Theory of Behavior,* which won him the Appleton-Century-Crofts Award for the 1963 Distinguished Contribution to Psychology. He has published and contributed to more than 100 journal articles, and served as coeditor of *Modern Therapies*.

RISK MANAGEMENT IN SPECIAL EDUCATION

Many times educational settings are unaware of the relationship between school practices and legal liability. Risk management is a proactive stance that attempts to identify potential areas of liability, evaluate current policy and standards, and provide workable strategies in an attempt to prevent injury and minimize liability (Phillips, 1990). In addition, risk management allows for consistent practices among school personnel covering a wide range of situations and circumstances.

Common risk management strategies in educational settings include appropriate documentation when altering a child's instructional curriculum, specified protocol when a student has expressed suicidal feelings, adherence to state regulations and guidelines in diagnostic assessments, informed consent procedures for parents and children regarding school counseling, and maintaining adequate liability coverage (Wood, 1988). Risk management strategies for school personnel include knowing and following ethical guidelines, and keeping current with professional development and standards of practice (Phillips, 1990).

REFERENCES

Phillips, B. N. (1990). Law, psychology, and education. In T. R. Kratochwill (Ed.), *Advances in School Psychology* (Vol. 7, pp. 79–130). Hillsdale, NJ: Erlbaum.

Wood, R. H. (1988). *Fifty ways to avoid malpractice*. Sarasota, Florida: Professional Resource Exchange.

LINDA M. MONTGOMERY
The University of Texas of the Permian Basin

RITALIN

Ritalin, the trade name for methylphenidate, is a central nervous system stimulant commonly prescribed for children with an abnormally high level of activity or with attention-deficit/hyperactivity disorder (ADHD). Ritalin is also occasionally prescribed for individuals with narcolepsy, mild depression, or withdrawn senile behavior (Shannon, Wilson, & Stang, 1995).

Although all the intricacies of Ritalin are not fully understood, it increases the attention span in ADHD children (Deglin & Vallerand, 1999). Ritalin stimulates the central nervous system with effects similar to weak amphetamines or very strong coffee. Its effects include (a) increasing attention and reducing activity in hyperactive children, apparently by stimulating inhibitory centers (NIDAInfofax, 1998); (b) diminishing fatigue is in individuals with narcolepsy; and (c) increasing motor activity and mental alertness in individuals exhibiting withdrawn senile behavior (Shannon et al., 1995).

All individuals need to be advised to take sustained released Ritalin as a whole tablet and never to crush or chew the pill. Ritalin should be taken at regular intervals during the day and only by the individual for whom it is prescribed (Deglin & Vallerand, 1999). As a stimulant medication, Ritalin may cause sleep disorders if taken late in the day (Skidmore-Roth & McKenry, 1997). To minimize insomnia, the last dose of Ritalin should be taken before 6:00 PM. Weight loss is another potential side effect of this medication, and individuals should be advised to weigh themselves at least twice weekly (Deglin & Vallerand, 1999). Because of the combined effects of multiple stimulants, all individuals should be informed that they should refrain from drinking any caffeine-containing beverages such as cola or coffee (Skidmore-Roth & McKenry, 1997). As with any continuous medication regime, school personnel should be notified of the medication and any other health-related concerns (Wong, 1995).

Stimulant medications such as Ritalin have strong potential for abuse, and the United States Drug Enforcement Administration (DEA) has placed numerous stringent controls on Ritalin's manufacture, distribution, and prescription. Ritalin is documented to be a strong, effective, and safe medication, but the potential risks in long-term usage need further investigation (NIDAInfofax, 1998).

REFERENCES

Deglin, J., & Vallerand, A. (1999). *Davis's drug guide for nurses* (6th ed.). Philadelphia: F. A. Davis. NIDAInfofax. (1998, February 27). http://www.nida.nih.gov/Infofax/ritalin.html.

Shannon, M., Wilson, B., & Stang, C. (1995). *Govoni & Hayes drugs and nursing implications* (8th ed.). Norwalk, CT: Appleton & Lange.

Skidmore-Roth, L., & McKenry, L. (1997). *Mosby's drug guide for nurses* (2nd ed.). St. Louis: Mosby-Year Book.

Wong, D. (1995). *Whaley & Wong's nursing care of infants and children* (5th ed.). St. Louis: Mosby-Year Book, Inc.

KARI ANDERSON
University of North Carolina at Wilmington

ATTENTION DEFICIT DISORDER-HYPERACTIVITY MEDICAL MANAGEMENT

ROBERTS APPERCEPTION TEST FOR CHILDREN (RATC)

The Roberts Apperception Test for Children (RATC) is a personality assessment technique designed for children ages 6 to 15. The RATC is an attempt to combine the flexibility of a projective technique with the objectivity of a standardized scoring system. Similar to the Thematic Apperception Test and the Children's Apperception Test, the RATC consists of a set of drawings designed to elicit thematic stories. The test consists of 27 cards, 11 of which are parallel forms for males and females. Thus 16 cards are administered during testing, which takes 20 to 30 minutes.

The RATC is said to have significant benefits over similar project measures (McArthur & Roberts, 1982). The test manual is well designed and includes substantial information on psychometric properties of the test, administration, and scoring, as well as several case studies. The picture drawings were designed specifically for children and young adolescents, and depict scenes designed to elicit common concerns. For example, specific cards portray parent/child relationships, sibling relationships, aggression, mastery, parental disagreement and affection, observation of nudity, school, and peer relationships. The test has a standardized scoring system, with scores converted to normalized T scores based on data from a sample of 200 well-adjusted children. The following information may be obtained from the RATC:

1. *Adaptive Scales.* Reliance on others, support for others, support for the child, limit setting, problem identification, resolution.
2. *Clinical scales.* Anxiety, aggression, depression, rejection, lack of resolution.
3. *Critical Indicators.* Atypical response, maladaptive outcome, refusal.
4. *Supplementary Measures.* Ego functioning, aggression, levels of projection.

A review of the RATC in the *Ninth Mental Measurements Yearbook* (Sines, 1985) describes four unpublished validity studies and concludes that the psychometric properties of the test are unimpressive. In perhaps the most substantial of these studies, 200 well-adjusted children were compared with 200 children evaluated at guidance clinics. The normal children scored higher than the children at clinics on all eight adaptive scales; however, the two groups could not be reliably differentiated on the clinical scales for anxiety, aggression, and depression.

Overall, the RATC appears to be a well-designed projective technique for children and young adolescents. The standardized scoring system, while lacking in evidence compared with purely objective measures of personality, appears to be relatively satisfactory compared with similar projective techniques.

REFERENCES

McArthur, D., & Roberts, G. (1982). *Roberts Apperception Test for Children: Test Manual*. Los Angeles: Western Psychological Services.

Sines, J. (1985). The Roberts Apperception Test for Children. In J. Mitchell (Ed.), *The ninth mental measurements yearbook*. Lincoln, NE: Buros Institute.

FRANCES F. WORCHEL
Texas A & M University

CHILD PSYCHOLOGY
PERSONALITY ASSESSMENT

ROBINOW'S SYNDROME

See RARE DISEASES

ROBINSON, HALBERT B. (1925–1981) AND ROBINSON, NANCY M. (1930–   )

Nancy and Hal Robinson have done extensive work in the areas of children with mental retardation, early child care, and gifted children. They coauthored *The Mentally Retarded Child: A Psychological Approach* (1976), an influential text defining the field of mental retardation and emphasizing its research base, and coedited the *International Monograph Series on Early Child Care* (1974), which offers descriptions of early child care options of nine nations, including the United States.

In 1966, with Ann Peters, Hal Robinson founded the Frank Porter Graham Child Development Center at the University of North Carolina (Robinson & Robinson, 1971), and in 1969 he accepted a position at the University of Washington, Seattle (UW) as a professor of psychology. While at UW, Hal also served as the principal investigator of the Child Development Research Group (CDRG, now the

Halbert Robinson Center for the Study of Capable Youth). Child Development Preschool, formerly a CDRG program (later independent of UW), focused on the identification and development of curriculum for children with advanced intellectual and academic skills (Roedell, Jackson, & Robinson, 1980), while the UW Early Entrance Program admitted middle school-age students to the University, depending on their readiness, prior to entering high school (Robinson & Robinson).

Of their many honors, the Robinsons received the Education Award of the American Association on Mental Deficiency (1982). Additionally, Nancy has served as editor of the *American Journal of Mental Deficiency*, and after Hal's death in 1981, she assumed the directorship of the Hal Robinson Center for the Study of Capable Youth, a position she holds today. She is also a professor of psychiatry and behavioral science at UW, and has continued to publish on important topics including the counseling of highly gifted children and mathematically gifted children (Robinson, 1996; Robinson, Abbot, Berninger, Busse, & Mukhopadhyay, 1997).

REFERENCES

Robinson, H. B., & Robinson, N. M. (1971). Longitudinal development of very young children in a comprehensive day care program: The first two years. *Child Development, 42,* 1673–1683.

Robinson, H. B., Robinson, N. M., Wolins, M., Bronfenbrenner, U., & Richmond, J. B. (1974). Early child care in the United States. In H. B. Robinson & N. M. Robinson (Eds.), *International monograph series on early child care*. London: Gordon, Breach.

Robinson, N. M. (1996). Counseling agendas for gifted young people: A commentary. *Journal for the Education of the Gifted, 20*(2), 128–137.

Robinson, N. M., Abbot, R. D., Berninger, V. W., Busse, J., & Mukhopadhyay, S. (1997). Developmental changes in mathematically precocious young children: Longitudinal and gender effects. *Gifted Child Quarterly, 41*(4), 145–158.

Robinson, N. M., & Robinson, H. B. (1976). *The mentally retarded child: A psychological approach* (2nd ed.). New York: McGraw-Hill.

Robinson, N. M., & Robinson, H. B. (1982). The optimal match: Devising the best compromise for the highly gifted student. In D. H. Feldman (Ed.), *Developmental approaches to giftedness and creativity*. San Francisco: Jossey-Bass.

Roedell, W. C., Jackson, N. E., & Robinson, H. B. (1980). *Gifted young children*. New York: Columbia University.

ANN E. LUPKOWSKI
Texas A & M University
First edition

TAMARA J. MARTIN
*The University of Texas of the
Permian Basin*
Second edition

ROBOTICS

A robot is a programmable multifunctional device that is capable of performing a variety of tasks, manipulations, and locomotions. Robots come in one of four configurations: rectangular, cylindrical, spherical, and anthropomorphic articulated (Yin & Moore, 1984). These electronic devices have five characteristics that set them apart from other devices: mobility, dexterity, payload capacity, intelligence, and sensory capability. The characteristics are found singly or in combination; however, at present there is no single system that integrates all of the characteristics.

Industrial robots are known for their payload capacity. For example, the large electronic arms used on the automotive assembly lines in Japan are capable of lifting enormous weights and performing the same routines tirelessly. Other robots are recognized for their sensory capability (e.g., to sense temperature or to recognize patterns). Educational robots usually have mobility and dexterity. For example, the Heath Company's robot Hero can be told to go forward, backward, left, or right. Hero's arm and hand can manipulate objects. The arm's five axes allow him to wave, gesticulate, lift objects, and drop them. Hero also speaks 64 phonemes, which means the robot can be programmed to speak almost any language. Hero can also respond to light, sound, and objects (Slesnick, 1984).

Turtle Tot is a small robot that can be programmed by young children to count, draw pictures, and move at various angles. A machine that has greater dexterity but less mobility is the Rhino XR II, which is used in college-level engineering classes. The arm is a five-axis manipulator that has a hip, shoulder, elbow, and hand. The hand is capable of pitch, roll, and grip (Shahinpoor & Singer, 1985).

In special education, robots offer the potential to perform two basic functions. First, they can serve as an extension of the teacher by interacting with students and providing instruction in a fascinating area of technology. Second, robots can be controlled by students to meet their personal needs and objectives. For handicapped individuals, robotics can help alleviate many of the restrictions imposed by limited mobility and dexterity. For the orthopedically disabled in particular, robotics may compensate for missing or impaired human functions (Kimbler, 1984). In the future, robotics may help compensate for visual and auditory disabilities. Scientists are working on robots that will respond to voice commands and have computerized vision.

REFERENCES

Kimbler, D. L. (1984, June). *Robots and special education: The robot as extension of self.* Paper presented at Special Education Technology Research and Development Symposium, Washington, DC.

Shahinpoor, M., & Singer, N. (1985). A new instructional laboratory. *T.H.E. Journal, 13,* 54–56.

Slesnick, T. (1984). Robots and kids. *Classroom Computer Learning, 4,* 54–59.

Yin, R. K., & Moore, G. B. (1984). *Robotics, artificial intelligence, computer simulation: Future applications in special education.* (Contract No. 300-84-0135). Washington, DC: U.S. Department of Education.

ELIZABETH McCLELLAN
*Council for Exceptional
Children*

**COMPUTER-ASSISTED INSTRUCTION
COMPUTER USE WITH THE HANDICAPPED**

ROBOTICS IN SPECIAL EDUCATION

Robotics in special education serves two potential functions. First, robotics can operate as an auxiliary to education by providing novel instruction to students, increasing motivation, and acting as an extension of the teacher in an instructional role. These auxiliary educational functions can be found in robots and robotic educational systems available today. They have been put to productive, albeit limited, use in special education. Little research has been conducted to test the efficacy of such uses.

A second, and perhaps potentially more dramatic, use of robotics for the handicapped concerns the robot as an extension of self. The robot is controlled by the individual to meet his or her personal needs and objectives and to control the environment. These functions demand a robot capable of a high level of sophistication in its logic and actions, a level not currently available in a single robotics unit (Kimbler, 1984). Nevertheless, the potential of the robot as an extension of the handicapped individual has prompted speculation concerning relevant applications and preliminary work on requisite performance characteristics.

Speculation on the usefulness of robotics has focused on handicapped conditions that limit mobility, dexterity, and interaction with the environment (Kimbler, 1984). The robot has been conceptualized as providing missing or impaired human functions under the direction of the disabled individual. Remote control devices have been used in this manner to some extent, and individual robots have been employed in restricted environments to perform limited functions such as serving meals. However, these applications have required modification of the environment. Ideally, the capacity of the robot would be more generalized; it would perform its functions by interacting with existing environments. A second major type of disability for which robotics applications have been conceptualized is sensory impairments, including visual and auditory disabilities. In these cases, the robot would provide sensory interaction as a mobile, dextrous adaptive device, permitting individuals to perceive the environment and then to operate on the setting directly or to control the robot to interact for them.

To support these functions, certain performance characteristics are necessary. For example, mobility under internal control to accomplish external demands is required. This movement needs to be smooth, to vary in speed from very slow to quick, and to react to novel environments through sensory systems. Robotics for these purposes require both payload, or strength and manipulation for that which needs to be carried, and dexterity dimensions to support varied and precise functions. The intelligence of the robot must allow reception and transmission of information through sensory apparatus, coordination of basic motion with its command and sensory input, communication in a conversational mode, and adaptation to new settings and uses. Finally, the robot must combine these characteristics with reasonable size; for acceptable and practical use, the robot must approximate the size of an average adult but maintain adequate bulk, stability, and power.

The robot that meets these requirements is complex and beyond current capabilities. Nevertheless, research on machine intelligence, performance characteristics, and integration proceeds. Work on artificial intelligence, expert systems, real-time computing, sensing capabilities, environmental mapping, conversational input and output, and power sources continues. The present state of technology in each of these areas supports feasibility of the robotic extension but requires packaging into a single working unit (Kimbler, 1984). Additionally, philosophical issues related to the cost of such technology must be addressed before applications of robotics to improve the ability of the handicapped to function in uncontrolled environments can be realized (Blaschke, 1984).

REFERENCES

Blaschke, C. (1984). *Market profile report: Technology and special education*. Falls Church, VA: Project Tech Mark, Education TURNKEY Systems.

Kimbler, D. L. (1984). Robots and special education: The robot as extension of self. In T. S. Hasselbring (Ed.), Toward the advancement of microcomputer technology in special education, *Peabody Journal of Education, 62,* 67–76.

LYNN S. FUCHS
Vanderbilt University

ROCHESTER METHOD

The Rochester method is an oral, multisensory procedure for instructing deaf children in which speech reading is simultaneously supplemented by finger spelling and auditory amplification. The language of signs is wholly excluded from this procedure of instruction. (Quigley & Young, 1965).

The Rochester method was established by Zenos Westervelt at the Rochester School for the Deaf, in Rochester, New York, in 1878. Westervelt was convinced that finger spelling was the best means of teaching deaf children grammatically correct language. He believed that the easy visibility of finger spelling could help in lip reading as well as in speech instruction (Levine, 1981). The Rochester method is directly related to the method used by Juan Pablo Bonet of Spain. He advocated the use of a combination of a one-handed alphabet and speech in his book *The simplification of sounds and the art of teaching mutes to speak,* published in 1620. This method had a resurgence in the Soviet Union in the 1950s under the name neo-oralism, and in the United States in the 1960s (Moores, 1982).

Various studies have assessed the effectiveness of the Rochester method as an educational tool. Reviewing these, Quigley and Paul (1984) reported that, in general, researchers concluded that deaf children exposed to the Rochester method performed better than comparison groups in finger spelling, speech reading, written language, and reading. They also found that, when good oral techniques are used in conjunction with finger spelling, there are no detrimental effects to the acquisition of oral skills.

REFERENCES

Levine, E. (1981). *The ecology of early deafness.* New York: Columbia University Press.

Moores, D. (1982). *Educating the deaf: Psychology, principles and practices.* Boston: Houghton Mifflin.

Quigley, S., & Paul, P. (1984). *Language and deafness.* San Diego, CA: College-Hill.

Quigley, S., & Young, J. (Eds.). (1965). *Interpreting for deaf people.* Washington, DC: U.S. Department of Health, Education, and Welfare.

ROSEMARY GAFFNEY
Hunter College

DEAF
SIGN LANGUAGE TRAINING
TOTAL COMMUNICATION

ROEPER REVIEW

The *Roeper Review,* published since 1977 by the Roeper City and Country School, is a journal on the education of gifted students. It originated as an information periodical for parents whose children attended the Roeper City and County School. The journal has three purposes: (1) presenting philosophical, moral, and academic issues that are related to the lives and experiences of gifted and talented persons; (2) presenting various views on those issues; and (3) translating theory into practice for use at school, at home, and in the general community (Staff, 1983, p. ii).

The audience and authors for *Roeper Review* include practicing teachers and administrators, teacher-educators, psychologists, and scientists. They are served by in-depth coverage of important topics in each issue. Some examples of issues discussed in past editions are teacher education for gifted education, social studies education for the gifted, special subpopulations among gifted students, and perceptions of gifted students and their education. The mailing address is *Roeper Review,* Box 329, Bloomfield Hills, MI 48013.

REFERENCE

Staff. (1983). Statement of purpose. *Roeper Review, 6,* ii.

ANN E. LUPKOWSKI
Texas A & M University

ROGER, HARRIET B. (1834–1919)

Harriet B. Roger began the first oral school for the instruction of the deaf in the United States in 1863 when she accepted a deaf child as a private pupil in her home. With published accounts of the instruction of the deaf in Germany to guide her, she taught herself how to instruct the child. Her success in this undertaking led to the admission of other deaf children. One of these was Mabel Hubbard, who became Mrs. Alexander Graham Bell and whose father, a prominent lawyer, obtained legislation for the creation of an oral school for the deaf in_Massachusetts. Hubbard formed this school by moving Rogers' school to Northampton, where, in 1867, they established the Clarke School for the Deaf, the second purely oral school for the deaf in the United States (the Lexington School for the Deaf having opened in New York City earlier that year). Rogers, the first teacher and the instructional leader of the Clarke School, remained there until her retirement in 1886.

REFERENCE

Lane, H. (1984). *When the mind hears.* New York: Random House.

PAUL IRVINE
Katonah, New York

Philip Roos

ROOS, PHILIP (1930–   )

Born in Brussels, Belgium, Philip Roos obtained his BS (1949) in biology and psychology with highest distinction from Stanford University, and from 1950 to 1951 did postgraduate work there in statistics and clinical and child psychology. He then earned his PhD (1955) in clinical psychology at the University of Texas, Austin. Roos is currently President of Roos & Associates in Hurst, Texas, a consulting firm providing training to business and industry, and he maintains a private clinical psychology practice as well.

Roos advocates the early use of behavior modification with institutionalized individuals with severe and profound retardation and adolescents with mild retardation who exhibit behavior disorders (Roos & Oliver, 1970). He is the originator of the Developmental Model, used for programming persons with mental retardation, emphasizing the potency of expectations in working with individuals with handicaps, and evaluating the impact of the interpersonal environment in shaping individual development. Roos' model has been the basis for many programs for those with mental retardation and a component of numerous national accreditation standards of agencies working with this population.

Roos has been an active advocate on behalf of children with handicaps and their families, assisting them in dealing with both emotional and practical frustrations, helping to individualize services, and aiding in the establishment of their rights (Roos, 1983). His service to the profession has included the positions of associate commissioner in the Division of Mental Retardation of the New York State Department of Mental Hygiene (1967–1968); national executive director of both the Association of Retarded Citizens (1969–1983) and Mothers Against Drunk Driving (1983–

1984); and a member of the board of directors of the Sunny Von Bulow Victim Advocacy Center (1986–1994). Roos has also been recognized in *Who's Who in America*, *Who's Who in the South and Southwest*, and *Who's Who in Medicine and Healthcare*.

REFERENCES

Roos, P. (1983). Advocate groups of the mentally retarded. In J. L. Matson & J. Mulick (Eds.), *Comprehensive handbook of mental retardation*. New York: Pergamon.

Roos, P., & Oliver, M. (1970). Evaluation of operant conditioning with institutionalized retarded children. *American Journal of Mental Deficiency, 74,* 325–330.

E. VALERIE HEWITT
Texas A & M University
First edition

TAMARA J. MARTIN
The University of Texas of the Permian Basin
Second edition

RORSCHACH

The Rorschach, developed by Hermann Rorschach in 1921, is generally regarded as the most widely used projective personality assessment technique (Lubin, Wallis, & Paine, 1971). Five distinct scoring systems developed following Rorschach's death in 1922. Exner's Comprehensive Rorschach System (Exner, 1974, 1978; Exner & Weiner, 1982) has provided the fragmented Rorschach community with a common methodology, language, and literature; it is one of the most frequently used systems.

The Rorschach test stimuli consist of 10 inkblots, half achromatic and half with different degrees of color. Cards are presented individually to subjects, who are allowed to give as many responses as they wish describing "what the cards might be." Determinants that are scored include location, form, color, shading, movement, and quality and quantity of responses. Information obtained from the scored protocol includes personality state and trait characteristics, coping style, extent and quality of self-focus, quality of reality testing, likelihood of suicidal ideation or schizophrenia, depression, maturity, and complexity of psychological operations. Scoring and interpretation of the Rorschach, which is time-consuming and detailed, requires that the examiner be thoroughly trained in Rorschach assessment.

Criticisms of the Rorschach include the length of the time needed for administration, scoring and interpretation, and the fact that accurate usage is highly dependent on the clinical skills of the administrator. When used to gather descriptive clinical information, the Rorschach is considered to be an empirically valid instrument (Maloney & Glasser, 1982; Parker, 1983). Gittelman-Klein (1978) has presented an in-depth review of the validity of projective techniques, with positive results.

REFERENCES

Exner, J. E. (1974). *The Rorschach: A comprehensive system. Vol. 1. Basic foundations*. New York: Wiley.

Exner, J. E. (1978). *The Rorschach: A comprehensive system. Vol. 2: Current research and advanced interpretation*. New York: Wiley.

Exner, J. E., & Weiner, I. B. (1982). *The Rorschach: A comprehensive system. Vol. 3: Assessment of children and adolescents*. New York: Wiley.

Gittelman-Klein, R. (1978). *Validity of projective tests for psychodiagnosis in children*. In R. L. Spitzer & D. F. Klein (Eds.), Critical issues in psychiatric diagnosis. New York: Raven.

Lubin, B., Wallis, R. R., & Paine, C. (1971). Patterns of psychological test usage in the United States: 1935–1969. *Professional Psychology, 2,* 70–74.

Maloney, M. P., & Glasser, A. (1982). An evaluation of the clinical utility of the Draw-A-Person test. *Journal of Clinical Psychology, 38,* 183–190.

Parker, K. A. (1983). A meta-analyses of the reliability and validity of the Rorschach. *Journal of Personality Assessment, 47,* 227–231.

CONSTANCE Y. CELAYA
FRANCES F. WORCHEL
Texas A & M University

RORSCHACH INKBLOT TEST

The Rorschach inkblot test is a widely-used projective personality assessment technique. The test is administered in a non-directive fashion (Exner, 1995). Respondents are asked to describe what he or she can see in a series of ten inkblots. Administration time with children is approximately 30 minutes, with interpretation taking 30 to 45 minutes. Examiners transcribe the respondent's words and identify the visual percepts, which are then coded and tabulated through an extensively researched, empirically-based system. Considerable examiner training is necessary to accomplish the administration, coding, and interpretation tasks.

The Comprehensive System (Exner, 1993) approach makes the Rorschach an objective multiscale performance and personality test. Its administration and coding standards, normative data, and accumulated research provide a sturdy empirical basis to the test. Test-retest reliability for children is as expected given developmental considerations: Some variables demonstrate relatively strong test-retest reliability for a year or two at a during the primary grade school years (Exner, Thomas, & Mason, 1985; Exner & Weiner, 1995). Test-retest reliability increases gradually, so that almost all measures of trait variables are relatively stable by age 18.

The test yields a large number of variables related to the domains of cognition, affect, interpersonal perception, self-perception, and coping styles, and also various characteristics related to diagnostic categories. Personality, coping, and problem-solving interpretations can be synthesized, along with observations about social, school, family, and problem behaviors, into a description of the psychological functioning of the child.

Criticism of the test has been a popular rallying cry, but empirical reports indicate adequate validity and utility, particularly for issues that are not readily accessible through self-report, brief interview, or observation (Exner, 1993; Viglione, in press). The fact that all responses are formulated by the subject without prefabrication from test developers allows the test to access personally meaningful information. For example, the Rorschach can shed light on issues that the respondent may be unwilling or unable to express. No other instrument yields such an efficient, yet comprehensive, empirically-based understanding of the individual. Criticism about the test may result from a misunderstanding of its so-called 'projective components'. This is not a test of imagination, and it goes far beyond projective processes, despite unfortunate and inaccurate characterizations (e.g., Dawes, 1994).

Rorschach variables have demonstrated concurrent and predictive validity for both academic achievement test scores and classroom performance by young children, even after the effects of intelligence were statistically removed (e.g., Russ, 1980, 1981; Wulach, 1977). These results support the belief that the Rorschach addresses cognitive motivational trends and real-life application of abilities.

As far as the special education evaluation goals of truly understanding a child, the Rorschach can help to identify the psychological factors associated with the expression of observed strengths and weaknesses. For example, the test can help to identify and to understand emotional and psychological disturbances that impede learning, difficulties with peer and authority relationships, inappropriate behaviors which interfere with school performance and socialization, and problem-solving styles which result in poor performance despite intellectual abilities. However, the use of the Rorschach remains controversial and an opposing view of its reliability and validity is available in Sechrest, Stickle, and Stewart (1998).

REFERENCES

Dawes, R. M. (1994). *House of cards: Psychology and psychotherapy built on myth*. New York: The Free Press.

Exner, J. E. (1993). *The Rorschach: A comprehensive system, Vol. 1: Basic foundations* (3rd ed.). New York: Wiley.

Exner, J. E. (1995). *A Rorschach workbook for the comprehensive system* (4th ed.). Asheville, North Carolina: Rorschach Workshops.

Exner, J. E., Thomas, E. A., & Mason, B. J. (1985). Children's Rorschachs: Description and prediction. *Journal of Personality Assessment, 49*, 13–20.

Exner, J. E., & Weiner, I. B. (1995). *The Rorschach: A comprehensive system, Vol. 3: Assessment of children and adolescent* (2nd ed.). New York: Wiley.

Russ, S. W. (1980). Primary process integration on the Rorschach and achievement in children. *Journal of Personality Assessment, 44*, 338–344.

Russ, S. W. (1981). Primary process integration on the Rorschach and achievement in children: A follow-up study. *Journal of Personality Assessment, 45*, 473–477.

Sechrest, L., Stickle, T., & Stewart, M. (1998). The role of assessment in clinical psychology. In C. R. Reynolds (Ed.), *Assessment*, Vol. 4 of A. Bellack & M. Hersen (Eds.), *Comprehensive Clinical Psychology* (pp. 1–32). Oxford: Elsevier Science.

Viglione, D. J. (in press). A review of recent research addressing the utility of the Rorschach. *Psychological Assessment*.

Wulach, J. S. (1977). Piagetian cognitive development and primary process thinking in children. *Journal of Personality Assessment, 41*, 230–237.

Donald J. Viglione
California School of Professional Psychology

ROSS INFORMATION PROCESSING ASSESSMENTS

The *Ross Information Processing Assessment–Second Edition* (RIPA–2) provides quantifiable data for profiling 10 key areas basic to communicative and cognitive functioning: Immediate Memory, Recent Memory, Temporal Orientation (Recent and Remote Memory), Spatial Orientation, Orientation to Environment, Recall of General Information, Problem Solving and Abstract Reasoning, Organization, and Auditory Processing and Retention. The RIPA–2 enables the examiner to quantify cognitive–linguistic deficits, determine severity levels for specific skill areas, and develop rehabilitation goals and objectives.

The study sample included 126 individuals with traumatic brain injury in 17 states and was representative of TBI demographics for gender, ethnicity, and socioeconomic status. Raw scores are converted to standard scores. Reliability and validity studies performed on individuals with traumatic brain injury (TBI) are reported. Internal consistency reliability was investigated, and the mean reliability coefficient for RIPA–2 subtests was .85, with a range of .67 to .91. Content, construct, and criterion-related validity are reported in the manual.

The earlier edition of RIPA–2 was reviewed in *Eleventh*

Mental Measurements Yearbook and *Test Critiques;* references for the newest edition of the instrument are unavailable because of its recent publication date. Franzen (1988) reported that the RIPA appeared to be a good beginning towards producing an instrument capable of profiling the different areas of information processing that might be affected by diffuse or right-hemisphere injury. Ehrlich (1992) felt that the instrument measured selected verbally mediated aspects and could be a useful tool in a clinical setting.

The *Ross Information Processing Assessment–Geriatric* (RIPA–G) is an adaptation that is designed for residents in skilled nursing facilities (SNFs), hospitals, and clinics. In addition to standard questions and stimulus items used for assessing cognitive-linguistic deficits, the RIPA–G incorporates questions from the Minimum Data Set used by nursing staffs in SNFs. These questions provide correlational data with nursing staff's assessments of patients' cognitive-linguistic abilities. Percentile ranks, standard scores, and composite quotients are provided for individual subtests, skill areas, and overall cognitive-linguistic functioning. Periodic retesting provides objective data to assess treatment efficacy and documents progress often required for Medicare and third-party payment. Internal consistency reliability coefficients of the RIPA–G were found to be .80 or greater.

The *Ross Information Processing Assessment–Primary* is designed for children ages 5 through 12 who have had a traumatic brain injury, experienced other neuropathologies such as seizure disorders or anoxia, or exhibit learning disabilities or weaknesses that interfere with learning acquisition. The eight subtests measure immediate and recent memory, spatial orientation, temporal orientation, organization, problem solving, abstract reasoning, and recall of general information.

The RIPA–P was standardized on 115 individuals ages 5 through 12. Reliability coefficients were found to be .81 or above, and more than a third of them were over .90. Validity studies show that the test discriminates between "normal" and LD or neurological problems. Item discrimination coefficients for the RIPA–P range from .39 to .94. Norms include children who have learning disabilities.

REFERENCES

Ehrlich, J. (1992). Review of the Ross Information Processing Assessment. In J. J. Kramer & J. C. Conoley (Eds.), *The eleventh mental measurements yearbook* (pp. 775–776). Lincoln: Buros Institute of Mental Measurements, University of Nebraska Press.

Franzen, M. D. (1988). Review of the Ross Information Processing Assessment. In D. J. Keyser & R. C. Sweetland (Eds.), *Test Critiques–Volume VII* (pp. 496–498). Austin, TX: Pro-Ed.

Ross-Swain, D. (1996). *Ross Information Processing Assessment–Second Edition.* Austin, TX: Pro-Ed.

Ross-Swain, D., & Fogle, P. (1996). *Ross Information Processing Assessment–Geriatric.* Austin, TX: Pro-Ed.

Ross-Swain, D. (1999). *Ross Information Processing Assessment–Primary.* Austin, TX: Pro-Ed.

Taddy Maddox
Pro-Ed, Inc.

ROSWELL-CHALL DIAGNOSTIC READING TEST OF WORD ANALYSIS SKILLS, REVISED AND EXTENDED

The Roswell-Chall Diagnostic Reading Test was developed to evaluate the word analysis and word recognition skills of pupils reading at the first- through fourth-grade levels. It may also be used with pupils who are reading at higher levels where there is a suspicion of decoding and word recognition difficulties or for research and program evaluation.

Two comparable forms of the test are available. Each is individually administered. The test has 10 main subtests and 4 extended evaluation subtests. All of the subtests or only those deemed appropriate may be given. The following skills are measured: high-frequency words, single consonant sounds, consonant diagrams, consonant blends, short vowel words, short and long vowel sounds, rule of silent e's, vowel diagrams, common diphthongs and vowels controlled by *r*, and syllabication (and compound words). The extended evaluation subtests include naming capital letters, naming lower-case letters, encoding single consonants, and encoding phonetically regular words.

The test takes approximately 10 minutes to administer, score, and interpret. Score interpretations are provided in the manual. The test has good reliability and validity. Users should be concerned about the size and somewhat limited nature of the norm sample, therefore, the administrator should be knowledgeable in the kinds of skills needed in most individual testing situations and, in order to interpret the test accurately, be a relatively skilled reading clinician.

REFERENCE

Manual of instructions: Roswell-Chall Diagnostic Reading Test of Word Analysis Skills, Revised and Extended. (1978). LaJolla, CA: Essay.

Ronald V. Schmelzer
Eastern Kentucky University

ROTHMUND-THOMPSON SYNDROME

See RARE DISEASES

Jean J. Rousseau

ROUSSEAU, JEAN J. (1712–1778)

Jean Jacques Rousseau, French-Swiss philosopher and moralist, revolutionized child-rearing and educational practices with the publication, in 1762, of *Emile,* a treatise on education in the form of a novel. Rousseau contended that childhood is not merely a period of preparation for adulthood to be endured, but a developmental stage to be cherished and enjoyed. He enjoined parents and educators to be guided by the interests and capacities of the child, and was the first writer to propose that the study of the child should be the basis for the child's education. Probably every major educational reform since the eighteenth century can be traced in some way to Rousseau, and indebtedness to him is clear in the works of Pestalozzi, Froebel, Montessori, and Dewey. An eloquent writer, Rousseau's works on man's relationship with nature, as well as his writings on social, political, and educational matters, were major contributions to the literature of his day.

REFERENCES

Boyd, W. (1963). *The educational theory of Jean Jacques Rousseau.* New York: Russell & Russell.

Rousseau, J. J. (1969). *Emile.* New York: Dutton.

PAUL IRVINE
Katonah, New York

RUBELLA

Postnatal rubella (German measles) is a relatively mild viral infection that is generally inconsequential. It was first differentiated from measles and scarlet fever by German workers in the latter part of the eighteenth century. German scientists termed the disease *Roethelm.* According to *Black's Medical Dictionary,* the term German measles has no geographical reference but rather comes from the word germane, meaning akin to. Rubella comes from the Latin word *rubellus* meaning red (*Black's,* 1984).

The postnatal rubella virus is transmitted through contact with blood, bodily waste excretions, nasopharyngeal secretions of infected persons, and, possibly, contact with contaminated clothing (*Professional Guide to Diseases,* 1984). Humans are the only known host for the rubella virus and the period of communicability lasts from about 10 days before the rash appears until about 5 days after it appears. When acquired postnatally, rubella is a self-limited viral infection. It appears most frequently in the late winter or spring, particularly in large urban communities. Rubella is distributed worldwide. Although major epidemics occur in intervals ranging from 10 to 30 years, sizable epidemics may occur every 6 to 9 years (Alford, 1976). The factors responsible for the continuation of the epidemics is unknown.

It is believed that the rubella virus enters the body through the upper respiratory tract, is transmitted to the blood system, and results in low levels of viral production from 9 to 11 days. After this time, virimic seeding results in viral excretion from the nasopharynx, urine, cervix, and feces. After the incubation period of 14 to 21 days, a red rash erupts. Enlargement of the lymph nodes, most easily identified on the face or the neck, is a hallmark of a rubella infection. The rash, which typically begins on the face, rapidly spreads to the trunk and other parts of the body. The rash may be accompanied by a low-grade fever (99 to rarely higher than 104). In adults, the rash may also be accompanied by headaches, joint pains, and conjunctivitis.

Because of the mild nature of rubella acquired postnatally, there is little concern for active treatment. The rash rarely requires topical ointments but aspirin may be taken to ease the discomfort associated with fever and body pains. Children or adults with postnatal rubella should be isolated owing to the threat of infecting newly pregnant mothers.

Congenital rubella is a concern because of the 20 to 30% chance of damage to the fetus when a mother contracts the infection during the first trimester of pregnancy (Bonwick, 1972). Catastrophic damaging effects were first reported by Sir Norman Gregg, an Australian ophthalmologist, 1941. The classic congenital rubella syndrome as described by Gregg consists of fetal anomalies, ocular defects, and hearing impairment. Mental retardation was also shown to be a common result of early damage to the fetus.

Shortly after the rubella virus was isolated in 1961, the first epidemic since 1940, and the last major epidemic to date, struck the United States. The results of the epidemic are reported by Rudolph and Desmond, 1972:

Some 30,000 pregnancies ended in miscarriage or stillbirth, and between 20,000 to 30,000 infants suffered from various defects . . . 8000 cases of deafness, 3600 cases of deafness and blindness, 1800 cases of mental retardation, and 6600 other malformations . . . 5000 therapeutic abortions and 2000 excess neonatal deaths. (p. 4)

It appears that circulation of the virus in the blood of the infected mother during the incubation period of her postnatal infection is the initial step in contraction of congenital rubella by the fetus. The virus is transferred from the mother's bloodstream to the placenta and then often to the fetal bloodstream. Although the exact reasons for this are not known, it is apparent that the earlier in the pregnancy the mother contracts the viral infection, the more pervasive the damage to the fetus. It is also apparent that congenital rubella is very different from postnatal rubella in that the former is widely disseminated throughout the body of the fetus.

Extensive investigations during the last 20 years have characterized congenital rubella as having pathologic potential much greater than was first assumed by Gregg. For instance, it is now hypothesized that congenital rubella, in addition to being responsible for the anomalies previously reported, may also be responsible for numerous abnormalities that appear later in life. These include dental problems, anemia, encephalitis, giant cell hepatitis, dermatitis, and diabetes.

Active prevention seems the key to reducing the impact of congenital rubella, as once the damage has been done in utero there appears to be little hope of reversing the effects. Of course, corrective surgery can be performed in cases where the fetus suffers cardiac damage or has cataracts, and hearing aids can be given to the hearing-impaired child, but the damage is not reversible.

Passive immunization procedures such as large doses of gamma globulin have been shown to be ineffective in preventing damage to the fetus once the mother has contracted the virus. Chemotherapeutic procedures also have proven inadequate as protection against the devastating effects of congenital rubella (Alford, 1976).

An active immunization program seems to hold the best promise to date to reducing the spread of rubella to pregnant females. Immunization with live virus vaccine RA27/3 is used in the United States. This preventive program is aimed at vaccinating large numbers of infants and young children in the hopes of reducing circulation of the virus in the general population and thus protecting females in the childbearing years. Some have advocated that all young girls between 11 and 14 years should be vaccinated if they have not had the disease. It is also advocated now that all young women of childbearing age who have not had the disease and who are not pregnant be vaccinated. In Europe immunization programs are directed toward young married women. This approach is not without its risks and questions (Alford, 1976). Certain guidelines for administering the vaccine are available (*Professional Guide to Diseases*, 1984).

Often the psychological impact of giving birth to a handicapped child can be as damaging as the virus itself. Parents of children with congenital rubella can obtain help and advice from the National Association for Deaf, Blind and Rubella Handicapped, 12 A Rosebery Avenue, London, England ECIR 4TD.

REFERENCES

Alford, C. A. (1976). Rubella. In J. S. Remington, & J. O. Klein (Eds.), *Infectious diseases of the fetus and newborn infant*. Philadelphia: Saunders.

Black's medical dictionary. (1984). Totowa, NJ: Barnes & Noble.

Bonwick, M. (1972). *Rubella and other intraocular viral diseases in infancy*. Boston: Little, Brown.

Professional guide to diseases. (1984). (pp. 384–386). Springhouse, PA: Springhouse.

Rudolph, A. J., & Desmond, M. M. (1972). Clinical manifestations of the congenital rubella syndrome. In M. Bonwick (Ed.), *Rubella and other intraocular viral diseases in infancy*. Boston: Little, Brown.

JULIA A. HICKMAN
University of Texas

CATARACTS
CONGENITAL DISORDERS
MENTAL RETARDATION

RUBENSTEIN-TAYBI SYNDROME

See RARE DISEASES

RURAL SPECIAL EDUCATION

Approximately 67% of the 16,000 public school districts in the United States are classified as rural because of sparse population or geographic location (Sher, 1978). According to Helge (1984), educational characteristics of rural areas are distinctly different from those of urban areas. Rural areas have higher poverty levels and serve greater percentages of handicapped children. Populations in rural areas are increasing, however, their tax bases are not. Education costs more in rural areas than in nonrural areas because of transportation requirements and scarce professional resources.

Because of the remoteness of the areas, assessing the effectiveness of special education services to handicapped and gifted children has been difficult. One reason for this, according to the director of the National Rural Research Project (Helge, 1984) has been the absence of a consistently applied definition of the term rural among federal agencies, educators, and professional organizations. The definition that is most commonly used is the one developed for the 1978 to 1983 research projects funded by the U.S. Office of Special Education Programs and conducted by the National Rural Research and Personnel Preparation Project. This definition reads:

> A district is considered rural when the number of inhabitants is fewer than 150 per square mile or when located in counties with 60% or more of the population living in communities not larger than 5000 inhabitants. Districts with more than 10,000 students and those within a Standard Metropolitan Statistical Area (SMSA), as determined by the U.S. Census Bureau, are not considered rural. (p. 296)

The National Rural Research and Personnel Preparation Project was funded (to be conducted in four phases from 1978 to 1981)

> to investigate state and local educational agencies nationwide in order to determine problems and effective strategies for implementing Public Law 94-142; and to develop profiles of effective special education delivery systems and strategies, given specific rural community and district subcultural characteristics. (p. 296)

Phase I, conducted during 1978 and 1979, focused on identifying facilitating and hindering factors that operate to determine the success or failure of rural local educational agency compliance with PL 94-142. Results of this phase showed that problems identified by state educational agencies were grouped in three categories: (1) staffing problems (recruiting and retaining qualified staff); (2) attitudinal variables (resistance to change, suspicions of outside interference, and long distances between schools); and (3) problems based on rural geography (fiscal problems, difficult terrain, and economic conditions). Phase II, conducted during 1979 and 1980, was designed to develop profiles interrelating community characteristics and school district characteristics with service delivery options proven viable in other local education agencies with similar characteristics. Phase III (1980) involved using Phase I and II data to develop interdisciplinary models of personnel preparation for effective service delivery to rural subcultures. Phase IV, conducted in 1980 and 1981, was designed to field test and disseminate the modules for use in preservice and in-service training programs (Helge, 1981).

A series of in-service training modules have been developed with topics that range from stress reduction to alternate rural service delivery systems. In addition, several preservice modules are presently being field tested in universities across the country. Topics of the modules include alternate instructional arrangements and delivery systems for low-incidence handicapped students in rural America; Warren Springs, Mesa: a rural preservice simulation; solving rural parent-professional related dilemmas; working with parents of rural handicapped students; involving citizens and agencies of rural communities in cooperative programming for handicapped students; working with peer professionals in rural environments; creative resource identification for providing services to rural handicapped students; solving educational dilemmas related to school administration; and personal development skills and strategies for effective survival as a rural special educator. These modules are available through the American Council on Rural Special Education.

In a report on the state of the art of rural special education (Helge, 1984), it was noted that major service delivery problems remained basically the same as in the initial study done in 1979. These problems were associated with funding inadequacies, difficulties in recruiting and retaining qualified staff, transportation inadequacies, problems with providing services to low-incidence handicapped populations, and inadequacies of preservice training. In addition, many of these inadequacies were seen as future problems.

In an effort to focus on rural special education and the identified service delivery problems, the American Council on Rural Special Education was founded in 1981. This nonprofit national membership organization is an outgrowth of the National Rural Development Institute, headquartered at Western Washington University in Bellingham. The organization is composed of approximately 1000 rural special educators and administrators, parents of handicapped students, and university and state department personnel. The specific purposes of the organization are to enhance direct services to rural individuals and agencies serving exceptional students; to increase educational opportunities for rural handicapped and gifted students; and to develop a system for forecasting the future for rural special education and planning creative service delivery alternatives.

The American Council on Rural Special Education (ACRES) serves as an advocate for rural special education at the federal, state, regional, and local levels; provides professional development opportunities, and disseminates information on the current needs of rural special education. The ACRES has established a nationwide system to link educators and administrators needing jobs with agencies having vacancies. The ACRES Rural Bulletin Board communicates to interested agencies information regarding rural special education issues and promising practices through SpecialNet, the electronic communication system operated by the National Association of State Directors of Special Education. ACRES publishes a quarterly newsletter and a journal the *Rural Special Education Quarterly*. These publications include up-to-date information on issues facing handicapped students in rural America, problem-solving strategies, pertinent legislation and conferences, and articles on rural preservice and in-service strategies. The ACRES also holds an annual conference each year in the spring, usually at the institute's headquarters. The conferences feature presentations to enhance services to rural handicapped and gifted children, media displays curriculum materials, and hardware and software exhibits.

REFERENCES

Helge, D. I. (1981). Problems in implementing comprehensive special education programming in rural areas. *Exceptional Children, 47,* 514–524.

Helge, D. I. (1984). The state of the art of rural special education. *Exceptional Children, 50,* 294–305.

Sher, J. P. (1978). A proposal to end federal neglect of rural schools. *Phi Delta Kappan, 60,* 280–282.

CECELIA STEPPE-JONES
*North Carolina Central
University*

RUSH, BENJAMIN (1745–1813)

Benjamin Rush, physician, teacher, reformer, and patriot, began medical practice in Philadelphia in 1769. He taught chemistry at the College of Philadelphia, and published the first American textbook on that subject. During the Revolutionary War, he served as surgeon-general of the Army and published a textbook on military medicine that was still in use at the time of the Civil War. Following his military service, Rush returned to the practice of medicine in Philadelphia, where he established the first free dispensary in the United States. He is believed to be the first physician to relate smoking to cancer and to advocate temperance and exercise to promote good health. An outspoken advocate of humane treatment for the mentally ill, in 1812 Rush published a work that would influence medical education for generations to come, *Medical Inquiries and Observations Upon the Diseases of the Mind.*

Despite his accomplishments as a physician, political and social issues were Rush's major interests. He was a member of the Continental Congress and a signer of the Declaration of Independence. He was active in the movement to abolish slavery, and was influential in the ratification of the federal Constitution in Pennsylvania. He involved himself in a number of educational causes, advocating improved education for girls and proposing a comprehensive system of public schools that would offer science and practical subjects as well as traditional academics.

REFERENCES

Hawke, D. (1971). *Benjamin Rush.* New York: Bobbs-Merrill.

Rush, B. (1962). *Medical inquiries and observations upon the diseases of the mind.* New York: Hafner.

PAUL IRVINE
Katonah, New York

RUSSELL-SILVER SYNDROME

See RARE DISEASES

RUSSIA, SPECIAL EDUCATION IN

Special education in Russia first developed from the then-progressive ideas of Vygotsky, Luria, Boskis, Pevzner, Levina, Rau and other behavioral researchers. They approached the education of a child with special needs while considering his or her complex psychophysiological development, with the most complete possible social rehabilitation of a child as a goal. During the Communist regime these ideas were replaced by a pedagogy that was less child-centered, isolating a child with special needs from society, and establishing several boarding institutions (van Rijswijk et al., 1996).

Recently, Russia has entered a new phase in its thinking and attitudes about special education. A return to the individual child-focus has been augmented by the ideal for full participation or integration in society. Social rehabilitation continues to be valued, but social participation is also highly valued.

The modern phase into which special education has recently entered was necessary because of the absence of protective legislation for the civil rights of children with handicaps or with other special needs. This modern phase of special education in Russia places new emphases on preschool interventions and on staff training of teachers, psychologists, social workers, and others.

Legal Bases for Special Education

During the Soviet period in the republics of the former USSR, the rights of the child (as indicated in the UNO Convention, the UNO Declaration on the rights of the invalids and the rights of the mentally handicapped people) were not well-observed. Within the last decade, Russia's central government has taken firm steps toward ratification and realization of these international documents. Nevertheless, still there is inadequate legislation for special education, although there is some progress in this direction (Aksenova, 1997). The new phase for special education was signaled in part by a landmark Law on Education (1992), which was considered one of the most democratic in the history of Russia. This law was followed four years later by several further insertions and improvements to "About the Education;" these went into effect January 5th, 1996.

The Law on Education significantly improves the state guarantee of a free, appropriate public education to people with disabilities. Particularly, Article 50, Point 10 of the Law foresees the establishment of the special (correctional) educational institutions for children and adolescents with special needs, where they can have treatment, upbringing, education, social adaptation, and integration into society. Note that social rehabilitation is emphasized more than social participation.

A second new law that marks the modern phase of special education in Russia is "On Social Care of Invalids," which went into effect on January 1st, 1996. Article 18 of this Law is dedicated to the upbringing and education of child invalids. According to the law, the educational institutions together with social and health care organizations must provide upbringing and education of children with disabilities, from preschool through secondary school, both within classrooms and outside, according to an individually defined program of rehabilitation. In both mainstream schools and special educational institutions, this education is free.

Another change in the modern phase is that the subjects of the Russian Federation (RF) have received the right to make legislation for solving their local problems, including the field of help and care of children and their families. This is appropriate because the financing of education, health, and other social services is carried out mainly at the expense of local budgets (which also brings about regional differences in type and quality of services). These legislative changes have encouraged public organizations to play a significant role in the improvement of children with special needs. In addition, public interest groups are beginning to attempt to influence regional decision-making in the field of special education. Newly active public organizations are representing the interests of children with disabilities and their families. However, the national networking and sharing of information is still minimal. For example, there is not a uniform data bank on children with disabilities and programs in operation, let alone data on program effectiveness.

Although the recent Russian legislation for the children with special needs is a major step forward, it touches only some aspects of special education. Now Russia must develop a new law specifically for special education; in fact, a draft has been worked out and is under consideration by the State Duma.

Structure of Special Education

In Russia, several ministries are responsible for children with special needs, which causes a number of difficulties. The interdepartmental barriers interfere with creation of an integrated, harmonious, and effective system of social care and support. There is a whole complex of problems: social, scientific, practical. The largest obstacle to progress is the absence of high-grade statistical information about such children; in the Russian Federation there is no uniform state system to account for them.

The system of special education in Russia is based on five age designations and the specific type of disability.

Age structure. The vertical structure consists of 5 levels:

- early childhood (from 0 to 3 years old);
- preschool period (from 3 to 7);
- compulsory education (from 7 to 16);
- comprehensive education and vocational training (from 15 to 18 and up to 21 for the blind, deaf, and physically handicapped);
- adults-invalid training.

During the period of early childhood (from the birth to 3) children are trained and brought up in home conditions, in establishments for infants, and in homes for children if the child is an orphan. Developmental and remedial work with children with developmental problems is carried out in various centers of early intervention and rehabilitation, in special groups and at psychological-medical-pedagogical consulting centers.

For children of pre-school age there are the following establishments:

- special kindergartens with day and day-night stay
- remedial homes for children
- special groups in regular kindergartens
- special rehabilitation centers
- preschool groups in special schools (for children with visual, hearing, emotional, and mental disorders).

Special (remedial) educational establishments for children with developmental problems offer programs of elementary regular education, general regular education, and general comprehensive regular education. These establishments must meet special state educational standards. They focus on special remedial work, education, treatment, social adaptation, and integration into the society.

Special education is offered within a variety of administrative structures:

- special (remedial) school (daily or evening)
- special boarding school
- rehabilitation centers
- special class at a regular educational establishment
- individually in a regular educational establishment
- home education
- external education
- education in a stationary medical establishment.

Persons with developmental problems may receive both a regular education and vocational training in:

- special average schools
- special industrial workshops

- centers of social-labor rehabilitation
- special vocational schools.

Disability-type (Horizontal) Structure

The horizontal structure of special education in Russia is by eight types of disability:

    I. for the deaf (classes for mentally retarded children)

    II. for the hard of hearing (classes for mentally retarded children)

    III. for the blind (classes for mentally retarded children)

    IV. for visually impaired (classes for mentally retarded children)

    V. with severe speech and language disorders

    VI. with emotional disabilities (classes for mentally retarded children)

    VII. with learning disabilities

    VIII. for mentally retarded (special classes for children with severe mental retardation, classes for children with multiple and complex disorders).

For children and teenagers with deviant behavior there exist three kinds of special educational establishments in Russia:

- special educational school
- special vocational technical school
- special (remedial) comprehensive school and special (remedial) professional technical school for children and teenagers with problems in development (learning disabilities, light forms of mental retardation) who commit socially dangerous actions.

In Russia, statistics on children with special needs were not available during most of the Communist era. But beginning from 1993 according to the Russian Governmental Decree N 848 (23.08.93), "About the Realization of the UNO Convention on the Rights of a Child" and "International Declaration about the Providing of the Surviving, Care and Development of Children," a governmental statistical report is published every year. Entitled "About the Situation of Children in the Russian Federation," it contains statistics related to demographics and legal mandates for service in Russia as a whole and specific Russian regions.

The number of special schools for children with developmental problems (see table) is annually increasing. Special (remedial) classes in the mainstream schools have also grown.

In Russia, there are no special schools for children with emotional and behavioral problems. Concerning the education of children with early infant autism, there was no specific approach until recently, when individual groups in special kindergartens and primary schools began to be created for such children. Children with moderate and severe mental retardation usually live in state-financed boarding schools or with families, where education is partial or nonexistent. Until recently such children were labeled incapable of studying. Improvements in the education of these children is slow, but there are increasing numbers of special developmental classes in the schools for the children with mild mental retardation.

Russia is still marked by the existence of large numbers of separate special education boarding schools, where the majority of children get psychological, medical and pedagogical help. Such boarding schools became popular for two reasons. First, because of Russia's large territory, in rural areas the school is usually situated so far from home that daily attendance is impossible. Secondly, many of these children do not have parents, have been given up for adoption, or have been refused by their parents, becoming wards of the state.

In Russia, approximately 1% to 2% of children from 6 to 16 years old attend special schools (and, more recently, special classes). Until recently in the Russian Federation, a significant number of children who needed special education could not get it because of the scarcity of special schools and personnel, especially in the regions of far North, Siberia, and rural districts. In remote areas, many children with disabilities received no help.

Integrated Education for Children with Special Needs

In the latter part of this decade, special education in Russia has been improving in two main ways. First, there has been improvement in the existing network of special education programs and their expansion. The second improvement has been in the integrated education of these children (Shipitsina, 1996). The first improvement in the type and extent of special services is noted in the table. Note that the number of special schools has increased gradually or been static. On the other hand, the number of special classes within regular public schools is expanding rapidly (see Table).

Undoubtedly, not all children with problems in development can be integrated into a regular school, but many more can than are presently doing so. The difficult problem is identifying those particular children with developmental problems who can be integrated and when is the best time to start their integrative education.

Generally, in Russia, there are few statistics about the number of children with visual, hearing, and other impairments educated in mainstream schools. We do know that the majority of such children do not get any special help in ordinary schools. In recent years in Moscow, Saint Peters-

Schools For Children With Mental and Physical Disorders in the Russian Federation (beginning of educational year)*

Types of establishments	Number of schools				Number of students (in thousands)			
	1990	1992	1994	1996	1990	1992	1994	1996
for children with mental or physical handicaps—Total	1817	1835	1848	1889	312.1	277.4	267.6	277.2
for mentally retarded	1452	1459	1443	1440	251.6	217.9	203.9	205.5
for the blind	20	19	18	20	3.7	3.3	2.9	3.4
for visually impaired	51	52	56	61	7.8	7.4	8.0	8.5
for the deaf (and mute)	82	81	85	84	12.5	11.9	12.0	11.3
for the hard of hearing	70	73	73	77	11.2	10.8	10.6	11.0
for children with consequences of poliomyelitis and cerebral palsy	40	40	43	52	6.5	6.0	6.1	6.7
for severe speech and language problems	61	61	61	62	10.8	11.0	11.5	11.9
for learning disabilities	41	50	65	71	8.0	9.1	12.1	13.4
for children with mental or physical disorders set up in regular schools					53.0	119.7	155.5	192.0
for mentally retarded in regular schools					7.1	10.7	10.6	14.7
for learning disabled in regular schools					44.9	103.2	141.9	175.9

*Data of the State Statistical Committee of Russian Federation.

burg, and some other big cities of Russia, research began on the practical psychological and pedagogical guidance of children with sensory and moving problems in the mainstream school.

So far in Russia, the attitude to integrative education is restrained. Parents of children with impairments are commonly advised to place their child in a special boarding home from his or her very early life. The justification is usually that mainstream schools do not have the special staff and that the children cannot receive necessary support in mainstream classes in these schools. Unfortunately, this argument is partly true, as regular schools lack resources, expertise and philosophies of integration. Usually the nature of integration is not questioned; the majority agree that it is good in the abstract, but that the practical obstacles are too great. Where attitudes are the problem, they usually come from the teachers in the mainstream schools (Makhortova, 1996).

Inclusive Education in the Regular Classroom

Children with different disabilities are included differentially in general education classrooms in Russia. Children with hearing impairments have only recently been in-

cluded. Today the process of integration of such children into mainstream establishments is steadily expanding (Shmatko, 1996). The integrated education of children with sight impairments in the mainstream school is a rare phenomenon, and most mainstream schools are not yet ready for it. Some of the hesitation is due to concern for the adjustment of the child with disabilities. Some contend that full integration may increase personal problems (Makhortova, 1996).

Special Classes in the Mainstream School

Today in Russia, one of the fastest growing models of integrative education is the organization of special classes in the mainstream school. They are organized:

—for the children with intellectual impairments (where there are not any special schools for this category of the children nearby), their number is rather small

—for the children with learning difficulties, the classes with special educational support or remedial classes

—for the children "of risk groups" (with learning difficulties, behavior problems, weak health), the classes of compensative education, special educational support, adaptation, and recreation.

In rare cases, due to the large distance from the special schools and unwillingness of the parents to refer their children to receive the education in the boarding schools, special classes or groups for children with sight, hearing, and speech impairments are organized in the mainstream kindergartens and schools.

Despite the positive results of the work of special classes in mainstream schools, serious problems are still not solved.

- First, students depend upon the existence of specialists (psychologists, speech therapists, special teachers), which are too few to service the children.

- Frequently, teachers refuse to work in special classes because of difficulties and lack of necessary knowledge about children with problems in development.

- Special classes often have a stigma attached, leading to aggressive social behavior and negative attitudes among peers.

- These classes promote the process of separating out children from the mainstream, permitting general educators to escape from their full responsibilities. Thus, the methods of selecting children for the special classed may be suspect.

- Mainstream education lacks the vocational training that many students with disabilities need in the secondary grades.

Despite all the problems and difficulties, it should be understood that in Russia the process of integration of the children with special needs into the mainstream schools is accelerating. Throughout the country, diverse models and forms of interaction between special and mainstream schools are developing; special schools are being deemphasized; and conditions for both social adaptation and personal development are being more closely approached that ever before.

REFERENCES

Aksenova, L. I. (1997). Legal bases of special education and social care of children with problems in development. *Journal Defectology, 1*, 3.

State Report about the Situation of Children in Russian Federation-1996. (1997). Moscow.

Makhortova, G. H. (1996). Problems of psychological adaptation of children with visual impairments in the mainstream schools, *Journal of Defectology, 4*, 45–50.

Shipitsina, L. M. (1996). The topical aspects of integrative education of children with problems in development in Russia. *Integrative Education: Problems and Prospects.*

Shmatko, N. D. (1996). Integrative approach to education of children with hearing impairments in Russia. *Integrative Education: Problems and Prospects.*

van Rijswijk, K., Foreman, N., & Shipitsina, L. M. (Eds.). (1996). *Special education on the Move.* Acco Leuven/Amersfoort.

Vygotsky, L. S. (1983). Principles of education of children with problems in physical development. *Complete works: Volume 5: Bases of defectology* (T. Vlasova, Ed.). Moscow.

LUDMILLA SHIPITSINA
RAOUL WALLENBERG
*International University for
Family and Child*

LURIA, A. R.
VYGOTSKY, L. S.

RUTTER, MICHAEL (1933–)

On completing his basic medical training at the University of Birmingham, England (1955), Michael Rutter took residencies in internal medicine, neurology, and pediatrics. His training in general and child psychiatry was done at Maudsley Hospital. Away on fellowship study for a year (1961–1962), Rutter returned to work in the Medical Research Council Special Psychiatry Research Unit. From 1965 to 1994, Rutter served as professor and head of the Department of Child and Adolescent Psychiatry at the University of London's Institute of Psychiatry. His distinguished appointments include honorary director of the Medical Research Council Child Psychiatry Unit (1984–1998); honorary director of the Social, Genetic and Developmental Psychiatry Research Centre (1994–1998); honorary consultant psychiatrist, Bethlehem and Maudsley Hospitals Trust; and research professor at the Institute of Psychiatry (1998).

Rutter's major fields of interest indicate a strong inter-

Michael Rutter

disciplinary approach, include schools as social institutions, and stress resilience in relation to developmental links between childhood and adult life, psychiatric genetics, neuropsychiatry, psychiatric epidemiology, and infantile autism. As a teacher and researcher, his work centers on building bridges between the areas of child development and clinical child psychiatry.

Rutter's major published contributions include *Child and Adolescent Psychiatry: Modern Approaches* (3rd ed.), *Depression in Young People: Developmental and Clinical Perspectives* (1986), *Antisocial Behavior By Young People* (1998), *Fifteen Thousand Hours: Secondary Schools and Their Effects On Children* (1994), and *Psychosocial Disorders in Young People* (1995). To date, he has written 36 books, 138 chapters, and 300 research articles and associated works.

In 1979 Rutter served as a fellow at the Center for Advanced Study in the Behavioral Sciences at Stanford. He is a Fellow of The Royal Society (FRS), London; Foreign Associate Member of the Institute of Medicine of the National Academy of Sciences, United States; Foreign Honorary Member of the American Academy of Arts and Sciences; Foreign Associate Member of the US National Academy of Education; Founding Member of Academia Europaea; and Fellow of the Academy of Medical Sciences. In addition, he has been a trustee of the Nuffield Foundation since 1992, and became governor of the Wellcome Trust in 1996.

The numerous honorary degrees bestowed upon Rutter include the University of Birmingham (1990), University of Edinburgh (1990), University of Chicago (1991), University of Ghent (1994), and University of Jyvaskyla, Finland (1996). He was knighted in January of 1992, and has re-ceived many prestigious awards, the most recent being the John P. Hill Award for Excellence in Theory Development and Research on Adolescence from the Society for Research on Adolescence (1992); the American Psychological Association Distinguished Scientists Award (1995); the Castilla del Pino Prize for Achievement in Psychiatry, Cordoba, Spain (1995); and the Helmut Horten Award for research in autism that has made a difference to clinical practice (1997). He is a member of the editorial boards of some 20 journals.

REFERENCES

Rutter, M. (1994). *Fifteen thousand hours: secondary schools and their effects on children*. London: P. Chapman.

Rutter, M., Giller, H., & Hagell, A. (1998). *Antisocial behavior by young people*. New York: Cambridge.

Rutter, M., & Hersov, L. (Eds.). (1985). *Child and adolescent psychiatry: Modern approaches*. Oxford: Blackwell.

Rutter, M., Izard, C., & Read, P. (1986). *Depression in young people: Developmental and clinical perspectives*. New York: Guilford.

Rutter, M., & Smith, D. J. (1995). *Psychosocial disorders in young people: Time trends and their causes*. New York: Wiley.

MARY LEON PEERY
Texas A & M University
First edition

TAMARA J. MARTIN
The University of Texas of the Permian Basin
Second edition

S

SABATINO, DAVID A. (1938–   )

David A. Sabatino obtained his BA (1960), MA (1961), and PhD (1966) from Ohio State University. He is currently a professor in the department of human development and learning at East Tennessee State University, Johnson City.

Sabatino's interests have focused on gifted children and adolescents, children with disabilities, and psychological assessment (Fuller & Sabatino, 1998; Sabatino, Miller, & Schmidt, 1981; Sabatino, Spangler, & Vance, 1995; Spangler & Sabatino, 1995). He views learning disabilities as complex problems associated with difficulty in information processing. As a complicated problem, Sabatino contends that no one professional, from any single discipline, can meet the needs of all children. Instead, he advocates input from any service provider that can assist a particular child with a handicap (Sabatino et al., 1981).

In his work, Sabatino noted that increasing numbers of children with handicaps were being neglected and secondary schools were ill-equipped to handle the influx, frequently stressing subject mastery rather than individual growth and learning. Thus, he advocated functional teaching, or teaching the necessary information in order for a child to function at a basic academic level. Teaching a child to read, if he or she does not know how to read, is preferable to labeling that child, according to Sabatino (Sabatino & Lanning-Ventura, 1982).

Sabatino continues his work involving programming for school-age children, recently investigating demographic and personality characteristics of at-risk high school students. This study indicated a prevalence of six factors, including defensiveness-hopelessness, attention seeking, and family relationship problems, as well as the predominant characteristics of absence of extra-curricular activities, a negative attitude toward school, and truancy. This research has important implications for programming at-risk students (Fuller & Sabatino, 1996).

REFERENCES

Fuller, C. G., & Sabatino, D. A. (1996). Who attends alternative high school? *High School Journal, 79,* 293–297.

Fuller, C. G., & Sabatino, D. A. (1998). Diagnosis and treatment considerations with comorbid developmentally disabled populations. *Journal of Clinical Psychology, 54,* 1–10.

Sabatino, D. A., & Lanning-Ventura, S. (1982). Functional teaching, survival skills and teaching. In D. A. Sabatino & L. Mann (Eds.), *A handbook of diagnostic and prescriptive teaching.* Rockville, MD: Aspen.

Sabatino, D. A., Miller, T. L., & Schmidt, C. R. (1981). *Learning disabilities: Systemizing teaching and service delivery.* Rockville, MD: Aspen.

Sabatino, D. A., Spangler, R. S., & Vance, H. B. (1995). The relationship between the Wechsler Intelligence Scale for Children-Revised and the Wechsler Intelligence Scale for Children-III scales and subtests with gifted children. *Psychology in the Schools, 32,* 18–23.

Spangler, R. S., & Sabatino, D. A. (1995). Temporal stability of gifted children's intelligence. *Roeper Review, 17,* 207–210.

E. Valerie Hewitt
Texas A & M University
First edition

Tamara J. Martin
The University of Texas of the Permian Basin
Second edition

SAFETY ISSUES IN SPECIAL EDUCATION

Accountability, malpractice, due process, and liability insurance are all terms familiar to special educators. For teachers to gain protection from legal situations it is critical that children's safety become a high priority. In particular, physically impaired and severely handicapped children are more prone to accidents, medical emergencies, and injuries. Therefore, teachers must take certain precautions to protect students and staff from unnecessary risks. Specifically, educators must consider many facets of the classroom program in order to create safe environments for children. Four major areas related to safety must be considered: (1) basic first aid skills, (2) emergency weather and fire drill procedures, (3) safe classroom environments, and (4) parent consent and involvement in classroom activities.

Many states require teachers to obtain certification in first-aid procedures before they are eligible to obtain a teaching certificate. In particular, teachers should be trained in cardiopulmonary resuscitation (CPR) and anti-choking procedures such as the Heimlich maneuver. For teachers working with children who have seizures, a clear understanding of first-aid procedures for managing seizures is critical. Furthermore, basic instruction on poison management, eye injuries, and contusions must be included in first-aid programs. In the same context, children on medication such as Ritalin, Phenobarbital, and Dilantin, must be carefully monitored for signs of over or under dosage. Teachers should never be left solely responsible for dispensing any medications to children without the assistance of a physician or school nurse.

Emergency weather and fire drill procedures should be clearly posted in all classrooms. For teachers in certain areas of the country, where tornados and hurricanes are likely, extra efforts must be taken to understand the civil defense procedures for the school. For teachers of the physically handicapped, visually impaired, and nonambulatory severely impaired, procedures should be established with the school principal for added assistance during civil defense drills and fire drills.

Much has been written on designing school facilities and classroom environments for handicapped students (Abend, Bednor, Froehlinger, & Stenzler, 1979; Birch & Johnstone, 1975; Forness, Gutherie, & MacMillan, 1982; Hutchins & Renzaglia, 1983; Zentall, 1983). Environmental designing of classrooms also involves a safety aspect for children in special education. For example, many classrooms for physically handicapped or blind students should have adequate storage space for bulky equipment (e.g., wheelchairs, walkers) and materials (e.g., braillers, books, canes). A classroom that is organized and neat ensures safety for children. Cabinets within the classroom holding harmful materials should be inaccessible to students in the classroom. Rossol (1982) discusses the possible hazards to students in special education using art materials.

Many of the activities developed for handicapped students involve out-of-school visits such as field trips, community-based training, and recreation/leisure trips. Parental consent would be critical if liability issues arose from one of these activities. Additionally, behavioral intervention programs that might appear intrusive (e.g., time-out, physical restraint, withholding food) must be discussed by the educational team and parents prior to implementation of any such procedures. Each school or district should have policies regarding corporal punishment. Those policies must be understood by all special education teachers and all parents.

In conclusion, safety in special education is a topic that is rarely found in the literature, yet it has enormous implications for teachers working with handicapped children. Although much of what has been discussed is commonsense, it is important to remind teachers of the many safety aspects in special education.

REFERENCES

Abend, A., Bednor, M., Froehlinger, V., & Stenzler, Y. (1979). *Facilities for special education services*. Reston, VA: Council for Exceptional Children.

Birch, J., & Johnstone, B. (1975). *Designing schools and schooling for the handicapped*. Springfield, IL: Thomas.

Forness, S., Guthrie, D., & MacMillan, D. (1982). Classroom environments as they relate to mentally retarded children's observable behavior. *American Journal of Mental Deficiency, 3,* 259–265.

Hutchins, M., & Renzaglia, A. (1983). Environmental considerations for severely handicapped individuals: The needs and the questions. *Exceptional Education Quarterly, 4,* 67–71.

Rossol, M. (1982). *Teaching art to high risk groups*. (ERIC Document Reproduction Service No. ED 224 182)

Zentall, S. (1983). Learning environments: A review of physical and temporal factors. *Exceptional Education Quarterly, 4,* 90–115.

Vivian I. Correa
University of Florida

ACCESSIBILITY OF PROGRAMS
LIABILITY OF TEACHERS IN SPECIAL EDUCATION
MEDICALLY FRAGILE STUDENT
RITALIN

SALVIA, JOHN (1941–)

John Salvia was born in St. Louis, Missouri. He obtained his BA (1963) in education and MEd (1964) in history from the University of Arizona, later earning his EdD (1968) in special education (with a minor in educational psychology) from Pennsylvania State University. Salvia is currently a professor of special education at Pennsylvania State University.

Early in his professional career, Salvia was a teacher of the educable mentally retarded. His interests have included color blindness in children with mental retardation and assessment in special education (Salvia, 1969; Salvia & Ysseldyke, 1978). His book, coauthored with Ysseldyke, *Assessment in Special and Remedial Education*, provided basic information regarding the assessment process and its resulting data to those who use and need the information but are not involved in the assessment process. His work in this area has also included assessment bias, comparison of test profiles of students with and without disabilities, and assessment strategies for use in instructional decisions (Salvia, 1988, 1990; Salvia & Meisel, 1980).

Salvia has been involved in a children's television workshop and a visiting professor at the University of Victoria, British Columbia, Canada. He was a Fulbright fellow at the University of São Paulo, Brazil, and has been recognized in *Leaders in Education*.

REFERENCES

Salvia, J. (1969). Four tests of color vision: A study of diagnostic accuracy with the mentally retarded. *American Journal of Mental Deficiency, 74*(3), 421–427.

Salvia, J. (1988). A comparison of WAIS-R profiles of nondisabled college freshmen and college students with learning disabilities. *Journal of Learning Disabilities, 21*(10), 632–636.

Salvia, J. (1990). Some criteria for evaluating assessment strategies. *Diagnostique, 16*(1), 61–64.

Salvia, J., & Meisel, C. J. (1980). Observer bias: A methodological consideration in special education research. *Journal of Special Education, 14*(2), 261–270.

Salvia, J., & Ysseldyke, J. E. (1978). *Assessment in special and remedial education.* Boston: Houghton Mifflin.

E. Valerie Hewitt
Texas A & M University
First edition

Tamara J. Martin
*The University of Texas of the
    Permian Basin*
Second edition

SAPIR, SELMA GUSTIN (1916–   )

Born in New York City, Selma Gustin Sapir obtained her BS (1935) in education and psychology from New York University and her MA (1956) in psychology from Sarah Lawrence College. She went on to earn her EdD (1984) in applied clinical psychology from Teachers College, Columbia University. Sapir organized and directed the Learning Disability Laboratory at Bank Street College, New York, a child demonstration center and interdisciplinary training project.

Sapir is the author of the Sapir Dimensions of Learning (1980), Sapir Learning Lab Language Scale (1979), and Sapir Self-Concept Scale, as well as other educational treatment methods combining psychological theory and practices with educational models for children with learn-

ing disabilities. Based on child development research, these models emphasize the continual nature of the development process, noting that when a change occurs in one dimension (e.g., social, emotional, or cognitive), growth in other areas takes place as well. Therefore, according to Sapir, recognizing and understanding the norms of development is crucial in this respect (Sapir, 1985).

Sapir advocates a broad theoretical understanding of individual differences, proposes generic training programs, and emphasizes training implications of interdisciplinary collaboration for personnel who work with children with learning disabilities (Sapir, 1986). Additionally, she has examined the concept of "reverse mainstreaming," with non-handicapped children, their parents, and teachers visiting the classes of children with handicaps and emphasizing social and physical integration of those with disabilities (Sapir, 1990). This experimental program increased the probability of successful mainstreaming as well as providing parents and students opportunities for mutual acceptance and perceptions based on experience.

Sapir has made numerous contributions to the field of special education, including the development of graduate programs in learning disabilities and special education in Mayaguez, Puerto Rico and Mons, Belgium. Her service to professional organizations includes United Nations delegate (1982); member of the board of directors (1985–1987) and president-elect (1996) of the International Council of Psychologists; and past president of the Multidisciplinary Academy of Educators.

REFERENCES

Sapir, S. G. (1985). *The clinical teaching model: Clinical insights and strategies for the learning disabled child.* New York: Brunner, Mazel.

Sapir, S. G. (1986). Training the helpers. *Journal of Learning Disabilities, 19*(8), 473–476.

Sapir, S. G. (1990). Facilitating mainstreaming: A case study. *Journal of Reading, Writing, & Learning Disabilities International, 6*(4), 413–418.

E. Valerie Hewitt
Texas A & M University
First edition

Tamara J. Martin
*The University of Texas of the
    Permian Basin*
Second edition

Selma Gustin Sapir

SARASON, SEYMOUR B. (1919–   )

Seymour B. Sarason was born in Brooklyn, New York. He received his BA (1939) from the University of Newark (now the Newark campus of Rutgers, The State University of New Jersey), later earning both his MA (1940) and PhD (1942) in psychology from Clark University. Sarason began his professional career in Connecticut as chief psychologist at the Southbury Training School for the Mentally Retarded and later joined the faculty at Yale University, where he retired in 1989 after two decades of directing the clinical training program.

As one of the first to argue social and cultural influences in the etiology of mental retardation, Sarason is regarded as a major figure in the field (Cherniss, 1991). His advocacy role included broadening society's conceptualization of the needs of those with mental retardation and emphasizing the ability to understand an individual from observation in noncontrived, naturally occurring situations as opposed to test scores obtained in an artificial setting.

As an author and guest lecturer, Sarason continues to be a leader in the field of psychology, writing extensively on school change and school governance (Sarason, 1996, 1997, 1998). A prevailing theme throughout his work is his view that the primary problem confronting our educational system is that schools are uninteresting places for both teachers and children (Cherniss, 1991). Charging the current educational system as incapable of reform, Sarason proposes a system in which adults, both teachers and parents, are responsible for the education of children.

Sarason is the recipient of the Gold Medal Award for Life Contribution by a Psychologist in the Public Interest (1996) awarded by the American Psychological Foundation. His major publications include *Psychological Problems in Mental Deficiency* (1969) and *Revisiting The Culture of School and the Problem of Change* (1996).

REFERENCES

Cherniss, C. (1991). Biography of Seymour Sarason. *Journal of Applied Behavioral Science, 27*(4), 407–408.

Sarason, S. B. (1969). *Psychological problems in mental deficiency* (4th ed.). New York: Harper, Row.

Sarason, S. B. (1996). *Revisiting the culture and the problem of change*. New York: Teachers College.

Sarason, S. B. (1997). *How schools might be governed and why*. New York: Teachers College.

Sarason, S. B. (1998). *Political leadership and educational failure. The Jossey-Bass education series*. San Francisco, CA: Jossey-Bass.

E. Valerie Hewitt
Texas A & M University
First edition

Tamara J. Martin
The University of Texas of the
Permian Basin
Second edition

Jerome M. Sattler

SATTLER, JEROME M. (1931–   )

Born in New York City, Jerome M. Sattler received his BA from the City College of New York in 1952. He went on to the University of Kansas and earned his MA in psychology in 1953 and PhD in psychology in 1959. As a professor of psychology at San Diego State University, Sattler's research has led him to become an authority in the areas of intelligence testing, interviewing, child maltreatment, racial experimenter effects, ethnic minority testing, and racial factors in counseling and psychotherapy. His introductory text, *Assessment of Children* (Third Edition), is a standard textbook used in the field of school psychology and clinical psychology, and it remains a classic reference text in the field of special education. He published another assessment text, *Clinical and Forensic Interviewing of Children and Families: Guidelines for the Education, Pediatric, and Child Maltreatment Fields*, in 1988.

Sattler was an expert witness and consultant to the California Attorney General's Office for the case of Larry P. v. Riles from September 1977 to April 1978; this was a landmark case in the area of cultural bias in assessment. In addition, he is a coauthor with R. E. Thorndike and E. Hagen of the Stanford–Binet Intelligence Scale, Fourth Edition, published in 1986.

Sattler was a Fulbright lecturer at the University of Kebangsaan, Malaysia, from 1972 to 1973, and an exchange professor at the Katholicke Universiteit, Instituut voor Orthopedagogiek, Nijmegen, Netherlands, from 1983 to 1984. He also was an exchange professor at University College Cork, in Cork, Ireland, from 1989 to 1990. In 1979 he was elected a fellow of the American Psychological Association. Sattler has published over 99 articles in the field of psychology and has been a special reviewer for over 70 books, articles, and grant proposals, as well as an editor for such journals as the *Journal of Consulting and Clinical Psychology, Psychology in the Schools, the Journal of Psychoeducational Assessment,* and *Psychological Reports.*

REFERENCES

Sattler, J. M. (1992). *Assessment of children* (3rd ed.). San Diego, CA: Sattler.

Sattler, J. M. (1998). *Clinical and forensic interviewing of children and families: Guidelines for the education, pediatric, and child maltreatment fields.* San Diego, CA: Sattler.

STAFF

SAVE THE CHILDREN FUND AND CHILDREN WITH DISABILITIES

Save the Children began when Eglantyne Jebb, the organization's founder, drew up the *Charter On the Rights of the Child* in 1919. Special mention was made of the disabled child, and this charter has now been enshrined in the UN Convention on the Rights of the Child. Disabled children are children first, and all articles in the convention that refer to children include disabled children.

Save the Children's current policy and practice on disabled children and education has developed from ongoing analytical reflection on a strong body of practical experience in a wide range of countries (in Asia, Africa, the Middle East, and Europe). Disabled children are defined as children with impairments (physical, mental, visual, hearing, speech, or multiple impairments) who are excluded or discriminated against in their local context and culture (Stubbs, 1997).

Beginning in 1960, for 30 years Save the Children supported a pioneering residential school for physically disabled children in Morocco. This was a residential institution that enabled a small group of academically able children to gain access to a high-quality education; many students went on to universities. However, this strategy did nothing for the majority of disabled children, who were still unable to access mainstream education; it did nothing to support parents or to change the negative attitudes of the majority; and it was also unsustainable financially. This concept of "special" and segregated education, while sometimes (not always) providing a quality education to a few, had many limitations.

Learning lessons from this experience, in 1987 Save the Children adopted a clear policy to promote the basic rights of the majority of disabled children, in the context of their family and community, rather than offering a privileged education to a few. Community-based rehabilitation (CBR) was promoted as a strategy to support the disabled child within his or her family and community, and CBR workers would work with the family, the child, and the local school to integrate the disabled child. For more severely disabled children, the focus was on providing daycare, support to parents, and education on activities of daily living in the home. This strategy of integrated education was sustainable, low-cost, and enabled children with disabilities to stay within their families and community. However, the strategy was very dependent on the goodwill of the local school and teachers, and relied largely on changing the child to fit a rigid system (which was not always possible) rather than changing the system to accommodate a variety of children.

In 1990, the Jomtien Conference promoted Education for All. It was followed by the Salamanca Conference in 1994, which drew attention to problems in the school system (methodology, curriculum, teacher skills, attitudes, environment, and so on) that resulted in the exclusion of large numbers of children: disabled children, street children, ethnic minorities, and girls. This was the concept of inclusive education, which differs from special or integrated education in that it places the responsibility on the system, not the child, and is based on a strong belief that children should receive appropriate and relevant education together with their peers in their own communities.

Save the Children's current policy and strategy is "towards inclusion," acknowledging that inclusion is an ideal, and that the vast majority of education systems are difficult to change. Interestingly, the increasing number of successful examples of progress towards inclusion are in the developing countries in Asia and Africa (Holdsworth & Thepphavongsa, 1996).

In a poor province in China with 56 million people, Save the Children supported a pilot project that integrated two children with mild to moderate mental disabilities into each class. This was achieved through training teachers in child-focused approaches, introducing flexible methodology such as team-teaching and group work, large scale awareness-raising, promoting parental involvement, and transforming the system from teacher-centered to child-centered. This project is extremely successful in that it not only allowed disabled children access to essential early childhood education, but also improved the system for all children. It has now been scaled up throughout the province with existing resources, as schools support each other.

In Lesotho, Save the Children supported a national inclusive education program, aiming to include all types of disabled children in existing primary schools. The project was piloted in one school in each district by providing in-service training to all teachers in each school, working with the national Disabled People's Organizations to develop knowledge and skills in braille and sign language, and by involving parents and the community. Now it is possible to visit schools where the class sizes are over 100 and to see children signing, visually impaired children sitting next to buddies who offer support, and children with learning difficulties in the front row where the teacher can give them extra support (Stubbs, 1995).

Many of the Western industrialized countries have a legacy of segregated special education provision and professional special educators. In many economically poorer countries, there is more expertise on managing sparse resources, more community solidarity, and a strong tradition and experience of self-reliance. It is Save the Children's experience that pioneers in inclusive education are increasingly found in developing countries, and that there are many "lessons from the south" that can inform the international community (Holdsworth & Kay, 1996; Stubbs, 1997).

REFERENCES

Holdsworth, J., & Kay, J. (Eds.). (1996). *Toward inclusion: SCF UK's experience in integrated education*. Discussion paper, N.I. SEAPRO Documentation Series. Save the Children Fund.

Holdsworth, J., & Thepphavongsa, P. (Eds.). (1996). *Don't use mature wood if you want to bend it: Don't pick old mushrooms if you want to eat them. Experiences of the Lao People's Republic in provision for children with disabilities using the kindergarten sector*.

Stubbs, S. (1995). *The Lesotho National Integrated Education Programme: A case study on implementation*. Master's thesis, University of Cambridge, England.

Stubbs, S. (1997). *Education and geopolitical change*. Presented at the Oxford International Conference on Education and Development, Great Britain.

SUE STUBBS
Save the Children Fund

SCALES OF INDEPENDENT BEHAVIOR–REVISED

The *Scales of Independent Behavior–Revised* (SIB–R; Bruininks, Woodcock, Weatherman, & Hill, 1996) is used to assess adaptive behavior and problem behavior. It includes three forms—a Full Scale, Short Form, and Early Development Form. A Short Form for the Visually Impaired is also available. Administration time ranges from 15 to 20 minutes for either the Short Form or Early Development Form to 45 to 60 minutes for the Full Scale. The SIB–R is norm-referenced and nationally standardized on 2,182 individuals. It is appropriate for use with individuals from birth to 80+ years.

The SIB–R is easier to administer than its predecessor, the original SIB. In addition to the structured interview procedure, a checklist procedure is now available. It is also easier to score. Age-equivalent scoring tables are included in the response booklets for each subscale. A significant feature is the addition of a Support Score, which predicts the level of support a person will require based on the impact of maladaptive behaviors and adaptive functioning. Another unique feature of the SIB–R is the functional limitations index, which can be used to define the presence and severity of functional limitations in adaptive behaviors.

The test manual contains internal consistency reliabilities (mid to high .90s), test-retest reliabilities for the adaptive behavior scales (.83–.97) and the maladaptive behavior indexes (.69–.90), and interrater reliabilities (most correlations in the .80s). Extensive validity studies reported in the Comprehensive Manual support the developmental nature of the SIB–R adaptive behavior scales. The SIB–R is strongly related to other adaptive behavior measures and highly predictive of placements in different types of service settings.

There is very little independent research on the SIB–R. This is unfortunate, because the comprehensiveness, usefulness, and psychometric qualities of this instrument are truly outstanding.

REFERENCE

Bruininks, R. K., Woodcock, R. W., Weatherman, R. F., & Hill, B. (1996). *Scales of Independent Behavior—Revised* (SIB–R). Itasca, IL: Riverside.

FREDRICK A. SCHRANK
The Riverside Publishing Company

ADAPTIVE BEHAVIOR

SCALES OF ORDINAL DOMINANCE

See ORDINAL SCALES OF PSYCHOLOGICAL DEVELOPMENT.

SCANDINAVIA, SPECIAL EDUCATION IN

Since the publication of the first edition of the *Encyclopedia of Special Education* (Braswell, 1987), Scandinavian perspectives on special education have changed in some respects. It is true that, in the terms of Braswell, Scandinavian countries "have been in the vanguard with respect to their concern for the social welfare for their citizens" (p. 1381), including those with disabilities. But it is also true that much social policy has been difficult to implement in practice, especially since 1986.

In all Scandinavian countries, special education reform has been dependent on reforms in regular education systems and schools. As part of ongoing globalization patterns, higher priority has been given to values such as competition and education for excellence. These values have been embraced in general education. The guiding perspective of special education policy is an inclusive one, with special education support as much as possible integrated into regular education frameworks. Sweden and Denmark have traditionally been considered leaders in inclusion, and Norway and Finland were seen as following behind (Tuunainen, 1994). This is no longer the case, at least regarding Norway. Decisions on school laws and curricula during the 1990s by Norway's Parliament are more radically inclusive than in the other Scandinavian countries.

As in Sweden, a few general societal policy conditions greatly influence special education. There is ongoing decentralization of decision power and responsibilities from the national level to local municipalities (less evident in Finland). This process is happening concurrent with the effects of an economic recession during most of the 1990s (less evident in Norway). In combination, these two circumstances have meant that responsibilities and decision-making power have been moved from national and/or central bodies to local municipalities and schools. In Sweden, Denmark, and Norway, there are little or no resources earmarked specifically for special education any longer. School laws and other official guidelines stress that schools shall give high priority to the fulfillment of students' special needs. These resource allocation decisions, made on local levels of the system, have had to be made at the same time as severe budget cuts during most of the 1990s. These matters have raised sincere questions about what is possible to spend on students with special needs, especially compared to other school and student needs. This is most evident in Sweden and Denmark and, to a lesser extent, in Norway. Norway still has some stipulations for resource allocation for guaranteed support to students with certain severe disabilities. This is a small proportion (only around 2%) of all students, though, and is also a small fraction of all students given special education support in the schools. According to results from an evaluation study (Skårbrevik, 1995), the support given in this way to students with severe disabilities also covers only 20% to 30% of their weekly hours in school. In Sweden and Denmark, this support has to be financed within the frameworks of regular school budgets.

The process of closing down special schools and institutions has continued, and very few special schools are now in use. Most of those are for students who are deaf or hard of hearing, or who have intellectual or multiple disabilities. Again, this closing is going on at a slower rate in Finland than in the other three countries. Many of the former institutions and special schools are in the process of developing into resource centers. Their responsibilities are first-hand competence development and consultant support to schools attended by students with severe disabilities. They also often give shorter, intensive training courses for students, family members, and school teachers. They are still

financed by government money, which is seen as necessary in order to guarantee qualified support to children with the greatest need, regardless of where they live or go to school. In most respects these resource centers and their consultant responsibilities are organized on a basis. At the national level, Sweden has a National Swedish Agency for Special Education, a separate administrative body parallel to the National Agency for Schools. In Norway, the same national administrative body monitors both regular and special education, as well as education for those with more severe disabilities.

In all countries, there is concern about the availability of qualified support given from resource centers to schools, and measures are continuously taken to satisfy necessary competence development. Especially in Norway, where special schools for students with intellectual disabilities have been closed, many resource centers will have to deal with new disability areas, and therefore develop broader and deeper competence. This is a need also in the other Scandinavian countries. In Sweden, this is a responsibility for the National Swedish Agency for Special Education and is financed within regular government budget framework. In Norway, where there is no such monitoring body between the national government ministry and resource centers, the ministry has used some of the financial resources saved by closing institutions toward competence development. A five-year research and development program (1993–98) and a three-year program of resource center development initiatives have both been implemented. In comparison to the other Scandinavian countries, this is a massive national government input for increasing the level of competence needed to guarantee the meeting of severe disability special needs, independent of geographic location. The research and development program in special education also means broadening the competence area through involvement of more academic disciplines and university departments. Over the last ten to fifteen years, it has been important to see special education as a more comprehensive domain than simply medical disability knowledge.

An inclusive education policy means demands on teacher education programs for both special educators and regular education professionals. In all Scandinavian countries, special education objectives are included in regular teaching training programs. This has proven difficult in all the countries, and too little has really been included. This prevents new teachers from being as well prepared as they should be for a job in an inclusive environment. These matters are of current concern, especially in Sweden and Denmark, where preparatory work for teacher training reforms is ongoing. Teacher training is clearly a field of many controversies, and it is not evident that inclusive education needs will be a part of the guidelines for future reforms training for regular education teachers. The continuous changes of special education teacher programs have been more successfully implemented, but this has caused increasing differences between programs at different universities, within Scandinavian countries and within the region of Scandinavia itself. This may be less the case in Finland, where special education programs are still more centralized, and where there are still specific programs for teaching in special classes or special schools.

Decreasing proportions of students attend special schools or special classes, usually less than 2% or 3% a year. It must be taken into account, though, that such proportion figures do not always give the full picture. This has to do with the decentralized and goal-based educational systems. Partly, this means that differences between local municipalities and schools are increasing, even affecting definitions for special education. There are some statistics from evaluation study reports on what could be a trend toward increasing proportions of students referred to special groups or schools again. For instance, clustering of special education resources sometimes means organization of special classes and schools turning up again on local or regional levels. This is the case in Sweden, according to special schools for students with intellectual disabilities, but corresponding trends are clearly seen in Denmark and, lately, Norway. One factor behind such trends is a lack of sufficient resources, which is related to elite and competitive values and priorities. Also, school officials hear parent worries and complaints that their disabled children are not being adequately supported in the integrated settings. Both circumstances lead to more segregated solutions.

Compulsory schooling is nine years in all countries, and in some special schools it may be extended to ten. But today there is generally a need for further education in order to meet the demands of employment and society. An increasing number of students have had to continue their educations and go on to upper secondary schools, and the current proportion of each age group doing so is between 95% to 98% in all of the Scandinavian countries. Although this schooling is officially voluntary, from the student point of view it has become obligatory. This is also the case for students with disabilities and learning difficulties. Consequently, special needs have also become important issues in these schools.

Adult education has a long tradition in the Scandinavian countries, and so has special education support within this education area. In Scandinavia, as elsewhere, lifelong learning has become a more commonly used concept in education policy and planning, especially during the 1990s. This has meant an expansion of adult education in many respects. Expansion of adult education has also been one of the most important measures taken toward increasing unemployment, especially in Sweden. Special education support within regular programs, as well as special courses for those with disabilities, have a long tradition. In colleges, universities, and the adult education system at large, support to meet special needs has been further developed in the past ten years.

From having been nearly culturally homogeneous until the 1960s, Scandinavia has become increasingly multicultural through immigration. During the first decades immigration was mostly a result of labor; more recently, immigrants have moved to Scandinavian countries as refugees for different reasons. This is so especially in Denmark, Sweden, and Norway, while Finland still has a comparatively small immigration rate. In many Danish and Swedish municipalities, the proportion of inhabitants with immigrant background reaches 30% or more, and there are schools in these places where the proportion of immigrant background students are up to 80% to 85%. This multicultural situation creates challenges for special education.

Scandinavian countries are still in the vanguard of special education development in inclusive education. However, there are many conflicting current trends and widening gaps between more privileged students and those who are less well off. The welfare state model, often thought of as guaranteed, has become at risk of being dismantled during the last decade. These trends also have great influence on education policies, and especially on special education policy and practice. Therefore, Scandinavia will continue to be a very interesting focus for studies of special education.

REFERENCES

Braswell, D. (1987). Scandinavia, special education in. In C. R. Reynolds & L. Mann (Eds.), *Encyclopedia of special education*. New York: Wiley.

Haug, P. (1997). *Integration and special education research in Norway*. Paper presented at the AERA 1997 Annual Conference, Chicago.

Skårbrevik, K. (1995). Spesialpedagogiske tiltak pa dagsorden. Evaluering av prosjektet "Omstrukturering av spesialundervisning." Volda: Høgskulen og Møreforsking, Forskingsrapport no. 14.

Tuunainen, K. (1994). Finland, Norway, and Sweden. In K. Mazurek & M. Winzer (Eds.), Comparative studies in special education. Washington, DC: Gallaudet University Press.

INGEMAR EMANUELSSON
Goteburg University

FRANCE, SPECIAL EDUCATION IN
WESTERN EUROPE, SPECIAL EDUCATION IN

SCAPEGOATING

A scapegoat is generally defined as a person or group that bears the blame for the mistakes of others. Typically, this is manifested as a group singling out an individual for unfair attack. In schools such systematic victimization of one child by a group of others can isolate the child from the social life of the class and cause the child to feel unworthy of inclusion in the peer group. At times handicapped children may be scapegoats, particularly those with low self-esteem, which is usual with handicapped children owing to academic, emotional, or physical problems (Gearheart, 1985).

Allan (1985) has reported that the scapegoating of one child by others is a common problem facing teachers and counselors. The scapegoats suffer from social isolation and poor self-concept. This type of environment can only have a negative effect on learning. This is especially true for children in classes for the handicapped. However, the disruptiveness caused by scapegoating is not only destructive to the scapegoat, but also to children who fear that they may become the next victim. These children may develop coping strategies to avoid that possibility. Such strategies may include ingratiating themselves with class leaders, mistreating scapegoats to prove that they are not scapegoats themselves, and refusing to associate with former friends who are now scapegoats.

Nonhandicapped children require help with social skills as they interact with handicapped peers in mainstreamed classrooms. One problem that may arise is the calling of names, which can be dealt with in a variety of ways. Salend and Schobel (1981) described one strategy that they implemented with a fourth-grade class. Discussion included the meaning of names, how names differ, and the positive and negative consequences of names. The last topic included a discussion of the negative effects of nicknames and the importance of considering another person's reaction to the nickname. It is obvious that educators must seriously consider the effects of scapegoating and must continue to develop strategies to counteract the negative effects of scapegoating on handicapped children.

REFERENCES

Allan, C. L. (1985). Scapegoating: Help for the whole class. *Elementary School Guidance and Counseling, 18,* 147.

Gearheart, B. R. (1985). *Learning disabilities.* St. Louis: Times Mirror/Mosby College Pub.

Salend, S. J., & Schobel, J. (1981). Coping with namecalling in the mainstream setting. *Education Unlimited, 3*(2), 36–38.

JOSEPH M. RUSSO
Hunter College

SELF-CONCEPT
SOCIAL SKILLS

SCHAEFER, EARL S. (1926–   )

A native of Adyeville, Indiana, Earl S. Schaefer received his BA (1948) in psychology from Purdue University, and later earned both his MA (1951) and PhD (1954) in psychology at the Catholic University of America. He is cur-

rently a professor in the department of maternal and child health in the School of Public Health, University of North Carolina, Chapel Hill. He is also senior investigator at the Frank Porter Graham Child Development Center at the University.

Schaefer's early research began with studies of parent attitudes and behavior as related to child development, resulting in the development of the Parental Attitude Research Instrument and an infant education program (Schaefer & Bell, 1958). This research was later extended to parent-child relationships, child social-emotional development, husband-wife relationships, and mental health of parents and children (Schaefer, 1991; Schaefer & Burnett, 1987; Schaefer & Edgerton, 1985). In his investigations, Schaefer has shown correlations between parental beliefs/values and a child's intellectual development, correlations between a parent's behavior and the child's school development, and the effects of a perceived marital relationship on individual adjustment. This research has important implications for the development of parent education programs.

Among his many honors, Schaefer is the recipient of the Research Scientist Award of the National Institute of Mental Health (1975–1979), and has served as consulting editor of the *American Journal of Mental Deficiency* and *Child Development.*

REFERENCES

Schaefer, E. S. (1991). Goals for parent and future-parent education: Research on parental beliefs. *Elementary School Journal, 91*(3), 239–247.

Schaefer, E. S., & Bell, R. Q. (1958). Development of a parental attitude research instrument. *Child Development, 29,* 339–361.

Schaefer, E. S., & Burnett, C. K. (1987). Stability and predictability of women's marital relationships and demoralization. *Journal of Personality and Social Psychology, 53*(6), 1129–1136.

Schaefer, E. S., & Edgerton, M. (1985). Parent and child correlates of parental modernity. In E. Sigel (Ed.), *Parental Belief Systems.* Hillsdale, NJ: Erlbaum.

E. VALERIE HEWITT
Texas A & M University
First edition

TAMARA J. MARTIN
*The University of Texas of the
    Permian Basin*
Second edition

SCHIEFELBUSCH, RICHARD L. (1918–   )

Richard Schiefelbusch received his BS (1940) from Kansas State Teachers College and his MA (1947) in speech pathol-

Richard L. Schiefelbusch

ogy and psychology from the University of Kansas. He went on to earn his PhD (1951) in speech pathology at Northwestern University. Schiefelbusch was director of the Bureau of Child Research at the University of Kansas from 1955 to 1990, and since 1989 has held the distinction of professor emeritus at that university.

Schiefelbusch has spent his career helping persons with disabilities. As director of the Bureau of Child Research, he conducted research related to language and communications programs for mentally retarded children and he was instrumental in discovering and developing effective applied behavior techniques for those with severe mental retardation. The studies conducted during his time there were designed to alter the range of educational and social activities of institutionalized children, demonstrating that children with no history of educational success could participate in productive instructional programs. This research was instrumental in the development of innovative treatment and training in language and social skills for children with severe and multiple handicaps. Schiefelbusch's work involving the language potential of people with severe mental retardation was a key element in the establishment of the constitutional right to education and the enactment of the Education of the Handicapped Act in 1966.

Among his numerous awards, Schiefelbusch is the recipient of the Distinguished Service award of the National Association for Retarded Citizens (1983) and the Distinguished Accomplishment award of the American Association of University Affiliated Programs (1987). His major publications include *Language Intervention Strategies* (1978) and *Communicative Competence* (1984).

REFERENCES

Schiefelbusch, R. L. (Ed.). *Language intervention strategies*. Baltimore: University Park Press.

Schiefelbusch, R. L., & Pickar, J. (Eds.). (1984). *Communicative competence: Acquisition and intervention*. Baltimore, MD: University Park Press.

E. VALERIE HEWITT
Texas A & M University
First edition

TAMARA J. MARTIN
The University of Texas of the Permian Basin
Second edition

SCHIZENCEPHALY

Schizencephaly is a disorder of grossly abnormal neuronal migration patterns with onset during fetal development. It is characterized by clefts in the parasylvian region of the brain along with additional openings in the regions of the pre- and postcentral gyri. These anomalies may or may not be symmetrical (Baron, Fennell, & Voeller, 1995). Other regions of the brain may also be involved in ways that are not predictable solely on the basis of the diagnosis of schizencephaly. The disorder is diagnosable via fetal ultrasound but CT and MRI studies after birth are necessary to view the extent of the abnormalities in brain structure.

Outcomes vary widely and may range from microcephaly and severe or profound levels of mental retardation to normal intelligence, although at least some neuropsychological impairment will always be present. Children with schizencephaly may have a variety of neurological problems including hydrocephalus, seizure disorders of various types, mental retardation, and coordination disorders of varying degrees of severity (Baron, Fennell, & Voeller, 1995). Special education programming will be necessary in virtually all cases, but only after careful assessment due to the highly variable expressivity of symptoms. As the child develops, the behavioral and mental symptom complex may change significantly and frequent, comprehensive neuropsychological examinations are recommended.

REFERENCE

Baron, I., Fennell, E., & Voeller, K. (1995). *Pediatric neuropsychology in the medical setting*. Oxford: Oxford University Press.

CECIL R. REYNOLDS
Texas A & M University

SCHIZOPHRENIA

See CHILDHOOD SCHIZOPHRENIA

SCHOOL ATTENDANCE OF HANDICAPPED

School attendance of students with disabilities, and of all children, is affected by the following factors: motivational level, home and community problems, levels of stress, academic underachievement, rate of failure, negative self-concept, social difficulties, external directedness, improper school placement, inconsistent expectations by parents and teachers, employment outside of school aversive elements in the school environment, and skill deficiencies (Grala & McCauley, 1976; Schloss, Kane, & Miller, 1981; Sing, 1998; Unger, Douds, & Pierce, 1978). Absenteeism is learned; as it becomes habitual, it increases and continues to reinforce itself (Stringer, 1973).

Since it is difficult to develop effective intervention strategies in academic, social, emotional, and vocational areas if children are not in school, attendance becomes a parallel goal to the successful completion of the handicapped student's individual educational plan (IEP). Various authors (Bosker & Hofman, 1994; Jones, 1974; Schloss, Kane, & Miller, 1981; Unger, Douds, & Pierce, 1978) have suggested programs for motivating or changing patterns of behavior of special education students to assist in increasing their school attendance.

Jones (1974) described the Diversified Satellite Occupations Program and Career Development, which allows the student to register in a less structured school setting from the one he or she normally attends, provides a curriculum with an emphasis on occupational guidance for all ages, and shortens the school day. The program was successful in decreasing truancy.

Schloss, Kane, and Miller (1981) evaluated factors related to adverse aspects of attending school and pleasant aspects of staying at home. An intervention program was individually developed to assist the student in increasing the amount of satisfaction received from going to school, decreasing the amount of satisfaction gained from staying home, and actively teaching skills that enhance the student's ability to benefit from going to school. Not only did school attendance improve, but test scores also increased. Unger, Douds, and Pierce (1978) described a program that taught students the skills necessary to succeed in school. Each student's attendance pattern was examined, reasons for truancy evaluated, and individual lessons devised. Students' attendance and attitudes toward school both improved.

School attendance for handicapped children is mandated by the Individuals with Disabilities Education Act (IDEA). It is extremely important that absenteeism be evaluated constantly by the local educational agency and that steps be undertaken to remediate the situation on an individual basis whenever possible.

REFERENCES

Bosker, R. J., & Hofman, W. H. A., (1994). School effects on dropout: A multi-level logistic approach to assessing school-level correlates of dropout of ethnic minorities. *Tijdschrift voor Onderwijsresearch, 19*(1), 50–64.

Grala, R., & McCauley, C. (1976). Counseling truants back to school: Motivation combined with a program for action. *Journal of Counseling Psychology, 23*, 166–169.

Jones, H. B. (1974). *Dropout prevention: Diversified Satellite Occupations Program and Career Development. Final report.* Washington, DC: Bureau of Adult, Vocational, and Technical Education.

Schloss, P. J., Kane, M. S., & Miller, S. (1981). Truancy intervention with behavior disordered adolescents. *Behavior Disorders, 6*(3), 175–179.

Sing, K. (1998). Part-time employment in high school and its effect on academic achievement. *Journal of Educational Research, 91*(3), 131–139.

Stringer, L. A. (1973). Children at risk 2. The teacher as change agent. *Elementary School Journal, 73*(8), 424–434.

Unger, K. V., Douds, A., & Pierce, R. M. (1978). A truancy prevention project. *Phi Delta Kappan, 60*(4), 317.

SUSANNE BLOUGH ABBOTT
*Bedford Central School District
Mt. Kiseo, New York*

**INDIVIDUALS WITH DISABILITIES EDUCATION ACT (IDEA)
PARENTS OF THE HANDICAPPED**

SCHOOL EFFECTIVENESS

School effectiveness is a term adopted in the late 1970s to refer to a body of research on identifying effective schools and the means for creating more of them. The movement to research effective schools has been driven largely by three principal assumptions. According to Bickel (1983), these are that: (1) it is possible to identify schools that are particularly effective in teaching basic skills to poor and minority children; (2) effective schools exhibit identifiable characteristics that are correlated with the success of their students and these characteristics can be manipulated by educators; and (3) the salient characteristics of effective schools form a basis for the improvement of noneffective schools.

Bickel (1983) has traced the origins of the school effectiveness movement to three factors. The first is the backlash that developed in response to the Coleman studies (and like research) of the 1960s. These studies left the unfortunate impression that differences among schools were irrelevant in the education of poor and minority children. The second basis, according to Bickel, was the general psychological climate of the 1970s. Principals, teachers, parents, and others seemed ready for a more positive, hopeful message, one that said schools could make a difference and that effective schools did exist in the real world. The final factor described by Bickel is the readiness of the educational research community to accept the findings that to date include such intuitively appealing variables as strong instructional leadership, an orderly school climate, high expectations, an emphasis on basic skills, and frequent testing and monitoring of student progress.

MacKenzie (1983) has noted broad, rapid agreement on the dimensions and fundamental elements of what constitutes effective schools. The Table, adapted from MacKenzie's (1983) excellent review, lists these various elements; however, as MacKenzie has discussed, the listing of attributes is truly misleading in this instance. The characteristics of effective schools are largely interactive, producing a circumstance that promotes learning that goes far beyond a summation of the parts. The effectiveness of a school cannot be predicted by determining the mere presence or absence of each of these factors—they must be assessed as they interact within the school under observation.

As can be seen from the elements of school effectiveness given in the Table, making schools particularly good learning environments is a total system effort. Elements are listed that affect the district level, building level, and classroom level. It is difficult to point to any one level as being the most crucial, even though schools are hierarchically arranged; however, if there is one level that deserves more emphasis, it is the classroom. The individual classroom is where instruction takes place; it will always be the key to the educational process. The classroom is affected by many elements that cannot be ignored. MacKenzie (1983) emphasizes:

> The classroom as a learning environment is nested in the larger environment of the school, which is embedded in a political-administrative structure through which it relates to the surrounding community. . . . It will be difficult if not impossible to provide effective classroom teaching in a disorderly, disorganized, and disoriented school environment, and it may be nearly as difficult to organize good schools in an atmosphere of political and managerial indifference. (p. 9) (Also see Purkey and Smith, 1982.)

Effective schools may have been thought, intuitively, by some to bring all students to some designated average level of performance. However, instead of causing students to cluster tightly about some central tendency, effective schools expand the differences among students rather than restrict them. Rich, facilitative environments en-

Dimensions of Effective School Research and Corresponding Elements of Effective Schools

Leadership Dimensions

Core Elements

1. Positive overall school and organizational climate
2. Activities focused toward clear, attainable, relevant, and objective goals
3. Teacher-directed classroom management
4. Teacher-directed decision making
5. In-service training designed to develop effective teaching

Facilitating Elements

1. Consensus among teachers and administrators on goals and values
2. Long-range planning
3. Stability of key staff
4. District-level support for school improvement

Efficacy Dimensions

Core Elements

1. Expectations for high achievement
2. Consistent press for excellence
3. Visible rewards for academic excellence
4. Group interaction in the classroom
5. Autonomy and flexibility to implement adaptive practices
6. Total staff involvement in school improvement
7. Teacher empathy, rapport, and interaction with students

Facilitating Elements

1 Emphasis on homework and study
2. Acceptance of responsibility for learning outcomes
3. Strategies to avoid nonpromotion of students
4. Deemphasis on ability grouping

Efficiency Dimensions

Core Elements

1. Amount and intensity of time engaged in learning
2. Orderly school and classroom environments
3. Continuous assessment, evaluation, and feedback
4. Well-structured classroom learning activities
5. Instruction driven by content
6. Schoolwide emphasis on basic and on higher order skills

Facilitating Elements

1. Opportunities for individualized work
2. Number and variety of opportunities to learn
3. Reduced class size

Source: After MacKenzie, 1983

hance the results of ability differences, allowing the maximum possible levels of growth; deprived, restrictive environments slow and constrain growth. This does not mean that group differences will necessarily increase. If schools and instruction are particularly effective for all groups, as should be the case, then the overall level of achievement should increase for all groups along with the within group dispersion. This, at least in theory, is currently being attempted in terms of school accountability movement, in which expectations for schools now include test results of special education students (CISP, 1998).

As promising as the school effectiveness literature appears to be, and even with the consensus on the core elements of school effectiveness, a variety of valid criticisms have been offered. These have been summarized and reviewed by Rowan, Bossert, and Dwyer (1983). The technical properties of the research have been criticized as (1) using narrow, limited measures of effectiveness that focus only on instructional outcomes; (2) using design that allows an analysis of relational variables from which cause and effect cannot be inferred; and (3) making global comparisons on the basis of aggregate data, without assessing intraschool variations in organizational climate or outcomes across classes within schools. Rowan, Bossert, and Dwyer (1983) also caution that the effect sizes present in this line of research are questionable. They have argued that the traditional methods of research in school effectiveness resemble "fishing expeditions" that spuriously inflate the probability of finding significant results. Despite these and other problems, the school effectiveness movement has rekindled optimism that schools can be organized and restructured to enhance student performance. As yet, the application of the methods and concepts of the school effectiveness literature have not been applied to special education programs. Special education programs are typically excluded from the data in such studies and desperately need to be assessed. It remains to be seen whether special education programs that can be identified as particularly effective in educating the handicapped are affected by the same variables and with the same form of interaction as are regular education programs. The time to apply the concepts and research methods of school effectiveness to special education is past due. It holds much promise for understanding what makes special education effective and how to effect such changes.

REFERENCES

Bickel, W. E. (1983). Effective schools: Knowledge, dissemination, inquiry. *Educational Researcher, 12*, 3–5.

Clark, T. A., & McCarthy, D. P. (1983). School improvement in New York City: The evolution of a project. *Educational Researcher, 12*, 17–24.

Consortium on Inclusive Schooling Practices. (1998). *Including students with Disabilities in Accountability Systems.* Issue brief. Pittsburgh, PA: Allegheny University of Health Sciences.

MacKenzie, D. E. (1983). Research for school improvement: An appraisal of some recent trends. *Educational Researcher, 12*, 5–19.

Purkey, S. C., & Smith, M. S. (1982). Too soon to cheer? Synthesis of research on effective schools. *Educational Leadership, 40*, 64–69.

Rowan, B., Bossert, S. T., & Dwyer, D. C. (1983). Research on effective schools: A cautionary note. *Educational Researcher, 12*, 24–32.

CECIL R. REYNOLDS
Texas A & M University

SPECIAL EDUCATION PROGRAMS
TEACHER EFFECTIVENESS

SCHOOL FAILURE

There are many reasons why children fail in school. In some cases, failure may be due to circumstances within the child's environment. In other cases, school failure may be the result of a physical problem originating before, during, or after birth. This section identifies and discusses some of the chief causes of failure in school.

Failure in school often occurs when children come from environments characterized by economic hardship, deprivation, neglect, trauma, divorce, death, foster parenting, drug abuse, poor school attendance, or lack of adequate instruction. Indeed, dyspedagogia carries more of a role in school failure simply because of the theoretical paradigm in Western schools of individualism as opposed to social/interactive paradigms such as those favored in Russian schools for so many years. Some change may be noted in the teacher preparation and involvement in inner-city schools (Yeo, 1997).

Cultural differences also contribute to school failure. When a language other than English is used in the home and children are limited in English proficiency, they do poorly in school. The cultural values held by students also affect how they perceive their school, their teachers, and their peer group. For example, students' values determine how much they will be motivated in class, how they perceive and respond to authority, and whether they will be highly competitive or more responsive to a cooperative approach to learning. When values differ widely from one culture to another, what is valued in one culture may serve as a barrier to learning in another (Saville-Troike, 1978).

Children who exhibit behavior problems in the classroom also experience school failure. Some children have conduct disorders in which they disrupt the class, constantly irritate the teacher, do not follow directions, are easily distracted, are impulsive, or fail to attend. Other students who are fearful, anxious, withdrawn, or immature have difficulty in responding freely in the classroom and fail to learn to the limits of their abilities. Children whose self-esteem is so low that they believe they are of little worth often learn to be helpless. These children stop trying in school because they think they cannot learn. When children with behavior problems do not conform to the standards of the school environment, they may become socially aggressive, reject the values of the school and society, and come into conflict with authorities. A student may openly confront teachers and administrators, begin using drugs or alcohol, join gangs, break laws, steal, and eventually be expelled from or drop out of school (Knoblock, 1983; Long, Morse, & Newman, 1980; Quay & Werry, 1979).

Children who have difficulty in seeing and hearing often fail in school. Although 1 child in 10 enters school with some degree of visual impairment, most of these problems can be corrected and have no effect on educational development. One child out of a thousand, however, has visual impairments so severe they cannot be corrected. Children who are hard of hearing or deaf have difficulty in learning to understand language. This causes difficulty in learning to speak, read, and write the English language (Barraga, 1983).

Mental retardation results in school failure. Mental retardation may range in severity from mild to moderate to severe to profound. Delayed mental development can contribute to failure in language acquisition and use, achievement in academic subjects, social adjustment, and becoming a self-supporting adult (Mittler, 1981).

Specific learning disabilities can result in failure in school. A learning disability is a dysfunction in one or more of the psychological processes that are involved in learning to read, write, spell, compute arithmetic, etc. In some cases, a child may have an attention disability and may not be able to direct attention purposefully, failing to selectively focus attention on the relevant stimuli or responding to too many stimuli at once. A memory disability is the inability to remember what has been seen or heard. Perceptual disabilities cover a wide range of disorders in which a child who has normal vision, hearing, and feeling may experience difficulty in grasping the meaning of what is seen, heard, or touched. An example is a child who has difficulty in seeing the directional differences between a "d" and a "b," or who requires an excessive amount of time to look at a printed word, analyze the word, and say the word. Thinking disabilities involve problems in judgment, making comparisons, forming new concepts, critical thinking, problem solving, and decision making. A disability in oral language refers to difficulties in understanding and using oral language. All of these specific learning disabilities might cause difficulty in learning to read, write, spell, compute arithmetic, or adopt appropriate social-emotional behaviors (Kirk & Chalfant, 1984). Recent research cites the need for school-family partnerships (Poole, 1997) and intensive case management (Reid, Bailey-Dempsey, Cain, & Cook, 1994).

REFERENCES

Barraga, N. (1983). *Visual handicaps and learning* (rev. ed.). Austin, TX: Exceptional Resources.

Kirk, S. A., & Chalfant, J. C. (1984). *Academic and developmental learning disabilities*. Denver, CO: Love.

Knoblock, P. (1983). *Teaching emotionally disturbed children*. Boston: Houghton Mifflin.

Long, N., Morse, W., & Newman, R. (Eds.). (1980). *Conflict in the classroom: The education of emotionally disturbed children* (4th ed.). Belmont, CA: Wadsworth.

Mittler, P. (Ed.). (1981). *Frontiers of knowledge in mental retardation: Vol. 1. Social educational and behavioral aspects; Vol. 2. Biomedical aspects*. Baltimore, MD: University Park Press.

Poole, D. L. The SAFE Project. *Health & Social Work, 22*(4), 282–289.

Quay, H., & Werry, J. (Eds.). (1979). *Psychopathological disorders of childhood* (2nd ed.). New York: Wiley.

Reid, W. J., Bailey-Dempsey, C. A., Cain, E., & Cook, T. V. (1994). Case incentives versus case management: Preventing School Failure? *Social Work Research, 18*(4), 227–236.

Saville-Troike, M. (1978). *A guide to culture in the classroom*. Rosslyn, VA: National Clearinghouse for Bilingual Education.

Yeo, F. (1997). Teacher preparation and inner-city schools: Sustaining educational failure. *Urban Review, 29*(2), 127–143.

JAMES CHALFANT
University of Arizona

EMOTIONAL DISORDERS
LEARNED HELPLESSNESS
LEARNING DISABILITIES
MENTAL RETARDATION

SCHOOL PHOBIA (SCHOOL REFUSAL)

School phobia has been the subject of hundreds of research studies and dozens of literature reviews over the past several decades. The phenomenon was first described in 1932 when Broadwin distinguished a type of school refusal from truancy by an anxiety component. The term school phobia was coined in 1941 (Johnson, Falstein, Szurek, & Svendson, 1941). A common definition of school phobia cited in the more recent literature includes the following characteristics:

Severe difficulty in attending school often amounting to prolonged absence.

Severe emotional upset shown by such symptoms as excessive fearfulness, undue temper, misery or complaints of feeling ill without obvious organic cause on being faced with the prospect of going to school.

Staying at home during school hours with the knowledge of the parents at some stage in the course of the disorder.

Absence of significant antisocial disorder, such as stealing, lying, wandering, destructiveness, or sexual misbehavior. (Berg, Nichols, & Pritchard, 1969, p. 123)

In contrast to school phobia, truancy is characterized by behaviors that are the opposite of the last two behaviors.

Contemporary writers who use the term school refusal generally describe it with the same set of characteristics that defines school phobia that lack intensity (Kearney, Eisen, & Silverman, 1995). An exception is the American Psychiatric Association's (1994) classification system (DSM-IV), which describes school refusal as one possible concomitant of separation anxiety disorder, while reserving the term school phobia for a fear of the school situation even when parents accompany the child.

The occurrence of school phobia is relatively rare when one considers the abundance of literature devoted to it. Estimates of the incidence of school phobia range from 3.2 to 17 per 1000 schoolchildren (Kennedy, 1965; Yule, 1979). The wide discrepancy may be due in part to the age at which children are sampled. Prevalence is thought to peak at three different ages: 5 to 7, on entry or shortly after entry to school; 11, around the time children change schools; and 14, often concomitant with depression (Hersov, 1977). Many writers consider school phobia to occur in three girls for every two boys (Wright, Schaefer, & Solomons, 1979). However, this ratio has not appeared in several studies of school phobics reported in the literature (Baker, & Wills, 1978; Berg et al., 1969; Hersov, 1960; Kennedy, 1965).

The causes of school phobia have been couched in psychoanalytic, psychodynamic, and social learning theory terms. The psychoanalytic focus frames school phobia within a mutually dependent and hostile parent-child relationship. Some psychoanalysts believe that the unconscious conflict resulting from this relationship leads the child to want to protect the mother, and hence, not leave her. Other psychoanalysts indicate that the conflict surrounding the hostile-dependent relationship with mother is displaced onto the school situation, which becomes the manifest phobic object. In any case, both agree that separation anxiety plays a key role in school phobia (Atkinson, Quarrington, & Cyr, 1985; Kelly, 1973).

An alternative theory that was intended to explain the occurrence of school phobia at later ages was postulated by Leventhal and Sills (1964). Kelly (1973) labeled this theoretical approach, which focuses on the school phobic's unrealistic self-image, as "nonanalytic psychodynamic." According to Leventhal and Sills (1964):

These children commonly overvalue themselves and their achievements and then try to hold onto their unrealistic self-image. When this is threatened in the school situation, they suffer anxiety and retreat to another situation where they can maintain their narcissistic self-image. This retreat may very well be a running to a close contact with mother. (p. 686)

Others have used the term fear of failure in referring to this theory (Atkinson et al., 1985).

Behavioral theories account for school phobia in terms of both classical and operant conditioning. The former model explains school phobia as a conditioned anxiety response elicited by the school situation or some other school-related event. For instance, an often cited case (Garvey & Hegrenes, 1966) involved a boy whose mother repeatedly told him as he was leaving for school that she might die while he was gone. Eventually, the thought of going to school led to fear of his mother's death. The operant model assumes that internal or environmental cues both trigger and maintain the school phobic behavior.

Atkinson et al. (1985) argued that the three perspectives differ more in focus than in substance because all can account for school phobia as a fear of separation, of the school situation, or of failures in school. For example, the child whose unrealistic self-image leads to a fear of failure in the school situation may be reinforced by parents for not attending school. Similarly, separation anxiety may be a component of school phobia triggered by a traumatic school event.

Coolidge, Hahn, and Peck (1957) were the first to describe subtypes of school phobia. Based on differences within a fairly small sample of 27 school phobics, they discussed neurotic and characterological types. The former were characterized by sudden onset after several years of normal school attendance while the latter were described as more severely disturbed, with the fear of school being only one fear among many in a generally fearful personality. Subsequent investigations by Kennedy (1965) and Hersov (1960) confirmed the general distinction between an acute form and a more pervasive disturbance. Kennedy (1965) elaborated 10 criteria that distinguished type 1 (neurotic) from type 2 (characterological) school phobics based on a sample of 50 children aged 4 to 16. Generally, the former was characterized by acute onset, a first episode, intact family relations, and occurrence in younger children. Type 2 was characterized as being chronic, often accompanied by a character disorder, unstable parental relationship, incipient onset, and a history of prior episodes.

Family relations have been investigated as a separate correlate of school phobia. Hersov (1960) described three patterns of parent-child relationships that characterized his sample of 50 school phobic children aged 7 to 16 years:

An overindulgent mother and an inadequate, passive father dominated at home by a willful, stubborn, and demanding child who is most often timid and inhibited in social situations.

- A severe, controlling, and demanding mother who manages her children without much assistance from her passive husband; a timid and fearful child away from home and a passive and obedient child at home, but stubborn and rebellious at puberty.

- A firm, controlling father who plays a large part in home management and an overindulgent mother closely bound to and dominated by a willful, stubborn, and demanding child, who is alert, friendly, and outgoing away from home. (p. 140)

The first two relationship types have been considered to be subtypes of characterological school phobia while the third seems more characteristic of the neurotic type (Atkinson et al., 1985). It should be noted that categorization based on a sample of 50 children needs further validation before conclusions are drawn about parent-child correlates. The same caution holds for Kennedy's classification system, particularly of type 2 school phobia, which was based on six children.

As Atkinson et al. (1985) noted in their review, the construct of school phobia is too heterogeneous to be described by a simple dichotomy. They examined five variables related to school phobia, some of which overlap more than others—extensiveness of disturbance, source of fear, mode of onset, age, and gender of the child. The extensiveness of fear can be conceptualized along a continuum with the dichotomies of neurotic/characterological or type 1/type 2 at the end points. Generally, acute or sudden onset is characteristic of type 1 and chronic or gradual onset is characteristic of type 2. When researchers have operationalized acute mode of onset as the occurrence of school phobia after 3 or more years of trouble-free attendance, other correlates emerge. For instance, chronic onset tended to be associated more than acute onset with poor premorbid adjustment, dependency on parents, low self-esteem, and a poor prognosis.

Similarly, source of fear, age, and gender do not bear a one-to-one correspondence with the dichotomous classifications. Generally, four sources of fear have been reported that correspond to the etiological approaches—fear of maternal separation, fear of something or someone at school, fear of failure, and a generally fearful disposition Atkinson et al. (1985) conclude that the fear sources are not mutually exclusive, and that fears surrounding separation may coincide with more general fearfulness. They caution, however, that conclusions relating the extensiveness of disturbance to a specific fear source are premature based on current studies. In contrast, extent of disturbance and age appear to be related, with older children generally exhibiting more severe disturbance. While Kennedy differentiated type 1 from type 2 phobics in part on age differences, there is no consistent finding that type 1 or acute type is more typical of younger children.

Both psychological and pharmacotherapy have been employed for children experiencing school phobia. We fo-cus here on psychological interventions only. The interested reader is referred to Gittelman and Koplewicz (1985) for an overview of pharmacotherapy of childhood anxiety disorders. Early treatments of school phobia stemmed from the psychoanalytic tradition and focused on resolving the mutual hostile-dependent relationship between the school phobic child and his or her parents. Typically, parallel treatment was carried out on mother and child, with one therapist using play therapy with the child and another therapist "treating" the mother. Johnson et al. (1941) describe treatment as "a collaborative dynamic approach . . . to relieve the guilt and tension in both patients" (p. 706). Treatment of eight cases reported in their seminal study of school phobia lasted from 5 months to over a year. There does not appear to be consensus among the psychoanalytic clinicians on whether gradual or immediate return is preferable.

The treatment that emerged from Leventhal and Sills' (1967) psychodynamic theory involves "outmaneuvering" the child. Unlike the psychoanalytic approach, rapid return rather than insight is the primary goal of treatment. Once parents are helped to see their complicity in maintaining school avoidance, the parent who is likely to stand firm is chosen to carry out the plan, which is essentially immediate, forced return to school. Kennedy (1965) also advocates forced return to school and described successful treatment of 50 cases of type 1 school phobia. He identified the following six components as essential to successful treatment: (1) good professional public relations; (2) avoidance of emphasis on somatic complaints; (3) forced school attendance; (4) structured interview with parents; (5) brief interview with child; and (6) follow-up (p. 287).

During the past 20 years a proliferation of behavioral treatments of school phobia have occurred. Yule (1979) and Trueman (1984) provide critical reviews of the behavioral treatment of school phobia. Trueman (1984) reviewed 19 case studies between 1960 and 1981 that used behavioral treatments based on classical, operant, or a combination of those techniques. Of the eight studies reviewed that used techniques based on classical conditioning, six used reciprocal, one used implosion, and one used emotive imagery. Six of the studies involved boys aged 10 to 17; two studies involved girls aged 8 and 9. Trueman noted considerable variation among the reciprocal inhibition treatments, making conclusions difficult concerning the most efficacious component. Additionally, he noted the difficulty in distinguishing between systematic densensitization and shaping.

Among the 10 case studies reviewed by Trueman that used operant procedures, five involved boys aged 7 to 12 and five involved girls aged 6 to 14. The change agents varied among studies as well as the specific techniques and the criteria for success. Thus comparisons between procedures are hard to make. The procedures included training parents in positive reinforcement methods, contingency contracting, prompting and shaping, and school-based contingencies. It is important that resolution is long-term for these cases, because longitudinal studies indicate life-long outcomes (Flakierska, Lindstroem, & Gillberg, 1997). Home-school collaboration essential (Jenni, 1997).

REFERENCES

American Psychiatric Association. (1980). *Diagnostic and statistical manual of mental disorders (3rd ed.)*. Washington, DC: Author.

Atkinson, L., Quarrington, B., & Cyr, J. J. (1985). School refusal: The heterogeneity of a concept. *American Journal of Orthopsychiatry, 55*, 83–101.

Baker, H., & Wills, U. (1978). School phobia: Classification and treatment. *British Journal of Psychiatry, 132*, 492–499.

Berg, I., Nichols, K., & Pritchard, C. (1969). School phobia—Its classification and relationship to dependency. *Journal of Child Psychology & Psychiatry, 10*, 123–141.

Broadwin, I. T. (1932). A contribution to the study of truancy. *American Journal of Orthopsychiatry, 2*, 252–259.

Coolidge, J., Hahn, P., & Peck, A. (1957). School phobia: Neurotic crisis or way of life. *American Journal of Orthopsychiatry, 27*, 296–306.

Flakierska, P. N., Lindstroem, M., & Gillberg, C. (1997). School phobia with separation-anxiety disorder: A comparative 20 to 29-year follow-up study of 35 school refusers. *Comprehensive Psychiatry, 38*, 17–22.

Garvey, W. P., & Hegrenes, J. R. (1966). Desensitization techniques in the treatment of school phobia. *American Journal of Orthopsychiatry, 36*, 147–152.

Gittelman, R., & Koplewicz, M. S. (1985). Pharmacotherapy of childhood anxiety disorders. In R. Gittelman (Ed.), *Anxiety disorders in children*. New York: Guilford.

Hersov, L. A. (1960). Refusal to go to school. *Child Psychology & Psychiatry, 1*, 137–145.

Hersov, L. A. (1977). School refusal. In M. Rutter & L. Hersov (Eds.), *Child psychiatry: Modern approaches* (pp. 455–486). Oxford England: Blackwell.

Jenni, C. B. (1997). School phobia: How home. School collaboration can tame this dragon. *School Counselor, 44*(3), 206–217.

Johnson, A. M., Falstein, E. J., Szurek, S. A., & Svendsen, M. (1941). School phobia. *American Journal of Orthopsychiatry, 11*, 702–711.

Kearney, C. A., Eisen, A. R., & Silverman, W. K. (1995). The legend and myth of school phobia. *School Psychology Quarterly, 10*(1), 65–85.

Kelly, E. W. (1973). School phobia: A review of theory and treatment. *Psychology in the Schools, 10*, 33–42.

Kennedy, W. A. (1965). School phobia: Rapid treatment of fifty cases. *Journal of Abnormal Psychology, 70*, 285–289.

Leventhal, T., & Sills, M. (1964). Self-image in school phobia. *American Journal of Orthopsychiatry, 34*, 685–694.

Leventhal, T., Weinberger, G., Stander, R. J., & Stearns, R. P. (1967). Therapeutic strategies with school phobics. *American Journal of Orthopsychiatry, 37*, 64–70.

Trueman, D. (1984). The behavioral treatment of school phobia: A critical review. *Psychology in the Schools, 21*, 215–223.

Wright, L., Schaefer, A., & Solomons, G. (1979). *Encyclopedia of pediatric psychology*. Baltimore, MD: University Park Press.

Yule, W. (1979). Behavioral approaches to the treatment and prevention of school refusal. *Behavioral Analysis & Modification, 3*, 55–68.

JANET A. LINDOW
THOMAS R. KRATOCHWILL
University of Wisconsin at Madison

RICHARD J. MORRIS
University of Arizona

CHILDHOOD NEUROSIS
PHOBIAS AND FEARS
SEPARATION ANXIETY AND THE HANDICAPPED

SCHOOL PSYCHOLOGY

Psychology is devoted to the goals of describing and explaining human behavior and promoting conditions that foster human development and welfare. School psychologists generally share these goals and strive to apply psychological theories, concepts, and techniques to facilitate growth and development through education and schools. The birth of psychology occurred about 100 years ago in Germany. Psychologists began working in U.S. schools about 20 years later as child study departments and clinics began to form.

The number of school psychology programs and students has increased during the last decade (Fagan, 1985). An estimated 2200 students graduate yearly from more than 200 school psychology programs (Brown & Lindstrom, 1978). Students seeking a specialist's degree frequently take 2 years of graduate work plus a full-time, yearlong internship. Those seeking a doctoral degree frequently take 3 years of graduate work and devote 1 or more years each to an internship and a dissertation. Thus, with 3 to 5 years of graduate preparation, school psychologists tend to be the most highly educated behavioral scientists employed by the schools.

Some (Brown, 1982) view school psychology as a profession separate and independent from the professions of psychology and education; others (Bardon, 1982) view school psychology as a specialty within the profession of psychology. In fact, most school psychologists straddle the professions of psychology and education. They provide many services that are unique and drawn from psychology as well as education. A comprehensive study of the expertise of school psychologists (Rosenfeld, Shimberg, & Thornton, 1983) found the practice of school psychology to be similar to the practice of clinical and counseling psychology. In fact, school psychologists devote considerable attention to assessment and organizational issues.

School psychological services differ between communities. Their character is influenced by many conditions: federal and state laws and policies; local institutional traditions, policies, and practices; financial resources and practices governing allocation; availability of psychologists and the nature of their professional preparation; and national, state, and local professional standards. Furthermore, the services often differ for elementary and secondary grades. Although the nature of their services differ, many school psychologists are guided by a scientist-practitioner model (Cutts, 1955), which holds that applications of psychology should be supportable empirically or theoretically and derived from a body of literature that is held in high esteem. Professionals are expected to have good command of this literature discussing the theoretical, empirical, and technical components of their specialties. They are also expected to deliver culturally competent services (Rogers & Ponterotto, 1997).

A comprehensive review of the school psychology literature (Ysseldyke, Reynolds, & Weinberg, 1984) identified the following 16 domains as ones in which school psychology has expertise: classroom management, classroom organization and social structure, interpersonal communication and consultation, basic academic skills, basic life skills, affective/social skills, parent involvement, systems development and planning, personnel development, individual differences in development and learning, school-community relations, instruction, legal, ethical, and professional issues, assessment, multicultural concerns, and research and evaluation.

While school psychology is a dynamic specialty and one not easily categorized or described, its work in five broad areas is described briefly. School psychologists frequently conduct psychoeducational evaluations of pupils needing special attention. The evaluations typically consider a student's cognitive (i.e., intelligence and achievement), affective, social, emotional, and linguistic characteristics, and use behavioral, educational, and psychological (including psychoneurological (D'Amato, Hammons, Terminie, & Dean, 1992) and psychoanalytic) techniques.

School psychologists also participate in planning and evaluating services designed to promote cognitive, social, and affective development. Their services can include teaching, training, counseling, and therapy. While their principal focus frequently is on individual pupils, they also work individually with parents, teachers, principals, and other educators.

School psychologists also offer indirect services to pupils through educators, parents, and other adults. Their indirect services typically involve in-service programs for teachers, parent education programs, counseling, consultation, and collaboration. Their consultative and collaborative activities involve them with groups composed of students, teachers, parents, and others. Their work as members of the education staff enables them to effect important changes in organizations by working on broad and important issues that impact classrooms, school buildings, districts, communities, corporations, or a consortium of districts and agencies.

School psychologists' knowledge of quantitive methods commonly used in research and evaluation often surpasses that of other educational personnel. Thus they frequently are responsible for conceptualizing and designing studies, collecting and analyzing data, and integrating and disseminating findings.

School psychologists also may supervise pupil personnel and psychological services. In this capacity, they are responsible for conceptualizing and promoting a comprehensive plan for these services, for hiring and supervising personnel, for promoting their development, and for coordinating psychological services with other services in the district or community.

School psychology, like other professions, has developed and promulgated a number of standards that exemplify the profession's values and principles and that serve the needs of service providers, clients, educators, society, and legal bodies (Oakland, 1986).

Most school psychologists work in the schools or within other organizational structures (e.g., mental health clinics, juvenile courts, guidance centers, private and public residential care facilities). State certification is important for these school psychologists. Forty-nine states presently certify school psychologists—an increase of 42 since 1946. Many school psychologists also want the option to practice privately. Although those who have doctoral degrees typically can be licensed by their states as psychologists, those holding subdoctoral degrees typically have been denied a license to practice psychology independently and increasingly are seeking the right to be licensed and to practice privately.

Five professional journals are devoted to advancing the knowledge and practice of school psychology: *Journal of School Psychology, Professional School Psychology, Psychology in the Schools, School Psychology International, and School Psychology Review.* An additional 16 secondary and 26 tertiary journals add to the literature (Reynolds & Gutkin, 1990). Persons interested in further information about school psychology are encouraged to consult the professional journals, *The Handbook of School Psychology* (Reynolds & Gutkin, 1990), textbooks discussing school psychology (Whelan & Carlson, 1980), and the National Association of School Psychologists (Dwyer, & Gorin, 1996).

REFERENCES

American Psychological Association. (1968). *Psychology as a profession*. Washington, DC: Author.

American Psychological Association. (1972). Guidelines for conditions of employment of psychologists. *American Psychologist*, 27, 331–334.

American Psychological Association. (1973). *Ethical principles in the conduct of research with human subjects*. Washington, DC: Author.

American Psychological Association. (1977). *Standards for providers of psychological services* (Rev. ed.). Washington, DC: Author.

American Psychological Association. (1980). *Criteria for accreditation of doctoral training programs and internships in professional psychology*. Washington, DC: Author.

American Psychological Association. (1981a). *Ethical principles of psychologists* (Rev. ed.). Washington, DC: Author.

American Psychological Association. (1981b). Specialty guidelines for the delivery of services by school psychologists. *American Psychologist*, 36, 639, 670–682.

American Psychological Association. (1985). *Standards for educational and psychological testing*. Washington, DC: Author.

Bardon, J. (1982). The psychology of school psychology. In C. R. Reynolds & T. B. Gutkin (Eds.), *The handbook of school psychology* (pp. 1–14). New York: Wiley.

Brown, D. (1982). Issues in the development of professional school psychology. In C. R. Reynolds & T. B. Gutkin (Eds.), *The handbook of school psychology* (pp. 14–23). New York: Wiley.

Brown, D. T., & Lindstrom, J. P. (1978). The training of school psychologists in the United States: An overview. *Psychology in the Schools*, 15, 37–45.

Cutts, N. E. (Ed.). (1955). *School psychology at mid-century*. Washington, DC: American Psychological Association.

D'Amato, R. C., Hammons, P. F., Terminie, T. J., & Dean, R. S. (1992). Neuropsychological training in American Psychological Association-accredited and non-accredited school psychology programs. *Journal of School Psychology*, 30(2), 175–183.

Dwyer, K. P., & Gorin, S. (1996). A national perspective of school psychology in the context of school reform. *School Psychology Review*, 25(4), 507–511.

Fagan, T. (1985). Quantitative growth of school psychology in the United States. *School Psychology Review*, 14, 121–124.

National Association of School Psychologists. (1978). *Standards for credentialing in school psychology*. Washington, DC: Author.

National Association of School Psychologists. (1984a). *Principles for professional ethics*. Washington, DC: Author.

National Association of School Psychologists. (1984b). *Standards for the provision of school psychological services*. Washington, DC: Author.

National Association of School Psychologists. (1984c). *Standards for training and field placement programs in school psychology*. Washington, DC: Author.

Oakland, T. (1986). Professionalism within school psychology. *Professional School Psychology*, 1, 9–27.

Reynolds, C. R., & Gutkin, T. B. (1990). *The handbook of school psychology*. (2nd ed.) New York: Wiley.

Rogers, M. R., & Ponterotto, J. G. (1997). Development of the multicultural school psychology counseling competency scale. *Psychology in the Schools*, 34, 211–217.

Rosenfeld, M., Shimberg, B., & Thornton, R. (1983). *Job analysis of licensed psychologists in the United States and Canada*. Princeton, NJ: Educational Test Service.

Stapp, J., & Fulcher, R. (1981). *Salaries in psychology*. Washington, DC: American Psychological Association.

Whelan, T., & Carlson, C. (1980). Books in school psychology: 1970 to present, *Professional School Psychology*, 1, 283–293.

THOMAS OAKLAND
University of Florida

EDUCATIONAL DIAGNOSTICIAN

PSYCHOLOGY IN THE SCHOOLS

SCHOOL PSYCHOLOGY DIGEST

See SCHOOL PSYCHOLOGY REVIEW.

SCHOOL PSYCHOLOGY REVIEW

School Psychology Review, first published in 1972 as *The School Psychology Digest*, is the official journal of the National Association of School Psychologists (NASP). In 1980, the name of the journal was changed to reflect the change from the publication of condensations of previously published articles to the publication of original research, reviews of theoretical and applied topics, case studies, and descriptions of intervention techniques useful to psychologists working in educational settings. Scholarly reviews of books, tests, and other psychological materials are also published occasionally. Portions of two or three issues each year are reserved for guest-edited miniseries on themes relevant to NASP membership, such as program evaluation, testing and measurement issues, psychological theories, and special education practices. These solicited theme issues differentiate the *Review* from other major school psychology journals.

The primary purpose of the *Review* is to impact the delivery of school psychological services by publishing scholarly advances in research, training, and practices. *School Psychology Review* is a quarterly publication with an editor and appointed editorial advisory board. Seven individuals have served as its editor (Shapiro, 1995). The founding editor was John Guidubaldi of Kent State University, and the current editor is Patti L. Harrison of the University of Alabama.

A content analysis of the *Review* indicates that approximately 10 to 20% of the articles concern professional issues in school psychology, 30 to 40% relate to interventions for academic and behavior problems of children, and 30 to 35% involve testing and measurement issues. The remaining articles cover a wide array of topics, including program evaluation, psychological theories, and special education practices.

The *School Psychology Review* enjoys the largest circulation (over 20,000 subscribers) of any of the journals representing the field of school psychology, and is the second most widely distributed journal in the entire discipline of psychology. *School Psychology Review* is published by the National Association of School Psychologists and is a benefit of membership; it may also be purchased separately.

REFERENCE

Shapiro, E. S. (1995). School Psychology Review: Past, present, and future revisited. *School Psychology Review, 24*, 529–536.

STEPHEN N. ELLIOTT
Louisiana State University
First edition

DONNA WALLACE
The University of Texas of the Permian Basin
Second edition

SCHOOL RECORDS

See FERPA (FAMILY EDUCATION & PRIVACY RIGHTS ACT).

SCHOOL REFUSAL

See SCHOOL PHOBIA.

SCHOOL STRESS

Stress is the nonspecific response of the human body to a demand. It is not simply nervous tension but a physiological response of the body. Stress occurs in all living organisms and is with us all the time (Selye, 1976). Stress comes from mental, emotional, and physical activity.

School stress results from the impact of the school environment on children. Physical stress is accompanied by feelings of pain and discomfort, but physical stress is seldom a major factor in school stress. In schools the stressors are most often psychological and result in emotional reactions with accompanying physiological changes in the body. Exceptional children experience more stress, less peer support, and poorer adjustment than peers without disabilities (Wenz-Gross & Siperstein, 1998).

In school stress, the demands usually result from significant others in the school, i.e., teachers and peers, or those who are expectant about school activities (e.g., par-

ents). School stress is dependent on cognitive processes that lead to emotional reactions and a form or style of coping behavior. The coping behavior may or may not be effective, or the coping behavior may only appear to be effective. When this is the case, the body has changed from a state of alarm and is in the resistance stage. When in the resistance stage, one's ability to deal effectively with other stressors is reduced. Resistance can be maintained only so long before physical or psychological problems occur (Selye, 1976). In the stage of resistance, the person is much more susceptible than when not defensive. In reacting to stress, individuals usually try harder with the coping skills they have or search for other techniques, but when stress is prolonged or is particularly frustrating, it may cause distress physically or mentally. If the stimuli continue to be perceived as stressful, the individual's reaction can be as debilitating as prolonged physical stress in other situations.

Some children are bothered much more than others by what appear to be the same stressors. The intensity of the demand as perceived by the individual and whether the individual is able to manage the stress are the most important factors. Teachers and principals often represent authority and generate the stress that goes with reacting to authority figures. They, and/or parents, often press children to achieve more (sometimes much more) than they are able to produce. School stress often comes from a lack of perceived success, but stress may come from any segment of the environment. Stress can come from those things that are novel, intense, rapidly changing, or challenging the limits of a child's tolerance. Some children pressure classmates to keep up (or to not work very hard regardless of what adults say), to speak as they do, to appear as they do, to disclose secret thoughts, etc. Sometimes stress comes from crowding, racial imbalance, the opposite sex, or facing separation from one or both parents or certain friends. Whether in school or out, many children are pressured to perform competitively. Some children thrive on pressure, others wilt and withdraw.

School stress can be prevented by intervening in the environment to eliminate or modify stress-producing situations before they have a chance to affect children; by intervening with children to protect them from the impact of stressors by building up their resistance and personal strength (i.e., self-concept); by intervening with children to increase their tolerance for stress; and by putting children who are adversely affected by stress in an environment that minimizes stress (Phillips, 1978). There are many techniques and strategies that can be used with children suffering from school stress. Most involve a focus on learning and motivational processes.

REFERENCES

Phillips, B. (1978). *School stress and anxiety*. New York: Human Sciences.

Selye, H. (1976). *The stress of life*. New York: McGraw-Hill.

Wenz-Gross, M., & Siperstein, G. N. (1998). Students with learning problems at risk in middle school: Stress social support, and adjustment. *Exceptional Children, 65*(1), 91–100.

JOSEPH L. FRENCH
Pennsylvania State University

SCHOOL PHOBIA
STRESS AND THE HANDICAPPED STUDENT

SCHOPLER, ERIC (1927–   )

Eric Schopler received his BA (1949) from the University of Chicago. He received an MA (1955) in psychiatric social work from the School of Social Service Administration, and his Ph.D. (1964) in clinical child development from the Committee on Human Development, University of Chicago. He is currently a professor of psychology and psychiatry, and the founder and co-director of the Division for the Treatment and Education of Autistic and related Communication handicapped CHildren (TEACCH), University of North Carolina, Chapel Hill.

Eric Schopler

Early experiences helped convince Schopler that Freudian theories applied to autism were mistaken (Schopler, 1993) and that parents were not the cause but, along with their children, the victims of a neurobiological disorder (1971, 1994). Schopler (1997) and colleagues identified principles for optimum education for children in the autism spectrum based on parent collaboration and including the use of a visually structured education (Schopler, Mesibov, & Hearsey, 1995).

Schopler initiated an effective statewide program with

unified parent-professional collaboration that focuses on family adaptation, school adjustment, and community relations (Schopler, 1986). TEACCH includes both strong research and professional training components. The organization's publications have been translated into many languages and the TEACCH program has served as a national and international model. In recognition of his contributions, Schopler has received the American Psychiatry Association (APA) Gold Achievement Award, the University of North Carolina's O. Max Gardner Award for Outstanding Contribution to Human Welfare (1985), the APA Award for Distinguished Public Service (1985), and the North Carolina Award (1993), the highest honor awarded by the state for achievements in public leadership.

REFERENCES

Schopler, E. (1986). Relationship between university research and state policy: Division TEACCH—Treatment and Education of Autistic and related Communication handicapped CHildren. *Popular Government, 51*(4), 23–32.

Schopler, E. (1993). The anatomy of a negative role model. In G. Brannigan & M. Merrens (Eds.),*The undaunted psychologist* (pp. 172–186). Philadelphia, PA: McGraw-Hill.

Schopler, E. (1994). Neurobiological correlates in the classification and study of autism. In S. Broman & J. Grafman (Eds.), *Atypical cognitive deficits in developmental disorders: Implication for brain function* (pp. 87–100). Hillsdale, NJ: Erlbaum.

Schopler, E. (1997), Implementation of the TEACCH philosophy. In D. J. Cohen & F. R. Volkmar (Eds.), *Handbook of autism and pervasive developmental disorders*. New York: Wiley.

Schopler, E., Mesibov, G. B., & Hearsey, K. (1995). Structured teaching in the TEACCH system. In E. Schopler & G. B. Mesibov (Eds.), *Learning and cognition in autism* (pp. 243–267). New York: Plenum.

STAFF

SCHWARTZ-JAMPEL SYNDROME

See RARE DISEASES

SCOLIOSIS

Scoliosis, a lateral curvature of the spine, is the most common type of spinal deformity. Functional scoliosis results from poor posture or a difference in length of the legs. It is not progressive and usually disappears with exercise. Structural scoliosis, however, is a more severe form, involving rotation of the spine and structural changes in the vertebrae (Ziai, 1984).

Most cases of structural scoliosis are idiopathic—of unknown cause (Benson, 1983). Idiopathic scoliosis occurs most frequently in adolescent females during the growth spurt, ages 12 to 16. If untreated, the condition progresses rapidly throughout the spinal growth period (ages 15 to 16 for girls and ages 18 to 19 for boys). Scoliosis can also accompany neuromuscular disorders such as cerebral palsy and muscular dystrophy, or can develop as a result of infection, trauma, or surgery.

Early diagnosis of scoliosis is essential to prevent progression of the curvature. Treatment varies with the type of scoliosis, the age of the child, and severity of deformity. Mild curvatures require only observation, while more pronounced curvatures require bracing and exercise. In severe cases, surgery is required. Recent treatment approaches have also included electrostimulation (Benson, 1983) and use of biofeedback techniques (Birbaumer, Flor, Cevey & Dworkin, 1994; Ziai, 1984).

REFERENCES

Birbaumer, N., Flor, H., Cevey, B., & Dworkin, B. (1994). Behavioral treatment of scoliosis and kyphosis. *Journal of Psychosomatic Research*, 38(6), 623–628.

Benson, D. R. (1983). The spine and neck. In M. E. Gershwin & D. L. Robbins (Eds.), *Musculoskeletal diseases of children* (pp. 469–538). New York: Grune & Stratton.

James, J. I. P. (1976). *Scoliosis* (2nd ed.). Edinburgh, Scotland: Churchill Livingstone.

Ziai, M. (Ed.). (1984). *Pediatrics* (3rd ed.). Boston: Little, Brown.

CHRISTINE A. ESPIN
University of Minnesota

CEREBRAL PALSY
MUSCULAR DYSTROPHY

SCOPE AND SEQUENCE

Scope and sequence information play an important role in the special education of exceptional individuals. In academic areas where curriculum is not readily available, the use of scope and sequence information and task analysis provides the special educator with ways of determining a set of skills (Hargrave & Poteet, 1984).

To provide appropriate programs, special educators need a clear understanding, in the form of a sequence of skills, of what each of the academic domains include. This array of skills is referred to as scope and sequence information. Scope and sequence charts provide schemata of an instructional domain. Scope refers to those skills that are taught; sequence refers to the order in which they are taught. Sequences may be determined from the work of others or may be synthesized by the special educator from experience (Wehman & McLaughlin, 1981).

Scope and sequence charts vary in structure and format among special educators and programs. Scope and sequence information provide a link between assessment and the specification of instructional goals and objectives (Wehman & McLaughlin, 1981). It is essential in developing individual educational programs. Knowledge of the scope and sequence of skills provides the teacher with a clearer profile of those skills that the student has acquired and those that he or she still needs to acquire (Mercer & Mercer, 1985).

REFERENCES

Hargrave, L. J., & Poteet, J. A. (1984). *Assessment in special education*. Englewood Cliffs, NJ: Prentice-Hall.

Mercer, C. D., & Mercer, A. R. (1985). *Teaching students with learning problems*. Columbus, OH: Merrill.

Wehman, P., & McLaughlin, P. J. (1981). *Program development in special education*. New York: McGraw-Hill.

ANNE M. BAUER
University of Cincinnati

SCOTT CRANIODIGITAL SYNDROME WITH MENTAL RETARDATION

Scott craniodigital syndrome with mental retardation is a rare, X-linked recessive genetic disorder. Children with this syndrome have mental retardation and various craniofacial and extremity abnormalities. Craniofacial features include a small, wide head; small, narrow nose; excessively small jaw; and eyes set far apart. Other head and facial characteristics include an extended hairline, thick eyebrows, and long eyelashes. A startled expression on their face is found among some children (National Organization for Rare Disorders [NORD], 1997).

Extremity abnormalities have also been found among these children, including webbing of their hands and feet. The heels of these children's feet are turned inward as well. Excessive hair growth on different parts of their body have also been reported (NORD, 1997).

Mental retardation is present; therefore, it will be important for the child to enter an early childhood intervention program at age 3, with continued special education services as the child progresses through school.

REFERENCE

National Organization for Rare Disorders (NORD). (1997). *Singleton-Merton syndrome*. New Fairfield, CT: National Organization for Rare Disorders, Inc.

PATRICIA A. LOWE
Texas A & M University

JOAN W. MAYFIELD
Baylor Pediatric Specialty Service

SCOUTING AND THE HANDICAPPED

The scouting movement for boys and girls has made a significant effort to involve youths with handicaps. This was not always the case (Stevens, 1995) but currently in America, all levels of scouting have provisions to mainstream scouts in community units and to develop specialized troops for youngsters with severe disabilities or unusual needs. Scouting organizations catering to members with given disabilities are capable of designing adapted activities. For example, Stuckey and Barkus (1986) reported that the Boy Scout Troop of the Perkins School for the Blind went on a special camping trip at the Philmont Scout Ranch in New Mexico.

The national scout offices coordinate their efforts with a variety of organizations serving and advocating for the handicapped. Leadership training materials that deal with issues in scouting for handicapped members and guidelines on adapting scouting activities are available, as are materials such as taped scout handbooks. A number of adapted merit badge programs allow impaired scouts to earn an award while knowing that they have truly met the requirements for a badge.

Scouting offers youths many opportunities for developing motor, cognitive, and social skills, increasing self-esteem and a sense of achievement, and obtaining a feeling of enjoyment. Boy Scout and Girl Scout programs have worked toward making these benefits available to all youths. Many publications and other materials are available to interested persons from the national offices of Girl Scouts and Boy Scouts and from various local scout executives.

REFERENCES

Stevens, A. (1995). Changing attitudes to disabled people in the Scout Association in Britain (1908–62): A contribution to a history of disability. *Disability & Society, 10*(3), 281–293.

Stuckey, K., & Barkus, C. (1986). Visually impaired scouts meet the Philmont challenge. *Journal of Visual Impairment & Blindness, 80,* 750–151.

Lee A. Jackson, Jr.
University of North Carolina at Wilmington

RECREATION, THERAPEUTIC

SECKEL SYNDROME

Seckel syndrome, also known as nanocephaly, is a genetic disorder. The incidence of Seckel syndrome is higher in females than males and is due to an autosomal recessive gene (Thoene, 1992). The primary characteristics of the disorder include a very small head (microcephaly); intrauterine and postnatal growth failure, resulting in dwarfism; and sharp facial features with an underdeveloped chin (Rudolph, 1991). Prominence of the midface is typical in children with Seckel syndrome. Children with this disorder have a beak-like nose, large, malformed eyes, and low-set ears without lobes. They are short in stature, ranging in height from 3 to 3½ feet as an adult (Jones, 1988). Other physical abnormalities may include permanent fixation of the fifth finger in a bent position, malformation of the hips, and dislocation of the radial bone in the forearm (NORD, 1998).

Children with Seckel syndrome have moderate to severe mental retardation (Jones, 1988). These children often exhibit hyperactive behavior and have attention and concentration difficulties (Jones, 1988). These children would benefit from a small group educational setting that provides one-on-one instruction and allows them to progress at their own speed. A structured, educational setting with expected rewards and consequences would be optimal. The standard treatment of Seckel syndrome is symptomatic and supportive. Parent training with a pediatric psychologist including behavioral management techniques may be beneficial. Genetic counseling may be helpful as well (Thoene, 1992).

REFERENCES

Jones, K. L. (Ed.). (1988). *Smith's recognizable patterns of human malformation* (4th ed.). Philadelphia, PA: W. B. Saunders.

Rudolph, A. M. (1991). *Rudolph's pediatrics-19th Edition.* Norwalk, CT: Appleton & Lange.

National Organization For Rare Disorders (NORD). (1998). *Seckel syndrome.* New Fairfield, CT: Author.

Thoene, J. G. (Ed.). (1992). *Physician's guide to rare diseases.* Montvale, NJ: Dowden Publishing.

Joan Mayfield
Baylor Pediatric Specialty Services

Patricia A. Lowe
Texas A & M University

SECOND LANGUAGE LEARNERS IN SPECIAL EDUCATION

Special education is a field addressing many challenges, one of them being working with second language learners. Today, many children across the United States come from countries and homes where English is not spoken or used as a language in which concepts are discussed. If, as projections suggest, 10% to 20% of any given population has some or several disabilities, then special education serves a number of these children. For many such students, English is their second language. This condition currently presents challenges to educators and service providers, impacting the outcomes of evaluations and interventions (Ortiz, 1997). Unlike a child brought up in an English-only environment, the learner of English as a second language shows developmental lags in articulation, vocabulary, insights on syntax, and comprehension of complex oral and printed texts. These conditions, coupled with limited understanding of the stages of second language acquisition, tends to promote overreferral to and placement in special education (National Coalition of Advocates for Schools, 1991). For example, Ochoa, Robles-Pina, Garcia, and Breunig's (in press) study across eight states with large populations of second language learners revealed that oral language-related factors (acquisition and/or delays) were the third most common reason for referral of second language learners. Further, Ochoa, Robles-Pina, Garcia, and Breunig (in press) state that eight of the top 13 most commonly cited reasons for referral of these learners could be linked to language; in their study, language reasons accounted for 54% of all responses provided. Equally, limited awareness of conditions that suggest a disability promote patterns of underreferral of this population among general educators who consider the students' problems as typical patterns of second language learners (De León & Cole, 1994).

Until recently, special education in general invested modest efforts attending to the specific communication needs of second language learners and their families, and most support focused on attending to their conditions or disabilities. However, literature within the last ten years reveals a change in this trend, the effects of which will be reviewed perhaps five years from now. Consequently, increasing research, training, and publication efforts raise awareness and educate professionals. For example, guidelines and recommendations based on best practices for children without disabilities are advocated for second language learners with disabilities (California Department of Education, 1997; Fernández, 1992; Gersten, Brengelman, & Jimenez, 1994). Currently, the literature reflects continuous appeals to special educators and speech clinicians to incorporate modified approaches like English as a second language (ESL) and/or Sheltered English into their practice (De León & Cole, 1994; Garcia & Malkin, 1993; Gersten, Brengelman, & Jimenez, 1994). However, the appropriateness and effectiveness of such practices are yet to be validated. The following sections address critical issues and challenges related to the education of second language learners with disabilities served in special education programs.

Heterogeneity

Diversity effectively describes the linguistic abilities of second language learners (SLLs) served in special educa-

tion programs. Different disabilities, cultural and socioeconomic backgrounds, communicative abilities, and degrees of exposure to English are interacting variables that easily confound design and outcomes of many studies involving SLLs. Surveys and studies involving teachers and other categories of service providers working in programs serving SLLs reveal limited knowledge of the stages of second language acquisition through which learners advance naturally (De León & Cole, 1994; Ochoa, Rivera & Ford, 1997; Ortiz & Yates, 1988). Common practice approaches this challenge by educating second language learners as if they were native speakers of English, promoting very few, if any, modifications to interventions (Fernández, 1992). For example, use of ESL or equally meaningful approaches for the instruction of SLLs is recommended in literature but seldom is practiced (De León & Cole, 1994). Quite often, focusing on the child's disability excludes other needs the learner might have related to his or her condition of being a second language learner (such a child is usually expected to perform like a native speaker of English). Furthermore, generic prescriptions studied and validated for children without disabilities continue to be proposed (Fueyo, 1997; Gersten, Brengelman, & Jimenez, 1994) for a population whose specific linguistic characteristics remain undefined.

Assessment

English language learners (ELLs)[1], as they are currently named, pose a challenge to those participating in the identification process. Unless their disability is obvious—e.g., orthopedic or visual impairment, or moderate to severe mental retardation—the question most evaluators encounter upon referral to assessment and possible placement is whether the learner has acquired English in all its linguistic and functional dimensions, or if the learner is advancing within the earlier stages of the long-term process of second language acquisition (Cummins & Sayers, 1995). Has the learner received appropriate instruction using methodology appropriate to the condition of learning English as a second language? Such information is critical to establish a distinction between poor performance due to ongoing development of linguistic competence, due to a disability, or a combination of both. Actually, Ochoa, Galarza, and Gonzalez (1996) found that only 6% of school psychologists conducting bilingual assessments of second language learners referred for special education actually implemented best practices that would enable them to obtain this critical information. Without establishing this distinction clearly, interpretation of current performance, prereferral strategies, assessment results, categorization, progress, and redesignation can be impacted negatively. Reports continue to emerge that question classification and disqualification for services and offer criticism on the interpretation of assessment data (Cheng, Ima, & Labovitz, 1994; Garcia & Malkin, 1993; Ochoa,

Galarza, and Gonzalez, 1996; Ochoa, Rivera, & Powell, 1997). These matters demand attention at policy, research, and practice levels given the increasing expectations that all children be educated to reach their potential, and barely anything is being done to monitor an appropriate, meaningful, and effective learning opportunity.

Access to the Curriculum

Reviews of policies and practices affecting second language learners in the United States reveals very limited focus on the specific instructional needs of ELLs with disabilities. Instead, most frequently, discussions on ELLs are embedded within references addressing diversity issues. Searches that include articles referring to culturally and linguistically diverse (CLD) learners with disabilities enables access to some of the scant literature on the pedagogy to educate second language learners in special education. Extracting information from reports is complex since, frequently, linguistic diversity is used to refer to second language learners, particularly Spanish speakers, when in reality linguistic diversity is larger than this subcategory. A plethora of articles focus on cross-cultural variations and culturally relevant interventions rather than on the study of the best, or most effective, instructional practices for children with disabilities requiring the support of instruction in English as their second language.

Comprehensible input facilitates access and consequently impacts learning (Fueyo, 1997). Methodologies designed to teach second language learners without disabilities offer a promising potential in facilitating access to the English curriculum for second language learners affected by one or several disabilities. Attending to the provision of comprehensible input is crucial. Instructional approaches such as English as a Second Language (ESL), the purpose of which is to promote effective early English language acquisition, and Sheltered English, which facilitates the development of higher levels of competence in English as a second language focusing on the development of reading and content-area skills (or academic courses) while strengthening emerging English skills, beg validation of their effectiveness for individuals with disabilities. Such approaches constitute common options recommended for linguistically appropriate individualized education programs (IEPs) for second language learners with limited English proficiency (California Department of Education, 1997; Gersten, Brengelman, & Jimenez, 1994; Ortiz, 1997; Ortiz & Garcia, 1990; Ortiz & Yates, 1988).

Opportunities to learn through the first language promise a greater degree of comprehension of the instructional content, but the literature reflects a paucity of studies documenting best practices where this approach is implemented (Cloud, 1993; Willig & Swedo, 1987). Ortiz and Wilkinson (1989) found that in only 2% of the 203 IEPs of second language learners they reviewed was the child's first language specified as the language of instruction. Fur-

thermore, research needs to document for which students this is an effective and valid option.

Professional Development

Most of the research efforts involving second language learners in special education throughout the last fifteen years have been dedicated to documenting disparity in identification, access to the curriculum, and appropriate services. Documentation reveals that programs are not responding to the individual needs of second language learners and that the number of teachers familiar with pedagogy that supports second language acquisition is extremely reduced, and in most cases, bilingual paraprofessionals are the ones with direct responsibility for the instruction of these students. As appropriate and effective research-based interventions are validated and cross-referenced with each learner's linguistic profiles, a priority needs to be established to support extended and comprehensive professional development related to the education of students with disabilities for whom English is the second, and often weakest language.

Research and Policy Agenda

A research agenda for the future demands attention to the identification of linguistic abilities, matching instruction to developmental stage, and documentation of effective interventions, with particular emphasis on methodology and support mechanisms to enhance the learning opportunity. A research agenda including attention both to the needs of individuals with moderate to severe disabilities, and to the effects of introduction of the second language for non-speakers or non-comprehenders of English with disabilities is equally crucial. As more is learned about the effects of modulating instructional practices for SLLs in special education, policies and practices need to respond to these research-based interventions. Ultimately, the role of the researcher, teacher, and service provider is to advocate for the study of a pedagogy that encompasses the range of abilities and competence within any classroom where second language learners are present, particularly those with a disability.

Conclusion

Much needs to be learned about effective interventions for children with disabilities who are learning or who have learned English as their second language. A research agenda must evolve from this critical need so that a solid understanding of appropriateness and effectiveness of recommendations can be developed.

NOTE

[1] The term ELL replaces LEP which is the most common in the literature when it deals with students learning English as their

second language. The new term is more inclusive of different levels of proficiency not just beginning levels.

REFERENCES

California Department of Education. (1997). *Guidelines for language, academic, and special education services required for limited-English-proficient students in California public schools, K–12.* Sacramento: Special Education Division.

Cheng, L., Ima, K., & Lobovitz, G. (1994). Assessment of Asian and Pacific Islander students for gifted programs. In S. B. Garcia (Ed.), *Addressing cultural and linguistic diversity in special education* (pp. 30–45). Reston, Va.: The Council for Exceptional Children.

Cloud, N. (1993). Language, culture and disability: Implications for instruction and teacher preparation. *Teacher Education and Special Education, 16,* 60–72.

Cummins, J., & Sayers, D. (1995). *Brave new schools: Challenging cultural illiteracy through global learning networks.* N.Y.: St. Martin's Press.

De León, J., & Cole, J. (1994). Service delivery to culturally and linguistically diverse exceptional learners in rural school districts. *Rural Special Education Quarterly, 13,* 37–45.

Fernández, A. T. (1992). Legal support for bilingual education and language appropriate related services for limited English proficient students with disabilities. *Bilingual Research Journal, 16,* 117–140.

Fueyo, V. (1997). Below the tip of the iceberg: Teaching language-minority students. *Teaching Exceptional Children, 30,* 61–65.

Garcia, S. B., & Malkin, D. H. (1993). Toward defining programs and services for culturally and linguistically diverse learners in special education. *Teaching Exceptional Children, 26,* 52–58.

Gersten, R., Brengelman, S., & Jiménez, R. (1994). Effective instruction for culturally and linguistically diverse students: A reconceptualization. *Focus on Exceptional Children, 27,* 1–16.

Ochoa, S. H., Galarza, A., & Gonzalez, D. (1996). An investigation of school psychologists' assessment practices of language proficiency with bilingual and limited English proficient students. *Diagnostique, 21*(4), 17–36.

Ochoa, S. H., Rivera, B. D., & Ford, L. (1997). An investigation of school psychology training pertaining to bilingual psychoeducational assessment of primarily Hispanic students: Twenty-five years after Diana v. California. *Journal of School Psychology, 35,* 329–349.

Ochoa, S. H., Rivera, B. D., & Powell, M. P. (1997). Factors used to comply with the exclusionary clauses with bilingual and L.E.P. pupils: Initial guidelines. *Learning Disabilities Research and Practice, 12,* 161–167.

Ochoa, S. H., Robles-Pina, R., Garcia, S. B., & Breunig, N. (in press). School psychologists' perspectives on referrals of language minority students. *Journal of Multiple Voices for Ethnically Diverse Exceptional Learners.*

Ortiz, A. A. (1997). Learning disabilities occurring concomitantly with linguistic differences. *Journal of Learning Disabilities, 30,* 321–332.

Ortiz, A. A., & Garcia, S. B. (1990). Using language assessment data for language and instructional planning for exceptional bilingual students. In *Teaching the bilingual special education student* (pp. 25–47). Norwood, N.J.: Ablex.

Ortiz, A. A., & Wilkinson, C. Y. (1989). Adapting IEP's for limited-English-proficient students. *Academic Therapy, 24*(5), 555–568.

Ortiz, A. A., & Yates, J. R. (1988). Characteristics of learning disabled, mentally retarded, and speech-language handicapped Hispanic students at initial evaluation and reevaluation. In A. A. Ortiz and B. R. Ramirez (Eds.), *Schools and the culturally diverse exceptional student: Promising practices and future directions* (pp. 51–62). Reston: The Council for Exceptional Children.

Willig, A. C., & Swedo, J. J. (1987, April). *Improving teaching strategies for exceptional Hispanic limited English proficient students: An exploratory study of task engagement and teaching strategies.* Paper presented at the annual meeting of the American Educational Research Association, Washington, DC.

ELBA MALDONADO-COLON
San Jose State University

SALVADOR HECTOR OCHOA
Texas A & M University

SECONDARY SPECIAL EDUCATION

Special education practice at the secondary level must account for different competencies and a different orientation than would be expected at the elementary level. The practitioner at the elementary level is able to communicate easily with regular classroom teachers because they share common training and a similar purpose in the instruction of basic language and math skills. The most common type of service delivery system in the elementary school seems to be the resource room. This arrangement is a natural extension of the regular classroom, with activities integrated with regular school curriculum. The result is a high degree of continuity from one area to another. Several problems are associated with using this approach at the secondary level. Teachers tend to be divided by areas of specialization and do not focus on individual differences of learners as readily as at the elementary level. This often results in the misinterpretation or misunderstanding of the value and nature of special education programming (Ysseldyke & Algozzine, 1984). This approach is not usually successful because it fails to involve many regular education classroom teachers and disregards the realities of the advanced secondary curriculum. The efforts of the special education practitioner should, therefore, be directed toward immediate problems of the learner and provide for close interaction with teachers and the specific course of study for each student.

Because few models for service delivery of secondary special education services exist, and university training programs have traditionally prepared teachers with an elementary emphasis, many secondary systems have relied on the elementary resource room as a model for service delivery. If the school adopts the philosophy of providing assistance only in the acquisition of basic skills in language and mathematics, then the traditional elementary model might be useful. If the school recognizes, however, the special demands and circumstances of the exceptional student as well as the unique problems associated with the onset of adolescence, then different programming is needed (Marsh, Gearheart, & Gearheart; 1978).

Lerner (1976) asserts that a secondary service delivery system in special education must account for several options in programming. For some students it may be desirable to offer a self-contained classroom, while for others a special resource room may be more beneficial because the teacher can act as a liaison between the regular education teacher, counselor, student, and parent. The school also may offer a variety of specially designed courses for students with learning problems. Lerner holds that resource room teachers in high school must be familiar with the entire curriculum of the school to be successful in remediating and programming for exceptional students. This familiarity would enable the teacher to assist the students in a variety of courses rather than in the remediation of specific academic skills. Remediation must be tied closely to what happens in the mainstream classroom.

Goodman and Mann proposed a different model in 1976. They theorized a basic education program at the secondary level that restricts the activities of the teacher to instruction of mathematics and language arts. Enrollment of students would be limited to those who lacked sixth-grade achievement. The goal for the secondary teacher in special education would be to remediate students to a sixth-grade level to allow for mainstreaming into regular education classes.

Program options, in fact, lie somewhere between the two extremes, with decisions regarding the thrust of programming often dictated by local custom and philosophy. The main objective should be to provide a system of instruction that reduces the complexity without sacrificing quality. A carefully balanced program should include the provision for specific remediation as well as assistance in addressing course work through the accommodation of individual needs. Equal opportunity should allow each student to benefit from academic training and career education to the fullest extent possible. Insufficiency in reading should not deny a student the opportunity to participate and learn in an academic class; nor should it limit the student to training that leads to entry-level skills in low-status jobs. The verbal bias evidenced in the instruction of many schools should not limit the pursuits of intelligent but inefficient learners.

REFERENCES

Goodman, L., & Mann, L. (1976). *Learning disabilities in the secondary school*. New York: Grune & Stratton.

Lerner, J. W. (1976). *Children with learning disabilities* (2nd ed.). Boston: Houghton Mifflin.

Marsh, G. E., Gearheart, C., & Gearheart, B. (1978). *The learning disabled adolescent*. St. Louis: Mosby.

Scranton, T., & Downs, M. (1975). Elementary and secondary learning disabilities programs in the U.S.: A survey. *Journal of Learning Disabilities, 8*(6), 394–399.

Ysseldyke, J. E., & Algozzine, B. (1984). *Introduction to special education*. Boston: Houghton Mifflin.

CRAIG D. SMITH
Georgia College

RESOURCE ROOM
RESOURCE TEACHER
VOCATIONAL TRAINING

SECTION 504 OF THE 1973 REHABILITATION ACT

See REHABILITATION ACT OF 1973.

SEEING EYE DOGS

See ANIMALS FOR THE HANDICAPPED; DOG GUIDES FOR THE BLIND.

SEGUIN, EDOUARD (1812–1880)

Edouard Seguin, who demonstrated to the world that mentally retarded individuals can be educated, studied medicine under Jean Marc Gaspard Itard in Paris, and applied the training methods of that famous physician and teacher to the education of the mentally retarded. In 1837 Seguin established the first school in France for the mentally retarded, with remarkable success. In 1848 he moved to the United States, where he practiced medicine, served as director of the Pennsylvania Training School, and acted as adviser to numerous state institutions. He was a founder and first president of the Association of Medical Officers of American Institutions for Idiotic and Feeble-Minded Persons, now the American Association on Mental Deficiency.

Seguin's methods, which provided the foundation for the movement for the education of the mentally retarded in the United States, were based on a number of principles:

that observation of the child is the foundation of the child's education; that education deals with the whole child; that the child learns best from real things; that perceptual training should precede training for concept development; and that even the most defective child has some capacity for learning. Seguin incorporated art, music, and gymnastics into the educational program, and emphasized the use of concrete materials in the classroom.

Seguin's influence on the early development of special education services can hardly be overstated. Samuel Gridley Howe, who was responsible for the formation of the first state school for mentally retarded children in the United States, obtained much of his methodology directly from Seguin. Maria Montessori gave credit to Seguin for the principles on which she based her system of education. Today, more than a century after his death. Seguin's influence is evident in the methods being used to instruct children with learning handicaps.

REFERENCES

Kanner, L. (1960). Itard, Seguin, Howe—Three pioneers in the education of retarded children. *American Journal of Mental Deficiency, 65,* 2–10.

Seguin, E. (1907). *Idiocy and its treatment by the physiological method.* New York: Teachers College, Columbia University.

Talbot, E. *Edouard Seguin: A study of an educational approach to the treatment of mentally defective children.* New York: Teachers College, Columbia University.

PAUL IRVINE
Katonah, New York

SEIZURE DISORDERS

Seizures are relatively common in children and are the most common basis for a referral to a pediatric neurologist (Haslam, 1996). A seizure is a "paroxysmal involuntary disturbance of brain function that may manifest in an impairment or loss of consciousness, abnormal motor activity, behavioral abnormalities, sensory disturbances, or autonomic dysfunction" (Haslam, 1996, p. 1686). In many cases, seizures can be directly related to head trauma resulting from brain injury or high fever. Approximately 8% of children can be expected to have at least one seizure before adolescence (Brown, 1997). Epilepsy may be diagnosed only in an individual who has a series of seizures. Although descriptions of childhood seizures by parents and others may be very helpful in diagnosis, some different seizures (for example, absence and complex partial) may present almost identically in different individuals. Thus, EEG records are an important aspect of diagnosis

(Haslam, 1996). Seizure disorders frequently occur in association with more severe degrees of mental retardation and cerebral palsy.

Classification of Seizures

The International Classification of Seizures divides seizures into two major categories: partial and generalized. Partial seizures begin in unilateral (focal or local) areas and may or may not spread bilaterally. Generalized seizures begin with immediate involvement of bilateral brain structures and are associated with either bilateral motor movements, changes in consciousness, or both.

Partial seizures

Partial seizures are divided into: (1) simple partial attacks that arise from a local area and do not impair consciousness and (2) complex partial attacks that begin in a local area but spread bilaterally and therefore impair consciousness. They are the most common type of seizure disorder, accounting for 40%–60% of all childhood seizures (Brown, 1997; Haslam, 1996). In simple partial types, consciousness is unimpaired; in complex partial types, degree of altered awareness or unresponsiveness is involved.

Simple partial seizures often exhibit primary neurologic symptoms that indicate the site of origin. Partial seizures involve motor activity from any portion of the body. They usually involve the limbs, face, or head, and sometimes cause speech arrest. Hallucinations and visual illusions may occur, depending on the site of the seizure. Partial seizures that progress with sequential involvement of parts of the body that are represented in contiguous cortical areas are termed Jacksonian. Benign rolandic epilepsy is common and may result in the child awakening from sleep and showing motor symptoms. Localized paralysis or weakness that may last for minutes or days sometimes occurs and indicates an underlying structural lesion. Partial motor seizures also can be continuous for extended periods of time.

Complex partial seizures, previously called psychomotor or temporal lobe seizures, are the most common shown in older children and adolescents and occur in over 50% of adults with seizure disorders. The seizures characteristically begin with emotional, psychic, illusory, hallucinatory, or special sensory symptoms. Sometimes, consciousness becomes impaired at the onset of the attack. After the aura, the individual becomes completely or partially unresponsive and may perform apparently purposeful activity. The seizure consists of involuntary motor movements such as eye blinking, lip smacking, facial grimaces, groaning, chewing and other automatisms, but more elaborate behavior can occur. In the state of depressed awareness, patients may actively resist efforts to restrain them. A complete attack usually lasts between 1 and 3 minutes; on recovery, there is complete amnesia for the attack except for the aura or partial motor onset. Complex partial seizures usually begin in the temporal lobe but may originate from the frontal, parietal, or occipital regions.

Generalized seizures

Generalized seizures involve bilateral brain regions and begin with immediate involvement of both hemispheres. Five types are recognized; (1) absence seizures with associated 3-Hz (cycles per second) generalized spike-and-wave discharges in the electroencephalogram (EEG); (2) atypical absence seizures; (3) myoclonic seizures; (4) tonic-clonic seizures; and (5) atonic seizures.

Absence seizures are not as common as other types of seizures, and account for only 5% of all seizure disorders. These seizures are short interruptions of consciousness that last from 3 to 15 seconds each. They are not associated with auras or other evidence of focal onset. Absence seizures begin and end abruptly and recur from a few to several hundred times per day. Ongoing behavior stops. While otherwise immobile, the individual may show inconspicuous flickering of the eyelids or eyebrows about three times per second; there may be simple automatic movements, such as rubbing the nose, putting a hand to the face, or chewing and swallowing. Falling does not occur because of the ability to retain muscle tone. Immediately following the short interruption of awareness, the individual is again mentally clear and fully capable of continuing previous activity. Patients with absence seizures of this type show bilaterally synchronous 3 Hz spike-and-wave discharges, usually occurring against an otherwise normal background activity. The age of onset of these short absence seizures is almost always after age 2; they almost never occur for the first time after age 20. Individuals with short absence seizures rarely have other neurological problems, but 40% to 50% of the patients have infrequent, easily controlled, generalized tonic-clonic seizures. Photic sensitivity is present in some cases.

Generalized tonic-clonic seizures occur at some time in most patients with seizure disorder regardless of the individual's usual pattern. This type of seizure can be triggered by many various events (e.g., fever, CNS infection, brain abnormality, and hereditary tendency) and also is commonly seen in childhood seizure disorders. A tonic-clonic seizure is classified under generalized seizures if the attack itself, the neurological examination, and the EEG all indicate that bilateral cerebral structures are simultaneously involved at the onset. A tonic-clonic seizure is classified as a partial seizure evolving to a secondarily generalized one if the same criteria indicate that the attack began in one hemisphere and then spread to produce a major generalized attack. Tonic-clonic convulsions usually last 3 to 5 minutes, and are characterized by a complex loss of consciousness and falling. As the patient falls, the body stiffens because of generalized tonic contraction of the limb and axial muscles. The legs usually extend and the arms flex partially. After the tonic stage, which usually lasts less than 1 minute, jerking or clonic movements occur in all four limbs for about 1 minute. Next, a period of unconsciousness follows (about 1 minute) during which the patient appears more relaxed. Consciousness then is regained and the patient usually is confused, sleepy, and uncooperative for several minutes prior to full recovery.

Atypical absence seizures generally result in blank stares that can last longer than the typical absence seizure. Atypical absence seizures are often associated with various types of seizure patterns including tonic-clonic, myoclonic, and atonic seizures. Atonic seizures usually begin in childhood and are characterized by sudden loss of postural tone which can cause slumping, a head drop, and even sometimes resulting in abrupt drops to the floor. These episodes occur without warning, are extremely short, and frequently cause injury. Myoclonic seizures are involuntary contractions of the limb and truncal muscles that are sudden, brief, and recurrent. Slight bilateral symmetric myoclonic movements often occur in persons who have absence seizures, but rarely are severe bilaterally symmetric myoclonic jerks the predominant symptoms of individuals with absence seizures.

Treatment

Seizure disorders can typically be treated with antiepileptic drugs (AEDs). In treating seizures, it is initially important to identify and eliminate factors that potentially cause or precipitate the attacks. Different medications are used for various types of seizures. Medications are used until seizure control is achieved or until toxic side effects limit further increments. In more severe cases, when pharmacological treatments prove completely ineffective, surgery is often the only alternative. Removing lesions or tumors from the brain is often risky and later impairs cognitive functioning. The anterior portion of the temporal lobe is the most frequent site of surgical excision in individuals with medically intractable seizures.

General Concerns

People, particularly children, with seizure disorders frequently and understandably are often fearful and feel that they have relatively little control. In addition to medical management, parents and children may need counseling. Rarely are any special restrictions on activity needed except during swimming and bathing, and parents should be encouraged to allow their children to behave as normally as possible.

An excellent source for further information is the Epilepsy Foundation of American, 4351 Garden City Drive,

Landover, MD 20785; phone: (800) EFA-1000; email: webmaster@efa.org; and website: http://www.efa.org/index.html.

REFERENCES

Brown, L. W. (1997). Seizure disorders. In M. L. Batshaw (Ed.), *Children with disabilities* (4th ed., pp. 553–593). Baltimore: Brookes.

Haslam, R. H. A. (1996). Seizures in childhood. In R. E. Behrman, R. M. Kliegman, & A. M. Arvin (Eds.), *Nelson textbook of pediatrics* (15th ed., pp. 1686–1699).

ROBERT T. BROWN
AIMEE R. HUNTER
*University of North Carolina at
Wilmington*

SELF-CARE SKILLS

See SELF HELP SKILLS.

SELF-CONCEPT

Self-concept is an individual's evaluation of his or her own abilities and attributes. It includes all aspects of an individual's personality of which he or she is aware. Although some authors have drawn distinctions between self-concept and self-esteem (Damon & Hart, 1982), the terms are frequently used interchangeably. Several theoretical models of self-concept exist in the literature. For example, Coopersmith (1967) has suggested that four factors contribute to an individual's self-concept: significance (feeling of being loved and approved of by important others), competence (ability to perform tasks considered important), virtue (adherence to moral and ethical principles), and power (the degree to which an individual is able to exert control over self and others). Recently, Harter (1982) found that self-concept can be broken down into three specific components, cognitive, social, and physical competence, and a general self-worth factor.

Children with a positive self-concept are described as imaginative, confident in their own judgments and abilities, assertive, able to assume leadership roles, less preoccupied with themselves, and able to devote more time to others and to external activities. Children with a negative self-concept are described as quiet, unobtrusive, unoriginal, lacking in initiative, withdrawn, and doubtful about themselves (Coopersmith, 1967). School progress and academic achievement are influenced by self-concept, as is vocational choice. Unfortunately, much of the research on the effects of self-esteem has been subject to methodological and theoretical criticism (Damon & Hart, 1982; Wylie, 1979).

Self-concept begins to develop early in life, with children as young as 18 to 24 months able to discriminate between self and others (Lewis & Brooks-Gunn, 1979). As children's thought processes become less concrete and more abstract, there are corresponding changes in self-concept. Younger children (e.g., 9 year olds) tend to describe themselves in categorical terms (name, age, gender, physical attributes, etc.), while older children take an increasingly abstract view, describing their personal and interpersonal traits, attitudes, and beliefs (Montemayor & Eisen, 1977). There is not, however, any consistent evidence of age-related changes in the level of self-esteem (how positively or negatively one views oneself). The one exception to this is a temporary decline in self-esteem around the time children enter their teens (Simmons et al., 1979).

A number of factors influence an individual's self-concept. Parents appear to play a particularly important role (Coopersmith, 1967). Children with high self-esteem tend to have parents who themselves have high self-esteem and who are warm, nurturing, and accepting of their children while setting high academic and behavioral standards. They set and enforce strict limits on their children and are fair, reasonable, and consistent in their use of discipline. Parents of low self-esteem children alternate unpredictably between excessive permissiveness and harsh punishment. A close relationship with the same-sex parent is typical among high self-esteem children. Findings of higher self-esteem in only children and first-born children suggest that parental attention is important. Other factors associated with high self-esteem include academic success, the presence of a close friendship, and the perceived opinions of others. Physical attractiveness and height are unrelated to self-esteem (Coopersmith, 1967). It is very important for educators to remember that different ethnic groups perceive self-concept and its measurement in different ways (Obiakor, 1992).

Instruments to measure self-concept include the Piers-Harris Children's Self-Concept Scale (Piers, 1969), the Coopersmith Self-Esteem Inventory (Coopersmith, 1967), the Perceived Competence Scale for Children (Harter, 1982), and the Preschool and Primary Self-Concept Scale (Stager & Young, 1982).

REFERENCES

Coopersmith, S. (1967). *Antecedents of self-esteem*. San Francisco: Freeman.

Damon, W., & Hart, D. (1982). The development of self-understanding from infancy through adolescence. *Child Development, 53*, 841–864.

Harter, S. (1982). The perceived competence scale for children. *Child Development, 53*, 87–97.

Lewis, M., & Brooks-Gunn, J. (1979). *Social cognition and the acquisition of self*. New York: Plenum.

Montemayor, R., & Eisen, M. (1977). The development of self-conceptions from childhood to adolescence. *Developmental Psychology, 13,* 314–319.

Obiakor, F. E. (1992). Self-concept of African-American students: An operational model for special education. *Exceptional Children, 59*(2), 160–167.

Piers, E. V. (1969). *The Piers Harris Children's Self-Concept Scale.* Nashville, TN: Counselor Recordings and Tests.

Simmons, R. G., Blyth, D. A., Van Cleave, E. F., & Bush, D. M. (1979). Entry into early adolescence: The impact of school structure, puberty, and early dating on self-esteem. *American Sociological Review, 44,* 948–967.

Stager, S., & Young, R. D. (1982). A self-concept measure for preschool and early primary grade children. *Journal of Personality Assessment, 46,* 536–543.

Wylie, R. C. (1979). *The self-concept: Theory and research on selected topics* (Vol. 2, Rev. ed.). Lincoln: University of Nebraska Press.

ROBERT G. BRUBAKER
Eastern Kentucky University

DEPRESSION
EMOTIONAL LABILITY
SELF-MANAGEMENT
SOCIAL SKILLS

SELF-CONTAINED CLASS

The first self-contained special classes were established in the late 1800s and early 1900s as public school classes for the moderately retarded, deaf, hard of hearing, blind, emotionally disturbed, and physically handicapped. Esten (1900) states that special classes for the mentally retarded were established to provide slow learners with more appropriate class placement. A self-contained classroom for the handicapped can be defined as one that homogeneously segregates different children from normal children. Children are usually segregated along categorical groupings. As a result of Dunn's (1968) article on the detrimental aspects of self-contained placements for the mildly handicapped, students receiving special education in self-contained classes today are usually "low-incidence," exhibiting more severe problems Dunn was later refuted by Walker and McLaughlin, (1992). However, Kirk and Gallagher (1983) report gifted students are also grouped into special classes according to interests and abilities.

A self-contained class is a place where special education students spend more than 60% of their school day and receive most of their academic instruction. Typically, caseloads are small, ranging from 5 to 10 students in a class. A wide variety of instructional materials are available to the students. The self-contained class provides the opportunity for highly individualized, closely supervised, special-ized instruction. The self-contained classroom is usually taught by one trained teacher who is certified according to the categories served. The self-contained classroom may be categorically specific (serving one population) or cross-categorically grouped (serving multicategorical populations).

Major purposes of a self-contained class as outlined by Sabatino, Miller, and Schmidt (1981) include providing the student with the social and personal adjustment skills necessary to promote school success, and maintaining a constant structure within the instructional environment to reduce distractibility, hyperactivity, restlessness, poor attention span, and control over the rate of information flowing to the learner. Additionally, the purposes include teaching the basic academic and social skills necessary for success in life and making cooperative arrangements based on adequate communication with parents (p. 321). It is possible that a student may be assigned to a self-contained classroom and receive additional resource room assistance or partake in inclusive programming. Placement depends on what is best for the students in terms of least restriction. Usually, students are mainstreamed into regular education for nonacademic subjects such as music, physical education, and art, or academic areas of proficiency.

REFERENCES

Dunn, L. M. (1968). Special education for the mildly handicapped: Is much of it justifiable? *Exceptional Children, 35,* 5–22.

Esten, R. A. (1900). Backward children in the public schools. *Journal of Psychoaesthenics, 5,* 10–16.

Kirk, S. A., & Gallagher, J. J. (1983). *Educating exceptional children* (4th ed.). Boston: Houghton Mifflin.

Sabatino, D. A., Miller, T. L., & Schmidt, C. R. (1981). *Learning disabilities: Systemizing teaching and service delivery.* Rockville, MD: Aspen Systems.

Walker, J. G., & McLaughlin, T. F. (1992). Self-contained versus resource room classroom placement: A review. *Journal of Instructional Psychology, 19*(3), 214–225.

MARIBETH MONTGOMERY KASIK
Governors State University

GROUPING OF CHILDREN
LEAST RESTRICTIVE ENVIRONMENT
RESOURCE ROOM
SPECIAL CLASS

SELF-CONTROL CURRICULUM

The self-control curriculum was a product of the work of Fagen, Long, and Stevens (1975). They contended that emotional and cognitive development are closely related and therefore both need to be addressed simultaneously in the instructional process. They held that learning is impaired when learners have negative feelings about themselves. Fagen et al. believed that in many cases of behavior disorders there was an inability on the part of the individual to exert self-control. The self-control curriculum had as its goals the development of self-control and positive feelings.

There were eight enabling skills in the self-control model. Four of these were in the cognitive area and four in the affective area. The eight skills are:

1. *Selecting*. Paying attention to directions/instruction.
2. *Storing*. Remembering directions/instructions.
3. *Sequencing and ordering*. Organizing materials/work areas to perform work.
4. *Anticipating Consequences*. Realizing that behavior has consequences and predicting those consequences.
5. *Appreciating Feelings*. Expressing feelings by words and actions.
6. *Managing Frustrations*. Behaviorally maintaining control in stressful situations.
7. *Inhibiting and Delaying*. Delaying actions and reflecting on consequences of possible actions even when excited.
8. *Relaxing*. Consciously relieving bodily tension.

The curriculum has pupil activities and guidelines for teachers for developing more lessons in each unit. The activities involve games, discussions, and role-playing activities. The position taken in the curriculum was that self-control must be taught just as any other subject. General recommendations throughout the curriculum were to proceed from easy to difficult, to proceed in small steps, to use repetition and provide practice, to make activities enjoyable, reinforce efforts, and provide opportunities to practice skills in new situations and settings. Little research has been conducted over the past years to validate the curriculum.

REFERENCE

Fagen, S. A., Long, N. J., & Stevens, D. (1975). *Teaching children self-control*. Columbus, OH: Merrill.

ROBERT A. SEDLAK
University of Wisconsin

SELF-MONITORING
SOCIAL BEHAVIOR OF THE HANDICAPPED
SOCIAL SKILLS TRAINING

SELF-FULFILLING PROPHECY

See PYGMALION EFFECT.

SELF-HELP TRAINING

The skill areas typically included under the domain of self-help are toileting, eating, dressing, and personal hygiene. An obvious reason for training the developmentally disabled in these skills is that there are widespread self-help skill deficits among this population. Another reason is that the acquisition of these skills represents a critical step in the developmental process and can increase self-esteem, promote positive social interaction, and maintain physical health and well-being (Kimm, Falvey, Bishop, & Rosenberg, 1995). Once the skills are acquired, the caregiver's time devoted to the routine maintenance of the developmentally disabled person is reduced. The acquisition of self-help skills can have meaningful social consequences. It can increase the possibility of gaining access to valued places and activities.

Probably the most significant development in the training of self-help skills is the application of behavior modification procedures. This has been referred to as one of the most influential factors in improving the care and training of the developmentally disabled in the last 20 years (Whitman, Sciback, & Reid, 1983).

Research in each of the self-help skill training areas has undergone a similar developmental sequence (Reid, Wilson, & Faw, 1980). Early research demonstrated that caregivers, after receiving in-service training, could train a number of developmentally disabled individuals in self-help skills. Even though this research lacked experimental rigor, it did show the usefulness of behavior modification and stimulated further research. Contemporary research has focused on individual skills and has been more methodologically rigorous. There has also been an effort by Azrin et al. (Azrin & Fox, 1971; Azrin & Armstrong, 1973; Azrin, Schaeffer, & Wesolowski, 1976) to develop an intensive training approach that is more comprehensive than previous approaches. Intensive training is intended to produce rapid learning that is resistant to extinction.

Each self-help skill area has some unique characteristics that have affected the direction of research and training in that particular area (Reid et al., 1980). Training in independent toileting has become more complex and focuses on a more naturally occurring sequence of toilet behaviors. Automatic devices are being used to signal trainers when a trainee is about to have a toileting accident or has eliminated into the toilet. Nighttime toileting skills have also been trained to reduce the frequency of enuresis (bed wetting).

It is believed that training independent eating through behavior modification procedures has been relatively successful because food is an inherent reinforcer. In addition to focusing on the acquisition of independent eating skills, researchers and practitioners have attempted to eliminate or reduce inappropriate mealtime behaviors (e.g., eating too quickly and stealing food).

As in training eating skills, dressing has focused on acquisition of appropriate skills and the reduction of inappropriate behaviors (e.g., public disrobing). The generalization of dressing skills to other contexts has been an issue when developing training programs because training typically occurs when dressing is not naturally required. Maintenance over time has also been an important training issue because dressing is less inherently reinforcing than toileting and eating.

It is unusual that little research has been conducted on personal hygiene skills considering their importance in improving independent functioning and helping the developmentally disabled to gain community acceptance. A current development in training personal hygiene skills is a packaged approach called independence training (Matson, DiLorenzo, & Esveldt-Dawson, 1981). This approach expands on the typical behavioral training strategy by having trainees evaluate their own progress (self-monitor) and give each other feedback.

There are several areas of concern for future research and practice (Whitman et al., 1983). Often there is a discrepancy between the development of an effective training technology and its day-to-day application by caregivers. Consequently, it is important to understand what factors contribute to caregivers' willingness to carry out training. A component analysis of the multifaceted training strategies, like the intensive training package, could assist practitioners in selecting the most effective and efficient training. As increasing numbers of developmentally disabled people live and work in the community, it will be necessary to train more advanced and complex skills in community contexts. It will also be necessary to determine the social validity of certain self-help skills, particularly in the areas of dressing and personal hygiene. By assessing social validity, practitioners will know what to teach in order to bring a skill into a socially acceptable range. Finally, effective and practical self-help training procedures need to be developed for the physically disabled.

REFERENCES

Azrin, N. H., & Armstrong, P. M. (1973). The "mini-meal." A method for teaching eating skills to the profoundly retarded. *Mental Retardation*, *11*, 9–13.

Azrin, N. H., & Fox, R. M. (1971). A rapid method of toilet training the institutionalized retarded. *Journal of Applied Behavior Analysis*, *4*, 89–99.

Azrin, N. H., Schaeffer, R. M., & Wesolowski, M. D. (1976). A rapid method of teaching profoundly retarded persons to dress by a reinforcement guidance method. *Mental Retardation*, *14*, 29–33.

Kimm, C. H., Falvey, M. A., Bishop, K. D., & Rosenberg, R. L. (1995). Motor and personal care skills. In M. A. Falvey (Ed.), *Inclusive and heterogeneous schooling: Assessment, curriculum, and instruction* (pp. 187–227).

Matson, J. L., DiLorenzo, T. M., & Esveldt-Dawson, K. (1981). Independence training as a method of enhancing self-help skills acquisition of the mentally retarded. *Behavior Research Therapy*, *19*, 399–405.

Reid, D. H., Wilson, P. G., & Faw, G. D. (1980). Teaching self-help skills. In J. L. Matson & J. A. Mulick (Eds.), *Handbook of mental retardation* (pp. 429–442). New York: Pergamon.

Whitman, T. L., Sciback, J. W., & Reid, D. H. (1983). *Behavior modification with the severely and profoundly retarded: Research and application*. New York: Academic.

JOHN O'NEILL
Hunter College

DAILY LIVING SKILLS
FUNCTIONAL SKILLS
HABILITATION
REHABILITATION

SELF-INJURIOUS BEHAVIOR

Self-injury is one of the most unusual and probably least understood form of aberrant behavior. It may take a variety of forms, including biting, head banging, face slapping, pinching, or slapping. Such behavior has been reported to affect approximately 4 to 5% of psychiatric populations. Approximately 9 to 17% of normal young children (9 to 36 months of age) also exhibit self-injurious behavior (Carr, 1977).

Carr (1977) has reviewed the hypothetical causes of self-injurious behavior. These include positive reinforcement (seeking of attention), negative reinforcement (attempting to escape), sensory input (gaining stimulation), and psychogenic (psychosis) and organic (genetic and biological) factors. Carr was able to support each of the hypotheses, except for the psychogenic and the organic, by restrospectively applying research to each of the causal explanations. Since then, Evans and Meyer (1985) have proposed one additional hypothesis, an absence of appropriate skills, which research appears to substantiate. Each of these hypotheses warrants examination because of the effect they have on the selection of interventions.

Prior to the mid-1960s, self-injurious behavior was thought to be a product of insane persons with deranged or psychotic minds (Lovaas, 1982). This thinking shaped the model mental health professionals used to intervene with persons who exhibited self-injurious behavior. This dictated the extensive reliance on psychotherapy, drugs, and physical restraint for control.

Through a series of unrelated, yet complementary, studies, researchers were able to demonstrate that self-injurious behavior is regulated by the same laws that affect other human behaviors. The data from these early studies clearly point to the validity of applying the learning theory model to the treatment of self-injurious behavior (Lovaas, 1982).

The etiology of self-injurious behavior has been in debate for some time. There appears to be an organic basis for some self-injurious behavior. There are data to support the contention that self-injurious behaviors are seen in the Lesch-Nyhan and de Langhe syndromes, which are both genetically caused. In Lesch-Nyhan syndrome, a rare form of X-linked cerebral palsy found in only males, there is repetitive biting of the tongue, lips, and fingers. It is thought that this behavior is biochemically related. Considerable research has gone into finding a chemical cure for these characteristics. In de Lange syndrome, which is also genetic in origin, a broad variety of self-injurious behaviors have been reported. A biochemical association has not been presented. Other organic origins of self-injurious behavior have been identified. These include elevated pain thresholds and painful and prolonged infections of the middle ear. The data on organic causes of self-injurious behavior are contradictory, and limited chemical and medical mediations have been found. Although there is limited substantiation of organic causes of self-injurious behavior, awareness that there is a possibility of such causal factors, even in a small percentage of the handicapped population, is important. Those who deal directly with handicapped individuals should recognize that medical screening is necessary at the onset of any treatment program, and in some cases medical intervention may be appropriate (Carr, 1977; Evans & Meyer, 1985).

The positive reinforcement hypothesis can be easily explained as the individual seeking attention through the use of self-injurious behavior. The caregivers, in turn, reinforce such behavior and allow it to continue or progress in intensity. Under such conditions, behavioral interventions that remove reinforcement (e.g., extinction or time out) from the individual would possess a high probability of being successful (Carr, 1977).

The negative reinforcement hypothesis is explained by the use of self-injurious behavior to escape demands being placed on the individual. By exhibiting this form of aberrant behavior, the handicapped person is often allowed by the caregiver or teacher to refrain from participating in a required activity. Appropriate treatment for self-injurious behavior exhibited under these conditions should include interventions that focus on continued demand. In so doing the individual is not allowed to escape the demand (Carr, 1977).

The sensory input hypothesis is based on finding behaviors that provide the handicapped person with input into sensory receptors that under average conditions receive limited amounts of stimulation. An example might be found in a blind student who eye gouges. Self-injurious behavior becomes self-reinforcing and in turn self-maintaining. Interventions for behavior motivated in this manner have taken several different directions, including limiting the input that the self-injurious behavior provides the individual. This is done by modifying the environment (e.g., by using padding or placing adaptive devices on the individual). Another intervention that has been successful is the provision of increased amounts of stimulation from other sources (e.g., a vibrator; Carr, 1977).

The absence of alternative skills hypothesis rests on the concept that the handicapped person has extremely limited skills. Self-injurious behavior is part of a behavior system of an individual who lacks appropriate behavior to meet functional needs. This hypothesis is probably a subset of one or more of the preceding explanations of self-injurious behavior; however, it implies a somewhat different treatment. Part of the intervention strategy for self-injurious behavior caused by lack of skills would include teaching appropriate skills to replace the self-injurious ones (Evans & Meyer, 1985; Gerra, Dorfman, Plaue & Schlachman, 1995; LeBlanc, 1993).

Iwata et al. (1982) have provided the practitioner with a method for functionally analyzing self-injurious behavior. Using this method it is possible to identify the specific motivational factors causing self-injury in many handicapped persons. Employing this approach requires observing the individual in four situations: under negative reinforcement, social attention, play, and alone. Mean levels of self-injurious behavior across each situation are determined. Specific patterns of behavior are manifested in a specific setting that often clearly reflects a specific motivational cause for the behavior.

As previously noted, medical interventions are occasionally appropriate and successful in reducing or eliminating self-injurious behavior. Psychotherapy and other psychological methods have also been used to treat self-injurious behavior. Clearly, the most successful and effective interventions have been behaviorally based. Such interventions should be selected on a least-restrictive model and monitored by systematic data collection procedures. Behaviorally based intervention strategies include the use of punishment. Punishment has been shown to be highly successful, at least on a short-term basis, for the treatment of self-injurious behavior. In cases of chronic self-injurious behavior, where life or irreversible damage is threatened, steps as drastic as electrical shock have been used (Lovaas, 1982). These procedures are generally used to suppress serious self-injurious behavior until other approaches can replace them.

Self-injurious behavior poses many problems to the practitioner in its treatment. Although often misunderstood, recent work has provided both a theoretical explanation and a new direction for finding practical, effective, treatment methods for self-injurious behavior (Symons, 1995).

REFERENCES

Carr, E. (1977). The motivation of self-injurious behavior: A review of some hypothesis. *Psychological Bulletin*, *84*, 800–816.

Evans, I. M., & Meyer, L. H. (1985). *An educative approach to behavior problems*. Baltimore, MD: Brooks.

Gerra, L. L., Dorfman, S., Plaue, E., & Schlachman, S. (1995). Functional communication as a means of decreasing self-injurious behavior. *Journal of Visual Impairment & Blindness*, *89*(4), 343–348.

Iwata, B. A., Dorsey, M. F., Slifer, K. J., Bauman, K. E., & Richman, G. S. (1982). Toward a functional analysis of self-injury. *Analysis and Intervention in Developmental Disabilities*, *2*, 3–20.

LeBlanc, R. Educational management of self-injurious behavior. *International Journal of Child & Adolescent Psychiatry*, *56*(2), 91–98.

Lovaas, O. I. (1982). Comments on self-destructive behaviors. *Analysis and Intervention in Developmental Disabilities*, *2*, 115–124.

Symons, F. J. Self-injurious behavior. *Developmental Disabilities Bulletin*, *23*(1), 90–104.

ALAN HILTON
Seattle University

APPLIED BEHAVIOR ANALYSIS
SELF-STIMULATION
STEREOTYPIC MOVEMENT DISORDERS

SELF-MANAGEMENT

Self-management, also termed self-control, self-regulation, and self-direction, refers to actions intended to influence one's own behavior. Individuals are taught techniques that can be used in a deliberate manner to change their thoughts, feelings, or actions. Students who engage in self-management may, for example, work longer, complete more problems, make fewer errors, engage in fewer aggressive outbursts, or behave appropriately when an adult is not present.

The traditional approach in education has emphasized external management of programming by the teacher. As noted by Lovitt (1973), "Self-management behaviors are not systematically programmed [in the schools] which appears to be an educational paradox, for one of the expressed objectives of the educational system is to create in-dividuals who are self-reliant and independent" (p. 139). Although frequently effective, use of external management procedures has several potential disadvantages (Kazdin, 1980). Implementation of procedures may be inconsistent as teachers may miss instances of behavior, or there may be problems with communication between change agents in different settings. A teacher may become a cue for particular behaviors, resulting in limited generalization to other situations in which that teacher is not present. Other potential disadvantages of external procedures include limited maintenance of behavior change, excessive time demands placed on educators, and the philosophic concern that the student has minimal involvement in the behavior change process.

Self-management procedures offset the concerns associated with external control and offer the possibility of improved maintenance and generalization of behavior change. The focus of self-management in special education is on teaching students to become effective modifiers of their own behaviors through use of such procedures as self-monitoring, self-evaluation, self-consequation, and self-instruction. Although each of these is discussed separately, in practice they frequently have been combined in self-management packages.

Self-monitoring refers to the observation, discrimination, and recording of one's own behavior. A child in the classroom, for example, may record on an index card each math problem completed. Self-monitoring has been demonstrated to have both assessment and therapeutic use with exceptional students who present a wide range of social and academic behaviors. Common problems associated with using self-monitoring as an assessment procedure include the inaccuracy and reactivity (spontaneous behavior change) of self-monitoring, both of which may result in a distorted picture of the initial levels of behavior. When self-monitoring is used as a treatment strategy, however, reactive effects are desired and inaccuracy may not interfere with obtaining this desired reactivity.

Self-evaluation, or self-assessment, is the comparison of one's own behavior against a preset standard to determine whether performance meets this criterion. Standards may be self-imposed or externally determined. In one study, special education students were asked to rate their behavior as "good," "okay," or "not good" when a timer rang at the end of 10-minute intervals. As is typical, self-evaluation was used as one component of a more comprehensive package; this resulted in reductions in disruptive behavior and increases in academic performance in these students (Robertson, Simon, Pachman, & Drabman, 1979).

Self-consequation refers to the self-delivery of positive consequences (self-reinforcement) or aversive consequences (self-punishment) following behavior. Self-reinforcement is preferred over self-punishment when possible and frequently is used in combination with other procedures. As an example, continued low levels of disruptive behavior or increased on-task behavior have been observed in special education students when self-reinforcement procedures were added to multicomponent programs (Shapiro & Klein, 1980).

Self-instruction is a process of talking to oneself to initiate, direct, or maintain one's own behavior. Children with attention deficit disorder, for example, may be taught specific coping self-statements that compete with such classroom problems as distractibility, overactivity, and off-task behavior. Typical training components include cognitive modeling, overt and covert rehearsal, graded practice on training tasks, and performance feedback (Meichenbaum, 1977).

Self-management training frequently combines these and other procedures in multicomponent self-management packages. In one example, disruptive developmentally disabled individuals were taught skills of self-monitoring, self-evaluation, self-consequation, and self-instruction that successfully reduced their chronic and severe conduct difficulties in a vocational training setting (Cole, Gardner, & Karan, 1985; Cole, Pflugrad, Gardner, & Karan, 1985).

Although total self-management is not possible for many special education students, most can be taught to be more self-reliant. Further, evidence suggests that self-management procedures are at least as effective as similar externally managed procedures in facilitating positive behavior change and in ensuring maintenance of this behavior change. Thus, in addition to its therapeutic effects, self-management offers economic, philosophic, legal, and professional benefits for use in special education.

REFERENCES

Cole, C. L., Gardner, W. I., & Karan, O. C. (1985). Self-management training of mentally retarded adults presenting severe conduct difficulties. *Applied Research in Mental Retardation, 6,* 337–347.

Cole, C. L., Pflugrad, D., Gardner, W. I., & Karan, O. C. (1985). *The self-management training program: Teaching developmentally disabled individuals to manage their disruptive behavior.* Champaign, IL: Research.

Kazdin, A. E. (1980). *Behavior modification in applied settings* (rev. ed.). Homewood, IL: Dorsey.

Lovitt, T. C. (1973). Self-management projects with children with behavioral disabilities. *Journal of Learning Disabilities, 6,* 15–28.

Meichenbaum, D. (1977). *Cognitive-behavior modification: An integrative approach.* New York: Plenum.

Robertson, S. J., Simon, S. J., Pachman, J. S., & Drabman, R. S. (1979). Self-control and generalization procedures in a classroom of disruptive retarded children. *Child Behavior Therapy, 1,* 347–362.

Shapiro, E. S., & Klein, R. D. (1980). Self-management of classroom behavior with retarded/disturbed children. *Behavior Modification, 4,* 83–97.

CHRISTINE L. COLE
*University of Wisconsin at
Madison*

**ATTENTION DEFICIT DISORDER
COGNITIVE BEHAVIOR MODIFICATION
SELF-CONTROL CURRICULUM
SELF-MONITORING**

SELF-MONITORING

Self-monitoring is one component of a more general process variously known as self-management, self-regulation, or self-control. The process of self-monitoring first involves a person's recognizing that a need exists to regulate his or her behavior. To recognize this need, the person must be observing his or her behavior and comparing it with some preset standard. This self-observation and assessment then combines with recording the behavior to create the self-monitoring component (Shapiro, 1981). Other components in the self-management process can include self-reinforcement, standard setting, self-evaluation, and self-instruction. These components have been used in various combinations with self-monitoring to modify many different types of behaviors (e.g., overeating, temper outbursts, negative statements, attending to task) in the developmentally disabled (Cole, Gardner, & Karan, 1983; Marion, 1994).

It has been shown that many different types of developmentally disabled individuals are capable of self-monitoring a range of behaviors in various settings. However, at least some of these individuals, particularly the mentally retarded, need training to acquire self-monitoring skills (Litrownik, Freitas, & Franzini, 1978; Shapiro, McGonigle, & Ollendick, 1980).

Self-monitoring among nondevelopmentally disabled people has a reactive or therapeutic effect: those behaviors being monitored tend to change in a desirable direction (McFall, 1977; Nelson & Hayes, 1981). The studies that have assessed the use of self-monitoring in developmentally disabled populations have also found therapeutic effects. For example, mentally retarded individuals have shown increases in the percent of housekeeping chores completed (Bauman & Iwata, 1977), the frequency of appropriate classroom verbalizations (Nelson, Lipinski, & Boykin, 1978) and the productivity of work (Zohn & Bornstein, 1980). Therapeutic decreases have also occurred in face-picking, head-shaking (Zegiob, Klukas, & Junginger, 1978), and tongue-protrusion behaviors (Rudrud, Ziarnik, & Colman, 1984). However, some studies conducted with the developmentally disabled (Horner & Brigham, 1979; Shapiro & Ackerman, 1983) have found the desirable effects of self-monitoring to be short-term or nonexistent, which is consistent with some research conducted on the nondisabled (Kazdin, 1974).

The variable results obtained with self-monitoring are probably due to several intervening factors that can impact on the reactivity or therapeutic value of self-monitoring (Nelson, 1977). The following comments are only suggestive, because the empirical evidence is limited and most of the supporting research has been done with nondevelopmentally disabled people. First, a behavior's valence or a person's desire to change the behavior can affect reactivity. Positively valenced behaviors tend to increase and negatively valenced behaviors to decrease. Generally, reactivity is enhanced by the frequency of self-monitoring; however, there are situations where the act of monitoring can interfere with reactivity, particularly with positively valenced behaviors. Reactivity also tends to be augmented when the recording device is visible and apparent to the person doing the self-monitoring. In addition, if several behaviors are monitored concurrently, the likelihood of change in any of them is suppressed. Finally, training in self-monitoring seems to enhance reactivity, particularly if the behavior is negatively valenced.

REFERENCES

Bauman, K. E., & Iwata, B. A. (1977). Maintenance of independent housekeeping skills using scheduling plus self-recording procedures. *Behavior Therapy, 8,* 554–560.

Cole, C. L., Gardner, W. I., & Karan, O. C. (1983). *Self-management training of mentally retarded adults with chronic conduct difficulties.* Madison WI: University of Wisconsin, Rehabilitation Research and Training Center, Waisman Center on Mental Retardation and Human Development.

Horner, R. H., & Brigham, T. A. (1979). The effects of self-management procedures on the study behavior of two retarded children. *Education & Training of the Mentally Retarded, 14,* 18–24.

Kazdin, A. E. (1974). Self-monitoring and behavior change. In M. J. Mahoney & C. E. Thoresen (Eds.), *Self-control: Power to the person.* Monterey, CA: Brookes/Cole.

Litrownik, A. J., Freitas, J. L., & Franzini, L. R. (1978). Self-regulation in mentally retarded children: Assessment and training of self-monitoring skills. *American Journal of Mental Deficiency, 82,* 499–506.

Marion, M. (1994). Encouraging the development of responsible anger management in young children. *Early Child Development & Care, 97,* 155–163.

McFall, R. M. (1977). Parameters of self-monitoring. In R. B. Stuart (Ed.), *Behavioral self-management.* New York: Brunner/Mazel.

Nelson, R. O. (1977). Methodological issues in assessment via self-monitoring. In J. D. Cone & R. P. Hawkins (Eds.), *Behavioral assessment: New directions in clinical psychology.* New York: Brunner/Mazel.

Nelson, R. O., & Hayes, S. C. (1981). Theoretical explanations for reactivity in self-monitoring. *Behavior Modification, 5,* 3–14.

Nelson, R. O., Lipinski, D. P., & Boykin, R. A. (1978). The effects of self-recorders' training and the obtrusiveness of the self-recording device on the accuracy and reactivity of self-monitoring. *Behavior Therapy, 9,* 200–208.

Rudrud, E. H., Ziarnik, J. P., & Colman, G. (1984). Reduction of tongue protrusion of a 24-year-old woman with Down's syndrome through self-monitoring. *American Journal of Mental Deficiency, 88,* 647–652.

Shapiro, E. S. (1981). Self-control procedures with the mentally retarded. In M. Hersen, R. M. Eisler, & P. M. Miller (Eds.), *Progress in behavior modification.* New York: Academic.

Shapiro, E. S., & Ackerman, A. (1983). Increasing productivity rates in adult mentally retarded clients: The failure of self-monitoring. *Applied Research in Mental Retardation, 4,* 163–181.

Shapiro, E. S., McGonigle, J. J., & Ollendick, T. H. (1980). An analysis of self-assessment and self-reinforcement in a self-managed token economy with mentally retarded children. *Applied Research in Mental Retardation, 1,* 227–240.

Zegiob, L., Klukas, N., & Junginger, J. (1978). Reactivity of self-monitoring procedures with retarded adolescents. *American Journal of Mental Deficiency, 83,* 156–163.

Zohn, C. J., & Bornstein, P. H. (1980). Self-monitoring of work performance with mentally retarded adults: Effects upon work productivity, work quality, and on-task behavior. *Mental Retardation, 18,* 19–25.

JOHN O'NEILL
Hunter College

IMPULSE CONTROL
SELF-CARE SKILLS
SELF CONTROL CURRICULUM
SELF-MANAGEMENT

SELF-SELECTION OF REINFORCEMENT

When the student involved in a contingency management program is permitted to choose a reinforcer or determine the cost of a reinforcer relative to a target behavior, the technique of self-selection of reinforcement is being used. It is one of several self-management methods. It may be used in isolation or in combination with self-recording or self-evaluation (Hughes & Ruhl, 1985). However, a recording and evaluation system (controlled by either the teacher or the student) must be in operation prior to implementing self-selection of reinforcement.

As with other self-management techniques, self-selection of reinforcement appears to be more effective with students previously exposed to a systematic, externally controlled reinforcement system. Consequently, it may function as a helpful transition step for students being weaned from externally controlled systems. Studies (Cosden, Gannon, & Haring, 1995; Dickerson & Creedon, 1981; Rosenbaum & Drabman, 1979) have indicated that student-selected reinforcers are more effective than those selected by the teacher. This may be true because students are more capable of identifying what is of value to them and what they are willing to work for.

According to Hughes and Ruhl (1985), the following

considerations and steps are helpful when teaching students to use self-selection of reinforcement:

1. Begin with a system of externally controlled contingencies.
2. Verify student understanding of ongoing recording and evaluation procedures and directly reteach if student understanding is in doubt.
3. List available reinforcers and have the student identify one for which he or she is willing to work.
4. Determine stringent performance standards for obtaining reinforcement with the student.
5. Establish a time or signal for administration of the reinforcer.

Stringent performance standards for reinforcement (i.e., those requiring a high rating or frequency for all, or almost all, evaluation periods) are important because they result in significantly better performance results than do lax standards (Alberto & Troutman, 1982). Because students tend to set performance standards that are more lenient than those established by teachers (Flexibrod & O'Leary, 1973, 1974; Frederiksen & Frederiksen, 1975), students should be prompted to set vigorous criteria. Verbal prompts, providing examples and rationales and praising acceptable performance standards, will assist the student in determining appropriate criteria. Examples of criteria for reinforcement include obtaining a specified number of tokens or time intervals with low rates of occurrence of an inappropriate behavior.

Regardless of who is recording or evaluating the behavior, a method for communicating the time for reinforcement should be established. For example, the self-selected reinforcement might come at the end of an academic period, after reading five pages of a text, or at the end of the school day when the school bell rings.

REFERENCES

Alberto, P. A., & Troutman, A. C. (1982). *Applied behavior analysis for teachers: Influencing student performance.* Columbus, OH: Merrill.

Cosden, M., Gannon, G., & Haring, T. G. (1995). Teacher-control versus student-control over chance of task and reinforcement for students with severe behavior problems. *Journal of Behavioral Education, 5*(1), 11–27.

Dickerson, A. E., & Creedon, C. F. (1981). Self-selection of standards by children: The relative effectiveness of pupil-selected and teacher-selected standards of performance. *Journal of Applied Behavior Analysis, 141,* 425–433.

Flexibrod, J. J., & O'Leary, K. D. (1973). Effects of reinforcement on children's academic behavior as a function of self-determined and externally imposed contingencies. *Journal of Applied Behavior Analysis, 6,* 241–250.

Flexibrod, J. J., & O'Leary, K. D. (1974). Self-determination of academic standards by children: Toward freedom from external control. *Journal of Educational Psychology, 66,* 845–850.

Frederiksen, L. W., & Frederiksen, C. B. (1975). Teacher-determined and self-determined token reinforcement in a special education classroom. *Behavior Therapy, 6,* 310–314.

Hughes, C. A., & Ruhl, K. L. (1985). Learning activities for improving self-management skills. In B. Algozzine (Ed.), *Educators' resource manual for management of problem behaviors in students.* Rockville, MD: Aspen.

Rosenbaum, M. S., & Drabman, R. S. (1979). Self-control training in the classroom. *Journal of Behavior Analysis, 12,* 467–485.

KATHY L. RUHL
Pennsylvania State University

APPLIED BEHAVIOR ANALYSIS
BEHAVIOR MODIFICATION
CONTINGENCY CONTRACTING
POSITIVE REINFORCEMENT

SELF-STIMULATION

Self-stimulation, also called stereotypic behavior, includes "highly consistent and repetitious motor posturing behaviors which are not outer directed in the sense of being explicitly disruptive and harmful to others" (Forehand & Baumeister, 1976, p. 226). Examples of self-stimulatory behavior include flapping the hands at the wrists, light gazing, excessive laughing, repetitive humming, head weaving, twirling in circles, hand staring, spinning or banging objects, finger posturing, and masturbation. Approximately two-thirds of the individuals living in institutions exhibit self-stimulatory behaviors (Snell, 1983).

Another class of self-stimulation is self-injurious behavior. This occurs when a person repeats a behavior that causes injury to himself or herself. Examples of self-injurious behaviors are eye gouging, head banging, self-biting, scratching or pinching, and face slapping. It has been estimated that between 4 and 10% of the institutionalized population engages in some form of self-injurious behavior (Snell, 1983).

Many variables can influence the frequency of self-stimulatory behavior. Environments interpreted as aversive may reinforce self-stimulatory behavior as a means of escape. A second variable that may influence self-stimulatory behavior is the reinforcing characteristic of the behavior itself. Self-stimulatory behavior is intrinsically reinforcing, and because it feels good, it increases the likelihood that the behavior will reoccur. Additionally, attention from others when the person is self-stimulating may increase the behavior's occurrence.

Ecological variables can also influence self-stimulatory behavior. For example, the number of people in the environment, the specific setting, the materials used for instruction, and the amount of nonstructured time available can influence the frequency of self-stimulation. In the past, institutions' characteristic lack of programming and staff contributed to the acquisition of self-stimulatory behaviors. Additionally, self-stimulatory behaviors are characteristic of persons with autism and severe and multiple handicaps.

Although not always disruptive to others in the environment, self-stimulatory behavior disrupts the individual's learning environment, precludes participation in normalized educational, vocational, and leisure activities, and, in the case of self-injurious behavior, poses a threat to physical well-being. Self-stimulatory behaviors, especially self-injurious behaviors, are high priorities for intervention.

Intervention techniques need to be carefully evaluated to determine their potential for alleviating a particular individual's self-stimulatory behavior. Before any behavioral or environmental intervention is begun, the medical status of the individual must be evaluated. Physical discomfort may be responsible for the self-stimulatory behavior. If no medical factors are revealed, other approaches should be explored.

The framework for selecting intervention techniques to reduce self-stimulatory behavior involves evaluating techniques along a continuum of least intrusive and most natural to most intrusive and least natural. According to Snell (1983), the degree of intrusiveness can be determined by evaluating

> the extent to which the procedure can be applied in the natural environment without interfering with learning, the necessity for involving artificial or prosthetic devices, the amount of staff time required, the potential for abuse of the technique, the potential for increasing appropriate behaviors as alternatives to the aberrant behavior, and the degree to which the people required to carry out the program feel comfortable with the techniques selected. (p. 325)

According to Alberto and Troutman (1982), the techniques of first choice are those that apply a positive approach to behavior reduction; i.e., strategies of differential reinforcement. The technique of second choice would be the use of extinction procedures or the withdrawing of reinforcers that maintain the behavior. Third choice employs a punishing consequence, in that a desirable stimulus is contingently removed in order to decrease behavior. Fourth choice is the application of unconditional or conditional aversive stimuli.

Interventions that have aversive consequences (e.g., physical punishment, noxious odors and liquids, electric shock) are interventions of last resort. These interventions may be justifiable when self-injurious behaviors are life-threatening and all other less intrusive techniques have failed. In cases where aversive techniques are used, continuous program monitoring is critical both for programming and for ethical and legal justification.

REFERENCES

Alberto, P. A., & Troutman, A. C. (1982). *Applied behavior analysis for teachers.* Columbus, OH: Merrill.

Forehand, R., & Baumeister, A. (1976). Deceleration of aberrant behavior among retarded individuals. In M. Hersen, R. M. Eisler, & P. M. Miller (Eds.), *Progress in behavior modification,* 2. New York: Academic.

Foxx, R. M. (1982). *Decreasing behaviors of severely retarded and autistic persons.* Champaign, IL: Research Press.

Snell, M. E. (1983). *Systematic instruction of the moderately and severely handicapped.* Columbus, OH: Merrill.

CAROLE REITER GOTHELF
Hunter College

AUTISTIC BEHAVIOR
SELF-INJURIOUS BEHAVIOR

SEMMEL, MELVYN I. (1931–   )

Melvyn I. Semmel was born and educated in New York City, receiving his BS (1955) and MS (1957) in special education from City College, City University of New York. He later earned his EdD (1963) in special education with a minor in psychology from George Peabody College. He is currently a professor of special education and director of the Special Education Research Laboratory in the Graduate School of Education, University of California, Santa Barbara.

Semmel's early teacher training led to his involvement with teacher preparation and research on special education methods. In 1968, he pioneered the development of the Computer-Assisted Teacher Training System (CATTS), and later directed the Center for Innovation in Teaching the Handicapped (CITH), a research and development center for alternative teacher training methods and instructional materials. During his tenure at CITH, the center was recognized as the outstanding organization of the year by the National Society for Performance and Instruction. Semmel's research work at the University of California has focused on issues such as use of microcomputers for learners with handicaps, development of new models for research teaching, and devising cognitively-oriented interventions for individuals with severe emotional disturbance. Recently, he and his colleagues have examined the effectiveness of special education for students with mild disabilities, finding that, based on student performance, no single factor (e.g., structure or organization of school environment) consistently indicated its relative effectiveness (Larrivee, Semmel, & Gerber, 1997).

Semmel has written over 100 books, research papers, articles, and chapters related to special education and educational psychology. He has been recognized in *Who's Who in American Education* and has been elected a life member and fellow of the American Association on Mental Deficiency for 30 years of continuous service to the field.

REFERENCE

Larivee, B., Semmel, M. I., & Gerber, M. M. (1997). Case studies of six schools varying in effectiveness for students with learning disabilities. *Elementary School Journal, 98*(1), 27–50.

E. VALERIE HEWITT
Texas A & M University
First edition

TAMARA J. MARTIN
*The University of Texas of the
    Permian Basin*
Second edition

SENF, GERALD M. (1942–   )

Gerald M. Senf graduated with honors from Yale University with a BA (1964) in psychology. He went on to earn his MA (1966) in experimental psychology and his doctorate in 1968 in experimental and clinical psychology from the University of California, Los Angeles. During his career, Senf has held the positions of professor of psychology at University of Iowa, associate professor of psychology at University of Illinois, evaluation research director of the Leadership Training Institute in Learning Disabilities, and associate professor of special education at the University of Arizona.

Senf has written extensively on the topics of cognitive functioning and research methodology associated with the study of learning disabilities, with his principal focus on information-processing skills and memory of those with learning disabilities (Senf, 1969, 1972, 1976, 1981, 1986). He has continued to study in the area of cognitive functioning, recently investigating the comparison of electrical brain activity in normal individuals to individuals with various cognitive impairments to assist the clinician in diagnosing and treating the patient (Senf, 1988).

Senf is coauthor of a screening test, has coedited several books, and has devised computer programs to assist the learning disabled.

REFERENCES

Senf, G. M. (1969). Development of immediate memory for bisensory stimuli in normal children and children with learning disorders. *Developmental Psychology Monograph, 1* (Pt. 2).

Senf, G. M. (1972). An information integration theory and its application to normal reading acquisition and reading disability. In N. D. Bryant & C. E. Kass (Eds.), *Leadership Training Institute in Learning Disabilities* (Vol. 2). Tucson: University of Arizona Press.

Senf, G. M. (1976). Some methodological considerations in the study of abnormal conditions. In R. Walsh & W. T. Greenough (Eds.), *Environment as therapy for brain dysfunction*. New York: Plenum.

Senf, G. M. (1981). Issues surrounding the diagnosis of learning disabilities: Child handicap versus failure of the child-school interaction. In T. R. Kratochwill (Ed.), *Advances in school psychology* (Vol. 1, pp. 83–131). Hillsdale, NJ: Erlbaum.

Senf, G. M. (1986). LD research in sociological and scientific perspective. In J. K. Torgesen & B. Wong (Eds.), *Psychological and educational perspectives on learning disabilities*. San Diego, CA: Academic.

Senf, G. M. (1988). Neurometric brainmapping in the diagnosis and rehabilitation of cognitive dysfunction. *Cognitive Rehabilitation, 6*(6), 20–37.

ROBERTA C. STOKES
Texas A & M University
First edition

TAMARA J. MARTIN
*The University of Texas of the
    Permian Basin*
Second edition

JOURNAL OF LEARNING DISABILITIES

SENSORINEURAL HEARING LOSS

A sensorineural hearing loss is a hearing impairment resulting from a pathological condition in the inner ear or along the auditory nerve (VIII cranial nerve) pathway from the inner ear to the brain stem. If the pathological condition or site of lesion is confined to the inner ear or cochlea, it is known as an inner ear or cochlea hearing loss. If the site of lesion is along the auditory nerve (as is the case with an acoustic nerve tumor), it is known as a retrocochlear hearing loss. Several audiological, medical, and radiological special tests have been developed to assist in the diagnosis of whether a sensorineural hearing loss is due to a cochlear or retrocochlear site of lesion.

An individual with a sensorineural hearing loss has reduced hearing sensitivity and lacks the ability to discriminate speech sounds, especially when listening in a noisy environment. Tinnitus is a common symptom of a sensorineural hearing loss. Tinnitus is any sensation of sound in the head heard in one or both ears. It may be described as a hissing, whistling, buzzing, roaring, or a high-pitched tone or noise. Dizziness is also a symptom of sensorineural hearing loss; it can range from light-headedness to a severe whirling sensation known as vertigo, that leads to nausea.

A sensorineural hearing loss can occur in varying degrees ranging from mild-moderate to severe-profound. The degree of sensorineural hearing loss is determined by averaging the decibel amount of hearing loss across the frequencies needed to hear and understand speech or the speech frequencies (500, 1000, and 2000 Hz). Individuals with a mild to severe hearing loss are usually classified as being hard of hearing, while individuals with a profound hearing impairment are classified as deaf. A sensorineural hearing loss can occur in just one ear (unilateral) or in each ear (bilateral). If the hearing loss occurs in each ear, one ear may be more affected than the other.

A sensorineural hearing loss can be caused by many factors, including genetic diseases (dominant, recessive, or sex-linked), diseases acquired during pre-, peri-, and postnatal periods, and childhood diseases. Adults can obtain sensorineural hearing loss from noise exposure, diseases, medication, and the aging process. Many sensorineural hearing losses are due to unknown etiology. A sensorineural hearing loss also may be part of a syndrome that affects the individual in other ways. A congenital sensorineural hearing loss is one that has existed or has an etiology from birth; an adventitious hearing loss is one that occurred after birth and in most cases is due to injury or disease. If the sensorineural hearing loss occurred prior to the development of speech and language skills, it is known as prelingual; if it occurred after the development of speech and language skills, it is known as postlingual. Standardized batteries of cognitive abilities and memory are currently being used to assess concurrent learning disabilities and skill strengths and weaknesses (Plapinger & Sikora, 1995; Sikora & Plapinger, 1994).

In children having sensorineural hearing losses, about half the cases are due to genetic causes and half to acquired causes. Meningitis and prematurity are the leading acquired causes of sensorineural hearing loss in children. For adults, the leading cause of sensorineural hearing loss is the aging process, known as presbyacusis, and excessive exposure to noise. Typically, the sensorineural hearing loss from presbyacusis or noise exposure is a progressive reduction of high frequency (1000 to 8000 Hz) hearing sensitivity that causes problems in understanding speech.

It is important that individuals with a sensorineural hearing loss have audiological and otological diagnosis and management. In almost all cases, there is no medical treatment for sensorineural hearing loss from a cochlear site of lesion. However, a retrocochlear lesion from a tumor, or some other growth along the auditory nerve may benefit

from an operation. Cochlear implants are now available, but their use is controversial (Carver, 1997).

Children and adults with cochlear sensorineural hearing loss can benefit through the use of hearing aids. Most children are fitted with a hearing aid for each ear (binaural amplification) and require auditory and speech reading training, speech and language therapy, and academic tutoring. Adults are usually fitted with either a hearing aid on one ear (monaural) or with binaural amplification. Generally, adults do not need specialized training; however, many adults benefit from speech-reading therapy. References for in depth discussion of sensorineural hearing loss are cited below.

REFERENCES

Carver, R. (1997). *Questions parents should ask about cochlear implants*. British Columbia, Canada: DCSD.

Gerber, S. E., & Mencher, G. T. (1980). *Auditory dysfunction*. San Diego, CA: College-Hill.

Jerger, J. (1984). *Hearing disorders in adults*. San Diego, CA: College-Hill.

Plapinger, D. S., & Sikora, D. M. (1995). The use of standardized test batteries in assessing skill development of children with mild to moderate sensorineural hearing loss. *Language, Speech & Hearing in Schools, 26*(1), 39–44.

Schubert, E. D. (1980). *Hearing: Its function and dysfunction*. New York: Springer-Verlag.

Schuknecht, H. F. (1974). *Pathology of the ear*. Cambridge, MA: Harvard University Press.

Sikora, D. M., & Plapinger, D. S. (1994). Using standardized psychometric tests to identify learning disabilities in students with learning disabilities. *Journal of Learning Disabilities, 27*(6), 352–359.

Wolstenholmer, G. E. W., & Knight, J. (1970). *Sensorineural hearing loss*. London: J. & A. Churchill.

Thomas A. Frank
Pennsylvania State University

DEAF
DEAF EDUCATION

SENSORY EXTINCTION

Sensory extinction is a procedure developed by Rincover (1978) for reducing various pathological behaviors in developmentally disabled children. It has been used to suppress self-stimulation (Maag, Wolchik, Rutherford, & Parks, 1986; Rincover, 1978), compulsive behaviors (Rincover, Newsom, & Carr, 1979), and self-injury (Rincover & Devaney, 1981). In a sensory extinction paradigm, stereotypy is considered operant behavior maintained by its sensory consequences. For example, repetitive finger flapping might be conceptualized as being maintained by the specific proprioceptive feedback it produces, while persistent delayed echolalia may be maintained by auditory feedback.

Sensory extinction involves masking, changing, or removing certain sensory consequences of behavior. If the sensory reinforcement received is removed, the behavior will be extinguished. For example, if a child continuously spins a plate on a table, a piece of carpet could be placed on the table to remove the auditory feedback resulting from this behavior. Similarly, the stereotypic behavior of a child who ritualistically switches a light on and off could be extinguished by either removing the visual feedback (if seeing the light were reinforcing) or removing the auditory feedback (if hearing the light switch click were reinforcing).

When sensory extinction is used to suppress stereotypy, the preferred sensory consequences of the behavior can be used to teach appropriate behaviors. For example, the child who spins plates could be taught to spin a top instead, since this would provide the same sensory consequences as the maladaptive behavior. Rincover, Cook, Peoples, and Packard (1979) found that children preferred to play with toys that provided sensory reinforcement similar to the sensory reinforcement previously found in the stereotypy.

While sensory extinction is a procedure in which multiple components are altered at the same time (Maag et al., 1986), it remains unclear as to the extent to which stimulus modality is an important factor (Murphy, 1982). Maag et al. found that isolating the sensory consequences for some forms of behavior can be impractical and/or time-consuming. In addition, Maag et al., point out that a cumbersome apparatus is sometimes necessary to mask some types of sensory feedback. This apparatus may restrict the child's ability to participate in activities and also be socially stigmatizing. Therefore, although sensory extinction may represent a viable set of procedures for reducing stereotypy, it should be assessed thoroughly to determine the appropriateness of this intervention for particular children.

REFERENCES

Maag, J. W., Wolchik, S. A., Rutherford, R. B., & Parks, B. T. (1986). Response covariation of self-stimulatory behaviors during sensory extinction procedures. *Journal of Autism & Developmental Disorders, 16,* 119–132.

Murphy, G. (1982). Sensory reinforcement in the mentally handicapped and autistic child: A review. *Journal of Autism & Developmental Disorders, 12,* 265–278.

Rincover, A. (1978). Sensory extinction: A procedure for eliminating self-stimulatory behavior in developmentally disabled children. *Journal of Abnormal Child Psychology, 6,* 299–310.

Rincover, A., Cook, R., Peoples, A., & Packard, D. (1979). Sensory extinction and sensory reinforcement principles for program-

ming multiple adaptive behavior change. *Journal of Applied Behavior Analysis, 12,* 221–233.

Rincover, A., & Devaney, J. (1981). The application of sensory extinction principles to self-injury in developmentally disabled children. *Analysis & Intervention in Developmental Disabilities, 4,* 67–69.

Rincover, A., Newsom, C. D., & Carr, E. G. (1979). Using sensory extinction procedures in the treatment of compulsive-like behavior of developmentally disabled children. *Journal of Consulting and Clinical Psychology, 47,* 695–701.

ROBERT B. RUTHERFORD, JR.
Arizona State University

BEHAVIOR MODIFICATION
SELF-STIMULATION

SENSORY INTEGRATIVE THERAPY

Sensory integrative therapy is a technique for the remediation of sensory integrative dysfunction developed by A. Jean Ayres (Ayres, 1972). Sensory integrative dysfunction is believed by Ayres and others (Quiros, 1976; Silberzahn, 1982) to be at the root of many learning disorders. Ayres uses the term sensory integrative dysfunction to describe children whose learning problems are due to the failure of the lower levels of the brain (particularly the midbrain, brain stem, and vestibular system) to use and organize information effectively. The principal objective of sensory integrative therapy is to promote the development and the organization of subcortical brain mechanisms as a foundation for perception and learning. Treatment procedures consist of the use of gross motor activities and physical exercise to achieve this goal. Sensory integrative therapy has gained its greatest popularity among occupational therapists.

The five key features of sensory integrative dysfunction follow (Silberzahn, 1982):

1. *Developmental Apraxia.* This is a problem in motor planning and is part of a complex that includes deficits in tactile functions. According to Ayres (1972), the fundamental problem lies in the difficulty in recognizing the time and space aspects of sensation and the relationships among body parts that are necessary for cortical planning of events.

2. *Tactile Defensiveness.* This represents a defensive or hostile reaction to tactile stimuli and it part of a complex believed, in sensory integrative therapy, to include hyperactivity, distractibility, and discrimination problems in most major sensory modalities.

3. *Deficits in Interhemispheric Integration.* These deficits are manifest in problems integrating the two

sides of the body. Ayres (1972) believes these deficits are common in children with reading problems and that they can be shown clinically as the child tends to use each side of the body independently and avoids crossing the midline.

4. *Visual and Space Perception Deficits*. These problems are typically associated with a more extensive problem that involves inadequate integration of vestibular, proprioceptive, tactile, and visual stimuli at the level of the brain stem. Developmental apraxia may also result.

5. *Auditory-Language Deficits*. These deficits are a result of problems in areas 3 and 4 and disrupt written and spoken language.

Sensory integrative therapy attempts to remediate these problems through the development of perception and learning via the enhancement of organizations and sensations at the brain stem level. Motor activities are the principal therapeutic media and center around activities that require the child to adapt and organize a variety of sensory motor experiences while taking an active role in each process. Coordinated use of the two sides of the body is promoted.

Carefully controlled studies of the outcome of sensory integrative therapy are lacking, particularly in regard to improvements in academic skills. The therapy is a deficit-centered approach to remediation, though not strictly a process approach. However, it seems unlikely that learning disabilities can be corrected through the use of gross motor activities and physical exercise.

REFERENCES

Ayres, A. J. (1972). *Sensory integration and learning disorders*. Los Angeles: Western Psychological Services.

Quiros, J. B. de. (1976). Diagnosis of vestibular disorders in the learning disabled. *Journal of Learning Disabilities*, 9, 39–47.

Silberzahn, M. (1982). Sensory integrative therapy. In C. R. Reynolds & T. B. Gutkin (Eds.), *The handbook of school psychology*. New York: Wiley.

CECIL R. REYNOLDS
Texas A & M University

AYRES, A. J.
DEFICIT MODELS OF REMEDIATIONS

SENSORY MOTOR INTEGRATION

See SENSORY INTEGRATIVE THERAPY.

SEPARATION ANXIETY AND CHILDREN WITH DISABILITIES

Separation anxiety is defined by Bowlby as anxiety about losing, or becoming separated from, someone loved. It is the usual response to a threat or some other risk of loss. This fear of abandonment can not only create intense anxiety, it can arouse anger of an intense degree, especially in older children and adolescents, and cause dysfunction (Bowlby, 1982). Adverse separation experiences have at least two kinds of effects: They make the individual more vulnerable to later adverse experiences and they make it more likely that the individual will have such experiences (Bowlby, 1982; Klein, 1995).

In infants and young children, separation anxiety is a normal part of the developmental process; it is related to the formation of positive attachment behavior. Sears (1972) says that attachment is completed during the second half of the first year of life, while separation anxiety appears after the child reaches 6 months of age. Ainsworth (1972) also states that an attachment if formed when definitive separation causes anxiety, although Yarrow (1972) believes that environmental conditions that influence the strength of positive attachment behaviors determine the strength and character of response to separation anxiety.

By observing the pattern of behavior shown in unfamiliar situations and in the episodes of reunion after separation, a child's response can be used in assessment procedures to measure the degree of positive attachment. Some danger signals of attachment quality include greater than average separation anxiety, shadowing of the caregiver, ignoring the caregiver, and continuing impulse-driven darting away, provoking the caregiver to pursuit (Mahler, 1979). Ainsworth (1979) identified eight patterns, but classed responses into three main groups. Group A was anxious/avoidant, where on separation, the child rarely cried and during reunion the child mingled proximity-seeking with avoidant behaviors, ignoring the caregiver. Group B was securely attached, but distressed by separation and seeking contact with the caregiver on reunion. Group C was anxious/resistant, and intensely distressed by separation and ambivalent about reunion episodes. In normal infants, it appears that differences in attachment behavior are attributable to caregiver behavior.

When the quality of attachment is poor, all subsequent development of personal relationships may be in jeopardy. In later development, Ainsworth (1979) found the securely attached infants more cooperative and affectively positive toward caregivers and other familiar adults, and more competent and sympathetic in interaction with peers. They were more curious, self-directed, and ego-resilient. Group A infants continued to be more aggressive, non-compliant, and avoidant, while group C emerged as more easily frustrated, less persistent, and generally less competent.

The presence of a handicap can put significant stress on the attachment process, increasing the vulnerability of both the infant and the caregivers (Ulrey, 1981). By viewing the attachment-separation process as a system, it follows that any change will produce disequilibrium, with different implications for various handicaps. A child with motor deficits may be at increased risk because the infant may not be able to adjust to the physical comforting offered by the parents, possibly minimizing parental contact. Abnormal muscle tone may influence the child's activity level and facial movements, affecting the child's emotional expressiveness, while other motor deficits may make it impossible for the child to physically move away from the caregivers, delaying the separation process. A visually handicapped child will develop attachments more slowly than a sighted child, but, once formed, attachments persist longer, delaying separation. Children with impaired hearing may also be at increased risk for disruption of the attachment process (Ulrey, 1981). A caregiver's anxiety about a child who is handicapped may make it difficult for appropriate interaction with the child to provide the stimulation necessary to form a quality attachment.

Separation anxiety has been linked to obsessive-compulsive disorder, panic attacks and life-long issues with separation. (Brynska & Wolanczyk, 1998; Klein, 1995).

REFERENCES

Ainsworth, M. D. S. (1972). Attachment and dependency: A comparison. In J. L. Gerwitz (Ed.), *Attachment and dependency* (pp. 97–139). New York: Winston/Wiley.

Ainsworth, M. D. S. (1979). Infant-mother attachment. *American Psychologist, 34,* 932–937.

Bowlby, J. (1969). *Attachment and loss: Vol. 1. Attachment.* New York: Basic Books.

Bowlby, J. (1982). Attachment and loss: retrospect and prospect. *American Journal of Orthropsychiatrics, 52,* 664–678.

Brynska, A., & Wolanczyk, T. (1998). Obsessive-compulsive disorder and separation anxiety. *Journal of the American Academy of Child & Adolescent Psychiatry, 37*(4), 350–351.

Klein, R. G. (1995). Is panic disorder with childhood separation anxiety disorder? *Child Neuropharmacology, 18*(2), 7–14.

Mahler, M. S. (1979). *The selected papers of Margaret S. Mahler, M. D.: Vol. 2. Separation-individuation.* New York: Aronson.

Sears, R. R. (1972). Attachment, dependency and frustration. In J. L. Gerwitz (Ed.), *Attachment and dependency* (pp. 1–28). New York: Winston/Wiley.

Ulrey, G. (1981). Emotional development of the young handicapped child. In N. J. Anastasiow (Ed.), *Socioemotional development: New directions for exceptional children* (No. 5, pp. 33–52). San Francisco: Jossey-Bass.

Yarrow, L. J. (1972). Attachment and dependency: A developmental perspective. In J. L. Gerwitz (Ed.), *Attachment and dependency* (pp. 81-96). New York: Winston/Wiley.

CATHERINE O. BRUCE
Hunter College

BORDERLINE PERSONALITY DISORDER
CHILD-CARETAKER
SCHOOL PHOBIA

SEPTO-OPTIC DYSPLASIA

Septo-optic dysplasia, also known as De Morsier syndrome, is a rare disorder characterized by visual impairments and pituitary deficiencies. The etiology of Septo-optic dysplasia is not known; however, this birth defect is found in a higher percentage of infants who are the first-born children of young mothers. Both genders are affected equally by this rare disorder.

Visual impairments include dimness in sight, especially in one eye (often referred to as lazy eye), and dizziness. These symptoms result from small, not-fully-developed optic disks associated with the visual system. In this disorder, the pupil (the opening in the eyeball through which light enters) does not respond appropriately. Instead of a consistent response, the pupil's response to light of the same intensity varies from one occasion to another. Occasional field dependence has also been noted. Besides visual impairments, an underactive pituitary gland is present either at birth or later in development. If left untreated, a child's growth is stunted. Jaundice may also be present at birth.

Standard treatment for Septo-optic dysplasia is symptomatic and supportive. Hormone replacement therapy is used to treat the pituitary hormone deficiencies. Children with Septo-optic dysplasia are usually of normal intelligence; however, mental retardation or learning disabilities may occur (Thoene, 1992). Occasional sexual precocity has been reported (Jones, 1988).

If a child experiences learning problems or developmental delays, a comprehensive neuropsychological evaluation is recommended to determine cognitive strengths and weaknesses. Based on those results, recommendations can be made, and an individualized educational plan can be developed and implemented in the schools.

REFERENCES

Jones, K. L. (Ed.). (1988). *Smith's recognizable patterns of human malformation* (4th ed.). Philadelphia, PA: W.B. Saunders.

Thoene, J. G. (Ed.). (1992). *Physician's guide to rare diseases.* Montvale, NJ: Dowden.

JOAN MAYFIELD
*Baylor Pediatric Specialty
Services*

PATRICIA A. LOWE
Texas A & M University

SEQUENCED INVENTORY OF COMMUNICATION DEVELOPMENT, REVISED

The Sequenced Inventory of Communication Development, Revised Edition (SICD-R; Hendrick, Prather, & Tobin, 1984) is a diagnostic assessment tool to evaluate the communication abilities of normal and retarded children, ages 4 months to 4 years. The SICD-R utilizes both parental report and observation of communication behaviors. The inventory includes 100 items which are broken into Receptive and Expressive Scales. Responses may also be recorded on the Behavioral Profile that examines awareness, discrimination, understanding, imitation, initiation, response, motor, vocal, and verbal areas. There is also a Process Profile that examines semantics, syntax, pragmatics, perceptual, and phonological areas.

The normative data are from a sample of 252 children, all Caucasian from monolingual homes, who were believed to have normal hearing, language, physical, and mental development. Additional data from a field study in Detroit are also reported; however, Pearson (1989) notes that these additional data do not provide answers to questions about reliability or validity of the SICD-R. Only 10 subjects are reported as a sample providing test-retest data and the reliability value reported was .93. Interrater reliability (based on 21 children) was reported to be 96% agreement between two raters. The reliability data must be viewed with caution because of the small number of subjects in the reliability studies (Mardell-Czudnowski, 1989; Pearson, 1989). Validity data are not complete enough to warrant the SICD-R's use for determining delays (Pearson, 1989).

In 1989, a version of the SICD-R was developed for adults and adolescents who do not possess any speech skills or who have only minimal skills. This version is titled the Adapted Sequenced Inventory of Communication Development (A-SICD; McClennen, 1989). The A-SICD allows examinees to respond through gestures, signing, picture board communication, or voice communication. Like the SICD-R, the A-SICD has both a Receptive and Expressive Scale.

Validation studies for the A-SICD were conducted with 40 subjects between the ages of 16 and 55. Interrater reliability was reported (N=10) to be 88% to 100% on the Receptive Scale and 90% to 100% on the Expressive Scale. Internal consistency was .78 for the Receptive Scale and .91 for the Expressive Scale. Because of the small sample size, the generalizability of these results is questionable. The A-SICD is not norm-referenced; thus, the examiner must use clinical judgement to interpret the inventory. Carey (1995) notes that much of the same information collected on the A-SICD could be obtained through structured observations of the examinee in educational, vocational, or home settings.

REFERENCES

Carey, K. T. (1995). Review of the Adapted Sequenced Inventory of Communication Development. In J. J. Kramer & J. C. Conoley (Eds.), *The twelfth mental measurements yearbook* (pp. 32–33). Lincoln, NE: Buros Institute of Mental Measurements.

Hendrick, D. L., Prather, E. M., & Tobin, A. R. (1984). *Sequenced Inventory of Communication Development*. Seattle, WA: University of Washington Press.

Mardell-Czudnowski, C. (1989). Review of the Sequenced Inventory of Communication Development. In J. J. Kramer & J. C. Conoley (Eds.), *The eleventh mental measurements yearbook* (pp. 740–742). Lincoln, NE: Buros Institute of Mental Measurements.

McClennen, S. E. (1989). *Adapted Sequenced Inventory of Communication Development*. Seattle, WA: University of Washington Press.

Pearson, M. E. (1989). Review of the Sequenced Inventory of Communication Development. In J. J. Kramer & J. C. Conoley (Eds.), *The eleventh mental measurements yearbook* (pp. 742–744). Lincoln, NE: Buros Institute of Mental Measurements.

ELIZABETH O. LICHTENBERGER
The Salk Institute

VERBAL DEFICIENCY
VERBAL SCALE IQ

SEQUENTIAL AND SIMULTANEOUS COGNITIVE PROCESSING

Sequential and simultaneous are two of many labels used to denote two primary forms of information coding processes in the brain. These coding processes are the primary functions of Luria's (1973) Block II of the brain (the parietal, occipital, and temporal lobes, also known as the association areas of the brain). They have been proposed as fundamental integration processes in Das, Kirby, and Jarman's (1979) model of Luria's fundamental approach to human information processing. Other labels commonly used to distinguish these forms of processing include successive versus simultaneous (Das et al., 1979), propositional versus appositional (Bogen, 1969), serial versus multiple or parallel (Neisser, 1967), and analytic versus gestalt/holistic (Levy, 1972).

No matter what label is applied, the descriptions of the processes corresponding to each label appear to be defining similar processes though some minor distinctions may exist. Thus sequential processing is defined as the processing of information in a temporal or serial order. Using this coding process, analysis of information proceeds in successive steps in which each step provides cues for the processing of later steps. This type of processing is generally employed, e.g., when an individual repeats a series of numbers that have been orally presented. Each stage of processing is dependent on the completion of the immediately preceding stage.

Simultaneous coding processes are used when all the pieces of information or all the stimuli are surveyable at one time and are thus available for processing at one time; i.e., at the analysis of parts of information can take place without dependence on the parts' relationship to the whole. When an individual discerns the whole object with only parts of the picture available, this is usually accomplished using simultaneous processing. The Figure presents an example of a strongly simultaneous processing task. See if you can determine what is pictured. Even with many of the parts missing and the pictured figure only in silhouette form, most individuals beyond the age of 10 to 12 years will recognize the figure to be a man on horseback. Some will have great difficulty or take a long time to rec-

ognize the figure; this is true especially if one takes a step-by-step approach to determining the identity of the picture, looking at individual pieces and trying to add them as a simple sum of the separate parts. While not impossible, such an approach is more difficult.

In the literature, several assumptions regarding these two forms of processing are presented. First, sequential and simultaneous processing are not hierarchical. That is, one form of processing does not appear to be more complex than the other. Both appear to require the transformation of stimulus material before synthesis of the information can occur (Das et al., 1979).

Second, determining whether to process information sequentially or simultaneously is not solely dependent on the presentation mode of the stimuli to be processed (e.g., visual or auditory). Rather, the form of processing used appears to be more dependent on the cognitive demands of

An example of a task that might be used to assess an individual's simultaneous cognitive processing skills; what do you think is pictured here? (The answer is in the text)

the task and the unique sociocultural history and genetic predisposition of the individual performing the task (Das et al., 1979; Kaufman & Kaufman, 1983). This may become habitual and individuals do develop preferred styles of information processing.

Third, sequential and simultaneous processing have been indirectly linked to various areas of the brain, but psychologists do not agree on the exact location of each of these functions. Some contend that processing abilities are best associated with the two hemispheres of the brain (Gazzaniga, 1975; Reynolds, 1981), with sequential processing being a left hemisphere function and simultaneous processing being a right hemisphere function. Luria (1973), on the other hand, located successive or sequential processing as a function of the frontal regions of the brain, with simultaneous processing carried out in the occipital-parietal or rear sections of the brain.

These forms of processing have traditionally been measured in nonbrain-damaged individuals with a battery of standardized tests, the components of which are certainly less than pure measures of process. Evidence of simultaneous processing abilities has been inferred from individuals' performance on such instruments as Raven's Progressive Matrices (Raven, 1956), Memory-for-Designs (Graham & Kendall, 1960), and Figure Copying (Ilg & Ames, 1964). Each of these tasks places a premium on visuo-spatial skills and the synthesis of information for successful performance.

Sequential processing abilities have typically been inferred from observing an individual's performance on such tasks as Digit Span (a purely auditory task), Visual Short-Term Memory, and Serial or Free Recall. It is apparent that it is not the mode of presentation but rather the cognitive demands of the task that are the major determining factors in what cognitive processing style is used.

Recently, the Kaufman Assessment Battery for Children (K-ABC; Kaufman & Kaufman, 1983) was introduced into psychological and educational circles. This instrument was designed as an individually administered intelligence test for children ages 2½ and 12½; it is composed of several subtests that according to factor analytic data, measure sequential and simultaneous processing abilities. Focused on process rather than content as the major distinction of how children solve unfamiliar problems, this instrument has resulted in more controversy and discussion than any intelligence test in recent history (Reynolds, 1985).

Controversy has arisen over the Kaufmans' assertion that knowledge about a child's information-processing abilities, as measured on the K-ABC, in conjunction with other sources of data, can more easily translate into educational programming for children with learning or behavioral problems than traditionally had been possible from data gathered on other, content-based intelligence tests. Primarily employing an aptitude ¥ treatment interaction (ATI) paradigm (Cronbach, 1975) and the habilitation phi-

losophy of neuropsychology (Reynolds, 1981), the Kaufmans propose using knowledge regarding a child's individual strengths in information processing (e.g., simultaneous processing) as the foundation for any remedial plans thus developed. The notion of a strength model of remediation is in direct contrast to the deficit-centered training models that have dominated special education remedial plans for years, but that have proven largely ineffective in improving academic abilities (Ysseldyke & Mirkin, 1982).

Although preliminary data seem encouraging regarding the efficacy of using knowledge of a child's individual processing style to remediate learning or behavioral difficulties (Gunnison, Kaufman, & Kaufman, 1983), the data are not sufficient to support this assumption unequivocably. Much research remains to be done in this area.

REFERENCES

Bogen, J. E. (1969). The other side of the brain: Parts I, II, & III. *Bulletin of the Los Angeles Neurological Society, 34,* 73–203.

Cronbach, L. J. (1975). Beyond the two disciplines of scientific psychology. *American Psychologist, 30,* 116–125.

Das, J. P., Kirby, J. R., & Jarman, R. F. (1979). *Simultaneous and successive cognitive processes.* New York: Academic.

Gazzaniga, M. S. (1975). Recent research on hemispheric lateralization of the human brain: Review of the split brain. *UCLA Educator, 17,* 9–12.

Graham, F. K., & Kendall, B. S. (1960). Memory-for-Designs Test: Revised general manual. *Perceptual & Motor Skills, 43,* 1051–1058.

Gunnison, J., Kaufman, N. L., & Kaufman, A. S. (1983). Reading remediation based on sequential and simultaneous processing. *Academic Therapy, 17,* 297–307.

Ilg, F. L., & Ames, L. B. (1964). *School readiness: Behavior tests used at the Gesell Institute.* New York: Harper & Row.

Kaufman, A. S., & Kaufman, N. (1983). *The Kaufman Assessment Battery for Children.* Circle Pines, MN: American Guidance Service.

Levy, J. (1972). Lateral specification of the human brain: Behavioral manifestations and possible evolutionary basis. In J. A. Kiger (Ed.), *Biology of behavior.* Cornallis: Oregon State University Press.

Luria, A. R. (1973). *The working brain: An introduction to neuropsychology.* London: Penguin.

Neisser, W. (1967). *Cognitive psychology.* New York: Appleton-Century-Crofts.

Raven, J. C. (1956). *Coloured progressive matrices: Sets A, Ab, B.* London: H. K. Lewis.

Reynolds, C. R. (1981). Neuropsychological assessment and the habilation of learning: Considerations in the search for the aptitude ¥ treatment interaction. *School Psychology Review, 10,* 343–349.

Reynolds, C. R. (Ed.). (1985). K-ABC and controversy [Special issue]. *Journal of Special Education, 18*(3).

Ysseldyke, J., & Mirkin, P. (1982). The use of assessment information to plan instructional interventions: A review of the research. In C. R. Reynolds & T. B. Gutkin (Eds.), *The handbook of school psychology*. New York: Wiley.

JULIA A. HICKMAN
University of Texas

INFORMATION PROCESSING
KAUFMAN ASSESSMENT BATTERY FOR CHILDREN
PERCEPTUAL TRAINING
REMEDIATION, DEFICIT-CENTERED MODELS OF

SEQUENTIAL ASSESSMENT OF MATHEMATICS INVENTORIES: STANDARDIZED INVENTORY

The Sequential Assessment of Mathematics Inventories: Standardized Inventory (SAMI; Reisman & Hutchinson, 1985) is designed to measure the achievement of specific mathematics content objectives and to compare students' performance to national norms. It may be used to assess children in kindergarten through the eighth grade.

The SAMI is presented to students in an easel format, with the questions read aloud by the examiner. Students respond by pointing, writing, or verbally responding. Nine scores are obtained on the SAMI: Mathematical Language (grades K–3 only), Ordinality (grades K–3 only), Number/Notation, Computation, Measurement, Geometric Concepts, Mathematical Applications (grades 4–8 only), Word Problems, and Total. Subtest standard scores have a mean of 10 and a standard deviation of 3.

The SAMI was normed on a sample of about 1,400 students in kindergarten through eighth grade. Test-retest reliability values over a 6-week interval ranged from .43 to .89 with a median of .66. However, five of the subtests have reliability values below .50. Internal consistency values range from .72 to .97 with a median of .93. Validity evidence is limited to one study comparing the SAMI and two standardized achievement tests, as well as the reported intercorrelation of subtests. Fleenor (1993) states that the SAMI has promise as a measure of mathematics performance, but needs more data supporting its reliability and validity.

REFERENCES

Fleenor, J. W. (1992). Review of the Sequential Assessment of Mathematics Inventories: Standardized Inventory. In J. J. Kramer & J. C. Conoley (Eds.), *The eleventh mental measurements yearbook* (pp. 817–819). Lincoln, NE: Buros Institute of Mental Measurements.

Reisman, F. K., & Hutchinson, T. A. (1985). *Sequential Assessment of Mathematics Inventories: Standardized Inventory*. San Antonio, TX: The Psychological Corporation.

ELIZABETH O. LICHTENBERGER
The Salk Institute

ASSESSMENT
MATHEMATICS, LEARNING DISABILITIES IN

SERIOUSLY EMOTIONALLY DISTURBED

The term seriously emotionally disturbed (SED) has been defined by federal legislation (IDEA) as a condition with one or more of the following characteristics occurring to a marked degree and over a long period of time: (1) inability to learn not explainable by health, intellectual, or sensory factors; (2) inability to develop or maintain appropriate interpersonal relationships with students and teachers; (3) inappropriate behaviors or feelings in normal circumstances; (4) a pervasive mood of depression; (5) a tendency to develop physical symptoms or fears in response to personal or school difficulties [Code of Federal Regulations, Title 34, Section 300. 7(b) (9)]. According to the legislative definition, the term specifically includes childhood schizophrenia but specifically excludes children who are socially maladjusted except when the maladjustment is accompanied by serious emotional disturbance. Although autism was originally included as a form of serious emotional disturbance, in the *Diagnostic and Statistical Manual of Mental Disorders* (DSM-III), autism was removed from classification as a psychosis and defined as a pervasive developmental disorder. This reclassification of autism was based on recent research that has established clear differences between autism and the childhood psychoses on a variety of dimensions, including symptomatology, age of onset, family history of psychopathology, language ability, intellectual functioning, and socioeconomic status.

The U.S. Department of Education (1997) reports that the incidence of emotional disturbance in children and youth served in the public schools for the 1995–96 school year was 438,217. The causes of emotional disturbance are varied and include factors such as genetics, trauma, diet, stress, social skills deficits, and family dysfunction. Children and youth exhibit psychiatric disorders in different ways than adults. Therefore, emotional disturbance may be seen in behaviors such as immaturity, hyperactivity, self-monitoring deficits, social skill deficits, learning difficulties and aggression or self-injurious behavior. Children with the most serious emotional disturbances may exhibit distorted thinking, extreme anxiety, abnormal mood swings, and other symptoms indicative of psychoses (NICHCY, 1998).

Children and youth with emotional disturbance are identified and referred to special education much in the same way as learning disabled or other exceptional students. Usually, the behaviors that are interfering with the student's ability to succeed in school have been longstanding and have not been responsive to preservice referral interventions by the teacher or school team. The student is assessed usually by the school psychologist who, through a process of inclusion and exclusion, assesses eligibility for services in special education. The assessment must have examined how the student is functioning across settings; have ruled out medical, neurological, and neuropsychological conditions; and have assessed the student across modalities and in an objective and comprehensive manner.

The entrance to special education for SED students has changed over the years to reflect the least restrictive environment (LRE) principle of IDEA and similar legislation. Placement of these students in psychiatric residential facilities has declined in recent years due to LRE and to financial constraints; however, the need for comprehensive treatment is still present. The inclusion movement has advocates that suggest that SED students are best served in the regular classroom with special education support. However, again, the least restrictive environment for SED students should be determined on a case-by-case method. What is least restrictive for one SED student may be a dangerous or nonadvantageous placement for another.

The difficulty of placement, treatment, and education for SED students has probably steered the field to look towards the identification of at-risk students and culturally competent intervention. Lago-Delello (1996) did a study of the differences between kindergarten and first-grade children identified as "at-risk" or "not-at-risk" for the development of severe emotional disturbance on selected factors of classroom dynamics. The comparison focused on teacher factors, classroom interactions, student factors, and instructional factors. Results indicated that at-risk students experienced a markedly different reality in the classroom than their not-at-risk peers. Four major findings emerged: (1) At-risk students were generally rejected by their teachers and not-at-risk peers were not; (2) At-risk students received significantly more negative or neutral teacher feedback statements than not-at-risk peers; (3) At-risk students spent significantly less time academically engaged than not-at-risk peers; and (4) teachers made few accommodations for these students and were generally resistant to making adjustments in tasks, materials, or teaching methods to meet the individual needs of at-risk students. Others (e.g., McKinney, Montague, & Hocutt, 1998) are developing screening instruments and procedures to identify students at risk for emotional disturbance.

Ongoing teacher training for regular and special educators has been identified on many levels; and much of it has targeted multicultural competencies (Singh, 1997). The more that SED students are included in regular education, the more competencies are essential for all personnel involved in the regular education process.

Outcomes for SED students are not as good as they are for students with some other disabilities. Greenbaum (1996) has found that serious problems in these students tend to be present even seven years after the initial identification. These problems many times become lifelong adjustment issues and are highly correlated with adult high-risk behaviors in crime and substance abuse. The magnitude of the problem with the SED population is supported by data on these students concerning academic outcomes, graduation rates, school placement, school absenteeism, dropout rates, encounters with the juvenile justice system, and identification rates of students of varying socioeconomic backgrounds. Seven interdependent strategic targets have been identified by the Chesapeake Institution (1994) to address the future of policy, funding, and treatment of SED by federal, state, and local agencies: (1) expand positive learning opportunities and results; (2) strengthen school and community capacity; (3) value and address diversity; (4) collaborate with families; (5) promote appropriate assessment; (6) provide ongoing skill development and support; and (7) create comprehensive collaborative systems. Three universal themes are also stressed: first, collaborative efforts must extend to initiatives that prevent emotional and behavioral problems from developing or escalating; second, services must be provided in a culturally sensitive and respectful manner; and third, services must empower all stakeholders and maintain a climate of possibility and accountability.

The federal government is currently revising the definition of SED (NICHCY, 1998). Hopefully, more emphasis will be placed on prevention. The identification of at-risk children is the key to preventing serious adjustment problems for many children and youth. The field is moving towards being able to identify, in an objective and a culturally competent manner, young students who are having problems meeting the demands of everyday living. Once identified, this population can receive sensitive programming that includes family participation. Together, the school and family can help those young children who have not yet developed serious emotional difficulties to adjust and to meet the demands of their age group. The alternative is the present situation, where hundreds of thousands of children and youth are already suffering and in serious jeopardy of losing their ability to receive the benefits of an appropriate education.

REFERENCES

American Psychiatric Association. (1980). *Diagnostic and statistical manual of mental disorders* (3rd ed.). Washington, DC: Author.

Chesapeake Institute. (1994). National agenda for achieving better results for children and youth with serious emotional disturbance. Washington, DC: Author.

Greenbaum, P. E. (1996). *National adolescent and child treatment study: Outcomes for children with serious emotional and behavioral disturbance.* (ERIC Clearinghouse No. EJ53063)

Lago-Delello, E. (1996). *Classroom dynamics and young children identified as at-risk for the development of serious emotional disturbance.* Paper presented at the Annual International

Convention of the Council for Exceptional Children, Orlando, Florida, April 1-5.

McKinney, J. D., Montague, M., & Hocutt, A. M. (1998). *A two year follow-up study of children at risk for developing SED: Implications for designing prevention programs*. Paper presented at the Annual Convention of the Council for Exceptional Children, Minneapolis, MN, April 16.

National Information Center for Children and Youth with Disabilities (NICHCY). (1998). *General information about emotional disturbance*. Fact Sheet Number 5 (FS5), Washington, DC: Author.

Singh, N. N. (1997). Value and address diversity. *Journal of Emotional & Behavioral Disorders, 5*(1), 24-35.

U.S. Department of Education. (1997). *Nineteenth annual report to Congress on the implementation of the Individuals with Disabilities Education Act*. Washington, DC: Author.

STAFF

CHILDHOOD PSYCHOSIS
CHILDHOOD SCHIZOPHRENIA
EMOTIONAL DISORDERS

SERVICE DELIVERY MODELS

Service delivery models are programs, processes, and safeguards established to ensure a free, appropriate public education for handicapped children and youths. The models that have been developed for the delivery of services to handicapped school-aged children generally reflect in their form and operation the influence of at least three factors: (1) the statutory requirements and congressional intent of Individuals with Disabilities Education Act (IDEA); (2) the nature of the particular state or local education agency providing the services in terms of physical size, population distribution, and, to some extent, the available fiscal and human resources; and (3) the specific needs of the children being served. IDEA requires that children with disabilities to the degree possible be educated with nonhandicapped children and that removal from the regular education environment occur "only when the nature or severity of the handicap is such that education in regular classes with the use of supplementary aids and services cannot be achieved satisfactorily" (U.S.C. 1412(5)(B)). The regulations for the Act elaborate on this condition and refer to a continuum of alternate placements that must include instruction in regular classes with access to resource room services or itinerant instruction if necessary, special classes, special schools, home instruction, and instruction in hospitals and institutions. The regulations also require assurance that the various alternative placements are available to the extent necessary to implement the individualized education program for each handicapped child. The congressional intent clearly was to ensure the design of models for the delivery of services to meet the instructional needs of each child with disabilities rather than to allow assignment of a child with disabilities to whatever special education services happen to be available at the time, unless those services also happen to meet the needs of the particular child as detailed in that child's individual education plan (IEP).

The continuum of alternative placements as listed in the U.S. Department of Education regulations together with the language of IDEA suggest the basic models for the delivery of special education and related services. The number of children placed in different educational settings are reported every year as seen in table 1 below for the 1994–95 school year. Reynolds (1962) originally laid out a chart showing various organizational patterns for instruction. His work was later modified by Deno and illustrates a cascade of services for handicapped children (Reynolds & Birch, 1982). The placements as shown in Figure 1 can be classified according to the amount of direct intervention provided by someone other than the regular classroom teacher; the more direct services necessary, the more a child moves away from the first level placement, the regular classroom. As the triangular shape of the illustration might suggest more children with special needs should be found in regular classrooms with access to consultant or itinerant support or resource room assistance and fewer in the special classes, special schools, residential schools, or placements outside the school setting. The figure has been adapted to include collaborative/consultative teaching arrangements that allow the special education student to remain in the regular education classroom with direct instruction from the regular and special education teachers.

IDEA and its regulations intend for regular class placement to be the goal for handicapped students. There will always be some students whose educational needs cannot be met in the regular class, however, without some adaptations, special equipment and/or materials, or extra help (Cartwright, Cartwright, & Ward, 1985). Because the regular class teacher may not be adequately trained to make those adaptations, secure the special equipment or materials, or provide the specialized instruction, full-time regular class placement for some children may be enhanced by the provision of consulting teachers who collaborate with regular class teachers and provide up to and including direct instruction.

Educators, parents, advocates, and others who promote appropriate inclusion of students with disabilities in general education classes believe that doing so will provide those students with greater access to the general education curriculum, appropriate education with their nondisabled peers, raise expectations for student performance, and improve coordination between regular and special educators. They also believe that greater inclusion will result

Table 1. Percentage of Children Ages 3–21 Served in Different Educational Environments Under IDEA, Part B, During the 1994–95 School Year

State	Regular Class	Resource Room	Separ Class	Public Separ Facil	Private Separ Facil	Public Resid Facil	Private Resid Facil	Home Hosp Envir
Alabama	44.36	37.73	15.28	1.23	0.17	0.61	0.20	0.41
Alaska	60.71	25.57	13.24	0.03	0.21	0.06	0.13	0.05
Arizona	40.67	36.35	19.82	1.64	0.92	0.19	0.21	0.20
Arkansas	41.13	38.84	14.19	0.29	2.90	0.01	1.11	1.52
California	51.54	19.40	25.09	1.38	1.58	0.20	0.31	0.50
Colorado	69.75	16.48	10.11	1.25	0.19	0.70	0.90	0.62
Connecticut	56.49	18.80	19.53	1.55	2.29	0.05	0.93	0.36
Delaware	26.93	60.21	7.66	4.58	0.01	0.05	0.09	0.47
District of Columbia	13.57	18.82	43.35	13.43	8.87	0.00	1.58	0.38
Florida	40.73	22.31	32.67	2.29	0.30	0.43	0.00	1.27
Georgia	42.38	31.03	25.46	0.67	0.14	0.01	0.10	0.20
Hawaii	43.49	32.24	22.97	0.38	0.06	0.04	0.10	0.72
Idaho	64.97	23.83	9.54	1.03	0.11	0.02	0.24	0.26
Illinois	27.46	33.96	31.17	4.18	2.00	0.42	0.30	0.51
Indiana	61.23	12.09	23.96	1.65	0.10	0.47	0.14	0.35
Iowa	60.77	26.01	10.14	1.65	—	0.90	0.19	0.33
Kansas	50.07	31.38	14.81	1.84	0.75	0.77	0.12	0.26
Kentucky	52.64	32.67	12.56	0.66	0.17	0.76	0.04	0.49
Louisiana	35.53	18.10	42.99	1.30	0.07	1.28	0.06	0.66
Maine	50.51	33.17	10.66	0.83	2.72	0.05	0.82	1.24
Maryland	49.09	19.40	24.36	3.77	1.93	0.65	0.42	0.38
Massachusetts	66.40	13.29	14.24	1.57	3.02	—	0.68	0.79
Michigan	45.10	24.89	22.36	5.50	—	0.20	0.10	1.86
Minnesota	60.06	22.75	10.30	4.70	0.39	0.83	0.26	0.72
Mississippi	34.39	37.25	25.81	0.88	0.18	0.67	0.05	0.76
Missouri	46.29	30.14	20.83	1.54	0.60	0.22	0.17	0.21
Montana	55.90	29.96	11.44	0.80	0.28	0.62	0.55	0.45
Nebraska	58.25	23.64	12.40	3.66	0.27	0.29	0.09	1.40
Nevada	42.18	36.88	17.39	3.28	0.00	0.00	0.03	0.25
New Hampshire	51.97	22.16	19.33	2.88	1.27	0.26	1.51	0.62
New Jersey	45.38	15.59	29.21	3.13	5.27	0.80	0.07	0.56
New Mexico	31.99	28.82	37.65	0.04	0.01	0.94	0.05	0.51
New York	38.82	14.62	35.02	7.42	2.18	0.64	0.52	0.80
North Carolina	58.63	20.75	17.45	1.55	0.46	0.67	0.01	0.47
North Dakota	75.10	12.56	8.98	1.78	0.22	0.52	0.46	0.38
Ohio	57.68	23.12	15.68	2.18	0.00	0.35	0.00	0.99
Oklahoma	49.39	32.96	15.60	0.93	0.09	0.53	0.09	0.40
Oregon	68.79	18.75	8.42	1.33	1.34	0.37	0.28	0.72
Pennsylvania	37.84	28.07	28.98	1.75	1.57	0.61	0.28	0.90
Puerto Rico	7.14	52.90	29.44	4.23	2.09	0.43	0.10	3.68
Rhode Island	51.03	18.76	24.63	0.79	2.67	0.00	1.38	0.73
South Carolina	36.80	36.47	24.26	1.59	0.04	0.48	0.03	0.34
South Dakota	60.81	23.70	11.67	0.58	0.76	0.69	1.63	0.15
Tennessee	49.70	28.79	17.75	0.93	0.80	0.47	0.43	1.13
Texas	27.40	46.78	23.88	0.52	0.03	0.13	0.01	1.26
Utah	40.20	34.98	20.04	2.79	0.00	1.67	—	0.34
Vermont	83.76	4.39	4.96	1.20	1.39	0.12	1.71	2.46
Virginia	38.36	31.14	26.65	1.10	0.73	0.67	0.25	1.09
Washington	50.14	29.22	18.57	1.03	0.32	0.20	0.01	0.51
West Virginia	9.98	70.10	18.32	0.43	0.08	0.57	0.03	0.49
Wisconsin	38.06	37.58	22.59	1.18	0.05	0.35	0.02	0.16
Wyoming	57.05	32.35	8.19	0.38	0.43	0.89	0.55	0.16
American Samoa	62.84	23.65	13.51	0.00	0.00	0.00	0.00	0.00
Guam	35.89	52.79	10.65	0.62	0.00	0.00	0.06	0.00
Northern Marianas	83.57	11.19	3.50	0.00	0.00	0.00	0.00	1.75
Palau	54.95	23.42	17.12	0.00	0.00	0.00	0.00	4.50
Virgin Islands	—	—	—	—	—	—	—	—
Bur. of Indian Affairs	24.49	58.75	14.90	0.22	0.24	0.90	0.40	0.09
U.S. and outlying areas	45.04	27.01	23.26	2.22	1.04	0.43	0.24	0.76
50 states, D.C., & P.R.	45.07	26.96	23.28	2.23	1.04	0.43	0.24	0.76

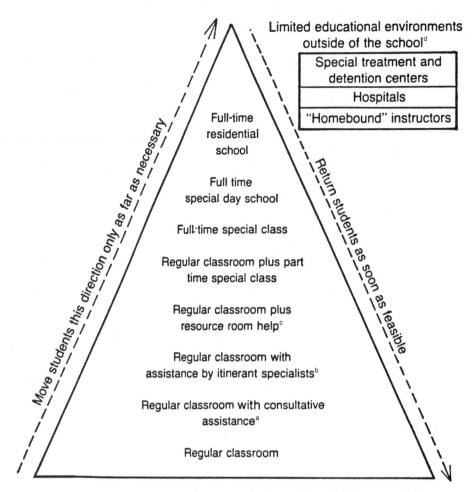

[a]Consultative assistance might be offered, for example, by school psychologists, consulting teachers, resource room teachers, supervisors or others. The term *consultative* denotes only *indirect* services such as prereferral interventions and no *direct* service or instruction to the child by the consultant.

[b]Direct instruction is provided by the regular and special education teacher in a variety of collaborative or consultative arrangements.

[c]Itinerant specialists commonly include speech and hearing therapists and mobility instructors for the blind, for example. They offer some *direct* instruction to the students involved.

[d]A resource classroom is a special station in a school building that is manned by a resource teacher who usually offers some direct instruction to selected students but also usually offers consulting services to regular teachers. Sometimes resource teachers are categorical (such as resource teacher for the blind) but increasingly resource teachers are employed for a more generic, noncategorical role.

[e]This special set of environments in included here in set-aside fashion because usually students are placed in these settings for reasons other than educational. for example, they go to detention centers on court orders for reason of conviction for some criminal offense; or they go to hospitals or are held at home because of health problems. Special educators often work in these *limited* ednvironments and some degree of specialization in education is required. But, in the main, there is strong preference, from an educational point of view, for return of the students to regular school environments as soon as feasible.

Figure 1. The original special education cascade. *Source:* Reynolds, M. C. and Birch, J. W. (1982). *Teaching exceptional children in all America's schools.* Reston, VA: Council for Exceptional Children, 39. Adapted by E. Fletcher-Janzen.

in increased school-level accountability for educational results (U.S. Department of Education, 1998).

In 1994–95, 2.2 million of the total 4.9 million students with disabilities ages 6 through 21 spent at least 80% of their school day in general education classes (See Table 1), and more than 95% of all students with disabil-

ities attended regular schools. The environments in which students receive services vary according to the individual needs of the child. Although 87% of students with speech and language impairments were served in regular classes for 80% or more of the school day, only 9.7% of those with mental retardation were served in regular class placements. Students ages 6–11 were more likely to receive services in regular class placements than students ages 12–17 or 18–21 (U.S. Department of Education, 1998).

A resource room program can enable some children who need more intensive instruction in some or all of the basic skills, or whose behavior at times goes beyond what is appropriate or tolerable in the regular class, to remain in the regular class except for limited periods of time each day or week. The resource room model has been particularly popular for learning-disabled students, although students with other handicapping conditions also profit from additional help provided by resource room teachers. Some resource room programs are organized by disability area while others, particularly in more recent years, accommodate children with a variety of handicapping conditions but whose instructional needs are similar.

Placement in a special class for all or part of the school day is considered necessary for some children. Frequently, the deciding factors for inclusive programming, resource room, part-time special class, or full-time special class placement are the amount of time the handicapped child can benefit from time in the regular class and the severity of the needs of that child. Interestingly, there seems to be considerable overlap in the types of students, the amount of time spent in the regular class, and the ways teachers actually use their time in resource room classes, self-contained special classes, and even residential classes, at least for emotionally disabled students (Peterson, Zabel, Smith, & White, 1983). This suggests some inconsistencies in determining appropriate placement for children and in defining responsibilities for special and regular education personnel.

Some children with disabilities are placed in special schools for their daily instructional programs. Such children, by the nature of their placement, have limited access to participation in social, academic, extracurricular, or spontaneous activities with nonhandicapped children. These children are, therefore to be placed in special schools and residential settings only when the severity of their conditions warrants such placement and only for so long as that placement is necessary. The same holds true for those students in settings such as hospitals, treatment centers, and detention facilities that are outside the educational system.

The overriding principle in selecting appropriate placement for a handicapped child who needs special education and related services is that of the least restrictive environment. No one placement or service delivery system described here can be cited as the best for all handicapped children, and that includes the regular classroom, although some proponents of full inclusion would argue this point. Rather, selection must be made on the basis of what setting permits the implementation of the IEP designed for a given child and allows for meaningful involvement with nonhandicapped children, if possible in the same community where the handicapped child would attend school if there were no handicapping condition necessitating a special education program.

While the service delivery models described represent the typical programs available for handicapped children, or those that should be available by law and regulation, the specific character of any particular program will be determined in part by the nature of the geography, size, population distribution, and resources available in the child's district of residence. Rural areas have special challenges to face, among which are transportation, length of time en route to programs, recruitment and retention of qualified personnel to serve children with low-incidence handicaps, smaller tax base, and in some communities, the power of tradition (Helge, 1984). Urban areas face another set of challenges that typically include transportation in densely populated areas, desegregation issues, and the problems that develop when large numbers of people with little in common must interact under crowded conditions.

In addition to these special urban and rural factors, there is the impact that access to special education programs in private schools can have. The laws and regulations are clear that handicapped children must be provided appropriate free public education in approved private day and residential schools only, and in accord with the principle of the least restrictive environment (Grumet & Inkpen, 1982; U.S. Office of Education, 1977). If parents wish their handicapped child to attend a private school program and place their child in that program themselves, then except for special circumstances, the parents are responsible for the cost of their child's education. But if the private day or residential school placement is recommended as the appropriate one for the child by the child's local school district, then the education program must be provided at no cost to the parents. Already complex issues regarding private school placement become even more complicated when out-of-state private schools offer programs considered appropriate for children with certain types of needs as, for example, multihandicapped children or deaf-blind children.

In summary, the cascade of service delivery models emphasizes the place where children with special needs might be assigned for instruction. These models have collected criticism because of their focus on placement more than program content. Inherent in the instructional cascade is the goal of equipping the regular classroom to be a learning environment where the diverse needs of many children, including handicapped, gifted, and handicapped gifted learners, can be accommodated (Reynolds & Birch, 1982).

Service delivery models in the context of special education have changed over the years as laws, the inclusion movement, court decisions, local needs, parental pressures, fiscal and human resources, and community concerns have made their influence felt. Ysseldyke and Algozzine (1982) have suggested that change will continue but primarily in response to economic needs. More recently, Crowner (1985) has presented a taxonomy of special education finance and an analysis of funding bases, formulas and types and sources of funds for special education. The balance between congressional intent and legal necessity, local control, fiscal reality, and administrative expediency is delicate at best. For the benefit of all children currently in school and those to come, efforts must continue to be directed at designing and operating service delivery systems that meet the needs of all children, those who have conditions requiring special education and those who do not.

REFERENCES

Cartwright, G. P., Cartwright, C. A., & Ward, M. E. (1985). *Educating special learners* (2nd ed.). Belmont, CA: Wadsworth.

Crowner, T. T. (1985). A taxonomy of special education finance. *Exceptional Children, 51*(6), 503–508.

Fox, W. L., Egner, A. N., Paolucci, P. E., Perelman, P. F., McKenzie, H. S., & Garvin, J. S. (1973). An introduction to a regular classroom approach to special education. In E. Deno (Ed.), *Instructional alternatives for exceptional children*. Reston, VA: Council for Exceptional Children.

Grumet, L., & Inkpen, T. (1982). The education of children in private schools: A state agency's perspective. *Exceptional Children, 49*(3), 200–206.

Haight, S. L. (1984). Special education teacher consultant: Idealism versus realism. *Exceptional Children, 50*(6), 507–515.

Helge, D. (1984). The state of the art of rural special education. *Exceptional Children, 50*(4), 294–305.

Peterson, R. L., Zabel, R. H., Smith, C. R., & White, M. A. (1983). Cascade of services model and emotionally disabled students. *Exceptional Children, 49*(5), 404–408.

Reynolds, M. C., & Birch, J. W. (1992). *Teaching exceptional children in all America's schools*. Reston, VA: Council for Exceptional Children.

Salund, S. J. (1984). Factors contributing to the development of successful mainstreaming programs. *Exceptional Children, 50*(5), 409–416.

U.S. Office of Education. (1977, August 23). Education of handicapped children: Implementation of Part B of the Education of the Handicapped Act. *Federal Register, 42*(163), 42474–42518.

U.S. Department of Education. (1998). Nineteenth Annual Report to Congress. Washington, DC: Author.

Ysseldyke, J., & Algozzine, B. (1982). *Critical issues in special and remedial education*. Boston: Houghton Mifflin.

MARJORIE E. WARD
The Ohio State University

CASCADE MODEL OF SPECIAL EDUCATION
INDIVIDUALS WITH DISABILITIES EDUCATION ACT
LEAST RESTRICTIVE ENVIRONMENT
RESOURCE ROOM
SELF-CONTAINED CLASSROOM

SEVERE DISCREPANCY ANALYSIS (SDA)

Severe Discrepancy Analysis (SDA) is a computer program developed by Reynolds and Stowe (1985) to assist in the diagnosis of learning disabilities. The program provides an analysis of the severe discrepancy component of the federal definition of learning disabilities, which is also one of the most prevalent of the five major components of definitions of learning disabilities nationwide. The program also strongly recommends that all remaining aspects of the definition be assessed prior to arriving at a diagnosis of learning disabilities.

The program performs the two fundamental analyses recommended in the Federal Work Group Report on Critical Measurement Issues in Learning Disabilities (Reynolds, 1984): it assesses (1) the statistical significance of the difference between the child's score on an aptitude measure and an achievement measure and (2) the relative frequency of occurrence of the difference between the child's current achievement level and the average achievement level of all other children at the same IQ level. These two analyses and the principles underlying them are explained in detail in Reynolds (1984, 1985).

The SDA is available for use on personal computers. It requires a disk drive and needs approximately 2 minutes per case to perform the various analyses. It will allow the adjustment of cutoff scores but defaults to the values recommended in the Federal Work Group Report. The program is designed for use with all major tests of achievement and aptitude that provide standard scores. Any future tests may be easily accommodated and can be entered by the user if standard scores are available. Grade equivalents and related types of scores cannot be used (Reynolds, 1981).

REFERENCES

Reynolds, C. R. (1981). The fallacy of "two years below grade level for age" as a diagnostic criterion for reading disorders. *Journal of School Psychology, 19,* 350–358.

Reynolds, C. R. (1984). Critical measurement issues in learning disabilities. *Journal of Special Education, 18,* 451–476.

Reynolds, C. R. (1985). Measuring the aptitude-achievement discrepancy in learning disability diagnosis. *Remedial & Special Education, 6,* 37–55.

Reynolds, C. R., & Stowe, M. (1985). *Severe discrepancy analysis.* Philadelphia: TRAIN.

CECIL R. REYNOLDS
Texas A & M University

GRADE EQUIVALENTS
LEARNING DISABILITIES, PROBLEMS IN DEFINITION OF
LEARNING DISABILITIES, SEVERE DISCREPANCY ANALYSIS IN

SEX DIFFERENCES IN LEARNING ABILITIES

Popular stereotypes and epidemiological research both suggest that boys have more learning and adjustment problems than girls. Boys are more readily referred for psychological services than girls with similar problems (Caplan, 1977). In addition, boys of all ages are more likely than girls to be evaluated or treated for learning problems (Eme, 1979). The reasons for apparent gender differences are widely debated. Some suggest that (1) boys are at some biological or developmental disadvantage that affects learning and adjustment (Ullian, 1981); (2) classrooms, teachers, or professionals are less tolerant of boys than girls (Pleck, 1981); and (3) the problems manifested by girls are perceived differently or considered to be less important. This debate leads one to question whether recognizable gender differences exist in children's learning abilities.

Many persons believe the cognitive abilities of boys and girls differ. The common notion is that boys have better developed quantitative abilities while girls are better in verbal areas. After reviewing literature on psychological gender differences, Maccoby and Jacklin (1974) conclude that three cognitive gender differences are well established: girls have greater verbal ability than boys, while boys have better visual-spatial and mathematical ability than girls. The authors further conclude that gender differences in verbal ability emerge after age 11, gender differences in quantitative (i.e., mathematical) abilities emerge at around 12, and gender differences in spatial ability emerge in adolescence.

Other investigations report gender differences in verbal and spatial abilities at earlier ages than those reported by Maccoby and Jacklin. A number of researchers have found that females as early as age 1 month and throughout the preschool years show some slight verbal advancement over males, an advancement that appears stronger and more reliable after age 10 or 11 (McGuinness & Pribram, 1979; Oetzel, 1966; Petersen & Wittig, 1979). While sex differences are seen more clearly during and after adolescence, male superiority in spatial performance may appear as early as age 6 (Harris, 1978; McGuinness & Pribram, 1979). The magnitude of differences between males and females depends in part on the type of spatial skill. Maccoby and Jacklin (1974) distinguish visual nonanalytic spatial skills (i.e., those solved without the use of verbal mediation) from visual analytic spatial skills (i.e., those solvable with verbal mediation). Postpubescent males score consistently higher than females on most spatial abilities, particularly nonanalytic visualization abilities (Maccoby & Jacklin, 1974; Petersen & Wittig, 1979).

Generalizations regarding gender differences in verbal, spatial, and quantitative areas do not go unchallenged. After reviewing the evidence on cognitive gender differences used by Maccoby and Jacklin, Sherman (1978) reported

the magnitude of the gender differences to be very small. Hyde (1981) also concludes from a meta-analysis of the data used by Maccoby and Jacklin that the gender differences in verbal ability, quantitative ability, visual-spatial ability, and field articulation are small. Sex differences appear to account for no more than 5% of the population variance. In general, gender differences in verbal ability are smaller and gender differences in spatial ability are larger. Hyde questions whether statistically significant sex differences in cognitive abilities are practically significant. In other words, the common notion that girls are better at verbal tasks while boys excel in spatial or mathematical areas largely is meaningless in terms of educational implications. Moreover, a close review of literature examining gender differences is likely to lead readers to conclude that boys and girls exhibit similarities more frequently than differences.

Do sex differences exist in school achievement? The evidence is contradictory. Few gender differences in learning were found in a five-year longitudinal study of students ages 5 through 9 (Anastas & Reinherz, 1984). However, a review of the cross-national data on gender differences in achievement found that boys' mathematics achievement is higher than that of girls at both the elementary and secondary levels, that boys score higher in all areas of science, and that girls have higher achievement in verbal areas involving reading comprehension and literature (Fennema, 1982; McGuinness, 1993).

Assuming achievement is affected by opportunities to learn (e.g., participation in courses, amount of instruction), and that boys generally have more opportunities to learn mathematics and science than girls (Finn, Dulberg, & Reis, 1979), we may conclude that girls perform lower in math and science because of fewer opportunities in these areas rather than intrinsic factors. While research infrequently has considered the extent to which differences in socialization and educational experiences may account for differential performance and attainment, many social scientists believe most or even all sex differences in ability and achievement are due to differing cultural and social opportunities and expectations for boys and girls (Levine & Ornstein, 1983). Still, we know little about the origins of sex differences. When gender differences appear, we should be cautious in speculating about their etiologies.

REFERENCES

Anastas, J. W., & Reinherz, H. (1984). Gender differences in learning and adjustment problems in school: Results of a longitudinal study. *American Journal of Orthopsychiatry, 54,* 110–122.

Caplan, P. (1977). Sex, age, behavior and school subject as determinants of report of learning problems. *Journal of Learning Disabilities, 10,* 314–316.

Eme, R. (1979). Sex differences in childhood psychopathology. A review. *Psychological Bulletin, 86,* 574–593.

Fennema, E. (1982, March). *Overview of sex-related differences in mathematics.* Paper presented at the annual meeting of the American Educational Research Association. New York.

Finn, J. D., Dulberg, L., & Reis, J. (1979). Sex differences in educational attainment: A cross-national perspective. *Harvard Educational Review, 49,* 477–503.

Harris, L. J. (1978). Sex differences in spatial ability: Possible environmental, genetic, and neurological factors. In M. Kinsbourne (Ed.), *Asymmetrical function of the brain.* London: Cambridge University Press.

Hyde, J. S. (1981). How large are cognitive gender differences? A meta-analysis using w^2 and d. *American Psychologist, 36,* 892–901.

Levine, D. U., & Ornstein, A. C. (1983). Sex differences in ability and achievement. *Journal of Research & Development in Education, 16,* 66–72.

Maccoby, E. E., & Jacklin, C. N. (1974). *Psychology of sex differences.* Stanford, CA: Stanford University Press.

McGuinness, D., & Pribram, K. H. (1979). The origins of sensory bias in the development of gender differences in perception and cognition. In M. Bortner (Ed.), *Cognitive growth and development.* New York. Brunner/Mazel.

McGuinness, D. Gender differences in cognitive style: Implications for mathematics performance and achievement. In L. A. Penner and G. M. Batsche (Eds.), *The Challenge in Mathematics and Science Education.* Psychology's Response (pp. 251–274). Washington, DC: APA.

Oetzel, R. (1966). Classified summary of research on sex differences. In E. E. Maccoby (Ed.), *The development of sex differences.* Stanford, CA: Stanford University Press.

Petersen, A. C., & Wittig, M. A. (1979). Sex differences in cognitive functioning: An overview. In M. A. Wittig & A. C. Petersen (Eds.), *Sex-related differences in cognitive functioning: Developmental issues.* New York: Academic.

Pleck, J. (1981). The myth of masculinity. Cambridge, MA: MIT Press.

Sherman, J. (1978). *Sex-related cognitive differences: An essay on theory and evidence.* Springfield, IL: Thomas.

Ullian, D. (1981). Why boys will be boys: A structural perspective. *American Journal of Orthopsychiatry, 51,* 493–501.

THOMAS OAKLAND
JEFF LAURENT
University of Texas

HEMISPHERIC ASYMMETRY, SEX DIFFERENCES IN

SEX EDUCATION OF THE HANDICAPPED

Many professionals and parents believe the sexual needs of the handicapped should be met (Craft & Craft, 1981; Fitz-Gerald & Fitz-Gerald, 1979; Love, 1983). The principle of normalization promoted in the United Nations Declaration of Rights of the Mentally Handicapped (United Nations, 1971) underscores this belief. The declaration states that handicapped people have the same basic rights as other citizens of the same country and the same age. In the United States, normalization is espoused in the Rehabilitation Act of 1973 (PL 93-380) and the Individuals with Disabilities Act (IDEA), which provide for the individualized education of the handicapped in accordance with the requirement of the least restrictive environment.

The advocacy of inclusion in school and the movement away from custodial institutional care and toward community living supply the impetus for focusing on the sexual rights of the handicapped (Bass, 1974; Jacobs, 1978; Shindell, 1975; Thornton, 1979). In conjunction with the philosophy of protecting basic human rights, sex education is advocated to achieve the same ends for the handicapped as for the nonhandicapped: to develop sexually fulfilled persons who understand themselves, their values, and resulting behaviors (Harris, 1974; Reich & Harshman, 1971). Moreover, many persons agree with Kempton (1977) that sex education is bound to the practical tasks of improving the social and sexual functions of the handicapped. The need to moderate educational goals on the bases of age, gender, type of handicap and severity of handicap is inherent in the nature of sex education of the handicapped.

Alongside the demands for individualization of instruction is a humanistic approach that advocates meeting the needs of persons while deemphasizing labels (Johnson, 1981). In contradiction to the rationale given in the past, this outlook maintains that sex education should not only respond to critical sexual problems as they arise, or to conditioning that seeks to prevent all sexual experiences (Craft & Craft, 1978, 1980; Edmonson & Wish, 1975; Gordon, 1971a, 1971b; Kempton, 1977, 1978). Implied in the normalization philosophy is the goal of working for the good of all by securing individual freedom since, with teaching, training, and the availability of specific support services, the handicapped are more likely to blend into society.

Notwithstanding the fact that the philosophy of normalization has impacted the literature, the topic of sex education for the handicapped is fraught with controversy. Issues and concerns presently being raised include improvement of curricula and resources, training and preparation of teachers, assessment of the effects of teaching, and involvement of the parents in sex education.

Great strides have been made in the individualization of sex education (Johnson & Kempton, 1981). A wealth of curriculum guides exists that identifies programs to meet the varied needs of the handicapped (see Edmonson, 1980, for a 30-reference list of programs and materials available for the blind, deaf, retarded, and emotionally impaired). Adapted sex education enables even the severely retarded to improve their sexual knowledge (Edmonson, 1980).

However, outdated sex laws and repressive social attitudes often prevent the optimal development and employment of instructional resources (Sherwin, 1981). Teaching materials aimed at compensating for specific handicaps (e.g., genital models for use with the blind) can run afoul of obscenity laws. Also, few legal principles protect sex educators, counselors, or therapists (Sherwin, 1981). Audiotactual sex education programs for blind children have been implemented successfully with the use of models, but touching the human body is seen as problematic (Knappett & Wagner, 1976; Tait & Kessler, 1976). Sex education programs for blind children should take into account the sexual taboos of our culture (Torbett, 1974). Fortunately, according to Johnson (1981), this negativism is lifting somewhat as judged by a shift from a position of elimination regarding the acceptance of the sexuality of the handicapped to a position of toleration. The recent evolution toward a more permissive attitude regarding sexual expression for recreational rather than procreational purposes has been conducive to this change. Still, sodomy laws in many states condemn all sexual activity as illegal except vaginal intercourse within marriage. These laws deny nonprocreative sex as a legitimate right. For a given handicapped person, this form of sexual expression may be the only one possible. In light of such social taboos and legal restraints, the development of appropriate programming to suit the individual needs of the handicapped is constrained.

Minimal attention is paid to sex education during the preparation of teachers for the handicapped. A survey indicated that, while 61% of student teachers in special education courses received some preparation in sex education, this preparation was either an elective option or a few hours of coverage subsumed under a different topic such as methods of teaching (May, 1980). This is regrettable because sex education courses in special education could help teachers overcome their discomfort in dealing with this subject (Blom, 1971). Professionals can increase their comfort with sexual matters as well as improve attitude and knowledge levels as a result of systematic training in sexuality and disability (Chubon, 1981). Kempton (1978) has proposed training professionals to provide services, as well as develop policies, regarding the sexual rights of the handicapped. She advises (1977) that successful programs be broadly conceived to prepare for skills for living in society.

A major obstacle to sex education of the handicapped has been the denial of their sexuality by parents and teachers, who are concerned that education could trigger sexual experimentation and appetite (Craft, 1983). However, experts in this field (Gordon, 1975; Kempton, 1978) have argued that sex education results in improved social behavior, increased self-respect, more openness, and fewer guilt feelings. On the other hand, withholding information fails to deter sexual activity, causes confusion, needless fears, inappropriate behaviors, and unwanted consequences such as pregnancy.

In spite of this authoritative stance, advocates for sex education have provided little evidence that sex education has changed sexual behavior patterns or identified the valid expectations and limitations of their procedures (Balester, 1971). The literature that examines specific sex education programs for the handicapped mainly presents theorizations rather than scientific data (Vockell & Mattick, 1972). Teaching the handicapped is a complex task owing to such factors as low cognitive abilities and academic skill, short attention span, and secondary handicaps of a sensory, physical, emotional, or behavioral nature. Therefore, restraints in setting educational goals have been recommended (Watson & Rogers, 1980). However, programs that facilitate specific abilities (e.g., contraceptive use or knowledge of sexually transmitted diseases) seem to represent too modest a first step toward devising an educational technology of sexual instruction that will empirically appraise the limits of sexual development and social awareness in this diverse population.

While many parents are interested in sex education for their handicapped youngsters, their sexual conservatism may severely limit the nature of the curriculum. For example, parents of sensorially impaired students give the highest rating to teaching less controversial topics such as cleanliness, knowledge of one's own body, venereal disease, dating, reproduction, pregnancy, marriage, and feelings about self and others. They frequently resist instruction regarding contraceptives, sexual intercourse, sexual deviancy, incest, divorce, masturbation, abortion, sterilization, and pornography (Love, 1983). Parental cooperation and support are crucial to program development and to the transfer of skills from school to home and community settings. Thus it remains essential to involve the parents in cooperative educational efforts by securing their agreement with expectations of instruction (Hamre-Nietupski & Ford, 1981; Kempton, 1975).

Normalization frequently entails the sexual development of the handicapped to enable them to assume more normal lives. While there has been progress in designing and offering sex education program for the handicapped, several areas of concern have hampered their acceptance. These include (1) constraints imposed on the design and implementation of curricula owing to legal and social restraints that pertain to sexual taboos; (2) neglect by teacher training institutes in the preparation of professionals in special education who are trained in sex education; (3) problems in assessing the effects of teaching because of the nature of affective instructional goals interacting with a diversity of abilities in this population; and (4) conservatism on the part of parents that tends to place limitations on expectations of instruction. These problems hinder but do not preclude change. Models for the successful institutionalization of sex education for the handicapped exist elsewhere, as in Sweden (Grunewald & Linner, 1979). Public policy regarding sex education for the handicapped is desirable given the obvious needs in this area (Craft, 1983). The handicapped should understand their sexuality, should be safe from sexual exploitation, and should become responsible in their sexual behavior (Cole, 1993; Craft, 1983).

REFERENCES

Balester, R. J. (1971). Sex education: Fact and fancy. *Journal of Special Education, 5,* 355–357.

Bass, M. S. (1974). Sex education for the handicapped. *Family Coordinator, 23,* 27–33.

Blom, G. E. (1971). Some considerations about the neglect of sex education in special education. *Journal of Special Education, 5,* 359–361.

Chubon, R. A. (1981). Development and evaluation of a sexuality and disability course for the helping professions. *Sexuality & Disability, 4,* 3–14.

Cole, S. S., & Cole, T. M. (1993). Sexuality, disability, and reproductive issues through the lifespan. *Sexuality & Disability, 11*(3), 189-205.

Craft, A. (1983). Sexuality and mental retardation: A review of the literature. In A. Craft & M. Craft (Eds.), *Sex education and counseling for mentally handicapped people.* Baltimore, MD: University Park Press.

Craft, A., & Craft, M. (1980). Sexuality and the mentally handicapped. In G. B. Simon (Ed.), *Modern management of mental handicap: A manual of practice.* Lancaster England MTP Press.

Craft, A., & Craft, M. (1981). Sexuality and mental handicap: A review. *British Journal of Psychiatry, 139,* 494–505.

Craft, M., & Craft, A. (1978). *Sex and the mentally handicapped.* London: Routledge & Kegan Paul.

Edmonson, B. (1980). Sociosexual education for the handicapped. *Exceptional Education Quarterly, 1,* 67–76.

Edmonson, B., & Wish, J. (1975). Sex knowledge and attitudes of moderately retarded males. *American Journal of Mental Deficiency, 80,* 172–179.

Fitz-Gerald, D., & Fitz-Gerald, M. (1979). Sexual implications deaf-blindness. *Sexuality & Disability, 2,* 212–215.

Gordon, S. (1971a). Missing in special education. Sex. *Journal of Special Education, 5,* 351–354.

Gordon, S. (1971b). Okay, let's tell it like it is (instead of just making it look good). *Journal of Special Education, 5,* 379–381.

Gordon, S. (1975). Workshop: Sex education for the handicapped. In M. S. Bass & M. Gelof (Eds.), *Sexual rights and responsibilities of the mentally retarded.* Proceedings of the Conference of the American Association on Mental Deficiency, Washington, DC: AAMD.

Grunewald, K., & Linner, B. (1979). Mentally-retarded: Sexuality and normalization. *Current Sweden,* 237–239.

Hamre-Nietupski, S., & Ford, A. (1981). Sex education and related skills: A series of programs implemented with severely handicapped students. *Sexuality & Disability, 4,* 179–193.

Harris, A. (1974). What does "sex education" mean? In R. Rogers (Ed.), *Sex education: Rationale and reaction.* Cambridge, England: Cambridge University Press.

Jacobs, J. H. (1978). The mentally retarded and their need for sexuality education. *Psychiatric Opinion, 15,* 32–34.

Johnson, W. R. (1981). Sex education for special populations. In L. Brown: (Ed.), *Sex education in the eighties.* New York: Plenum.

Johnson, W. R., & Kempton, W. (1981). *Sex education and counseling of special groups.* Springfield, IL: Thomas.

Kempton, W. (1975). Sex education: A cooperative effort of parent and teacher. *Exceptional Children, 41,* 531–535.

Kempton, W. (1977). The mentally retarded person. In H. Gochros & J. Gochros (Eds.), *The sexually oppressed.* New York: Association.

Kempton, W. (1978). The rights of the mentally ill and mentally retarded: Are sexual rights included? *Devereux Forum, 13,* 45–49.

Knappett, K., & Wagner, N. N. (1976). Sex education and the blind. *Education of the Visually Handicapped, 8,* 1–5.

Love, E. (1983). Parental and staff attitudes toward instruction in human sexuality for sensorially impaired students at the Alabama Institute for Deaf and Blind. *American Annals of the Deaf, 128,* 45–47.

May, D. C. (1980). Survey of sex education coursework in special education programs. *Journal of Special Education, 14,* 107–112.

Reich, M., & Harshman, H. (1971). Sex education for the handicapped youngsters, reality or repression? *Journal of Special Education, 5,* 373–377.

Sherwin, R. (1981). Sex and the law on a collision course. In W. R. Johnson (Ed.), *Sex in life.* Dubuque, IA: Brown.

Shindell, P. E. (1975). Sex education programs and the mentally retarded. *Journal of School Health, 45,* 88–90.

Tait, P. E., & Kessler, C. (1976). The way we get babies: A tactual sex education program. *New Outlook for the Blind, 70,* 116–120.

Thornton, C. E. (1979). A nurse-educator in sex and disability. *Sexuality & Disability, 2,* 28–32.

Torbett, D. S. (1974). A humanistic and futuristic approach to sex education for blind children. *New Outlook for the Blind, 68,* 210–215.

United Nations. (1971). *Declaration of general and special rights of the mentally handicapped.* New York: UN Department of Social Affairs.

Vockell, E. L., & Mattick, P. (1972). Sex education for the mentally retarded: An analysis of problems, programs, and research. *Education & Training of the Mentally Retarded, 7,* 129–134.

Watson, G., & Rogers, R. S. (1980). Sexual instruction for the mildly retarded and normal adolescent: A comparison of educational approaches, parental expectations and pupil knowledge and attitude. *Health Education Journal, 39,* 88–95.

JACQUELINE CUNNINGHAM
THOMAS OAKLAND
University of Texas

PEDIATRIC AIDS
SEX DISTURBANCES IN THE HANDICAPPED
SOCIAL BEHAVIOR OF THE HANDICAPPED
SOCIAL DEVELOPMENT
SOCIAL ISOLATION
SOCIAL SKILLS TRAINING

SEX INFORMATION AND EDUCATION COUNCIL OF THE UNITED STATES (SIECUS)

The Sex Information and Education Council of the United States (SIECUS) is a nonprofit, voluntary health organization dedicated to the establishment and exchange of information about human sexual behavior. The council is funded primarily by foundation grants and individual contributions. The SIECUS provides information and responds to requests for consultation from churches, communities, school boards, and any other national or international health or educational organizations interested in establishing or improving their sex education programs. As a part of this concern, SIECUS developed a policy and resource guide concerning sex education for the mentally retarded individual (SIECUS, 1971).

The guide begins by observing that the mentally retarded individual has sexual feelings similar to those of all humans, but that because of possible confusion and misunderstanding, the mentally retarded student may need sexual guidance and education to understand sex and his or her own sexuality. The SIECUS provides instructional, curricular, and counseling information in the guide that will be useful in helping the mentally retarded individual to achieve this understanding. Finally, information is provided regarding printed materials, films and filmstrips, tapes, and other teaching aids that may be useful in sex education for the mentally retarded individual.

SIECUS also presents a listing of sexuality and disability materials published between 1982 and 1992 (Shortridge, Steele-Clapp, & Lamin, 1993).

REFERENCE

SIECUS. (1971). *A resource guide in sex education for the mentally retarded.* New York: Author.

Shortridge, J., Steele-Clapp, L., & Lamin, J. (1993). Sexuality and disability: A SIECUS annotated bibliography of available print materials. *Sexuality & Disability, 11*(2), 159–179.

JOHN R. BEATTIE
University of North Carolina at Charlotte

SEX RATIOS IN SPECIAL EDUCATION

As concern grows about sexual bias in society and its effect on children, attention is focusing on the classroom. Sex bias in education is of particular concern to the field of special education. Research indicates that more males than females are served in special education programs, and that the sex label has been recognized as having a profound impact on the education of handicapped children. Gillespie and Fink (1974) report that the mere identification of exceptional children as either male or female results in arbitrary practice and discriminatory judgments, and in intervention decisions that limit opportunities for personal and vocational development of those children and youths.

There is a belief among educators that boys are more in need of special services than girls; consequently, more male students are provided with special education services. Boys are much more likely to be referred and treated in all the major areas of exceptionality; they are more likely to be identified as exhibiting reading problems, learning disabilities, and mental retardation (Gillespie & Fink, 1974). However, female students are shown to be more in need of special education assistance on the basis of standardized test data (Sadker, Sadker, & Thomas, 1981).

Caplan (1977) suggests that girls with learning disabilities are less likely than learning-disabled boys to be identified as learning disabled or to participate in special education programs. It is generally accepted among special educators that the male to female ratio in special education is about 3:1. Norman and Zigmond (1980) confirm that learning disabilities usually are identified as a male disorder; they find a ratio of 3.7:1. The authors report that the ratio is similar to the 3:1 ratio suggested by Kirk and Elkins (1975) and the 4.6:1 ratio reported by Lerner (1976). This has not been supported by recent research on reading disorders (Flynn, & Rahbar, 1994).

Rubin and Balow (1971), in a longitudinal study of 967 kindergarten through third grade students, discovered that educationally defined behavior problems were exhibited by 41% of the children participating in their study. When results were reported by sex, the number of boys far exceeded the number of girls; boys were reported to have more attitude and behavior problems, to be receiving more special services, and to be repeating more grades. The authors suggested that teachers accept only a narrow range of behaviors, and that deviations outside this range are viewed as cause for intervention. This is supported by later research (Callahan, 1994).

Further evidence for the disproportionate number of males in special education comes from a study reported in Young, Algozzine, and Schmid. McCarthy and Paraskevopoulos (1969) examined behavior patterns of average, emotionally disturbed, and learning-disabled children, and found that boys outnumbered girls 8:1 in the emotionally disturbed sample and 9:1 in the learning-disabled sample.

Mirkin, Marston, and Deno (1982) investigated the referral-placement process and discovered that males were referred far in excess of females; however, this was true only for teacher judgment referrals. For referrals based on academic screening using curriculum-based tasks, no significant differences were found in the number of males versus females referred for special education. Furthermore, females who had been referred by teachers were rated as more problematic than the females referred by the screening tests.

A variety of theories have been proposed to account for the sex ratio discrepancy in special education. Caplan (1977) suggested that the boy/girl learning problem report ratio is aggravated by behavioral differences. Caplan and Kinsbourne (1974) discovered that girls who fail in school tend to behave in socially acceptable ways, but their male counterparts tend to react punitively and aggressively. On the basis of this discovery, the authors suggested that because teachers view aggression as the most disturbing type of behavior, they would be more likely to notice boys who are failing in school than their well-behaved, silent female counterparts. Consequently, boys would be more likely to be recognized as needing special attention, if only to get them out of the classroom.

Physiological explanations for the higher incidence of males in special education also have been offered; several categories of exceptionality such as that of learning disabilities have been explained on the basis of sex-linked genetic traits (Rossi, 1972). However, according to Singer and Osborn (1970), there are no known physiological causes to explain the higher number of males treated for mental retardation. Singer and Osborn explain the high ratio of males to females receiving treatment as stemming from sociocultural expectations such as behavior differences and less societal tolerance for boys with academic problems.

Whatever the cause of the unbalanced ratio of males to females in special education, it is apparent that a bias exists. Special educators must recognize this discrepancy, establish its causes, and make the delivery of special education services more equitable.

REFERENCES

Callahan, K. (1994). Causes and implications of the male dominated sex ratio in programs for students with emotional and behavioral disorders. *Education and Treatment of Children, 17*(3), 228–243.

Caplan, P. J. (1977). Sex, age, behavior and school subject as determinants of report of learning problems. *Journal of Learning Disabilities, 5,* 314–316.

Caplan, P. J., & Kinsbourne, M. (1974). Sex differences in response to school failure. *Journal of Learning Disabilities, 4,* 232–235.

Flynn, J. M., & Rahbar, M. H. (1994). Prevalence of reading failure in boys compared with girls. *Psychology in the Schools, 3,* 1, 66–71.

Gillespie, P. H., & Fink, A. H. (1974). The influence of sexism on the education of handicapped children. *Exceptional Children, 41,* 155–161.

Mirkin, P., Marston, D., & Deno, S. L. (1982). *Direct and repeated measurement of academic skills: An alternative to traditional screening, referral, and identification of learning disabled students* (Research Report No. 75). Minneapolis: University of Minnesota, Institute for Research on Learning Disabilities.

Norman, C. A., & Zigmond, N. (1980). Characteristics of children labeled and served as learning disabled in school systems affiliated with child service demonstration centers. *Journal of Learning Disabilities, 13*(9), 16–21.

Rossi, A. O. (1972). Genetics of learning disabilities. *Journal of Learning Disabilities, 5,* 489–496.

Rubin, R., & Balow, B. (1971). Learning and behavior disorders: A longitudinal study. *Exceptional Children, 38,* 293–299.

Sadker, D., Sadker, M., & Thomas, D. (1981). Sex equity and special education. *Pointer, 26*(1), 33–37.

Schlosser, L., & Algozzine, B. (1979). The disturbing child: He or she? *Alberta Journal of Educational Research, 25*(1), 30–36.

Singer, B. D., & Osborn, R. W. (1970). Special class and sex differences in admission patterns of the mentally retarded. *American Journal of Mental Deficiency, 75,* 162–190.

Young, S., Algozzine, B., & Schmid, R. (1979). The effects of assigned attributes and labels on children's peer accepted ratings. *Education & Training of the Mentally Retarded, 12,* 257–261.

KATHLEEN RODDEN-NORD
GERALD TINDAL
University of Oregon

PRE-REFFERAL INTERVENTION
SEX DIFFERENCES IN LEARNING DISABILITIES

SEXUAL DISTURBANCES IN HANDICAPPED CHILDREN

Most of the research and study concerning sexual disturbances in handicapped individuals has focused on those persons with physical disabilities and/or mental retardation in institutional settings. Sexual problems also exist in other special populations but they are less well documented.

Monat (1982) outlines a number of problems found in the mentally retarded population, including excessive and harmful masturbation, same-sex mutual masturbation, opposite-sex, mutual masturbation, bestiality (especially in rural areas), sodomy, indecent exposure, child sexual abuse, lewd and lascivious behavior, and statutory rape.

Undesired pregnancy is also a problem with the mentally retarded, though not necessarily a sexual disturbance.

The approaches recommended today for dealing with sexual disturbances in the mentally retarded ask that professionals who attempt to intervene be both knowledgeable about sex and sexuality and comfortable with this knowledge and their own sexuality. Recognition must be given to differing levels of cognitive ability with the mentally retarded population that lead to variable levels of conceptual understanding and to the likelihood of different sexual behaviors and problems at different levels of functioning. In the past, especially in residential facilities, excessive reliance on moralization, punishment, and sterilization (Haavik & Menninger, 1981) colored attempts to deal with sexual matters. Current approaches generally focus on staff training for desensitization, concrete sex education (including on birth control, marriage, and parenthood), the dispelling of sexual myths, the importance of personal choice and responsibility, the appropriateness of personal social behavior, and the concept of privacy. The staff needs to follow through and review to be certain learning has occurred and the information has been retained. Sex counseling, which is designed to deal with the values and feelings surrounding sexuality, is now more readily available to complement sex education (which is more concerned with the transfer of relevant information).

In examining sexual disturbances, the type of living environment involved is important. With the present preference for community living and independence for the handicapped, greater emphasis must be placed on appropriate community behavior, the legality of different sexual behaviors, personal choices, and the acceptance of responsibility. The handicapped adolescent or adult moving to a less restrictive setting must be aware of the dangers of venereal disease, acquired immune deficiency syndrome (AIDS), prostitution (Monat, 1982). For some, especially those leaving certain residential facilities or protected home settings, community living arrangements, community-based training centers, or job sites of any type may offer the first true coeducational experiences. It has been shown that the knowledge of even noninstitutionalized mentally retarded young men and women is often severely limited (Brantlinger, 1985). West (1979) characterized the observed sexual behavior of institutionalized severely retarded adolescents and adults as essentially normal and appropriate, though sometimes socially improper. He noted that the residents' "sexual activity was very often the only spontaneous cooperative mutual behavior observed and the only interresident interaction apart from aggression."

Attitudes have always played a large part in viewing the sexuality of the handicapped. Sexual disturbances or problems of physically handicapped individuals, especially those with essentially normal intelligence whose physical disability resulted from postnatal accident, injury, or trauma, have been something of an exception among the general handicapped population. Professionals, and probably society in general, seem more willing to recognize the sexual rights of this group and to provide the understanding, support, and even the aids or prostheses to help them regain normal sexuality (Thorn-Gray & Kern, 1983). This view is markedly different than that found when dealing with mentally retarded persons.

Where education has been unsuccessful in preventing sexual disturbances or counseling has been ineffective in eliminating inappropriate sexual behaviors, a variety of behavioral approaches have been found to be successful in individual cases. Hurley and Sovner (1983) describe case reports on the effective use of response cost procedures, aversive conditioning, overcorrection, in vivo desensitization, and positive reinforcement in dealing with problems such as exhibitionism, public masturbation, public disrobing, and fetishism. Assaultive and inappropriate interpersonal sexual behaviors were successfully eliminated in an adolescent male with Down's syndrome through a combination of differential reinforcement of other behaviors and naturalistic social restitution. The control of this behavior was able to be generalized to the student's teachers (Polvinale & Lutzker, 1980).

Sexual problems noted in learning-disabled populations have often been attributed to conceptual difficulties, disinhibition, or inadequate impulse control. Insights into sex-related difficulties in blind and visually impaired persons can be found in Mangold and Mangold (1983) and in Welbourne et al. (1983). Information on sex deafness can be found in *Sexuality and Deafness* (Gallaudet College, 1979).

REFERENCES

Brantlinger, E. A. (1985). Mildly mentally retarded secondary students' information and attitudes toward sexuality and sex education. *Education & Training of the Mentally Retarded, 20,* 99–108.

Gallaudet College. (1979). *Sexuality and deafness.* Washington, DC: Outreach Services.

Haavik, S. F., & Menninger, K. A. (1981). *Sexuality, law, and the developmentally disabled person: Legal and clinical aspects of marriage, parenthood and sterilization.* Baltimore, MD: Brookes.

Hurley, A. D., & Sovner, R. (1983). Treatment of sexual deviation in mentally retarded persons. *Psychiatric Aspects of Mental Retardation Newsletter, 2*(4), 13–16.

Mangold, S. S., & Mangold, P. N. (1983). The adolescent visually impaired female. *Journal of Blindness & Visual Impairment, 77*(6), 250–255.

Monat, R. K. (1982). *Sexuality and the mentally retarded.* San Diego, CA: College-Hill.

Polvinale, R. A., & Lutzker, J. R. (1980). Elimination of and inappropriate sexual behavior by reinforcement and social restitution. *Mental Retardation, 18*(1), 27–30.

Thorn-Gray, B. E., & Kern, L. H. (1983). Sexual dysfunction associated with physical disability: A treatment guide for the rehabilitation practitioner. *Rehabilitation Literature, 44*(5–6), 138–144.

Wellbourne, A., Lifschitz, S., Selvin, H., & Green, R. (1983). A comparison of the sexual learning experiences of visually impaired and sighted women. *Journal of Blindness & Visual Impairment, 77*(6), 256–261.

West, R. R. (1979). The sexual behaviour of the institutionalised severely retarded. *Australian Journal of Mental Retardation, 5,* II–L3.

JOHN D. WILSON
Elwyn Institutes

MASTURBATION, COMPULSIVE
MENTAL RETARDATION
SELF STIMULATION

SHELTERED WORKSHOPS

The concept of the sheltered workshop was introduced in the United States in 1838 by the Perkins Institute for the Blind. The early workshop programs that followed provided sheltered employment for those whose handicapping conditions precluded competitive employment.

Federal involvement with sheltered workshops came about 100 years later. In an effort to help sheltered workshops compete with other businesses for contracts, the 1938 amendments to the Vocational Rehabilitation Act (PL 75-497) allowed workshops to pay below-minimum wages to employees.

With the passage of the Vocational Rehabilitation Act of 1943 (PL 78-113), persons with mental retardation and mental illness were considered eligible for rehabilitation services. This initiated a change in rehabilitation programs in the United States. For the first time, there was recognition of persons who had never been employed.

The Vocational Rehabilitation Act amendments of 1965 (PL 89-333) expanded the definition of "gainful employment" to include not only competitive but also sheltered employment. There was an emphasis on the provision of services that would lead toward gainful sheltered employment for more severely handicapped individuals. According to Snell (1983):

> Sheltered employment is when an individual is receiving subsidized wages or working for less than minimum wage, with handicapped co-workers at a job that provides limited advancement to competitive work settings and that is organized primarily for therapeutic habilitation or sheltered production. (p. 504)

The Rehabilitation Act of 1973 (PL 93-112) and the continuation amendments up to 1992 emphasized the provision of services that would lead toward gainful sheltered employment for persons with severe handicaps and the transition from school work.

Special education programs help prepare young adults with disabilities to work in sheltered workshops. According to Bigge (1982), the special education curriculum should include transition skills, work evaluation, work adjustment, work experience, vocational skills, and on-the-job training programs.

The sheltered workshop is the most widely used type of vocational training facility for adults with handicaps. Sheltered workshops can be classified into three general types: regular program workshops; work activities centers; and adult day programs. Regular program workshops (or transitional workshops) provide therapies and work intended to foster readiness for competitive employment. The Department of Labor requires that workers earn no less than 50% of minimum wages. Work activities centers (WACs) provide training, support, and extended employment in a sheltered environment to more severely handicapped adults. A wage ceiling of 50% of minimum wage has been set for WACs clients. The Fair Labor Standards Act, as amended in 1966, defines regular program workshops and work activities centers. Both are monitored by the Department of Labor. Adult day programs, managed by state developmental disabilities agencies, provide nonvocational services such as socialization, communication skills, and basic work orientation. The primary goal of adult day programs is the acquisition of basic living skills, leading to a decrease in maladaptive behavior and movement toward more vocationally oriented programs.

A sheltered workshop operates as a business. It generally engages in one of three types of business activities: contracting, prime manufacturing, or reclamation. In contracting, there is an agreement that a sheltered workshop will complete a specified job within a specified time for a given price. Workshops bid competitively for each job. Prime manufacturing is the designing, producing, marketing, and shipping of a complete product. A reclamation operation is one in which a workshop purchases or collects salvageable material, performs a reclamation operation, and then sells the reclaimed product. Recently, sheltered workshops have been closing and competitive employment (supported employment, for example) has been substituted. The closure of some workshops has created a division of scholars as to what is the best interests of persons with disabilities' employment (Block, 1997).

REFERENCES

Bigge, J. L. (1982). *Teaching individuals with physical and multiple disabilities* (2nd ed.). Columbus, OH: Merrill.

Block, S. R. Closing the sheltered workshop. Toward competitive employment opportunities for persons with developmental disabilities. *Journal of Vocational Rehabilitation, 9*(3), 267–275.

Heward, W. L., & Orlansky, M. D. (1984). *Exceptional children.* (2nd ed.). Columbus, OH: Merrill.

Lynch, K. P., Kiernan, J. A., & Stark, J. A. (1982). *Prevocational and vocational education for special needs youth.* Baltimore, MD: Brookes.

Mori, A. A., & Masters, L. F. (1983). *Teaching the severely mentally retarded.* Germantown, MD: Aspen.

Schreerenberger, R. C. (1983). *A history of mental retardation.* Baltimore, MD: Brookes.

Snell, M. A. (1983). *Systematic instruction of the moderately and severely handicapped* (2nd ed.). Columbus, OH: Merrill.

CAROLE REITER GOTHELF
Hunter College

VOCATIONAL REHABILITATION
VOCATIONAL TRAINING OF THE HANDICAPPED

SIBLINGS OF THE HANDICAPPED

Siblings of the handicapped have received little research attention compared with the literature available on the effects of a handicapped child on parents (Crnic, Friedrich, & Greenberg, 1983; Drew, Logan, & Hardman, 1984; Trevino, 1979). The available research, however, suggests that nonhandicapped siblings are a population at risk for behavioral problems, the degree to which is influenced by a number of variables and factors (Crnic et al., 1983; Gargiulo, 1984; Trevino, 1979). Specific factors that appear to interact and contribute to sibling adjustment include the number of normal siblings in the family (Powell & Ogle, 1985), the age and gender of siblings (Crnic et al., 1983; Grossman, 1972), and parental response and attitude toward the handicapped child (Trevino, 1979). Trevino (1979) reports that prospects for normal siblings having difficulty in adjusting increase when (1) there are only two siblings in the family, one who is handicapped and one who is not; (2) the nonhandicapped sibling is close in age to or younger than the handicapped sibling or is the oldest female child; (3) the nonhandicapped child and the handicapped child are the same sex; and (4) the parents are unable to accept the handicap. Schwirian (1976), Farber (1959), and Cleveland and Miller (1977) found that the female sibling's role demanded more parent-surrogate duties as she was expected to help care for the disabled child when she was at home. In addition, sibling literature emphasizes healthy and honest parental attitudes and behaviors toward the handicapped child as essential to the siblings positive growth and development.

Grossman (1972) found that socioeconomic status (SES) can also affect sibling responses to a handicapped child. Middle-class families and those from higher SES families tended to be more financially secure and better prepared to use outside resources such as respite care services, thus lessening a youngster's responsibility of caring for a handicapped sibling.

The emotional responses of siblings of the handicapped have been reported to include hostility, guilt, fear, shame, embarrassment, and rejection. Crnic et al. (1983) found that the presence of a retarded child has a detrimental effect on a nonretarded sibling's (particularly a female's) individual functioning. This involves high degrees of anxiety, conflicts with parents, and problems in social and interpersonal relationships. On the other hand, Farber (1960) reported, after an extensive study, that many siblings adopted life goals toward dedication and sacrifice (Crnic et al., 1983).

Although the concerns of siblings vary according to the nature and degree of severity of their handicapped sibling's disability, key concerns, such as how to deal with parents, what to tell friends, and what kind of future they can expect for their handicapped sibling, appear to be similar across types of impairments (Murphy, 1979). If the needs and concerns of siblings are not met, they may result in problems and negative feelings.

The psychological and behavioral problems that may result from having a handicapped sibling is a reality that must be dealt with by parents and professionals. Siblings can benefit from the experience of having a handicapped sibling if they are introduced to the situation in an understanding and compassionate way. Siblings and parents should seek support from family counselors, religious organizations, nonprofit agencies, and sibling support groups that focus on the individual needs, attitudes, concerns, and feelings of the nonhandicapped sibling. Teachers should be alerted to the child's family situation to provide additional support and information.

REFERENCES

Cleveland, D. W., & Miller, N. (1977). Attitudes and life commitments of older siblings of mentally retarded adults; An exploratory study. *Mental Retardation, 15,* 38–41.

Crnic, K. A., Friedrich, W. N., & Greenberg, M. T. (1983). Adaptation of families with mentally retarded children: A model of stress, coping and family ecology. *American Journal of Mental Deficiency, 88,* 125–139.

Drew, C. J., Logan, D. R., & Hardman, M. L. (Eds.). (1984). *Mental retardation: A life cycle approach* (3rd ed.). St. Louis: Times/Mirror Mosby.

Farber, B. (1959). Effects of a severely mentally retarded child on family integration. *Monographs of the Society for Research in Child Development, 24,* (whole No. 71).

Farber, B. (1960). Family organization and crisis: Maintenance of integration in families with a severely retarded child. *Mono-*

graphs of the Society for Research in Child Development, 25,
1–95.

Gargiulo, R. M. (1984). Understanding family dynamics. In R. M.
Gargiulo (Ed.), *Working with parents of exceptional children*
(pp. 41–64). Boston: Houghton Mifflin.

Grossman, F. K. (1972). *Brothers and sisters of retarded children:
An exploratory study* Syracuse, NY: Syracuse University Press.

Murphy, A. T. (1979). Members of the family: Sisters and brothers
of the handicapped. *Volta Review, 81,* 352–354.

Powell, T. H., & Ogle, P. A. (1985). *Brothers and sisters in the family system.* Baltimore, MD: Brookes.

Schwirian, P. M. (1976). Effects of the presence of a hearing impaired pre-school child in the family on behavior patterns of
older "normal" siblings. *American Annals of the Deaf, 121,*
373–380.

Trevino, F. (1979). Siblings of handicapped children: Identifying
those at risk. *Social Casework: Journal of Contemporary Social Work, 62,* 488–493.

MARSHA H. LUPI
Hunter College

FAMILY RESPONSE TO HANDICAP
RESPITE CARE

SICARD, ABBÉ ROCHE AMBROISE CUCURRON (1742–1822)

Abbé Roche Ambroise Cucurron Sicard, educator of the
deaf, studied with Abbé Epée at the National Institution
for Deaf-Mutes in Paris and, in 1782, opened a school for
the deaf at Bordeaux. Sicard succeeded Epée at the National Institution and, except for a few years during the
French Revolution, served as its director until his death in
1822. Sicard made many improvements in Epée's educational methods. His most important publication was a dictionary of signs, a work begun by Epée.

The beginning of education for the deaf in the United
States was greatly influenced by Sicard. He invited
Thomas Gallaudet, who was planning the first school for
the deaf in the United States, to observe the methods employed at the National Institute in Paris, with the result
that Gallaudet became proficient in Sicard's methods. In
addition, Sicard provided Gallaudet with his first teacher,
Laurent Clerc.

REEFERENCES

Bender, R. E. (1970). *The conquest of deafness.* Cleveland, OH:
Case Western Reserve University Press.

Lane, H. (1984). *When the mind hears.* New York: Random House.

PAUL IRVINE
Katonah, New York

SICKLE-CELL DISEASE

Sickle-cell disease is an inherited blood disorder that occurs as two conditions, sickle-cell anemia (SCA) and sickle-
cell trait (SCT). Sickle-cell anemia is the more serious
of the two conditions; it can be defined as an abnormality
of the hemoglobin molecule, the oxygen-carrying protein in
the red blood cells. Oxygen-carrying red blood cells are
usually round and flexible. Under certain conditions, the
red blood cells of a person with sickle-cell anemia may
change into a crescent or sickle cell. This unusual shape
causes the cells to adhere in the spleen and other areas,
leading to their destruction. This results in a shortage of
red blood cells, which has serious consequences for the individual with SCA (Haslam & Valletutti, 1975; March of
Dimes, 1985). These consequences include fever, abdominal discomfort, bone pain, damage to the brain, lungs, and
kidneys, and, for some, death in childhood or early adulthood (Haslam & Valletutti, 1975; March of Dimes, 1985;
National Association for Sickle Cell Disease [NASCD],
(1978). Individuals with SCA will experience episodes of
pain known as sickle-cell crisis. During these periods, the
sickled cells become trapped in tiny blood vessels. This
blocks other red blood cells behind them, which lose oxygen
and become sickle-shaped, totally blocking the vessels.
When the bone marrow inadequately produces red blood
cells, the child experiences an aplastic crisis and requires
blood transfusion (Weiner, 1973). These crises and their effects vary greatly from person to person. Most people with
SCA enjoy reasonably good health much of the time (March
of Dimes, 1985; NASCD, 1978).

Sickle-cell anemia occurs when a sickle-cell gene is inherited from each parent. A person with sickle-cell anemia
has sickle cells in the bloodstream and has sickle-cell disease. The second condition, sickle-cell trait (SCT), occurs
when a sickle-cell gene is inherited from one parent and a
normal gene from the other. A person with sickle-cell trait
does not have sickle cells in the bloodstream and does not
have sickle-cell disease. Persons with SCT may pass the
sickle-cell gene on to their offspring (March of Dimes,
1985; NASCD, 1978; Whitten, 1974). As an autosomal recessive disorder, children of parents who both carry the
sickle-cell gene have a 50% chance of inheriting SCT, a
25% chance of being a carrier, and a 25% chance of having
SCA (Whitten, 1974).

In the United States, sickle-cell disease occurs most frequently among blacks and Hispanics of Caribbean ancestry. About 1 in every 400 to 600 blacks and 1 in every 1000
to 1500 Hispanics inherit sickle-cell disease (March of
Dimes, 1985). Approximately 1 in 12 black Americans
carry a gene for sickle-cell trait (NASCD, 1978). Less commonly affected peoples include those whose ancestors lived
in countries bordering on the Mediterranean Sea (Greeks,
Maltese, Portuguese, Arabians; NASCD, 1978).

There is no known cure for sickle-cell anemia. However,

a number of new therapies for reducing the severity and frequency of crises are being tried (March of Dimes, 1985; Weiner, 1973). A blood test for sickle-cell anemia and its trait is readily available; it is called hemoglobin electrophoresis. There is also a prenatal test to determine whether the fetus will develop sickle anemia or be a carrier.

The child with SCA may need to be placed in an educational program that is geared to his or her physical capabilities. Services may assist the child and family in many areas such as adaptation to chronic illness and pain management (Conner-Warren, 1996). Since many individuals with SCA tire easily, children should be encouraged to participate in most school activities of other children their age with the understanding that they may rest more frequently. If communication between the child and family has been open and honest concerning SCA, then the child can develop healthy social attitudes and self-reliance (NASCD, 1978).

REFERENCES

Conner-Warren, R. L. (1996). Pain intensity and home pain management of children with sickle-cell disease. *Issues in Comprehensive Pediatric Nursing, 19*(3), 183–195.

Haslam, R. M. A. and Valletutti, P. J. (1975). *Medical problems in the classroom.* Baltimore, MD: University Park Press.

March of Dimes. (1985). *Genetics series: Sickle cell anemia.* White Plains, NY: Author.

National Association for Sickle Cell Disease. (1978). *Sickle cell disease: Tell the facts, quell the fables.* Los Angeles: Author.

Weiner, F. (1973). *Help for the handicapped child.* New York: McGraw-Hill.

Whitten, C. F. (1974). Fact sheet on sickle cell trait and anemia. Los Angeles: National Association for Sickle-Cell Disease.

MARSHA H. LUPI
Hunter College

GENETIC DISORDERS

SIDIS, WILLIAM JAMES (1898–1944)

William James Sidis was a famous child prodigy of the early twentieth century who came to a tragic end after leading a short, largely unfulfilled life. Sidis's history and early demise are often cited in early literature opposing acceleration and other aspects of special education for the intellectually gifted. Much of Sidis's life has been distorted in various informal accounts. Montour (1977) has characterized the use of Sidis's story deny acceleration to intellectually advanced children as the Sidis fallacy. Simply stated, the Sidis fallacy denotes "early ripe, early rot."

In 1909, at the age of 11, Sidis entered Harvard College. A year later he lectured on higher mathematics at the Harvard Mathematical Club. Sidis had performed remarkably in intellectual endeavors throughout his life. By Montour's (1977) account, by the age of 3 he read fluently with good comprehension; he was writing with a pencil 6 months later. By age 4, Sidis was a fluent typist. When he was 6, Sidis could read English, Russian, French, German, and Hebrew; he learned Latin and Greek shortly thereafter. At the age of 8, Sidis passed the entrance exam at the Massachusetts Institute of Technology, developed a new table of logarithms employing base 12 instead of base 10, and passed the Harvard Medical School exam in anatomy. He was well qualified to enter Harvard at that time but was denied entrance based on his age. Sidis earned his BA in 1914, although it has been reported that he completed his work for the degree 2 years earlier. Sidis pursued some graduate study in several fields, including a year in law school, but never earned an advanced degree. He spurned academia after an unsuccessful year as a professor at Rice University at age 20. He became sullen, cynical, and withdrawn from society (Montour, 1977). Sidis chose to live as a loner, working at low-level clerical jobs until his death in 1944, at the age of 46, from a stroke.

Sidis's academic contributions were limited to two books. In 1926 he published *Notes on the Collection of Transfers.* A more serious volume, published in 1925 (but written in 1919 and 1920), *The Animate and Inanimate,* was devoted to a proof of James's theory of reserve energy.

Sidis's turn against academia and his choice to drop out of society seems related to his intellectual talent and precocity only in the most indirect fashion; it was certainly not a result of his academic acceleration. Montour (1977) argues credibly that it was the result of a rebellion against an overbearing, domineering, but emotionally barren father who rejected Sidis at the first sign of any weakness. Although the Sidis's case is often cited in opposition to academic acceleration, there is little to support such a position on the basis of Sidis's history. In fact, far more cases of successful acceleration are present with outcomes strongly supportive of acceleration programs. Norbert Wiener (a classmate of Sidis), John Stuart Mill, Merrill Kenneth Wolf, David Noel Freedman, and John Raden Platt are but a few of many such successes (Montour, 1977). Indeed, educational acceleration will be the method of choice for the education of many intellectually precocious youths.

"It was not extreme educational acceleration that destroyed William James Sidis emotionally and mentally, but instead an interaction of paternal exploitation and emotional starvation" (Montour, 1977, p. 276). The events of Sidis's life are often exaggerated and misstated. The Sidis fallacy has restricted the education of the gifted and persists in some educational programs even today; it is yet another myth that afflicts programs for the gifted.

REFERENCES

Montour, K. (1977). William James Sidis, the broken twig. *American Psychologist, 32,* 265–279.

Sidis, W. J. (1925). *The animate and inanimate.* Boston: Badger.

Sidis, W. J. (1926). *Notes on the collection of transfer.* Philadelphia: Dorrance.

Cecil R. Reynolds
Texas A & M University

ACCELERATED PLACEMENT OF GIFTED CHILDREN STUDY OF MATHEMATICALLY PRECOCIOUS YOUTH

SIDIS FALLACY

See SIDIS, WILLIAM JAMES.

SIECUS

See SEX INFORMATION AND EDUCATION COUNCIL OF THE UNITED STATES.

SIGHT-SAVING CLASSES

For much of the present century it was common to educate children with low vision in "sight-saving classes". This was done in public schools as well as in residential facilities. Such classes for partially sighted children were begun in public schools as far back as 1913 (Livingston, R.).

The notion behind these sight-saving classes was that a low-vision child's residual vision would be damaged by overuse. The emphasis, thus, was on conserving the child's vision as far as possible. This meant that children whose vision was impaired but still usable were removed from presumably visually stressful situations by reducing visual demands made on them. Some were even educated in dark rooms or blindfolded. The situation today is dramatically altered. It is now believed that all children, including visually handicapped ones, benefit from using their visual abilities as much as possible.

REFERENCE

Livingston, R. (1986). Visual impairments. In N. G. Haring & L. McCormick (Eds.), *Exceptional children and youth* (4th ed., pp. 398–429). Columbus, OH: Merrill.

Mary Murray
Journal of Special Education

LOW VISION PARTIALLY SIGHTED

SIGN LANGUAGE

Sign language is a general term that refers to any gestural/visual language that makes use of specific shapes and movements of the fingers, hands, and arms, as well as movements of the eyes, face, head, and body. There is no international system that is comprehensible to all deaf people. There exists a British Sign Language, a Spanish Sign Language, an Israeli Sign Language, and probably a sign language in every country where deaf people have needed to communicate among themselves rapidly, efficiently, and visually without the use of pad and pencil.

American Sign Language, sometimes called Ameslan or ASL, was created over the years by the deaf community in the United States. In American Sign Language, one hand shape frequently denotes a concept. American Sign Language must be differentiated from finger spelling or dactylology, which is the use of hand configurations to denote the letters of the alphabet. In finger spelling, one hand shape stands for one letter. Sometimes finger spelling is used to spell out the English equivalent for a sign (especially proper nouns) when ASL is used. In ASL, interpreters frequently finger spell the word for a technical or uncommon sign the first time it is used during a conference. Finger spelling with speech and speech reading for additional acoustic and visual cues is called the Rochester method (Quigley & Paul, 1984).

Total communication is the use of signs, finger spelling, speech, speech reading, and, in reality, any and all modes of communication to ensure effective communication with hearing-impaired people. Although it is possible for ASL to be used as the manual component of total communication, the two terms are not synonymous.

Signed English, developed in the 1960s under the direction of Harry Bornstein of Gallaudet College, is a manually coded system of English used in conjunction with speech. It was devised to facilitate the acquisition of English by young deaf children. It incorporates special signs to indicate affixes (prefixes like un-, and suffixes like -s and -ment) and verb tense. Signed English is basically an educational tool used in some schools for deaf students. Its use of the specific tense and affix markers slows down the communication process considerably (Schlesinger & Namir, 1978).

Research into the linguistic nature of American Sign Language has shown that the grammar of ASL, like the grammar of all languages, consists of a finite set of rules with which an infinite number of sentences can be created or generated. Deaf children and hearing children of deaf parents who use ASL acquire these rules in much the same way that hearing children abstract linguistic rules from the spoken language to which they are exposed (Bellugi & Klima, 1985). Courses in sign language are offered in many colleges, schools for deaf students, centers for continuing education, and some public libraries. Courses in sign language for hearing learners may also enhance language acquisition because of the multimodal advantage (Daniels, 1994).

REFERENCES

Bellugi, U., & Klima, E. (1985). The acquisition of three morphological systems in American Sign Language. In F. Powell (Ed.), *Education of the hearing-impaired child*. San Diego, CA: College Hill.

Daniels, M. (1994). The effect of sign language on hearing children's language development. *Communication Education, 43*(4), 291–298.

Quigley, S., & Paul, P. (1984). *Language and deafness*. San Diego, CA: College Hill.

Schlesinger, I., & Namir, L. (1978). *Sign language of the deaf*. New York: Academic.

ROSEMARY GAFFNEY
Hunter College

**LIPREADING/SPEECHREADING
ROCHESTER METHOD
TOTAL COMMUNICATION**

SIMULTANEOUS PROCESSING

See SEQUENTIAL AND SIMULTANEOUS COGNITIVE PROCESSING.

SINGLE-SUBJECT RESEARCH DESIGN

Increasingly, researchers are recognizing the importance of single-case investigations for the development of a knowledge base in psychology and education. Single-case time series designs involve observations before, during, and after interventions in order to describe changes in selected dependent variables. The development of time-series methodology, especially single-subject design, has been advantageous for researchers for several reasons. First, single-case research designs provide an important knowledge base that is unobtainable through traditional large-N between-group designs in clinical research. Single-subject designs are uniquely suited to evaluation of treatments involving a single client, a characteristic that is important given that it often is impossible to conduct

group comparative outcome studies because of the limited number of subjects for a particular type of disorder or problem.

Another major advantage of single-case designs is that they provide an alternative to traditional large-N group designs about which various ethical and legal considerations are often raised (Hersen & Barlow, 1976). These concerns include the ethical objections of withholding treatment from clients in a no-treatment control group or randomly assigning clients to a particular treatment type.

Single-subject designs have been important in promoting the development of a measurement technology that can be used repeatedly throughout the intervention process. For example, various outcome measures such as direct observation, rating scales and checklists, self-monitoring, standardized tests, and psychophysiological recordings, can be used as ongoing measures of client functioning over the course of a research program. Such repeated measures taken over time allow for an analysis of individual variability as well as monitoring of potential response covariation within a single client. Perhaps the most important aspect of repeated measurement technology is its flexibility in the modification of treatment if the data indicate that this modification is necessary.

Single-case research strategies have also provided options for practitioners to be involved in research and evaluation of practice. There are differences of opinion, however, as to how feasible it is to implement well-controlled designs while providing clinical services. Carefully constructed single-case designs are usually difficult to implement (Kratochwill & Piersel, 1983). The use of a particular design may compromise the on-line clinical intuition of the therapist, yielding either a threat to internal validity of the evaluation or less appropriate treatment of the client. Finally, while clinicians may be concerned with the potential threats to being most responsive to patient needs, others may take the position that formal evaluation increases efficacy of the intervention itself (Barlow, Hayes, & Nelson, 1984). By implementing careful observation and measurement of behavior change, the therapist can measure type and degree of improvement and also know whether the treatment is responsible for change. The issues are readily subject to debate.

As single-subject strategies become more prevalent in the educational literature, it becomes important to discuss some design types. Three basic design types have been described in the literature (Barlow et al., 1984); they include within-, between-, and continued-series strategies.

In within-series designs, changes observed within a series of data points across time on a single measure or set of measures are analyzed. Each data point is analyzed in the context of those that immediately precede and follow it. Each consistent condition constitutes a phase in the series. Phases also are evaluated in the context of phases that precede and follow them. The researcher establishes internal validity in within-series designs by replicating effects of the independent variable across the phases.

One type of within-series design is the withdrawal procedure, that is used to assess whether responses are maintained under different conditions rather than to demonstrate the initial effects of an intervention in altering behavior (Kazdin, 1982). Typically, an A-B-A-B paradigm is used in which the intervention is introduced following a baseline, withdrawn for a phase, and then reintroduced. The withdrawal design seems best suited for evaluating the controlling effects of a reversible procedure, that is defined as one that would not produce a permanent change in the dependent variable. Withdrawal of the procedure would result in a return to baseline measures.

An example of the A-B-A-B withdrawal design is offered by Powers and Crowel (1985). They studied the effectiveness of a positive practice overcorrection procedure to decrease stereotypic vocal behavior produced by an 8-year-old autistic male. A baseline level of the child's percent of 10-second intervals of stereotypic vocalizations was obtained over 9 days. Treatment was then introduced and implemented for 7 days, withdrawn for 17 days, and reimplemented for 7 more days. Figure 1 illustrates the effects of the positive practice overcorrection procedure on the stereotypic vocalizations produced by the subject. During the initial baseline, the vocalizations averaged about 69%. During treatment, the percent of intervals of stereotypic vocalizations decreased to an average of about 17%. Withdrawal of the treatment resulted in a return to initial baseline levels of vocalizations, while reintroduction of the treatment resulted in another decrease in average levels of the stereotypic behavior.

Since the A-B-A-B design is generally not appropriate for irreversible procedures (Hersen & Barlow, 1976), there are a number of considerations regarding its use. First, ethical decisions need to be made regarding withdrawal of treatment in any therapy program. Complicated decisions need to be made regarding the relative importance and overall advantages of obtaining reliable data about treatment efficacy as against withdrawing treatment from the client. Second, practical limitations may prevent one's choice of an A-B-A-B design. Often there is not enough time to institute two or more withdrawal phases. A third issue pertains to one's philosophy of intervention. In remediation of certain disorders, it might be argued that the client will not reverse to previous states once an intervention is introduced.

The withdrawal design might also be implemented in evaluating components of a treatment package. Specific aspects of a particular approach may be investigated by manipulating one variable at a time between adjacent phases in a withdrawal design. This type of strategy has been described in detail by several authors in their discussions of interaction designs (Barlow et al., 1984; Kratochwill, 1978; McReynolds & Kearns, 1983). Interaction designs examine the interactions of two or more variables over time in a basic within-series procedure. The purpose is to evaluate additive, subtractive, and interactive effects of individual components of a treatment.

If the researcher is interested in the effect of two independent variables but without evaluation of the individual contributions of B and C, the design would follow the classic A-B-A design, but it would specify the existence of the two variables. The design would be represented as A-BC-A-BC. However, if the investigator is interested in the relative contribution of B and C, and the interactive effects of

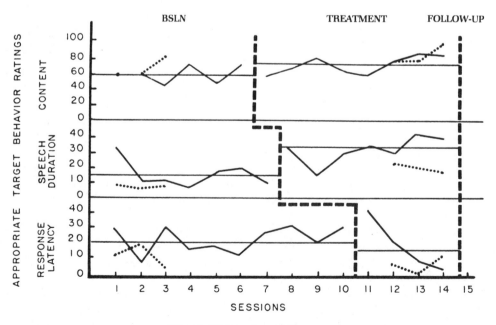

Figure 1. BSLN treatment follow-up.

both, each variable must be evaluated alone and in conjunction with the other. The design may be represented as A-B-BC-B-BC. In this format, the effect of B alone is tested as well as the effect of BC together.

It should be noted that only one variable is manipulated at a time and each variable to be evaluated must be adjacent to the rest. Unless the components are in adjacent phases (e.g., B-BC-B) the investigator cannot determine the effects of either component alone. For example, if one used an A-B-BC-A-B design, comparison of the behavior in B with the behavior in BC is confounded because of the intervening A phase. An A-B-A-B-BC design is often mistakenly interpreted as revealing interactive and relative effects. The final two phases (B-BC) form an uncontrolled A-B design and, therefore, are descriptive rather than experimental.

The interaction design may be time consuming since all the phases need to be completed. Also, there is a threat of sequence effects as one phase follows another. To control for order effects, the researcher would need to increase the number of subjects and implement counterbalancing and replication.

Other variations of the withdrawal design may be applicable. Maintenance of a behavior may be studied following a successful treatment package. A sequential withdrawal design might be implemented in which different components of the treatment package are gradually withdrawn while observations are made to see whether the behavior is maintained. A partial withdrawal design is another strategy that is used to evaluate maintenance. It consists of withdrawing a component of the treatment package from one of several different baselines, or from one of several subjects. This design would be readily applicable to many situations where one is interested in whether target behaviors measured during treatment are likely to be maintained if the treatment package or components are withdrawn.

Another within-series procedure is the changing criterion design. This design can be used to evaluate the effects of treatment on a single gradually acquired behavior. It is appropriate for studying the effectiveness of shaping behavior. The effect of the intervention is demonstrated by showing that behavior changes gradually over the course of treatment. Rather than withdrawing or withholding treatment, the design uses several subphases within the intervention phase. In each subphase a different criterion for performance is specified. When performance meets the criterion, more stringent criteria are set. This is done repeatedly over the course of the design.

During the baseline phase a single behavior is monitored until a stable response rate is achieved. Baseline data are used to establish an initial criterion level and treatment is initiated and continued until the target behavior stabilizes at that level. Both reinforcement schedules and criterion levels are then increased. The remainder of the phase progresses in a steplike manner, with each criterion adjustment more closely approximating a terminal level.

Many aspects and variations of the design are important in its use, including phase length, number and magnitude of criterion shifts, directionality of change, and potential data ambiguity. This design is most appropriate for behaviors acquired gradually; it does not require withdrawal or reversal of treatment. Only one behavior is selected for treatment, allowing inferences to be made about the efficacy of the treatment for that specific behavior. Possible confounding because of order effects and counterbalancing is also avoided in this design. This design ishwell suited for examining generalization across settings, subjects, and time.

Between-series designs allow comparisons of two or more treatments or conditions in order to examine relative effectiveness on a given behavior. There are two basic types of between-series designs: the alternating treatment design and the simultaneous treatment design (Barlow, Hayes & Nelson, 1984). The alternating treatment design involves the rapid alternation of two or more conditions. It exposes the subject to the separate treatment components for equal periods of time. The treatment may be alternated from one session to another or across two sessions each day, with sequence being determined randomly or through counterbalancing. Differences between the two treatments are examined rather than any differences over time within one condition. For example, an alternating treatment design was used to study the effects of teacher-directed versus student-directed instruction and cues versus no cues for improving spelling performance (Gettinger, 1985). Nine children received four alternating experimental treatments during a 16-week spelling program. The two cuing procedures (cues vs. no cues) were alternated weekly while the student-directed and teacher-directed components were alternated biweekly. Mean pretest, posttest, and retention scores were obtained for each treatment condition; they indicated improved spelling accuracy for all four conditions. The data also demonstrated that a student-directed procedure incorporating visual and verbal cues produces the highest posttest accuracy scores.

The simultaneous treatment design differs from the alternating treatment design in that the treatments (or conditions) are available simultaneously. The purpose of the design is to measure subject "preference" rather than the treatment efficacy (Barlow et al., 1984). For example, a simultaneous treatment design might be employed to determine which type of reinforcement is most preferred by a client. That particular reinforcement could then be incorporated into a remediation program.

Potential problems exist for the use of these designs in some areas of research. The interactive effects of two treatments or conditions would be difficult to ascertain, especially in patients exhibiting cognitive or language deficits.

Carryover or generalization effects of one intervention may confound inferences that might be made with regard to the other treatment or condition. Both alternating treatment and simultaneous treatment designs depend on showing changes for a given behavior across sessions or time periods. The need for behavior to shift rapidly dictates both the type of interventions and the behaviors that can be studied in multiple treatment designs. Interventions suitable for these designs may need to show rapid effects initially and to have little or no carryover effects when terminated. If the effects of the first intervention linger after it is no longer presented, the intervention that follows would be confounded by the previous one.

In addition to alternating and simultaneous treatment designs, one other strategy has been employed when withdrawal and reversal designs are not feasible. These are multiple baseline designs that combine within and between series strategies with regard to inference.

The methodology for multiple baseline designs is relatively straightforward. Baseline data are collected on two or more units (e.g. subjects, settings, behaviors, or time). After performance is stable for all the units, treatment is applied to the first; measurements continue to be taken across all. The researcher's expectation is that changes will be seen quickly in the treated unit while the others remain stable at baseline levels. After performance again stabilizes across all the units, the treatment is applied to the second and continued on the first. Data continue to be taken across all units. This process is repeated until all units have been treated. The effect of the intervention is evaluated on whether the series remains stable at baseline levels until treatment, at which time a change is seen. Each time an intervention is introduced, a test is made between the level of performance during the intervention and the projected level of the previous baselines. A unique feature of this design is the testing of predictions across different units; these units serve as control conditions to evaluate what changes can be expected without the application of the treatment.

An example of the use of a multiple baseline design is offered in Figure 2, that illustrates the results of a study designed to test the effectiveness of social skills training for improving the social behaviors of a 17-year-old deaf female (Lemanek & Gresham, 1984). A multiple baseline design across behaviors was used to examine the effect of treatment on three dependent variables (duration of communications, response latency, and content).

Figure 2 illustrates the baseline measures across all three dependent variables, with treatment initiated on the first behavior (content) at session seven. Baseline measures continued to be taken on the second and third behaviors (speech duration and response latency). Treatment was then initiated on the second behavior, and at session 11, on the third behavior. Visual inspection of the data indicates a slight improvement in appropriate content during treatment. Speech duration increased significantly from baseline to treatment. Decreases in response latency occurred from baseline throughout treatment and follow-up.

Several variations of the multiple baseline design are often used, applying the strategy across subjects, or across situations, settings, and time (Kazdin, 1982). In the variation across subjects, baseline data are gathered for a specific behavior across two or more subjects. A selected treatment is then applied in sequence across the matched subjects, just as in the multiple baseline across behaviors.

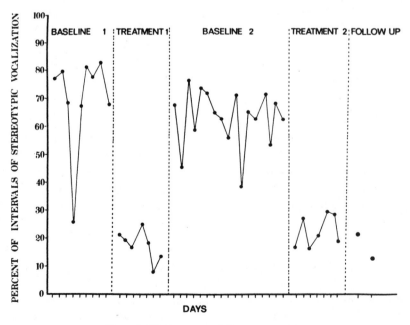

Figure 2. BSLN treatment follow-up 1 and 2.

Preferably, the subjects are exposed to identical environmental conditions. In the variation across settings, a treatment variable is applied sequentially to the same behavior in the same subject across different and independent settings. The same procedures apply for introducing the treatment after the stabilization of behavior across each setting for each baseline.

Many issues that are important to the implementation of this design are beyond the scope of this presentation. However, among the more salient are that at least two baselines should be used and that more are preferable. Issues such as length of phase and counterbalancing are important in these designs as well, and should be taken into account. It also should be noted that the use of this design across subjects or behaviors could result in withholding treatment from a particular subject for a longer period of time than might be judged clinically appropriate.

In multiple baseline designs across behaviors, the assumption is that the targeted behaviors are independent from one another. In some disorders, it is reasonable to assume that targeted behaviors may covary. As a result, the controlling effects of the treatment variables are subject to question.

A particular problem with implementing many single-case time-series designs in applied settings is the amount of time required for appropriate baseline measures. Often the subject cannot handle a long treatment session, or is frustrated by repeated attempts at a difficult treatment. A balance must be reached between the amount of data needed to demonstrate experimental control and the practical aspects of working with the client. One design that has been offered to alleviate this problem is the multiple-probe design. This design is a combination of multiple baseline design and probe procedures.

A probe is defined as an intermittent assessment of selected target behaviors under nontreatment conditions. The nature of the probes depends on behaviors being investigated and practical considerations. There are three primary features of the multiple-probe design. First, there is an initial probe of every step in a chain or successive approximation. Second, a probe is conducted on each step in the treatment sequence after criterion is achieved on any one step. Third, a series of probes or real baselines are conducted immediately before the initiation of treatment on any given step in the sequence. Only probes following the completion of all prerequisite steps and immediately before intervention are considered a true measure of the subject's ability to perform a given step.

Experimental control can be shown despite less baseline data as long as the pretreated probe and true baseline data are stable and a consistent change with introduction of treatment is shown. Graphic representation of the data would resemble that of multiple baseline studies. Probes and true baselines along the abscissa can be examined to determine whether the behavior remained stable until intervention was initiated at each step in the training sequence.

In the multiple-probe design, similar but independent behavior must be chosen to maintain experimental control, as the design is not appropriate for studying steps that are truly interdependent. The multiple-probe design avoids problems of extinction, fatigue, and distraction that can occur as a result of continuous baseline testing. The design is a potentially efficient means of evaluating the effects of training on sequential steps in a treatment program for behaviors that are not totally interdependent.

Time-series designs, especially single-subject investigations, are increasingly recognized as important methodologies for the evaluation of the efficacy of treatment. Within-, between-, and combined-series designs each provide internally valid methods for answering questions regarding the effects of a particular treatment, or the relative effects of different treatments or conditions. The use of single-subject time-series designs offers the educational researcher a valid way of answering questions about the nature of the intervention offered clients.

REFERENCES

Barlow, D. H., Hayes, S. C., & Nelson, R. O. (1984). *The scientist practitioner: Research and accountability in clinical and educational settings*. New York: Pergamon.

Gettinger, M. (1985). Effects of teacher-directed versus student-directed instruction and cues versus no cues for improving spelling performance. *Journal of Applied Behavior Analysis, 18*, 167–171.

Hersen, N., & Barlow, D. H. (1976). *Single case experimental designs: Strategies for studying behavior change*. New York: Pergamon.

Kazdin, A. E. (1982). *Single-case research designs: Methods for clinical and applied settings*. New York: Oxford University Press.

Kratochwill, T. R. (Ed.) (1978). *Single-subject research: strategies for evaluating change*. New York: Academic.

Kratochwill, T. R., & Piersel, W. C. (1983). Time-series research: Contributions to empirical clinical practice. *Behavioral Assessment, 5*, 165–176.

Lemanek, K. L., & Gresham, P. M. (1984). Social skills training with a deaf adolescent. Implications for placement and programming. *School Psychology Review, 13*, 385–490.

McReynolds, L., & Kearns, K. (1983). *Single subject experimental designs in communicative disorders*. Baltimore, MD: University Park Press.

Powers, M. D., & Crowel, R. L. (1985). The educative effects of positive practice overcorrection: Acquisition, generalization, and maintenance. *School Psychology Review, 14*, 360–372.

EDYTHE A. STRAND
THOMAS R. KRATOCHWILL
*University of Wisconsin at
Madison*

APPLIED BEHAVIOR ANALYSIS
RESEARCH IN SPECIAL EDUCATION

SINGLETON-MERTON SYNDROME

Singleton-Merton syndrome is a rare disorder of unknown etiology. The primary features of this syndrome include aortic calcification, dental abnormalities, and osteoporosis. Children with Singleton-Merton syndrome have abnormal accumulations of calcium deposits in their aorta, the major artery in the human body, and valves of their heart. Progressive calcification of the aorta and heart valves is life-threatening, as heart block or heart failure may result. In contrast, progressive loss of protein of the bones, resulting in osteoporosis, occurs in individuals with this disorder. Dental abnormalities in the form of poorly developed teeth and/or premature loss of primary teeth are seen in children with this syndrome as well (National Organization for Rare Disorders [NORD], 1997).

Other features of the disorder include generalized muscular weakness and hip and foot abnormalities. Motor delays are not uncommon. These children tend to be relatively short in stature due to growth retardation. Skin lesions, especially on their fingers, are also common among these children (Gay & Kuhn, 1976; NORD, 1997).

Physical therapy and occupational therapy may help motor development and increase muscle strength. Children may receive these support services through the school based on an Other Health Impaired diagnosis.

REFERENCES

Gay, B. B., Jr., & Kuhn, J. P. (1976). A syndrome of widened medullary cavities of bone, aortic calcification, abnormal dentition, and muscular weakness (the Singleton-Merton syndrome). *Radiology, 118*(2), 389–395.

National Organization for Rare Disorders (NORD). (1997). Singleton-Merton syndrome. New Fairfield, CT: National Organization for Rare Disorders, Inc.

PATRICIA A. LOW
Texas A & M University

JOAN W. MAYFIELD
*Baylor Pediatric Specialty
Services*

SIX-HOUR RETARDED CHILD

The term 6-hour retardate first appeared in the report of the Conference on Problems of Education of Children in the Inner City (President's Committee on Mental Retarda-

tion, 1969). The conference was charged with developing a new set of recommendations regarding the problems of mentally retarded children living within the ghettos of U.S. cities. After reviewing the papers of the 92 participants, 7 major recommendations were developed: (1) provide early childhood stimulation education as part of the public education program; (2) conduct a study of histories of successful inner-city families who have learned to cope effectively; (3) restructure education of teachers, administrators, and counselors; (4) reexamine present systems of intelligence testing and classification; (5) commit substantial additional funding for research and development in educational improvement for the disadvantaged; (6) delineate what constitutes accountability and hold the school accountable for providing quality education for all children; and (7) involve parents, citizens, citizen groups, students, and general and special educators in a total educational effort. However, one outcome overshadowed all of these recommendations. It was the conclusion that "we now have what may be called a 6-hour retarded child—retarded from 9 to 3, 5 days a week, solely on the basis of an IQ, without regard to his adaptive behavior, which may be exceptionally adaptive to the situation and community in which he lives."

The concept of the 6-hour retarded child survived into the mid 1980s. Today many psychologists and educators have accepted as a given that children identified as mildly retarded during the school-age years manifest retarded functioning only in the school setting, and that outside of school, during childhood and in their work lives as adults, they function successfully. Often their retardation is invisible to their employers, families, neighbors, and friends.

The conclusion of the conference participants was not inconsistent with case studies and some published reports of the adult lives of the mildly retarded. Although observations of the mildly retarded as children led many to believe that as adults they would fail in community adaptation, many investigators observed a high proportion of the adult retarded who achieved satisfactory adjustment, even when a variety of criteria were used.

The results of these early conclusions were confounded by subsequent reports showing that success in adult adaptation was equivocal, at best. The challenge of a more definitive portrayal of the adult lives of the mildly retarded was undertaken by the Socio-Behavioral Research Group at UCLA, who produced several informative studies of mildly retarded children as adults. Edgerton (1984) and Koegel and Edgerton (1984) used a holistic natural approach rather than measures of discrete adult outcomes. They conducted extensive ethnographic participant research studies of several aspects of the adult behavior of individuals who had been mildly retarded as children.

One of their studies centered on the functioning of blacks who had been classified as educable mentally retarded (EMR) as children, an adult sample of those who were the object of concern in the 1969 Conference on Problems of Education of Children of the Inner City. They identified 45 residents in a black community who had attended EMR classes and who represented the broad range of competencies and lifestyles found among mildly retarded adults in the black community. The 12 subjects who were selected for their study satisfied one criterion: field researchers, during the course of their first visits, expressed serious doubt that they were, in fact, retarded. These 12 individuals, when compared with the remainder of the sample, clearly led more normal lives. They had mean IQ scores of 62, 33% were married, and 42% were competitively employed. For 1 year a staff of black ethnographic field researchers maintained regular contact with the 12 participants, visiting them for 1 to 4 hours a day on an average of 12 separate occasions. The visits took place in homes, at work sites, and schools, during leisure activities, shopping expeditions, and job searches. Both parents and subjects were interviewed regarding any limitations they perceived, as well as their experiences in various aspects of their adult lives.

Although the adult lives of the participants were varied, none of them had "disappeared" into his or her community as a normal person. All 12 were seen by others close to them as limited or handicapped and most of the 12 participants acknowledged their own limitations. The participants continued to be troubled by the same problems that characterized them during their formal schooling—problems with reading, numerical concepts, and everyday tasks such as shopping, applying for jobs, travelling around the city, eating out in restaurants, making ends meet, etc.

Their problems transcended those associated with academic or intellectual pursuits. Their case histories included difficulties arising from poor judgment, vulnerability to exploitation and victimization, need for help in rearing their children, and an inability to comprehend satisfactorily their everyday experiences.

This study and several others of the adult lives of mildly retarded adults raise serious doubts regarding the efficacy and use of the concept of the 6-hour retarded child. The lives of these participants sometimes paralleled those of the nonretarded in the community, but never completely. Even though they were no longer receiving services as adults, they continued to face the same kinds of problems they did as children.

The contrast between the expectancies of the conference participants in 1969 and some of the recent studies such as the work by Edgerton et al. suggests that regular and special education programs should attend to preparing children with limited potential for the roles they will engage in as adults. Moreover, no one concerned about the future of the mildly retarded pupil can be content in the belief that their problems exist only in school, and that outside of this setting they function as capably as their age mates.

REFERENCES

Edgerton, R. B. (Ed.). (1984). *Lives in process: Mildly retarded adults in a large city.* Washington, DC: American Association on Mental Deficiency.

Koegel, P., & Edgerton, R. B. (1984). Black "six hour retarded" children as young adults. In R. B. Edgerton (Ed.), *Lives in process: Mildly retarded adults in a large city.* Washington, DC: American Association on Mental Deficiency.

President's Committee on Mental Retardation. (1969). *The six hour retarded child.* Washington, DC: Bureau of Education for the Handicapped, Office of Education, U.S. Department of Health, Education, and Welfare.

NADINE M. LAMBERT
University of California

EDUCABLE MENTALLY RETARDED
MENTAL RETARDATION

SKEELS, HAROLD M. (1901–1970)

Harold M. Skeels, pioneer researcher in the field of mental retardation, was responsible for a large number of studies of institutional populations during the 1930s and early 1940s. These studies showed that children placed in unstimulating institutional environments failed to develop normally, and that the longer they remained, the greater their deficits became. Skeels reached the conclusion that it is possible to improve intellectual functioning through early stimulation, and he advocated early adoption as an alternative to institutionalization. His findings set off a nature-nurture controversy, and Skeels and his associates were the targets of vehement attacks.

Following service in the armed forces during World War II, and subsequent employment with the U.S. Public

Harold M. Skeels

Health Service and the National Institute of Mental Health, Skeels made a follow-up study of some of the subjects of his earlier research. The results showed dramatically the long-term effects of differences in childhood environments. By the time his report was published, many of Skeels's concepts from the 1930s had become commonplace: adoption at an early age had become routine, institutional placements were decreasing, and a variety of early childhood services had been developed, including some programs, like Head Start, aimed specifically at early stimulation of disadvantaged and handicapped children.

REFERENCES

Crissey, M. S. (1970). Harold Manville Skeels. *American Journal of Mental Deficiency, 75,* 1–3.

Skeels, H. M. (1966). Adult status of children with contrasting early life experiences. *Monograph of the Society for Research in Child Development, 33,* 1–65.

Skeels, H. M., & Dye, H. B. (1939). A study of the effects of differential stimulation. *Proceedings of the American Association on Mental Deficiency, 44,* 114–136.

Paul Irvine
Katona, New York

HEAD START
NATURE VERSUS NURTURE

SKILL TRAINING

The skill training model rests on the premise that assessment of a student's performance should focus on classroom tasks. Such assessment is usually tied to some hierarchy of skills. Instruction, then, follows directly from the results of the hierarchical assessment, and often uses direct instruction skills (Mercer, 1983).

Skill training is a commonly used approach in special education. It provides the teacher with an opportunity to evaluate specific skills, skills that are of immediate and direct concern to classroom instruction. The skill training process usually begins with the administration of a criterion-referenced or teacher-made assessment device. The analysis of the results of the assessment provides the teacher with additional information that is specifically related to classroom interventions. That is, the analysis, focusing on a hierarchy of skills, helps to pinpoint the specific error the student is making, allowing a more precise instructional decision to be made. This instructional decision will usually result in the teacher using some direct instructional technique, concentrating the teaching efforts on a specific academic skill (Gable & Warren, 1993). Pupil progress is continuously measured to ensure that instruc-

tion continues to focus on appropriate skills. On mastery of one skill, the teacher and student progress to the next hierarchical skill.

REFERENCES

Gable, R. A., & Warren, S. F. (Eds.). (1993). *Strategies for teaching students with mild to severe mental retardation.* Baltimore, MD: Brookes.

Mercer, C. D. (1983). *Students with learning disabilities* (2nd ed.). Columbus, OH: Merrill.

John R. Beattie
University of North Carolina at Charlotte

MASTERY LEARNING

SKINNER, BURRHUS FREDERICK (1904–1990)

B. F. Skinner was born in northeastern Pennsylvania in 1904. He continued to write and work until his death on August 18, 1990. Skinner studied English and classics at Hamilton College where he received his AB (1926) in literature. After his aspirations of becoming a writer were discouraged, he entered the graduate program in psychology at Harvard, earning his MA in 1930 and his PhD under E. G. Boring in 1931. Regarded as a classic, his dissertation reflected his theory that a reflex arc, a then widely-debated concept, was nothing more than the relationship between a stimulus and a response. He argued that all be-

Burrhus Frederick Skinner

havior, in fact, could be explained by looking at the stimuli that result in its occurrence. These themes were the root of his theoretical orientation throughout his distinguished and remarkable career.

Skinner completed several post-doctoral fellowships after leaving graduate school, subsequently accepting the position of assistant professor at the University of Minnesota (1936–1945). He was a Junior Fellow in the Society of Fellows of Harvard University from 1933 to 1936. After spending a short time at Indiana University as chairman of the department psychology (1945–1947), he returned to Harvard as William James Lecturer, where he remained as professor and ultimately, professor emeritus of psychology until his death in 1990.

Skinner is considered by many to be the most important figure in 20th century psychology. In the field of education, he is perhaps best known for the development of programmed instruction and teaching machines as well as his behavior modification techniques. These areas allow the special educator to analyze and develop a systematic and situation-specific plan of instruction for learning or behavior. He denounced theoretical explanations of psychology, viewing the discipline as scientific and empirically driven, concerned with the observation of behaviors and the stimuli that bring them about. This Radical Behaviorism, as it has been termed, involves strict adherence to behavioral principles.

Skinner's concept of behaviorism, known as operant conditioning, as well as the results of numerous experiments, were outlined in his first major publication, *The Behavior of Organisms* (1938). The term *operant* refers to the identification of behavior which is traceable to reinforcing contingencies rather then to eliciting stimuli. Skinner believed speculation about what intervenes between stimulus and response or between response and reward to be superfluous.

The idea of creating a utopian community using his principles of conditioning, controlling all aspects of life using positive reinforcement, continued to interest him throughout his life. The notion of this ideal community was delineated in his 1948 novel, *Walden Two*. Another of his major books, *Science and Human Behavior* (1952), dealt with the application of behavioral principles to real-life situations including social issues, law, education, and psychotherapy. In this work, he postulated that the human organism is a machine like any other, thus behaving in lawful, predictable ways in response to external stimuli.

His notorious *Verbal Behavior* was published in 1957. This analysis of human language behavior was roundly criticized, most notably by linguist Noam Chomsky in a devastating review published in 1959. It is generally believed that neither Skinner nor his advocates ever responded successfully to the criticisms raised in this review, often noted as the beginning of the decline in influence of behavioral psychology.

Skinner advanced behaviorism by distinguishing between two types of behavior, respondent and operant, and showing how varying contingencies of reinforcement can be employed to modify or control any type of behavior. Controversy was raised once again by his publication of *Beyond Freedom and Dignity,* a 1971 book in which he dealt with the application of these principles. In this book, he interprets concepts of freedom, value, and dignity in objective terms, suggesting a society designed by shaping and controlling the behavior of citizens with a planned system of rewards (reinforcements). Among his numerous publications, *The Technology of Teaching* (1968) and his autobiographical trilogy (the last part, *A Matter of Consequence,* published in 1983) are of particular interest.

Skinner's contributions to psychology were recognized in 1958 by the American Psychological Association's (APA) Distinguished Scientific Award and again, just before his death, with a Lifetime Achievement Award. Other honors include the National Medal of Science (1968), the gold medal from the APA (1971), and his portrayal on the cover of *Time* magazine (1971).

In later years, Skinner extended his studies to psychotic behavior, instructional devices, and the analysis of cultures. Despite the criticisms and his unwavering position on a broad range of issues, his significant influence and impact on contemporary psychology assures him a place in its history.

REFERENCES

Skinner, B. F. (1938). *The behavior of organisms: An experimental analysis.* New York: Appleton-Century.

Skinner, B. F. (1948). *Walden two.* New York: Macmillan.

Skinner, B. F. (1953). *Science and human behavior.* New York: Macmillan.

Skinner, B. F. (1957). *Verbal behavior.* New York: Appleton-Century-Crofts.

Skinner, B. F. (1968). *The technology of teaching.* New York: Appleton-Century-Crofts.

Skinner, B. F. (1971). *Beyond freedom and dignity.* New York: Bantam.

Skinner, B. F. (1984). *A matter of consequences.* Washington Square, NY: New York University.

ELAINE FLETCHER-JANZEN
University of Northern Colorado
First edition

TAMARA J. MARTIN
The University of Texas of the Permian
Second edition

BEHAVIOR MODIFICATION
OPERANT CONDITIONING

SKINNER'S FUNCTIONAL LEARNING MODEL

B. F. Skinner's functional learning model, known as operant conditioning, describes the relationship between behavior and the environmental events that influence it. The basic principles of operant conditioning include reinforcement, punishment, extinction, and stimulus control. These principles describe the functionality of events that precede or follow behavior. Reinforcement, for example, serves the function of increasing the strength of behavior. Skinner (1953) described two types of reinforcement. Positive reinforcement refers to the presentation of an event, commonly called a reward, following behavior. For example, a teacher smiles and says, "Good work" following completion of a child's assignment. Negative reinforcement refers to the removal of an event presumed to be unpleasant following behavior. For example, a child's aggressive behavior may cause a teacher to remove an unpleasant request. In both cases, the effect of reinforcement is the same—the child is more likely to engage in that behavior (assignment completion or aggressive behavior) under similar conditions in the future.

The application of operant conditioning to special education involves the arrangement of contingencies of reinforcement to ensure effective learning. Skinner (1968) noted that although students obviously learn outside the classroom without such systematic procedures, "teachers arrange special contingencies which expedite learning, hastening the appearance of behavior which would otherwise be acquired slowly or making sure of the appearance of behavior which might otherwise never occur" (p. 65). Operant techniques have been applied in classrooms more than in any other setting and have been extremely successful in improving a variety of academic and social behaviors in diverse student populations (Kazdin, 1978).

REFERENCES

Kazdin, A. E. (1978). *History of behavior modification: Experimental foundations of contemporary research.* Baltimore, MD: University Park Press.

Skinner, B. F. (1953). *Science and human behavior.* New York: Free Press.

Skinner, B. F. (1968). *The technology of teaching.* Englewood Cliffs, NJ: Prentice-Hall.

CHRISTINE L. COLE
University of Wisconsin at Madison

BEHAVIOR MODIFICATION
CONDITIONING
OPERANT CONDITIONING
SKINNER, B. F.

SLINGERLAND SCREENING TESTS

The Slingerland screening tests are comprised of four forms with designated grade levels (Form A, grades 1 and 2; Form B, grades 2 and 3; Form C, grades 3 and 4; Form D, grades 5 and 6) (Slingerland & Ansara, 1974; Slingerland, 1974). There are eight subtests for Forms A, B, and C that may be either group or individually administered. These subtests require the students to copy letters and words from a board, copy from a page, perform visual matching exercises by selecting a stimulus word from an array of distractor words with various letter reversals, copy words presented in flashcard fashion, write dictated words, and detect initial and final sounds. For children that exhibit difficulties with portions of the eight subtests, there are individually administered auditory tests designed to assess auditory perception and memory. The student is asked to repeat individual words and phrases, to complete sentences with a missing word, and to retell a story. With the exception of additional subtests assessing personal orientation, Form D is comparable to the other three forms of the test. As noted by Fujiki (1985) and Sean and Keough (1993), the purpose of the Slingerland is not to identify linguistically handicapped children, but to assess auditory, visual, and motor skills associated with learning to read and write.

Local norms are advocated to interpret the results of students' test performance. This recommendation is necessary because of the notable omission of adequate normative data. Also absent in the manuals is an adequate discussion of reliability, stability, or validity.

REFERENCES

Fujiki, M. (1985). Review of Slingerland Screening Tests for identifying children with specific language disabilities. In J. V. Mitchell (Ed.), *The ninth mental measurements yearbook* (Vol. 2, pp. 1398–1399). Lincoln, NE: University of Nebraska Press.

Sean, S., & Keough, B. (1993). Predicting reading performance using the Slingerland procedures. *Annals of Dyslexia, 43,* 78–79.

Slingerland, B. H. (1974). *Teacher's manual to accompany Slingerland Screening Tests for Identifying Children with Specific Language Disability-Revised Edition* (Form D). Cambridge, MA: Educators.

Slingerland, B. H., & Ansara, A. S. (1974). *Teacher's manual to accompany Slingerland Screening Tests for Identifying Children with Specific Language Disability-Revised Edition* (Forms A, B and C). Cambridge, MA: Educators.

JACK A. CUMMINGS
Indiana University

ASSESSMENT
BASIC ACHIEVEMENT SKILLS
LANGUAGE DISORDERS

SLOSSON INTELLIGENCE TEST (SIT)

First published in 1961 by Slosson Educational Publications, the Slosson Intelligence Test (SIT) is a highly verbal, brief screening measure of intelligence intended to approximate the lengthier Stanford-Binet Intelligence Scale. A second edition was published in 1981. The SIT is a popular screening measure used by many special educators. Unfortunately, its use for any purpose is largely unsupportable on psychometric grounds and its status as a brief screening test precludes use in placement decisions.

The 1981 norming sample was drawn entirely from the New England states, and no attempt was made to select children randomly or to otherwise mimic the general population with whom the test is intended to be used. Attempts were made to develop deviation IQs that are equated to Stanford-Binet (1972 norms) IQs. Even this effort was seriously flawed as many extrapolations were made as well as interpolations between extrapolations. Internal consistency reliability estimates are not reported and the few reliabilities given are likely inflated owing to collapsing across four and five age ranges.

With the publication of the Stanford-Binet Fourth Revision in 1985, any remaining justification for the use of the SIT is eliminated. Given the number of well-standardized, sophisticated, and psychometrically sound measures of intelligence now available, there are no longer any reasons for the use of poorly normed scales. Whenever a brief screening measure of intelligence is desired, the use of short forms of major scales such as the WISC-III and the K-ABC is best.

CECIL R. REYNOLDS
Texas A & M University

DEVIATION IQ
KAUFMAN ASSESSMENT BATTERY FOR CHILDREN
STANFORD-BINET INTELLIGENCE TEST
WECHSLER INTELLIGENCE SCALE FOR
    CHILDREN—THIRD EDITION

SLOW LEARNER

Historically, the slow learning child has been described in numerous ways. Ingram's (1960) book, the *Education of the Slow-Learning Child*, discussed the education of the educable mentally retarded child. Johnson (1963) noted that "slow learners compose the largest group of mentally retarded persons" (p. 9). Today, however, the term slow learner most accurately describes children and adolescents who learn or underachieve, in one or more academic areas, at a rate that is below average yet not at the level considered comparable to that of an educable mentally re-

tarded student. Intellectually, slow learners score most often between a 75 and a 90 IQ—between the borderline and low-average classifications of intelligence.

It is unusual to find the slow learner discussed in the standard special education textbook. Indeed, slow learners are not special education students. There is no individuals with disabilities education act (IDEA) label or definition of slow learner, and these students are not eligible for any monies or services associated with that law. When slow learners receive additional supportive services, it is typically in the regular classroom or in remedial classes that may be supported by federal title funds or programs. These remedial classes are not conceptualized as alternative educational programs; they are used to reinforce regular classroom curricula and learning. Some slow learners are inappropriately labeled learning disabled to maintain the enrollment (and funding) of some special education classrooms, or because they would otherwise fail in the regular classroom, despite not having special education needs.

There is no consensus on a diagnostic or descriptive profile that characterizes the slow learner. Indeed, there is very little contemporary research with samples specifically labeled as slow learners. Many slow learners are now described by their specific academic weaknesses; research and/or remedial programs are applied to these academic areas—not to the slow learner labels. Because of this shift in emphasis, earlier research describing slow learners as being from low socioeconomic and minority family backgrounds, academically and socially frustrated, and devalued by teachers and peers, and as having low self-concepts, do not apply (Cawley, Goodstein, & Burrow, 1972).

REFERENCES

Cawley, J. F., Goodstein, H. A., & Burrow, W. H. (1972). *The slow learner and the reading problem*. Springfield, IL: Thomas.

Ingram, C. P. (1960). *Education of the slow-learning child* (3rd ed.). New York: Ronald.

Johnson, G. O. (1963). *Education for slow learners*. Englewood Cliffs, NJ: Prentice-Hall.

HOWARD M. KNOFF
University of South Florida

CLASSIFICATION, SYSTEMS OF
EDUCABLE MENTALLY RETARDED

SMITH-LEMLI-OPITZ SYNDROME

Smith-Lemli-Opitz syndrome is a genetic disorder due to an autosomal recessive gene. A larger number of males are affected by the syndrome than females (Jones, 1988). Smith-Lemli-Opitz syndrome is characterized by facial, limb, and genital abnormalities. Children with Smith-Lemli-Opitz syndrome have small heads; long, narrow faces; slanted or low-set ears; heavy or thick upper eyelids; anteverted nostrils; and small jaws. Squinting of the eyes is also a common characteristic found among these children. These children tend to be short in stature as well. On the palms of their hands and soles of their feet, simian creases are present and webbing often appears between their toes (Jones, 1988; Thoene, 1992). Some children with Smith-Lemli-Opitz syndrome experience seizures, and have cardiac anomalies, abnormal EEGs, kidney defects, and cataracts (Jones, 1988).

There are two forms of Smith-Lemli-Opitz syndrome: types I and II. Type II, also known as Lowry-Miller-Maclean syndrome, is a more severe form of the disorder. Stillbirth is a common characteristic of the type II form. Those who do survive have a low birth weight and failure to thrive. A shrill cry, vomiting, and feeding problems are typical in early infancy.

Moderate to severe mental retardation is evident among these children (Thoene, 1992). Special education programs focusing on life-skill training would be beneficial.

REFERENCES

Jones, K. L. (Ed.). (1988). *Smith's recognizable patterns of human malformation* (4th ed.). Philadelphia, PA: W.B. Saunders.

Rudolph, A. M. (1991). *Rudolph's pediatrics-19th edition.* Norwalk, CT: Appleton & Lange.

Thoene, J. G. (Ed.). (1992). *Physician's guide to rare diseases.* Montvale, NJ: Dowden.

JOAN MAYFIELD
Baylor Pediatric Specialty Services

PATRICIA A. LOWE
Texas A & M University

RARE DISEASES

SNELLEN CHART

The Snellen chart is a measuring device used to determine an individual's central distance visual acuity. The chart contains eight rows of letters of the alphabet in graduated sizes. There is a version for young children and for people who cannot read that replaces the alphabet with the letter E in different orientations and sizes. The letter sizes on the chart correspond to the estimate of the ability of a typical person to read the material. It is constructed so that at a distance of 20 ft, a person reading the figures on the chart corresponding to what a normal eye sees at 20 ft is said to have 20/20 vision (Bryan & Bryan, 1979). A person with 20/20 vision and both eyes working in a coordinated fashion is considered to be normally sighted. When a person

sees at 20 ft what a normal person sees at 70 ft or 200 ft, that person has 20/70 or 20/200 vision. Individuals who have low vision or who are visually limited may be legally blind (visual acuity of 20/200 or less), or partially sighted (visual acuity between 20/70 and 20/200; DeMott, 1982).

The Snellen chart is widely used as a screening device for detecting eye problems because of the ease and speed with which it can be administered, its low cost, and its wide range of applicability. When compared with the Orthorater vision tester, Johnson and Caccamise (1983) found the Snellen chart to be an "acceptable, less expensive alternative" (p. 406). It can be used with young children as well as adults. However, because the Snellen measures only central visual acuity, it should be combined with other procedures in screening. The Snellen chart gives no indication of near-point or peripheral vision, convergence ability, fusion ability, or muscular imbalance.

Bryan and Bryan (1979) list three shortcomings of the Snellen chart:

1. It is not a good predictor of competence in visual processing of objects and tasks.

2. It does not tell how a child uses vision in terms of discriminating light or darkness, estimating size, or determining spatial location.

3. The results are not translatable into educational programs. Children with the same visual acuity may respond differently to school tasks, and, therefore, require different programming.

However, DeMott (1982) holds that the most important initial screening device for detecting eye problems is one that measures central visual acuity. Combining results from the Snellen chart with other screening measures is important for early diagnosis and remediation of eye problems.

REFERENCES

Bryan, J. H., & Bryan, L. H. (1979). *Exceptional Children.* Sherman Oaks, CA: Alfred.

Getman, G. N. (1985). A commentary on vision-training. *Journal of Learning Disabilities, 18*(9), 505–512.

DeMott, R. M. (1982). Visual impairments. In N. G. Haring (Ed.), *Exceptional children and youth.* Columbus, OH: Merrill.

Johnson, D. D., &,Caccamise, F. (1983). Hearing impaired students: Options for visual acuity screening. *American Annals of the Deaf, 128*(3), 402–406.

Kirk, S. A. (1962). *Educating exceptional children.* Boston: Houghton Mifflin.

NANCY J. KAUFMAN
University of Wisconsin at Stevens Point

VISUAL ACUITY
VISUALLY IMPAIRED

SOCIAL BEHAVIOR OF THE HANDICAPPED

Evidence from Lerner (1985) and Stephens, Hartman, and Lucas, (1983) has clearly documented that many exceptional children experience difficulty in the area of social skills. This difficulty could range from mild problems to severe disorders. Minskoff (1980) considers social perceptual difficulties as among the more serious problems of learning-disabled children. Drew, Logan, and Hardman (1984) indicate that retarded students often have a higher incidence of emotional problems than nonretarded students. Lerner (1985) identified six characteristics of social behavior that are common among disabled children and youths: (1) lack of judgment, (2) difficulties in perceiving others, (3) problems in making friends, (4) poor self-concept, (5) problems involving family relationships, and (6) social difficulties in the school setting.

In most instances, children who are receiving special education services have more than one problem and disabilities produce different behaviors in different children (Cartwright, Cartwright, & Ward, 1984). Bloom (1956) proposes a system whereby all education-related activities would fall into three major domains—affective, psychomotor, and cognitive. Cartwright et al. (1984) define the affective domain as the social domain; this deals with an individual's social abilities, such as establishing and maintaining satisfactory interpersonal skills, displaying behavior within reasonable social expectations, and making personal adjustments. Social skills and the ability to get along with others are just as important to the handicapped student as they are to the nonhandicapped student. In fact, these social skills are even more critical to the person who is handicapped because the handicapped are often compared with the norm and must compete for grades, social status, and employment.

Wallace and Kauffman (1986) indicate that social behavior development is inseparable from the student's acquisition of academic skills and that "inappropriate behavior limits the student's chances for success in school: conversely, school failure often prompts undesirable behavior" (p. 165). Wallace and Kauffman (1986) strongly suggest that the remediation of students' social behavior problems is just as important as the remediation of their academic problems.

Social skills have been hard to define and even more difficult to measure according to Wallace and Kauffman (1986), and Strain, Odom, and McConnell (1984). Direct observation is perhaps one of the most reliable methods used in assessment of social skills problems. Other procedures used to assess competence in social behavior are self-reporting and screening instruments, clinical judgment, analysis of antecedent events, interviews, sociometric procedures, behavior and rating scales. However, when assessing an individual's social skills, one must be aware of the situations and circumstances in which the behavior occurs. Social and emotional problems may not be the primary difficulties facing most exceptional children; nevertheless, except for behavior-disordered or seriously emotionally disturbed students, these problems are present.

Eleas and Maher (1983) suggest that well-adjusted children have certain social and academic skills that many mildly handicapped students do not possess. Such skills as sensitivity to others' feelings, goal-setting persistence, and an adequate behavior repertoire are just a few mentioned. Many more social skills deficits that often plague students with disabilities such as poor self-concept, withdrawal, rejection, attention problems, compound the academic problems. School personnel need to address these social skill problems of the handicapped student. Mercer and Mercer (1985) indicate that teachers can "help foster the student's emotional development as well as the acquisition of social skills" (p. 132). Wallace and Kauffman (1986) and Mercer and Mercer (1985) believe that direct instruction may be the best method for remediating problems associated with social skills deficits. In addition to direct instruction, there are instructional materials and kits available commercially that are designed for teaching social skills. However, many of these kits have little validity data and vary widely in terms of the populations with which they have been used.

Perhaps social competence might be a better term to describe the skills necessary to get along with others. Schulman (1980) defines social competence as "getting along with people, communicating with them and coping with the frustrations of social living" (p. 285) Girls tend to achieve social competence more frequently than boys (Merrell, Merz, Johnson, & Ring, 1992). Nearly all of us need to feel accepted and socially competent. However, many handicapped students and adults have difficulty, to some degree, in developing those skills necessary for adequate social acceptance.

REFERENCES

Bellach, A. S. (1983). Recurrent problems in the behavior assessment of social skills. *Behavior Research & Therapy, 21,* 29–41.

Bloom, B. (1956). *Taxonomy of educational objectives: The classification of educational goals.* New York: Longman.

Cartwright, C. P., Cartwright, C. A., & Ward, M. E. (1984). *Educating special learners.* Belmont, CA: Wadsworth.

Eleas, M. J., & Maher, C. A. (1983). Social and effective development of children: A programmatic perspective. *Exceptional Children, 4,* 339–346.

Drew, C. J., Logan, D. R., & Hardman, M. L. (1984). *Mental retardation: A life cycle approach* (3rd ed.). St. Louis: Mosby.

Lerner, J. (1985). *Learning disabilities: Theories, diagnosis, and teaching strategies* (4th ed.). Boston: Houghton Mifflin.

Mercer, D. D., & Mercer, A. R. (1985). *Teaching students with learning problems* (2nd ed.). Columbus, OH: Merrill.

Merrell, K. W., Merz, J. M., Johnson, E. R., & Ring, E. N. Social competence of students with mild handicaps and low achievement: A comparative study. *School Psychology Review, 21*(1), 125–137.

Minskoff, E. H. (1980). Teaching approach for developing non-verbal communication skills in students with social perception deficits. *Journal of Learning Disabilities, 13*, 118–126.

Schulman, E. D. (1980). *Focus on retarded adults: Programs and services.* St. Louis: Mosby.

Stephens, T. M., Hartman, A. C., & Lucas, V. H. (1983). *Teaching children basic skills: A curriculum handbook* (2nd ed.). Columbus, OH: Merrill.

Strain, P. S., Odom, S. L., & McConnell, S. (1984). Promoting social reciprocity of exceptional children: Identification, target behaviors selection, and intervention. *Remedial & Special Education, 1,* 21–28.

Wallace, G., & Kauffman, J. M. (1986). *Teaching students with learning and behavior problems* (3rd ed.). Columbus, OH: Merrill.

HUBERT R. VANCE
East Tennessee State University

ADAPTIVE BEHAVIOR
SOCIAL SKILLS
SOCIAL SKILLS TRAINING
SOCIOGRAM

SOCIAL COMPETENCE

See ADAPTIVE BEHAVIOR.

SOCIAL DARWINISM

Social Darwinism, a social philosophy that was developed in the latter half of the nineteenth century, was based on the application of Darwin's principles of natural selection and survival of the fittest to the problems of society. Mental retardation, insanity, epilepsy, alcoholism, and other disorders were explained in terms of heredity, genetics, and Darwinian principles. Adams (1971) describes social Darwinism as follows: "the people of above average intelligence by previous standards become the norm in the next evolutionary phase, and the slow ones drop back to become the social casualties of the new order." Social Darwinism was also associated with attempts to interpret mental retardation as deviance rather than incompetence (Farber, 1968).

When Western Europe and North America became industrialized, environmental conditions that hindered the intellectual development of normal children resulted. Industrialization also led to health hazards that were responsible for the birth of biologically deficient children. At the same time, correlations were found between intellectual and social deficits that stimulated a variety of explanatory efforts. According to the principle of social Darwinism, human deficiencies were caused by evolutionary obstacles or the degeneration of genetic matter. The historical perspective of social Darwinism and its relation to the eugenics movement are central to understanding the treatment of disabled individuals from the 1850s to the 1950s.

In the 1850s, even before Darwin published his findings and theories, Morel speculated that all varieties of mental illnesses were related and were due to hereditary factors. Noting an association between mental retardation and sterility, he further postulated that these illnesses became more profound with each succeeding generation, leading ultimately to, sterility and extinction. Morel suggested that mental illnesses were caused by physical diseases, alcoholism, and social environments, and called for more adequate food, housing, and working conditions as preventive measures. Concurrently, with evidence of a genetic inheritable component of intelligence mounting, mental health professionals were becoming convinced that institutional segregation of the disabled was necessary, thus abandoning their efforts to return handicapped individuals to the community. Darwinism reached a height of popularity in England in the 14-year period from 1858 to 1872, but its effects were felt until the turn of the century. In the United States, Darwinian doctrine provided justification for the existing status structure prior to and during the Civil War. Darwinian proponents contended that foreigners and members of lower socioeconomic levels were distinct races that were inferior and might justifiably be subjugated. However, the North's victory strengthened the position of the anti-Darwinian proponents (Farber, 1968).

The optimism that characterized the treatment and care of the disabled in the early portion of the nineteenth century began to disappear in the latter half of the century. Institutions began moving away from treatment programs, replacing them with basic care and maintenance services. The emphasis on rehabilitation and education degenerated into support for terminal institutional placement (Hardman, Drew, & Egan, 1984). In the early portion of the twentieth century, with the introduction of mental tests, researchers found that a large proportion of prison inmates could be classified as feebleminded. Mentally retarded women were believed to be promiscuous, burdening society with many illegitimate offspring. It was estimated that criminals and unmarried mothers constituted 40 to 45% of the mentally retarded population. Furthermore, Tredgold and his followers contended that 90% of mental deficiency was due to hereditary factors. The feebleminded were regarded as unable to sustain gainful employment and a danger to the community and the "race." The solutions that were proposed most often were segregation and sterilization (Farber, 1968).

The "eugenic scare" of the early 1900s has been described as a shift in focus from the protection of the mentally handicapped from a cruel and exploitative society to the protection of society from contamination by inferior mental stock (Adams, 1971). With social Darwinism setting the stage, the eugenic movement was fed by the alarming increase in pauperism, vagrancy, alcoholism, and delinquency in society, and the association of low mentality and sociopathic behavior within identified families (e.g., the Jukes and the Kallikaks) whose genetic lines had been traced. The eugenic position was manifested in legislation for sterilization and the proposal to extend custodial care to all the retarded in the United States during their childbearing years. The first sterilization law was passed in Indiana in 1907, followed by similar legislation in seven other states soon thereafter. (Adams, 1971).

By the 1920s, pessimistic forecasts appeared to have been vindicated in England, where the incidence of mental deficiency was sharply increasing. Although eugenicists strove to win the debate on mental deficiency during the period from 1900 to 1940, their efforts were hindered by their inability to identify the unfit, to prove causation, and to limit fertility (Macnicol, 1983). In reality, the concept of total social control over the retarded was never much more than an idea, and neither wholesale institutional commitment nor sterilization was implemented. Providing institutional care to segregate a large portion of society at public expense proved to be highly impractical. Nevertheless, by associating mental defects with genetic factors, the social forces that were causing pathological living conditions among the poor were neglected and the economic causes for social maladjustment were ignored (Adams, 1971). Recently, the negative side effects of involuntary sterilization of retarded persons have been documented. Low self-esteem, feelings of failure, a sense of helplessness, and social isolation have all been associated with forced sterilization (Roos, 1975).

Social Darwinism and related social movements have had a profound impact on the treatment of the mentally retarded and other disabled individuals. However, not all of the effects of the social Darwinism movement were negative. Its popularity, along with the development of special educational services, has been credited with providing an impetus for the systematic study of the prevalence of mental retardation (Farber, 1968).

REFERENCES

Adams, M. (1971). *Mental retardation and its social dimensions.* New York: Columbia University Press.

Farber, B. (1968). *Mental retardation: Its social context and social consequences.* Boston: Houghton Mifflin.

Hardman, M. L., Drew, C. I., & Egan, M. W. (1984). *Human exceptionality: School, society, and family.* Boston: Allyn & Bacon.

Macnicol, J. (1983). Eugenics, medicine and mental deficiency: An introduction. *Oxford Review of Education, 3,* 177–180.

Roos, P. (1975). Psychological impact of sterilization on the individual. *Law & Psychology Review, 1,* 45–56.

GREG VALCANTE
University of Florida

EUGENICS
HEREDITY
JUKES AND THE KALLIKAKS

SOCIAL INTEGRATION OF HANDICAPPED IN SCHOOL

See INCLUSION.

SOCIAL ISOLATION

Social isolation has been subsumed under the rubric of social skills or social competence. The problem of defining social isolation in children, specifically, is consonant with the problem of defining social skills or social competence in general. Children labeled as social isolates do not appear to constitute a homogeneous or clearly defined group, and several descriptors have been used in the literature as labels (e.g., shy, isolated, withdrawn, anxious-withdrawn). Social isolation is a behavior pattern that occurs across various categories of children such as autistic, mentally retarded, schizophrenic, severe visual impaired, (Gourgey, 1998) and normal.

There is a lack of agreement among investigators regarding the specific behaviors that need to be performed to indicate social skillfulness or competence, and the appropriate behaviors that are not performed, or the inappropriate behaviors that are performed, that indicate a lack of social skillfulness or competence. The contribution of several variables such as age, sex, social status, and situationally specific factors, in determining the presence or absence of social competence is poorly understood. Also, the criterion measures used to assess social isolation (behavioral observations, peer sociometric ratings, teacher ratings) may affect what is labeled as social isolate behavior (Conger & Keane, 1981). These criterion measures may not tap the same dimensions of behavior and may identify different subtypes of children (Gottman, 1977). The behaviors that have been selected as indicators of social isolate behavior have not been empirically determined. They have been chosen on the basis of the face validity of their relationship to the behavior pattern of social isolation, and single measures of social isolation typically have been employed (Conger & Keane, 1981). Additionally, little or no relationship has been found between the two main types of criterion measures used to assess social isolate behavior when they have been compared (i.e., global peer sociometric ratings of acceptance or rejection and behavioral observations of rate of discrete social interactions; Gottman, 1977).

The principal approaches in the conceptualization of social isolation in childhood have been in terms of withdrawal indicated by low rates of social interaction relative to other children and rejection or lack of acceptance by peers (Gottman, 1977). These two groups of social isolates may represent different populations; however, the infrequent use of both methods of assessment with the same groups of children does not allow for a determination of how well these measures agree on or discriminate among different subtypes of children. Also, given the lack of agreement on what behaviors or lack of behaviors are related to social isolation, it is unclear whether low rates of social interaction imply a lack of social skills or a lack of exhibiting social skills that the child possesses. In terms of peer acceptance or rejection, it is not clear whether this is based on a lack of social skills or on behaviors perceived as negative by peers such as aggressiveness. The grouping together of various behaviors within the category of social isolate behavior obscures assessment and intervention efforts and reduces the likelihood of heterogeneous grouping.

The development of positive social relationships with peers is an important developmental achievement. Typically, social interaction increases and relationships become more stable as children grow older (Asher, Oden, & Gottman, 1977). Thus social isolation may represent a significant deviation in social development. Gronlund (1959) reports that 6% of a sample of grades 3 to 6 had no classroom friends, and 12% had only one friend. A study of elementary age problem children identified 13.95% of the children referred by teachers for psychological services as withdrawn (Woods, 1964; as cited in Woods, 1969). Strain, Cook, and Apolloni (1977) estimate that 15% or more of children referred for psychological services exhibit social withdrawal as a major presenting symptom. Once a pattern of withdrawal behavior is established, it may persist through childhood and adolescence (Branson, 1968). The evidence for the carryover of social isolation into adulthood is beset with methodological problems and conflicting results that limit generalizations. It does appear, however, that adults with certain psychiatric disabilities were socially isolated as children, but that not all socially isolated children develop psychiatric disabilities as adults (Strain et al., 1977). Hops, Walker, & Greenwood (1979) note that children referred for psychological services because of social isolate behavior appear to lead quiet, retiring lives, with some restriction in social contacts.

Intervention approaches used with socially withdrawn children increasingly emphasize the training of social skills. Social learning procedures (Coombs & Slaby, 1977) have constituted major treatment methods for teaching social skills to socially isolated children (Conger & Keane, 1981; Hops, 1983). The use of instructional packages with multiple components appears to be the best method for teaching social skills. The packages may include a combination of shaping, modeling, coaching, and reinforcement. Cognitively oriented interpersonal problem-solving interventions have also been employed; they emphasize the training of cognitive processes to mediate performance across a range of situations rather than discrete behavioral responses to various situations (Urbain & Kendall, 1980). The cognitive-behavioral approach uses many of the same instructional methods as the social learning approach, but it focuses on teaching problem-solving strategies and verbally mediated self-control (e.g., self-instruction). Music therapy has also been used successfully (Gourgey, 1998).

The evidence to date suggests that interventions have demonstrated modest to moderate effects in teaching social skills to socially isolated children. Also, there are problems in establishing training effects that generalize beyond the treatment setting and maintain over time. Given the importance of positive social relationships with peers, efforts need to be continued to overcome conceptual, methodological, and assessment problems. Advances in these areas may further improve intervention efforts with children for whom peer relationships are problematic.

REFERENCES

Asher, S. R., Oden, S. C., & Gottman, J. M. (1977). Children's friendship in the school setting. In L. G. Katz (Ed.), *Current topics in early education* (Vol. 1). Norwood, NJ: Ablex.

Bronson, W. C. (1968). Stable patterns of behaviors: The significance of enduring orientations for personality development. In J. P. Hill (Ed.), *Minnesota symposia on child psychology* (Vol. 2). Minneapolis, University of Minnesota Press.

Conger, J. C., & Keane, P. (1981). Social skills intervention in the treatment of isolated or withdrawn children. *Psychological Bulletin, 90*(3), 478–495.

Coombs, M. L., & Slaby, D. (1977). Social skills training with children. In B. B. Lahey & A. E. Kazdin (Eds.), *Advances in clinical child psychology* (Vol. 1). New York: Academic.

Gottman, J. M. (1977). Toward a definition of social isolation in children. *Child Development, 48,* 513–517.

Gourgey, C. (1998). Music therapy in the treatment of social isolation in visually impaired children. *REView, 29*(4), 157–162.

Gronlund, N. E. (1959). *Sociometry in the classroom.* New York: Harper.

Hops, H. (1983). Social skills training for socially withdrawn/isolate children. In P. Karoly & J. J. Steffen (Eds.), *Improving children's competence.* Lexington, MA: Lexington.

Hops, H., Walker, H. M., & Greenwood, C. R. (1979). PEERS: A program for remediating withdrawal in school. In L. A.

Hamerlynck (Ed.), *Behavioral systems for the developmentally disabled: In school and family environments.* New York: Brunner/Mazel.

Strain, P. S., Cooke, T. P., & Apolloni, T. (1976). *Teaching exceptional children: Assessing and modifying social behavior.* New York: Academic.

Urbain, E. S., & Kendall, P. C. (1980). Review of social-cognitive problem-solving interventions with children. *Psychological Bulletin, 88*(1), 109–143.

HAROLD HANSON
PAUL BATES
Southern Illinois University

SOCIAL BEHAVIOR
SOCIAL BEHAVIOR OF THE HANDICAPPED
SOCIOGRAM

SOCIAL LEARNING THEORY

Social learning theory is one of the most well known and most influential models for understanding human behavior. In explaining this theory, it is helpful to describe what it is not, because social learning theory grew out of a reaction to other theoretical orientations. First, social learning theory does not view human behavior as purely a result of internal cognitive thoughts or feelings. Freud, for example, viewed human behavior as mediated by thoughts, wishes, self-concepts, impulses, etc. Neither does social learning theory view behavior as strictly a function of environmental events. Thus social learning theory is not a model of human behavior based strictly on the principles of operant conditioning developed by B. F. Skinner. Skinner and others believe that behavior is purely a function of environmental events.

Social learning theory does, however, provide an integration of previous theories such as Freud's and Skinner's. Although social learning theory is closely related to Skinner's principles of operant conditioning, the major difference is the incorporation of internal events as controlling stimuli. Social learning theorists recognize that an individual's thoughts and feelings have a significant impact on behavior.

Social learning theory is a term that has been applied to the views of a relatively wide range of theorists and researchers. Without question, the theorist who has done the most to conceptualize and advance the ideas of social learning theory is Albert Bandura of Stanford University. His more recent work has moved away from the early environmental determinism that characterized behavioristic social learning theory. His most comprehensive presentation is in his 1986 book in which he extensively details his social cognitive theory. No socialization theory has as much careful empirical support as social cognitive theory. Bandura has added significant arguments for why internal evaluative processes must be included in any behavioral theory. At the core of Bandura's theory is the concept of reciprocal determinism. Similar to but more limited than Bronfenbrenner's ecological model, reciprocal determinism conceptualizes behavior as a continuous reciprocal interaction between an individual's thoughts, behaviors, and environmental factors.

This triadic model views human functioning as a three-way interaction among behavior (B), cognitions and other internal events that affect perceptions and actions (P), and a person's external environment (E). An interesting aspect of this view is that each element of the triad affects the other two elements. Thus, not only do internal and environmental events affect behavior, but behavior also affects internal events and the environment in reciprocal fashion.

Bandura's (1986) emphasis on internal mediators can be seen in work on observational learning, enactive learning, predictive knowledge and forethought, interpretations of incentives, vicarious motivators, self-regulatory mechanisms, self-efficacy, and cognitive regulators. Bandura demonstrates how cognitive factors determine what we observe, how we evaluate our observations, and how we use this information in the future. For example when students take tests, they read the questions, answer according to their interpretations of what the teacher wants, receive feedback in the form of grades, and then adjust depending on how successfully they believe they answered the questions graded by the teacher. No behavior occurs in a vacuum without prior internal processes and external effects.

A key component in most social learning theories is observational learning, which is based on the process of modeling. Through modeling, children learn a wide array of complicated skills, such as language and social interaction. Moreover, these skills are learned without reinforcement. This is in stark contrast to radical behavioral theory, which posits that complex behaviors are learned through the reinforcement of gradual changes in molecular response patterns. Teachers make use of observational learning many times a day. For example, some teachers will verbally reinforce a child who is behaving appropriately just so other children will be encouraged to imitate the modeled behavior. Most socialization is the result of observational learning, because it is much more efficient and realistic than the step-by-step shaping advocated by radical behaviorists.

Another key component that has received considerable research attention is the concept of self-efficacy. Self-efficacy is a complex process in which persons assess the likelihood of successfully performing a task based upon their previous mastery (e.g., training), vicarious experience (e.g., modeling of others), verbal persuasion (e.g., encouragement), physiological condition (e.g., health), and affective state (e.g., happy). Persons high in self-efficacy will make realistic judgments of their abilities to perform tasks, will tend to seek appropriately difficult tasks, and will persist in them until completed (Bandura, 1997). Teachers with high teacher self-efficacy will be more likely to believe they can teach a classroom of difficult children. In special education classes, high teacher self-efficacy will result in greater progress and competence in the students.

Social learning theory has also emphasized the concept of internal dialogues. These dialogues, or internal speeches, are used by people to learn information (e.g., to rehearse a phone number), for self-instruction (e.g., "Now what do I do next?"), and for self-reinforcement (e.g., "Way to go!"). These internal dialogues fit in nicely with Vygotsky's developmental theory postulating a cognitive self-guidance system in which these dialogues eventually become silent or inner speech. Teaching internal dialogues to children with learning disabilities may help them become better problem solvers (Berk, 1992).

Because social learning theory has incorporated internal variables (e.g., thoughts and feelings) that are not directly observable, it has been criticized by radical behaviorists. Similarly, the emphasis within social learning theory on environmental factors and the lack of emphasis on cognitive development has caused it to be questioned by developmentalists. Freudian psychologists are dissatisfied with the lack of strong emotional components. Despite these detractors, social learning theory has enormous appeal to a wide variety of professionals. The reason for this appeal is the testability of the theory and the broad coverage of internal and external factors. Social learning theory is seen by many as being very comprehensive in its ability to handle a diverse range of human experiences and problems.

REFERENCES

Bandura, A. (1986). *Social foundations of thought and action: A social cognitive theory.* Englewood Cliffs, NJ: Prentice-Hall.

Bandura, A. (1997). *Self-efficacy: The exercise of control.* New York, NY: Freeman.

Berk, L. E. (1992). Children's private speech: An overview of theory and the status of research. In R. M. Diaz & L. E. Berk (Eds.), *Private speech: From social interaction to self-regulation.* Hillsdale, NJ: Erlbaum.

SPENCER THOMPSON
*The University of Texas of the
Permian Basin*

BANDURA, A.
IMPULSE CONTROL
MEDIATIONAL DEFICIENCIES
MEDIATORS
OBSERVATIONAL LEARNING
RECIPROCAL DETERMINISM

SOCIAL MATURITY

See ADAPTIVE BEHAVIOR.

SOCIAL SECURITY

Social Security is based on the concept of providing income and health maintenance programs for families in such instances as retirement, disability, poor health, or death. In general, to be eligible for Social Security a person must first pay into Social Security by working and allowing a certain amount of income to be deducted from earnings. Sixteen percent (over 3 million people) of the population in the United States receive Social Security checks. Individuals over 65 (about 25 million) are covered under health insurance called Medicare. In the category of disability, the number receiving benefits are about 3 million.

The Social Security Act of 1935 consisted of three broad areas: (1) Social Security insurance, which included old age, survivors, disability, and hospital insurance (DASDHI), unemployment insurance, workman's compensation, compulsory temporary disability insurance, and railroad retirement system and railroad unemployment and temporary disability insurance; (2) government sponsorship of government or farm workers under civil service retirement, national service life insurance, federal crop insurance, public assistance (which is based on need), and veterans benefits; and (3) social assistance (welfare), which includes public assistance, national assistance, old-age assistance, unemployment assistance, and social pension programs that provide cash payments and other benefits to individuals based on need. Owing to the many changes in our society since 1935 such as demographic shifts, changes in values and attitudes, and inflation the Social Security system has been revised.

To be considered disabled under Social Security law a person must have a physical or mental condition that prevents that person from doing any substantial gainful work. The condition must be expected to last for at least 12 months, or expected to result in death. Examples of such conditions include diseases of the heart, lungs, or blood vessels that have resulted in serious loss of heart or lung reserves or serious loss of function of the kidneys; diseases of the digestive system that result in severe malnutrition, weakness, and anemia; and damage to the brain that has resulted in severe loss of judgment, intellect, orientation, or memory. The World Health Organization revised the mental health aspects of the International Classification of Impairments, Disabilities, and Handicaps (ICIDH) in 1995 to assist in the planning of care. Children of individuals who are eligible disabled persons can receive benefits if they are under 18 or 19, still in high school full time, or disabled before age 22, unmarried, and living at home. If an individual is blind, there are special considerations such as a disability freeze on income averaging for retirement purposes. Work situations for all individuals must require skills and abilities that are comparable to those of the individual's previous work history. If, however, the person is disabled before 22 and the parents are paying into Social Security, they can receive disability benefits. In order to qualify, the person must be unable to work in gainful employment and the person under whose credits they are applying must be retired, disabled, deceased, or fully insured under Social Security.

Another federal program administered by the Social Security Administration for low-income individuals is Supplemental Security Income (SSI). Supplemental security income is not based on work credits. Eligibility is based on age (over 65), income guidelines, and disability at any age for persons who earn below a specific income. In general, individuals living in institutions are not eligible for SSI unless they are classified under the four exceptions listed by the Social Security Administration (1986):

1. A person who lives in a publicly operated community residence that serves no more than 16 people may be eligible for SSI payments.
2. A person who lives in a public institution primarily to attend approved educational or vocational training provided in the institution may be eligible if the training is designed to prepare the person for gainful employment.
3. If a person is in a public or private medical treatment facility and Medicaid is paying more than half the cost of his or her care, the person may be eligible, but the SSI payments limited to no more than $25 per month.
4. A person who is a resident of a public emergency shelter throughout a month can receive SSI payments for up to 3 months during any 12-month period. (pp. 9–10)

In the early 1990s the eligibility for SSI based on childhood disability was expanded because of a Supreme Court decision in Zebley v. Sullivan (Ford & Schwann, 1992).

To receive SSI under a disability option, the individual must have a physical or mental disability that prevents him or her from gainful employment. The disability must be one that will last at least 12 months or be expected to end in death. For individuals under age 18, the decision is based on whether the disability would not allow the person to work if he or she were an adult.

REFERENCES

Ford, M. E., & Schwann, J. B. (1992). Expanding eligibility for SSI based on childhood disability: The Zebley decision. *Child Welfare, 71*(4), 307–318.

Uestuen, C., van Duuren-Kristen, S., & Kennedy, C. (1995). Revision of the ICIDH: Mental health aspects. *Disability & Rehabilitation: An International Multidisciplinary Journal, 17,* 3–4.

JANICE HARPER
*North Carolina Central
University*

**DISABILITY
LEGISLATION REGARDING THE HANDICAPPED
REHABILITATION
SOCIOECONOMIC STATUS**

SOCIAL SKILLS/COMPETENCE TRAINING

Social skills training is a method of teaching children effective social coping strategies. It is used as an intervention to manage disruptive behavior, a method to prevent future disruptions, and a tool to foster emotional growth in children (Gresham & Elliott, 1984). The adjustment problems of many children with disabilities have been related to social skills deficits; social skills training attempts to address these dysfunctional areas. Drawing from behavioral, cognitive, and humanistic theories of psychology, social skills training employs an educational approach to remediating behavior problems.

Social skills have been described in various terms. Eisenberg and Harris (1984) have defined them as a set of developmentally related abilities that contribute to an overall level of social competence. The component skills include role or perspective taking, interpersonal problem solving, moral judgment, self-control, and communication facility. Kratchowill and French (1984) view social skills as learned verbal and nonverbal behaviors that are performed within a specific social context. Gerber (1983) has discussed social skills in relation to an individual's social perceptual accuracy (i.e., the ability to understand subtle nuances and define critical elements in the social environment). Rathjen (1984) defines social skills within the context of an aggressiveness-shyness continuum, and views adjustment in relation to an individual's awareness of socially accepted limits. Erin, Dignan & Brown (1991) have worked with blind and visually impaired students and define social skills as having three components: 1) assertiveness training; 2) interactional skills; and 3) physical communication.

An individual's social skills determine important social outcomes such as peer acceptance and ascribed personality characteristics. Those children with poor self-control may learn inappropriate social strategies because their behavior leads to peer rejection (Gresham & Elliott, 1984). Socially incompetent children are reported to continue having socialization difficulties through adulthood (Rathjen, 1984).

In a review of a number of social skills training programs, Baskin and Hess (1980) reported that programs designed with cognitive and behavioral objectives were effective in increasing children's understanding of social causation, improving peer relations, decreasing discipline referrals, and improving behavioral adjustment ratings made by teachers. Successful training programs appear to balance content flexibility with skill sequence and structure (Shure & Spivack, 1981). They stimulate thought and discussion around the types of interpersonal problems with which participants can identify. Effective programs also allow for repetition and practice of learned skills. Meichenbaum (1983) states that training materials should be drawn from the child's natural play environment when possible. He also finds that children are able to incorporate material when they brainstorm as a group. Finally, program effectiveness is enhanced when trainers are highly energetic and capable of acting at the child's level.

A number of social skills training programs are available as commercial packages; others are offered as models and techniques. Shure and Spivack (1981) designed a program to improve behavior-disordered children's interpersonal cognitive problem solving skills. Children are trained to examine their behavior in terms of possible outcomes. They are then guided to consider alternate behaviors that might be substituted for the present one. Next, predicted outcomes for these alternate behaviors are explored. Finally, the children are taught to weigh the various outcomes in terms of desirability and to choose the behavior most likely to produce the desired effect.

Cognitive behavior modification (CBM), a technique developed by Donald Meichenbaum, is an approach to social skills training that has been used with impulsive, aggressive, and hyperactive children (Meichenbaum, 1983). The CBM focuses on generalizable strategies that children can use across a variety of situations. The training consists of guided rehearsal and modeling, in which the children work with mediating adult to establish covert verbal control over their disruptive behaviors. The turtle technique, a method based on CBM, has been found effective in reducing impulsive children's aggressive responses to frustration (Schneider, 1974). This procedure teaches children to respond to a verbal cue by relaxing, pausing, and implementing problem-solving techniques such as visualizing the consequences of a proposed action and its alternatives.

Elardo and Cooper (1977) developed AWARE, a four-step social skills training program. First, children are helped to formulate rules for their group meetings. Next, they are taught to become more aware of their feelings and the feelings of others. Third, the children are encouraged to explore unique aspects of their own personalities and to recognize the uniqueness of others. Finally, the children are encouraged to explore real-life difficulties and to solve them in a peaceful and mutually beneficial manner. The teacher's duties in the AWARE program include leading discussions, carrying through ideas in daily practice, asking questions, and providing a warm and supportive environment.

Handicapped students with inadequate social perception need training in basic interpersonal skills (Speer & Douglas, 1981; Swanson, 1992). They may need to learn appropriate social gestures such as smiling and making eye contact. Learning-disabled children may also need instruction in interpreting and labeling facial expressions, and in moderating their verbal behavior. Language-deficient children must be taught appropriate verbal responses in social conversation. Communication training for language-impaired youngsters should teach them to be aware of four critical factors: personalities and roles of the participants, setting, topic, and objectives (Minskoff, 1982). Reality therapy, an approach to social skills training that stresses the relationship between behavior and natural consequences, has been used to encourage emotionally disturbed children to use more effective interpersonal strategies (Fuller & Fuller, 1982).

Social skills training has also been used with retarded children. Meisgeier (1981) has outlined a program stressing problem solving, personal responsibility, and communication skills. Students are taught to replace aggressive behaviors with assertive ones. The program consists of a series of structured success experiences stressing positive self-statements and relaxation.

Social skills training has been employed to increase the probability of mainstreaming and inclusion (Iannaccone & Hwang, 1998) effectiveness, and to help nonhandicapped children to accept their handicapped peers (Gresham, 1982). Gresham suggests that social skills assessments be included in all mainstreaming decisions.

As critics (Gerber, 1983) have argued that social skills training takes up valuable academic learning time, Shure and Spivack (1981) suggest that evaluation components be integrated into all social skills training programs to judge student growth and program effectiveness. One commonly used instrument is the Means-Ends Problem Solving measure (Platt, Spivack, and Bloom, 1971). This consists of a set of hypothetical social problems in which children are required to formulate a variety of possible solutions. Ratings can be made on the quantity and quality of these proposed solutions. Another popular evaluation approach uses sociometric procedures. Sociometric data are gathered by asking peers to rate each other in terms of popularity and desirability. Behavior rating scales also offer a means of assessing social skills. These scales attempt to define skills in terms of observable behavior, and are usually completed by the classroom teacher.

REFERENCES

Baskin, E. J., & Hess, R. D. (1980). Does affective education work? A review of seven programs. *Journal of School Psychology, 18*(1), 40–50.

Eisenberg, N., & Harris, J. D. (1984). Social competence: A developmental perspective. *School Psychology Review, 13*(3), 267–277.

Elardo, P., & Cooper, M. (1977). *AWARE: Activities for social development.* Menlo Park, CA: Addison-Wesley.

Erin, J. N., Dignan, K., & Brown, P. A. (1991). Are social skills teachable? A literature review. *Journal of Visual Impairment & Blindness, 85*(2), 58–61.

Fuller, G. B., & Fuller, D. L. (1982). Reality therapy: Helping LD children make better choices. *Academic Therapy, 17*(3), 269–277.

Gerber, M. M. (1983). Learning disabilities and cognitive strategies: A case for training or constraining problem solving. *Journal of Learning Disabilities, 16*(5), 255–260.

Gresham, F. M. (1982). Misguided mainstreaming: The case for social skills training with handicapped children. *Exceptional Children, 48*(5), 422–433.

Gresham, F. M., & Elliott, S. M. (1984). Assessment and classification of children's social skills: A review of methods and issues. *School Psychology Review, 13*(3), 292–301.

Iannaccone, C. J., & Hwang, Y. G. (1998). Transcending social skills oriented instruction within integrated classrooms. *Emotional and Behavioral Difficulties, 3*(1), 25–29.

Kratchowill, T. R., & French, D. C. (1984). Social skills training for withdrawn children. *School Psychology Review, 13*(3), 339–341.

Meichenbaum, D. (1983). Teaching thinking: A cognitive-behavioral perspective. In S. Chipman and J. Segal (Eds.), *Thinking and learning skills: Current research and open questions.* Hillsdale, NJ: Erlbaum.

Meisgeier, C. (1981). A social/behavioral program for the adolescent student with serious learning problems. *Focus on Exceptional Children, 13*(9), 1–13.

Minskoff, E. H. (1982). Training LD students to cope with the everyday world. *Academic Therapy, 17*(3), 311–316.

Platt, J. J., Spivack, G., & Bloom, M. R. (1971). *Means-ends problem solving procedure (MEPS): Manual and tentative norms.* Philadelphia: Hahnemann Medical College and Hospital.

Rathjen, D. P. (1984). Social skills training for children. Innovations and consumer guidelines. *School Psychology Review, 13*(3), 302–310.

Schneider, M. R. (1974). Turtle technique in the classroom. *Teaching Exceptional Children, 7,* 22–24.

Shure, M. B., & Spivack, G. (1981). The problem solving approach to adjustment: A competency-building model of primary prevention. *Prevention in Human Services, 1*(1-2), 87–103.

Speer, S. K., & Douglas, D. R. (1981). Helping LD students improve social skills. *Academic Therapy, 17*(2), 221–224.

Swanson, H. L., & Malone, S. (1992). Social skills and learning disabilities: A meta-analysis of the literature. *School Psychology Review, 21*(3), 427–443.

GARY BERKOWITZ
Temple University

BEHAVIOR MODELING
DEVELOPING UNDERSTANDING OF SELF AND OTHERS

SOCIAL VALIDATION

In an educational context, social validation is the philosophy of providing psychological services that emphasize the importance of the student's or teacher's subjective opinions about intervention methods. Social validity differs from the statistical notion of validity in several aspects. Statistical validity refers to how well treatment results correlate with an objective set of criteria or other treatment methods. Social validity is concerned with the subjective opinions of teachers, parents, and/or students and how these subjective opinions affect the overall treatment outcomes. In social validity it is assumed "that if the participants don't like the treatment then they may avoid it, or run away, or complain loudly. And thus, society will be less likely to use our technology, no matter how potentially effective and efficient it might be" (Wolf, 1978, p. 206).

Social validity can be assessed on at least three levels (Wolf, 1978). First, we can evaluate the social significance of the treatment goals. Here we consider whether desired outcomes are of any real value to teachers, students, or society in general. The second level of assessment of social validity questions the social appropriateness of the treatment procedures. At this level, teachers and students are asked how acceptable the treatment methods are (i.e., whether the results of the treatment justify the methods used). "Judgements of acceptability include whether a treatment is appropriate for the problem, whether it is fair, reasonable, or intrusive, and whether it is consistent with conventional notions of what treatment should be" (Kazdin, 1980, p. 330). The treatment acceptability paradigm has been used with students and teachers in clinical settings (Kazdin, French, & Sherick, 1981); university settings (Kazdin, 1980); and primary and secondary school settings (Elliott, Witt, Galvin, & Moe, 1986; Turco, Witt, & Elliott, in press). In the final level of social validation evaluation, teachers and students report their satisfaction with the methods used (i.e., How important are the effects of the treatment methods? Are the teachers and students satisfied with the results, even the unplanned ones?; Wolf, 1978).

Consumer satisfaction differs from treatment acceptability mainly in the timing of the measurements. Treatment acceptability requires teachers and students to judge treatments before they begin. Consumer satisfaction requires teachers and students to judge treatments during the treatment or after the treatment is over. In applied behavior analysis, it is believed that the outcomes of treatments are easily judged based on behavioral changes from baseline measurements. However, according to the social validity paradigm, the usefulness of school interventions can only be judged by the subjective evaluations of the teachers and students participating in the treatment program.

REFERENCES

Elliott, S. N., Witt, J. C., Galvin, G. A., & Moe, G. L. (1986). Children's involvement in intervention selection: Acceptability of interventions for misbehaving peers. *Professional psychology: Research and practice, 17*(3), 235–241.

Kazdin, A. E. (1980). Acceptability of alternative treatments for deviant child behavior. *Journal of Applied Behavior Analysis, 13,* 259–273.

Kazdin, A. E., French, N. H., & Sherick, R. B. (1981). Acceptability of alternative treatments for children: Evaluations by inpatient children, parents, and staff. *Journal of Consulting and Clinical Psychology, 49,* 900–907.

Turco, T. L., Witt, J. C., & Elliott, S. N. (in press). Factors influencing teachers' acceptability of classroom interventions for deviant student behavior. *Monograph on secondary behavioral disorders.* Reston, VA: Council for Exceptional Children.

Wolf, M. M. (1978). Social validity: The case for subjective measurement or how applied behavior analysis is finding its heart. *Journal of Applied Behavior Analysis, 11,* 203–214.

TIMOTHY L. TURCO
STEPHEN N. ELLIOTT
Louisiana State University

APPLIED BEHAVIOR ANALYSIS
TEACHER EXPECTANCIES

SOCIAL WORK

Social work in special education traditionally falls within the realm of the school social worker. The functions performed by social workers within the school include individual and family casework, individual and group work with students, and community liaison services. School social workers have stated their goals as helping students to maximize their potential, developing relationships between the school and other agencies, and offering a perspective of social improvement in the education of students (Costin, 1981).

In 1975, PL 94-142 and subsequent amendments resulting in IDEA mandated free and appropriate education for all students; social work falls under the section providing for related services (Hancock, 1982). The school social worker often participates as a member of an interdisciplinary team, and in some states assumes a permanent position on a child study team. Local boards of education determine the specific roles of team members (Winters & Easton, 1983). As a team member, the social worker may be responsible for gathering family information, coordinating team meetings, developing individualized educational programs, and monitoring services.

The school social worker often participates in the evaluation of students who are being considered for special education. In this regard, the case history is an extremely important tool that the social worker uses to gain environmental, developmental, social, and economic information about the student.

To work effectively with a special population, the school social worker must have several basic competencies. Dickerson (1981) includes counseling, crisis intervention, knowledge of related services, and understanding of adapted curricula and techniques as required skills. To be effective, the school social worker must also hold the belief that special-needs children are entitled to the same rights and privileges as those afforded to their mainstreamed peers.

Often, family members of the children with disabilities need support from the social worker in their efforts to program for their impaired youngsters. The primary goal of the social worker in providing services to family members of the handicapped is to help them face and accept the limiting condition (Dickerson, 1981). The family is encouraged to follow through on recommendations designed to enhance their child's functioning. The social worker helps the family to recognize that the problem is real and that it can be helped by the development of an accepting, positive attitude about the child.

The school social worker may provide a number of different services to the family. Hancock (1982) writes that one role for the school social worker is to support parents in their efforts to become more active participants in school decisions regarding their children. Social workers may contribute information regarding home versus institutional care for severely impaired children. The social worker may also provide direct counseling services to the family, or act as a link to other supportive services. For example, parents might be encouraged to find a support or advocacy group. Ensuring that families receive the financial support to which they are entitled is another important function.

Pupil services such as counseling, sex education, prevocational development, and child advocacy are often performed by the school social worker. As an advocate, the social worker attempts to create systemic changes that improve the quality of the impaired child's school life. The social worker may assume responsibility for shaping a school system's attitudes to reflect more adaptive, relevant, and socially responsible positions (Lee, 1983).

School social workers may be responsible for developing communication links within the school so that teachers, administrators, and other staff can exchange information necessary for student programming. They may also plan in-service workshops in areas related to student welfare. Future trends in special education social work will continue to expand the systems approach to service delivery. To this end, an increase in coordinator and liaison roles for special education social workers is predicted (Randolph, 1982), and mandated in inclusive programming (Pryor, Kent, McGunn, & LeRoy, 1996).

REFERENCES

Costin, L. B. (1981). School social work as specialized practice. *Social Work, 26,* 36–44.

Dickerson, M. O. (1981). *Social work practice and the mentally retarded.* New York: Free Press.

Hancock, B. L. (1982). *School social work.* Englewood Cliffs, NJ: Prentice-Hall.

Lee, L. J. (1983). The social worker in the political environment of a school system. *Social Work, 28*(4), 302–307.

Pryor, C. B., Kent, C., McGunn, C., & LeRoy, B. (1996). Redesigning social work in inclusive schools. *Social Work, 41*(6), 668–676.

Randolph, J. L. (1982). School social work can foster educational growth for students. *Education, 102,* 260–265.

Winters, W. G., & Easton, F. (1983). *The practice of social work in the schools.* New York: Free Press.

GARY BERKOWITZ
Temple University

MULTIDISCIPLINARY TEAMS
PERSONNEL TRAINING IN SPECIAL EDUCATION

SOCIODRAMA

Sociodrama is a group-therapy technique developed by J. L. Moreno (1946) as an extension of a group-therapy technique, also devised by Moreno, known as psychodrama. (Moreno is often credited with having initiated group therapy in Vienna just after the beginning of the twentieth century.) Though he developed the technique, Moreno did little with sociodrama, preferring to continue his efforts in the development and application of psychodrama. E. Paul Torrance, a psychodramatist who studied with Moreno, later reconceptualized and refined sociodrama as a group problem-solving technique based on Moreno's early work but also incorporating the creative problem-solving principles of Torrance (1970) and Osborn (1963). Sociodrama can be used with all ages from preschool through adulthood.

The primary uses of sociodrama, largely reflecting Torrance's interests and influence, have been in primary prevention of behavior problems with the disadvantaged and other high-risk populations. Sociodrama has also been used in specific treatment programs with adolescents who engage in socially deviant behaviors and with status offenders. Sociodrama seems particularly helpful in introducing and teaching new social behaviors as well as in improving the problem-solving skills of the youngsters involved, giving them more behavioral options.

During sociodrama, a problem or conflict situation that is likely to be common to the group is derived from group discussion. Members of the group are cast into roles, which they play as the situation is acted out. Many production techniques are brought into play to facilitate solution of the conflict; these include the double, the soliloquy, direct presentation, mirror, and role reversal.

The director's role is to keep the action moving in the direction of a resolution, or, preferably, multiple resolutions of the conflict. Each session should end with a series of potential resolutions that can be discussed by the group. Appropriate behaviors can also be practiced. By teaching participants to brainstorm alternative behaviors and to rehearse for real-life problem situations, sociodrama has proved a useful method for treatment and prevention of behavior problems in children and adolescents. Torrance (1982) provides a more detailed presentation of the techniques of sociodrama.

REFERENCES

Moreno, J. L. (1946). *Psychodrama.* Beacon, NY: Beacon House.

Osborn, A. F. (1963). *Applied imagination* (3rd ed.). New York: Scribner's.

Torrance, E. P. (1970). *Creative learning and teaching.* New York: Dodd, Mead.

Torrance, E. P. (1982). Sociodrama: Teaching creative problem-solving as a therapeutic technique. In C. R. Reynolds & T. B. Gutkin (Eds.), *The handbook of school psychology.* New York: Wiley.

CECIL R. REYNOLDS
Texas A & M University

GROUP THERAPY
PSYCHODRAMA

SOCIOECONOMIC IMPACT OF DISABILITIES

There is a well-established relationship between parents' socioeconomic status and children's school performance, (Barona, 1992). Caldwell (1970) reports that many of the children from lower socioeconomic classes live in restricted and nonstimulating environments. As a result, low socioeconomic profile is one factor that is significantly related to poor cognitive functioning. There are many more children from lower socioeconomic classes with poor cognitive functioning than from higher socioeconomic classes.

An investigation analyzing the extent to which parental social status influences the decisions made in reference to potentially handicapped students was conducted by Ysseldyke et al. (1979). Individuals involved in decision making were given identical data on students referred for evaluation. All data were samples of normal or average performance. The decision makers were told in half of the cases that the child's father was a bank vice president and the mother a real estate agent. The other half were told that the child's father was a janitor at the bank and the mother a clerk at a local supermarket. As a result of knowledge of the parents' socioeconomic status, the decision makers made different placement and classification decisions for the children. This has been supported in later research (Podell & Scodlak, 1993).

There are many factors associated with socioeconomic status that are considered contributing factors to some disabilities. These include poor health care, inadequate pre- and postnatal care, improper diet, and lack of early stimulation. Zachau-Christiansen and Ross (1975) state that infants from lower socioeconomic families are at greater risk for experiencing or being exposed to conditions that may hinder development. These conditions include low birth weight, lead poisoning, malnutrition, and maternal infections during pregnancy. Kagan (1970) discusses other psychological differences between lower class and more privileged children. The differences are evident during the first 3 years of life and tend to remain stable over time. Variables include language, mental set, attachment, inhibition, sense of effectiveness, motivation, and expectancy of failure. All of the factors play a crucial role in influencing school performance. Deficits in any of these areas limits the child's ability in various cognitive skills. Young children raised in an environment lacking in stimulation and healthy interaction with adults will often be retarded in motor, language, cognitive, and social skills.

Lack of proper nutrition can negatively affect the maturation of the brain and central nervous system. Malnutrition affects brain weight and tends to have lasting effects on learning and behavior. It has a very damaging effect during the first 6 months of life owing to the rate of brain cell development during this period. In the area of mental retardation and learning disabilities, the majority of the students tend to be from lower socioeconomic status homes and racial and cultural minorities. In many cases, the poor achievement of the socioculturally different individual is related to lack of proper nutrition and medical care. Kavale (1980) reports that almost all complications of prenatal life, pregnancy, labor and delivery, and postnatal diseases that are potentially damaging to the infant's brain development are disproportionately high among low socioeconomic groups.

Many other correlates of low socioeconomic status are associated with poor school learning. Some of these correlates are delayed development of language; greater impulsivity; lower intelligence on standard intelligence tests that predict success in standard curricula; lower parental educational levels; families with children over five; poor home climate; lack of variety in sensory stimuli; minimal encouragement of scholastic success within the home; and less time spent on tasks in the classroom and on homework.

An area that is crucial to academic performance is language development. Jensen (1968) lists several factors associated with language development as sources of social class differences and intellectual achievement. In the lower classes, early vocalization by infants is less likely to be rewarded; the child is less likely to have a single mother-child relationship in the early years; there is less verbal interaction and verbal play in response to early vocalizations; and speech tends to be delayed. In the early stages of speech, there is less shaping of speech sounds, in which parents reinforce approximations of adult speech, and much vocal interaction with slightly older siblings whose own speech is only slightly more advanced and who do not systematically shape behavior.

According to MacMillian (1982), the physical environment of lower class homes tends to be related to cultural familial retardation. When compared with middle-class households, lower class households tend to have the father absent from the home, crowded living conditions, poor nutrition and medical care, large family size, dilapidated living environment, and high ratio of children to adults. These factors have a negative impact on the child and his or her social, emotional, and educational adjustment. In many instances, the lower classes are less likely to vote and participate in political or social activities.

MacMillian (1982) has emphasized the dangers of class stereotyping. Determining socioeconomic status and the relationship between the ratings and developmental outcomes can be misleading; there are some exceptions to every rule. It is very important that special education personnel are trained in cultural awareness programming that includes socioeconomic variables. The major concern should be placed on the overall impact of socioeconomic factors in preventing or enhancing the possibility of physical, social, emotional, and intellectual disabilities.

REFERENCES

Barona, A., & Faykus, S. P. (1992). Differential effects of sociocultural variables on special education eligibility categories. *Psychology in the Schools, 29*(4), 313–320.

Caldwell, B. (1970). The rationale for early intervention. *Exceptional Children, 36*, 717–727.

Jensen, A. R. (1968). Social class, race, and genetics: Implications for education. *American Educational Research Journal, 5*, 1–412.

Kagan, J. (1970). On class differences and early development. In V. Denenberg (Ed.), *Education of the infant and young child.* New York: Academic.

Kavale, K. A. (1980). Learning disability and cultural-economic disadvantage: The case for a relationship. *Learning Disability Quarterly, 3*, 97–112.

MacMillian D. L. (1982). *Mental retardation in school and society.* (2nd ed.). Boston: Little, Brown.

Podell, D. M., & Soodlak, L. C. (1993). Teacher efficacy and bias in special education referrals. *Journal of Educational Research, 86*(4), 247–253.

Ysseldyke, J. E., Algozzine, B., Regan, R., Potter, M., Richey, L., & Thurlow, M. L. (1979). *Psychoeducational assessment and decision making: A computer-simulated investigation* (Research Report No. 32). Minneapolis: University of Minnesota Institute for Research on Learning Disabilities.

Zachau-Christiansen, B., & Ross, E. M. (1979). *Babies: Human development during the first year.* Chichester, England: Wiley.

Zigler, E. (1970). Social class and the socialization process. *Review of Educational Research, 40,* 87–110.

JANICE HARPER
*North Carolina Central
University*

CULTURALLY/LINGUISTICALLY DIVERSE STUDENTS
GIFTED AND TALENTED MINORITIES
SOCIOECONOMIC STATUS

SOCIOECONOMIC STATUS (SES)

Davis (1986) defines socioeconomic status (SES) as a person's position in the community. There are many factors involved in determining SES. These factors include income, employment, location and cost of home, and social status of the family. Socioeconomic status influences various behavior patterns. For example, the number of children, the year and model of the family car, and the number of vacations per year will vary according to SES.

Society places a high value on wealth and material possessions. There is a tendency to rank individuals based on their wealth and power within the community. Wealth is highly correlated with education, income, and occupation. Studies of social classes in the United States report five or six classes. Hodges (1964) has developed a system of six social classes. The first is the upper-upper class, which represents 1 to 2% of the community. This group includes people with wealth, power, and a family name that is prominent. Individuals can only be born into this class, with the exception of a few marrying into it. The lower-upper class also represents 1 to 2% of the community. This class does not have a prominent family name and their money is fairly new. However, they have wealth and power. The upper-middle class represents 10 to 12% of the community. These people have college degrees, are usually professionals and successful merchants. The lower-middle class represents 33% of the community. These people are usually small business people, salespeople, clerks, and forepeople. They tend to have average income and education, with high value placed on family, religion, thrift, and hard work. The upper-lower class also represents 33% of the community. In many cases they are employees rather than employers. The lower-lower class represents 15 to 20% of the population. These people are unskilled workers. Many are not high-school graduates and may frequently be unemployed.

Socioeconomic status has a direct relationship to the length and quality of life. The lower-lower classes do not live as long as members of the upper class. The poor are more likely to suffer from chronic and infectious diseases and are less likely to see a physician or a dentist. This may be a result of lack of money to pay for medical expenses. However, it has also been found that minor illnesses such as fevers, have a low priority in poverty-stricken homes. Other factors such as child-rearing practices, are affected by socioeconomic status of the family. Middle-class parents tend to be more permissive, while lower class parents are more rigid (Bassis, Gelles, & Levine, 1980).

Kohn (1969) states that middle-class mothers value self-control, dependability, and consideration, while lower class mothers value obedience and the ability to defend oneself. The middle-class family raises the child in an environment where achievement and getting ahead are encouraged. The lower class family raises the child in an environment that emphasizes the immediate and the concrete. The child is taught to shy away from the new or unfamiliar. According to Boocock (1972), the family characteristic that is the most powerful predictor of school performance is socioeconomic status. More specifically, the higher the socioeconomic status of the family, the higher the child's academic achievement. Socioeconomic status also predicts the number and type of extracurricular activities the child will be involved in and social and emotional adjustment to school. Other areas highly correlated with socioeconomic status include grades, achievement test scores, retentions at grade level, course failures, truancy, suspensions from school, dropout rates, college plans, and total amount of schooling.

REFERENCES

Bassis, M. S., Gelles, R. J., & Levine, A. (1980). *Sociology: An introduction* (2nd ed.). New York: Random House.

Boocock, S. S. (1972). *An introduction to the sociology of learning.* Dallas: Houghton Mifflin.

Davis, W. E. (1986). *Resource guide to special education* (2nd ed.). Boston: Allyn & Bacon.

Hodges, H. M. (1964). *Social stratification.* Cambridge, MA: Schenkman.

Kohn, M. (1969). *Class and conformity.* Homewood, IL: Dorsey.

JANICE HARPER
*North Carolina Central
University*

SOCIOECONOMIC IMPACT OF DISABILITIES

SOCIOGRAM

A sociogram (Moreno, 1953) is a graphic display of inter-personal relationships within a group. It is considered one of the most common sociometric techniques used by teachers. In most instances, a sociometric test is administered to a group of children by asking each child who he or she would like to work with on a particular activity. The sociogram displays a diagram of students with whom other students prefer to study, play, or work. It also displays a diagram of students who are rejected and tend to be isolates. Each child is asked such questions as, With which three students would you prefer to study? Which three students do you like best? Which two students do you prefer to play with at recess? Which three students are your best friends? The students' responses to these types of questions are used to construct the sociogram.

There are two types of sociograms: the graphic and the target diagram. The graphic sociogram assigns initial letters of the alphabet (such as A, B, C) to the most popular students. These students appear in the center of the chart. The isolates are assigned middle letters (such as H, I, J), and appear on the edges of the diagram. Stanley and Hopkins (1972) listed the limitations of this chart as difficulty in reading with 30 or more students and requiring a great deal of practice to learn the most effective placement. The target diagram consist of circles, with the most popular students placed in the center and the isolated students placed on the outer edges. According to Stanley and Hopkins (1972), this diagram is more productive for teachers with large classrooms.

The information obtained from a sociogram can be used for assessing students who may be isolated, socially immature, unhappy, and who have disabilities (Conderman, 1995). Once this information has been obtained from the sociogram, the teacher may begin to ask questions to determine why some students are considered isolates and often rejected. This information can assist the teacher with assigning students to groups for class projects and making changes in classroom relationships. It may also alert the teacher to the possibility of an existing or potential handicapping condition. Almost 40% of all teachers use sociometric techniques (Vasa, Maag, Torrey, & Kramer, 1994).

REFERENCES

Conderman, G. (1995). Social status of sixth- and seventh-grade students with learning disabilities. *Learning Disability Quarterly. 18*(1), 13–24.

Moreno, J. L. (1953). *Who shall survive? Foundations of sociometry, group psychotherapy, and sociodrama* (2nd ed.). New York: Beacon House.

Stanley, J. C., & Hopkins, K. D. (1972). *Educational and psychological measurement and evaluation.* Englewood Cliffs, NJ: Prentice-Hall.

Vasa, S. F., Maag, J. W., Torrey, G. K., & Kramer, J. J. (1994). Teachers' use of and perceptions of sociometric techniques. *Journal of Psychoeducational Assessment, 12*(2), 135–141.

JANICE HARPER
*North Carolina Central
University*

SOCIAL SKILLS
SOCIAL SKILLS AND THE HANDICAPPED

SOCIOMETRIC TECHNIQUES WITH THE HANDICAPPED

Sociometric techniques originated by Moreno (1953) are a set of questions used to determine the social organization of a group. There are various types of sociometric techniques that are used with the handicapped. The two most common forms are peer nomination and roster and rating methods. Most peer nomination techniques ask questions such as, With whom would you most like to study? Who would you most like to sit with at lunch? Who would you most enjoy working with on an art project? Who would you most enjoy being with during break? (Mercer & Mercer, 1981 p. 109).

Other forms of peer nomination techniques may ask students questions relating to attitudes and behavior: Which students are very popular? Which students does the teacher like most? Which students cause a lot of trouble? Which students are selfish? (Mercer & Mercer 1981 p. 110). The rating scales usually lists all students in the class along with the rating scale (e.g., 1 = low and 10 = high) and ask each student to rate each person in the class. A score is determined for each child based on the average of their ratings.

Another common sociometric technique is the use of the sociogram, which is a visual display of the interrelationships within a group. The sociogram clearly shows which child is popular and which child is isolated by their positions on a diagram. There are teacher-made sociometric techniques and commercially produced sociometric techniques. The commercially produced techniques include the Ohio Social Acceptance Scale, which is designed for children in grades three through six. There are six headings: (1) my very best friends; (2) my other friends; (3) not friends, but okay; (4) don't know them; (5) don't care for them; (6) dislike them. The children are asked to write the names of their classmates under each of the headings (Wallace & Larsen 1978).

Another commercial technique is the Peer Acceptance Scale, which is used to obtain social status scores of children. This test uses stick figures of two children playing ball together, which is labeled friend; two children at a blackboard, which is labeled all right; and two children with their backs to each other, which is labeled wouldn't like. The students are read a list of names of classmates they are familiar with and asked to circle the figure that best describes how they feel about the student (Goodman, Gottlieb, & Harrison, 1972). The information from these sociometric techniques may be helpful to the teacher for the following activities: (1) assigning instructional groups and peer tutors; (2) planning affective development activities; (3) identifying potential groups; (4) predicting interpersonal difficulties within the group; and (5) measuring change in social adjustment (Marsh, Price, & Smith, 1983, p. 51).

With handicapped children social acceptance is considered a very important aspect of school adjustment and educational achievement. Sociometric techniques may help the teacher determine whether the handicapped child is accepted by his or her nonhandicapped peers (Conderman, 1995). If the child is not accepted, the next step is to decide which interventions will help to improve the child's social status.

REFERENCES

Conderman, G. (1995). Social status of sixth- and seventh-grade students with learning disabilities. *Learning Disability Quarterly, 18*(1), 13–24.

Goodman, H., Gottlieb, J., & Harrison, H. (1972). Social acceptance of EMRs integrated into a nongraded elementary school. *American Journal of Mental Deficiency, 76,* 412–417.

Marsh, G. E., Price, B. J., & Smith, T. E. (1983). *Teaching mildly handicapped children: Method and materials.* St. Louis: Mosby.

Mercer, C. D., & Mercer A. R. (1981). *Teaching students with learning problems.* Columbus, OH: Merrill.

Moreno, J. L. (1953). *Who shall survive? Foundations of sociometry, group psychotherapy and sociodrama* (2nd ed.). New York: Beacon House.

Wallace, G., & Larsen, S. (1978). *Educational assessment of learning problems: Testing for teaching.* Boston: Allyn & Bacon.

JANICE HARPER
*North Carolina Central
University*

SOCIAL SKILLS
SOCIOGRAM

SOCIOPATHY/ANTISOCIAL
PERSONALITY DISORDER

Sociopathy is a diagnostic label applied to adults of 18 years or older who exhibit a lifelong pattern of conduct problems or antisocial behavior. About 1800, Philippe Pinel coined the term *manie sans délire* to designate those individuals who exhibit deviant social behavior but lack many of the cardinal manifestations of a mental disorder such as delusions, hallucinations, or bizarre behavior. The category was narrowed when Prichard used the term moral insanity in the mid-nineteenth century. By the turn of the twentieth century, the label psychopathic inferiority was introduced by Koch; it is still reflected in the current usage of psychopathic personality disorder, psychopathic character, and psychopath. The *Diagnostic and Statistical Manual* (DSM) which was published in 1952, substituted the term sociopathic personality to underscore the etiological importance of environmental factors and to rid the concept of its moralistic flavor. The subsequent four editions of the DSM have favored the term antisocial personality disorder.

Behavioral characteristics of sociopaths can be observed in their work history, drug use (including alcohol), social and familial relationships, and illegal activities. Sociopaths frequently show a checkered employment history with significant unemployment, absenteeism, or frequent job changes. Their functioning as parents is often inadequate as evidenced by gross financial, medical, and emotional neglect of their children. An arrest record is not uncommon because sociopaths fail to accept norms. In addition, they exhibit difficulty in maintaining close relationships and interpersonal affairs and are often exploitive and blatantly manipulative. Sociopaths are remarkable for their lack of empathy and an absence of genuine remorse or guilt for their transgressions. Many sociopaths display a superficial charm and are highly skilled in conveying the appearance of sincerity; this makes them all the more successful in "conning" others. Some successful politicians, professionals, and business-people evidence aspects of sociopathy but are not likely to meet the current DSM-IV criteria for classification, particularly in the areas of employment history, poor school achievement, and delinquency. DSM-IV has been criticized for bringing the criteria for antisocial personality dangerously close to criminality in general (Davison & Neale, 1982). Contrary to popular myth, sociopaths are not of superior intelligence. Also, chronic criminal activity during adolescence or adulthood is not necessarily indicative of sociopathy. However, a random sample of the prison population would yield a higher percentage of sociopaths than would a random sample of the general population; that is why much of the research on sociopathy is conducted in prisons. The disorder is much more frequently diagnosed in males.

The most valid predictor of sociopathy is antisocial behavior in childhood. Fighting, stealing, persistent lying, delinquency, and chronic violations of rules at home serve as markers for the disorder. Conduct problems at school are chronic. It is not uncommon for these children to have a sociopathic father. In fact, irrespective of socioeconomic status, the more family relatives that display antisocial behavior, the greater the likelihood that the child will engage in antisocial acts (Robins, 1972).

As is true for most psychological disorders, specific patterns of parenting or family dynamics have not been clearly identified as leading to sociopathy. Nonetheless, several authors have noted two styles of child rearing that may contribute to the development of the syndrome (Meyer, 1980). One consists of cold, aloof parents that fail to demonstrate, and thus inculcate, a sense of empathy and a capacity for intimacy. The other parental style is characterized by a lack of consistency in administering reinforcement and punishment. The child then fails to learn abstract rules of right and wrong and instead responds to short-term consequences, fails to trust, and does not react to interpersonal consequences such as disapproval. In addition, exposure to an antisocial adult, usually a male, provides a model for nonnormative behavior.

Unfortunately, there is no widely accepted, experimentally based theory of sociopathy. Several biological and behavioral correlates have been observed but they have not as yet been integrated into a formulation that accounts for the development of the disorder. There is suggestive evidence that a biological predisposition may be of etiological significance. Research in Denmark by Hutchings and Mednick (1974) with criminals, and Schulsinger (1972) with sociopaths, revealed a higher rate of criminality and sociopathy in biological relatives. Research in the United States with adopted children has shown similar results (Cadoret, 1978; Crowe, 1974).

During the 1960s it was hypothesized that males who possessed an extra male Y chromosome were predisposed to violent activity. In fact, lawyers for the mass murderer Richard Speck tried unsuccessfully to use the XYY syndrome as the basis for an insanity plea. Ten years later, a large-scale study in Denmark (Witkin, et al., 1976) found the prevalence of this syndrome to be 2.9 per thousand. Of 12 XYY men, 5 (42%) had already been convicted of criminal offenses. Only 9.3% of a comparison group of XY men had been convicted of a crime. This would seem to lend support to the XYY syndrome hypothesis. However, it was found that only one of the XYY men had been convicted of a violent crime. Moreover, the average IQ of XYY males is lower than that of XY males. Thus it is plausible that men with subnormal intelligence are predisposed to criminal activity or are less successful in escaping apprehension for illegal activities.

Several studies have found electroencephalogram (EEG) abnormality in 31 to 58% of sociopaths. The most common abnormality is nonlocalized slow-wave activity, typical of infants and young children (Ellingson, 1954). Among extremely impulsive and aggressive sociopaths, temporal lobe EEG abnormalities have been found and positive spikes of 6 to 8 cycles per second (cps) and 14 to 16 cps have been observed (Hill, 1952; Syndulko, 1978). These data are difficult to interpret as causal factors in sociopa-

thy because not all sociopaths show such brain wave activity. Perhaps there are subtypes of this personality disorder that when identified will allow for a different etiological theory of each type. Nevertheless, Hare (1970) has speculated that slow wave brain activity is indicative of a dysfunction in behavioral inhibitory mechanisms. This is consistent with the belief that sociopaths have difficulty in learning from experience, and despite social or physical punishment continue their maladaptive behavior.

Based on early observations by Cleckley (1976) that sociopaths are seldom anxious, manifest a cool demeanor in the face of threat, and seem not to be regulated by the social consequences of their misbehavior, Lykken (1957) hypothesized that the sociopath's low level of anxiety is responsible for a lack of behavioral inhibition. In one study, in an experimental task, subjects were required to learn a sequence of 20 correct lever presses. Feedback was delivered that indicated when a response was correct or incorrect; some of the incorrect lever presses were followed by shock. Since the threat of shock induces anxiety and anxiety usually facilitates the learning of avoidance behavior, it was predicted that sociopaths would be less successful in learning to avoid the electric shock. When compared with a group of college students and nonsociopathic prison inmates, the results supported the hypothesis. Sociopaths received significantly more shocks than college students and their inmate counterparts, although the latter comparison only approached significance. A replication study by Schachter and Latané (1964) found clear differences among the groups, providing further support for the hypothesis. Moreover, when sociopaths were injected with adrenalin, their avoidance learning improved. Anxiety is mediated by the sympathetic branch of the autonomic nervous system and the effects of adrenalin mimic sympathetic activity, thus creating an increase in anxiety, particularly when the subject is unaware that he is receiving adrenalin, as was true in the study (Schachter & Singer, 1962).

An interesting study by Schmauk (1970) qualifies these findings by showing that sociopaths do not evidence impaired avoidance learning when the punisher is loss of money rather than shock. Thus it appears that the failure to learn from experience notion needs to be revised. While behavioral consequences such as physical punishment and social disapproval have less effect in controlling the behavior of sociopaths in comparison with nonsociopaths, consequences that are meaningful within the value system of the sociopath serve as effective motivators and do control their behavior, albeit the means used to avoid these punishers or acquire reinforcers may be antisocial.

Despite the protestations of some that sociopathy is a wastebasket category, the concept is considered meaningful by most clinicians (Gray & Hutchinson, 1964) and is reliably diagnosed. Indeed, interrater agreement for this disorder exceeds that commonly found for most other categories in the *Diagnostic and Statistical Manual* (Spitzer, Cohen, Fliess, & Endicott, 1967). No doubt the definitional criteria for antisocial personality will continue to shift, most likely in the direction of subtypes, as researchers continue to bring this complex syndrome into focus. It is hoped that these efforts will also lead to effective measures for prevention and treatment. With the exception of isolated reports (Meyer, 1980), the most optimistic prognostic statement is that the sociopathic behavior pattern seems to lessen as the person reaches middle age. However, special education personnel must deal with the conduct-disordered youth and hopefully prevent the antisocial adult from developing.

REFERENCES

Cadoret, R. J. (1978). Psychopathology in adopted-away offspring of biologic parents with antisocial behavior. *Archives of General Psychiatry, 35,* 176–184.

Cleckley, H. (1976). *The mask of insanity* (5th ed.). St. Louis: Mosby.

Crowe, R. R. (1974). An adoption study of antisocial personality. *Archives of General Psychiatry, 31,* 785–791.

Davison, G. C., & Neale, J. M. (1982). *Abnormal psychology.* New York: Wiley.

Ellingson, R. (1954). Incidence of EEG abnormality among patients with mental disorders of apparently nonorganic origin: A criminal review. *American Journal of Psychiatry, 111,* 263–275.

Gray, H., & Hutchinson, H. C. (1964). The psychopathic personality: A survey of Canadian psychiatrists' opinion. *Canadian Psychiatric Association Journal, 9,* 450–461.

Hare, R. D. (1970). *Psychopathy: Theory and research.* New York: Wiley.

Hill, D. (1952). EEG in episodic psychotic and psychopathic behavior: A classification of data. *EEG & Clinical Neurophysiology, 4,* 419–442.

Hutchings, B., & Mednick, S. A. (1974). Registered criminality in the adoptive and biological parents of registered male adoptees. In S. A. Mednick, F. Schulsinger, J. Higgins, & B. Bell (Eds.), *Genetics, environment and psychopathology.* New York: Elsevier.

Lykken, D. T. (1957). A study of anxiety in the sociopathic personality. *Journal of Abnormal and Social Psychology, 55,* 6–10.

Meyer, R. G. (1980). The antisocial personality. In R. H. Woody (Ed.), *Encyclopedia of clinical assessment.* San Francisco: Jossey-Bass.

Robins, L. N. (1972). Follow-up studies of behavior disorders in children. In H. C. Quay & J. S. Werry (Eds.), *Psychopathological disorders in childhood.* New York: Wiley.

Schachter, S., & Latané, B. (1964). Crime, cognition, and the autonomic nervous system. In D. Levine (Ed.), *Nebraska symposium on motivation* (Vol. 12). Lincoln: University of Nebraska Press.

Schachter, S., & Singer, J. E. (1962). Cognitive, social and physiological determinants of emotional state. *Psychological Review, 69,* 379–399.

Schmauk, F. J. (1970). Punishment, arousal, and avoidance learning in sociopaths. *Journal of Abnormal Psychology, 76,* 443–453.

Schulsinger, F. (1972). Psychopathy: Heredity and environment. *International Journal of Mental Health, 1,* 190–206.

Spitzer, R., Cohen, J., Fliess, J., & Endicott, J. (1967). Quantification of agreement in psychiatric diagnosis: A new approach. *Archives of General Psychiatry, 17,* 83–87.

Syndulko, K. (1978). Electrocortical investigations of sociopathy. In R. D. Hare & D. Schalling (Eds.), *Psychopathic behavior: Approaches to research.* New York: Wiley.

Witkin, H. A., Mednick, S. A., Schulsinger, F., Bakkestrom, E., Christiansen, K. O., Goodenough, D. R., Hirschhorn, K., Lundsteen, C., Owen, D. R., Philip, J., Rubin, D. B., & Stocking, M. (1976). Criminality in XYY and XXY men. *Science, 193,* 547–555.

LAURENCE G. GRIMM
University of Illinois

CONDUCT DISORDER
DRUG ABUSE

SOFT (NEUROLOGICAL) SIGNS

Neurological soft signs are defined by Shaffer, O'Connor, Shafer, and Prupis (1983) as "non-normative performance on a motor or sensory test identical or akin to a test of the traditional neurological examination, but a performance that is elicited from an individual who shows none of the features of a fixed or transient localizable neurological disorder" (p. 145). Some sources (e.g., Buda, 1981; Gaddes, 1985) suggest soft signs have a strong age-related component, in that many of the behaviors judged to represent soft signs in children of a certain age would be considered within the range of normal behavior for chronologically younger children (Ardilla & Rosselli, 1996). The term is contrasted with hard neurological signs, which are medically documented symptoms of neurologic disease.

The concept of neurological soft signs developed during the 1960s in conjunction with the non-defunct description of the minimal brain dysfunction (MBD) syndrome (Spreen et al., 1984). Although there were behavioral differences observed in children described as having MBD syndrome, hard neurologic findings were not demonstrated in the population. The vague, inconsistent behaviors that were observed were called soft neurological signs. To be considered a soft sign, Shaffer et al. (1983) state there should be no association between the observed behavior and a positive history of neurologic disease or trauma. Furthermore, clusters of neurological soft signs should not be pathognomonic of neurologic disease or encephalopathy. Soft signs, by definition, are not indicative of specific central nervous system pathology. Soft signs are not additive in the traditional sense: "the presence of more than one soft sign does not make a hard sign" (Spreen et al., 1984, p. 246).

The generalizability of data from studies of neurological soft signs has been complicated by inconsistency across studies in the specific signs tested. Soft signs have been categorized into three different types: those that may suggest immaturity or developmental delay; those that are mild expressions of classic hard neurological signs, which are difficult to elicit and may be inconsistent; and behaviors that may be associated with nonneurologic causes (Spreen et al., 1984). Testing a population of children for soft signs of the type associated with the first category may identify a different subgroup than would testing for signs associated with the others.

Nearly 100 different neurological soft signs have been identified (Spreen et al., 1984). Such signs encompass a wide variety of behaviors, including impulsivity (Vitello, Stoff, Atkins, & Mahoney, 1990) attention, concentration, fine motor speed, activity level, and affect. Gaddes (1985) lists the following as among the most common neurologic soft signs: motor clumsiness, speech and language delays, left-right confusion, perceptual and perceptual-motor deficits, and deficient eye-hand coordination. Soft signs may occur in conjunction with hyperactivity and specific learning disabilities, but the presence should not be considered pathognomonic of these conditions (Gaddes, 1985).

The relationship between neurologic soft signs and learning and behavior disorders in children has been investigated widely. In a comprehensive review of studies of children conducted prior to 1983, Shaffer et al. (1983) reported these investigations demonstrated consistent relationships between neurological soft signs and IQ scores, as well as diagnosed psychiatric disturbances and behavior problems. The authors described a study of 456 children participating in the Collaborative Perinatal Project of the National Institute of Neurological and Communicative Disorders and Stroke (NINCDS). The subjects were examined for the presence or absence of 18 neurological soft signs at age 7. Specific signs included movement disorders (e.g., tics, tremors, mirror movements) and coordination difficulties (e.g., dysmetria, dysdiadochokinesia). Subjects were rated blind on 15 behaviors (e.g., fearfulness, verbal fluency, cooperativeness, attention span). As in previous studies, the authors reported increased incidence of cognitive dysfunction, learning problems, and behavior disorders in children who exhibited neurologic soft signs.

The etiology of neurological soft signs has not been delineated clearly, and it is likely there are multiple causes. Soft signs may constitute one end of a continuum of neurologic signs, and thus may be a result of mild central nervous system impairment. For other individuals, soft signs may represent a genetic variation (Shaffer et al., 1983). The high incidence of neurologic soft signs in the general population suggests that caution should be exercised when interpreting their significance.

REFERENCES

Ardilla, A., & Rosselli, M. (1996). Soft neurological signs in children: A normative study. *Developmental Neuropsychology, 12*(2), 181–200.

Buda, F. B. (1981). *The neurology of developmental disabilities.* Springfield, IL: Thomas.

Gaddes, W. H. (1985). *Learning disabilities and brain function: A neuropsychological approach* (2nd ed.). New York: Springer-Verlag.

Shaffer, D., O'Connor, P. A., Shafer, S. Q., & Prupis, S. (1983). Neurological "soft signs": Their origins and significance for behavior. In M. Rutter (Ed.), *Developmental neuropsychiatry* (pp. 144–163). New York: Guilford.

Spreen, O., Tupper, D., Risser, A., Tuokko, H., & Edgell, D. (1984). *Human developmental neuropsychology.* New York: Oxford University Press.

Vitello, B., Stoff, D., Atkins, M., & Mahoney, A. (1990). Soft neurological signs and impulsivity in children. *Journal of Developmental & Behavioral Pediatrics, 11*(3), 112–115.

CATHY F. TELZROW
*Cuyahoga Special Education
Service Center*

LATERALIZATION
NEUROPSYCHOLOGY
VISUAL-MOTOR AND VISUAL-PERCEPTUAL PROBLEMS

SOMPA

See SYSTEM OF MULTICULTURAL PLURALISTIC ASSESSMENT.

SONICGUIDE

The Sonicguide is a mobility aid and environmental sensor for the visually handicapped. It operates on the principle of reflected high-frequency sound, which, when converted into audible stereophonic signals, provides the user with information about the distance, position, and surface characteristics of objects within the travel path and immediate environment. Users of all ages (Hill, Dodson-Burk, Hill, & Fox, 1995) learn to locate and identify objects up to a distance of approximately 5 meters.

A transmitter in the center of a spectacle frame radiates ultrasound (high-frequency sound inaudible to the human ear) in front of the wearer. When the ultrasound hits an obstruction such as a wall, a person, or a tree, it is reflected to the aid and received by two microphones below the transmitter. The microphones transform the reflected signals into electrical signals, which are shifted to a much lower range of frequency and converted into audible sounds by two small earphones in the arms of the spectacle frame. The sounds are then directed to each ear by small tubes. These tubes do not interfere with normal hearing and the user learns to integrate the sounds of the Sonicguide with natural sounds to enhance a concept of the environment. The microphones are deflected slightly outward so that sounds produced by objects to either side of the user will be louder in the ear nearer to the object. This process of sound localization occurs in normal hearing and therefore is a natural indication of direction. The pitch of the signal indicates the approximate distance of a reflecting object; it is highest at the maximum range of the aid and gradually reduces as the object comes closer. By interpreting the comparative loudness at each ear of the signal and its pitch and tonal characteristics, the user is able to judge the direction, distance, and surface qualities of reflecting objects.

The electronics of the aid are contained in a control box that is attached by a cable to the spectacle frame. The battery that powers the aid is attached under the control box and the complete unit can be carried in a pocket, at the belt, or on a shoulder strap. The aid's sensors are built into a spectacle frame to encourage the user to develop the same head movements and posture as a sighted person. When the skills of the aid are mastered, safer and more confident travel and a heightened awareness of the environment is assured. In outdoor situations, the device is to be used in conjunction with a long cane or guide dog, unless the area of travel is both familiar and free from hazards at ground level, which the Sonicguide may not detect.

REFERENCE

Hill, M. M., Dodson-Burk, B., Hill, E. W., & Fox, J. (1995). An infant sonicguide intervention program for a child with a visual disability. *Journal of Visual Impairments, 89*(4), 329–336.

MONIQUE BAUTERS
*Centre d'Etude et de
Reclassement*

**BLIND
ELECTRONIC TRAVEL AIDS
VISUAL TRAINING**

SOUTH AFRICA, SPECIAL EDUCATION IN

Introduction

Special education provision during the period prior to 1994 (commonly referred to as the apartheid era) is character-ized by disparate provision of services in terms of race. As a result of apartheid policy the state classified four groups Africans, Coloreds, Whites, and Indians, who were exposed to different education systems that were controlled by the Apartheid State. During this period there were 17 different education departments in South Africa.

The 17 departments include those that were created in homelands. "The homelands or Bantustan policy was an important part of the National Party's (White minority ruling party) plan for South African development, and its accompanying ideology...the homeland policy would reduce the numbers of permanently settled blacks in urban areas, and provide an alternative basis for the supply and control of black labor" (Christie & Collins, 1990, p. 172). Thus, large numbers of Africans were moved to homelands that were self-governing but controlled by the apartheid state. There were 10 of these states, each with a separate education department. The provision of services in special schools in self-governing states was minimal. For example, in two of these states, KaNgwane and KwaNdebele, there were no special schools. In KwaZulu, there were 7 special schools and the total school enrollment of these children was 15.9% of the total school enrollment in the country (National Education Policy Investigation into Education Support Services, 1992). There were 89 special schools for White children, and they only constituted 9.7% of the total school enrollment (National Education Policy Investigation into Education Support Services, 1992).

Generally, fiscal allocation for the provision of education was skewed towards Whites, and consequently White children enjoyed a much better service delivery. For example, government expenditure on auxiliary services (school health, school guidance and counseling, and special education) for White children amounted to 30% of the total budget. They constituted 9.7% of the total school enrollment. The remaining 70% had to be shared between classified Africans, Coloreds, and Indians who made up 79.2%, 8.7%, and 2.4% of total school enrollment respectively (National Education Policy Investigation into Education Support Services, 1992).

As a result of wide-scale inequalities and the inevitability of a new democratic order in South Africa, policy initiatives were begun as early as 1990, with a goal of establishing ways of redressing historical imbalances and creating an equitable dispensation for all South Africans.

Policy Initiatives in Special Education

Between December 1990 and August 1992, the National Education Policy Investigation into Education Support Services was conducted. This was a component of a wider investigation that included all areas of education with the aim of building a unitary and efficient education system for all South Africans.

Besides providing policy options that suggested equality in special education provision for all South Africans, this policy investigation challenged the conceptualization of special education need (SEN). The challenge centered around the lack of consideration of extrinsic factors as a possible cause of SEN. The report indicated that by locating the problem within the learner and ignoring societal factors, the system "perpetuates categorization, labeling, and separation of the child from mainstream education and community life" (National Policy Investigation into Education Support Services, 1992:78). This statement was particularly significant because the majority of Black children in South Africa face adverse social conditions that could result in a breakdown in learning (Naicker, 1995). As a result, many universities and colleges of education injected a sociological dimension in SEN preservice and in-service teacher training courses to provide a more comprehensive understanding, thus ensuring more appropriate intervention strategies. In 1992, the National Party Government, after an investigation into all areas of education, presented the Education Renewal Strategy (ERS). With regard to special education, the report called mainly for an equitable dispensation for all South Africans (ERS, 1992). There were no significant shifts in conceptualization.

After the advent of the new democratic order in 1994, the National Ministry of Education transformed the 17 education departments into a single system of education for all South Africans. As part of the transformation initiative, the National Ministry of Education appointed a National Commission for Special Education Needs and Training (NCSNET) and the National Committee for Education Support Services (NCESS) in 1996. Both NCSNET and NCESS were charged with the task of making recommendations on all aspects of special needs and support services in education and training in South Africa. As part of its terms of reference, the NCSNET and NCESS were to appropriate the principles of the Constitution of South Africa, the White Paper on Education and Training, and major international declarations, such as the Salamanca Statement, that were underpinned by a rights culture. With regards to a rights culture, the new Constitution in South Africa states very clearly that nobody should be discriminated against on the basis of race, disability, or gender (Constitution of South Africa, 1996).

The investigation was completed in the latter part of 1997 and the report was submitted to the National Minister of Education in November of the same year. The recommendations of the NCSNET and NCESS were radically different from previous policy initiatives. While other policy investigations focused on equity and minor conceptual shifts, the central thrust of the recommendations was a move away from a dual system of education to a single one. "Key strategies to achieve the vision include: transforming all aspects of the education system, developing an integrated system of education, and infusing 'special needs and support services' throughout the system. It also has

the strategy of the holistic development centers of learning to ensure a barrier-free physical environment and a supportive and inclusive psychosocial learning environment, and developing a flexible curriculum to ensure access to all learners. By promoting the rights and responsibilities of parents, teachers and learners, it provides effective development programs for educators, support personnel, and other relevant human resources. While fostering holistic and integrated support provision (intersectoral collaboration), it develops a community-based support system which includes a preventative and developmental approach to support, and developing funding strategies that ensure redress, sustainability, and ultimately access to education for all learners" (NCSNET & NCESS report, 1997, p. xi).

Therefore, the recommendations of both NCSNET and NCESS suggest that education centers (schools) should have the capacity to respond to diversity. Further, those barriers to learning should be identified and broken down. More emphasis should be placed on the limitations of the system instead of the deficits in individuals. For example, a learner who is physically disabled and uses a wheelchair would gain access to mainstream schools by removing the barrier of lack of access (since no ramps are provided). It also suggests a range of learning contexts offering diversity in terms of the curriculum, and that 'high need' support (severe difficulties) to a small percentage of learners should be made available, taking into account the need to promote their full participation and inclusion in the education process and in society at large (NCSNET & NCESS, 1997). In order to bring about these radical changes, the NCSNET and NCESS recommended that the implementation plan will be put into place over a 10-year period.

Current State of Special Education

The recommendations of NCSNET and NCESS have resulted in the appointment of a three-person committee to pursue the drafting of a White Paper in 1998 that captures the work of the commission. When completed, the White Paper will be circulated for comment. Thereafter, legislation will be drafted and tabled in Parliament. It is expected that this process will be completed at the end of 1999 (Report of NCSNET & NCESS). In the interim, while there are many difficulties associated with transformation, the nine provinces in South Africa are compelled through legislation to ensure that there is no racial discrimination concerning provision of special education services. Many of the difficulties relate to lack of resources, poorly trained and unqualified Black teachers, resources being located in more privileged areas, and unwillingness amongst those privileged in the past to share in the notion of change. The dual systems of regular and special education are still in place. It is anticipated that once legislation is passed in Parliament, the ten-year plan of the NCSNET and NCESS for the transformation from a dual to a single system of education will be initiated with a massive financial injection.

REFERENCES

Christie, P., & Collins, C. (1990). Bantu education: Apartheid and labour reproduction. In P. Kallaway, (Ed.), *Apartheid and education.* Johannesburg: Raven Press.

Department of National Education. (1992). *Education renewal strategy.* Pretoria: Government Printer.

Department of Education. (1997). *Report of the National Commission on Special Needs in Education and Training and National Committee for Education Support Services.* Pretoria: Government Printer.

Naicker, S. M. (1995). The politics of special education. *Perspectives in Education, 16*(1), 163–172.

Naicker, S. M. (1995). The need for a radical restructuring of special education need in South Africa. *British Journal of Special Education, 22*(4), 152–154.

National Education Policy Investigation. (1992). *Support services.* Cape Town: Oxford University Press.

Parliament of South Africa. (1996). *The Constitution of South Africa.* Pretoria: Government Printers.

SIGAMONEY NAICKER
*Western Cape Educational SI
Department*

SOUTH AMERICA

See ARGENTINA, SPECIAL EDUCATION IN; MEXICO, SPECIAL EDUCATION IN; PERU, SPECIAL EDUCATION IN.

SOUTHERN AND EASTERN AFRICA, SPECIAL EDUCATION IN

A brief history, statements on current status, and the future prospects of special education in twelve East and Southern African countries are presented here. The countries discussed include Botswana, Ethiopia, Eriteria, Kenya, Lesotho, Malawi, Namibia, Swaziland, Tanzania, Uganda, Zambia, and Zimbabwe. The availability of information on the aforementioned topics and between these countries differs widely. Thus, some countries are discussed in greater detail (Tanzania, Uganda, and Zimbabwe) than others (Eriteria, Malawi, and Swaziland).

Incidence of Handicapping Conditions within This Region

Reliable data on the incidence of childhood disorders within this region are unavailable. Various problems associated with incidence surveys preclude obtaining accurate data. Parents may need to register their disabled children in special centers, and they often are reluctant to admit their children display handicapping conditions (Kisanji, 1997; Whyte & Ingstad, 1995). Also, community attitudes toward the handicapped often are negative (Devlieger, 1995; Jackson & Mupedziswa, 1989). These and other qualities are believed to contribute to grossly underestimated incidence figures for handicapping conditions.

This large region in East and Southern Africa is home to an estimated 59,800,000 children. Population details for children ages 5 to 16 years for the year 1996 are provided below (UNICEF, 1996):

Botswana	700,000
Ethiopia	15,600,000
Eritrea	1,600,000
Kenya	12,100,000
Lesotho	600,000
Malawi	3,200,000
Namibia	700,000
Tanzania	8,700,000
Uganda	10,500,000
Zambia	2,900,000
Zimbabwe	3,200,000

If we accept the World Health Organization's general incidence estimate that 10% of a country's population is likely to be handicapped, almost six million children in this region can be expected to have one or more handicapping conditions. We believe this estimate substantially underestimates the number of handicapped children, given the region's sub-standard medical, health, and early childhood education facilities. Among children with handicaps, less than 1% attend formal school (Tungaraza, 1994; Kann, Mapolelo, & Nleya, 1989).

General History of Educational Services for Handicapped Children

The availability of special education services and other resources for children with physical, sensory, and cognitive disabilities occurred recently. Historically, native African societies integrated learning and other developmental activities within their everyday home and community activities (Kisanji, 1997). Home- and community-based activities provide various advantages: a favorable ratio between the young and elders, accommodations to match the child's developmental levels, and utilization of the child's natural milieu within which to promote development and transfer of training. The extent to which homes and communities provide appropriate adaptations to accommodate children with disabilities is unknown. The beneficial effects that professional services can have on children with disabilities are well-established.

The introduction and evolution of professional services for these children in East and Southern Africa closely follows a pattern found in other developing areas: first, national or regional institutions, often residential in nature and initiated by religious, humanitarian, and philanthropic agencies, are established. Professional services for middle-class children then develop in metropolitan centers. The widespread provision of services to children with disabilities in public schools occurs only after general education services, at least through the elementary level, are well-developed and nationally available. Children with handicapping conditions who reside in rural areas are least likely to receive professional services. Stronger special education services generally are found in countries with stronger and well-established regular education programs (Saigh & Oakland, 1989).

The majority of countries in this region have inadequate basic education programs (UNICEF, 1991, 1994), lack formal special education policies, and experience school dropout rates in the range of 15% to 60% involving disadvantaged children, which includes those with disabilities (Kann, Mapolelo, & Nleya, 1989; Stubbs, 1997; UNICEF, 1994).

The Role of Missionaries

Christian missionaries, often from Western Europe, initiated and provided almost all formal education within African communities during the colonial period. The development of special education services in this region is closely associated with their work. Trends in the development of special education facilities within individual countries generally followed a consistent pattern: Services were provided first for those with visual handicaps, and then for those with auditory, physical, and mental handicaps. This trend probably reflected the missionaries' beliefs as to the resources (like teaching expertise and materials) needed to serve each of these groups, as well as the family's willingness to admit one or more members have a disability. Because of their normal hearing ability, persons with visual impairments may have been thought to respond more favorably to the use of conventional instructional methods.

In Botswana, German missionaries opened special schools for the visually handicapped at Linchwe (in Mochudi) and the hearing impaired at Ramotswa (in Ramotswa) in the 1950s. A German couple opened residential centers named Rankoromane based on the Waldorf School model to educate children with mental handicaps in a number of towns in the late 1960s (Ingstad, 1995).

In Ethiopia, the Christofeblinden Mission opened a school for the blind and a training program for teachers of the visually handicapped in the early 1950s. Finnish missionaries were involved in developing Ethiopia's special education programs, and they opened a school for the deaf at Keren in the 1950s. The Church of Christ established

the Mekanissa School for the Deaf in 1964. The Baptist Mission created the Alpha School for the Deaf in Addis Ababa in 1967. The Ethiopian Evangelical Mekaneyesus Church started the Hossana School for the Deaf in 1981.

In Eriteria, French Catholic, Swedish Lutheran and Italian Catholic churches provided school education to the natives since 1890 (Miran, 1998). The role of these organizations in founding schools for persons with disabilities could not be established. Eriteria, now an independent nation, was once a province of Ethiopia.

The first school in Kenya for the visually impaired, the Thika School, was opened by the Salvation Army in 1946 (Kristensen, 1987). Kenya's first full-time program to prepare teachers of students with visual handicaps and a school for deaf-blind children were founded by the Christofeblinden Mission in the 1980s.

In Malawi, education for the blind was started during the early 1940s when two primary residential special schools were established by missionaries at Kasungu and Lulwe. The Catholic Order of the Immaculate Conception (of the Netherlands) developed a program in 1964 that integrated students with and without visual impairments into regular classrooms within ordinary schools; resource rooms provided supportive services to the visually impaired. Fourteen resource rooms serving about 100 blind students were in operation by 1983 (Ross, 1988). The program at Montfort College, organized by the Catholic teaching brothers of the Order of the Immaculate Conception, prepared teachers for students with auditory and visual impairments for Malawi and some neighboring countries (namely, Lesotho, Swaziland, Tanzania, Zimbabwe, and Zambia) in the 1970s.

Tanzania established its first special education facility in 1950 when the Anglican Church opened a school for the blind, the Buigiri School. Two additional schools for the blind followed this school, one opened by the Swedish Free Mission, the Furaha, in 1962, and another by the Lutheran Church, the Irente School, in Lushoto in 1963. The first Tanzanian school for the hearing impaired, the Tabora Deaf-Mute Institute, was opened by the Roman Catholic Church in 1963. The Salvation Army opened the first school in Tanzania for the physically handicapped in 1967.

In Zambia, missionaries again pioneered special education services in the region (Csapo, 1987a). The Dutch Reformed Church established the first school for the deaf (Sichula, 1990) and one for the blind (Csapo, 1987a) at Magwero Mission in 1955. The Christian Mission of Zambia opened another school for the blind at Mambiling soon after. Other special schools were opened by missionaries and continue to exist today.

In Zimbabwe, the Dutch Reformed Church opened the Margaret Hugo School for The Blind, at Masvingo in 1927 (Peresuh, Adenigba, & Ogonda, 1997). Two schools for the hearing impaired opened in 1947, one in Loreto and another in Pamushana, founded by the Catholic Dominican Sisters and the Dutch Reformed Church respectively (Chimedza, 1994).

Information on missionary work and the opening of special education facilities in Lesotho, Namibia, Swaziland, and Uganda could not be located. However, the Dutch Reformed Church appears to have been involved in Namibia, and the Roman Catholic Church and Church of Uganda may have been involved in Uganda. Margaret Brown of the Church Missionaryf Society initiated Uganda's in-service teacher education for children with hearing impairment in 1962. Although Islam has a substantial following in some East African countries (namely, Tanzania, Uganda, Kenya, and Ethiopia), its role in establishing special education facilities in these countries could not be ascertained.

The Role of International Nongovernmental Organizations and Local Organizations

International nongovernmental organizations and local organizations advocating on behalf of students with disabilities also have had strong roles in developing and providing special education services. Their importance exceeds that of the colonial governments. The Danish International Development Agency (DANIDA), UNESCO Sub-Regional Project for Special Education in Eastern and Southern Africa, Swedish International Development Agency (SIDA), Royal Commonwealth Society for the Blind (now called the Sight Savers), International League for Persons with Mental Handicaps, and the British Red Cross are among the international agencies that have played significant roles in establishing special education programs in East and Southern Africa. DANIDA has been actively involved in promoting special education advising in Kenya, Uganda, and Zimbabwe for at least the past decade. SIDA has been involved in developing special education programs in all twelve Eastern and Southern African countries which comprise the focus of this paper. It helped establish Braille printing presses in Tanzania in 1971 (Tungaraza, 1994) and in Zimbabwe in 1994. In the early 1960s the Royal Commonwealth Society for the Blind started a rehabilitation center at Salama (in Uganda) for adults with visual impairments (Onen & Njuki, 1998).

Information on the involvement of local organizations in founding special education facilities in the East and Southern African countries is quite sparse. The Botswana Red Cross, with support from the Norwegian Red Cross, established a vocational training center for persons with physical disabilities in 1981. The Botswana Council for the Disabled has been unable to implement programs that enable children with disabilities to attend school (Ingstad, 1995). In Ethiopia, the Haile Selassie One Foundation established two special schools for blind students. They became government schools in the 1980s.

In Kenya, local voluntary organizations established two special schools for the mentally handicapped at St.

Nicholas and Aga Khan in the late 1950s. These schools amalgamated in 1968 to form the Jacaranda School (Ross, 1988). The Kenya Society for the Mentally Handicapped and The Parents and Friends of Handicapped Children were formed by parents of children with disabilities to promote the education of persons with disabilities, improve the preparation for teachers of children with disabilities, and consolidate schools. The Tanzania Society for the Deaf established the first school for the hearing impaired at Buguruni in 1974. In 1955, the first school for children with visual impairment and blindness was started at Madera in Eastern Uganda by the joint effort of the then-local education committee (Teso education committee), the Ministry of Education, and Uganda Foundation for the Blind. The Uganda government later asked the Catholic Church to administer the school.

With the assistance of the Uganda Society for the Deaf, Sherali Bendali Jafer, Peter Ronald, and Mr. Semmpebwa were closely involved in developing awareness throughout Uganda of the need to educate children with hearing impairment (Onen & Njuki, 1998). As a result of their efforts, an integration unit for children with hearing impairment was started at Mengo Primary School. Subsequently, the Uganda School for the Deaf was started on Namirembe Hill in 1968. The following year, Ngora School for the Deaf was established.

Ugandan educational services for children with physical disabilities and mental handicaps both began in 1968, and both were largely the results of efforts of local self-help organizations. For instance, the Uganda Spastic Society was formed in 1968. Its membership consisted mainly of parents of children with spastic conditions and polio, and medical professionals. The society played a key role in the establishment of a school for the physically handicapped at Mengo (Onen & Njuki, 1998). Services for children with mental disabilities were available through the Uganda Association for Mental Health (UAMH). This association, established in 1968 by the Ministry of Health, had a short life due to the political turmoil in the country at the time and in subsequent years. In 1983, the Uganda Association for the Mentally Handicapped was founded, and it has been instrumental in the founding of many resource units for children with mental handicaps.

In Zimbabwe, the Jairos Jiri Association founded the Narran Center School for the Deaf and the Blind in Gweru in 1968, a school for the visually impaired at Kadoma in 1981, and a number of other schools for children with various physical, mental, and multiple handicaps at Bulawayo, Gweru, and Harare in the 1970s (Farquar, 1987). Zimbabwe's Council for the Blind has been involved in providing structural facilities and equipment to school-based integration units for children with visual disabilities since about 1980. Its Zimcare Trust has been actively involved in providing education for Zimbabwean children with mental handicaps since the 1980s.

Zambia's Council for the Handicapped has conferred with teachers and the Zambian government to promote effective ways of teaching children with disabilities since the 1970s. However, its role in the establishment of special education facilities in that country is unclear.

Information on the involvement of international nongovernmental agencies and local organizations advocating for those with disabilities and the establishment of special education facilities in Eriteria, Malawi, Namibia, and Swaziland could not be located.

The Role of Postcolonial Governments

Support for the development of special education by the postcolonial governments in each of the twelve East and Southern African countries differs widely. Support is strongest when elementary and secondary education is widely available and a commitment to the principle of universal education is widely held. Countries recently ravaged by civil war (Uganda, Eriteria, Ethiopia) currently are attempting to re-establish basic elementary and secondary education programs. Their programs in special education are in initial stages of development and support. In contrast, countries that have enjoyed relative political stability (Kenya, Tanzania, Zimbabwe) tend to have stronger regular education programs, as well as a longer history and stronger support for special education programs.

Although Botswana's National Development Plans (1973–1978; 1991–1997) identify the needs of disabled persons as a national priority (Ingstad, 1995), the government historically has viewed educational support to children with disabilities as a family responsibility rather than a state obligation (Ingstad, 1995; Kann et al., 1989). Children with disabilities are conspicuous in their absence from Botswana schools (Kann et al, 1989). Nonetheless, a special education unit was established within the Botswana Ministry of Education in 1984 with the support of SIDA. The University of Botswana has complemented government efforts by offering a two-year diploma course for specialist teachers for children with mental, visual, hearing, and learning handicaps, and is expected to launch a bachelor's degree in special education in August, 1998 (Abosi, C., pers. comm., February 2, 1998).

The Kenya government, through the Kenya Institute of Education, launched special needs teacher education programs at Jacaranda and Highridge Teachers Colleges in 1966–67 (Peresuh et al., 1997). The Kenya Institute of Special Education (KISE), founded by the Kenyan government with the assistance of DANIDA, has assumed responsibility for these programs. More than one thousand teachers have graduated from the KISE teacher education programs since 1987. KISE also is responsible for the educational placement of children with disabilities, community education, and teacher in-service education programs on disabilities.

Lesotho's government became involved in special education in 1987 when its Ministry of Education, with the financial support from the United States Agency for International Development (USAID), commissioned a comprehensive study of its special education programs and accompanying guidelines for its development (Csapo 1987b). The report recommended the infusion of special needs components to both pre- and in-service teacher preparation programs, adoption of an integration (resource room) model for educating children with special needs, and full community involvement in establishing and supporting special education facilities. The Lesotho Ministry of Education, Lesotho National Federation of Disabled People, Ministry of Social Welfare and Health, and Save the Children Fund (UK) created ten integration units. A special education unit was established in the Lesotho Ministry of Education in 1991 to coordinate the opening of integration units. The Lesotho National Teacher Training College assumed responsibility for introducing special education components in its pre-service programs in 1996, and the abovementioned special education unit within the Ministry of Education assumed responsibility for in-service education programs for teachers (Pholoho, Mariga, Phachaka, & Stubbs, 1995).

Namibia became politically independent in 1990 after a legacy of colonial rule under apartheid from South Africa, which left most of its Blacks with little or no education. Thus, the history of educating children with disabilities in Namibia is recent and short. According to Bruhns et al. (1995), Namibia established its first school for children with disabilities, the Dagbreek Special School, in 1970 as a racially segregated facility for White children. The school opened its doors to disabled students of other races after Namibia become independent. The Eluwa School for blind and deaf students was established at Ongwediva in 1973 with 20 deaf and 20 blind students. By 1995 the school enrolled 172 deaf, 70 blind, and eight physically disabled students. The Moreson School for children with severe learning difficulties was established by the Association of the Handicapped in 1976 and became a government school in 1990. It had 60 students along with seven teachers in 1995.

The Tanzania government, with the help of the Royal Commonwealth Society for the Blind, established the country's first integrated education program for children with visual handicaps, Uhuru Co-education School, in 1966, followed by a similar program for children with mental handicaps in 1982 (Tungaraza, 1994). The government also established a diploma-level teacher education program in 1976 and one for teachers of pupils with mental handicaps in 1983 at the Tabora Teacher Training College. In addition, the Mpwapwa Teacher Training College prepares teachers to work with students with visual handicaps. The number of special needs teachers who have graduated from the two Tanzania colleges could not be established.

Uganda's government involvement in special education came earlier than others in the region because of the lobbying efforts of Sr. Andrew Cohen, then-Governor of Uganda, to educate a blind relative (Atim, 1995). Government support to educate the blind was established through an act of Parliament in 1952. The first trial to integrate children with visual impairment was launched in 1962 at Wanyange Girls School in Eastern Uganda. In July 1973, a department of special education was established at the Uganda Ministry of Education headquarters in Kampala. This department was created to coordinate special education services in the Ministry and to work with other governmental and nongovernmental organizations providing services for persons with disabilities. The head start Uganda enjoyed in developing its special education programs was severely thwarted during two decades of dictatorships and civil war. Special education programs in Uganda began to rebuild after 1991.

The Ugandan government, with the help of DANIDA, founded the Uganda National Institute of Special Education (UNISE) in 1991 and save it the responsibility for co-ordinating the country's special education programs and teacher education programs at certificate, diploma, and degree levels. So far, about 255 teachers have received specialist training and attended awareness seminars, which are offered to ordinary primary school teachers in the districts throughout the country. The Special Education/Educational Assessment and Resource Services of Uganda (EARS-U) was formed in 1992. EARS-U, a division within the Uganda Ministry of Education, is responsible for evaluating programs for children with hearing, speech, learning, visual, mental, and physical impairments. EARS-U also is responsible for coordinating educational placements of children with disabilities, counseling services to their parents, community education, and prevention programs.

The Zimbabwe government, with the assistance of SIDA, established a Department of Special Education within the Ministry of Education in 1982, with its primary responsibility being educational placement of children with disabilities, pre-service and in-service training of teachers on special educational needs, and community education programs on disabilities. A teacher education program for teachers of children with visual, mental, hearing, and speech and language impairments was established by the government at the United College of Education in Bulawayo in 1983. About 300 special needs teachers graduated from the United College of Education since the establishment of its special education teacher education program. A two-year, post-diploma bachelor's degree in special education was launched at the University of Zimbabwe in 1993 and has graduated about 75 teachers of special needs children. The Zimbabwe Ministry of Education also has issued a number of documents to guide special education programs in the schools (Mpofu & Nyanungo, in press).

Government involvement in special needs programs in Zambia, Ethiopia, Eriteria, Malawi, and Swaziland could not be ascertained. However, respondents to a recent survey of special needs experts in these countries suggested that special education facilities in these countries are quite limited (Mpofu, Zindi, Oakland, & Peresuh, 1997).

Current Status of Special Education in East and Southern Africa

Special education services in East and Southern Africa generally follow a functional integration (resource room) model in which children with disabilities attend class part-time to full-time with their non-disabled peers and receive support of a full-time specialist teacher (Charema & Peresuh, 1997). Specialist teachers maintain the resource room, provide intensive individualized instruction to children with disabilities, and work closely with mainstream teachers in planning and effecting integration strategies for children with disabilities. A functional integration model generally is preferred for children with mild to moderate sensory, physical, and cognitive handicaps. Children with more severe handicaps generally attend special schools and rehabilitation centers, typically those residential in nature, which provide more specialized resources. With few exceptions, most integration units for the visually handicapped and hearing impaired are residential, whereas those for children with moderate to mild physical and cognitive handicaps are nonresidential.

Compared to current needs and potential demand, special education facilities in the twelve East and Southern countries of this survey are severely limited. Botswana has approximately 20 special schools and resource units for children with visual, auditory, mental, and physical handicaps (Abosi, C. O., pers. comm., February 2, 1998). Current enrollment figures by handicapping condition were unavailable. However, previous enrollment was vision (35 students), hearing (88), mental (176), and physical (18) (Kann et al., 1989). There are no facilities in the country for children with severe disabilities.

Lesotho has twelve special schools (Stubbs, 1997). Enrollment figures by handicapping condition were unavailable. Lesotho's Ministry of Education, with support from international nongovernmental organizations and United Nations agencies, recently opened integration units for children with a variety of handicaps in eight of the country's ten districts.

Namibia's school for children with visual impairments has 71 students and its school for the hearing impaired has 185 students (Bruhns et al., 1995). Twenty-four specialist teachers work in these schools. Two schools and 15 specialist teachers serve 125 children with severe learning disabilities. Two additional schools staffed by 67 teachers provide instruction to 733 children with mild learning difficulties. Twelve schools and 16 teachers offer remedial education to 385 children with specific learning disabilities. Namibia also has 28 integration units attended by 507 children with moderate to mild disabilities and taught by 40 teachers.

In Tanzania, services for students with visual impairments are provided in twelve special schools and 23 integrated (18 primary, 5 secondary) schools that offer education to 979 children with visual disabilities (Possi & Mkaali, 1995; Tungaraza, 1994). Sixty-four specialist teachers and 157 regular education teachers provide education to children with visual handicaps. Services for children with auditory impairments are provided through 14 special schools and three integrated primary (one residential and two nonresidential) schools to approximately 980 pupils and staffed by 100 specialist and 26 regular class teachers. In addition, 6 schools serve 305 deaf-blind students. About 930 children with physical disabilities attend 61 specialist and integration units staffed by 185 specialist and regular class teachers. The vast majority of children with physical disabilities either attend schools in their communities or do not attend school at all. Tanzania also has four residential special schools for children with moderate mental handicaps and 15 nonresidential integrated units that serve 980 children with moderate to mild mental handicaps. Sixty-seven specialist and 128 regular class teachers teach these children. Twelve children with autism and 14 with cerebral palsy attend four units taught by 6 specialist teachers. Thousands of children with severe mental handicaps do not receive any schooling. In contrast, more than 90% of Tanzanian children with epileptic conditions attend ordinary schools (Whyte, 1995).

Uganda has at least 6 special schools and one integration unit which serve about 500 children with visual impairments, two special schools for 150 children with hearing impairments, and one special school for 124 students with physical handicaps (Ross, 1988). An estimated 32,134 children with mild to moderate disabilities are attending ordinary schools (Onei & Njuki, 1998). The Ugandan government's goal was to have the country's estimated 325,000 children with disabilities attend school in 1997 (Kristensen, 1997; Uganda Ministry of Education, 1992). However, the country lacked the resources for meeting this highly ambitious target then, and it still does today (Mpofu et al., 1997).

Zimbabwe's twenty special schools provide educational and rehabilitation services to 5,000 children with visual, hearing, physical, and mental disabilities. The country also has 162 integrated resource units: 69 for those with hearing disabilities, 46 with mental disabilities, and 47 with visual disabilities. A total of 1,315 children with disabilities are served by the integrated resource units: 552 with hearing impairments, 409 with mental impairments, and 354 with visual impairments. Additionally, about 4,300 children with moderate to mild generalized learning difficulties attend 270 part-time special classes in regular education settings. At least 50,000 children with learning difficulties receive part-time remedial education in classes or clinics in general education schools.

The current status of special education programs in Swaziland, Eriteria, Kenya, and Zambia is unknown. However, information from respondents to a survey on school psychology practices in these countries (Mpofu et al., 1997) suggests special education programs may be better established in Kenya than in other East and Southern African countries. Such programs generally are limited to urban areas in Zambia, and may not exist to any significant degree in Swaziland and Eriteria.

Although the need for more special education facilities in all of the East and Southern African countries is quite apparent, a paradox exists in that attendance is below capacity in many existing special education schools and units in some countries, including Tanzania and Lesotho (Kisanji, 1995; Stubbs, 1997). This under-utilization exists because the facilities are not well-known to parents of children with disabilities and parents in some rural communities are suspicious of their intended purposes. In addition, government departments and international aid agencies often established special education schools and units in certain communities in response to requests by local politicians or parochial interest groups, but without adequate consultation with traditional and other community leaders. Thus, resistance to utilizing these facilities often occurs regardless of their need.

Some countries in this region have mounted comprehensive community outreach programs aimed at educating citizens on the nature of disabilities, their prevention, and appropriate educational interventions. In addition, teachers have walked from village to village to locate children with disabilities to attend school (Kisanji, 1995). The teachers' door-to-door, village-to-village approach can effectively reach families and significant community leaders, and it often yielded larger enrollments of children with disabilities in areas that seem to have few if any such children.

Future Prospects of Special Education in East and Southern Africa

Nearly all countries in East and Southern Africa provide some forms of special education programs. The work of Christian missionaries and nongovernmental agencies often resulted in the establishment of special education programs. The continued involvement of missionaries, although desired, is unlikely to match prior levels of involvement. Nongovernmental agencies increasingly are recognized by international agencies (like the United Nations and the World Bank) as effective implementers of needed social programs. Although their involvement is likely to continue for some years, their resources also are limited in time. Thus, special education programs in this large and important region must depend more heavily, if not exclusively, on local and regional resolve and resources.

A government's involvement in special education programs and teacher preparation programs (through policies enacted and funded by its legislature and implemented by its ministries of education) provides demonstrable evidence that they support special education as an essential component of its national education program. Although the degree to which federal governments are involved in special education programs differs among the twelve countries within this region, all are involved to some degree. However, beneficial policies often are enacted and either not funded or not implemented by ministries of education. For example, the governments of Uganda and Botswana both established policy underscoring the importance of school attendance among children with disabilities as a national priority. However, this policy remains to be implemented.

The adoption of the principle of universal primary education by these governments implicitly recognizes children with disabilities as having the right to education. This, and other positive trends in educational thinking, eventually can be expected to translate into more favorable policies and practices governing special education programs. Moreover, most governments continue to support the further development of their elementary and secondary regular education programs—conditions prerequisite to the strong support of special education programs. Thus, prospects for the continued growth and availability of special education programs in these countries are somewhat encouraging.

However, one should not underestimate impediments to the further development of sustainable special education programs in East and Southern Africa. These impediments include inadequate personnel and financial resources for the provision of basic and regular education and inadequate leadership from advocacy groups.

Given other pressing responsibilities, federal governments in this region are unlikely to prioritize special education programs without some form of external support. Uncertainty exists as to the willingness and commitment of some governments to fund special education programs at current or higher levels than that currently provided by international development agencies (like DANIDA and SIDA).

The sustainability of donor-supported special education programs in East and Southern Africa will depend on the extent to which donor agencies build into their aid packages policies and practices that cultivate a cadre of local personnel willing to lobby for future programs, to implement genuine partnerships with federal and regional government to establish and maintain special education programs, to employ phased donor-funding withdrawal, and to help developing vibrant self-advocacy organizations at

the local and national levels. For example, the Swedish Federation for the Blind has financed an advisory project in Eastern Africa aimed at improving the organization and self-advocacy of persons with disabilities (Ross, 1988).

Greater involvement of parents and community members in founding special education schools and integration units would strengthen a sense of ownership for special education facilities in communities, leading to greater attendance and school retention. In addition, the importance of community education programs on disabilities to the future of special education programs in East and Southern Africa cannot be over-emphasized. Most parents of children with disabilities are not involved with any special interest groups or agencies providing special education services (Kisanji, 1995; Ross, 1988).

The significantly limited material and manpower resources within most of these countries constrain the establishment and growth of special education programs (Tungaraza, 1994; Ross, 1988). Most countries are grappling with the provision of basic education and health facilities. The countries have very few personnel specifically prepared to work with children with disabilities in either special or mainstream school settings. The future of special education programs in the region could be considerably enhanced if countries pooled resources to promote professional preparation and research on effective methods to promote basic education of students in special education.

REFERENCES

Atim, S. (1995). *Special education in Uganda.* Paper presented at the South-South-North Workshop. Kampala, Uganda.

Bruhns, B., Murray, A., Kanguchi, T., & Nuukuawo, A. (1995). *Disability and rehabilitation in Namibia: A national survey.* Windhoek: The Namibian Economic Policy Research Unit.

Farquhar, J. (1987). *Jairos Jiri–the man and his works.* Gweru: Mambo.

Charema, J., & Peresuh, M. (1997). Support services for special needs educational needs: Proposed models for countries south of the Sahara. *African Journal of Special Needs Education, 1,* 76–83.

Chimedza, R. (1994). Bilingualism in the education of the hearing impaired in Zimbabwe: Is this the answer? *Zimbabwe Bulletin of Teacher Education, 4,* 1–11.

Csapo, M. (1987a). *Perspectives in education and special education in southern Africa.* Vancouver: Center for Human Development and Research.

Csapo, M. (1987b). *Basic, practical, cost-effective education for children with disabilities in Lesotho.* Vancouver: University of British Columbia.

Devlieger, P. (1995). Why disabled? The cultural understanding of physical disability in an African society. In B. Ingstad & S. R. Whyte (Eds.), *Disability and culture* (pp. 94–106). Berkeley: University of California Press.

Ingstad, B. (1995). Public discourses on rehabilitation: From Norway to Botswana. In B. Ingstad & S. R. Whyte (Eds.), *Disabil-*

ity and culture (pp. 174–195). Berkeley: University of California Press.

Jackson, H., & Mupedziswa, R. (1989). Disability and rehabilitation: Beliefs and attitudes among rural disabled people in a community based rehabilitation scheme in Zimbabwe. *Journal of Social Development in Africa, 1*, 21–30.

Kann, U., Mapolelo, D., & Nleya, P. (1989). *The missing children: Achieving basic education in Botswana*. Gaborone: NIR, University of Botswana.

Kisanji, J. (1997). The relevance of indigenous customary education principles in the education of special needs education policy. *African Journal of Special Needs Education, 1*, 59–74.

Kisanji, J. (1995). Interface between culture and disability in the Tanzania context: Part 1. *International Journal of Disability, Development and Education, 42*, 93–108.

Kristensen, K. (1997). School for all: A challenge to special needs education in Uganda–A brief country report. *African Journal of Special Needs Education, 2*, 25–28.

Miran, J. (1998). *Missionaries, education and the state in the Italian colony of Eriteria 1980–1936*. Paper presented at the Third Annual Midwest Graduate Student Conference in African Studies. University of Wisconsin-Madison, February 27–March 1.

Mpofu, E., & Nyanungo, K. R. (in press). Educational and psychological testing in Zimbabwean schools: Past, present and future. *European Journal of Psychological Assessment*.

Mpofu, E., Zindi, F., Oakland, T., & Peresuh, M. (1997). School psychological practices in East and Southern Africa. *Journal of Special Education, 31*, 387–402.

Murray, J. L., & Lopez, A. D. (1996). *Global health statistics: A compendium of incidence, prevalence and mortality estimates for over 200 conditions*. Cambridge: Harvard University Press.

Onen, N., & Njuki, E. P. (1998). *Special education in Uganda*. Unpublished manuscript.

Peresuh, M., Adenigba, S. A., & Ogonda, G. (1997). Perspectives on special needs education in Nigeria, Kenya, and Zimbabwe. *African Journal of Special Needs Education, 2*, 9–15.

Pholoho, K., Mariga, L., Phachaka, L., & Stubbs, S. (1995). Schools for all: National planning in Lesotho. In B. O'Tootle & R. McConkey (Eds.), *Innovations in developing countries for people with disabilities*. Lancashire, England: Lisieux Hall Publications.

Possi, M. K., & Mkaali, C. B. (1995). *A brief report on special education services in Tanzania*. Paper presented at the South-South-North Workshop. Kampala, Uganda.

Ross, D. H. (1988). *Educating handicapped young people in Eastern and Southern Africa*. Paris: UNESCO.

Saigh, P. A., & Oakland, T. (Eds.). (1989). *International perspectives on school psychology*. Hillsdale, NJ: Erlbaum.

Sichula, B. (1990). *East African sign language report*. Helsinki, Finland: Finnish Association of the Deaf.

Stubbs, S. (1997). Lesotho integrated education programme. *African Journal of Special Needs Education, 1*, 84–87.

Tungaraza, F. D. (1994). The development and history of special education in Tanzania. *International Journal of Disability, Development, and Education, 41*, 213–222.

Uganda Ministry of Education. (1992). *Government white paper on the education policy review commission report*. Kampala, Uganda: Author.

UNICEF. (1996). *The state of the world's children: 1996*. Oxford: Oxford University Press.

UNICEF. (1994). *The state of the world's children: 1994*. Oxford: Oxford University Press.

UNICEF. (1991). *Children and women in Zimbabwe: A situation analysis update, July 1985–July 1990*. Republic of Zimbabwe: Author.

Whyte, S. R. (1995). Constructing epilepsy: Images and contexts in East Africa. In B. Ingstad & S. R. Whyte (Eds.), *Disability and culture* (pp. 226–245). Berkeley: University of California Press.

Whyte, S., & Ingstad, B. (1995). Disability and culture: An overview. In S. Whyte & B. Ingstad (Eds.), *Disability and culture* (pp. 3–32). Berkeley: University of California Press.

ROBERT CHIMEDZA
ELIAS MPOFU
University of Zimbabwe

THOMAS OAKLAND
University of Florida

SOVIET EDUCATION

Soviet Education is a journal of English-language translations that started publication in 1959. It made Soviet education literature available through English-language translations for the first time. The founding editors of *Soviet Education* were Myron Sharpe, Murray Yanowitch, and Fred Ablin. From 1967 through 1969, Seymour Rosen served as editor, followed by Harold Noah in 1970. The editorial load was shared with Beatrice Szekely, who assumed the full role of editor in the late 1970s.

A topical journal, *Soviet Education* draws material from Russian-language books and works in teacher training texts, educational psychology, sociology, comparative education, and educational administration. The journal tends to focus on educational policy issues. It is published monthly.

ROBERTA C. STOKES
CECIL R. REYNOLDS
Texas A & M University

SOVIET UNION AND EASTERN EUROPE, SPECIAL EDUCATION IN THE

See RUSSIA SPECIAL EDUCATION IN.

SPACHE DIAGNOSTIC READING SCALE

See DIAGNOSTIC READING SCALE.

SPAN OF APPREHENSION

See PERCEPTUAL SPAN.

SPASTICITY

Spasticity is a type of cerebral palsy involving a lack of muscle control. Spastic children make up the largest group of the cerebral palsied, constituting 40 to 60% of the total.

Another term that has been used to refer to spastic cerebral palsy is pyramidal. This term was coined because the nerves involved are shaped like pyramids. Spastic cerebral palsy is produced by damage sustained to the nerve cell that is found in the motor cortex. The motor cortex is the gray matter of the brain containing nerve cells that initiate motor impulses to the muscles. The nerve cells have tracts that extend from the neuron in the cortex to the spinal cord. These cells eventually connect with nerve tracts that innervate the limb so that muscle movement can be carried out. If these nerve cells or tracts are injured, spasticity results.

Because spasticity can affect one or all four extremities, it is subdivided into several types. Monoplegia involves one extremity only, either an arm or leg. This type is extremely rare. Triplegia involves the impairment of three extremities; it is an unusual occurrence. Hemiplegia means that the abnormality is confined to half of the body, either the right or left side with the arm more involved than the leg. This is the most common locus of involvement. Bilateral hemiplegia or double hemiplegia involves weakness or paralysis of both sides of the body with the arms compromised more than the legs. Another type, quadriplegia, occurs in all four extremities with more disability of the legs than the arms. Diplegia means that all four limbs are affected, with minimal involvement of the arms. Paraplegia is neurologic dysfunction of the legs only. Spastic hemiplegias are the most common group, representing approximately 40% of the total cerebral palsied population, while spastic quadriplegias represent 19% of the total (Capute, 1978).

In mild cases, the spastic child has an awkward gait and may extend his or her arms for balance (Kerrigan & Annaswamy, 1997). In moderate cases, the child may bend the arms at the elbow and hold both arms close to the body with the hands bent toward the body. The legs may be rotated inwardly and flexed at the knees; this causes a "scissoring gait." In severe cases, the child may have poor body control and be unable to sit, stand, and walk without the support of braces, crutches, a walking frame, or other support (Kirk & Gallagher, 1979).

REFERENCES

Capute, A. (1978). Cerebral palsy and associated dysfunctions. In R. Haslam & P. Valletutti (Eds.), *Problems in the classroom* (pp. 149–163). Baltimore, MD: University Park Press.

Kerrigan, D. C. & Annaswammy, T. M. (1997). The functional significance of spasticity as assessed by gait analysis. *Journal of Head Trauma Rehabilitation, 12*(6), 29–39.

Kirk, S., & Gallagher, J. (1979). *Educating exceptional children* (3rd ed.). Boston: Houghton Mifflin.

CECELIA STEPPE-JONES
North Carolina Central University

CEREBRAL PALSY
PHYSICAL DISABILITIES

SPEARMAN, C. E. (1863–1945)

C. E. Spearman grew up in an English family of established status and some eminence; he became an officer in the regular army. He remained in the army until the age of 40, attaining the rank of major. He then obtained his PhD in Wundt's laboratory at Leipzig in 1908 at the age of 45. He was appointed to an academic position at University College, London, where he remained for the rest of his career.

Spearman is known for his theory of general intelligence and for a number of contributions to statistical methodology, including factor analysis, the Spearman rank correlation, and the Spearman-Brown prophecy formula. Spearman's primary interest was in the study of general intelligence, which he preferred to call g. His methodological innovations were directed toward the better definition and measurement of g.

Spearman conceived of intelligence as a general capability involved in the performance of almost all mental tasks, although he saw some tasks as more dependent on g than others. Thus the variance of any mental test may be divided into two parts: a part associated with individual differences in g and a part specific to the test in question. Since the correlation coefficient indicates the proportion of shared variation of two variables, Spearman was able to develop methods of analyzing a matrix of correlations among tests to determine the presence of a general factor and to calculate the g loading for a test, its correlation with the underlying general factor. The conception of intelligence as g provided an objective method of defining intelligence and of evaluating the adequacy of any proposed measure of intelligence.

Spearman's original two-factor theory (Spearman, 1904) included only g and a factor specific to each task. Subsequently, he expanded the theory to include group factors, which are factors common to a group of tasks independent of g. However, his major emphasis was always on g (Spearman, 1927). Subsequent development and mathematical refinement of factor analysis by Thurstone and others emphasized the group factors; g became obscured in the correlation among the primary factors. Today g is recognized as a second order factor accounting for the correlations among the primaries. There is still disagreement concerning its importance.

REFERENCES

Spearman, C. E. (1904). "General intelligence" objectively determined and measured. *American Journal of Psychology, 15,* 201–293.

Spearman, C. E. (1927). *The abilities of man: Their nature and measurement.* London: Macmillan.

ROBERT C. NICHOLS
DIANE JARVIS
State University of New York at Buffalo

g **FACTOR THEORY**
INTELLIGENCE
REACTION TIME

SPECIAL CLASS

The first special classes were established in the late 1800s and early 1900s as public school classes for the moderately retarded, deaf, hard of hearing, blind, emotionally disturbed, and physically handicapped. Esten (1900) stated that special classes for mentally retarded were established to provide slow-learning children with more appropriate class placement.

A special classroom for the exceptional can be defined as one that homogeneously segregates different children from normal children. Children are usually segregated along categorical groupings. As a result of Dunn's (1968) article on the detrimental aspects of special class placements for the mildly handicapped, students receiving special education in self-contained special classes today are usually those with more severe problems. However, Kirk and Gallagher (1983) report gifted exceptional students are also grouped into special classes according to interests and abilities. As low-incidence students demonstrate proficiency in specific skill areas, they are mainstreamed into regular classes.

Other types of service delivery for special education students (e.g., resource rooms) do not fall under the label special class. Resource rooms usually provide service for high-incidence populations. Special classes, on the other hand, usually service low-incidence populations. In addition, there are four different types of resource rooms: categorical, serving one population; noncategorical, serving more than one population itinerant; and teacher-consultant. There is usually only one type of special class, self-contained.

REFERENCES

Dunn, L. M. (1968). Special education for the mildly handicapped: Is much of it justifiable? *Exceptional Children, 35,* 5–22.

Esten, R. A. (1900). Backward children in the public schools. *Journal of Psychoaesthenics, 5,* 10–16.

MARIBETH MONTGOMERY KASIK
Governors State University

CASCADE OF SERVICES
INCLUSION
RESOURCE ROOM
SELF-CONTAINED CLASS
SERVICE DELIVERY MODELS

SPECIAL EDUCATION, EFFECTIVENESS OF

See EFFECTIVENESS OF SPECIAL EDUCATION.

SPECIAL EDUCATION, FEDERAL IMPACT ON

The impact of the federal government on special education occurs through two independent, but overlapping, functions: (1) the administration and development of programs, and (2) the compliance monitoring of state education agencies. The administration and development of programs involves the disbursement of discretionary grants and contracts as well as the disbursement of formula grant funds under Part B of the Individuals with Disabilities Education Act (IDEA) and under Part H and the Preschool Grant Program. Discretionary grants are awarded to individuals and organizations in states and territories on a competitive basis. Depending on the specific program for which awards are made, these funds are to be used for research, program/materials development, technical assistance, demonstration, or training. For the most part, these projects do not directly serve handicapped children and youths, but rather, are intended to support existing programs, demonstrate new or more effective ways of delivering services, train special education and re-

State Grant Awards Under IDEA, Part B, Preschool Grant Program and Part H

Appropriation Year 1996
Allocation Year 1996–1997

State	IDEA Part B	Preschool Grant Program	Part H
Alabama	40,895,889	5,640,150	4,483,470
Alaska	7,445,561	1,322,423	1,545,710
Arizona	30,926,630	5,149,246	5,306,409
Arkansas	21,767,818	4,947,109	2,549,297
California	228,622,421	36,022,407	41,438,233
Colorado	28,189,964	4,694,437	3,972,753
Connecticut	31,009,767	5,254,252	3,378,163
Delaware	6,415,559	1,273,857	1,545,710
District of Columbia	3,133,152	253,984	1,545,710
Florida	125,183,617	17,772,314	14,722,619
Georgia	54,500,058	8,737,835	8,226,009
Hawaii	6,468,961	857,114	1,569,551
Idaho	9,586,202	2,011,527	1,545,710
Illinois	103,277,776	16,385,574	13,785,909
Indiana	54,064,193	8,046,763	6,065,530
Iowa	26,735,870	3,830,760	2,712,211
Kansas	21,632,619	4,026,335	2,716,195
Kentucky	33,452,225	9,636,295	3,876,538
Louisiana	36,749,462	6,292,502	5,023,051
Maine	12,862,856	2,331,796	1,545,710
Maryland	40,707,760	6,228,185	6,148,806
Massachusetts	64,529,602	9,346,216	8,621,533
Michigan	76,182,721	11,971,373	10,071,913
Minnesota	39,676,213	7,075,455	4,873,116
Mississippi	26,960,663	4,336,103	3,120,649
Missouri	48,997,264	5,509,548	5,422,619
Montana	7,447,163	1,189,852	1,545,710
Nebraska	15,863,867	2,173,630	1,689,626
Nevada	11,381,723	2,077,812	1,783,636
New Hampshire	10,206,502	1,424,148	1,545,710
New Jersey	79,530,001	10,919,997	8,497,315
New Mexico	19,201,461	2,994,648	2,045,597
New York	159,349,369	31,853,656	20,119,188
North Carolina	59,357,530	10,940,998	7,582,020
North Dakota	5,044,365	767,202	1,545,710
Ohio	91,825,830	11,947,090	11,402,583
Oklahoma	29,633,498	3,486,209	3,381,056
Oregon	26,241,486	4,001,396	3,086,097
Pennsylvania	86,078,620	13,510,371	12,702,122
Puerto Rico	18,127,953	2,326,545	4,549,818
Rhode Island	10,118,522	1,531,123	1,568,805
South Carolina	34,921,251	6,775,530	3,852,059
South Dakota	6,432,855	1,428,085	1,545,710
Tennessee	51,036,950	6,661,992	5,414,050
Texas	178,197,295	21,173,206	23,718,333
Utah	21,172,943	3,190,222	2,768,788
Vermont	4,539,452	797,391	1,545,710
Virginia	57,509,947	8,676,144	6,930,714
Washington	43,138,514	8,246,275	5,664,434
West Virginia	18,358,789	3,177,753	1,798,698
Wisconsin	42,946,007	8,889,438	5,553,755
Wyoming	5,064,508	1,021,186	1,545,710
American Samoa	2,546,094	34,783	514,925
Guam	6,151,324	122,726	1,140,327
Northern Marianas	1,570,112	23,626	342,733
Palau	552,502	5,120	78,014
Virgin Islands	4,663,611	87,286	671,647
Bur. of Indian Affairs	28,408,765		3,864,276
U.S. and outlying areas	2,316,593,632	360,409,000	315,754,000
50 states, D.C., and P.R.	2,272,701,224	360,135,459	309,142,078

State grants awards are initial allocations for the 1996 appropriation.
October 1, 1996

lated services personnel, or increase our knowledge of current or promising components of special education (i.e., research efforts). Following is a list of State Grant Awards under IDEA Part B, Part H; and Preschool Grant Programs.

In addition to discretionary grant awards and contracts, states also receive annual funds based on the total number of handicapped children and youths receiving special education and related services. The history of funding for the PART B entitlement program under IDEA, state grant program from 1977 to 1996, is shown in the table below:

IDEA, Part B State Grant Program: Funds Appropriated, 1977–96

Appropriation Year	IDEA, Part B State Grants[a]	Per Child Allocation[b]
1977	$ 251,770,000	$ 71
1978	566,030,000	156
1979	804,000,000	215
1980	874,190,000	227
1981	874,500,000	219
1982	931,008,000	230
1983	1,017,900,000	248
1984	1,068,875,000	258
1985	1,135,145,000	272
1986	1,163,282,000	279
1987	1,338,000,000	316
1988	1,431,737,000	332
1989	1,475,449,000	336
1990	1,542,610,000	343
1991	1,854,186,000	400
1992	1,976,095,000	410
1993	2,052,730,000	411
1994	2,149,686,000	413
1995	2,322,915,000[c]	418
1996	2,323,837,000	413[d]

[a]The figures from 1977 through 1994 include amounts appropriated to the Federated States of Micronesia and the Republic of the Marshall Islands. In 1995, those entities received no appropriations.
[b]The per child allocation excludes children and funds for the Outlying Areas and Bureau of Indian Affairs (BIA) and is based on the child count information available as of July 1 of the fiscal year.
[c]This amount includes $82,878,000 added to the Grants to States appropriation because of the elimination of the Chapter 1 Handicapped Program.
[d]This allocation was derived by dividing the total appropriations for the 50 States, District of Columbia, Outlying Areas, and BIA by the total number of children served in all of those areas.
Source: U.S. Department of Education, Office of Special Education Programs, Data Analysis System (DANS).

Each state education agency (SEA) must distribute at least 75% of the total funds to local education agencies to be used directly for the education of handicapped students. The remaining funds may be used by the SEA, with some portion going toward administrative costs. Thus federal funds are used to offset some of the additional costs associated with educating handicapped students.

Until 1994, children and youth with disabilities were also served under the Chapter 1 Handicapped Program. In October 1994, the Improving America's School Act (IASA) was enacted, which reauthorized the Elementary and Secondary Education Act of 1965 (ESEA). However, the Chapter 1 Handicapped Program was not reauthorized. Beginning with the FY 1995 appropriation, all children with disabilities were served under programs authorized by IDEA. The IASA included a number of amendments to IDEA to provide for a smooth transition to serving all children. (U.S. Department of Education, 1997).

Part H of the Individuals with Disabilities Education Act (IDEA) was adopted by Congress in 1986. Part H was designed to address the needs of infants and toddlers with disabilities and their families through a "statewide system of coordinated, comprehensive, multidisciplinary, interagency programs providing appropriate early intervention services to all infants and toddlers with disabilities and their families" (20 U.S.C. §1476 (a)). Figure I shows the number of infants and toddlers with disabilities served under PART H from 1992 to 1995.

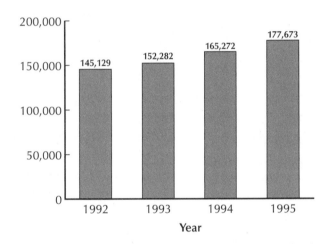

Figure 1 Number of infants and toddlers with disabilities served under IDEA, Part H. Source: U.S. Department of Education, Office of Special Education Programs, Data Analysis System (DANS).

The increase in the number of infants and toddlers served under PART H (22.4 percent) since 1992 has been greater than the growth in the number of children served under Part B. The growth rate is, however, comparable to the number of 3-5 year olds served under Part B (U.S. Dept. of Education, 1997).

Thus one of the primary ways special education is impacted by the federal government is through a direct infusion of funds that assist state and local educational agencies in offering special education and related services, or through efforts that further state and local programs (discretionary grants and contracts).

The second major area in which the federal government

impacts special education is through compliance monitoring. To accomplish this objective, special education programs engage in program administrative reviews that involve on-site and off-site reviews of information. Where deficiencies are found, corrective actions are requested from the SEA. The corrective actions report includes a description of the steps to be taken by the SEA, timelines for completion, and the documentation to be submitted verifying that deficiencies have been corrected. Should substantial noncompliance be noted, the U.S. Department of Education is authorized to withhold federal funds. Considerable leeway exists within the department's administration of its compliance monitoring efforts to ensure that each state receives funding. Nevertheless, the possibility that a state may not receive federal funds can be persuasive in altering special education programs in that state. Thus this is one further way in which special education is impacted.

Audette and Algozzine have suggested that the dearth of legislation monitoring, and regulations from the federal level have increased bureaucratic paperwork and procedures to the point of being a major hindrance: That special education is "costly rather than free." (Audette & Algozzine, 1997).

REFERENCES

Audette, B., & Algozzine, B. (1997). Re-inventing government? Let's re-invent special education. *Journal of Learning Disabilities, 30*(4), 378–383.

U.S. Department of Education. (1997). Nineteenth Annual Report to Congress on the Implementation of the Individuals with Disabilities Education Act. Washington DC: Author.

MARTY ABRAMSON
University of Wisconsin at Stout

DEMOGRAPHY OF SPECIAL EDUCATION
POLITICS AND SPECIAL EDUCATION
SPECIAL EDUCATION PROGRAMS

SPECIAL EDUCATION, GENERIC

See GENERIC SPECIAL EDUCATION.

SPECIAL EDUCATION, HISTORY OF

See HISTORY OF SPECIAL EDUCATION.

SPECIAL EDUCATION, HUMANISTIC

See HUMANISTIC SPECIAL EDUCATION.

SPECIAL EDUCATION, PHILOSOPHERS' OPINIONS ABOUT

See PHILOSOPHY OF EDUCATION FOR THE HANDICAPPED.

SPECIAL EDUCATION, PROFESSIONAL STANDARDS FOR

See PROFESSIONAL STANDARDS FOR SPECIAL EDUCATORS.

SPECIAL EDUCATION, RACIAL DISCRIMINATION IN

See RACIAL DISCRIMINATION IN SPECIAL EDUCATION.

SPECIAL EDUCATION, SUPERVISION IN

See SUPERVISION IN SPECIAL EDUCATION.

SPECIAL EDUCATION, TEACHER TRAINING IN

The training and practice of special educators have undergone rapid development and change over the past three decades. In recognition of the small number of individuals who were prepared to conduct research and train teachers to educate the retarded, PL 85-926 was passed in 1958. With the passage of this law, funds were allocated to establish university, doctoral-level training programs in the area of mental retardation. These training programs, along with a robust postwar economy, resulted in a decade characterized by a proliferation of programs for exceptional children (Tawney & Gest, 1984). The need for trained individuals to run public and private school programs has preceded a clear understanding of what and how to teach children with various handicapping conditions. The first special education curricula were watered-down or slowed-down adaptations of regular class programs; they underscored the absence of empirical data in the field. Training, for the most part, focused on how to control children's behavior. The hope was that a child controlled was a child ready to learn.

The 1970s saw a continuance of the optimism of the 1960s and a period of advocacy and activism. Public Law 94-142, a civil rights bill for the handicapped, guaranteed a "free and appropriate" education for exceptional children. At the same time, it called on special educators to document, as precisely as possible, children's progress. For the first time in public education, teachers were called on to be accountable. Practically, concerns for accountability meant that the field moved to replace the generalized curricula of the 1960s with more individualized curricula focused on matching instructional strategies to individual learner characteristics. Tawney and Gest (1984) pointed out that "the cumulative effect of the developmental efforts of the 1970s, then, was to set the stage for a new era of intensive programming for handicapped students in the 1980s" (p. 5). Problems with a worsening economy in the late 1970s, however, shifted attention from the problems of the handicapped to more personal priorities.

The reality of the 1990s is essentially economic in character. Given the increase in the number of children being served and the fact that federal, state, and local budgets do not have unlimited resources, the 1990s have become a period of retrenchment and uncertainty in special education. There is a clear and pressing need to increase the number of teachers qualified to work with handicapped children, but at the same time newly trained teachers are being asked to do more with less. Teachers in special education are being called on to be more resourceful, more organized, and more precise in creating, planning, and executing instructional interventions and more directly involved in general or regular education.

In addition to these broad political and economic factors, the quantity and quality of research in human learning and development and pedagogy has had an impact on the preparation of teachers for handicapped pupils. Out of the massive research and development efforts with handicapped and nonhandicapped children that began in the 1960s, special educators have acquired a substantial base of knowledge concerning effective instructional practices. With this large and growing body of information and the complex roles that special education teachers are currently being asked to assume, effective training of special educators in the 1990s and beyond will require greater breadth and depth of preparation than ever before.

While there is a lack of agreement concerning specific knowledge and skills that teachers of the handicapped should possess, there is a growing consensus among regular and special educators concerning the general characteristics of a professional teacher and the framework for teacher preparation programs. The general parameters include the following. First, teachers need a firm foundation in general literacy and in the basic disciplines of the humanities, liberal arts, and sciences as prerequisite to entering the teaching profession (Denemark & Nutter, 1980). Second, special education teachers must be well versed in general education requirements as well as those specific to special education; i.e., they must be education generalists as well as education of the handicapped specialists

(Reynolds, 1979). Their training should include acquiring knowledge of school development, basic academic skill curricula, instructional methods, including the effective use of computer-assisted instruction, and instructional and behavioral management strategies. In return, the inclusion movement has mandated that general educators have same training in special education. General education teacher license requirements in 22 states include a requirement that teachers have some coursework related to students with disabilities. Eleven states require some practical work with students as well as coursework (U.S. Dept. of Education, 1997).

Third, as a key to participation in inclusion efforts, special education teachers must function as team members and as consultants, providing interaction with the general education faculty on questions concerning handicapped pupils. Fourth, regardless of the nature and severity of a pupil's disability, all special education teachers must possess effective communication skills to work with parents of handicapped children. These include a working knowledge of the motivational, cognitive, and social consequences associated with their pupils' handicapping conditions. Special educators should also be able to assess pupils' current levels of functioning, select and implement instructional strategies based on youngsters' learning characteristics, and evaluate the effectiveness of their instructional procedures.

Lastly, teacher training programs should provide extensive practical experience for their students. This practical experience should be initiated early in the students' training, with greater amounts of professional practice provided as students progress through the program (Scannell & Guenther, 1981). As researchers have recognized that the first year of teaching is critical for the maintenance and development of effective teaching skills, a year-long paid and supervised internship has been recommended as the culminating training experience of a preservice program. For student-teachers to gain the most from these practica, they should be closely monitored and effective models of teaching should be provided. Training that includes the previously noted components cannot be provided in an undergraduate teacher preparation program. The American Association of Colleges of Teacher Education Commission of Education for the Profession argues that the presently constituted teaching profession is, at best, a semiprofession (Howsam, Corrigan, Denemark, & Nash, 1976). The commission recommends a 5-year initial teacher preparation program combining the bachelor's and master's degrees, plus a sixth year of supervised internship to improve the quality of teacher education. Such an effort would enhance the profession of teaching and lead to outstanding pupil achievement. In view of these collective recommendations, it appears that preparation of special education teachers will require the extension of teacher education into graduate training.

Unfortunately, due to declining enrollments in teacher preparation programs and reductions in university budgets, few university faculties have decided to make their programs more rigorous by incorporating the recommendations of leaders in the area of teacher education and special education.

Attrition of special education teachers has been a major concern nationally. Moreover, lack of quality in preservice training has been related to teacher attrition rates. With the extensive and culturally competent (Miller, Miller, & Schroth, 1997) course work, practica, and internship training required in new programs, graduates will be better prepared to meet the challenges and demands of special education instruction. As a consequence, they may continue to teach handicapped youngsters for a longer period of time and in a more effective manner.

REFERENCES

Denemark, G., & Nutter, N. (1980). *The case for extended programs of initial teacher preparation*. Washington, DC: ERIC Clearinghouse on Teacher Education.

Howsam, R. B., Corrigan, D. C., Denemark, G. W., & Nash, R. J. (1976). *Education as a profession: Report of the Bicentennial Commission on Education for the Profession of Teaching of the American Association of Colleges for Teacher Education*. Washington, DC: American Association of Colleges for Teacher Education.

Keogh, B. K. (1985). *Learning disabilities: Diversity in search of order*. Paper prepared for the Pittsburgh Research Integration Project, University of Pittsburgh.

Miller, S. Miller, K. L., & Schroth, G. (1997). Teacher perceptions of multicultural training in preservice programs. *Journal of Instructional Psychology, 24*(4), 222–232.

Palmer, D. J., Anderson, C., Hall, R., Keuker, J., & Parrish, L. (1985). *Preparation of special educators: Extended generic special education training program* (Report to the U.S. Department of Education, Special Education Programs, Division of Personnel Preparation)

Reynolds, M. (1979). *A common body of practices for teachers: The challenge of Public Law 94-142 to teacher education*. Minneapolis, MN: The National Support System Project.

Scannell, D., & Guenther, J. E. (1981). The development of an extended program. *Journal of Teacher Education, 32*, 7–12.

Tawney, J. W., & Gest, D. L. (1984). *Single subject research in special education*. Columbus, OH: Merrill.

U.S. Department of Education. (1997). *Nineteenth Annual Report to Congress on the Implementation of the Individuals with Disabilities Act* (IDEA). Washington DC: Author.

DOUGLAS J. PALMER
ROBERT HALL
Texas A & M University

HUMAN RESOURCE DEVELOPMENT
TEACHER BURNOUT
TEACHER EFFECTIVENESS

SPECIAL EDUCATION, TELECOMMUNICATION SYSTEMS IN

See TELECOMMUNICATION SYSTEMS IN SPECIAL EDUCATION.

SPECIAL EDUCATION AND POLITICS

See POLITICS AND SPECIAL EDUCATION.

SPECIAL EDUCATION INSTRUCTIONAL MATERIALS CENTERS (SEIMCs)

More than a decade before the passage of the Education for All Handicapped Children Act, the United States Office of Education recognized that one of the main obstacles to education of quality for handicapped students was the dearth of appropriate instructional materials and services both for the students and for those responsible for their education (Alonso, 1974). The federal government hoped to have established a network of service centers to address this problem by 1980.

The initiation of this effort began in 1963, when two projects were funded—one at the University of Southern California and the other at the University of Wisconsin— to serve as demonstration models for the development and dissemination of effective instructional materials and methods. From this modest beginning was to come 13 regional special education instructional materials centers (SEIMCs); four regional media centers for the deaf and hearing impaired (RMCs); a Clearinghouse on Handicapped and Gifted Children in the Educational Resources Information Center (ERIC) Network; an Instructional Materials Reference Center at the American Printing House for the Blind; and a National Center on Education Media and Materials for the Handicapped (NCEMMH).

The role of SEIMCs, some of which in various funding periods were also called regional Resource Centers (RRCs) and Area Learning Resource Centers (ALRCs), would change somewhat over the decade of their existence. During the experimental phase, which ran from 1964 to 1966, the two centers were expected to develop appropriate materials and methods for handicapped children, transform them into workable curricula, and disseminate the results, along with other information, to the field. The early centers were also charged with the exploration of new technologies for instructional purposes as well as for information dissemination (Langstaff & Volkmor, 1974).

The official scope of the centers was not strictly defined by the government. It was acknowledged that needs varied widely from one service area to another, and each program was encouraged to respond to its local situation appropriately and to take full advantage of the special strengths of its staff. In general, however, the activities tended to break down into three categories. The first involved identifying, collecting, evaluating, circulating, and, when necessary, developing or stimulating the development of instructional materials. The second category consisted of field services of various sorts: the training of teachers in the choice, evaluation, and use of instructional media and materials; coordination activities that established or improved the delivery of services to special educators and their students; and technical assistance to state departments of education to ensure the institutionalization of ongoing support services within each state. Finally, the centers were all involved to some extent in the systematic dissemination of information regarding current research, methods, and materials for special education.

REFERENCES

Alonso, L. (1974). *Final technical report of the Great Lakes region special education instructional materials center* Washington, DC: Bureau of Education for the Handicapped. (ERIC Document Reproduction Service No. ED 094 507)

Langstaff, A. L., & Volkmor, C. B. (1974). *Instructional materials center for special education: Final technical report* Washington, DC: Bureau of Education for the Handicapped. (ERIC Document Reproduction Service No. ED 107 086)

JANET S. BRAND
Hunter College

**ON-LINE DATABASES FOR SPECIAL EDUCATION
SPECIAL NET**

SPECIAL EDUCATION IN THE UNITED KINGDOM

See UNITED KINGDOM, SPECIAL EDUCATION IN THE.

SPECIAL EDUCATION PROGRAMS (SEP)

In 1982 Special Education Programs (SEP) succeeded the Office of Special Education as the primary federal agency responsible for overseeing federal initiatives in the education of the handicapped. Although SEP's mission has basically remained the same since the creation of the Bureau of Education for the Handicapped in 1966, its organizational structure has changed. Special Education Programs is divided into five divisions.

The Division of Assistance to States (DAS) has four areas of responsibility. Its primary function is to monitor the extent to which states are implementing the requirements of PL 94-142 and PL 89-313 state-operated programs. The DAS is also SEP's liaison with the Office for Civil Rights when parent complaints are received. The DAS provides technical assistance to states either directly through its program officers or through a national network of regional resource centers. Finally, DAS oversees the awarding of grants to centers that serve the deaf-blind.

The Division of Innovation and Development (DID) carries out SEP's mission for generating new information to help the handicapped. The DID administers several grant competitions. Field-initiated research allows any investigator to suggest a project and student projects are the most widely known. The DID has the U.S. Department of Education's responsibility for conducting the PL 94-142, Section 618, evaluation of the implementation of programs for the handicapped whose results appear in the *Annual Reports to Congress* (U.S. Department of Education, 1986).

The Division of Personnel Preparation administers grant programs to prepare special educators and related services personnel, parents of handicapped children, and doctoral-level professionals, among others, to serve the needs of handicapped students.

The Division of Educational Services is responsible for grant projects that develop model programs in the areas of early childhood education, youth employment, services for the severely handicapped, transitional services for students changing their least restrictive environment placement, and captioning of films for the hearing impaired.

The Division of Program Analysis and Planning has responsibility for managing the planning and budgetary processes within SEP. It also coordinates the efforts of other divisions when changes are proposed and made to regulations in the administration of PL 94-142, PL 89-313, and the various grant and contract programs.

The current address of SEP is U.S. Department of Education, Special Education Programs, 400 Maryland Avenue, SW, Washington, DC 20202.

REFERENCE

U.S. Department of Education. (1986). *Eighth annual report to Congress on the implementation of Public Law 94-142: The Education for All Handicapped Children Act*. Washington, DC: Author.

ROLAND K. YOSHIDA
Fordham University

OFFICE OF SPECIAL EDUCATION

SPECIALNET

SpecialNet, the largest education-oriented computer-based communication network in the United States, is operated by the National Association of State Directors of Special Education. SpecialNet makes it possible for its more than 2000 subscriber agencies to use the system to send electronic mail (messages, forms, reports, questions, and answers) instantaneously to one or many participants. The system also contains electronic bulletin boards, which are topical displays of various information bases, administered by content experts around the country. Nearly 30 such bulletin boards are currently available; they include coverage of personnel development, early childhood education, computers and other technologies, program evaluation, promising practices, federal news, gifted education, parent programs, educational policy, vocational education, and many other topics.

SpecialNet can be accessed on any computer. Access through a local or toll-free 800 number is available nationwide via the GTE Telenet public data network, through which SpecialNet information is transmitted and stored. Access to SpecialNet is obtained through an annual subscription fee. Further charges accrue for on-line time spent accessing the system. SpecialNet may be contacted at LRP Publications, 747 Dresher Road, Suite 500, Horsham, PA, 19044; 1-800-341-7874, or http://www.lrp.com.

JUDY SMITH-DAVIS
Counterpoint Communications Company

ON-LINE DATA BASES FOR SPECIAL EDUCATION SPECIAL EDUCATION INSTRUCTIONAL MATERIALS CENTERS

SPECIAL OLYMPICS

See OLYMPICS, SPECIAL.

SPECIAL SERVICES IN THE SCHOOLS (SSS)

Published by Haworth Press (New York City), *Special Services in the Schools (SSS)* is a quarterly, refereed journal with an applied focus. It is now in its seventh volume. The *SSS* is intended to be read by multidisciplinary professional audiences who provide special services in schools and related educational settings, including school psychologists, guidance counselors, consulting teachers, social workers, and speech and language clinicians. It is the journal's policy to disseminate available information of direct relevance to these professionals. As such, information published in *SSS* includes reviews of relevant research and literature, descriptions and evaluations of programs, viewpoints on latest trends in policy development, and guidelines for designing, implementing, and evaluating special service programs.

The issues of the journal are organized in a sequence whereby thematic and general issues alternate. Thematic issues have focused on topics such as microcomputers and exceptional children, health promotion strategies, new directions in assessment of special learners, and international perspectives on facilitating cognitive development of children. Articles in general issues have included topics such as evaluation of programs of children of divorce, staff stress and burnout, curricula and programs for pregnant and parenting adolescents, and involving parents in the education of their handicapped children.

Articles are aimed at being informative and instructive to special educators, psychologists, counselors, nurses, social workers, speech and language clinicians, physical and occupational therapists, and school supervisors and administrators. The material is intended to assist these professionals in performing a wide range of service delivery tasks. These include:

Assessing individual pupils and groups to determine their special educational needs

Designing individualized and group programs

Assisting regular and special classroom teachers in fostering academic achievement and functional living for special students

Enhancing the social and emotional development of pupils through preventive and remedial approaches

Helping school administrators to develop smoothly functioning organizational systems

Fostering the physical well being of special students

Involving parents and families in special programs

Educating and training school staff to more effectively educate special needs students

Manuscripts that focus on the topical areas and service delivery tasks noted are routinely considered for publication. All manuscripts undergo blind review by editorial consultants.

CHARLES A. MAHER
Rutgers University

LOUIS J. KRUGER
Tufts University

SPECIFIC LEARNING DISABILITIES

See LEARNING DISABILITIES.

SPEECH

In the context of special education, the word speech may have two different meanings. Sometimes, it is used to refer to the whole of linguistic skills. Such is the case in compounds such as speech pathologist and speech therapy. In other cases, the meaning is narrower, with the word referring to spoken language. The use of the word speech to denote the whole of verbal abilities is indicative of the cardinal importance of spoken language. Oral language is by far the most frequently used form of verbal communication. It is also the first linguistic ability to be acquired by the child.

Speech (i.e., spoken language) is produced by means of the speech organs. These organs make up parts of the respiratory system and the digestive tract. Usually, expiratory air is used to generate audible speech sounds. If air from the lungs activates the larynx, voiced sounds such as vowels or voiced consonants are produced. If the vocal cords are kept apart and consequently do not vibrate during exhalation, egressive air is turned into voiceless consonants (such as /s/ or /f/). Speech movements are rapid, complex, and finely timed sequences of gestures. Therefore, it takes the child several years to learn to perform them.

Since speech is ordinarily produced on exhalation, air is taken in just prior to starting to speak. Inspiration is caused by a contraction of the diaphragm and of the external intercostal muscles. When it contracts, the diaphragm flattens out and goes down. When the external intercostals contract, they lift up the rib cage. A membrane called parietal pleura is attached to both the diaphragm and the rib cage. When the diaphragm goes down and the rib cage goes up, the parietal membrane follows them. This enlarges the interpleural space, which is the closed space between the parietal membrane and the visceral membrane. The latter membrane enwraps each of the two lungs. Because the interpleural space becomes larger, the pressure in this space drops. Residual air (even after the most forcible expiration possible, some air remains in the lungs; this air is called residual) forces the expansible lungs to dilate so that the visceral pleura can follow the parietal pleura and annihilate the negative pressure in the interpleural space. In the expanded lungs the pressure is now negative and external air flows in via the nose (or mouth), larynx, and trachea to annihilate it (Kaplan, 1971).

Once the diaphragm starts to relax, the lower part of the parietal pleura is sucked upward by the retractile lungs. Similarly, the upper part of the pleura is sucked downward once the external intercostals start to relax. The retraction of the lungs increases the air pressure in them and air escapes via the upper respiratory tract. If, at some point, the relaxation pressure becomes insufficient to produce audible speech, expiratory muscles, mainly the internal intercostals, are used to draw the rib cage further in (Perkins & Kent, 1985).

On its way out, egressive air passes the larynx. This organ comprises a vertical tube in which a V-shaped horizontal narrowing, called the glottis, is found. The sides of the glottis are formed by two ligaments, which together with the muscle fibers behind them constitute the vocal folds. If the vocal folds are approximated during expiration, the glottis is closed and the air can no longer flow out of the trachea. As a result, the air pressure in the trachea increases. At some point, the pressure is such that it blows the vocal folds apart. Some air escapes through the glottis. As a consequence, the pressure in the trachea diminishes. Moreover, a Bernoulli effect is created in the glottis. The Bernoulli effect is the negative pressure on the sides of a bottleneck when a gas or a liquid flows through it. The glottis forms a bottleneck between the trachea and the pharynx. As a consequence, when air escapes through the glottis, the vocal folds are sucked toward one another. The Bernoulli effect and the temporary decrease in tracheal air pressure enable the elastic vocal folds to come together again. Since the glottis is now closed again, pressure builds up in the trachea until it blows the vocal cords apart, etc. In this way, the column of pulmonary air is divided into a quick succession of puffs that are fired into the supraglottal cavities (pharynx, mouth, and nasal cavity). The puffs of air hit the air mass present in the supraglottal cavities, causing it to vibrate. These vibrations, leaving the mouth of the speaker, propagate themselves in the air until they reach the ears of a listener, who perceives them as voice. The form of the individual vocal waves varies with the form of the supraglottal cavities (Zemlin, 1968). In this way, it is possible to produce vocal waves that sound like /a/, /u/ or any other vowel.

The puffs of air from the larynx not only hit the mass of air in the supraglottal cavities, but also move it forward. This forward movement can be used to form consonants. These consonants are voiced since their generation is synchronous with voice production. If, on the contrary, the vocal folds are kept in an abducted position and consequently do not vibrate, air from the lungs flows directly into the supraglottal cavities, where it can be molded into voiceless consonants. The shaping of the vocal waves and the molding of egressive air into speech sounds is performed by the articulators. The main articulators are the tongue and the velum. The latter moves upward and shuts off the nasal cavity from the oropharyngeal cavity during articulation of oral sounds. In English, most speech sounds are articulated with the velum in a raised position. Failure of the velum to occlude the passage of air to the nose results in hyperrhinolalia, i.e., nasalized speech.

REFERENCES

Kaplan, H. (1971). *Anatomy and physiology of speech*. New York: McGraw-Hill.

Perkins, W., & Kent, R. (1985). *Textbook of functional anatomy of speech, language, and hearing*. Philadelphia: Taylor & Francis.

Zemlin, R. (1968). *Speech and hearing science: Anatomy and physiology.* Englewood Cliffs, NJ: Prentice-Hall.

YVAN LEBRUN
School of Medicine, V.U.B.

LANGUAGE DISORDERS
SPEECH DISORDERS

SPEECH, ABSENCE OF

Many children use their first recognizable word at age one and by two are using some type of sentence. When a child has not started speaking by age two, parents often become concerned about the child's development. However, it is not unusual for the normally developing child not to use his or her first word until some time after the second birthday. However, if a child has no speech by age five, it is likely that a serious difficulty exists (Bloodstein, 1984).

The most common cause of a lack of speech is an intellectual disability. While many children exhibiting severe intellectual disabilities have the potential to develop some language, those with a profound disability are likely to have no speech throughout their lives (Robinson & Robinson, 1976). Intellectual disabilities may sometimes be due to genetic factors. In other instances, traumatic brain injuries are the known cause of intellectual difficulty. Children with intellectual disabilities who do develop language typically do so in much the same manner as normally developing children but slower (Naremore & Dever, 1975; Van Riper & Erickson, 1996). They do, however, tend to exhibit limitations in their vocabulary and syntax usage.

Congenital deafness is another possible cause of a child exhibiting no speech. When a child is born with a profound hearing loss, he or she does not generally develop speech without special intervention. A number of children are born with some degree of hearing loss, but the impairment is not so severe that they cannot use hearing for the development of speech and language. However, a child with profound deafness typically experiences severe problems in developing speech because they have no way of monitoring their own speech production. Surprisingly, a profoundly deaf child's difficulty with hearing is often not noticed until the child is about age two and has not spoken his or her first word. This is due in part to the fact that many children with hearing impairments appear to go through the babbling stage in much the same way that children with hearing do.

Once a hearing loss is identified, most children with hearing impairments are fitted with a hearing aid. If the child has more than a 90 dB loss, he or she will probably not learn speech and language through hearing alone. The speech and language training of some children begins with the oral method, where language instruction is carried out primarily by requiring the child to lip read and speak. During the last 20 to 25 years, however, language instruction for children who are deaf has changed. Now most children are exposed to a sign language system once they are identified. For children who are born with a profound hearing loss, only a small percentage attain speech that is intelligible to a stranger. However, many do attain a fairly high level of intelligibility to those who are familiar with the speech patterns of individuals who are deaf. It is important to make a distinction between speech and language when referring to children with hearing impairments because many children with profound deafness acquire language without having usable speech.

Another cause of absence of speech is cerebral palsy (Cruickshank, 1976; Pausewang Gelfer, 1996). Cerebral palsy is caused by brain damage occurring at or near the time of birth. Cerebral palsy can be of the type and of such severity that the child will not have sufficient control of the speech mechanism to produce intelligible speech. Some children, as their speech mechanism matures, can learn to produce intelligible speech with the help of specialists. However, other children can communicate only through other means such as communication boards and computers. Because of the physical disability and difficulty in communicating, the intelligence of children with cerebral palsy is often considerably underestimated.

An additional problem that can cause an absence of speech is the presence of social/emotional disturbances, specifically childhood schizophrenia and early infantile autism (Van Riper & Erickson, 1996). Typically, a child with schizophrenia appears to develop normally for the first few years of life, and then begins to regress, possibly losing all language and speech. Schizophrenia, characterized by periods of remission, has been found to be resistant to treatment. Unlike schizophrenia, autism seems to be present in a child from birth. Infants with autism often withdraw from social contact, not looking into the eyes of adults and not leaning on the person carrying them. As they grow, their behavior may be characterized by obsessive actions, with play appearing to be stereotyped. Many children with autism fail to develop language. Language usage that does develop can be quite deviant. Some children with autism have been known to speak fully formed sentences, but only once or twice in their lifetimes. Others develop what is known as echolalic speech, where they parrot back what is spoken to them. These utterances do not appear to be used meaningfully. Other children do use some sentences meaningfully, but these seem to be memorized strings of words and are often simple demands. A smaller percentage of children with autism eventually attain a fair degree of speech and language.

Social deprivation can also be a cause of language acquisition problems. However, deprivation must be extremely severe for the child to acquire no speech whatsoever. Human beings appear to have a strong predisposition for learning language. Only minimal conditions of exposure to language need be present for the child to learn to speak. However, there are a few isolated cases of children who apparently have had no exposure to language and therefore do not develop language (e.g., Fuller, 1975). In some cases where a child is consistently deprived of attention, severe language delay may occur. For example, some children who were institutionalized received no attention except for feeding and being kept clean. In such situations, many children experienced severe delays in the acquisition of language.

Occasionally, a clinician will see a child who understands language but does not speak at all. No cause can be found. Previously, it was thought that these children were suffering from maternal overprotection: Because the mother anticipated the child's needs, the child did not learn to speak. Over time, however, clinicians expressed doubt about attributing the lack of language usage to the behavior of the mother. While it was true that the mother often responded to the nonverbal cues of the child, it was generally recognized that the mother did this to alleviate severe frustration on both their parts. The mother's behavior is now seen as a response rather than as a cause. Children exhibiting this disorder frequently develop normal language over a period of time.

In the past, many children who did not acquire speech were institutionalized, receiving little or no educational services. With the advent of PL 94-142, many of these children were able to live at home and were provided schooling on a regular basis. Continued refinement of public educational laws (e.g., Individual with Disabilities Education Act Revisions of 1997) and a broader base of services have resulted in marked improvement in the communication skills of a number of who have difficulty in this area.

REFERENCES

Bloodstein, O. (1984). *Speech pathology: An introduction*. Boston: Houghton Mifflin.

Cruickshank, W. M. (1976). *Cerebral palsy: A developmental disability* (3rd ed.). Syracuse, NY: Syracuse University Press.

Fuller, C. W. (1975). Maternal deprivation and developmental language disorders. *Speech & Hearing Review: A Journal of New York State Speech & Hearing Association, 7*, 9–23.

Naremore, R. C., & Dever, R. B. (1975). Language performance of educable mentally retarded and normal children at five age levels. *Journal of Speech & Hearing Research, 18*, 92.

Pausewang Gelfer, M. (1996). *Survey of communication disorders: A social and behavioral perspective*. New York: McGraw-Hill.

Robinson, N. M., & Robinson, H. B. (1976). *The mentally retarded child* (2nd ed.). New York: McGraw-Hill.

Van Riper, C., & Erickson, R. L. (1996). *Speech correction: An introduction to speech pathology and audiology* (9th ed.). Boston: Allyn & Bacon.

CAROLYN L. BULLARD
Lewis & Clark College
First edition

ROBERT L. RHODES
New Mexico State University
Second edition

AUTISM
ELECTIVE MUTISM
MUTISM
SPEECH THERAPY

SPEECH AND LANGUAGE HANDICAPS

See COMMUNICATION DISORDER; LANGUAGE DISORDERS.

SPEECH-LANGUAGE PATHOLOGIST

Speech-language pathologist is the recognized title of a professional who evaluates and treats persons with speech and/or language disorders. There is some confusion about this title because there are other equivalent titles for speech-language pathologist including speech (-language) therapist, speech pathologist, and speech (-language) clinician. In addition, speech-language pathologists sometimes use the informal abbreviated title of SLP. Different titles are used depending on the preferences of speech-language pathologists as well as the particular work settings (schools vs. hospitals, etc.). Different titles do *not* necessarily reflect any differences in educational or skill levels.

Speech-language pathologist is the title officially recognized by the American Speech-Language-Hearing Association (ASHA), a professional organization whose members include speech-language pathologists and audiologists (Van Riper & Erickson, 1996). Although not all speech-language pathologists and audiologists are members of ASHA, many of its members earn ASHA's Certificate of Clinical Competence (CCC), given to persons who hold a Master's degree in speech-language pathology.

Speech-language pathologists must also sometimes be licensed by individual jurisdictions (e.g., states or provinces) before being permitted to do speech or language therapy in those jurisdictions. Speech-language pathologists work in schools, universities, hospitals, rehabilitation centers, and other institutions which serve the communicatively disabled.

REFERENCE

Van Riper, C., & Erickson, R. L. (1996). *Speech correction: An introduction to speech pathology and audiology* (9th ed.). Boston: Allyn & Bacon.

EDWARD A. SHIRKEY
New Mexico State University

COMMUNICATION DISORDERS
SPEECH THERAPY

SPEECH-LANGUAGE SERVICES

The provision of services to children and adults who have speech and/or language disorders is a complex problem. According to Cleland and Swartz (1982), delivery of services includes such factors as funding, transportation, and consumer resistance, in addition to problems of keeping service providers up to date in the latest techniques and tools. Speech and language services are provided in a variety of settings (Van Riper and Erickson, 1996), but always by professionals trained as speech pathologists having appropriate certification or a state license. All clinically certified speech-language pathologists are capable of providing a complete range of services. Some choose to specialize, but all have knowledge across a variety of speech and language disorders. The greatest number of speech pathologists are employed in school settings, ranging from preschool through high school. Services provided include screening for speech and hearing disorders, diagnosis, treatment, and referral for more complex disorders. Since children make up the caseload in public schools, the majority of disorders treated are those concerning speech, language, voice, and stuttering. Many hospitals provide speech and language services. Speech clinics are usually established in rehabilitation departments. Speech-language pathologists work with occupational and physical therapists to treat people with physical disorders. Sometimes hospitals also provide services for children, thus offering an alternative to the free services of public schools.

There are speech-language clinics in many large metropolitan areas. Some of these clinics are private; others are associated with hospitals or universities. These clinics usually provide a wide range of services while at the same time being used as a training base for future speech language professionals. Privately funded or publicly funded health service agencies may also provide speech-language services. These agencies provide speech-language services to people from less privileged socioeconomic backgrounds. Speech clinicians employed by these agencies usually are itinerant: They go to the home of the client to provide the speech-language service. Clinics run by these agencies also provide a wide range of clinical services. There is a trend for speech-language pathologists to establish their own speech-language services rather than work for a school, hospital, clinic, or public agency. These individuals set up offices and see clients there. Occasionally, they hire other speech pathologists and enlarge their caseloads to the point where they can call their practice a clinic. Again, services are provided across the full range of speech and hearing disorders. Occasionally, speech-language pathologists are employed by industry. In these settings, the pathologists usually serve a diagnostic function only. In summary, speech-language services cover a wide range of diagnostic and therapeutic treatments in a variety of settings. These settings include public schools, hospitals, private speech clinics, university speech clinics, health service agencies, and private practices.

REFERENCES

Cleland, C. C., & Swartz, J. E. (1982). *Exceptionalities through the lifespan.* New York: Macmillan.

Van Riper, C., & Erickson, R. L. (1996). *Speech correction: An introduction to speech pathology and audiology* (9th ed.). Boston: Allyn & Bacon.

EDWARD A. SHIRKEY
New Mexico State University

SPEECH THERAPISTS
SPEECH THERAPY

SPEECH SYNTHESIZER

A speech synthesizer is an electronic device that attempts to duplicate the human voice. Essentially, it allows a machine to talk to a human being. Of course, a human being must program the synthesizer and tell it what to say.

There are two different techniques for producing speech output that account for almost all the current synthesizer designs. The first is called linear predictive coding (LPC), which attempts to make an electronic model of the human voice. It creates tones much like those of the human vocal folds. These tones are passed through a set of filters that shape the tones into sounds the way that the articulators (tongue, lips, teeth, etc.) shape tones into sounds. This is a popular technique because it requires only enough computer memory to store the filter configurations and therefore is relatively inexpensive to make. Sound quality is acceptable but not realistic because the modeling of the voice is not exact enough to duplicate all the subtle vocal characteristics of human speech. The result is a machinelike speech quality.

The second method of producing speech is referred to as digitized speech. Actually, digitized speech is not synthesized speech. In digitized speech, the sound waves of the speech signal rather than the throat positions are recorded. These waves are then digitized—converted to digital codes and played back when needed. The advantage to this method is that the speech quality is good, sounding like a high-quality tape recorder. Nonetheless, it still takes time for the average listener to adjust and understand synthesized speech (Venkatagiri, 1994). The disadvantage is that great amounts of memory are required to store the speech waves.

Aside from the industrial application of speech synthesizers, the synthesizers are being used as communication devices for nonspeaking handicapped individuals and to prompt handicapped individuals using remediation software (Lundberg, 1995).

REFERENCES

Lundberg, I. (1995). The computer as a tool of remediation in the education of students with reading disabilities. *Learning Disability Quarterly*, 18(2), 89–99.

Venkatagiri, H. S. (1994). *Effect of sentence length and exposure on the intelligibility of synthesized speech*. American Journal of Speech-Language Pathology, 4, 4, 36–45.

FREDERICK F. WEINER
Pennsylvania State University

AUGMENTATIVE COMMUNICATION SYSTEMS
COMPUTER USE WITH THE HANDICAPPED

SPEECH THERAPY

Speech therapy includes all efforts to ameliorate disordered speech. Treatment activities include attempts to improve the speech of persons who have never spoken normally (habilitation) as week as to improve the speech of persons who formerly had normal speech (rehabilitation). A variety of treatment approaches are used, depending on the speaker's age, speech disorder, and the professional training and experience of the speech pathologist. Speech therapy usually includes teaching a person with a speech disorder to speak differently. Concerning adults and older children, however, therapy may consist of play activities during which treatment is indirect.

Although many research investigations have been conducted into the nature and treatment of speech (and language) disorders, much remains unknown. Therapy remains, therefore, often more of an "art" than a science. The speech pathologist must often rely more on intuition and experience than on research results. Often, no attempt is made to determine the cause of the speech disorder because, in most cases, the cause(s) cannot be found (e.g., Van Riper and Erickson, 1996). Although some speech disor-

ders can be completely "cured" so that no traces of the original behavior remain, some speech disorders cannot be completely eradicated. For instance, some children and adults who stutter will continue to have vestiges of stuttering despite successful speech therapy.

Clients receive therapy in group and/or individual sessions, and therapy may be short-term (a few sessions) or long-term (several years), depending on the nature and severity of the disorder. The length and frequency of therapy sessions also depend on a variety of factors. (The terms client, patient, and student are all variously used to refer to the person being treated for a speech disorder, depending on the treatment setting).

Speech-language pathologists typically assess clients before therapy actually begins, although a period of "diagnostic therapy" may also be used to help determine the nature of the disorder. Sometimes, clients are referred to other professionals by the speech-language pathologist (e.g., audiologists, dentists, physicians.).

REFERENCE

Van Riper, C., & Erickson, R. L. (1996). *Speech correction: An introduction to speech pathology and audiology*. Boston: Allyn and Bacon.

EDWARD A. SHIRKEY
New Mexico State University

AUGMENTATIVE COMMUNICATION SYSTEMS
COMMUNICATION DISORDERS
SPEECH-LANGUAGE PATHOLOGIST

SPELLING DISABILITIES

Spelling is a traditional element of the elementary school curriculum and an integral part of the writing process. The primary goal of spelling instruction for both handicapped and nonhandicapped students is to make the act of correctly spelling words so automatic that it requires only a minimal amount of conscious attention. If students master the ability to spell words with maximum efficiency and minimum effort, it is assumed that they will be able to devote more of their attention, and consequently more of their effort, to higher order writing processes such as purpose, content, and organization (Graham, 1982).

It is commonly believed that the majority of students who are labeled handicapped exhibit spelling problems. This is particularly the case for handicapped students with reading difficulties (Lennox & Siegal, 1993). For instance, MacArthur and Graham (1986) found that learning-disabled students made spelling errors in approximately 1 out of every 10 words that they used when writing a short story. Although similar spelling difficulties have been reported for other handicapping conditions (Graham & Miller, 1979), it is important to note that our present understanding of spelling difficulties and handicapped students' development of spelling skills is incomplete.

One development of particular interest in the area of spelling disabilities is the formulation of various systems for classifying spelling problems. Poor spellers who are also poor readers have frequently been classified as dyslexic, while poor spellers who possess normal reading skills have been labeled dysgraphic. In addition, many of the classification schemes presently available represent an attempt to interpret various spelling errors and difficulties as evidence of neurological dysfunction.

Spelling instruction for the handicapped has, in large part, been based on the use or modification of traditional spelling procedures and techniques. Although handicapped students may not progress as rapidly through the spelling curriculum or master all of the skills taught to normally achieving students, their spelling programs commonly emphasize the traditional skills of (1) mastering a basic spelling vocabulary; (2) determining the spelling of unknown words through the use of phonics and spelling rules; (3) developing a desire to spell words correctly; (4) identifying and correcting spelling errors; and (5) using the dictionary to locate the spelling of words. There is considerable controversy, however, surrounding the issue of which skills should receive primary emphasis. Some experts, for example, recommend that a basic spelling vocabulary should form the core of the spelling program, while others have argued that spelling instruction should take advantage of the systematic properties of English orthography and stress the application of phonics and spelling rules (Graham, 1983).

Although spelling instruction for handicapped students has received little attention in the research literature, experts generally agree that these students should be taught a systematic procedure of studying unknown spelling words. Effective word study procedures usually emphasize careful pronunciation of the word, visual imagery, auditory and/or kinesthetic reinforcement, and systematic recall (Graham & Miller, 1979). Additional instructional procedures that are considered desirable for use with handicapped students include using a pretest to determine which words a student should study; presenting and testing a few words on a daily basis; interspering known and unknown words in each spelling test; requiring students to correct their spelling tests under the guidance of a teacher; periodically reviewing to determine whether spelling skills have been maintained; and using spelling games to promote interest and motivation.

A final point concerns the use of behavioral and cognitive procedures. Although the evidence is not yet conclusive, spelling procedures based on behavioral and/or cognitive principles appear to be particularly effective with handicapped students. McLaughlin (1982) found, for example, that the spelling accuracy of students in a special class improved as a result of group contingencies. In terms of cognitive procedures, Harris, Graham, and Freeman (1986) found that strategy training improved learning disabled students' spelling performance and, in one study condition, improved their ability to predict how many words would be spelled correctly on a subsequent test. Others have found that computers assist in spelling skill acquisition in a meaningful way (Gordon, Vaughn, Schumon & Shay, 1993; Van Daal & Van der Leij, 1992).

REFERENCES

Gordon, J., Vaughn, S., & Schumon, J. S. (1993). Spelling in instruction: A review of literature and implications for instruction for student with learning disabilities. *Learning Disabilities Research and Practice, 8*(3), 175–181.

Graham, S. (1982). Composition research and practice: A unified approach. *Focus on Exceptional Children, 14*, 1–16.

Graham, S. (1983). Effective spelling instruction. *Elementary School Journal, 83*, 560–568.

Graham, S., & Miller, L. (1979). Spelling research and practice: A unified approach. *Focus on Exceptional Children, 12*, 1–16.

Harris, K., Graham, S., & Freeman, S. (1986). *The effects of strategy training and study conditions on metamemory and achievement.* Paper presented at the American Educational Research Association, San Francisco.

Lennox, C., & Siegal, L. S. (1993). Visual and phonological spelling errors in subtypes of children with learning disabilities. *Applied Psycholinguistics, 14*(4), 473–488.

MacArthur, C., & Graham, S., (1986). *LD students' writing under three conditions: Word processing, dictation, and handwriting.* Paper presented at the American Educational Research Association, San Francisco.

McLaughlin, T. (1982). A comparison of individual and group contingencies on spelling performance with special education students. *Child and Family Behavior Therapy, 4*, 1–10.

Van Daal, V. H., & Van der Leij, A. (1992). Computer-based reading and spelling practice for children with learning disabilities. *Journal of Learning Disabilities, 25*(3), 186–195.

STEVE GRAHAM
University of Maryland

WRITING REMEDIATION
WRITTEN LANGUAGE OF THE HANDICAPPED

SPERRY, ROGER W. (1913–1994)

Fifty years of systematic and ingenious research resulted in Roger Sperry's development of novel ideas about the nervous system and mind. Born to a middle class family in Hartford, Connecticut on August 20, 1913, Sperry dedicated his professional life to understanding two basic ques-

Roger W. Sperry

tions in psychology: 1) what is consciousness? and 2) what roles do nature and nurture play in the regulation of behavior? Educated at Oberlin College in Ohio (BS in English and MS in psychology), Chicago (PhD in Zoology), and Harvard (post-doctoral fellowship in psychology), Sperry always went against the conventional wisdom of his day, tending to question established fact through simple but brilliant studies. Most of his important studies were completed as Hixson Professor of Psychobiology at the California Institute of Technology.

He indicated that his work could be divided into phases. The first phase, developed at Oberlin and continued through his Chicago years, focused on determining whether the nervous system was malleable or amenable to change through learning. After interchanging nerve fibers in rats, initially motor ones and later sensory ones also, he concluded that the nervous system was more hard-wired than we had previously thought. These experiments were later replicated in a variety of amphibians and mammals, using both motor and sensory fibers. It was during this time that he developed the theory of chemoaffinity of nerve fibers. He proposed that if nerve fibers were cut, they would grow back to their original site using chemically-induced growth.

During the 1950s, Sperry began to question whether this hard-wired concept was also found inside the brain (since he had previously worked with fibers in the peripheral nervous system). Initially working with cats and later with monkeys, Sperry began cutting the largest nerve tract in the brain, the corpus callosum. It had been previously thought that this fiber tract's role was essentially to hold the two sides of the brain together. His initial studies reflected that the two sides appeared to have different functions. However, he believed that humans could provide more accurate information regarding the perceived differences.

Together with surgeons Joseph Bogen and Phillip Voegl, Sperry designed a series of studies aimed at discovering the functions of the two sides of the brain and if the brain was as hard-wired as the peripheral nervous system. About a dozen patients with intractable epilepsy had their corpus callosum severed in what is now called "split-brain" preparation. Over numerous studies, some of which are still are still being carried out, it was discovered that the brain was indeed hard-wired, much like the peripheral nervous system. Further, it was found that the left hemisphere was primarily responsible for verbal information while the right hemisphere controlled visual information.

Additional studies revealed that the patients had two separate minds. Hence, their behavior was not integrated. After further study, Sperry concluded that consciousness was a function of the integration of both sides of the brain simultaneously. Also, he believed that the consciousness emerged from brain function and, in turn, had a downward control on the brain function from which it had been produced.

In his later years, Sperry became interested in the notion that specific value systems, as found in conscious thought, had an effect on the global situation. Specifically, he believed that appropriate values (reduction in overpopulation and pollution) were the solution to the modern problems facing society.

For his scientific work, Sperry shared the 1981 Nobel Prize in Medicine and received the highest awards in the disciplines he worked in, including psychology, neuroscience, and philosophy with over 300 publications, close to 100 students doing research in 9 different continents, Sperry's contributions extend way beyond his half century of research and modern-day psychology. He died at the age of 80 in Pasadena, California from complications of ALS. He is survived by his wife and two children.

REFERENCES

Puente, A. E. (1995). Roger Sperry (1913–1994). *American Psychologist*.

Sperry, R. W. (1952) Neurology and the mind-brain problem. *American Scientist, 40,* 2910312.

Sperry, R. W. (1982). Some effects of disconnecting the cerebral hemispheres. *Science, 217,* 1223–1226.

ANTONIO E. PUENTE
University of North Carolina at Wilmington

SPINA BIFIDA

Spina bifida (myelomeningocele) is a congenital abnormality present at birth. The defect begins early in embryogenesis (the first 30 days of gestation), as the central nervous system is developing with a failure of the spinal cord to close over the lower end (Haslam & Valletutti, 1975). Without such closure, normal development of the spinal column cannot occur; the spinal cord and covering membranes bulge out and block further development.

It is a fairly common developmental anomaly present in .2 to .4 per 1000 live births (Haslam & Valletutti, 1975). The risks increase dramatically to 1/20 to 1/40 following the birth of one affected infant. It is possible to test for spina bifida through amniocentesis. The amniotic fluid is analyzed by testing for abnormally high alpha fetal protein and acetyl cholinesterase levels. Both are normally present in the fetal cerebrospinal fluid, which, in myelomeningocele, leaks into the amniotic fluid (Behrman & Vaugh, 1983).

Detection at birth is due to the presence of a large bulging lesion or swelling, with or without a skin covering, at the lower part of the back (lumbosacral region). It is the damage to or the defect of the spinal cord that results in a variety of handicapping conditions. Eighty percent of children with spina bifida have hydrocephalus, a condition caused by the accumulation of fluid in the ventricles of the brain (Haslam & Valletutti, 1975). If left untreated, hydrocephalus can result in severe mental retardation. Treatment consists of diverting the cerebrospinal fluid to some other area of the body, usually the atria of the heart or the abdominal cavity (Wolraich, 1983).

Paraplegia resulting from the disruption of the motor tracts from the brain to the muscles at the spinal cord level leads to weakness and paralysis of muscles. The degree of paralysis depends on the location and extent of spinal cord damage. Bladder and bowel control is often absent and may present one of the biggest obstacles to a child's participation in a regular school program.

Children with spina bifida will require extensive medical, orthopedic, and educational services. This is often expensive and time consuming, creating frustration and financial hardship for the family. Educational programming for these children must consider the need for personnel trained in toileting techniques and physical therapy. While some children with spina bifida may require a self-contained special education class setting, others who are less severely impaired cognitively may be able to perform successfully in a mainstream classroom with support services.

Incidence of spina bifida can be significantly reduced owing to the discovery of a strong link between neural tube defects in general and folic acid deficiency. Folic acid is now known to protect against such defects, although the mode of action is not clear. Women who have had one child with spina bifida who take folic acid supplements during subsequent pregnancies have a 70% reduction in recurrence. Further, folic acid supplements can reduce incidence of new cases of spina bifida by 50%. Thus, all women who may become pregnant are advised to take daily folic acid

supplements both before and during the first 12 weeks of pregnancy. Such supplements are now planned for common foods such as bread, flour, and rice (Liptak, 1997).

REFERENCES

Behrman, R. E., & Vaughn, V. C. (1983). Defects of closure tube. In W. B. Nelson (Ed.), *Nelson's textbook of pediatrics* (pp. 1560–1561). Philadelphia: Saunders.

Haslam, R. A., & Valletutti, P. J. (1975). *Medical problems in the classroom: The teacher's role in diagnosis and management.* Baltimore, MD: University Park Press.

Liptak, G. S. (1997). Neural tube defects. In M. L. Batshaw (Ed.) *Children with disabilities* (4th ed.) (pp. 529–552). Baltimore Brookes.

Wolraich, M. (1983). Myelomeningocele. In J. A. Blackman (Ed.), *Medical aspects of developmental disabilities in children birth to three: A resource for special service providers in the educational setting.* Iowa City: University of Iowa.

MARSHA H. LUPI
Hunter College

HYDROCEPHALUS

SPINAL CORD INJURY

Damage to the spinal cord frequently, but not always, result in paralysis or paresis to the extremities. The specific impairment or dysfunction that occurs in the extremities depends on the corresponding spinal level and the severity of the injury. In some situations, the injury may be only temporary and the individual may not experience any permanent effects. More often, the injury results in permanent damage and loss of function in the involved extremities.

The most common causes of spinal cord injury are accidents in or about the home, falls, bullet wounds, sports injuries, or motor vehicle accidents. The injury is often associated with fractured bones of the spinal column but also may occur from dislocation of one or more of these bones on the other. When the spinal cord is damaged, the nervous pathways between the body and the brain are interrupted. All forms of sensation (e.g., proprioception, touch, temperature, pain) and muscular control are typically lost below the level of the damage. Although nerves outside the spinal cord may be repaired or heal spontaneously, damaged nerves within the spinal cord will not regenerate. If the injury is low on the spinal cord (usually below the first thoracic vertebra), only the lower extremities are involved. This type of injury is called paraplegia. If the injury is higher on the spinal cord (cervical level), all four extremities and the trunk may be involved; this condition is referred to as quadriplegia. Injury to the highest levels of the cervical spine may cause death because of the loss of innervation to the diaphragm. Occasionally, only one side of the cord is damaged. This type of condition is called Brown-Sequard syndrome. Loss of proprioception and motor paralysis occur on the same side as the injury, while loss of pain, temperature, and touch sensations occur on the opposite side.

Immediate treatment after a spinal injury or suspected injury is immobilization. Immobilization prevents further shearing of the spinal column, which may result in further or more permanent damage to the spinal cord. If there is any doubt about a possible spinal cord injury, the injured person should not be moved until trained assistance arrives. Once the injured person has been transported to an appropriate medical facility, the course of treatment varies, depending on the nature of the injury.

During the initial stage of spinal cord trauma, autonomic and motor reflexes below the level of the injury are suppressed. This flaccid paralysis is called spinal shock and may last from several hours to 3 months. As the spinal shock recedes, spinal reflexes return in a hyperactive state. This spasticity or muscular hypertonicity may vary initially at different times of the day or in response to different stimuli, but it becomes more consistent within one year of the injury. The most common form of acute treatment is traction to the spinal column to bring about a realignment and healing of the fractured or displaced vertebrae. Special beds may be used to permit people in traction to be turned from their back to their abdomen, thereby reducing the chance of pressure sores (decubitus).

Artificial ventilation usually is necessary for persons with injuries at or above the level of the third cervical vertebra (C3). Decreased respiratory capacity is present in injuries from C4 through T7 (the seventh thoracic vertebra), making coughing difficult and often necessitating suctioning when the patient gets a respiratory infection. Dizziness or blackout may occur from pooling of blood in the abdomen and lower extremities when a person is first brought to an upright position following a period of immobilization. This is a normal reaction and is avoided through the aid of a reclining wheelchair or a tilt table that allows gradual adjustment to a full upright position. Numerous other secondary conditions or complications may occur for several months or years following a spinal cord injury. These include muscle contracture or shortening, loss of sexual functioning in males, impaired bowel or bladder control, kidney or urinary tract infections, or psychological reactions, to name but a few.

Rehabilitation procedures begin within a few days of the injury and usually continue for several weeks or months after the healing process is complete. The general goal of rehabilitation is to improve the physical capacities and develop adapted techniques to promote as independent a lifestyle as possible. Unfortunately, rehabilitation's goals all too often focus on participation rather than performance (Dudgeon, Massagli, & Ross, 1997). Educational performance for a person with a spinal cord injury is hampered only by the individual's physical limitations. However, the individual may have problems with self-image, coping strategies, accessibility support, and unresolved feelings, all of which may affect educational performance (Mulcahey, 1992). Persons with high-level injuries may require numerous assistive devices such as an electronic typewriter with mouthstick or mechanical page turner. Persons with low-level injuries may not require any specialized assistance to benefit from education. Counseling to help a person adjust to new physical impairments and to develop future vocational pursuits may also be in order.

REFERENCES

Dudgeon, B. J., Massagli, T. L., & Ross, B. W. (1997) Educational participation of children with spinal cord injury. *American Journal of Occupational Therapy, 51*(7), 553–561.

Hanak, M., & Scott, A. (1983). *Spinal cord injury: An illustrated guide for health care professionals*. New York: Springer-Verlag.

Long, C. (1971). Congenital and traumatic lesions of the spinal cord. In T. H. Krusen, F. H. Kottke, & P. M. Ellwood (Eds.), *Handbook of physical medicine and rehabilitation* (2nd ed., pp. 475–516). Philadelphia: Saunders.

Mulcahey, M. J. (1992). Returning to school after spinal cord injury: Perspectives from four adolescents. *American Journal of Occupational Therapy, 46*(4), 305–312.

Trombly, C. A. (1984). Spinal cord injury. In C. A. Trombly (Ed.), *Occupational therapy for physical dysfunction* (3rd ed.), Baltimore: Williams & Wilkins.

Wilson, D. J., McKenzie, M. W., Barber, L. M., & Watson, K. L. (1984). *Spinal cord injury: A treatment guide for occupational therapists*. Thorofare, NJ: Slack.

DANIEL D. LIPKA
*Lincoln Way Special Education
Regional Resource Center*

PARAPLEGIA
QUADRIPLEGIA

SPINOCEREBELLAR DEGENERATION

See FRIEDREICH'S ATAXIA.

SPITZ, HERMAN (1925–   )

Herman Spitz was born on March 2, 1925 in Paterson, New Jersey. He is a noted psychologist and researcher in the field of mental retardation. Spitz obtained his BA at Lafayette College (1948) and PhD at New York University (1955). He was an assistant psychologist (1951–1955) and chief psychologist (1955–1957) at Trenton State Hospital. From 1957 to 1989, Spitz was affiliated with the E. R.

Johnstone Training and Research Center, initially as a research associate, and beginning in 1962, as the director of research.

As an author of over 90 publications, Spitz has written extensively on the subject of mental retardation, particularly as related to assessment, intervention (both cognitive and behavioral), and causes (Spitz, 1986a, 1986b, 1994). He has also shown an interest in the unconscious, and has recently authored a book on the topic, exploring how nonconscious movements can influence our expression of ideas, inner conflicts, and wishful thinking, and particularly serving to facilitate communication of individuals who are severely and profoundly retarded or autistic (Spitz, 1997).

Spitz has served as a consulting editor for several professional journals, including the *American Journal of Mental Deficiency* and *Memory and Cognition*. He is a fellow of the American Psychological Association and the American Psychological Society and member of the American Academy on Mental Retardation. In recognition of his research contributions, Spitz has served as an invited lecturer and consultant to numerous institutions, including Alabama University, Columbia University, George Peabody College for Teachers, and the Medical Research Council, London.

REFERENCES

American Men of Science. (1962). (10th edition). Tempe, AZ: Jaques Cattell.

Spitz, H. H. (1986a). Disparities in mentally retarded persons' IQ derived from different intelligence tests. *American Journal of Mental Deficiency, 90*(5), 588–591.

Spitz, H. H. (1986b). Preventing and curing mental retardation by behavioral intervention: An evaluation of some claims. *Intelligence, 10*(3), 197–207.

Spitz, H. H. (1994). Fragile X syndrome is not the second leading cause of mental retardation. *Mental Retardation, 32*(2), 156.

Spitz, H. H. (1997). *Nonconscious movements: From mystical messages to facilitated communication.* Mahwah, NJ: Erlbaum.

IVAN Z. HOLOWINSKY
Rutgers University
First edition

TAMARA J. MARTIN
*The University of Texas of the
Permian Basin*
Second edition

SPITZ, RENE ARPAD (1887–1974)

Rene Arpad Spitz, educated in his native Hungary and in the United States, was a leading representative of psychoanalysis in the United States. He served on the faculty of the New York Psychoanalytic Institute, was professor of psychiatry at City College, City University of New York and the University of Colorado, and was clinical professor of psychiatry at Lenox Hill Hospital in New York City. The author of some 60 monographs and papers, Spitz is best known for his extensive studies of infant development.

REFERENCES

Spitz, R. A. (1962). *A genetic field theory of ego formation.* New York: International Universities Press.

Spitz, R. A., & Cobliner, W. G. (1966). *The first year of life.* New York: International Universities Press.

PAUL IRVINE
Katonah, New York

SPLINTER SKILL

See IDIOT SAVANT.

SPLIT-BRAIN RESEARCH

The technique of cerebral commissurotomy (split-brain surgery) was first introduced by Van Wagenen in 1940 as a surgical solution for severe and intractible forms of epilepsy. Van Wagenen performed the operation on approximately 2 dozen cases, hoping to be able to restrict the abnormal electrical activation characteristic of epilepsy to a single hemisphere. Unfortunately, the early operations were not successful and the procedure was largely abandoned until the early 1960s, when it was taken up by Roger Sperry working in collaboration with Joseph Bogen and Philip Vogel (Beaumont, 1983). The refined operation proved to be effective in many cases and, more important from scientific perspective, the procedure allowed a unique opportunity to study cerebral organization. Sperry's work with split-brain patients was deemed so important that he shared the Nobel Prize in Medicine in 1984. This award appropriately reflects the tremendous advances that were made in the neurosciences following this seminal work.

The technique of cerebral commissurotomy involves the complete section of the corpus callosum, including the anterior and hippocampal commissures in the massa intermedia. This technique effectively isolates each half of the cortex and prevents transfer of information from one side of the brain to the other. Despite the operation's dramatic nature, postsurgical patients appear to function quite well. Fairly sophisticated testing procedures are necessary to isolate and identify the effects of surgery.

Detailed study of postsurgical split-brain patients reveals that, in fact, a number of problems do exist for these patients (Springer & Deutsch, 1981). The patients frequently report trouble with associating names and faces. This may be due to the differential loci for naming and facial recognition, with the assignment of names occurring in the left hemisphere and the recognition of faces more intimately linked to the right hemisphere. Patients also report difficulty with geometry, and many complain of memory loss. Finally, many postsurgical patients report cessation of dreaming; however, this has not been supported empirically and these patients continue to show REM sleep postsurgically.

Sperry has consistently maintained that the operation produces two separate minds within one body, each with its own will, perception, and memories. This is supported by numerous anecdotes of conflict between the hemispheres or between the body parts controlled by the respective hemispheres. These reports, albeit fascinating, are largely anecdotal and appear to be somewhat exaggerated. In general, while early studies and writers emphasized the division and uniqueness of the two hemispheres, recent research has been devoted to how the brain works as a whole and how the hemispheres cooperate in transferring information back and forth. Zaidel (1979) has compared performance of each hemisphere operating singly with performance of the brain operating as a whole. He has found that much better results are evident when the brain is working as a whole with the hemispheres serving in tandem. In addition, it is important not to forget that both cortical structures are intimately linked to an integrated subcortical substrate with a number of linked bilateral structures (Corballis, 1998).

Eccles (1977) has reviewed the split-brain research and has argued that it suggests consciousness is intimately linked to speech and therefore must reside in the dominant left hemisphere. However, all such generalizations from split-brain research are limited by the fact that the brains studied are clearly pathological specimens and may not represent normal cognitive functioning.

One of the interesting findings that has emerged from split-brain research is that rudimentary language perception skills have been associated with the right cerebral hemisphere. Recognition of nouns by the right hemisphere appears to be easier than recognition of verbs (Gazzaniga, 1970). This difference is especially marked when a rapid response is required. If patients are given maximum time to respond, the noun-verb distinction is less apparent.

Levy and her colleagues have completed a number of studies with split-brain patients employing chimeric stimulae (Levy, Trevarthen, & Sperry, 1972). These are stimulus items that are composed by joining two half-stimuli. The stimuli are presented in such a way that each half goes to the isolated contralateral hemisphere. On the basis of these studies, Levy has argued that the left hemisphere is best described as analytic while the right is best described as holistic.

Split-brain patients make ideal subjects for dichotic listening experiments in which different stimuli are presented simultaneously in each ear. In addition, for those patients who receive a commissurotomy, divided visual field studies can be employed with less concern for saccadic eye movements. However, considerable experimental skill is necessary to avoid the phenomenon of cross-cuing. This occurs when a patient deliberately or inadvertently develops strategies for delivering information to both hemispheres simultaneously. For example, a subject who is palpating a comb may rub the teeth of the comb with the left hand. Although the tactile information will reach only the right hemisphere in the split-brain patient, the associated sound goes to both ears and may reach the left hemisphere and allow for linguistic identification.

Increasingly, neurosurgeons are performing partial commissurotomies with good success. These procedures allow still more detailed information about the localization of transference fibers in the corpus callosum. For example, it has become clear that somatosensory information is transmitted via the anterior corpus callosum while the rear portion, the splenium, transfers visual information. In addition, there is an indication that some perceptual judgements may be made sub-cortically (Corballis, 1994).

The work done to date on split-brain patients may offer important clues to help the teacher better understand and educate the child with special needs. Levy (1982) has used split-brain data to develop a model of handwriting posture; Obrzut and Hynd (1981) have applied these findings on cerebral lateralization to children with learning disabilities; and Hartlage (1975) has developed a plan for predicting the outcome of remedial educational strategies based on a model of cerebral lateralization. Perhaps it is only through understanding how each half of the brain works that we will ever approach an understanding how it works as a whole: a concept supported fully by Sperry (Corballis, 1998).

REFERENCES

Beaumont, J. G. (1983). *Introduction to neuropsychology*. New York: Guilford.

Corballis, M. C. (1994). Split decisions: Problems in the interpretation of results from commissurotomized subjects. *Behavioral Brain Research, 64*(1), 163–172.

Corballis, M. C. (1998). Sperry and the age of Aquarius: Science values and the split brain. *Neuropsychologies, 36*(10), 1083–1087.

Eccles, J. C. (1977). *The understanding of the brain* (2nd ed.). New York: McGraw-Hill.

Gazzaniga, M. S. (1970). *The bisected brain*. Englewood Cliffs, NJ: Prentice-Hall.

Hartlage, L. C. (1975). Neuropsychological approaches to predicting outcome of remedial educational strategies for learning disabled children. *Pediatric Psychology, 3*, 23–28.

Levy, J. (1982). Handwriting posture and cerebral organization: How are they related? *Psychological Bulletin, 91*, 589–608.

Levy, J., Trevarthen, C., & Sperry, R. W. (1972). Perception of bilateral chimeric figures following hemispheric disconnection. *Brain, 95*, 61–78.

Obrzut, J. E., & Hynd, G. W. (1981). Cognitive development and cerebral lateralization in children with learning disabilities. *International Journal of Neuroscience, 14*, 139–145.

Springer, S. P., & Deutsch, G. (1981). *Left brain, right brain.* San Francisco: Freeman.

Zaidel, E. (1979). Performance on the ITPA following cerebral commissurotomy and hemispherectomy. *Neuropsychologia, 17*, 259–280.

DANNY WEDDING
Marshall University

CEREBRAL DOMINANCE
LEFT BRAIN, RIGHT BRAIN

SPORTS FOR THE HANDICAPPED

The origin of sports adapted to the needs of the handicapped can be traced to the end of World War II, when thousands of physically handicapped veterans joined already existing groups of people with congenital and traumatic handicaps. In 1948 Stoke Mandeville Hospital in Aylsburg, England, first introduced an organized wheelchair sports program for patients; the first international games were held there in 1952 (Wehman & Schleien, 1981). This use of sports in rehabilitation was the stimulus for the growth of the international sports for the disabled movement that is prevalent today (DePauw, 1984).

From the beginning it was apparent that adaptations of rules and equipment were going to be necessary for sports programs, and many of the adaptations were the result of the imaginative efforts of the participants themselves. In addition, the participants joined together with others who needed the same adaptations, and through their activities were able to participate within the wider community. For some disabled persons, a sports program means competition; in other situations, the aim of sports is to meet therapeutic needs; for others the objective of sports involvement is to fulfill leisure-time pursuits (Adams et al., 1982).

Currently, federal mandates regulate physical education services and sports opportunities for individuals with disabilities. IDEA requires a free appropriate public school education, which includes instruction in physical education, in the least restrictive environment. Section 504 of the Rehabilitation Act, specifies nondiscrimination on the basis of handicap, and states that equal opportunity and equal access must be provided for handicapped persons, specifically including physical education services, intra-murals, and athletics. The most direct mandate for sports opportunities is the Amateur Sports Act of 1978 (PL 95-606) (DePauw, 1984).

As a result of this law, the U.S. Olympic Committee initiated a Handicapped in Sports Committee, which changed its name to the Committee on Sports for the Disabled (COSD) in 1983 (DePauw, 1984). Committee membership consists of two representatives from each major national organization in the United States offering sports opportunities for disabled individuals. At least 20% of COSD members must be, or have been, actively participating disabled athletes.

There are seven organizations designated as members of COSD. The National Association of Sports for Cerebral Palsy is a program of United Cerebral Palsy providing competitive sports opportunities for individuals with cerebral palsy and similar physically disabling conditions (Adams, 1984). The American Association for the Deaf sanctions and promotes state, regional, and national basketball, softball, and volleyball tournaments, the World Games for the Deaf, the AAD Hall of Fame, and the Deaf Athlete of the Year (Ammons, 1984). The National Handicapped Sports and Recreation Association is unique in the world of sports groups in that its members possess a variety of physical and mental disabilities (Hernley, 1984). The National Wheelchair Athletic Association organizes and conducts competition in seven different Olympic sports, and also in wheelchair slalom, involving a race against time over a series of obstacles to challenge a competitor's wheelchair handling and speed skills (Fleming, 1984). The United States Amputee Athletic Association has grown from a small group of competitors in 1981 to a national organization which sponsors annual games (Bryant, 1984). The major purpose of the U.S. Association for Blind Athletes is to develop individual independence through athletic competition without unnecessary restrictions (Beaver, 1984).

Founded in 1968 by Eunice Kennedy Shriver, the first International Special Olympics was a single track and field event with about a thousand participants. Today over 1 million mentally handicapped children and adults from around the world take part in Special Olympics; it is the biggest sports event in which handicapped children are likely to be involved. Sports activities range from events in swimming, gymnastics, and bowling, to basketball, track and field, and soccer. Racewalking has been adopted as a new sport, and equestrian sporting events are now being offered as demonstration sports.

Sports activities for the handicapped are sponsored by many nonschool groups, however, guarantees of equal opportunities for disabled students require that educators and psychologists give more attention to school-sponsored sports programs (Ashen, 1991). Unique and innovative approaches are needed so that these individuals can participate in sports within the schools. One possibility is to have special sections for the disabled as part of regular track, swimming, and gymnastic meets. It also may be possible to mix people with different handicapping conditions with able-bodied individuals in some sports programs. One promising program is the Paralympic movement. The paralympic games as one of the largest sporting events in the world (Steadward, 1996.)

REFERENCES

Adams, C. (1984). The National Association of Sports for Cerebral Palsy. *Journal of Physical Education, Recreation & Dance, 55,* 34–35.

Adams, R. C., David, A. N., McCubbin, J. A., & Rullman, L. (1982). *Games, sports and exercises for the physically handicapped* (3rd ed.). Philadelphia: Lea & Febiger.

Ammons, D. C. (1984). American Athletic Association for the Deaf, *Journal of Physical Education, Recreation and Dance, 55,* 36–37.

Ashen, M. J. (1991). The challenge of the physically challenged: Delivering sport psychology services to physically disabled athletes. *Sport Psychologist, 5*(4), 370–381.

Beaver, D. P. (1984). The United States Association for Blind Athletes. *Journal of Physical Education, Recreation & Dance, 55,* 40–41.

Bryant, D. C. (1984). United States Amputee Athletic Association. *Journal of Physical Education, Recreation, and Dance, 55,* 40–41.

DePauw, K. P. (1984). Commitment and challenges, sport opportunities for athletes with disabilities. *Journal of Physical Education, Recreation & Dance, 55,* 34–35.

Fleming, A. (1984). The National Wheelchair Association. *Journal of Physical Education, Recreation & Dance, 55,* 38–39.

Hernley, R. (1984). National Handicapped Sports and Recreation Association. *Journal of Physical Education, Recreation & Dance, 55,* 38–39.

Steadward, R. D. (1996). Integration and sport in the paralympic movement. *Sport Science Review, 5*(1), 26–41.

Wehman, P., & Schleien, S. (1981). *Leisure programs for handicapped persons, adaptations techniques and curriculum.* Baltimore, MD: University Park Press.

CATHERINE O. BRUCE
Hunter College

OLYMPICS, SPECIAL
RECREATIONAL THERAPY

STAFF DEVELOPMENT

Staff development represents the professional growth of persons toward observable and measurable objectives that benefit an organization and its members. Professional and personal growth are necessary if an organization is to maintain its performance standards, develop a feeling of pride, stimulate its membership, and generate a creative work environment, all of which contribute to personal and corporate well being.

Staff development is necessary to improve the product of an organization by raising the skill level and awareness of the human resources of that organization. In the public schools, the product is education. Teachers design and deliver the product; students consume; and the public evaluates the product based on their observations of its effects on the consumers (children). Education must be accepted as meaningful and pertinent to the children before they learn. The motivating and technical skills of teachers, as salespersons, are vital to the success of the enterprise. The delivery of the product—instruction—requires teacher performance, materials, physical plant, technology, and student motivation. These variables determine the amount of the product the consumers buy or, in some cases, refuse. The teacher's skills, as those of the producer and delivering agent, are the key input in the process. Because of the importance of those skills, development of the staff as a key resource should be continuous and planned, as with any of the other resources of an organization. Development must be perceived as required, meaningful, and attainable by the staff.

Initial planning may begin by determining the needs of the organization and its membership. Needs surveying instruments are designed for that purpose. A staff development plan will fulfill those preferred needs that have been identified. The staff may contribute by assembling a list of requirements that can be collectively prioritized with regard to an organization's needs. This allows for all staff to feel a part of the planning process. Communication of the results of the needs survey should follow.

Another component of basic staff development is the creation of a supportive environment. To establish this environment there are several desirable elements that an administrator should provide, including teaching assignments, scheduling, released time, and special instructional supplies. Administrators must also be sensitive to personal needs and personalities of the staff, supporting them with concern, sincerity, and other humanizing factors. Developing support groups among teachers, organizing functional committees, and being a public relations agent for the school are indicative of a supportive environment. Praising and supporting teachers in the community when adversarial situations are apparent is also important in providing a supportive environment.

The administration should develop a plan for the enhancement of the school's staff resource. The plan may encompass several areas: curriculum; instruction; personal skills; licensure; advanced education; stress management; work environment; administrative support; school, home, community relations; student management; and school organization. Once the needs of the organization have been identified, each staffer's part in the scheme is drawn up and agreed to. The individual's role is contracted for and evaluated in the routine teacher evaluation process. Methods for enhancing the skill level of the organization may include professional in-service training, team teaching, internships, remedial plans of development, individual guided education units, school visitations, outside instruction, and role modeling.

Once needs are identified, a positive environment established, and a plan designed and implemented, monitoring of the professional staff is recommended. Positive feedback to personnel regarding their teaching performance is essential for it identifies the organizational expectations. Monitoring/supervising can be the same activity. Being visible, asking curriculum-directed questions, acknowledging instructional changes, encouraging staff reviews and faculty support groups, organizing creative instructional changes, providing evaluative feedback, and holding teacher conferences are all supervisory techniques under the heading of monitoring. Classroom visitations are important to monitoring. These activities deliver a clear message of administrative interest. When these components are addressed, an environment of trust develops. The teaching staff becomes more accepting of staff development programs once positive staff development has occurred in the school among the staff.

Need identification, planning and implementation, support and monitoring are basic staff development and personal growth activities. Before the typical staff development plans are initiated, these components should be communicated to and experienced by the staff. Teaching personnel need to know their needs have been identified by the administration as part of the organization's requirements. They should realize that the administration wants to provide a supportive, positive, professional working environment and that a system of consistent, fair, sincere supervision/monitoring is in place. Before outside resources are brought to the organization, in-house staff development should be established on a continuing basis. Staff development strategies can fall on deaf ears unless teachers are in an accepting, creative, and productive atmosphere cultivated by involvement in the building's own program.

The administrator is the key person in preparing the staff for a resourceful plan, but only after the staff has been provided the opportunity for in-house planning and leadership. The assets of an organization, human and physical, must be known. A development system can allow for a committee of teachers to help decide in-service and other needs. As the human resources are assessed, staff should be placed in positions where personal/professional talents are best used. An extension of the effort can complete the plan for achievement of the overall objective of the organization.

ANN SABATINO
Hudson, Wisconsin

PERSONNEL TRAINING IN SPECIAL EDUCATION SUPERVISION IN SPECIAL EDUCATION

STANDARD DEVIATION

The standard deviation is a measure of the dispersion of sample or population scores around the mean score. It is the most important and most widely used measure of dispersion for quantitative variables when the distribution is symmetric. We compute the standard deviation for a population of n scores by first averaging squared deviations of scores (X) from the mean population (m) using Equation 1:

$$\sigma^2 = \frac{\sum_{i=1}^{n}\left(X_i - \mu\right)^2}{n} \tag{1}$$

This yields the variance of the scores, s2. The square root of this value, s, is the population standard deviation. For a sample of n scores, the variance is computed using Equation 2:

$$s^2 = \frac{\sum_{i=1}^{n}\left(X_i - \bar{X}\right)^2}{n - 1} \tag{2}$$

where

$\bar{X}$ is the mean sample score. Here we use $(n - 1)$ as the divisor instead of n because this produces an unbiased sample estimate of σ2. Dividing by n produces a biased estimate. The square root of this value, s, is the standard deviation of the scores in the sample; i.e., the average dispersion of the scores around the mean score.

This measure of dispersion is widely used in the behavioral sciences to describe the spread of scores around the mean score when the distribution of scores is normal. Then we can state the proportion of scores that fall above or below any given value or between any two values by first converting the value(s) to z score units using

$$z_1 = \frac{X_i - \bar{X}}{s} \quad \text{or} \quad z_i = \frac{X_i - \mu}{\sigma} \tag{3}$$

for a sample or population. For example, for a sample of scores with computed statistics
$\bar{X} = 40$ and $s = 5$, the value $X_i = 50$ is two standard deviations above the mean. Thus from a normal table, we find that 97.72% of the scores fall below 50 while 0.28% are larger than 50.

The size of the standard deviation also indicates the relative spread of two comparable distributions. For example, given that $s = 3$ for males and $s = 5$ for females on a given test, where the mean score, 15, is the same for either group, we can tell that the female scores span a wider range than the male scores, with 16% of the females scoring at least 20 while only 5% of the males obtain this score or higher.

In addition to describing a distribution of scores, the standard deviation is used widely in inferential statistics for describing the spread of the sampling distribution. For example, the standard deviation of the sampling distribution of the sample mean, $\overline{X}$, is given by ($\sigma/\sqrt{n}$, where s is defined in Equation 2. We may also obtain the standard deviation of the sample proportion, variance, correlation coefficient, or any other statistic. When so used, the standard deviation is called the standard error of estimate of the statistic. Further, in regression estimation procedures, the standard deviation of the errors of prediction is used to judge the precision of the predicted values. This measure is called the standard error of estimate of prediction. In measurement, we define the standard deviation of the errors of measurement, the standard error of measurement, and use it to infer the value of true scores (Hopkins & Stanley, 1981). Further information on the standard deviation is found in the following references.

REFERENCES

Glass, G. V., & Hopkins, K. D. (1984). *Statistical methods in education and psychology* (2nd ed.). Englewood Cliffs, NJ: Prentice-Hall.

Hays, W. L. (1981). *Statistics* (3rd ed.). New York: Holt, Rinehart, and Winston.

Hopkins, K. D., & Stanley, J. C. (1981). *Educational and psychological measurement and evaluation* (6th ed.). Englewood Cliffs, NJ: Prentice-Hall.

Kirk, R. E. (1984). *Elementary statistics* (2nd ed.). Monterey, CA: Brooks/Cole.

GWYNETH M. BOODOO
Texas A & M University

CENTRAL TENDENCY
NORMAL CURVE EQUIVALENT

STANDARDS FOR EDUCATIONAL AND PSYCHOLOGICAL TESTING (SEPT)

The Standards for Educational and Psychological Testing (SEPT) is a joint effort of the American Psychological Association, the American Educational Research Association, and the National Council on Measurement in Education. The most recent revision of these standards (Committee to Review the Standards for Educational and Psychological Testing, 1985) is an update of the 1974 standards. It represents an evolution of formal standards for testing, beginning with the Technical Recommendations for Psychological Tests and Diagnostic Techniques published by the American Psychological Association in 1954. The document is now under continuing review by the committee

and will undergo periodic revision. Information on and copies of the most recent SEPT are available from the American Psychological Association.

The SEPT is divided into four major sections: technical standards for test construction and evaluation; professional standards for test use; standards for particular applications (including testing language minorities and testing individuals with handicapping conditions); and standards for administrative procedures. The principal purposes for the SEPT are to provide criteria for the evaluation of tests, testing practices, and the effects of test use. While these evaluations depend an the judgment of professionals with appropriate training and certification/licensure for the use and construction of test, the SEPT provides the key frame of reference and ensures that all relevant areas are addressed in making such judgments. Tests and testing are rapidly changing and the SEPT does not provide precise numbers or cutoffs for meeting the various standards. Rather, the SEPT requires that specific types of information be reported so that appropriate evaluations can be made on the basis of evidence and not various fallacies such as the "expert opinion" or appeal to authority.

The SEPT sets several relatively specific requirements for evaluating new tests or testing programs. The SEPT states that:

> When judging the short-term acceptability of a test or program under development or redevelopment, the test user should determine that the test is on a par with readily available alternatives. In addition, the test developers or publishers should determine that (1) advertising for a test or program recommends only applications supported by a test's research base; (2) necessary cautions are given in the manual or elsewhere to encourage sufficiently limited reliances on test results, particularly when the use of the new test will have significant impact on the test takers; and (3) there is clear indication of continuing and significant improvement in the research base directed toward observation of the standards. (p. 3)

While spelling out the responsibilities of the test author and test publishers, the SEPT is prominent in pointing out that the ultimate responsibility for appropriate test use lies with the users of the test.

Though all sections of the SEPT are relevant to the testing of children and adolescents for special education placement and program planning, the 1985 SEPT, for the first time, places special emphasis on this process by devoting an entire chapter to testing people who have handicapping conditions. This has been supported by IDEA amendments and regulations that mandate culturally competent assessment practices and standards.

The SEPT is a document that all test users and consumers of test results should have intimate knowledge of and should apply in practice. Tests not reporting the required information or conforming to the standards should not be used because their appropriateness cannot be evaluated adequately.

REFERENCE

Committee to Review the Standards for Educational and Psychological Testing. (1985). *Standards for educational and psychological testing*. Washington, DC: American Psychological Association.

CECIL R. REYNOLDS
Texas A & M University

BUROS MENTAL MEASUREMENT YEARBOOK
TEST IN PRINT

STANFORD-BINET INTELLIGENCE SCALE: FOURTH EDITION

The Stanford-Binet Intelligence Scale: Fourth Edition (Thorndike, Hagen, & Sattler, 1986) is an individually-administered intelligence test appropriate for ages 2 to young adult. It consists of fifteen tests designed to appraise four major areas of cognitive ability: Verbal Reasoning, Abstract/Visual Reasoning, Quantitative Reasoning, and Short-Term Memory. Each individual test has a Standard Age Score (SAS) mean of 50 and a standard deviation of 8. The Area Scores and the total test Composite SAS have a mean of 100 and a standard deviation of 16. The total test Composite SAS provides the best measure of general reasoning ability, or *g*.

The Stanford-Binet traces its origins to Lewis M. Terman's 1916 Stanford Revision and Extension of the Binet-Simon Scale. Major revisions of the Stanford-Binet were completed in 1937, 1960, and 1986. Historically, the Stanford-Binet has had its leading applications in the assessment of preschool cognitive-intellectual functioning, mental retardation, learning problems, and intellectual giftedness.

The Stanford-Binet offers an adaptive testing format, in which the main focus is on quick and efficient administration of tasks most closely suited to the examinee's ability. Testing time is typically within 60 to 90 minutes, usually taking less than 70 minutes to administer (Camara, Nathan, & Puente, 1998). The Stanford-Binet also offers a six-test General Purpose Abbreviated Battery which requires about 30 to 40 minutes of testing time and which provides a good estimate of overall cognitive abilities. The age-scale format from previous editions has been replaced by a point-scale format, in which all items from a given test are administered before proceeding to the next test.

Extensive validity, reliability, and fairness studies have been published in the Technical Manual (Thorndike, Ha-gen, & Sattler, 1986) and professional journals. Validity studies reported in the technical manual document factor analytic investigations, correlations with other measures of intelligence (e.g., Stanford-Binet Form L-M, Wechsler intelligence scales, K-ABC), and mean test performance among several exceptional samples (e.g., individuals who are designated by their schools as intellectually gifted, learning disabled, or mentally retarded). Studies of test score reliability in the Technical Manual show internal consistency reliabilities typically in the .80s and .90s, with the total test Composite SAS having a median KR-20 reliability of .98 across ages. Abbreviated versions (six tests, four tests, or two tests) of the full Stanford-Binet also yield median reliabilities above .90. Test-retest scoring stability over an average of four months yields median total test Composite SAS reliabilities at or above .90, with the stability of the four Area Scores ranging from .51 to .88. Fairness studies reported in the Technical Manual include expert bias and sensitivity reviews of items and procedures, as well as quantitative studies of item properties using both traditional and Rasch procedures. A more extensive report of statistical analyses of the test's fairness in terms of sex, race, and ethnic membership is available from Riverside Publishing.

Critiques of the Stanford-Binet have generally noted its "high level of technical quality" (Anastasi, 1989) while suggesting that its clinical utility and advantages over other intelligence tests remain to be established (e.g., Anastasi, 1989; Cronbach, 1989). The discontinuation of the traditional age-scale format, in which all items of any type for a given age are administered before proceeding to the next set of items for adjacent ages, has led some reviewers to note that the Stanford-Binet may be "less game-like" (e.g., Cronbach, 1989) than previous editions and other tests. Even with these limitations, contemporary test usage surveys show that the Stanford-Binet ranks as the second most commonly used intelligence test among school psychologists after the Wechsler scales (Reschly, 1998).

REFERENCES

Anastasi, A. (1989). Review of the Stanford-Binet Intelligence Scale, Fourth Edition. In J. C. Conoley & J. J. Kramer (Eds.), *The tenth mental measurements yearbook* (pp. 771–773). Lincoln, NE: Buros Institute of Mental Measurements.

Camara, W., Nathan, J., & Puente, A. (1998). *Psychological test usage in professional psychology*: Report to the APA Practice and Science Directorates. Washington, DC: American Psychological Association.

Cronbach, L. J. (1989) Review of the Stanford-Binet Intelligence Scale, Fourth Edition. In J. C. Conoley & J. J. Kramer (Eds.), *The tenth mental measurements yearbook* (pp. 773-775). Lincoln, NE: Buros Institute of Mental Measurements.

Reschly, D. J. (1998). School psychology practice—Is there change? Paper presented at the Annual Convention of the American Psychological Association, San Francisco.

Thorndike, R. L., Hagen, E. P., & Sattler, J. M. (1986). *Stanford-Binet Intelligence Scale: Fourth Edition technical manual.* Itasca, IL: Riverside Publishing.

JOHN WASSERMAN
The Riverside Publishing Company

ASSESSMENT
BINET, A.
INTELLIGENCE TESTING
MENTAL RETARDATION

STANFORD DIAGNOSTIC MATHEMATICS TEST—FOURTH EDITION (SDMT4)

The Stanford Diagnostic Mathematics Test—Fourth Edition (SDMT4, 1996) is designed to measure which areas of mathematics are of specific difficulty to a student. The test is intended to be used for diagnostic purposes as well as to help create appropriate intervention. The test may be administered from grade one through community college. Two response formats are provided: multiple choice and free response. A group or individual format may be used in administration.

The content of the items varies across the various age levels. For example, for grades 6 and 7 numeration, graphs and tables, statistics and probability, and geometry are included in the Concepts section. For the Computation section at this level, addition and subtraction of whole numbers, multiplication facts and operations, and division facts and operations are included. Norm-referenced (scaled scores and percentile ranks) and criterion-referenced scores (cut scores) are provided.

The standardization sample of the SDMT4 involved over 40,000 students that were representative of the US school population. Internal reliability coefficients were generally above .80, and interrater reliability for the free-response items is very good (above .95). Evidence for validity was provided by correlations with the Otis-Lennon School Ability test, with correlations among the two instruments in the .60s and .70s.

Generally, the SDMT4 has been favorably reviewed (e.g., Lehmann, 1998; Poteat, 1998). It provides much detail in terms of diagnostic information. The psychometric qualities are strong, and lead to obtained scores that are reliable and valid. The SDMT4 is not useful for simply obtaining achievement test norms. It also does not provide information about algebraic operations. It is best used for assessing students that are below average, rather than those that are at or above average functioning.

REFERENCES

Lehmann, I. J. (1998). Review of the Stanford Diagnostic Mathematics Test, Fourth Edition. In J. C. Impara & B. S. Plake (Eds.), *The thirteenth mental measurements yearbook* (pp. 932–936). Lincoln, NE: Buros Institute of Mental Measurements.

Poteat, G. M. (1998). Review of the Stanford Diagnostic Mathematics Test, Fourth Edition. In J. C. Impara & B. S. Plake (Eds.), *The thirteenth mental measurements yearbook* (pp. 937–938). Lincoln, NE: Buros Institute of Mental Measurements.

Stanford Diagnostic Mathematics Test—Fourth Edition. (1996). Cleveland, OH: Harcourt Brace Jovanovich.

ELIZABETH O. LICHTENBERGER
The Salk Institute

ARITHMETIC INSTRUCTION
ASSESSMENT
MATHEMATICS, LEARNING DISABILITIES AND

STANFORD DIAGNOSTIC READING TEST—FOURTH EDITION (STRT4)

The Standford Diagnostic Reading Test—Fourth Edition (SDRT4; Karlsen & Gardner, 1996) is intended to diagnose students' strengths and weaknesses in the major components of the reading process. There are several components that are specifically assessed: Phonetic Analysis, Vocabulary, Comprehension, and Scanning. The SDRT4 may be administered in a group or individual format. Students may be assessed with the SDRT4 from the end of grade one through the first semester of college. In addition to assessment of reading, the SDRT may be used to develop strategies for teaching reading or may be used to challenge students who are doing well.

The SDRT4 is a diagnostic test, not an achievement test, and as such it provides more detailed coverage of reading skills and places a greater emphasis on measuring the skills of low achieving students. Both norm-referenced and criterion-referenced information is available on reading skills. The normative sample was based on data collected from approximately 53,000 examinees from 1994 to 1995. The sample was found to closely match the total US school enrollment statistics. The criterion-referenced scores include raw scores and Progress Indicator Cut scores. Process Indicator Cut Scores are used to classify students that have demonstrated their competence in specific areas of reading. However, Engelhard (1998) notes that these scores should be used with great caution because insufficient detail is provided on how the cut scores were set and by whom. Engelhard (1998) evaluated the reliability statistics in the SDRT4 manual and found that the use of the shorter subtests for the diagnosis of an individual's strengths and weaknesses is not recommended. No evidence for stability of scores over time is provided.

Overall, the SDRT4 is found to be a sound measure of reading. It provides adequate traditional psychometric information, clear administration directions, and scoring strategies. Teaching suggestions are also described, but the base of the interventions is not clear. Interpretation and intervention based on the SDRT4 should be done by those with specialized knowledge in clinical practices in reading.

REFERENCES

Engelhard, G. (1998). Review of the Stanford Diagnostic Reading Test, Fourth Edition. In J. C. Impara & B. S. Plake (Eds.), *The thirteenth mental measurements yearbook* (pp. 939–941). Lincoln, NE: Buros Institute of Mental Measurements.

Karlsen, B., & Gardner, E. F. (1996). *Stanford Diagnostic Reading Test—Fourth Edition*. Cleveland, OH: Harcourt Brace Jovanovich.

ELIZABETH O. LICHTENBERGER
The Salk Institute

READING

STANLEY, JULIAN C. (1918–   )

Julian C. Stanley received his BS (1937) from what is now Georgia State University and his EdM (1946) and EdD (1950) in experimental educational psychology from Harvard University. Stanley is widely known for his work in test theory, experimental design (Campbell & Stanley, 1963), and statistics, but he is perhaps best known for his study of gifted students. Since 1971, he has been director of the Study of Mathematically Precocious Youth (SMPY) and professor of psychology at Johns Hopkins University.

Stanley's interest in the intellectually talented began in 1938, a year after he became a high school science teacher while enrolled in a tests and measurements course at the University of Georgia. He pursued his career as a research methodologist in education and psychology until a grant from the Spencer Foundation enabled him to create SMPY at Johns Hopkins in 1971 (Benbow & Stanley, 1983; Stanley, Keating, & Fox, 1974; Stanley, 1997).

The goals of SMPY include identifying mathematically able youngsters and enabling them to learn mathematics and related subjects faster and better than they might in the usual school curriculum. Some young people who participate in SMPY score a minimum of 700 before the age of 13 on the mathematics portion of the Scholastic Aptitude Test, a score achieved by only about 1 in 10,000 youngsters of their age group. The talent-search concept, covering the entire United States, is conducted at the Institute for the Academic Advancement of Youth (IAAY) at Johns Hopkins and in programs at Duke University, the University of Denver, and the University of Washington.

Known nationally and internationally, Stanley has been a Fulbright research scholar at the University of Louvain (1958-1959) and a Fulbright-Hays lecturer in Australia and New Zealand (1974). He served as president of the American Educational Research Association (AERA) from 1965 to 1966, and has been the recipient of numerous awards, including the AERA Award for Distinguished Contributions to Research in Education (1980).

Julian C. Stanley

REFERENCES

Benbow, C. P., & Stanley, J. C. (1983). *Academic precocity: Aspects of its development*. Baltimore, MD: Johns Hopkins University.

Campbell, D. T., & Stanley, J. C. (1963). Experimental and quasi-experimental designs for research on teaching. In N. L. Gage (Ed.), *Handbook of research on teaching* (pp. 171–246). Chicago: Rand McNally.

Stanley, J. C. (1997). Varieties of intellectual talent. *Journal of Creative Behavior, 31*, 93–130.

Stanley, J. C., Keating, D. P., & Fox, L. H. (1974). *Mathematical talent: Discovery, description, and development*. Baltimore, MD: Johns Hopkins University.

ANN E. LUPKOWSKI
Texas A & M University
First edition

TAMARA J. MARTIN
The University of Texas of the Permian Basin
Second edition

STUDY OF MATHEMATICALLY PRECOCIOUS YOUTH

STEINART'S DISEASE (MYOTONIC DYSTROPHY)

Steinart's disease (myotonic dystrophy) appears to be caused by an autosomal dominant characteristic that results in varying degrees of mental retardation, poor muscle development, bilateral facial paralysis, and general muscular wasting. Overt myotonic does not usually occur in early infancy. Most often, it manifests itself in late childhood or adolescence. Many children display behavioral characteristics of suspiciousness and moroseness and are asocial and submissive in treatment needs. Mental retardation is often present; although it may vary from mild to severe, it tends to be severe, particularly with early onset of the disease (Carter, 1978).

The older toddler or young child with myotonic dystrophy may have muscular weakness and wasting with psychomotor delay, drooping eyelids, and an open, drooling mouth. Cataracts are present in most individuals. High-arched palates and weak tongues are seen, as is an open, drooling mouth, even in older children. Children often have difficulty in feeding and swallowing. Abnormal curvature of the neck and back is seen. Atrophy of the extremities is often seen and clubfoot may be present. Premature baldness is also seen. Hypogonadism causes premature loss of libido or impotence in affected males. Nasal speech and articulation problems are common, as are vision problems associated with cataracts. Diabetes, heart arrhythmias, and cardiac abnormalities may be present, as well as increased incidence of diabetes mellitus (Lemeshaw, 1982).

Educational planning will often include categorical placement in classes for students with mild mental retardation; however, this disorder may not manifest itself until much later in life but then will remain constant (Tuikka, Laaksonen, & Somer, 1993). For this reason, educational placement will vary with the individual. Health problems may affect education and physical education programs. Speech services will commonly be needed, as will vision services. Orthopedic defects will often necessitate physical and occupational therapy as well as specialized adaptive educational materials. With young children having swallowing and feeding problems, an aide may be required.

REFERENCES

Carter, C. (Ed.). (1978). *Medical aspects of mental retardation.* (2nd. ed.). Springfield, IL: Thomas.

Lemeshaw, S. (1982). *The handbook of clinical types in mental retardation.* Boston: Houghton Mifflin.

Menolascino, F., & Egger, M. (1978). *Medical dimensions of mental retardation.* Lincoln: University of Nebraska Press.

Tuikka, R. A., Laaksonen, R. K., & Somer, H. V. K. (1993). Cognitive function in myotonic dystrophy: A follow-up study. *European Neurology, 33*(6), 436–441.

SALLY L. FLAGLER
University of Oklahoma

DIABETES
MENTAL RETARDATION
MUSCULAR DYSTROPHY

STELAZINE

Stelazine is the trade name for the generic antipsychotic agent Trifluoperazine. It is of the class of drugs known as phenothiazines and demonstrates many of the expected side effects. The piperazine subgroup of phenothiazines is very potent in its actions. In relation to Thorazine (Chlorpromazine), the dose/response ratio is approximately 20 to 1. Stelazine also appears to be more long-acting than Thorazine; thus fewer administrations are necessary to maintain therapeutic blood level.

In addition to the general side effects produced by phenothiazines, the piperazine subgroup has been related to a consistent pattern of extrapyramidal symptoms called the Rabbit syndrome, owing to distinctive facial movements (Bassuk & Schoonover, 1977). These side effects are reported most commonly in women over age 45. Characteristic symptoms include tremor of the lips and masticatory muscles that resembles a rabbit chewing. In contrast to tardive dyskinesia, tongue movements do not appear to be involved.

REFERENCE

Bassuk, E. L., & Schoonover, S. C. (1977). *The practitioner's guide to psychoactive drugs.* New York: Plenum Medical.

ROBERT F. SAWICKI
*Lake Erie Institute of
Rehabilitation*

THORAZINE

STEREOTYPIC BEHAVIORS

Stereotypic behaviors are variously defined in the literature. Terms are used to describe animal as well as human behaviors in developmental stages and in some abnormal or pathological situations (Berkson, 1983). Stereotyped behaviors are highly persistent and repetitious motor or posturing behaviors that seem to have little or no functional significance (Baumeister & Forehand, 1973). They are rhythmic movements that are coordinated and apparently intentional. They are repeated in the same fashion for long periods, often an hour or more at a time (Mitchell & Etches, 1977). Stereotyped movements are voluntary, brief, or prolonged habits or mannerisms that often are experienced as pleasurable (American Psychiatric Association, 1994). Stereotypic behaviors result from conditioning (in some form) and appear to be related to the achievement of homeostasis (Nijhof, Joha, & Pekelharing, 1998). Sometimes present in children of normal intelligence, they are most common among individuals with mental retardation or autism. The stereotyped behaviors, mainly seen in infancy and early childhood, may persist into adolescent and adult life, especially in institutionalized retarded persons.

The most typical movements are head rolling, head banging, and body rocking. Other rhythmic repetitive movements have been described as foot kicking, hand shaking, hand rotation, finger and toe sucking, lip biting, and tooth grinding. Nail biting is frequently associated with emotionally disturbed children. According to Sallustro and Atwell (1978) and Mitchell and Etches (1977), head rolling from side to side on the pillow occurs mainly before the infant falls asleep, but it also may be seen during sleep and while awake; it is usually encountered in early infancy up to the first 2 to 3 years of life. Head banging, seen more often in the sitting position but sometimes on hands and knees or even standing, typically starts toward the end of the first year. It sometimes follows head rolling and ceases before the age of 4 years. The child repeatedly and monotonously bangs the head against the pillow or the bars of the cot, and sometimes against a wall or the floor. This generally occurs before sleep, but it may be seen at any time of the day or night, may continue for an hour or longer, and may alternate with other rhythmic movements. Body rocking, the most frequent stereotyped behavior, is a slow, rhythmical backward and forward swaying of the trunk, usually while in the sitting position, beginning in the first year of life (Sallustro & Atwell, 1978). It can persist in normal children, but it is very common in children and adults with Down's syndrome or other types of mental handicaps.

Various theories and opinions are presented in the literature regarding the origin, the mechanisms, and the significance of repetitive stereotyped behaviors. Rhythmicity is a characteristic and fundamental attribute of all life. Thelen (1979) showed in her studies of the development of normal infants during their first year of life that groups of stereotypies involving particular parts of the body or postures have characteristic ages of onset and peak performance and decline, and are highly correlated with motor development. As maturation enlarges processing capacity, repetitive behaviors are normally inhibited or incorporated into more complex behavior patterns. For many authors, the stereotypic behaviors represent a developmental disorder, as they are already seen in normal infants in relation to motor growth and maturity but they remain longer in the repertoire and persist into adolescent and adult life in mentally defective individuals. Their maintenance in some normal children might be due to personal or familial predisposition to rhythmic patterns, as head rolling and body rocking sometimes are present in one of the parents and are more frequent among other members of the family. However, the transformation of natural repetitive movements into pathological stereotypies is not clearly understood.

Many other authors believe that the movements are deliberate and purposeful, pleasurable, and self-stimulatory in character (Berkson, 1983), and that they supply compensatory satisfaction by relief of sensory monotony, body tension, discomfort, apprehension, frustration, anger, or boredom. None of the hypotheses presented explain why some of the stereotypies, like head banging and biting, are self-injurious and dangerous to the individual's well being, while others are not (e.g., head rolling, body rocking, complex hand and finger movements).

The true significance of these movements is still unknown as to their anatomical and functional levels. Their high frequency among severely mentally handicapped children suggests the failed development of cortical control and that most of these movements are probably infracortical in origin. The element of volition appears to indicate participation of the cerebral cortex in their initiation and maintenance. La Grow and Repp (1984) have reviewed various treatments and strategies used to suppress the stereotyped patterns from the behavior repertoire.

REFERENCES

American Psychiatric Association. (1994). *Diagnostic and statistical manual of mental disorders* (4th ed.). Washington, DC: Author.

Baumeister, A. A., & Forehand R. (1973). Stereotyped acts. In N. R. Ellis (Ed.), *International review of research in mental retardation* (Vol. 6). New York: Academic. p. 55–96.

Berkson, G. (1983). Repetitive stereotyped behaviors. *American Journal of Mental Deficiency, 88,* 239–246.

La Grow, S. J., & Repp, A. C. (1984). Stereotypic responding: A review of intervention research. *American Journal of Mental Deficiency, 88,* 595–609.

Mitchell, R. G., & Etches, P. (1977). Rhythmic habit patterns (stereotypies). *Developmental Medicine and Child Neurology, 19,* 545–550.

Nijhof, G., Joha, D., & Pekelharing, H. (1998). Aspects of stereotypic behavior among autistic persons: A study of the literature. *British Journal of Developmental Disabilities, 44*(86) 3–13.

Sallustro, F., & Atwell, C. W. (1978). Body rocking, head banging, and head rolling in normal children. *Journal of Pediatrics, 93,* 704–708.

Thelen, E. (1979). Rhythmical stereotypies in normal human infants. *Animal Behavior, 27,* 699–715.

HENRI B. SZLIWOWSKI
Hôpital Erasme

JEANNIE BORMANS
Center for Developmental Problems

AUTISM
MENTAL RETARDATION
SELF-INJURIOUS BEHAVIOR
SELF-STIMULATION

STEREOTYPISM

People generally are classified and fit into molds or groups that have certain attributable characteristics. With handicapped individuals, the characteristics especially focused on are disabilities rather than abilities. Labeling an individual or fitting a person into a specific handicapped group or category according to certain characteristics has a few advantages and many disadvantages. The traditional handicapping labels are basically used to explain a medical problem or to aid in educational intervention, but the result generally is stereotyping of individuals, which may lead to misleading and inhumane side effects.

Throughout history, we can see that the treatment and attitudes toward those persons classified as different or abnormal have slowly changed (Kirk, 1972). Frampton and Gall (1955) recognized three stages: pre-Christianity, when the handicapped were mistreated, neglected, or killed; the Christian era, when they were pitied and protected; and the present era. In recent years, the handicapped are being accepted, educated, and integrated more and more into society.

During the early years (before present enlightenment), terms such as idiot, mad, crazy, moron, and imbecile were used to describe people who differed from the norm (Snell, 1978). These terms carried negative connotations and caused great misconceptions of what handicapped individuals are really like. People were actually afraid of these individuals because of the mystery surrounding their handicaps. The fear was due partly to lack of knowledge about the causes of these deviations and partly to lack of exposure to individuals with these characteristics. At first, the handicapped were put away in institutions, basements, or closets. Later, they were allowed to be kept in homes but away from schools. Even when education programs became prominent, the special education classrooms were in environments different from other children's. The first special education classrooms in regular schools were in the basement or away from the regular students.

Today, misconceptions arise from stereotyping the handicapped. Although many visually handicapped individuals have no mental retardation, the term visually handicapped often carries the connotation that these individuals are physically disabled and severely mentally deficient (Hollinger & Jones, 1970). Goffman (1963) and Edgerton (1967) write extensively of the negative stereotypes and stigmata associated with the mentally retarded. People with cerebral palsy may have an IQ of average or above average, but their physical rigidity and slurred speech often make people talk to them as if they were un-

able to understand. The hearing impaired have fought against the stereotype of being deaf and dumb. People interacting with blind individuals believe they have to talk loudly in order to be heard. Learning-disabled students and students with attentional problems (Cornett-Ruiz & Hendricks, 1993) are frequently associated with the retarded even though their mental capacities are generally average or above. The emotionally disturbed are thought to be crazy or mad.

The misconceptions have caused many sociological, economic, and other types of barricades for the handicapped. These individuals have been denied access to a life that is as normal as possible, not only in the physical environment but also in the social environment. Many of the handicapped are still isolated, laughed at, and criticized. Their problems may be increased because of added emotional stress.

We have come a long way toward bringing positive images of the handicapped to the fore. The Special Olympics, media reports of accomplishments of individuals physically or mentally disabled, and improved school programs have helped to eliminate some barriers. Making the public more knowledgeable about definitions of handicapping terminology has improved public opinion. Movies or television shows about deformed or retarded individuals have switched to positive and inspiring messages. As the exceptional person becomes more prevalent in restaurants, stores, schools, etc., the public becomes educated.

A reversal of roles would be an ideal way for the general public to learn about and relate to individuals with handicapping conditions. Spending a few hours in a wheelchair, with a blindfold on, or with mittens on, would help one to see what it is like to be handicapped. It would be important for one to experience the difficulties of having the handicap and to feel the stares and other negative attitudes of those more fortunate.

School intervention has changed greatly for the better. Education programs are now a great source for informing the public. Mainstreaming has helped regular classroom students to better understand special education students; mainstreaming has also helped special education students to develop feelings of belonging and self-worth. Exposure to the regular classroom student has given the special education student a model from which to learn.

If less negative labels were used, and if the educational programs were fit to the handicapped individual's needs, there would be less stereotyping (Reger, Schroeder, & Uschold, 1968). It is hoped that as the positive trends continue to grow, the stigmata will be replaced with understanding and acceptance.

REFERENCES

Cornett-Ruiz, S., & Hendricks, B. (1993). Effects of labeling and ADHD behaviors on peer and teacher judgments. *Journal of Educational Research*, *86*(6), 349–355.

Frampton, M. E., & Gall E. D. (1955). *Special education for the exceptional* MA: Porter Sargent.

Goffman, E. (1963). *Notes on the measurement of spoiled identity.* Englewood Cliffs; NJ: Prentice-Hall.

Hollinger, C. S., & Jones, R. L. (1970). Community attitudes toward slow learners and mental retardates: What's in a name? *Mental Retardation, 8,* 19–13.

Kirk, S. A. (1972). *Educating exceptional children.* Boston: Houghton-Mifflin.

Reger. R., Schroeder, W., & Uschold, K. (1968). *Special education children with learning problems.* New York: Oxford University Press.

Snell, M. E. (1978). *Systematic instruction of the moderately and severely handicapped.* Columbus, OH: Merrill.

DONNA FILIPS
Steger, Illinois

**ATTITUDES TOWARD THE HANDICAPPED
FAMILY RESPONSE TO A HANDICAPPED CHILD
HISTORY OF SPECIAL EDUCATION**

STERN, WILLIAM (1871–1938)

William Stern, German psychologist and pioneer in the psychology of individual differences, introduced the concept of the intelligence quotient, in 1912. This quotient, used to express performance on intelligence tests, is found by dividing the subject's mental age as determined by the test performance by the chronological age and multiplying by 100. In the United States, the intelligence quotient, or IQ, was used by Lewis M. Terman in his 1916 Stanford Revision of the Binet Scales.

REFERENCES

Murchison, C. (Ed.). (1961). *A history of psychology in autobiography.* New York: Russell & Russell.

Stern, W. (1914). *The psychological methods of intelligence testing.* Baltimore, MD: Warwick & York.

PAUL IRVINE
Katonah, New York

STIGMATIZATION

See LABELING.

STIMULANT DRUGS

Stimulant drugs are a commonly used class of medications for the treatment of inattention, impulsivity, and restlessness in school-age children and adolescents, and, less often, for the treatment of narcolepsy and drowsiness or disorders of arousal in the elderly. Children and adolescents having an attention deficit disorder (American Psychiatric Association, 1994) are the ones most often given these medications because of the significant effects of the drugs on sustained attention. In fact, stimulants are the most commonly prescribed psychotropic medications in child psychiatry (Wilens, & Biederman, 1992). The drugs are so named because of their stimulation of increased central nervous system activity, presumably by way of their effects on dopamine and norepinephrine production, and reuptake at the synaptic level of neuronal functioning (Cantwell & Carlson, 1978). The drugs may also have effects on other central neurotransmitters as well as on peripheral nervous system activity. The changes in central neurotransmitter activity result in increased alertness, arousal, concentration, and vigilance or sustained attention, as well as reductions in impulsive behavior and activity or restlessness that is irrelevant to particular tasks (Barkley, 1977, 1981). While a number of substances such as caffeine fall into this class of medications, those most typically used with children and adolescents are methylphenidate (Ritalin), d-amphetamine (Dexedrine), a mixture of dextroamphetamine and racemic amphetamine salts (Adderall, Popper, 1994) and pemoline (Cylert). Despite similar behavioral effects and side effects, the mechanism of action of each of these stimulants is somewhat different, and that for pemoline is not well specified.

The stimulants are relatively rapid in their initiation of behavioral changes and in the time course over which such changes are maintained. Most stimulant drugs, taken orally, are quickly absorbed into the bloodstream through the stomach and small intestine and pass readily across the blood-brain barrier to affect neuronal activity. Behavioral changes can be detected within 30 to 60 minutes after ingestion and may last between 3 and 8 hours, depending on the type of stimulant and preparation (regular or sustained release) employed. Traces of medication and their metabolites in blood and urine can be detected up to 24 hours after ingestion, perhaps corresponding to the clinical observation of persisting side effects after the desired behavioral effects are no longer noticeable.

Approximately 70% or more of children over 5 years of age, adolescents, and young adults display a positive behavioral response to the stimulants. Children below age 3 are much less likely to respond well to medication, and the drugs have not been approved by the Food and Drug Administration for children younger than 6 years. The best predictor of a positive response is the degree of inattention before treatment, while that for a poor response is the presence and severity of pretreatment anxiety and emotional disturbance (Barkley, 1976; Loney, 1986; Taylor, 1983).

The medications are taken one to three times per day, with some children taking them only on school days while others remain on medication throughout the week. Medication is often discontinued during summer vacations from school to permit a rebound in appetite and growth that may have been mildly suppressed during treatment. Children having more severe, pervasive, developmental disorders such as autism or severe behavioral disorders, however, may remain on medication throughout the year (Aman, 1996). The average length of treatment with stimulants is typically 3 to 5 years, but this may increase in the future because of reports of equally positive effects with adolescents and young adults having significant inattention, impulsivity, and restlessness (Woods, 1986).

The most commonly experienced side effects are diminished appetite, particularly for the noon meal, and insomnia, although these are often mild, diminish within several weeks of treatment onset, and are easily managed by reductions in dose where problematic. Increases in blood pressure, heart rate, and respiration may occur, but they are typically of little consequence (Hastings & Barkley, 1978). Other side effects of lesser frequency are sleeplessness (Day & Abmayr, 1998), irritability, sadness or dysphoria, and proneness to crying, especially during late afternoons, when the medication is "washing out" of the body (Cantwell & Carlson, 1978). Some children experience heightened activity levels during this washout phase. Headaches and stomach aches are infrequently noted and, like all side effects, appear to be dose related. Temporary suppression of growth in height and weight may be noted in some children during the first 1 to 2 years of treatment with stimulants, but there appear to be few lasting effects on eventual adult stature. Between 1 and 2% of children and adolescents may experience nervous tics while on stimulant medication, but these diminish in the majority of cases with reduction in dose or discontinuation of medication. A few cases of Gilles de la Tourette's syndrome (multiple motor tics, vocal tics, and, in some cases, increased utterance of profanities) have been reported after initiation of stimulant medication (Barkley, 1987). Children with a personal or family history of motor/vocal tics should use these drugs only with caution because of the possible emergence or exacerbation of their tic conditions, observed in more than 50% of such children.

The medications appear to improve fine motor agility, planning, and execution, as well as reaction time, speech articulation (in children having mild delays in fine motor control of speech), and handwriting, in some children. Increases in academic productivity, short-term memory, simple verbal learning, and drawing and copying skills frequently are noted, but little, if any, change is seen on tests of intelligence, academic achievement, or other complex cognitive processes (Barkley, 1977). Despite generally positive behavioral improvements in most children with attention-deficit/hyperactivity disorder taking stimulants, these drugs have shown little, if any, significant, lasting effect on the long-term outcome of such children in late adolescence or young adulthood once medication has been discontinued.

REFERENCES

Aman, M. G. (1996). Stimulant drugs in the developmental disabilities revisited. *Journal of Developmental & Physical Disabilities, 8*(4), 347–365.

American Psychiatric Association. (1994). *Diagnostic and statistical manual of mental disorders* (4th ed.). Washington, DC: Author.

Barkley, R. (1976). Predicting the response of hyperactive children to stimulant drugs: A review. *Journal of Abnormal Child Psychology, 4,* 327–348.

Barkley, R. (1977). A review of stimulant drug research with hyperactive children. *Journal of Child Psychology & Psychiatry, 18,* 137–165.

Barkley, R. A. (1981). *Hyperactive children: A handbook for diagnosis and treatment.* New York: Guilford.

Barkley, R. A. (1987). Tic disorders and Tourette's syndrome. In E. Mash & L. Terdal (Eds.), *Behavioral assessment of childhood disorders* (2nd ed.). New York: Guilford.

Cantwell, D., & Carlson, G. (1978). Stimulants. In J. Werry (Ed.), *Pediatric psychopharmacology.* New York: Brunner/Mazel.

Day, H. D., & Abmayr, S. B. (1998). Parent reports of sleep disturbances in stimulant-medicated children with attention-deficit/hyperactivity disorder. *Journal of Clinical Psychology, 54*(5), 701–716.

Hastings, J., & Barkley, R. (1978). A review of psychophysiological research with hyperactive children. *Journal of Abnormal Child Psychology, 7,* 413–447.

Loney, J. (1986). Predicting stimulant drug response among hyperactive children. *Psychiatric Annals, 16,* 16–22.

Popper, C. W. (1994). The story of four salts. *Journal of Child & Adolescent Psychopharmacology, 4*(4), 217–223.

Taylor, E. (1983). Drug response and diagnostic validation. In M. Rutter (Ed.), *Developmental neuropsychiatry* (pp. 348–368). New York: Guilford.

Wilens, T. E., & Biederman, J. (1992). The stimulants. *Psychiatric Clinics of North America, 15*(1), 191–222.

Woods, D. (1986). The diagnosis and treatment of attention deficit disorder, residual type. *Psychiatric Annals, 16,* 23–28.

RUSSELL A. BARKLEY
*University of Massachusetts
Medical Center*

**ATTENTION DEFICIT HYPERACTIVITY DISORDER
DOPAMINE
HYPERACTIVITY
NOREPINEPHRINE
RITALIN
TOURETTE'S SYNDROME**

STIMULUS DEPRIVATION

Stimulus deprivation refers to an increase in reinforcer effectiveness that occurs following a reduction in the availability of or access to that reinforcing event. The effectiveness of reinforcers, especially of primary reinforcers such as food, depends greatly on the deprivation state of the individual. Using edible reinforcers with a student who has just returned from lunch probably will not be as effective as using the same reinforcers immediately prior to lunch, when the student is more likely to be in a state of deprivation for food. Most stimulus events serve as effective reinforcers only if the individual has been deprived of them for a period of time prior to their use. In general, the longer the deprivation period, the more effective the reinforcer (Martin & Pear, 1983).

The magnitude or amount of a reinforcer required to change behavior is less when the individual is partially deprived of the event (Kazdin, 1980). For example, students who are temporarily deprived of teacher attention may require less attention to maintain behavior than students who have frequent access to teacher attention. If a potential reinforcer is provided in limited quantities, thus creating a partial state of deprivation, that event is more likely to maintain its effectiveness as a reinforcer.

A state of deprivation may be created intentionally by the educator to increase the value of reinforcing events. This procedure is especially valuable with events that previously were effective reinforcers but temporarily show a satiation effect. Using the principle of deprivation, the reinforcer is withheld or reduced in availability for a period of time as a means of increasing the state of deprivation. If free time, listening to music, or a particular edible item show satiation effects, the teacher may wish to reduce or remove these for a period of time. As students become deprived, these reinforcers can once again be introduced with increased effectiveness.

Ethical and legal issues should be considered prior to use of a deprivation procedure. Major objections typically focus on deprivation of essential primary reinforcers (e.g., food, water, shelter, human contact) on the basis that it constitutes a violation of basic human rights. As noted by Kazdin (1980), however, deprivation is a natural part of human existence. All people are, in some ways, deprived by society of self-expression in such areas as free speech and sexual behavior. Certainly, special education students who demonstrate academic and behavioral difficulties frequently are deprived of access to employment or other economic opportunities as a result of their characteristics. Thus the negative effects of social deprivation that special education students normally experience as a result of their deficits must be weighed against any temporary negative effects associated with stimulus deprivation used as a treatment strategy (Baer, 1970). A decision to use deprivation, or any other aversive technique, requires careful consideration of the kind of deprivation, the duration of the program, the availability of alternative treatment strategies, and the demonstrable benefits resulting from its use (Kazdin, 1980). As a precautionary measure when using a deprivation procedure, an individual should never be completely deprived of the reinforcing event for a lengthy period of time.

Fortunately, intentional deprivation of reinforcers usually is not necessary, as the natural deprivation that occurs in the course of an individual's daily activities often is sufficient to increase reinforcer effectiveness. Since children in the classroom, for example, do not have unlimited access to free time, they normally experience a mild form of deprivation during the course of a school day. As another example, when using small amounts of edible reinforcers to increase appropriate responding, the only deprivation required may be the natural deprivation that occurs between meals. Thus a variety of events may serve as effective reinforcers simply as a result of natural deprivation without the introduction of more formal deprivation procedures.

REFERENCES

Baer, D. M. (1970). A case for the selective reinforcement of punishment. In C. Neuringer & J. L. Michael (Eds.), *Behavior modification in clinical psychology.* New York: Appleton-Century-Crofts.

Kazdin, A. E. (1980). *Behavior modification in applied settings* (revised ed.). Homewood, IL: Dorsey. Martin, G., & Pear, J. (1983). *Behavior modification: What it is and how to do it* (2nd ed.). Englewood Cliffs, NJ: Prentice-Hall.

CHRISTINE L. COLE
University of Wisconsin at Madison

BEHAVIOR MODIFICATION
OPERANT CONDITIONING
STIMULUS SATIATION

STIMULUS SATIATION

Stimulus satiation refers to the reduction in reinforcer effectiveness that occurs after a large amount of that reinforcer has been obtained (usually within a short period of time). Thus an event that initially shows reinforcing qualities may become ineffective or even aversive for a period of time if experienced too frequently or excessively. Teacher praise may be effective the first few times if it is provided in the morning, but may gradually diminish in value with additional use during the day. Treats and certain activities may be highly reinforcing if used sparingly but may lose their effectiveness if used frequently. The special educator should be sensitive to the principle of satiation and provide alternative reinforcing events when loss of effectiveness is noted (Gardner, 1978).

Satiation is especially common with primary reinforcers such as food. These reinforcers, when provided in excessive amounts within a short period, may lose their reinforcing properties relatively quickly. To prevent or delay satiation, only a small amount of the reinforcer should be provided at any one time. Satiation of primary reinforcers is usually temporary, as these events regain their reinforcing value as deprivation increases.

Secondary reinforcers such as praise, attention, and recognition are less likely than primary reinforcers to be influenced by satiation effects. The category of secondary reinforcers called generalized reinforcers is least-susceptible to satiation. This is due to the fact that the reinforcers themselves (e.g., tokens, grades, money) can be exchanged for a variety of other reinforcing events called back-up reinforcers. Thus satiation of generalized reinforcers is not likely to occur unless the individual becomes satiated with the items or events offered as back-up reinforcers. The greater the number and range of back-up reinforcers available, the less likelihood that satiation will occur (Kazdin, 1980). This would suggest that teachers consider the use of tokens, exchangeable for a wide variety of back-up reinforcers, when tangible events are required to ensure effective learning and behavior (Gardner, 1978).

The principle of satiation may also be used as an intervention tactic to reduce the value of events that appear to serve as reinforcers for maladaptive behavior. In a stimulus satiation procedure, the individual is provided with a reinforcing event with such frequency or in such large quantities that the event loses its reinforcing qualities for a period of time; the result is that the behavior maintained by that reinforcer is weakened. In a frequently cited example, Ayllon (1963) used a stimulus satiation procedure with a hospitalized psychiatric patient who hoarded large numbers of towels in her room. Although many efforts had been made to discourage hoarding, these had proved to be unsuccessful and the staff had resorted to simply removing on a regular basis the towels she had collected. With the stimulus satiation procedure, the staff provided her with large numbers of towels without comment. After a few weeks, when the number of towels in her room reached 625, she began to remove a few and no more were given to her. The patient engaged in no towel hoarding during the subsequent year.

The purpose of such a stimulus satiation procedure is to reduce or remove the reinforcing qualities of the event serving to maintain the maladaptive behavior. In the Ayllon study (1963) this loss of reinforcer effectiveness was reflected in the patient's comments: "Don't give me no more towels. I've got enough. . . . Take them towels away. . . . Get these dirty towels out of here" (p. 57). Apparently, as the number of towels increased to an excessive level, they were no longer reinforcing and even became aversive to her.

Although long-term maintenance of behavior change was obtained in this case, the effects of stimulus satiation procedures typically are temporary. This is especially true if the reinforcer is highly valuable to the individual. Educators can enhance the effects of a satiation procedure by ensuring that, during the interim period in which the maladaptive behavior is absent or of low strength, other more appropriate replacement behaviors are taught and strengthened (Gardner, 1978).

REFERENCES

Ayllon, T. (1963). Intensive treatment of psychotic behaviour by stimulus satiation and food reinforcement. *Behaviour Research & Therapy, 1,* 53–61.

Gardner, W. I. (1978). *Children with learning and behavior problems: A behavior management approach* (2nd ed.). Boston: Allyn & Bacon.

Kazdin, A. E. (1980). *Behavior modification in applied settings* (Rev. ed.). Homewood, IL: Dorsey

CHRISTINE L. COLE
*University of Wisconsin at
Madison*

APPLIED BEHAVIOR ANALYSIS
BEHAVIOR MODIFICATION
STIMULUS DEPRIVATION

STRABISMUS, EFFECT ON LEARNING OF

Strabismus, also called heteropia, is a visual condition in which the two eyes are not parallel when viewing an object. While one eye is fixed on an object, the other eye will be directed elsewhere. Strabismus can be classified in two ways. The first concerns the angle of separation. In concomitant strabismus, the angle of separation is fixed; in noncomitant strabismus the angle between the eye that is fixed and the deviant eye varies. Strabismus also can be classified as to whether the visual paths of the two eyes converge or diverge (Harley & Lawrence, 1977).

The effect of strabismus on learning is closely tied to its age of onset. If it occurs later in childhood (Flax, 1993), after other visual reflexes have developed, it can result in double vision (diplopia), which can be stressful and lead to learning disabilities. Lipton (1971) noted significant correlations between strabismus and neurotic traits, character disorders, and learning problems. Haskell (1972), on the other hand, showed no relationship between strabismus and academic achievement.

If the onset of strabismus occurs before the age of two, the effects are not as severe because other visual reflexes are not as developed. However, early onset of strabismus can lead to the development of ambliopia, a condition in which the brain suppresses the signals coming from the deviant eye. If not corrected, the brain can permanently lose the ability to process a 20/20 image from this eye.

Some form of strabismus occurs in approximately 5% of

all children. The percentage increases to 40 to 50% for children with cerebral palsy; it is noted in as many as 60% of the children who are visually impaired at birth as a result of their mother's having contracted rubella during pregnancy.

Strabismus can be corrected through lenses if it is detected early in a child's life. Freeman, Nguyen, & Jolly (1996) suggest that amblyopia and strabismus deviation are the major components of visual acuity, loss and should be reduced by whatever means are available. Additionally, some doctors recommend eye exercises as a way to correct the condition. This recommendation is controversial. Eden (1978) notes that strabismus often starts early in life, before the child is capable of following any rigorous exercise schedule. Once the child is capable of following such a schedule, permanent visual damage may already have occurred. In school, close work should be limited for students with strabismus, and these students should be given frequent rest periods.

REFERENCES

Eden, J. (1978). *The eye book*. New York: Viking.

Flax, N. (1993). The treatment of strabismus in the four to ten year old child. *Child and Adolescent Social Work Journal*, *10*(5), 411–416.

Freeman, A. W., Nguyen, V. A., & Jolly, N. (1996). Components of visual acuity loss in strabismus. *Vision Research*, *36*(5), 765–774.

Harley, R. K., & Lawrence, G. A. (1977). *Visual impairment in the schools*. Springfield, IL: Thomas.

Haskell, S. H. (1972). Visuoperceptual, visuomotor, and scholastic skills of alternating and uniocular squinting children. *Journal of Special Education*, *6*, 3–8.

Lipton, E. L. (1971). Remarks on the psychological aspects of strabismus. *Sight-Saving Review*, *4*, 129–138.

THOMAS E. ALLEN
Gallaudet College

AMBLIOPIA
BLIND
CATARACTS
LIBRARIES FOR THE BLIND AND PHYSICALLY HANDICAPPED

STRAUSS, ALFRED A. (1897–1957)

Alfred A. Strauss was born in Germany and received his medical degree and subsequent training in psychiatry and neurology there. He left Germany in 1933, became visiting professor at the University of Barcelona, and helped to establish Barcelona's first child guidance clinics. In 1937

Alfred A. Strauss

Strauss joined the staff of the Wayne County (Michigan) School, where he served as research psychiatrist and director of child care. In 1947 Strauss founded the Cove School in Racine, Wisconsin, a residential institution that gained an international reputation for its pioneering work with brain-injured children. Strauss served as president of the school until his death.

Strauss made major contributions in the areas of diagnosis and education of brain-injured children. He developed tests for diagnosing brain injury. His studies of children without intellectual deficit who showed characteristics of brain injury in learning and behavior resulted in the first systematic description of a new clinical entity, minimal brain dysfunction. His 1947 book, *Psychopathology and Education of the Brain-Injured Child*, written with Laura Lehtinen, was the major guide for many of the numerous school programs for minimally brain-injured children that came into existence during the 1950s and 1960s.

REFERENCES

Gardiner, R. A. (1958). Alfred A. Strauss, 1897–1957. *Exceptional Children*, *24*, 373.

Lewis, R. S., Strauss, A. A., & Lehtinen, L. E. (1960). *The other child*. New York: Grune & Stratton.

Strauss, A. A., & Kephart, N. C. (1955). *Psychopathology and education of the brain-injured child* (Vol. 2). New York: Grune & Stratton.

Strauss, A. A., & Lehtinen, L. E. (1947). *Psychopathology and education of the brain-injured child* (Vol. 1). New York: Grune & Stratton.

PAUL IRVINE
Katonah, New York

BIRTH INJURIES

STRAUSS SYNDROME

The term Strauss syndrome was coined by Stevens and Birch (1957) to focus on an expanded set of behavioral characteristics of children who could not learn and did not easily fit into other classification systems. It also extended the work of a leading pioneer in the field, Alfred Strauss. Strauss's ideas regarding the education of brain-injured, perceptually handicapped children were presented in works coauthored first with Laura Lehtinen (1947) and later with Newell Kephart (1955).

The term Strauss syndrome was introduced to describe the brain-injured child who evidenced (1) erratic and inappropriate behavior on mild provocation; (2) increased motor activity disproportionate to the stimulus; (3) poor organization of behavior; (4) distractibility of more than an ordinary degree under ordinary conditions; (5) persistent hyperactivity; and (6) awkwardness and consistently poor motor performance (Stevens & Birch, 1957).

Despite the importance of the works of Strauss et al., it became apparent that their description of the brain-injured child pertained only to a certain portion of the total group having neurogenic disorders of learning. Major objections to the term brain-injured child were presented by Stevens and Birch (1957). They concluded that:

1. The term is an etiological concept and does not appropriately describe the symptom complex. This is important because the condition that prevails is viewed in terms of symptoms rather than etiology.

2. The term is associated with other conditions, some of which have no relation to the symptom complex commonly referred to as brain injury.

3. The term does not help in the development of a sound therapeutic approach.

4. The term is not suited for use as a descriptive one because it is essentially a generic expression, the use of which results in oversimplification (p. 349).

REFERENCES

Stevens, G., & Birch, J. (1957). A proposal for clarification of the terminology used to describe brain-injured children. *Exceptional Children, 23*, 346–349.

Strauss, A., & Kephart, N. (1955). *Psychopathology and education of the brain-injured child* (Vol. 2). New York: Grune & Stratton.

Strauss, A., & Lehtinen, L. (1947). *Psychopathology and education of the brain-injured child* (Vol. 1). New York: Grune & Stratton.

CECILIA STEPPE-JONES
*North Carolina Central
University*

BRAIN DAMAGE
ETIOLOGY

LEARNING DISABILITIES
LESIONS
MINIMAL BEGIN DYSFUNCTION

STRENGTH MODELS OF REMEDIATION

See REMEDIATION, DEFICIT-CENTERED MODELS OF.

STREPHOSYMBOLIA

Strephosymbolia is a Greek term that literally means twisted symbol. Originally used by Samuel T. Orton, strephosymbolia is most commonly used in discussions regarding dyslexia. Orton and others noticed that when certain children read, they often reverse letters, syllables, or words. These children see all parts of a word, but not in the accepted order. So, instead of "pebbles," a strephosymbolic child might see "pelbbse" (Johnson, 1981). This twisting of reading material is viewed as a primary symptom of dyslexia (Clarke, 1973).

Orton believed that strephosymbolia resulted from a failure to establish cerebral dominance in the left hemisphere of the brain (Lerner, 1985). The reversals that resulted from the lack of cerebral dominance were due to failure to erase memory images from the nondominant side of the brain (Kessler, 1980). These memory images were projected to the dominant side of the brain as mirror images, resulting in the reversals of letters and/or words (Kessler, 1980).

Currently, Orton's theory has little credibility as there has been no substantiation that mirror images are projected onto the brain (Kessler, 1980). Mercer (1983) notes that these difficulties are referred to as severe reading disabilities and are treated according to the specific difficulty.

REFERENCES

Clarke, L. (1973). *Can't read, can't write, can't talk too good either*. New York: Walker.

Johnson, C. (1981). *The diagnosis of learning disabilities*. Boulder, CO: Pruett.

Kessler, J. W. (1980). History of minimal brain dysfunction. In H. E. Rice & E. D. Rice (Eds.), *Handbook of minimal brain dysfunction: A critical review*. New York: Wiley.

Lerner, T. (1985). *Learning disabilities: Theories, diagnosis and teaching strategies* (4th ed.). Boston: Houghton Mifflin.

Mercer, C. D. (1983). *Students with learning disabilities* (2nd ed.). Columbus, OH: Merrill.

JOHN R. BEATTIE
*University of North Carolina at
Charlotte*

DYSLEXIA
READING DISORDERS

STRESS AND THE HANDICAPPED STUDENT

Stress results when physical and psychological demands on an individual exceed personal coping skills. Stress is activated when a threat to security, self-esteem, or safety is perceived. Schultz (1980) suggests that stress is often triggered by environmental interactions, which may be more problematic for handicapped children than for nonhandicapped ones. Handicapped children may also develop stress reactions to personal thoughts.

In regard to the development of stress, Schultz has suggested a pattern of (1) occurrence of an event, (2) internal assignment of the meaning of the event, and (3) occurrence of internal and external responses to the event depending on the assigned meaning.

Rutter (1981) suggests resilience is demonstrated by young people who succeed despite stress, but that children who have handicapping conditions may be constitutionally less resilient. Particularly stressful periods for handicapped children include school entry, change of school, and last years of school. The uncertainties present during these periods are exacerbated because of the handicapped child's lack of resilience (Kershaw, 1973).

Low-achieving individuals demonstrate more stress than their better achieving peers. Lower functioning handicapped students are subject to more stress in childhood than higher functioning individuals (Westling, 1986). This increased stress may be due to social rejection and parental overprotection concurrent with the children's reduced capacity for coping with various situations.

Mainstreaming and inclusive practices may produce increased social stress in the handicapped student. Tymitz-Wolf (1984) analyzed mildly mentally handicapped students' worries about mainstreaming as related to academic performance, social interactions, and the transitions inherent in split placement. A range of worries were reported in all three areas, with worries concerning transitions being the most prevalent.

Schultz (1980) contends that stress-management programs for handicapped students should emphasize instruction in adaptive coping skills, including relaxation training. Relaxation training has been used to decrease stress in learning-disabled students (Hegarty & Last, 1997; Omizo, 1981).

In addition, it has been found that parental support is very important and can be enhanced by the school providing parent support and parent support training for students (Volenski, 1995).

REFERENCES

Hegarty, J. R., & Last, A. (1997). Relaxation training for people who have severe/profound and multiple learning disabilities. *British Journal of Developmental Disabilities*, *43*(85), 122–139.

Kershaw, J. D. (1973). *Handicapped children in the ordinary school: Stresses in children*. New York: Crane & Russak.

Omizo, M. M. (1981). Relaxation training and biofeedback with hyperactive elementary school children. *Elementary School Guidance & Counseling*, *15*(4), 329–332.

Rutter, M. (1981). Stress, coping, and development: Some issues and some questions. *Journal of Child Psychology & Psychiatry*, *22*, 323–356.

Schultz, E. (1980). Teaching coping skills for stress and anxiety. *Teaching Exceptional Children*, *13*(3), 12–15.

Tymitz-Wolf, B. (1984). An analysis of EMR children's worries about mainstreaming. *Education & Training of the Mentally Retarded*, *19*, 157–168.

Volenski, L. T. (1995). Building support systems for parents of handicapped children: The parent education and guidance program. *Psychology in the Schools*, *32*(2), 124–129.

Westling, D. L. (1986). *Introduction to mental retardation*. Englewood Cliffs, NJ: Prentice-Hall.

ANNE M. BAUER
University of Cincinnati

SELF-CONCEPT
SOCIAL SKILLS

STRONG INTEREST INVENTORY

The Strong Interest Inventory (SVIB-SCII, Fourth Edition; Hansen & Campbell, 1985) assesses an individual's interests in occupations, hobbies, leisure activities, and school subjects. The test has a long history, with its first edition, the Strong Vocational Interest Blank, being published over 70 years ago. There have been major changes since the SVIB, most notably a gender equity process that began in 1971. Also, a theoretical framework, Holland's hexagonal model of career types, was incorporated into the test. The most recent revision occurred in 1985 and with it came 17 new vocational-technical occupational groups, 6 newly emerging professional occupations, and updated norms.

The SVIB-SCII is a paper-and-pencil measure in which the respondent is asked to indicate "Like," "Dislike," or "Indifferent" to the items. The test takes an average of 30 minutes to complete and was designed for use with adults and 16–18 year olds with a 6th grade reading ability. The SVIB-SCII is machine-scored and responses are compared to the interests of people in a wide variety of jobs. The test yields five types of information: scores on 6 General Occupational Themes, 23 Basic Interest Scales, and 207 Occupational Scales. Additionally there are 2 Special Scales (Academic Comfort and Introversion-Extroversion), and Administrative Indexes (validity scales). Interpretive information includes a profile with an optional interpretive report.

The psychometric properties of the SVIB-SCII are excellent. Over 48,000 people taken from 202 occupational samples were used to construct the Occupational Scales. The fourth edition of the *Manual for the SVIB-SCII* describes the reliability, validity and sampling procedures for all the scales in detail.

The SVIB-SCII is easy to administer and provides easily understood interpretive results. Critiques of the inventory praise its outstanding interpretive information and excellent psychometric properties (Busch, 1995). One issue with the test is the authors' failure to report response rates for the occupational samples; response rates can affect the representativeness of the sample, and thus the predictive validity of the scales (Busch, 1995; Worthen & Sailor, 1995). However, despite the concern, the SVIB-SCII has been described as "by far the best available interest inventory" (Worthen & Sailor, 1995).

REFERENCES

Busch, J. C. (1995). In J. C. Conoley & J. C. Impara (Eds.), *The twelfth mental measurements yearbook*. Lincoln, NE: Buros Institute of Mental Measurements.

Hansen, J. C. & Campbell, D. P. (1985). Manual for the *Strong Interest Inventory* (4th ed.). Stanford, CA: Stanford University Press.

Worthen, B. R. & Sailor, P. (1995). In J. C. Conoley & J. C. Impara (Eds.), *The twelfth mental measurements yearbook*. Lincoln, NE: Buros Institute of Mental Measurements.

DEBRA Y. BROADBOOKS
*California School of
Professional Psychology*

**HABILITATION
VOCATIONAL REHABILITATION**

STRUCTURE OF INTELLECT

J. P. Guilford (1967), in his work *The Nature of Human Intelligence*, developed a model of intelligence based on his factor analysis of human intellect. The structure of intellect theory (SI) grew out of experimental applications of the multivariate method of multiple-factor analysis. The basic research was carried out on a population of young adults but successive investigations have substantiated Guilford's initial findings with subject samples ranging in age from 5 to 15 years. Implications from this theory and its concepts have led to many new interpretations of al-

ready known facts of general significance in psychology.

The major aim of the structure of intellect theory is to give the concept of intelligence a firm, comprehensive, and systematic theoretical foundation. A second aim is to put intelligence within the mainstream of general psychological theory. For his frame of reference, Guilford has chosen what he terms a morphological, as opposed to hierarchical, model. His model, which he also refers to as the "three faces of intellect," includes three categories along with their subclassifications. The three dimensions are content, referring to types of information that are discriminable by the individual; products, the outcomes of intellectual operations; and operations, referring to the primary kinds of intellectual activities or processes.

The model or cube is a three-dimensional diagram. The operations dimension is broken down into five subclassifications: evaluation, convergent production, divergent production, memory, and cognition. The six types of products are units, classes, relations, systems, transformations, and implications. The four types of content are figural, symbolic, semantic, and behavioral. The complete schema is diagrammed as an array of 120 ($5 \times 4 \times 6$) predicted cells of intellectual abilities. The 120 types of abilities are derived from the intersection of the three-way classification system. Of the 120 discrete factors, at least 82 have been demonstrated; others are still under investigation.

Although Guilford's model has not been widely used, it has pointed to a theory that has been lacking from the beginning of the era of mental testing—i.e., to give the concept of intelligence a firm, comprehensive, and systematic theoretical foundation. Guilford maintains that a firm foundation must be based on detailed observation; that the theory itself should include all aspects of intelligence; and that the result must be systematic, embracing numerous phenomena within a logically ordered structure. The outcome is his structure of intellect.

REFERENCE

Guilford, J. P. (1967). *The nature of human intelligence*. New York: McGraw-Hill.

CECELIA STEPPE-JONES
*North Carolina Central
University*

**INTELLIGENCE
INTELLIGENCE TESTING**

STUDY OF MATHEMATICALLY PRECOCIOUS YOUTH (SMPY)

The Study of Mathematically Precocious Youth (SMPY) was officially begun on September 1, 1971, by Julian Stanley. Stanley had become intrigued by a 13½-year-old boy who scored extremely well on several standardized mathematics tests. A fear that students such as this one might fail to be identified and appropriately served led Stanley to devise the SMPY at Johns Hopkins University.

The SMPY is geared to the top 1 to 3% of mathematics students in U.S. junior high schools (Johnson, 1983). These students often display swift and comprehensive reasoning, an inclination to analyze mathematical structure, a tendency to deal in the abstract, and an untiring approach to working on mathematics (Heid, 1983). Indeed, students accepted into SMPY are so mathematically advanced that they must score at least 700 on the math portion of the Scholastic Aptitude Test (SAT-M) before their thirteenth birthday (Stanley & Benbow, 1983). Allowances are made for those students who are over 13 years of age. They must score an additional 10 points on the SAT-M for each month of age over 13 years. For example, a student who is 13 years, 2 months, must score at least 720 on the SAT-M before being considered for the SMPY (Stanley & Benbow, 1983).

Once the students have been selected, the goal of the program is to accelerate learning in mathematics. Stanley & Benbow (1982) note that there is no sense in allowing precocious students to languish in slow-paced math classes. Math classes, they feel, should be taught according to individual students' abilities and achievements. Consequently, precocious students should spend less time in math classes, allowing for potential concentration on related topics such as physics (Tursman, 1983). Additionally, by spending less time in math class, mathematically precocious students would spend less time in school. This would allow them to take college courses while still in high school and to enter college at an earlier age (Stanley & Benbow, 1982). This is a goal of SMPY and is strongly emphasized by Stanley as a way to get these students quickly into the work force (Stanley, 1997).

The SMPY is essentially a summer program. Students are identified, evaluated, and selected for the program throughout the year. Once selected, students participate in an eight-week program, meeting one day a week for slightly less than 5 hours per day. Throughout the instruction, the student-teacher ratio never exceeds 1:5 (Stanley, 1980). All instructors are former SMPY graduates and usually range in age from 13 to 20. During this approximately 35-hour program, students will typically demonstrate mastery of material 2 school years beyond where they began (Stanley, 1980).

To achieve such dramatic results, SMPY uses a "diagnostic testing followed by prescriptive instruction" method of instruction (Stanley, 1980; Stanley & Benbow, 1983). An evaluation determines what the student does not know. The instructors then help the student learn the information without taking an entire course (Stanley & Benbow, 1982).

REFERENCES

Heid, M. K. (1983). Characteristics and special needs of the gifted students in mathematics. *Mathematics Teacher, 76*, 221–226.

Johnson, M. L. (1983). Identifying and teaching mathematically gifted elementary school children. *Arithmetic Teacher, 30*, 55–56.

Stanley, J. C. (1980). On educating the gifted. *Educational Researcher, 9*, 8–12.

Stanley, J. C. (1997). Varieties of intellectual talent. *Journal of Creative Behavior, 31*(2), 93–119.

Stanley, J. C., & Benbow, C. P. (1982). Educating mathematically precocious youth: Twelve policy recommendations. *Educational Researcher, 11*, 4–9.

Stanley, J. C., & Benbow, C. P. (1983). SMPY's first decade: Ten years of posing problems and solving them. *Journal of Special Education, 17*, 11–25.

Tursman, C. (1983). Challenging gifted students. *School Administrator, 40*, cover, 9–10, 12.

JOHN R. BEATTIE
University of North Carolina at Charlotte

ACCELERATION OF GIFTED CHILDREN
ADVANCED PLACEMENT PROGRAM
GIFTED AND TALENTED CHILDREN

STUTTERING

Stuttering is the most common of several disorders of fluency (Manning, 1996), all of which affect the rhythm or "flow" of speech. All speakers are sometimes disfluent, though not all speakers stutter. The causes of stuttering remain unknown despite decades of research. Recent speculations (e.g., Guitar, 1998) are that stuttering probably has several causative factors, including genetic predisposition, as well as neurophysiological and psychological influences. Research has consistently shown that more boys stutter than girls, a fact which has sometimes been used as evidence of a biological explanation.

Stuttering has both overt and covert aspects. The overt dimensions of the disorder include part-word repetitions, sound prolongations, and a variety of so-called "secondary" (learned struggle and avoidance) behaviors. The covert or hidden aspects of stuttering include word and situation avoidances, and feelings of anxiety, embarrassment, fear, and frustrations.

Although many preschool children eventually "outgrow" their early disfluencies without needing formal treatment, those children who do continue to stutter usually begin doing things to avoid it. A child's earliest stuttering is typically characterized by unstruggled ("easy") part-word repetitions. However, as children get older, they often begin reacting to their stuttering which leads to struggle and avoidance behaviors, both of which can become a greater problem than the stuttering itself.

Treatment for stuttering varies depending on the age of the person and the severity of the disorder, as well as the training and orientation of the speech-language pathologist. Therapies designed for young children who stutter include working with the child's parents to help reduce stressors, reducing the parents' speaking rate, discovering and eliminating fluency disruptors, and teaching the child a slower and "easier" way to speak.

Treatments for older children and adults tend to fall into one of two large categories. The first group of therapies is the "stuttering modification" or "stutter-more-fluently" therapies. Stutterers are encouraged to confront their fears and to stop avoiding their stuttering. They learn how to stutter in a more fluent and controlled manner. The emphasis is on reducing the struggling and the abnormality of the disorder rather than on trying to eliminate the stuttering.

The second family of therapies is the "fluency shaping" or "speak-more-fluently" therapies. Using slow speech and other methods, stutterers are taught to speak fluently (i.e., without stuttering), first in the therapy room and later in other speaking situations. Maintaining fluent speech has been the greatest challenge to therapists who use fluency shaping therapies.

Both types of treatments are effective with at least some stutterers, and, recently, speech-language pathologists have begun combining aspects of stuttering modification and fluency shaping therapies (e.g., Guitar, 1998). As yet, however, there is no single, accepted treatment for stuttering. As with the cause of stuttering, its treatment remains controversial.

REFERENCES

Guitar, B. (1998). *Stuttering: An integrated approach to its nature and treatment* (2nd ed). Baltimore: Williams and Wilkins.

Manning, W. (1996). *Clinical decision making in the diagnosis and treatment of fluency disorders*. Albany, NY: Delmar.

Van Riper, C. (1982). *The nature of stuttering* (2nd ed.). Englewood Cliffs, NJ: Prentice Hall.

EDWARD A. SHIRKEY
New Mexico State University

SPEECH INSTRUCTION
SPEECH THERAPY

SUBSTANCE ABUSE

Substance abuse is often said to be one of the major public health concerns in this country. The term "substance abuse" describes abusive or harmful use of any substance. A drug is any substance that crosses from the bloodstream into the brain and that somehow changes the way the brain is functioning. By this definition, some common substances such as alcohol, nicotine, and even caffeine are considered "drugs." Although caffeine, nicotine, and alcohol are by far the most common drugs in the United States, some other drugs of abuse include marijuana, cocaine, amphetamines ("speed"), heroin and other opiates, hallucinogens (LSD, psilocybin mushrooms, peyote), depressants (barbiturates, benzodiazepines, or "downers"), and prescription drugs. In recent years, the development of "designer" drugs and newer chemical compounds has gotten a good deal of media attention. Such substances as the "date rape drugs," including Rohypnol and GHB, have been gaining in popularity in recent years. Although the use and abuse of these drugs are not nearly as prevalent as some other substances, they are causing some alarm within the community of substance-abuse treatment professionals.

Many drugs are synthesized in a laboratory. Some of the synthetic, or man-made, drugs include prescription drugs such as tranquilizers, barbiturates, sedatives, narcotics, pain medications, and some hallucinogens (LSD). Although some of these drugs are indeed chemical substances, others such as marijuana, opium, peyote, psilocybin mushrooms, and coca leaves are natural, organic compounds. Further, some organic plants may be chemically processed to make them more usable to the human body. For example, opium and coca leaves can be processed into heroin and cocaine respectively (Maisto et al., 1995).

Substance abuse is not a recent phenomenon. Evidence indicates that the production of beer began in ancient Egypt as early as 5000 BCE. Within this country alone, the use and abuse of various substances has reached epidemic proportions at a number of different periods. Tobacco use by Native Americans was apparent long before the arrival of Europeans in the Americas. In the 19th century, morphine and opium were commonly available without a prescription. With the invention of the hypodermic needle in 1840, morphine became even more common for use as a pain medication, fueling a higher prevalence of morphine addiction. Amphetamine, inhalant, hallucinogen, and marijuana use have all been prevalent at different times during our history. Alcohol was prohibited at one time in our society because of its detrimental effects, only to be legalized and taxed several years later. Although many people consider alcohol prohibition to have been a failure in terms of an overall method of drug control, it did lead to a marked decrease in alcohol use. Lawsuits against the major tobacco companies and efforts to curb tobacco use in the United States may lead to decreases in tobacco use (Maisto et al., 1995).

The effects of different substances depend on a number of biological and psychological factors. Of course, the type of drug that is being used will affect people's experience.

Individuals' biological characteristics, such as weight, gender, and initial sensitivity to a substance may affect people's reaction to given a particular substance (Maisto et al., 1995). The setting in which the substance is used also affects how an individual will experience the effect of the substance (Maisto et al., 1995). Finally, people's expectations or beliefs about how the substance will affect them plays a role in their reaction to a particular substance (Goldman, Brown, & Christiansen, 1995).

Although neither necessary nor sufficient for a diagnosis of substance abuse or dependence, tolerance and withdrawal are key indicators of problematic use or addiction. Tolerance and withdrawal may indicate that the individual's body has become physically dependent on the drug. Tolerance basically means that the individual's body has become accustomed to the substance, such that larger and larger amounts of the substance are required to produce the same effect. Tolerance is generally developed through repeated exposure to a particular substance. However, some substances with similar actions may have what is known as cross-tolerance, in which an individual who has developed a high tolerance for a particular substance may also have a high tolerance for other similar substances, even if the substance has not actually been used. Regular use of most substances results in tolerance, at least to some degree.

Depending on the particular substance, abrupt cessation of the substance after a high tolerance has developed may result in withdrawal symptoms. Withdrawal symptoms from any particular drug are experienced most commonly as the direct opposite of the initial effect of the substance and can be psychological, physiological, or both, depending on the substance. Substances such as marijuana and hallucinogens cause no marked physical withdrawal symptoms, but abrupt cessation of use may result in psychological distress that may be severe. Other substances, especially compounds like alcohol, barbiturates, tranquilizers, and some pain medications, cause severe physical pain as well as psychological distress. Although withdrawal from some substances leads to serious enough consequences such as severe distress, painful withdrawal symptoms, and impairment in functioning, withdrawal from other substances may lead to seizures, coma, and even death.

In addition to tolerance and withdrawal, many users may become preoccupied with a substance, focusing much of their time and attention on finding, purchasing, and using it. Many people experience craving, or an intense desire to use the substance, when they stop using. Furthermore, some users become so preoccupied with using a substance that they are unable to function in their normal everyday lives.

A number of variations of substance abuse are included in the Diagnostic and Statistical Manual of Mental Disorders-Fourth Edition (DSM-IV; American Psychiatric Asso-ciation, 1994). Criteria are specified in DSM-IV for substance intoxication, withdrawal, abuse, and dependence. The major criterion for diagnosis of substance abuse according to the DSM-IV is identified as "a maladaptive pattern of substance use manifested by recurrent and significant adverse consequences related to the repeated use of substances." A child or adolescent who is abusing a substance may show a number of behavior changes, including failure to complete school work, marked decreases in academic performance, behavior problems at school and home, problems with the legal system, fighting, arguing, and problems with peers. Substance dependence, by contrast, is more severe than substance abuse. According to the DSM-IV, substance dependence is indicated by at least three of the following symptoms: marked tolerance, withdrawal symptoms, using more of the substance than was intended, inability to control or stop using, a desire to stop using, disruption in normal everyday functioning and activities, and continuing to use the substance even after knowing that the use is causing physical or psychological problems. Note that while tolerance and withdrawal are typical "hallmarks" of addiction, these criteria are neither necessary nor sufficient to indicate substance dependence. One of the reasons that these criteria are not necessary for a diagnosis of substance dependence is the fact that some substances, such as marijuana and most hallucinogens, cause few marked physiological withdrawal symptoms. Thus, substance dependence may be indicated by a disruption in functioning in a number of areas of an individual's life (American Psychiatric Association, 1994).

Although many people assume that the highest rates of substance abuse are in adults, the highest rates of heavy alcohol use and of marijuana use are in those of ages 18–25 years (U.S. Department of Health and Human Services, 1993; American Psychiatric Association, 1994). The initial substance use that may eventually lead to abuse or dependence generally begins in adolescence. Adolescents who show symptoms of abuse or dependence are less likely to complete school than those who do not (American Psychiatric Association, 1994). Therefore, and obviously, educators and health professionals need to pay particular attention to the problem of substance abuse in adolescence and young adulthood.

Apparently, little research is available on substance abuse in children enrolled in special education programs. One study on the possible association between special education status and substance abuse yielded alarming results. Gress and Boss (1996) surveyed students from grades 4–12 and found differences in substance use between students in special education and noncategorical classes, especially for students in intermediate (4–6) and junior high (7–8) grades. Some of the most striking differences were found between students in the intermediate grades. For instance, 20% of severely behaviorally-handicapped but only 2.3% of noncategorical students used marijuana. Interestingly, whereas a high percentage of students with severe behavioral handicaps and specific learning disabilities used alcohol, amphetamine, and inhalants, a lower, percentage of students with developmental disabilities used these substances than did noncategorical students. The authors suggest that substance abuse among students in special-education programs is related to several factors, including unmet needs for attachment and close relationships, difficulty establishing a "self-identity," a need to have a certain image within the eyes of their peers, and a need for immediate gratification. Common to all children, these factors may be especially important to students in special education who want to "fit in." Gress and Boss (1996) suggest that students with serious handicaps may lack some of the necessary internal skills to deal with unmet needs. Risk of substance abuse may increase as a result of psychological, emotional, and social problems related to their specific disabilities (Gress & Boss, 1996).

Since substance use begins to be a problem for many people when they are children and adolescents, many educators and substance-abuse professionals focus on prevention of substance use and abuse in this population. A number of different models are in place for prevention of substance use with children and teenagers. One that has gained recent popularity is a social norms approach, in which prevention campaigns are designed to change people's attitudes about social norms regarding substance use. Other methods of substance abuse prevention efforts geared toward children and adolescents include restricting the availability of particular substances, drink/drug refusal training, providing substance-free activities, mentoring programs, values clarification, and the development of appropriate stress management and social skills (Maisto, Galizio, & Connors, 1995).

Many different treatment methods exist to help people with substance abuse problems. Formal counseling or psychological treatment is available for individuals with substance abuse problems in inpatient, outpatient, and day treatment facilities, depending on the needs of the individual. Many people choose to attend self-help groups, such as Alcoholics Anonymous, Narcotics Anonymous, Women for Sobriety, or Rational Recovery.

Important to note is that although many people in the United States experience substance abuse problems, many others are affected by another person's substance abuse. Many children are affected by the substance abuse of their parents, siblings, extended family members, or friends. Educators should be familiar with issues related to substance abuse and able to listen to nonjudgmentally to the concerns of their students. When a child is experiencing difficulty as a result of either his or her own substance abuse or that of another person, the child should have access to a school counselor, psychologist, or social worker who can provide counseling and resources for the student.

REFERENCES

American Psychiatric Association. (1994). *Diagnostic and statistical manual of mental disorders fourth edition (DSM-IV).* Washington, DC: Author.

Goldman, M., Brown, S., Christiansen, B., & Smith, G. (1991). Alcoholism and memory: Broadening the scope of alcohol-expectancy research. *Psychological Bulletin, 110,* 137–146.

Gress, J., & Boss, M. (1996). Substance abuse differences among students receiving special education services. *Child Psychiatry and Human Development, 26,* 235–236.

Maisto, S., Galizio, M., & Connors, G. (1995). *Drug use and abuse.* Orlando, FL: Harcourt Brace College Publishers.

U.S. Department of Health and Human Services (USDHHS). (1993). *Alcohol and Health.* Rockville, MD: Author.

PAMELA M. RICHMAN
ALISON SHANER
*University of North Carolina at
Wilmington*

**CHEMICALLY DEPENDENT YOUTH
DRUG ABUSE**

SUBSTANTIA NIGRA

The substantia nigra houses the cell bodies of dopamine containing neurons that project to the striatum (putamen and caudate nucleus). This the so-called nigrostriatal pathway is the major dopamine pathway in the brain. The substantia nigra is a midbrain structure and is darkly pigmented, hence its name (i.e., black substance or black body). The nigrostriatal pathway is an important pathway in the extrapyramidal motor system, which controls background movement. Because of the importance of dopamine in the regulatory control of motor as well as emotional functioning, the nigrostriatal system has been implicated in a variety of neurobehavioral disorders (Andreasen, 1984). In particular, a breakdown of normal functioning of the dopaminergic system has been strongly implicated in schizophrenia (Andreasen, 1984). Also, other lines of investigation have suggested that dopamine plays a role in hyperactivity and attention deficit disorder (Shaywitz, Shaywitz, Cohen, & Young, 1983) and Rett syndrome (Segawa, 1997). The motor maladroitness frequently seen in learning-disabled children may be related in some fashion to basal ganglia/nigrostriatal irregularities (Duane, 1985; Rudel, 1985). The prototype neurologic disorder with primary substantia nigra involvement, and hence dopamine loss, is Parkinson's disease (Kolb & Whishaw, 1985).

REFERENCES

Andreasen, N. C. (1984). *The broken brain.* Cambridge, England. Harper & Row.

Duane, D. (1985). Written language underachievement: An overview of the theoretical and practical issues. In F. H. Duffy & N. Geschwind (Eds.), *Dyslexia: A neuroscientific approach to clinical evaluation*. Boston: Little, Brown.

Kolb, B., & Whishaw, I. Q. (1985). *Fundamentals of human neuropsychology*. New York: Freeman.

Rudel, R. G. (1985). The definition of dyslexia: Language and motor deficits. In F. H. Duffy & N. Geschwind (Eds.), *Dyslexia: A neuroscientific approach to clinical evaluation*. Boston: Little, Brown.

Segawa, M. (1997). Pathophysiology of Rett syndrome from the standpoint of early catecholamine disturbance. *European Child & Adolescent Psychiatry, 6*(1), 56–60.

Shaywitz, S. E., Shaywitz, B. A., Cohen, D. J., & Young, J. G. (1983). Monoaminergic mechanisms in hyperactivity. In M. Rutter (Ed.), *Developmental neuropsychiatry*. New York: Guilford.

ERIN D. BIGLER
Austin Neurological Clinic
University of Texas

DOPAMINE
PUTAMEN

SUBTEST SCATTER

Subtest scatter refers to the variability of an individual's subtest scores. The highs and lows of the profile indicate strengths and weaknesses on specific subtests. Differences between composite scores for an individual also are termed scatter. While the term subtest scatter may be aptly applied to any multiple subtest battery of basic skills, reading achievement, adaptive behavior, or other tests, the term has been popularized by its association with intellectual assessment. Exactly what role scatter has in diagnosing and differentiating among populations has not been determined. Is scatter a valid indicator for diagnostic purposes, or is it limited to identifying a subject's abilities and achievements in various areas? The believers in the significance of scatter have developed several diagnostic schemes that can be used to differentiate among populations.

Kaufman (1994) points out that scatter, significant differences in abilities measured by the Wechsler Intelligence Scale for Children (WISC-III), occurs frequently in the normal population. On the basis of this finding, he emphasizes the importance of being certain that the intersubtest variability is indeed rare in comparison with that of normal children before associating the scatter with abnormality. However, certain characteristic scatter has been consistently found for specific groups. Low scores on arithmetic, coding, information, and digit span subtests of the WISC-III have been shown to characterize the performance of many groups of learning-disabled children. This recently has been refuted (Dumont & Willis, 1995). It has been concluded however, that learning disabilities are more likely to be indicated by intraindividual differences than by set profiles.

Scatter has been applied to problems other than learning disabilities. Different types of mental deficiencies have been described in terms of scatter (Roszkowski & Spreat, 1982). Organically caused mental deficiency exhibited more scatter in Wechsler Adult Intelligence Scale (WAIS) scores than environmentally caused deficiency, but not to a significant degree. Greater scatter may be linked to lower functioning individuals. Large amounts of scatter on intelligence tests can also be associated with high degrees of maladaptive behaviors (Roszkowski & Spreat, 1983) and social-emotional problems (Greenwald, Harder, & Fisher, 1982). Thus scatter can be associated with behavioral, emotional, and organic disorders, as well as with the more commonly thought of learning disabilities.

There may be evidence linking scatter to various disorders, but it is questionable whether it is strong enough to warrant its use as a diagnostic tool. The greatest portion of the evidence says no (Kavale & Forness, 1984). Subtest scatter may be useful in specifying particular strengths and weaknesses of an individual's performance, and in educational intervention planning. Caution is needed with interpretation of scatter and profile analysis, and flexibility is recommended when selecting tests for a particular population (Kamphaus, 1985).

REFERENCES

Bannatyne, H. (1971). *Language, reading, and learning disabilities*. Springfield, IL: Thomas.

Decker, S. A., & Corley, R. P. (1984). Bannatyne's "genetic dyslexic" subtype: A validation study. *Psychology in the Schools, 21*, 300–304.

Dumont, R., & Willis, J. O. (1995). Intrasubtest scatter on the WISC-III for various clinical samples vs. the standardization sample: An examination of the WISC folklore. *Journal of Psychoeducational assessment, 13*(3), 271–285.

Greenwald, D. F., Harder, D. W., & Fisher, L. (1982). WISC scatter and behavioral competence in high-risk children. *Journal of Clinical Psychology, 38*, 397–401.

Kamphaus, R. W. (1985). Perils of profile analysis. *Information/Edge: Cognitive Assessment & Remediation, 1*, 1–4.

Kaufman, A. S. (1994). *Intelligence testing with the WISC-III*. New York: Wiley.

Kavale, K. A., & Forness, S. (1984). A meta-analysis of the validity of Wechsler scale profiles and recategorizations: Patterns or parodies? *Learning Disability Quarterly, 7*, 136–156.

Roszkowski, M., & Spreat, S. (1982). Scatter as an index of organicity: A comparison of mentally retarded individuals experiencing and not experiencing concomitant convulsive disorders. *Journal of Behavioral Assessment, 4*, 311–315.

Roszkowski, M., & Spreat, S. (1983). Assessment of effective intelligence: Does scatter matter? *Journal of Special Education*, 17, 453–459.

LISA J. SAMPSON
Eastern Kentucky University

FACTOR ANALYSIS
INTELLIGENCE
INTELLIGENT TESTING
PROFILE ANALYSIS
TEST SCATTER
WISC-III

SUICIDE

There has been much concern about the adolescent suicide rate that dramatically increased from 1950 to 1990. Seven percent of high school students attempt suicide in a one-year period, and 60% of them use handguns (O'Donnell, 1995).

The origins of suicide in children and adolescents have been cited as (1) lack of stable support in a home or family situation; (2) family problems that lead the young person to feel powerless and without control of his or her own life; (3) lack of supportive social relationships; and (4) inability to successfully solve problems (Wagner, 1997; Weiner, 1982). Clearly, these factors, singly or in concert, are likely to affect many exceptional children and youths, particularly those who experience institutionalization or social stigmatization. In addition, there are clear parallels between these factors and theories of learned helplessness and depression (Steer, Kumar, & Beck, 1993). Seligman (1975) has defined learned helplessness as the belief that one's actions do not affect or shape one's destiny. It has been further hypothesized that children who grow up with the sense of having little control over their own lives typically feel unable to cope with problem situations and become depressed (Dweck, 1977; Miller & Seligman, 1975).

Recent research dealing with affective disorders among the mentally retarded suggests low levels of social support do lead to depression and learned helplessness within this group (Reiss & Benson, 1985). Reynolds and Miller (1985), in an initial investigation, found educable mentally retarded (EMR) adolescents to be more depressed than their nonretarded peers. In addition, higher than normal rates of suicide have been reported among other exceptional groups, including persons with alcohol and drug abuse problems, for which children and adolescents are at increasingly high risk (Farmer, 1978; McIntire & Angle (1980), and mental illness (Dunham, 1978; Wagner, 1997) a disorder for which the retarded are at high risk (Lewis & MacLean, 1982; Szymanski, 1980).

These factors clearly indicate that exceptional youths constitute a high-risk group for suicide, particularly during mid to late adolescence. Age, the social/familial conditions and absence of control that often develop in consonance with physical or developmental disorders (e.g., living away from home, lack of a supportive peer group, not being involved in making decisions affecting one's life), and the coexistence of additional problems such as mental illness, each place the exceptional child at high risk. For the individual for whom several risk factors occur, the possibility of depression and/or suicide is magnified proportionally.

To reduce the risk of suicide among exceptional children and adolescents, intervention must occur on a basic level, addressing those needs that have been identified as preceding learned helplessness, depression, and suicide. The construction of stable family or familylike support groups, the involvement of the exceptional individual in planning and control of his or her own life, assistance in forming supportive peer and social relationships, training in problem solving and coping skills, and appropriate treatment for related disorders such as alcohol, drug abuse, or mental illness should substantially reduce the risk of suicide in this population.

REFERENCES

Dunham, C. S. (1978). Mental illness. In R. M. Goldenson, J. R. Dunham, & C. S. Dunham (Eds.), *Disability and rehabilitation handbook*. New York: McGraw-Hill.

Dweck, C. S. (1977). Learned helplessness: A developmental approach. In J. G. Schulterbrandt & A. Raskin (Eds.), *Depression in childhood*. New York: Raven.

Farmer, R. H. (1978). Drug-abuse problems. In R. M. Goldenson, J. R. Dunham, & C. S. Dunham (Eds.), *Disability and rehabilitation handbook*. New York: McGraw-Hill.

Lewis, M. H., & MacLean, W. E., Jr. (1982). Issues in treating emotional disorders. In J. L. Matson & R. P. Barrett (Eds.), *Psychopathology in the mentally retarded* (pp. 1–36). New York: Grune & Stratton.

O'Donnell, C. R. (1995). Firearm deaths among children and youth. *American Psychologist*, 50(9), 771–776.

McIntire, M. S., & Angle, C. R. (1980). *Suicide attempts in children and youth*. New York: Harper & Row.

Miller, W., & Seligman, M. E. P. (1975). Depression and learned helplessness in man. *Journal of Abnormal Psychology*, 84, 228–238.

Reiss, S., & Benson, B. A. (1985). Psychosocial correlates of depression in mentally retarded adults: I. Minimal social support and stigmatization. *American Journal of Mental Deficiency*, 89, 331–337.

Reynolds, W. M., & Miller, K. L. (1985). Depression and learned helplessness in mentally retarded and nonmentally retarded adolescents: An initial investigation. *Applied Research in Mental Retardation*, 6, 295–306.

Seligman, M. E. P. (1975). *Helplessness: On depression, development, and death*. San Francisco: Freeman.

Steer, R. A. Kumar, G., & Beck, A. T. (1993). Self-reported suicidal ideation in adolescent psychiatric inpatients. *American Psychologist, 61*(6), 1096–1099.

Szymanski, L. S. (1980). Individual psychotherapy with retarded persons. In L. S. Szymanski & R. E. Tanguay (Eds.), *Emotional disorders of mentally retarded persons*. Baltimore, MD: University Park Press.

Wagner, B. M. (1997). Family risk factors for child and adolescent suicidal behavior. *Psychological Bulletin, 121*(2), 246–298.

Weiner, I. B. (1982). *Child and adolescent psychopathology*. New York: Wiley.

LAURA KINZIE BRUTTING
J. TODD STEPHENS
University of Wisconsin at Madison

DEPRESSION
EMOTIONAL DISORDERS
LEARNED HELPLESSNESS

SULLIVAN, ANN

See MACY, ANN SULLIVAN.

SULLIVAN PROGRAMMED READING

The Sullivan Programmed Reading system comprises an individualized programmed workbook approach to teaching reading to students in grades one through three. The sequence of the three-year system extends from Reading Readiness through Series III, with diagnostic prescriptive teaching aids and student activities that are designed to optimize individual pacing. Pupils systematically progress from letter discrimination to word recognition or to reading sentences and stories. The first ten weeks of the program are spent in the development of a basic vocabulary and the acquisition of skills that are necessary for the use of programmed material. This part of the series is teacher directed or oriented and must be done as a class or group. Afterward, the program allows each pupil to progress according to his or her own rate of learning. The pupil is provided with a minimal amount of information, a problem is posed, a response is solicited, and the response is corrected or reinforced. The child makes the response, then checks his or her answer against the correct response that is revealed as a slider moves down the page to reveal the next frame (Hafner & Jolly, 1972; Moyle & Moyle, 1971; Scheiner, 1969; Sullivan Associates, 1968).

The Reading Readiness and Programmed Readers Series I, II, and III provide sequential instruction in consonants, vowels, sight words, punctuation, suffixes, contractions, possessives, capitals, and comprehension. Placement tests indicate at which point in the series to enter a pupil who begins in the system after first grade. The Programmed Reading Program is comprised of 23 levels, with one book per level. Pupils progress through each book and are expected to pass an end-of-book test before proceeding to the next book. A total of 3266 words are introduced in the complete program (Hafner & Jolly, 1972; Sullivan Associates, 1968).

The following components of the Sullivan Associates system may be ordered as kits or separately. Reading Readiness consists of two kits, each of which contain two full-color, 72-page Big Books, two comprehensive teacher guides, two hour-long tape cassettes, a set of Webstermasters, and a wire easel and alphabet strips. On completion of the prereading stage, the child should master (1) the names of letters; (2) how to write letters; (3) the sounds that represent letters; (4) left to right sequencing; (5) the concept that words are formed from groups of letters; and (6) the ability to read the words *yes* or *no* in sentences. Series I, II, and III Programmed Readers Books 1 to 23 provide logical linguistic progression, constant reinforcement, colorful art, and stimulating story content. By the end of the eighth book in Series I, 14 vowels and 23 consonant classes will have been mastered; in addition, children will know approximately 450 words phonetically and 10 sight words. On completion of Series III, 25 more vowels and consonant classes, a total of 3200 new words, and 40 more sight words, will have been mastered.

Two sets of seven filmstrips that are primarily designed to introduce the readers to new words supplement Books 1 to 14. Each filmstrip reviews material from the previous level and presents new vocabulary and characters. Three sets of Activity Books reinforce ideas provided by the programmed series through cutout patterns for characters, puppets, and games. Webstermasters allow duplications to supplement each series of programmed readers. Read and Think Series are provided for Series I and II and are to be read after completion of the programmed text to motivate children to read for enjoyment. Achievement tests (criterion-referenced) measure student progress in terms of predetermined behavioral objectives for each series. There is an item-by-item analysis of the skills tested and specific remediation for each item that is missed. Word cards and response booklets allow pupils to write their answers using a wax pencil or crayon, making the tests reusable. Teachers' guides are organized by book, skill, and unit. An overview of decoding and comprehension information, and a listing of the sound-symbol and vocabulary progression and content summary, are outlined. Each grade also contains a reading aloud, dictation, creative writing, and test section for each book level, and specific item-by-item instructions for both with remediative recycling options (Sullivan & Associates, 1968). For uses with exceptional children, see Lerner (1985).

REFERENCES

Hafner, L., & Jolly, H. (1972). *Patterns of teaching reading in the elementary school*. New York: Macmillan.

Lerner, J. (1985). *Learning disabilities: Theories, diagnosis and teaching strategies* (4th ed.). Dallas: Houghton Mifflin.

Moyle, D., & Moyle, L. (1971). *Modern innovations in the teaching of reading*. London: University of London Press.

Scheiner, L. (1969). *An evaluation of the Sullivan Reading Program (1967–1969) Rhoads Elementary School*, Washington D.C.: U.S. Department of Health, Education and Welfare. (ERIC Document Reproduction Service ED 002 362).

Sullivan Associates. (1968). *Sullivan Associates programmed reading Sullivan Press*. New York: McGraw-Hill.

FRANCES T. HARRINGTON
Radford University

READING DISORDERS
READING REMEDIATION

SUMMER SCHOOL FOR THE HANDICAPPED

Extended-year programs for individuals with handicapping conditions have been a highly debated issue for many years. The position of many individuals is that extended school year programs are needed for students with handicapping conditions to prevent the loss of existing skills, accelerate the acquisition of new skills, and provide recreational programming and respite care for the parents. There are several main questions for which there are no appropriate answers: (1) Do extended school year programs accomplish instructional objectives and, if so, how much? (2) If students do learn something, is it additive to what is learned during the school year? (3) Do students without extended school years lose skills or do they increase maladaptive (i.e., irritant) responding? (4) Do students without extended school years catch up to students who do experience extended school year programming and thus negate the effect of the extended year? (5) If students with extended school years do have additive learning, is the cost effectiveness of that learning acceptable? (6) What types of extended school years (e.g., school, school plus recreational, recreational, short programs, long programs) have what types of effects, and what are the desired effects (e.g., retention, gain, degree of gain)? (7) What are the "do-ability" variables (e.g., What teachers and aides will be involved? Is burnout an issue? Who will supervise? (8) How will documentation be provided? (9) Is there student burnout, etc.

There are some other questions that do have answers.

First, do handicapped students have a right to a public education? Public Law 94-142, and Section 504 of the Rehabilitation Act of 1973, have defined the right of handicapped children to a free appropriate public education. Second, do specific classes of handicapped students have a right to an extended school year? The courts have substantiated the right of specific classes of handicapped children to extended (over 180-day) school year programs in a number of court cases (e.g., *Armstrong* v. *Kline*, 1979). Additional cases are currently pending throughout the United States. Therefore, while there is growing educational and legal support for extended-year programming, many questions still need to be addressed.

Empirical support for the current policy on extended-year programs for individuals with handicaps is difficult to find in the literature. Browder, Lentz, Knoster, and Wilansky (1984) found that the primary methodology for determining both eligibility for and effectiveness of extended-year programs was the subjective judgments of teachers and parents (Bahling, 1980; McMahon, 1983). This information, while not surprising, does not provide empirical support for extended school year programming. Ellis (1975a) studied the effects of a summer program on possible regression of 16 multihandicapped blind children, and found that none of the students had regressed in eight target skill areas (e.g., communication skills). In a second study, Ellis (1975b) examined the skill levels of 145 physically and neurologically handicapped students and found a significant improvement in skill areas for the summer program participants. In contrast, Edgar, Spence, and Kenowitz (1977), in a study that examined the findings of 18 summer programs, found that the data (e.g., teacher observations, rating scales) did not strongly support the premise that such programs facilitated the maintenance of skills. However, these results are possible when there is not a coherence between the school year objectives and those of the summer program. Therefore, there are conflicting data concerning the effectiveness of extended-year programming in either maintaining or extending the learning repertoire of handicapped students.

In a recent study, Zdunich (1984) reported on data gathered on extended-year programs in Canada. This study examined the effects of four types of summer programming (short programs, high-structure, low-structure, and medium-structure programs). A control group that received no summer programming was also used in the study. While the study's sample size was relatively small (overall *n* = 186), its results were interesting. First, the study found that maladaptive behaviors had been significantly reduced only in the high- and medium-structure programs and that students in the other conditions increased maladaptive responding. Second, skill development (e.g., communication, self-help, fine motor skills) was significantly greater in high- and medium-structure programs. Other types of summer experiences showed relative maintenance of skills with some small amount of skill regression. In addition, the skill acquisition data held constant over the following academic year. The study also examined many variables related to each of these two major concerns. It should provide a substantial increase in our database on the educational and social impact of extended school year programming.

REFERENCES

Bahling, E. (1980). *Extended school year program, Intermediate Unit #5, June–August, 1980*. Paper presented at the annual international convention of Council for Exceptional Children, Philadelphia. (ERIC Document Reproduction Service No. 208 609)

Browder, D. M., Lentz, F. E., Knoster, T., & Wilansky, C. (1984). *A record based evaluation of extended school year eligibility practice*. Unpublished manuscript.

Edgar, E., Spence, W., & Kenowitz, L. (1977). Extended school year for the handicapped: Is it working? *Journal of Special Education, 11,* 441–447.

Ellis, R. S. (1975a). Summer pre-placement program for severely multihandicapped blind children. *Summer 1975, Evaluation Report*. New York City Board of Education. (ERIC Document Reproduction Service No. ED136489)

Ellis, R. S. (1975b). Summer education program for neurologically and physically handicapped children *Summer 1975, Evaluation Report*. New York City Board of Education. (ERIC Document Reproduction Service No. ED136489)

McMahon, J. (1983). Extended school year programs. *Exceptional Children, 49,* 457–460.

Zdunich, L. (1984). *Summer programs for the severely handicapped*. Edmonton, Alberta, Canada: Alberta Education.

LYLE E. BARTON
Kent State University

TUTORING

SUPERVISION IN SPECIAL EDUCATION

Current emphasis in special education is on the employment of a program administrator specifically for exceptional children. Other titles used are special education director and supervisor of exceptional children's programs. For most states, the administrator or director of special education must have an academic degree at the master's level in the education of exceptional children or a related field. Owing to the nature of the position, it is also helpful if this person completes the requirements for a supervisor's or administrator's certificate in addition to the master's degree in special education. The educational program for the preparation of exceptional children's program administrators is basically the same as for preparing general school administrators. The major difference in their preparation is in the specific exceptional children's program content requirement.

The exceptional children's program administrator has been identified by the North Carolina Division for Exceptional Children as

one who plans, develops, coordinates, supervises, administers, and evaluates the effectiveness of local educational agency's educational programs. The program administrator provides guidance and leadership to all exceptional children program personnel. The role is performed under the general supervision of the superintendent or designee. The program administrator maintains a cooperative relationship with principals, other school personnel, other related service agencies, and parents. The administrator is responsible for maintaining the program within local, state, and federal guidelines, rules, regulations, and laws which govern exceptional children.

Program administrators should have competencies in the administration of exceptional children's programs, including assessment; planning and implementing programs; budgeting; communicating with parents, central office staff, principals, other service providers, and state and local agencies; staff development; and program evaluation. Another area of expertise necessary for program administrators is the application of school law administration of exceptional children's programs. This includes knowledge of legislation about the handicapped as it relates to IDEA other state and federal statutes; confidentiality guidelines; due process procedures; procedures for auditing and evaluating compliance; authority of the hearing officer; and schools' responsibility for various placements, transportation, suspension and expulsion, related services, competency tests, and evaluations.

Program administrators should be well versed in supervision of instruction centered around personnel management. He or she should be able to interview and select qualified exceptional children's teachers, observe and evaluate teachers to identify teaching strengths and weaknesses, and develop professional growth plans for teachers and support staff. The administrator should be able to design instructional units that specify performance objectives, instructional sequences, learning activities, and materials and evaluation processes, and prepare an educational plan that includes curriculum content and level, activities, alternative teaching strategies, and evaluation of learning outcomes (Sage & Burrello, 1994). The program administrator should also be able to evaluate the quality, utility, and availability of learning resource materials.

REFERENCES

Comprehensive system of personnel development report. (1984, August). Raleigh: Division for Exceptional Children, North Carolina Department of Public Instruction.

Competencies and guidelines for approved teacher education programs. (1983, September). Raleigh: Division for Exceptional Children, North Carolina Department of Public Instruction.

Sage, D. D., & Burrello, L. C. (1994). *Leadership in educational reform: An administrator's guide to changes in special education.* Baltimore, MD: Brookes.

CECELIA STEPPE-JONES
*North Carolina Central
University*

ADMINISTRATION OF SPECIAL EDUCATION POLITICS, SPECIAL EDUCATION AND

SUPPORT, BEHAVIORAL

Behavioral support is the outcome of a collaborative process of systematically creating comprehensive and effective behavior support plans for individuals with severe behavioral challenges. Behavior support plans typically focus on data from functional assessments that result in environmental modifications and specific instructional procedures that teachers, family, and support personnel can implement which decrease the problem behavior, increase alternative behaviors, and result in attributions of self-determination, inclusion, and independence for the person of concern (Field, Martin, Miller, Ward, & Wehmeyer, 1998; O'Neill et al., 1997; Sugai & Horner, 1994; Turnbull & Turnbull III, 1990). Behavioral support planning is a nonaversive approach for reducing challenging behaviors that incorporates systems-level change and skill development based on an understanding of the purpose or function of the problem behavior within the context of targeted environments (Horner et al., 1990; Sugai & Horner, 1994; Turnbull, Turnbull, Shank, & Leal, 1999). O'Neill et al. (1997) write that the outcome of behavioral support is "not just to define and eliminate undesirable behavior but to understand the structure and function of those behaviors in order to teach and promote effective alternatives" (p. 8). An additional outcome of behavioral support is the promotion of durable and generalizable change that positively affects each individual's access to the general education curriculum, community settings, and preferred activities and persons across environments (Horner et al., 1990).

Behavioral support planning is predicated on an accurate functional assessment of the purpose or function that the problem behavior serves for the individual. Functional assessment is defined as a systematic process for gathering information about the contextual factors that predict and/or maintain persistent problem behavior. Data from functional assessments are used to develop comprehensive behavior support plans that outline the hypothesized function or purpose that a targeted problem behavior serves for

an individual. This includes data of any distal and immediate predictors that occasion the behavior and/or consequent events that are hypothesized to maintain the problem behavior. The behavior support plan also outlines proposed environmental modifications, curricular adaptations, and instructional strategies for teaching the person replacement responses that serve the same function or purpose of the problem behavior, but are more socially acceptable given the individual's home, school, and work environments. O'Neill et al. (1997) conclude that the ultimate purpose of functional assessment is to "increase the effectiveness and efficiency of behavior support plans" (p. 65).

Because schools are dynamic and complex social systems, policies and procedures need to be in place to promote effective behavioral support across settings, faculty, staff, and students (Sugai & Horner, 1994). Within the context of schools, four major subsystems have been identified that should be considered when addressing the behavioral support needs of all learners. These subsystems include school-wide behavioral support systems, setting-specific behavioral support systems, classroom-specific behavioral support systems, and individual student behavioral support systems (Sugai, 1996). Each of the subsystems listed above incorporate (a) procedures for teaching expected behaviors to all students, (b) procedures for monitoring and evaluating student progress using both formative and summative assessments, and (c) procedures for accessing local behavioral expertise (e.g., Behavior Support Team) so that teachers can receive assistance and support in the areas of functional assessment and behavioral support planning (Colvin, Kameenui, & Sugai, 1993; Sugai & Horner, 1994).

O'Neill et al. (1997) offers four considerations for building effective behavioral support plans. Behavioral support plans should describe our behavior; that is, behavioral support planning is a process of examining the changes that teachers, family, and support personnel will make across environments with the intent of teaching the student more effective alternatives to the problem behavior. Behavior support plans also should always build upon the results of comprehensive functional assessments; that is, the behavior support team should incorporate both indirect and direct functional assessment methodologies as a means to understand the purpose or function that the problem behavior serves for the individual. Behavior support plans should be technically sound; that is, effective behavioral support plans should include strategies that make the problem behavior irrelevant, inefficient, and ineffective by implementing empirically-validated behavioral principles across settings, persons, and time. Behavior support plans should also fit the setting where they will be implemented; that is, the behavior support plan should provide a good fit for the behavior support team and the person of concern by taking into account the values, time, and resources of those that will implement the procedures. In summary, effective behavioral support is a process of creating responsive environments that take into account the preferences, strengths, and needs of the person with severe challenging behaviors in their current environments by incorporating data from functional assessments, by promoting systems-level change across environments and persons, and through skill development activities that teach the individual effective alternatives to the targeted problem behaviors (Sugai & Horner, 1994; Turnbull, Turnbull, Shank, & Leal, 1999).

REFERENCES

Colvin, G., Kameenui, E. J., & Sugai, G. (1993). Reconceptualizing behavior management and school-wide discipline in general education. *Education and Treatment of Children, 16,* 361–381.

Field, S., Martin, J., Miller, R., Ward, M., & Wehmeyer, M. (1998). *A practical guide for teaching self-determination.* Reston, VA: The Council for Exceptional Children.

Horner, R. H., Dunlap, G., Koegel, R. L., Carr, E. G., Sailor, W., Anderson, J., Albin, R. W. & O'Neill, R. E. (1990). Toward a technology of "nonaversive" behavioral support. *The Journal of the Association for Persons with Severe Handicaps, 15,* 125–132.

O'Neill, R. E., Horner, R. H., Albin, R. W., Sprague, J. R., Storey, K., & Newton, J. S. (1997). *Functional assessment and program development for problem behavior: A practical handbook* (2nd ed.). Pacific Grove, CA: Brooks/Cole.

Sugai, G. (1996, Winter). Providing effective behavioral support to all students: Procedures and processes. *SAIL, 11*(1), 1–4.

Sugai, G., & Horner, R. (1994). Including students with severe behavior problems in general education settings: Assumptions, challenges, and solutions. In J. Marr, G. Sugai, & G. Tindal (Eds.), *The Oregon Conference Monograph* (pp. 102–120). Eugene, OR: University of Oregon.

Turnbull, A. P. & Turnbull, H. R., III. (1990). A tale about lifestyle changes: Comments on "toward a technology of 'nonaversive' behavioral support." *The Journal of the Association for Persons with Severe Handicaps, 15,* 142–144.

Turnbull, A., Turnbull, R., Shank, M., & Leal, D. (1999). *Exceptional lives: Special education in today's schools* (2nd ed.). Upper Saddle River, NJ: Merrill.

RANDALL L. DE PRY
University of Colorado
Colorado Springs

FUNCTIONAL ASSESSMENT

SUPPORTED EMPLOYMENT

Supported employment is a vocational alternative that has been described in rules published by the U.S. Department of Education in the *Federal Register* (June 18, 1985) as "paid work in a variety of integrated settings, particularly regular work sites, especially designed for severely handicapped individuals irrespective of age or vocational potential." Traditionally, individuals with severe disabilities have been served in day activity centers in which the intended goal is to prepare these clients for vocational rehabilitation services and, ultimately, employment. However, this readiness model of service delivery has not prepared these individuals successfully for vocational rehabilitation services or employment. Supported employment provides employment opportunities to those individuals with mental and physical disabilities so severe that they are not eligible for vocational rehabilitation services.

Supported employment (Will, 1985) includes four characteristics that differentiate it from vocational rehabilitation services and traditional methods of providing day activity services. First, the service recipients are those typically served in day activity centers who do not have the potential for unassisted competitive employment and thus are ineligible for vocational rehabilitative services. Second, ongoing support, which is unavailable in a traditional day activity program, as well as supervision and ongoing training is involved. Supported employment is not designed to lead to unassisted competitive work as are vocational rehabilitation programs. Third, the employment focus of supported employment provides the same benefits typically obtained by people from work (e.g. income, security, mobility, advancement opportunities, etc.). It does not seek to identify and teach prerequisite skills and behaviors needed for employment as is usually done in day activity centers. Last, there is flexibility in support strategies to assist individuals with severe disabilities in obtaining and maintaining employment. This may include the provision of a "job coach" by a community agency. The coach provides training and supervision at an individual's work site, direct support to employers to offset training and special equipment costs, or salary supplements to coworkers who provide regular assistance in the performance of personal care activities while at work.

Federal initiatives have provided the impetus for the development of supported employment programs. These programs vary according to client characteristics, community resources, and employment opportunities. Options for supported employment are flexible owing to the wide range of community jobs and the variety of ways to provide support to individuals with severe disabilities (McCarthy, Everson, Moon, Barcus, 1985). The features common to various supported employment program options are emphasis on paid employment, ongoing support and training that enables individuals with severe handicaps to get and keep a job, and social integration in which these individuals are provided with opportunities to work and interact with coworkers, supervisors, and other nondisabled individuals (Mark, O'Neill, & Jensen, 1998; Password, 1985). Examples of four supported employment options are enclaves, mobile work crews, specialized industrial programs, and supported competitive employment. A brief discussion of each follows.

An enclave is an industry-based option that relies on private and public sector cooperation to create an organizational structure that supports the employment of individuals with severe disabilities. While a wide range of alternatives is possible with this service model, an enclave is a group of individuals with disabilities who are provided training and support by a third-party public organization among nonhandicapped workers in a private company. Rhodes and Valenta (1985) describe the ideal enclave as having the following characteristics. Enclave employees are located in physical proximity to coworkers and represent approximately 1% of the total work force. Enclave employees perform the same work, have the same work routines (work hours, breaks, lunch), and are supervised in the same manner as their nonhandicapped coworkers. They are employed by the host company and arrive at work via car pools with coworkers or public or company transportation. Finally, the support organization maintains low visibility and intervenes only when necessary to maintain and support employment.

Mobile work crews are community-based employment groups that usually involve four to six individuals and a crew supervisor working together on various job sites (Bourbeau, 1985). As the title indicates, these work crews operate out of a vehicle and move from one work site to the next. The work performed by the crews is specific to community needs any may entail a variety of jobs such as janitorial work or grounds maintenance (Bourbeau, 1985). Since the job site is in the community, integration and interaction is fostered (interaction with people in the community, eating in community restaurants, etc.).

Another supported work option is described by O'Bryan (1985), the benchwork model. This model was developed at the University of Oregon in 1973 as a small, nonprofit business and since has been replicated at 17 sites. The benchwork model shares many of features and constraints with traditional sheltered workshops, although it is designed for persons with more severe disabilities. The major differences are the size and location of the operation. Only 15 individuals with severe or profound disabilities are employed. The location in the community close to stores and restaurants provides the opportunity for regular participation in the surrounding community. Training in skills that relate to a typical working day are provided with the major foci on those skills necessary to experience the regular daily, weekly, and monthly rhythms of the community. One of the major constraints, however, is that job security, benefits, and integration depend on the organization's commercial success.

The fourth option, a supported competitive employment program, has been defined by Wehman (1985) as real work at the federal minimum wage at a job with predominantly nonhandicapped workers. The provision of specialized assistance in locating an appropriate job, intensive job-site training, and permanent ongoing support at the level required by the individual are components of this option.

Supported work options have been initiated at state and local levels to meet the vocational needs of individuals with severe disabilities. The purpose of these work options is to provide these individuals with real work opportunities and the support necessary for them to keep their jobs. Supported work has been found to be cost-effective (McCoughvin, Ellis, Rusch, & Heal 1993). The assumption is that all persons, regardless of the severity of their disabilities, have the ability to work as long as appropriate, ongoing services are provided.

REFERENCES

Bourbeau, P. E. (1985). Mobile work crews: An approach to achieve long-term supported employment. In P. McCarthy, J. Everson, S. Moon, & M. Barcus (Eds.), *School-to-work transition for youth with severe disabilities* (pp. 151–166). Richmond, VA: Rehabilitation Research and Training Center; Virginia Commonwealth University.

Mark, D., O'Neill, C. T., & Jensen, R. (1998). Quality in supported employment: A new demonstration of the capabilities of people with severe disabilities. *Journal of Vocational Rehabilitation*, *11*(1), 83–95.

McCarthy, P., Everson, J., Moon, S., & Barcus, M. (Eds.). (1985). *School-to-work transition for youth with severe disabilities*. Richmond, VA: Rehabilitation Research and Training Center, Virginia Commonwealth University.

McCoughvin, W. B., Ellis, W. K., Rusch, F. R., & Heal, L. W. (1993). Cost-effectiveness of supported employment. *Mental Retardation*, *31*(1), 41–48.

O'Bryan, A. (1985). The specialized training program (STP) benchwork model. In P. McCarthy, J. Everson, S. Moon, & M. Barcus (Eds.), *School-to-work transition for youth with severe disabilities* (pp. 183–194). Richmond, VA: Rehabilitation Research and Training Center, Virginia Commonwealth University.

Password. (1985, Autumn). *Office of Special Education and Rehabilitative Services (OSERS) News in Print*, *1*(1), 2.

Rhodes, L. E., & Valenta, L. (1985). Enclaves in industry. In P. McCarthy, J. Everson, S. Moon, & M. Barcus (Eds.), *School-to-work transition for youth with severe disabilities* (pp. 129–149). Richmond, VA: Rehabilitation Research and Training Center, Virginia Commonwealth University.

Wehman, P. (1985). Supported competitive employment for persons with severe disabilities. In P. McCarthy, J. Everson, S. Moon, & M. Barcus (Eds.), *School-to-work transition for youth with severe disabilities* (pp. 167–182). Richmond, VA: Rehabilitation Research and Training Center, Virginia Commonwealth University.

Will, M. (1985, Autumn). Supported employment programs: Moving from welfare to work. *Office of Special Education and Rehabilitative Services (OSERS) News in Print*, *1*(1), 8–9.

EILEEN F. MCCARTHY
University of Wisconsin at Madison

TRANSITION
VOCATIONAL REHABILITATION

SURROGATE PARENTS

The Individuals with Disabilities Education Act (IDEA) included parental participation as a major component in the educational planning for children with disabilities. The purpose of including parents was to ensure that the rights of the child and the parents are protected. This component of IDEA officially recognized the parents as a crucial and viable force in the life of their child and required their input in the educational planning and decision-making process. However, there are instances when a handicapped child's parents, for various reasons, are unable to represent him or her in the educational decision-making process. This is when the public agency responsible for educating the child appoints a surrogate parent. According to federal regulations, a surrogate parent is appointed when (1) no parent can be identified; (2) the public agency, after reasonable efforts, cannot discover the whereabouts of a parent; or (3) the child is a ward of the state under the laws of that state (*Federal Register*, 1977 p. 42496).

Surrogate parents are individuals who are responsible for ensuring that the handicapped child receives a free appropriate education in the least restrictive environment. The surrogate parents' role is limited to the educational needs of the child. However, more and more grandparents are taking on this role (Rottenberg, 1996). Specifically, the role of the surrogate parents, based on the federal regulations, relates to

> (1) The identification, evaluation, and educational placement of the child. . . .

> (2) The provision of a free appropriate education to the child. . . . The public agency may select a surrogate parent in any way permitted by state law. The public agencies shall insure that a person selected as surrogate has no interest that conflicts with the interests of the child he or she represents; and has knowledge and skills that ensure adequate representation of the child. The person who is appointed as a surrogate parent cannot be an employee of the public agency that is directly involved in the education and care of the child. (*Federal Register*, 1977 p. 42496)

Shrybman (1982) listed the following rights of surrogate parents:

1. Review all written records regarding the child's education
2. Take part in the evaluation and development of the individual education plan (IEP)
3. Reject, accept, or recommend changes in the IEP
4. Request and/or initiate a second evaluation
5. Initiate mediation, hearing, or appeals procedures
6. Receive legal help at no cost if such assistance is necessary in the furtherance of the surrogate's responsibilities
7. Monitor the child's program
8. Recommend changes in the pupil's placement
9. Take advantage of all the rights afforded to natural parents in the special education decision-making process (pp. 267–268)

Each state is required to develop specific requirements for the selection of the surrogate parents. Once the need has been proven by the local agency, the criteria and responsibilities are specifically defined. A surrogate parent does not have to be a professional person; however, it is important that the surrogate have a general knowledge of state and federal laws relating to the handicapped. In addition, knowledge of the rules and regulations of the public school system and specific information about the child's handicap and educational needs are crucial areas. The state is responsible for education and training of the surrogate parent to ensure adequate representation of the child.

The surrogate parent has many responsibilities that must be understood and explained by the local agency. Knowledge of these responsibilities are essential if the educational needs of the child are to be met in the least restrictive environment. A surrogate parent may be dismissed from his or her role if the local agency determines that the roles and responsibilities outlined by federal and state regulations have been neglected, or the well being of the child is at risk. Shrybman (1982) listed the responsibilities of surrogate parents of handicapped children: to attend any training program the local agency offers; to be sure there are no areas of interest that conflict with their responsibilities to the child; to be involved in identification, evaluation, program development, initial placement, review placement, and reevaluation; to be knowledgeable of the child's educational needs, wishes, and concerns; to maintain confidentiality of all records; to be aware of support provided by human services in the community; and to be sure the child is receiving special education in the least restrictive environment.

REFERENCES

Federal Register. (1977). Washington, DC: U.S. Government Printing Office.

Rothenberg, D. (1996). *Grandparents as parents: A primer for schools*. (ERIC Digest No. ED401044).

Shrybman, J. A. (1982). *Due process in special education*. Rockville, MD: Aspen.

JANICE HARPER
*North Carolina Central
University*

INDIVIDUALS WITH DISABILITIES EDUCATION ACT
PARENT EDUCATION
PARENTS OF THE HANDICAPPED

SURVIVAL SKILLS

Survival skills are essential components of functional teaching. Many educators use the terms survival skills and functional teaching synonymously. Heward and Orlansky (1984) define functional skills as skills that are "frequently demanded in a student's natural environment" (p. 340). Cassidy and Shanahan (1979) suggest the term survival emphasizes the need to develop skills that will help individuals to attain personal goals and social responsibilities. A few examples of survival skills include balancing a checkbook, riding a bus, completing a job application, reading a menu, and shopping for groceries (Alcantara, 1994). Survival skills have also been extended to self-management skills in the classroom (Synder & Bambara, 1997).

Sabatino (1982) emphasized the importance of the functional curriculum model to prepare the handicapped youth for a vocational career. Examples of survival skills from this model include a word list from a driver's manual, social skills training, and using technical terms to understand career information. McDowell (1979) further stressed the need for handicapped adolescents to exhibit specific behaviors to help them function successfully in today's society and on the job. These behaviors include showing respect for others, demonstrating good manners, knowing when certain behaviors are appropriate, and learning to accept and follow directions.

Sabatino and Lanning-Ventura (1982) state that there is an important question that must be addressed by teachers of educationally handicapped students at the secondary level. When should the educational program focus on survival skills and not on overcoming educational handicaps? The answer to this question should be based on the individual characteristics of the student. However, functional teaching is most appropriate when the chances for academic gains are limited.

An essential component of survival skills in the area of reading is selection of materials. Cassidy and Shanahan (1979) identified the three basic criteria for selection as relevance, necessity, and frequency. Relevance implies considering the student's age, current level of functioning, and geographical area when selecting materials. In terms of geographical area, using materials such as a phone book or a bus schedule from a student's hometown is more appropriate than using commercial materials. Necessity suggests selecting materials that are representative of tasks required in the real world. Frequency deals with the number of times the student will deal with the materials selected. Activities such as reading menus and container labels occur often in the real world.

Potential strengths of the functional curriculum model identified by Alley and Deshler (1979) include the following: (1) students are equipped to function independently, at least over the short term in society; (2) students may be better prepared to compete for specific jobs on graduation from high school; and (3) instruction in the functional curriculum may have particular relevance for the high school junior or senior who is severely disabled (p. 50).

REFERENCES

Alcantara, P. R. (1994). Effects of videotape instructional package on purchasing skills of children with autism. *Exceptional Children*, *61*(1), 40–55.

Alley, G., & Deshler, D. (1979). *Teaching the learning disabled adolescent: Strategies and methods*. Denver: Love.

Cassidy, J., & Shanahan, T. (1979). Survival skills: Some considerations. *Journal of Reading*, *23*, 136–40.

Heward, H. L., & Orlansky, M. D. (1984). *Exceptional children*. Columbus OH: Merrill.

McDowell, R. L. (1979, May). *The emotionally disturbed adolescent* (PRISE Reporter, No. 3) (pp. 1–2). King of Prussia, PA: Pennsylvania Resource and Information Center for Special Education.

Sabatino, D. A. (1982). An educational program guide for secondary schools. In D. A. Sabatino & L. Mann (Eds.), *Diagnostic and prescriptive teaching*. Rockville, MD: Aspen.

Sabatino, D. A., & Lanning-Ventura, S. (1982). Functional teaching: Survival skills and tutoring. In D. A. Sabatino & L. Mann (Eds.), *Diagnostic and prescriptive teaching*. Rockville, MD: Aspen.

Synder, M. C., & Bambara, L. M. (1997). Teaching secondary students with learning disabilities to self-manage classroom survival skills. *Journal of Learning Disabilities*, *30*(5), 534–543.

JANICE HARPER
*North Carolina Central
University*

DAILY LIVING SKILLS
FUNCTIONAL INSTRUCTION
FUNCTIONAL SKILLS

SWEDEN, SPECIAL EDUCATION IN

See SCANDINAVIA, SPECIAL EDUCATION IN.

SWITZERLAND, SPECIAL EDUCATION IN

Education in Switzerland

Switzerland is a confederation of 26 cantons which include 2,929 political municipalities. The cantons are autonomous states. Their population varies from 14,100 to 1,178,800 citizens. For further statistic key data, refer to the internet (http://www.admin.ch/bfs/).

Switzerland does not have national school/educational legislation. The cantons remain the highest authority in this area, except for certain fields of vocational education. Article 69 of the Swiss Federal Constitution specifies the responsibilities of the 26 cantons for an adequate, sufficient, and free compulsory education. Compulsory education (pre-school, primary school, lower secondary school) is subordinate to the Cantonal Departments of Public Education. Each canton is highly independent with regard to school administration and organization, which leads to an extreme decentralization of the school authority in Switzerland. Only few institutions on the tertiary level (e.g. universities, advanced vocational training, higher vocational schools) are administered and supported by the Federal Government. The Federal Government also promotes and supports the cooperation and coordination between the cantons.

Figure 1 shows the diagram of the basic structure of the various cantonal school systems. It reveals the differences in the organization of the primary and the secondary level of compulsory education. In some cantons the decision for secondary school has to be made much earlier than in others, and depending on the canton, education on the lower secondary level lasts for three, four, or five years. On the lower secondary level, schools in most cantons provide three to four streams for pupils with different abilities and competences.

Common to all 26 educational systems are:

- *the basic structure:* pre-school (kindergarten), primary level, lower secondary level. The possibilities for educational courses on the upper secondary level, as well as on the tertiary level, depend on the size of the respective canton.
- *the compulsory education:* For all children between 6 to 7 years and 15 to 16 years, school attendance is compulsory on the primary and on the lower secondary level. Preschool is mandatory only in some cantons, but on a national level, children attend kindergarten almost without exception. Depending on the canton, preschool lasts one to two years.
- *the beginning of the school year:* All over Switzerland, the school year begins in late summer.

According to the constitution, the Swiss Conference of Cantonal Directors of Education has to guarantee a minimal intercantonal coordination. Members of the conference are the cantonal directors of education and/or other responsible representatives. The conference employs a few collaborators on a full-time basis, but mostly it mandates numerous commissions to prepare and elaborate different papers and documents. The Conference of Cantonal Directors of Education cannot promulgate any laws, it can only elaborate recommendations on behalf of the cantons.

The cantonal autonomy, mentioned above, has some

clear advantages in the field of education. On one hand, it preserves the political and cultural diversity. One example is the Romansch speaking part of Switzerland: In a country with a strictly centralistic government, Romansch would probably not have become one of the official languages at school and it would have died out sooner or later. On the other hand, it is questionable whether this strong decentralization is really necessary and whether it is still appropriate at the end of the 20th century. How is it useful to maintain a special department of education for as small units as some of the Swiss cantons? And how can school reforms be effected on a Swiss level if federalism is of such high importance? It often takes years to come to an agreement on a Swiss level, even for simple reforms like the beginning of the school year or the five-day school week.

Such examples emphasize the difficulty to effect more extensive reforms such as the integration of children with special needs, reforms which can hardly be realized in a federalistic state like Switzerland.

The Education of Children with Special Educational Needs

Pre-school Level

Small children with disabilities and/or developmental problems are taken care of by early childhood special education services. Early education of children with special needs can be extended from birth to kindergarten, special kindergarten, or the start of school. The most common kind of early childhood interventions are the mobile education programs: They take place at the child's home where the specialist works with the child and the family in their usual environment once or twice a week. In some cases, early childhood education programs take place in institutions or a clinic where the child lives. Most services are staffed with professionals with a degree in special education; some services also employ other specialists such as speech therapists, physiotherapists, or specialists for the education of children with sensory impairments. Costs for early childhood special education are borne to a great extent by the Federal Disability Insurance. Cantons, municipalities, or other public or private responsible bodies contribute according to specific agreements.

Compulsory Education Level

If a child needs special help, it usually attends a special class (tied to the regular school) or a special school (managed partly by private organizations and partly by the canton, subsidized by Federal Disability Insurance). Thus, children with special educational needs are mostly segregated from the regular school (see Figure 1). Actually, 5.6% of all school-age children are schooled in classes with a special curriculum (Bundesamt für Statistik, 1997). A good

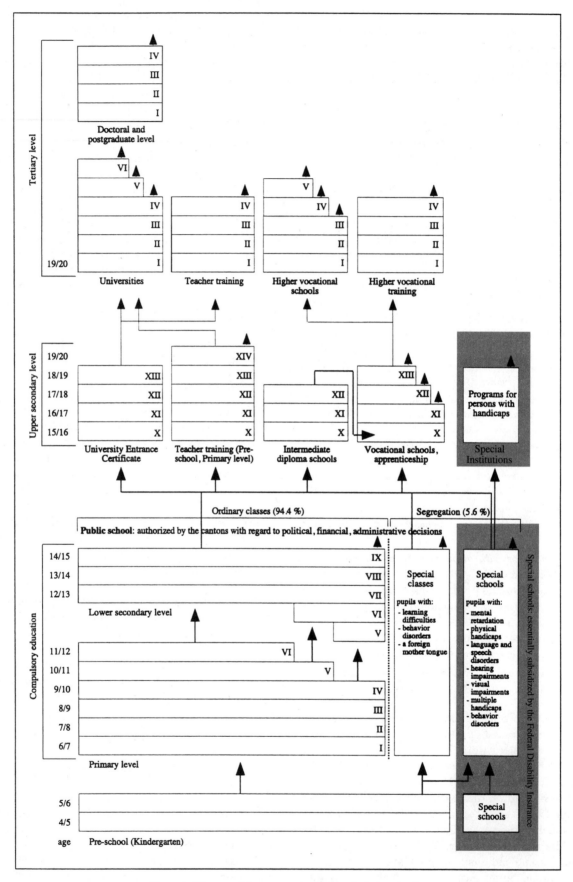

Figure 1. Diagram of the system of education in Switzerland.

number of children in regular classes, special classes, and special schools get additional support and assistance from itinerant support services (between 10% to 20%, depending on the area they live). These services mostly provide psychological counseling, speech/language and psychomotor therapy. School services also includes school medical service, school dental service, vocational counseling, and support teaching for immigrant children with a foreign mother tongue. Over the past 15 years, an increasing trend towards the integration of children with special educational needs into the regular school system can be observed; in some cantons, a restricted kind of integration is already practiced. As mentioned above, special schooling embraces all the school- and education-oriented endeavours for children and youths with special needs. On the compulsory education level, this function is assumed by special classes and special schools.

Special classes are small classes which contain no more than 12 children with relatively minor disabilities (learning difficulties, mild emotional disturbances, and mild sensory and speech/language disorders). Due to the structure and the grouping of these classes, they practice segregation, although they are mostly located in public schools and are under the political and financial authority of the Cantonal Departments of Education. Apart from the special classes for children with learning difficulties, many cantons also provide special classes for pupils with behavior disorders, speech/language impairments, physical handicaps, or a foreign native language. According to their special concept and the group of pupils, such classes should be taught by special teachers with a degree in special education. Unlike the regular classes, special classes are not homogeneous with regard to the age of their pupils. Depending on the number of pupils, they are grouped on four levels, which cover the compulsory education span: introduction classes or lower level, middle level, upper level, and vocational classes on the lower secondary level.

Special schools are open to all children with severe sensory, physical, and/or mental handicaps who benefit from Federal Disability Insurance. They hold their own school facilities, mostly connected to a residential home. Special schools are managed partly by private organizations and funds under cantonal authority and partly by the canton, and they are subsidized by the Federal Disability Insurance (IV). Special schools are relatively autonomous. IV-supported special schools are classified as follows: special schools for children and youths with severe emotional and behavior disorders, with mental and multiple handicaps, with physical handicaps, with severe visual and hearing impairments, and with specific speech/language impairments. Not all these types of special schools are run by every canton, but there are contractual agreements for intercantonal cooperation.

Most cantons have their own legal provisions for their special classes and special schools. Due to its high financial commitment, the Federal Disability Insurance has an important influence on the organization and the development of the special schools to which almost 2.5% of all Swiss pupils are referred.

Post-school Level

This level is particularly dominated by the vocational training, although part of the vocational education already takes place on the secondary level I. On the lower secondary school level, programs include early vocational exposure/choice, vocational counseling and vocational preparation courses. Schools on this level maintain a close cooperation with vocational guidance services.

After their compulsory education, a good part of those exiting special classes take up vocational training (apprenticeship) or they enter an individualized vocational program which takes into account the trainee's difficulties and problems. The vocational training runs on a dual basis: The young people are trained in practical work in a particular enterprise 3 to 4 days a week; and 1 to 2 days a week they go to a vocational training school, where they attend general education classes as well as specific classes referring to their professional field. The training ends with a Federal diploma. Some of the young persons with minor disabilities do not go through a vocational training, but they might work on their parents' farms or carry out some unskilled work.

Young people who have difficulties training for a job in the free market because they suffer from physical handicaps (visual or—rarely—hearing impairments) get their training in specialized institutions. Many of the youths with mental retardation are occupied in sheltered workshops. On their way towards professional life, young persons with disabilities are supported by professionals of the vocational guidance services, run by the Federal Disability Insurance. For further information on special education in Switzerland refer to Bürli (1993).

A Challenge for Educational Policy: The Integration of Children with Special Educational Needs into Regular Classes

Except for the integration of the increasing number of immigrant children within the Swiss educational system, the integration of children with special educational needs is one of the most difficult and intriguing challenges for school authorities in Switzerland. Looking back on the educational policy of the past years, the Swiss school authorities have made many efforts to establish and develop a highly differentiated network of special schools and special classes. Towards the end of the seventies, this differentiation reached its high actual standard.

Integration is defined as the common schooling and education of handicapped and nonhandicapped pupils in ordinary classes of the public school system, with an adequate support for the children with special educational needs. This definition does not include the school settings which only practice a more or less close cooperation between special classes and ordinary classes, even if both types of classes are located under the same roof, which may allow regular interactions between handicapped and non-handicapped pupils. Real integration is characterized by common instruction of all pupils.

How Has Integration been Implemented up to This Day?

Most of the pupils with special educational needs in regular classes in Switzerland are children with speech and language disorders. The schooling of this category of pupils in ordinary classes should rather be seen as nonsegregation than integration. Despite their special therapeutic needs, these pupils have never been systematically segregated. In Switzerland, pupils with specific, as well as complex, speech and language disorders usually remain in their regular classes, because the Swiss public school system can provide a dense network of special logopedic support. Only about 5% to 10% of the children with speech and language disorders are referred to a special school. Most of them suffer not only from speech/language impairments, but also from behavior disorders and/or learning difficulties.

The most remarkable development towards mainstreaming can be observed in the field of learning difficulties. About 15 years ago, pupils with learning difficulties could remain in their ordinary class for the first time. Besides the instruction based on the regular curriculum, they did get special assistance by a support teacher. At present, approximately 300 Swiss schools practice this kind of integration. About 8% to 12% of all pupils with learning difficulties are integrated in ordinary classes. This seems to be quite a low quota, but with regard to Swiss standards it can be considered as a rather high proportion (Bless 1995, p. 61–64).

Pupils with a foreign native language attend ordinary classes in most Swiss cantons. Usually, they get special support for improving their knowledge of the standard school language. Several cantons with a high density of population run special classes for these pupils, but they aim to integrate them in ordinary classes as soon as possible. But despite these integrative tendencies, the statistics plainly show a growing number of pupils with a foreign mother tongue in special classes (Kronig, 1996).

Pupils with physical handicaps or with hearing and visual impairments are integrated on a small scale. Two preconditions are essential for their mainstream placement. On one hand, these pupils have to be able to achieve the academic standard of their class without a differentiation of the regular curriculum. On the other hand, the schools have to be able to make available the necessary therapeutic support on their premises.

Despite the limited attempts to implement integration in Switzerland, several encouraging projects have been initiated lately. Some special schools apply new methods: They provide support for pupils with special educational needs who attend ordinary schools. For example, the staff of a special school support several mentally handicapped children attending the kindergarten of their residential area. One special school for pupils with hearing and language impairments did transform its division for the hearing impaired into a support and advisory center. They closed down their special classes, integrated the pupils in ordinary classes, and granted them a systematic regular support. These individual cases should not be overvalued, but they can give signals for further attempts.

A look back on the evolution of mainstreaming in Switzerland proves that two conditions are essential for integration:

1. *Integration must not cause any further expenses.*

   The Federal Disability Insurance (IV) is of high importance for the development of integration. The IV has an impeding influence on all integrative efforts, as it only subsidizes education of pupils with special educational needs in special schools and classes. As the Federal Disability Insurance contributes largely to school tuition, board, and lodging, the cantons—which are responsible for the schooling and education of mentally handicapped children—are not interested in integrating these pupils. However, some of the enactments of the Federal Disability Insurance make it possible to provide an integrative pedagogic and therapeutic care for pupils who need speech therapy, psychomotor therapy, or training in hearing and lip-reading. As long as integrative measures do not cause any further expenditures, the cantons are willing to back them up. If integrative measures exceed regular expenses, the cantons stop such efforts. For example, the integration of pupils with learning difficulties does not cause any problems because the cantons finance both ordinary classes and special classes (see figure 1); therefore it does not matter in what classes these pupils are schooled. Pupils with speech and language impairments can be mainstreamed, because the Federal Disability Insurance Days for their special support without having these pupils referred to a special school.

2. *Integration must not disturb the regular teaching in the classroom.*

   As long as classroom instruction can be accomplished in its regular way, integration is accepted. As soon as teachers have to individualize their lessons beyond a certain degree, integration does not have a good chance. For instance, pupils with hearing impairments and additional severe learning difficulties are rarely taught in ordinary classes, because integrating these children asks for a high degree of differentiation and individualization.

How Can the Actual and the Future Development of Integration Be Assessed?

If we take into consideration the amount of integrated pupils, we can observe neither a slowdown nor a standstill. If we consider the categories of pupils who are integrated into mainstream education, integration seems to have come to a standstill, because many groups of children with special educational needs—particularly the mentally handicapped pupils—are excluded from integrative schooling. As long as the financial conditions and structures for the disabled in Switzerland are not fundamentally changed, true and real integration—that means common education and schooling of all children—will never be possible. Only a basic reorganization of the financial system can open the way to school reforms which aim at integration in the true sense of the word.

The following determinants do or may obstruct a further reorganization of the Swiss system of education in favor of true integration:

- A political system with 26 autonomous Ministries of Education is not very flexible with regard to a reorganization of the educational system within a useful period.
- On an all-Swiss level, there is no strong political will to support integration.
- Financial resources set a limit to integration. The structures of financing the disabled in Switzerland have been drawn up in view of segregation. They corroborate the segregation of the disabled and they

place at a disadvantage all the cantons which strive for an extensive integration.

- Unlike the advocates for integration, the special schools can rely on an efficient lobby. Most of the boards of directors of special schools can count on the honorary support of popular politicians and of other well-known personalities of regional or cantonal importance.
- Generally, the attitude of the majority of teachers towards integration is rather ambivalent. Basically, teachers recommend and support integrative ideas and efforts, but when it comes to realize such ideas and efforts, they are rather cautious and reserved.
- Compared to Germany, Austria, or other countries, Switzerland does not have any serious parents' movement in favor of the handicapped.

An extensive evaluation of integrative trends and tendencies within the Swiss educational system cannot be restricted to listing and classifying specific cases of realized integration. Such an approach to integration is liable to consider only one specific aspect of the reality. Another important aspect is the constant study of the relevant statistic data (Bundesamt für Statistik, 1997). Contrary to the widespread view of numerous politicians and professionals or specialists in the field of education, the Swiss educational system has become more and more intolerant towards children with specific educational needs. Figure 2 shows a continuous increase of segregated children since the school year 1983/84 (4.26%). In 1995/96, their number

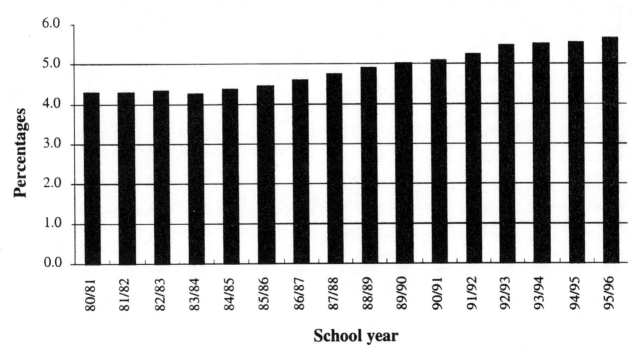

Figure 2. Percentage quota of segregated pupils in special classes and schools from 1980/81 to 1995/96, calculated on the basis of the total number of pupils of the primer and the lower secondary level (compulsory education).

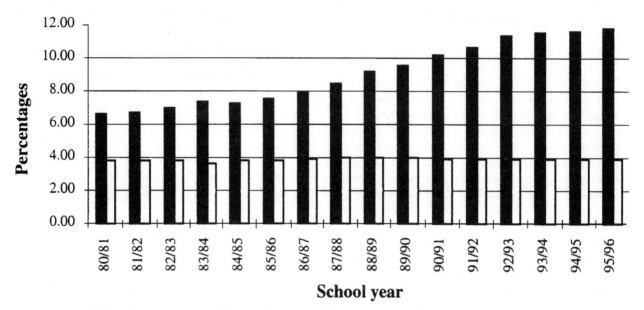

Figure 3. Percentage quota of Swiss children and children of immigrant families in special classes and schools from 1980/81 to 1995/96, calculated on the basis of the total number of pupils in compulsory education.

equaled 5.63%. It is remarkable that the number of segregated children increases parallel to the beginning and intensifying discussion on integration.

How can this increasing quota of segregated pupils be explained? Up to this day, no special school and only few special classes have been closed down, despite all integrative efforts. Thus, the special institutions remain an option for the education of children with special needs. It is true that more and more of these children are integrated into the regular schools, but, on the other hand, the loss of such children is offset by segregating other groups of pupils, mostly children of immigrant families (see figure 3).

Special classes and schools are still used—or misused—to normalize the regular school. But over the past years, the segregation policy has changed. Actually, more immigrant children are referred to special classes, which initially had been set up for children with minor disabilities.

To sum up the latest developments in the field of special education, we notice that the schools have considerable trouble managing the growing diversity of their pupils. Despite the intensified discussion on integration of the past years, our schools are still not apt to more integration. On the contrary, they have even become more intolerant of children who do not comply with their standards.

REFERENCES

Bless, G. (1995). *Zur Wirksamkeit der Integration. Forschungsüberblick, praktische Umsetzung einer integrativen Schulform, Untersuchungen zum Lernfortschritt.* BernStuttgart-Wien: Haupt-Verlag.

Bless, G. (1997). *Integration in the ordinary school in Switzerland.* In OECD (Organisation for Economic Cooperation and Development), *Implementing Inclusive Education.* OECD Proceedings—Centre for Educational Research and Innovation. Paris.

Bundesamt für Statistik. (1997). *Schülerinnen, Schüler und Studierende 1995/96.* Bern. Bundesamt für Statistik (BFS).

Bürli, A. (1993). *Special Education in Switzerland.* Aspects 50. Lucerne: Edition SZH. Swiss Institute for Special Education.

Kronig, W. (1996) *Besorgniserregende Entwicklungen in der schulischen Zuweisungspraxis bei ausländischen Kindern mit Lernschwierigkeiten.* Vierteljahresschrift für Heilpädagogik und ihre Nachbargebiete (VHN).

OECD (Organization for Economic Cooperation and Development). (1997). *Education at a Glance 1997: OECD Indicators.* Paris.

GÉRARD BLESS
University of Fribourg

WESTERN EUROPE, SPECIAL EDUCATION IN

SYDENHAM'S CHOREA

Sydenham's chorea is more commonly known as St. Vitus' Dance, but it also may be called minor chorea, rheumatic chorea, or acute chorea. It is generally regarded as an inflammatory complication of rheumatic fever, tonsillitis, or other infection; it also can be associated with pregnancy (chorea gravidarum). The condition is most prevalent in young girls between the ages of 5 and 15 and more common in temperate climates during summer and early fall. The condition has declined substantially in recent years owing to a similar decline in rheumatic fever. It is characterized by involuntary choreic movements throughout the body and occurs in about 10% of rheumatic attacks.

Choreic movements are rapid, purposeless, short lasting, and nonrepetitive. The movements usually begin in one limb and flow to many different parts of the body; they may resemble athetoid cerebral palsy. Fidgety behavior, clumsiness, dropping of objects, facial grimacing, awkward gait, and changes in voice or slurred speech are common symptoms that may occur at onset. A month or more may pass before medical attention is sought because these symptoms initially may be mild. Anxiety, irritability, and emotional instability also may occur because of the uncontrolled movements. The involuntary motions disappear during sleep and occasionally are suppressed by rest, sedation, or attempts at voluntary control. Sydenham's chorea is nonfatal and recovery usually occurs within 2 to 6 months. Recurrence may happen two or three times over a period of years in almost one-third of the people affected.

Differential diagnosis depends on ruling out other causes through history and laboratory studies. There are no characteristic laboratory abnormalities, and pathologic studies suggest scattered lesions in the basal ganglia, cerebellum, and brain stem. No deficits in muscle strength or sensory perception are found during neurologic examination. The course of the impairment is variable and difficult to measure because of its gradual diminution.

There is no specific treatment, but some medications (phenobarbital, diazepam, perphenazine, or haloperidol) can be effective in reducing chorea. In most situations, the person with Sydenham's is encouraged to return to school or work, even if residual symptoms continue. In severe cases, protection from self-injury by using restraints may be necessary. The prognosis for recovery is variable but the condition inevitably subsides. Reassurance that the condition is self-limiting and eventually will decline without residual impairment is in order for people with Sydenham's, their families, teachers, and classmates. Behavioral problems, mild motor abnormalities, and poor performance in psychometric testing have been reported after the chorea dissipates. It is important that affected individuals receive Therapeutic Support (Moore, 1996).

REFERENCES

Berkow, R. (Ed.). (1982). *Merck Manual* (14th ed.) (pp. 87–88). Rahway, NJ: Merck, Sharp, & Dohme Research Laboratories.

Bird, M. T., Palkes, H., & Prensky, A. L. (1976). A follow-up study of Sydenham's chorea. *Neurology, 26*, 601–606.

Fahn, S. (1985). Neurologic and behavioral diseases. In J. Wyngaarden & L. Smith, Jr. (Eds.), *Cecil textbook of medicine* (17th ed., pp. 2074–2075). Philadelphia: Saunders.

Magalini, S., & Scarascia, E. (1981). *Dictionary of medical syndromes* (2nd ed., pp. 882–883). Philadelphia: Lippincott.

Merritt, H. H. (1979). *A textbook of neurology* (6th ed.). Philadelphia: Lea & Febiger.

Moore, D. (1996). Neuropsychiatric aspects of Sydenham's chorea: A comprehensive review. *Journal of Clinical Psychiatry, 57*(9), 407–414.

Nuasieda, P. A., Grossman, B. J., Koller, W. C., Weiner, W. J., & Klawans, H. L. (1980). Sydenham's chorea: An update. *Neurology, 30*, 331–334.

DANIEL D. LIPKA
*Lincoln Way Special Education
Regional Resource Center*

CHOREA
HUNTINGTON'S CHOREA

SYNAPSES

The synapse is the structure that mediates the effects of a nerve impulse on a target cell, permitting communication among nerve cells, muscles, and glands. It is a synapse that joins the terminal end of an axon of one neuron with the dendrites or cell body of another. The synapse was first described by Sir Charles Sherrington in 1897. The word itself means connection.

Messages arrive at the synapse in the form of action potentials. Synaptic potentials are triggered by action potentials; they in turn trigger subsequent action potentials, continuing the neural message on to its destination. While action potentials vary in frequency, they do not vary in form or magnitude. It is the synaptic potential that is responsible for variance in the nervous system.

The synaptic terminals on the end tips of axons take on various forms such as ball-like endings (boutons), nobs, spines, and rings. These terminals almost, but not quite, make contact with a part of another neuron (usually a dendrite or occasionally an axon or cell body). The space between the terminal of one neuron and the other neuron is called the synaptic cleft. This cleft is miniscule, typically on the order of about 200 angstroms. Transmission time across the synaptic cleft is approximately .3 to 1.0 msec.

Synaptic transmission can be electrical or chemical, although the former is uncommon in the mammalian brain (Gazzaniga, Steen, & Volpe, 1979). With chemical transmission, one cell, the presynaptic, secretes molecules that cross a synaptic cleft and join with a postsynaptic cell. The presynaptic cell endings contain mitochondria and synaptic vesicles that hold various neurotransmitters. The neurotransmitter substances are released in tiny packettes called quanta. These substances can serve excitatory or inhibitory purposes, and not all are currently identified. However, major excitatory neurotransmitters include acetylcholine, noradrenalin, seratonin, and dopamine. Important inhibitory transmitters include gamma-aminobutric acid (GABA) and glutamate. Specific receptor molecules that receive these neurotransmitters have been identified on the postsynaptic cell.

Synapses generally are classified as axiodendritic or axiosomatic. The typical pattern is axiodendritic; this pattern occurs when an axon meets a dendrite. Somewhat less common is the axiosomatic pattern, in which an axon meets a cell body.

REFERENCES

Barr, M. D. (1979). *The human nervous system: An anatomic viewpoint* (3rd ed.). New York: Harper & Row.

Gazzaniga, M., Steen, D., & Volpe, B. T. (1979). *Functional neuroscience.* New York: Harper & Row.

DANNY WEDDING
Marshall University

DENDRITES
DOPAMINE

SYNTACTIC DEFICIENCIES

See CHILDHOOD APHASIA, LANGUAGE DISORDERS EXPRESSIVE; LANGUAGE DISORDERS.

SYSTEMS OF CLASSIFICATION

A system of classification can be developed in an effort to identify individuals as members of one of the major handicapping conditions (e.g., learning disabilities), or it may be used to provide a subclassification within a major area of exceptionality (e.g., Down's syndrome as a subcategory of mental retardation). Contemporary special education services rely heavily on the classification of general handicapping conditions and, to lesser extent, on subclassifications.

The historical origins of the use of classification systems are dominated by two events. First, special education represents a unique educational development derived from the discipline of psychology. As such, it emerged in light of that discipline's intense interest in the measurement and study of individual differences. Subsequent refinements in measurement, including the development of classification

systems based on reliable individual differences, were transferred to special education practice in the first part of the twentieth century. A second related influence arose from the attempts of early special educators to provide a science of treatment. That is, the study of individual differences led to the acceptance of a nosological orientation in treatment. Long practiced in medicine, the nosological orientation presumes that disorders can be isolated with reference to etiology, that etiology can ultimately be treated, and that subsequent cases can be similarly addressed (i.e., treatment proceeds from symptom to diagnosis of etiology to specification of treatment). In this approach, the development of a precise system of classification and subclassification is essential.

Possibly the most influential classification system now in effect is that provided within Individuals with Disabilities Education Act. Ysseldyke and Algozzine (1984) indicate that through this legislation, the U.S. Department of Education recognizes 11 categories of exceptionality, although some states recognize more or less categories. In most states, the categories represent an effective determinant of service: If an individual is not a member of the specified handicapping condition, services are not mandated. Thus, systems of classification, and related entry procedures, are essential in the selection process that ultimately determines entrance to special education.

A number of subclassification systems exist within the broad categories of exceptionality. Most of these attempt to suggest, if not prescribe, the general course of diagnosis and treatment. Two well-known systems typify this approach. The *Diagnostic and Statistical Manual of Mental Disorders* (fourth edition; DSM IV) is a psychiatrically derived classification system for use with children and adults with emotional disorders. The DSM IV is the standard classification system within mental health facilities in the United States, though it has far less official influence in public education. In DSM IV, disorders are grouped into five major divisions (intellectual, behavioral, emotional, physical, and developmental). Each division is further partitioned into specific disorders as defined by rigid diagnostic criteria. Individuals thus receive codes that indicate the diagnosed handicaps. Recent criticisms suggest that this system is archaic and needs to be redefined. Psychiatric classification of personality disorders, for example, could be classified in terms of severity and subtype (Tyrer, 1996).

A second classification system is used in the diagnosis and treatment of mental retardation. The American Association on Mental Deficiency classification system (Grossman, 1983) is based on a number of factors, including intelligence and adaptive behavior. In this system, the degree of retardation is specified as mild, moderate, severe, or profound. The intent of the system is clearly to specify training and structural support needs.

It is erroneous to conclude that these two well-accepted classification systems are acceptable to all agencies, that alternatives are nonexistent, or that particular systems are not revised over time. For example, DSM IV is in the fourth substantially revised edition and tends not to be used in schools; alternatives such as Quay's (1964) system are often favored. Nor is there a paucity of systems. MacMillan (1982) reports at least 10 systems have been used in the twentieth century with the mentally retarded. Of these, four are now in common use. Clearly, classification systems are modified in response to the influence of social pressures, research bases, and professional opinions.

A number of theoretical and pragmatic pitfalls are evident in current classification systems. Three are particularly germane. First, the fact that multiple classification systems exist and are endorsed by various agencies creates opportunities for classification and service provision irregularities. Second, there is question as to whether behavioral diagnostic techniques possess the necessary reliability and validity to provide precise classification; error in measurement and misassignment to categories is possible (Salvia & Ysseldyke, 1985). Third, the significance of classification systems based on etiology may prove to be less important to the behavioral than the medical sciences. That is, treatment links have generally not been established between etiological diagnosis and behavioral treatment. Such links may prove difficult or impossible to achieve (Neisworth & Greer, 1975).

Despite these criticisms, classification systems remain an important consideration for special education. Kauffman (1977) provided a rationale for the continuation of attempts to classify behavior: classification is a fundamental aspect of any developing science of behavior; classification is of importance in organizing and communicating information; and classification systems, if scientifically investigated, may ultimately assist in the prediction of behavior and offer insights into the preferred method of treatment. As noted by Kauffman (1977), the alternative to continued development of classification systems is "an educational methodology that relies on attempts to fit interventions to disorders by random choice, intuition, or trial and error" (p. 27).

REFERENCES

American Psychiatric Association. (1994). *Diagnostic and statistical manual of mental disorders* (4th ed.). Washington, DC: American Psychiatric Association.

Grossman, H. J. (Ed.). (1983). *Manual on terminology and classification in mental retardation* (3rd ed.). Washington, DC: American Association on Mental Deficiency.

Kauffman, J. M. (1977). *Characteristics of children's behavior disorders*. Columbus, OH: Merrill.

MacMillan, D. L. (1982). *Mental retardation in school and society* (2nd ed.). Boston: Little, Brown.

Neisworth, J. T., & Green, J. G. (1975). Functional similarities of learning disabilities and mild retardation. *Exceptional Children, 42*, 17–21.

Quay, H. C. (1964). Dimensions of personality in delinquent boys as inferred from factor analysis of case history data. *Child Development, 35*, 479–484.

Salvia, J., & Ysseldyke, J. E. (1985). *Assessment in special and remedial education* (3rd ed.). Boston: Houghton Mifflin.

Tyrer, P. (1996) New ways of classifying personality disorder. *Psychiatrist, 7*(1), 43–48.

Ysseldyke, J. E., & Algozzine, B. (1984). *Introduction to special education*. Boston: Houghton Mifflin.

Ted L. Miller
University of Tennessee

DIAGNOSTIC AND STATISTICAL MANUAL OF MENTAL DISORDERS (DSM IV)
LEARNER TAXONOMIES

SYSTEM OF MULTICULTURAL PLURALISTIC ASSESSMENT (SOMPA)

The System of Multicultural Pluralistic Assessment (SOMPA) (Mercer & Lewis, 1979) was designed to provide a comprehensive measure of the cognitive abilities, perceptual-motor abilities, sociocultural background, and adaptive behavior of children ages 5 through 11 years. It employs three models of assessment and attempts to integrate them into a comprehensive assessment: (1) the medical model, defined as any abnormal organic condition interfering with physiological functioning; (2) the social system model, determined principally from labeling theory and social deviance perspectives taken from the field of sociology, which attempts to correct the "Anglo conformity" biases of the test developers who have designed IQ tests for the last 80 years; and (3) the pluralistic model, which compares the scores of a child with the performance levels of children of a similar ethclass (that is, the same demographic, socioeconomic, and cultural background) correcting for any score discrepancies with the white middle class. English and Spanish language versions of the scale are available.

The SOMPA is a complex and somewhat innovative system of assessment designed to ameliorate much of the conflict over assessment in the schools. The senior author, Mercer, a sociologist, conceptualized SOMPA in the late 1960s and early 1970s from her work in sociology's labeling theory and her sociological surveys and studies of mental retardation, particularly mild mental retardation, as a sociocultural phenomenon. The SOMPA has been extensively reviewed and debated (Humphreys, 1985; Nuttall, 1979; Reynolds, 1985; Reynolds & Brown, 1984; Sandoval, 1985). Unfortunately, presentation of the SOMPA for clinical application as opposed to pure research appears to have been premature. Major conceptual and technical issues pertaining to the scale have not been resolved adequately, even considering that a complete resolution of most of these issues is not possible. As a result, the SOMPA has contributed to the controversy over assessment practices in the schools rather than moved the field closer to a resolution. Even though controversy frequently can be stimulating to a discipline, in many ways, SOMPA has polarized the assessment community.

One of the major conceptual problems of the SOMPA centers around its primary underlying assumption. Mercer developed the SOMPA in response to her acceptance of the cultural test bias hypothesis. Briefly stated, this hypothesis contends that all racial, ethnic, socioeconomic, or other demographically based group differences on mental tests are due to artifacts of the tests themselves and do not reflect real differences. According to Mercer and Lewis, this is due to the extent of Anglocentrism (degree of adherence to white middle-class values, norms, and culture) apparent in most, if not all, mental measurements. In accepting this hypothesis as fundamentally correct, Mercer relies primarily on the mean differences definition of bias, which states that any differences in mean levels of performance among racial or ethnic groups on any mental scale is prima facie evidence of bias. The principal purpose of the SOMPA is to remove this bias by providing a correct estimate of intellectual abilities, an estimated learning potential (ELP). While adding a "correction factor" to the obtained IQs of disadvantaged children is not a new idea, the SOMPA corrections are unique in their objectivity and in having a clearly articulated, if controversial, basis. The corrections are based on the child's social-cultural characteristics and equate the mean IQs of blacks, whites, and Hispanics with varying other cultural characteristics such as family structure and degree of urban acculturation.

Unfortunately for the SOMPA, its underlying assumption that mean differences among sociocultural groups indicate cultural bias in tests is the single most rejected of all definitions of test bias by serious psychometricians researching the cultural test bias hypothesis (Jensen, 1980; Reynolds, 1982). The conceptual basis for the SOMPA is far more controversial than it appears in the test manuals and is indeed open to serious question. If other approaches to the cultural test bias hypothesis had demonstrated the existence of bias, then the need for a resolution to the problem such as proposed by Mercer would remain tenable. However, the large body of evidence regarding the cultural test bias hypothesis, gathered primarily over the last decade, has failed to substantiate popular claims of bias in the assessment of native-born, ethnic minorities. For the most part, the psychometric characteristics of well-designed and carefully standardized tests of intelligence such as the Wechsler scale have been shown to be substantially equivalent across ethnic groups (Jensen, 1980; Reynolds, 1982).

If this argument is dismissed and Mercer's contentions regarding test bias accepted, other serious conceptual is-

sues remain. The ELP, a regression-based transformation of Wechsler IQs, is said to provide a good estimate of the child's innate intelligence or potential to profit from schooling. Such a claim is difficult to support under any circumstances. It is unlikely that we will ever be able to assess innate ability since environment begins to impact the organism at the moment of conception. We are left only with the possibility of observing the phenotypic construct. Furthermore, as of this writing, no evidence exists relating ELP to any other relevant criteria (Reschly, 1982).

Others have noted substantial agreement in criticisms of the SOMPA ELP, particularly regarding its construct validity (Humphreys, 1985; Reschly, 1982). Humphreys, (1985) argues that "Estimated learning potential is a thoroughly undesirable construct. Many people want to hear and believe the misinformation furnished by ethclass norms, but this is dangerous for it solves no real problems. It is conceivable, of course, that several generations from now black and Hispanic performance on standard tests of intelligence and achievement might equal the white majority. In this limited sense, ethclass norms might not misinform, but an inference that requires 50 years or more to validate helps little in dealing with today's children. They need higher scores on measures of reading, listening, writing, computing, mathematics, and science, not ethclass IQs" (p. 1519). The ELP may in fact be misleading and result in a denial of special education services to children who are seriously at risk of academic failure or already experiencing such failure. As Reschly has stated, "All of the direct uses of ELP at present and in the foreseeable future are questionable" (p. 242). Equally controversial, even in Mercer's home field of sociology, is labeling theory, another important concept in the establishment of the need for a system like SOMPA. If we accept the contention that false negatives are more desirable than false positives in the diagnosis of mental retardation, a check on the utility function tells us that it would most likely be best to diagnose no children as mentally retarded since the incidence in Mercer's model in particular is far less than 3%.

Technical problems are also evident in the development and application of the concept of ELP. As noted, the ELP is a regression-based transformation of Wechsler IQs to a scale with a mean of 100 and standard deviation of 15 independent of a child's sociocultural characteristics. These transformations are made on the basis of the SOMPA sociocultural scales. Based on data derived during the norming of the SOMPA, regression equations were derived for determining the ELP. The stability of these regression equations and their generalizability to children outside the standardization sample have been called into question. Since the SOMPA was not normed on a stratified random sample of children nationwide, but rather on a sampling restricted to California, generalizability studies received some priority on the measure's publication. Regression equations derived from samples from other states, notably

Texas and Arizona, have not been at all similar to the original equations; even the multiple R between the various sociocultural variables and Wechsler IQ varies substantially (i.e., from .30 to .60 in some cases) across states and across ethnic groups (Reschly, 1982). Given the state of contemporary applied psychometrics and the sophisticated normative sampling of such scales as the Wechsler series and the recent Kaufman Assessment Battery for Children, the failure to provide an adequate standardization sample for the SOMPA is inexcusable and not characteristic of the publisher.

The reliability of the ELP will also be dependent to a large extent on the stability of the sociocultural scales from which the corrections to the obtained Wechsler IQs are derived. The stability of these scores has been seriously questioned in at least one recent study. Over a 4-year period, Wilkinson and Oakland (1983b) report test-retest correlations that range from .39 to the high .90s across scales. Within scales and across demographic groupings such as race, sex, and socioeconomic status, the correlations also vary considerably, pointing up the real possibility of bias in the SOMPA. Apparently the ELP can change dramatically for individual children over a 4-year period (given that half of the stability coefficients reported for the SOMPA sociocultural scales are below .80), a result that seems antithetical to the entire concept of the ELP.

Stability of other SOMPA scales that should be relative stable has also been questioned. The SOMPA health history inventory shows test-retest reliability coefficients minus ranging from −.08 (!) to .96. Considerable differences are evident within scales across demographic groupings as well. The trauma scale shows a stability coefficient of .23 for males and .74 for females (Wilkinson & Oakland, 1983a). Prepostnatal scores show a stability of .78 for whites and .96 for blacks, a scale that should remain highly stable since the SOMPA begins at age 5 years.

These are but a few of the conceptual and technical issues plaguing the SOMPA. Much work was needed on the SOMPA prior to its presentation for practical application, work that was not done. The conceptual issues in particular needed clarification. Nevertheless, the SOMPA does have one component that may be useful.

There are relatively few good measures of adaptive behavior available to clinicians. The Adaptive Behavior Inventory for Children (ABIC), developed to accompany the SOMPA as an integral part of the scale, is one of the promising current adaptive behavior measures for children ages 5 to 11 years. Though lengthy, somewhat cumbersome, and suffering from a lack of high-quality normative data, the ABIC may be useful in a comprehensive assessment, especially when mental retardation or emotional disturbance are viable possibilities. However, the scaling of the ABIC does leave something to be desired. The use of a scaled score system with a mean of 50 and a standard deviation of 15 adds to the difficulty of using the whole system; a well-known or common scale such as T-scores (mean = 50, standard deviation = 10), or an IQ-based scale (mean = 100, standard deviation = 15), would have enhanced its interpretability. Though Mercer and Lewis recommend that only the complete SOMPA should be used, the ABIC is able to stand on its own and can (and should) be abstracted from the SOMPA and used in the assessment of adaptive behavior. Those who do not wish to violate the author's recommendation in this regard should consider the AAMD Adaptive Behavior Scale, public school version, or the 1984 revision of the Vineland Social Maturity Scales (VABS) as excellent alternatives. The ABIC does need much more validity data, however, and until it is available, these alternative measures may be more desirable; though the VABS was published in 1984, it already has more available data than the ABIC.

On another level, the SOMPA must be questioned as an assessment system for children especially. The SOMPA is designed primarily as a means of providing a fairer scheme of classifying children into diagnostic categories. It has clearly not been validated adequately for this purpose. However, a more far-reaching concern to the clinician working with children experiencing school failure is the development of programs for the habilitation of learning. The SOMPA, outside of the ABIC, provides no real clues to the development of such interventions. This is especially damaging to practical applications of the SOMPA because it requires a substantial investment of professional time to be properly administered. The commitment of so much time and effort to an assessment system that does not provide considerable help with the development of individual educational programs cannot be justified in any kind of cost-benefit analysis. The emphasis on prevention-intervention-habilitation is more in keeping with the needs of the field.

The SOMPA cannot be recommended for use at this time. Its conceptual, technical, and practical problems are simply too great. Nevertheless, it was an innovative, gallant effort at resolving the conflict over assessment practices in the schools. Current evidence would point to failure; however, it may serve as a springboard in some ways for future assessment systems if we attend to the problems inherent in this scale.

REFERENCES

Humphreys, L. G. (1985). Review of System of Multicultural Pluralistic Assessment. In J. V. Mitchell (Ed.), *Ninth mental measurements yearbook*. Lincoln, NE: Buros Institute.

Jensen, A. R. (1980). *Bias in mental testing*. New York: Free Press.

Mercer, J., & Lewis, J. (1979). *System of Multicultural Pluralistic Assessment*. New York: The Psychological Corporation.

Nuttall, E. V. (1979). Review of System of Multicultural Pluralistic Assessment. *Journal of Educational Measurement, 16,* 285–290.

Reschly, D. J. (1982). Assessing mild mental retardation: The influence of adaptive behavior, sociocultural status, and prospects for nonbiased assessment. In C. R. Reynolds & T. B. Gutkin (Eds.), *The handbook of school psychology*. New York: Wiley.

Reynolds, C. R. (1982). The problem of bias in psychological assessment. In C. R. Reynolds & T. B. Gutkin (Eds.), *The handbook of school psychology*. New York: Wiley.

Reynolds, C. R. (1985). Review of System of Multicultural Pluralistic Assessment. In J. V. Mitchell (Ed.), *Ninth mental measurements yearbook*. Lincoln, NE: Buros Institute.

Reynolds, C. R., & Brown, R. T. (Eds.). (1984). *Perspectives on bias in mental testings*. New York: Plenum.

Sandoval, J. (1985). Review of System of Multicultural Pluralistic Assessment. In J. V. Mitchell (Ed.), *Ninth mental measurements yearbook*. Lincoln, NE: Buros Institute.

Wilkinson, C. Y., & Oakland, T. (1983a, August). *Stability of the SOMPA's health history inventory*. Paper presented to the annual meeting of the American Psychological Association, Anaheim, CA.

Wilkinson, C. Y., & Oakland, T. (1983b, August). *Stability of the SOMPA's sociocultural modalities*. Paper presented to the annual meeting of the American Psychological Association, Anaheim, CA.

CECIL R. REYNOLDS
Texas A & M University

ADAPTIVE BEHAVIOR
CULTURAL BIAS IN TESTING
MERCER, JANE R.
VINELAND ADAPTIVE BEHAVIOR SCALES

T

TACHISTOSCOPE

The tachistoscope, or t-scope, is an instrument for presenting visual stimuli for very brief times at a controlled level of illumination (Stang & Wrightsman, 1981). The t-scope may be a self-contained unit or mounted on a slide projector.

Often the goal of tachistoscopic presentation is to determine the threshold at which subjects verbally report recognition of a stimulus. Research using the tachistoscope also has been carried out concerning the existence of subliminal perception where stimuli are said to affect behavior below the conscious threshold of perception.

Reading involves very briefly viewing words; the tachistoscopic task was broadly assumed to mimic the requirements faced by skilled readers. Despite questions of the applicability of t-scope research to everyday reading tasks, a variety of components of reading have been examined in the presence of varying speeds of presentation and levels of illumination. The threshold of word recognition can be determined and models of skilled reading can be constructed (Carr & Pollatsek, 1985; Gough, 1984; Mewhort & Campbell, 1981). The performance of skilled and disabled readers can be compared to determine the differences that might be diagnostically significant (Pirozzollo, 1979).

REFERENCES

Carr, T., & Pollatsek, A. (1985). Recognizing printed words: A look at current models. In D. Besner, T. G. Waller, & G. E. Mackinnon (Eds.), *Reading research: Advances in theory and practice* (Vol. 5, pp. 2–82). Orlando, FL: Academic.

Gough, P. B. (1984). Word recognition. In P. D. Pearsen (Ed.), *Handbook of reading research* (pp. 225–291). New York: Longman.

Mewhort, D. J. K., & Campbell, A. J. (1981). Toward a model of skilled reading performance: An analysis of performance in tachistoscopic tasks. In G. E. Mackinnon & T. G. Waller (Eds.), *Reading research: Advances in theory and practice* (Vol. 1.3, pp. 39–118). New York: Academic.

Pirozzolo, F. J. (1979). *The neuropsychology of developmental reading disorders*. New York: Praeger.

Stang, D., & Wrightsman, L. (1981). *Dictionary of social behavior and social research methods*. Monterey, CA: Brooks–Cole.

LEE ANDERSON JACKSON, JR.
University of North Carolina at Wilmington

PERCEPTUAL SPAN

TAIWAN, SPECIAL EDUCATION IN

Historical Overview

The early development of special education in Taiwan has its root in the tenets of Confucianism: "education for all" and "instruction by potential." In this context, efforts are made both by government agencies and private sectors to ensure that all exceptional individuals are entitled to a right to appropriate education. The protocol of educational alternatives for students with disabilities in Taiwan can be traced back to the late years of the nineteenth century. Interestingly, early attempts to educate the individuals with disabilities were inaugurated by the clergy. To illustrate, the first special day school (built in 1886 for children who are deaf and mute) was funded by English churches and staffed by ministers. This day school served as a catalyst for establishment of similar facilities throughout the island. Public schools did not provide special education programs until 1961, when the Dong-Men elementary school of Taipei developed the first self-contained class of its kind for children with emotional disturbances.

Educational programs for children with mental retardation (MR) have played a major role in the development of special education within the public schools. Actually, special education and classes for students with MR were considered one and the same. The confusion was attributed to overemphasis on developing programs for MR children and the lack of programs for other exceptional children and youth, which in turn was associated with the overrepresentation of students with mental retardation.

Few efforts had been organized before the 1980s to fight for the rights of populations with disabilities. The stimulus for increased public interest in and governmental attention to the welfare of people with disabilities is attributed in part to political parties and academic scholars who had their advanced studies abroad. In the late 1970s as the major opposition political party emerged, the rights movement for people with handicaps became overwhelming. The outcome has been passage of the Special Education Act of 1984 and similar legislation, plus significant changes in schools and communities.

The Special Education Act of 1984 provides the framework for special education policies and its regulations delineate a broad guideline for criteria for the identification, placement, and delivery of educational services for children with special needs. Specifications of the regulations include classroom organization, instructional objectives, and teaching methods and materials. Much of the impetus for the laws passed in the 1980s stems from issues surrounding education of children with MR, including (a) the assumed negative impact of labels, (b) expansion of special class placement, and (c) excessive reliance on single assessment measures—primarily the intelligence test.

In each locality, the Ministry of Education develops a Special Education Coordination Committee in charge of programming and monitoring of enforcement of laws and regulations associated with special education. The local government designates the Identification, Placement and Consultation Committee (IPC) to deal with special education practices in schools. The revised Special Education Act of 1997 is characterized by an addition of zero rejects to the array of special services and an extension of children from school-aged to preschool. Specifically, public schools are now open by law to all children and youths with disabilities aged 3 to 18.

Current Status

Currently, each county develops the IPC Committee. Homeroom teachers refer students with special needs. Referral is delivered to the committee, which initiates assessments and makes the final decision. The committee also recommends (based on the least-restrictive principle) the placement options ranging from regular classes to institutions. Children with disabilities come in the following categories: mental retardation, visual impairments, hearing impairments, language disorders, physical handicaps, health impairments, behavioral disorders, learning disabilities, and multiple handicaps. The current policy mandates that students with mild disabilities are placed in the regular classes with resource room services; those with moderate impairments are placed in the self-contained classes; and those with severe and profound handicaps are recommended to special schools and institutions respectively.

To reduce stigmatization to the minimum, schools have long adopted terms with educational implications. The *wisdom-developing* designation, for example, is used to refer to education associated with MR, *illumination-developing* designation for visual impairments and *love-developing* for physical handicaps. Thus, not only do we have *Taipei Wisdom-Developing School* and *Tainan Illumination-Developing School,* but in the regular school there are *audition-developing* classes for students with hearing impairments.

Prospectus

Many educational problems of exceptional children and youth can be prevented or minimized through the provision of comprehensive services. The revised Special Education Act of 1997 applies to handicapped individuals ages 3–18. Many more special needs children are eligible for special education services. The role of the public school has been extended both in the nature of services and the ages of students served. Identification of exceptional children and high-risk children as infants or preschoolers has become a widespread practice, and early childhood programs designed to enhance development of the handicapped and prepare them for school have been demonstrated to be effective. Several metropolitan cities have already mandated the provision of preschool programs for children with disabilities. Career programs designed specifically for post-junior-high adolescents are under assessment across the island and the programs are gaining in popularity. Community resources are being applied to help young adults with handicaps establish themselves as active members of the community.

While full inclusion is in practice in the West, it appears that Taiwan has a long way to go yet. Quite against the worldwide trend of normalization, special day schools are recently flourishing in Taiwan. There were only two special day schools here for children with MR in 1980, but in ten years, eight new schools have been added to the list, at the increase rate of one school each year. A few more are either on blueprints or under construction.

It is hoped that the Office of Special Education will be soon established both in central and local governments such that to coordinate policies and practices in special education. Many issues in the field of special education in Taiwan remain unresolved, but the prospect is promising, with the government starting to play the key role in setting the stage for further development.

REFERENCES

Ministry of Education. (1984). *Special Education Act.* Taiwan: Author.

Ministry of Education. (1997). *Revised Special Education Act.* Taiwan: Author.

JENGJYH DUH
National Taiwan Normal University

TALENTED CHILDREN

See SPECIFIC TALENT, E.G., ACADEMICALLY TALENTED CHILDREN.

TALKING BOOKS

Talking books are books recorded on vinyl disks or, more often the case in recent years, on cassette tapes that are used principally by the blind. These modified records are played on special talking book machines and recorded on modified machines as well. Talking books and the modified recorders are available to all visually impaired students registered through the American Printing House for the Blind. Severely reading impaired students with a diagnosis of dyslexia may also qualify for the use of talking books.

STAFF

AMERICAN PRINTING HOUSE FOR THE BLIND

TASH

Formerly the Association for Persons with Severe Handicaps, TASH is an international advocacy association of people with disabilities, their family members, other advocates, and professionals working toward a society in which inclusion of all people in all aspects of community is the norm. The organization is comprised of members concerned with human dignity, civil rights, education, and independence for all individuals with disabilities. Creating, disseminating, and implementing programs useful for the education and independent lifestyles of persons who are severely handicapped is a primary objective of TASH.

Formed in 1975, TASH is a membership-supported, not-for-profit association with chapters in 34 states and members in 35 countries. Current membership includes professionals, paraprofessionals, parents, and medical and legal personnel. The organization's mission is to stretch the boundaries of what is possible through building communities in which no one is segregated and everyone belongs, forging new alliances that embrace diversity, advocating for opportunities and rights, and eradicating injustices and inequities. In addition, TASH strives to actively support research, disseminate knowledge and information, and support progressive legislation and litigation. Promoting excellence in services and inclusive education for all individuals is another aim of the association.

TASH seeks to promote the full participation of people with disabilities in integrated community settings that support the same quality of life available to people with disabilities. This task is accomplished through its facilitation of training in best practices, systems change, Americans with Disabilities Act (ADA), and Individuals with Disabilities Education Act (IDEA). TASH also strives to provide information, linkage with resources, legal expertise, and targeted advocacy. The organization accomplishes its work by disseminating information via a monthly newsletter covering current disability-related issues and a quarterly academic journal containing cutting-edge research. TASH also sponsors an annual conference and topical workshops, and advocates on behalf of people with disabilities and their families through building grassroots coalitions.

TASH'S central office is located at 29 W. Susquehanna Avenue, Suite 210, Baltimore, Maryland, 21204. The association can be reached via telephone (410-828-8274), fax (410-828-6706), TDD (410-828-1306), e-mail (info@tash.org), or by visiting TASH's web site at www.tash.org

TAMARA J. MARTIN
*The University of Texas of the
Permian Basin*

TASK ANALYSIS

Task analysis is a teaching strategy that encompasses the breaking down and sequencing of goals into teachable subtasks. Moyer and Dardig (1978) noted it is a critical component of the behavioral approach and it serves a dual role in the instruction of learners with handicaps. First, it serves an effective diagnostic function by helping teachers pinpoint a student's individual functioning levels on a specific skill or task. Second, it provides the basis for sequential instruction, which may be tailored to each child's pace of learning. A thorough task analysis results in a set of subtasks that form the basic steps in an effective program. In essence, task analysis is both an assessment and a teaching tool (Ysseldyke & Elliott, 1999).

Task analysis has been acclaimed to be an effective strategy for the mildly handicapped learner (Bateman, 1974; Siegel, 1972; Tawney, 1974). Gold (1976) applied this technique to the education of severely handicapped learners with great success and Williams, Brown, and Certo (1975) stated that task analysis is critical to teachers of severely handicapped learners since programmatic steps must be sequenced with precision and care.

According to Mithaug (1979), the procedures that define task analysis have evolved from Frederick Taylor's work measurement studies and Frank and Lillian Gilbreth's motion studies conducted in the late 1800s. Motion analysis was the precursor of today's task analysis, although many elements critical to motion analysis have not been included in the educational applications of task analysis. The term task analysis came into increasing use during the 1950s, whenever tasks were identified and examined for their essential components within the workplace. This foreshadowed subsequent applications of task analysis to teach individuals with disabilities in the late 1960s.

Guidelines for designing and implementing task analysis programs have been suggested (Moyer & Dardig, 1978; Siegel, 1972). These are:

Limit the scope of the main task

Write subtasks in observable terms

Use terminology at a level understandable to potential users

Write the task in terms of what the learner will do

Focus attention on the task rather than the learner

In choosing a method of task analysis, Moyer & Dardig (1978) noted that all tasks, whether from the psychomotor, cognitive, or affective domains, can be broken down into simple units of performance. However, there is no foolproof strategy for selecting the appropriate method of analysis for a given task. It is helpful first to identify the domain of the learning task and then to apply the appropriate task analysis procedure. They suggest several possible methods of task analysis that may be adopted by the special education teacher:

1. Watch a master perform. This requires watching and writing down all the steps that are required to perform the task as it is performed by someone adept at it.

2. In a variation of the first method, have the teacher perform the task, making note of the required steps. Sometimes this is difficult in that performing the task may interfere with recording the steps.

3. Work backward from the terminal objective, making note of the required steps.

4. Brainstorm. This entails writing down all the component steps without regard to order. Then, once all steps have been identified, arrange them into some logical order.

5. Make the conditions under which the task is completed progressively more simple. As the learner gains proficiency, slowly change the simplified conditions (e.g., trace name; gradually remove the model: dark model, light model, dotted model, etc.).

The ability to analyze tasks, a skill that can be acquired by any teacher, enables the detection of trends in a student's performance and the modification of task compo-

nents during an instructional session (Junkala, 1973). Thus it is an extremely effective instructional method and diagnostic tool in special education.

REFERENCES

Bateman, B. D. (1974). Educational implications of minimum brain dysfunction. *Reading Teacher, 27,* 662–668.

Gold, M. C. (1976). Task analysis of a complex assembly task by the retarded blind. *Exceptional Children, 43,* 78–84.

Junkala, J. (1973). Task analysis: The processing dimension. *Academic Therapy, 8*(4), 401–409.

Mithaug, D. E. (1979). The relation between programmed instruction and task analysis in the pre-vocational training of severely and profoundly handicapped persons. *AAESPH Review, 4*(2), 162–178.

Moyer, J. R., & Dardig, J. C. (1978). Practical task analysis for special educators. *Teaching Exceptional Children, 11*(1), 16–18.

Siegel, E. (1972). Task analysis and effective teaching: *Journal of Learning Disabilities, 5,* 519–532.

Tawney, J. W. (1974). *Task analysis.* Unpublished manuscript, University of Kentucky.

Williams, W., Brown, L., & Certo, N. (1975). Basic components of instructional programs for the severely handicapped students. *AAESPH Review, 1*(1), 1–39.

Ysseldyke, J., & Elliott, J. (1999). Effective instructional practices: Implications for assessing educational environments. In C. R. Reynolds & T. B. Gutkin (Eds.), *The Handbook of School Psychology* (3rd ed.). New York: Wiley.

EILEEN F. MCCARTHY
University of Wisconsin at Madison

BEHAVIOR ASSESSMENT
BEHAVIOR MODIFICATION
BEHAVIORAL OBJECTIVES

TAT

See THEMATIC APPERCEPTION TEST.

TAXONOMIES

Taxonomy is the science of systematics. It incorporates the theory and practice of classification, or sorting and ordering significant similarities and differences among members of a system to facilitate precise communication about members, enhance understanding of the interrelationships among members, and suggest areas where additional relationships might be discovered. Early attempts to design taxonomies date back to the third century BC and Aristotle's efforts to classify animals as warm- or cold-blooded. Theophrastus, Aristotle's pupil, concentrated on a system for sorting plants. In the eighteenth century in Sweden, Linnaeus designed a classification system for botany that has served as a basis for almost all subsequent systems.

Among the more commonly used taxonomies today are the Library of Congress and Dewey Decimal systems for the classification of books and the taxonomies developed for the classification of plants and animals. The latter contains categories that permit the identification of individual organisms according to species, genus, family, order, class, phylum, and kingdom.

In the late 1940s, members of the American Psychological Association who were concerned about the problems of precise communication among college examiners and researchers involved in testing and curriculum development began work on the classification of educational objectives. The result was the preparation of taxonomies of educational objectives or intended student outcomes in the cognitive, affective, and psychomotor domains (Bloom, 1956; Harrow, 1972; Krathwohl, Bloom, & Masia, 1964). The major classes in these three taxonomies are presented in Figure 1. All three reflect an emphasis on the intended outcomes of instruction and the student behaviors that would demonstrate achievement of each outcome.

Stevens (1962) developed a taxonomy for special education that focuses on physical disorders. He observed that classification systems then in use were typically based on a medical model with an emphasis on disease, etiology, and symptomatology. His intent was to improve communication regarding educationally relevant attributes or somatopsychological or body disorders and the special education procedures students with such disorders might require. Stevens stressed the differences among the terms impairment, disability, and handicap and provided for attributes that carried significance for planning special education programs. Figure 2 lists Stevens' classes.

More recently the World Health Organization (WHO) has published its *International Classification of Impairments, Disabilities, and Handicaps* (1980). This publication relates consequences of disease to circumstances in which disabled persons are apt to find themselves as they interact with others and adapt to their physical surroundings. The purpose of WHO's efforts, which are summarized in Figure 3, was to prepare a taxonomy that would ease the production of statistics regarding the consequences of disease, facilitate the collection of statistics useful in planning services, and permit storage and retrieval of information about impairments, disabilities, and handicaps (WHO, 1980). Diagnosis, a useful precursor to treatment, is a form

Cognitive Domain
1. Knowledge
2. Comprehension
3. Application
4. Analysis
5. Synthesis
6. Evaluation

Affective Domain
1. Receiving/attending
2. Responding
3. Valuing
4. Organization
5. Characterization

Psychomotor Domain
1. Reflex movement
2. Basic fundamental movement
3. Perceptual abilities
4. Physical abilities
5. Skilled movements
6. Nondiscursive movements

Figure 1. Taxonomies of educational objectives for the cognitive, affective, and psychomotor domains (Bloom, 1956; Harrow, 1972; Krathwohl, Bloom, & Masia, 1964).

of taxonomic classification (e.g., see Kamphaus, Reynolds, & McCammon, 1999).

Ultimately, taxonomies should be comprehensive, improve communication, stimulate thought, and be accepted by professionals in the field for which they were designed (Bloom, 1956). Whether the taxonomies available for special educators lead to the achievement of these goals remains to be seen, but without taxonomies as a guide, com-

1. *Somatopsychological variants*
  1.1 Handicap
  1.2 Disability
  1.3 Impairment
2. *Educationally significant attributes of somatopsychological disorders*
  2.1 Nature of condition
  2.2 Nature of therapeutic process
  2.3 Psychological aspects
  2.4 School considerations
  2.5 Cultural considerations
  2.6 Etc.
3. *Special education procedures*
  3.1 Modification of laws
  3.2 Finance
  3.3 Instructional modifications
  3.4 Noninstructional services
  3.5 Administrative modifications
  3.6 Ancillary services
  3.7 Etc.

Figure 2. Taxonomy in special education for children with body disorders (Steven, 1962).

Impairments
1. Intellectual
2. Other psychological
3. Language
4. Aural
5. Ocular
6. Visceral
7. Skeletal
8. Disfiguring
9. Generalized, sensory, and other

Disabilities
1. Behavior
2. Communication
3. Personal care
4. Locomotor
5. Body disposition
6. Dexterity
7. Situational
8. Particular skill
9. Other activity restrictions

Handicaps
Survival roles
1. Orientation
2. Physical independence
3. Mobility
4. Occupational
5. Social integration
6. Economic self-sufficiency
Other handicaps
7. Other handicaps

Figure 3.   WHO classification of impairments, disabilities, and handicaps (WHO, 1980).

munication would be surely impaired (Kamphaus, Reynolds, & McCammon, 1999).

REFERENCES

Bloom, B. S. (Ed.). (1956). *Taxonomy of educational objectives: The classification of educational goals: Handbook I. Cognitive domain.* New York: McKay.

Harrow, A. J. (1972). *A taxonomy of the psychomotor domain: A guide for developing behavioral objectives.* New York: McKay.

Kamphaus, R. W., Reynolds, C. R., & McCammon, C. (1999). Roles of diagnosis and classification in school psychology. In C. R. Reynolds & T. B. Gutkin (Eds.), *The Handbook of School Psychology* (3rd ed.) New York: Wiley.

Krathwohl, D. R., Bloom, B. S., & Masia, B. B. (1964). *Taxonomy of educational objectives: Classification of educational goals: Handbook II. Affected domain.* New York: McKay.

Stevens, G. D. (1962). *Taxonomy in special education for children with body disorders.* Pittsburgh, PA: Department of Special Education and Rehabilitation, University of Pittsburgh.

World Health Organization. (1980). *International classification of impairments, disabilities, and handicaps.* Geneva, Switzerland: Author.

Marjorie E. Ward
The Ohio State University

TAY-SACHS SYNDROME

Tay-Sachs disease is a disorder of fat metabolism that results in loss of visual function and progressive mental deterioration. It is one of a variety of demyelinating diseases of the nervous system characterized by cerebral macular degeneration. The disorder is named after Warren Tay, an English physician (1843–1927), and Bernard Sachs, an American neurologist (1858–1944). The disorder is transmitted by an autosomal recessive gene and is found with dramatically increased frequency among Jewish infants of eastern European origin. Approximately 90% of cases of Tay-Sachs syndrome can be traced to Lithuanian or Jewish ancestry.

The disorder typically first manifests itself in infants between the ages of 4 and 8 months. Early signs include an abnormal startle response to acoustic stimulation, delay in psychomotor development or regression with loss of learned skills (e.g., loss of the ability to roll over), spasticity, and cherry red spots in the retinas, the result of degeneration of retinal ganglion cells. Head size typically increases in the second year while the cerebral ventricles remain relatively normal. There are frequently tonic-clonic seizures and blindness may occur. Infants typically become weak and apathetic. Death usually occurs at 3 to 5 years. At autopsy, the appearance of the brain is one of widespread atrophy. Treatment is aimed at the symptoms of the disease with anticonvulsant medications used to suppress seizures.

REFERENCE

Adams, R. A., & Victor, N. (1977). *Principles of neurology.* New York: McGraw-Hill.

Danny Wedding
Marshall University

TEACCH

Treatment and Education of Autistic and related Communication handicapped Children (TEACCH) is a unique program offering comprehensive services, research, and professional training for autistic children of all ages, and their families, in the state of North Carolina. TEACCH is a division of the psychiatry department of the University of North Carolina School of Medicine, Chapel Hill.

The program was founded in 1966 by Eric Schopler and Robert J. Reichler as a research project supported in part by the National Institute of Mental Health. Its purpose was to investigate the following misconceptions about autism: (1) that the syndrome is primarily an emotional disorder that causes children to withdraw from their hostile and pathological parents; (2) that these parents are educationally privileged and from an upper social class; and (3) that autistic children had potential for normal or better intellectual functioning. The research results clarified these misconceptions by demonstrating that autism is a developmental disability rather than an emotional illness; that parents come from all social strata and, like their children, are the victims rather than the cause of this disability; and that in spite of peak skills, mental retardation and autism can and do coexist.

These empirical research findings led to the development of the TEACCH program based on the following principles:

1. Parents should be collaborators and cotherapists in the treatment of their own children.

2. Treatment should involve individualized teaching programs using behavior theory and special education.

3. Teaching programs should be based on individualized diagnosis and assessment.

4. Implementation should be by psychoeducational therapists or teachers who function as generalists rather than specialists in a technical field such as physical therapy or speech therapy. Treatment outcome is evaluated according to the interaction between improved skills and environmental adjustments to deficits.

The TEACCH program provides comprehensive services, including professional training and research efforts that are integrated with clinical services. Training is provided for various specialists, including teachers, psychologists, psychiatrists, pediatricians, speech pathologists, and social workers. The main emphasis is on the involvement of parents in all facets of the program directed toward adjustment in all areas of the child's life—home, school, and the community.

Home adjustment is facilitated at five regional TEACCH centers, each located in a city housing a branch of the state university system to facilitate both research and training. The centers' main function is to provide diagnosis and individualized assessment involving family and school. Parents are trained to function as cotherapists using behavior management and special education techniques. The centers' staff provide professional training and consultation.

School adjustment is fostered through special education classrooms in the public schools that include four to eight children with a teacher and an assistant teacher. These classrooms (about 54 currently) are under TEACCH direction according to individual school contracts. TEACCH functions often include hiring teachers, intensive in-service training of teachers, diagnosis and placement of children, and ongoing classroom consultation for behavior problems and special curriculum issues.

Community adaptation is facilitated through parent groups. Each center and class has a parent group affiliated with the North Carolina Society for Autistic Adults and Children, and a chapter of the National Society. The main goal of this collaboration is to improve community understanding of the client's special needs and to develop new and cost-effective services. In recent years, this involved services for the older age group, including group homes, respite care, summer camps, vocational training, social skills training, and the development of a learning-living community program.

The outcome studies of various TEACCH services have shown that autistic children learn better in a structured setting, and that with appropriate training, parents become effective in teaching and managing their own children. Such gains carry over into the home situation. Moreover, when the North Carolina rate of institutionalized autistic children is compared with the rate reported from other states and countries, it is less than one-fifth, demonstrating that a strong community support program can improve the quality of life for handicapped children and adults at a fraction of the cost incurred by institutional warehousing.

ERIC SCHOPLER
*University of North Carolina at
Chapel Hill*

AUTISM
FILIAL THERAPY
JOURNAL OF AUTISM AND DEVELOPMENTAL
  DISORDERS

TEACHER BURNOUT

Increased public demands on education have produced additional pressures and stresses on teachers. Needle, Griffin, Svendsen, and Berney (1981) report that teaching ranks third in the hierarchy of stressful professions. Studies conducted by teachers' unions and other educational agencies support the notion that many teachers are currently "burning out" (Cichon & Koff, 1980; Wilson & Hall, 1981). Special educators in particular may be at high risk for burnout and its consequences (Bradfield & Fones, 1985).

Burnout has been defined in a variety of ways in the literature during its nearly 10-year history (Gold, 1985). Weiskopf (1980) defines burnout by its relationship to six categories of stress often found at the teaching work place. They include work overload, lack of perceived success, amount of direct contact with children, staff-child ratio, program structure, and responsibility for others. Freudenberger (1974) and Maslach (1977) find the general theme of burnout to be "emotional and/or physical exhaustion resulting from the stress of interpersonal contact." It can be viewed as a gradual process with stages ranging from mild to severe (Spaniol & Caputo, 1979).

Burnout seems to affect people working in the human social services professions particularly because of the degree of intimacy that they experience with their clients and the extended period of time that they work with them. Moreover, many of the recipients of human services do not respond to the efforts of professionals, causing disillusionment and frustration (Pines & Maslach, 1977). This may be particularly true for special education teachers because of the unique nature of their teaching responsibilities (Bradfield & Fones, 1985).

Many causes for burnout in the helping professions have been proposed. In education, occupational burnout may arise from the failure of the work environment to provide the teacher with the support and encouragement needed and expected (Needle, Griffin, Svendsen, & Berney, 1981). Bensky et al. (1980) point out that often teachers are not given clearly defined job descriptions and receive additional job responsibilities for which they are unprepared or to which they are unaccustomed. Role ambiguity, if not clarified as part of the education process, is likely to lead to an increase in job-related stress and dissatisfaction (Coates & Thoresen, 1976; Greenberg & Valletutti, 1980). Many teachers have cited violence, vandalism, disruptive students, inadequate salaries, lack of classroom control, lack of job mobility, and fear of layoffs as reasons for burnout (Gold, 1985).

The effects of burnout vary from individual to individual depending on such variables as personality, age, sex, and family history. Physiological manifestation may include such reactions as migraine headaches, ulcers, diarrhea, muscle tension, and heart disease. Emotional manifestations include such reactions as depression, anxiety, irritability, and nervousness. Behavioral manifestations generally include excessive smoking or overeating (American Academy of Family Physicians, 1979).

The ways in which teachers may manifest specific responses to burnout on the job is cause for concern. Spaniol and Caputo (1979) have formulated a list of symptoms that may indicate that a teacher is experiencing burnout: a high level of absenteeism, lateness for work, a low level of enthusiasm, decline in performance, lack of focus, a high level of complaints, lack of communication, and a lack of openness to new ideas.

The implications of teacher burnout are grave and broadly based. They include the individual's own personal dissatisfaction, his or her family's unhappiness, chronic health problems, problems with colleagues and school administrators, and, ultimately, ineffective teaching. Sparks and Ingram (1979) reported that the teachers from whom students learn the most are reasonable, relaxed, enthusiastic, and interested in their students. Teachers who are consistently feeling stressed have been described as irritable, tense, humorless, depressed, self-involved, and unable to perform their job well. In general, Needle et al. (1981) found that job stress affects the classroom environment, the teaching/learning process, and the attainment of educational goals and objectives.

To reduce the possibility of teacher burnout, teachers must be provided with knowledge and information on effective methods of coping with stress in the environment. One popular method has been involvement in stress management workshops (Betkouski, 1981). These workshops have been effective in providing teachers with strategies for coping with stress such as forming support groups, reviewing exercise and nutrition patterns, developing hobbies and interests outside the work environment, and practicing relaxation techniques (Shannon & Saleeby, 1980). The prevention of burnout in teaching, however, must first and foremost involve a serious commitment to improving the quality and circumstances under which teachers work.

REFERENCES

American Academy of Family Physicians. (1979). *A report on the lifestyles/personal health in different occupations: A study of attitudes and practices.* Kansas City: Research Forecasts.

Bensky, J., Shaw, S. F., Gouse, A. S., Bates, H., Dixon, B., & Beane, W. (1980). Public law 94-142 and stress: A problem for educators. *Exceptional Children, 47*(1), 24–29.

Betkouski, M. (1981 March). On making stress work for you: Strategies for coping. *Science Teacher, 48,* 35–37.

Bradfield, R. H., & Fones, D. M. (1985). Stress and the special teacher: How bad is it? *Academic Therapy, 20*(5), 571–577.

Cichon, D. J., & Koff, R. H. (1980, March). Stress and teaching. *National Association of Secondary School Principals Bulletin,* 91–103.

Coates, T. J., & Thoresen, C. E. (1976). Teacher anxiety: A review with recommendations. *Review of Educational Research, 46,* 159–184.

Freudenberger, H. J. (1974). Staff burn-out. *Journal of Social Issues, 30*(1), 159–165.

Gold, Y. (1985). Burnout: Causes and solutions. *Clearinghouse, 58,* 210–212.

Greenberg, S. F., & Valletutti, P. J. (1980). *Stress and the helping professions.* Baltimore, MD: Brookes.

Maslach, C. (1977). Job burnout: How people cope. *Public Welfare, 36,* 61–63.

Needle, R., Griffin, T., & Svendsen, R., & Berney, M. (1981). Occupational stress: Coping and health problems of teachers. *Journal of School Health, 51,* 175–181.

Pines, A., & Maslach, C. (1977, April). *Detached concern and burnout in mental health professions.* Paper presented at the

2nd National Conference on Child Abuse and Neglect, Houston, TX.

Shannon, C., & Saleeby, D. (1980). Training child welfare workers to cope with burnout. *Child Welfare, 59*(8), 463–468.

Spaniol, L., & Caputo, J. (1979). *Professional burnout: A personal survival kit.* Boston: Human Services Associates.

Sparks, D., & Ingram, M. J. (1979). Stress prevention and management: A workshop approach. *Personnel & Guidance Journal, 59,* 197–200.

Weiskopf, P. A. (1980). Burn-out among teachers of exceptional children. *Exceptional Children, 47*(1), 18–23.

Wilson, C. F., & Hall, D. L. (1981). *Preventing burnout in education.* La Mesa, CA: Wright Group.

Marsha H. Lupi
Hunter College

TEACHER EFFECTIVENESS
TEACHER EXPECTANCIES

TEACHER CENTERS (TC)

A teacher center represents a centralized setting that facilitates teacher development, in-service programs, and the exchange of ideas (Hering, 1983). Initially, TCs were funded directly with federal dollars. The basis for this funding was the passage in 1976 of PL 94-482. Approximately 110 TCs were directly supported by the federal government. However, as noted by Edelfelt in 1982, "The categorical assignment of funds for teacher centers . . . [was] terminated in the fiscal year 1982 federal budget" (p. 393). The majority of TCs have continued as a result of their funding from other local and state sources. Their continuation supports the contention that the original concepts that premised their initiation are still valid.

A primary factor that led to the origination of TCs in the United States in the mid-1970s was the interest of teachers in being in charge of their own in-service training and to keep up with new educational trends and curricular concepts. The idea was that TC in-service programs were to depart from the traditional and standard in-service programs, e.g., one-time sessions on a given topic such as discipline or learning activities for the talented and gifted. In contrast, the intent of established TC in-service programs was to be innovative and to influence professional development; those goals are still desirable today.

Another of the original precepts was that TCs would have a full-time director who was both an administrator and a teacher. The director would then become the nucleus of a governing board that was to consist of local citizens. Boards with an efficient mix of leadership, inspiration, and idealism were and are in a position effectively to institute needed changes. Weiler (1983) has outlined a blueprint for the establishment of new TCs that make needed changes possible.

Researchers (Commission on Reading, 1984; Committee on Education and Labor, 1984; Kozal, 1984; Tunley, 1985; Zorinsky, 1985) estimate that 12 to 18% of the teenage and adult population groups are functionally illiterate. There are 25 to 40 million Americans who are handicapped with depressed literacy skills in the primary academic areas of reading, writing, and arithmetic. This instructional need is one that active TCs can legitimately embrace through the initiation of planned in-service programs that retrain teachers to be more efficient in their instruction.

Beyond the need for TC to endorse direct instructional intervention to improve the efficiency of classroom instruction, Hering (1983) identified a composite of five major functions that TCs can attend to: (1) assist teachers in their more immediate awareness of changes in instructional knowledge as it appears in educational literature; (2) assist teachers to be more efficient in meeting the social educational goals of students that society expects its nation's schools to attend to; (3) assist teachers to be more effective in their classrooms in attending to their students' developmental and remedial instructional needs; (4) assist teachers in achieving increased social and psychological competence; and, (5) assist teachers as a faculty group to be more responsible to the needs of the group.

The history of TCs (Edelfelt, 1982) has had its share of developmental setbacks. However, as Hering (1983) has pointed out, TCs that work toward a quality program of instruction for all students will simultaneously attain from the community and the school board recognition of the worth and the work of teachers. Teacher centers that are influential in achieving quality instruction for any one group or classification of students have the probability of doing the same for any other group or classification of students, including the special education student.

REFERENCES

Commission on Reading. (1984). *Becoming a nation of readers.* Washington, DC: U.S. Department of Education.

Committee on Education and Labor. (1984). *Illiteracy and the scope of the problem in this country.* Washington, DC: U.S. Government Printing Office.

Edelfelt, R. A. (1982, September). Critical issues in developing teacher centers. *Education Digest, 48,* 28–31.

Hering, W. M. (1983). *Research on teachers' centers: A summary of fourteen research efforts.* Washington, DC: National Institute of Education.

Kozal, J. (1984). *Illiterate america.* Garden City, NY: Doubleday.

Tunley, R. (1985, September). America's secret shame. *Reader's Digest,* 104–108.

Weiler, P. (1983, September). Blueprint for a teacher center. *Instructor, 93,* 146–148.

Zorinsky, E. (1985). The National Commission on Illiteracy Act. *Congressional Record, 131*(41). Washington, DC: U.S. Government Printing Office.

ROBERT T. NASH
University of Wisconsin at Oshkosh

IN SERVICE TRAINING OF SPECIAL EDUCATION TEACHERS
INSTRUCTIONAL MEDIA CENTER

TEACHER EDUCATION AND SPECIAL EDUCATION

Teacher Education and Special Education is the official journal of the Teacher Education Division (TED) of the Council for Exceptional Children (CEC). The purposes of *Teacher Education and Special Education* are to support goals of the TED, and to stimulate thoughtful consideration of the critical issues that are shaping the future of teacher education.

The journal is published four times a year and the first issue of each volume is a potpourri issue that includes articles dealing with a wide range of topics. The second issue focuses on either preservice, in-service, or doctoral preparation. The third issue focuses on a topic of timely interest in personnel preparation. The last issue focuses on research and/or evaluation activities related to personnel preparation.

REBECCA BAILEY
Texas A & M University

COUNCIL FOR EXCEPTIONAL CHILDREN

TEACHER EFFECTIVENESS

Over the last several decades, field-based studies have been conducted on the teaching process that related specific teaching behaviors to student achievement outcomes. The results of the early studies (Crawford et al., 1978; Anderson, Evertson, & Brophy, 1979; Fisher et al., 1978; Good & Grouws, 1977, 1979; Stallings, Needles, & Strayrook, 1979) were that there is a common set of process variables that can be observed or documented in effective teachers across grade and subject areas. It is further indicated that less effective teachers do not demonstrate these same behaviors to the appropriate degree. Continued research demonstrated clearly that teachers do make a difference in children's lives, especially with regard to classroom learning (see review by Gettinger & Stoiba, 1999).

The body of this research clearly speaks to a technology of teaching, making it increasingly clear that teachers and what they do are important determinants of student achievement. We know that effective teachers (1) optimize academic learning time; (2) reward achievement in appropriate ways; (3) use interactive teaching practices; (4) hold and communicate high expectations for student performance; and (5) select appropriate units of instruction. There are, of course, exceptions to these and other principles, and as such, teachers need to be adaptable. The research does not say that there is one best system of teaching but rather that the teacher must constantly be analyzing the feedback from students and performance data and making decisions to modify the instruction. Therefore, the findings from the teacher effectiveness studies and related research should be viewed as road maps with the teacher constantly making decisions regarding the best route to pursue and sometimes alter the selected route based on new information. In general, the literature strongly addresses the need to train teachers as accurate decision makers. It is not level of effort or the aspiration to teach well that differentiates effective instruction; it is rather knowledge, skill, and confidence (Elmore et al., 1996).

Changing teachers' behaviors has not been found to be as difficult a task as first believed (Good, 1979). Studies have examined the amount of intervention needed to create a change that will affect teacher effectiveness (Coladarci & Gage, 1984; Good, 1979; Mohlman, Coladarci, & Gage, 1982). Coladarci and Gage (1984) found that there is a lower limit in regard to how little can be done while still achieving a meaningful change in behavior. Periodic direct observation of teachers appears to be one component that facilitates adoption of the practices. An enthusiastic presentation of the information to the teachers and a spirit of support for the practices also appear to be important. Mohlman et al. (1982) found that teacher acceptance of change to the use of effective teaching practices was based on (1) teaching recommendations being stated in explicit, easily understood language; (2) a philosophical acceptance of the suggested practice on the part of the teacher; and (3) teachers' perceived view of the cost in terms of time and effort and a belief that the investment in time and effort was worth the payoff in expected student achievement.

Mohlman et al. (1982) also found that teacher acceptance of the innovations is more important than understanding of the innovations. One other finding from the research is that teachers who were trained in effective teaching practices either by workshop, summaries, or workbooks are much more likely to use these practices in their classrooms than teachers who were not provided with such information.

Various authors have separated the major components of effective teaching practices into different configurations.

One possible organization places these practices under the domains of management, decision making, time utilization, and instruction, all of which interact with each other and result in the development of a supportive classroom climate. These domains and their subdomains are based on the experimental and correlational research reported regularly in journals on studies involving instructional strategies.

Effective teachers use effective classroom management. Effective classroom management means (1) organizing the physical classroom to minimize disruptions; (2) establishing teaching rules and procedures and adhering to those rules and procedures; and (3) anticipating problem situations and having action plans to prevent problems or deal with them when they occur. Effective teachers have a strong command of their subject matter and a keen awareness of how children think and learn (Elmore et al., 1996).

Management has repeatedly been demonstrated as a critical element of effective teaching in major studies, including *The First Grade Reading Group Study* (Evertson et al., 1981) and *The Study of a Training Program in Classroom Organization and Management for Secondary School Teachers* (Fitzpatrick, 1982). Management includes the establishment and teaching of rules and procedures, specification of consequences, physical organization of the classroom, and behaviors on the part of the teacher that prevent disruptive behavior. Good room management eliminates potential distractions for students and minimizes opportunities for students to disrupt others. Students' desks are arranged so that students can easily see instructional displays and visuals and so that students can be easily monitored by the teacher. Students are seated so as to eliminate "action zones." These zones are created when students select seating locations. There is a tendency in self-selection for high-ability learners to sit together in the front and low-ability students to sit at the back or side. The more effective teacher will intermingle with these students. When hand raisers are spread throughout the room, it will enable the teacher to spread his or her attention more evenly and become sensitized to low responders.

Rules govern student behaviors such as talking and respect for property. Effective teachers have only three to six rules stated in generic language. These are posted and taught through examples to students at the beginning of the school year. Merely posting rules is less effective than posting and teaching the rules. Established procedures and routines are time-saving mechanisms. When procedures are established, students know when to use the bathroom, how to head papers, how to distribute and collect assignments, how to ask for help, and so on. Without such established procedures, time is lost in explanations, or students disrupt the classroom by not knowing the procedures.

Consistency in enforcing the rules is a hallmark of effective teachers. Effective teachers have a hierarchy of consequences they follow to maintain the rules. Eye contact, moving closer to a student, or a pointed finger might be the first level of intervention. Withholding a privilege, assigning detention, conferencing with a student, or having a student restate a broken rule might be the second level. Contacting parents, behavioral contracting, or outside assistance might constitute the third level. In all cases, the teacher should remain calm when enforcing a rule.

Prevention of problems is largely brought about by advanced planning. A teacher can help prevent behavior problems by staying in close proximity to students while frequently teaching and monitoring them. A teacher should plan positive comments that can be used with students to establish a positive mood. Finally, a teacher should formulate plans to handle hypothetical disciplinary situations.

One major reason why management is such a critical variable in the teaching process is because of its relationship to instructional time. Instructional time is highly related to academic achievement. Walberg's (1982) review of studies involving time and achievement found correlation ranges from .13 to .71 with a median of .41. Ninety-five percent of the 25 studies reviewed as "time-on-learning" reported positive effects. Instructional time is lost for members of a class where students are disruptive, procedures are not readily available for teaching, and students do not understand the behavioral expectations of the teacher.

Decision making is generally an unobservable phenomenon, but the products of the decision are observable. Teachers regularly make decisions on content, time allocations, pacing, grouping, and class activities. If the content is not taught, then students generally do not learn. The literature uses the term "opportunity to learn" when describing this phenomenon. According to Berliner (1985), teachers make content decisions based on (1) the amount of effort required to teach the subject, (2) the perceived difficulty for the students, and (3) the teacher's personal feelings of enjoyment. In making content decisions, knowledge of the subject discipline appears to be of importance. The teacher's philosophy also enters into content decisions. Research from teacher effectiveness studies shows wide variability between the subject matter content covered by teachers of the same subject and grade.

Time allocation decisions involve time allotted across the school day and within a curriculum area. Observational studies on teacher behavior indicate that less than 1% of the time available in reading classes focuses on the teaching of reading comprehension (Pearson & Gallagher, 1983). Fisher et al. (1978) found some teachers of the same grade level allocated 16 minutes of instruction in math each day while others were allocated 51 minutes. The basic principle that evolves from this data is that teachers' time allocation decisions can affect students' opportunity to learn.

Pacing involves the rate at which a teacher covers the course or subject material. The more material that is covered, the more opportunity to learn is given; hence, each student attains a higher achievement level. The corollary to the pacing principle is that students need to be learning the material at the pace that is followed. More effective teachers solicit regular feedback from students by frequent tests and questioning; they use that information to gauge the pace of the instruction. Sometimes the textbooks impose a pace. Why do students learn to spell 20 new words each week? Because the textbooks are set up to teach 20 words a week. Some students could learn 40, others only 10. Teachers need to be aware of how materials may put limitations on pacing.

If grouping is to be done, the teacher must base the grouping on objective criteria related to a valid achievement measure and must frequently reassess the value of the grouping. A problem inherent in grouping is the possible increased gap that can be created among different groups based on a difference in pacing. Grouping decisions cannot be taken lightly, and alternatives to grouping and differential pacing might be explored by teachers prior to a grouping decision. Teachers need to understand the consequences of grouping decisions as reflected in subsequent student achievement.

Appropriate use of time is a third component in a teaching effectiveness model. Research by Stallings et al. (1979), and Walberg (1979), and many others has revealed that time use is more important than time per se. Time can be conceptualized according to the activities being conducted. Berliner (1984) has identified the following components of time: allocated time, engaged time, time related to outcome, and academic learning time. Academic learning time (ALT) is most related to student achievement. The key is to increase the amount of ALT within the time allocated for instruction. Strategies related to room arrangement, minimizing transition time, and teaching material at the conceptual level of students all need to be addressed to increase ALT. Research on effective teachers reveals that they plan the use of their school day, allocate a greater percent of the school day to the basic subjects, and teach in groups so that students can get more instructional time. They spend 50% of their reading periods actually engaged in reading instruction. They use short periods of time (not over 30 seconds) to assist individual students with problems in seat work. They circulate among the students doing seat work to ensure a high degree of on-task behavior.

Most research on teacher effectiveness has been done with students in the elementary grades; some has been done at the junior high or secondary level. All have come to similar conclusions about effective teaching (Lightfoot, 1981; Stallings, 1981). MacKinzie (1983) has noted, however, that while the core principles are the same, their expression in actual practice are different. High-school faculties are content specialists who hold little investment in basic skills.

Teaching strategies are the final component of the model. They represent a wide variety of specific procedures. These strategies are based on basic principles of learning and the interaction of those principles with student characteristics. Teaching requires knowledge, explanation, elaboration, and clarification. Sequence, order, modeling, appropriate practice, goal setting, basic concept development, feedback, questioning, and a host of procedures and learning principles can be collapsed under this heading. The critical feature is to train teachers in the effective use of these procedures and in making decisions on when to best use each.

Effective teachers practice effective instruction a large percentage of the day. Instruction requires explanation, demonstration, and clarification. Effective instruction requires that material be explained and reviewed so that new material can be linked to old. Using demonstration and practice while focusing attention on the relevant dimension of a concept is a teaching art. The science of instruction followed by effective teachers is comprised of modeling, questioning, providing prompts and cues, providing feedback, and providing opportunities to practice newly learned skills. Students in classes taught by effective teachers know the goals and the expectations of the teachers for meeting those goals. Finally, research substantiates that effective teachers are people who believe they can make a difference in student achievement.

REFERENCES

Anderson, L. M., Evertson, C. M., & Brophy, J. E. (1979). An experimental study of effective teaching in first-grade reading groups. *Elementary School Journal, 79,* 193–222.

Berliner, D. C. (1984). The half-full glass: A review of research in teaching. In P. L. Hosford (ed.), *Using What We Know about Teaching.* Alexandra, VA: Association for Supervision and Curriculum Development.

Caladarci, T., & Gage, N. L. (1984). Effects of minimal intervention on teacher behavior and student achievement. *American Educational Research Journal, 21*(3), 539–555.

Crawford, et al. (1978). *An experiment on teacher effectiveness and parent assisted instruction in the third grade* (3 vols.). Stanford, CA: Center for Educational Research at Stanford.

Elmore, R., Peterson, P., & McCarthey, S. (1996). *Restructuring in the classroom: Teaching, learning, and school organization.* San Francisco: Jossey-Bass.

Emmer, E., Evertson, C., Sanford, J., Clements, B., & Worsham, M. (1982). *Organizing and managing the junior high classroom.* Austin: Research and Development Center for Teacher Education, University of Texas.

Evertson, C., Emmer, E., Clements, B., Sanford, J., Worsham, M., & Williams, E. (1981). *Organizing and managing the elementary school classroom.* Austin: Research and Development Center for Teacher Education, University of Texas.

Fisher, et al. (1978). *Teaching behaviors, academic learning time, and student achievement: Final report of Phase III-B, Begin-*

ning Teacher Evaluation Study (Technical Report V-1). San Francisco: Far West Regional Laboratory for Educational Research and Development.

Fitzpatrick, K. (1981). *Successful management strategies for the secondary classroom.* Downers Grove, IL.

Gettinger, M., & Stoiba, K. (1999). Excellence in teaching: Review of instructional and environmental variables. In C. R. Reynolds & T. B. Gutkin (Eds.), *The Handbook of School Psychology* (3rd ed.). New York: Wiley.

Good, T., & Grouws, D. (1977). Teaching effects: A process-product study in fourth-grade mathematics classrooms. *Journal of Teacher Education, 28,* 49–54.

Good, T. L. (1979). Teacher effectiveness in the elementary school: What we know about it. *Journal of Teacher Education, 30,* 52–64.

Good, T. L., & Grouws, D. A. (1979). The Missouri mathematics effectiveness project. *Journal of Educational Psychology, 71,* 355–382.

Lightfoot, S. L. (1981). Portraits of exemplary secondary schools: Highland Park. *Daedalus, 110*(4), 59–80.

Mackinzie, D. E. (1983). Research for school improvement: An appraisal of some recent trends. *Educational Researcher, 12*(4), 5–17.

Mohlman, G., Caladarci, T., & Gage, N. L. (1982). Comprehension and attitude as predictors of implementation of teacher training. *Journal of Teacher Education, 33,* 31, 36.

Pearson, P. D., & Gallagher, M. C. (1983). The instruction of reading comprehension. *Contemporary Educational Psychology, 8,* 317–344.

Stallings, J. A. (1981). *What research has to say to administrators of secondary schools about effective teaching and staff development.* Paper presented at the Conference Creating the Conditions for Effective Teaching, Center for Educational Policy and Management, Eugene, OR.

Stallings, J., Needles, M. & Strayrook, N. (1979). *The teaching of basic reading skills in secondary schools, Phase I and Phase II.* Menlo Park, CA: Stanford Research Institute.

Walberg, H. J. (1979). *Educational environments and effects: Evolution, policy, and productivity.* Berkeley, CA: McCutchon.

Walberg, H. J. (1982). What makes schooling effective? A synthesis and a critique of three national studies. *Contemporary Education: A Journal of Reviews, 1*(1), 22–34.

ROBERT A. SEDLAK
University of Wisconsin at Stout

TEACHER BURNOUT
TEACHER EXPECTANCIES
TEACHING STRATEGIES

TEACHER EXPECTANCIES

The general area of teacher expectancies involves investigating the effects of teachers' perceptions, beliefs, or attitudes about their students. Rosenthal and Jacobson (1968) tested kindergarten through fifth-grade children and then randomly identified some of them by telling their teachers that they had the greatest potential to show significant academic achievement over the school year. Results demonstrating that these children made significantly greater IQ gains than the control groups were interpreted to suggest that the teachers' expectations for the higher potential children influenced their teaching interactions with them, positively affecting the children's learning, as manifested in the higher scores. These results and interpretations were rejected by some owing to methodological flaws; e.g., the failure to measure the teachers' changed expectations and their teaching interactions. Later studies (Hall & Merkel, 1985) failed to replicate these results and indicated that teachers base their expectations for the most part on criteria relevant to academic performance and that they do not bias children's education.

With respect to the handicapped, teacher expectations have been discussed mostly in conjunction with the effects of labeling. Within this field, there is a fear that children's special education labels will cause teachers, parents, and others to lower their expectations for these children's academic and social development. The term self-fulfilling prophecy has been used to describe teachers' expectations and resulting instructional interactions that reinforce handicapped children to act in a manner consistent with the stereotypical characteristics of their handicap. There is the possibility that these children will have difficulty in learning because "they are handicapped," and may master skills only up to a level popularly ascribed to their handicap. This self-fulfilling prophecy, then, might lower teachers' and others' expectations for handicapped children, lower the children's expectations for themselves, and significantly limit the educational opportunities for them because they are not exposed to more advanced work or complex learning situations.

The research investigating teacher expectancies with handicapped individuals has been inconclusive. While some studies have demonstrated that labels do affect teacher perceptions and expectations of handicapped children, others have shown no significant negative effects. MacMillan (1977) appropriately concludes:

> Although it [the evidence] does not demonstrate convincingly that calling attention to people with [for example] intellectual deficiencies by giving them special attention is always a bad thing, the controversy over labeling should make us all more sensitive to its potential hazards. (p. 245)

Hobbs (1975), who coordinated a national study on the effect of labels and their resulting expectancy effects, similarly noted no simple solution to the issues as long as labels are required for entrance into special education programs and for the reimbursement of federal and state funds to finance these programs. What appears necessary are ways to minimize the potential expectancy effect of labels while permitting their continued use in the field.

REFERENCES

Hall, V. C., & Merkel, S. P. (1985). Teacher expectancy effects and educational psychology. In J. B. Dusek (Ed.), *Teacher expectancies* (pp. 67–92). Hillsdale, NJ: Erlbaum.

Hobbs, N. (1975). *The future of children.* San Francisco: Jossey-Bass.

MacMillan, D. L. (1977). *Mental retardation in school and society.* Boston: Little, Brown.

Rosenthal, R., & Jacobson, L. (1968). *Pygmalion in the classroom.* New York: Holt, Rinehart, & Winston.

HOWARD M. KNOFF
University of South Florida

PYGMALIAN EFFECT

TEACHING AND CONSULTATION

Consultation as one of the methods of delivering services to exceptional children was recognized by Reynolds (1962) in his Hierarchy of Services for Special Education Services. In this hierarchy, it was recognized that the majority of students classified as exceptional should and could be served in general education classrooms with consultation being one of the support services. Deno (1970) also recognized the teacher consultant as part of a "cascade of services." Kirk and Gallagher (1979) indicated that to facilitate mainstreaming, school systems might provide consultation services to regular teachers in the form of special education teachers, psychologists, social workers, and medical personnel. They go on to indicate that consultants are available to regular teachers when they have questions about a child or when they need advice concerning special materials and methods of instruction. Thomas, Correa, and Morsink (1995) provide an extensive look at the historical and legal foundations of consultation, collaboration, and teaming in special education beginning with the Deno model.

A number of definitions of and terms for consultation have been formulated. The terms include triadic process (Tharp, 1975), developmental and problem-centered consultation (Bergan, 1977), and collaborative problem solving (Medway, 1979). In special education Idol, Paolucci-Whitcomb, and Nevin (1986) defined collaborative consultation as "an interactive process that enables people with diverse expertise to generate creative solutions to mutually defined problems." Dettmer, Thurston, and Dyck (1995) defined school consultation and the role of the consultant as an "activity in which professional educators and parents collaborate within the school context by communicating, cooperating and coordinating their efforts as a team to serve the learning and behavioral needs of students." It also is important to note what consultation is not. Pryzwansky (1974) pointed out that consultation should not be an "expert" providing some type of prescription. Other cautions include one for a distinction between a medical model and a behavioral approach and one for the differences between consultation and counseling and consultation and collaboration.

Three of the most popular models of consultation in special education are triadic, organizational, and behavioral. In the triadic model there is a target (person with problem), a mediator (person with means to influence change), and a consultant (person with knowledge to mobilize mediator's influence.) Thomas et al. describe the collaborative consultation model of Idol et al. as an extension of the triadic model in which the target is the student with a problem, the mediator is the general education teacher and the consultant is the special educator or other professional. Organizational consultation focuses on interactions, interrelationships, shared decision making, and communication skills. The emphasis is on change with an organization or group. The consultant's role is primarily that of facilitator. Behavioral consultation emphasizes student behavior change. This model uses direct observation, identification of target behavior for change, and data-based interventions and assessment. Gutkin and Curtis (1982) identified characteristics present in the majority of consultation models they reviewed. These include indirect service delivery, consultant-consultee relationship, coordinate status, involvement of consultee in the consultation process, consultee's right to reject consultant suggestions, voluntary nature of consultation, and confidentiality.

The process of consultation is summarized by Thomas et al. in eight steps which are listed below:

1. establishing the relationship
2. gathering information
3. identifying the problem
4. stating the target behavior
5. generating interventions
6. implementing interventions
7. evaluating the interventions
8. withdrawing from the consultative relationship

A concept closely related to consultation is teaming. Teams within special education are generally thought of as organized groups of professionals from different disciplines. Their common goal is cooperative problem solving. Combining collaboration and teamwork builds on the strengths of both approaches. Teaming models include the multidisciplinary team, the interdisciplinary team, and the transdisciplinary team. The multidisciplinary team concept evolved from the medical model, in which experts in various fields shared their observations and generally reported them to one person. The interdisciplinary team is similar to the multidisciplinary team, but generally the team members evaluate a child and meet to share their observations. The transdisciplinary team model is a combination of the two previously mentioned and attempts to reduce fragmentation. It is viewed as an education/treatment model that integrates assessment, program goals, and objectives from various disciplines. Its characteristics, according to Lyon and Lyon (1980), are a joint team and professional development approach and implementation of role release. Orelove and Sobsey (1991) identify other characteristics as an indirect therapy approach, multiple lines of communication, and integration of services.

Consultation, collaboration, teaming, and family involvement have been stressed in special education (especially since the passage of PL 94-142), and these concepts have been strengthened with each amended or reauthorized version of this law. Teachers and other school personnel are recognizing the importance of shared decision making as the needs of children become increasingly complex. The emphases on effective schools, total quality management, site based management, comprehensive schools, and inclusion are providing the impetus for a model combining the salient features of previously identified consultation, collaboration, and teaming approaches. Thomas et al. proposed such a model, which they describe as interactive teaming. Interactive teaming is defined as a mutual or reciprocal effort among and between members of a team to provide the best possible educational program for a student. This model has ten elements drawn from previous research of models and programs with interactive teaming components. These are the elements which must be present for the model to be effective.

Legitimacy and autonomy

Purpose and objectives

Competencies of team members and clarity of roles

Role release and role transitions

Awareness of the individuality of team members

Process of team building

Attention to factors that affect team functioning

Leadership styles

Implementation procedures

Commitment to common goals

Consultation in special education has evolved from the concept of a professional sharing expertise with a regular classroom teacher to one of the special educator being a member of a team in which all individuals have critical roles.

REFERENCES

Bergan, J. R. (1977). *Behavioral consultation.* Columbus, OH: Merrill.

Deno, E. (1970). Special education as developmental capital. *Exceptional Children, 37,* 229–237.

Dettmer, P., Thurston, L. P., & Dyck, N. (1995). *Consultation, collaboration, and teamwork for students with special needs.* Boston: Allyn & Bacon.

Gutkin, T. B., & Curtis, M. J. (1982). School-based consultation. In C. R. Reynolds & T. B. Gutkin (Eds.), *The handbook of school psychology.* New York: Wiley.

Idol, L., Paolucci-Whitcomb, P., & Nevin, A. (1986). *Collaborative consultation.* Rockville, MD: Aspen Systems Corporation.

Kirk, S. A., & Gallagher, J. J. (1972). *Educating exceptional children* (2nd ed.). Boston: Houghton Mifflin.

Kirk, S. A., & Gallagher, J. J. (1979). *Educating exceptional children* (3rd ed.). Boston: Houghton Mifflin.

Kirk, S. A., & Gallagher, J. J. (1983). *Educating exceptional children* (4th ed.). Boston: Houghton Mifflin.

Lyon, S., & Lyon, G. (1980). Team functioning and staff development: A role release approach to providing integrated educational services for severely handicapped students. *Journal of the Association for the Severely Handicapped, 5,* 250–263.

Medway, F. J. (1979). How effective is school consultation? A review of recent research. *Journal of School Psychology, 17,* 285–282.

Orelove, F. P., & Sobsey, D. (1991). *Educating children with multiple disabilities: A transdisciplinary approach* (2nd ed.). Baltimore: Brookes.

Pryzwansky, W. W. (1974). A reconsideration of the consultation model for delivery of school-based psychological services. *Journal of Orthopsychiatry, 44,* 579–583.

Reynolds, M. C. (1962). A framework for considering some issues in special education. *Exceptional Children, 29,* 147–169.

Tharp, R. G. (1975). The triadic model of consultation: Current considerations. In C. A. Parker (Ed.), *Psychological consultation: Helping teachers meet special needs.* Reston, VA: Council for Exceptional Children.

Thomas, C. C., Correa, V. I., & Morsink, C. V. (1995). *Interactive teaming: Consultation and collaboration in special programs* (2nd ed.). Englewood Cliffs, NJ: Merrill.

ELEANOR BOYD WRIGHT
CAROL CHASE THOMAS
University of North Carolina at Wilmington

TEACHING EXCEPTIONAL CHILDREN (TEC)

Teaching Exceptional Children (*TEC*) is a professional journal that is a joint production of the Council for Exceptional Children Information Center and the Instructional Materials Centers Network for Handicapped Children and

Youth. It was first published in 1968 and now has a circulation of 55,000.

Edited by Dave L. Edyburn, TEC's objective is "to disseminate practical and timely information to classroom teachers working with exceptional children and youth." Published quarterly the journal deals with various topic areas such as practical classroom procedures for use with the gifted and handicapped, educational-diagnostic techniques, evaluation of instructional material, new research findings, and reports of educational projects in progress.

The *TEC* is designed to garner feedback from readers and allow for professional input through features such as "The Teacher Idea Exchange," "Questions and Answers," "Teacher Write In," and "Letters to the Editor."

Information concerning subscriptions or manuscripts should be referred to Publication for Council for Exceptional Children, 1920 Association Drive, Reston, VA 22091.

RICK GONZALES
Texas A & M University

COUNCIL FOR EXCEPTIONAL CHILDREN

TEACHING: INCLUSION AND CO-TEACHING

Co-teaching is a form of instruction in which a general education teacher and special education teacher work together in an inclusive classroom consisting of students with and without disabilities. Typically, the types of students with disabilities found in a co-teaching environment are students considered to have mild disabilities (i.e., learning, behavioral, and speech/language disabilities). Because students with mild disabilities bring a number of general and specific weaknesses to classrooms that may be structurally rigid and where information may be poorly organized, too abstract, uninteresting, and assumes a great deal of prior knowledge, a teacher who specializes in learning processes is a critical support.

Two issues emerge, however: (a) How do teachers teach together to facilitate more successful learning by students with and without disabilities?, and (b) What kinds of teacher and student outcomes can be expected?

What Does Research Say about Co-Teaching?

The literature on co-teaching or collaborative instruction has primarily described barriers to collaboration (e.g., Johnson, Pugach, & Hammittee, 1988; Phillips & McCullough, 1990), types of collaborative relationships (e.g., Bauwens, Hourcade, & Friend, 1989; Dettmer, Thurston, & Dyck, 1993), and a variety of collaborative skills and roles (e.g., Friend & Cook, 1992a; Knackendoffel, Robinson, Deshler, & Schumaker, 1992), and provided little data

on the instructional dynamics of two teachers teaching students with and without disabilities or the performance of the students in inclusive classes (e.g., Idol, Nevin, & Paolucci-Whitcomb, 1994; Reeve & Hallahan, 1994).

In one of the few existing data-based reports on co-teaching, Hudson (1990) described gains for one group of elementary children with and without mild disabilities in grade-point average, achievement test scores, number of academic objectives mastered, adaptive behavior ratings, peer status, and school attendance when they were enrolled in two classrooms employing the Class-Within-a-Class Model for collaborative teaching. Schulte, Osborne, and McKinney (1990) discovered that students with mild disabilities who received some instruction from the special education teacher in general education settings made greater overall gains on a standardized achievement test as compared to students receiving resource room support for one period per day, and as compared to students in the general education classroom where consultation was only provided by the general education teacher. There were no significant differences on a criterion-referenced test, however.

Another study on collaborative instruction in an elementary setting provided negative results. Zigmond and Baker (1990) observed teachers and students with learning disabilities in inclusive classrooms where a combination of collaborative instruction and consultation took place. They concluded that the types of support and kinds of instruction by teachers were essentially "business as usual." Students did not make significant gains on a standardized achievement test, they earned lower grades, and curriculum-based measures showed only minimal progress. Boudah, Schumaker, and Deshler (1997) found that teachers could learn to teach together, but that teacher change translated to only minimal change in student engagement and use of learning strategies. Students also continued to perform poorly on unit tests & quizzes.

Descriptions from these and other studies indicate several other characteristics of co-teaching. Many co-teaching relationships are arranged by building administrators (Boudah, Schumaker, & Deshler, 1997). Perhaps because of such arrangements and little training, the special education teacher also typically functions in one of two roles: (a) provider of indirect services to students through consultation with the general education teacher (e.g., Peck, Killen, & Baumgart, 1989; Tindal, Shinn, Walz, & Germann, 1987); or (b) provider of at least some direct services within general education classrooms, but primarily or exclusively to students with disabilities and with apparently few interactions between the two teachers (e.g., Givens-Olge, Christ, & Idol, 1991; Hudson, 1990). Thus, in the second role, the special education teacher functions more like an instructional aide than a specialist or teacher of at least equivalent instructional status. In addition, many collaboratively taught classes may include a large number of students with disabilities and thus operate like "low-track" classes (Boudah & Knight, 1999). Such efforts then may lead to ceiling effects on teacher instructional change and student performance (Boudah, Schumaker, & Deshler, 1997).

What Might Co-Teaching Look Like?

The keys to two teachers working in the same classroom are the interactions between the teachers as well as the interactions between the teachers and students (Boudah, Schumaker, & Deshler, 1997). Thus, there are several possible models for co-teaching (e.g., Bauwens & Hourcade, 1997; Burrello, Burrello, & Friend, 1996). Some of the models may be called (a) teach and circulate or observe, (b) station teaching, (c) alternative teaching, and (d) team teaching.

In the first model (*teach and circulate or observe*), one teacher would present the content material (e.g., a lesson on the geography of France), and the other teacher would circulate among the students to assist as needed, or collect observation data on student behavior and performance. Teachers might use *station teaching* in order to individualize support for groups of students. For instance, one teacher may need to reteach material to one group of students who were absent the previous day, the other teacher may need to review material for a group with learning disabilities, and another group of students may work independently on an assignment. In *alternative teaching,* a small group of students might sit with one teacher in a corner of the room for additional review, reteaching, enrichment, or help completing an assignment or test.

Team teaching is more dynamic. During class instruction, teachers function in two primary roles: presenter and enhancer. During whole group instruction, the *presenter* presents content information such as facts, rules, concepts, and themes in a subject area such as social studies, math, science, or English. Meanwhile, the *enhancer* arbitrates between students and the content material being presented in class. For instance, in one instructional sequence, a science teacher might talk about a specific concept while the special education teacher simultaneously summarizes the most important points by writing bulleted statements on the chalkboard; later, the special education teacher might talk about another part of the science concept while the science teacher elaborates by providing some specific examples or an analogy. The sequence may finish with both teachers functioning as enhancers, one prompting students to summarize a chronology of facts or events while the other interjects by prompting students to predict what would happen if a different order of events had occurred. Therefore, while the presenter teaches *what* to learn, the enhancer, in essence, teaches *how* to learn the material (Boudah, Schumaker, & Deshler, 1997).

At least initially, the general education teacher may function in the presenter role more often, and the special education teacher commonly may function in the enhancer role. This is for obvious reasons: the general education teacher is likely to be more knowledgeable about the content being presented, and the special education teacher's strength is usually related to teaching skills or strategies for learning. Eventually, however, the general education teacher and the special education teacher may function equally as presenter and enhancer, and both teachers may function as presenter or enhancer at any given time during a lesson. Thus, through this kind of instructional process, the special education teacher and general education teacher can complement and support each other, like partners who are dancing together (Adams, Cessna, & Friend, 1992).

In summary, in co-teaching, both teachers should be actively engaged in teaching students. Both teachers should monitor and enhance student understanding of information and concepts presented in class. Teachers can help each other expand and clarify information and concepts, teach strategies, and enhance, rather than "water down," content. Either teacher can provide whole group or individualized instruction, and both teachers are responsible for managing student behavior and evaluating performance.

Where Do Teachers Start?

As with any method for delivering instructional services to students with disabilities, it is important to focus first on the needs of individual students and decide which students would benefit from co-teaching in inclusive classes. This may not include every student or even every student with a particular disability classification. Once those decisions have been made, clustering a small number of students with disabilities in an inclusive class may not only be instructionally effective, but also may be a more efficient way for special education teachers to serve students.

In addition, co-teaching is often a change in the typical operations of a school. Therefore, co-teachers need to build their plans and schedules with the principal. In order to set up successful experiences, teachers also should be allowed to decide who will teach together. Special education teachers who are trying to facilitate inclusion may need to target general education teachers who may have some special education experience, background, and/or exposure. These teachers are most likely to understand the needs of students with disabilities and be adaptable to instructional change.

Next, co-teachers may want to conduct observations in each others' classes so that they become familiar with their partner's teaching styles and routines. Observations can provide opportunities to think about appropriate co-teaching models and ways to modify and adapt instructional methods. Co-teachers also may find that it is worthwhile to pilot one class for a period of time, develop a relationship, plan as a team, teach as a team, and evaluate team performance before committing to co-teaching for a longer period of time.

Co-teachers should seek out training experiences on specific collaborative skills as well as ways of building shared expectations. Committing to a regular team planning time can also help clarify expectations. Team planning and organization also should lead to more dynamic teaching in the classroom.

School restructuring efforts often highlight coordination and collaboration as important dimensions of the delivery of educational services for children in a broad array of programs including gifted education, English as a Second Language (ESL), Chapter 1 (Association for Supervision and Curriculum Development, 1991), as well as special education. Such integration of services necessarily requires the collaboration of those assigned to work with such a diversity of students. Co-teaching is one way for teachers to collaborate in order to provide a free and appropriate education to some students with disabilities in general education classrooms.

REFERENCES

Adams, L., Cessna, K., & Friend, M. (1992, October). *Co-teaching: Honoring uniqueness and creating unity.* Presentation made at the Annual Conference of the Council for Learning Disabilities, Kansas City, MO.

Bauwens, J., & Hourcade, J. J. (1997). Cooperative teaching: Pictures of possibilities. *Intervention in School and Clinic, 33*(2), 81–85, 89.

Bauwens, J., Hourcade, J. J., & Friend, M. (1989). Cooperative teaching: A model for general and special education integration. *Remedial and Special Education, 10,* 17–22.

Boudah, D. J., Schumaker, J. B., & Deshler, D. D. (1997). Collaborative instruction: Is it an effective option for inclusion in secondary classrooms? *Learning Disability Quarterly, 20*(4), 293–316.

Burrello, L. C., Burrello, J. M., & Friend, M. (Producers). (1996). *The power of 2: Making a difference through co-teaching* [Film]. Indiana University Television Services and Elephant Rock Productions. (Available from CEC Resources, Association Drive, Reston, VA)

Dettmer, P., Thurston, L. P., & Dyck, N. (1993). *Consultation, collaboration, and teamwork for students with special needs.* Boston: Allyn and Bacon.

Friend, M., & Cook, L. (1992a). *Interactions: Collaboration skills for school professionals.* New York: Longman.

Givens-Olge, L., Christ, B. A., & Idol, L. (1991). Collaborative consultation: The San Juan Unified School District project. *Journal of Educational and Psychological Consultation, 2*(3), 267–284.

Hudson, F. (1990). *Research reports for Kansas City, Kansas public schools division of special education on CTM-collaborative teaching model at Stony Point South Elementary School,* *1989–90.* Kansas City, KS: University of Kansas Medical Center, Department of Special Education.

Idol, L., Nevin, A., & Paolucci-Whitcomb, P. (1994). *Collaborative consultation* (2nd ed.). Austin, TX: Pro-Ed.

Johnson, L. J., Pugach, M. C., & Hammittee, D. J. (1988). Barriers to effective special education consultation. *Remedial and Special Education, 9,* 41–47.

Knackendoffel, E. A., Robinson, S. M., Deshler, D. D., & Schumaker, J. B. (1992). *Collaborative problem solving: Team teaching series.* Lawrence, KS: Edge Enterprises, Inc.

Peck, C. A., Killen, C. C., & Baumgart, D. (1989). Increasing implementation of special education instruction in mainstream preschools: Direct and generalized effects of nondirective consultation. *Journal of Applied Behavior Analysis, 2*(2), 197–210.

Phillips, V., & McCullough, L. (1990). Consultation-based programming: Instituting the collaborative ethic in schools. *Exceptional Children, 56,* 291–304.

Reeve, P. T., & Hallahan, D. P. (1994). Practical questions about collaboration between general and special educators. *Focus on Exceptional Children, 26*(7), 1–12.

Schulte, A. C., Osborne, S. S., & McKinney, J. D. (1990). Academic outcomes for students with learning disabilities in consultation and resource programs. *Exceptional Children, 57*(2), 162–171.

Staff. (1991). Resolutions 1991. *Association for Supervision and Curriculum Development.*

Tindal, G., Shinn, M. R., Walz, L., & Germann, G. (1987). Mainstream consultation in secondary settings: The Pine County model. *The Journal of Special Education, 21,* 94–106.

Zigmond, N., & Baker, J. (1990). Mainstream experiences for learning disabled students (Project MELD): Preliminary report. *Exceptional Children, 57*(2), 176–185.

Daniel J. Boudah
Texas A & M University

TEACHING STRATEGIES

Teaching strategies are those activities that are conducted by a teacher to enhance the academic achievement of students. A teaching strategy is based on a philosophical approach that is used in conjunction with a learning strategy. Teachers generally choose a particular approach based on their educational background and training, their personal beliefs, the subject being taught, the characteristics of the learner, and the degree of learning required.

Training backgrounds of special educators can range from the behavioral to the process-oriented. Teachers with behavioral backgrounds will use approaches that are task specific and focus on observable behaviors. Those coming from a process background are more inclined to follow approaches that focus on underlying processes. They try to treat the hypothesized cause of the problem or deficit rather than the observable behavior. Approaches such as perceptual-motor training or cognitive training may be followed by teachers with process orientations. Perceptual-motor training approaches are controversial and have questionable effectiveness in regard to academic achievement (Arter & Jenkins, 1979; Kavale & Forness, 1999; Sedlak & Weener, 1973). Cognitive training approaches focus on thinking skills and learning how to learn rather than specific content skills. The research on this approach is promising. Examples of behavioral approaches are direct instruction and applied behavior analysis. These approaches focus on identifying the specific content to be taught and teaching that content in a systematic fashion using a prescribed system of learning strategies. There are also subject specific approaches. For example, in reading, some of the different approaches available are the linguistics approach, phonics, sight word, Fernald, multisensory, language experience, and the neurological impress method. These approaches focus on the organization of the materials needed for instruction and also prescribe, in some cases, specific strategies to be used.

In addition to an approach, the application of a learning strategy to a situation is needed to create a teaching strategy. A learning strategy becomes a teaching strategy when the teacher systematically plans, organizes, and uses a learning strategy with a student to achieve a specific outcome. In many texts, these learning strategies are referred to as generic strategies or principles of instruction. These strategies generally are used in conjunction with a particular phase of learning (e.g., acquisition, retention, or transfer), or for a particular type of learning (e.g., discrimination, concept, rule, problem solving). Generic strategies used for the acquisition phase include giving instruction (verbal, picture, modeling or demonstration, reading), revealing objectives to the learner, providing appropriate practice on a skill, providing feedback to the learner, organizing material into small steps and in sequential order, checking on student comprehension through questions, and offering positive and negative examples of concepts. However, it is also important for students to learn to teach others through the development of their own strategic and skillful processing of information (Alexander & Murphy, 1999).

The generic strategies that can be used to maintain skills already acquired are overlearning, reminiscence, and spaced review. To teach for transfer, multiple examples of the application of the skill or concept are needed, along with teaching the skill with the appropriate cues in the setting in which it is to be practiced. Gradually fading artificial cues and relying on natural cues in the environment is another strategy used by teachers to facilitate transfer. Some other examples of teaching strategies are the use of mnemonics, peer teaching, assigned homework, graded homework, cooperative learning, mediated instruction, and computer-assisted instruction. In strategies such

as these, a variety of learning strategies are organized and used.

REFERENCES

Alexander, P., & Murphy, P. (1999). What cognitive psychology has to say to school psychology. In C. R. Reynolds & T. B. Gutkin (Eds.), *The Handbook of School Psychology* (3rd ed.). New York: Wiley.

Arter, J. A., & Jenkins, J. R. (1979). Differential diagnosis—Prescriptive teaching: A critical appraisal. *Review of Educational Research, 49,* 517–555.

Kavale, K., & Forness, S. (1999). The effectiveness of special education. In C. R. Reynolds & T. B. Gutkin (Eds.), *Handbook of School Psychology* (3rd ed.). New York: Wiley.

Sedlak, R. A., & Weener, P. (1973). Review of research on the Illinois Test of Psycholinguistics Abilities. In L. Mann & D. Sabatino (Eds.), *The first review of special education.* Philadelphia: JSE.

Robert A. Sedlak
University of Wisconsin at Stout

**ABILITY TRAINING
APPLIED BEHAVIOR ANALYSIS
DIRECT INSTRUCTION
MNEMONICS
TEACHER EFFECTIVENESS**

TECHNIQUES: A JOURNAL FOR REMEDIAL EDUCATION AND COUNSELING

Techniques originated in July 1984 with Gerald B. Fuller and Hubert Vance as coeditors. The journal provides multidisciplinary articles that serve as an avenue for communication and interaction among the various disciplines concerned with the treatment and education of the exceptional individual and others encountering special problems in living. The orientation is primarily clinical and educational, and reflects the various types of counseling, therapy, remediation, and interventions currently employed. The journal does not mirror the opinion of any one school or authority but serves as a forum for open discussion and exchange of ideas and experiences.

The specific sections in *Techniques* represent the following content areas:

1. *Educational and Psychological Materials.* This section helps the professional to keep current by evaluating, critiquing, comparing, and reviewing educational, counseling, and psychological materials (e.g., programs, kits) that are being proposed or used in applied settings.

2. *Research Studies*. This section offers empirical research, case studies, and discussion papers that focus on specific counseling, therapy, and remediation techniques that cut across various disciplines.

3. *Practical Approaches in the Field*. This section provides a description of hands-on techniques or approaches that the author(s) have used and found to be successful within their field.

4. *Parent Education*. This section provides comprehensive treatment of such topics as disruptive children and youths, single-parent families, reconstituted families, and prevention and treatment of child abuse and neglect.

5. *Bibliotherapy*. This is a compilation of books that are useful for the child and parent as well as the practitioner. The topics are practical and address such issues as divorce, self-concept, and drug abuse.

6. *What's New in the Field*. This section provides current information in the areas of remedial programs and counseling techniques, and includes reviews of current software programs.

GERALD B. FULLER
Central Michigan University

TECHNOLOGY FOR THE DISABLED

If there is one word that summarizes the impact of technology in the last 25 years, it is zeitgeist, the spirit of the time. The inculcation of silicon chips and microprocessors into our everyday lives irrevocably changed us from an industrial society to an informational society (Toffler, 1982). If disabled persons are to function fully in this society, they must have access to the myriad technologies that can improve communication, information processing, and learning. While technological advances are making in-roads in the reduction of the impact of motoric, sensory, and cognitive disabilities, the real potential is yet to be met. The following section is an introduction to some of the technologies that are currently affecting the lives of disabled persons. It also offers an overview of some of the technologies that have yet to fulfill their promise.

The computer is second only to the printing press in its impact on the way in which humans acquire and distribute information. As computers are reduced in size and cost, their impact is multiplied geometrically. The computer has two characteristics that are particularly significant for disabled individuals: (1) as hardware decreases in size, it generally increases in capacity; and (2) the more sophisticated computers become, the easier they are to use. These characteristics are very important for handicapped individuals in several respects. First, as computers become smaller, they also become more portable. For example, hand-held microcomputers can be attached to wheelchairs to improve mobility. Second, as computers become easier to use, they are more accessible to the handicapped. For example, reducing the number of keystrokes required to perform certain computer functions has greatly facilitated their use.

Microprocessor-based technology facilitates communication in two ways: as a compensatory device for sensory disabilities and as an assistive device for individuals whose physical impairments make communication difficult. Examples of compensatory devices include talking computer terminals that can translate text into speech (Stoffel, 1982); special adaptive devices for microcomputers that can provide visual displays of auditory information by translating sound into text (Vanderheiden, 1982); and Cognivox, an adaptive device for Apple personal computers that combines the capabilities of voice recognition and voice output (Murray, 1982).

For individuals with motoric disabilities, communication aids have been developed that allow them to operate computers with single-switch input devices. These devices may be as simple as game paddles and joysticks or as sophisticated as screen-based optical headpointing systems. Keyboard enhancers and emulators help individuals with restricted movement by reducing the number of actuations necessary for communication. For example, Minispeak is a semantic compaction system that can produce thousands of clear, spoken sentences with as few as seven keystrokes (Baker, 1982). Adaptive communication devices can also be linked with microcomputers to help the disabled control their living environments (e.g., by running appliances, answering the telephone, or adjusting the thermostat).

The term telecommunication means communication across distance. It is a means of storing text and pictures as electronic impulses and transmitting them via telephone line, satellite, coaxial and fiber optic cables, or broadcast transmission. Telecommunication offers several advantages over traditional means of communication. First, telecommunication is relatively inexpensive when spread across time and users. Also, telecommunicating helps alleviate the problems associated with geographic remoteness or the isolation imposed by limited mobility. Information-gathering and dissemination need not be limited to schools. It can occur in the home or office; a local area network (LAN) can link several microcomputers or terminals to a computer with expanded memory. Such a system permits several operators to use the same software and data simultaneously. A wide-area network links computers from distant geographic regions. Examples of this networking capability can be found in several states where all of the local agencies are linked to the state agency. Statewide systems greatly reduce the time and paperwork necessary for compliance with special education legislation.

SpecialNet is another example of a wide-area network. Subscribers use it primarily to access electronic bulletin boards and to send messages through electronic mail. Electronic bulletin boards function much the same as traditional corkboards found in most schools. Users can post messages to obtain information, or they can read messages to find out the latest information about a given topic. For example, the employment bulletin board on SpecialNet posts vacancies in special education and related services. The Request for Proposals (RFP) bulletin board has information on the availability of upcoming grants and contracts. The exchange bulletin board is for users to post requests for information. Electronic mail, as the name implies, is a system whereby computer users can send and receive messages through their computers. On the SpecialNet system, each subscriber is given a special name that identifies his or her mailbox; with the aid of word processing and telecommunication software, users can send short or long documents in a matter of seconds.

In addition to capabilities offered by electronic bulletin boards and electronic mail, individuals with telecommunication hookups have access to information from large electronic libraries that store, sort, and retrieve bibliographic information. For example, the Educational Resources Information Center (ERIC), operated by the Council for Exceptional Children, is the largest source of information on handicapped and gifted children. Other important sources of information are the Handicapped Exchange (HEX), which contains information on handicapped individuals, and ABLEDATA, which is a catalog of computer hardware, software, and assistive devices for the handicapped.

Another important form of telecommunication is teletext, a one-way transmission to television viewers. Teletext uses the vertical blanking interval (VBI), the unused portion of a television signal, to print information on television screens. Applications of teletext include news headlines, weather forecasts, and information on school closings. Closed captioning is a form of teletext that allows hearing-impaired individuals to see dialogue (JWK International, 1983). Experiments are now under way to use teletext to transmit instructional material. Broadcasters can transmit public domain software into homes and schools that have microcomputers and special transmission decoding devices.

A videodisk is a tabletop device that is interfaced with a monitor to play video programs stored on 12-inch disks. When interfaced with a microcomputer, the videodisk becomes interactive, and thus becomes a powerful instructional tool. Part of the videodisk's power comes from its storage capacity; it can hold 54,000 frames of information, including movies, filmstrips, slides, and sound. When combined with the microcomputer's branching capacity, videodisks allow students to move ahead or go back according to the learner's needs. Information can also be shown in slow motion or freeze frame. One of the earliest educational videodisks was the First National Kidisc, a collection of games and activities for children. The California School for the Deaf in Riverside also developed a system to use the videodisk to teach language development and reading. With this system, students use light pens to write their responses on the screen (Wollman, 1981). In the past, videodisk technology has been very expensive because of the cost in developing the disks. Now, however, educators and other service providers can have customized disks made at relatively low cost.

Artificial intelligence refers to the use of the computer to solve the same types of problems and to make the same kinds of decisions faced by humans (Yin & Moore, 1984). Because scientists do not fully understand how humans solve problems and make decisions, they have debated whether true artificial intelligence is possible. So far, the closest they have come is the development of expert systems, natural systems, and machine vision. Expert systems are computer programs that use knowledge and inference strategies to solve problems. The systems rely on three kinds of information: facts, relations between the facts, and methods for using the facts to solve problems (D'Ambrosio, 1985). An example of an expert system is Internist, which makes medical diagnoses. Natural language processing is the use of natural speech to communicate with computers and to translate foreign language texts. Machine vision takes advantage of sensory devices to reproduce objects on the computer screen. These technological applications, like many others, offer potential benefits to disabled individuals, but their use for physical or cognitive prostheses hinges on the commitment of vast resources for their development.

A robot is a device that can be programmed to move in specified directions and to manipulate objects. What distinguishes a robot from other technologies and prosthetic devices is its capacity for locomotion. Robotic arms can pick up and move objects, assemble parts, and even spray paint. Robots of the future will not only be able to move, they will also be able to sense the environment by touch, sight, or sound. More important, the robot will be able to acquire information, understand it, and plan and implement appropriate actions (Yin & Moore, 1984). While robots offer great potential as prosthetic devices for the disabled, their current use is limited primarily to research and manufacturing. To some extent, robots are being used in classrooms to teach computer logic.

Specific technologies are in use today in special education classrooms for nearly all categories of disabling conditions, including communication disorders, health impairments, hearing impairments, visual impairments, and students with learning disabilities in particular (e.g., see Cartwright, Cartwright, & Ward, 1995). Technology is growing most rapidly in areas where it was first used and seems to have the greatest impact on quality of life issues in the sensory impairments and communication disorders.

Computer-aided instruction is on the rise as well, especially with children with learning disabilities, but is a latecomer. As recently as 1990, the major textbook in learning disabilities (Myers & Hammill, 1990) makes no mention of technology for learning disability interventions.

REFERENCES

Baker, B. (1982). Minispeak: A semantic compaction system that makes self-expression easier for communicatively disabled individuals. *Byte, 7,* 186–202.

Cartwright, P., Cartwright, C., & Ward, M. (1995). *Educating special learners* (4th ed.). Boston: Wadsworth.

D'Ambrosio, B. (1985). Expert systems—Myth or reality? *Byte, 10,* 275–282.

JWK International. (1983). *Teletext and videotex* (Contract No. 300-81-0424). Washington, DC: Special Education Programs Office.

Murray, W. (1982). The Cognivox V10-1003: Voice recognition and output for the Apple II. *Byte, 7,* 231–235.

Myers, P., & Hammill, D. (1990). *Methods for learning disorders* (4th ed.). Austin, TX: Pro-Ed.

Pfaehler, B. (1985). Electronic text: The University of Wisconsin experience. *T.H.E. Journal, 13,* 67–70.

Stoffel, D. (1982). Talking terminals. *Byte, 7,* 218–227.

Toffler, A. (1982). *The third wave.* New York: Bantham.

Vanderheiden, G. (1982). Computers can play a dual role for disabled individuals. *Byte, 7,* 136–162.

Wollman, J. (1981). The videodisc: A new educational technology takes off. *Electronic Learning, 1,* 39–40.

Yin, R. K., & Moore, G. B. (1984). *Robotics, artificial intelligence, computer simulation: Future applications in special education.* Washington, DC: U.S. Department of Education.

ELIZABETH MCCLELLAN
*Council for Exceptional
Children*

COMPUTER USE WITH THE HANDICAPPED
ROBOTICS
SPECIALNET

TECSE

See EARLY CHILDHOOD SPECIAL EDUCATION, TOPICS IN.

TEGRETOL

Tegretol (carbamazepine) is an anticonvulsant medication indicated for the treatment of various types of seizure disorders. In addition, Tegretol may also be prescribed for the treatment of manic-depressive disorders, resistant schizophrenia, rage outburst, or alcohol withdrawal management (Shannon, Wilson, & Stang, 1995).

Tegretol should be taken with food to minimize gastric irritation. All individuals need to be advised to take sustained released Tegretol as a whole tablet and never crush or chew the pill. Tegretol must be taken at regular intervals during the day and exactly as ordered by the physician (Deglin & Vallerand, 1999). Abrupt discontinuation may result in severe seizure activity and is not recommended (Shannon, Wilson, & Stang, 1995). Possible side effects include dizziness or drowsiness, and those starting treatment should take great care to avoid operating any machinery or driving a vehicle until their response to Tegretol is analyzed (Deglin & Vallerand, 1999). Since photosensitivity reactions also may occur, excessive sunlight should be avoided and sunscreen protection routinely used (Shannon, Wilson, & Stang, 1995).

Tegretol may cause breakthrough bleeding in women taking oral contraceptives (McKenry & Salerno, 1998). Women should be instructed to use other birth control methods as Tegretol may interfere with the effectiveness of their oral contraceptives. Tegretol is also excreted in breast milk and is not recommended in nursing mothers (McKenry & Solerno, 1998). Tegretol, along with other anticonvulsant medications such as phenytoin, (Dilantin), valproic acid (Depakene/Depakote), primidone (Mysoline), and phenobarbitol, appears to have teratogenic effects, and prenatal exposure to multiple ones appears to increase risk to the fetus (Jones, 1997). Women with seizure disorders who are at risk for pregnancy should be tested to determine if medication can be suspended if they have been seizure free for two years or at least maintained on a low dose. The conflict between potentially adverse effects of seizures on mother and fetus and medication on the fetus may be difficult to resolve.

An individual taking Tegretol should be advised that a medical alert identification card, bracelet, or necklace should be with the person at all times to alert health care providers of the medications that the person is taking as well as any pertinent medical history (Skidmore-Roth & McKenry, 1997). With any continuous medication regime, school personnel should be notified of this medication and any other health related concerns (Wong, 1995).

REFERENCES

Deglin, J., & Vallerand, A. (1999). *Davis's drug guide for nurses* (6th ed.). Philadelphia: F. A. Davis.

Jones, K. L. (1997). *Smith's recognizable patterns of human malformation* (5th ed.). Philadelphia: W. B. Saunders.

McKenry, L., & Salerno, E. (1998). *Pharmacology in nursing* (20th ed.). St. Louis: Mosby-Year Book, Inc.

Shannon, M., Wilson, B., & Stang, C. (1995). *Govoni & Hayes drugs and nursing implications* (8th ed.). Norwalk, CT: Appleton & Lange.

Skidmore-Roth, L., & McKenry, L. (1997). *Mosby's drug guide for nurses* (2nd ed.). St. Louis: Mosby-Year Book.

Wong, D. (1995). *Whaley & Wong's nursing care of infants and children* (5th ed.). St. Louis: Mosby-Year Book.

KARI ANDERSON
University of North Carolina at Wilmington

ABSENCE SEIZURES
ANTICONVULSANTS
GRAND MAL SEIZURES

TELECOMMUNICATION DEVICES FOR THE DEAF (TDDs; TTYs)

Telecommunication devices for the deaf (TDDs or TTYs) make communication by telephone available to the hearing-impaired population by providing video or printed modes of communication across regular phone lines. Using a modem, or acoustic coupler, a TDD user types out a message to another user. This message either moves across a video display screen or is typed on a roll of paper. In this fashion, conversations can be held and information exchanged as far as telephone wires extend.

A TDD uses a regular or slightly modified keyboard. Some special terminology is used to facilitate ease of transmission. GA, for go ahead, indicates to one user that the other is waiting for a reply. SK, for stop keying, denotes the completion of a conversation. Often a Q is typed to imply a question.

The number of TDDs in public and private use is increasing rapidly. Public service agencies such as libraries, schools, and airlines are using TDDs to enable the hearing-impaired population to use their services (Low, 1985). Police and fire departments use TDDs to ensure the safety of hearing-impaired individuals. The TDD has been hailed as a great contributor to the independence of hearing-impaired persons.

REFERENCE

Low, K. (1985). Telecommunication devices for the deaf. *American Libraries, 16*, 746–747.

MARY GRACE FEELY
School for the Deaf

DEAF
ELECTRONIC COMMUNICATION AIDS

TELECOMMUNICATIONS SYSTEMS IN SPECIAL EDUCATION

The use of telecommunication technology for special education mirrors the explosion of technology in society. In the same way that commercial electronic network services such as Compu-Serve and The Source have become widely known to the general public, SpecialNet is an electronic mail service and information source specifically for special educators. Similarly, transformation of the telephone system from copper to fiber optic wire will facilitate rapid data transmission for any use, including perhaps transfer of data on special education students as they move from district to district.

Certain types of telecommunication technologies (e.g., computer-assisted instruction) delivered over telephone lines from a central location, as in the University of Illinois' PLATO system, are being made obsolete as modifications are made for personal computers, thus reducing the costs of instruction delivery. Other technologies involving electronic memory and telephone transmission are expanding, notably ABLEDATA, a bibliographic source of information on assistive devices for the disabled.

Telecommunications technology, currently in a period of rapid change, may transform special education practice in much the same way that it is transforming communication worldwide. However, in contrast to other technologies developed specifically for the disabled, special education will benefit from technological advances for all citizens. Thus the average modern family may use a personal computer, modem, and telephone line as a link to specialized news sources, stock quotes and discount brokers, specialized electronic news services, and targeted mailboards or electronic mailboxes. Disabled persons, using the same systems, may communicate with other persons with similar interests, scan specialized information sources, work in competitive employment from their homes, and avail themselves of services provided for all citizens. Special educators in public schools and higher education may use telecommunications for much the same purposes, targeting their efforts toward the acquisition of information from rapidly expanding specialized information networks.

JAMES W. TAWNEY
Pennsylvania State University

COMPUTER-ASSISTED INSTRUCTION
ELECTRONIC COMMUNICATION AIDS

TEMPERAMENT

Individual differences in temperament have been recognized for centuries. The Greeks talked of four basic dispositions, Kretschmer (1925) and Sheldon (1942) related personality to body types, and Eysenck (1967) linked constitutional and personality variables. Yet, the notion of constitutional contributions to behavior received only limited formal attention from American psychologists and educators until relatively recently. Major impetus to the study of temperament has come from the work of psychiatrists Alexander Thomas and Stella Chess and their colleagues (Thomas & Chess, 1977; Thomas, Chess, Birch, Hertzig, & Korn, 1963), but independent support for the notion of temperament may be found in pediatric and psychiatric research (Carey, 1981, 1982, 1985a; Graham, Rutter, & George, 1973; Rutter, 1964; Rutter, Tizard, & Whitmore, 1970), in longitudinal studies of development (Lerner & Lerner, 1983; Werner & Smith, 1982), in research on infants (Bates, 1980, 1983; Rothbart & Derryberry, 1981) and on child-family interactions (Dunn & Kendrick, 1982; Hinde, Easton, Meller, & Tamplin, 1982; Stevenson-Hinde & Simpson, 1982), in twin studies (Goldsmith & Gottesman, 1981; Matheny, Wilson, & Nuss, 1984; Wilson, 1983; Wilson & Matheny, 1983), and in work in behavioral genetics (DeFries & Plomin, 1978; Plomin, 1982; Torgersen, 1982). Temperament is an important area of concern from both research and applied perspectives. Its relevance to special education and the development and adjustment of handicapped children is increasingly recognized.

Definitions. Although intuitively appealing, temperament has somewhat different definitions, depending on the investigator. Thomas and Chess (1977) view temperament as a stylistic variable. They consider that temperament describes how an individual behaves, not what an individual does or how well he or she does it. Thomas and Chess identified nine dimensions of temperament or behavioral style: activity level, adaptability, approach/withdrawal, attention span and persistence, distractibility, intensity of reaction, quality of mood, rhythmicity (regularity), and threshold of responsiveness. The dimensions were derived in part from Thomas and Chess's clinical observations, and were formalized in major longitudinal research, the New York Longitudinal Study (NYLS). In Thomas and Chess's view, these temperamental variations are, in part, constitutional in base.

The constitutional or biological anchoring of temperament is apparent in other definitions. Buss and Plomin (1975, 1984) propose that to be considered a temperament, a behavioral predisposition must meet criteria of developmental stability, presence in adulthood, adaptiveness, and presence in animals, and must have a genetic component. They define four dimensions that, in their view, meet these criteria: emotionality, activity, sociability, and impulsivity. Rothbart and Derryberry (1981), based primarily on their studies of human infants, suggest that temperament is best conceptualized as individual differences in reactivity and regulation that are presumed to be constitutionally based. Their formulation emphasizes arousal (or excitability) and the neural and behavioral processes that regulate or modulate it, a formulation consistent with that of Strelau (1983). Goldsmith and Campos (1986) adopt a somewhat different perspective, defining temperament as individual variation in emotionality, including differences in

the primary emotions of fear, anger, sadness, pleasure, etc., as well as in a more general arousal; they consider both temperament and intensive parameters. It should be noted that a major definitional issue relates to distinctions between temperament and personality (Goldsmith & Campos, 1982; Rutter, 1982). Many investigators consider temperament a constitutional and genetic component of personality. This view is well reflected in the definition that emerged from the 1980 New Haven Temperament Symposium: "Temperament involves those dimensions of personality that are largely genetic or constitutional in origin, exist in most ages and in most societies, show some consistency across situations, and are relatively stable, at least within major developmental areas" (Plomin, 1983, p. 49). Thus, despite differences in specific components and in emphases, there is some consensus that temperament is an individual difference that has its basis in biological or constitutional makeup, has some stability across setting and time, and is linked to differences in behavioral or expressive styles (Bouchard, 1995).

Measurement. Adequacy of measurement has been a persistent problem for researchers of temperament (Hubert, Wachs, Peters-Martin, & Gandour, 1982; Plomin, 1982; Rothbart, 1981; Rothbart & Goldsmith, 1985; Rutter, 1982). Rothbart and Goldsmith (1985) note that the three most commonly used data-gathering techniques for infant temperament studies are questionnaires, home observations, and laboratory observations. With older children there has been reliance primarily on parent, caretaker, or teacher reports gathered through interviews or questionnaires. Measures designed for use with adults (Burks & Rubenstein, 1979; Guilford & Zimmerman, 1949; Lerner, Palermo, Spiro, III, & Nesselroade, 1982) are usually self-report formats. In addition to issues of psychometric adequacy of scales, individual investigators have developed measuring instruments and techniques that are consistent with their own conceptualizations of temperament. Thus scales differ in the number of dimensions identified and in the content of those dimensions. As an example, the Thomas and Chess scale taps nine dimensions, the Buss and Plomin (EASI) scale taps four. Similarly, behavior observations in natural and laboratory settings vary according to project and investigator. The consequence has been continuing concern about constructs and measures (Baker & Velicer, 1982; Bates, 1980, 1983; Plomin, 1982; Rothbart, 1981; Thomas, Chess, & Korn, 1982; Vaughn, Deinard, & Egeland, 1980; Vaughn, Taraldson, Crichton, & Egeland, 1981). Given the importance of Thomas and Chess's influence on this field, and the relevance of their work to clinical and educational practice, their questionnaires will be described in more detail.

Thomas and Chess developed a Parent Temperament Survey (PTS) and a Teacher Temperament Survey (TTS). The PTS contains 72 items, 8 for each of the 9 hypothesized dimensions of temperament. The TTS, similar in format, contains 64 items (the dimension of rythmicity is not included). Items were selected to describe behavioral expressions of the various temperament dimensions (e.g., "When first meeting new children, my child is bashful"; from the TTS: "Child will initially avoid new games and activities, preferring to sit on the side and watch"). Items are rated 1 (hardly ever) to 7 (almost always). Dimensional scores (means of the items in each dimension) are assumed to be independent. Factor studies and qualitative analyses within the NYLS suggested three temperamental constellations that described two-thirds of the sample: the easy child, characterized as regular or rhythmic, positive in approach to new stimuli, adaptable to change, and mild or moderately intense and positive in mood; the difficult child, described as irregular, negative in response to new stimuli, low or slow in adaptability, and intense, often negative in mood; and the slow-to-warm-up child, viewed as mildly intense in reactivity, slow to adapt, but given time, positive in involvement.

A number of investigators have modified the PTS and TTS but have maintained Thomas and Chess's conceptual framework. Keogh, Pullis, and Cadwell (1980, 1982) reduced both parent and teacher scales to 23 items each, and identified simpler factor structures. The three primary factors in the TTS were task orientation, personal-social flexibility, and reactivity, an essentially negative factor. The PTS yielded two multidimensional factors and two single-dimension factors: social competence and reactivity, and mood and persistence. These factors are generally consistent with those identified by Windle and Lerner (1985) in their life-span research and with those defined by Martin and his colleagues (Martin, 1984a; Paget, Nagle, & Martin, 1984) in work with schoolchildren. Also working within the Thomas and Chess framework, Carey, Fox and McDevitt (1977) have done extensive scale development. Their questionnaires cover infancy through the elementary school years and include the Infant Temperament Questionnaire (ITQ; Carey, 1970; Carey & McDevitt, 1978), the Toddler Temperament Scale (Fullard, McDevitt, & Carey, 1978), the Behavioral Styles Questionnaire (McDevitt & Carey, 1978), and the Middle Childhood Temperament Questionnaire (Hegvik, McDevitt, & Carey, 1982). These instruments are similar in format, describe behaviors that are age and setting appropriate, and have good reliability and internal consistency. Each scale contains approximately 100 items and requires about 30 minutes for a parent to complete. Thus there are a number of instruments designed to capture parents' and teachers' views of children's temperamental characteristics. Despite their clinical appeal and usefulness, many of the questionnaires have been challenged on a number of counts: lack of independence of items and dimensions, item unreliability or bias, unknown factorial organization across developmental periods, or situational specificity of behaviors. Clearly, there are real and continuing uncertainties in the measurement of temperament that mandate caution in interpreting temperament findings. Yet, there is also considerable consistency of findings across studies and approaches, which argues for the robustness of temperament variables.

Clinical Applications. There are increasing numbers of reports of the importance of temperament in pediatric and psychiatric settings. Pediatricians Carey (1981, 1985a, 1985b, 1985c) and Weissbluth (1982, 1984; Weissbluth et al.; Weissbluth, Brouillette, Kiang, & Hunt, 1985; Weissbluth & Green, 1984) emphasize that temperament is an influence on children's development and adjustment, specifically linking infants' temperamental characteristics to a variety of pediatric problems (e.g., colic, sleep difficulties). In recent work, Carey (1985b) suggests that temperament may also be viewed as an outcome or consequence of various clinical conditions e.g., pre-, post-, and perinatal conditions or insults. From psychiatric and psychological perspectives, there has also been a continuing interest in temperament as a predisposing factor for behavioral and emotional or adjustment problems (Barron & Earls, 1984; Cameron, 1977; Chess & Korn, 1970; Earls, 1981; Graham et al., 1973; Rutter, 1964; Thomas & Chess, 1977; Thomas, Chess, & Birch, 1968). Maziade et al., (1985) found difficult temperament predicted psychiatric diagnosis in later childhood, and Kolvin, Nichol, Garside, Day, and Tweddle (1982) reported relationships between temperament and aggression in clinic referred boys. Although the processes linking temperament and problems in behavior and adjustment are not yet explicit, there appears to be enough evidence to infer a relationship.

Educational Applications. The formal application of temperament constructs to educational practice is relatively recent but is growing. As part of the NYLS, Gordon and Thomas (1967) reported that children's temperament influenced teachers' estimates of their school abilities, and Carey, Fox, and McDevitt (1977) identified relationships between parents' ratings of children and adjustment in school. A number of investigators report relationships between temperamental patterns and academic performance in school (Chess, Thomas, & Cameron, 1976; Hall & Cadwell, 1984; Hegvik, 1984, 1986; Keogh, 1982a; Keogh & Pullis, 1980; Lerner, 1983; Lerner, Lerner, & Zabski, 1985; Martin, 1984b, 1986; Martin, Nagle, & Paget, 1983; Pullis, 1979; Pullis & Cadwell, 1982; Skuy, Snell, & Westaway, 1985). It should be noted that in general, there are non-significant or marginally significant relationships between temperament and cognitive ability as indexed by IQ (Keogh, 1982a, 1982c; Pullis, 1983), although Martin (1985) identified moderate and significant relationships between temperament attributes of adaptability, approach/withdrawal, and persistence and IQ in a sample of grade 1 pupils. Overall, the evidence suggests that temperament and cognitive ability are partially independent contributors to educational achievement.

In addition to achievement in academic content, there is considerable evidence to suggest that temperamental variations are related to children's personal and social adjustment in school. Billman (1984), Carey et al. (1977), Chess et al. (1976), Feuerstein and Martin (1981), Hall and Keogh (1978), Keogh (1982a, 1982b, 1982c), Kolvin et al. (1982), Lerner (1983), Lerner at al. (1985), Martin (1985), Paget et al. (1984), Terestman (1980), and Thomas and Chess (1977) have linked children's temperament and behavior and adjustment problems. The impact of temperament may be particularly powerful where children have other handicapping or problem conditions (Keogh, 1982c), although there are temperamental differences within groups of handicapped children (Hanson, 1979). Field and Greenfield (1982) suggest that temperament patterns may be associated with particular handicapping conditions, and Chess, Korn, and Fernandez (1971) report a high number of behavior disorders related to difficult temperament patterns in a group of young congenital rubella children; the latter findings were consistent with the relationship between temperament and behavior problems in a group of mentally delayed children (Chess & Korn, 1970). In a series of ongoing studies, (Keogh, Bernhemier, Pelland, and Daley, 1985) confirmed links between developmentally delayed children's temperament and their behavior problems and adjustment. Lambert and Windmiller (1977) found strong correlations between selected temperament attributes and hyperactivity in a large group of at-risk elementary school children. There also is some tentative evidence linking temperament to adjustment and achievement problems of learning-disabled pupils (Keogh, 1983; Pullis, 1983; Scholom & Schiff, 1980).

Temperament may contribute to school achievement and adjustment in several ways (Keogh, 1986) and is related to intellectual performance (Brebner & Stough, 1995). It may be a factor in a generalized response set; i.e., some temperaments may fit well with the complex and changing demands of school whereas others do not. Temperament may affect a child's specific preparation for learning by allowing activity and attention to be modulated and directed easily and quickly. Temperament may interact with particular subject matter to facilitate or impede learning. Individual differences in temperament are also significant contributors to children's personal-social adjustment in school. Intuitively, at least, interpersonal problems have a strong foundation in child-peer and child-teacher interactions. Thus, personal style, or temperament, may be a major factor in problem behavior. If the relationship between children's temperament and their achievement and behavioral adjustment in school is considered within Thomas and Chess's "goodness of fit" notion, then both child characteristics and setting or task demands and conditions must be taken into account. Goodness of fit has important implications for identification, diagnosis, intervention, and treatment.

REFERENCES

Baker, E. H., & Velicer, W. F. (1982). The structure and reliability of the Teacher Temperament Questionnaire. *Journal of Abnormal Child Psychology, 10*(4), 531–546.

Barron, A. P., & Earls, F. (1984). The relation of temperament and social factors to behavior problems in three-year-old children. *Journal of Child Psychology & Psychiatry, 25*(1), 23–33.

Bates, J. E. (1980). The concept of difficult temperament. *Merrill-Palmer Quarterly, 26*(4), 299–319.

Bates, J. E. (1983). Issues in the assessment of difficult temperament: A reply to Thomas, Chess, and Korn. *Merrill-Palmer Quarterly, 29*(1), 89–97.

Billman, J. (1984, October). *The relationship of temperament traits to classroom behavior in nine year old children: A follow-up study.* Paper presented at the Conference on Temperament in the Educational Process, St. Louis, MO.

Bouchard, T. (1995). Longitudinal studies of personality and intelligence. In D. Saklofske & M. Zeidner (Eds.), *International handbook of personality and intelligence,* NY: Plenum.

Brebner, J., & Stough, C. (1995). Theoretical and empirical relationships between personality and intelligence. In D. Saklofske & M. Zeidner (eds.), *International handbook of personality and intelligence.* New York: Plenum.

Burks, J., & Rubenstein, M. (1979). *Temperament styles in adult interaction: Application in psychotherapy.* New York: Brunner/Mazel.

Buss, A. H., & Plomin, R. (1975). *A temperament theory of personality development.* New York: Wiley.

Buss, A. H., & Plomin, R. (1984). *Temperament: Early developing personality traits.* Hillsdale, NJ: Erlbaum.

Cameron, J. R. (1977). Parental treatment, children's temperament, and the risk of childhood behavioral problems: Initial temperament, parental attitudes, and the incidence and form of behavioral problems. *American Journal of Orthopsychiatry, 48,* 140–147.

Carey, W. B. (1970). A simplified method for measuring infant temperament. *Journal of Pediatrics, 77,* 188–194.

Carey, W. B. (1981). The importance of temperament-environment interaction for child health and development. In M. Lewis & L. A. Rosenblum (Eds.), *The uncommon child.* New York: Plenum.

Carey, W. B. (1982a). Clinical use of temperament data in pediatrics. In R. Porter & G. M. Collins (Eds.), *Temperament differences in infants and young children* (pp. 191–205). London: Pitman.

Carey, W. B. (1985a). Clinical use of temperament data in pediatrics. *Developmental & Behavioral Pediatrics, 6*(3), 137–142.

Carey, W. B. (1985b). Interactions of temperament and clinical conditions. In M. Wolraich & D. K. Routh (Eds.), *Advances in developmental and behavioral pediatrics* (Vol. 6, pp. 83–115). Greenwich, CT: JAI.

Carey, W. B. (1985c). Temperament and increased weight gain in infants. *Development & Behavioral Pediatrics, 6*(3), 128–131.

Carey, W. B., Fox, M., & McDevitt, S. C. (1977). Temperament as a factor in early school adjustment. *Pediatrics, 60*(4), 621–624.

Carey, W. B., & McDevitt, S. C. (1978). Revision of the Infant Temperament Questionnaire. *Pediatrics, 61,* 735–739.

Chess, S., & Korn, S. (1970). Temperament and behavior disorders in mentally retarded children. *Archives of General Psychiatry, 23,* 122–130.

Chess, S., Korn, S., & Fernandez, P. (1971). *Psychiatric disorders of children with congenital rubella.* New York: Brunner/Mazel.

Chess, S., Thomas, A., & Cameron, M. (1976). Temperament: Its significance for early schooling. *New York University Education Quarterly, 7*(3), 24–29.

DeFries, J. C., & Plomin, R. (1978). Behavioral genetics. *Annual Review of Psychology, 29,* 473–515.

Dunn, J., & Kendrick, C. (1982). Temperamental differences, family relationships, and young children's responses to change within the family. In R. Porter & G. M. Collins (Eds.), *Temperamental differences in infants and young children* (pp. 87–105). London: Pitman.

Earls, F. (1981). Temperament characteristics and behavior problems in three-year-old children. *Journal of Nervous & Mental Disease. 169,* 367–387.

Eysenck, H. J. (1967). *The biological basis of personality.* Springfield, IL: Thomas.

Feuerstein, P., & Martin, R. P. (1981, April). *The relationship between temperament and school adjustment in four-year-old children.* Paper presented at the annual meeting of the American Educational Research Association, Los Angeles.

Field, T., & Greenberg, R. (1982). Temperament ratings by parents and teachers of infants, toddlers, and preschool children. *Child Development, 53,* 160–163.

Fullard, W., McDevitt, S. C., & Carey, W. B. (1978). *The Toddler Temperament Scale.* Unpublished manuscript, Temple University, Philadelphia.

Goldsmith, H. H., & Campos, J. J. (1982). Toward a theory of infant temperament. In R. M. Emde & R. J. Harmon (Eds.), *The development of attachment and affiliative systems* (pp. 161–193). New York: Plenum.

Goldsmith, H. H., & Campos, J. J. (1986). Fundamental issues in the study of early temperament: The Denver twin temperament study. In M. E. Lamb & A. L. Brown (Eds.), *Advances in developmental psychology* (pp. 231–283). Hillsdale, NJ: Erlbaum.

Goldsmith, H. H., & Gottesman, I. I. (1981). Origins of variation in behavioral style: A longitudinal study of temperament in young twins. *Child Development, 52,* 91–103.

Gordon, E. M., & Thomas, A. (1967). Children's behavioral style and the teacher's appraisal of their intelligence. *Journal of School Psychology, 5*(4), 292–300.

Graham, P., Rutter, M., & George, S. (1973). Temperamental characteristics as predictors of behavior disorders in children. *American Journal of Orthopsychiatry, 43*(3), 328–339.

Guilford, J. P., & Zimmerman, W. (1949). *The Guildford-Zimmerman Temperament Survey.* Beverly Hills, CA: Sheridan Supply.

Hall, R. J., & Cadwell, J. (1984, April). *Temperament influences on cognition and achievement in children with learning disabilities.* Paper presented at the annual conference of the American Educational Research Association, New Orleans, LA.

Hall, R. J., & Keogh, B. K. (1978). Qualitative characteristics of educationally high-risk children. *Learning Disability Quarterly, 1*(2), 62–68.

Hanson, M. J. (1979). A longitudinal description study of the behaviors of Down's syndrome infants in an early intervention program. *Monographs of the Center on Human Development.* Eugene, University of Oregon.

Hegvik, R. L. (1984, October). *Three year longitudinal study of temperament variables, academic achievement, and sex differences.* Paper presented at the Conference on Temperament in the Educational Process, St. Louis, MO.

Hegvik, R. L. (1986, May). *Temperament and achievement in school.* Paper presented at the sixth occasional Temperament Conference, Pennsylvania State University.

Hegvik, R. L., McDevitt, S. C., & Carey, W. B. (1982). The middle childhood temperament questionnaire. *Developmental & Behavioral Pediatrics, 3,* 197–200.

Hinde, R. A., Easton, D. F., Meller, R. E., & Tamplin, A. M. (1982). Temperamental characteristics of 3–4 year olds and mother-child interactions. In R. Porter & G. M. Collins, *Temperamental differences in infants and young children* (pp. 66–86). London: Pitman.

Hubert, N. C., Wachs, T. D., Peters-Martin, P., & Gandour, M. J. (1982). The study of early temperament: Measurement and conceptual issues. *Child Development, 53,* 126–132.

Keogh, B. K. (1982a). Children's temperament and teachers' decisions. In R. Porter & G. M. Collins (Eds.), *Temperamental differences in infants and young children* (pp. 269–279). London: Pitman.

Keogh, B. K. (1982b). *Temperament and school performance of preschool children* (Technical report, Project REACH). Los Angeles: University of California, Los Angeles.

Keogh, B. K. (1982c). Temperament: An individual difference of importance in intervention programs. *Topics in Early Childhood Special Education, 2*(2), 25–31.

Keogh, B. K. (1983). Individual differences in temperament: A contribution to the personal-social and educational competence of learning disabled children. In J. D. McKinney & L. Feagens (Eds.), *Current topics in learning disabilities* (pp. 33–55). Norwood, NJ: Ablex.

Keogh, B. K. (1986). Temperament and schooling: What is the meaning of goodness of fit? In J. V. Lerner & R. M. Lerner (Eds.), *New directions for child development: Temperament and social interaction in infants and children.* San Francisco: Jossey-Bass.

Keogh, B. K., Bernheimer, L., Pelland, M., & Daley, S. (1985). *Behavior and adjustment problems of children with developmental delays* (Technical report). Los Angeles: University of California, Los Angeles, Graduate School of Education.

Keogh, B. K., & Pullis, M. E. (1980). Temperamental influences on the development of exceptional children. In B. K. Keogh (Ed.), *Advances in special education: Vol. 1. Basic constructs and theoretical orientations* (pp. 239–276). Greenwich, CT: JAI.

Keogh, B. K., Pullis, M. E., & Cadwell, J. (1980). *Project REACH* (Technical report). Los Angeles: University of California, Los Angeles.

Keogh, B. K., Pullis, M. E., & Cadwell, J. (1982). A short form of the Teacher Temperament Questionnaire. *Journal of Educational Measurement, 29*(4), 323–329.

Kolvin, I., Nicol, A. R., Garside, R. F., Day, K. A., & Tweddle, E. G. (1982). Temperamental patterns in aggressive boys. In R. Porter & G. M. Collins (Eds.), *Temperamental differences in infants and young children* (pp. 252–268). London: Pitman.

Kretschmer, E. (1925). *Physique and character.* New York: Harcourt.

Lambert, N. M., & Windmiller, M. (1977). An exploratory study of temperament traits in a population of children at risk. *Journal of Special Education, 11*(1), 37–47.

Lerner, J. V. (1983). The role of temperament in psychosocial adaptation in early adolescents: A test of a "goodness of fit" model. *Journal of Genetic Psychology, 143,* 149–157.

Lerner, J. V., & Lerner, R. M. (1983). Temperament and adaptation across life: Theoretical and empirical issues. In P. B. Baltes & O. G. Brim (Eds.), *Lifespan development and behavior* (Vol. 5). New York: Academic Press.

Lerner, J. V., Lerner, R. M., & Zabski, S. (1985). Temperament and elementary school children's actual and rated academic performance: A test of a "goodness of fit" model. *Journal of Child Psychology and Psychiatry, 26,* 125–136.

Lerner, R. M., Palermo, M., Spiro, A., & Nesselroade, J. (1982). Assessing the dimensions of temperamental individuality across the life-span: The dimensions of temperament survey (DOTS). *Child Development, 53,* 149–160.

Martin, R. P. (1984a). *The Temperament Assessment Battery (TAB).* Atlanta: University of Georgia, Department of School Psychology.

Martin, R. P. (1984b, October). *A temperament model for education.* Paper presented at the Conference on Temperament in the Educational Process, St. Louis, MO.

Martin, R. P. (1985, July). *Child temperament and educational outcomes: A review of research.* Paper presented at the Symposium on Temperament, Leiden, the Netherlands.

Martin, R. P. (1986, May). *Context influences on the expression of temperament.* Paper presented at the sixth occasional Temperament Conference, Pennsylvania State University.

Martin, R. P., Nagle, R., & Paget, K. (1983). Relationships between temperament and classroom behavior, teacher attitudes, and academic achievement. *Journal of Psychoeducational Assessment, 1,* 377–386.

Matheny, A. P., Jr., Wilson, R. S., & Nuss, S. M. (1984). Toddler temperament: Stability across settings and over ages. *Child Development, 55,* 1200–1211.

Maziade, M., Caperaa, P., Laplante, B., Boudreault, M., Thivierge, J., Cote, R., & Boutin, P. (1985). Value of difficult temperament among 7-year-olds in the general population for predicting psychiatric diagnosis at age 12. *American Journal of Psychiatry, 142*(8), 943–946.

McDevitt, S. C., & Carey, W. B. (1978). The measurement of temperament in 3–7 year old children. *Journal of Child Psychiatry & Psychology, 19*(3), 245–253.

Paget, K. D., Nagle, R. J., & Martin, R. P. (1984). Interrelationships between temperament characteristics and first-grade teacher-student interactions. *Journal of Abnormal Child Psychology, 12*(4), 547–560.

Plomin, R. (1982). Behavioral genetics and temperament. In R. Porter & G. M. Collins (Eds.). *Temperamental differences in infants and young children* (pp. 155–167). London: Pitman.

Plomin, R. (1983). Childhood temperament. In B. B. Lahey & A. E. Kazdin (Eds.), *Advances in clinical child psychology* (Vol. 6, pp. 45–92). New York: Plenum.

Pullis, M. E. (1979). *An investigation of the relationship between children's temperament and school adjustment.* Unpublished doctoral dissertation, University of California, Los Angeles.

Pullis, M. E. (1983). *Temperament influences of teachers' decisions in regular and mainstreamed classes.* Paper presented at the meeting of the American Educational Research Association, New York.

Pullis, M. E., & Cadwell, J. (1982). The influence of children's temperament characteristics on teachers' decision strategies. *American Educational Research Journal, 19*(2), 165–181.

Rothbart, M. K. (1981). Measurement of temperament in infancy. *Child Development, 52,* 569–578.

Rothbart, M. K., & Derryberry, D. (1981). Development of individual differences in temperament. In M. E. Lamb & A. L. Brown (Eds.), *Advances in developmental psychology* (Vol. 1, pp. 37–86). Hillsdale, NJ: Lawrence Erlbaum.

Rothbart, M. K., & Goldsmith, H. H. (1985). Three approaches to the study of infant temperament. *Developmental Review, 5,* 237–260.

Rutter, M., (1964). Temperament characteristics in infancy and the later development of behavior disorders. *British Journal of Psychiatry, 110,* 651–661.

Rutter, M. (1982). Temperament: Concepts, issues and problems. In R. Porter & G. C. Collins (Eds.), *Temperamental differences in infants and young children* (pp. 1–19). London: Pitman.

Rutter, M., Tizard, J., & Whitmore, K. (1970). *Education, health, and behavior: Psychological and medical study of childhood development.* New York: Wiley.

Scholom, A., & Schiff, G. (1980). Relating infant temperament to learning disabilities. *Journal of Abnormal Child Psychology, 8,* 127–132.

Sheldon, W. (1942). *The varieties of temperament: A psychology of constitutional differences.* New York: Harper.

Skuy, M., Snell, D., & Westaway, M. (1985). Temperament and the scholastic achievement and adjustment of black South African children. *South African Journal of Education, 5*(4), 197–202.

Stevenson-Hinde, J., & Simpson, A. E. (1982). Temperament and relationships. In R. Porter & G. M. Collins (Eds.), *Tempera-*

mental differences in infants and young children (pp. 51–65). London: Pitman.

Strelau, J. (1983). *Temperament-personality-activity.* New York: Academic Press.

Terestman, N. (1980). Mood quality and intensity in nursery school children as predictors of behavior disorder. *American Journal of Orthopsychiatry, 50,* 125–138.

Thomas, A., & Chess, S. (1977). *Temperament and development.* New York: Brunner/Mazel.

Thomas, A., Chess, S., & Birch, H. G. (1968). *Temperament and behavior disorders in children.* New York: New York University Press.

Thomas, A., Chess, S., Birch, H. G., Hertzig, M., & Korn, S. (1963). *Behavioral individuality in early childhood.* New York: New York University Press.

Thomas, A., Chess, S., & Korn, S. J. (1982). The reality of difficult temperament. *Merrill-Palmer Quarterly, 28*(1), 1–20.

Torgersen, A. M. (1982). Influence of genetic factors on temperament development in early childhood. In R. Porter & G. M. Collins (Eds.), *Temperamental differences in infants and young children* (pp. 141–154). London: Pitman.

Vaughn, B., Deinard, A., & Egeland, B. (1980). Measuring temperament in pediatric practice. *Journal of Pediatrics, 96,* 510–514.

Vaughn, B., Taraldson, B., Crichton, L., & Egeland, B. (1981). The assessment of infant temperament: A critique of the Carey Infant Temperament Questionnaire. *Infant Behavior & Development, 40,* 1–17.

Weissbluth, M. (1982). Plasma progesterone levels, infant temperament, arousals from sleep, and the sudden infant death syndrome. *Medical Hypotheses, 9,* 215–222.

Weissbluth, M. (1984). Sleep duration, temperament, and Conners' ratings of three-year-old children. *Developmental & Behavioral Pediatrics, 5*(3), 120–123.

Weissbluth, M., Brouillette, R. T., Kiang, L., & Hunt, C. E. (1982). Clinical and laboratory observations: Sleep apnea, sleep duration and infant temperament. *Journal of Pediatrics, 101*(2), 307–310.

Weissbluth, M., & Green, O. C. (1984). Plasma progesterone concentrations and infant temperament. *Developmental & Behavioral Pediatrics, 5*(5), 251–253.

Weissbluth, M., Hunt, C. E., Brouillette, R. T., Hanson, D., David, R. J., & Stein, I. (1985). Respiratory patterns during sleep and temperament ratings in normal infants. *Journal of Pediatrics, 106*(4), 688–690.

Werner, E. E., & Smith, R. S. (1982). *Vulnerable, but invincible: A longitudinal study of resilient children and youth.* New York: McGraw-Hill.

Wilson, R. S. (1983). The Louisville twin study: Developmental synchronies in behavior. *Child Development, 54*(2), 298–316.

Wilson, R. S., & Matheny, A. P. (1983). Assessment of temperament in infant twins. *Developmental Psychology, 19,* 172–183.

Windle, M., & Lerner, R. M. (1985). *Reassessing the dimensions of temperamental individuality across the life span: The Revised Dimensions of Temperament Survey* (DOTS-R). Unpublished manuscript, Johnson O'Connor Research Foundation, Chicago.

BARBARA KEOGH
University of California

BODY IMAGE
HYPERACTIVITY
LEARNED HELPLESSNESS
PERSONALITY ASSESSMENT
TEACHER EXPECTANCIES

TEMPER OUTBURST

The temper outburst or temper tantrum, as it may be referred to more frequently, is familiar to any professional who works with children. The temper tantrum occurs more frequently among younger children who exhibit a variety of learning, physical, or emotional problems. In almost every instance where a temper tantrum occurs, it is obvious to the attending adults that the child is attempting to gain some personal objective(s) through this staged outburst.

The temper tantrum is usually easily recognizable because it is characterized by explosive kinds of behavior. Such behaviors as cursing, kicking, hitting, biting, destruction of property, and related behaviors that may be dangerous to those around as well as to furnishings. The wild rage and anger, the intense yelling and crying signify a child that is out of control emotionally. It often appears that the usual defenses of the child have fallen apart and that he or she can only vent intense, uncontrollable rage.

In general, the temper outburst seems to occur only when the child is in the presence of an adult in charge. Typically, this behavior may occur in the presence of the parent, but it may also occur with teachers or in an institutional setting with child-care workers. Trieschmann, Whittaker, and Bendro (1969) present a comprehensive treatment of the nature, causes, and possible treatments for temper tantrums. In general, the authors view the temper tantrum as an effort by the child to gain control and deal with developmental problems.

In many instances, the parent or child-care worker reports that there seems to be no reason for or warning that the child is going to erupt into wild, uncontrollable anger. However, most educators and psychologists who have made a thorough investigation of children's temper tantrums discover that there are precipitating or contingent factors. For example, the child usually exhibits tantrum behavior only around adults and always around other people. Usually, the child receives an intense amount of attention, albeit negative. In fact, adults present will often need to exhibit a great deal of attention (e.g., restraint) to prevent the child from hurting others or from destroying property. Mullen (1983) provides an extensive description of the occurrences of temper tantrums among children institutionalized in a youth development center. Some of these children are strong teenagers who can, and do, inflict injury on professional child-care workers. A temper outburst in this setting is characterized by fear on the part of other children and the staff. In all cases, the person having a temper tantrum captures the attention of others.

Less attention has been paid to temper tantrums in the literature in the last 10 years; that may be due in part to our success in extinguishing this behavior in some children. The key to its elimination often appears to be the reduction of attention from significant others following the temper tantrum. Graham and Doubleday (1984) report that children from ages 6 to 11 agree that anger is an emotion that they can control. This was in contrast to pity and guilt, for example, which they believed they could not control. Relying on the notion of self-control for temper tantrums, many professionals have succeeded in extinguishing temper tantrums completely. Zarski (1982) reports on the successful elimination of temper tantrums by a 5-year-old cerebral palsied child. This behavior began with the parents in their efforts to get the child to develop greater physical strength and skills. The successful plan of extinction was to tell the child that it was all right to have tantrums but that he must always have them in one specific room. The child was always taken to that room and encouraged to continue to have the tantrums while he was there. Within 2 months, the temper outbursts stopped completely. Carlson, Arnold, Becker, and Madsen (1968) report similar success with an 8-year-old girl in an elementary classroom. Her chair was placed in the back of the room and she was held in the chair (which she resented) until the temper outburst subsided. All other children in the classroom were rewarded for not noticing her outbursts. Her behavior improved although the temper outbursts were not completely controlled that year. Although psychologists and educators continue to expand their understanding and techniques for controlling temper tantrums, they remain an attempt by children to gain control in certain social situations.

REFERENCES

Carlson, C. S., Arnold, C. R., Becker, W. C., & Madsen, C. H. (1968). The elimination of tantrum behavior of a child in an elementary classroom. *Behavioral Research & Therapy, 6,* 117–119.

Graham, S., & Doubleday, C. (1984). The development of relations between perceived controllability and the emotions of pity, anger, and guilt. *Child Development, 55,* 561–565.

Mullen, J. K. (1983). Understanding and managing the temper tantrum. *Child Care Quarterly, 12,* 59–70.

Trieschmann, A. E., Whittaker, J. K., & Bendro, L. K. (1969). *The other 23 hours: Child care work in a therapeutic milieu.* Chicago: Aldine.

Zarski, J. A. (1982). The treatment of temper tantrums in a cerebral palsied child: A paradoxical intervention. *School Psychology Review, 11,* 324–328.

BERT O. RICHMOND
University of Georgia

BEHAVIOR MODIFICATION
BEHAVIOR OBSERVATION
RESTRAINT

TERATOGEN

The word teratogen drives from the Greek *teras,* signifying a marvel, prodigy, or monster; thus, by definition, a teratogen is an agent that causes developmental malformations or monstrosities (Duke-Elder, 1963). The causes can be environmental, genetic, multifactorial, maternal-fetal, or unknown. Environmental agents include drugs and similar agents (e.g., alcohol, anticonvulsants, LSD), hormones, infections (e.g., cytomegalic inclusion disease, influenza, mumps, rubella, syphilis, toxoplasmosis), radiation, mechanical trauma, hypotension (low blood pressure), vitamin deficiency or excess (hypervitaminosis A), and mineral deficiency (zinc). Genetic causes include chromosomal abnormality (e.g., Down's syndrome, trisomy 13) and various hereditary patterns—sporadic, dominant, recessive, and polygenetic. Maternal-fetal interactions are exemplified by advanced maternal age and maternal hypothyroidism. Finally, a variety of dysmorphic syndromes are undetermined as to etiology. Many congenital abnormalities may be detected prior to birth. The primary means for such diagnosis has been through amniocentesis. Additionally, imaging systems such as ultrasonography demonstrate relatively gross abnormalities late in development (Spaeth, Nelson, & Beaudoin, 1983).

The timing of development helps to clarify the spectrum of associated malformations. Injuries prior to the fifteenth day of gestation affect development of primary germ layers; such abnormalities are usually so global that survival of the fetus is unusual. Between weeks two and seven, insults cause major abnormalities that affect whole organ systems. Following the first trimester (the period of differentiation of organ detail and organ interrelationship), abnormalities tend to be more limited and specific. While timing of embryonic or fetal insult relates closely to manifest anomaly, certain substances may cause varying malformations, though the time of insult is constant.

REFERENCES

Duke-Elder, S. (1963). *System of ophthalmology: Vol. III, Part 2. Congenital deformities.* St. Louis, MO: Mosby.

Spaeth, G. L., Nelson, L. B., & Beaudoin, A. R. (1983). Ocular teratology. In T. D. Duane & E. A. Jaeger (Eds.), *Biomedical foundations of ophthalmology* (Vol. 1, pp. 6–7). Hagerstown, MD: Harper & Row.

GEORGE R. BEAUCHAMP
Cleveland Clinic Foundation

CENTRAL NERVOUS SYSTEM GENETIC VARIATIONS

TERMAN, LEWIS M. (1877–1956)

Lewis M. Terman received his PhD in education and psychology from Clark University, where he studied under G. Stanley Hall. Experienced as a schoolteacher, principal, and college instructor, in 1910 he joined the faculty of Stanford University, where he served as head of the psychology department from 1922 until his retirement in 1942.

With an interest in mental tests dating from his graduate studies at Clark University, Terman became a leading figure in the newly born testing movement, developing dozens of tests during his career. The best known and most widely used of his tests were the Stanford-Binet tests of intelligence, which he adapted from the Binet-Simon Scale of Intelligence in 1916 and revised in 1937. He also developed the Army Alpha and Beta tests (the first group intelligence tests) for use in classifying servicemen during World War I. With the publication of the Stanford-Binet tests in 1916, Terman introduced the term intelligence quotient

(IQ), a term that quickly became a part of the general vocabulary.

In 1921 Terman initiated the first comprehensive study of gifted children. His staff tested more than 250,000 schoolchildren to identify 1,500 with IQs above 140. This sample of boys and girls was studied intensively and followed up periodically in a study that continues today. Terman found that, contrary to the popular belief at the time, children with high IQs tend to be healthier, happier, and more stable than children of average ability. In addition, they are more successful in their personal and professional lives. Terman, who can be credited with founding the gifted child movement, used his findings to promote the provision of special educational programs for able students.

REFERENCES

Fancher, R. E. (1985). *The intelligence men.* New York: Norton.

Hilgard, E. (1957). Lewis Madison Terman: 1877–1956. *American Journal of Psychology, 70,* 472–479.

Murchison, C. (Ed.). (1961). *A history of psychology in autobiography.* New York: Russell & Russell.

PAUL IRVINE
Katonah, New York

STANFORD-BINET INTELLIGENCE SCALE

TERMAN'S STUDIES OF THE GIFTED

In 1911, while at Stanford University, Lewis M. Terman began a systematic collection of data on children who achieved exceptionally high scores on the Stanford-Binet Intelligence Test. In the early 1920s, working with Melita Oden, he administered the Stanford-Binet test to students referred to by teachers as being "highly intelligent." Studies of their traits and the extent to which they differed from unselected normal children were begun in 1925.

Terman's subjects were in a 1500-child sample (800 boys and 700 girls) that was in the top 1% of the school population in measured intelligence; i.e., they possessed tested IQs of 140 or higher (Terman & Oden, 1925).

Terman and Oden (1951) summarized the characteristics of the students in their gifted sample as (1) slightly larger, healthier, and more physically attractive; (2) superior in reading, language usage, arithmetical reasoning, science, literature, and the arts; (3) superior in arithmetical computation, spelling, and factual information about history and civics (though not as markedly as in the areas covered in (2); (4) spontaneous, with a variety of interests; (5) able to learn to read easily, and able to read more and better books than average children; (6) less inclined to

Lewis M. Terman

boast or overstate their knowledge; (7) more emotionally stable; (8) different in the upward direction for nearly all traits.

Follow-up studies in 1947, 1951, and 1959 were completed to obtain a comparison between promise and performance. Follow-up studies by other authors have obtained less "perfect" findings, in that not all of the subjects were found to be geniuses in the sense of transcendent achievement in some field (Feldman, 1984). Recent studies have supported Terman's findings on emotional stability (Schlowinski & Reynolds, 1985), spontaneity and creativity in play (Barnett & Fiscella, 1985), and reading aptitude (Anderson, Tollefson, & Gilbert, 1985).

The entire set of data sources for Terman's original group is maintained in closed files at Stanford University. It is estimated that less than half of the coded responses of this source of data have been transferred to tabulation sheets.

REFERENCES

Anderson, M. A., Tollefson, N. A., & Gilbert, E. C. (1985). Giftedness and reading: A cross sectional view of differences in reading attitudes and behavior. *Gifted Child Quarterly, 29*(4), 86–189.

Barnett, L. A., & Fiscella, J. (1985). A child by any other name. . . . A comparison of the playfulness of gifted and non-gifted children. *Gifted Child Quarterly, 29*(2), 61–66.

Feldman, D. H. (1984). A follow-up of subjects scoring about 180 IQ in Terman's "Genetic Studies of Genius." *Exceptional Children, 50*(6), 518–523.

Schlowinski, E., & Reynolds, C. R. (1985). Dimensions of anxiety among high IQ children. *Gifted Child Quarterly, 29*(3), 125–130.

Sears, P. S. (1979). The Terman genetic studies of genius, 1922–1972. In A. H. Passow (Eds.), *The gifted and talented.* Chicago: National Society for the Study of Education.

Terman, L. M., & Oden, M. H. (1925). *Genetic studies of genius: Mental and physical traits of a thousand gifted children.* Stanford, CA: Stanford University Press.

Terman, L. M., & Oden, M. H. (1951). The Stanford studies of the gifted. In P. A. Witty (Ed.), *The gifted child.* Boston: D. C. Heath.

ANNE M. BAUER
University of Cincinnati

GIFTED CHILDREN
GIFTED CHILDREN AND READING

TEST ANXIETY

Test anxiety is such a universal phenomenon that it hardly requires general definition. In school, on the job, or for various application procedures, tests are required. Performance on a test can impact negatively on the test-taker. Thus an essential component for an anxiety arousal state exists when the individual is placed in a test-taking situation. Test situations are specific and thus present an opportunity to investigate the nature of anxiety.

Test anxiety is usually regarded as a particular kind of general anxiety. Ordinarily, it refers to the variety of responses—physiological, behavioral, and phenomenal (Sieber, 1980)—that accompany an individual's perceptions of failure. The person experiencing test anxiety often has a fear of failure as well as a high need to succeed. Both the fear of failure and the drive for success may be internalized. In some instances, either may seem more of a desire on the part of the test-taker to please a parent or other significant individual. Regardless of the originating causes of test anxiety, it can be a debilitating state of arousal.

One of the major challenges for theorists and researchers on test anxiety is to ascertain why anxiety appears to motivate some persons yet limits seriously the performance of others. Findings from several researchers suggest that the individual's expectations of success or failure on a test are strongly correlated to the development of test anxiety (Heckhausen, 1975; Weiner, 1966). For example, it may be argued that those who are low in motivation to succeed attribute failure to a lack of ability whereas those who are high in motivation to succeed see failure as emanating more from a lack of effort. Heckhausen (1975) cites data showing that those persons with a high fear of failure tend to attribute success more to good luck than those persons with a high expectation of success. Thus, for those who expect to succeed, anxiety may be more of a motivating force than for those who fear failure. For the latter group, initial anxiety may become a debilitating form of test anxiety.

Another avenue of investigation seeks to understand the affective value of test-taking in the context of its social significance. For some persons, test anxiety is heightened if it occurs where there is an observer of the test-taking performance (Geen, 1979; Geen & Gange, 1977). Test anxiety may then be heightened if there are judges, monitors, or others with whom the test-taker must interact. Some persons may, therefore, find an oral or observed performance type of test more anxiety producing than a written test. For such persons, it appears that test anxiety is more a response to their need for and perceptions of social approval than it is to an internalized need to demonstrate competence.

In summary, much of the available research and numerous self-reports suggest that test anxiety is a recurring problem for children and adults. Moreover, test anxiety often appears to inhibit the usual maximal level of performance of the individual. Thus if a test situation is to be used as an effective means of assessing human potential, it is important that we understand more fully the origin of test anxiety as well as its impact on individual performance.

REFERENCES

Dew, K. M. H., Galassi, J. P., & Galassi, M. D. (1984). Math anxiety: Relation with situational test anxiety, performance, physiological arousal, and math avoidance behavior. *Journal of Counseling Psychology, 31,* 480–583.

Geen, R. G. (1979). The influence of passive audiences on performance. In P. Paulus (Ed.), *The psychology of group influence.* Hillsdale, NJ: Erlbaum.

Geen, R. G., & Gange, J. J. (1977). Drive theory of social facilitation: Twelve years of theory and research. *Psychological Bulletin, 84,* 1267–1288.

Heckhausen, H. (1975). Fear of failure as a self-reinforcing motive. In I. G. Sarason & C. D. Spielberger (Eds.), *Stress and anxiety* (Vol. 2). Washington, DC: Hemisphere.

Sieber, J. E. (1980). Defining test anxiety: Problems and approaches. In I. G. Sarason (Ed.), *Test anxiety: Theory, research, and applications.* Hillsdale, NJ: Erlbaum.

Weiner, B. (1966). The role of success and failure in the learning of easy and complex tasks. *Journal of Personality & Social Psychology, 3,* 339–344.

BERT O. RICHMOND
University of Georgia

ANXIETY
STRESS AND THE HANDICAPPED STUDENT

TEST EQUATING

Test equating is a technique for making the characteristics of two tests similar or identical, if possible, so that an individual's scores on the two tests mean the same thing. This process is accomplished currently through statistical means. There are two different problems associated with test equating. One is the problem of equating scores on two tests that were designed to be of the same difficulty, for the same kind of student, with the same content. This is called horizontal equating. The other problem is how to equate tests that were designed for different populations, often younger and older students, in which the content overlaps. In this case, one test will be hard for the younger students and the other will be quite easy for the older. This is called vertical equating.

Horizontal equating, while by no means completely solved as a statistical problem, is the better developed and studied of the two. The problem is best stated as follows: For a student with ability A, the relative placement of his or her score on test 1 is identical to the relative score on test 2 if the two tests have been perfectly equated. Mathematically, the two frequency distributions must be equal in normalized form. This means that a youngster's score on test 1 is the same number of standard deviations from the mean and exceeds the same percent of other scores as on test 2. There are three major techniques for achieving horizontal equating.

The first method of horizontal equating is called the equipercentile method. It is the most widely used and seems to be the most robust method under a variety of conditions. Simply put, observed score distributions are matched for percentile points. That is, the score at the first percentile point in test 1 is equated to the score at the first percentile point for test 2. This is done for all percentile points up to 99 or perhaps 99.9. There is a smoothing of the equated scores so that there are no abrupt jumps in scores from one percentile to the next. This procedure has been shown by Petersen, Marco, and Stewart (1982) to be not as good as linear equating, the next technique covered, in which the tests are similar and linear in relationship to each other. When there is a nonlinear relationship between the tests, the equipercentile technique is superior. This case is not common.

Linear equating is the application of a straight line equation of the form $Y = aX + b$. The parameters are functions of the means and standard deviations of the two tests (Braun & Holland, 1982). Not surprisingly, it works best when there is just a simple linear relation between true test scores.

The third technique for equating tests horizontally consists of a number of related techniques grouped under the heading item-characteristic curve (ICC) techniques. These techniques generally make somewhat stronger assumptions about the nature of the test and the test-taker than do the other two methods. They are based on a model that allows estimation of a test-taker's ability. $T1$ on test 1 and $T2$ on test two. These two scores then are equated, and the observed score from which they have been estimated can be calculated. Thus we can begin with either test, estimate the student's underlying ability on the test, and use that ability score on the other test to calculate an equivalent observed score. Since the procedure works both ways, it is hoped that the tests give similar results between calculated and actual observed scores. In general, such procedures have proven inferior to linear or equipercentile methods for large-scale standardized tests, which are carefully constructed. The ICC methods may be better for smaller, experimentally oriented tests, but their restriction to large samples makes this a rare usage.

Vertical equating is a more difficult problem, conceptually and statistically. The primary techniques used have been based on ICC models. They have not proven satisfactory to date. If two tests are given to a student, one that is hard for him or her and one that is easy (or easier), the ICC methods tend to overpredict ability score on the easy test and underpredict it on the hard test (Kolen, 1981).

REFERENCES

Braun, H. I., & Holland, P. W. (1982). Observed-score test equating: A mathematical analysis of some ETS equating procedures. In P. W. Holland & D. B. Rubin (Eds.), *Test Equating* (pp. 9–49). New York: Academic.

Kolen, M. J. (1981). Comparison of traditional and item response theory methods for equating tests. *Journal of Educational Measurement, 19,* 279–293.

Petersen, N. S., Marco, G. L., & Stewart, E. E. (1982). A test of the adequacy of linear score equating models. In P. W. Holland & D. B. Rubin (Eds.), *Test Equating* (pp. 71–135). New York: Academic.

VICTOR L. WILLSON
Texas A & M University

ASSESSMENT
MEASUREMENT

TEST FOR AUDITORY COMPREHENSION OF LANGUAGE—THIRD EDITION (TACL-3)

The *Test for Auditory Comprehension of Language—Third Edition* (TACL-3) is an individually-administered measure of receptive spoken language that assesses a subject's ability to understand the following categories of English language forms: Vocabulary, Grammatical Morphemes, and Elaborated Phrases and Sentences. The TACL-3 consists of 142 items, divided into three subtests, each of which corresponds to a category of language form. Each item is composed of a word or sentence and a corresponding picture plate that has three full-color drawings.

Percentile ranks, standard scores, and age equivalents are available for children ages 3–0 through 9–11. The TACL-3 provides a variety of norm comparisons based on a standardization sample of 1,102 children, relative to socioeconomic factors, ethnicity, gender, and disability that are the same as those estimated for the year 2000 by the U.S. Bureau of the Census. Studies have shown the absence of gender, racial, disability, and ethnic bias. Reliability coefficients are computed for subgroups of the normative sample (e.g., individuals with speech disabilities, African Americans, European Americans, Hispanic Americans, females) as well as for the entire normative group.

Earlier editions of the TACL were reviewed extensively; references for the newest edition of this instrument are unavailable because of its recent publication date. A review of the TACL-R by Schmitt (1987) concluded that the instrument can be considered both a valid and reliable test for determining an individual's knowledge of the test's constructs. Bankson (1989) reported that the TACL-R could be particularly useful as part of a comprehensive language evaluation of children referred for language disorders.

Haynes (1989) felt the test was a well-designed and psychometrically sound instrument for evaluating limited aspects of comprehension.

REFERENCES

Bankson, N. W. (1989). Review of the Test for Auditory Comprehension of Language—Revised. In J. C. Conoley & J. J. Kramer (Eds.), *The tenth mental measurements yearbook* (pp. 822–824). Lincoln: Buros Institute of Mental Measurements, University of Nebraska Press.

Carrow-Woolfolk, E. (1999). *Test for Auditory Comprehension of Language—Third Edition.* Austin, TX: Pro-Ed.

Haynes, W. O. (1989). Review of the Test for Auditory Comprehension of Language—Revised. In J. C. Conoley & J. J. Kramer (Eds.), *The tenth mental measurements yearbook* (pp. 824–826). Lincoln: Buros Institute of Mental Measurements, University of Nebraska Press.

Schmitt, J. F. (1987). *Test Critiques: Volume VI* (pp. 586–593). Austin, TX: Pro-Ed.

TADDY MADDOX
Pro-Ed, Inc.

AUDITORY PROCESSING

TEST OF ADOLESCENT AND ADULT LANGUAGE–THIRD EDITION (TOAL-3)

The *Test of Adolescent and Adult Language–Third Edition* (TOAL-3; Hammill, Brown, Larsen, & Wiederholt, 1994) is a revision of the Test of Adolescent Language originally published in 1981 and revised in 1987. A major improvement in the test is the extension of the norms to include 18- through 24-year-old persons enrolled in postsecondary education programs. This improvement required that the name of the test be changed to indicate the presence of the older population in the normative sample. TOAL-3 yields 10 composite scores: Listening—the ability to understand the spoken language of other people; Speaking—the ability to express one's ideas orally; Reading—the ability to comprehend written messages; Writing—the ability to express thoughts in graphic form; Spoken Language—the ability to listen and speak; Written Language—the ability to read and write; Vocabulary—the ability to understand and use words in communication; Grammar—the ability to understand and generate syntactic and morphological structures; Receptive Language—the ability to comprehend both written and spoken language; and Expressive Language—the ability to produce written and spoken language. The Overall Language Ability quotient and the other 10 composite quotients have a mean of 100 and a standard deviation of 15.

The normative sample exceeded 3,000 persons in 22

states and 3 Canadian provinces. It was representative of the U.S. population according to 1990 U.S. Census percentages for region, gender, race, and residence; the sample is stratified by age. Internal consistency, test-retest, and score reliability were investigated. All reliability coefficients exceed .80. Content, criterion-related, and construct validity have been thoroughly studied. In addition, the TOAL-3 scores distinguished between groups known to have language problems and those known to have normal language. Evidence is also provided to show that TOAL-3 items are not biased with regard to race or gender.

From its beginning the TOAL has been reviewed widely. Most reviewers have praised the test's statistical properties, theoretical base, and clearly written manual (McLoughlin & Lewis, 1990; Shapiro, 1989; Stinnett, 1992; Williams, 1985). Several reviewers, however, think the test is too long, yields too little useful information, and has old normative data (Richards, 1998; MacDonald, 1998).

REFERENCES

MacDonald, J. (1998). Review of the Test of Adolescent Language–Third Edition. In J. C. Impara & B. S. Plake (Eds.), *The thirteenth mental measurements yearbook* (pp. 1018–1019). Lincoln: Buros Institute of Mental Measurements, University of Nebraska Press.

McLoughlin, J. A., & Lewis, R. B. (1990). *Assessing special students* (3rd ed.). Columbus, OH: Merrill.

Richards, R. A. (1998). Review of the Test of Adolescent Language–Third Edition. In J. C. Impara & B. S. Plake (Eds.), *The thirteenth mental measurements yearbook* (pp. 1019–1021). Lincoln: Buros Institute of Mental Measurements, University of Nebraska Press.

Shapiro, D. A. (1989). Review of the Test of Adolescent Language-2. In J. C. Conoley & J. J. Kramer (Eds.), *The tenth mental measurements yearbook* (pp. 828–830). Lincoln: Buros Institute of Mental Measurements, University of Nebraska Press.

Stinnett, T. A. (1992). Test reviews. *Journal of Psychoeducational Assessment, 10,* 182–189.

Williams, R. T. (1985). Review of the Test of Adolescent Language. In J. V. Mitchell (Ed.), *The ninth mental measurements yearbook* (pp. 1549–1551). Lincoln: Buros Institute of Mental Measurements, University of Nebraska Press.

TADDY MADDOX
Pro-Ed, Inc.

TEST OF EARLY MATHEMATICAL ABILITY–SECOND EDITION (TEMA-2)

The *Test of Early Mathematical Ability–Second Edition* (TEMA-2; Ginsburg & Baroody, 1990) measures the mathematics performance of children between the ages of 3–0

and 8–11 years. Items are specifically designed to measure the following domains: concepts of relative magnitude, reading and writing numerals, counting skills, number facts, calculation, calculational algorithms, and base-ten concepts.

The TEMA-2 standardization sample was composed of 896 children representing 27 states. The characteristics of the sample approximate those in the 1980 U.S. Census. The results of the test, which takes approximately 5 to 15 minutes to administer, may be reported as standard scores, percentiles, or age equivalents. Reliabilities are in the .90s; validity has been experimentally established. Test results are reported in terms of a standard score (M = 100, SD = 15) and a percentile rank. The TEMA-2 now includes a book of remedial techniques for improving skills in the areas assessed on the test.

All reviewers (Cohen & Spenciner, 1998; Johnson, 1992; McLarty, 1992; Taylor, 1997) recommend additional reliability and validity evidence. Taylor (1997), along with Johnson (1992), notes that one advantage of the TEMA-2 is the companion book of remedial techniques.

REFERENCES

Cohen, L. G., & Spenciner, L. J. (1998). *Assessment of children and youth.* New York: Longman.

Ginsburg, H. P., & Baroody, A. J. (1990). *Test of Early Mathematical Ability, Second Edition.* Austin, TX: Pro-Ed.

Hammill, D. D., Brown, L., & Bryant, B. R. (1992). *A consumer's guide to tests in print* (2nd ed.). Austin, TX: Pro-Ed.

Johnson, J. (1992). Review of the Test of Early Mathematical Ability, Second Edition. In J. J. Kramer and J. C. Conoley (Eds.), *The eleventh mental measurements yearbook* pp. 939–141. Lincoln: Buros Institute of Mental Measurements, University of Nebraska Press.

McLarty, J. R. (1992). Review of the Test of Early Mathematical Ability, Second Edition. In J. J. Kramer and J. C. Conoley (Eds.), *The eleventh mental measurements yearbook* (pp. 141–142). Lincoln: Buros Institute of Mental Measurements, University of Nebraska Press.

Taylor, R. L. (1997). *Assessment of exceptional students.* Boston: Allyn and Bacon.

WAYNE P. HRESKO
Journal of Learning Disabilities

TEST OF EARLY READING ABILITY, SECOND EDITION (TERA-2)

The *Test of Early Reading Ability, Second Edition* (TERA-2; Reid, Hresko, & Hammill, 1991) measures the actual reading ability of young children from ages 3–0 to 9–11. Items measure knowledge of contextual meaning, alphabet knowledge, and book and print conventions.

Performance is reported as a standard score (M = 100; SD = 15), percentile, or normal curve equivalent. The TERA-2 has two alternate, equivalent forms. Although subtests are not provided, items can be profiled to reflect abilities in the areas of contextual meaning, alphabet knowledge, and book and print conventions. The TERA-2 was standardized on a national sample of 1,454 children. Normative data are given for every 6-month interval. Both internal consistency and test-retest reliability are reported in the test manual. In all instances, coefficients approach or exceed .80. Validity coefficients are available based on correlations of the TERA-2 with other tests of reading, language, intelligence, and achievement. The TERA-2 Picture Book is in an easel format. A computer scoring system is available.

Hiltonsmith (1992) refers to the TERA-2 as a "thoughtful and generally well-constructed" measure of early reading. Beck (1992) questioned the interpretation of some items and suggested additional reliability data at young ages. Taylor (1997) thought additional validity evidence at some ages was needed.

REFERENCES

Barnett, R. M., & Barnett, D. W. (1992). Test reviews. *Journal of Psychoeducational Assessment, 10,* 384–388.

Beck, M. D. (1992). Review of the *Test of Early Reading Ability - 2.* In J. J. Kramer & J. C. Conoley (Eds.), *The eleventh mental measurements yearbook* (pp. 942–944). Lincoln, NE: The University of Nebraska Press.

Hammill, D. D., Brown, L., & Bryant, B. R. (1992). *A consumer's guide to tests in print* (2nd ed.). Austin, TX: Pro-Ed.

Hiltonsmith, R. W. (1992). Review of the *Test of Early Reading Ability - 2.* In J. J. Kramer & J. C. Conoley (Eds.), *The eleventh mental measurements yearbook* (pp. 944–946). Lincoln, NE: The University of Nebraska Press.

Reid, D. K., Hresko, W. P., & Hammill, D. D. (1991). *Test of Early Reading Ability, Second Edition.* Austin, TX: Pro-Ed.

Taylor, R. L. (1997). *Assessment of exceptional students* (4th ed.). Boston: Allyn & Bacon.

WAYNE P. HRESKO
Journal of Learning Disabilities

TEST OF EARLY WRITTEN LANGUAGE, SECOND EDITION (TEWL-2)

The *Test of Early Written Language, Second Edition* (TEWL-2; Hresko, Herron, & Peak, 1996) measures early writing ability in children from ages 3–0 to 10–11. It includes two forms, each with a Basic Writing and Contextual Writing subtest. The Basic Writing subtest requires responses to specific items (spelling, capitalization, punctuation, sentence construction, and metacognitive knowl-

edge) while the Contextual Writing subtest depends on the authentic assessment (story format, cohesion, thematic maturity, ideation, and story construction) of a writing sample. Detailed scoring instructions are provided. Each subtest measures conventional, linguistic and conceptual components of writing. Further, each subtest may be given independently.

Three quotients (Basic Writing, Contextual Writing, and Global Writing) are provided each based on a mean of 100 and a standard deviation of 15. The TEWL-2 norms represent more than 1400 children from 33 states. Normative information is reflective of the nation as a whole with respect to gender, race, ethnicity, geographic region, and urban/rural residence. Internal consistency and reliability coefficients all exceed .90. Substantial content-description procedures, criterion-prediction procedures, and construct-identification procedures are presented.

Hurford (1998) commends the authors of the TEWL-2, noting that it possesses an excellent conceptual framework and content-appropriate tasks. He also stresses the need for continued research into reliability and validity evidence related to group differentiation. Trevisan (1998) stresses the strong reliability and validity evidence and recommends the TEWL-2 without reservation.

REFERENCES

Hresko, W. P., Herron, S. R., & Peak, P. K. (1996). *Test of Early Written Language, Second Edition.* Austin, TX: Pro-Ed.

Hurford, D. P. (1998). Review of the Test of Early Written Language, Second Edition. In J. C. Impara & B. S. Plake (Eds.), *The thirteenth mental measurements yearbook* (pp. 1027–1030). Lincoln, NE: The Buros Institute of Mental Measurements, The University of Nebraska Press.

Trevisan, M. S. (1998). Review of the Test of Early Written Language, Second Edition. In J. C. Impara & B. S. Plake (Eds.), *The thirteenth mental measurements yearbook* (pp. 1027–1030). Lincoln, NE: The Buros Institute of Mental Measurements, The University of Nebraska Press.

WAYNE P. HRESKO
Journal of Learning Disabilities

TEST OF LANGUAGE DEVELOPMENT–PRIMARY: THIRD EDITION

Originally published in 1997, the *Test of Language Development–Primary* (TOLD; Newcomer & Hammill, 1997) is now in its third edition. It is a nine subtest, individually administered test designed to measure a child's language ability relative to three types of linguistic systems (listening, organizing, speaking) and three types of linguistic features (semantics, syntax, phonology). The results of the subtests are combined to form six clinically useful composite scores, one for each of the systems and features listed above. The test is for children ages 4–0 through 8–11 and takes about an hour to give. A companion test (*Test of Language Development-Intermediate*) also by Hammill and Newcomer (1997) is available for children aged 8–12.

The test was normed on 1,000 children in 28 states. The sample was stratified by age and was found to be representative of the nation's school-age population as reported in the *Statistical Abstract of the United States* (U.S. Bureau of the Census, 1997) regarding gender, race, ethnicity, family income, education of parents, and disability.

The test is widely used by speech and language pathologists and educational diagnosticians who need to obtain a normative comparison of a child's language skills. Because the third edition of the TOLD has just been published, no reviews of the test are available. However, reviewers of earlier editions have generally found the norms and reliability of the test to be adequate. References to these reviews are listed below.

REFERENCES

Casey, A., & Holman, R. (1990). The Test of Language Development-2: Primary. *Journal of Psychoeducational Assessment, 8,* 94–97.

Compton, C. (1996). *A guide to 100 tests for special education.* Upper Saddle River, NJ: Globe Fearon Educational.

Hammill, D. D., & Newcomer, P. (1997). *Test of Language Development–Intermediate* (3rd ed.). Austin, TX: Pro-Ed.

McLaughlin, J. A., & Lewis, R. B. (1994). *Assessing special students* (4th ed.). New York: Merrill.

Newcomer, P., & Hammill, D. D. (1997). *Test of Language Development–Primary* (3rd ed.). Austin, TX: Pro-Ed.

Salvia, J., & Ysseldyke, J. E. (1998). *Assessment* (7th ed.). Boston: Houghton-Mifflin.

DONALD D. HAMMILL
Pro-Ed, Inc.

LANGUAGE DISORDERS

TEST OF MEMORY AND LEARNING (TOMAL)

The TOMAL (Reynolds & Bigler, 1994a) is a comprehensive battery of 14 memory and learning tasks (10 core subtests and 4 supplementary subtests) normed for use from ages 5 years 0 months 0 days through 19 years 11 months 30 days. The 10 core subtests are divided into the content domains of verbal memory and nonverbal memory that can be combined to derive a Composite Memory Index. A Delayed Recall Index is also available that requires a repeat recall of the first four subtests' stimuli 30 minutes after their first administration.

Memory may behave in unusual ways in an impaired

brain and traditional content approaches to memory may not be useful. The TOMAL thus provides alternative groupings of the subtests into the Supplementary Indexes of Sequential Recall, Free Recall, Associative Recall, Learning, and Attention and Concentration. These Supplementary Indexes were derived by having a group of "expert" neuropsychologists sort the 14 TOMAL subtests into logical categories (Reynolds & Bigler, 1994b). To provide greater flexibility to the clinician, a set of four purely empirically derived factor indexes representing Complex Memory, Sequential Recall, Backward Recall, and Spatial Memory have been made available as well (Reynolds & Bigler, 1996).

Table 1 summarizes the names of the subtests and summary scores, along with their metric. The TOMAL subtests

Table 1. Core and Supplementary Subtests and Indexes Available for the TOMAL

	M	SD
Core subtests		
Verbal		
Memory for Stories	10	3
Word Selective Reminding	10	3
Object Recall	10	3
Digits Forward	10	3
Paired Recall	10	3
Nonverbal		
Facial Memory	10	3
Visual Selective Reminding	10	3
Abstract Visual Memory	10	3
Visual Sequential Memory	10	3
Memory for Location	10	3
Supplementary subtests		
Verbal		
Letters Forward	10	3
Digits Backward	10	3
Letters Backward	10	3
Nonverbal		
Manual Imitation	10	3
Summary scores		
Core indexes		
Verbal Memory Index (VMI)	100	15
Nonverbal Memory Index (NMI)	100	15
Composite Memory Index (CMI)	100	15
Delayed Recall Index (DRI)	100	15
Supplementary indexes (expert derived)		
Sequential Recall Index (SRI)	100	15
Free Recall Index (FRI)	100	15
Associative Recall Index (ARI)	100	15
Learning Index (LI)	100	15
Attention Concentration Index (ACI)	100	15
Factor scores (empirically derived)		
Complex Memory Index (CMFI)	100	15
Sequential Recall Index (SRFI)	100	15
Backwards Recall Index (BRFI)	100	15
Spatial Recall Index (SMFI)	100	15

are scaled to the familiar metric of mean equaling 10 and a standard deviation of 3 (range 1 to 20). Composite or summary scores are scaled to a mean of 100 and standard deviation of 15. All scaling was done using the method of rolling weighted averages and is described in detail in Reynolds and Bigler (1994b).

TOMAL Subtests

The ten core and four supplementary TOMAL subtests require about 60 minutes for a skilled examiner if the delayed recall subtests are also administered. The subtests were chosen to provide a comprehensive view of memory functions and, when used together, provide the most thorough assessment of memory available (Ferris & Kamphaus, 1995). The subtests are named and briefly described in Table 2.

The TOMAL subtests systematically vary the mode of presentation and response so as to sample verbal, visual,

motoric, and combinations of these modalities in presentation and in response formats (Reynolds & Bigler, 1997). Multiple trials to a criterion are provided on several subtests, including selective reminding, so that learning or acquisition curves may be derived. Multiple trials [at least five are necessary according to Kaplan (1996) and the TOMAL provides up to eight] are provided on the selective reminding subtests to allow an analysis of the depth of processing. In the selective reminding format (wherein examinees are reminded only of stimuli "forgotten" or unrecalled), when items once recalled are unrecalled by the examinee on later trials, problems are revealed in the transference of stimuli from working memory and immediate memory to more long-term storage. Cueing is also provided at the end of certain subtests to add to the examiner's ability to probe depth of processing.

Subtests are included that sample sequential recall (which tends strongly to be mediated by the left hemisphere, especially temporal regions; e.g., see Lezak, 1995)

Table 2. Description of TOMAL Subtests

Core

Memory for Stories. A verbal subtest requiring recall of a short story read to the examinee. Provides a measure of meaningful and semantic recall and is also related to sequential recall in some instances.

Facial Memory. A nonverbal subtest requiring recognition and identification from a set of distractors: black-and-white photos of various ages, males and females, and various ethnic backgrounds. Assesses nonverbal meaningful memory in a practical fashion and has been extensively researched. Sequencing of responses is unimportant.

Word Selective Reminding. A verbal free-recall task in which the examinee learns a word list and repeats it only to be reminded of words left out in each case: tests learning and immediate recall functions in verbal memory. Trials continue until mastery is achieved or until eight trials have been attempted: sequence of recall unimportant.

Visual Selective Reminding. A nonverbal analogue to WSR where examinees point to specified dots on a card, following a demonstration of the examiner, and are reminded only of items recalled incorrectly. As with WSR, trials continue until mastery is achieved or until eight trials have been attempted.

Object Recall. The examiner presents a series of pictures, names them, has the examinee recall them, and repeats this process across four trials. Verbal and nonverbal stimuli are thus paired and recall is entirely verbal, creating a situation found to interfere with recall for many children with learning disabilities but to be neutral or facilitative for children without disabilities.

Abstract Visual Memory. A nonverbal task. AVM assesses immediate recall for meaningless figures when order is unimportant. The examinee is presented with a standard stimulus and required to recognize the standard from any of six distractors.

Digits Forward. A standard verbal number recall task. DSF measures low-level rote recall of a sequence of numbers.

Visual Sequential Memory. A nonverbal task requiring recall of the sequence of a series of meaningless geometric designs. The ordered designs are shown followed by a presentation of a standard order of the stimuli and the examinee indicates the order in which they originally appeared.

Pair recall. A verbal paired-associative learning task is provided by the examiner. Easy and hard pairs and measures of immediate associative recall and learning are provided.

Memory for Location. A nonverbal task that assesses spatial memory. The examinee is presented with a set of large dots distributed on a page and asked to recall the locations of the dots in any order.

Supplementary

Manual Imitation. A psychomotor, visually based assessment of sequential memory where the examinee is required to reproduce a set of ordered hand movements in the same sequence as presented by the examiner.

Letters Forward. A language-related analogue to common digit span tasks using letters as the stimuli in place of numbers.

Digits Backward. This is the same basic task as Digits Forward except the examinee recalls the numbers in reverse order.

Letters Backward. A language-related analogue to the Digits Backward task using letters as the stimuli instead of numbers.

and free recall in both verbal and visual formats to allow localization; purely spatial memory tasks are included that are very difficult to confound via verbal mediation to assess more purely right hemisphere functions.

Well-established memory tasks (e.g., recalling stories) that also correlate well with school learning are included along with tasks more common to experimental neuropsychology that have high (e.g., Facial Memory) and low (e.g., Visual Selective Reminding) ecological salience; some subtests employ highly meaningful material (e.g., Memory for Stories) while some use highly abstract stimuli (e.g., Abstract Visual Memory).

Aside from allowing a comprehensive review of memory function, the purpose for including such a factorial array of tasks across multiple dimensions is to allow a thorough, detailed analysis of memory function and the source of any memory deficits that may be discovered. The task of the neuropsychologist demands subtests with great specificity and variability of presentation and response and that sample all relevant brain functions in order to solve the complex puzzle of dysfunctional brain-behavior relationships. Kaufman (1979) first presented a detailed model for analyzing test data in a comprehensive format (later elaborated by Kaufman, 1994) that likens the task of the clinician to that of a detective. The thoroughness, breadth, and variability of the TOMAL subtests, coupled with their excellent psychometric properties, make the TOMAL ideal for use in an "intelligent testing" model and particularly in the analysis of brain-behavior relationships associated with memory function (Reynolds & Bigler, 1997).

Standardization

The TOMAL was standardized on a population-proportionate stratified (by age, gender, ethnicity, socioeconomic status, region of residence, and community size) random sample of children throughout the United States. Standardization and norming was conducted for ages 5 up to 20. Details of the standardization and specific statistics on the sample are provided in Reynolds and Bigler (1994b).

Reliability

The TOMAL subtests and composite indexes show excellent evidence of internal consistency reliability. Reynolds and Bigler (1994b) report coefficient alpha reliability estimates that routinely exceed 0.90 for individual subtests and 0.95 for composite scores. Stability coefficients are typically in the 0.80s.

Validity

Reynolds and Bigler (1994b) review a series of prepublication studies that demonstrate evidence for the validity of the TOMAL as a measure of memory functioning. The

TOMAL scores correlate around 0.50 with measures of intelligence and achievement, indicating the TOMAL is related to but not the same as these measures. Measures of intelligence typically correlate with one another (around 0.75 to 0.85) and with measures of achievement (around 0.55 to 0.65).

Since publication of the TOMAL, several studies have provided evidence of convergent and divergent validity of the TOMAL subtests as measures of various aspects of memory by examining patterns of correlations among TOMAL subtests and the Rey Auditory Verbal Learning Test and the Wechsler Memory Scale-Revised. The verbal components of the TOMAL correlate well with these measures but the nonverbal sections are relatively independent (Barker et al., 1994; Mueller et al., 1994; Russo et al., 1994). The TOMAL nonverbal subtests, unlike a number of other purportedly visual and nonverbal memory tests, are difficult to encode verbally, making the TOMAL nonverbal subtests more specific and less contaminated by examinees' attempts at verbal mediation. On the nonverbal or visual memory portions of existing memory batteries, examiners should expect larger differences across tests than on verbal memory measures.

Validity is a complex concept related to the interpretation of scores on tests and many approaches to the question of meaning of performance on tests such as the TOMAL are appropriate. Case studies, group comparisons, and views of the internal structure of tests all add to this knowledge. These are provided in Reynolds and Bigler (1997).

REFERENCES

Barker, L. H., Mueller, R. M., Russo, A. A., Lajiness-O'Neill, R., Johnson, S. C., Anderson, C., Norman, M. A., Sephton, S., Primus, E., Bigler, E. D., & Reynolds, C. R. (1994, November). *The Word Selective Reminding subtest of the Test of Memory and Learning (TOMAL): A concurrent and construct validity study using the Rey Auditory Verbal Learning Test (RAVL) and the Wechsler Memory Scale-Revised (WMS-R)*. Paper presented at the annual meeting of the National Academy of Neuropsychology, Orlando.

Ferris, L. M., & Kamphaus, R. W. (1995). Review of the Test of Memory and Learning. *Archives of Clinical Neuropsychology, 10*(6).

Kaplan, E. (1996, March). Discussant. Symposium presented at the annual meeting of the National Association of School Psychologists, Atlanta.

Kaufman, A. S. (1979). *Intelligent testing with the WISC-R*. New York: Wiley-Interscience.

Kaufman, A. S. (1994). *Intelligent testing with the WISC-3*. New York: Wiley-Interscience.

Lezak, M. D. (1995). *Neuropsychological assessment* (3rd ed.). London: Oxford University Press.

Mueller, R. M., Russo, A. A., Barker, L. H., Lajiness-O'Neill, R., Johnson, S., Anderson, C., Norman, M. A., Sephton, S., Primus, E., Bigler, E. D., & Reynolds, C. R. (1994, November).

Memory testing and memory for sentences: Concurrent and construct validity of the Test of Memory and Learning (TOMAL) utilizing the Wechsler Memory Scale-Revised (WMS-R). Paper presented at the annual meeting of the National Academy of Neuropsychology, Orlando.

Reynolds, C. R., & Bigler, E. D. (1994a). *Test of Memory and Learning.* Austin, TX: Pro-Ed.

Reynolds, C. R., & Bigler, E. D. (1994b). *Manual for the Test of Memory and Learning.* Austin, TX: Pro-Ed.

Reynolds, C. R., & Bigler, E. D. (1996). Factor structure, factor indexes, and other useful statistics for interpretation of the Test of Memory and Learning. *Archives of Clinical Neuropsychology, 11*(1), 29–43.

Reynolds, C. R., & Bigler, E. D. (1997). Clinical assessment of child and adolescent memory with the Test of Memory and Learning. In C. Reynolds & E. Fletcher-Janzen (Eds.), *The Handbook of Clinical Child Neuropsychology* (pp. 296–319). New York: Plenum.

Russo, A. A., Barker, L. H., Mueller, R., Lajiness-O'Neill, R., Johnson, S. C., Anderson, C. V., Norman, M. A., Sephton, S., Primus, E., Bigler, E. D., & Reynolds, C. R. (1994, November). *Memory and digit span: Concurrent and construct validity of the Test of Memory and Learning (TOMAL) using the Wechsler Memory Scale-Revised (WMS-R).* Paper presented at the annual meeting of the National Academy of Neuropsychology, Orlando.

CECIL R. REYNOLDS
Texas A & M University

TEST OF NONVERBAL INTELLIGENCE–THIRD EDITION (TONI-3)

The *Test of Nonverbal Intelligence–Third Edition* (TONI-3; Brown, Sherbenou, & Johnsen, 1998), a major revision of the popular TONI-2, was designed to be a language-free measure of abstract-figural problem solving for children and adults ages 6–0 to 89–11. The TONI-3 measures a specific component of intelligent behavior by testing an individual's ability to solve problems without overtly using language. The directions, content, and responses of the test are all language-free, which makes the TONI-3 an ideal test for those who are deaf, language disordered, non-English speaking, or culturally different.

The abstract-figural content of the test ensures that each item presents a novel problem. The TONI-3 items contain no words, numbers, familiar pictures, or symbols. The drawings in the TONI-3 Picture Book have been substantially improved in this revision. Because the TONI-3 has 2 equivalent forms, it is ideal for situations where both pre- and post-measures are desirable. Each 45 item form contains problem-solving tasks that progressively increase in complexity and difficulty. Raw scores are converted to

percentile ranks and to deviation quotients that have a mean of 100 and a standard deviation of 15 points.

The TONI-3 was normed over 3,000 subjects tested in 1995 and 1996. Their demographic characteristics matched those of the United States population according to the 1996 Census data. The normative group was stratified on the basis of age, gender, race, ethnic group membership, geographic location, community size, principal language spoken in the home, and socioeconomic status as indicated by educational attainment and family income.

Almost 20 years of research has established the test's reliability and validity. Extensive research is reported in the manual, including the authors' own research and all published research conducted by independent investigators since the test was first published in 1980. Considerable validity data are reported as well. These data document the test's relationship to other measures of intelligence, its relationship to measures of achievement and personality, its efficiency in discriminating groups appropriately, and its factor structure. The potential bias of test items was studied and found to be insignificant.

In this revision of TONI, the authors made improvements suggested by reviewers of the previous editions (Aiken, 1996; McLoughlin & Lewis, 1994; & Murphy, 1992). Earlier editions of the TONI were reviewed extensively; references for the newest edition of the test (TONI-3) are unavailable because of its recent publication date.

REFERENCES

Aiken, L. R. (1996). *Assessment of intellectual functioning* (2nd ed.). New York: Plenum Press.

Brown, L., Sherbenou, R. J., & Johnsen, S. J. (1997). *Test of Nonverbal Intelligence–Third Edition.* Austin, TX: Pro-Ed.

McLoughlin, J. A., & Lewis, R. B. (1994). *Assessing special students* (4th ed.). Columbus, OH: Merrill.

Murphy, K. R. (1992). Review of the Test of Nonverbal Intelligence, Second Edition. In J. J. Kramer & J. C. Conoley (Eds.), *The eleventh mental measurements yearbook* (pp. 969–970). Lincoln: Buros Institute of Mental Measurements, University of Nebraska Press.

TADDY MADDOX
Pro-Ed, Inc.

TEST OF PHONOLOGICAL AWARENESS (TOPA)

The *Test of Phonological Awareness* (TOPA; Torgesen & Bryant, 1994) measures young children's awareness of the individual sounds in words. The TOPA can be used to identify children in kindergarten who may profit from instructional activities to enhance their phonological awareness in preparation for reading instruction. The Early Elementary version of the TOPA can be used to determine if first-

and second-grade students' difficulties in early reading are associated with delays in development of phonological awareness.

The TOPA is provided in a Kindergarten version (measuring same and different beginning sounds) suitable for administration any time during the kindergarten year and in an Early Elementary version (measuring same and different ending sounds) suitable for first- and second-grade children. Both versions can be administered either individually or to groups of children, with group administration taking about 20 minutes. The test has been standardized on a large sample of children representative of the population characteristics reported in the U.S. census. The manual provides information to generate percentiles and a variety of standard scores. Internal consistency reliabilities range from .89 to .91 at different ages. Evidence of content, predictive, and construct validity also is provided in the manual.

Long (1998) finds the TOPA test format simple and reports that administration should be completed rapidly in most instances. McCauley (1998) feels that the TOPA makes a substantial contribution to the group assessment of phonological awareness in young school-aged children. She states that evidence of reliability and validity is generally quite adequate.

REFERENCES

Long, S. H. (1998). Review of the Test of Phonological Awareness. In J. C. Impara & B. S. Plake (Eds.), *The thirteenth mental measurements yearbook* (pp. 1049–1050). Lincoln: Buros Institute of Mental Measurements, University of Nebraska Press.

McCauley, R. (1998). Review of the Test of Phonological Awareness. In J. C. Impara & B. S. Plake (Eds.), *The thirteenth mental measurements yearbook* (pp. 1050–1052). Lincoln: Buros Institute of Mental Measurements, University of Nebraska Press.

Torgesen, J. K., & Bryant, B. R. (1994). *Test of Phonological Awareness*. Austin, TX: Pro-Ed.

TADDY MADDOX
Pro-Ed, Inc.

TEST OF WORD FINDING (TWF)

The *Test of Word Finding* (TWF; German, 1989) assesses an important expressive vocabulary skill. An examiner can diagnose word-finding disorders by presenting five naming sections: Picture Naming: Nouns; Picture Naming: Verbs; Sentence Completion Naming; Description Naming; and Category Naming. The TWF includes a special sixth comprehension section that allows the examiner to determine if errors are a result of word-finding problems or are due to poor comprehension. The instrument provides formal and informal analyses of two dimensions of word finding: speed

and accuracy. The formal analysis yields standard scores, percentile ranks, and grade standards for item response time. The informal analysis yields secondary characteristics (gestures and extra verbalization) and substitution types. Speed can be measured in actual or estimated item response time.

The TWF is an individually administered test consisting of a primary form (80 items) for grades 1 and 2, and an intermediate form (90 items) for grades 3 through 6. Administration time is between 20 and 30 minutes. Age norms for ages 6–6 to 12–11 and grade norms for Grades 1 through 6 are available.

The instrument was nationally standardized on 1,200 individuals residing in 18 states. The sample was stratified based on the 1980 census. Reliability and validity are reported in the technical manual.

Weinberg (1992) reported in her review that the TWF is a well-conceived and psychometrically sound measure of word-finding problems in children. Weismer (1992) summarized that the TWF is a reliable and valid assessment instrument for evaluating children's word-finding abilities.

REFERENCES

German, D. J. (1989). *Test of Word Finding*. Austin, TX: Pro-Ed.

Weinberg, S. L. (1992). Review of the Test of Word Finding. In J. J. Kramer & J. C. Conoley (Eds.), *The eleventh mental measurements yearbook* (pp. 976–978). Lincoln: Buros Institute of Mental Measurements, University of Nebraska Press.

Weismer, S. E. (1992). Review of the Test of Word Finding. In J. J. Kramer & J. C. Conoley (Eds.), *The eleventh mental measurements yearbook* (pp. 978–979). Lincoln: Buros Institute of Mental Measurements, University of Nebraska Press.

TADDY MADDOX
Pro-Ed, Inc.

APHASIA
LEARNING DISABILITIES

TEST OF VARIABLES OF ATTENTION

The Test of Variables of Attention (TOVA; Greenberg, 1989/1996) is an individually-administered visual continuous performance test. It is designed primarily for diagnosing children with attentional disorders and for monitoring the effectiveness of medication in treating attentional disorders. The TOVA is a 23-minute computerized test that requires neither language skills nor recognition of letters or numbers. The task is relatively simple: one of two easily discriminated visual stimuli is presented for 100 milliseconds at 2-second intervals, and the subject is required to click a button whenever the target appears, but must inhibit responding whenever the non-target appears. The target stimulus is a small square adjacent to the top of a larger square and the non-target stimulus is a small square adjacent to the bottom of a larger square. There are two conditions during the test: 1) infrequent presentation of targets that is designed to measure attention; and 2) frequent presentation of targets that is designed to measure impulsivity.

Seven scores are obtained on the TOVA: errors of omission, errors of commission, mean correct response time, variability, anticipatory responses, multiple responses, and post-commission response time. The TOVA kit provides a manual for interpretation of test results and the test itself provides computerized test interpretations. The TOVA kit also provides two videotapes that demonstrate how the TOVA may be used to screen for ADHD, to predict response to medication, and to monitor the psychopharmacological treatment.

Norms for the TOVA are based on a total of 1,590 subjects ages 4 through 80. The manual does not provide extensive data on the characteristics of the sample; the subjects are only described as "normal." The evidence for test-retest reliability is based on a study (no citation is provided) that reports no significant differences between testings for a randomly selected group of normal children, ADHD subjects, and normal adults. The validity data are not adequate for the TOVA. There is question about the content validity of the measure (i.e., whether a small sample of behavior is a valid estimate of characteristic behavior for the individual), as a very limited research base is provided (Hagin & Dellabella, 1998). In terms of providing an accurate assessment of the presence or absence of ADHD, the TOVA produces fairly high rates of misclassification (15% false positive rate and 28% false negative rate; Stein, 1998). Overall the technical characteristics of reliability and validity are not adequately provided in the TOVA manual (Hagin & Dellabella, 1998; Stein, 1998). The TOVA can be used as a *part* of a diagnostic battery for purposes of diagnosing attentional disorders, but should be done so with caution until more normative information is available (Stein, 1998).

REFERENCES

Greenberg, L. M. (1996). Test of Variables of Attention. Los Alamitos, CA: Universal Attention Disorders, Inc. (Original work published 1988).

Hagin, R. A., & Dellabella, P. (1998). Review of the Test of Variables of Attention. In J. C. Impara & B. S. Plake (Eds.), *The thirteenth mental measurements yearbook* (pp. 1058–1060). Lincoln, NE: Buros Institute of Mental Measurements.

Stein, M. B. (1998). Review of the Test of Variables of Attention. In J. C. Impara & B. S. Plake (Eds.), *The thirteenth mental measurements yearbook* (pp. 1060–1062). Lincoln, NE: Buros Institute of Mental Measurements.

ELIZABETH O. LICHTENBERGER
The Salk Institute

TEST OF WRITTEN LANGUAGE—THIRD EDITION (TOWL-3)

The *Test of Written Language—Third Edition* (TOWL-3) measures language in spontaneous and contrived formats. Using a pictorial prompt, the student writes a passage that is scored on Contextual Conventions (capitalization, punctuation, and spelling), Contextual Language (vocabulary, syntax, and grammar), and Story Construction (plot, character development, and general composition). The contrived subtests (Vocabulary, Spelling, Style, Logical Sentences, and Sentence Combining) measure word usage, ability to form letters into words, punctuation, capitalization, ability to write conceptually sound sentences, and syntax. Composite quotients are available for overall writing, contrived writing, and spontaneous writing.

The TOWL-3 was standardized on a 26-state sample of more than 2,000 public and private school students in grades 2 through 12. These students have the same characteristics as those reported in the 1990 Statistical Abstract of the United States. Percentiles, standard scores, and age equivalents are provided. Internal consistency, test-retest with equivalent forms, and interscorer reliability coefficients approximate .80 at most ages, and many are in the .90s. The validity of the TOWL-3 was investigated and relevant studies are described in the manual, which has a section that provides suggestions for assessing written language informally and that gives numerous ideas for teachers to use when remediating writing deficits. In addition, the TOWL-3 is shown to be unbiased relative to gender and race and can be administered to individuals or small groups. Because two equivalent forms (A and B) are available, examiners can evaluate student growth in writing using pretesting and posttesting that is not contaminated by memory.

The instrument was reviewed in *The Thirteenth Mental Measurements Yearbook*. Hansen (1998) summarized by reporting that the TOWL-3 based in a strong conceptual model of writing and is most useful in identifying student writers who are performing substantially below their peers. Bucy and Swerdlik (1998) feel that the TOWL-3 meets a need for a measure of written language for both diagnostic and research purposes.

REFERENCES

Bucy, J. E., & Swerdlik, M. E. (1998). Review of the Test of Written Language—Third Edition. In J. C. Impara & B. S. Plake (Eds.), *The thirteenth mental measurements yearbook* (pp. 1072–1074). Lincoln: Buros Institute of Mental Measurements, University of Nebraska Press.

Hammill, D. D., & Larsen, S. C. (1996). *Test of Written Language—Third Edition*. Austin, TX: Pro-Ed.

Hansen, J. B. (1998). Review of the Test of Written Language—Third Edition. In J. C. Impara & B. S. Plake (Eds.), *The thirteenth mental measurements yearbook* (pp. 1070–1072). Lincoln: Buros Institute of Mental Measurements, University of Nebraska Press.

TADDY MADDOX
Pro-Ed, Inc.

TEST SCATTER

Individuals who take intelligence, achievement, and other educational and psychological tests seldom, if ever, earn precisely the same score on all tests or even on the subparts of one test. This variation in performance across tests by individuals is known as test scatter. There are three principal measures of test scatter present in the testing literature: the range, the number of deviant signs, and profile variability.

The range is simply the highest minus the lowest score for an individual on a battery of tests once the scores have been placed on a common scale such that the means and standard deviations are equal. The Wechsler Intelligence Scale for Children-Revised (WISC-R) has 10 regularly administered subtests and two supplementary subtests. As one index of test scatter, one might locate the highest subtest score and the lowest subtest score for a particular child and then subtract the two. The resulting number is the range. The range for a particular child can be compared with the average range of scores for individuals in the standardization sample of the tests or some other relevant reference group to determine the degree of "usualness" of the observed range of scores. Sometimes, as with the WISC-R verbal and performance scales, a range will be calculated with only two scores.

The number of deviant signs (NDS) refers to the number of subtests or other component parts or a battery of tests that deviate at a statistically significant level (typically, $p \leq .05$) from the mean score of the individual across all tests taken or at least all of those used in the comparisons. Six subtests constitute the WISC-R verbal scale. It may be of interest of know whether the number of subtests that differ significantly from a child's own mean subtest score is unusual or whether it is a common occurrence to show so many strengths and weaknesses in an ability profile. Normative comparisons would again be made.

Profile variability is another prominent index of test scatter and one that appears to be the most stable. Profile variability is simply the variance of a set of scores for one individual, i.e., the average squared deviation from the mean score of all the scores.

Since perhaps the inception of the field of learning disabilities, learning-disabled (LD) children have been characterized as having a large or unusual amount of intra- and intertest scatter (Chalfant & Scheffelin, 1969). Until the mid-1970s, this assumption was made largely in igno-

rance of the degree of test scatters that characterizes the test performance of normal children. Although normative data on test scatter for the WISC had been presented as early as 1960, these data went largely ignored until Kaufman's studies of the WISC-R were published in 1976 (Kaufman, 1976a, 1976b). Prior to his examination of test scatter for the 2200 normal children in the WISC-R standardization sample, myths regarding such indexes abounded.

In an informal survey, Kaufman (1976a) reported that when asked to estimate the range of subtest scores on the WISC-R for normal children, most practicing psychologists and other diagnosticians suggested a range of only two to four points. The mean range for normal children in the WISC-R standardization sample turned out to be more than seven points, more than twice the typical estimate. A similar phenomenon occurred with regard to verbal-performance IQ differences on the WISC-R.

Conventional diagnostic beliefs, prior to the publication of Kaufman's work, held that a verbal-performance IQ difference of 15 points or more was a primary indication of learning disability. Even Wechsler (1974) indicated that this degree of scatter was of clinical significance and deserving of follow-up study. At it turns out, approximately 35% of the population of normal children have a verbal-performance IQ difference of 12 or more points, representing a statistically significant difference between the two scores, and 24%, or nearly one out of four, of normal children demonstrate a difference of 15 or more points. These data are extremely similar to those reported in 1960 for the WISC.

A complete tabulation of Kaufman's (1979) findings regarding verbal-performance IQ differences is presented in the Table.

Since these seminal studies, a number of authors have investigated test scatter for normal children on such widely used tests as the Wechsler Preschool and Primary Scale of Intelligence (Reynolds & Gutkin, 1981) and the Kaufman Assessment Battery for Children (Chatman, Reynolds, & Willson, 1983). It is now clear that normal children exhibit much variation in their abilities, exploding the myth of the normal child's "flat" ability profile and that only exceptional children show large amounts of test scatter. Recent revisions of the Wechsler scales including the WISC-III and WAIS-III continue to show distributions of test scatter similar to what was seen in Kaufman's (1979) early work.

Large amounts of scatter in the profiles of normal children do not negate the importance of variation in children's test scatter. If the differences among a child's test scores are large enough to be considered real (reliable), then chances are that real differences exist among the child's cognitive skills and abilities, differences that mandate attention and that have relevance to the development of instructional strategies. Unusual differences among test

Percentage of Normal Children Obtaining WISC-R V-P Discrepancies of a Given Magnitude or Greater, by Parental Occupation

Size of V–P Discrepancy (Regardless of Direction)	Parental Occupation					
	Professional and Technical	Managerial, Clerical, Sales	Skilled Workers	Semiskilled Workers	Unskilled Workers	Total Sample
9	52	48	48	46	43	48
10	48	44	43	41	37	43
11	43	40	39	36	34	39
12	40	35	34	31	29	34
13	36	33	31	28	26	31
14	32	29	29	25	24	28
15	29	25	26	21	22	24
16	26	22	22	19	19	22
17	24	19	18	15	16	18
18	20	16	16	14	15	16
19	16	15	13	12	14	14
20	13	13	12	10	13	12
21	11	11	8	9	10	10
22	10	9	7	7	9	8
23	8	8	6	6	8	7
24	7	7	5	5	6	6
25	6	6	4	4	5	5
26	5	5	3	3	4	4
27	4	4	2	2	3	3
28–30	3	3	1	1	2	2
31–33	2	2	<1	<1	1	1
34+	1	1	<1	<1	<1	<1

Source: Kaufman, Alan S. Intelligent testing with the WISC-R. © 1979, New York: Wiley.

scores will continue to have diagnostic use as well, but only when determined with regard to normative standards.

REFERENCES

Chalfant, J. C., & Scheffelin, M. A. (1969). *Central processing dysfunctions in children* [NINDS Monograph No. 9]. Bethesda, MD: U.S. Department of Health, Education, and Welfare.

Chatman, S. P., Reynolds, C. R., & Willson, V. L. (1983). Multiple indexes of test scatter on the Kaufman Assessment Battery for Children. *Journal of Learning Disabilities, 17,* 523–531.

Kaufman, A. S. (1976a). A new approach to the interpretation of test scatter on the WISC-R. *Journal of Learning Disabilities, 9,* 160–168.

Kaufman, A. S. (1976b). Verbal-performance IQ discrepancies on the WISC-R. *Journal of Consulting & Clinical Psychology, 44,* 739–744.

Kaufman, A. S. (1979). *Intelligent testing with the WISC-R.* New York: Wiley-Interscience.

Reynolds, C. R., & Gutkin, T. B. (1981). Test scatter on the WPPSI: Normative analyses of the standardization sample. *Journal of Learning Disabilities, 14,* 460–464.

Wechsler, D. (1974). *Wechsler intelligence scale for Children-revised.* New York: The Psychological Corporation.

CECIL R. REYNOLDS
Texas A & M University

PROFILE VARIABILITY
VERBAL-PERFORMANCE IQ DISCREPANCIES

TESTS IN PRINT

Tests in Print (Buros, 1961, 1974; Mitchell, 1983; Murphy, Conoley, & Impara, 1994) are volumes that provide a comprehensive index of commercially available educational and psychological tests in English-speaking countries. The volumes contain descriptive information about each test (e.g., the age or grade levels for which the test is designed, author, publishing company, scale scores); literature related to the specific test; an index to all reviews of the test in previous Buros *Mental Measurement Yearbooks*; and references to test descriptions and related literature cited in previous *Test in Print* volumes.

The most current, *Tests in Print IV* (Murphy, Conoley, & Impara, 1994), contains thousands of descriptions of commercially available tests; references for specific tests; an alphabetical listing of test names, a directory of publishers with addresses and an index to their tests; a title index showing both in print and out-of-print tests since previous listings a name index for test authors, reviewers, and authors of references; and a classified subject index for quickly locating tests in particular areas.

REFERENCES

Buros, O. K. (1961). *Tests in print.* Highland Park, NJ: Gryphon.

Buros, O. K. (1974). *Tests in print II.* Highland Park, NJ: Gryphon.

Mitchell, J. V., Jr. (1983). *Test in print III.* Lincoln, NE: Buros Institute of Mental Measurements.

Murphy, L. L., Conoley, J. C., Impara, J. C. (1994). *Test in print IV.* Lincoln, NE: Buros Institute of Mental Measurements.

JANE CLOSE CONOLEY
University of Nebraska
First edition

ELIZABETH O. LICHTENBERGER
The Salk Institute
Second edition

BUROS MENTAL MEASUREMENTS YEARBOOK

TESTS

See SPECIFIC TEST.
Also See MEASUREMENT.

TEST-TEACH-TEST PARADIGM

The Test-Teach-Test Paradigm (TTT-P) is representative of an instructional concept that is similar to the concept of teaching students how to read by using the phonics approach. To conceptualize the TTT-P, we need to review some other terms: direct instruction, model-lead and test, criterion assessment, criterion instruction and appropriate practice.

Fundamentally, the TTT-P represents an instructional sequence. The portrayal that follows (Nash, 1985) is an adaptation of the instructional sequencing suggested by Bateman (1971) and Engelmann and Bruner (1969). In the course of this portrayal, some of the other terms referred to above will be employed. The instructional concept and postures of both Bateman and Engelmann are regarded by many as representing a kind of pioneering methodology of the 1970s that distinguished special educational instruction from regular education.

A. *The initial testing part of the TTT-P*

 In a reading test with beginning second-grade students, all of the students misread the word *blew.*

B. *The teaching part of the TTT-P*

1. The teacher begins by saying, "We are going to learn to read the word *blew* by use of sounds using a simultaneous multisensory instructional procedure."
2. Next, the teacher directs the students to copy down the word that has been written out on the blackboard in front of the students.
3. Then the teacher models for the students what it is that they are to do.
   a. The teacher states that this word has three sounds. The teacher says the sounds, /b/, /l/, and /ew/, and simultaneously underlines each of them while doing so, *b l ew.*
   b. Next, the teacher, using a lead, says, "We, all of us, will now individually underline the three sounds that this word has—simultaneously saying the sound of the letter or letters as we do so." The teacher and the students all together and in an audible voice do so, *b l ew.*
   c. The teacher, using an intervening test, says, "Your turn—reunderline each sound saying each sound out loud as you do so." The students do so, *b l ew.*
   d. Next, the teacher, using another model, says, "I will now loop and say in an audible voice the sounds in this word, *b l ew.*"
   e. Then, using another lead, the teacher says, "We will now all together loop and say the sounds in this word." Students and teacher do so, *b l ew.*
   f. Next, the teacher, using another intervening test, says, "Your turn, now all by yourself you loop and say out loud the sounds in this word." The students do so, *b l ew.*
   g. The teacher, using another lead, says, "We will now underline and say the word rapidly." The teacher and the students do so, *b l ew.*
   h. Then the teacher, using another intervening test, says, "Your turn—now all by yourself, you are to underline and say the word rapidly." The students do so, *b l ew.*
   i. Last, the teacher says, "All of you have just read the word *blew* correctly."

C. *The test part to the TTT-P*

This last phase of step in the TTT-P is the simplest part to do and can be attended to in a number of ways. Using our example word, a teacher could offer repeated appropriate practice experiences in reading this particular word.

 The process of the TTT paradigm as exemplified can be replicated across any and all instruction, be it initial or advanced, and across any and all tasks, with spelling as one of the more obvious ones. In the course of doing so, the teacher will automatically be involved with these initial concepts (Nash, 1986):

1. Direct instruction: The precise identification of what

the student is to learn and how he or she is going to do so.

2. Model-lead-and test: While carrying out any given bit of instruction, the teacher can model what the student is to do and simultaneously follows this with a lead; i.e., doing the task with the student. At this point, the teacher can employ a simple test of what it is that the student knows.

3. Criterion assessment (CA): Both of the test parts of the TTT-P are examples of CA. The first part tests what it is the teacher is to teach if the student fails the test; the second test of the TTT-P is simply a reaffirmation and check on what the teacher intended to teach.

4. Criterion instruction (CI): The teaching part of the TTT-P represents CI because there is an intended 1:1 correlation between the first test and the subsequent needed instruction.

5. Appropriate practice. In the execution of the instruction associated with the TTT-P, the teacher will be implementing the model-lead-test concept automatically and involving the student in the necessary practice.

Instruction that implements the concepts reviewed is instruction that guarantees student success. These patterns can be repeated as often as student errors dictate.

REFERENCES

Bateman, B. D. (1971). *The essentials of teaching.* Sioux Falls, SD: Adapt.

Engelmann, S., & Brunder, E. (1969). *Distar reading.* Chicago: Science Research.

Nash, R. T. (1985). Remediation courses. Project Success, University of Wisconsin-Oshkosh. Unpublished raw data.

Nash, R. T. (1986). *Manual for remediating the reading and spelling deficits of elementary, secondary and post-secondary students.* Flossmoor, IL: Language Prescriptions, Inc.

ROBERT T. NASH
University of Wisconsin at Oshkosh

DIAGNOSTIC-PRESCRIPTIVE TEACHING

THALIDOMIDE

Thalidomide was among the first drugs for which teratogenicity was established. A teratogen is a chemical agent that can cross the placenta and cause congenital malformations. Effective as a sedative and a tranquilizer, thalidomide is an example of a teratogen that had positive effects on the mother but devastating consequences for the embryo. Even after decades of study, the mechanism by which thalidomide causes deformities is not understood (T.J., 1999).

Teratogenicity became suspected with the birth of a relatively large number of babies with phocomelia (seal-flipper limbs) and a variety of other deformities in Europe in the late 1950s and early 1960s. Phocomelia is a condition in which arms and/or legs are drastically shortened or absent and fingers/toes extend from the foreshortened limbs or the trunk. Thalidomide was widely distributed in Europe, where it is estimated to have affected over 7,000 individuals. It was withdrawn from the market in late 1961 before it passed Food and Drug Administration approval in the United States (Moore, 1982). Teratogenicity was unusually high; over 90% of women who took thalidomide during a particular period in pregnancy had infants with some type of defect (Holmes, 1983).

Thalidomide is the only drug whose timing of harmful effects has been well-established, causing defects only if taken by the mother when the embryo was 34 to 50 days old; earlier or later consumption had no adverse effects (Holmes, 1983). Individual defects can be traced to particular days when the mother took the drug. The specificity of the embryo's age for thalidomide effects provides a particularly dramatic example for a critical period.

The particular complex of effects is sometimes termed the thalidomide syndrome (Landau, 1986). Phocomelia is the most common and pronounced sign, but absent or deformed ears and digits are common, and malformations of forehead, heart, and digestive system occasionally occur. Generally, overall intelligence is unaffected, but some language deficits have been reported (Holmes, 1983; Landau, 1986; Moore, 1982). Because thalidomide has teratogenic but not mutagenic qualities, thalidomide-syndrome individuals would be expected to have normal children.

Despite the horrific consequences of prenatal exposure to thalidomide, research on its potential benefits began again shortly after it was withdrawn from the market. In 1964, thalidomide was given to a patient with leprosy because of evidence of the drug's anti-inflammatory benefits; within days the patient's symptoms subsided and stayed reduced with continued use of thalidomide (Blakeslee, 1998). It has received FDA approval for use in treatment of leprosy, and may be of benefit in treatment of a number of other diseases, including brain and other forms of cancer, inflammatory disease, and autoimmune disorders. Thalidomide is now being used experimentally with AIDS, and appears to relieve symptoms such as oral ulcers and severe weight loss. Some research suggests that thalidomide may inhibit HIV replication (Blaney, 1995). Thalidomide has been said to be non-toxic among those taking the drug; researchers have yet to find a lethal dose (Blakeslee, 1998).

However beneficial, thalidomide remains a major human teratogen and therefore its use must be carefully monitored in order to avoid any recurrence of the severe malformations seen in children whose mothers were some of thalidomide's first users.

REFERENCES

Blakeslee, D. (1998). Thalidomide. *Journal of the American Medical Association* [HIV/AIDS Information Center]. http://www.ama-assn.org/special.hiv.newsline.briefing.thalido.htm [11/15/98].

Blaney, C. (1995). Second thoughts about thalidomide. *Medical Sciences Bulletin.* http://pharminfo.com/pubs.msb/thalidomide.html

Holmes, L. B. (1983). Congenital malformations. In R. E. Behrman & V. C. Vaughn (Eds.), *Nelson textbook of pediatrics* (12th ed.) Philadelphia: W.B. Saunders.

Landau, S. I. (1986). *International dictionary of medicine and biology.* New York: Wiley.

Moore, K. L. (1982). *The developing human* (3rd ed.) Philadelphia: Saunders.

T. J. (Feb 20, 1999). Theorizing about the dark side of thalidomide. *Science News, 155*(8), 124–125.

ROBERT T. BROWN
AIMEE R. HUNTER
University of North Carolina at Wilmington

EARLY EXPERIENCE AND CRITICAL PERIODS
ETIOLOGY
TERATOGENS

THEIR WORLD

Their World is the annual publication of the Foundation for Children with Learning Disabilities (FCLD). The FCLD was founded in 1977 and began publication of *Their World* in 1979. The publication is presented each year at FCLD's annual benefit in New York City. *Their World* is a public awareness vehicle, intended to educate the public about learning disabilities generally while emphasizing the accomplishments of the learning disabled. *Their World* publishes real-life stories about the way families cope with learning-disabled children. *Their World* supports after school, summer, athletic, and creativity programs as a support network for the learning disabled and their families. The publication is distributed to over 75,000 parents, educators, legislators, and professionals each year.

CECIL R. REYNOLDS
Texas A & M University

FOUNDATION FOR CHILDREN WITH LEARNING
   DISABILITIES

THEMATIC APPERCEPTION TEST (TAT)

The Thematic Apperception Test (TAT) is a projective assessment instrument developed by Henry Murray (1938) as a means of investigating his theory of personality. Designed for use with subjects ages 7 and older, TAT has become one of the most widely used assessment techniques. The test materials consist of 31 black and white pictures depicting characters in various settings. Each picture is designed to elicit particular themes or conflicts. Subsets of pictures (typically 8 to 10) are selected for administration depending on the individual's age and sex and the nature of the presenting problem. Subjects are asked to tell a story about each picture as it is presented. Typical instructions stress that subjects use their imagination and include in their response a description of what the characters in the scene are doing, thinking, and feeling, the preceding events, and the outcome. Responses are recorded verbatim by the examiner. An inquiry is usually conducted after all pictures have been presented.

The TAT has also been presented in group form; this requires the subject to provide written responses. Murray and others (Groth-Marnat, 1984) have devised scoring systems for TAT; however, in clinical practice, such systems are rarely used (Klopfer & Taulbee, 1976). Variations on the TAT include the Children's Apperception Test and the Senior Apperception Test (Bellack, 1975), which include stimulus materials believed to be more relevant to children and the elderly, respectively.

REFERENCES

Bellack, L. (1975). *The TAT, CAT and SAT in clinical use* (3rd ed.). New York: Grune & Stratton.

Groth-Marnat, G. (1984). *Handbook of psychological assessment.* New York: Van Nostrand Reinhold.

Klopfer, W. G., & Taulbee, E. S. (1976). Projective tests. In M. R. Rosenzweig & L. W. Porter (Eds.), *Annual review of psychology, 17,* 543–567.

Murray, H. A. (1938). *Explorations in personality.* New York: Oxford University Press.

ROBERT G. BRUBAKER
Eastern Kentucky University

EMOTIONAL DISORDERS
PERSONALITY ASSESSMENT

THEORY OF ACTIVITY

The theory of activity is a general theoretical paradigm for psychological and developmental research that has its historical roots in work carried out in the Soviet Union between 1925 and 1945 by L. S. Vygotsky, A. R. Luria, A. N. Leont'ev, and their colleagues (Leont'ev 1978, 1981; Minick, 1985; Wertsch, 1981, 1985). Activity theory is among the most important intellectual forces in contemporary Soviet psychology, providing a unifying conceptual framework for a wide range of psychological theory, research, and practice. As a consequence of linguistic, political, and conceptual barriers, however, it was only in the late 1970s that psychologists and social scientists in Western Europe and the United States began to become aware of activity theory.

The theory of activity is the product of an effort by Vygotsky's students and colleagues to extend the theoretical framework Vygotsky had developed between 1925 and his death in 1934. Vygotsky had been concerned with two fundamental limitations in the psychological theories of his time. First, he felt that many psychologists had underestimated or misrepresented the influence of social and cultural factors on human psychological development. He was particularly concerned with the failure to clarify the mechanisms of this influence. Second, Vygotsky felt that the disputes between the traditional psychology of mind and the behaviorist theories that were emerging in the 1920s reflected a widespread tendency in psychology and philosophy to represent mind and behavior in conceptual isolation from one another rather than as connected aspects of an integral whole (Davydov & Radzikhovskii, 1985; Minick, in press). Vygotsky's work and the subsequent emergence of activity theory were attempts to develop a theoretical paradigm that would overcome these limitations in existing theory.

A central premise of the theory of activity is that human psychological development is dependent on a process in which the individual is drawn into the historically developed systems of social action that constitute both society and the life of the mature adult. Within this framework, psychological development or change is dependent on the individual's progressively more complete participation in social life. Modes of organizing and mediating cognitive activity are mastered and the relationship to the external world of objects and people is defined in this process.

Three additional characteristics of activity theory are also extremely important to any effort to understand it. First, the concepts, constructs, and laws that provide the basic content of psychological theory developed within this framework and that determine how psychological characteristics and their development are conceptualized are represented and defined in such a way that a connection is consistently maintained between psychological characteristics and the organization of social action (Minick, 1985). For example, Leont'ev (1978) defines personality as a system of hierarchically related goals and motives that derives its structure from (1) the objective relationships among the actions that constitute the social system; (2) the objective relationships among the actions that constitute

the life of the individual; and (3) the subjective relationships among these actions that are defined by the individual's values and beliefs. With this approach to the definition of scientific constructs in psychology, it becomes impossible to conceptualize the psychological characteristics of the individual or the laws of psychological functioning and development apart from the organization of concrete social systems and the individual's place in them (Minick, 1985). This can be contrasted with theoretical frameworks in which key constructs are defined in ways that conceptually isolate the psychological (e.g., reversible operations, traits, or associative networks) and the social (e.g., social roles, social norms, or social organization).

Second, the goal-oriented action serves as the central analytic object in activity theory (Davydov & Radzikhovskii, 1985; Leont'ev, 1978; Zinchenko, 1985). To analyze psychological characteristics and psychological processes in connection with socially organized action systems, one has to identify an appropriate analytic unit for the development of theory and research. As a basic unit both of the psychological life of the individual and of the organization of society, the goal-oriented action has assumed this role in activity theory.

Third, the theory of activity is based on a schema that emphasizes the importance of considering three levels of analysis in studying the goal-oriented action and the psychological processes that function and develop in connection with it (Leont'ev, 1978). At the level of activities, general yet socially and culturally defined motives are considered. For example, there are important differences in the organization of actions and goals in western systems of formal schooling and in more traditional apprenticeship systems. In formal schooling, education and learning are the motives that provide the general organizing framework for concrete goal-oriented actions. In apprenticeship, these motives are subordinated to the economic motives connected with the production of products for use or sale. At the level of operations, the impact of the object world on the way an action is carried out is considered. Under different conditions, a single set of motives may lead to the emergence of different concrete goals or to different ways of performing actions in order to realize those goals. This system of analytic levels (i.e., activity-motive, action-goal, and operation-condition) has provided activity theory with a useful framework for analyzing psychological functioning and development without losing sight of its connections with the physical and social environment in which it occurs.

As a general perspective on psychology and psychological development, the theory of activity has had an important impact on theory and practice in the broad domain of special education in the Soviet Union. While a detailed discussion of the nature of this impact is impossible in this context, a useful illustration is available in the English translation of a volume by Alexander Meshcheryakov in which he reviews his work with deaf and blind children (Meshcheryakov, 1979).

REFERENCES

Davydov, V. V., & Radzikhovskii, L. A. (1985). Vygotsky's theory and the activity-oriented approach in psychology. In J. V. Wertsch (Ed.), *Culture, communication, and cognition: Vygotskian perspectives* (pp. 35–65). New York: Cambridge University Press.

Leont'ev, A. N. (1978). *Activity, consciousness, and personality.* Englewood Cliffs, NJ: Prentice-Hall.

Leont'ev, A. N. (1981). *Problems of the development of mind.* Moscow: Progress Publishers.

Meshcheryakov, A. N. (1979). *Awakening to life: Forming behavior and the mind in deaf-blind children.* Moscow: Progress Publishers.

Minick, N. (1985). *L. S. Vygotsky and Soviety activity theory: New perspectives on the relationship between mind and society.* Unpublished doctoral dissertation, Northwestern University, Evanston, IL.

Minick, N. (in press). *The development of Vygotsky's thought. Introduction to L. S. Vygotsky, Collected works: Problems of general psychology* (Vol. 1). New York: Plenum.

Vygotsky, L. S. (in press). Thinking and speech. In V. V. Davydov (Ed.), *L. S. Vygotsky, Collected works: General Psychology Vol. 1* (N. Minick Trans.). New York: Plenum.

Wertsch, J. V. (Ed.). (1981). *The concept of activity in Soviet psychology.* New York: Sharpe.

Wertsch, J. V. (1985). *Vygotsky and the social formation of mind.* Cambridge, MA: Harvard University Press.

Zinchenko, V. P. (1985). Vygotsky's ideas about units for the analysis of mind. In J. V. Wertsch (Ed.), *Culture, communication, and cognition: Vygotskian perspectives* (pp. 94–118). New York: Cambridge University Press.

NORRIS MINICK
Center for Psychosocial Studies,
The Spencer Foundation

VGOTSKY, L. S.
ZONE OF PROXIMAL DEVELOPMENT

THERAPEUTIC COMMUNITY

The therapeutic community as a model for psychosocial rehabilitation was developed following World War II by Maxwell Jones, a psychiatrist, in Great Britain. This approach developed out of Jones's experience in working with soldiers on a psychiatric unit who had suffered emotional trauma and with persons with personality problems. Jones's approach was a reaction to the traditional psychiatric hospital practice that produced dependent patients who needed resocialization in addition to treatment of their illness if they were to be discharged. He believed the hospital could be purposefully employed as a significant therapeutic milieu by facilitating full social participation by the patients (Main, 1946). Providing appropriately organized social environments, rather than just psychotherapeutic or medical approaches, was the method of effecting change in patients. Jones's work was significant for the development of social psychiatry, in which emphasis is placed on the environmental sources of stress that cause persons to learn maladaptive ways of coping rather than on illness or deviancy, the traditional psychiatric emphases.

Jones initially presented the principles and practices of the therapeutic community in *Social Psychiatry: A Study of Therapeutic Communities* (1952), but the book was limited in detail. A clearer explication of the underlying themes that guided and shaped the social interactions in the therapeutic community was provided by R. N. Rapoport, an anthropologist, in *Community as Doctor* (1960). Themes identified by Rapoport were those of (1) democratization—an equal sharing among community members of the power in decision making about community affairs; (2) permissiveness—the toleration of a wide degree of behavior from members of the community; (3) communalism—the free exchange of information and observations among all members of the community, including patients and staff; and (4) reality confrontation—the continuous presentation to the patients of interpretations of their behavior from the perspective of other members of the therapeutic community.

The principal social methods used in the therapeutic community were the discussion of events that occurred within the context of frequent community group meetings by all community members; the facilitation of exchange of information among members of the community; the development of relationships between staff and clients that emphasized their status as peers in learning through interacting with each other; the provision of frequent situations in which patients could learn more adaptive ways to cope with problematic situations by interacting with community members; and the continued examination by community members, especially staff members, of their roles to find more effective ways of functioning.

The ideology of the therapeutic community was never completely operationalized, and some found it extremely difficult to implement (Manning, 1975). Rapoport (1960) offered reasons for the difficulty in implementing Jones's ideology and explanations of why later therapeutic movements used many but not all of the principles. First, there were limits set by the local community on the extremes in democracy or permissiveness that would be tolerated; second, communalism encouraged communication in groups rather than between individuals; third, conflicts arose between ideological themes such as when excessively dominant behavior is permissively tolerated but might be anti-democratic; and fourth, there was an unresolved conflict between the rehabilitation goals that required the hospital to approximate the conditions of life outside the hospital and the treatment goals that required different conditions for the recovery of the patient than those in which the problems developed. About the same time that development of therapeutic communities was taking place, psychotropic medications were introduced into psychiatric practice. This resulted in the obscuring of the effects of the therapeutic community as psychotropic medications were often used with persons who were also in therapeutic communities. In addition, no satisfactory study of the efficacy of the therapeutic community as a treatment approach was ever conducted, though it had wide support among mental health clinicians.

The therapeutic community as developed by Jones declined from the period of the late 1950s (Manning, 1975). Other therapeutic community movements have developed that serve persons with drug, alcohol, and social adjustment problems, and persons in correctional settings. These movements have developed some distinctive characteristics in their approach to treatment but have been greatly influenced by the work of Jones.

REFERENCES

Jones, M. (1952). *Social psychiatry: A study of therapeutic communities.* London: Tavistock.

Main, T. F. (1946). The hospital as a therapeutic institution. *Bulletin of the Menniger Clinic, 10,* 66–70.

Manning, N. (1975). What happened to the therapeutic community. In K. Jones & S. Baldwin (Eds.), *The yearbook of social policy in Britain.* London: Routledge & Kegan Paul.

Rapoport, R. N. (1960). *Community as doctor.* London: Tavistock.

HAROLD HANSON
PAUL BATES
Southern Illinois University

COMMUNITY RESIDENTIAL PROGRAMS
PSYCHONEUROTIC DISORDERS
SOCIAL BEHAVIOR OF THE HANDICAPPED

THERAPEUTIC RECREATION

See RECREATION, THERAPEUTIC.

THINK ALOUD

Think Aloud is a cognitive behavior modification program designed to improve social and cognitive problem-solving skills in young children. Based on the pioneering work of

Meichenbaum, Goodman, Shure, and Spevak, and tied to theory regarding development of self-control. Think Aloud was conceived as a training program to decrease impulsivity, encourage consideration of alternatives, and plan courses of action. It emphasizes the use of cognitive modeling as a teaching tool in which teachers model their own strategies for thinking through problems. Students are then encouraged to "think out loud" while systematically approaching each problem through asking and answering four basic questions: What is my problem? How can I solve it? Am I following my plan? How did I do?

The original small group (two to four students) program (Camp & Bash, 1985) was tested on 6- to 8-year-old boys identified as hyperaggressive by teachers. In the hands of trained teachers, improvement in cognitive impulsivity was demonstrated across several trials, as was improvement in prosocial classroom behavior. Although significant decreases in aggressive behavior were also observed, this was not significantly more than observed in attention-control groups. A refresher course 6 to 12 months after the original program supported previously developed skills and led to significant decreases in hyperactivity and increases in friendliness.

With some demonstrated success in altering thinking and behavior patterns in aggressive boys in the small group situation, the authors reasoned that a more "dilute" program such as found in a large classroom should benefit a broader range of children with mild to moderate deficits in social and cognitive problem skills. In addition, availability of a classroom version of the program would help regular classroom teachers to support skills learned in the small group program. Consequently, they began in 1976 to build Think Aloud Classroom Programs spanning grades 1 to 6 (Bash & Camp, 1985a, 1985b; Camp & Bash, 1985).

Development and study of these programs was supported in part by ESEA Title IV grants to the Denver public schools. Few of the classroom program studies could be conducted with random assignment to experimental or traditional teaching programs. However, within limitations imposed by a nonequivalent control group design, children in the Think Aloud classrooms improved on measures of both social and cognitive problem-solving skills more than children in nonprogram classrooms at all grade levels. Cognitive differences between children in the Think Aloud classroom programs and comparison children were most reliable for the program for grades 1 and 2 and the program for grades 5 and 6. Differences in social problem-solving skills were reliable at all grade levels. The classroom programs can easily be adapted for use in an individual or tutorial program to intensify and individualize the experience. The materials now provide challenge to children over a broad range of developmental levels, making them suitable for special education classrooms as well as regular classrooms, for some middle school children, and for children with special needs for social skills training or assistance in curbing impulsivity.

REFERENCES

Bash, M. A. S., & Camp, B. W. (1985a). *The Think Aloud Classroom Program for Grades 3 and 4*. Champaign, IL: Research.

Bash, M. A. S., & Camp, B. W. (1985b). *The Think Aloud Classroom Program for Grades 5 and 6*. Champaign, IL: Research.

Camp, B. W., & Bash, M. A. S. (1985). *The Think Aloud Classroom Program for Grades 1 and 2*. Champaign, IL: Research.

STAFF

CAMP, BONNIE
IMPULSE CONTROL

THINKING CENTERS

See CREATIVE STUDIES PROGRAM.

THORAZINE

Thorazine is the trade name for the generic antipsychotic agent chlorpromazine. Though Thorazine was among the first synthesized drugs that were found effective in the control of behavioral symptoms associated with psychotic disorders, it is no longer as widely prescribed as it was 30 years ago. However, Thorazine is still used as a benchmark against which new antipsychotic agents are compared in terms of frequency of side effects and efficacy. Thorazine is of the drug class phenothiazine and tends to produce the classic panorama of side effects associated with the phenothiazine group.

In addition to use as a major tranquilizer with psychotic individuals, Thorazine also is used in emergency situations to limit the effects of LSD and to control prolonged behavioral reactions after intoxication with other hallucinogens. One of the major criticisms of Thorazine as a therapeutic agent has been its reported abuse as a chemical restraint (Leavitt, 1982).

In use with children, several cautions must be considered: children are more likely to show side effects; dose-related attentional problems can develop and thus create interference in learning (Seiden & Dykstra, 1977); and seizures may be potentiated in children with a preexisting seizure disorder (Bassuk & Schoonover, 1977).

REFERENCES

Bassuk, E. L., & Schoonover, S. C. (1977). *The practitioner's guide to psychoactive drugs*. New York: Plenum Medical.

Leavitt, F. (1982). *Drugs and behavior*. New York: Wiley.

Seiden, L. S., & Dykstra, L. A. (1977). *Psychopharmocology: A biochemical and behavioral approach*. New York: Van Nostrand Reinhold.

ROBERT F. SAWICKI
Lake Erie Institute of Rehabilitation

STELAZINE

THORNDIKE, EDWARD L. (1847–1949)

E. L. Thorndike was an early theorist and writer who applied psychology to education. He was educated at Wesleyan, Harvard, and Columbia universities, with most of his professional career spent at Teachers' College, Columbia University. He is best known for his contributions to learning theory (Thorndike, 1905, 1931, 1932, 1935, 1949) and intellectual assessment (Thorndike, 1901, 1926, 1941).

Thorndike's major contribution to learning theory, termed the Law of Effect, is well known as a basic behavioral principle. The Law of Effect states; "any act which in a given situation produces satisfaction becomes associated with that situation, so that when the situation occurs, the act is more likely to recur also" (Thorndike, 1905, p. 203). His theory of connectionism was cognitively oriented, and viewed both physical and mental acts as involving the establishment of neural pathways. Learning was viewed as taking place when pathways were established through repetition.

Thorndike's measurement interests were diverse, as reflected by his famous dictum, "If anything exists, it exists in some amount. If it exists in some amount, it can be measured" (Thorndike, 1926, p. 38). His multifactored approach to measurement viewed intelligence as comprising abstract, mechanical, and social abilities. Intellectual assessment to Thorndike also involved the dimensions of attitude, breadth, and speed (i.e., level of difficulty, number of tasks, and rate of completion, respectively). This multifactored approach was in contrast to the approach of others of his time, who viewed intelligence as a general or unitary factor. Thorndike developed many tests, especially college entrance and achievement tests.

REFERENCES

Thorndike, E. L. (1901). *Notes on child study*. New York: Macmillan.

Thorndike, E. L. (1905). *The elements of psychology*. New York: Seiler.

Thorndike, E. L. (1926). *The measurement of intelligence*. New York: Teacher's College, Columbia University.

Thorndike, E. L. (1931). *Human learning.* New York: Century.

Thorndike, E. L. (1932). *Fundamentals of learning.* New York: Columbia University.

Thorndike, E. L. (1935). *The psychology of wants, interests and attitudes.* New York: Appleton-Century.

Thorndike, E. L. (1940). *Human nature and social order.* New York: Macmillan.

Thorndike, E. L. (1941). Mental abilities. *American Philosophical Society, 84,* 503–513.

Thorndike, E. L. (1949). *Selected writings from a connectionist's psychology.* New York: Appleton-Century-Crofts.

Thorndike, E. L., Bregman, E. O., Cobb, M. V., & Woodyard, E. (1925). *The measurement of intelligence.* New York: Columbia University.

Thorndike, E. L., & Lorge, I. (1944). *The teacher's wordbook of 30,000 words.* New York: Teacher's College, Columbia University.

JOSEPH D. PERRY
Kent State University

MEASUREMENT

THOUGHT DISORDERS

In the diagnosis of a psychiatric illness, it is common to evaluate disturbances in the following areas: consciousness, emotion, motor behavior, perception, memory, intelligence, and thinking (Ginsberg, 1985). Disorders in thinking, although most commonly associated with schizophrenia, may also occur in paranoid disorders, affective disorders, organic mental disorders, or organic delusional syndromes such as those owed to amphetamine or phencyclide abuse (*Diagnostic and Statistical Manual of Mental Disorders* [DSM IV], 1994). Schizophrenic patients, however, tend to show more severe and specific forms of thought disorders, and may continue to show some degree of idiosyncratic thinking when not in the acute phase of the disease (Ginsberg, 1985). According to DSM IV (1994), at some point, schizophrenia always involves delusions, hallucinations, or certain disturbances in the form of thought most often expressed by the patient in disorganized speech. A thought disorder is but one of the criteria needed for a diagnosis of schizophrenia; the illness is also characterized by disorganization in perceptions, communication, emotions, and motor activity. The term thought disorder encompasses a large array of dysfunctions, including disturbances in the form of thought, structure of associations, progression of thought, and content of thought.

Disturbances in Form of Thought. Thinking in a healthy individual occurs in a rational, orderly way. A thought might be stimulated by unconscious or conscious impulses, affective cues, or biological drives, yet the thinking process itself is directed by reason and results in a reality-oriented conclusion. As characterized by Ginsberg (1985), disturbances in the form of thought result in sequences that are no longer logical. In formal thought disorders, thinking is characterized by loosened associations, neologisms, and illogical constructs. In illogical thinking, thinking contains erroneous conclusions or internal contradictions. In dereism, there is mental activity not concordant with logic or experience. In autistic thinking, thinking gratifies unfilled desires but has no regard for reality (p. 500).

Disturbances in Structure and Progression of Associations. In DSM IV, these disturbances are included under the Form of Thought category. However, as described by both Ginsberg (1985) and Kolb (1968), a division of this category is warranted. In a healthy individual, each separate idea is logically linked with ideas both preceding and following that idea. This progression occurs in a coherent fashion and at a relatively steady, moderate rate of speech. In severe cases of disorder, however, speech becomes so disjointed as to be incomprehensible. It then includes

1. Flight of ideas—an extremely rapid progression of ideas with a shifting from one topic to another so that a coherent whole is not maintained and considerable digression occurs from the beginning to the ending of the story. There is generally some association between thoughts; e.g., a single word in one sentence will lead to a following sentence. Flight of ideas is associated with a lack of goal directed activity and with heightened distractibility and an accelerated inner drive. A patient might respond to the question, "What is your name?" with, "My name is David. David was in the *Bible* which is a religious document written many years ago. I feel that religion leads to persecution for many important citizens as a result of their beliefs which have been well thought out; however, thought is a very abstract concept as might be noted of music and art."

2. Clang associations—similar to flight of ideas. With clang associations, the stimulus that prompts a new thought is a word similar in sound, but not in meaning, to a new word.

3. Retardation—speech becomes slow and labored; often a lowered tone of voice is used. The patient may relate that his or her thoughts come slowly or that it is very difficult to concentrate or think about a topic.

4. Blocking—an unconscious interruption in the train of thought to such an extent that progression of thought comes to a complete halt. This is usually temporary, with thought processes resuming after a short time.

5. Pressure of speech—an excessive flow of words to such an extent that it becomes difficult to interrupt the speaker.

6. Perseveration—an occurrence in which the patient uses the same word, thought, or idea repeatedly, often in response to several different questions. One patient, when being diagnosed with the Rorschach Inkblot Test, responded to all 10 separate cards, "That looks like a man's genitals. Why are you showing me all these pictures of the same thing?"

7. Circumstantiality—the patient is eventually able to relate a given thought or story, but only after numerous digressions and unnecessary trivial details. This occurs largely in persons who are not able to distinguish essential from nonessential details. It is often observed in persons of low intelligence, in epileptics, and in cases of advanced senile mental disorder.

8. Neologism—when entirely new words are created by the patient.

9. Word salad—an incoherent mixture of words and phrases.

10. Incoherence—similar to word salad, the difference being that incoherence is generally marked by illogically connected phrases or ideas. Word salad generally consists of illogically connected single words or short phrases. A patient speaking incoherently may state, "Yes, this is the great reason for truth and validity as you must know and we all must know in times of need all great men who have an interest in greatness, perhaps, yes, cold is a very nice color, but, not inconsequentially as we have every reason to believe that our President is for better or worse, no, yesterday."

11. Irrelevant answer—an answer that has no direct relevance to the question asked.

12. Derailment—gradual or sudden deviation in one's train of thought without blocking.

Disturbances in Content of Thought. The most common disturbance in the content of thought involves a delusion, which is an idea or system of beliefs that is irrational, illogical, and with little or no basis in fact. In normal, healthy individuals, fantasy, daydreaming, rationalization, or projection can be used as effective ways to handle stress. Delusions appear to be an exaggerated form of this type of thinking. Delusions, however, are indicative of severe psychopathology in that they are patently absurd, and the patient cannot be argued out of his or her beliefs despite overwhelming evidence refuting the delusions. There are several different types of delusions, based on the specific thought content:

1. Delusions of grandeur—belief that an individual is special, important, or in some way superior to others. In many instances the patient may actually believe that he or she is someone else, e.g., God.

2. Delusions of reference—belief that innocent remarks or actions of someone else are directed exclusively at the patient. One hospitalized patient explained that whenever carrots were served at dinner, it meant that she was to take two baths that night; whenever ham was served, it meant that she was to avoid speaking to anyone until the following day.

3. Delusions of persecution—the belief that others are spying on, plotting against, or in some way planning to harm the patient.

4. Delusions of being controlled—the belief that one's thoughts and actions are imposed by someone else. Similar to this are thought broadcasting (the belief that one's ideas are broadcast to others); thought insertion (the belief that ideas are being inserted into one's head); and thought withdrawal (the belief that ideas are being removed from one's head).

Other less common delusions include self-accusation, sin, guilt, somatic illness, nihilism, religiosity, infidelity, and poverty (DSM IV, 1994; Ginsberg, 1985; Kolb, 1968; MacKinnon & Michels, 1971).

Several theories have been advanced to account for the existence of thought disorders. The more psychogenic of these theories point to inadequate ego functioning, such that the patient creates his or her own reality to cope with overwhelming stress and anxiety. Biological theories view thought disorders as being genetically transmitted. Research in this area has focused on chemical neurotransmitters such as dopamine; it found differing levels of such chemicals in disturbed and healthy individuals. The effectiveness of drug therapy in treating thought disorders lends credence to biological theories. Other theories such as learning, cognitive, and family approaches are more environmentally based, and hold that persons with thought disorders may learn maladaptive ways of thinking or acting in response to live circumstances or unhealthy family situations (Worchel & Shebilske, 1983).

REFERENCES

American Psychiatric Association. (1994). *Diagnostic and statistical manual of mental disorders* (4th ed.). Washington, DC: Author.

Ginsberg, G. (1985). The psychiatric interview. In H. Kaplan & B. Sadock (Eds.), *Comprehensive textbook of psychiatry/IV* (Vol. 1, pp. 500–501). Baltimore, MD: Williams & Wilkins.

Kolb, L. (1968). *Noye's modern clinical psychiatry* (7th ed.). Philadelphia: Saunders.

MacKinnon, R., & Michels, R. (1971). *The psychiatric interview.* Philadelphia: Saunders.

Worchel, S., & Shebilske, W. (1983). *Psychology: Principles and applications.* Englewood Cliffs, NJ: Prentice-Hall.

FRANCES F. WORCHEL
Texas A & M University

DIAGNOSTIC AND STATISTICAL MANUAL OF MENTAL DISORDERS (DSM IV)
EMOTIONAL DISORDERS

TICS

Tics are recurrent, rapid, abrupt movements and vocalizations that represent the contraction of small muscle groups in one or more parts of the body. Motor tics may include eye blinking, shoulder shrugging, neck twisting, head shaking, or arm jerking. Vocal tics frequently take the form of grunting, throat clearing, sniffing, snorting, or squealing. These abnormal movements and sounds occur from once very few seconds to several times a day, with varying degrees of intensity. Although tics are involuntary, they often can be controlled briefly. However, temporary suppression results in a feeling of tension that can be relieved only when the tics are allowed to appear. Tics increase with anxiety and stress and diminish with intense concentration (Shapiro & Shapiro, 1981). The prevalence for tic disorders is 1.6% or about 3.5 million individuals in the United States. Boys are affected more frequently than girls (Baron, Shapiro, Shapiro, & Ranier, 1981).

The *Diagnostic and Statistical Manual of Mental Disorders,* fourth edition, delineates three major tic disorders that are based on age of onset, types of symptoms, and duration of the condition: transient tic disorder, chronic motor tic disorder, and Tourette syndrome (American Psychiatric Association, 1994). Familial studies suggest that these classifications may not represent distinct disorders but, rather, reflect a continuum of severity of the same disorder (Golden, 1981). The transient tic disorder or "habit spasm" is the mildest and most common of the disorders. Symptoms develop during childhood or adolescence and usually are observed in the face, head, or shoulders. Vocal tics are uncommon. Tic frequency, as well as intensity, generally fluctuates during the course of the disorder. Such childhood tics are transient and benign, disappearing after several months to 1 year.

Symptoms of the chronic motor tic disorder, which appear either in childhood or after the age of 40, are similar to those associated with the transient tic disorder. Vocalizations develop infrequently. When they are present, they tend to be grunts or other noises caused by contractions of the abdomen or diaphragm. The severity, intensity, and type of involuntary movement persist unchanged for years.

Tourette syndrome, the most severe condition, is differentiated from the other tic disorders by the presence of both motor and vocal tics and a pattern of symptoms that waxes and wanes as the tics slowly move from one part of the body to another. Complex movements such as jumping and dancing are often exhibited. Not always present, but confirmatory of Tourette syndrome, are echolalia (repetition of words or phrases spoken by others), palilalia (repetition of one's own words), coprolalia (involuntary swearing), echopraxia (imitation of the movement of others), and copropraxia (obscene gesturing). Although the nature and severity of these symptoms vary over time, the disorder rarely remits spontaneously and usually remains throughout life (Shapiro, Shapiro, Bruun, & Sweet, 1978).

REFERENCES

American Psychiatric Association. (1994). *Diagnostic and statistical manual of mental disorders* (4th ed.). Washington, DC: Author.

Baron, M., Shapiro, A. K., Shapiro, E. S., & Rainer, T. D. (1981). Genetic analysis of Tourette syndrome suggesting major gene effect. *American Journal of Human Genetics, 33,* 767–775.

Golden, G. S. (1981). Gilles de la Tourette's syndrome. *Texas Medicine, 77,* 6–7.

Shapiro, A. K., & Shapiro, E. S. (1981). The treatment and etiology of tics and Tourette syndrome. *Comprehensive Psychiatry, 22,* 193–205.

Shapiro, A. K., Shapiro, E. S., Bruun, R. D., & Sweet, R. D. (1978). *Gilles de la Tourette's syndrome.* New York: Raven.

MARILYN P. DORNBUSH
Atlanta, Georgia

ECHOLALIA
ECHOPRAXIA
TOURETTE SYNDROME

TIME ON TASK

The amount of time that students spend on task has been an issue that concerns teachers in all fields, not just those involved with special education. Squires, Huitt, and Segars (1981) have identified three measures of student involvement that may be used to determine time on task. The first, allocated time, is simply the amount of time that is planned for instruction. Obviously, students will probably not be on task for the entire time that has been allocated. The second measure, which addresses this observation, is known as engagement rate. It is defined as the percent of allocated time that students actually attend to the tasks they are assigned. The third measure, engaged time, is the number of minutes per day students spend working on specific academic or related tasks; it is an integration of allocated time and engagement rate. Stallings and Kaskowitz (1974) found that, given certain maximum time limits based on a child's age and the subject matter at hand, engaged time is the most important variable that is related to student achievement. Given this finding, many researchers have focused on increasing time on task.

As an example, Bryant and Budd (1982) used self-instruction training with three young children who had difficulties in attending to task in kindergarten or preschool. The researchers trained the children to verbalize five separate types of self-instruction: (1) stop and look; (2) ask questions about the task; (3) find the answers to the questions posed in (2); (4) give instructions that provide guidance; and (5) give self-reinforcement for accomplished tasks. The results indicated an increase in on-task behavior for two of the children and, when used in combination with an unintrusive classroom intervention of reminders and stickers, all three of the children exhibited marked increases in their engaged time.

A somewhat different approach to the study of on-task behaviors was undertaken by Whalen et al. (1979), who examined the effects of medication (Ritalin) on the on- and off-task behaviors of children identified as hyperactive. They found clear differences in a maladaptive direction in the behaviors of their subjects who had been diagnosed as hyperactive under placebo conditions when compared with peers who had no diagnoses of hyperactivity. However, while the authors acknowledged that the medication did result in more on-task and prosocial behaviors in many of their subjects, they cautioned against a wholesale reliance on medications since many long-term effects had not yet been studied. Rather, the researchers felt that careful study of all variables in individual situations (e.g., teacher tolerance, cost effectiveness, environmental adaptations) must be undertaken when making treatment decisions.

REFERENCES

Bryant, L. E., & Budd, K. S. (1982). Self-instruction training to increase independent work performance in preschoolers. *Journal of Applied Behavior Analysis, 15,* 259–271.

Squires, D., Huitt, W., & Segars, J. (1981). Improving classrooms and schools: What's important. *Educational Leadership, 39,* 174–179.

Stallings, J. A., & Kaskowitz, D. (1974). *Follow through classroom observation evaluation, 1972–1973.* Menlo Park, CA: Stanford Research Institute.

Whalen, C. K., Henker, B., Collins, B., Finck, D., & Dotemoto, S. (1979). A social ecology of hyperactive boys: Medication effects in structured classroom environments. *Journal of Applied Behavior Analysis, 12,* 65–81.

ANDREW R. BRULLE
Eastern Illinois University

**ATTENTION DEFICIT DISORDER
ATTENTION SPAN
HYPERACTIVITY**

TIME-OUT

Time-out is an individual behavior management technique typically used to reduce or eliminate inappropriate attention-getting behaviors of children and sometimes adults (institutionalized disturbed). Time-out occurs when access to reinforcement is removed contingent on the emission of a response (Sulzer-Azaroff & Mayer, 1986).

The reductive effect is best demonstrated when time-out is implemented as follows:

Total removal of opportunities for reinforcement (e.g., removal from the reinforcing environment and placement in a nonstimulating environment).

Time-out durations of short to medium length (e.g., 3 to 10 minutes following the cessation of the inappropriate behavior).

Clear communication of conditions to the subject prior to use of time-out (e.g., the inappropriate behavior that will occasion time-out).

Consistent use of time-out after each occurrence of the inappropriate behavior until reduction has been maintained.

Reinforcement of desirable alternative behaviors to the inappropriate behavior to occur in conjunction with the use of time-out once the subject has returned to the natural environment.

In addition to its reductive effect on inappropriate behaviors, time-out allows for management of behaviors without the application of aversive stimuli. However, the incorrect use of time-out (e.g., extended durations of isolation) may prove ineffective as well as unethical (Hall & Hall, 1980). Sulzer-Azaroff and Mayer (1986) and Walker and Shea (1984) provide a more detailed description of time-out.

REFERENCES

Hall, R. V., & Hall, M. C. (1980). *How to use time-out.* Lawrence, KA: H & H Enterprises.

Sulzer-Azaroff, B., & Mayer, G. R. (1986). *Achieving educational excellence using behavioral strategies.* New York: Holt, Rinehart, & Winston.

Walker, J. E., & Shea, T. M. (1984). *Behavior management: A practical approach for educators* (3rd ed.). St. Louis: Mosby.

MARGARET LYONS
LOUIS J. LANUNZIATA
University of North Carolina at Wilmington

**AVERSIVE STIMULUS
BEHAVIOR MODIFICATION
PUNISHMENT**

TIME SAMPLING

Time sampling is an intermittent means of recording behavior by observing the subject at certain prespecified times and recording his or her behavior in a manner prescribed by the time sampling method in use. According to Arrington (1943), the major impetus to developing various time sampling procedures was provided by the National Research Council between 1920 and 1935. The council, which controlled many research fund allocations, had become concerned because the diary records typically used in research on the behavior of children were neither comparable nor exact. This group began to encourage research that used quantifiable and replicable methods of data collection. One of the first researchers to accept the challenge was F. L. Goodenough (1928), whose technique involved dividing an observation session into a series of short intervals and recording whether or not the target behavior occurred during each of those intervals. Other researchers in child development and psychology (e.g., Arrington, 1932; Bindra & Blond, 1958; Olson, 1929; Parten, 1932) adopted and refined these procedures.

In more recent times, a common terminology has developed that defines the various types of time sampling methods. In a landmark study, Powell et al. (1977) discussed three different types of time sampling procedures: (1) whole interval recording, (2) partial interval recording, and (3) momentary time sampling. In all of these procedures, the observation session is divided into a series of intervals. When the intervals are equal, the procedure is known as fixed interval (e.g., every 30 seconds). When the interval lengths are assigned at random but still average to the desired length (e.g., on the average, every 30 seconds), the procedure is known as variable interval.

In whole interval time sampling, the behavior is scored as having occurred only if it has endured for the entire interval; in partial interval time sampling the behavior is recorded as having occurred if it occurs at all (even for an instant) during the interval. In the technique known as momentary time sampling (MTS), the data collector records what behavior is occurring exactly at the end of each interval.

Repp et al. (1976) demonstrated conclusively that partial interval time sampling was not an accurate means of recording behaviors when frequency was the dimension of interest. Powell et al. (1977) conducted a study on the accuracy of all of these procedures and concluded that, when used to estimate the duration of a behavior, whole interval time sampling generally provided an underestimate while partial interval recording provided an overestimate. Momentary time sampling procedures both over- and underestimated the true duration of the behavior but, when averaged, provided the most accurate measure. The researchers felt that MTS interval lengths as long as 60 seconds could be used to collect accurate data. In an extension of this study, Brulle and Repp (1984) demonstrated that MTS procedures provide an accurate estimate of the duration of the behavior when averaged, but that each data entry, even when intervals are as short as 30 seconds, is subject to considerable error. They recommended that only very short intervals be used if averages are not acceptable.

The Student Observation Scale (SOS) of the Behavior Assessment System for Children is an example of a standardized time-sampling procedure that uses a fourth approach successfully. The SOS employs brief intervals, and at the end of each, the examiner/observer records all behaviors occurring at any time during the 3-second observation (Reynolds & Kamphaus, 1992). After recording, behavior is again observed, and the process is repeated for a 15 minute total time sample.

REFERENCES

Arrington, R. E. (1932). Interrelations in the behavior of young children. *Child Development Monographs,* No. 8.

Arrington, R. E. (1943). Time sampling in studies of social behavior: A critical review of techniques and results with research suggestions. *Psychological Bulletin, 40,* 81–124.

Bindra, D., & Blond, J. (1958). A time-sample method for measuring general activity and its components. *Canadian Journal of Psychology, 12,* 74–76.

Brulle, A. R., & Repp, A. C. (1984). An investigation of the accuracy of momentary time sampling procedures with time series data. *British Journal of Psychology, 75,* 481–488.

Goodenough, F. L. (1928). Measuring behavior traits by means of repeated short samples. *Journal of Juvenile Research, 12,* 230–235.

Olson, W. C. (1929). A study of classroom behavior. *Journal of Educational Psychology, 22,* 449–454.

Parten, M. B. (1932). Social participation among preschool children. *Journal of Abnormal Social Psychology, 57,* 243–269.

Powell, J., Martindale, B., Kulp, S., Martindale, A., & Bauman, R. (1977). Taking a closer look: Time sampling and measurement error. *Journal of Applied Behavior Analysis, 10,* 325–332.

Repp, A. C., Roberts, D. M., Slack, D. J., Repp, C. F., & Berkler, M. S. (1976). A comparison of frequency, interval, and time-sampling methods of data collection. *Journal of Applied Behavior Analysis, 9,* 501–508.

Reynolds, C. R., & Kamphaus, R. W. (1992). *Behavior assessment system for children.* Circle Pines, MN: American Guidance Service.

ANDREW R. BRULLE
Eastern Illinois University

BEHAVIORAL CHARTING
BEHAVIOR ASSESSMENT
BEHAVIOR ASSESSMENT SYSTEM FOR CHILDREN
BEHAVIOR MODIFICATION

TOFRANIL

Tofranil is the proprietary name for the drug Imipramine, which primarily is used in the treatment of major depression and nocturnal enuresis. It has been suggested that Tofranil may be useful in the treatment of school phobia (Hersov, 1985).

Though Tofranil has proved to be an effective treatment

for major depression in adults (AMA Drug Evaluations, 1983), its use with children is questionable. Shaffer (1985) reports that there have been few well-designed studies of the effectiveness of Tofranil and childhood depression. In one reported study in which Tofranil was compared double blind with a placebo, a 60% response rate was reported in both groups. In adults, Tofranil has a mild sedative effect that serves to lessen anxiety, though it is not intended to be used for this symptom. It has been suggested that it is this anxiety effect that may be helpful in a multidisciplinary approach toward school refusal (Hersov, 1985). In the 1990s, use of Tofranil has declined in favor of selective serotonin reuptake inhibitor, such as Prozac and Zoloft.

In children, Tofranil is most frequently used to ameliorate nocturnal enuresis. Numerous studies have demonstrated Tofranil's effectiveness in decreasing nighttime enuresis in most children (Shaffer, Costello, & Hill, 1968). The effect is seen rapidly, and almost always within the first week of treatment (Williams & Johnston, 1982). Unfortunately, research also has suggested that once the medication is withdrawn, many of these children begin wetting again. The effects of long-term treatment have not been studied (Shaffer, 1985). The relapse rate following cessation of the drug compares unfavorably with the withdrawal of the pad and bell procedure. The mode of action of Tofranil in decreasing nocturnal enuresis is not understood. An adverse side effect of Tofranil may be increased restlessness, agitation, and confusion.

REFERENCES

AMA Drug Evaluations (5th ed.). (1983). Philadelphia: Saunders.

Hersov, L. (1985). School refusal. In M. Rutter & L. Hersov (Eds.). *Child and adolescent psychiatry: Modern approaches* (2nd ed., pp. 382–399). St. Louis: Blackwell Scientific.

Shaffer, D. (1985). Enuresis. In M. Rutter & L. Hersov (Eds.), *Child and adolescent psychiatry: Modern approaches* (2nd ed., pp. 465–481). St. Louis: Blackwell Scientific.

Shaffer, D., Costello, A. J., & Hill, I. D. (1968). Control of Enuresis with Imipramine *Archives of diseases in childhood, 43,* 665–671.

Williams, D. I., & Johnston, J. H. (1982). *Pediatric urology* (2nd ed.). London: Butterworth Scientific.

Greta N. Wilkening
Children's Hospital

DEPRESSION
ENURESIS

TOKEN ECONOMICS

A token economy is basically a miniature monetary system in which clients work for generalized, secondary reinforcers that are exchangeable for a variety of backup reinforcers. The token economy was first described in detail in the late 1960s (Ayllon & Azrin, 1965, 1968); it has since become one of the most popular means of providing reinforcers in special education settings. Successful token economies have been documented with such diverse populations as psychiatric patients (Ayllon & Azrin, 1965), sheltered workshop clients (Welch & Gist, 1974), and students in special education classes (Heward & Eachus, 1979).

When developing a token economy, the service provider needs to consider a number of different points. First, the token itself must be established. Just about anything can be used, however, some of the most popular items are plastic chips, check marks, and points. What is important in deciding what to use for tokens is that the tokens be easily administered and not easily counterfeited. A second consideration is the choice of backup reinforcers and their token prices. These reinforcers must be desirable for the clients and reasonably priced. A wide choice and constant variation of backup reinforcers will make the system appealing. A third consideration is access to the purchase of backup reinforcers. Regular times that provide access to the reinforcers on at least a weekly schedule are desirable. A fourth consideration is the record-keeping system devised by the service provider. Both clients and teachers should be aware of storage options or means of recording tokens earned. Finally, as with any behavioral procedure, the service provider must ensure that tokens are administered consistently. The clients and teachers must be clearly aware of what behaviors can earn tokens and what behaviors can result in fines, and these rules must be strictly enforced.

Kazdin (1982) and Kazdin and Bootzin (1972) have provided reviews of token economy systems. Most recently, Kazdin (1982) has commented on the progress within the profession on four critical issues (enhancing effects of token economies, staff training, client resistance to the program, and long-term effects) and has identified three emergent areas of concern (integrity of treatment, administrative and organizational issues, and dissemination of the token economy). In the first area of progress, enhancing effects, Kazdin (1982) notes that varying the strength of the reinforcers, emphasizing the economic aspects of the token system, and involving peers have all been helpful in improving the efficiency of token systems. Second, Kazdin (1982) points out that a number of studies have focused on effective means of training staff to administer token programs. Generally, training that includes several facets (e.g., modeling and informative feedback) has been most effective. When clients resist the program, Kazdin (1982) feels that providing opportunities that are not usually available (e.g., negotiating reinforcers) might help to reduce negative behaviors. As the final point of progress, Kazdin (1982) stresses that many descriptions of token programs are now providing follow-up data on their clients and that these data are necessary parts of the reporting process.

The emerging issues discussed by Kazdin (1982) are generally administrative in nature and focus on (a) whether or not the program was conducted as intended, (b) how various organizational variables (e.g., authority to make decisions) affect the token program, and (c) how well program methodologies and results are shared with others. Kazdin (1982) feels that currently, methodology for token economies has been well established, and that "the next step for research is to explore and evaluate procedures to integrate token economies routinely into settings where programs are likely to be of use" (p. 441–442).

For further information on the development of a token system, please consult Alberto and Troutman (1982) and for an in-depth review of the issues, Kazdin (1982) is an excellent source.

REFERENCES

Alberto, P. A., & Troutman, A. C. (1982). *Applied behavior analysis for teachers.* Columbus, OH: Merrill.

Ayllon, T., & Azrin, N. H. (1965). The measurement and reinforcement of behavior of psychotics. *Journal of the Experimental Analysis of Behavior, 8,* 356–383.

Ayllon, T., & Azrin, N. H. (1968). *The token economy: A motivational system for therapy and rehabilitation.* New York: Appleton-Century-Crofts.

Heward, W. L., & Eachus, H. T. (1979). Acquisition of adjectives and adverbs in sentences written by hearing impaired and aphasic children. *Journal of Applied Behavior Analysis, 12,* 391–400.

Kazdin, A. E. (1982). The token economy: A decade later. *Journal of Applied Behavior Analysis, 15,* 431–445.

Kazdin, A. E., & Bootzin, R. R. (1972). The token economy: An evaluative review. *Journal of Applied Behavior Analysis, 5,* 343–372.

Welch, M. W., & Gist, J. W. (1974). *The open token economy system: A handbook for a behavioral approach to rehabilitation.* Springfield, IL: Thomas.

ANDREW R. BRULLE
Eastern Illinois University

APPLIED BEHAVIOR ANALYSIS
BEHAVIORAL CHARTING
BEHAVIOR MODIFICATION

TONI

See TEST OF NON-VERBAL INTELLIGENCE.

TONIC NECK REFLEX, ASYMMETRICAL

See ASYMMETRICAL TONIC NECK REFLEX.

TOPICS IN EARLY CHILDHOOD SPECIAL EDUCATION

Topics in Early Childhood Special Education (TECSE) is a refereed, quarterly journal publishing articles on timely issues in early childhood special education. Three issues per year are topical; one is nontopical. The topical issues address an identified problem, trend, or subject of concern and importance to early intervention. Persons interested in services provided to infants, toddlers, and preschoolers who display developmental delays and disabilities and the families of such youngsters will find *TECSE* informative. *TECSE* has been published continuously since 1981. Pro-Ed, Inc. purchased the journal from Aspen Press in 1983.

JUDITH K. VORESS
Pro-Ed, Inc.

TOPICS IN LANGUAGE DISORDERS

Topics in Language Disorders, an interdisciplinary journal that is published quarterly, addresses topics within the general fields of language acquisition, language development, and language disorders. Contributors include speech and language pathologists, psycholinguists, pediatricians, neurologists, and special educators, especially remedial reading and learning disabilities teachers. This journal originated in 1980 to meet the need for published interactions across professional boundaries on specific topics.

As the title implies, each journal presents a variety of issues surrounding one topic. A guest editor is responsible for soliciting manuscripts; in doing so, he or she seeks equality among disciplines as well as several views. Both clinical and educational application are sought with balance between theory and practice.

Members of the American Speech and Hearing Association may earn continuing education credits by reading each volume and responding to the questions at the end of the volume. Responses are then submitted to the address included in the journal.

ANNE CAMPBELL
Purdue University

TORCH COMPLEX

TORCH complex is a phrase used by some authors (e.g., Nahmias & Tomeh, 1977; Thompson & O'Quinn, 1979) to group a set of maternal infections whose clinical manifestations in children are so similar that differentiation among them on the basis of those symptoms alone may not be possible. TORCH stands for *TO*xoplasmosis, *R*ubella, *C*ytomegalovirus, and *H*erpes. Generally speaking, with the exception of herpes, the infections have only mild and transitory effects on the mother, but through pre- or perinatal transmission, they may produce severe and irreversible damage to offspring. The major manifestations are visual and auditory defects and brain damage, which may result in mental retardation. The infections generally destroy already formed tissue rather than interfering with development; infants are frequently born asymptomatic, but gradually develop symptoms in the early years of life.

Although the major symptoms of the members of the TORCH complex are similar, the detailed symptoms, mechanisms of action, and times of major action differ.

REFERENCES

Nahmias, A. J., & Tomeh, M. O. (1977). Herpes simplex virus infections. In A. M. Rudolph (Ed.), *Pediatrics* (16th ed.). Englewood Cliffs, NJ: Prentice-Hall.

Thompson, R. J., & O'Quinn, A. N. (1979). *Developmental disabilities*. New York: Oxford University Press.

ROBERT T. BROWN
University of North Carolina at Wilmington

CYTOMEGALOVIRUS
HERPES SIMPLEX I AND II
RUBELLA
TOXOPLASMOSIS

TORRANCE, ELLIS PAUL (1914–   )

Ellis Paul Torrance earned his AA at Georgia Military College (1936), his BA at Mercer University (1940), his MA at the University of Minnesota (1944), and his PHD at the University of Michigan. Since 1966, he has served as professor of educational psychology and as department chairman at the University of Georgia. Although formally retired in 1984, Torrance continues to be active through the Georgia Studies of Creative Behavior.

Torrance is widely recognized for his voluminous contributions to the field of creative, gifted, and future education. At the heart of his philosophy is the impetus to change the goals, needs, and concepts in education. Future educational institutions will need to cultivate not only learning, but thinking. As a means of teaching versatility in thinking, Torrance reconceptualized and refined sociodrama as a group creative problem-solving technique. In addition, his efforts to identify gifted people from different cultures and all ages produced the Torrance Tests of Creative Thinking (TTCT). He has also produced Thinking Creatively in Action and Movement (TCAM), Sounds and

Ellis Paul Torrence

Images, What Kind of Person are You?, the Creative Motivation Scale, and Style of Learning and Thinking (SOLAT).

Torrance has contributed to over 2000 publications and over 40 books, including *Guiding Creative Talent, Education and the Creative Potential, Creative Learning and Teaching, Gifted and Talented Children in the Regular Classroom,* and *Making the Creative Leap Beyond.* He has directed 118 doctoral dissertations and 39 masters' theses.

Torrance and his late wife Pansy are the founders of the Future Problem Solving Program (1974), which teaches problem-solving skills to thousands of children in America and abroad. His many honors and awards include being appointed Alumni Foundation Distinguished Professor in 1973, being awarded a grant by the Japan Society for the Promotion of Science to study creativity and creative instruction within Japanese educational institutions, and receiving the Life Creative Achievement Award from the American Creativity Association in 1994.

REFERENCES

Torrance, E. P. (1962). *Guiding creative talent*. Englewood Cliffs, NJ: Prentice Hall.

Torrance, E. P. (1963). *Education and the creative potential*. Minneapolis: University of Minnesota.

Torrance, E. P., & Safter, H. T. (1998). *Making the creative leap beyond*. Buffalo, NY: Creative Education Foundation.

Torrance, E. P., & Sisk, D. A. (1965). *Gifted and talented children in the regular classroom*. Buffalo, NY: Creative Education Foundation.

STAFF

CREATIVITY TESTS
TORRANCE CENTER FOR CREATIVE STUDIES

TORRANCE CENTER FOR CREATIVE STUDIES

The Torrance Center for Creative Studies is a research center dedicated to investigations of the development of creative potential. Its research and development program honors and builds on the legacy of Ellis Paul Torrance, a native Georgian and a University of Georgia Alumni Foundation distinguished professor emeritus. This legacy is best reflected in the following statement:

> In almost every field of human achievement, creativity is usually the distinguishing characteristic of the truly eminent. The possession of high intelligence, special talent, and high technical skills is not enough to produce outstanding achievement. . . . It is tremendously important to society that our creative talent be identified, developed, and utilized. The future of our civilization—our very survival—depends upon the quality of the creative imagination of our next generation. (Torrance, 1959, p. 1)

Torrance, a pioneer in research on the identification and development of creative potential, is best known for his work in the development and refinement of the Torrance Tests of Creative Thinking (TTCT), the most widely used tests of creativity in the world.

The goals of the research and instructional program of the Torrance Center are to investigate and evaluate techniques and procedures for assessing creative potential and growth; to develop, apply, and evaluate strategies that enhance creative thinking; and to facilitate national and international systems that support creative development.

Four components—assessment, development, education, and evaluation—provide the organizational structure for the research and instructional programs of the center. Each component has been designed to contribute research that verifies and expands our understanding of creativity as a major ingredient in the development of human ability and that carries out the further development of instructional and evaluation technology to enhance the development of that ability.

Research on instruments and procedures to assess creative potential and to evaluate creative growth form the basis of the assessment component. Research on tests developed by Torrance, including validity studies, refinement of administration and scoring procedures, and interpretation of test results, and on the effects of strategies to develop creative ability, are coordinated through the center in conjunction with Scholastic Testing Service, the publishers of the Torrance tests and the Georgia Studies of Creative Behavior.

Two programs to investigate and evaluate techniques that facilitate or inhibit creative thinking and to determine the nature of systems and activities that support and encourage creative growth form the basis of the development component. The Future Problem Solving Program (FPS), founded in 1974 by E. Paul and J. Pansy Torrance, involves a deliberately interdisciplinary approach to studying and solving problems. It was motivated by a belief that we have reached a point in civilization at which education must devote a considerable part of the curriculum to helping students enlarge, enrich, and make more accurate their images of the future (Torrance, 1980). The FPS program is now international. Its headquarters are at St. Andrews College, Laurinburg, North Carolina. Anne Crabbe is the director. The Georgia FPS program is coordinated through the Torrance Center.

A major program initiative of the Torrance Center is the Torrance Creative Scholars Program. This program provides educational services to those individuals who score in the top 1½% of the national population on the TTCT, verbal and/or figural. The program is consistent with Torrance's assertions (1984) that

> a common characteristic of people who have made outstanding social, scientific, and artistic contributions has been their creativity. Since we are living in an age of increasing rates of change, depleted natural resources, interdependence, and destandardization, there are stronger reasons than ever for creatively gifted children and adults to have a fair chance to grow. We must find these "world treasures" and give them support so that they can give society those things it so desperately needs.

A unique aspect of the Torrance Creative Scholars Program is its use of a mentoring component. This component provides a year-round mentoring network for the creative scholars. Individuals selected by Torrance are designated Torrance creative scholar-mentors; they provide mentoring services to the scholars in a variety of ways. These mentors are also eligible to become Torrance creative scholars and to receive the services of the program.

Scoring and validation of scores on the TTCT for the Torrance Creative Scholars Program are coordinated through Scholastic Testing Service. Programs and services are developed and implemented through the Torrance Center.

The third component, education, provides training for educators interested in creativity. This component operates in conjunction with the degree programs (master's, sixth year, and doctoral) offered through the department of educational psychology at the University of Georgia. Training programs offered through the center include the Torrance Center Summer Creativity Institute, the Challenge Program for preschool through fifth graders, and the Visiting Scholars Program for national and international scholars. In addition, there is the annual E. Paul Torrance Lecture and the library and archives donated to the university by Torrance. A future goal of the Torrance Center is to endow an E. Paul Torrance Research Professor Chair. The final component, evaluation, focuses on quantitative and qualitative evaluations of assessment techniques, educational strategies, and support systems for the various programs of the center.

The Torrance Center for Creative Studies was formally established at the University of Georgia in the spring of 1984 by Mary M. Frasier. It is located in the department of educational psychology, College of Education, 422 Aderhold Hall, University of Georgia, Athens, GA 30602.

REFERENCES

Torrance, E. P. (1959). *Understanding creativity in talented students.* Paper prepared at the Summer Guidance Institute Lecture Series on Understanding the Talented Student, University of Minnesota.

Torrance, E. P. (1980). Creativity and futurism in education: *Retooling Education, 100,* 298–311.

Torrance, E. P. (1984). *The search for a nation's treasure* (Keynote address). St. Louis: National Association for Gifted Children.

MARY F. FRASIER
University of Georgia

CREATIVITY
CREATIVITY TEST
TORRANCE, ELLIS PAUL

TORRANCE TESTS OF CREATIVE THINKING

The Torrance Tests of Creative Thinking (figural form) can be used from kindergarten to graduate school (Torrance, 1974). Thinking Creatively with Words is useful from fourth grade to graduate school. Thinking Creatively in Action and Movement is designed for 3- to 8-year-olds. The test's author defines creativity as a process of becoming sensitive to problems, deficiencies, gaps in knowledge, or missing elements.

The Torrance Tests of Creative Thinking (figural forms A and B) use tasks that require drawing. They report scores in terms of fluency—the ability to think of many ideas for a given topic; originality—the ability to think of new and unusual ideas; abstractness of titles—the ability to sense the essence of a problem and know what is essential; elaboration—the ability to add details to a basic idea; and resistance to premature closure—the ability to "keep open" in processing information and to consider a wide variety of information. The Torrance Test of Creative Thinking (verbal forms A and B) require written responses and report scores in terms of fluency, originality, and flexibility (the ability to shift thinking and produce ideas in different categories). Thinking Creatively in Action and Movement uses action, movement, and verbal responses to test creative thinking ability. It measures this in terms of fluency, originality, and imagination.

Test results indicate an individual's creative thinking as compared with other adults or children in the same grade. In addition, the test results may be used to give additional insight into a student's style of thinking, learning, and creating. Several studies indicated that the Torrance Tests of Creative Thinking (figural and verbal) and Thinking Creatively in Action and Movement show no sexual, racial, or socioeconomic bias (Torrance, 1962, 1971, 1973, 1974). The Torrance Tests of Creative Thinking are not used prevalently today.

REFERENCES

Torrance, E. P. (1962). Guiding creative talent. Engelwood Cliffs, NJ: Prentice Hall.

Torrance, E. P. (1971). Are the Torrance tests of creative thinking biases against or in favor of disadvantaged groups? *Gifted Child Quarterly, 15,* 75–80.

Torrance, E. P. (1972). Predictive validity of the Torrance tests of creative thinking. *Journal of Creative Behaviors, 6,* 236–252.

Torrance, E. P. (1973). Assessment of disadvantaged minority group children. *School Psychology Digest, 4,* 3–10.

Torrance, E. P. (1974). *Norms-technical manual: The Torrance Test of Creative Thinking.* Lexington, MA: Personnel Press/Ginn.

JUNE SCOBEE
University of Huston
First edition

ELIZABETH O. LICHTENBERGER
The Salk Institute
Second edition

GIFTED AND TALENTED CHILDREN
INSIGHT
TORRANCE, E. PAUL

TORSIONAL DYSTONIA

The term "dystonia" was first used by H. Oppenheim in 1911 to denote the coexistence of muscular hypotonia and hypertonia. Since that time, the term has been used to describe a symptom of abnormal muscle contraction, a syndrome of abnormal involuntary movements, and a disease that has either a genetic or ideopathic origin. Torsional dystonia is commonly referred to as a progressive disorder characterized by slow, twisting movements that ultimately may result in bizarre, twisting postures of the extremities or trunk. Some causes of torsional dystonia are identifiable while other causes remain unknown, making classification of the condition difficult.

The disorder has a gradual onset, beginning between the ages of 5 and 15, and commonly involves the foot or leg. Torsional dystonia may spread to several parts or all of the body, but the condition is not present during sleep. Contractures or permanent muscle shortening and joint deformity ultimately occur. Hereditary forms of torsional dystonia are more common than ideopathic forms; one hereditary form is found most often in Ashkenazic Jews. The diagnosis of dystonia is based on clinical signs because diagnostic laboratory or biopsy findings are not known. The symptoms suggest dysfunction in the extrapyramidal system, since temporary drug-induced symptoms have occurred from medications that have a known effect on the basal ganglia of the extrapyramidal system.

Treatment of torsional dystonia generally has been disappointing. Medications such as diazepam (Valium), carbamazepine (Tegretol), haloperidol, and, in some cases, levodapa or anticholinergic drugs have been helpful in reducing the severity of the symptoms; but none of these medications has been consistently effective. Various neurosurgical or biofeedback procedures have resulted in isolated improvement but consistent benefits have not been achieved through these approaches.

REFERENCES

Berkow, R. (Ed.). (1982). *The Merck Manual* (14th ed., p. 1363). Rahway, NJ: Merck, Sharp, & Dohme.

Fahn, S. (1985). The extrapyramidal disorders. In J. Wyngaarden & L. Smith, Jr. (Eds.), *Cecil textbook of medicine* (17th ed., pp. 2077–2078). Philadelphia: Saunders.

Fahn, S., & Roswell, E. (1976). Definition of dystonia and classification of the dystonic states. In R. Eldridge & S. Fahn (Eds.), *Advances in neurology* (Vol. 14, pp. 1–5). New York: Raven.

Magalini, S., & Scarascia, E. (1981). *Dictionary of medical syndromes* (2nd ed.). Philadelphia: Lippincott.

Marsden, C. D. (1976). Dystonia: The spectrum of the disease. In M. D. Yahr (Ed.), *Basil ganglia* (pp. 351–365). New York: Raven.

Marsden, C. D., Harrison, M. J. G., & Bundey, S. (1976). Natural history of idiopathic torsion dystonia. In R. Eldrige & S. Fahn (Eds.), *Advances in neurology* (Vol. 14, pp. 177–187). New York: Raven.

Zeman, W. (1976). Dystonia: An overview. In R. Eldrige & S. Fahn (Eds.), *Advances in neurology* (Vol. 14, pp. 91–101). New York: Raven.

DANIEL D. LIPKA
Lincoln Way Special Education
Regional Resource Center

PHYSICAL ANOMALIES
PHYSICAL HANDICAPS

TOTAL COMMUNICATION

The expression total communication can be used in the general sense of communication through all possible chan-nels, not only vocal (including verbal) communication, but also communication provided by such other means as mimicry, gestures, etc. Recently, total communication has been used mainly in a more restricted field, namely the education of deaf children. It presents itself not as a method, but as "a philosophy incorporating the appropriate aural, manual, and oral methods of communication in order to ensure effective communication with and among hearing impaired persons" (Garretson, 1976, p. 300). It advocates the use of various modes of communication, such as speech (which should not be neglected, as the deaf live among a majority of hearing people), written language (reading and writing), sign language, finger spelling, pantomime, etc.

In recent years, methods of teaching deaf children applying this philosophy have been used in a steadily increasing number of schools in the United States and in Europe. These schools gave up the oral method that had prevailed since the end of the nineteenth century, mainly in Europe, where the resolutions of the International Congress held in Milan in 1880 were accepted and recommended almost unanimously (Lane, 1980).

According to the defenders of total communication, the oral approach, including lip reading, gives unsatisfactory results as far as linguistic and cognitive development are concerned (Conrad, 1979). It is argued that even if the hearing loss is discovered early, poor parent-infant communication delays the acquisition of language considerably and irretrievably, except with children whose residual hearing is sufficient to make communication possible. Ensuing education in specialized institutions is slower and less differentiated than with hearing children and, instead of reducing the gap, increases the retardation of the deaf children.

Total communication advocates the use of signing as the most appropriate mode of early communication between parents and hearing-impaired children. The double exposure to sign and speech (about 9 out of 10 deaf children have hearing parents) should allow partially hearing children equipped with appropriate audiological aids to be educated together with their hearing peers; children whose residual hearing is insufficient should be educated through a wide network of activities, of which "spoken language, finger spelling, signing, and written language constitute the linguistic core. Being capable of consistent transmission and internal symbolization of linguistic signals, these are the media of special relevance to linguistic and cognitive growth" (Evans, 1982, p. 91).

Evans (1982) shows three problematic issues for total communication: (1) the way the linguistic competence in sign language, with its own lexical, morphological, and syntactic characteristics, is to be transferred to linguistic competence in the spoken language of the community in which the deaf person is living; (2) the necessity for a specific training or recycling of teachers in total communication; and (3) the role of the (hearing) parents, who being confronted suddenly with the deafness of their baby, are obliged to learn the sign language in which they are going to communicate with the child in a very short time.

The philosophy of total communication remains unaltered in a variant in which the exposure to speech and sign is replaced by cued speech. The deaf child is taught to perceive the spoken language through a combination of residual hearing, lip reading, and a limited number of disambiguating signs near the speaker's face (Cornett, 1967).

Opponents of total communication think that signing may prove harmful and impede the acquisition of a spoken language and that too much time spent on teaching signs (finger spelling, etc.) could be used more appropriately to teach the spoken language. They stress the fact that some deaf children, albeit a minority, educated through the oral method succeed in obtaining a satisfactory level in spoken language perception and production.

REFERENCES

Conrad, R. (1979). *The deaf schoolchild: Language and cognitive functioning.* London: Harper & Row.

Cornett, O. (1967). Cued speech. *American Annals of the Deaf, 112,* 3–13.

Evans, L. (1982). *Total communication: Structure and strategy.* Washington, DC: Gallaudet College Press.

Garretson, M. D. (1976). Total communication. In R. Frisina (Ed.), A bicentennial monograph on hearing impairment: Trends in the U.S.A. *Volta Review, 78.*

Lane, H. (1980). A chronology of the oppression of sign language in France and the United States. In H. Lane & F. Grosjean (Eds.), *Recent perspectives on american sign language.* Hillsdale, NJ: Erlbaum.

S. DE VRIENDT
Vrije Universiteit Brussel

AMERICAN SIGN LANGUAGE
DEAF EDUCATION

TOURETTE SYNDROME

Tourette syndrome is a tic disorder characterized by the appearance between the ages of 2 and 15 of involuntary muscular movements. A single, simple tic is generally the initial symptom and takes the form of an eye blink, head shake, or nose twitch. However, the symptoms gradually change over time, becoming more complex and involving other body parts. Complicated movements of the entire body are often observed, including kicking, jumping, and turning in circles. Vocalizations such as throat clearing, coughing, grunting, or barking are present. Later these noises may change into words and phrases. Echolalia (repetition of phrases made by others), palilalia (repetition of one's own words), coprolalia (utterance of obscene words), echopraxia (imitation of the movement of others), and copropraxia (obscene gesturing) frequently accompany the disorder.

While the frequency and severity of the symptoms fluctuate over time, the disorder is chronic and rarely remits spontaneously (Shapiro, Shapiro, Bruun, & Sweet, 1978). Associated features often include obsessive-compulsive behaviors, an attention deficit disorder with hyperactivity, school-related problems, and an increased incidence of learning disabilities (Jagger et al., 1982). The etiology of Tourette syndrome remains unknown. However, the discovery of the efficacy of haloperidol in the treatment of the disorder has led researchers to postulate that Tourette syndrome may result from a biochemical imbalance in the nervous system (Snyder, Taylor, Coyle, & Meyerhoff, 1970). This hypothesis is further substantiated by the tendency of families of individuals with the disorder to have a positive history of Tourette syndrome or simple motor and vocal tics (Shapiro & Shapiro, 1982).

REFERENCES

Jagger, J., Prusoff, B. A., Cohen, D. J., Kidd, K. K., Carbonari, C. M., & John, K. (1982). The epidemiology of Tourette syndrome: A pilot study. *Schizophrenia Bulletin, 8,* 267–278.

Shapiro, A. K., & Shapiro, E. S. (1982). Tourette syndrome: Clinical aspects, treatment, and etiology. *Seminars in Neurology, 2,* 373–385.

Shapiro, A. K., Shapiro, E. S., Bruun, R. D., & Sweet, R. D. (1978). *Gilles de la Tourette's syndrome.* New York: Raven.

Snyder, S. H., Taylor, K. H., Coyle, J. T., & Meyerhoff, J. L. (1970). The role of brain dopamine in behavioral regulation and the action of psychotropic drugs. *American Journal of Psychiatry, 127,* 199–207.

MARILYN P. DORNBUSH
Atlanta, Georgia

ECHOLALIA
ECHOPRAXIA
TICS
TOURETTE SYNDROME ASSOCIATION

TOURETTE SYNDROME ASSOCIATION

The Tourette Syndrome Association, a voluntary nonprofit organization, was founded for the purpose of assisting individuals with Tourette syndrome, their families, friends, and concerned professionals. The primary objectives of the association include disseminating information regarding symptomatology and treatment of Tourette syndrome and raising funds to encourage and support scientific research into the nature and causes of the disorder.

In an effort to promote understanding of Tourette syndrome, the organization publishes quarterly newsletters, pamphlets, medical reprints, and films, and publicizes the disorder in newspapers, magazines, radio, and television. It provides support groups at a regional level for sharing current information about research, treatment, and management of Tourette syndrome. Information may be obtained from the Tourette Syndrome Association, Bell Plaza Building, 42-40 Bell Boulevard, Bayside, NY, 11361.

MARILYN P. DORNBUSH
Atlanta, Georgia

TICS
TOURETTE SYNDROME

TOXOPLASMOSIS

Toxoplasmosis is caused by an intracellular protozoan, Toxoplasma gondii, which is transmitted via the blood to the prenatal fetus. This congenital infection causes mild to severe mental and motor retardation. The largest number of newborns will be asymptomatic in the neonatal period so they must be observed for ocular and central nervous system disability. The newborn with symptomatic toxoplasmosis will present at birth with one or more of the following: head abnormalities (large or small), cerebral calcifications, brain damage, muscle spasticity, convulsions and seizures, visual and hearing impairments, and eye infections. An enlarged liver and spleen, which cause an extended abdomen, are often present. Rashes and jaundiced skin may be seen in infants. Motor impairment as a result of brain damage may be seen. Prognosis is poor; death occurs in 10 to 15% but a high percentage of children have neuromotor defects, seizure disorders, mental retardation, and damaged vision (Behrman, 1977; Carter, 1978).

Many children with toxoplasmosis may need to be placed in a fairly restrictive setting because of mental retardation and visual, hearing, and motor impairments. Children often need self-help skills training (including feeding and toileting) from an early age. Related services may be required for speech, vision, and hearing deficits. Physical and occupational therapy may also be needed. Since a variety of health problems may be present, a medical consultation will probably be needed. Team placement and management will be necessary for adequate educational programming.

REFERENCES

Behrman, R. (Ed.). (1977). *Neo-natal-perinatal diseases of the fetus and infant* (2nd ed.). St. Louis: Mosby.

Carter, C. (Ed.). (1978). *Medical aspects of mental retardation.* (2nd ed.). Springfield, IL: Thomas.

Hunt, M., & Gibby, R. (1979). *The mentally retarded child: Development, training and education* (4th ed.). Boston: Allyn & Bacon.

SALLY L. FLAGLER
University of Oklahoma

FUNCTIONAL SKILLS
MENTAL RETARDATION

TOY LENDING LIBRARIES

Toy libraries, occasionally named a Toybrary, are lending libraries with a broad range of toys, learning materials, and equipment appropriate for young children. Many traditional public libraries offer a toy section that includes puzzles, games, stuffed animals, blocks, etc., that can be checked out and taken home by children and adults. However, the real growth in toy lending libraries is as a part of the increasing need for child care outside the traditional home setting. Toy lending libraries and resource centers are becoming more common across the country as child-care needs and services grow and as people become more interested and involved in meeting the needs of children and those who care for them. Such libraries allow the various child-care programs in a specific geographic area to pool their resources and share equipment, as well as to exchange ideas and information. These libraries are particularly useful to people in isolated areas or those who work alone. When these libraries limit their use to certified day-care providers, they may also serve as a motivating force that results in a greater pool of licensed and certified day-care providers.

Types of equipment typically found in such libraries include recreational equipment, sand and water play sets, transportation equipment, farm and animal sets, blocks and other manipulatives, housekeeping materials, make believe materials, infant toys, puzzles, perception, alphabet, and math materials, and large and small motor toys. Funding for toy lending libraries comes from a number of sources. The most common would be government (national, state, or local) grants, foundation awards, local United Ways, and dues from members. Special groups such as state (Councils for Exceptional Children) have also been known to provide start-up funds for such libraries.

DENISE M. SEDLAK
*United Way of Dunn County,
Menomonie, Wisconsin*

DAY-CARE CENTERS
PLAY

TRACE MINERALS

Trace minerals are minerals found in very small quantities in the human body but having significant relationships to certain metabolic events necessary for normal function. Severe deficiencies of trace minerals can result in a variety of handicaps, including orthopedic and learning disabilities. Some minerals and their relative levels in the body affect memory and attention as well. An overabundance or improper metabolism of some minerals also may produce problems. Depending on the particular mineral and the chronicity of the deficiency (or oversupply), mineral-related handicaps may or may not be reversible, though all are treatable to a large extent.

STAFF

ETIOLOGY
NUTRITIONAL DISORDERS

TRAINABLE MENTALLY RETARDED

Trainable mentally retarded (TMR) was a diagnostic category in the 1960s and 1970s, referring to those people whose IQ scores ranged between 25 and 50 (based on the IQ tests of those days; Smith, 1998), and who were believed unable to benefit from the standard educational curriculum. This group represents roughly 10% of the mentally retarded population.

The term "trainable" is outdated and misleading, since it implies that the person is unable to profit from educational efforts. Most people with this level of mental retardation learn communication skills during early childhood, can benefit from vocational and occupational skills training, and usually adjust well to community life, generally in supervised settings.

The most appropriate diagnostic category currently is "moderate mental retardation," which requires an IQ score within the 35–55 range, as well as impairments in adaptive behavior that adversely affect the person's ability to perform ordinary, everyday activities of living (American Psychiatric Association, 1994).

REFERENCES

Smith, D. D. (1998). *Introduction to special education: Teaching in an age of challenge.* Boston, MA: Allyn and Bacon.

American Psychiatric Association. (1994). *Diagnostic and statistical manual of mental disorders* (4th ed.). Washington, DC: Author.

KAY E. KETZENBERGER
The University of Texas of the
Permian Basin

ARC, THE
MENTAL RETARDATION

TRAINING FOR EMPLOYMENT IN TRADITIONAL SETTINGS

Mildly and moderately handicapped students can be educated or trained to succeed as adult workers in many vocations. The vocational program that prepares handicapped students will be similar to regular vocational education; however, unique components should be evidenced.

All vocational preparation programs should begin with an assessment phase. Students' job interests, abilities, and readiness will be evaluated. For many special education students, this assessment procedure will be their first directed opportunity to examine their own capabilities and limitations as they relate to employment (Weisgerber, 1978).

The assessment phase should be comprehensive in order to provide information that will help the instructors and students to set appropriate vocational goals. Also, adequate assessment data will ensure that the subsequent training program will be effective. Specific job skills capabilities should be identified, as well as appropriate interpersonal relationship skills. More handicapped workers are dismissed from their employment because of lack of social skills than lack of job skills (Weisgerber, Dahl, & Appleby, 1981).

The primary goal of the training phase of a vocational program for handicapped students will be to prepare them for successful employment. To accomplish this goal, several components must be integrated into the total program (Weisgerber, Dahl, & Appleby, 1981).

The faculty responsible for these programs must continually be aware of the limitations and capabilities of the students and the employment community. Job analyses that include data concerning vocational opportunities, employers attitudes toward the handicapped, and the community's receptivity to accommodating the handicapped should be conducted periodically.

An amicable relationship among special education teachers, vocational education faculty, and community employers will facilitate successful employment of handicapped graduates. Teachers who are knowledgeable about their students' work abilities can be effective advocates for these students when they are seeking employment.

Vocational training programs should use technology to assist their students in increasing their abilities and reducing the effects of their handicapping conditions. Familiarity with new devices will enable the faculty to share this knowledge with prospective employers to promote employment of the handicapped in traditional settings.

Securing realistic work sites either at school or in businesses and factories will increase the effectiveness of a special education vocational program. By practicing specific job skills that will be used in a vocation, students will not have to be retrained when they become employed, saving the employers time and money.

Teachers who advocate employment of handicapped students should have expertise in the area of adaptations for job sites. Alteration of the work place and occasionally the work routine may enable the handicapped worker to become more productive. In these instances, it is the environment that is handicapping rather than the physical or mental limitations of the worker (Wade & Gold, 1978).

REFERENCES

Wade, M. G., & Gold, M. W. (1978). Removing some of the limitations of mentally retarded workers by improving job design. *Human Factors, 20,* 339–348.

Weisgerber, R. A. (Ed.). (1978). *Vocational education: Teaching the handicapped in regular classes.* Reston, VA: Council for Exceptional Children.

Weisgerber, R. A., Dahl, P. R., & Appleby, J. A. (1981). *Training the handicapped for productive employment.* Rockville, MD: Aspen.

JONI J. GLEASON
University of West Florida

COMMUNITY PLACEMENT
HABILITATION
PROFOUNDLY HANDICAPPED, COMPETENCIES OF
 TEACHERS OF
REHABILITATION
VOCATIONAL TRAINING

TRAINING IN THE HOME

Literature relating to child development frequently states that parents and other family members are the primary teachers of infants and young children. A great deal of the teaching and learning of young children in the home occurs during everyday activities such as watching TV and completing daily chores. As a result of the parent's role in teaching and socializing young children, it is essential to include the family and the home environment in any intervention plan for young children at risk (Fallen & Umansky, 1985). According to Cartwright, Cartwright, and Ward (1995) many handicapped children tend to have problems generalizing from the specific teaching setting to other settings. Therefore, an advantage of home-based training is that many opportunities are available for the parents to apply learning to life activities.

One home-based approach to early education is the Portage project. This project was designed to meet the needs of young children in rural Wisconsin. Emphasis was placed on the skills of parents in teaching their handicapped children. A teacher would visit the home and provide the parents with the necessary materials, written instructions, and forms for record keeping. Some of the basic assumptions that this project was developed around are that parents are concerned about their children and want them to develop to their maximum potential; that parents can, with assistance, learn to be effective teachers; that the socioeconomic and educational levels of the parents are no indication of the willingness to help or the amount of gains the children will achieve; and that precision teaching maximizes the chances of success for children and parents. Research has shown that when parents are involved in their children's treatment and education, children do better. The family is considered the most effective system for fostering the development of the child (Shearer, 1974).

On the other hand, there are some educators who strongly suggest that parents should leave teaching of academics to the schools. Lerner (1981) states that when learning-disabled children are tutored by their parents, it makes the children feel stressed. This is because there is a good chance that the children will feel like failures in front of the most important people in their lives. This stress tends to have a negative effect on the parent-child relationship. Lerner emphasized that parents should concentrate on teaching children domestic tasks and helping them develop a good self-image. Barsch (1969) feels that parents do not have the patience to teach their children. He lists several reasons why parents should not teach academics. They include the following:

1. Parents lack essential teaching skills.
2. The parent-child instructional session often results in frustration and tension for both members.
3. Most parents and children wish that academics could be accomplished during the school day.
4. Most teachers do not have the time to guide the parent.
5. When both the home and school stress academics, the child finds little rest.
6. Parents differ greatly in their competence as teachers.
7. Parents may feel guilty if they do not find the time to tutor their child regularly.

It has been established that some parents can successfully tutor their children. Therefore, the parents' decision to tutor or not should be made on an individual basis. According to Kronick (1977), a major question that should be addressed in terms of whether to tutor or not is whether tutoring can be accomplished without depriving any family member of resources that assist in maintaining a well-balanced life. If the parents decide to teach their children at home, Lovitt (1977) has suggested four guidelines for parents. They should establish a specific time each day for the tutoring sessions; keep sessions short; keep responses to the child; and keep a record.

REFERENCES

Barsch, R. H. (1969). *The parent teacher partnership.* Reston, VA: Council for Exceptional Children.

Cartwright, G. P., Cartwright, C. A., & Ward, M. E. (1995). *Educating special needs learners* (4th ed.). Boston: Wadsworth.

Fallen, N. H., & Umansky, W. (1985). *Children with special needs* (2nd ed.). Columbus, OH: Merrill.

Kronick, D. (1977). A parent's thoughts for parents and teachers. In N. G. Haring & B. Bateman (Eds.), *Teaching the learning disabled child.* Englewood Cliffs, NJ: Prentice-Hall.

Lerner, J. W. (1981). *Learning disabilities: Theories, diagnosis and teaching strategies* (3rd ed.). Boston: Houghton Mifflin.

Lovitt, T. C. (1977). *In spite of my resistance . . . I've learned from children.* Columbus, OH: Merrill.

Shearer, M. S. (1974). A home based parent training model. In J. Grim (Ed.), *First chance for children: Training parents to teach: Four models* (Vol. 3, pp. 49–62). Chapel Hill: Technical Assistance Development System, North Carolina University.

JANICE HARPER
North Carolina Central University

FAMILY RESPONSE TO A HANDICAPPED CHILD
HOMEBOUND INSTRUCTION
HOMEWORK
TUTORING

TRAINING SCHOOLS

Training schools were an intricate part of the larger multipurpose residential facilities known as the "colony plan" that were established in the late 1800s. These schools served children and adolescents who were not considered eligible for public school education because of their unique educational needs.

The evolvement of the training school concept was based on earlier work by Samuel Gridley Howe (1801–1876). Howe's Perkin School for the Deaf (1848) led to the development of other self-contained schools (e.g., Massachusetts School for Idiots and Feeble-Minded Youth, 1855). Although Howe's 10-bed unit was the first residential facility established, it was not until 1848 that the first large facility, the Syracuse Institution of the Feeble-Minded was developed. Harvey B. Wilbur (1820–1883), a physician, became the first superintendent of this facility. Like Howe,

Wilbur was very much influenced by the philosophy and principles of Edward Seguin; he placed a great deal of emphasis on education.

Although institutions for exceptional individuals were initially viewed as beneficial by many throughout history, their purpose, programs, and administration changed drastically. The small homelike educational establishment was replaced by the larger, overcrowded, and underfinanced multipurpose facility that would typify institutions for generations to come.

Initially, training schools in institutions were intended to serve school-aged exceptional needs children and adolescents. As years passed, it became increasingly clear that individuals who reached the age limit for school programming had few choices for continued educational services. Typically, these adults were sent to almshouses or other similar institutions.

Though educational programs continued in institutions, there was a growing emphasis on vocational training. Most of the basic operations in running these large facilities were the sole responsibility of the individuals who resided at the facility. Therefore, skills that were taught to the residents had a direct application toward the continued function of the institution.

By 1890 the school facilities of the 1850s evolved into larger facilities intended to serve four distinct groups of residents. The colony plan was developed to serve (1) the teachable portion of a school-attending group, (2) the helpless, deformed, epileptic, and unteachable, (3) the male adults who had reached school age but were unable to become self-supportive, and (4) the female adults who at that time needed close supervision. The colony plan included training schools as well as an industrial, custodial, and farm department.

As early as the 1860s, however, advocacy of education in public schools was being heard. Although it is difficult to determine precisely when the first public school special education program was initiated, credit is usually given to the public school system of Providence, Rhode Island. An auxiliary school for 15 mentally retarded students opened in December 1896 (Woodhill, 1920). By 1898 the city of Providence established three more auxiliary schools and one special education classroom in a public school.

Other cities soon followed Providence's example. By the turn of the century, special education provisions for the mentally retarded shifted from total residential training schools to generally accepted, though not always implemented, education in public school systems.

REFERENCES

Kanner, L. (1964). *A history of case and study of the mentally retarded.* Springfield, IL: Thomas.

Scheerenberger, R. C. (1983). *The history of mental retardation.* Baltimore, MD: Brookes.

Woodhill, E. (1920). Public school clinics in connection with a state school for the feeble-minded. *Journal of Psycho Asthenics, 25,* 14–103.

Michael G. Brown
*Central Wisconsin Center for the
Developmentally Disabled*

HISTORY OF SPECIAL EDUCATION
HUMANISTIC SPECIAL EDUCATION

TRANQUILIZERS

The term tranquilizer is a superordinate that may be applied to two general classes of psychoactive drugs: antipsychotic agents (major tranquilizers) and antianxiety agents (minor tranquilizers). Both major and minor tranquilizers produce sedative effects, though to different degrees. Minor tranquilizers tend to produce fewer neurotoxic side effects, but appear to be more likely candidates for abuse (Blum, 1984). The following table summarizes the two groups of tranquilizers.

The major tranquilizers were developed in an attempt to humanize the treatment of psychotic individuals, who were being given long-term treatment in psychiatric hospitals. The drugs were developed based on observations of related agents that produced calming effects on wild animals. Like the minor tranquilizers, the major tranquilizers have not been found to be physically addictive. Abrupt withdrawal, however, has been reported to induce insomnia, anxiety, and gastrointestinal symptoms (Brooks, 1959). (See Table.)

In terms of the general public, the minor tranquilizers are more familiar and also show more pervasive, popular use. The benzodiazapines are often used to reduce the effects of chronic stress, tension, and emotional discomfort. Valium has been described as the most prescribed drug in the United States, with 75% of the prescriptions being issued by nonpsychiatrists (Blum, 1984). Blum also reports that annual revenue of the antianxiety drug market in the United States is approximately $500 million. When added together, the prescriptions for Librium and Valium would account for approximately one out of five American adults (Blum, 1984).

In addition to more general stress-reducing effects, Valium is also a drug of abuse. Dosages of 100 to 500 mg produce intoxication (Patch, 1974). Valium also is used by substance abusers to deal with the frightening effects of a "bad trip" after hallucinogen (e.g., LSD) ingestion or to diminish the hangover effects after amphetamine intoxication (Blum, 1984). Therapeutically, Valium has been found to produce symptomatic relief for tension and anxiety states, free-floating agitation, mild depressive symptoms, fatigue, and short-term treatments of insomnia (Katzung, 1982). In addition, benzodiazapines have been used as adjuncts in the treatment of seizure disorders, since administration tends to raise the seizure threshold (Katzung, 1982). Valium also has been used to relieve skeletal muscle spasms, whether induced by local reactions or trauma, and spasticity secondary to upper motor neuron disorders (Blum, 1984).

Effects commonly reported owing to drug sensitivity or to intoxication include anticholinergic effects. In addition, lethargy, headache, slurred speech, tremor, and dizziness also have been reported (Blum, 1984). Paradoxical reactions including acute periods of increased excitability, increased anxiety, hallucinations, insomnia, rage, and increased muscle spasticity also have appeared in the literature (Blum, 1984). Though severe overdose of Valium is uncommon, symptoms include somnolence, confusion, coma, and blunted reflexes (Blum, 1984). The minor tranquilizers have not been found to be physically addictive; however, habituation (psychosocial accommodation to the effects of the drugs) has been reported frequently.

REFERENCES

Blum, K. B. (1984). *Handbook of abusable drugs.* New York: Gardner.

Brooks, G. W. (1959). Withdrawal from neuroleptic drugs. *American Journal of Psychiatry, 115,* 931.

Katzung, B. G. (1982). *Basic and clinical pharmocology.* Los Altos, CA: Lange Medical.

Patch, V. D. (1974). The dangers of diazepam: A street drug. *New England Journal of Medicine, 190,* 807.

Robert F. Sawicki
*Lake Erie Institute of
Rehabilitation*

MELLARIL
STELAZINE
THORAZINE

Tranquilizers

Major	Minor
Phenothiazines	*Benzodiazapines*
Thorazine (Chlorpromazine)	Valium (Diazepam)
Stelazine (Trifluoperazine)	Librium (Chlordiazepoxide)
Mellaril (Thioridazine)	Dalmane (Flurazepam)
Prolixin (Fluphenazine)	Tranxene (Chlorazepate)
Thioxanthenes	*Meprobamate*
Navane (Thiothixene)	
Butyrophenones	
Haldol (Haloperidol)	

TRANSDISCIPLINARY MODEL

Originally conceived by Hutchison (1974), the transdisciplinary model is one of several team approaches for the delivery of educational and related services to handicapped students. The other team models are the multidisciplinary model and the interdisciplinary model. In a multidisciplinary model, team members maintain their respective discipline boundaries with only minimal, if any, coordination, collaboration, or communication (McCormick, 1984). The interdisciplinary model differs from the multidisciplinary model in that there is some discussion among the involved professionals after their individual assessments have been completed and at least an attempt to develop a coordinated service delivery plan. However, the programming recommendations are often not realistic. The teacher may not have the skills to implement the recommendations or the authority to arrange for their provision (Hart, 1977). Another problem is the lack of provision for follow-up and feedback in the interdisciplinary model.

The transdisciplinary model is the only one of the three models to adequately address the issue of coordinated service delivery. This model suggests specific procedures for sharing information and skills among professionals and across discipline boundaries. It is differentiated from the other models by its emphasis on coordination, collaboration, and communication among the involved discipline representatives and its advocacy of integrated services.

The transdisciplinary model assumes the following: (1) joint functioning (team members performing assessment, planning, and service delivery functions together; (2) continuous staff development (commitment to expansion of each team member's competencies); and (3) role release (sharing functions across discipline boundaries; (Lyon & Lyon, 1980). The professional makeup of a transdisciplinary team varies depending on the needs of the student. It may include few or many professionals, but whenever possible they coordinate their assessment procedures and plan as a group for the student's daily programming.

Transdisciplinary team members are accountable for seeing that the best practices of their respective disciplines are implemented (McCormick & Goldman, 1979). However, their responsibility does not stop there. They are also responsible for monitoring program implementation, training others if necessary, and revising programs when evaluation data indicate that the procedures are not working. The teacher is usually coordinator and manager of team processes so that there is no duplication of efforts or splintering of services.

REFERENCES

Hart, V. (1977). The use of many disciplines with the severely and profoundly handicapped. In E. Sontag, J. Smith, & N. Certo (Eds.), *Educational programming for the severely and pro-* *foundly handicapped.* Reston, VA: Council for Exceptional Children, Division of Mental Retardation.

Hutchison, D. (1974). *A model for transdisciplinary staff development* (United Cerebral Palsy: Technical Report No. 8).

Lyon, S., & Lyon, G. (1980). Team functioning and staff development: A role release approach to providing integrated educational services for severely handicapped students. *Journal of the Association for Severely Handicapped, 5*(3), 250–263.

McCormick, L. (1984). Extracurricular roles and relationships. In L. McCormick & R. Schiefelbusch (Eds.), *Early language intervention.* Columbus, OH: Merrill.

McCormick, L., & Goldman, R. (1979). The transdisciplinary model: Implications for service delivery and personnel preparation for the severely handicapped. *AAESPH Review, 4*(2), 152–161.

LINDA McCORMICK
University of Hawaii

ITINERANT SERVICES
MULTIDISCIPLINARY TEAM

TRANSFER OF TRAINING

Transfer of training, also referred to as stimulus generalization or generalization, takes place when a behavior that has been reinforced in the presence of one stimulus event occurs in the presence of different but similar stimuli. Using the behavior analytic $S > R > C$ paradigm, the emphasis of this learning construct is on (1) the characteristics of the events that precede a behavior, and (2) the relationship of these characteristics to the occurrence of the behavior under similar stimulus conditions.

From this viewpoint, increasing similarities in events that precede a behavior result in an increased likelihood of stimulus generalization. Conversely, there is a decreased likelihood of the trained behavior occurring as these preceding events become more dissimilar. Applied to educational programming, the influence of these similarities might be beneficial or problematic. Thus a student may be trained to respond to questions asked by an adult male teacher by raising his or her hand. If this student responds likewise in other classroom settings to questions asked by female adults, a beneficial transfer of training has occurred. However, if the student responds to his father's inquiry, "Why are you late?" by raising his or her hand, the transfer of training that has taken place might be viewed as potentially problematic.

This example highlights some of the problems that relate to transfer of training and also touches on the fundamental role of this learning explanation in the educational process. Almost without exception, students are exposed to information and material with specific stimulus characteristics or in specific stimulus settings. Traditionally, this stimulus-specific training is assumed to automatically transfer to similar stimulus events. The accuracy of this assumption is highly questionable when teaching the learner with exceptional needs. As the severity of an individual's learning problems increase, so does the need for implementation of more specific interventions that are geared toward systematically promoting transfer of training.

A variety of approaches and procedures have been applied in order to increase the positive transfer of training. These attempts have been effective to varying degrees in achieving this purpose. Specific recommendations for achieving transfer of training have been offered by Martin and Pear (1983) and Stokes and Baer (1977). These recommendations include (1) training the skills in the situation where the behavior is to occur, (2) presenting a variety of stimulus events, (3) programming common stimulus characteristics across settings, and (4) training with sufficient examples.

Training the skill in the situation where it is expected to occur addresses the relationship between the training efforts extended to develop a student's skills in one setting and the implicit desire to have that student perform those skills in another setting. The use of this tactic requires the development of as many similarities as possible between the two settings, or actual skill training in the targeted situation. Therefore, if a student is being taught to locate the correct restroom using international door symbols, as much of the training as possible should take place in similar (analogue) or actual (in vivo) settings.

Another technique for promoting transfer of training is the presentation of a variety of stimulus events. Also referred to as training loosely, this tactic involves providing the student with a wide variety of stimuli to allow practicing of the response under different but similar conditions. Accordingly, training situations might involve different trainers, differing verbal requests, etc., each serving as a stimulus event for the same desired student response.

Programming of common stimuli is another tactic used to promote transfer of training. Alternatively referred to as the "don't teach basketball with a football" technique, this procedure focuses on the establishment of stimulus bridges between the training setting and the goal environment. Thus students are taught to respond to the materials, statements, or other stimulus events that will actually be present in the goal environment.

The final tactic suggested by these authors involves the presentation of representative stimulus events during training. In contrast to teaching a student to respond by presenting all possible stimulus options (e.g., every possible configuration of the word poison), the emphasis of "training sufficient examples" is on the use of stimulus events that encourage responses to example stimuli. Application of this technique in teaching a student to respond

to teacher greetings might involve training the student to say "hi" to one teacher and priming generalization of the response by rewarding the student's response to another teacher.

The effectiveness of education to a large extent relates to the amount of training that is transferred from one stimulus event to another similar events or settings. With the exceptional learner, this transfer must often be directly encouraged. For a comprehensive explanation of transfer of training and related teaching considerations, the reader is referred to texts by Sulzer-Azaroff and Mayer (1977) and Alberto and Troutman (1977).

REFERENCES

Alberto, P. A., & Troutman, A. C. (1977). *Applied behavior analysis for teachers: Influencing student performance.* Columbus, OH: Merrill.

Stokes, T. F., & Baer, D. M. (1977). An implicit technology of generalization. *Journal of Applied Behavior Analysis, 10,* 349–367.

Sulzer-Azaroff, B., & Mayer, G. R. (1977). *Applying behavior-analysis procedures with children and youth.* New York: Holt, Rinehart, & Winston.

J. TODD STEPHENS
University of Wisconsin at Madison

GENERALIZATION
TRANSFER OF LEARNING

TRANSFORMATIONAL GENERATIVE GRAMMAR

In 1957 Noam Chomsky revolutionized the field of English grammar and research with the publication of the book *Syntactic Structures.* Chomsky, considered the father of the theory of transformational grammar, proposed a finite set of operations (called transformations) that produce (or generate) sentences of infinite number and variety without producing nonsentences. These operations are acquired during the first few years of life through exposure to conversation rather than through formal study. They are internalized by the speaker without his or her being aware of or able to state them.

Chomsky's theory describes the language people do use rather than the language they ought to use (Cattell, 1978). It focuses on competence, the ideal speaker-listener's complete command of language, as opposed to performance, the actual use of language in concrete situations as affected by imperfection and inconsistency. Unlike the traditional grammarian who deals with sentence form, or surface structure, Chomsky distinguishes between surface structure and its underlying meaning or deep structure. This is the level at which grammatical relationships are preserved. By way of example, Quigley, Russell, and Power (1977) present the sentences "John is easy to please" and "John is eager to please." These two sentences are identical to one another in surface structure but completely different in deep structure. Muma (1978) elaborates by pointing out that the sentence "I bes here" (nonstandard dialect) is not inferior to the sentence "I am here" (standard dialect), as both are identical at the deep structure level.

Deep structures are turned into surface structures through transformations that expand, delete, and reorder sentence constituents, or component parts. These operations may be applied to all sentences without changing their meanings. Examples of transformations applied to the sentence "boys like girls" would include question (do boys like girls?), negation (boys don't like girls), and passive voice (girls are liked by boys) (Quigley, Russell, & Power, 1977).

Transformational grammarians view the sentence as a hierarchical organization of constituents. By applying a series of rewriting rules of increasing specificity, it is possible to analyze sentence structure, working backward through the derivation of a sentence to discover the initial transformational rule by which it was generated. These rewriting rules enable linguists to describe sentences pictorially using tree diagrams. Crystal, Fletcher, and Gorman (1977) point out that the easiest and best known of these rules is represented by the formula S Æ NP + VP, or rewrite the sentence as a noun phrase and a verb phrase.

Transformational generative grammar has been applied successfully to research into language function (Dever, 1971), language development and delay, dialectic differences, and ESL studies (Quigley, Russell, & Power, 1977). Its detractors have noted that the distinction between language competence and performance is minimal at best when dealing with individuals with language disorders (Crystal, Fletcher, & Gorman, 1977). Akmajian, Demers, and Harnish (1980) note that Chomsky's model has been challenged at every level, resulting in numerous changes since the mid-1960s.

REFERENCES

Akmajian, A., Demers, R. A., & Harnish, R. M. (1980). *Linguistics: An introduction to language and communication.* Cambridge, MA: MIT Press.

Cattell, N. R. (1978). *The new English grammar.* Cambridge, MA: MIT Press.

Chomsky, N. (1957). *Syntactic structures.* The Hague: Mouton.

Chomsky, N. (1965). *Aspects of the theory of syntax.* Cambridge, MA: MIT Press.

Crystal, D., Fletcher, P., & Gorman, M. (1977). *The grammatical analysis of language disability: A procedure for assessment and remediation.* London: Arnold.

Dever, R. B. (1971). The case for data gathering. *Journal of Special Education, 5,* 119–126.

Muma, J. R. (1978). *Language handbook: Concepts, assessment, intervention.* Englewood Cliffs, NJ: Prentice-Hall.

Quigley, S. P., Russell, W. K., & Power, D. J. (1977). *Linguistics and deaf children.* Washington DC: A. G. Bell Association.

SUSAN SHANDELMIER
Eastern Pennsylvania Special Education Regional Resource Center

CHOMSKY, A. N.
LANGUAGE DEFICIENCIES AND DEFICITS
LINGUISTIC DEVIANCE

TRANSITION

Transition is the process of changing from one condition or place to another; it is common to individuals at various times throughout their lives. Transition from preschool to school environments as well as transition from school to postschool environments present problems for the young child and the adolescent. For individuals with special needs who are graduating or leaving school, this process is frequently more difficult than for others. The entitlement to a free appropriate public education may not necessarily culminate in opportunities for employment, integration into the community, or adult services. In recognition of the concerns of parents, educators, and service providers regarding the futures of handicapped students leaving publicly supported education programs, a national priority on transition from school to work for all individuals with disabilities was announced by the Office of Special Education and Rehabilitation Services (OSERS) in 1983. The need for transitional services and the provision of some degree of financial support for these activities are addressed in PL 98-199, the Education for All Handicapped Children Amendments, and in IDEA.

Will (1984) has defined transition from school to work as "an outcome-oriented process encompassing a broad array of services and experiences that lead to employment" (p. 2). Transition refers to the period between school and work, and transitional services encompass both ends of a continuum between educational and adult services. The transition period includes the high school years, postsecondary services, and the first few years of employment. The goal of transition is meaningful paid employment and successful community functioning for individuals with disabilities. To obtain this goal, a restructuring and rethinking of the roles and responsibilities of various agencies at the federal, state, and local levels is necessary so as to ensure appropriate, nonduplicated services delivery (Vocational Transition, 1986).

The transition from school to work and adult life requires careful, systematic preparation and planning in the secondary school; cooperative support of interagency teams on graduation; and awareness and support of multiple employment options and services as needed by the community and professionals.

Generally, the difficulty in transition to postsecondary environments increases with the severity of the disability, Wilcox and Bellamy (1982) include the prevention of institutionalization in their definition of transition. They have suggested guidelines for effective transition of the more severely handicapped; these include using a case management approach to develop a comprehensive transition plan that is individualized, starts in the last years of school, has links with adult services, is locally designed, and ensures continuity of services without interruption. Preparation for the next environment should be stressed, as well as advocacy and family preparation.

Transition services may be grouped into three classes that reflect the nature of the public services used to provide support as the passage is completed: (1) transition with no special services—vocational technical schools and work experience; (2) transition with time-limited services—vocational rehabilitation, Job Training Partnership Act; and (3) transition with ongoing services—supported work environments for individuals with severe disabilities (Will, 1984).

Finally, one of the major issues surrounding transition is the lack of information about the status of special education graduates. Hasazi et al. (1985) cited the need to develop a body of data regarding the employment status of these individuals for use as a basis for future planning regarding transition activities.

REFERENCES

Hasazi, S. B., Gordon, L. R., & Roe, C. A. (1985). Factors associated with the employment status of handicapped youth exiting high school from 1979 to 1983. *Exceptional Children, 51,* 455–469.

Vocational transition: A priority for the '80s. (1986). *Project-Tie,* *1*(1).

Wilcox, B., & Bellamy, G. T. (1982). *Design of high school programs for severely handicapped students.* Baltimore, MD: Brookes.

Will, M. (1984). *OSERS programming for the transition of youth with disabilities: Bridges from school to working life.* Washington, DC: Office of Special Education and Rehabilitative Services.

EILEEN F. MCCARTHY
University of Wisconsin at Madison

VOCATIONAL REHABILITATION
VOCATIONAL TRAINING OF HANDICAPPED

TRANSITION PLANNING FOR CULTURALLY AND LINGUISTICALLY DIVERSE STUDENTS

National concern for transition issues began in the 1980s. Transition was addressed in the Education of the Handicapped Act Amendments of 1983 and Madeline Will, former assistant secretary for special education and rehabilitative services, Office of Special Education and Rehabilitative Services, issued a policy paper regarding transition from school to work. As transition became a national priority, transition programs and models for transition were developed and evaluated across the country. Transition programs focus on employment, residential, transportation, and recreational issues. Components of model programs include functional curricula, integrated school services, community-based instruction, comprehensive individual transition plans, interagency cooperation, and follow-up of students. In addition to including these components, successful programs provide early planning and early experiences in competitive employment for their students. Parent involvement and student self-determination are considered critical aspects of successful transition planning.

Components of Transition Planning

Transition planning involves decision-making about major life considerations related to employment, education, residence, and recreation/leisure activities. Students' vocational aptitude and interests are assessed to help provide guidance in career planning. Typically, these decisions are made by the student him or herself, his or her family, educators, and adult service agency personnel in the transition planning meeting. The transition planning team works together to set goals, which the student will work to attain during his or her secondary education. That aspects of transition planning might differ when working with culturally and linguistically diverse students is a relatively new concept.

Assessment

It is important to note that assessment results, which are used in transition planning, may not be valid for culturally and linguistically diverse students or for students with disabilities. Therefore, professionals must use caution in making decisions based on results of these assessments. According to Szymanski (1994), assessment that is not culturally valid can disempower culturally diverse students in the transition process. When possible, it is recommended that authentic assessment be used, to ensure that valid information is used to make important life decisions (Harry et al., 1995).

Self-Determination

Increasingly, individuals with disabilities are being encouraged to take charge of their own lives; this is referred to as self-determination. In some schools, with guidance from educators, students are conducting their own transition planning meetings. In encouraging students from culturally and linguistically diverse backgrounds to be more self-determined, it is critical to understand their unique family characteristics. Families either facilitate or impede student self-determination (Morningstar, Turnbull & Turnbull, 1995), and this effect is often culture-related. If educators encourage a student to have a goal of independently living in an apartment, but his or her family believes that their role is to care for their child for his or her lifespan, conflict will occur. Parents are a member of the transition planning team and their support is necessary for successful transition to occur; parent values and beliefs also greatly influence their children's vision of the future (Morningstar, Turnbull, & Turnbull, 1995). Finally, if the purpose of self-determination is to help students "to intentionally create experiences in their lives that are consistent with their unique beliefs, needs, and preferences," cultural and linguistic backgrounds need to be respected (Field, Martin, Miller, Ward, & Wehmeyer, 1998, p. 143).

Parent Involvement

In planning a student's transition from school to work, the involvement of the student him- or herself and his or her parents can impact the success of the plan. Although parents have the right to participate, actual parent participation in the special education process is very limited (Gartner & Lipsky, 1987). In addition to being limited, participation decreases as the age of the child increases (Cone, Delawyer, & Wolfe, 1985; Salisbury & Evans, 1988). In a survey of parents of 129 graduates of high school special education programs, only 34% of the parents perceived themselves as being actively involved in their child's school program; 43% perceived themselves as somewhat involved (attending meetings, etc.) and 23% perceived that they were not involved at all (Haring, Lovett, & Saren, 1991). This limited involvement could reflect a lack of effort on the part of school personnel, or a choice made by the parents. In addition, it is common for Hispanic families to defer all educational decisions to "experts" in the school (Lynch & Stein, 1987); this is a sign of respect, rather than an indication of disinterest. While there are differing opinions regarding the need for parent involvement, there are

definite benefits, such as providing input regarding their years of experience with the child, providing continuity to the child's program, setting appropriate goals for the child, and serving as an advocate for the child. Professionals need to empower parents from culturally diverse backgrounds by showing them the value of their input in making decisions for their child.

Participation has been found to differ according to ethnicity of parents (Stein, 1983; Lynch & Stein, 1987). Hispanic parents, while satisfied with their level of involvement, are less able to be involved in their child's education program and participate less actively. Both Hispanics and African Americans are less aware of services included in the Individual Education Program (IEP) than are Anglos; however, African Americans participate more actively than do Hispanics in the IEP development and assessment process. Major barriers identified in preventing Hispanic parents from participating in their child's program were work and lack of bilingual communication.

According to Turnbull and Turnbull (1982), for various reasons parents may choose not to be involved in educational decision making for their child with disabilities. They maintain that parents should not be expected to have the equivalent of a master's level training in special education. While some parents choose to be actively involved in their children's special education, some prefer to leave the educational decisions to the educational specialists. The individual needs of the parents need to be considered as well as the individual needs of the child. Professional roles should not be forced upon parents (Allen & Hudd, 1987). Parents should be given an opportunity to be informed of educational goals and objectives and allowed to participate to the degree they choose, but parental involvement should not be mandatory (Turnbull & Turnbull, 1982; MacMillan & Turnbull, 1983).

When schools do involve parents in their children's special education, often the emphasis is on obtaining signatures for documentation that required procedures were followed (Shevin, 1983). In a survey of 145 special education teachers, while 51% viewed the IEP meeting as an opportunity for parent involvement, 44.3% perceived it as merely a formality (Gerber, Banbury, Miller, & Griffin, 1986). Although legal mandates are being followed, the intent of the law is not followed if parents and/or students do not understand because of cultural or language barriers. At the same time, parents often lack the confidence to persist in their efforts to formulate their children's educational programs (Shevin, 1983). Parents not only need to be given the opportunity to be involved in educational planning for their children with disabilities, they need to be informed.

Even when professionals involve parents according to the law, often their participation is perceived as less valuable. Parents receive the message that their input is given a lower priority than that of professionals (Harry, Allen, & McLaughlin, 1995). Parents from linguistically different backgrounds may use different terms to identify and/or describe their child's characteristics, while they may be perceived as not accepting the child's limitations, thus devaluing their input in the eyes of professionals, often the difference is merely in the language used to describe the disability (Harry, 1992b). It is important to remember that although parents may interpret their child's disability differently, they still may be very perceptive regarding the disability and can be important contributors to educational planning.

Parent Education

For parents to become active members of their children's transition planning teams, education and training regarding transition issues will have to be provided. In a survey of parents of students with severe disabilities, only 65% of the 203 respondents reported having received any information about post-school services available in their community (McDonnell, Wilcox, Boles, & Bellamy, 1985). Without this information, parents cannot effectively plan for their children's transitions. A survey of parents of young adults with mild disabilities revealed that parents were hindered in providing support for transition by a lack of information regarding issues such as knowledge of vocational abilities and limitations, potential employment opportunities for their children, and post-secondary services available (Tilson & Neubert, 1988). It is particularly important to provide information in the parents' dominant language; language usage and professional jargon are often a barrier to parent participation (Congress, 1997).

Setting Goals

In setting goals, educators must remember that norms differ across cultures (Harry et al., 1995); terms such as "work" and "independent living" are culturally-based, and families may interpret these terms differently than professionals in schools. Parents can be very effective members of their children's educational planning team; however, sensitivity to cultural differences must be considered when presenting different options within these three domains. According to Kelker et al. (1986), parents can serve various roles in transition planning, including providing information, sharing values and concerns about the student, helping to set priorities, acting as case manager, serving as an advocate for services, and providing role models. Again, professionals need to consider the cultural background and values of each family when recommending roles for them to take. It is also necessary to avoid assuming that parents are aware of the transition options within the community; individuals from culturally diverse backgrounds

may be less knowledgeable than their Anglo counterparts in certain areas (Lynch & Stein, 1987).

Goodall and Bruder (1986) maintain that parents are the ultimate advocates and case managers, as they are "the one constant in a lifetime of changing services and providers" (p. 23). After the students leave high school, the parents will be responsible for them obtaining the necessary services; parental involvement in transition planning, therefore, is critical. Problems may occur in transition planning when parents' goals and aspirations are different from the potential of the child as perceived by professional educators. For example, educators may aspire for their students' competitive employment, independent living, and integrated leisure activities. However, in a close-knit Hispanic family, the parents may wish for their child to stay at home, unemployed, participating in the community as a member of their family only (Lynch, 1992).

Opportunities for persons in rural areas are limited. This includes Native Americans who live on reservations. Transition planning will be more challenging for these students, because there will not be the same array of services available to facilitate transition. The distance between the family's residence and the nearest services may result in families refusing services, even though educators believe the services to be in the best interest of the child. It is important for the educator to be aware that this refusal is a result of a cultural difference rather than an uncaring attitude about the child.

Increasing Parent Involvement

Increasing parent involvement in special education can result in positive outcomes (Boone, 1992). This may be accomplished by scheduling meetings beyond school hours, conducting meetings at a neutral site, providing additional opportunities for parental input to educational planning, providing follow-up telephone calls after meetings, and introducing parents to support groups (Gress & Carroll, 1985). At meetings, there should be enough time to allow parents and educators to share and discuss ideas (Witt, Miller, McIntyre, & Smith, 1984).

Parents can also be involved in the implementation of their children's education plans (Izzo, 1987); in teaching functional living goals, educators can discuss with parents which skills or competencies will be stressed at school and which will be taught at home by parents. Parents can be invited and encouraged to visit job sites and vocational training programs (Lehmann, Deniston, & Grebenc, 1989). Parents who are aware of what is occurring in their child's education will be able to be more involved with their child.

Stein (1983) offers the following suggestions for increasing involvement of Hispanic parents:

- conduct meetings and present school communications in the language of the home;

- encourage families to ask questions, offer suggestions, and provide information about their child;
- train bilingual parent facilitators to assist parents in becoming partners;
- consider and respect cultural differences and similarities, while also opening discussions about the consequences of such differences and similarities;
- not expect parents to permeate the "walls" of the school but to open the doors wider and encourage parents to come in;
- help teach parents how to participate in their children's special education program by explaining clearly and accurately parental rights and responsibilities as well as available educational processes and services;
- provide necessary transportation and child-care services when parent participation at a school meeting is required; and
- frequently survey the Hispanic community and work with Hispanic community agencies to develop strategies to more actively involve Hispanic citizens (p. 438).

Although these suggestions are particular to the involvement of Hispanic parents, they apply in general to any parent of a different culture of ethnicity. Lynch and Stein (1987) recommend the following for involving families of diverse cultural backgrounds:

- conduct a study of parent involvement to determine the differences and needs within the community;
- develop a concise position paper which addresses the importance of parental involvement in special education decision making;
- develop grant applications which support the hiring and training of parents from various cultural groups to become liaisons between the school system and other parents;
- work with other community groups and organizations to provide training about special education programs and services to individuals in the various cultural communities who have direct contact with families;
- develop training packages for parents from diverse cultures about special education programs, services, and processes;
- provide inservice education to school personnel which describes cultural and linguistic differences and sensitizes all school staff to the values and beliefs of the families whom they serve; and
- continue to recruit and hire school personnel who represent a wide range of cultural and linguistic backgrounds (p. 110).

Awareness and sensitivity to cultural diversity and the involvement of representatives of different cultures in developing strategies to increase parent involvement within their cultures can be as effective for other groups as well as Hispanics.

Parents need to be empowered with knowledge regarding the transition process and post-secondary options for their children with disabilities to improve services available through adult agencies, as well as specific training in implementing their children's transition plans (Lehmann, Deniston, & Grebenc, 1989). McDonnell and Hardman (1985) report that for parents to be successfully involved in transition planning, they need information regarding the components of effective high school programs, the characteristics of adult service programs, criteria for evaluating post-school service programs, potential service alternatives, and the status of services in the local community. They suggest that schools can provide this information through conducting inservice training sessions for parents and through the development of a transition planning guide for parents.

Guidelines for Transition Planning

Although broad generalizations regarding different cultures have been presented, it is extremely important to recognize that each student and his or her family have unique characteristics all their own and there is no "recipe" for transition planning based on an individual's ethnic background. For example, one might assume that Asian American families have high expectations for their children and would steer their child toward a scientific or technological career. This is a stereotype that will not hold true for all Asian American families. What is important is to be aware that different families have different values and goals for their individual members. In assisting students from culturally and linguistically diverse backgrounds as they transition from school to work, it is essential that educators seek to know each student and his or her family individually and take their values, goals, and so on into consideration. Harry and colleagues (1995) claim that "shared cultural, educational, social, and linguistic experiences allow parents and professionals to proceed more directly to special education matters" (p. 102). The following general guidelines will facilitate the understanding of each family's unique culture (U.S. Department of Education, 1997; Greene, 1996; Harry et al., 1995; Harry, 1992a; Harry, 1992c; Inger, 1992; Lynch, 1992).

1. Home visits can be a valuable means for developing understanding of a family's culture and background. They offer the added advantage of meeting a family on their own turf, in comfortable surroundings. To develop a collaborative relationship with a family, educators must understand the family's perspective.

2. Ask, rather than assume, what language is spoken in the home and by what members of the family. Also, ascertain the literacy level of different family members. Take this information into consideration in all communications with the family.

3. Providing written material is not enough; it needs to be discussed verbally and explained. The transition process needs to be explained, and written materials used as a reminder, not a primary source. The most successful approach in communicating is face-to-face, in a person's native language.

4. Parent involvement, particularly in attending meetings, can be greatly enhanced by flexibility in accommodating parents' schedules, providing transportation, and altering the site of the meetings. Important information should be presented in the parents' dominant language. Positive interactions should be fostered at all meetings to ensure continued participation.

5. There is a need for improved communication regarding parent training meetings. Input from parents needs to be obtained to determine why parents do not attend and why they seem to perceive that the districts are lacking in this area. Communication can then be improved.

6. Districts need to provide inservice meetings for special education teachers to familiarize them with aspects related to the cultural diversity of the students they serve. Teachers or special education personnel responsible for transition need to have more intensive sessions specifically related to transition; however, all teachers need to be familiar with the process and know how to direct parents' questions.

7. Finally, transition councils and parent advisory groups can be effectively used to develop the transition process and facilitate collaboration between professionals and culturally and linguistically diverse families. Obtaining input from those with whom the district will be working in transition planning and service provision is a very effective way to encourage their involvement.

REFERENCES

Allen, D. A., & Hudd, S. S. (1987). Are we professionalizing parents? Weighing the benefits and pitfalls. *Mental Retardation, 25*(3), 133–139.

Boone, R. (1992). Involving culturally diverse parents in transition planning. *Career Development for Exceptional Individuals, 15*(2), 205–221.

Congress, E. P. (Ed.). (1997). *Multicultural perspectives in working with families.* New York: Springer.

Cone, J. D., Delawyer, D. D., & Wolfe, V. V. (1985). Assessing parent participation: The parent/family involvement index. *Exceptional Children, 51*(5), 417–424.

Field, S., Martin, J., Miller, R., Ward, M., & Wehmeyer, M. (1998). *A practical guide for teaching self-determination.* Reston, VA: Council for Exceptional Children.

Gartner, A., & Lipsky, D. K. (1987). Beyond special education: Toward a quality system for all students. *Harvard Educational Review, 57*(4), 367–385.

Gerber, P. J., Banbury, M. M., Miller, J. H., & Griffin, H. C. (1986). Special educators' perceptions of parental participation in the individual education plan process. *Psychology in the Schools, 23*(2), 158–163.

Goodall, P., & Bruder, M. B. (1986). Parents & the transition process. *Exceptional Parent, 16*(2), 22–28.

Greene, G. (1996). Empowering culturally and linguistically diverse families in the transition planning process. The *Journal for Vocational Special Needs Education, 19*(1), 26–30.

Gress, J. R., & Carroll, M. E. (1985). Parent-professional partnership and the IEP. *Academic Therapy, 20*(4), 443–449.

Haring, K. A., Lovett, D. L., & Saren, D. (1991). Parent perceptions of their adult offspring with disabilities. *Teaching Exceptional Children, 23*(2), 6–10.

Harry, B. (1995). Developing culturally inclusive services for individuals with severe disabilities. *JASH, 20*(2), 99–109.

Harry, B. (1992a). *Cultural diversity, families, and the special education system.* New York: Teachers College Press.

Harry, B. (1992b). Making sense of disability: Low-income, Puerto Rican parents' theories of problems. *Exceptional Children, 59*(1), 27–40.

Harry, B. (1992c). Restructuring the participation of African-American parents in special education. *Exceptional Children, 59*(2), 123–131.

Harry, B., Allen, N., McLaughlin, M. (1995). Communication versus compliance: African-American parents' involvement in special education. *Exceptional Children, 61*(4), 364–377.

Inger, M. (1992). Increasing the school involvement of Hispanic parents. ERIC Clearinghouse on Urban Education. (*ERIC Digest Number 80,* 24–25)

Izzo, M. V. (1987). Career development of disabled youth: The parents' role. *Journal of Career Development, 13*(4), 47–55.

Kelker, K., Mcrae, T., Faught, K., Allard, G., Hagen, M., & Offner, R. (1986). *Planning for transition: An implementation guide for administrators and teachers.* Billings, MT: The Montana Center for Handicapped Children.

Lehmann, J. P., Deniston, T., & Grebenc, R. (1989). Counseling parents to facilitate transition: The difference parents make. *The Journal for Vocational Special Needs Education, 11*(3), 15–18.

Lynch, E. W., & Stein, R. C. (1987). Parent participation by ethnicity: A comparison of Hispanic, Black, and Anglo families. *Exceptional Children, 54*(2), 105–111.

Lynch, P. S. (1992). Parents' perceptions of their involvement in planning the transition from school to work for their children with disabilities in Texas.

Macmillan, D. L., & Turnbull, A. P. (1983). Parent involvement with special education: Respecting individual preferences. *Education and Training of the Mentally Retarded, 18*(1), 4–9.

McDonnell, J., & Hardman, M. (1985). Planning the transition of severely handicapped youth from school to adult services: A framework for high school programs. *Education and Training of the Mentally Retarded, 10*(1), 17–21.

McDonnell, J. J., Wilcox, B., Boles, S. M., & Bellamy, G. T. (1985). Transition issues facing youth with severe disabilities: Parents' perspective. *Journal for the Association for Persons with Severe Handicaps, 10*(1), 61–65.

Morningstar, M. E., Turnbull, A. P., & Turnbull, H. R. (1995). What do students with disabilities tell us about the importance of family involvement in the transition from school to adult life? *Exceptional Children, 62*(3), 249–260.

Shevin, M. (1983). Meaningful parental involvement in long-range educational planning for disabled children. *Education and Training of the Mentally Retarded, 10*(1), 17–21.

Stein, R. C. (1983). Hispanic parents' perspectives and participation in their children's special education program: Comparisons by program and race. *Learning Disability Quarterly, 6*(4), 432–438.

Szymanski, E. M. (1994). Transition: Life-span and life-space considerations for empowerment. *Exceptional Children, 60*(5), 402–410.

Tilson, G. P., & Neubert, D. A. (1988). School-to-work transition of mildly disabled young adults. *The Journal for Vocational Special Needs Education, 11*(1), 33–37.

Turnbull, A. P., & Turnbull, H. R. (1982). Parent involvement in the education of handicapped children: A critique. *Mental Retardation, 20*(3), 115–122.

U.S. Department of Education. (1997). *Nineteenth annual report to Congress on the Implementation of the Individuals with Disabilities Education Act.* Washington, DC: Author.

Witt, J. C., Miller, C D., McIntyre, R. M., & Smith, D. (1984). Effects of variables on parental perceptions of staffings. *Exceptional Children, 51*(1), 27–32.

PAT LYNCH
Texas A & M University

BROOKE DURBIN
Texas A & M University

CULTURALLY/LINGUISTICALLY DIVERSE STUDENTS

TRANSPORTATION OF HANDICAPPED STUDENTS

Transportation of handicapped students is usually viewed as an administrative requirement to ensure access to public education. It is seldom viewed as an opportunity to teach students community mobility skills. However, community mobility is the dynamic concept within the issue of transportation of handicapped students. The ability of an individual to participate independently or semiindependently in all aspects of community life (e.g., domestic, recreational, and vocational) is dependent on community mobility (Wehman, Renzaglia, & Bates, 1985). Community mobility refers to movement from one place to another within a particular setting and travel between two community locations. The concept of community mobility was originally developed in program practice and literature related to working with visually handicapped individuals. In this literature, community mobility is referred to as orientation and mobility training.

For visually impaired individuals, orientation and mobility training has long been a well-respected component of the curriculum. As the rights of all citizens to participate in the least restrictive environment have been acknowledged, the concept of community mobility has been broadened to include the physically handicapped, mentally retarded, emotionally disturbed, and other special education consumers. Assurances for meeting the basic transportation needs to and from school have been established within PL 94-142 for all special education students. However, the transportation needs of handicapped students are complex.

The ability of a person to be independently mobile is dependent on several factors. One of the primary factors that influences the degree of mobility attained by handicapped individuals is the opportunity for travel from one place to another. Opportunity for mobility can be restricted by both physical and attitudinal barriers. In many communities, extensive physical modifications have been made, including construction of ramps, widening of doorways, installment of elevators, cutting out of curbs, and purchase of lift buses. Although these modifications have removed many barriers to independent mobility, obstacles still exist in all communities. Realistically, many of these obstacles are not going to be eliminated. Some of these obstacles are outside of the control of engineers and educators (e.g., weather conditions, natural terrain). Since mobility obstacles are likely to remain in every community, efforts must be directed toward teaching individuals to overcome these problems. By combining environmental changes with specific instruction programs, handicapped citizens are provided easier access as well as more skills for traveling independently within their communities. Community mobility training programs should reflect this dual concern for improving physical accessibility and training skills that compensate for various environmental barriers.

Attitudinal barriers can severely restrict a person's chances for learning independent mobility skills in an even more devastating way than physical obstacles. These barriers result from a combination of overprotectiveness and lowered expectations. Parents and professionals have contributed to this problem. According to Perske (1972), "such overprotection endangers the client's human dignity, and tends to keep him from experiencing the risk taking of ordinary life which is necessary for normal growth and development" (p. 29).

Overprotectiveness and lowered expectations can combine to present attitudinal barriers that severely limit a person's opportunity to acquire independent living skills. However, the development of responsible and effective community mobility training programs can alleviate fears and concerns regarding safety and consequently raise the expectations of parents and professionals for independent living by handicapped individuals. The development of such programs will significantly increase the opportunity an individual will have to acquire independent living skills.

Recently, more community mobility training programs have began to emphasize the functional relationship between public transportation and access to community services. For example, Sowers, Rusch, and Hudson (1979) used systematic training procedures to teach a severely retarded adult to complete the following 10-behavior sequence to ride the city bus to and from work: (1) cross controlled intersections, (2) cross unmarked intersections, (3) use bus tickets, (4) walk to bus, (5) identify the correct bus, (6) board, (7) ride, (8) depart, (9) transfer, and (10) walk to work. Further, Marholin, O'Toole, Touchette, Berger, and Doyle (1979) taught four moderately and severely retarded adults to use public bus transportation to travel between a public institution and various community locations for shopping and eating in a restaurant.

The responsibility of public schools for transporting handicapped students to and from school programs must be expanded to include greater sensitivity to the unique community mobility needs of individual students. In meeting these responsibilities, educators should promote the development of a normalized repertoire of transportation skills. At a basic level, this could involve assistance that enables handicapped students to use the same transportation system in association with their nonhandicapped peers. At a more complex level, this would require a commitment to teaching a variety of mobility skills that would enhance a person's ability to access community activities throughout his or her lifetime.

REFERENCES

Marholin, D., Touchette, P., Berger, P., & Doyle, D. (1979). I'll have a Big Mac, Large Fries, Large Coke, and Apple Pie—of teaching adaptive community skills. *Behavior Therapy, 10,* 236–248.

Perske, R. (1972). The dignity of risk. In W. Wolfensberger (Ed.), *The principle of normalization in human services.* Toronto, Ontario: National Institute on Mental Retardation.

Sowers, J., Rusch, F. R., & Hudson, C. (1979). Training a severely retarded young adult to ride the city bus to and from work. *AAESPH Review, 4,* 15–22.

Wehman, P., Renzaglia, A., & Bates, P. (1985). *Functional living skills for the moderately and severely handicapped.* Austin, TX: Pro-Ed.

PAUL BATES
Southern Illinois University

ELECTRONIC TRAVEL AIDS
MOBILITY TRAINING
TRAVEL AIDS FOR HANDICAPPED

TRAUMATIC BRAIN INJURY AND SCHOOL REENTRY

Traumatic brain injury (TBI) involves a physical injury to the brain caused by an external force, resulting in diminished consciousness or coma (Stratton & Greogory, 1994). There are two types of traumatic brain injuries: open and closed-head injuries. Open head injuries occur when an object (e.g., a bullet or shell fragment) penetrates the skull and produces damage to the brain. The damage tends to be localized about the path of the penetrating object (Lezak, 1995). In contrast, closed head injuries are more common than open head injuries and are more likely to produce diffuse damage (Begali, 1992). A blow to the head without penetrating the skull is an example of a closed head injury. In closed head injuries, the direct impact causes the brain, which is floating in cerebrospinal fluid within the skull, to strike the inside of the skull in one or more places. The movement of the brain within the skull causes shearing and tearing of nerve fibers and contusions (i.e., bruising; Lezak, 1995). In addition to the primary effects (e.g., the bruising, shearing, and tearing), secondary effects are often present in the form of brain swelling and hemorrhaging. The secondary effects compound the damage, resulting in a wide variety of neural structures being affected (Stratton & Gregory, 1994). As a result, diversity in behavioral sequelae (i.e., consequences) in TBI patients is the norm rather than the exception. Impairments in cognition, language, memory, attention/concentration, conceptual functions, abstract reasoning, judgment, academic achievement or new learning, and perception have been reported in traumatic brain injured children and adolescents. Motor and sensory deficits have also been noted along with behavioral and socioemotional problems (Begali, 1992). For additional information on the sequelae associated with TBI, see the entry on traumatic brain injury in children.

Head injury is a common occurrence among children and adolescents. It is the leading cause of death and disability in children (Begali, 1992). Approximately one million children in the United States experience a head injury each year (Research and Training Center in Rehabilitation and Childhood Trauma, 1993). Of these one million, 165,000 children and adolescents are hospitalized with a traumatic brain injury yearly (National Information Center for Children & Youth with Disabilities [NICCYD], 1993). Although most of these children and adolescents will enjoy a substantial recovery, 16,000 to 20,000 of these individuals will have moderate to severe injuries producing long-term effects (Clark & Hostetter, 1995).

Children with TBI are not new to the schools; however, the number of severely injured children surviving and returning to schools has grown. Sophisticated medical technology has resulted in an increased survival rate among children following a traumatic brain injury (Rapp, 1999).

Federal law mandates that these children are to be served by the schools; however, educators and parents often lack the knowledge on how to best serve these students (Blosser & DePompei, 1991).

In 1990, traumatic brain injury was added to the list of eligibility categories under the Individuals with Disabilities Education Act (IDEA). IDEA, or Public Law 101-476, is the major special education law in the United States. P.L. 101-476, now P.L. 105-17, defines a traumatic brain injury as:

> An acquired injury to the brain caused by an external force, resulting in total or partial functional disability or psychosocial impairment, or both, that adversely affects a child's educational performance. The term applies to open or closed head injuries resulting in impairments in one or more areas, such as cognition; language; memory; attention; reasoning; abstract thinking; judgment; problem-solving; sensory, perceptual and motor abilities; psychosocial behavior; physical functions; information processing; and speech. The term does not apply to brain injuries that are congenital or degenerative, or injuries induced by birth trauma (Federal Register, 1992, p. 44802).

According to the federal law, children and adolescents who experience a brain injury resulting from internal as opposed to external trauma are excluded from this definition and services. In other words, children whose injuries are caused by internal events, such as brain tumors, cerebral vascular accidents, exposure to environmental toxins, or central nervous system infections cannot be served under the TBI category, but may be eligible for services under another special education category (e.g., Other Health Impaired). Some states, however, have opted to identify, classify, and serve a broader range of children whose injuries are the result of either external or internal trauma (Rapp, 1999). State rules and regulations should be consulted to determine whether children whose brain injury is the result of internal trauma are eligible for services under the TBI category.

To be eligible for services under the TBI category of IDEA, children's educational performances must be adversely affected by their injury. For those individuals with TBI who are not eligible for special education and related services under IDEA, Section 504 of the Vocational Rehabilitation Act of 1973, a civil rights law, may provide sufficient services and protections in the general education classroom. Section 504 outlines the school district's responsibility to provide educational accommodations and related services to allow disabled students to have equal access to all publicly funded programs available to their nondisabled peers. In either case, the federal law is quite clear. Children with TBI who are eligible under IDEA or Section 504 must be served. Thus, plans must be developed and services implemented in order to successfully reintegrate these children into the classroom following their injury.

A number of resources must be mobilized and activities planned and implemented prior to a child's return to school to ensure successful school reentry, including assignment of a case manager, formation of a school or interdisciplinary team, inservice training for school personnel, family education, peer education, notification to the State's Vocational Rehabilitation Office, and collaboration among the systems (home, school, hospital/rehabilitation unit). Successful school reintegration is dependent upon collaboration and open communication among the family, school, and hospital/rehabilitation systems. Open communication is imperative in all stages of recovery. Information exchanged should begin immediately following the injury, when the child is first admitted to the hospital (Clark, 1997); however, controversy exists as to which system is responsible for making the initial contact. Haak and Livingston (1997) suggest the school should take the initiative and contact the parents to obtain permission to contact the medical facility. Opening communication channels helps ensure that the child will be appropriately served.

The school should appoint a representative (i.e., a case manager), who is knowledgeable about TBI, to serve as a liaison among the different systems. The case manager's role should be to establish and maintain communication and coordinate services among the systems on behalf of the child. The case manager should relay information to the school from the hospital regarding the severity of child's injury, current behavior, medication management (Clark, 1997), progress, and expected discharge and school reentry dates (Haak & Livingston, 1997). Through the case manager, assessment results and the hospital/rehabilitation unit's recommendations can be forwarded to the school. The case manager provides the medical facility, on the other hand, with information from the school regarding the child's educational history, any preinjury assessment results, classroom assignments, and the school's progress in preparing for the child's reentry (Clark, 1997); for example, removal of architectural barriers, if needed. The case manager also communicates with the parents to obtain information about the child's current status and any problems the child may be experiencing.

Family education is also critical to a child's successful school reentry. The child's family needs to receive general information on TBI and TBI sequelae. They also need to be informed about the child's specific needs (e.g., educational needs) and abilities. Medical professionals and the case manager can help educate the family in these areas. Medical professionals can also provide the family with information on TBI and TBI sequelae, whereas the case manager can provide the family with information on IDEA and Section 504. The child's family needs to know what services are available in a school district, eligibility criteria to receive these services, process to obtain these services, and child and family's rights in relation to these services under the federal law (Ylvisaker, Hartwick, & Stevens, 1991).

Inservice training is another essential activity needed to facilitate a child's successful reentry back into the school setting. Common reactions of school personnel about a child preparing to return to school are either sheer panic or overconfidence. Panic may result because of the school personnel's lack of knowledge on how best to serve the child, whereas the staff's overconfidence may be based on the assumption that the child is fully recovered and educational programming can begin where it had abruptly ended at the time of the accident. These reactions are typical, but unnecessary (Rapp, 1999). Inservice training can inform and address the issues and concerns of the school staff. Inservice training conducted by an individual with expertise on TBI (e.g., a rehabilitation professional) can provide general information about TBI and TBI sequelae. The professional with expertise on TBI should provide information on the specific needs and abilities of the child as well (Ylvisaker et al., 1991). Information about intervention strategies that may be beneficial to the child in and outside the classroom should also be included (Clark, 1997).

Besides inservice training, in-class meetings should be held between the case manager and the child's peers to educate classmates about TBI and discuss the child's condition and possible changes in his/her behavior (e.g., changes in personality). A discussion with the student's classmates about the child with his/her permission (Ylvisaker et al., 1991) may help peers to develop a better understanding of the situation and support for the student.

The state's Office of Vocational Rehabilitation should also be contacted in the likelihood that a child with TBI will need their services in order to obtain employment upon graduation from high school. Many vocational rehabilitation offices have tracking systems. Notification results in the youth's name being entered into the vocational rehabilitation system for future services. In addition, the school counselor and vocational liaison specialist for the school district should be made aware of the need to develop community-based work experiences for the child. On-site training will help the individual with TBI develop work skills needed to succeed in a competitive employment market (Ylvisaker et al., 1991).

Before the child with TBI is discharged from the medical facility, the formation of a school or interdisciplinary team is needed to develop a plan for school reentry. The team is composed of a variety of professionals, the child's parents, and the child. The team usually consists of a general education teacher, special education teacher, case manager, school psychologist, parent, and student. Other team members may include a neuropsychologist, counselor, rehabilitation specialist, speech pathologist, physical therapist, and occupational therapist. The team's composition is dependent upon the child's needs (Clark, 1997). The team develops a tentative plan consisting of accommodations and intervention strategies and addresses the possibility that special education and related services will be needed.

Transitions from the medical facility to home and from home to school, along with the injury and its aftermath, are stressful periods for most children with TBI and their families. Guidelines exist to assist families with these transitions (e.g., Cohen, Joyce, Rhoades, & Welks, 1985). For example, Cohen et al. provide guidelines to help families and school personnel determine when a child is ready to return to school and will benefit from the school experience. According to Cohen and colleagues, a child is ready to return to school when he/she is able to attend for 10–15 minutes at a time, tolerate 20–30 minutes of classroom stimulation, function in a group setting, follow simple directions, engage in meaningful communication, and demonstrate some degree of learning. These guidelines are means of helping families reduce the stress associated with the transitions.

For the child with TBI, the transition and return to school can be very stressful and upsetting. The return to school highlights the losses in cognitive abilities, academic skills, physical functioning, and changes in behavior. These losses and changes can be demoralizing to the child and make the child a target of misperceptions. An increase in risk-taking behavior (Begali, 1992), social isolation, and withdrawal may result. Classmates' understanding and support are essential during these critical periods.

The transition from home to school can result in parental frustration and stress as well. In her review, Begali (1992) reported that common parental frustrations have been found, including lack of teacher understanding about TBI, reduced parental contact with support networks, inappropriate class placements, and social isolation of the child. For the family of a child with TBI, the injury and recovery process never occur in an interpersonal vacuum. Brain injury affects both the child and his or her family (Haak & Livingston, 1997). The family may have difficulty accepting their child's limitations and possible changes in personality. Moreover, financial difficulties, injury to other family members, and weariness may exist as the result of the accident. Schools can assist the family in the aftermath of TBI by empowering the family to play an active role in their child's education, teaching the family about TBI, and offering support and counsel. Family stress and frustration highlights the importance of developing a school reintegration plan and the value of having a knowledgeable and well-prepared school staff (Begali, 1992).

When a child with TBI returns to school, questions arise concerning the most appropriate placement for the child to receive his or her education. Not all children with TBI will require special education. Some students will need only monitoring in the classroom with slight adjustments made in the curriculum based on teacher observations. Others, on the other hand, will require special education and related services. To receive these services, a student must be "educationally diagnosed" (Begali, 1992). In other words, an evaluation needs to be conducted to determine a child's eligibility for special education.

Assessment plays a prominent role in determining eligibility and treatment of traumatic brain injured children and adolescents (Begali, 1992). Assessment results provide invaluable information and help determine educational placement, related services, and instructional goals. Psychoeducational, ecological, neuropsychological, and neurological evaluations should be conducted and results should be integrated in order to determine appropriate accommodations and modifications needed in the school environment to provide optimal learning experiences for children and adolescents with TBI. Standardized testing supplemented with testing of the limits and process procedures will provide invaluable information for designing appropriate accommodations and interventions (Kaplan, 1988).

A standard psychoeducational evaluation consists of an intelligence test, achievement test, and behavioral rating scales (Rapp, 1999). A psychoeducational evaluation can predict future learning potential and learning disabilities; however, children and adolescents with TBI are more likely to have problems with attention or concentration, memory, new learning, problem solving, and socioemotional behavior, which will not be appropriately assessed using only a standard psychoeducational battery (Rapp, 1999; Reitan & Wolfson, 1992). Therefore, other evaluation procedures are needed.

In contrast, a neuropsychological evaluation assesses a broad range of brain-behavior relationships, current cognitive strengths and weaknesses, and new learning. Educational and vocational program goals can be developed based on these assessment results. Neuropsychological evaluations and neurological evaluations, consisting of physical assessments conducted by medical specialists, should be used to augment standard psychological assessments (Goldstein, 1984). A neuropsychological evaluation should be conducted before the child reenters school and reevaluations should be conducted frequently during the first year (Rapp, 1999). Begali (1992) recommends conducting a reevaluation every three to six months for the first two years postinjury. Following the first or second year postinjury, reevaluations should be conducted before major school transitions, when new problems arise, or when lack of educational progress is reported (Rapp, 1999).

Ecological evaluations consist of observations of children or adolescents in a variety of settings. Students with TBI usually have difficulty monitoring and regulating their own behavior in the real world, generalizing skills and abilities, and cognitive organization. Formal testing cannot assess these skills with any degree of accuracy, nor does formal testing have any resemblance to the real world or classroom environment. Thus, observations complement formal testing. Observations of children and adolescents with TBI provide a means of monitoring these students' progress and evaluating educational programs and interventions (Rapp, 1999). Observations should be conducted on a frequent basis.

Informal testing such as curriculum-based and criterion-based assessment is also recommended. Curriculum-based and criterion-based assessment may be used to guide instructional efforts and provide feedback. Program deficiencies can be identified and revisions of instructional objectives can be made. The main point to remember in the assessment of children with TBI is that frequent formal and informal testing will be needed to monitor these children's progress, as these children can recover substantial cognitive, physical, and behavioral functioning in short periods of time (Clark, 1997).

If a child is found to be eligible for special education based on assessment results and other relevant information, the Individualized Education Program (IEP) team, the members of the school, or interdisciplinary team will develop an IEP. The IEP is a document stating the educational goals and objectives and specific educational and related services that will be provided. The IEP is required to address the child's current level of educational performance in the areas affected by the disability (Clark, 1997). This requirement can be a challenge to the IEP team, as dramatic changes are seen in individuals with TBI during the first three months of recovery (Lezak, 1995). Thus, constant review and updating of educational goals and objectives is needed to keep pace with the child's recovery. A review of the IEP within three months of its implementation is recommended. After the initial review, the IEP should be reviewed periodically thereafter (Clark, 1997). For those who do not qualify for special education and related services under IDEA, but do qualify for services under Section 504, the school's 504 team will need to develop a plan to ensure that children with TBI are adequately served as well.

Because of the dramatic changes seen in children with TBI during the recovery process and the fact that no two traumatic brain injuries are alike, educational programs for children with TBI must be individualized, flexible, and delivered in a timely manner. Educational programs for children with TBI should ensure that professional training, instructional methods, and program practices parallel the state-of-the-art in head trauma rehabilitation. Quality educational programs should include the following options: environmental control, low student-to-teacher ratio, individualized and intensive instructional techniques (Begali, 1992), flexible class scheduling, and community-based experiences.

Some children with TBI need a more controlled environment in the schools, such as a self-contained placement. Common characteristics found among children with TBI are their limited ability in interpreting environmental cues and responding to these cues in socially appropriate ways (Wood, 1990), hypersensitivity and hyposensitivity to sensory stimuli (Savage & Wolcott, 1994), and difficulty remembering class schedules and organizing their materials. Temporary placement in a self-contained classroom may provide these individuals with the time needed to develop coping strategies to interact appropriately and to handle the less predictable and more demanding general educational environment (Begali, 1992).

Flexible class scheduling is another mark of a quality educational program for children and adolescents with TBI. Children with TBI often lack the stamina needed to attend school on a full-time basis when they first return. Shortened school days and reduction in class load and number of classes may be needed to combat fatigue. Appointments with specialists, such as an occupational or physical therapist, may need to be scheduled into the school day as well. Thus, the actual time spent in the classroom may be very limited upon initial reentry (Begali, 1992).

Small classes where the student-to-teacher ratio is low may be beneficial to some children with TBI, especially those with severe head injuries. In these smaller classes, children with TBI can receive more intensive training, closer supervision, and more frequent feedback. In addition, distractions in these classes are more likely to be held to a minimum in comparison to the larger regular education classes (Begali, 1992).

Individual and intensive instructional opportunities are other key features of quality education programs for children with TBI. Children with TBI may need individual instruction or additional instructional assistance due to cognitive impairments, problems with new learning, loss of specific skills, or behavioral problems. Remediation, compensation, and accommodation strategies may be helpful in addressing these children's difficulties. For learned maladaptive behaviors, changes in the environment and setting clear limits may be beneficial. Accommodation strategies are often the initial intervention methods used when children with TBI return to the classroom. Remediation of specific lost skills is also an appropriate strategy to use with children with TBI. Practice, repetition, and more time to relearn specific lost skills are examples of remediation strategies. Teaching compensatory strategies is another set of intervention methods that may be used to circumvent cognitive impairments. With compensatory strategies, such as the use of mnemonics, new ways of performing and learning tasks are acquired (Rapp, 1999). To maximize instructional time, limits on transitional time and extracurricular classes may be set. Attendance in an extended school program during the summer months, if eligible, may be helpful in preventing regression in learning. Due to the rapid changes in cognitive, physical, and behavioral skills and abilities, dynamic and responsive instructional approaches tailored to the individual will be required (Begali, 1992). For additional information on more specific intervention strategies to use with students with TBI, see the entry on traumatic brain injury in children.

Community-based work experience is another indicator of a quality educational program for children with TBI. In 1990, IDEA required school districts to provide students in special education with transitional services. Children with TBI who are in special education and are 14 years of age or older qualify for these services. Participation in community-based work experiences occurs during the school day. These students go to work sites located in their community to receive on-the-job training. These work experiences are arranged to help students develop good work skills, work habits, and social skills needed in today's competitive employment market. The goal of the school-to-work experience is for students to develop the skills needed to obtain meaningful employment and to have independent living opportunities upon graduation (Haak & Livingston, 1997).

School reentry is a challenging experience for the student, family, and school. At present, limited information exists on school reentry programs for children with TBI. In addition, empirical research demonstrating the effectiveness of school reentry programs for children with TBI is lacking. Collaboration among the systems (home, school, medical, and community) and drawing upon the technical expertise of these resources are needed in order to assist these children on their road to recovery.

REFERENCES

Begali, V. (1992). *Head injury in children and adolescents.* Brandon, VT: Clinical Psychology Publishing Company.

Blosser, J. L., & DePompei, R. (1991). Preparing education professionals for meeting the needs of students with traumatic brain injury. *Journal of Head Trauma Rehabilitation, 6*(1), 73–82.

Clark, E. (1997). Children and adolescents with traumatic brain injury: Reintegration challenges in educational settings. In E. D. Bigler, E. Clark, & J. E. Farmer (Eds.), *Childhood traumatic brain injury: Diagnosis, assessment, and intervention.* Austin, TX: Pro-Ed.

Clark, E., & Hostetter, C. (1995). *Traumatic brain injury: Training manual for school personnel.* Longmont, CO: Sopris West.

Cohen, S., Joyce, C., Rhoades, K., & Welks, D. (1985). Educational programming for head injured students. In M. Ylvisaker (Ed.), *Head injury rehabilitation: Children and adolescents* (pp. 383–411). San Diego: College-Hill Press.

Diamond, R. (1987). Children and head injury. In A. Thomas & J. Grimes (Eds.), *Children's needs: Psychological perspectives.* Washington D.C.: The National Association of School Psychologists.

Federal Register. (1992, September 9). Individual with Disabilities Education Act. (IDEA), U.S. Department of Education Regulations. Washington, DC: U.S. Government Printing Office.

Goldstein, G. (1984). Neuropsychological assessment. In G. Goldstein & M. Hersen (Eds.), *Handbook of psychological assessment* (pp. 181–211). New York: Pergamon.

Haak, R. A., & Livingston, R. B. (1997). Treating traumatic brain injury in the school: Mandates and methods. In C. R. Reynolds & E. Fletcher-Janzen (Eds.), *Handbook of clinical child neuropsychology* (2nd ed., pp. 482–505). New York: Plenum.

Kaplan, E. (1988). A process approach to neuropsychological assessment. In T. Boll & B. K. Bryant (Eds.), *Clinical neuropsychology and brain function: Research, measurement, and practice* (pp. 129–167). Washington D.C.: American Psychological Association.

Lezak, M. D. (1995). *Neuropsychological assessment* (3rd ed.). New York: Oxford.

National Information Center for Children and Youth with Disabilities. (1993). *Traumatic brain injury.* Fact sheet number 18 (FS 18). Washington, DC: NICCYCD.

Rapp, D. L. (1999). Interventions for integrating children with traumatic brain injuries into their schools. In C. R. Reynolds & T. B. Gutkin (Eds.), *The handbook of school psychology* (3rd ed., pp. 863–884). New York: Wiley.

Reitan, R. M., & Wolfson, D. (1992). *Neuropsychological evaluation of older children.* South Tucson, AZ: Neuropsychology Press.

Research and Training Center in Rehabilitation and Childhood Trauma (1993). *National Pediatric Trauma Registry.* Boston, MA: Tufts University School of Medicine, New England Medical Center.

Savage, R. C. & Wolcott, G. F. (Eds.). (1994). *Educational dimensions of acquired brain injury.* Austin, TX: Pro-Ed.

Stratton, M. C. & Gregory, R. J. (1994). After traumatic brain injury: A discussion of consequences. *Brain Injury, 8*(7), 631–645.

Wood, R. L. (1990). Neurobehavioral paradigm for brain injury rehabilitation. In R. Wood (Ed.), *Neurobehavioral sequelae of traumatic brain injury* (pp. 3–17). New York: Taylor & Frances.

Ylvisaker, M., Hartwick, P., & Stevens, M. (1991). School reentry following head injury: Managing the transition from hospital to school. *Journal of Head Trauma Rehabilitation, 6,* 10–22.

PATRICIA A. LOWE
CECIL R. REYNOLDS
Texas A & M University

TRAUMATIC BRAIN INJURY AND SPECIAL EDUCATION SERVICES

Traumatic brain injury (TBI) involves an insult to the brain, not of a degenerative or congenital nature, but or caused by an external physical force of sufficient magnitude producing a diminished or altered state of consciousness and/or associated neurological or neurobehavioral dysfunction (Begali, 1992). Mild to severe structural or physiological changes in the neural tissue of the brain resulting from TBI may cause transient to permanent changes in behavior (Begali, 1992; Salvage & Wolcott, 1994). Tissue abnormalities and neural damage resulting from TBI may be due to the direct impact following an accident involving the head or may be due to secondary effects (i.e., secondary damage or metabolic changes) associated with the trauma (Begali, 1992).

TBIs may be classified into two types, open and closed head injuries. Open head injuries involve the penetration of the skull and brain by a foreign object. The agents commonly responsible for open head injuries include bullets, shell fragments, knives, rocks, and blunt instruments. Gunshot wounds account for the majority of open head injuries, although knife and scissor wounds are frequently reported as well (Ward, Chisholm, Prince, Gilmore, & Hawkins, 1994). Open head injuries result in an increased risk of infection, bleeding, and seizures, as bone fragments or shattered pieces of shells or bullets penetrate the brain (Rapp, 1999). Primary damage, however, tends to be localized about the path of the penetrating object. As a result, cognitive losses and changes in behavior due to the localized damage are relatively circumscribed and predictable. Depending on the location of the injury, open head injuries may result in specific intellectual impairments and behavioral changes, memory deficits, slower information processing, attention and concentration difficulties, and changes in the ability to deal with everyday cognitive demands (Begali, 1992).

Closed head injuries, on the other hand, are more common and more diffuse in comparison to open head injuries (Lezak, 1995). Closed head injuries result from a direct impact to the brain, such as a blow to the head, without penetration of the skull. There are three types of closed head injuries (Reynolds, pers. comm., June 6, 1997) produced by two mechanical factors; namely, direct contact forces and inertial forces (Begali, 1992; Katz, 1992). An acceleration injury occurs when an individual's head accelerates too quickly (e.g., when a child's head is hit with a baseball bat). In an acceleration injury, the child's skull, which surrounds the brain (a gelatin-like substance supported and floating in cerebrospinal fluid), compresses against the brain and forces the brain to move to the opposite side of the initial point of impact where the brain hits the inside of the skull again. The point of initial impact is called the coup, whereas the secondary point of impact, orthogonal to the plane (i.e., opposite side) of the initial point of impact, is called the counter coup. Damage to the brain in an acceleration injury occurs at both the coup and counter coup, with more severe damage at the coup.

In contrast, a deceleration injury occurs when an individual's head decelerates or stops too quickly (e.g., when an adolescent's head strikes an immovable or stationary object, such as a car's dashboard during a motor vehicle accident). Under these circumstances, the brain moves forward and strikes the inside of the skull (coup) and then moves in the opposite direction (backwards) and strikes the inside of the skull again (counter coup). In a deceleration injury, brain damage is more severe at the site of the counter coup than the coup.

A pinball injury is a third type of closed head injury. A pinball injury may also occur during a motor vehicle accident when the individual's head strikes the dashboard and then the individual is thrown from the vehicle and lands on the ground, hitting the side of his/her head. A pinball injury results in multiple points of impact producing damage at a number of coup and counter coup sites.

Coup and counter coup damage is the product of direct contact forces. Inertial forces, on the other hand, generate other types of injuries, such as shearing and tearing of nerve fibers. Shearing and tearing of nerve fibers occur in acceleration, deceleration, and pinball closed head injuries. Shearing and tearing result from brain movement and rotation of the brain within the skull. Tearing injuries are likely to occur when nerve fibers projecting from the base of the brain are stretched to their limit, resulting in their snapping or tearing. In contrast, shearing injuries may occur, for example, when association fibers, which connect different areas of the brain together, scrape against the bony ridges of the inside of the skull. This scraping movement results in the removal of layers of association fibers.

Brain damage typically occurs in two stages; namely, the primary and second injury. The primary injury is the damage that occurs at the time of the injury, whereas the second injury results from the damage incurred from the primary injury (Lezak, 1995). Primary injuries in closed head injuries include skull fractures, concussions, contusions, and shearing and tearing injuries. A skull fracture is a crack in the cranium (i.e., the skull) surrounding the brain. The skull fracture may vary in size or severity. A contusion occurs when the brain strikes the inside of the skull (i.e., a coup or counter coup), resulting in bruising of the brain. Blood vessels may also rupture during the accident or shortly thereafter, causing extensive bleeding. Bleeding within the cranium is dangerous and possibly fatal, as the blood accumulates in this case surrounding the brain with no place to go. As a result, pressure mounts inside the cranium. This pressure can be fatal. In contrast, a concussion occurs when the brain strikes the inside of the skull, resulting in a period of confusion or loss of consciousness. A variety of primary injuries are possible when a closed head injury occurs. Thus, each closed head injury is unique and is dependent upon the physical characteristics of the insult and the movement of the brain within the skull (Begali, 1992).

Secondary damage or the second injury develops after the insult in either an open or closed head injury. Secondary complications include (a) edema (brain swelling due to an increase in fluid content); (b) infarction (loss of brain tissue due to blood deprivation); (c) increased cranial pressure (buildup of pressure in the cranium); (d) hypoxia (oxygen deprivation); (e) hemorrhage (rupture of blood ves-

sels in the brain); (f) hematoma (collection of blood in the brain tissue); and/or (g) infection (Pang, 1985). Secondary damage may also result from metabolic change (North, 1984), damage to the pituitary gland and hypothalamus, electrolyte disturbance (a chemical imbalance in the blood), and/or hyperventilation (excessive breathing; Pang, 1985).

Head injury is a common occurrence among children and adolescents; however, prevalence rates and incidence of TBI have been difficult to ascertain, as incongruities in classification procedures and methodological weaknesses in epidemiological studies have been reported (Lehr, 1990). It has been estimated that more than one million children in the United States sustain a mild to severe traumatic brain injury each year (Research and Training Center in Rehabilitation and Childhood Trauma, 1993). Researchers have estimated that 10 out of every 100,000 children die as a result of brain injury yearly (Luerssen, 1991). Pediatric patients account for approximately 40% of the TBI cases reported on an annual basis, which translates, based on different estimates, into 200,000 to 600,000 TBI child and adolescent cases each year that come to the attention of medical professionals (Brandstater, Bontke, Cobble, & Horn, 1991; Crouchman, 1990). The majority of these TBI cases occur in youth between the ages of 15 and 19 years due to automobile accidents (Farmer & Peterson, 1995). Many of these individuals will require educational support once they return to school. Approximately 50% of the children and adolescents who sustain a traumatic brain injury need educational support during the first year following their injury (Donders, 1994). It is estimated that 8% to 20% of the special education population is believed to have suffered a traumatic brain injury (Savage, 1991).

Gender differences have also been reported. Males are twice as likely as females to sustain a traumatic brain injury at all ages, except in infancy and the senior years of life (Lezak, 1995). This gender differential is found to be the greatest during the peak trauma years, the 15–24 year age range (Naugle, 1990), when males are four times more likely than females to suffer an injury (Vernon-Levett, 1991). Males also tend to sustain more severe brain injuries than females, with the male to female mortality ratio being 4:1 (Frankowski, Annegers, & Whitman, 1985).

The external forces that produce TBIs tend to vary with the age of the individual (Farmer & Peterson, 1995; Goldstein & Levin, 1990). Infants, toddlers, and preschoolers are more likely to acquire TBIs due to falls, physical abuse, and vehicular accidents (Rapp, 1999). Physical abuse, such as shaken baby or thrown infant syndrome, is the leading cause of traumatic brain injury among infants. Sixty-six percent of the infants who are physically abused sustain a brain injury as a result of the abuse (Bruce & Zimmerman, 1989). Falls, on the other hand, are the major source of TBI among children under age five and account for more than 50% of the injuries in the toddler and preschool population

(Kraus et al., 1984). After age 5, pedestrian and bicycle injuries increase, with motor vehicle accidents, falls, recreation and sports injuries, and assaults contributing to the rate of injury (Mira, Tucker, & Tyler, 1992). Not surprisingly, adolescents and young adults are at the greatest risk of any age group for acquiring TBIs (Savage & Wolcott, 1994), primarily through motor vehicle accidents but also from sports injuries and assaults (Rapp, 1999). During adolescence, the combination of increased risk-taking behaviors and learning how to drive often lead to an increase in motor vehicle accidents. Automobile accidents account for three deaths and 260 injuries among children and adolescents each day (Brain Injury Association, 1997). Overall, moving vehicle accidents and falls are the major causes of head trauma (Lezak, 1995). Moreover, the risk of sustaining a brain injury increases dramatically with each successive TBI an individual experiences (Brain Injury Association, 1997).

There are many factors that influence the outcomes of traumatic brain injury in children: child, family, medical, school, and community factors (Farmer, 1997). A level of influence within these factors either increases the risk of poor outcomes, or creates a buffer or offers protection, and thus maximizes optimal outcomes. For example, child factors can serve as either risk or protective factors that influence TBI outcomes. Child factors include preinjury characteristics, age/developmental stage at onset, type and persistence of impairments, postinjury adjustment, and severity of injury. Type and persistence of impairments are determined by the nature of the injury, such as a closed versus open head injury, and the location and severity of the injury (Warzak, Mayfield, & McAllister, 1998). Postinjury adjustment, on the other hand, is dependent upon the child and family's coping resources and the child's social acceptance by others (Wade, Taylor, Drotar, Stancin, & Yeates, 1996). Preinjury characteristics include genetics and the child's preexisting medical, behavioral, and affective status. Harrington (1990) reported that children with TBI with above-average intelligence, academic skills, and social skills tend to have a better prognosis than those individuals with TBI with below average skills. Students with TBI, however, are more likely to have preexisting academic problems and prior behavioral problems in comparison to their classmates (Farmer, Clippard, Wieman, Wright, & Owings, 1997).

Another potential differentiating factor that influences TBI outcomes is the age of onset or the child's developmental stage at the time of the injury. The relationship between age of onset and recovery from brain injury, however, is complex and is not well understood (Dalby & Obrzut, 1991). Early research suggested a high degree of plasticity in the brains of young children (i.e., children's brains had the ability to compensate for some injuries by reorganizing neural function). In other words, a young child's brain was thought to be more resilient in response to injury, as other brain structures spared of injury assumed the function of the damaged areas (Farmer & Peterson, 1995). Subsequent studies, however, have indicated young children's superior recovery from head trauma cannot be presumed (Farmer, 1997). In fact, recent studies have found just the opposite (i.e., more unfavorable outcomes) in younger children who have experienced a brain injury in the areas of language development (Ylvisaker, 1993), attention (Kaufmann, Fletcher, Levin, Miner, & Ewing-Cobbs, 1993), intellectual and behavioral functioning (Michaud, Rivara, Jaffe, Fay, & Dailey, 1993), and problem solving (Levin et al., 1994).

Preliminary evidence suggests preschool children may be at greatest risk (Farmer & Peterson, 1995). Disruption of primary skills (e.g., sensory, motor, language, behavioral, and social skills) in early childhood may result in changes in learning, such as the order, rate, and level of learning, and development of higher order skills, such as self-regulation of behavior and planning ability (Farmer, 1997). In addition, some research (e.g., Lehr & Savage, 1990) suggests early brain injury may result in delayed, late-onset effects in which a child who appears to be fully recovered shows a marked decline in functioning over time.

Brain injury severity is another factor that influences TBI outcomes. Severity is medically diagnosed using the terms mild, moderate, and severe. Classification of brain injury severity is based on three critical factors. These three critical factors include an individual's level of consciousness, degree of posttraumatic amnesia experienced, and physical findings. In general, severity of head trauma serves as a good prognosticator of behavioral and neuropsychological outcomes (Kreutzer, Devany, Myers, & Marwitz, 1991), with more long-lasting changes in physical, cognitive, and behavioral functioning occurring with more severe TBI cases (Fay et al., 1993; Jaffe et al., 1993). Although children and adolescents who sustain severe TBIs are more likely to experience chronic effects, individual differences must be taken into account. Some individuals with severe head injuries have not encountered significant disability, whereas some children and adolescents with mild brain injuries have symptoms that cause significant and lasting impairments (Farmer, 1997; Fay et al., 1993).

Diminished or altered level of consciousness is one of the most commonly used indicators of brain trauma. The Glasgow Coma Scale (GCS; Teasdale & Jennett, 1974) is a means of assessing an individual's level of consciousness following a brain injury. The GCS is routinely used to measure the degree and duration of altered consciousness within 24 hours of the trauma and to periodically monitor changes in consciousness during the early stages of recovery (Teasdale & Jennett, 1974). A GCS score is obtained through observing, evaluating, and summarizing the patient's best-rated responses, ranging from 1 to 6 in motor movements, 1 to 5 in verbal functioning, and 1 to 4 in eye movements. Possible scores range from 3 to 15. Coma is diagnosed when there is no eye opening, inability to obey commands, and inability to speak. One critical limitation of the GCS, however, is its development and use almost exclusively with adults and older adolescents. Thus, the clinical utility of the GCS with the younger child population is questionable, as the presentation of coma differs across young children and adults (Lehr, 1990). In response to the limited utility of the GCS, alternative measures for use with comatose pediatric patients have been developed, such as the Children's Coma Scale (CCS; Raimondi & Hirschauer, 1984). The CCS has been used to assess the level of consciousness in infants and toddlers up to age 3. Possible scores range from 3 to 11 and are not interchangeable with the GCS. The CCS, however, has its limitations as well, as the predictive validity of this scale has not been examined due to limited use (Lehr, 1990).

The degree of posttraumatic amnesia (PTA) is another indicator of brain injury severity. Posttraumatic amnesia refers to the period of time when an alert individual who has experienced a brain injury has "persistent difficulties retaining new information" (Farmer & Peterson, 1995, p. 233). Estimates of brain injury severity based on PTA duration vary from less than five minutes to more than four weeks (Bigler, 1990). PTA duration correlates well with GCS ratings, with the exception of extreme GCS scores (Bigler, 1990), as PTA duration typically lasts four times longer than the period of unconsciousness or coma (Lezak, 1995). Children's Orientation and Amnesia Test (Ewing-Cobbs, Levin, Fletcher, Miner, & Eisenberg, 1989) or structured parent interviews (Rutter, Chadwick, Shaffer, & Brown, 1980) have been used to assess PTA in children. PTA is difficult to assess in young children, as children's memories are less reliable and accurate than adults. As a result, PTA is usually not assessed and reported in children under the age of nine (Lehr, 1990).

A third indicator of injury severity is gauged by examining physical findings through a variety of medical procedures. Physicians conduct neurological examinations to assess sensory deficits, reflexes, and the motor system. Medical professionals also use a variety of technologically advanced medical procedures to assess the degree of damage sustained. Computerized tomography, magnetic resonance imagery, functional magnetic resonance imagery, single-photon emission computer tomography, positron emission tomography, regional cerebral blood flow, and brain electrical activity mapping have proven to be useful, some procedures more than others (Lezak, 1995), in evaluating the severity of injury.

Although assessment of the level of brain injury severity has its limitations, the three critical factors (i.e., level of consciousness, duration of posttraumatic amnesia, and physical findings) offer a means of predicting TBI outcomes. A mild brain injury has been defined as a GCS score of 13 to 15, which suggests little or no impairment in speaking and motor and eye movement. A PTA of less than one hour occurs and no known structural damage to the brain is evident (Binder, 1986). Approximately 75% to 90% of all head trauma falls into this category (Alves & James, 1985). Students who sustain a mild brain injury often make good academic recovery but may experience attention and concentration difficulties, fatigue, and deficits in retaining new information. Deficits following a mild TBI tend to be subtle but may have considerable impact on social, familial, academic, and occupational functioning (Lezak, 1995). The term "walking wounded" used to describe these individuals seems appropriate, as the effects of the disability often go unnoticed (Wade et al., 1996). Clusters of symptoms in affective, social, cognitive, somatic, and sensory areas may persist following a mild TBI (Warzak et al., 1998).

Moderate brain injury has been defined as a GCS score of 9 to 12 and a PTA duration of one to twenty-four hours (Bigler, 1990). Eight to ten percent of all head injuries fall into this category (Lezak, 1995). An individual with a GCS score of 9 to 12 is able to open his or her eyes, flex his or her muscles, and speak intelligibly, but is unable to sustain a conversation. Significant residual impairments often result due to the trauma. Persistent headaches, memory deficits, and difficulties with adaptive living skills have been reported (Lezak, 1995; Warzak et al., 1998). If frontal lobe damage is sustained (i.e., damage to the anterior portion of the brain), more impulsive behavior and temper outbursts or affective muting may be exhibited, whereas damage to the temporal lobe, located near the middle to top half of one's ears, may result in a true learning disorder. Planning ability and self-monitoring are frequently compromised as well. Students who have experienced a moderate brain injury may require special education and related services.

A severe head injury has been defined as a GCS score of 3 to 8 and a PTA duration of more than 24 hours (Bigler, 1990). When an individual has a GCS of 3 to 8, the ability to open one's eyes, obey commands, or utter recognizable words may be absent. Fewer than 10% of head trauma victims fall into the severely injured category (Lezak, 1995). Attention deficits, behavioral slowing (i.e., both mental processing and response), memory impairments, diminished awareness of one's deficits, and impaired reasoning and verbal fluency are common (Mitiguy, Thompson, & Wasco, 1990). Insight and empathy may be compromised as well. Perseverative behavior may be displayed. Moreover, planning ability and ability to choose among alternatives may be impaired. Acting-out behavior and apathy may be exhibited and social isolation is common (Lezak, 1995). Students who experience a severe brain injury will require a variety of special services. These individuals are highly unlikely to return to the general education classroom without considerable support (Warzak et al., 1998).

Children and adolescents with TBI represent a heterogeneous group with regard to neurobehavioral characteristics and outcomes. These individuals may display a wide variety of difficulties or deficits. The difficulties or deficits may occur in one or more of the following areas: physical functioning, cognitive functioning, behavioral control, and socioemotional functioning.

Physical sequelae (i.e., consequences) associated with traumatic brain injury in children and adolescents include motor deficits, sensory deficits, speech/language dysfunction, seizure disorders, postconcussive syndrome, and fatigue. Motor deficits vary in degree depending upon the site and extent of the damage to the brain. Deficits range from fine volitional movements to severe paralysis. Motor deficits may include hemiplegia (paralysis on one side of the body), hemiparesis (weakness affecting one side of the body), hypotonicity (low muscle tone of trunk and extremities), rigidity, spasticity, tremors, ataxia (inability to coordinate voluntary muscles), and apraxia (problems in planning and executing sequential movement; Begali, 1992; Savage & Wolcott, 1994). Prognosis for a full motor recovery is relatively good in TBI patients and is better than a prognosis for full cognitive recovery. Recovery of motor functions in TBI accidents follows a predictable course with lower limb functioning returning sooner and more completely than upper limb functioning, and proximal (trunk) movements returning sooner and more completely than distal (extremity) movements. Moreover, children with TBI may lose functional use of their dominant hand and will need to learn how to write and perform various hand activities with their nondominant hand. Recovery and refinement of balance reactions or proper weight shifting and control may not occur, however, until after youngsters are discharged to their homes and schools. Thus, physical rehabilitation may be needed in the school setting (Begali, 1992).

Sensory impairments associated with TBI vary in degree depending on the extent of damage to the brain. Sensory deficits may include visual field deficits (i.e., restriction of an individual's field of vision), squinting, defects in color vision, double vision, and tracking disorders (Begali, 1992). Reduced auditory acuity and impaired ability to taste or smell have also been reported (Savage & Wolcott, 1994). Hypersensitivity and hyposensitivity to sensory stimuli have been noted as well (Begali, 1992; Savage & Wolcott, 1994).

Speech/language dysfunction may occur with TBI. Dysarthia characterized by poor phonation skills, hypernasality, poor articulation, slow rate of speech, and monotonic speech is found in some children and adolescents following TBI. Apraxia and aphasia may also result from brain injury. Apraxia involves the inability to execute preplanned, purposeful sequences for oral communication, whereas aphasia results in partial or complete impairment in language comprehension. Aphasic individuals are able to comprehend one or two words or short phrases rather than lengthy discourse (Begali, 1992).

Epilepsy may also occur following a traumatic brain injury. Penetrating head injuries are more likely to produce epilepsy than closed head injuries (Lezak, 1995). Approximately 5% of children and adolescents who experience a closed head injury will develop epilepsy within four years after the injury (Begali, 1992). Seizures are more likely to occur in children under 5 years of age or children who have a severe injury. Seizures usually appear in the first few weeks of recovery after the head trauma. Seizures may have a delayed onset as well and begin approximately 3 months after the injury (Hauser & Hersdorffer, 1990). On the other hand, individuals who experienced a TBI and have had seizures in the past but have been seizure-free for three years can be 95% certain that they will not experience another seizure (Parker, 1990). Antileptic drugs, such as phenytoin, phenobarbital, carbamazepine, and valproate have been prescribed, however, these medications do have negative side effects. Negative side effects vary depending on the medication used and individual. Side effects include sedation, speech disturbances, dizziness, and cognitive impairment (Bagby, 1991).

Besides seizures, a head injury, and specifically a mild head injury, may result in postconcussive syndrome. Approximately 50% of individuals who experience a mild traumatic brain injury report symptoms associated with a postconcussive syndrome three or more months after the injury (Rutherford, 1989). Fatigue, dizziness, headache, and memory deficits are the most common symptoms (Edna & Cappelen, 1987). The syndrome tends to remit with time; however, 4% of the individuals who experience this syndrome report persistent memory problems and 20% report persistent headaches one year after the injury (Wilberger, 1993). Students with postconcussive syndrome may be viewed as lacking in motivation or being noncompliant or defiant in the school setting, when in reality they have attention, concentration, and memory problems.

Chronic fatigue and hypersensitivity to noise are complications that often occur as a result of head trauma (Lezak, 1995). Chronic fatigue prevents individuals with TBI from functioning at their premorbid pace. Shortened school days and reduced course loads are often implemented to combat fatigue. On the other hand, hypersensitivity to noise may produce stress in children with TBI. Certain times of the school day may be overtaxing to these children, such as lunchtime or recess. Thus, reintegration into the more stimulating or hectic parts of the school day must be done gradually.

Cognitive deficits are among the most common sequelae of TBI (Lezak, 1995); however, the pattern of impairment will vary from individual to individual (Crosson, 1992). Intelligence, attention/concentration, language functions, memory, abstract reasoning and judgment, academic achievement and new learning, visual-motor skills, and perception are highly susceptible to dysfunction (Begali, 1992).

A direct relationship between the severity of TBI and degree of cognitive/intellectual impairment has been reported (Oddy, 1993). Drops of 10 points in mean verbal IQ and 30 points in performance IQ on intelligence tests have been noted in children with severe head injuries (Chadwick, Rutter, Shaffer, & Shrout, 1981). Children and adolescents with TBI show more pronounced and persistent deficits in performance IQ than in verbal IQ. As a result, individuals who have experienced a brain injury are more likely to have difficulties learning new skills and solving problems than performing well-learned skills or retrieving factual information. Viewed another way, visual-perceptual and visual-motor skills are less likely to recover fully in comparison to verbal abilities in children with TBI (Begali, 1992). Location of the injury, however, has an effect, as verbal and academic skills tend to be more impaired following left hemisphere damage, whereas visuospatial skills tend to be more impaired following right hemisphere lesions (Wilkening, 1989).

Attention and concentration difficulties are common problems among children and youth following a traumatic brain injury (Lezak, 1995). A poor attention span is not conducive to school learning and is related to a slower rate of information processing (van Zomeren & Brouwer, 1994). Difficulties with sustained attention, selective attention, switching attention, and divided attention have been reported (Haak & Livingston, 1997). These attention difficulties contribute to a variety of cognitive problems including memory, learning, language problems, and social interactions. Off-task behavior is common among these individuals, especially in unstructured classroom settings (Begali, 1992).

Significant expressive and receptive language deficits may follow a severe closed head injury, with expressive language abilities being more affected than receptive (Wilkening, 1989). Two-thirds of the individuals with language deficits, however, recover fully or at least improve to the point where only word-finding or word-naming ability is impaired (Begali, 1992). Verbal fluency, reading comprehension, and writing may also be affected (Lezak, 1995). The speed and ease of verbal production (fluency) and reading comprehension may be hindered. Moreover, students, especially younger students, may struggle with their writing as they are unable recall letter-form movements, how to spell words correctly, or put words together to form sentences (Ewing-Cobbs & Fletcher, 1990). Auditory comprehension may be impaired as well in either a global or selective manner. Specifically, comprehension of classes of words may be affected, such as colors or prepositions (Begali, 1992). Moreover, conversational skills, which require the integration and interplay of linguistic, cognitive, and social skills, are highly susceptible to disruption following TBI in children (Russell, 1993).

Memory disorders are the most common and persistent sequelae of traumatic brain injury (Levin, 1985). When memory deficits persist, these deficits interfere with academic progress. Deficits in new learning or recent memory are more likely to be affected than rote memory. During the early stages of recovery, long-term memory or memory for earlier events return first, followed by memory for events occurring closer to the time of the injury (Lezak, 1995). Retrograde amnesia, a loss of memory for events preceding the injury, may also occur if an individual is rendered unconscious by the head trauma (Begali, 1992). Overall, memory following TBI may be less complete and show less improvement than other cognitive skills.

Conceptual functions, abstract reasoning, and judgment may also be impaired as a result of head trauma. Children who have experienced a mild to severe brain injury or have experienced diffuse damage tend to do poorly on measures of abstract thinking (Lezak, 1995). These individuals have difficulty distinguishing relevant from irrelevant material and essential from nonessential detail. Children and adolescents may have difficulty categorizing and generalizing information or applying rules, such as social rules or rules associated with grammar or mathematics. They may misinterpret social cues, make inappropriate remarks, or miscommunicate their intentions (Begali, 1992).

Academic achievement or new learning may also be affected by head injuries. Inconsistency in academic proficiency has been reported (Begali, 1992). Children with TBI may perform new learned skills accurately one day but are unable to perform the skills correctly the next day. For example, the steps learned to perform long division with precision are forgotten when the child is required to perform the task again on another occasion.

Visual-motor and visual-perceptual problems are also common among children and adolescents who have experienced a brain injury. Visual-motor and visual-perceptual difficulties may include problems with directions, misperceptions, and configural distortions (Lezak, 1995). The ability to attend to detail and part-to-whole conceptualization is likely to be poor. Visual-motor dexterity tends to be slow as well.

Behavioral and socioemotional difficulties are common sequelae following TBI in children and adolescents. These difficulties may be the most prominent features associated with the injury (Oddy, 1993). The behavioral and socioemotional disturbances often exist as premorbid characteristics or tendencies that are exacerbated in response to the injury (Lezak, 1995). Although a well-defined pattern of behavioral and socioemotional difficulties does not exist, there are certain constellations of problems that occur more frequently than others (Haak & Livingston, 1997). Begali (1992) and Savage & Wolcott (1994) reported increases in overactive/hyperactive behavior, impulsivity, aggression, agitation/frustration, disinhibition, oppositional behavior, dependency, and lack of motivation among children and adolescents following TBI. Psychological adjustment difficulties have also been noted, including emotional lability (mood swings), anger, anxiety, withdrawal, and depression. Children and adolescents with TBI may experience difficulty in reading social cues and have poor interpersonal skills. Self-esteem issues may arise as these individuals become aware of or recognize the changes and deficits associated with their injury.

As noted, severity of the injury is related to cognitive deficits; however, the relationship between injury severity and behavioral adjustment is more complex and less understood (Ewing-Cobbs & Fletcher, 1990). Besides severity of the injury and premorbid characteristics, type of damage, site and laterality of lesion, age of onset, gender (Begali, 1992), family adaptation (Wade et al., 1996), and environmental factors influence behavioral outcomes (Farmer & Peterson, 1995).

Initial recovery following a traumatic brain injury tends to occur in a predictable series of stages, ranging from a coma to more purposeful and appropriate behavior (Farmer & Peterson, 1995). An eight-stage scale, the Rancho Los Amigos Level of Cognitive Functioning Scale (Hagen, Malkmus, & Durham, 1981), is used in rehabilitation settings to describe an individual's progress during the early stages of recovery. Children with more severe brain injuries are found at the lower levels of this scale and usually progress more slowly than individuals with less severe head injuries. Individual differences in recovery rates, however, must be taken into consideration, with some individuals recovering more rapidly and others remaining indefinitely at earlier stages of recovery. Attainment of the highest level on the Rancho Los Amigos scale does not necessarily indicate a full recovery to premorbid levels of functioning. Thus, students at each stage of recovery will need support and assistance from the schools.

Recovery from a TBI typically occurs most rapidly during the first 6–12 months following injury. Many children continue to show improvement in abilities 18–36 months postinjury. In some cases, progressive improvement has been observed beyond the 36-month postinjury mark (Boyer & Edwards, 1991).

In 1990, the Individuals with Disabilities Education Act (IDEA), Public Law 101-476 (P.L. 101-476), the main special education law in the United States, added traumatic brain injury as a separate eligibility category. Under this law, children with TBI whose educational performance is adversely affected by their disability are entitled to receive appropriate special education and related services necessary to meet their individual needs. According to P.L. 101-476, now P.L. 105-17, TBI is defined as follows:

Traumatic brain injury means an acquired injury to the brain caused by an external physical force, resulting in total or partial functional disability or psychosocial impairment, or both, that adversely affects a child's educational performance. The term applies to open or closed head injuries resulting in impairments in one or more areas, such as cognition; language; memory; attention; reasoning; abstract thinking; judgment; problem-solving; sensory, perceptual and motor abilities; psychosocial behavior; physical functions; information processing; and speech. The term does not apply to brain injuries that are congenital or degenerative, or brain injuries induced by birth trauma (Federal Register, 1992, p. 44802).

IDEA requires the child's brain injury to be caused by an external physical force not internal trauma (e.g., a stroke or a brain tumor) in order for the student to meet eligibility requirements. Professionals continue to debate the appropriateness of excluding children whose brain injuries are the result of internal trauma. Some states, however, have opted to identify and classify a broader range of children and adolescents whose injuries are the result of either an external physical force or internal trauma (Rapp, 1999). Thus, a significant amount of variability exists across states regarding educational policy and eligibility criteria for students with TBI (Katsiyannis & Conderman, 1994). State rules and regulations should be consulted to determine whether children whose brain injuries are the result of internal trauma are eligible for services under the TBI category or the more generic IDEA category of Other Health Impaired (OHI).

Whatever the etiology, children with brain injuries whose educational performance is adversely affected by their injuries are entitled to an evaluation to assess eligibility for special education. If eligible for special education and related services under the TBI or OHI category, an individualized educational program (IEP) must be developed. The purpose of the IEP is to specify the student's short- and long-term educational needs.

For those individuals with TBI who are not eligible for special education and related services under IDEA, Section 504 of the Vocational Rehabilitation Act of 1973, a civil rights law, may provide sufficient services and protections in the school setting. Section 504 outlines the school district's responsibility to provide educational accommodations and related services to enable disabled students to have equal access to all publicly funded programs available to their nondisabled peers. Through a written plan, the school's 504 team outlines the educational accommodations and related services necessary, so a disabled student will be able to access and benefit from his or her educational program.

Assessment plays a prominent role in determining eligibility and in the treatment paradigm of traumatic brain injured children and adolescents (Begali, 1992). Assessment results provide invaluable information and help determine educational placement, related services, and instructional goals. Psychoeducational evaluations, ecological evaluations, neuropsychological evaluations, and neurological evaluations should be conducted and results should be integrated in order to determine appropriate accommodations and modifications needed in the school environment to provide optimal learning experiences for children and adolescents with TBI. Standardized testing supplemented with testing of the limits and process procedures will provide invaluable information for designing appropriate accommodations and interventions (Kaplan, 1988).

A standard psychoeducational evaluation consists of an intelligence test, achievement test, and behavioral rating scales (Rapp, 1999). A psychoeducational evaluation can predict future learning potential and learning disabilities under normal circumstances; however, children and adolescents with TBI are more likely to have deficits in attention and concentration (Kaufmann, Fletcher, Levin, Miner, & Ewing-Cobb, 1993), retaining and retrieving new learning (Jaffe et al., 1993), organization and problem solving (Levin et al., 1988), and changes in behavior (Deaton, 1994), which will not be appropriately assessed using only a standard psychoeducational battery (Reitan & Wolfson, 1992). A psychoeducational evaluation may be appropriate and useful, however, in determining whether a student has lost any previous learned information (Rapp, 1999).

In contrast, a neuropsychological evaluation assesses a broad range of brain-behavior relationships, current cognitive processes, and new learning. Individual strengths and weaknesses can be identified, and degree of deficits approximated. Educational and vocational program goals can be developed, and practical implications of brain injury upon everyday functioning can be assessed. Neuropsychological evaluations as well as neurological evaluations, consisting of physical assessments conducted by medical specialists, should be used to augment standard psychological assessments (Goldstein, 1984). A neuropsychological evaluation should be conducted before the child reenters school and reevaluations should be conducted frequently during the first 18–24 months following the injury (Rapp, 1999). Begali (1992) recommends conducting a reevaluation every three to six months for the first two years postinjury. Following the first or second year postinjury, reevaluations should be conducted before major school transitions, when new or different problems arise, or lack of educational progress is reported (Rapp, 1999).

Ecological evaluations consist of observations of children or adolescents in a variety of settings. Students with TBI usually have difficulty monitoring and regulating their own behavior in the real world, generalizing skills and abilities, and cognitive organization. Formal testing conducted in a structured setting cannot assess with any degree of accuracy any difficulties in the aforementioned areas nor does formal testing have any resemblance to the real world or classroom environment. Thus, real world observational assessments complement formal testing. Observations of children and adolescents with TBI provide a means of monitoring these students' progress and evaluat-

ing the appropriateness of educational programs and interventions developed for these individuals (Rapp, 1999). Observations should be conducted on a frequent basis.

Informal testing such as curriculum-based and criterion-based assessment is also recommended. Curriculum-based and criterion-based assessment may be used to guide instructional efforts and provide feedback. Program deficiencies can be identified and revision of instructional objectives may be made based on the results of frequent informal testing in the classroom.

In the classroom, a child or adolescent with TBI can be a real challenge. Educators may feel stymied in their efforts to reintegrate the child or adolescent with TBI into the school setting. Educational success for a child with TBI depends not only on the child but also on the teacher who is knowledgeable about brain injury, has a feeling of self-efficacy or self-competence in the classroom, and fosters a positive teacher-student relationship with the child (Farmer & Peterson, 1995).

Many schools have adopted home-school consultation models to address the educational needs of children with TBI. In home-school consultation (e.g., Conjoint Behavioral Consultation; Sheridan, Kratochwill, & Bergen, 1996), a consultant (i.e., a school psychologist) works with consultees (i.e., teachers and parents) to address the difficulties encountered by the child. Through collaborative consultation, parents and the school engage in a mutual process that leads to a reorganization around the child who has a brain injury. An empowerment model is adopted where parents take an active and central role in the educational programming for their child, including programs to meet their child's academic, social, emotional, behavioral, and vocational needs. Parents and school personnel share equally in the identification and prioritization of issues to be addressed through individual interventions. Parents and teachers along with school specialists develop and implement intervention strategies to address the issues of concern. The child's progress is monitored and modifications are made when needed. Continued dialogue between the school and home is encouraged to ensure the best possible treatment regimen for the child (Conoley & Sheridan, 1997).

Classroom placement is one of the first questions raised when a child with TBI is discharged from the hospital or rehabilitation unit. School placement may range from participation in the regular education classroom with no special supports to residential placement, depending on the child's age and learning needs (Savage, 1991). Initially, a self-contained classroom may be needed to prevent overstimulation and to increase teacher contact. Shorter school days and a reduced workload may also be needed to offset fatigue (Farmer & Peterson, 1995).

Limited research exists on the best instructional methods to use with traumatic brain injured children. Thus, sound teaching practices used with other disabled learners is what is currently recommended for use with this heterogeneous group of learners (Begali, 1992). Systematic and structured programs and compensatory training are recommended. Direct instruction in the students' most intact sensory modality is suggested to optimize children's learning. Tape recording of materials or duplicates of other students' notes may be helpful when poor note-taking skills exist. To monitor progress in learning, assignment notebooks reviewed on a regular basis by teachers and parents may also be helpful. Extended deadlines, breakdown of tasks into smaller units, reduced workload, and alternate means of assessment may need to be implemented. Establishment of routine in the classroom is extremely important and will be required, as TBI children need consistency (D'Amato & Rothlisberg, 1997). For reading recovery, material should be presented initially in a vertical format with a gradual transition to a horizontal presentation. Graph or lined paper turned sideways is suggested for youngsters who are having difficulties with mathematical computations due to visual-spatial or graphomotor difficulties. Multiple choice formats or matching formats are recommended for students with memory problems, whereas oral exams are suggested for children with problems in written expression (Begali, 1992).

As noted earlier, attention/concentration difficulties affect a number of children with TBI. A variety of intervention strategies have been suggested to address attention/concentration difficulties, including environmental modifications, behavioral approaches, direct retraining approaches, biofeedback training, metacognitive and self-regulatory strategies (Mateer, Kerns, & Eso, 1997) and stimulant medication (Begali, 1992). Perhaps the simplest approach to help children with TBI attend in the classroom is to make environmental modifications. Environmental modifications may be as simple as having preferential seating arrangements, cueing/redirecting a child when off-task, or presenting information in smaller units with multiple repetition. Behavioral approaches to increase attending may involve the implementation of a response-cost program in which privileges are taken away for lack of attending. Examples of direct retraining approaches are computer-based activities, pencil and paper exercises, and other manipulatives to allow children to practice and exercise a variety of attention-dependent skills or processes. Self-monitoring, on the other hand, falls under the rubric of self-regulatory strategies where children monitor their own attending behaviors.

A variety of strategies have also been suggested to remedy memory deficits. Memory deficits are one of the major cognitive sequelae associated with traumatic brain injuries. Internal strategies such as mnemonics, verbal strategies, and visual imagery may prove to be beneficial. External aids may also be helpful, as they may be used to extend or supplement the internal storage mechanisms. Examples of external aids include computer-based systems, paging systems, electronic organizers, and memory notebooks (Mateer et al., 1997). Direct instruction that is presented in a logical and unambiguous format using behavioral techniques, such as task analysis, modeling, shaping, reinforcement of appropriate responses, and continuous assessment have proven to be effective with a wide range of learners, including students with TBI (Colvin, 1990).

Motor deficits, sensory deficits, language/speech difficulties, and perceptual problems have also been reported as common sequelae of traumatic brain injured children. Microcomputer-assisted training, paper and pencil cancellation tasks, mazes, visual closure worksheets, and eye-hand retraining techniques may be useful in addressing perceptual problems (Begali, 1992). In contrast, strategies to address language-processing problems may include pairing verbal with written instructions, avoiding figurative language, providing ample time to process information, and varying one's voice and intonation when repeating instructions (Blosser & DePompei, 1989). Direct remediation of specific language/speech deficits or compensatory training may also be needed. Consultation with medical specialists, however, may be the best strategy to use to address sensory deficits. Likewise, consultation with physical and occupational therapists is recommended to address motor deficits.

Social functioning may be impaired when individuals experience a brain injury. TBI can interfere with social functioning for a variety of reasons, including poor communication skills, limited mobility, decreased social cognition, and aggressive behavior. Social skills training and group activities such as cooperative learning activities may be beneficial in helping children with TBI to improve their social competency and acceptance by peers (Farmer & Peterson, 1995).

Behavioral sequelae following TBI are diverse. Both externalizing (e.g., aggression, noncompliance, and anger outbursts) and internalizing (e.g., anxiety and depression) behaviors have been reported (Begali, 1992). Intervention strategies to address externalizing behaviors in the classroom environment include public posting of classroom rules and applying appropriate consequences for compliant and noncompliant behavior. Other classroom management strategies that have proven effective in reducing externalizing behaviors include teacher reprimands, precision requests, and time out. Effective use of teacher praise, on the other hand, can increase the frequency of appropriate behaviors (Kehle, Clark, & Jenson, 1997).

The predominant psychological issue faced by children and adolescents with TBI and their families is loss (Begali, 1992). The family may mourn the loss of the individual they once knew (Lezak, 1995). In other words, personality changes often accompany a traumatic brain injury. The child or members of the child's family may display shock, denial, grief, depression, and anxiety as a result of the changes. Thus, education about TBI, individual counseling for the child, family support and advocacy, and/or family therapy for the entire family, including siblings, may be needed to help the child and family cope with the changes that have occurred in the aftermath of the injury (Conoley & Sheridan, 1997).

A traumatic brain injury can be devastating not only to the child but also to the child's family. Following traumatic brain injury, a child's reintegration into the school setting can be a challenging experience. Comprehensive assessment and intervention strategies are needed to enhance the child's outcome in all areas of functioning. Collaboration among parents, educators, hospital/rehabilitation staff, and community members is needed in order to help these children and adolescents achieve independence, reach their academic potential, and lead satisfying and quality lives (Farmer & Peterson, 1995).

REFERENCES

Alves, W. M., & James, J. A. (1985). Mild brain injury: Damage and outcome. In D. P. Beck & J. T. Povlishock (Eds.), *Central nervous system trauma: Status report-1985*. Washington, DC: National Institutes of Health.

Bagby, G. (1991). Advances in anticonvulsant therapy. *Headlines*, 2–5, 7–8.

Begali, V. (1992). *Head injury in children and adolescents*. Brandon, VT: Clinical Psychology Publishing Company.

Bigler, E. D. (1990). *Traumatic brain injury*. Austin, TX: Pro-Ed.

Binder, L. M. (1986). Persisting symptoms after mild head injury: A review of the postconcussive syndrome. *Journal of Clinical and Experimental Neuropsychology, 8*(4), 323–346.

Blosser, J., & DePompei, R. (1989). The head injured student returns to school: Recognizing and treating deficits. *Topics in Language Disorders, 9*(2), 67–77.

Boyer, M. G., & Edwards, P. (1991). Outcome 1 to 3 years after severe traumatic brain injury in children and adolescents. *Injury, 22*(4), 315–320.

Brain Injury Association. (1997). *Pediatric brain injury*, [fact sheet]. Alexandria, VA: Author.

Brandstater, M. E., Bontke, C. F., Cobble, N. D., & Horn, L. J. (1991). Rehabilitation in brain disorders: Specific disorders. *Archives of Physical Medicine and Rehabilitation, 72*, S332–S340.

Bruce, D. A., & Zimmermann, R. A. (1989). Shaken impact syndrome. *Pediatric Annals, 18*, 482–494.

Chadwick, O., Rutter, M., Shaffer, D., & Shrout, P. E. (1981). A prospective study of children with head injuries: IV. Specific cognitive deficits. *Journal of Clinical Neuropsychology, 3*, 101–120.

Colvin, G. (1990). Procedures for preventing serious acting-out behavior in the classroom. *Direct Instruction Newsletter, 9*, 27–30.

Conoley, J. C., & Sheridan, S. M. (1997). Pediatric traumatic brain injury: Challenges and interventions for families. In E. D. Bigler, E. Clark, & J. E. Farmer (Eds.), *Childhood traumatic*

brain injury: Diagnosis, assessment, and intervention (pp. 177–189). Austin, TX: Pro-Ed.

Crosson, B. A. (1992). *Subcortical functions in language and memory*. New York: Guilford.

Crouchman, M. (1990). Head injury: How community pediatricians can help. *Archives of Diseases in Children, 65*, 1286–1287.

Dalby, P. R., & Obrzut, J. E. (1991). Epidemiological characteristics and sequelae of closed head-injured children and adolescents: A review. *Developmental Neuropsychology, 7*, 35–68.

D'Amato, R. C., & Rothlisberg, B. A. (1997). How education should respond to students with traumatic brain injury. In E. D. Bigler, E. Clark, & J. E. Farmer (Eds.), *Childhood traumatic brain injury: Diagnosis, assessment, and intervention* (pp. 213–237). Austin, TX: Pro-Ed.

Deaton, A. V. (1994). Changing the behaviors of students with acquired brain injuries. In R. C. Savage & G. F. Wolcott (Eds.), *Educational dimensions of acquired brain injury* (pp. 257–275). Austin, TX: Pro-Ed.

Donders, J. (1994). Academic placement after traumatic brain injury. *Journal of School Psychology, 32*, 53–65.

Edna, T. H., & Cappelen, J. (1987). Late post-concussional symptoms in traumatic head injury. An analysis of frequency and risk factors. *Acta Neuropsychologica, 86*, 12–17.

Ewing-Cobbs, L., & Fletcher, J. M. (1990). Neuropsychological assessment of traumatic brain injury in children. In E. D. Bigler (Ed.), *Traumatic brain injury* (pp. 107–128). Austin, TX: Pro-Ed.

Ewing-Cobbs, L., Levin, H. S., Fletcher, J. M., Miner, M. E., & Eisenberg, H. M. (1989). Posttraumatic amnesia in head-injured children: Assessment and outcome. *Journal of Clinical and Experimental Neuropsychology, 11*, 58.

Farmer, J. E. (1997). Epilogue: An ecological systems approach to childhood traumatic brain injury. In E. D. Bigler, E. Clark, & J. E. Farmer (Eds.), *Childhood traumatic brain injury: Diagnosis, assessment, and intervention* (pp. 261–275). Austin, TX: Pro-Ed.

Farmer, J. E., Clippard, D. S., Wiemann, Y. L., Wright, E., & Owings, S. (1997). Assessing children with traumatic brain injury during rehabilitation: Promoting school and community reentry. In E. D. Bigler, E. Clark, & J. E. Farmer (Eds.), *Childhood traumatic brain injury: Diagnosis, assessment, and intervention* (pp. 33–62). Austin, TX: Pro-Ed.

Farmer, J. E., & Peterson, L. (1995). Pediatric traumatic brain injury: Promoting successful school reentry. *School Psychology Review, 24*(2), 230–243.

Fay, G. C., Jaffe, K. M., Polissar, N. L., Liao, S., Martin, K. M., Shurtleff, H. A., Rivara, J. B., & Winn, H. R. (1993). Mild pediatric traumatic brain injury: A cohort study. *Archives of Physical Medicine and Rehabilitation, 74*, 895–901.

Federal Register. (1992, September 9). Individuals with Disabilities Education Act (IDEA), U.S. Department of Education Regulations. Washington, DC: U.S. Government Printing Office.

Frankowski, R. F., Annegers, J. F., & Whitman, S. (1985). Epidemiological and descriptive studies: Part I. In D. Becker & J. T. Povlishock (Eds.), *Central nervous system trauma: Status report* (pp. 33–45). Bethesda, MD: National Institutes of

Health, National Institute of Neurological and Communicative Disorders and Stroke.

Goldstein, F. C., & Levin, H. S. (1990). Epidemiology of traumatic brain injury: Incidence, clinical characteristics, and risk factors. In E. D. Bigler (Ed), *Traumatic brain injury* (pp. 51–67). Austin, TX: Pro-Ed.

Goldstein, G. (1984). Neuropsychological assessment. In G. Goldstein & M. Hersen (Eds.), *Handbook of psychological assessment* (pp. 181–211). New York: Pergamon Press.

Haak, R. A., & Livingston, R. B. (1997). Treating traumatic brain injury in the school: Mandates and methods. In C. R. Reynolds & E. Fletcher-Janzen (Eds.), *Handbook of clinical child neuropsychology* (2nd ed., 482–505). New York: Plenum.

Hagen, C., Malkmus, D., & Durham, P. (1981). *Rancho los amigos: Levels of cognitive functioning*. Downey, CA: Professional Staff Association.

Harrington, D. (1990). Educational strategies. In M. Rosenthal, E. Griffith, M. Bond, & J. E. Miller (Eds.), *Rehabilitation of the adult and child with traumatic brain injury* (2nd ed., pp. 476–492). Philadelphia: Davis.

Hauser, W. A., & Hesdorffer, D. C. (1990). *Epilepsy: Frequency, causes and consequences*. Landover, MD: Epilepsy Foundation of America.

Jaffe, K. M., Fay, G. C., Polissar, N. L., Martin, K. M., Shurtleff, H., Rivara, J. B., & Winn, H. R. (1993). Severity of pediatric traumatic brain injury and neurobehavioral recovery at one year-A cohort study. *Archives of Physical Medicine and Rehabilitation, 74*, 587–595.

Kaplan, E. (1988). A process approach to neuropsychological assessment. In T. Boll & B. K. Bryant (Eds.), *Clinical neuropsychology and brain function: Research, measurement, and practice* (pp. 129–167). Washington, DC: American Psychological Association.

Katsiyannis, A., & Conderman, G. (1994). Serving students with traumatic brain injury: A national survey. *Remedial and Special Education, 15*, 319–325.

Katz, D. I. (1992). Neuropathology and neurobehavioral recovery from closed head injury. *Journal of Head Trauma Rehabilitation, 7*, 1–15.

Kaufmann, P. M., Fletcher, J. M., Levin, H. S., Miner, M. E., & Ewing-Cobbs, L. (1993). Attentional disturbance after pediatric closed head injury. *Journal of Child Neurology, 8*, 348–353.

Kehle, T. J., Clark, E., & Jenson, W. R. (1997). Interventions for students with traumatic brain injury: Managing behavioral disturbances. In E. D. Bigler, E. Clark, & J. E. Farmer (Eds.), *Childhood traumatic brain injury: Diagnosis, assessment, and intervention* (pp. 135–152). Austin, TX: Pro-Ed.

Kraus, J. F., Black, M. A., Hessol, N., Ley, P., Rokaw, W., & Sullivan, C. (1984). The incidence of acute brain injury and serious impairments in a defined population. *American Journal of Epidemiology, 119*, 186–201.

Kreutzer, J. S., Devany, C. W., Myers, S. L., & Marwitz, J. H. (1991). Neurobehavioral outcome following brain injury. In J. S. Kreutzer & P. H. Wehman (Eds.), *Cognitive rehabilitation for persons with traumatic brain injury: A functional approach*. Baltimore: Brookes.

Lehr, E. (1990). Incidence and etiology. In E. Lehr (Ed.), *Psychological management of traumatic brain injuries in children and adolescents* (pp. 1–98). Rockville, MD: Aspen.

Lehr, E., & Savage, R. (1990). Community and school integration from a developmental perspective. In J. Kreutzer & P. Wehman (Eds.), *Community integration following traumatic brain injury* (pp. 301–310). Baltimore: Brookes.

Levin, H. S. (1985). Outcome after head injury: Part II. In D. Becker & J. T. Povlishock (Eds.), *Central nervous system trauma: Status report* (pp. 281–303). Bethesda, MD: National Institutes of Health, National Institute of Neurological and Communicative Disorders and Stroke.

Levin, H. S., High, W. M., Ewing-Cobbs, L., Fletcher, J. M., Eisenberg, H. M., Miner, M. E., & Goldstein, F. C. (1988). Memory functioning during the first year after closed head injury in children and adolescents. *Neurosurgery, 22*, 1043–1052.

Levin, H. S., Mendelsohn, D., Lilly, M. A., Fletcher, J. M., Culhane, K. A., Chapman, S. B., Harward, H., Kusnerik, L., Bruce, D., & Eisenberg, H. M. (1994). Tower of London performance in relation to magnetic resonance imaging following closed head injury in children. *Neuropsychology, 8*, 171–179.

Lezak, M. D. (1995). *Neuropsychological assessment* (3rd ed.). New York: Oxford.

Luerssen, T. G. (1991). Head injuries in children. *Neurosurgery Clinics of North America, 2*, 399–410.

Mateer, C. A., Kerns, K. A., & Eso, K. L. (1997). Management of attention and memory disorders following traumatic brain injury. In E. D. Bigler, E. Clark, & J. E. Farmer (Eds.), *Childhood traumatic brain injury: Diagnosis, assessment, and intervention* (pp. 153–175). Austin, TX: Pro-Ed.

Michaud, L. J., Rivara, F. P., Jaffe, K. M., Fay, G., & Dailey, J. L. (1993). Traumatic brain injury as a risk factor for behavioral disorders in children. *Archives of Physical Medicine and Rehabilitation, 74*, 368–375.

Mira, M. P., Tucker, B. F., & Tyler, J. S. (1992). *Traumatic brain injury in children and adolescents: A sourcebook for schools*. Austin, TX: Pro-Ed.

Mitiguy, J. S., Thompson, G., & Wasco, J. (1990). *Understanding brain injury: Acute hospitalization*. Lynn, MA: New Medico.

Naugle, R. I. (1990). Epidemiology of traumatic brain injury in adults. In E. D. Bigler (Ed.), *Traumatic brain injury*. Austin, TX: Pro-Ed.

North, B. (1984). *Jamieson's first notebook of head injury* (3rd ed.). London: Butterworths.

Oddy, M. (1993). Head injury during childhood. *Neuropsychological Rehabilitation, 3*, 301–320.

Pang, D. (1985). Pathophysiologic correlations of neurobehavioral syndromes following closed head injury. In M. Ylvisaker (Ed.), *Head injury rehabilitation: Children and adolescents* (pp. 3–71). San Diego, CA: College-Hill Press.

Parker, R. S. (1990). *Traumatic brain injury and neuropsychological impairment: Sensorimotor, cognitive, emotional and adaptive problems of children and adults*. New York: Springer-Verlag.

Raimondi, A. J., & Hirschauer, J. (1984). Head injury in the infant and toddler. *Child's Brain, 11*, 12–35.

Rapp, D. L. (1999). Interventions for integrating children with

traumatic brain injuries into their schools. In C. R. Reynolds &
T. B. Gutkin (Eds.), *The handbook of school psychology* (3rd
ed., pp. 863–884). New York: Wiley.

Reitan, R. M., & Wolfson, D. (1992). *Neuropsychological evaluation of older children*. South Tucson, AZ: Neuropsychology
Press.

Research and Training Center in Rehabilitation and Childhood
Trauma. (1993). *National pediatric trauma registry*. Boston:
Tufts University of Medicine, New England Medical Center.

Russell, N. K. (1993). Educational considerations in traumatic
brain injury: The role of the speech-language pathologist. *Language, Speech, and Hearing Services in the Schools, 24,*
267–275.

Rutherford, W. H. (1989). In H. S. Levin, H. M. Eisenberg, & A. L.
Benton (Eds.), *Mild head injury*. New York: Oxford University
Press.

Rutter, M., Chadwick, O., Shaffer, D., & Brown, G. (1980). A
prospective study of children with head injuries: I. Design and
methods. *Psychological Medicine, 10,* 633–645.

Savage, R. C. (1991). Identification, classification, and placement
issues for students with traumatic brain injuries. *Journal of
Head Trauma Rehabilitation, 6*(1), 1–9.

Savage, R. C., & Wolcott, G. F. (Eds.). (1994). *Educational dimensions of acquired brain injury*. Austin, TX: Pro-Ed.

Sheridan, S. M., Kratochwill, T. R., & Bergen, J. R. (1996). *Conjoint behavioral consultation: A procedural manual*. New York:
Plenum.

Teasdale, G., & Jennett, B. (1974). Assessment of coma and impaired consciousness: A practical scale. *Lancet, 2,* 81–84.

VanZomeren, A. H., & Brouwer, W. H. (1994). *Clinical neuropsychology of attention*. London: Oxford University Press.

Vernon-Levett, P. (1991). Head injuries in children. *Critical Care
Nursing Clinics of North America, 3,* 411–421.

Wade, S. L., Taylor, G., Drotar, D., Stancin, T., & Yeates, K. O.
(1996). Childhood traumatic brain injury: Initial impact on the
family, *Journal of Learning Disabilities, 29*(6), 652–661.

Ward, J. D., Chisholm, A. H., Prince, V. T., Gilman, C. B., &
Hawkins, A. M. (1994). Penetrating head injury. *Critical Care
Nursing Quarterly, 17,* 79–89.

Warzak, W. J., Mayfield, J., & McAllister, J. (1998). Central nervous system dysfunction: Brain injury, postconcussive syndrome, and seizure disorder. In T. S. Watson & F. Gresham
(Eds.), *Handbook of child behavior therapy* (pp. 287–309). New
York: Plenum.

Wilberger, J. E. (1993). Minor head injuries in American football:
Prevention of long term sequelae. *Sports Medicine, 15,* 338–343.

Wilkening, G. N. (1989). Techniques of localization in child neu-
ropsychology. In C. R. Reynolds & E. Fletcher-Janzen (Eds.),
Handbook of clinical child neuropsychology (pp. 291–310).
New York: Plenum.

Ylvisaker, M. (1993). Communication outcome in children and
adolescents with traumatic brain injury. *Neuropsychological
Rehabilitation, 3,* 367–387.

PATRICIA A. LOWE
CECIL R. REYNOLDS
Texas A & M University

TRAUMATIC BRAIN INJURY IN CHILDREN

Incidence & Problems

Traumatic brain injury (TBI) in children remains as a major health problem and has been reported to be the leading
cause of death between the ages of 2 to 44 (Hay, 1967). Actual incidence records are only available for those with
more severe injuries who sought medical treatment but it
is estimated that approximately 15,000 suffer severe traumatic brain injury in the US each year (Di Scala et al.,
1991). Severe TBI produces many observable changes, and
even more changes in a child's cognitive functions. In less
severe TBI, or later in the recovery, the child may appear
to be functioning normally but subtle cognitive deficits
may remain which influence behavior in diffuse ways or
which remain unnoticed until later stages of development
are reached.

Assessment of the nature and extent of the consequences of TBI in children is more difficult and challenging
than with adults, yet effective treatment and remediation
requires an objective appraisal of cognitive strengths and
weaknesses. Underestimating the capacity of recovery
may lead to delayed rehabilitation with efforts aimed at
the consequences of the injury rather than at preventative
therapy (Stover & Zeiger, 1976). On the other hand, underestimating the extent of the impairment may lead to excessive stress or difficulty in emotional adjustment (Taylor
et al., 1995). Clearly, even mild head injury can become a
significant disruptive event to a child and his or her family
unless the consequences are properly evaluated and effective rehabilitation is instituted.

Development and Time to Recovery

For a time it was generally believed that TBI sustained
early in life was associated with less deleterious effects
(Kennard principle). Children were thought to have a more
resilient nervous system since they appear to recover more
rapidly than adults, experience less persistent symptoms
(Black et al., 1969), and seldom report post-concussion
symptoms (Rutter et al., 1983). However, this notion is at
best only partially accurate (Bolter & Long, 1985). Recent
research has suggested that the likelihood of residual cognitive deficits is greater with early injury (Max et al. 1997;
Taylor & Alden, 1997).

Children can "grow out" of some early deficits, but not
others. In some cases, dysfunction may only appear later
in the course of development (Teuber & Rudel, 1962; Goldman, 1971, 1972, 1974; Wrightson et al., 1995). For example, damage to the immature frontal lobes of a young
child may not produce behavioral manifestations until
much later in development when those cortical areas
would normally assume functional prominence (Russell,
1959). It is likely that the effects of head injury in children

combine with other functions in their development and may have widespread effects (Korkman, 1980). Age is only one variable of importance in determining the extent of recovery. In addition to age, one must consider location, nature, and the extent of the injury in order to determine the effects of the injury upon subsequent behavior.

Severity of Injury

The pathophysiology of brain injury is similar in children and adults. Severity of injury is usually measured by duration of coma and/or post-traumatic amnesia (PTA), although both are difficult to assess in younger children (Leigh, 1979). As a general guide, children experiencing coma of over 7 days seldom recover to their pre-injury level. Even coma of less than 7 days or PTA of less than 3 weeks is usually associated with permanent cognitive impairment (Stover & Zeiger, 1976).

Cognitive Consequences

After severe head injury, obviously impaired physical functions tend to improve rapidly, whereas cognitive dysfunction may resolve less quickly. Head injury frequently affects intelligence, memory, speech, language, and other functions. The effects upon cognitive functions are pervasive during the first 6 months following injury (Levin & Eisenberg, 1979). Later in recovery, the effects are often characterized by slowed information processing, poor problem solving ability, impulsivity, distractibility, and poor stress tolerance with irritability and emotional lability. In addition, researchers have documented memory impairment, decreased visuospatial processing (Lord-Maes & Obrzut, 1996) and decreased attentional shift (Ewing-Cobbs et al. 1998). Common behavioral symptoms also include hyperkinesis (32%), discipline problems (10%), and lethargy (87%; Black, 1969), as well as ADHD (Max et al., 1998). These effects are observed in school performance and in neuropsychological testing. More important is the finding that children suffering even mild head trauma, with little or no coma and/or PTA, demonstrate attenuated cognitive abilities.

Children are undergoing significant developmental changes and even mild TBI can cause developmental setbacks leading to immature behaviors. Such damage may cause a loss of previously mastered skills and compromise future ability for the acquisition of new skills.

Emotional and Social Factors

In addition to physical impairment and cognitive dysfunction, the brain injured child is at risk for the development of emotional problems (Max et al., 1998). The risks are greater in those with low premorbid I.Q., from low socioeconomic class, or from broken homes (Rutter et al., 1983).

Pre-injury family environment has also been shown to affect recovery (Yeates et al., 1997). Survivors of TBI are at a greater risk of developing psychiatric disorders as well, which is positively correlated with injury severity (Max et al., 1997, 1998).

Assessment Strategies

Proper assessment strategies leading into the development and enactment of an individually-tailored intervention plan are critical in facilitating the successful reentry of the brain injured child into his premorbid environment. These assessment strategies focus on cognitive, emotional, and environmental factors which interact and shape subsequent behavior. Initial assessment should focus on the neuropsychological consequences of the injury. This assessment examines the relationship between the functioning of the brain and the cognitive processing abilities exhibited by the child. This assessment of cognitive abilities, coupled with a consideration of the type and severity of injury, developmental factors, and emotional functioning of the child, affords a view of basic strengths and weaknesses in cognitive functioning which can serve to identify initial intervention strategies.

Repeated neuropsychological assessments are not necessary in most cases. Rather, a psychoeducational assessment should be of greater value later in recovery. Aptitude and achievement tests are not sensitive to the impact of a brain injury on functioning immediately following a TBI. However, they become critical components later in the assessment process for evaluating the impact of the child's processing strengths and weakness on school performance. The comparison of performance on aptitude and achievement tests given before and after the injury is valuable in evaluating changes in the child's ability to acquire and retain new information.

The child's emotional functioning and reaction to the environment in daily life is another key component of the assessment process. Observation of the child at home, within class, while interacting with peers, and so on is most likely to add to an understanding of the child's problems within these environments. Other assessment strategies include interviewing and utilizing scales of adaptive and emotional functioning. Evaluation of the appropriateness of the child's environment to his level of cognitive ability, emotional functioning, and behavioral control is needed.

Intervention Strategies

Examination of interacting cognitive, emotional, and environmental factors should be considered in the development of treatment plans. Traditional behavior management strategies may be helpful, but not completely adequate, for aiding the recovery of function in children with TBI. Because individuals with TBI often exhibit impaired concentration and memory and also have a low tolerance for frustration, environmental considerations must be made. Children with TBI should be afforded less distracting and more structured environments for study. Allowing children more time to complete their tasks can combat slowed processing. The lowered stamina of a child with TBI can be accommodated by providing frequent breaks and shortening the school day. The child's reentry into the normal school situation should be a gradual process. Care should be taken to insure that they are working at a level that will produce some successes. Resources such as special education and speech/language specialists should be utilized as needed. Additionally, consideration of emotional functioning should determine the need for psychological intervention. The reader is referred to a more extensive discussion of an ecological model of assessment and intervention (Farmer & Peterson, 1995, Long & Ross, 1992, Sbordone & Long, 1996).

REFERENCES

Black, P., Jeffries, J. J., Blumer, D., Wellner, A., & Walker, A. E. (1969). The postraumatic syndrome in children. In A. E. Walker, W. F. Caveness, & M. Critchley, (Eds.), *Late effects of head injury* (pp. 142–149). Springfield, Illinois: Thomas.

Bolter, J. F., & Long, C. J. (1985). Methodological issues in research in developmental neuropsychology. In L. C. Hartlage & C. F. Telzrow (Eds.), *The neuropsychology of individual differences* (pp. 41–59). New York: Plenum.

Di Scala, C., Osberg, J. S., Gans, B. M., Chin, L. J., and Grant, C. C. (1991). Children with traumatic head injury: morbidity and postacute treatment. *Archives of Physical Medicine and Rehabilitation, 72,* 662–666.

Ewing-Cobbs, L., Prasad, M., Fletcher, J. M., Levin, H. S., Miner, M. E., & Eisenberg, H. M. (1998). Attention after pediatric traumatic brain injury: a multidimensional assessment. *Child Neuropsychology, 4*(1), 35–48.

Farmer, J. E., & Peterson, L. (1995). Pediatric traumatic brain injury: promoting successful school reentry. *School Psychology Review, 24*(2), 230–243.

Goldman, P. (1971). Functional development of the prefrontal cortex in early life and the problem of neuronal plasticity. *Experimental Neurology, 3,* 366–387.

Goldman, P. S. (1972). Developmental determinants of cortical plasticity. *Acta Neurobiologica Experimentalis, 32,* 495–511.

Goldman, P. (1974). An alternative to developmental plasticity: Heterology of CNS structures in infants and adults. In D. Stein, J. Rosen, & N. Butters (Eds.), *Plasticity and recovery of function in the central nervous system* (p. 109). New York: Academic.

Hay, R. (1967). Head injuries. *Canadian Medical Association Journal, 97,* 1364–1368.

Korkman, M. An attempt to adapt methods of Luria for diagnosis of cognitive deficits in children. Convention paper INS, 1980.

Kraus, J. F. (1995). Epidemiological features of brain injury in children: Occurrence, children at risk, causes and manner of injury, severity, and outcomes. In S. H. Broman & M. E. Michel (Eds.), *Traumatic head injury in children* (pp. 22–39). New York: Oxford University Press.

Leigh, D. (1979). Psychiatric aspects of head injury. *Psychiatric Digest,* 21–34. Levin, H. S. & Eisenberg, H. M. (1979). Neuropsychological impairment after closed head injury in children and adolescents. *Journal of Pediatric Psychology, 4,* 389–402.

Long, C. J., & Ross, L. K., (1992). *Handbook of head trauma: Acute care to recovery.* New York: Plenum.

Lord-Maes, J., & Obrzut, J. E. (1996). Neuropsychological consequences of traumatic brain injury in children and adolescents. *Journal of Learning Disabilities, 29*(6), 609–617.

Max, J. E., Lindgren, S. D., Knutson, C., Pearson, C. S., Ihrig, D., & Welborn, A. (1997). Child and adolescent traumatic brain injury: Psychiatric findings from a pediatric outpatient specialty clinic. *Brain Injury, 11*(10), 699–711.

Max, J. E, Koele, S. L., Smith, W. L., Sato, Y., Lindgren, S. D., Robin, D. A., & Arndt, S. (1998). Psychiatric disorders in children and adolescents after severe traumatic brain injury: A controlled study. *Journal of the American Academy of Child and Adolescent Psychiatry, 37*(8), 832–840.

Max, J. E., Arndt, S., Castillo, C. S., Bokura, H., Robin, D., Lindgren, S. A., Smith, W. L., Sato, Y., & Mattheis, P. J. (1998). Attention-deficit hyperactivity symptomatology after traumatic brain injury: a prospective study. *Journal of the American Academy of Child and Adolescent Psychiatry, 37*(8), 841–847.

Russell, W. R. (1959). *Brain, memory, learning: A neurologist's view.* Oxford: Clarendon.

Rutter, M., Chadwick, O., & Shaffer, D. (1983). Head injury. In M. Rutter (Ed), *Developmental neuropsychiatry* (pp. 83–111). New York: Guilford.

Rutter, M., Chadwick, O., Shaffer, D., & Brown, G. (1980). A prospective study of children with head injuries: I. Design and methods. *Psychological Medicine, 10,* 633–645.

Rutter, M. D. (1981). Psychological sequelae of brain damage in children. *American Journal of Psychiatry, 138,* 1533–1544.

Sbordone, R. J., & Long, C. J. (1996). *Ecological validity of neuropsychological testing.* Delray Beach, Florida: St. Lucie.

Stover, S. L., & Zeiger, H. E. (1976). Head injury in children and teenagers: Function/recovery correlated with the duration of coma. *Archives of Physical Medicine and Rehabilitation, 57,* 201–205.

Taylor, H. G., & Alden, J. (1997). Age-related differences in outcome following childhood brain insults: An introduction and overview. *Journal of the International Neuropsychological Society, 3,* 555–567.

Taylor, H. G., Drotar, D., Wade, S., Yeates, K., Stancin, T., & Klein, S. (1995). Recovery from traumatic brain injury in children: The importance of the family. In S. H. Broman & M. E. Michel (Eds.), *Traumatic head injury in children* (pp. 188–216). New York: Oxford University Press.

Teuber, H. L., & Rudel, R. G. (1967). Behavior after cerebral lesions in children and adults. *Developmental Medicine and Child Neurology, 4,* 3–20.

Wrightson, P., McGinn, V., & Gronwall, D. (1995). Mild head injury in preschool children: evidence that it can be associated with a persistent cognitive defect. *Journal of Neurology, Neurosurgery, and Psychiatry*, 59(4), 375–380.

Yeates, K. O., Taylor, H. G., Drotar, D., Wade, S. L., Klein, S., Stancin, T. & Schatschneider, C. (1997). Preinjury family environment as a determinant of recovery from traumatic brain injuries in school-age children. *Journal of the International Neuropsychological Society*, 3(6), 617–630.

CHARLES J. LONG
JOY O'GRADY
MICHELLE RIES
The University of Memphis

TRAVEL AIDS, ELECTRONIC

See ELECTRONIC TRAVEL AIDS.

TRAVEL AIDS FOR INDIVIDUALS WITH DISABILITIES

The United States Department of Justice provides a guide to disability rights and laws to ensure equal opportunities for people with disabilities. Encompassed within this document are guidelines for access to public transportation, public accommodation, and air carriers (Disability Rights Section, 1996). America adheres to these guidelines and provides disabled travelers with various options for traveling. Numerous opportunities for accessible travel by car, boat, train, or airplane are available to those with handicaps. Airlines have made themselves more accessible by arranging for an aisle seat (many of which have removable arms for easier access), notifying the crew that a special needs traveler will be on board, and meeting special requests such as dietary needs or supplemental oxygen. Wheelchairs may be gate-checked for easier accessibility as they will be the first items offloaded at the traveler's destination or at any change of planes. Travelers with disabilities should ask the airlines or their travel agent to make reservations for the most direct route and to allow ample time to change planes if necessary.

Train travel is another option for the handicapped traveler. Amtrak provides information and details about station accessibility along its routes. Train aisles are narrow, so wheelchair access may be limited. However, often meals are served at the handicapped person's seat. Conductors give hearing-impaired travelers necessary announcements in writing. Guide dogs travel free, and most trains are equipped with signs in braille.

Avis Rent-a-Car and Hertz Car Rental companies offer hand-control cars if reserved well in advance. Other car companies also have vehicles to offer special needs clients, including wheelchair-accessible vans.

If traveling by ship, the handicapped traveler should check accessibility before making a reservation. Most major cruise lines have handicapped accessible cabins and public areas, but some small ships have limited access. The special needs traveler should check with each ship to find out what provisions have been made for the disabled and if specific needs can be met.

Quick handicapped travel answers can be found from sources such as Fodor's Great American Vacations for Travelers with Disabilities (1994). The internet also provides multiple sites providing travel information and answering specific questions. Project Action (1999) has a comprehensive database with city and state listings of accessible travel options. National 800 numbers are listed on the Project Action website with public transportation, airport transportation, hotel shuttles, private bus, and even tour companies' information links. Information can be located online.

Access Amtrak
400 N. Capital Street, NW
Washington, DC 20001

American Foundation for the Blind
Travel Concessions for Blind Persons
15 W. 16th Street
New York, NY 10011

Centers for the Handicapped, Inc.
10501 New Hampshire Avenue
Silver Springs, MD 20903 (301-445-3350)

Diabetes Travel Service
349 E. 52nd Street
New York, NY 10022

INTERMEDIC
777 Third Avenue
New York, NY 10007

International Association for Medical Assistance for Travelers
350 5th Avenue, Suite 5620
New York, NY 10001

National Easter Seals Society
Information Center
2023 W. Ogden, Avenue
Chicago, IL 60612

Society for the Advancement of Travel for the Handicapped (SATH)
"The United States Welcomes Handicapped Visitors"
(cassette or braille available)
5014 42nd Street, NW
Washington, DC 20016 (202-966-3900)

Travel Tips for the Handicapped
U.S. Travel Service
Department of Commerce
Washington, DC 20230

Wheelchair Wagon Tours
P.O. Box 1270
Kissimmee, FL 32741 (305-846-7175)

Whole Person Tours
137 W. 32nd Street
Bayonne, New Jersey 07002 (201-858-3400)

REFERENCES

Fodor's great American vacations for travelers with disabilities. (1994). New York: Fodor's Travel Publications.

Project Action. (1999). http://projectaction.org/paweb/index.htm.

Reamy, L. (1978). *Travel ability.* New York: Macmillan.

Rosenburg, M. (1985, August 25). *Aid for handicapped traveler grows. Minneapolis Star and Tribune.*

US Department of Justice. (1996). *Disability rights section.* Http://www.pueblo.gsa.gov/cic_prog/disability-law/disrits.html.

Sue A. Schmitt
University of Wisconsin at Stout
First edition

Kari Anderson
University of North Carolina at Wilmington
Second edition

TREACHER-COLLINS SYNDROME

See RARE DISEASES

TREATMENT ACCEPTABILITY

Treatment acceptability is a form of social validation that asks consumers how they feel about treatment methods prior to treatment. "Judgments of acceptability are likely to embrace evaluation of whether treatment is appropriate for the problem, whether treatment is fair, reasonable, and intrusive, and whether treatment meets with conventional notions about what treatment should be" (Kazdin, 1980, p. 259). The most basic assumption of the acceptability hypothesis is that the acceptability of a treatment method will influence the overall efficacy of the treatment. Methods that consumers feel are the most acceptable will be more effective than methods that are judged to be unacceptable. As Wolf (1978) stated, "If the participants don't like the treatment then they may avoid it, or run away, or complain loudly. And thus, society will be less likely to use our technology, no matter how potentially effective and efficient it might be" (p. 206).

Research efforts in treatment acceptability have followed the same general procedures. Subjects receive written, audio, oral, or audiovisual descriptions of problem behaviors and procedures for treating the problem behaviors. Then the subjects answer a number of questions designed to assess how acceptable the treatment is for improving the problem behavior. A number of scales of similar format have been developed for assessing treatment acceptability in different target populations. The Treatment Evaluation Inventory (TEI; Kazdin, 1980) has 15 questions scored on a seven-point Likert scale used with children and adults. The TEI requires subjects to make judgments about how acceptable an intervention is, how suitable the intervention is, how much the intervention is liked, and so on. The Intervention Rating Profile (IRP; Witt & Martens, 1983) has 20 questions scored on a six-point Likert scale; the questions were specifically written to assess teachers' acceptability judgments of interventions in classroom situations. The IRP has been used to delineate a number of treatment variables that effect teachers' acceptability ratings (Turco, Witt, & Elliott, in press; Witt, Elliott, & Martens, 1984). The Children's Intervention Rating Profile (CIRP; Elliott et al., 1986) has seven questions scored on a six-point Likert-scale. The CIRP has been used by a number of researchers (Elliott et al., 1986; Turco & Elliott, 1986; Turco, Elliott, & Witt, in press) to assess children's treatment acceptability.

REFERENCES

Elliott, S. N. (1986). Children's ratings of the acceptability of classroom interventions for misbehavior: Findings and methodological considerations. *Journal of School Psychology, 24,* 23–35.

Elliott, S. N., Witt, J. C., Galvin, G. A., & Moe, G. L. (1986). Children's involvement in intervention selection: Acceptability of interventions for misbehaving peers. *Professional Psychology: Research and Practice, 17,* 235–241.

Kazdin, A. E. (1980). Acceptability of alternative treatments for deviant child behavior. *Journal of Applied Behavior Analysis, 13,* 259–273.

Turco, T. L., & Elliott, S. N. (1986). Assessment of students' acceptability of teacher-initiated interventions for classroom misbehaviors. *Journal of School Psychology, 24,* 277–283.

Turco, T. L., Elliott, S. N., & Witt, J. C. (in press). Children's involvement in treatment selection: A review of theory and analogue research on treatment acceptability. *Monograph on Secondary Behavioral Disorders.* Reston, VA: Council for Exceptional Children.

Turco, T. L., Witt, J. C., & Elliott, S. N. (in press). Factors influencing teachers' acceptability of classroom interventions for deviant student behavior. *Monograph on Secondary Behavioral Disorders.* Reston, VA: Council for Exceptional Children.

Witt, J. C., Elliott, S. N., & Martens, B. K. (1984). Factors affecting teachers' judgments of the acceptability of behavioral interventions: Time involvement, behavior problem severity, and type of intervention. *Behavior Therapy, 15*, 204–209.

Witt, J. C., & Martens, B. K. (1983). Assessing the acceptability of behavioral interventions. *Psychology in the Schools, 20*, 570–577.

Wolf, M. M. (1978). Social validity: The case for subjective measurement or how applied behavior analysis is finding its heart. *Journal of Applied Behavior Analysis, 11*, 203–214.

TIMOTHY L. TURCO
STEPHEN N. ELLIOTT
Louisiana State University

TEACHER EFFECTIVENESS
TEACHER EXPECTANCIES

TRIARCHIC THEORY OF INTELLIGENCE

Traditional views of intelligence have either argued for an all-encompassing general factor (e.g., Spearman, 1946), two types of intelligence (e.g., the Crystallized and Fluid theory, Horn & Cattell, 1966), or, more recently, for a wide variety of multiple intelligences (Gardner, 1983). Sternberg's (1984, 1985, 1988) triarchic theory of intelligence, however, is one of the few theories that has had an impact on education and also is supported by empirical research.

The triarchic theory of intelligence is founded in the notion that intelligence has three primary aspects: analytical intelligence, practical intelligence, and creative intelligence. Analytical intelligence involves the ability to analyze, to make judgments and comparisons, and to evaluate. Practical intelligence is similar to "street smarts"—the ability to apply one's knowledge in a hands-on, real-world manner. Creative intelligence, finally, is the ability to create, to be imaginative, and to discover. However, all three of these intelligences work together (Sternberg, 1999).

Sternberg (1993) developed the Sternberg Triarchic Abilities Test, which measures these three intelligences; examining the different types of items used in the test can help define the three intelligences. The practical intelligence subtests include such tasks as route planning (reading maps and finding the shortest route from one place to another) and everyday verbal reasoning. Questions of the latter type require solving problems such as: How can a would-be college student who needs $1000 per year to supplement her scholarship obtain money yet remain financially independent? How can a teen-age boy who just moved from Arizona to Iowa, who has had a hard time making friends, and who enjoys writing stories, best solve his problem? Analytical intelligence questions include some interesting variations on traditional intelligence test items. An analogies subtest, for example, includes a "pretend" statement, such as "Money falls off trees." The subject must "pretend" the sentence is true, and then complete the statement: "snow is to shovel as dollar is to." The correct answer, hidden among words like "bank" and "bill," is "rake." Another analytical subtest invents algebraic operations such as "graf" and "flix," which take on specific meanings. The creative intelligence part includes such subtests as sentences that include nonsense words, such as "yip" or "tems," that have specific meanings that can be figured out from the context of the sentence. All three components are also measured via essay questions (Sternberg, 1993).

Neither creative nor practical intelligence have been shown to be highly correlated with IQ (Sternberg & Kaufman, 1996, 1998), which leads to a central implication of the triarchic theory: Two-thirds of a child's capacities are not being adequately measured by schools. In addition, because nearly all standardized tests focus on analytical intelligence, schools often over-reward students who are high on analytical intelligence while penalizing low-analytical students who may be quite intelligent in practical or creative abilities. Teachers may end up presenting their lectures and materials in an analytical manner, hoping (consciously or subconsciously) that students will be helped on the analytic-oriented standardized tests. But through this process, students who excel in other areas are unfairly penalized.

Sternberg (1998) suggests that teachers use a variety of activities, exercises, and lecture styles that emphasize each of the different patterns of abilities. Indeed, student performance was enhanced when the teaching style matched their abilities—even if the performance was measured by a traditional test (Sternberg, Ferrari, Clinkenbeard, & Grigorenko, 1996). Another study by Sternberg, Torff, and Grigorenko (1998) found that when students were taught to use all three aspects of their intelligence (analytical, practical, and creative), their school performance improved, regardless of their particular ability patterns. Sternberg (1998) is not necessarily suggesting that instruction should only aim at a student's strengths—for without struggling in weak areas, students would not learn to compensate and balance. However, he does believe that teaching should strive for uniformity across these abilities, allowing students to exercise their analytical, creative, and practical abilities, as well as improve their memory skills.

One final aspect of Sternberg's triarchic theory is his theory of mental self-management. In this conceptual framework, considered part of his theory of a triarchic mind, there are three mental processes used in thinking: metacomponents, performance components, and knowledge-acquisition components. Metacomponents, or "white collar" intelligence, are higher-order processes that are similar to analytical intelligence, while performance components, or "blue collar" intelligence, are lower-order processes that are similar to practical intelligence. Knowledge-acquisition components, finally, involve the process of learning and acquiring knowledge (Sternberg, 1988, 1999).

REFERENCES

Gardner, H. (1983). *Frames of mind: The theory of multiple intelligences*. New York: BasicBooks.

Horn, J. L., & Cattell, R. B. (1966). Refinement and test of the theory of fluid and crystallized general intelligences. *Journal of Educational Psychology, 57*(5), 253–270.

Spearman, C. (1946). Theory of general factor. *British Journal of Psychology, 36,* 117–131.

Sternberg, R. J. (1984). Toward a triarchic theory of human intelligence. *Behavioral and Brain Sciences, 7,* 269–287.

Sternberg, R. J. (1985). *Beyond IQ: A triarchic theory of human intelligence.* New York: Cambridge University Press.

Sternberg, R. J. (1988). *The Triarchic mind: A new theory of human intelligence.* New York: Viking.

Sternberg, R. J. (1993). STAT: Sternberg Triarchic Abilities Test. Unpublished test.

Sternberg, R. J. (1998). Applying the triarchic theory of human intelligence in the classroom. In R. J. Sternberg & W. M. Williams (Eds.), *Intelligence, instruction, and assessment* (p. 1–17). Mahweh, NJ: Erlbaum.

Sternberg, R. J. (1999). *Cognitive Psychology* (2nd ed.). New York: Harcourt Brace.

Sternberg, R. J., & Ferrari, M., Clinkenbeard, P., & Grigorenko, E. L. (1996). Identification, instruction, and assessment of gifted children: A construct validation of triarchic model. *Gifted Child Quarterly, 40,* 129–137.

Sternberg, R. J., & Kaufman, J. C. (1996). Innovation and intelligence testing: The curious case of the dog that didn't bark. *European Journal of Psychological Assessment, 12,* 175–182.

Sternberg, R. J., & Kaufman, J. C. (1998). Human abilities. *Annual Review of Psychology, 49,* 479–502.

Sternberg, R. J., Torff, B., & Grigorenko, E. L. (1998). Teaching for successful intelligence raises school achievement. *Phi Delta Kappan, 79*(9), 667–669.

JAMES C. KAUFMAN
Yale University

tion programs, it is most often encountered among mentally retarded populations. Incidences of trichotillomania have also been reported in conjunction with episodes of child abuse. Incidence is generally greater in females than males.

A variety of treatment approaches have been attempted with this unusual disorder, including psychoanalysis, traditional psychotherapies, hypnotherapy, and a variety of operant and other behavior modification techniques. Generally, the earlier the age of onset, the greater the likelihood of successful treatment (Sorosky & Sticker, 1980). Behavioral techniques appear to be the most successful methods of treating trichotillomania and trichophagia, particularly when competing responses can be developed, although success has been reported with a variety of techniques and the role of spontaneous remission is not known. Sources of treatment information include Azrin and Nunn (1973), Bayer (1972), and Mannino and Delgado (1969).

Some recent animal research suggests that a variety of self-injurious behaviors, including trichotillomania and trichophagia, may, in some cases, be of neurological origin. Relationships to damage of cells around the substantia nigra have been suggested.

REFERENCES

Azrin, N. H., & Nunn, R. G. (1973). Habit reversal: A method of eliminating nervous habits. *Behavior Research & Therapy, 11,* 619–628.

Bayer, C. A. (1972). Self-monitoring and mild aversion treatment of trichotillomania. *Journal of Behavior Therapy & Experimental Psychiatry, 3,* 139–141.

Mannino, F. C., & Delgado, R. A. (1969). Trichotillomania in children: A review. *American Journal of Psychiatry, 4,* 229–246.

Sorosky, A. D., & Sticker, M. B., (1980). Trichotillomania in adolescence. *Adolescent Psychiatry, 8,* 437–454.

CECIL R. REYNOLDS
Texas A & M University

SELF-INJURIOUS BEHAVIOR

TRICHOTILLOMANIA

Trichotillomania is a low-incidence disorder (occurring in less than 1% of pediatric referrals) of self-injurious behavior that consists of pulling out one's hair; it is often accompanied by trichophagia, subsequent eating of the hair. The etiology of trichotillomania is unknown, but it has long been held to be of a psychoanalytic or Freudian nature. It occurs most often in conjunction with a major psychological or psychiatric disorder, particularly schizophrenia and lower levels of mental retardation, though it also occurs with narcissistic personality disorders. In special educa-

TRICHORHINOPHALANGEAL SYNDROME

Trichorhinophalangeal syndrome is a relatively rare hereditary condition which is traced to a defect on chromosome 8. Children born with this disorder have thin, sparse hair; thick, heavy eyebrows along the bridge of the nose, thinning out toward the distal portions of their faces; a pear-shaped or bulbous nose; large eyes; thin upper lip; small and/or extra teeth; small jaw; and a horizontal groove under their chin. These children are short in stature and have thin fingernails. Abnormalities of the skeletal system, including short, stubby fingers and toes, are common. Problems in bone growth appear around age 3 or 4 years and persist and worsen until adolescent growth is completed. Degenerative hip disease may develop in the young adult and senior years (Rudolph, 1991; Jones, 1988).

Trichorhinophalangeal syndrome comes in two forms: Types I and II, with Type II more severe than Type I. Besides the degree of severity, other distinguishing characteristics of Type II include a smaller head circumference and susceptibility to upper respiratory infections. Moreover, these children have mild to moderate mental retardation and delayed onset of speech. Children with Type I are usually of normal intelligence. Some children with Type II may have a hearing loss. Standard treatment for the syndrome is symptomatic and supportive. Surgery may be performed to correct limb and extremity abnormalities. Genetic counseling may also be helpful (Thoene, 1992).

For children who are mentally retarded or speech delayed, it will be important to begin services through an Early Childhood Intervention (ECI) program. Based on the child's progress and development, he/she may continue to require additional support through special education or speech therapy.

REFERENCES

Jones, K. L. (Ed.). (1988). *Smith's recognizable patterns of human malformation* (4th ed.). Philadelphia, PA: W.B. Saunders.

Rudolph, A. M. (1991). *Rudolph's pediatrics-19th edition*. Norwalk, CT: Appleton & Lange.

Thoene, J. G. (Ed.). (1992). *Physician's guide to rare diseases*. Montvale, NJ: Dowden.

JOAN MAYFIELD
Baylor Pediatric Specialty Services

PATRICIA A. LOWE
Texas A & M University

TRISOMY 18

As indicated by its name, trisomy 18 is a congenital disease owed to the presence of three chromosomes 18 instead of two. Trisomy 18 symptomatology was first described by Edwards et al. (1960); therefore, the term Edwards syndrome is sometimes used instead of trisomy 18. As in many autosomal trisomies, severe polymalformations are observed. Moreover, affected patients show many common features, so that trained physicians are able to diagnose the syndrome on clinical inspection. Generally, trisomy 18

newborns are postmature (42 weeks of pregnancy), but nevertheless show a birth weight below 2500 g (Hamerton, 1971); hydramnios (too much amniotic fluid) is the rule. An elongated skull with prominent occiput is noted, together with microcephaly. Micrognatia (small mandible), low-set ears, short neck, short sternum, prominent abdomen with umbilical hernia, and narrow hips are usual findings. The extremities are also characteristic: fingers are in forced flexion, very difficult to unfold, and deviated so that the third one is recovered by the second and the fourth. Arches are present in most, if not all, fingers. These dermatoglyphic configurations are rare in normal people or in those with other chromosome diseases. Clubfoot is frequent, and the big toe is in dorsiflexion. Internal malformations include severe congenital heart anomalies in more than 95% of all cases, either intraventricular, septal defects or patent ductus arteriosus. Indeed, premature death can be related to these heart defects. Failure to thrive is the rule and, despite palliative treatment, death occurs in a mean time of 70 days (Hamerton, 1971). Developmental retardation is always observed, but accurate testing is difficult.

From a cytogenetic point of view, standard trisomy 18 concerns more than 80% of all cases. Mosaicism trisomy 18/normal cell line occurs in less than 10% of patients; survival may be longer and symptomatology less severe. Trisomy 18 from a transmitted translocation by one of the parents is rare. Incidence is situated around 1 in 10,000 births (Hook & Hamerton, 1977). This is much less than in trisomy 21; the symptoms are more severe, and many affected embryos are spontaneously aborted early in pregnancy. Interestingly, 80% of all newborn cases are female, suggesting a strong lethality in the male. Some authors (Conen & Erkman, 1966) have also reported on a different survival rate depending on whether the baby is a girl (294 days) or a boy (96 days). Maternal age is above average (32 years), but the relationship is not as clear, as in trisomy 21. In the presence of a small fetus showing few movements and severe hydramnios, it may be profitable to have a late prenatal diagnosis, during the seventh or eighth month of pregnancy. This may avoid a caesarean section for the mother.

REFERENCES

Conen, P. E., & Erkman, B. (1966). Frequency and occurrence of chromosomal syndromes. II. E-trisomy. *American Journal of Human Genetics, 18*, 387–398.

Edwards, J. H., Harnden, D. G., Cameron, A. H., Crosse, V. M., & Wolff, O. H. (1960). A new trisomic syndrome. *Lancet, 1*, 787–790.

Hamerton, J. L. (1971). *Human cytogenetics* (Vol. 2). New York: Academic.

Hook, E. B., & Hamerton, J. L. (1977). The frequency of chromosome abnormalities detected in consecutive newborn studies—Differences between studies—Results by sex and by severity of phenotypic involvement. In E. B. Hook & I. A. Porter (Eds.),

Population cytogenetics—Studies in Human. New York: Academic.

L. KOULISCHER
Institut de Morphologie
Pathologique

CHROMOSOMAL ABNORMALITIES GENETIC COUNSELING

TRISOMY 21

Trisomy 21 or Down's syndrome is a combination of birth defects characterized by mental retardation, abnormal facial features, heart defects, and other congenital disorders. Approximately one in 800 to one in 1,000 infants is born with this disorder (March of Dimes, 1997). Trisomy 21 occurs in all races and economic levels; however, incidence is highest among Caucasians. Over 250,000 individuals with Trisomy 21 (March of Dimes, 1997) live in the United States. Life expectancy and quality of life has greatly increased over the past twenty years due to improved treatment of related complications and better developmental educational programs (Ball & Bindler, 1999). Mortality rates for infants with Trisomy 21 and congenital heart defects remain high at 44%. However, overall life expectancy among adults has improved to over 55 years (March of Dimes, 1997).

The cause of Trisomy 21 is unknown. A number of theories including genetic predisposition, radiation exposure,

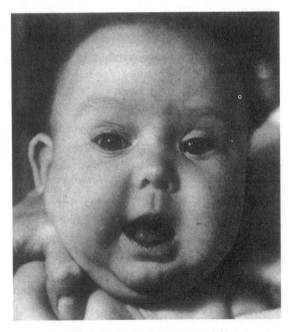

Characteristic facies of a trisomic 21 child.

environmental factors, viruses, and even infections have been proposed (Wong, 1995). Trisomy 21 does result from an aberration in chromosome 21 in which three copies instead of the normal two occur due to faulty meiosis (nondisjunction) of the ovum or, sometimes, the sperm. This results in a karyotype of 47 chromosomes instead of the normal 46. The incidence of nondisjunction increases with maternal age and the extra chromosome originates from the mother about 80% of the time (Wong, 1995). Mothers over the age of 35 years are at the greatest risk for rearrangement of their chromosomes and their risk of having a child with Trisomy 21 increases greatly with age. At age 35, the risk is calculated to be 1 in 385 births, at age 40, the risk increases to 1 in 106 births, and at age 49, the risk of having a baby with Trisomy 21 is 1 in 11 (Wong, 1995). Prenatal testing through amniocentesis or chorionic villus identifies Trisomy 21 (March of Dimes, 1997). Both procedures carry a risk of infection and miscarriage. Genetic counseling is available for couples with a known family history of genetic birth defects and is also indicated for mothers over the age of 35 (March of Dimes, 1997).

The physical signs of Trisomy 21 are apparent at birth. The newborn is lethargic and has difficulty eating. Trisomy 21 newborns have almond-shaped eyes with epicanthal folds, a protruding tongue, a small mouth, a single palmar crease (simian crease), small white spots on the iris of the eye (Brushfield spots), a small skull, a flattened bridge across the nose, a flattened profile, small and low-set ears, and a short neck with excess skin (Wong, 1995). Slowed growth and development are characteristic of this syndrome, especially in speech formation. Other physical abnormalities include dry, sensitive skin with decreased elasticity, short stature, broad hands and feet, abnormal fingerprints, and hypotonic limbs (Ball & Bindler, 1999). Premature dementia similar to Alzheimer's disease usually occurs during the fourth decade of life, and an increase in leukemia, diabetes mellitus, thyroid disorders, and chronic infections are all common in individuals with Trisomy 21 (Wong, 1995).

The degree of mental retardation with Trisomy 21 varies greatly and ranges from mild to profound. Although children with Trisomy 21 can usually do most things that any child can learn to do (walking, talking, dressing, self-feeding, and toileting), they develop at a slower rate and at a later age (March of Dimes, 1997). The exact age of achievement of developmental milestones and skills cannot be predicted. However, early intervention programs beginning in infancy encourage these special children to reach their greatest potential.

Special education programs are available around the country with many children fully integrated into regular classroom situations (March of Dimes, 1997). The future for special children with Trisomy 21 is brighter than twenty years ago. Many will learn to read, write, take care of themselves, and hold partially supported employment while living semi-independently in group homes (March of Dimes, 1997).

REFERENCES

Ball, J., & Bindler, R. (1999). *Pediatric nursing: Caring for children* (2nd ed.). Stamford, CT: Appleton & Lange.

March of Dimes. (1997). *Down syndrome: Public education information sheet.* http://www.noah.cuny.edu/prenancy/march_of_dimes/birth_defects/downsynd.html

Wong, D. (1995). *Whaley & Wong's nursing care of infants and children* (5th ed.). St. Louis: Mosby-Year Book.

KARI ANDERSON
University of North Carolina at Wilmington

CHROMOSOMAL ABNORMALITIES
DOWN'S SYNDROME
GENETIC COUNSELING

TUBERCULOSIS

See CHRONIC ILLNESS IN CHILDREN.

TUBEROUS SCLEROSIS

Tuberous sclerosis is an inherited disorder transmitted as an autosomal dominant trait with variable penetrance affecting the skin, brain, retina, heart, kidneys, and lungs. It belongs to the group of diseases called phakomatoses, characterized by malformations, the presence of birthmarks, and the tendency to tumor formation in the central nervous system, skin, and viscera. The estimated frequency of occurrence is 1 per 30,000 live births (Berg, 1982). About 25% of the patients are sporadic owing to new mutations.

Tuberous sclerosis is a protean disorder chiefly manifested by epilepsy, mental deficiency, and cutaneous lesions. Convulsions are the most frequent initial symptom (up to 88%), presenting often in early life as infantile spasms (about 70%), usually between the fourth and sixth months of life. The convulsions later become generalized grand mal epilepsy and focal or akinetic seizures (Gomez, 1979; Hunt, 1983; Jeavons & Bower, 1964; Pampiglione & Moynahan, 1976). Mental retardation, when present, is usually severe; one-third of the patients may have normal intelligence (Gomez, 1979). Only 12 to 15% of affected subjects are free of epilepsy and mental retardation. The cutaneous lesions are multiple. Adenoma sebaceum is the characteristic sign of the disease. It appears in the face between 1 and 5 years of age (usually after 4 years), starting as a macular rash over the cheeks in a butterfly appearance, then increasing in size and covering the nose, lips, and chin with a granular aspect. Those adenoma named Pringle's are seldom absent but they may grow very slowly. Hypopigmented leaf-shaped spots called white or achromatic spots or depigmented nevi are the most frequent sign in up to 95% of cases (Hunt, 1983); they are disseminated over the trunk and the limbs and are present at birth (Gold & Freeman, 1965), but they increase in number during the first 2 years of life. They appear more numerous under Wood's light and may be demonstrable in clinically asymptomatic parents. Shagreen patches are thickenings of skin best seen in the lumbos-acral region. Periungueal fibroma (Koenen tumors) are more often present on the toes than on the fingers and appear after the first decade and in adults; they may be the only sign in parents of an affected child.

The pathology in the nervous system shows the presence of cortical malformations, variable in size (called tubers), that contain neurons, astrocytic nuclei, and giant cells. The tubers also can be located in the subependymal area and contain calcium deposits that can be identified on X-rays or CAT scans. They may grow into the ventricles, interfering with cerebral spinal fluid circulation, blocking the foramen of Monro or the aqueduct of Sylvius, and producing hydrocephalus and signs of raised intracranial pressure. Tumors can also be present in the heart, the lungs, and the kidneys, but they can be discovered easily by ultrasound examination showing angiomyolipoma or even cystic tumors (Avni et al., 1984). The examination of the ocular fundus may reveal tumoral lesions at the nerve head or about the disk, even in the absence of vision complaints.

Diagnosis of the disease is based on the association of epilepsy, mental retardation, and skin lesions. It can be made very early in life on the presence of infantile spasms and achromatic spots in correlation with the cerebral calcifications seen on CAT scans of the brain (Lee & Gawler, 1978).

REFERENCES

Avni, E. F., Szliwowski, H., Spehl, M., Lelong, B., Baudain, P., & Struyven, J. (1984). Renal involvement in tuberous sclerosis. *Annales de Radiologie, 27,* 2–3, 207–214.

Berg, B. O. (1982). Neurocutaneous syndromes. In K. F. Swaiman, & F. S. Wright (Eds.), *The practice of pediatric neurology.* New York: Mosby.

Gold, A. P., & Freeman, J. M. (1965). Depigmented nevi: The earliest sign of tuberose sclerosis. *Pediatrics, 35,* 1003–1005.

Gomez, M. R. (1979). Clinical experience at the Mayo Clinic. In M. R. Gomez (Ed.), *Tuberous sclerosis* pp. 16–20. New York: Raven.

Hunt, A. (1983). Tuberous sclerosis: A survey of 97 cases. *Developmental Medicine and Child Neurology, 25,* 346–357.

Jeavons, P. M., & Bower, B. D. (1969). Infantile spasms. *Clinics Developmental Medicine, 15*, London: Sime/Heinemann.

Lee, B. C., & Gawler, J. (1978). Tuberous sclerosis. Comparison of computed tomography and conventional neuroradiology. *Radiology, 127*(2), 403–407.

Pampiglione, G., & Moynahan, E. I. (1976). The tuberous sclerosis: Clinical and EEG studies in 100 children. *Journal Neurology Neurosurgery & Psychiatry, 39*, 666–673.

HENRI B. SZLIWOWSKI
Université Libre de Bruxelles
Hôpital Erasme

TURKEY, SPECIAL EDUCATION IN

Turkey has a centralized education system. The Ministry of Education has an Office of Special Education which monitors all special education services in Turkey. These special education services are regulated by the new Special Education Law (KHK/573), which replaced the old law in 1997. Basic principles of special education, as cited in the new Special Education Law, are as follows:

1. All special needs individuals should be provided special education services according to their interests, desires, sufficiencies, and abilities.

2. Special education should be started as early in one's life as possible.

3. Special education services should be planned and administered without segregating the special needs individuals from their social and physical environments to the greatest extent possible.

4. Priority should be given to educating special needs individuals with other individuals (i.e., in regular education environments) by considering their educational performances and modifying the instructional goals, contents, and processes.

5. Collaboration should be made with other organizations and institutions providing rehabilitation services in order to prevent the interruption of services.

6. Individualized education plans should be developed and education programs should be individualized for special needs individuals.

7. Families should be encouraged to take part in every process of special education actively.

8. Opinions of nongovernment organizations of special needs individuals should be considered in developing special education policies.

9. When planning special education services, elements should be included to facilitate special needs individuals' interactions with and adaptation to society.

There are guidance and research centers affiliated with the Office of Special Education in every major town to monitor the local special education services in Turkey. Main responsibilities of the guidance and research centers are as follows:

- to accept referrals from schools and conduct assessments
- to identify special needs individuals
- to place identified individuals in regular or special education environments
- to follow-up the special needs individuals
- to conduct inservice training to education personnel.

There are 99[1] guidance and research centers all around Turkey at present. Personnel of these centers include special education teachers as well as counselors, which total 606 at press time.

There are various placement alternatives for special needs students in Turkey. Until 1997, most special needs students were placed in special schools or special classes where available; they were integrated in regular classes when special education placement was not available. In a sense, special students used to be integrated whenever they did not have a chance to be segregated. However, the new Special Education Law has a principle mandating integration to be considered as the preferred option for special needs students. Hence, this principle is expected to facilitate special education placements according to the "least restrictive environment" concept.

The number of special needs students from various disability categories enrolled in special schools, special classes and regular classes in 1997–98 in Turkey is 31,215. When all special needs students are considered, it is observed that 41% of them are educated in special schools, 26% of them are educated in special classes, and 33% of them are educated in regular classes.

The total number of students enrolled in elementary and secondary education programs is 11,355,736 (according to the records of the Ministry of Education). These data show that 0.3% of all students are special needs students. This means that the percentage of special needs children receiving special education services is rather low in Turkey.

The new Special Education Law mentions the need for special education support services for the integrated special needs students. Integration was started in Turkey without providing any support services to the integrated students and/or to their teachers. Therefore, integration did not prove to be a successful placement for many special needs students in the past. Now that special education support services are considered in the Special Education Law, regular schools are expected to have support personnel for providing services such as teacher consultations, in-class support, or resource room services when necessary.

Special education is a rather new and rare professional discipline in Turkey. Special education teacher training programs exist in only three universities, Abant Izzet Baysal University, Anadolu University, and Gazi University. The oldest of these programs, Anadolu University Special Education Teacher Training Program, started to graduate special education teachers in 1987. Thus, many teachers working with special needs students were originally trained as regular teachers and completed special education certificate programs, which are no longer offered.

Special education teacher training programs offer BA degrees in three special needs categories: developmental disabilities, hearing impairments, and visual impairments. Teacher training programs for the developmentally delayed have a behavioral orientation and emphasize direct instruction for teaching concepts and skills. Teacher training programs for the visually impaired aim to equip their students with knowledge necessary for teaching partially sighted and blind students. In teacher training programs for the hearing impaired, the auditory-oral approach is followed. Most of the graduates of special education teacher training programs apply to the Ministry of Education to be appointed as a special education teacher in a school or a guidance and research center, and some graduates choose to work in private schools. The total number of teachers working in special schools and special classes is 2653 at present, 435 of which are special education teachers.

Regarding special education research in Turkey, in addition to the quantitative methodologies, single-subject and qualitative research methodologies are two popular trends of the past few years. Although these research methodologies differ remarkably in terms of philosophical orientations as well as data collection/data analysis procedures, both are perceived to be very appropriate for improving special education knowledge and practices. Accordingly, the number of research projects, theses, and dissertations conducted qualitatively or by single-subject designs is increasing considerably in Turkey.

NOTES

¹All quantitative data are obtained from the Office of Special Education except where indicated.

GONAL KIRCAALI-IFTAR
Anadolu University

TURNBULL, ANN P. (1937–   )

An Alabama native, Ann P. Turnbull received her BSEd from the University of Georgia, her MEd from Auburn University (1971), and her EdD from the University of Alabama. Her formal education emphasized special educa-

tion of children with mental retardation, and early practical experience was gained as a teacher of children with mild mental retardation at schools in La Grange, Georgia (1968–1970). She is currently codirector of the Beach Center on Families and Disability and a professor in the department of special education at The University of Kansas.

Turnbull's research focuses on family systems and family-centered services, and includes programmatic implementation of policy requirements associated with PL 94-142. Parental involvement in educational decision-making and the development of a conceptual framework for family research and intervention based on family systems theory has been a major interest of Turnbull. Her focus on policy issues includes exploring government-provided services for enhancing the ability of families to provide care for their members with disabilities.

In 1988, Turnbull was a Joseph P. Kennedy, Jr. Policy Fellow working with the US House of Representatives Select Committee on Children, Youth, and Families, and in 1990 she was selected as one of three women from the international field of mental retardation to receive the Rose Fitzgerald Kennedy Leadership Award. Among her many leadership roles in professional and family organizations, she has served as chair of the family committee for the International League of Societies for Persons with Mental Handicaps and member of the board of directors of the American Association on Mental Retardation. She is currently a member of the board of directors of Zero to Three of the National Center for Clinical Infant Programs and the Autism National Committee. Turnbull was inducted as a member of The University of Kansas Women's Hall of Fame in 1994.

Turnbull has been the principal investigator on over 20 federally-funded research grants, and has authored 12 books and over 100 articles, chapters, and monographs. Her books include *Cognitive Coping, Families, and Disability* (1993); *Exceptional Lives: Special Education in Today's Schools* (1995); and *Families, Professionals, and Exceptionality: Collaborating for Empowerment* (1997).

Ann P. Turnbull and H. R. Turnbull

REFERENCES

Turnbull, A. P., Patterson, J. M., Behr, S. K., Murphy, D. L., Marquis, J. G., & Blue-Banning, M. J. (Eds.). (1993). *Cognitive coping, families, and disability.* Baltimore: Brookes.

Turnbull, A. P., & Turnbull, H. R. (1997). *Families, professionals, and exceptionality: Collaborating for empowerment* (3rd ed.). Columbus, OH: Merrill/Prentice Hall.

Turnbull, A. P., Turnbull, H. R., Shank, M., & Leal, D. (1995). *Exceptional lives: Special education in today's schools.* Columbus, OH: Merrill/Prentice Hall.

E. Valerie Hewitt
Texas A & M University
First edition

Tamara J. Martin
The University of Texas of the Permian Basin
Second edition

TURNBULL, H. RUTHERFORD (1937–)

H. Rutherford Turnbull received his BA in political science from Johns Hopkins University in 1959 and his LLB/JD from the University of Maryland Law School in 1964. He later attended Harvard Law School, earning his LLM in the Urban Studies program in 1969. As the father of an adult son with mental retardation and autism, Turnbull has specialized in law and public policy affecting persons with mental and developmental disabilities. He is currently codirector of the Beach Center on Families and Disability and professor of special education and courtesy professor of law at The University of Kansas.

Turnbull concentrates his research and training in four areas: special education law and policy, mental disability law and policy, public policy analysis, and ethics as related to disability policy and service provision. His initial work in the areas of special education law and rights of institutionalized persons led him to concentrate on issues that define and redefine the concepts of consent, least restriction, and parent participation in the education of children with disabilities. His work with policymakers and professional caregivers has focused on issues concerning the treatment of infants with disabilities and the restructuring of Medicaid financing of residential and other services for persons with mental retardation.

Turnbull's service in elected and appointed leadership includes president of the American Association on Mental Retardation (1985–1986), director of The Association for Retarded Citizens of the United States (1981–1983), chairman of the American Bar Association Commission on Mental and Physical Disability Law (1992–1995), and trustee of the Judge David Bazelon Mental Health Law Center (1993–1997).

Since developing his specialization in the mid-1970s while professor of public law and government at the Institute of Government of The University of North Carolina in Chapel Hill (1969–1980), Turnbull has authored over 125 articles, book chapters, monographs, technical reports, reviews, and commentaries related to disability issues. His major works include *Consent Handbook* (1978), *Free Appropriate Public Education: Law and the Education of Children with Disabilities* (1997), and *Exceptional Lives: Special Education in Today's Schools* (1998). He has been "of counsel" on amicus briefs in two disability cases heard by the United States Supreme Court as well as author and draftsman of North Carolina's special education law and limited guardianship law and P.L. 100-407, Assistive Technology for Individuals with Disabilities Act of 1988.

Turnbull was recognized in *Who's Who in America* in 1995, 1996, and 1997. His honors include the National Public Service Award of the International Council for Exceptional Children (1996) and the National Leadership Award of the American Association on Mental Retardation (1997).

REFERENCES

Turnbull, H. R. (1978). *Consent Handbook.* Washington, DC: American Association on Mental Retardation.

Turnbull, H. R. (1997). *Free appropriate public education: Law and the education of children with disabilities* (Rev. ed.). Denver, CO: Love.

Turnbull, A. P., Turnbull, H. R., Shank, M. S., & Leal, D. J. (1998). *Exceptional lives: Special Education in today's schools.* Columbus, OH: Merrill/Prentice Hall.

Tamara J. Martin
The University of Texas of the Permian Basin

TURNER'S SYNDROME

Turner's syndrome is a sex chromosome abnormality characterized by the absence of all or part of one X chromosome in females (Reed, 1975). That is, rather than having the two sex chromosomes of the normal female (XX), about 80% of females with Turner's syndrome have only one X chromosome, symbolized as XO. The remainder have a variety of mosaic patterns involving variability in cells with chromosome deletions or translocations (Bender, Puck, Salbenblatt, & Robinson, 1984). Physical and developmental stigmata are less pronounced for some of the mosaic types (Bender et al., 1984). Only a small percentage of fetuses with abnormal sex chromosomes result in live births and the estimated incidence of all types of Turner's syndrome is 1 out of 2500 female live births (Reed, 1975). Physical sequelae often associated with this syndrome are short stature, webbing of the neck, deformity of the elbow (i.e., cubitus valgus), sexual immaturity, and congenital heart defects (Park, Bailey, & Cowell, 1983). Medical treatment primarily involves estrogen replacement during adolescence.

Learning disorders have been consistently associated with Turner's syndrome. While earlier studies reported a greater risk for mental retardation (Haddad & Wilkins, 1959), several recent studies have replicated a finding that only visual-motor abilities rather than verbal and global cognitive skills are decreased (Bender et al., 1984). Children and adolescent girls have been found to have lower performance than verbal IQs on the Wechsler Intelligence Scale for Children Revised. Neuropsychological studies have reported reduced capabilities in the right cerebral hemisphere and particularly the right parietal lobe (Money, 1973). Hence girls with Turner's syndrome appear to have a particular risk for the neuropsychological learning disorder type of visual-spatial dyslexia. There has been no particular vulnerability to general behavioral problems or psychopathology other than attention deficit disorder with hyperactivity (Hier, Atkins, & Perlo, 1980).

The primary implication for special education practitioners is that girls with Turner's syndrome should receive a comprehensive psychoeducational and perhaps neuropsychological evaluation to detect possible learning disorders. Behavioral practitioners also could provide anticipatory guidance to the child and family regarding such issues as sterility.

REFERENCES

Bender, B., Puck, M., Salbenblatt, J., & Roninson, A. (1984). Cognitive development of unselected girls with complete or partial X monosomy. *Pediatrics, 73,* 175–182.

Haddad, H. M., & Wilkins, L. (1959). Congenital anomalies associated with gonadal aplasia: Review of 55 cases. *Pediatrics, 23,* 885–902.

Hier, D., Atkins, L., & Perlo, V. (1980). Learning disorders and sex chromosome aberrations. *Journal of Mental Deficiency Research, 24,* 17–26.

Money, J. (1973). Turner's syndrome and parietal lobe functions. *Cortex, 9,* 385–393.

Park, E., Bailey, J. D., & Cowell, C. A. (1983). Growth maturation of patients with Turner's syndrome. *Pediatric Research, 17,* 1–7.

Reed, E. W. (1975). Genetic abnormalities in development. In F. D. Horowitz (Ed.), *Review of child development research* (Vol. 4, pp. 283–318). Chicago: University of Chicago Press.

JOSEPH D. PERRY
Kent State University

GENETIC VARIATIONS
KLEINFELTER'S SYNDROME
MOSAICISM

TUTORING

Tutoring is a method of instruction in which one or a small group of students (tutees) receive personalized and individualized education from a tutor. Tutoring is widely used with students of all ages and all levels of ability. However, in elementary and secondary schools, it is most often used as an adjunct to traditional classroom instruction: (1) to provide remedial or supplementary instruction to students who have difficulty learning by conventional methods, including mainstreamed, handicapped children; (2) to provide students with increased opportunities to actively participate in the learning process and receive immediate feedback; and (3) to help relieve the classroom teacher of instructional and noninstructional duties.

In most cases, tutoring is provided to students by someone other than the regular teacher. This may be an adult who volunteers or is paid, a college student, a programmed machine or computer, or, in many cases, another student. The term peer tutoring is used when children serve as tutors to others close to their age who are functioning at a lower level. The term cross-age tutoring is used when older children or adolescents work with tutees who are several years younger than themselves.

The practices of peer and cross-age tutoring were recorded as early as the first century AD by Quintilian in the *Institutio Oratoria.* However, the practice was not formalized and instituted on a widespread basis until the late eighteenth century by Andrew Bell in India and later by William Lancaster in England. Tutoring was standard practice in the one-room schoolhouses of America until graded classes helped reduce the heterogeneity of student ability. Renewed interest in children teaching children began in the early 1960s because of shortages in professional teachers. Educators argued that disadvantaged children might learn more from a peer than from an adult. Several large-scale tutoring programs in New York City, Washington, DC, Chicago, Michigan, and California were successful (Allen, 1976).

Since 1970, numerous research studies and anecdotal reports have documented the benefits of tutoring for both the tutee and the tutor. Both have been found to benefit in terms of increases in achievement, school attitudes, peer acceptance, and self-image (Devin-Sheehan, Feldman, & Allen, 1976). Successful outcomes of tutoring have been reported for nonhandicapped tutees, tutees in special education including the moderately retarded, and those with aggressive behavior disorders (Maher, 1982).

Research further indicates that the effectiveness of tutoring depends greatly on how it is organized and structured and the nature of the relationship between the tutor and tutee. Some guidelines for developing a successful tutoring program follow.

Tutors must be carefully selected, trained, and supervised. Prospective tutor recruits must be dependable, responsible, and knowledgeable in the skill to be taught. They must be trained in tutoring skills (e.g., praising, task analysis, direct instruction, communication) and be provided with specific materials. A designated tutor supervisor must be available. Tutors and tutees should be matched carefully so that they have good rapport and work together conscientiously. Contracts are helpful in spelling out the responsibilities of each. If possible, tutoring should be held twice weekly for at least 30 minutes each session over a minimum of 10 weeks. The program should be continually monitored to determine its effectiveness. Meetings should be scheduled separately with the tutors and tutees to discuss any problems.

Extensive descriptions of tutorial procedures can be found in Allen (1976) and Ehly and Larsen (1980). The use of handicapped students as tutors for the nonhandicapped has been discussed by Osguthorpe (1984).

REFERENCES

Allen, V. L. (1976). *Children as teachers: Theory and research on tutoring*. New York: Academic.

Devin-Sheehan, L., Feldman, R. S., & Allen, V. L. (1976). Research on children tutoring children: A critical review. *Review of Educational Research, 46*, 355–385.

Ehly, S. W., & Larsen, S. C. (1980). *Peer tutoring for individualized instruction*. Boston: Allyn & Bacon.

Maher, C. A. (1982). Behavioral effects of using conduct problem adolescents as cross-age tutors. *Psychology in the Schools, 10*, 360–364.

Osguthorpe, R. T. (1984). Handicapped students as tutors for nonhandicapped peers. *Academic Therapy, 19*, 473–483.

FREDERIC J. MEDWAY
University of South Carolina

TEACHING STRATEGIES

TWINS

Twins may pose a number of educational problems because of their close relationship and their strong attachment to one another. For instance, they often show language delay. Because they are content with each other's company and consequently socialize less with other children and adults than singletons, they tend to be less influenced by the linguistic environment (Luchsinger, 1961). Indeed, they may develop a jargon that enables them to communicate with one another but that is incomprehensible to others. This private idiom is called cryptophasia. Cryptophasia is not a language sui generis (as some have thought it was), but a sort of pidgin based on the language of the adults (Lebrun, 1982). Despite reduced vocabulary and absence of grammar, it makes communication possible between the twins; they have so many affinities that they can understand one another with just a few words. To improve the twins' language command, speech therapy may be necessary. Moreover, it may be desirable to separate them part of the day so that they can learn to socialize.

REFERENCES

Lebrun, Y. (1982). Cryptophasie et retard de langage chez les jumeaux. *Enfance* (3), 101–108.

Luchsinger, R. (1961). Die Sprachentwicklung von ein- und zweiengen Zwillingen und die Vererbung von Sprachstörungen in den ersten drie Lebensjahren. *Folia Phoniatrica* (13), 66–76.

YVAN LEBRUN
School of Medicine, V.U.B.

U

ULCERS AND HANDICAPPED CHILDREN

While little empirical evidence exists to substantiate the relationship between ulcers and handicapped conditions, it appears that handicapped children may be more predisposed to ulceration than their nonhandicapped peers. Kim, Learman, Nada, & Thompson (1981) found that 5.4% of the residents in a large institution for mentally retarded children had peptic ulcers.

Other factors often associated with handicapping conditions also appear to lead to ulceration. For example, ulcers are more likely to occur in children with lower IQs (Christodoulou, Garigoulos, Poploukas, & Marinopoulou, 1977; Kim et al., 1981). Additionally, ulcers occur more often in children who are withdrawn and less likely to express their feelings or frustrations (Chapman & Loeb, 1967; Christodoulou et al., 1977), similar to some emotionally handicapped children. Finally, children who come from extended family situations (e.g., divorced or separated parents) are more likely to have ulcers, a factor that has been shown to be more likely to occur in handicapped children than in their nonhandicapped peers (Beattie & Maniscalco, 1985).

Particular types of ulcer's, particularly ulcerative colitis, may result in growth retardation and cosmetic problems that may lead to eligibility for services under the IDEA (Gillman, 1994; McClung, 1994).

REFERENCES

Ackerman, S. H., Manaker, S., & Cohen, M. I. (1981). Recent separation and the onset of peptic ulcer disease in older children and adolescents. *Psychosomatic Medicine, 43,* 305–310.

Beattie, J., & Maniscalco, G. (1985). Special education and divorce: Is there a link. *Techniques, 1,* 342–345.

Chapman, A. H., & Loeb, D. G. (1967). Psychosomatic gastrointestinal problems. In I. Frank & M. Powell (Eds.), *Psychosomatic ailments in childhood and adolescence.* Springfield, IL: Thomas.

Christodoulou, G. N., Gargoulas, A., Poploukas, A., & Marinopoulou, A. (1977). Primary peptic ulcers in childhood: Psychosocial, psychological and psychiatric aspects. *Acta Psychiatrica Scandinavica, 56,* 215–222.

Gillman, J. (1994). Inflammatory bowel diseases: Psychological issues. In R. Olsen, L. Mollins, J. Gillman, & J. Chaney (Eds.), *Pediatric psychology.* Boston: Longwood.

Kim, M., Learman, L., Nada, N., & Thompson, K. (1981). The prevalence of peptic ulcer in an institution for the mentally retarded. *Journal of Mental Deficiency Research, 25,* 105–111.

McClung, H. (1994). Inflammatory bowel diseases: Medical issues. In R. Olsen, L. Mullins, J. Gillman, & J. Chaney (Eds.), *Pediatric psychology.* Boston: Longwood.

Mylander, M. (1982). *The great American stomach book.* New Haven, CT: Tichnor & Fields.

JOHN R. BEATTIE
*University of North Carolina at
Charlotte*

ANTISOCIAL BEHAVIOR
DIVORCE AND SPECIAL EDUCATION
EMOTIONAL DISORDERS

ULTIMATE INSTRUCTION FOR THE SEVERE AND PROFOUNDLY RETARDED

The criterion of ultimate functioning (Brown, Nietupski, & Hamre-Nietupski, 1976) refers to a method of prioritization that may be used in developing programs for the severely or profoundly handicapped learner. Although the type of handicapping condition may vary, this program development philosophy has most often been applied to individuals who have been classified as mentally retarded.

Use of this type of rationale to develop curricula for such persons extends from three major assumptions (Brown et al., 1976). First, the exceptional needs learner should be taught skills that increase the student's independence in and access to less restrictive environments. Second, transfer of training, response generalization, and response maintenance cannot be assumed to occur with such learners. Third, programming efforts with the severely or profoundly handicapped learner should address the wide variety of individual learning characteristics of this group. Thus application of the criterion of ultimate functioning in developing curricula for these students requires that the skills and behaviors taught to such individuals should relate directly to the behaviors that will be expected of them in nonschool environments.

Brown et al. (1976) developed the concept of the criterion of ultimate functioning in response to inadequacies of educational programs that had been generated based on alternative curriculum philosophies. With the severely or profoundly handicapped learner, these philosophies have often been either developmental or nontheoretical in nature (Haring & Bricker, 1976).

The developmental approach to curriculum delination reflects adherence to a stage or hierarchical explanation of learning. From this perspective, the skills that are taught the severely or profoundly handicapped learner are dictated by the normal pattern of development that often takes place with the nonhandicapped child. Moving from the simple to the complex, the skills that are taught in developmentally oriented curricula might include teaching a student to vocalize before teaching words or teaching visual orientation before teaching word recognition. Proponents of a developmental approach to education feel that the simpler tasks must be mastered before the more complex skills are taught. Actual applications of a developmental orientation to the education of the severely or profoundly handicapped learner have often been criticized because of their inflexibility (e.g., "John is stabilized at the preoperational level") and lack of direct relationship to the teaching of immediately relevant skills (e.g., teaching object use through picture matching).

An alternative approach that has been used to develop curricula for the severely or profoundly handicapped learner has been referred to as nontheoretical (Haring & Bricker, 1976). This orientation develops curriculum content based on teacher-specified individual needs of the student. The emphasis of these types of programs has been on the use of specific methodologies that effectively teach the student new and increasingly complex skills. These skills do not reflect a particular developmental progression but instead are those skills that are relevant for the student as decided by the teacher. Although the emphasis on methodological consistency apparent in curricula of this type has often led to impressive skill acquisition, these skills have, at times, reflected teacher priorities that are not necessarily consistent with the best interests of the student (e.g., sitting quietly but not necessarily completing a task).

In response to the potential limitations of these curriculum development approaches, the criterion of ultimate functioning (Brown, et al., 1976) suggests teaching skills that are (1) relevant to student needs in light of individual learning characteristics; (2) immediately useful in terms of the environment(s) in which the student functions; and (3) able to increase the independence and ability of the student to attain access to more normative social environments. The teaching methods that are used from this perspective are based on specific analysis of the skills of the student and the requirements of the environment. Differences between these two assessment areas become the teaching objectives.

The criterion of ultimate functioning, used as a ration-

ale for curriculum development with the severely or profoundly handicapped learner, breaks with the traditional developmental curriculum orientation. The skills that are taught are directly relevant in terms of the environments in which the student does, or is expected to, function. Building on techniques that emphasize specific analysis of student behaviors and environmental requirements, this approach systematically teaches the exceptional needs student skills that increase independence in and access to less restrictive settings. In contrast with the nontheoretical approach mentioned previously, this focus on independence and normative (chronologically age-appropriate) environments reflects a view of the student as an integral part of society. Theoretically, the degree to which the student might access social environments is a direct function of teaching the skills necessary for effective adaptation to those environments. Accordingly, the skills that are taught address not only the immediate relevance of learning experiences but also the long-term relevance of such skills.

REFERENCES

Brown, L., Nietupski, J., & Hamre-Nietupski, S. (1976). The criterion of ultimate functioning. In M. A. Thomas (Ed.), *Hey! Don't forget about me*. Reston, VA: Council for Exceptional Children.

Haring, H., & Bricker, D. (1976). *Overview of comprehensive services for the severely/profoundly handicapped*. New York: Grune & Stratton.

J. Todd Stephens
University of Wisconsin at Madison

CURRICULUM FOR THE SEVERLY HANDICAPPED PROFOUNDLY RETARDTED

UNITED CEREBRAL PALSY (UCP)

United Cerebral Palsy (UCP) is a national voluntary association comprised of state and local affiliates and the national organization, United Cerebral Palsy Associations (UCPA), which is headquartered in New York City. A governmental affairs office is located in Washington, DC. Local affiliates provide direct services to individuals with cerebral palsy and their families, including special education, transitional services, and community living facilities. State affiliates coordinate the programs of local affiliates, provide services to areas not covered by locals, and work with agencies at the state level to further UCP goals. United Cerebral Palsy Associations assists state and local affiliates by formulating national policies on which affiliates are organized, managed, and supported. It also represents the UCP on a national level.

There are five district offices: UCP of Northeast in New York City; UCP of Midwest in Des Plaines, Illinois; UCP of southwest in Dallas, Texas; UCP of Western in Burlingame, California; and UCP of Southeast in East Point, Georgia. United Cerebral Palsy Associations' district offices were established to bring national services closer to affiliates and to transmit affiliate needs quickly to the national organization.

The UCP began as a parent group organized to improve services and educational programming for children with cerebral palsy. One of the first formal units was the Association for Cerebral Palsy, established in 1942 in California. In 1946, a parent group formed the New York State Association for Cerebral Palsy. These groups, along with others like them, evolved into a national agency that provides advocacy for legislative efforts, research and training, and direct services to clients. On August 12, 1948, the national organization was established as the National Foundation for Cerebral Palsy, a nonprofit membership corporation located in New York City. On August 12, 1949, the corporate name was changed to United Cerebral Palsy Associations, Inc. By 1952, more than 100 affiliates were linked with the national organization. As of September 1983, there were 228 local affiliates and 46 state affiliates.

UCPA works in many ways to generate new programs and services. In representing UCP in national affairs, UCPA cooperates with federal government agencies that administer programs that affect individuals with cerebral palsy. In addition, UCPA articulates UCP's positions on national issues such as national health services and transportation for people with disabilities. The UCPA develops model services for people with disabilities that are designed to be replicated in local communities (Cohen & Warren, 1985). The UCPA also supports national standards for the conduct of community programs. Through the UCP Research and Educational Foundation, UCPA promotes research into the causes of cerebral palsy, means of prevention, training of medical and allied personnel, and biomedical technology to improve mobility and communication. In addition, UCPA supports professional education by granting clinical fellowships and student traineeships and by running conferences and institutes. The UCPA uses national communications media to educate the public about cerebral palsy and to raise funds (e.g., public service messages are contributed to UCPA by television networks, radio and press syndicates, and national magazines). Public education and information materials are available from UCPA.

REFERENCES

Cohen, S., & Warren, R. (1985). *Respite care: Principles, programs, and policies.* Austin, TX: Pro-Ed.

Nielsen, C. (1978). *The cerebral palsy movement and the founding of UCPA, Inc.* Unpublished manuscript.

United Cerebral Palsy Associations. (1983). *Annual report 1983.* New York: Author.

United Cerebral Palsy Association. (undated). *Meet your national organization.* New York: Author.

CAROLE REITER GOTHELF
Hunter College

ADVOCACY FOR THE HANDICAPPED
CEREBRAL PALSY

UNITED KINGDOM, SPECIAL EDUCATION IN THE

To suggest that special education is undergoing change in the United Kingdom is an understatement. The rethinking of policies and practices in dealing with children with problems since the publication of the Warnock report in 1978 has produced massive changes, both tangible and attitudinal. Policy has altered from one of removal from normal schooling to one that attempts to integrate. A new set of procedures designed to keep children within the mainstream of society has been developed.

The United Kingdom has had special schools for over 200 years and legislation for special education since 1893. The principles of this education provision have been sound in their concern for children and their potential. Educational provision has been based on an extension of a medical model in which assessment allows diagnosis, which in turn leads to treatment. Following the medical model, it is the individual who is treated. For children in the United Kingdom, this has meant screening, diagnosis, and classification into groups such as deaf, blind, educationally subnormal, maladjusted, delicate, physically handicapped, autistic, and so on. In turn, the classification has led to segregation, partly to regularize ordinary schools and partly to provide special treatment in institutions. It is only since 1971 that all children have been included within the education system. Prior to that date, there was a further classification of ineducable. Severely mentally handicapped children were kept at home, in hospitals, or in junior training centers.

By the mid-1970s, the climate of opinion had changed sufficiently for there to be a major rethinking of this approach (Brennan, 1981, Fish, 1985). Pressures from parents, the mainstreaming lobby, sociological theorists, and the report of the Warnock Committee (1978) produced a new Education Act in 1981 that rejected the previous classifications in favor of "children with special educational needs":

A child has 'special educational needs' if he has a learning difficulty which calls for special education provision to be made for him. . . . A child has a 'learning difficulty' if: (a) he has a significantly greater difficulty in learning than the majority of children of his age; or (b) he has a disability which either prevents or hinders him from making use of educational facilities of a kind generally provided in schools within the area of the local authority concerned, for children of his age. (1981 Education Act)

By the time this Education Act came into force, provision was being made for 156,384 children in the United Kingdom (Fish, 1985). Of these, 45% were children with moderate learning difficulties, 20% had severe learning difficulties, 14% were maladjusted, 9% were physically handicapped, 5% were partially hearing or deaf, and 2% were partially sighted or blind. Following 1981 legislation, these categories were no longer used except where they would aid in the specification of need.

The Education Act requires local education authorities to be responsible for educational provision from birth if the parents request it and for the discovery of special educational needs from the age of 2. In addition, the procedures require parents to be active participants in every aspect of their child's assessment and placement. Within the school, procedures may be implemented differently from area to area but they must largely observe the following pattern:

1. The teacher concerned with pupil progress or behavior implements a program to assess and then develop those areas where problems arise.
2. Where change does not occur, alternative possibilities for the child are discussed at school meetings.
3. The parents are involved in these discussions.
4. Continuing difficulty leads, with the parents' permission, to outside professional involvement.
5. No progress leads to a full statement prepared on the child.
6. The local education authority acts on the basis of the statement in conjunction with the parents to place the child in a setting where special educational needs, as specified, can be met.
7. Reviews occur at least annually.

The central feature is the statement. This is the official document containing the local education authority's proposed placement of the child. In theory, the statement enforces multidisciplinary assessment of the child and allows the parents to offer evidence as well as their own opinions. In an ideal setting, the parents have considerable power in this process, as they must be consulted at every stage. The proposals for placement of the child and the statement of special education needs will be couched in positive terms to allow parents and education authorities to monitor progress and determine whether the child's needs are being met. Often, however, parents' involvement is small de-spite receiving written details on their rights. The proportion of parents offering evidence on their child is still very low. In effect, parents may not feel any more involved than before.

While a brief description of current practice is appropriate, it is also important to consider the main issues in special education in the United Kingdom today.

Not surprisingly, the first major issue is integration or mainstreaming. The Warnock report (1978) was widely taken as a charter for integration of the handicapped even though legislation had existed for this since 1976 and even though the report itself dealt warily with the issue. In essence, the report suggested that mainstreaming was less of an issue than might be imagined. This argument was based on simple arithmetic: around 16% of children have special educational needs at any one time in the United Kingdom; only 3% are receiving special educational provision (both integrated and segregated); therefore, the majority of children with needs are already in mainstream education. Nevertheless, better assessment is required to identify the missing 13% and better resources are required to provide for their special educational needs. Booth and Potts (1983) draw together many of the major themes: the need for a comprehensive schooling environment, reallocation of resources, clear policy and curriculum, support from the community, and, perhaps the most essential, a sense of group responsibility for all children.

There has been limited research on the effects of integration (Cave & Maddison, 1978) and it is likely that more integration could be taking place (Hegarty & Pocklington, 1982; Farrell, 1995). There appears to have been an increase in segregated education in the last 15 years in the United Kingdom (Booth, 1981). The most common way to discuss integration has been as a managerial and administrative problem (Fish, 1985) rather than as an issue in the broader educational sense. It is relatively easy to highlight the different possible patterns of integration, from total integration with limited teacher support through partial integration (on-site units and specialist teacher support) to minimal integration (special schools). To implement provision on a regional basis requires consideration of factors that concern the location of resources and the allocation of funds. However, integration issues tend to have been submerged under the weight of the administrative load, with mainstreaming decisions made according to existing resources rather than with any dynamic concept of special needs. The result has been a lack of change in curriculum everywhere except in special schools. Swann (1983) has shown how the curriculum itself must change to meet the goals of integration, not just in title but in delivery to students. This is happening only to a limited extent. In practice, children with special needs are being required to adapt to normal curricula. When this is difficult and the children fail, they are shifted into low-ability groups or manual- or craft-oriented areas of the curriculum.

However, alteration of curriculum requires an alteration of attitude. Potts (1983) comments, "Facilitating integration involves a reassessment of the dominant values of selection, competition, specialization." It requires a different view about children and their active contribution in education; it requires an examination of teacher-pupil relations that in the past have been simply the transfer of knowledge from one to the other. In a fully integrated system, children need to contribute to their own learning and the responsibility for learning must be shared. This dissolves competitiveness in the acquisition of knowledge and allows for the fact that people learn differently, according to their needs and according to their capabilities.

Perhaps the most powerful criticism of special education in recent times has been from the discipline of sociology. Tomlinson (1982) is one of the severest critics:

> But it is important to recognize that the recognition, classification, provision for, or treatment of children who have been at various times defined as defective, handicapped, or as having special needs may very well be enlightened and advanced but it is also a social categorization of weaker social groups. (p. 5)

The whole process whereby professionals assess and deliver special education has been questioned. In effect, it has been proposed that those involved have had a vested interest in maintaining levels of provision that highlight their own roles. As a result, what is determined as need is what can be catered to by that group of professionals. This criticism strikes a chord with the increasingly heard views of people who have come through the system. Campling (1981), using self-assessment by disabled people, shows the strength of group identity. Thomas (1982), in examining how the experience of disability affects a person's ability to contribute to society, indicates how a special education system maintains the lower social status of disabled people. There is no simple response to criticism in this area since it is an attack on the most fundamental aspects of special education itself. It does require a response, however, and as yet there has been none that would lead to more positive integration and a more sensitive education system.

The special education of minority groups has become a much wider issue in education as a result of the Swann report (1985) on multicultural education. We know that the underachievement of children in some minority groups pushes them toward the special educational needs area. However, even if we were in an equitable system where all minorities were proportionally represented, we would still face major problems for remediation. In a multicultural system, the values of the minority are respected and their cultural norms recognized in the education system. When special educational needs are specified, the question must be, "To which cultural norms should the child be directed?" For example, if a child has a speech or literacy problem,

should speech therapy or remedial reading be directed at the Gujerati spoken at home or the English valued in school? Do teachers understand adequately the requirements of a child with special educational needs when they do not understand the culture and cannot communicate with the parents? As one might expect, the response has been to call for more training or for a statement requiring English monocultural curricular values to be maintained. The solution is not yet in sight.

There has already been radical reorganization of services throughout the United Kingdom in the wake of the 1981 Education Act. It is not surprising that the discussion of special educational provision has meant a clarification of the respective roles of different agencies. In the preschool years, which for children with severe problems means only up to age 3, there has been greater cooperation between educational and medical professions. Legally, education can begin at birth if the parents or health services request it. This requires increased contact between health personnel and education services and should provide a much higher level of response to children and their families. In the school years, the peripatetic teams support not only the child, but also the teacher. In fact, the job of educating the classroom teacher about disability has largely fallen on the support teaching service.

In the postschool period, there has been greater attention to the child's transition to membership in adult society and continuing education for special needs. The former has meant the development of new curricula for young adults that are more relevant to society's demands. The latter has simply extended all special education issues into the areas of further education and adult education. The questions of integration and minority provision are no more easily answered in a college of further education than in an ordinary school.

While the 1981 act did not discuss teacher training in special education, at the center of all these issues are the teachers themselves. The structure of special education training is now undergoing marked change, with an increase in control from government (Galloway, 1998). All initial teacher training programs throughout the United Kingdom now include a special education component. To teach as a specialist in special education now requires additional second-tier training in special education. Training for work with special handicaps such as teaching the deaf or blind may ultimately become a third tier rather than the second tier it is at present. The picture is one of more extensive and more thorough training for all teachers at both the initial and in-service stages, but these changes will take many years to affect the system.

The current bureaucracy of professional practice in Britain prevents educational psychologists from paying any more than lip service to cultural diversity, parent involvement, and child-centered services (Galloway, 1998). Many are being used as consultants rather than in assessment (Marsh, Jacobsen, & Kanen, 1997). The latter may well be a reflection of tasks suggested by the Warnock Committee and realized in integration and inclusive practices taking place and succeeding (McNeill, 1996).

REFERENCES

Booth, T. (1981). Demystifying integration. In W. Swann (Ed.), *The practice of special education.* Oxford, England: Blackwell.

Booth, T., & Potts, P. (1983). *Integrating special education.* Oxford, England: Blackwell.

Brennan, W. (1981). *Changing special education.* Milton-Keynes, England: Open University Press.

Campling, J. (1981). *Images of ourselves.* London: Routledge & Kegan Paul.

Cave, C., & Maddison, P. (1978). *Research on special education.* Slough, England: National Foundation for Educational Research.

Farrell, P. (1995). The impact of normalisation on policy and provision for people with learning difficulties. *Issues in Special Education & Rehabilitation, 10*(1), 47–54.

Fish, J. (1985). *Special education: The way ahead.* Milton Keynes, England: Open University Press.

Galloway, D. (1998). Special education in the United Kingdom: Educational psychologists and the effectiveness of special education. *Educational & Child Psychology, 15*(1), 100–108.

Hegarty, S., & Pocklington, K. (1982). *Integration in action.* Slough, England: National Foundation for Educational Research-Nelson.

Marsch, A. J., Jacobsen, E., & Kanen, L. (1997). The impact of new legislation on school psychology in the United Kingdom. *School Psychology International, 18*(4), 299–324.

McNeill, B. (1996). Behavior support in a mainstream school. *Support for Learning, 11*(4), 181–184.

Potts, P. (1983). Summary and prospect. In T. Booth & P. Potts (Eds.), *Integrating special education.* Oxford, England: Blackwell.

Swann, W. (1983). Curriculum principles for integration. In T. Booth & P. Potts (Eds.), *Integration in action.* Oxford, England: Blackwell.

Thomas, D. (1982). *The experience of handicap.* London: Methuen.

Tomlinson, S. (1982). *A sociology of special education.* London: Routledge & Kegan Paul.

BENCIE WOLL
University of Bristol

FRANCE, SPECIAL EDUCATION IN
WESTERN EUROPE, SPECIAL EDUCATION IN

UNITED STATES OFFICE OF EDUCATION

The United States Office of Education, a precursor to the current federal Department of Education, was created by an act of Congress in 1867. Its original mission was to collect and disseminate information on the condition of education in the states and U.S. territories. According to Campbell et al. (1975), the Office of Education was responsible for establishing a system to identify and advance promising educational practices in school districts throughout the country.

During the nineteenth and early twentieth centuries, the Office of Education was located within the U.S. Department of the Interior. In 1939 the office was transferred to the jurisdiction of the Federal Security Agency. Its final home prior to achieving Cabinet level (departmental) status was with the U.S. Department of Health, Education, and Welfare (1953–1980).

Public Law 96-88, passed by Congress and signed by President Carter in 1979, created the U.S. Department of Education. The new department assumed all of the functions previously assigned to the Office of Education, and also included education-related programs and functions previously administered by other entities within HEW such as rehabilitation. Soll (1984) suggests that the rapid proliferation of social programs and the political mobilization of various educational constituencies combined to stimulate the creation of a Cabinet-level Department of Education.

Although exercising a modest role in American education during its first century of existence, the federal-level education agency has assumed an increasingly important role in administering national education initiatives. Recently (since the mid-1960s), the federal Office (now Department) of Education has been charged with (1) the collection and dissemination of educationally relevant national data; (2) the support of educational research; and (3) the financial and technical support of programs in compensatory education, special education, rehabilitation, higher education, vocational and adult education, and student financial assistance. The 1986 budget for all activities administered by the U.S. Department of Education was approximately $19 billion.

REFERENCES

Campbell, R. F., Cunningham, L. L., Nystrand, R. O., & Usdan M. D. (1975). *The organization and control of American schools.* Columbus, OH: Merrill.

Soll, C. D. (1984). The creation of the Department of Education. In R. J. Stillman (Ed.), Public administration: Concepts and cases *(3rd ed.)* (pp. 370–377). Boston: Houghton Mifflin.

GEORGE JAMES HAGERTY
Stonehill College

POLITICS AND SPECIAL EDUCATION

UNIVERSAL NONVERBAL INTELLIGENCE TEST

The Universal Nonverbal Intelligence Test (UNIT; Bracken & McCallum, 1998) is an individually administered instrument for children and adolescents ages 5 through 17 years. Although the UNIT can be administered whenever an intellectual assessment is warranted, the test was designed to be useful particularly when a traditional language-loaded intelligence test would create an unfair disadvantage for examinees. That is, the UNIT is especially useful when assessing students who are limited English proficient, speak English as a second language, deaf, hearing impaired, linguistically learning disabled, selective mute, or autistic.

The UNIT assesses intelligence through six culture-reduced subtests that combine to form two Primary Scales (Reasoning and Memory), two Secondary Scales (Symbolic and Nonsymbolic), and a Full Scale. Each of the UNIT subtests (i.e., Symbolic Memory, Cube Design, Spatial Memory, Analogic Reasoning, Object Memory, and Mazes) are administered in a totally nonverbal format (i.e., no receptive or expressive language is required of either the examiner or examinee) through the use of eight standardized gestures, task demonstration, and sample items. The six UNIT subtests and the primary and secondary scales to which they contribute are shown in the figure.

Three administration options can be employed with the UNIT, depending on the referral reason and examiner need. A two subtest Abbreviated Battery (10–15 minute administration time) is useful when intellectual screening is desired; a four subtest Standard Battery (30 minutes) is used for eligibility and placement decision-making; and a six subtest Extended Battery (45 minutes) is intended when additional diagnostic assessment is desired.

The UNIT was held to a high standard of technical adequacy for floors, ceilings, item gradients, internal consistency, stability, and validity (Bracken, 1987). Additionally, UNIT fairness was demonstrated for gender, race, ethnicity, language, hearing impairment, and color blindness. Average internal consistency and stability, respectively, for the Full Scale IQ were .91 and .83 for the Abbreviated Battery, .93 and .88 for the Standard Battery, and .93 and .85 for the Extended Battery. Scale internal consistencies ranged from .86 to .91 for the Standard and Extended Batteries; stability coefficients of the scales ranged from .78 to .87. Validity was examined through a variety of concurrent, contrasted-groups, construct, and predictive validity studies. Consistent with its reduced cultural content and elimination of receptive and expressive language in the test administration, the UNIT produced smaller mean score differences for African Americans, Asian Americans, Native Americans, and deaf examinees as compared to the

performance of these populations on traditional language-loaded intelligence tests (e.g., Suzuki & Valencia, 1997).

In one cross-cultural study reported in the Examiner's Manual, the UNIT was administered to 30 Spanish speaking students in Ecuador. The Ecuadorian sample was matched on the basis of age, sex, and parent education level with 30 English speaking students from the US standardization sample. The two samples, which differed in geographic location, language and culture, produced FSIQ mean scores that differed by 2.73 points for the Abbreviated Battery, 5.33 points for the Standard Battery, and 3.26 points for the Extended Battery. Across the three batteries, both samples produced mean FSIQs in the Average range (98–101, Ecuadorian; 102–104, US) and differed by only one-fifth to one-third standard deviations. These minimal differences between the two samples illustrate the potential utility of the UNIT for cross-cultural, cross-linguistic intellectual assessment. It should be recognized, however, that because the UNIT is a recently published instrument, independent validation studies have only begun (e.g., Maller, 1998). Many more studies are needed to assess the validity of this instrument, and its usefulness with specific populations.

REFERENCES

Bracken, B. A. (1987). Limitations of preschool instruments and standards for minimal levels of technical adequacy. *Journal of Psychoeducational Assessment, 5,* 313–326.

Bracken, B. A., & McCallum, R. S. (1998). *Universal Nonverbal Intelligence Test.* Itasca, IL: Riverside Publishing.

Maller, S. J. (1998). An investigation of differential item functioning in the Universal Nonverbal Intelligence Test. Paper presented at the annual meeting of the American Educational Research Association, April, 1998, San Diego, CA.

Suzuki, L. A., & Valencia, R. R. (1997). Race—ethnicity and measured intelligence: Educational implications. *American Psychologist, 52,* 1103–1114.

BRUCE A. BRACKEN
University of Memphis

UNIVERSITY AFFILIATED FACILITIES (UAF)

Today's network of university affiliated facilities (UAFs) grew out of the recommendations of the 1962 President's Panel on Mental Retardation, which stressed the need for a "continuum of care" for mentally retarded persons, parents, and volunteers. In the following year, federal funds for construction of facilities to house services affiliated with universities or hospitals were authorized in PL 88-164. Maternal and Child Health, now the Division of Maternal and Child Health (DMCH), was the first agency to provide program support. In keeping with the mandate of this agency, funding was limited to support for faculty po-

Figure 1. UNIT Subtests and Scales

Scale	MEMORY	REASONING
SYMBOLIC	Symbolic Memory Object Memory	Analogic Reasoning
NONSYMBOLIC	Spatial Memory	Cube Design Mazes

sitions and trainees within the traditional maternal and child health disciplines that focused on children's services. The UAFs were the first major federally backed initiative to provide interdisciplinary training and diverse health care for persons with mental retardation.

The developmental disabilities legislation in 1979 expanded the scope of concern to include other disabilities, and the Developmental Disabilities Act (administered by what is now the ADD [the Administration on Developmental Disabilities]) provided core support for administrative costs of UAFs. Today, 19 programs receive DMCH funding for training and ADD core support goes to 36 UAFs and 7 satellite programs. Additional support is generated in each UAF from a variety of federal, state, and local sources. In addition to the DMCH and ADD-funded UAFs, 5 programs have elected to become members of the national association of UAFs, so that the present network of UAFs includes 55 programs in 38 states and the District of Columbia.

The mission of the UAFs includes four major elements: interdisciplinary training, exemplary services, applied research, and technical consultation/dissemination. The UAFs reduce both the incidence and the impact of mental retardation and developmental disabilities through a range of activities designed to prevent these disabilities or to enable persons who have these conditions to achieve their fullest potential. The latter is accomplished through early diagnosis, treatment, training in self-help and employment-related skills, and education tailored to specific needs and capabilities. These goals are pursued through four distinct programmatic activities that are the components of the mission: (1) interdisciplinary training for professional, administrative, technical, direct-care, and other specialized personnel to work with children and adults who are mentally retarded or developmentally disabled or at risk for developing such conditions; (2) a continuum of a full range of services; (3) technical assistance and dissemination of information to state, regional, and community-service programs through in-service training, continuing education, publications, development and dissemination of training materials, and conferences; and (4) applied research into related disorders and the efficiency of prevention, treatment, and remedial strategies.

JAMES BUTTON
United States Department of Education

MENTAL RETARDATION

V

VAKT

VAKT is a multisensory method of instruction that uses visual, auditory, kinesthetic, and tactile senses to reinforce learning (Richek, List, & Lerner, 1983). Unlike most other teaching strategies, the VAKT method emphasizes the kinesthetic sensory input provided by tracing and the tactile sensory input provided through varying textures of stimuli. The VAKT method is based on the principle that some children learn best when redundant cues are provided through many sensory channels (Mercer & Mercer, 1985). During instruction, the student sees the stimulus, listens to the teacher pronounce the stimulus, and then traces the stimulus over some textured material (e.g., sandpaper, corduroy, Jello). Thorpe and Sommer-Border (1985) contend that the kinesthetic-tactile component increases students' attention to the task. Under VAKT instruction conditions, students are more likely to attend selectively to distinctive features of the target letters and words. In addition, they tend to persevere or stay on task for longer periods of time at higher rates of engagement.

Many variations in the types of sensory activities have been devised. Depending on the style of learning of individual students, emphasis may be on one sensory channel over another. Some students may need more involved sensory experiences. More potent stimulation may be provided by such activities as tracing stimuli in sand trays, cornmeal, or Jello. Other activities include tracing in air, tracing in air while blindfolded, and tracing over raised stimuli of varying textures. Since the activities used with the VAKT method are time-consuming, it has been recommended they be used particularly in cases of severe learning deficits (Richek et al., 1983). However, VAKT activities can be used with milder deficits or even everyday learning.

Two instructional systems used for teaching word recognition that highlight the VAKT methodology are the Fernald method (Fernald, 1943) and the Gillingham method (Gillingham & Stillman, 1968). The Fernald method combines the VAKT methods with a whole-word, language experience approach; the Gillingham method combines VAKT with a synthetic phonics approach.

The Fernald method consists of four learning stages through which students must pass. Each stage has specific procedures for teaching word recognition. As the student passes through the sequential stages, instruction entails less use of the kinesthetic and tactile senses. Words are chosen by the student for study based on stories generated by the student and written down by the teacher. This language experience approach is used to maintain student interest. Stage one emphasizes tracing and writing from memory individual words selected by the student. The teacher writes down a selected word on a large card and pronounces it while writing. Next, the student traces over the word with one or two fingers while saying the word. Word tracing is repeated until the student believes that the word can be written accurately from memory. The student now writes the word without looking at it and pronounces it while writing. If the word is written correctly from memory, it is stored in a word bank. If the student cannot write the word, the tracing procedure is repeated (Richek et al., 1983).

Stage two learning is initiated when the teacher believes that the student no longer needs to trace words for learning. Instruction differs from stage one in two ways: the words are presented on smaller cards and tracing is eliminated. As in stage one, words are selected from student-generated stories. A selected word is printed on a card; the student looks at it and says the word. The student then attempts to write the word from memory (Richek et al., 1983).

During stage three, the student begins to read from textbooks. Students can read from any material that they desire. Words are selected from the text, but are no longer written on cards. Instead, the student looks at the word in the text, says the word, then writes it down from memory (Richek et al., 1983).

Stage four is characterized by the student being able to read a word in context, say it, and remember it without having to write it. The student is taught to decode unknown words by associating them with known words or by using contextual cues. The student writes down for further review, the words that he or she cannot figure out using these means (Richek et al., 1983).

The Gillingham method is a highly structured phonics approach that uses the VAKT methods to enhance learning. The method is based on the work of Orton (1937) dealing with the relationship between cerebral dominance and reading and language disorders. A series of associative processes are used to link the names and sounds of phonemes with their written symbols. Six fundamental associations are used in instruction: (1) visual-auditory (V-A), (2) auditory-visual (A-V), (3) auditory-kinesthetic (A-K), (4) kinesthetic-auditory (K-A), (5) visual-kinesthetic, and (6) kinesthetic-visual (K-V) (Mercer & Mercer, 1985).

Instruction begins with the student learning letters and their sounds. Letter names are taught by the teacher showing the student a letter and saying the name (V-A). The student then repeats the letter name (A-K). The sounds of letters are taught next using the same procedures. The teacher prints the letter and explains its formation. The student then traces over the letter, copies the letter, and writes the letter from memory (A-K; K-A). The next stage involves reading words. The first set of words contains the vowels (V) a and i and consonants (C) b, g, h, j, k, n, p, and t. Sound blending is taught using letter patterns such as CVC, CVCe, etc. After a basic set of words is learned, words are combined into simple sentences and stories from which the student reads. Instruction proceeds with extensive use of spelling and dictation exercises (Mercer & Mercer, 1985; Richek et al., 1983).

REFERENCES

Fernald, G. M. (1943). *Remedial techniques in basic school subjects.* New York: McGraw-Hill.

Gillingham, A., & Stillman, B. (1968). *Remedial teaching for children with specific disability in reading, spelling, and penmanship.* Cambridge, MA: Educator's.

Mercer, C. D., & Mercer, A. R. (1985). *Teaching students with learning problems* (2nd ed.). Columbus, OH: Merrill.

Orton, S. T. (1937). *Reading, writing, and speech problems in children.* New York: Norton.

Richek, M. A., List, L. K., & Lerner, J. W. (1983). *Reading problems: Diagnosis and remediation.* Englewood Cliffs, NJ: Prentice-Hall.

Thorpe, H. W., & Sommer-Border, K. (1985). The effect of multisensory instruction upon the on task behavior and word reading accuracy of learning disabled children. *Journal of Learning Disabilities, 18,* 279–286.

LAWRENCE J. O'SHEA
University of Florida

FERNALD METHOD
GILLINGHAM-STILLMAN APPROACH
MULTISENSORY INSTRUCTION

VALETT DEVELOPMENTAL SURVEY OF BASIC LEARNING ABILITIES

The Valett Developmental Survey of Basic Learning Abilities was developed in 1966 by Robert E. Valett. The survey is designed to emphasize the use of psychoeducational diagnosis and evaluation to ascertain specific learning and behavioral problems in children ages 2 to 7 (Valett, 1967). A total of 53 learning behaviors that may appear in a deficit form have been grouped under seven major areas of learning as follows: motor integration and physical development (e.g., "Throw me the ball"); tactile discrimination (e.g., "Put your hand in the bag and find the spoon"); auditory discrimination (e.g., "Say, we are going to buy some candy for mother"); visual motor coordination (e.g., "Draw me a picture like this"); visual discrimination (e.g., "Show me one like this"); language development and verbal fluency (e.g., "What burns?"); and conceptual development (e.g., "Give me two pennies"). A graded range of one to four items for a particular age level constitutes a 233-task survey. Each of the seven major areas is operationally defined and arranged developmentally in ascending order of difficulty (Southworth, Burr, & Cox, 1980; Valett, 1967; Mann, 1972; Roger, 1972). The instrument, educational rationale for remedial programming, and remedial materials are presented in a loose-leaf workbook format that are number-keyed to the major areas and subtasks (Mann, 1972; Valett, 1966). Scoring is based on correct, incorrect, or partial development. The range of developmental levels and strengths and weaknesses are noted for the purpose of planning remedial programming (Southworth, Burr, & Cox, 1980). Program suggestions that relate directly to the 53 learning behaviors are provided by Valett's (1968) *Psychological Resource Program.*

REFERENCES

Buros, O. K. (1972). *The seventh mental measurements yearbook.* Highland Park, NJ: Gryphon.

Johnson, S. K., & Marasky, R. L. (1980). *Learning disabilities* (2nd ed.). Boston: Allyn & Bacon.

Mann, L. (1972). Review of the Valett Developmental Survey of Basic Learning Abilities. In O. Buros (Ed.), *The seventh mental measurements yearbook.* Highland Park, NJ: Gryphon.

Mitchell, J. V. (1983). *Tests in print III: An index to tests, test reviews and the literature on specific tests.* Lincoln: University of Nebraska Press.

Roger, R. A. (1972). Review of the Valett Developmental Survey of Basic Learning Abilities. In O. Buros (Ed.), *The seventh mental measurements yearbook.* Highland Park, NJ: Gryphon.

Southworth, L. E., Burr, R. L., & Cox, A. E. (1980). *Screening and evaluation in the young child: A handbook of instruments to use from infancy to six years.* Springfield, IL: Thomas.

Valett, R. E. (1966). The Valett Developmental Survey of Basic Learning Abilities. Palo Alto, CA. Consulting Psychologist Press.

Valett, R. E. (1966). A psychoeducational profile of basic learning abilities. *Journal of School Psychology, 4,* 9–24.

Valett, R. E. (1967). A developmental task approach to early childhood education. *Journal of School Psychology, 2,* 136–147.

Valett, R. E. (1968). *Psychological resource program.* Belmont, CA: Fearson.

FRANCES HARRINGTON
Radford University

PSYCHOEDUCATIONAL METHODS
REMEDIAL INSTRUCTION

VALIUM

Valium (diazepam) may be used for the management of anxiety disorders or for the short-term relief of the symptoms of anxiety. It also is used for the relief of skeletal muscle spasms or for spasticity caused by upper motor neuron disorders such as cerebral palsy; thus, it may be used for some children in special education classes. In some cases, it also may be used as an adjunct in status epilepticus and severe recurrent epileptic seizures. It has a central nervous system depressant effect, and is thought to act on parts of the limbic system, the thalamus, and hypothalamus. Side effects may include drowsiness and fatigue, with less frequent reactions of confusion, depression, headache, hypoactivity, and slurred speech. Overdosage may produce somnolence, confusion, or coma, and withdrawal symptoms such as convulsions, cramps, and tremor may occur following abrupt discontinuance.

A brand name of Hoffman-LaRoche, Inc., it is available in tablets of 2, 5, and 10 mg and in 2 ml ampuls for injection. Recommended dosages for children over 6 months of age is 1 to 2½ mg three to four times daily, with gradual increase of dosage as needed and tolerated; in the injectable form, dosages of up to 5 mg for children under 5 years of age and up to 10 mg for children over 5 years of age.

REFERENCE

Physicians' desk reference. (1984). (pp. 1671–1674). Oradell, NJ: Medical Economics.

LAWRENCE C. HARTLAGE
Evans, Georgia

ANTICONVULSANTS
DRUG THERAPY

VALPROIC ACID

Valproic acid is the recommended nonproprietary name for dipropylacetic acid. The common (proprietary) name for this drug is Depakene. In the United States and Europe, the sodium salt of dipropylacetic acid is used. In South America, the magnesium salt of dipropylacetic acid also is marketed.

Valproic acid is effective in the treatment of absence seizures. It is considered of some use in the treatment of myoclonic seizures, and in tonic-clonic seizures (Dreiffus, 1983). It is also used to treat certain forms of bipolar disorder, cyclothymia, and may be used with ADHD children who are unresponsive to or have problems with stimulant medication. The major side effects that are reported are drowsiness, gastrointestinal discomfort, and changes in appetite. The Committee on Drugs of the American Academy of Pediatrics lists valproic acid as having minimal adverse effects on cognitive functioning (Pruitt et al., 1985). The most significant and rare side effect of valproic acid is hepatic failure.

REFERENCES

Dreifuss, F. E. (1983). How to use valproate. In P. L. Morselli, C. E. Pippenger, & J. K. Penry (Eds.), *Antiepileptic drug therapy in pediatrics* (pp. 219–227). New York: Raven.

Pruitt, A. W., Kauffman, R. E., Mofenson, H. C., Roberts, R. J., Rumack, B. H., Singer, H. S., & Speilberg, S. S. (1985). Behavioral and cognitive effects of anticonvulsant therapy. *Pediatrics, 76,* 644–646.

Simon, S., & Penry, J. K. (1975). Sodium di-N-propylacetate (DPA) in the treatment of epilepsy. *Epilepsia, 16,* 549–573.

GRETA N. WILKENING
Children's Hospital

DEPAKANE

VALUES CLARIFICATION

Values clarification, an approach to moral instruction used with both handicapped and nonhandicapped pupils, stems from the humanistic education movement of the 1960s. Students trained in values clarification are taught to investigate the facts pertinent to a moral issue and to examine their feelings in a systematic manner. Values clarification teaches students the process of obtaining values and encourages them to explore personally held values and examine how they affect their decision-making processes (Casteel & Stahl, 1975). Rather than defining values in terms of good or bad, students learn to see values as guiding principles that affect choices. Critics of this approach have argued that values cannot be taught from a relativist position, and have questioned the appropriateness of using schools as settings for the teaching of values. As a result, values clarification started to lose its popularity as an educational force by the late 1970s (Brummer, 1984).

Raths, Harmin, and Simon (1978) outlined a seven-step process common to many values clarification curricula: (1) students are helped to examine and choose from alternative opinions; (2) they are assisted in weighing these alternatives in a thoughtful manner; (3) students are helped to see the value of making a free choice; (4) students are encouraged to prize their choices; (5) they are provided with an opportunity to publicly acclaim their chosen values; (6) students are encouraged to act on their choices; and (7) they are helped to establish behavior patterns that are consistent with their chosen values.

Students who are exposed to values clarification training become better consumers of information by learning to ask appropriate questions. Junell (1979) states that students' involvement and identification are heightened when values are taught in the context of an emotionally charged environment. As they develop their ability to integrate factual content with emotional responses, the trained students come to understand how they assign meaning and values to problems.

Values clarification activities might include rank ordering of preferential activities, sensitivity training, and listening skills development. Simulations are commonly employed to provide students with practice in values application. Social or philosophical dilemmas, based on real or hypothetical issues, are often presented as problems to be solved. Lockwood (1976) discusses the efficacy of using examples from other cultures when devising materials. The issues may be discussed in large or small groups, and students are encouraged to invoke their social decision-making skills in developing possible solutions.

Special education students are often faced with value decisions relating to their handicaps. For example, vocational programs for special education students may rule out certain academic options. The handicapped adolescent, limited in career opportunity, needs to explore the implications of vocational choices. Values clarification can help these youngsters to pick appropriate career directions and to learn decision-making principles necessary for adequate socialization at the work place (Miller & Schloss, 1982).

Some emotionally disturbed and learning-disabled children have been found to act without carefully considering the implications of their behaviors (Miller & Schloss, 1982). Values clarification provides a structure within which behaviorally disturbed children may find consistency. Thompson and Hudson (1982) found values clarification effective in reducing the maladaptive behavior of emotionally disturbed children. These children were also reported to be happier and less anxious.

Values clarification has also been used to help regular education students accept mainstreamed handicapped pupils. Simpson (1980) trained students to examine the effects of social influence and group affinity, and found that it eased the mainstreaming transition for both regular and handicapped students. Future research might focus on the long-range effects of values education on the attitudes of the general population toward handicapped individuals.

REFERENCES

Brummer, J. J. (1984). Moralizing and value education. *Educational Forum, 48*(3), 263–276.

Casteel, J. D., & Stahl, R. J. (1975). *Value clarification in the classroom: A primer.* Santa Monica, CA: Goodyear.

Junell, J. S. (1979). *Matters of feeling: Values education reconsidered.* Phi Delta Kappa Foundation.

Lockwood, A. L. (1976). *Values education and the study of other cultures.* Washington DC: National Educational Association.

Miller, S. R., & Schloss, P. J. (1982). *Career-vocational education for handicapped youths.* Rockville, MD: Aspen Systems.

Raths, L. E., Harmin, M., & Simon, S. B. (1978). *Values and teaching.* Columbus, OH: Merrill.

Simpson, R. L. (1980). Modifying the attitudes of regular class students toward the handicapped. *Focus on Exceptional Children, 13*(3), 1–11.

Thompson, D. G., & Hudson, G. R. (1982). Value clarification and behavioral group counseling with ninth grade boys in a residential school. *Journal of Counseling Psychology, 29*, 394–399.

GARY BERKOWITZ
Temple University

CONSCIENCE, LACK OF IN HANDICAPPED

MORAL REASONING

VAN DIJK, JAN (1937–   )

Jan van Dijk is world known for his work with rubella deaf-blind children. In 1958 he became a teacher of normal prelingual profoundly deaf children at the Institute for the Deaf, St. Michielsgestel, the Netherlands. His interest in the deaf-blind department led him to study at the Perkins Institute for the Blind, Watertown, Massachusetts, where he received the Inis Hall Award for his thesis. He continued his studies in education and special education at the Catholic University of Nijmegen and completed his doctoral program with the publication of *Rubella Handicapped Children* (1982), an extensive study of rubella children in Australia. Van Dijk continues his work at the institute as the director of the Deaf-Blind School and the Dyspraxic Deaf School. For his important contributions to the education of deaf-blind children, he received the Ann Sullivan Award in 1974. Van Dijk is currently with the Institute for the Deaf in St. Michielsgestel, Netherlands (Van Dijk, 1991).

Educational programming begins with a differential diagnosis for each child, not only for appropriate placement within the nine schools at the institute, but also to determine the child's learning style. This diagnosis is accomplished through the clinical use of such instruments as the Test of Development of Eupraxia in Hands and Fingers in Young Children, Test for Finger Eupraxia for Intransitive Movements, Bergs-Lezine Test for Imitation of Simple Gestures, Rhythm Test of Hand and Mouth for Prelingually Deaf Preschool Children, Finger Block Test, Hiskey Nebraska Test for Learning Aptitude, Reynell-Zinkin Scales, Denver Developmental Screening Test, and an adaptation of the Rimland Diagnostic Checklist for Behavioral Disturbed Children (van Dijk, 1982).

The guiding principle of the method is that the child is in the central position. The teacher "follows" the child and "seizes," in a natural way, what the child is trying to express. In order to do this, a close attachment or bond must be developed between child and teacher so that the teacher can be sensitive to the slightest nuance of the child's expression. This guiding principle precludes the use of a teacher-developed curriculum. Rather, the curriculum develops from the child's interests and desires. As the environment responds, the child feels the sense of mastery or competency necessary to reach out into the world.

Because the deaf-blind child is deprived of the organizing senses of vision and hearing, the world appears chaotic and meaningless. Meaning is developed by ordering and structuring the child's day in place and time, and with people. At first, the activities are similar to those of normal mother-child activities. The teacher creates enjoyable situations that encourage the child to initiate activities. The child learns it is nice to do something together with someone else. Initially, he or she may need to be taken through the activities passively (resonance). Then the child begins to move together with the adult (coactive movement) until the activity is done successively rather than together (imitation).

As the child's day becomes ordered around activities of interest, ideas are formed. The child anticipates events and may express this anticipation through "signal behavior" or body language. As the teacher responds, the child realizes that these signals produce a positive reaction. They then form the child's idiosyncratic lexicon known and responded to by all adults associated with the child. Drawings and objects are also used to represent, or signal, activities (objects of reference). Gradually the drawings and objects become more and more abstract until the child is ready to use formal symbolic language systems.

The special quality of the van Dijk method is that language is not taught as a labeling process, but as a social interaction between two people having a conversation about objects, activities, and emotions of mutual interest. Results with this method may not be as immediate as with a stimulus-response program, for example. It may be several years before the child develops signal behavior. However, there is a possibility of reaching high levels of language performance. Although this method has been developed primarily for deaf children who have language potential

based on a differential diagnosis, professionals working with the severely and profoundly handicapped are seeing value in it for their populations as well (Sternberg, Battle, & Hill, 1980).

REFERENCES

Hammer, E. (1982). The development of language in the deaf-blind multihandicapped child: Progression of instructional methods. In D. Tweedie & E. Shroyer (Eds.), *The multihandicapped hearing impaired: Identification and instruction.* Washington DC: Gallaudet College Press.

Sternberg, L., Battle, C., & Hill, J. (1980). Prelanguage communication programming for the severely and profoundly handicapped. *Teacher Education & Special Education, 3,* 224–233.

van Dijk, J. (1982). *Rubella handicapped children.* Lisse, the Netherlands: Swets & Zeitlinger.

van Dijk, J. (1986). An educational curriculum for deaf-blind multihandicapped persons. In D. Ellis (Ed.), *Sensory impairments in mentally handicapped people.* San Diego, CA: College Hill.

van Dijk, J., Carlin, R., & Hewitt, H. (1991). *Persons handicapped by rubella: Victors and victims—A follow-up study.* Amsterdam, Netherlands: Swets & Zeitlinger.

van Uden, A. (1977). *A world of language for deaf children. Part I: Basic principles.* Lisse, the Netherlands: Swets & Zeitlinger.

Visser, T. (1985). A development program for deaf-blind children. *Talking Sense, 31*(3), 6–7.

PEARL E. TAIT
Florida State University

RUBELLA
THEORY OF ACTIVITY

VAN RIPER, CHARLES (1905–1991)

A native of Champion, Michigan, Charles Van Riper received both his BA (1926) and MA (1930) from the University of Michigan, and his PhD (1934) from the University of Iowa. His degrees are in speech pathology and psychology. He is a professor in the department of speech pathology and audiology of Western Michigan University. He also has been the director of the Speech and Hearing Clinic at that University since 1936.

One of the premier authorities in the field of speech correction, Van Riper contributed to the theory and correction of stuttering and has developed methods for understanding, evaluating, and altering speech behavior. In 1978 the sixth edition of his textbook, *Speech Correction: Principles and Methods*, was published.

Van Riper was concerned with involving the family in the therapy of any child with a speech problem. He believes that parents who know what they are doing are frequently better speech therapists than formally trained therapists.

He began his book *Your Child's Speech Problems* (1961) with the statement that "once parents understand what the speech problem (of their child) is and what should be done, they can do great deeds" (p. xi).

A member of Phi Beta Kappa, Van Riper received the honors of the Association of the American Speech and Hearing Association. He has been included in *Leaders in Education, Who's Who in the South and Southwest,* and *American Men and Women of Science.*

REFERENCES

Van Riper, C. (1961). *Your child's speech problems.* New York: Harper & Row.

Van Riper, C. (1978). *Speech correction: Principles and methods* (6th ed.). Englewood Cliffs, NJ: Prentice-Hall.

E. Valerie Hewitt
Texas A & M University

SPEECH AND LANGUAGE HANDICAPS
SPEECH DISORDERS

VELO-CARDIO-FACIAL SYNDROME (SHPRINTZEN SYNDROME)

This is the syndrome most commonly associated with cleft palate. The symptoms of this autosomal dominant syndrome may include: small stature, slender and long hands and digits, cleft palate, pharyngeal hypotonia, velopharyngeal incompetence, structural facial anomalies, microcephaly, cardiac anomalies, pulmonary atresia, seizure disorder, personality disorder, intelligence ranging from normal to below normal (McWilliams, Morris, & Shelton, 1990). These symptoms result in speech problems which reduce intelligibility such as nasal resonance disorders due to a velopharyngeal valving deficit and articulation problems due to motor speech disorder. Hearing function is often impaired by conductive hearing loss associated with the occurrence of cleft palate, deficits in the muscles which dilate the Eustachian tube and structural narrowing of the Eustachian tube itself. Feeding difficulties can be present during infancy. Language development is frequently delayed and subsequent language deviations appear. Learning disability is a common outcome for this population.

The variety and range of severity of symptoms in Velo-Cardio-Facial syndrome complicates diagnosis and often delays effective treatment. Due to the wide range of medical and behavioral deviations, transdisciplinary team management is recommended for intervention with an individual who is diagnosed with this syndrome (Shprintzen & Bardach, 1995).

REFERENCES

McWilliams, B. J., Morris, H. L., & Shelton, R. L. (1990). *Cleft palate speech* (2nd ed.). Philadelphia: B.C. Decker Inc.

Shprintzen, R. J., & Bardach, J. (1995). *Cleft palate speech management: A multidisciplinary approach.* St. Louis: Mosby.

Staff

VELOPHARYNGEAL INADEQUACY (VPI)

Velopharyngeal inadequacy (VPI) is an inclusive term which refers to deficiencies in structure or function of the velopharyngeal mechanism. Such deficiencies result in loss of control of nasal resonance in speech. This can significantly affect intelligibility and may also cause swallowing dysfunction. The velopharyngeal mechanism includes the velum (soft palate) and posterior and lateral walls of the uppermost portion of the pharynx. The role of the velopharyngeal mechanism is to perform a sphincter-like maneuver which can disconnect the upper airway (nasopharynx and nasal cavities) from the vocal tract by forming a tight seal. The sphincter can also relax to allow the free flow of air or sound into the nasal area. This action produces the differentiation of oral speech sounds such as the vowels and most consonants from nasal sounds such as n, m and -ing in English. Another commonly used generic term is velopharyngeal dysfunction (VPD).

One problem area subsumed under VPI is anatomical structure anomalies, termed velopharyngeal insufficiency. In this case, there may be a lack of tissue in the velum which means it is too small to make contact with the posterior pharyngeal wall, thus compromising the seal necessary for disconnecting the nasal area. Another structural problem may involve interference from or loss of tonsilar tissue. Large palatine tonsils can obstruct the movements of the velum or lateral pharyngeal walls. In addition, pharyngeal tonsils (adenoids) can temporarily reduce the distance to be covered by velar elevation and their disappearance, due to surgery or maturation, may reveal a latent velar insufficiency. Finally, oral surgery techniques used to correct craniofacial deficiencies (e.g., maxillary advancement) may increase the diameter of the velopharyngeal portal beyond the capability of the existing velopharyngeal mechanism.

VPI also encompasses the term velopharyngeal incompetence. This term describes physiological dysfunction affecting movement of the velum or pharyngeal walls. The muscle fibers in these structures can be misdirected so that appropriate movement, such as medial motion in the lateral pharyngeal walls or elevation of the velum, is impossible. Muscle pairs may be asymmetric or asynchronous in their contraction response. Nervous supply to the muscles may be deficit, resulting in paralysis or paresis (weakness).

Velopharyngeal inadequacy can also describe the mislearning of the nasal/oral balance of specific speech sounds that occurs in the presence of hearing impairment and deafness. In addition, idiosyncratic phonological development or dialectical differences can also produce nonstandard nasal resonance patterns during speech.

Differential diagnosis of this condition involves perceptual and acoustic analysis of speech, examination of oral motor structures and functions and visualization of the velopharyngeal mechanism using videofluoroscopy and/or endoscopy. VPI can be reduced or corrected with surgical or behavioral intervention. Determination of the best treatment options for an individual can best be made by consulting a Cleft Palate Team which includes surgical and speech-language pathology professionals.

REFERENCES

Johnson, A. F., & Jacobson, B. H. (Eds.). (1998). *Medical speech-language pathology: A practitioner's guide.* New York: Thieme.

Shprintzen, R. J., & Bardach, J. (1995). *Cleft palate speech management: A multidisciplinary approach.* St. Louis: Mosby.

STAFF

VERBAL DEFICIENCY

Verbal deficiency is a term with multifaceted meaning in the field of special education. It refers to the use and understanding of language and indicates abilities that are either deficient in terms of an individual's overall level of functioning or clearly below the norm for individuals of a certain age. Frequently, verbal deficiency is diagnosed when a child's verbal IQ on an individually administered intelligence measure such as the Wechsler Intelligence Scale for Children-III, is significantly lower than performance IQ (Kaufman, 1994). Verbal deficiency is also inferred from a child's relative difficulty on those portions of group-administered standardized achievement tests that rely heavily on verbal skills. Parents and educators often note that a child's verbal skills are not age appropriate. A child may exhibit difficulty in following directions given orally or comprehending information presented orally. The child also may have difficulty with verbal expression. Language arts skills such as reading, composition, and spelling may be impaired. Speech pathologists working with children may use the term verbal deficiency when referring to subnormal development of language structures, verbal fluency, and knowledge of vocabulary.

A verbal deficiency may have roots and causes that are primarily medical. Hearing impairment, especially if mild, can be an undetected cause of verbal deficiency. A history of chronic otitis media (middle ear inflammation) and re-

sulting intermittent hearing loss can be a factor as well. Neurological impairment can result in deficiencies in verbal skills while leaving other areas of functioning relatively intact. Although mentally retarded children often show depressed functioning in all areas, this possible cause must be considered when a child presents with verbal deficiency.

It is sometimes possible to infer through evaluation and testing specific developmental difficulties that lead to verbal deficiency. These include expressive or receptive language deficiencies or a central auditory processing disorder. A learning disability (as defined by failure to learn at a normal rate despite average intellectual ability) in the language arts area also can be associated with a verbal deficiency.

Emotional factors also must be considered in understanding the concept of verbal deficiency in children. Physical or emotional abuse in the home as well as specific emotional disorders can affect the development of verbal skills. Sociocultural factors, some more readily apparent than others, may also play a role in the development of verbal deficiency. Manni, Winikur, and Keller (1984) provide discussion on this topic. English may not be the child's native language and may not be spoken in the home at all. Different dialects of the English language may be spoken at home. Educational level of the adult in the home, as well as the amount of time spent with the child on verbal tasks, may affect verbal development. Chronic school absenteeism, for medical or other reasons, can result in verbal deficiency.

Sattler (1982) and Kaufman (1994, 1979) provide a more detailed discussion of the nature and causes of verbal deficiency. A single or combination of causes may be present with a child presents with verbal deficiency. Causes not described here may exist as well in individual cases.

REFERENCES

Kaufman, A. S. (1979). WISC-R research: Implications for interpretation. *School Psychology Digest, 8,* 5–27.

Kaufman, A. S. (1994). *Intelligent testing with the WISC-III.* New York: Wiley.

Manni, J. L., Winikur, D. W., & Keller, M. R. (1984). *Intelligence, mental retardation, and the culturally different child.* Springfield, IL: Thomas.

Sattler, J. M. (1982). *Assessment of children's intelligence and special abilities* (2nd ed.). Boston: Allyn & Bacon.

MELISSA M. GEORGE
*Montgomery County
Intermediate Unit,
Norristown, Pennsylvania*

**EXPRESSIVE LANGUAGE DISORDERS
RECEPTIVE LANGUAGE DISORDERS**

VERBALISMS

Verbalisms is a term coined by Cutsforth (1932) to describe the use of words by the blind that represent terms or concepts with which the blind could not have had first-hand experience. Color words are one example. Blind children learn quickly that sighted individuals refer to green grass, blue sky, and a bright orange sun and use such terms freely in their own language although they never experience these colors. The development of verbalisms is important to the mastery of language and communication by the blind; however, the blind should also be encouraged not to rely exclusively on verbal learning.

REFERENCE

Cutsforth, T. D. (1932). The unreality of words to the blind. *Teachers Forum, 4,* 86–89.

CECIL R. REYNOLDS
Texas A & M University

BLIND

VERBAL-PERFORMANCE IQ DISCREPANCIES

When interpreting the results of any of the three Wechsler scales, WAIS-R, WISC-R, or WPPSI, particular attention is focused on whether or not a discrepancy exists between the verbal (V) and performance (P) composite IQs. Other intelligence tests (e.g., McCarthy Scales of Children's Abilities) yield similar verbal and performance IQs. Tests assessing only verbal or nonverbal (performance) intelligence are also available. Although this discussion will focus on interpreting V and P discrepancies of the commonly used Wechsler scales, much of content is also applicable to these other intelligence tests.

The interpretation of IQ test data often focuses initially on the V-P discrepancy because it possesses particular diagnostic and/or prognostic value. The value lies in indicating particular strengths and weaknesses of the examinee as they apply to present or future educational or vocational pursuits (Kaufman, 1979, 1994; Sattler, 1982).

When considering a V-P IQ discrepancy, the test user must determine whether the observed discrepancy reflects a real difference rather than one that could be attributed to chance error. Sattler (1982) and the individual test manuals of many of the intelligence tests provide useful tables to allow the examiner to associate critical magnitudes of V-P IQ discrepancies with their levels of statistical significance. For the purpose of interpretation and planning appropriate remediation programs, the 95% (.05) level of confidence is recommended to determine whether a V-P IQ difference is real or should be attributed to chance (e.g., error measurement; Kaufman, 1979).

In addition to the determination of the statistical significance of an observed V-P IQ discrepancy, the clinical or practical importance of such information must also be assessed. A method to evaluate the value of a particular V-P IQ discrepancy involves determining how common or rare the discrepancy is for normal individuals. This is accomplished by calculating how often V-P IQ discrepancies of a given magnitude occurred in the test's standardization sample comprised of normal individuals. By inference, this information provides data or base rates as to how often particular discrepancies occur in the general population. For example, Kaufman (1976) reported that as many as 50% of normal children in the WISC-R standardization sample had V-P IQ discrepancies of 9 points or greater and 34% of the sample obtained V-P IQ discrepancies of 12 points or greater. One out of every four children in the standardization sample earned V-P discrepancies of one standard deviation (15 points) or greater. Matarazzo and Herman (1984) presented similar base rates for the WAIS-R standardization sample. These statistics suggest that although statistically significant, discrepancies of these magnitudes are relatively common. Kaufman (1979) provides the following implications for interpreting both statistical and meaningful (i.e., base rate) significance that can be applied to all Wechsler scales:

> When a verbal-performance difference is significant, examiners have a basis for making remedial suggestions; when it is both significant and abnormal (i.e., occurring infrequently in the normal population), they also may have a basis for interpreting the test information in the context of other test scores and clinical evidence to reach a diagnostic hypothesis. (p. 52)

Based on analyses of the various standardization samples for the different Wechsler scales, equal percentages of subjects earn V greater (>) than P IQ discrepancies and P > V differences. Further, no pattern of V-P discrepancies were observed based on age, race, or sex. However, V-P IQ differences were related to overall IQ level (full-scale IQ) and background characteristics including parental occupation and socioeconomic status (SES). More V > P discrepancies were found at the higher IQ levels (average and above average) and for those from advantaged backgrounds, including individuals from professional families. Based also on standardization sample data, P > V discrepancies were more frequent in the lower IQ ranges (below average) and for those from lower SES backgrounds, including children of unskilled workers. These findings suggest that an examinee's background experiences help to influence the development of verbal and performance (nonverbal) cognitive skills. Also related to interpretation, the statistics suggest that a P > V discrepancy is particularly noteworthy for an individual from a professional, high SES background and a V > P difference is unusual for an examinee from a low-SES environment.

Extensive research has been conducted on the psychological significance of V-P discrepancies. Studies have reported a P > V discrepancy pattern for samples of delinquents and criminals, sociopaths, the poorly educated, disabled and underachieving readers, newly diagnosed pediatric cancer patients, the mentally retarded with familial and undifferentiated etologies, and various racial/ethnic groups, including Chicanos and Native Americans Indians. The V > P IQ discrepancies have been found among the mentally retarded with known organic etiologies and other brain-injured examinees, including children with minimal brain dysfunction, and various groups with personality and psychiatric disorders such as schizophrenics and those with depression. Although the results of a number of research studies support the use of V-P IQ discrepancies as useful diagnostic indicators, generally the findings are contradictory and point to an inability to reliably identify V-P discrepancy patterns for various groups. Currently, psychologists do not possess the ability to diagnose reliably various handicapping conditions based solely on V-P IQ discrepancy data (House & Lewis, 1985; Kaufman, 1979; LaGreca & Stringer, 1985; Sattler, 1982).

The primary use of investigating V-P IQ discrepancies lies in the ability of the test user to generate various hypotheses or explanations for the observed V-P IQ discrepancy. These hypotheses are then confirmed or refuted through examiner observations while assessing such activities as the subject's work habits and response style (e.g., lengthy explanations of verbal items). Additional diagnostic testing and testing of the limits (e.g., readministering timed items without a time limit) also contribute to selecting the most reasonable explanation for an observed V-P discrepancy. An examinee's age, overall ability level, and relevant background characteristics such as SES and other case history information, must be considered when choosing among various alternative explanations. A discussion of a number of alternative hypotheses or explanations follow and are based on the work of Kaufman (1979), Lutey (1977), and LaGreca and Stringer (1985).

Most individual IQ tests assessing verbal intelligence are comprised of items administered orally (auditorily) with the subject responding vocally. Performance IQ tests typically emphasize visual-motor channels, with most items visually presented and the subject performing a motor response. Undetected vision or hearing loss could represent a significant contributing factor to an observed V-P IQ discrepancy and should be ruled out prior to considering any alternative explanations.

A V-P IQ discrepancy may suggest an important intraindividual difference in style of thinking and learning. This explanation suggests that the V-P difference could reflect a meaningful difference in an individual's ability to express intelligence vocally in response to verbal stimuli; in the ability to think with words compared with expressing intelligence through manipulating visual concrete stimuli; or in the ability to think with symbols. Kaufman (1979) reviews the research speculating that this learning style difference can be traced to brain functioning with the left hemisphere being specialized in processing language/linguistic stimuli and the right hemisphere designed to handle visual-spatial stimuli. According to this explanation, a V-P IQ discrepancy suggests that one hemisphere is better developed than another.

Crystallized and fluid ability (Cattell, 1971) is yet another possible explanation for an observed V-P IQ discrepancy. Crystallized ability refers to those cognitive skills that are greatly influenced by specific training, education, and acculturation experiences. Often referred to as scholastic or academic ability, these verbal cognitive skills or crystallized abilities have a strong association with achievement. Crystallized ability is further characterized by more retrieval and application of general knowledge and is most strongly associated with verbal IQ scales. Fluid ability is related to the cognitive skills required in adaptation to new situations and solving novel problems that typically involve spatial, figural, or other nonverbal stimuli. Greater adaptiveness and flexibility in problem solving and a strong association with performance IQ scales also characterize fluid ability. Dependent on the particular direction of a V-P IQ discrepancy, a strength of weakness in either crystallized or fluid ability could be indicated.

A V-P IQ discrepancy can also reflect a psycholinguistic deficiency (Kirk & Kirk, 1971). The verbal scale emphasizes the auditory-vocal channel of communication while the performance scale involves the visual-motor modality such as visual reception.

Research also has been directed at the effects of bilingualism on observed V-P IQ discrepancies. Examinees who are bilingual and adept at speaking English frequently exhibit a significant P > V IQ discrepancy. It remains unclear whether the verbal IQ deficit associated with bilingualism is related to the language ability, cultural, or cognitive structure characteristics of individual subjects (LaGreca & Stringer, 1985). Also related to language, a V > P IQ discrepancy pattern characteristic of many black subjects has been hypothesized to be associated with their unique language development. This language development is reflected in the unique pronunciations, grammatical structures, and vocabulary that characterize black English. Jensen (1980) argues against black children possessing a language different from standard English that would contribute to a V-P IQ discrepancy. Jensen presents evidence that black youngsters do not perform at a higher level on nonverbal/performance tests. Despite these conflicting arguments, the language ability of black subjects exhibiting significant V-P IQ discrepancies must be considered (Kaufman, 1979, 1994).

Many performance IQ tests consist of items that demand responses involving some degree of fine motor coordination. For example, WISC-R subtests require the examinee to manipulate plastic blocks and jigsaw-type puzzle pieces and to copy geometric forms with a pencil. A V > P IQ discrepancy may reflect a deficit in fine motor coordination and should be confirmed through careful observation of the examinee's pencil grip, motor movements, and pattern of scores on performance scale subtests. As an example of a pattern of scores on the WISC-R, the amount of fine motor coordination required is approximately inversely proportional to the order of administration of the performance scale subtests.

Many performance IQ test items are timed and often include the awarding of bonus points for quick performance. An examinee's negative reaction to working under time pressure is another possible explanation for an observed V-P IQ discrepancy. Additional evidence related to this hypothesis can be obtained by observing the subject's performance on the same items with and without time limits. Further, a particular V-P IQ discrepancy may be explained by an examinee's immaturity or lack of appreciation of the implications of observing the examiner using a stopwatch. The subjects may also be overly slow and deliberate, impulsive or reflective, anxious, or compulsive in their work approach. Compulsiveness in responding to verbal items can also contribute to V > P IQ score discrepancies as extra points can often be earned on verbal test items for elaborate verbal responses (LaGreca & Stringer, 1985).

Field independence/dependence (Witkin et al., 1974) represents another alternative explanation for an observed V-P IQ discrepancy. Field independence is associated with a P > V score discrepancy and field dependence is related to higher scores on the verbal scale. Guilford's (1967) operation of evaluation refers to the ability to make judgments related to a known standard and is required for successful completion of many performance scale items. A more complete discussion of the relationships between field independence/dependence and Guilford's operation of evaluation and V-P IQ discrepancies can be found in Kaufman (1979).

Further research is necessary to generate additional and refine existing hypotheses or explanations for observed V-P IQ discrepancies. However, it rests with the competent test user to combine observed V-P IQ discrepancy data with additional relevant assessment information to gain a further understanding of a particular client's unique abilities and limitations. This information can represent a significant contribution to more efficient present and future educational and/or vocational planning for children and adults.

REFERENCES

Cattell, R. B. (1971). *Abilities: Their structure, growth, and action.* Boston: Houghton Mifflin.

Guilford, J. P. (1967). *The nature of human intelligence.* New York: McGraw-Hill.

House, A. E., & Lewis, M. L. (1985). Wechsler Adult Intelligence Scale-Revised. In C. C. Newmark (Ed.), *Major psychological assessment instruments* (pp. 323–379). Boston: Allyn & Bacon.

Jensen, A. (1980). *Bias in mental testing.* New York: Free Press.

Kaufman, A. S. (1976). Verbal-Performance IQ discrepancies on the WISC-R. *Journal of Consulting & Clinical Psychology, 44,* 739–744.

Kaufman, A. S. (1979). *Intelligent testing with the WISC-R.* New York: Wiley.

Kaufman, A. S. (1994). *Intelligent testing with the WISC-III.* New York: Wiley.

Kirk, S. A., & Kirk, W. D. (1971). *Psycholinguistic learning disabilities.* Urbana: Illinois University Press.

LaGreca, A. M., & Stringer, S. A. (1985). The Wechsler Intelligence Scale for Children-Revised. In C. S. Newmark (Ed.), *Major psychological assessment instruments* (pp. 277–321). Boston: Allyn & Bacon.

Lutey, C. (1977). *Individual intelligence testing: A manual and source book* (2nd ed.). Greeley, CO: Author.

Matarazzo, S. D., & Herman, D. O. (1984). Clinical uses of the WAIS-R: Base rates of differences between VIQ and PIQ in the WAIS-R standardization sample. In B. B. Wolman (Ed.), *Handbook of intelligence: Theories, measurements, and applications.* New York: Wiley.

Sattler, J. M. (1982). *Assessment of children's intelligence and special abilities* (2nd ed.). Boston: Allyn & Bacon.

Witkin, H. A., Faterson, H., Goodenough, D. R., & Karp, S. A. (1974). *Psychological differentiation.* Potomac, MD: Erlbaum.

MARK E. SWERDLIK
Illinois State University

INFORMATION PROCESSING
INTELLIGENCE TESTING
RIGHT BRAIN, LEFT BRAIN
WECHSLER SCALES

VERBAL SCALE IQ

The verbal scale IQ is a standard score (with mean of 100 and a standard deviation of 15) derived from a combination of five of the six subtests that comprise the verbal scale of the Wechsler Intelligence Scales. Every subtest on the verbal scale requires that the examinee listen to an auditorily presented verbal stimulus and respond verbally. The abilities measured include vocabulary, general information, verbal reasoning, and auditory-verbal memory. The verbal scale IQ is interpreted as a good indicator of verbal comprehension and expressive language skills. It is also considered to be an indicator of "crystallized" ability or intellectual functioning on tasks calling on previous training, education, and acculturation. Auditory attention is also reflected in the score.

Because of the verbal orientation of most American schools, the verbal scale IQ is by far the best predictor of academic achievement for students. Persons for whom English is a second language, or those from a low socioeconomic background or minority culture often earn a verbal scale IQ that is lower than their actual intellectual ability. Significant differences between verbal scale IQs and performance scale IQs are often used to document the presence of a learning or language disability.

REFERENCES

Kaufman, A. S. (1994). *Intelligent testing with the WISC-III.* New York: Wiley.

Sattler, J. M. (1982). *Assessment of children's intelligence and special abilities.* Boston: Allyn & Bacon.

Wechsler, D. (1967). *Manual for the Wechsler Preschool and Primary Scale of Intelligence.* New York: Psychological Corporation.

Wechsler, D. (1974). *Manual for the Wechsler Intelligence Scale for Children—Revised.* New York: Psychological Corporation.

Wechsler, D. (1981). *Manual for the Wechsler Adult Intelligence Scale—Revised.* New York, Psychological Corporation.

LIZANNE DESTEFANO
University of Illinois

VERBAL-PERFORMANCE IQ DISCREPANCIES WECHSLER SCALES

VERBO-TONAL METHOD (VTM)

The verbo-tonal method (VTM) is primarily an auditory method for the education of deaf children. It was developed by Petar Guberina in Zagreb, Yugoslavia (Guberina, Skaric, & Zaga, 1972) and reformulated by Asp and Guberina (1981). The term verbo-tonal was first coined to characterize an original audiometric technique that measured the perception of speech segments called logatomes (hence the term *verbo*) of variable main frequency spectrum (hence the word *tonal*) from the low, such as *bru-bru,* to the high such as *si-si.*

Guberina insists on the importance of the suprasegmental, or prosodic, features of spoken language: rhythm, pitch variations, and stress. He considers that all deaf children and adults have some hearing capacities, not only inferior but also different from those of the normally hearing. Those whose cochlear function is completely lost can still perceive speech sounds through their vibro-tactile sensitivity. For every deaf individual, therefore, it is pos-

sible to determine an optimal field (OF) for speech reception, characterized by those frequencies of the speech spectrum in which residual hearing, and/or vibro-tactile perception, are most efficient. The OF can be limited to the low frequencies (including impulses of infrasound frequency perceptible by tactile sensation) or to the high frequencies. It also can be discontinuous, consisting of two restricted frequency bands, one low, one high. Having observed that better speech perception could be achieved by amplifying only the OF frequencies and eliminating the others, Guberina devised special apparatus capable of selecting distinct frequency bands.

Besides the technical equipment, specific training procedures characterize the VTM. Individual work consists of auditory and speech training. For speech correction, particular attention is given to the analysis of faults. Following this, the therapist modifies his or her own speech to counteract the erroneous perception that has led to faulty production. Several modifications of pitch, tension, duration, phonetic context, and even phonetic structure are used. The visual channel of speech reception, lip reading, is not trained specifically.

Body rhythm is based on the concept that speech is a function of the whole body, and that appropriate macromotricity movements involving the body will facilitate the finer micromotricity movements of speech organs. Specific movements based on the phonetic features of the various speech sounds are executed simultaneously with their utterance. The deaf child, equipped with appropriate amplification, first watches and listens to the therapist, then is asked to reproduce the associated speech and body movements with the control of the residual hearing.

Musical rhythm aims at sensitizing the deaf child to the rhythm and changing intonation pattern of normal speech, while simultaneously training him or her to perceive and reproduce every phoneme in its different positions: initial, intermediate, or terminal. This is accomplished by presenting to the child a series of comptines, each constructed with a limited number of repetitive nonsense syllables, allowing for easy identification and reproduction.

Phonetic graphism, a later adjunct to the verbo-tonal method was developed by Gladic (1982). This technique is based on coordination between the fine hand movements of painting and writing and the subtle vocal tract motricity of the speech act.

Although devised for the education of the deaf, VTM has been adapted to the rehabilitation of children with a wide variety of language and personality disorders (Asp & Guberina, 1981). First developed in Zagreb in the 1950s, VTM was shortly thereafter introduced in France. In the beginning of the 1960s, it was demonstrated in several other western European countries, the United States, Canada, and some Latin American countries. It has since developed worldwide, gaining variable degrees of acceptance among oralist-oriented educators and parents of deaf children.

REFERENCES

Asp, C., & Guberina, P. (1981). *The verbo-tonal method.* New York: World Rehabilitation Fund Monographs.

Gladic, V. A. (1982). *Le graphisme phonétique.* Brussels, Belgium: Labor.

Guberina, P., Skaric, I., & Zaga, B. (1972). *Case studies in the use of restricted bands of frequencies in auditory rehabilitation of the deaf.* Zagreb, Yugoslavia: Institute of Phonetics, Faculty of Arts.

OLIVIER PÉRIER
Université Libre de Bruxelles
Centre Comprendre et Parler

DEAF
DEAF EDUCATION

VERSABRAILLE

Versabraille, a device for the blind, is a microcomputer with a braille keyboard. In lieu of a screen, there are 20 electronic braille cells, each containing the usual six dots that can be selectively raised to form braille characters. After a period of machine familiarization, reading speed on the 20-cell display is comparable to paper braille reading rates.

One of the main advantages of this system is that it can store much braille information on small floppy disks. Furthermore, it does not necessitate any printing on paper, and makes word processing and the production of tables and charts possible.

MICHEL BOURDOT
Centre d'Etude et de
Reclassement

BLIND
BRAILLE

VIDEOFLUOROSCOPY

Videofluoroscopy is a method of obtaining fluorographic/ radiographic and images of anatomical structure and physiological function. This procedure offers the benefits of low radiation levels, synchrony of visual and sound data for speech, and multiple viewing planes. The procedure requires an interface between common medical fluoroscopy equipment and a video recorder. The patient is observed in multiple positions to produce different views of the area of interest. A barium solution is administered to highlight soft tissue structures. The procedure is usually conducted by a team composed of a speech-language pathologist, radiologist, and an imaging technician. Two common applications of this procedure are to observe the functioning of the velopharyngeal mechanism during speech production and to track the movement of food and liquid during swallowing (Skolnick & Cohn, 1989).

Velopharyngeal inadequacy (VPI) may be suspected because an individual's speech contains inappropriate nasal resonance (i.e. hypernasality, hyponasality, assimilative nasality, cul de sac resonance). Videofluoroscopy is then used to evaluate the structure and function of the velopharyngeal mechanism while the individual produces selected speech samples which stress the valving capability of the mechanism. The information gained during this procedure aids in differential diagnosis, supports decisions regarding the efficacy of surgical or prosthetic and/or behavioral management of VPI, and can indicate the course of therapy.

Another form of the videofluoroscopy procedure, a modified barium swallow (MBS) study, can be used where neuromuscular problems have resulted in problems with swallowing. The MBS study is utilized to identify specific points of dysfunction in the upper gastrointestinal tract during eating and swallowing. The occurrence of foreign material entering the airway (aspiration) is of particular interest during the MBS study since this condition can lead to aspiration pneumonia. During this procedure, the patient is fed different consistencies and amounts of food/liquid containing a barium trace. The information gained includes how the individual is able to organize material in his or her mouth, prepare to swallow it, and how that material moves through the pharynx towards the esophagus and stomach. A treatment regimen, which can include dietary management, postural changes, and muscle stimulation, will result from an MBS study. The procedure is usually conducted by a speech-language pathologist, a radiologist, and an imaging technician, and the results are presented to a team of professionals for recommendations and followup.

REFERENCE

Skolnick, M. L., & Cohn, E. R. (1989). *Studies of speech in patients with cleft palate.* New York: Springer-Verlag.

STAFF

VIDEOTAPING IN SPECIAL EDUCATION

Videotaping is a feedback technique that has been derived from the field of interaction analysis (Amidon & Hough, 1967; Flanders, 1970; Webb, 1981). In special education, it is often used as a training system that permits special education teachers to monitor and modify their own teaching behavior (Shea, 1974). A student teacher teaches a lesson, is critiqued, shown a videotape, and reteaches the lesson (Koetting, 1985). The interaction analysis technique allows the teacher to employ various schemes for identifying units of behavior and mapping the relationships of the behaviors in time and space.

Procedurally, an observer (special education teacher, student teacher, supervisor, or principal) sits in a classroom and views a videotape. As the observer follows the flow of events, he or she identifies specific units of behavior and makes notations of their occurrences. Identification of each unit is based on a set of descriptive categories; the resultant series of notations provides the "map," which is subject to interpretation and analysis.

The use of videotaping has improved many observation problems inherent in evaluating complex interactions of the teaching-learning process. In classrooms for the emotionally handicapped, videotaping provides a method of permanently recording and stimulating teacher-pupil interactions for professional preparation. It also provides the opportunity for immediate feedback, immediate and repetitive replay, accurate recording, and availability for analysis (Fargo, Fuchigami, & Cagauan, 1968; Haring & Fargo, 1969).

Birch (1969) demonstrated that categorizing and recording the frequency of one's own verbal behaviors may be a powerful training procedure leading to changes in recorded preservice teacher behaviors. Thomas's (1972) research supported Birch's findings that the self-monitoring procedure, viewing videotapes of one's own teaching and categorizing the behaviors observed, can have an effect on the behavior of teachers who are already teaching and who have had as many as 15 years of teaching experience.

Research also indicates that 4-minute videotape segments may provide the best, most practical diagnostic tool available to supervisors in both preservice and in-service programs (Hosford & Neuenfeldt, 1979).

Videotaping for improving target behaviors with various special education populations is reported throughout the literature. Bricker, Morgan, and Grabowski (1972) used taped recordings of cottage attendant behavior to increase the time and quality of interactions with developmentally delayed children on a ward in a residential facility. The use of commercial trading stamps as token reinforcers in combination with an on-ward training program was used. The results demonstrated increases in interaction time associated with a progressive increase in the suitability of tasks selected by the attendants across four intervention phases if training was paired with viewing the videotapes and the delivery of trading stamps.

Gilbert et al. (1982) studied the effects of a peer modeling film on anxiety reduction and skill acquisition with children with health-related disabilities who were learning to self-inject insulin. The modeling film had no effect on reducing anxiety but the girls viewing the peer modeling film showed greater skill in self-injection.

Performance training methods such as live modeling, videotaped modeling, and individual video feedback has been proven effective in altering parent-child behaviors and attitudes (O'Dell, Mahoney, Horton & Turner, 1979; Webster-Stratton, 1981). However, these studies addressed only the short-term effectiveness of videotape training methods. Webster-Stratton (1982) studied whether changes brought about by videotape modeling are maintained over longer periods of time with 35 mothers and their 3- to 5-year-old children who exhibited inappropriate behaviors. The results of this study indicated that most of the behavioral changes noted during the short evaluation were maintained. At 1-year follow-up, mother-child interactions were significantly more positive and significantly less negative, nonaccepting, and domineering than at baseline assessment. A significant reduction in behavior problems at 1-year follow-up compared with baseline also was noted. There was a notable drop, however, in mother-child positive affect behaviors (showing lack of confidence and inability to manage problem behaviors).

The positive effects of using videotaping as a training tool for special education personnel, teachers in training, and special learners and their parents is clearly supported in the literature. The opportunity to emit behaviors and obtain feedback on performance are crucial variables of the technique.

REFERENCES

Amidon, E. J., & Hough, J. B. (Eds.). (1967). *Interaction analysis: Theory, research and application.* Reading, MA: Addison-Wesley.

Birch, D. R. (1969). *Guided self-analysis and teacher education.* Unpublished doctoral dissertation, University of California, Berkeley.

Bricker, W. A., Morgan, D. G., & Grabowski, J. G. (1972). Development and maintenance of a behavior modification repertoire of cottage attendants through tv feedback. *American Journal of Mental Deficiency, 77,* 128–136.

Fargo, C., Fuchigami, R., & Cagauan, C. A. (1968). An investigation of selected variables in the teaching of specified objectives to mentally retarded students. *Education & Training of the Mentally Retarded, 3,* 202–208.

Flanders, N. A. (1970). *Analyzing teaching behavior.* Reading, MA: Addison-Wesley.

Gilbert, B. O., Johnson, S. B., McCallum, M., Silverstein, J. H., & Rosenbloom, A. (1982). The effects of a peer-modeling film on children learning to self-inject insulin. *Behavior Therapy, 13,* 186–193.

Haring, N. G., & Fargo, G. A. (1969). Evaluating programs for preparing teachers of emotionally disturbed children. *Exceptional Children, 36,* 157–162.

Hosford, P., & Neuenfeldt, J. (1979). Teacher evaluation via videotape: Hope or heresy? *Educational Leadership, 36,* 418–422.

Koetting, J. R. (1985). *Video as a means for analyzing teaching: A process of self-reflection and critique.* Paper presented at the annual convention of the Association for Educational Communications and Technology, Anaheim, CA.

O'Dell, S. L., Mahoney, N. D., Horton, N. G., & Turner, P. E. (1979). Media assisted parent training: Alternative models. *Behavior Therapy, 10,* 103–110.

Shea, T. M. (1974). *Special education microteaching clinic: Final report* (Report No. 020533). Edwardsville: Southern Illinois University, Special Education Microteaching Clinic. (ERIC Document Reproduction Service No. ED 126 665)

Thomas, D. R. (1972). *Self-monitoring as a technique for modifying teaching behaviors.* Unpublished doctoral dissertation, University of Illinois, Urbana-Champaign.

Webb, G. (1981). An evaluation of techniques for analyzing small group work. *Programmed Learning and Educational Technology, 18,* 64–66.

Webster-Stratton, C. (1981). Videotape modeling: A method of parent education. *Journal of Clinical Child Psychology, 10,* 93–98.

Webster-Stratton, C. (1982). The long-term effects of a videotape modeling parent training program: Comparison of immediate and 1-year follow-up results. *Behavior Therapy, 13,* 702–714.

DEBORAH A. SHANLEY
Medgar Evers College

SUPERVISION IN SPECIAL EDUCATION
TEACHER EFFECTIVENESS
TEACHER TRAINING

VINELAND ADAPTIVE BEHAVIOR SCALES (VABS)

The Vineland Adaptive Behavior Scales (VABS; Sparrow, Balla, & Cicchetti, 1984), a revision of Doll's Vineland Social Maturity Scale, is an individually-administered questionnaire given to a person familiar with the individual being tested. The purpose of this scale is to assess personal and social sufficiency of people from birth to adulthood in a variety of settings, including clinical, research, and treatment planning. The Vineland is available in three forms including Survey, Expanded, and Classroom editions. Administration time of the VABS depends on the form used; however, it ranges from 20 to 90 minutes.

Four domains exist within this Scale: Communication, involving the skills needed for receptive, expressive, and written language; Daily Living Skills, including the practical skills that are needed to take care of oneself; Socialization, pertaining to those skills a person needs to get along with others; and Motor Skills, including how the individual uses his/her arms and legs for movement, coordination, and manipulation of objects. The Adaptive Behavior Composite is derived from these domains. The VABS also contains a Maladaptive Behavior domain, which assesses the presence of problematic behaviors interfering with an individual's ability to function effectively. Percentile ranks and age equivalent scores can also be obtained.

The examiner's manual offers information regarding technical aspects such as norming, reliability, and validity. Stratified using sex, race, size of community, region of the country, and level of parental education, a nationwide sample of 3,000 people was used for the Survey and Expanded forms. The Classroom edition was standardized using 2,984 children ranging from 3 years to 12 years, 11 months and was stratified using the same variables (sex, race, size of community, and so on). In terms of reliability, split-half, test-retest, and interrater were reported for the Survey form. Median split-half reliability coefficients range from .70 to .98. Median test-retest reliability coefficients range from .80 to .90. Finally, interrater reliability coefficients range from .62 to .75. With regard to validity, concurrent validity was established using such assessment tools as the Kaufman Assessment Battery for Children (K-ABC), the Peabody Picture Vocabulary Test—Revised (PPVT-R), Hayes-Binet, and Wechsler Intelligence Scale for Children (WISC and WISC-R). These coefficients range from .28 (PPVT-R) to .82 (Hayes-Binet).

Although the VABS is a useful assessment tool for adaptive behaviors, problems still exist. The questionnaires and scoring are long and time-consuming. Silverstein (1986) specifies problems with norming procedures. Means and standard deviations of the Standard scores fluctuate according to age group, specifically with mentally retarded individuals. In addition, difficulties framing questions, eliciting appropriate responses, and scoring responses exist (Sattler, 1992). Research into the area of adaptive behavior is quite extensive and has illustrated that adaptive behavior is related to intelligence, school achievement, and vocational performance (Harrison, 1987).

REFERENCES

Harrison, P. L. (1987). Research with adaptive behavior scales. *The Journal of Special Education, 21*(1), 37–68.

Sattler, J. M. (1992). *Assessment of children: Revised and updated third edition.* San Diego: Sattler.

Silverstein, A. B. (1986). Nonstandard standard scores on the Vineland Adaptive Behavior Sales: A cautionary note. *American Journal of Mental Deficiency, 89,* 301–303.

Sparrow, S. S., Balla, D. A., & Cicchetti, D. V. (1984). *Vineland Adaptive Behavior Scales.* Circle Pines, MN: American Guidance Service.

DARIELLE GREENBERG
*California School of
Professional Psychology*

ADAPTIVE BEHAVIOR
MENTAL RETARDATION
VINELAND SOCIAL-EMOTIONAL EARLY CHILDHOOD SCALES

VINELAND SOCIAL-EMOTIONAL EARLY CHILDHOOD SCALES

The Vineland Social-Emotional Early Childhood Scales (SEEC; Sparrow, Balla, Cicchetti, 1998) is designed to measure the emotional functioning of children from birth to 5 years, 11 months. The SEEC scales were derived from the Socialization domain of the Vineland Adaptive Behavior Scales. There are three scales on the SEEC: Interpersonal Relationships, Play and Leisure Time, and Coping Skills. A Social-Emotional Composite score is also available. The types of behaviors assessed include those such as paying attention, entering social situations, understanding emotional expression, developing relationships, and developing self-regulatory behaviors. The scales are designed to help develop early intervention plans and to chart developmental progress in preschool and kindergarten programs.

Administration of the SEEC Scales is done via a semistructured interview with a child's caregiver. Items are scored based on how often a child is reported to perform a certain behavior: a score of 2 indicates that the child "usually performs," a score of 1 indicates that a child "sometimes or partially performs," and a score of 0 indicates that a child "never performs." Age-based standard scores (M=100, SD=15), percentile ranks, and descriptive categories are obtained from the scales. The entire SEEC Scales administration time is usually 15 to 25 minutes.

The norms of the SEEC scales were computed from the normative data of the Vineland Adaptive Behavior Scales (Sparrow et al., 1998). The standardization sample was comprised of 1,200 children from birth to age 5 years, 11 months. Median internal consistency reliability coefficients for each of the scales ranged from .80 for Play and Leisure Time to .91 for Coping Skills. The median internal consistency value for the Composite was .93. Interrater reliability values ranged from .47 to .60. Validity studies reported the correlation between the SEEC Scales and the Early Development Scale of the Scales of Independent Behavior to be .63. In addition to the convergent validity information, a number of studies have indicated that the Vineland Socialization Domain differentiates between normal children and developmentally delayed children.

REFERENCE

Sparrow, S. S., Bala, D. A., & Cicchetti, D. V. (1998). *Vineland Social-Emotional Early Childhood Scales*. Circle Pines, MN: American Guidance Service.

ELIZABETH O. LICHTENBERGER
The Salk Institute

ADAPTIVE BEHAVIOR
VINELAND ADAPTIVE BEHAVIOR SCALES

VINELAND TRAINING SCHOOL

The Training School at Vineland, New Jersey, has had a long and influential role in the history of mental retardation in the United States. Originally founded in 1888 by Olin S. Garrison as a private school and institution for the "feebleminded," the Training School maintained a reputation for high standards of care and for pioneering experimental and research work. Rather than being a medical setting, it was designed to provide care and research within a psychological-educational context.

In 1901 Edward R. Johnstone became director of the Training School, a position he held until 1943. The genesis of many of the institution's later activities was the establishment in 1902 of the Feebleminded Club by a group of interested professionals and financial backers (Doll, 1972). In 1904 Johnstone started the summer school, one of the first programs designed to provide training for teachers of the mentally retarded. This program subsequently established university affiliations, and many leaders in the field were graduates of the program. In 1913 the Department of Extension was founded to publicize findings in the field. This led in 1914 to the Committee on Provisions for the Feebleminded, which undertook the first organized efforts of national scope to promote better state laws and increased institutional care for the retarded.

In 1906 the first psychological laboratory for the study of mental retardation was established at the Training School and Henry H. Goddard was appointed director of research. It was here that Goddard did his most famous work, translating and adapting the Binet intelligence scales, helping develop World War I army tests, and conducting extensive research on mental retardation. Goddard's (1912) study of the family history of Deborah Kallikak, a resident of the institution, became one of the most widely read research projects of the day; it gave impetus to the eugenics movement.

The laboratory Goddard directed continued to be considered a center for research on mental retardation for decades after his resignation in 1918. As director of research from 1925 to 1949, Edgar A. Doll made several important contributions, the most well known of his efforts being the establishment of criteria of social functioning. In the early 1960s the Training School changed its name to the American Institute for Mental Studies and in 1981 the Elwyn Institute assumed management responsibility for the facility.

REFERENCES

Doll, E. A. (1972). A historical survey of research and management of mental retardation in the United States. In E. P. Trapp & P. Himelstein (Eds.), *Readings on the exceptional child: Research and theory* (2nd ed., pp. 47–97). New York: Appleton-Century-Crofts.

Goddard, H. H. (1912). *The Kallikak family*. New York: Macmillan.

TIMOTHY D. LACKAYE
Hunter College

HISTORY OF SPECIAL EDUCATION
MENTAL RETARDATION

VISION TRAINING

Optometric visual training (vision therapy) is the art and science of developing visual abilities to achieve optimal vision performance and comfort. Training techniques are used in the prevention of the development of vision problems, the enhancement of visual efficiency, and the remediation and correction of existing visual problems.

Visual training encompasses orthoptics, which is a nonsurgical method of treating disorders of binocular vision. Orthoptic techniques were used as early as the seventh century by a Greek physician, Paulus Aeginaeta, who used a mask with small perforations to correct strabismus. The mask was still in use in 1583 by George Bartisch, the founder of German ophthalmology.

In the early eighteenth century, Buffon advocated occlusion of the good eye to improve vision in the poorer eye. This was followed by Wheatstone's mirror invention of the stereoscope, which was employed to correct postoperative divergence of the eyes. Brewster modified the stereoscope, which is still in use in visual training programs today, with lenses.

In 1864 Javal founded orthoptics and demonstrated that binocular vision could be recovered with the use of a stereoscope. Orthoptics took a step forward in 1903 when Worth established a fusion theory, classified binocular vision into three grades, developed the amblyoscope, and devised the four-dot test to detect suppression. Worth, who headed up the English orthoptic school, which stressed fusional capacity, stated that the essential cause of squint is a defect of the fusional faculty. Worth believed that the weak fusion could be reeducated.

Optometric vision training techniques were developed by Arneson, who used the principle of peripheral stimulation with a circular disk of 30 inches in diameter. Patients were asked to fixate a rotating jewel on the Arneson rotator "to aid central fixation and fusion through motion." This was the first of many techniques that were developed by optometrists to modify visual behavior by changing the accommodative convergence relationship. In 1932 two optometrists, Crow and Fuog, published a series of visual training papers that introduced the concept of visual skills.

In addition, lens application, especially at the near point to enhance visual comfort, began to play an important role in the 1930s when Skeffington developed the analytical examination with a group of optometrists from the optometric extension program. Harmon further demonstrated that "appropriate lens for near point would reduce physiological stress." A plus lens is therefore prescribed as a single vision or bifocal during or after a program of optometric vision training.

The need for visual training is established with the objective and subjective findings of the visual analysis and an evaluation of the ocular motility, accommodative facility, eye teaming ability, and visual perception. The visual analysis includes a detailed ocular, medical, and genetic history followed by distance and near visual acuity determination, external evaluation of the eyes, and cover test to determine eye position. Pupillary reflexes, keratometry, objective and subjective refraction, distance and near acuity, horizontal and vertical ductions, fusional amplitudes, and accommodative tests precede any visual training therapy. Additional testing procedures evaluate suppressions, stereopsis, eye preference, macular integrity, and foveal fixation.

Visual symptoms indicating the possible need for visual training include crossed eyes, headaches, head tilt, short attention span, rubbing and constant blinking of the eyes, poor hand-eye coordination, blurring of vision, holding of books close to the eyes, double vision, word and letter reversals, covering an eye, losing the place when reading, or the avoidance of near work.

Many of the current visual training techniques developed by Brock, Nichols, Getman, MacDonald, Schrock, Kraskin, and Greenstein emphasize development of smooth eye movement skills (fixation ability). These include pursuit, the ability of the eyes to smoothly and accurately track a moving object or read a line of print, and saccadic movement, the ability to move the eyes from one object or word accurately.

Additional skills emphasized in visual training are eye-focusing skills, eye-aiming skills, eye-teaming skills (binocular fusion), eye-hand coordination, visualization, visual memory, visual imagery, and visual form perception. These techniques have been found to be effective in eliminating or reducing visual symptoms even when the visual acuity is 20/20 at distance and near on the Snellen acuity charts.

Techniques employing lenses, prisms, the steroscope, and rotator are used to align the eyes and maximize optimal visual efficiency. Visual training procedures also are used when there are overt eye turns such as those encountered in constant, intermittent, or alternating strabismus (esotropia or exotropia). Prism therapy is often used in conjunction with lens therapy in the correction of horizontal and vertical deviations of the eye.

Visual training techniques also have been used in the treatment of amblyopia, learning-related problems, and juvenile delinquency; in sports training programs; and with older adults and workers having visual difficulties on the job.

The optometrist often works on a multidisciplinary team that includes the educator, psychologist, social worker, rehabilitation specialist, orientation and mobility instructor, and child development specialist who specializes in the remediation of the child, teen, or adult with a learning or visual disability. These methods are effective only if learning problems are related to vision system problems as opposed to a central processing dysfunction.

REFERENCES

American Optometric Association. (1985). *Vision therapy news backgrounder.* St. Louis: Author.

Borish, I. (1970). *Clinical refraction* (3rd ed.). Chicago: Professional.

Griffin, J. R. (1982). *Binocular anomalies procedures for vision therapy* (2nd ed.). Chicago: Professional.

Harmon, D. B. (1945). *Lighting and child development.* Philadelphia: Illuminating Engineering.

Hurtt, R. N., Rasicovici, A., & Windsor, C. (1952). *Comprehensive review of orthoptics and ocular motility.* St. Louis: Mosby.

McDonald, L. W. (1970). *Optometric visual training—Its history and development.* St. Louis: American Optometric Association.

Richman, J. E., Cron, M., & Cohen, E. (1983). *Basic vision therapy, A clinical handbook.* Ferris, MI:

Skeffington, A. M. (1946). *Visual rehabilitation, analytical optometry.* Duncan, OK: Occupational Education Programs.

Skeffington, A. M. (1959). *The role of a convex lens.* St. Louis: American Optometric Association.

Von Norden, G., & Maumenee, A. E. (1967). *Atlas of strabismus.* St. Louis: Mosby.

BRUCE P. ROSENTHAL
State University of New York

DEVELOPMENTAL OPTOMETRY
OPTOMETRISTS
VISUAL ACUITY
VISUALLY IMPAIRED

VISUAL ACUITY

Visual acuity refers to the degree to which the human eye can distinguish fine detail at varying distances. It is dependent on the eye's ability to bend light rays and focus them on the retina (Cartwright, Cartwright, & Ward, 1994). Tests of visual acuity provide measures of the smallest retinal formed images distinguishable by someone's eyes. The results of such tests are influenced by such factors as the area of retina stimulated, the intensity and distribution of illumination, the amount of time of exposure,

the effects of movement, and whether the visual acuity test is conducted with each of the eyes separately or both together (Duke-Elder, 1968).

Distance visual acuity is usually measured with a Snellen chart (first published in 1862) and according to Snellen's formula (based on use with this chart). In this formula, $V = d/D$, with V standing for visual acuity; d representing the distance at which test types are read on the chart; and D representing the distance at which the letters subtend an overall angle of 5 minutes on the Snellen chart (Jan, Freeman, & Scott, 1977). Thus, if at a distance (d) of 20 feet a child can identify letters on the 20 line (D) of a Snellen chart, his or her visual acuity (V) is 20/20, which is considered to be normal vision.

If a child's visual acuity is assessed as 20/200 in the better eye without correction, the child is only able to see images at a distance of 20 feet that a person with normal vision can see at 200 feet. Such a child would be classified as legally blind. Some low-vision children are able to see images at distances no farther than a few feet. If a child has a visual acuity measurement of 5/40, it means that he or she can see the 40 line (D) on the Snellen chart from a distance of 5 feet (d). Since such a rating is an equivalent of 20/160, it would also classify such a child as legally blind (Jan et al., 1977). Below measurements of 20/400, visual acuity is usually assessed by having the subject count fingers seen at short distances. LP noted for an eye examination means that the child can only perceive light.

When assessing children's visual acuity, particularly those with low vision, it is important to use visual displays with high-contrast letters and to avoid glare and visual distractions. In instances where a child has difficulty in localizing the symbols to be discriminated, e.g., when testing a child with cognitive difficulties, it may be necessary to occlude parts of the chart (Jose, 1983).

When assessing young children, those who are learning disabled, or those who have multiple handicaps that limit their ability to identify the letters on the Snellen chart, it may be necessary to use alternate methods to assess visual acuity. One of these methods, the Snellen E, requires the student to indicate the position of the E symbol (whether left, right, up, or down). Caution must be used in administering this test since a grasp of directionality and some eye-hand coordination is required to succeed; some training of the child may facilitate the application.

Other methods of approximating visual acuity include the use of an optokinetic drum, Sheridan's Stycar miniature toys, the Rosenbaum Dot Test, and the New York Lighthouse Symbol Flashcards. The last test employs three symbols, a house, an umbrella, and an apple, that conform to the sizes of the Snellen letters. The child can identify the symbols on the chart by naming them in any understandable way or by pointing to a symbol placed in front of the table where the child is seated (Faye, Padula, Gurland, Greenberg, & Hood, 1984).

In addition to testing for distance visual acuity, it is important to assess a child's near distance acuity because so many school and work-related tasks are performed at close distances. Near tasks, required in much of school learning, are usually performed from a distance of 14 to 16 inches. A major problem confronting the assessment of near vision is the lack of standardization in the types of chart systems that are currently used for this purpose. The Snellen near-point card uses the metric system to indicate close distance visual acuity. The Jaeger consists of 20 different type sizes in increasing graduations; it indicates the type sizes that the student is able to identify. The Point system uses type sizes in which one point equals $\frac{1}{72}$ of an inch. Thus a student who can read newspaper print has a near point Snellen equivalent of 20/40, a Jaeger recording of J4-5, and a Point recording of 8; a student who can only read newspaper headlines has a Snellen rating of 20/100, a Jaeger recording of J17, and a Point recording of 18 (Jose, 1983). A lay person may find it difficult to reconcile such diverse findings. For them to be understood by teachers and parents, the visual examiner should explain their nature and implications. Information respecting the visual acuity, both far and near, of all children, but particularly the handicapped, is an essential guide for children's instruction.

REFERENCES

Cartwright, G. P., Cartwright, C. A., & Ward, M. J. (1994). *Educating exceptional learners 4th ed.* Boston: Wadsworth.

Duke-Elder, S. A. (1968). *Systems of opthalmology.* St. Louis: Mosby.

Faye, E. E., Padula, W. V., Padula, J. B., Gurland, J. E., Greenberg, M. L., & Hood, C. M. (1984). The low vision child. In E. E. Faye (Ed.), *Clinical low vision* (pp. 437–475). Boston: Little, Brown.

Jan, J. E., Freeman, R. D., & Scott, ER. P. (1977). *Visual impairment in children & adolescents.* New York: Grune & Stratton.

Jose, R. T. (1983). *Understanding low vision.* New York: American Foundation for the Blind.

EMILY WAHLEN
Hunter College

VISUALLY IMPAIRED
VISUAL-MOTOR AND VISUAL-PERCEPTUAL PROBLEMS
VISUAL TRAINING

VISUAL EFFICIENCY

Visual efficiency, as defined by Barraga (1970, 1976, 1980, 1983), relates to a variety of visual skills including eye movements, adapting to the physical environment, attending to visual stimuli, and processing information with speed and effectiveness.

In keeping with this definition is Barraga's (1983) definition of the visually handicapped child as a child whose visual impairments limit his or her learning and achievement unless there are adaptations made in the way that learning experiences are presented to the child and effective learning materials are provided in appropriate learning environments.

The basic idea behind the notion of visual efficiency is that children learn to see best by actively using their visual abilities. As applied to the visually handicapped (i.e., low-vision children), this means that they should be provided with such opportunities for learning and should be taught in such ways that they learn effectively to use their residual vision. Low-vision children, without proper opportunities and training, may not be able to extract much useful information from their visual environments simply by being provided with appropriate visual environments, but they can learn to use their visual information with proper opportunities and training so that they eventually can make sense out of what were previously indistinct, uncertain visual impressions. Barraga's program to develop efficiency in visual functioning, intended for the training of low-vision children (1983), is one that emphasizes structured training for visual efficiency.

Associated with the idea of visual efficiency is the concept of functional vision. This concept is concerned with the ways that children use their vision rather than with their physical visual limitations, although the latter improves with specific training as well (Cartwright, Cartwright, & Ward, 1994).

REFERENCES

Barraga, N. C. (1970). *Teacher's guide for development of visual learning abilities and utilization of low vision.* Louisville, KY: American Printing House for the Blind.

Barraga, N. C. (1976). *Visual handicaps and learning: A developmental approach.* Belmont CA: Wadsworth.

Barraga, N. C. (1980). *Source book on low vision.* Louisville, KY: American Printing House for the Blind.

Barraga, N. C. (1983). *Visual handicaps and learning.* Austin, TX: Exceptional Resources.

Cartwright, G. P., Cartwright, C. A., & Ward, M. J. (1994). *Educating exceptional learners 4th ed.* Boston: Wadsworth.

Heward, W. L., & Orlansky, M. D. (1984). *Exceptional children: An introductory survey of special education.* Columbus, OH: Merrill.

JANET S. BRAND
Hunter College

FUNCTIONAL VISION

VISUAL IMPAIRMENT

Godfrey Stevens, in his study on *Taxonomy in Special Education for Children with Body Disorders* (1963), used the term impairment to mean any deviation from the normal. Thus impairment was interpreted by many to mean a disorder at the tissue level. Visual impairment, therefore, would mean the medical cause of the handicap. For example, cataract would be the impairment; diminished eyesight would be the disability or handicap. It would, therefore, be correct to refer to individuals with visual impairments.

In recent years, however, the term visual impairment has taken on a broader meaning. In many cases it denotes visual loss other than total blindness, such as the "blind" *and* the visually impaired, thereby separating the functionally blind from those who have some remaining vision. It is common also for experts in the field to refer to an individual with a visual impairment as anyone with a measured loss of any of the visual functions such as acuity, fields, color vision, or binocular vision (Barraga, 1983). Used in this context, visual impairment almost becomes synonymous with visual disability or visual handicap.

REFERENCES

Barraga, N. C. (1983). *Visual handicaps and learning* (rev. ed.). Austin, TX: Exceptional Resources.

Stevens, G. D. (1962). *Taxonomy in special education for children with body disorders.* Pittsburgh: Department of Special Education & Rehabilitation.

GIDEON JONES
Florida State University

VISUAL PERCEPTION AND DISCRIMINATION
VISUAL TRAINING

VISUAL-MOTOR AND VISUAL-PERCEPTUAL PROBLEMS

Many researchers have emphasized the importance of perceptual-motor skills to the development of children. Piaget and Inhelder (1956) stated that early sensory-motor experiences are basic to more advanced mental development, and Sherrington (1948) proposed that the motor system is the first neurological system to develop and the foundation for later perceptual growth. The concern for perceptual-motor development is a recurring theme in many areas of the history of special education (Lerner, 1976). While this perceptual-motor framework can be used to discuss all areas of perception that relate to motor responses—auditory, visual, haptic, olfactory, etc.—the relationships between visual-motor perception and discrimination and learning problems have received the greatest attention. The interest in visual motor perceptual problems in the United States can be traced back to the early research of Werner and Strauss (1939) and Strauss and Lehtinen (1947) with brain-damaged children. They noted that disturbances in visual perception and visual motor perceptual functioning often accompany central nervous system damage. Their work also fostered the rapid growth and development of several visual motor training programs by theorists such as Barsch, Frostig, Getman, and Kephart.

Although early researchers reported that visual-perceptual and visual-motor problems were evident in individuals with brain damage, a distinction between these two types of disturbances was not always made. While Goldstein and Scheerer (1959) considered visual-motor and visual-perceptual deficits as separate entities, Bartley (1958) viewed perception as being either experiental or motor. Some of the assessment instruments used to measure visual perception are actually visual-motor copying tasks; for example, the Bender Gestalt Test, the coding subtest of the Wechsler scales of intelligence, and the developmental test of visual motor integration, all require motor responses.

The failure to differentiate between visual-perceptual and visual-motor tasks may have far-reaching consequences. Perception is most directly tested when objects or pictures of various shapes, positions, or sizes are matched, or in some other way differentiated; it is then a task of interpreting what is seen. When the difficulty is demonstrated in a task that requires reproducing designs or spatial relationships, it is described as a visual-motor difficulty; i.e., the acts of perceiving and reproducing an object are combined. It may be possible that the child who displays a visual-motor difficulty also has a perceptual problem, although that inference cannot be made on the basis of a reproduction task. In normal development, visual perception of form precedes the visual motor reproduction of the form (Piaget & Inhelder, 1956), and copying requires skills of an order different from perceiving (Abercrombie, 1964).

Children who have visual-motor problems have difficulty coordinating their movements with what they see. Kirk and Chalfant (1984) reported that breakdowns in three areas may occur when a child displays problems in visual-motor perception and discrimination. First, a child may have problems with laterality, or lateral dominance. This type of problem becomes apparent when both sides of the body perform the same act at the same time when that is not part of the task, or when a child uses only one side of his or her body when two sides are called for. Second, a child may have a directional disability. Directional disabilities manifest themselves when the child fails to develop an awareness of basic directions such as right from left, up from down, and front from back. Very young children will have problems in directionality; this is normal during the early stages of development, but as the child matures, this problem usually corrects itself. If these difficulties continue, the child may have problems in learning. Finally, a child is said to have a breakdown in visual-motor perception when the child's development is limited to the stage where the hand leads the eye. As visual-motor perception is refined, the eye should lead the hand.

Problems in visual-motor perception and discrimination can be seen in both academic and nonacademic tasks. In particular, visual-motor difficulties are most evident when children are involved in pencil and paper activities, play with or manipulate toys and objects, or catch or throw a ball, or when they are involved in any tasks that require good eye-hand coordination.

Many educators and psychologists have believed for years that adequate visual-motor development is directly related to academic achievement. As a result of this belief, a number of standardized tests were developed to assess children's visual-motor performance. Unfortunately, the use of these tests has not been supported by the literature. Visual-motor tests have been shown to be unreliable and theoretically or psychometrically unsound (Salvia & Ysseldyke, 1985). These inadequacies raise the question as to their usefulness, and whether or not they should be used in planning educational programs for children.

Despite the inadequacies of visual-motor tests, they are still being used in the schools. Advocates of visual-motor testing use these assessment instruments to diagnose brain injury, to identify children with visual-motor problems so that training programs can be established to remediate learning disabilities, and to determine the degree to which visual-motor perception and discrimination problems may be interfering with academic achievement. Some of the most common assessment devices used to measure visual-motor skills include the Bender-Gestalt Test, the Developmental Test of Visual Motor Integration, and the Purdue Perceptual Motor Survey.

The methods used in visual-motor training programs are generally developmental and emphasize the importance of early motor learning and visual-spatial development in children. While many of the advocates of visual-motor training programs have slightly different rationales for their programs, the basic perceptual-motor orientation and the recommended training activities are very similar. Barsch, Getman, Frostig, and Kephart all propose techniques for working with children with learning problems (Myers, & Hammill, 1990).

One of the areas of controversy that surrounds the use of these training programs is the emphasis on training visual-motor perception processes to improve a child's skills in academic areas such as reading. Hammill and Larsen (1974) have argued that there is no evidence to support the assumption that academic learning is dependent on these types of psychological processes. However, unfortunately, both the critics and advocates of these training programs have based their arguments on highly questionable research reports (Hallahan & Kauffman, 1976). Detailed, recent meta-analyses demonstrate no real benefit to academic learning with perceptual-motor training programs (Kavale & Forness, 1999).

REFERENCES

Abercrombie, M. (1964). *Perceptual and visuo-motor disorders in cerebral palsy*. London: Heinemann.

Bartley, S. (1958). *Principles of perception*. New York: American Orthopsychiatric Association.

Goldstein, K., & Scheerer, M. (1959). Abstract and concrete behavior: An experimental study with special tests. *Psychological Monographs, 83*.

Hallahan, D., & Kauffman, J. (1976). *Introduction to learning disabilities*. Englewood Cliffs, NJ: Prentice-Hall.

Hammill, D., & Larsen, S. (1974). The relationship of selected auditory perceptual skills and reading ability. *Journal of Learning Disabilities, 7*, 429–436.

Kavale, K., & Forness, S. (1999). The effectiveness of special education. In R. Reynolds & T. B. Gutkin (Eds.), *The Handbook of School Psychology* (3rd ed.). New York: Wiley.

Kirk, S., & Chalfant, J. (1984). *Academic and developmental learning disabilities*. Denver: Love.

Myers, P., & Hammill, D. (1990). *Methods for learning disorders*. Austin, TX: PRO-ED Publishing.

Piaget, J., & Inhelder, B. (1956). *The child's concept of space*. London: Routledge & Kegan Paul.

Salvia, J., & Ysseldyke, J. (1985). *Assessment in special and remedial education* (3rd ed.). Boston: Houghton Mifflin.

Sherrington, C. (1948). *The integrative action of the nervous system*. New Haven, CT: Yale University Press.

Strauss, A., & Lehtinen, L. (1947). *Psychopathology and education of the brain injured child*. New York: Grune & Stratton.

Werner, H., & Strauss, A. (1939). Types of visuo-motor activity and their relation to low and high performance ages. *Proceedings of the American Association of Mental Deficiency, 44*, 163–168.

DEBORAH C. MAY
State University of New York at Albany

DONALD S. MAROZAS
State University of New York at Geneseo

PERCEPTION
PERCEPTUAL MOTOR DIFFICULTIES
PERCEPTUAL REMEDIATION
VISUAL-MOTOR INTEGRATION

VISUAL-MOTOR INTEGRATION

Visual-motor integration, also referred to as visual-motor association, denotes the ability to relate visual stimuli to motor responses in an accurate, appropriate manner. Historically, visual-motor problems have been associated with learning disabilities and, within a diagnostic-remedial intervention model, visual-motor skills have been taught to learning-disabled pupils as a prerequisite to academic skills (Lerner, 1985). This interest in visual-motor development within the learning disabilities field can be traced to the early work of Strauss and Werner (1941), who studied the visual-motor problems of mentally retarded students and believed that faulty visual-motor coordination was a behavioral symptom of brain damage. Werner and Strauss popularized the notion that adequate conceptual development is dependent on perceptual and motor development.

A prominent proponent of the importance of visual-motor integration to academic success is Getman. His visuomotor theory (Getman, 1965; Getman, Kane, & McKee, 1968) outlines the successive stages of visual-motor integration, including innate response, general motor systems, special motor systems, ocular motor systems, speech motor systems, visualization systems, vision or perception, and cognition. Each of these levels is conceptualized as more precise and exacting than the preceding one, with complete mastery at each stage required before completion of subsequent systems can be achieved. Therefore, within this model, academic learning must be preceded by extensive and successful motor learning. The implication is that learning-disabled children need exercise in the base levels of motor and visual-motor development before academics can be addressed.

Another proponent of the relation between learning disabilities and visual-motor integration is Kephart (1960, 1971), who theorized that breakdowns may occur at three key points in the development of visual-motor coordination. A child may fail to develop (1) an internal awareness of laterality of the left and right sides of the body and their differences; (2) left-right awareness within the body, which could lead to directionality problems; and (3) visual-motor coordination at the stage when the hand leads the eye. As Getman, Kephart believes that the education of the perceptually motor-disabled child must address motoric and visual development before conceptual skills.

Several teaching programs based on visual-motor integration theory have been designed, including Getman's Developing Learning Readiness: A Visual-Motor Tactile Skills Program. This program comprises activities in six areas: general coordination, balance, eye-hand coordination, eye movement, form recognition, and visual memory. Additionally, tests addressing visual-motor integration have been developed. One widely used measure, Beery and Buktenica's Developmental Test of Visual Motor Integration (1967), which requires examinees to reproduce geometric forms, is a norm-referenced test of the degree to which visual perception and motor behavior are integrated in young children.

Visual-motor integration assessment and remediation have been the focus of research. Results indicate the inability of visual-motor assessment to elucidate etiology of or instructional procedures for learning disabilities. Additionally, research has failed to support the effectiveness of visual-motor training for improving academic learning (Kavale & Forness, 1999).

REFERENCES

Beery, K. D., & Buktenica, N. A. (1967). *Developmental Test of Visual-Motor Integration Student Test Booklet.* Chicago: Follett.

Getman, G. N. (1965). The visuomotor complex in the acquisition of learning skills. In J. Hellmuth (Ed.), *Learning disorders* (Vol. 1). Seattle, WA: Special Child.

Getman, G. N., Kane, E. R., & McKee, G. W. (1968). *Developing learning readiness: A visual-motor tactile skills program.* Manchester Webster Division, McGraw-Hill.

Kavale, K., & Forness, S. (1999). The effectiveness of special education. In C. R. Reynolds & T. B. Gutkin (Eds.), *The Handbook of School Psychology* (3rd ed.). New York: Wiley.

Kephart, N. C. (1960). *The slow learner in the classroom.* Columbus, OH: Merrill.

Kephart, N. C. (1971). *The slow learner in the classroom* (2nd ed.). Columbus, OH: Merrill.

Lerner, J. W. (1985). *Learning disabilities: Theories, diagnosis, and teaching strategies* (4th ed.). Boston: Houghton Mifflin.

Strauss, A. A., & Werner, H. (1941). The mental organization of the brain injured mentally defective child. *American Journal of Psychiatry, 97,* 1194–1202.

LYNN S. FUCHS
DOUGLAS FUCHS
Vanderbilt University

DIAGNOSTIC PRESCRIPTIVE TEACHING
DYSLEXIA
VISUAL-MOTOR AND VISUAL-PERCEPTUAL PROBLEMS

VISUAL PERCEPTION AND DISCRIMINATION

Visual perception is a difficult concept to define and measure because it involves complex interactions between the individual and the environment. Basically, visual perception and discrimination is the ability to interpret what is seen. Frostig and Horne (1973) describe it as the ability to recognize stimuli and to differentiate among them.

Visual-perceptual problems are concerned with disabilities that occur despite the fact that a child has physiologically healthy eyes. A child may have 20/20 visual acuity and adequate eye muscle control, and still have visual perceptual problems. These disabilities may include problems in form perception: discriminating the shapes of letters, numbers, pictures, or objects; position in space: discriminating the spatial orientation—left/right, top/bottom, etc.—of letters or words; visual closure: discriminating pictures or words with parts missing; and figure-ground discrimination: the ability to perceive a figure as distinct from the background (Hallahan, Kauffman, & Lloyd, 1985). A child who has problems with visual perception and discrimination may have difficulty in school because most academic activities require good visual-perceptual skills. In particular, the areas of math and reading will be difficult for the child who cannot distinguish between a multiplication and an addition sign, or who has difficulty discriminating pictures, letters, numbers, or words. During the early stages of a child's development, these problems are normal, but as a child matures, parents and teachers should become concerned if these difficulties persist.

The measurement of visual perception is complicated since many of the instruments used require a copying or drawing response. Tests such as the Bender-Gestalt Test, the coding subtest of the Wechsler Scales, and the Developmental Test of Visual-Motor Integration all require motor responses and are based on the assumption that the reproduced form is indicative of the individual's visual perception of the shape. However, Goldstein and Scheerer (1959) consider visual-perceptual and visual-motor deficits as separate entities. According to this perspective, if a child copies a figure incorrectly, a teacher cannot assume that the child has a visual-perceptual problem; additional information is needed. When a child copies a figure incorrectly, but can correctly select a picture of the figure from a group of choices, then there is an indication that the problem may be a visual-motor one. However, if the child selects an incorrect choice, then there is evidence that there may be a visual-perceptual difficulty (Hallahan et al., 1985). Some tests that measure visual perception and discrimination without requiring a drawing response include the Motor-Free Visual Perceptual Test, the Visual Reception and Visual Closure subtests of the Illinois Test of Psycholinguistic Abilities, the discrimination of forms and mutilated pictures subtests of the Stanford-Binet, and the Position in Space subtest of the Frostig Developmental Test of Visual Perception.

REFERENCES

Frostig, M., & Horne, D. (1973). *Frostig program for the development of visual perception.* Chicago: Follett.

Goldstein, K., & Scheerer, M. (1959). Abstract and concrete behavior: An experimental study with special tests. *Psychological Monographs, 83.*

Hallahan, D., Kauffman, J., & Lloyd, J. (1985). *Introduction to learning disabilities* (2nd ed.). Englewood Cliffs, NJ: Prentice-Hall.

DEBORAH C. MAY
State University of New York at Albany

DONALD S. MAROZAS
State University of New York at Geneseo

**BENDER-GESTALT TEST
DEVELOPMENTAL TEST OF VISUAL PERCEPTION-2
ILLINOIS TEST OF PSYCHOLINGUISTIC ABILITIES
VISUAL-MOTOR PERCEPTION AND DISCRIMINATION**

VISUAL TRAINING

See VISION TRAINING.

VISUOMOTOR COMPLEX

Visuomotor complex is a term used by Getman (1965) to describe his model of the development of the visuomotor system and its relationship to the acquisition of learning skills. This model reflects Getman's training as an optometrist by emphasizing the visual aspects of perception. It illustrates the developmental sequences that a child progresses through while acquiring visual-perceptual and motor skills, and emphasizes that each successive stage is dependent on earlier stages of development.

The six systems of learning levels in this model are (from the lowest to the highest) the innate response system, the general motor system, the special motor system, the ocular motor system, the speech-motor system, and the visualization system. These systems all contribute to vision or the perceptual event that results in cognition when many perceptions are integrated (Lerner, 1971).

This visuomotor complex requires solid learning at each level before proceeding to the next level. Getman believes that children will not succeed in educational programs if they do not have adequate experiences in the lower systems of development. A teaching program, Developing Learning Readiness: A Visual-Motor Tactile Skills Program (Getman, Kane, & McKee, 1968), is based on this model.

This visuomotor model has been criticized for simplifying learning, overemphasizing the role of vision, neglecting the role of language, speech, and feedback, and not providing empirical evidence for the theory (Lerner, 1971; Myers & Hammill, 1969).

REFERENCES

Getman, G. (1965). The visuomotor complex in the acquisition of learning skills. In J. Hellmuth (Ed.), *Learning disorders* (Vol. 1, pp. 49–76). Seattle, WA: Special Child.

Getman, G., Kane, E., & McKee, G. (1968). *Developing learning readiness: A visual-motor tactile skills program.* Manchester, MO: Webster Division, McGraw-Hill.

Lerner, J. (1971). *Children with learning disabilities.* Boston: Houghton Mifflin.

Myers, P., & Hammill, D. (1969). *Methods for learning disorders.* New York: Wiley.

DEBORAH C. MAY
State University of New York at Albany

VISUAL PERCEPTION AND DISCRIMINATION
VISUAL TRAINING

VOCABULARY DEVELOPMENT

The knowledge of vocabulary, that is, the ability to recognize words and understand their meanings, is recognized as possibly the most important factor in being able to use and understand spoken and written language. Vocabulary knowledge is very closely associated with the ability to comprehend what is heard or read, and may be related to general intelligence and reasoning ability.

According to Harris (1970), children develop a variety of types of vocabulary knowledge in a developmental sequence. First they develop a hearing vocabulary, or the ability to respond to spoken words even before they themselves are able to use speech. For a number of years children are able to respond to more words that they hear than words that they are able to use themselves. Following the appropriate development of a hearing vocabulary, children begin to acquire emerging reading skills and a reading vocabulary—words that they are able to recognize in print and know the meanings of in context. Gradually, the developing reader is able to recognize more words in print and is able to use more words than in the speaking and writing vocabulary. Harris has explained that a child's total vocabulary involves all of the words that he or she can eventually understand and use in all the communications skills, including listening, speaking, reading, and writing.

The significance of a varied and well-developed vocabulary cannot be overemphasized, according to Johnson and Pearson (1984). They have identified and explained the reading process as a communication between an author and a reader. That communication is successful only when the reader is able to understand the author's original intent by recognizing and understanding the vocabulary that the author uses. It follows, then, that in order to be a fluent, proficient, and successful reader, it is necessary to possess a rich and varied vocabulary and word knowledge background.

General vocabulary development, and the ability to recognize words either in isolation or in context, have a common link in the diversity of words that the reader can both understand and use. Many of the words that the developing learner and reader uses and understands have been with him or her from early years; other words are learned and developed as they are used in the context of school-related activities. Therefore, while a rich experiential background during the preschool years is certainly a requisite for later vocabulary learning, much of the vocabulary development that the child experiences is accomplished in school. According to Smith and Johnson (1980), Stauffer (1969), and Johnson and Pearson (1984), a meaningful vocabulary is developed through reading- and writing-related activities in a variety of ways. These include the development of a basic sight vocabulary, various word identification strategies, including phonics, structural analysis, context clues, and instruction in understanding the deeper meanings of words. Through the activities outlined in basal reading programs, and occasionally through the use of content area materials, students are taught to use and understand synonyms, antonyms, homophones, and multiple meaning words. They also are taught to use the various resources such as dictionaries and thesauruses for determining word meaning.

One of the best ways to learn new words and what they mean is to become involved with reading and listening. Moffett and Wagner (1983) have stated that children need to become habitual readers. They must immerse themselves in a variety of reading and listening activities that will enable them to experience words in a variety of contexts and allow them to make generalizations about the meanings of words and how they may be used. Particularly during the elementary years, they argue, much of schooling must be involved with providing children with a variety of language-related situations that require them to be actively engaged in the production and reception of language in both oral and written forms. As the child becomes more engaged in reading and writing activities, preferably related to different content areas, not only is general vocabulary knowledge increased, but reasoning ability and conceptual development are enhanced.

The essence of reading and writing is communication, and the crucial variable in communication seems to be vocabulary knowledge. What distinguishes the fluent, successful reader from the poor reader seems to be a knowledge of words and what they mean. A successful and appropriate program of vocabulary development in the school, coupled with the child's preschool experiential background, may provide that key ingredient to becoming a successful language user. Johnson and Pearson (1984) give a complete and detailed account of how to provide an appropriate program of vocabulary development in school.

REFERENCES

Harris, A. J. (1970). *How to increase reading ability* (5th ed.). New York: McKay.

Johnson, D. D., & Pearson, P. D. (1984). *Teaching reading vocabulary* (2nd ed.). New York: Holt, Rinehart, & Winston.

Moffett, J., & Wagner, B. J. (1983). *Student centered language arts and reading, K–13: A handbook for teachers* (3rd ed.). Boston: Houghton Mifflin.

Smith, R. J., & Johnson, D. D. (1980). *Teaching children to read* (2nd ed.). Reading, MA: Addison-Wesley.

Stauffer, R. G. (1969). *Directing reading maturity as a cognitive process*. New York: Harper & Row.

JOHN M. EELLS
Souderton Area School District,
Souderton, Pennsylvania

INTELLIGENCE
READING
READING REMEDIATION

VOCATIONAL EDUCATION

The goal of vocational education programs is to prepare students to enter the world of work. Astuto (1982) described vocational programs as focusing on the development of basic academic skills, good work habits, personally meaningful work values, self-understanding and identification of preferences, skills and aptitudes, occupational opportunities, the ability to plan and make career decisions, and the locating and securing of employment.

The basic program components for vocational education are recognized as remedial basic skills, specific job training, personal and social adjustment skills, career information, modified content in subject areas, and on-the-job training. Further, Ondell and Hardin (1981) delineated four types of occupational activities that would be part of a vocational program: paid work experience during the day, paid work experience after school hours, unpaid work observation, and in-school vocational laboratory.

From a historical perspective, the first piece of legislation to address the vocational educational needs of the handicapped was the Vocational Education Act of 1963 (PL 88-210). The Educational Amendments of 1976 (PL 94-482) strengthened provisions for handicapped youths in vocational education.

According to Ondell and Hardin (1981), legislation promoting vocational education and the rights of the handi-

capped has included the Smith-Hughes Act of 1917, which provided funds for vocational education in public schools; the Civilian Rehabilitation Act of 1920, which assigned responsibility for the administration of vocational rehabilitation to state boards of vocational education; the Vocational Rehabilitation Amendments of 1943, which expanded the 1920 act to include mentally and emotionally handicapped persons; the Vocational Education Act of 1963, which provided occupational training for persons with special needs and allowed some of a state's allotment to be used in funding these programs; the Vocational Amendments of 1965, which removed the responsibility for administration of these programs from state boards; and the Vocational Amendments of 1968, which included more specific terminology and specified that 10% of the monies received by the state be set aside for the vocational education of the handicapped. With these monies many specifically designed programs for the handicapped were started, thus expanding the area of vocational education to encompass special groups (pp. 2–3).

The Vocational Education Act, as amended in 1976 (PL 94-482, Title II), designated vocational education for handicapped persons as a national priority. This mandated that 10% of federal monies be used, in part, to pay up to 50% of the cost of additional services handicapped students need to succeed in vocational education.

Public Law 94-142 has unequivocally established that every handicapped youth be given the opportunity to participate in free and appropriate vocational education programs. According to Greenan (1982), the law states that

> Vocational education means organized education programs which are directly related to the preparation of individuals for paid or unpaid employment, or for additional preparation for a career requiring other than a baccalaureate or advanced degree. (121a.14(b)(3))

And in addition

> vocational education is "included as special education" if it consists of specially designed instruction, at no cost to the parents, to meet the unique needs of a handicapped child. [121.14(a)(3)]

The Carl D. Perkins Vocational Education Act, PL 98-524, replaced the Vocational Education Act of 1963. The new act ordered federal involvement in vocational education around two broad themes. First, equal access to vocational education must be provided to handicapped persons. Second, the quality of vocational education must be improved. The act specifies that 10% of its funds must be allocated for vocational education services and activities designed to meet the special needs of, and enhance the participation of, handicapped individuals. This is accomplished through allotments to local school districts on a formula basis. Each local school district has to comply with five prescriptive requirements. The first of these is to provide information to handicapped students and parents concerning opportunities available in vocational education at least 1 year before the student enters the grade in which vocational education programs are first generally available, but in no event later than the beginning of ninth grade. Each handicapped student who enrolls in a vocational education program shall receive an assessment of his or her interests, abilities, and special needs; special services, including adaptation of curriculum; guidance, counseling, and career development activities conducted by professionally trained counselors; and counseling services designed to facilitate the transition from school to postsecondary environments.

Vocational education for students with disabilities generally entails at least two different approaches, depending on the severity of the disability. A major thrust at the state level has been to provide the necessary supportive services to handicapped persons enrolled in regular vocational education programs.

A leading example of a vocational education framework for youngsters with severe disabilities can be found in the Madison Metropolitan School District. Since 1976 severely handicapped students have been provided with systematic vocational training in nonsheltered community sites. There are two principles on which this framework was developed: that vocational training should occur in nonsheltered, nonschool environments and that all students must be taught to engage in meaningful work (Sweet et al., 1982).

In summary, Astuto (1982) discussed six aspects that defined excellence in vocational education programs: career exploration; vocational assessment/evaluation; training; work experience; follow-up with on-the-job placement; and advocacy. Also of importance were partnerships between vocational and special education as well as interagency agreement.

REFERENCES

Astuto, T. A. (1982). *Vocational education programs and services for high school handicapped students*. Bloomington: Council of Administrators of Special Education, Indiana University.

Brown, L., Shirago, B., Ford, A., Van Deventer, P., Nisbet, S., Loomis, R., & Sweet, M. (1983). Teaching severely handicapped students to perform meaningful work in nonsheltered vocational environments. In L. Brown, A. Ford, S. Nisbet, M. Sweet, B. Shiraga, & R. Loomis (Eds.), *Educational programs for severely handicapped students* (Vol. 13, pp. 1–100). Madison, WI: Madison Metropolitan School District.

Greenan, J. P. (1982). State planning for vocational/special education personnel development. *Teacher Education & Special Education, 5*(4), 69–76.

Ondell, J. T., & Hardin, L. (1981). *Vocational education programming for the handicapped*. Bloomington: Council of Administrators of Special Education, Indiana University.

Sweet, M., Shiraga, B., Fred, A., Nisbet, J., Graff, S., & Loomis, R. (1982). Are ecological strategies applicable for severely multihandicapped students? In L. Brown, J. Nisbet, A. Ford, M. Sweet, B. Shiraga, & L. Gruenewald (Eds.), *Educational programs for severely handicapped students* (Vol. 12, pp. 99–130). Madison, WI: Madison Metropolitan School District.

EILEEN MCCARTHY
University of Wisconsin at Madison

REHABILITATION
VOCATIONAL EVALUATION
VOCATIONAL TRAINING OF THE HANDICAPPED

VOCATIONAL EDUCATION ACT OF 1963

Public Law 88-210, the Vocational Education Act of 1963, provided priority allotments of state funds for vocational education programs for the handicapped. Under 20 USCS, Section 2310, for each fiscal year, at least 10% of each state's allotments under Section 103 (20 USCS Section 2303) from appropriations made under Section 102(a) (20 USCS, Section 2303(a)) shall be used to pay up to 50% of the cost of programs, services, and activities under Subpart 2 (20 USCS, Section 2330 et seq.) and of program improvement and support services under Subpart 3 (20 USCS, Section 2350 et seq.) for handicapped persons.

DANIEL R. PAULSON
University of Wisconsin at Stout

REHABILITATION
VOCATIONAL TRAINING OF THE HANDICAPPED

VOCATIONAL EVALUATION

Vocational evaluation is a term that encompasses the processes undertaken in determining eligibility and appropriate program plans for students entering vocational education. Specific components and processes used in vocational evaluation include assessment of skills, aptitude, interests, work behaviors, social skills, and physical capabilities (Leconte, 1985; Levinson & Capps, 1985; Peterson, 1985; Rosenberg & Tesolowski, 1982). The area of vocational assessment is affected by the Carl Perkins Vocational Education Act of 1984, which mandates that schools provide each handicapped or disadvantaged student who enrolls in a vocational education program an assessment of the individual's interests, abilities, and special needs with respect to the successful completion of the vocational education program (Cobb and Larkin, 1985).

The terms vocational evaluation and vocational assessment are often used interchangeably. Although Leconte (1985) indicated that the Division on Career Development (DCD) of the Council for Exceptional Children (CEC) does not discriminate between vocational evaluation and vocational assessment, he differentiated between the two terms as follows: vocational assessment is an on-going process carried out by professionals from many different disciplines, and information from vocational assessment is incorporated into a student's total educational program; vocational evaluation is an in-depth process conducted by a trained vocational evaluator, usually in a vocational evaluation center.

School personnel have not been able to agree on a term or title to represent the realm of student assessment in vocational education. When first introduced into school settings, programs were called vocational evaluation based on the service's origin in vocational rehabilitation. After PL 94-142, the service was aligned with services for special education and different forms of evaluation were frequently referred to as vocational assessment. In essence, vocational evaluation has been delineated as a more intensive, time-limited service than vocational assessment. Although the term vocational evaluation represents the broad umbrella under which vocational assessment is subsumed, for our purposes the terms will be referred to as vocational evaluation/assessment.

The purposes and goals are well defined and agreed on throughout the literature. Vocational assessment is a process that

> Measures skills, attitudes, interests, and physical abilities
>
> Predicts success in occupational placements
>
> Prescribes the necessary program plan needed to reach the objectives
>
> Explores interests and matches them with abilities
>
> Observes behavioral changes

Levinson and Capps (1985) discussed vocational assessment as a process that yields critical information with which vocational programming decisions may be made. They include the identification of appropriate goals and instructional methods in the process.

Peterson (1985) suggested six guidelines for effective vocational assessment: (1) use trained personnel; (2) develop and use locally developed work samples; (3) obtain access to a vocational evaluation center; (4) plan to develop and expand vocational assessment in phases with a team; (5) ascertain that vocational assessment is instructionally relevant and useful; and (6) ensure that the vocational assessment is used for vocational guidance and the identification of appropriate career and vocational service.

Peterson (1985) stated that vocational assessment can be "a powerful tool in the education of special students" since it can provide a link between special education or Chapter 1 services and vocational education. The challenge to fully operationalize these services with respect to students with disabilities remains.

REFERENCES

Cobb, R. B., & Larkin, D. (1985). Assessment and placement of handicapped pupils into secondary vocational education programs. *Focus on Exceptional Children, 17*(7), 1–14.

Leconte, P. (1985, December). *Vocational assessment of the special needs learner: A vocational education perspective.* Paper presented at the meeting of the American Vocational Association Convention, Atlanta, GA.

Levinson, E. M., & Capps, C. F. (1985). Vocational assessment and special education triennial reevaluations at the secondary school level. *Psychology in the Schools, 22,* 283–292.

Peterson, M. (1985, December). *Vocational assessment of special students: A comprehensive developmental approach.* Paper presented at the meeting of the American Vocational Association Convention, Atlanta, GA.

Rosenberg, H., & Tesolowski, D. G. (1982). Assessment of critical vocational behaviors. *Career Development for Exceptional Individuals, 5,* 25–37.

EILEEN F. MCCARTHY
University of Wisconsin at Madison

VOCATIONAL REHABILITATION
VOCATIONAL REHABILITATION COUNSELOR
VOCATIONAL TRAINING OF THE HANDICAPPED

VOCATIONAL REHABILITATION ACT OF 1973

Section 504 of what is commonly called the Rehabilitation Act is frequently cited as an important precursor to the passage of PL 94-142 two years later (Reschly & Bersoff, 1999). Section 504, among other things, protects the rights of handicapped children and precludes discrimination in employment and education. The stipulations of the Rehabilitation Act apply to the programs receiving federal financial assistance.

The Rehabilitation Act was cited in the noted *Larry P.* v. *Riles* decision by Judge Peckham in 1979. This decision cited the state as being in noncompliance with Section 504 in its use of intelligence tests for making placement decisions in special education. Certainly, the Rehabilitation Act of 1973 has had an important impact on special education practice by encouraging more sophisticated and humane treatment of handicapped children.

REFERENCE

Reschly, D., & Bersoff, D. N. (1999). Law and school psychology. In C. R. Reynolds & T. B. Gutkin (Eds.), *The handbook of school psychology* (3rd ed.). New York: Wiley.

RANDY W. KAMPHAUS
Eastern Kentucky University

EDUCATION FOR ALL HANDICAPPED CHILDREN ACT OF 1975
INDIVIDUALS WITH DISABILITIES EDUCATION ACT
LARRY P.

VOCATIONAL REHABILITATION COUNSELING

According to the 1984–1985 edition of the *Occupational Outlook Handbook,* "Rehabilitation counselors assist physically, mentally, emotionally, or socially handicapped individuals to become self-sufficient and productive citizens." While this general definition is correct, the actual activities engaged in by rehabilitation counselors and the resources available to them vary considerably depending on their work setting.

Today there are approximately 19,000 rehabilitation counselors in the United States, over half of whom work in agencies supported by federal and state funds (Wright, 1980). The prototypical rehabilitation counselor works for one of the state Department of Vocational Rehabilitation (DVR) agencies and places primary emphasis on the vocational adjustment of disabled clients who are adjudged to have the potential for gainful employment. Rehabilitation counselors also work in a wide variety of allied settings such as sheltered workshops, centers for the developmentally disabled, rehabilitation centers, Veterans' Administration programs, employment services, alcohol and drug abuse programs, halfway houses, insurance companies, and private for-profit organizations that specialize in the rehabilitation of industrially injured clients. New developments in the rehabilitation counselor's role are seen in recent movements to provide independent living skills to the severely disabled and assistance to disabled youths as they make the transition from school to the world of work.

The profession of rehabilitation counseling emerged with the passage of PL 236 (Smith-Fess Act) in 1920, which established the civilian vocational rehabilitation program in the United States. However, it was not until the passage of PL 565 in 1954 that federal funds were available to encourage formal academic training for rehabilitation personnel. There are now approximately 90 master's degree programs in rehabilitation counseling offered by universities and colleges throughout the country (Rubin & Roessler, 1983). There are also numerous bachelor's and doctoral programs available in rehabilitation. Today the professional identity of the rehabilitation counselor is well established and there is consensus regarding an appropriate educational curriculum. The knowledge base and competencies for this profession are reflected in the following core subjects that are taught in most rehabilitation counselor training programs: history and philosophy of rehabilitation, vocational and personal counseling, physical disabilities, mental retardation, mental illness, psychosocial implications of disability, psychological testing, vocational evaluation, occupational information and employment trends, community resources, job placement, and supervised internships.

The most prominent professional organizations for rehabilitation counselors are the National Rehabilitation Association, the National Rehabilitation Counseling Association, and the American Rehabilitation Counseling Association. Within the past decade, certification procedures for rehabilitation counselors have been established through the efforts of various professional organizations. Certification is based on a combination of education, experience, and the successful completion of a national examination. While certification procedures do guarantee minimum standards of competency, they may be criticized for restricting entrance into the profession by those who are otherwise qualified but lack formal credentials. Many rehabilitation employers expect applicants to be certified, but this is by no means universal and the eventual status of certification is unclear at present.

The high social validity of rehabilitation counseling is indicated by the continuing bipartisan congressional support that rehabilitation legislation has enjoyed for over 65 years. Studies estimate that once disabled persons return to work they earn, and pay taxes on, between 8 and 33 times the amount of money that was spent on their rehabilitation (Bitter, 1979). Additional economic benefits accrue to society from the reductions in welfare, disability, and medical assistance payments after the disabled person enters the work force. In human terms, state DVR agencies rehabilitate between 300,000 and 400,000 handicapped persons per year. The dignity and self-esteem these individuals feel when they become contributing members of society cannot be measured in dollars.

REFERENCES

Bitter, J. A. (1979). *Introduction to rehabilitation.* St. Louis: Mosby.

Bureau of Labor Statistics. (1984). *Occupational outlook handbook: 1984–1985 edition (Bulletin 2205).* Washington, DC: U.S. Department of Labor.

Rubin, S. E. & Roessler, R. T. (1983). *Foundations of the vocational rehabilitation process* (2nd ed.). Austin, TX: Pro-Ed.

Wright, G. N. (1980). *Total rehabilitation.* Boston: Little, Brown.

JOHN D. SEE
University of Wisconsin at Stout

VOCATIONAL EVALUATION
VOCATIONAL TRAINING OF HANDICAPPED

VOCATIONAL TRAINING OF HANDICAPPED

See VOCATIONAL EDUCATION.

VOCATIONAL VILLAGE

A vocational village is a cloistered community in which handicapped and nonhandicapped persons live and work. It is often referred to as a sheltered village. There is a strong work ethic in the community. The setting is not usually designed for transition but rather as a permanent living/working arrangement for the handicapped. There is usually a deep religious undertone in such villages and a majority of the time they are church sponsored. The nonhandicapped residents of the village are often volunteer workers who have made a long-term commitment to the village. There are also some nonhandicapped workers who are students working in practium arrangements or in work-study activities. Baker, Seltzer, and Seltzer (1977) explain that

> common to all sheltered villages is the segregation of the retarded person from the outside community and the implicit view that the retarded adult is better off in an environment that shelters him/her from many of the potential failures and frustrations of life in the outside community. (p. 109)

It is a delivery model that espouses the principle of separate but equal.

REFERENCE

Baker, B. L., Seltzer, G. B., & Seltzer, M. M. (1977). *As close as possible: Community residences for retarded adults.* Boston: Little, Brown.

ROBERT A. SEDLAK
University of Wisconsin at Stout

COMMUNITY PLACEMENT
COMMUNITY RESIDENTIAL PROGRAMS
SHELTERED WORKSHOPS

VOICE DISORDERS (DYSPHONIA)

Aronson (1985) says that, "A voice disorder exists when quality, pitch, loudness, or flexibility differs from the voices of others of similar age, sex and cultural group." What constitutes an abnormal voice is a relative judgment which is made by the speaker, the listener, and professionals who may be consulted. Causes of voice disorders are usually classified as either organic (physical) or functional (behavioral). Recent studies report the incidence of voice disorders in the U.S. population of school-aged children to be between 6–9% (Aronson, 1985). The parameters by which a voice can be judged as abnormal are considered in context. For example, a voice that is so hoarse that it distracts the listener or interferes with intelligibility can be identified as disordered and in need of treatment. The pitch of a female voice considered to be appropriate during her school-aged years may be too high for effective function as she enters the business world. The person who cannot produce a voice loud enough to be heard in a typically noisy classroom or one whose voice is so inflexible that the speaker seems emotionless may also be identified as abnormal. In some cases, such abnormal voice symptoms indicate the presence of an underlying illness which is in need of medical diagnosis and treatment. If a hoarse voice quality exists for an extended period of time (i.e. longer than two weeks), it could indicate the presence of a mass lesion in the larynx (voice box) which could be benign or malignant. An inability to alter pitch or loudness to convey meaning could signal a neuromuscular problem associated with incipient neurological disease. An inappropriately high pitch, used habitually, might point to endocrine dysfunction or to psychosocial issues which require attention (Colton & Casper, 1990).

Evaluation and treatment of voice disorders requires the combined efforts of the speech-language pathologist and an otolaryngologist (ENT). These professionals will examine the physical status of the larynx, velopharyngeal mechanism, and supporting respiratory system and will analyze the voice both perceptually and acoustically to determine if a clinically significant disorder exists. They will then attempt to identify the etiological factors underlying any abnormalities and prescribe a course of treatment. Often, the first choice for treatment is behavioral modification to eliminate factors contributing to the voice disorder and to establish good vocal hygiene. Less frequently, voice problems require physical management which might include medication, for example, in allergy therapy, or a more invasive treatment, such as surgery.

REFERENCES

Aronson, A. (1985). *Clinical voice disorders.* New York: Thieme.
Colton, R. H., & Casper, J. K. (1990). *Understanding voice problems.* Baltimore: Williams & Wilkins.

STAFF

SPEECH

VOLTA REVIEW, THE

The Volta Review was founded in 1898. It is published four times a year, with a monograph issue in September. The publication is a product of the Alexander Graham Bell Association for the Deaf, a nonprofit organization founded by Alexander Graham Bell in 1890 that serves as an information center for people with hearing impairment. Bell believed that people with hearing losses could be taught to speak and, through lip reading, could learn to understand others.

Only articles devoted to the education, rehabilitation, and communicative development of individuals with hearing impairment are published by *The Volta Review*. The target audience includes teachers of the hearing impaired; professionals in the fields of education, speech, audiology, language, otology, and psychology; parents of children with hearing impairments; and adults with hearing impairments. The articles are peer-reviewed for possible publication and vary in length, and the journal includes advertisements as well as illustrations. Topics include issues related to hearing impairment such as language development, parental concerns, medical/technical and psychosocial issues, teaching, and computers.

REBECCA BAILEY
Texas A & M University
First edition

TAMARA J. MARTIN
*The University of Texas of the
Permian Basin*
Second edition

DEAF
DEAF EDUCATION

VOLUNTARY AGENCIES

Voluntary agencies are those agencies that use volunteers to deliver services or to serve on decision-making boards. Volunteers are those members of the community who give their time on a nonpay basis to agencies that serve particular groups in an area. Approximately 84 million Americans serve as volunteers in such agencies each year (Shtulman, 1985). Women have provided a large portion of volunteer service but the entry of large numbers of women into the work force has limited their availability for volunteer service. However, an increasingly active senior citizen population is providing a pool of dependable, dedicated volunteers. Another developing source is through the work place. Some firms make it possible for their employees to have released time for community service; these firms say that this "loaned executive" program contributes to a better work force through the opportunity for workers to apply or develop skills, a lower rate of absenteeism, and increased productivity (United Way, 1985).

Volunteers on agency governing boards make decisions on the purchase of property and capital equipment, organizational policy, specific human services that will be available in the community, allocation of funds to other agencies (United Way, foundations, etc.) or within their own agency, and fund-raising.

REFERENCES

Shtulman, J. (1985). *A question-and-answer session on voluntarism*. Holyoke, MA: Transcript-Telegram.

United Way. (1985). *Volunteer notes*. Alexandria, VA: United Way of America.

DENISE M. SEDLAK
*United Way of Dunn County,
Menomonie, Wisconsin*

ADVOCACY FOR HANDICAPPED CHILDREN
LIBRARY SERVICES FOR THE HANDICAPPED

VON RECKLINGHAUSEN, FRIEDRICH (1833–1910)

Friedrich von Recklinghausen, a German pathologist, was a major contributor to the development of pathological anatomy as a branch of medicine. He is best known for his description, in 1863, of neurofibromatosis, or von Recklinghausen's disease, characterized by multiple small tumors affecting the subcutaneous nerves. The disease is hereditary and is associated with mental retardation.

REFERENCES

Talbott, J. H. (1970). *A biographical history of medicine*. Orlando, FL: Grune & Stratton.

von Recklinghausen, F. (1962). Multiple fibromas of the skin and multiple neuromas. In E. R. Long (Trans.), *Selected readings in pathology* (2nd ed.). Springfield, IL: Thomas.

PAUL IRVINE
Katonah, New York

NEUROFIBRAMATOSIS
MENTAL RETARDATION

VYGOTSKY, LEV S. (1896–1934)

Lev S. Vygotsky was a Soviet psychologist and semiotician. His work had a tremendous impact on the development of psychology in the Soviet Union and is currently attracting a great deal of interest outside the Soviet Union as well (Wertsch, 1985a, 1985b).

In the West, Vygotsky is known primarily for his work on the relationship between the development of thinking and speech in ontogenesis (Vygotsky, 1962, 1978, in press a). In Vygotsky's view, the more complex forms of human thinking, memory, and attention depend on the individual's mastery of historically and culturally developed means of organizing and mediating mental activity. Vygotsky argued that words and speech are first used in social interaction to organize and mediate the mental activity of several individuals working cooperatively on a task, and that these same linguistic means are later appropriated by the individual and internalized to be used in organizing and mediating his or her mental activity when working alone on similar tasks. In this sense, Vygotsky felt that certain kinds of social interaction between children and adults (or more competent peers) can create a "zone of proximal development" that raises the level of the child's cognitive functioning in the context of social interaction and helps move the child toward the next or proximal stage of independent functioning.

For Vygotsky, however, this work was only part of a much broader program of theory and research that was concerned with the relationships between historically developed modes of social behavior and the psychological development of the individual in all its aspects (Minick, 1987). In the decade following his death, the efforts of his colleagues and students to develop this broader theoretical framework led to the emergence of what is known as the theory of activity, a theoretical and research paradigm that illuminates the work of many contemporary Soviet psychologists.

Vygotsky had a lifelong interest in developing theory, research, and practical intervention techniques relevant to abnormal psychological functioning and development in both children and adults. He wrote extensively on these topics (Vygotsky, 1987) and founded several institutes that continue to play an important role in Soviet work in this area. Through this work and that of colleagues and students such as A. R. Luria (Luria, 1979), Vygotsky played a central role in the development of Soviet work in this domain.

REFERENCES

Luria, A. R. (1979). *The making of mind: A personal account of Soviet psychology*. Cambridge, MA: Harvard University Press.

Minick, N. (in press). The development of Vygotsky's thought. *Introduction to L. S. Vygotsky, Collected works: Problems of general psychology* (Vol. 2) (N. Minick, Trans.). New York: Plenum.

Vygotsky, L. S. (1962). *Thought and language* (E. Hanfmann & G. Vakar, Eds. and Trans.). Cambridge, MA: MIT Press. (Original work published 1934).

Vygotsky, L. S. (1978). *Mind in society* (M. Cole, V. John-Steiner, S. Scribner, & E. Souberman, Eds.). Cambridge, MA: Harvard University Press.

Vygotsky, L. S. (1987). Thinking and speech. In V. V. Davydov (Ed.), *L. S. Vygotsky, Collected works: General Psychology* (Vol. 2) (N. Minick, Trans.). New York: Plenum. (Original work published 1934).

Vygotsky, L. S. (1978). (1987). In A. V. Zaporozhets (Ed.), *L. S. Vygotsky, Collected works: The foundations of defectology* (Vol. 5) (J. Knox, Trans.). New York: Plenum.

Wertsch, J. V. (1985a). *Vygotsky and the social formation of mind*. Cambridge, MA: Harvard University Press.

Wertsch, J. V. (Ed.). (1985b). *Culture, communication, and cognition: Vygotskian perspectives*. New York: Cambridge University Press.

Norris Minick
*Center for Psychosocial Studies,
The Spencer Foundation*

THEORY OF ACTIVITY
ZONE OF PROXIMAL DEVELOPMENT

W

WAIS-III

See WECHSLER ADULT INTELLIGENCE SCALE—THIRD EDITION.

ASSESSMENT
BEHAVIORAL ASSESSMENT

WALKER PROBLEM BEHAVIOR IDENTIFICATION CHECKLIST (WBPIC)

The Walker Problem Behavior Identification Checklist (WBPIC) was published in 1983 (Walker, 1983). This edition consists of a teacher problem behavior rating scale for preschool through grade 6. The 50-item checklist contains six scales: acting-out, withdrawal, distractibility, disturbed peer relations, immaturity, and total. Separate forms are provided for boys and girls. The checklist is to be completed by a teacher who has known the child for at least a 2-month period. Raw scores on each scale are converted to T-scores for interpretation. The latest version was standardized on a sample of 1855 children from sites in Oregon and Washington. Norms are presented separately for males and females. The demographic characteristics of the norm group (e.g., socioeconomic status) are not specified in the manual.

Test-retest reliability coefficients for the six scales ranged from .43 to .88. No evidence of interrater agreement is reported. Validity data on the WBPIC are meager, although some discussion of content validity, the degree to which the items are of import to teachers, is presented. Mace (1985), in a review of the WBPIC, cites numerous shortcomings of the psychometric properties of the scales but concludes that it "may be useful for screening and target behavior selection."

REFERENCES

Mace, F. C. (1985). Review of the Walker Problem Behavior Identification Checklist. In J. W. Mitchell (Ed.), *The ninth mental measurements yearbook*. Lincoln: University of Nebraska Press.

Walker, H. M. (1983). *Walker Problem Behavior Identification Checklist*. Los Angeles: Western Psychological Services.

RANDY W. KAMPHAUS
Eastern Kentucky University

WALLIN, JOHN EDWARD (J. E.) WALLACE (1876–1969)

J. E. Wallace Wallin, a pioneer in the fields of special education and clinical psychology, was born in Page County, Iowa on January 21, 1876 to Henry and Emma M. (Johnson) Wallin, originally from Sweden. Wallace was the third of nine children. He attended the public schools of Stanton, Iowa. On June 21, 1913, at the age of 37, he married his wife, Frances Geraldine Tinsley. The couple had two daughters, Geraldine Tinsley Wallin Sickler (1919), and Virginia Stanton Wallin Obrinski (1915), who also became a psychologist.

Wallin obtained his BA degree in 1897 from Augustana College in Rock Island, Illinois. He attended Yale and studied under Dr. Edward W. Scripture and George Trumbull

John Edward Wallace Wallin

Ladd. Scripture had done his own thesis under "the great German psychologist," Wilhelm Wundt. While at Yale, Wallin completed an MA degree in 1899, and a PhD in 1901. Wallin also worked as an assistant to Dr. G. Stanley Hall at Clark University in Worcester, Massachusetts. Wallin served as head of the psychology department and vice-president of the East Stroudsburg State Teachers College in Pennsylvania. While at Stroudsburg, he taught courses in physiological, child, genetic, educational, and abnormal psychology and mental retardation. Wallin held numerous positions in the following years. He was the head of the department of psychology and education at the Normal Training School at Cleveland, Ohio, from 1909 to 1910, where he developed the field of special education, psychoclinical examinations, and one of the first group intelligence tests. By 1912, he established a psychoeducational clinic at the University of Pittsburgh, which was one of the first such clinics in the country. Wallin went on to become the director of numerous other clinics and special schools and affiliated with more than 25 colleges and universities (Wallin, 1958).

Outspoken, argumentative, critical, and at times cantankerous, Wallin was a crusader and a pioneer for disabled children. He was a leading advocate for the use of clinical psychology in education, especially as it relates to identification, diagnosis, and prescription for handicapped children (P.I., 1979), and was a strong advocate for the proper training of clinicians. He worked to establish the principle that all children would benefit from an education, regardless of degree of handicap, and helped to establish special classes in Western Pennsylvania, Ohio, Missouri, and Delaware. Wallin also made extensive contributions to the area of special education and the field of psychology by publishing over 30 books and 350 articles throughout his career, including psychological textbooks. He was a political activist for policies, regulations, and change to ensure appropriate education for children with special needs. He was a member of numerous professional organizations and served on many committees such as the secretary of the committee on special education for the White House Conference on Child Health and Protection from 1929–1930. He continued to write into his 90s. Wallin died on August 5, 1969.

REFERENCES

P. I. (1979). John Edward Wallace Wallin (1876–1969). A biographical sketch. *Journal of Special Education, 13,* 4–5.

Wallin, J. E. W. (1955). *The odyssey of a psychologist: Pioneering experiences in special education, clinical psychology, and mental hygiene with a comprehensive bibliography of the author's publications.* Wilmington, DE: Author.

Kim Ryan-Arredondo
Texas A & M University

John B. Watson

WATSON, JOHN B. (1878–1958)

John B. Watson developed and publicized the basic concepts of behaviorism, which in the 1920s became one of the major schools of psychological thought. Watson obtained his PhD at the University of Chicago and continued there as an instructor until 1908, when he accepted a professorship at Johns Hopkins University. Watson's behaviorism explained human behavior in terms of physiological responses to environmental stimuli and psychology as the study of the relationship between the two. Watson sought to make psychology "a purely objective experimental branch of natural science," with conditioning as one of its chief methods.

Watson's zealous environmentalism led him into some extreme positions, such as his assertion that he could train any healthy infant, regardless of its heredity, to become any type of person he might designate: "doctor, lawyer, artist, merchant-chief, and . . . even beggar-man and thief." Hyperbole aside, Watson's behaviorism was a dominant force in American psychology for decades and underlies many of today's behaviorally oriented instructional approaches. Watson eventually left the academic world, completing his career as an executive in the field of advertising.

REFERENCES

Skinner, B. F. (1959). John Broadus Watson, behaviorist. *Science, 129,* 197–198.

Watson, J. B. (1919). *Psychology from the standpoint of a behaviorist.* Philadelphia: Lippincott.

Paul Irvine
Katonah, New York

**BEHAVIOR MODIFICATION
CONDITIONING**

WECHSLER, DAVID (1896–1981)

Known primarily as the author of intelligence scales that played, and continue to play, a critical role in the lives of millions of individuals throughout the world, David Wechsler had a humanistic philosophy about testing as a part of assessment. His professional writing includes more than 60 articles and books that emphasize the importance of motivation, personality, drive, cultural opportunity, and other variables in determining an individual's functional level.

Born in Rumania, Wechsler moved with his family of nine to New York City at age 6. At 20 he completed a BA degree at City College (1916) and an MA the following year at Columbia University under Robert S. Woodworth. The next few years were spent with the armed forces, where Wechsler helped evaluate thousands of recruits, many of whom could not read English and who had little formal schooling. Near the end of his Army tour he studied with Charles Spearman and Karl Pearson in London and then, on a fellowship, with Henri Pieron and Louis Lapique in Paris. These studies provided the foundation for his continuous enthusiasm for the "nonintellective" components of intelligence.

While completing his PhD at Columbia (1925), Wechsler worked as a psychologist in New York City's newly created Bureau of Child Study. After serving as secretary for the Psychological Corporation (1925–1927) and in private clinical practice (1927–1932), Wechsler became chief psychologist at New York's Bellevue Hospital, a post he held for 35 years. In that position he developed the tests that carried both his and the hospital's name in the early editions: the Wechsler-Bellevue Intelligence Scale I (1939) and Scale II (1942), the Wechsler Intelligence Scale for Children (1949), the Wechsler Adult Intelligence Scale (1955), and the Wechsler Preschool and Primary Scale of Intelligence (1967). He continued to help with the revision of his scales in retirement. The utility of the scales has warranted periodic updating by the publisher.

Wechsler believed his most important work to be his article "The Range of Human Capacities" (1930), the seminal work for his book by the same name that was published in 1935 and revised in 1971. A more popular contribution is the concept of a deviation quotient used for reporting adult intelligence test scores in place of mental age and ratio IQ used with the Binet tests for children and youths. Today nearly all cognitive ability tests use standard scores patterned after the deviation IQ.

The many honors Wechsler received from professional groups and universities around the world include the Distinguished Professional Contribution Award from the American Psychological Association (APA) (1973), similar awards from APA's Division of Clinical Psychology (1960)

and Division of School Psychology (1973), and an honorary doctorate from the Hebrew University in Jerusalem.

JOSEPH L. FRENCH
Pennsylvania State University

ASSESSMENT
INTELLIGENCE TESTING

WECHSLER ADULT INTELLIGENCE SCALE— THIRD EDITION

The Wechsler Adult Intelligence Scale—Third Edition (WAIS-III) is the newest member of the Wechsler family of tests. It is an instrument for assessing the cognitive abilities of individuals ages 16 to 89. The WAIS-III has fourteen subtests that yield three IQ scores (Verbal, Performance, and Full Scale) and four factor indexes (Verbal Comprehension, Perceptual Organization, Working Memory and Processing Speed). Each of the IQs and factor indexes are standard scores with a mean of 100 and a standard deviation of 15. The subtests on the WAIS-III provide scaled scores with a mean of 10 and a standard deviation of 3.

The Verbal IQ is comprised of six verbal subtests (Vocabulary, Similarities, Arithmetic, Digit Span, Information, and Comprehension). In addition to these Verbal subtests, a new supplementary subtest (Letter-Number Sequencing) has been added which may substitute for Digit Span if necessary. The Performance IQ is comprised of five non-verbal subtests (Picture Completion, Picture Arrangement, Block Design, Matrix Reasoning, and Digit Symbol-Coding). In addition, there are two supplementary subtests on the Performance scale: Symbol Search (may be used to replace Digit Symbol-Coding) and Object Assembly (which is an optional subtest that may be used to replace any Performance subtest for individuals younger than 75) (Kaufman & Lichtenberger, in press; 1998). The Digit Symbol-Coding subtest also has new optional procedures, called Digit Symbol-Incidental Learning and Digit Symbol-Copy, that may be used to help the examiner rule out the cause of poor performance.

The following tables provide a brief description of each of the scales and subtests on the WAIS-III (Kaufman & Lichtenberger, in press).

The WAIS-III was standardized on 2,450 subjects stratified according to age, gender, race/ethnicity, geographic region, and educational level. This sample was selected to match basic demographic characteristics provided in the 1995 US Census data. An additional 200 African American and Hispanic individuals were administered the WAIS-III without discontinue rules during the process of normative

Verbal Scale

This scale measures verbal comprehension and expression, verbal reasoning and memory.

Verbal Comprehension

This factor index measures verbal knowledge, expression and Comprehension.

Vocabulary. Examinee orally defines a series of orally and visually presented words.

Similarities. Examinee explains how two common words are conceptually alike.

Information. Examinee answers a series of questions tapping knowledge of common events, objects, places, and people.

Comprehension. (Note that this subtest is only used in calculation of VIQ, not VC Index). Examinee answers questions that require an understanding of social rules and concepts or solutions to everyday problems.

Working Memory Index

This factor index measures number ability, sequential processing and verbal short-term memory.

Arithmetic. Examinee mentally solves a series of arithmetic problems.

Digit Span. Examinee repeats a list of orally presented numbers forward and backward.

Letter-Number Sequencing. Examinee remembers and repeats a series of orally presented sequences of letters and numbers.

Performance Scale

This scale measures nonverbal reasoning, visual motor cooordination, and processing speed.

Perceptual Organization

This factor index measures nonverbal thinking, reasoning, and visual motor coordination.

Picture Completion. Examinee determines which part of an incomplete picture is missing.

Block Design. Examinee replicates geometric patterns with red and white colored cubes.

Matrix Reasoning. Examinee completes a series of incomplete gridded patterns by pointing to one of five possible choices.

Object Assembly. (Optional subtest that can be substituted for a subtest in PIQ). Examinee assembles puzzle pieces into a meaningful whole.

Processing Speed

This factor index measures response speed.

Digit Symbol-Coding. Examinee uses a key to write symbols underneath corresponding numbers.

Symbol Search. Examinee indicates, by marking a box, whether a target symbol appears in a series of symbols.

---

data collection, in order to perform item bias analyses (The Psychological Corporation, 1997).

The reliability data for the WAIS-III are strong. The average split-half reliability coefficients, across the different age groups, were 0.97 for the Verbal IQ, 0.94 for the Performance IQ, and 0.98 for the Full Scale IQ. Numerous factor analytic studies were reported in the WAIS-III manual (The Psychological Corporation, 1997). The underlying four-factor structure of the WAIS-III was validated. However, one important exception to this finding should be noted: in the 75 to 89 age range, more subtests loaded on the Processing Speed factor the Perceptual Organization factor (Kaufman & Lichtenberger, in press). Only one Performance subtest, Matrix Reasoning, had a factor loading above 0.40 on the Perceptual Organization factor for the oldest age group.

The relationship between the WAIS-R (Wechsler, 1981) and the WAIS-III was examined to see how well the old and new versions of the test related. Subjects tended to perform about 2.9 points lower on the WAIS-III Full Scale IQ than on the WAIS-R Full Scale IQ. This would be predicted based on work done by Flynn (1984) that has shown similar patterns from the WAIS to WAIS-R. The overall correlations between the WAIS-III and WAIS-R were high: 0.94 for the Verbal IQ, 0.86 for the Performance IQ, and 0.93 for the Full Scale IQ (Kaufman & Lichtenberger, 1998).

Many improvements were made in this latest edition of the WAIS. Administration is not difficult with the clear and easy to read WAIS-III manual, in addition to the record form with ample space and visual icons (Kaufman & Lichtenberger, in press). The floor and ceiling of the WAIS-III were extended from its earlier version, providing better assessment of high and low functioning individuals. The WAIS-R's method of using a reference group (ages 20–34) to determine everyone's scaled scores was not retained in the development of the WAIS-III, which is also an improvement. The four-factor structure of the WAIS-III is a strength of the instrument that may aid in interpretation. The addition of Matrix Reasoning and Letter-Number Sequencing to the overall battery have made assessment of abilities such as fluid reasoning and working memory possible (Kaufman & Lichtenberger, in press). Although there are still a few areas that could be improved, Kaufman and Lichtenberger (in press) note that the WAIS-III's strengths seem to outweigh its weaknesses. The WAIS-R has proven itself as a leader in the field of assessment, and the WAIS-III is likely to follow suit.

REFERENCES

Flynn, J. R. (1984). The mean IQ of Americans: Massive gains 1932 to 1978. *Psychological Bulletin, 95,* 29–51.

Kaufman, A. S., & Lichtenberger, E. O. (in press). *Essentials of WAIS-III Assessment.* New York: Wiley.

Kaufman, A. S., & Lichtenberger, E. O. (1998). Intellectual Assessment. In A. S. Bellack & M. Hersen (Series Eds.), & C. R. Reynolds (Vol. Ed.), *Comprehensive clinical psychology: Volume 4. Assessment* (pp. 203–238). Oxford, England: Elsevier Science Ltd.

The Psychological Corporation. (1997). *Technical manual for the Wechsler Adult Intelligence Scale—Third Edition.* San Antonio, TX: The Psychological Corporation.

Wechsler, D. (1997). *Administration and scoring manual for the Wechsler Adult Intelligence Scale—Third Edition.* San Antonio, TX: The Psychological Corporation.

Wechsler, D. (1981). *Administration and scoring manual for the Wechsler Adult Intelligence Scale—Revised.* San Antonio, TX: The Psychological Corporation.

ELIZABETH O. LICHTENBERGER
The Salk Institute

INTELLIGENCE TESTS
STANFORD BINET
WISC/WISC-R
WPPSI

WECHSLER INTELLIGENCE SCALE FOR CHILDREN—THIRD EDITION

The Wechsler Intelligence Scale for Children—Third Edition (WISC-III) is an instrument for assessing the cognitive abilities of children and adolescents ages 6 to 16.

The WISC-III, like the WISC-R, is easily the most popular and widely researched test of children's intelligence. The WISC-III has thirteen subtests that yield three IQ scores (Verbal, Performance, and Full Scale) and four factor indexes (Verbal Comprehension, Perceptual Organization, Freedom from Distractibility and Processing Speed). Each of the IQs and factor indexes are standard scores with a mean of 100 and a standard deviation of 15. The subtests on the WISC-III provide scaled scores with a mean of 10 and a standard deviation of 3.

The five subtests that comprise the Verbal IQ include Vocabulary, Similarities, Arithmetic, Information, and Comprehension. In addition to these Verbal subtests, a supplementary Verbal subtest (Digit Span) is also administered and may substitute for other Verbal subtests if necessary. The five non-verbal subtests that comprise the Performance IQ include Picture Completion, Picture Arrangement, Block Design, Object Assembly, and Coding. In addition, there are two supplementary subtests on the Performance scale: Symbol Search (may be used to replace Coding) and Mazes (which is an optional subtest that may be used to replace any Performance subtest; Kaufman & Lichtenberger, 1998). Because of the significantly stronger psychometric properties of Symbol Search in comparison to Coding, Kaufman (1994) strongly recommends that Symbol Search be routinely substituted for Coding as part of the regular battery and in calculation of the Performance IQ.

The following provides a brief description of each of the scales and subtests on the WISC-III.

Verbal Scale	*Performance Scale*
This scale measures verbal comprehension and expression, verbal reasoning, and memory.	This scale measures nonverbal reasoning, visual motor cooordination, and processing speed.

Verbal Comprehension Index. This factor index measures verbal knowledge, expression and conceptualization.

- *Vocabulary.* Child orally defines a series of orally and visually presented words.

- *Similarities.* Child explains how two common words are conceptually alike.

- *Information.* Child answers a series of questions tapping knowledge of common events, objects, places, and people.

- *Comprehension.* Child answers questions that require an understanding of social rules and concepts or solutions to everyday problems.

Freedom from Distractibility Index. This factor index measures number ability, sequential processing and verbal short-term memory.

- *Arithmetic.* Child mentally solves a series of arithmetic problems.

- *Digit Span.* Child repeats a list of orally presented numbers forward and backward.

Perceptual Organization Index. This factor index measures nonverbal thinking, reasoning, and visual motor coordination.

- *Picture Completion.* Child determines which part of an incomplete picture is missing.

- *Block Design.* Child replicates geometric patterns with red and white colored cubes.

- *Picture Arrangement.* Child rearranges a set of pictures into a logical story sequence.

- *Object Assembly.* Child assembles puzzle pieces into a meaningful whole.

Processing Speed Index. This factor index measures response speed.

- *Digit Symbol-Coding.* Child uses a key to write symbols underneath corresponding numbers.

- *Symbol Search.* Child indicates, by marking a box, whether a target symbol appears in a series of symbols.

The WISC-III was standardized on 2,200 subjects stratified according to age, gender, race/ethnicity, geographic region, and educational level. This sample was selected to match basic demographic characteristics provided in the 1988 US Census data. The excellence of the WISC-III's norms have been noted by several reviewers (e.g., Braden, 1995; Kaufman, 1993; Sandoval, 1995).

The reliability data for the WISC-III are strong. The average split-half reliability coefficients for individual subtests, across the different age groups, ranged from 0.69 to 0.87. The average reliability values for the IQs and indexes were 0.95 for the Verbal IQ, 0.91 for the Performance IQ, 0.96 for the Full Scale IQ, 0.94 for the Verbal Comprehension Index, 0.90 for the Perceptual Organization Index, 0.87 for the Freedom from Distractibility Index, and 0.85 for the Processing Speed Index (Wechsler, 1991). Factor analytic studies were performed for four age groups: ages 6 to 7, ages 8 to 10, ages 11 to 13, and ages 14 to 16. The underlying four-factor structure of the WISC-III was validated, and provides evidence of the WISC-III's construct validity. Descriptions of what each of the four factors measure are listed along with descriptions of the subtests above. Substantial loadings on the large unrotated first factor also provide support for the construct of general intelligence (*g*) underlying the Full Scale IQ.

How to interpret or clinically use WISC-III results is not clearly delineated in the WISC-III manual, but there are many sources for obtaining such information (e.g., Kaufman, 1994; Prifitera & Sakolfske, 1998). The process of WISC-III profile interpretation is a complex one. It is recommended that individual subtests not be evaluated in isolation; rather, subtests should be grouped and combined with other supportive information in order to make hypotheses (Kaufman, 1994). Differences between the Verbal IQ and Performance IQ are regularly evaluated by examiners, but with the WISC-III, it may at times be more beneficial to compare differences between the factor indexes (i.e., Verbal Comprehension and Perceptual Organization; see Kaufman, 1994 for a detailed explanation). To best interpret a child's scores, the context of the referral question, background information, behavioral observations during the testing, and situational factors must all be considered together.

The WISC-III has obtained very favorable reviews (Braden, 1995; Sandoval, 1995). The improvements from the WISC-R include updating the testing materials and artwork, reducing item biases, and others. The norms for the WISC-III are excellent and its psychometric properties overall are very strong (Braden, 1995; Sandoval, 1995). However, Mazes is considered a weak subtest on the WISC-III, with an average stability coefficient of 0.57. This subtest is so poor psychometrically that Kaufman (1994) has stated that it should have been dropped. The addition of the Symbol Search subtest to the WISC-III was a good addition as it has allowed the four-factor structure. Some

reviews of the WISC-III have been mixed, but it continues to be one of the most frequently used tests in the field of children's intelligence testing (Kaufman & Lichtenberger, 1998).

REFERENCES

Braden, J. P. (1995). Review of the Wechsler Intelligence Scale for Children, Third Edition. In J. C. Conoley & J. C. Impara (Eds.), *The twelfth mental measurements yearbook* (pp. 1098–1103). Lincoln, NE: Buros Institute of Mental Measurement.

Kaufman, A. S. (1993). King WISC the third assumes the throne. *Journal of School Psychology, 31,* 345–354.

Kaufman, A. S. (1994). *Intelligent testing with the WISC-III.* New York: Wiley.

Kaufman, A. S., & Lichtenberger, E. O. (1998). Intellectual Assessment. In A. S. Bellack & M. Hersen (Series Eds.), & C. R. Reynolds (Vol. Ed.), *Comprehensive clinical psychology: Volume 4. Assessment* (pp. 203–238). Oxford, England: Elsevier Science Ltd.

Prifitera, A., & Saklofske, D. (Eds.). (1998). *WISC-III clinical use and interpretation.* San Diego: Academic.

Sandoval, J. (1995). Review of the Wechsler Intelligence Scale for Children, Third Edition. In J. C. Conoley & J. C. Impara (Eds.), *The twelfth mental measurements yearbook* (pp. 1103–1104). Lincoln, NE: Buros Institute of Mental Measurement.

Wechsler, D. (1991). *Wechsler Intelligence Scale for Children—Third Edition.* San Antonio, TX: The Psychological Corporation.

ELIZABETH O. LICHTENBERGER
The Salk Institute

ASSESSMENT
INTELLIGENCE TESTING
WAIS-III

WECHSLER PRESCHOOL AND PRIMARY SCALE OF INTELLIGENCE—REVISED

The Wechsler Preschool and Primary Scale of Intelligence–Revised (WPPSI-R; Wechsler, 1989) is a measure of cognitive functioning of children from ages 2 years, 11 months to 7 years, 3 months. The WPPSI-R overlaps with the Wechsler Intelligence Scale for Children—Third Edition (WISC-III) in the age 6 to 7 range. Examiners are likely to find the WPPSI-R a better measure for low functioning children in this age range, but the WISC-III a better instrument for normal or high functioning children in this age range.

The WPPSI-R is comprised of two scales: Performance and Verbal. Each provides standard scores with a mean of 100 and a standard deviation of 15. Mainly motor re-

Performance subtests	Verbal Subtests
Object Assembly. Child is required to fit puzzle pieces together to form a meaningful whole.	*Information.* Child must either point to a picture or verbally answer brief oral questions about commonplace objects and events.
Geometric Design. In the first part of the task, the child must look at a design and point to a matching design from an array of four. In the second part, child copies a drawing of geometric figure.	*Comprehension.* Child verbally responds to questions about consequences of events.
Block Design. Child reproduces patterns made from flat, red and white colored blocks.	*Arithmetic.* Child demonstrates ability to count and solve more complex quantitative problems.
Mazes. Child solves paper-and-pencil mazes of increasing difficulty.	*Vocabulary.* Child names pictured items and provides verbal definitions of words.
Picture Completion. Child identifies what is missing from pictures of common objects.	*Similarities.* Child chooses which pictured objects share a common feature or child completes a sentence that contains a verbal analogy.
Animal Pegs (Optional subtest). Child places pegs of the correct colors in the holes below a series of pictured animals.	*Sentences* (Optional subtest). Child repeats verbatim a sentence that is read aloud.

sponses are required on the Performance Scale (pointing, placing, or drawing) and spoken responses are required on the Verbal scale. The two scales are each comprised of five subtests, plus one optional subtest. Each of the subtests provides scaled scores with a mean of 10 and a standard deviation of 3. The section below lists and describes each of the WPPSI-R subtests.

The WPPSI-R was standardized on a sample of 1,700 children who were chosen to closely match the 1986 US Census data. The reliability and validity information are presented in the WPPSI-R Manual (Wechsler, 1989). The average internal consistency coefficients are 0.95 for the Verbal IQ, 0.91 for the Performance IQ, and 0.96 for the Full Scale IQ. Internal consistency values for individual subtests ranged from 0.54 to 0.93 (median = 0.81). The WPPSI-R is a fairly stable instrument with test-retest reliabilities of 0.90, 0.88, and 0.91 for the Verbal, Performance, and Full Scale IQs, respectively. Construct validity of the WPPSI-R is supported by the factor analytic studies described in the manual. Validity is further supported by strong correlations with other instruments such as the Stanford Binet-Fourth edition.

The original version of the WPPSI was criticized because of its drab color and lack of appropriate preschool activities. However, the WPPSI-R is more suitable for young children, and includes simplified directions (Bracken,

1992). Although the floor of the WPPSI-R for young, low-functioning children is weak, Bracken (1992) notes that it is generally stronger than many similar instruments. Another weakness of the WPPSI-R is the lack of information provided in the manual on interpretation. Kaufman (1992) notes that there is age-inappropriate stress on solving problems with great speed on the WPPSI-R. Overall, the WPPSI-R is a useful assessment tool, but it possesses certain strengths and weaknesses that should be considered upon deciding to use it.

REFERENCES

Bracken, B. (1992). Review of the Wechsler Preschool and Primary Scale of Intelligence—Revised. In J. J. Kramer & J. C. Conoley (Eds.), *The eleventh mental measurements yearbook* (pp. 1027–1029). Lincoln, NE: Buros Institute of Mental Measurements.

Kaufman, A. S. (1992). Evaluation of the WISC-III and WPPSI-R for gifted children. *Roeper Review, 14,* 154–158.

Wechsler, D. (1989). *Wechsler Preschool and Primary Scale of Intelligence—Revised.* San Antonio, TX: The Psychological Corporation.

ELIZABETH O. LICHTENBERGER
The Salk Institute

ASSESSMENT
INTELLIGENCE
INTELLIGENCE TESTS
KAUFMAN ASSESSMENT BATTERY FOR CHILDREN
STANFORD-BINET INTELLIGENCE TESTS
WISC-III

WELSH FIGURE PREFERENCE TEST

The Welsh Figure Preference Test (FPT) was developed by George Welsh in 1949, for his doctoral thesis, as a projective assessment of psychopathology. More recently, it has been used as a measure of creativity more than as a diagnostic tool for the evaluation of psychopathology.

The Welsh FPT (Welsh, 1959) consists of a booklet containing 400 black and white line drawings. Examples of items from the Welsh FPT are shown in the Figure. The scale was revised by Welsh in 1980. It is designed for use with individuals aged 6 years and up. It requires nearly an hour to complete and, despite being intended as a projective, provides objective scoring. Instructions to the test taker are simple. Individuals are asked to view each drawing and indicate on an answer sheet whether they like or dislike the drawing. The intent was to provide nonlanguage stimulus materials suitable for a wide range of individuals who could not be assessed with language-laden measures such as the MMPI, or projective measures such as the TAT, requiring extensive verbal expression.

Examples of "like" and "don't like" items from the Welsh Figure.

The Welsh FPT can separate artists from nonartists, as can many other tests; it can also separate clinical from nonclinical populations. However, it has not been extensively researched considering its publication date. Welsh (1986) contends that the Welsh FPT is useful as a measure of creativity; it has been used in creativity research since at least 1965. Its uses in creativity research seem well established at this time, but its validity as a measure of psychopathology is questionable.

REFERENCES

Welsh, G. S. (1949). *A projective figure-preference test for diagnosis of psychopathology: I, A preliminary investigation.* Doctoral thesis, University of Minnesota, Minneapolis.

Welsh, G. S. (1959). *Welsh figure preference test.* Palo Alto, CA: Consulting Psychologists.

Welsh, G. S. (1980). *Welsh Figure Preference Test, revised edition.* Palo Alto, CA: Consulting Psychologists.

Welsh, G. S. (1986). Positive exceptionality: The academically gifted and the creative. In R. T. Brown & C. R. Reynolds (Eds.), *Psychological perspectives on childhood exceptionality: A handbook.* New York: Wiley-Interscience.

CECIL R. REYNOLDS
Texas A & M University

CREATIVITY

WEPMAN'S AUDITORY DISCRIMINATION TEST, SECOND EDITION

The second edition of Wepman's Auditory Discrimination Test (ADT; Reynolds, 1986; Wepman, 1975) is a revised version of the Auditory Discrimination Test, first published in 1958. The ADT is a measure of a child's auditory discrimination that can be used as a reliable screening measure to identify children with problems in the areas of auditory, cognition, speech, and language abilities. The test is designed to be administered to children ages 4 to 8 years, 11 months who are suspected of having auditory discrimination problems.

The ADT contains 40 pairs of words: 30 pairs that differ in a single phoneme and 10 same-word pairs. The word pairs are read aloud to the child with the child's back to the examiner, so that visual cues cannot be used in responding. The demands of the ADT are minimal; the child may respond yes or no either verbally or nonverbally. The number of correct responses on 30 different-word pair items yields the total raw score. The same-word pairs serve as control items for checking the validity of the test. The test is considered invalid if a child scores 9 or less in the different-word pairs category or a score of 6 or less in the same-word pairs category. Raw scores may range from 10 to 30 and these are converted into a qualitative score, a standard score (T-score), and percentile ranks.

The ADT-Second Edition manual (Reynolds, 1986) reports reliability and validity statistics based on a standardization sample of 1,800 normally developing children. Internal consistency values based on the KR-20 procedure ranged from .74 to .82. However, a decrease was seen in the reliability scores for children ages 7 to 8 years, 11 months due to a ceiling effect. Reported test-retest reliability values ranged from .88 to .96. There are two ADT forms available and the alternate forms reliability reported is .92. The manual reports numerous criterion-related validity studies that reflect a moderate degree of relationship.

Reviews of the ADT have noted that it would be beneficial if the ADT had audiotapes available for administration to further standardize the pronunciation of the words (Bhat, 1992). The ADT is an easily administered test and is also easy to score (Bhat, 1994; Pannbacker & Middleton, 1992). However, Pannbacker and Middleton (1992, p. 1032) caution that "major management decisions should not be based on this test." Their reasons were that data on examiner reliability and listening conditions are lacking and that the empirical basis for testing auditory discrimination is not strong.

REFERENCES

Bhat, V. K. (1994). Wepman's Auditory Discrimination Test, Second Edition. In D. Keyser & R. Sweetland (Eds.), *Test Critiques, Volume X* (pp. 799–803). Austin, TX: Pro-Ed.

Pannbacker, M. & Middleton, G. (1992). Review of Wepman's Auditory Discrimination Test, Second Edition. In J. J. Kramer & J. C. Conoley (Eds.), *The eleventh mental measurements year-*

book (pp. 1031–1032). Lincoln, NE: Buros Institute of Mental Measurements.

Reynolds, W. M. (1986). *Manual for Wepman's Auditory Discrimination Test* (2nd ed.). Los Angeles: Western Psychological Services.

Wepman, J. M. (1975). *Auditory Discrimination Test manual*. Los Angeles: Western Psychological Services.

ELIZABETH O. LICHTENBERGER
The Salk Institute

AUDITORY DISCRIMINATION GOLDMAN, FRISTOE, WOODCOCK TEST OF AUDITORY DISCRIMINATION

WERNER, HEINZ (1890–1964)

Heinz Werner received his PhD from Vienna University in 1914 with highest honors. Perhaps the beginning of his scholarly career began when he read about the evolution of animals, man, and the cosmos. He became increasingly interested in philosophy and psychology while at the University of Vienna. His work in the field of psychological phenomena is relevant to psychologists, educators, anthropologists, students of animal behavior, and scholars investigating aesthetic phenomena.

His contributions to the field have been many. He has published over 15 books and monographs and more than 150 articles within a 50-year period. His principal publications include *Comparative Psychology of Mental Development* and *Developmental Processess: Heinz Werner's Selected Writings*. His selected writings include his general theory and perceptual experiences in Volume I; Volume II focuses on cognition, language, and symbolization.

Werner was a great teacher and researcher, and he inspired others to follow his example in the search for understanding of psychological phenomena. His theory was interdisciplinary because all of his developmental principles apply to all the life sciences. He founded an Institute for Human Development at Clark University in 1958. This institute made Clark an "international center directed toward the developmental analysis of phenomena in all the life sciences" (Werner, 1978). Werner's contributions to the field of developmental psychology are steadily gaining recognition.

REFERENCES

Werner, H. (1940). *Comparative psychology of mental development*. New York: Harper & Brothers.

Werner, H. (1978). *Developmental processes: Heinz Werner's selected writings*. New York: International Universities Press.

REBECCA BAILEY
Texas A & M University

WERNICKE'S APHASIA

Wernicke's aphasia is one of several subdivisions of fluent aphasia. This is the first type of aphasia described, and it is one in which the localization description still holds true in terms of the symptoms correlating with damage to particular location in the brain. Those possessing communicative deficits consistent with Wernicke's aphasia have pathology in the dominant superior temporal gyrus. A lesion in the superior posterior temporal is obligatory for Wernicke's aphasia.

Major language characteristics of Wernicke's aphasia are defective auditory comprehension; disturbed reading and writing; defective repetition of words and sentences with speech which is incessant at normal prosody with a rapid rate; good articulation but paraphasic speech, containing semantic and literal paraphasias and possible extra syllables added to words (Graham-Keegan & Caspari, 1997; Hegde, 1994). Other types of fluent aphasia include:

Transcortical Sensory

Here, the lesion is most frequently in the temporoparietal region but the precise Wernicke's area is spared. Damage to the posterior portion of the middle temporal gyrus is often seen; with some cases, the angular gyrus and visual and auditory association cortex are also involved.

Major language characteristics are very similar to those of Wernicke's aphasia with the difference being that in transcortical sensory aphasia repetition is intact (this skill is impaired in Wernicke's).

Conduction

This rare disorder is also called central aphasia. The neuroanatomical basis is very controversial, but consistent with the newer model of viewing the brain as a total system whose symptoms from impairment reflect impairments not only in specific locations within the brain but also in pathways and synergistic interactions. The most frequent theory of location of damage for this type of fluent aphasia is damage to the supramarginal gyrus and the arcuate fasciculus that connects Broca's area with Wernicke's area.

The major distinguishing language characteristic of conduction aphasia is severe impairment in repetition (repetitions may contain added or deleted phonemes); function words are more difficult to repeat. Individuals with conduction aphasia may comprehend problems in repeating sentences.

REFERENCES

Chapey, R. (1994). *Language intervention strategies in adult aphasia* (3rd ed.). Baltimore: Williams & Wilkins.

Graham-Keegan, L., & Caspari, I. (1997). Wernicke's aphasia. In L. L. LaPointe (Ed.), *Aphasia and related neurogenic language disorders* (pp. 42–62). New York: Thieme.

Hegde, M. (1994). *A coursebook on aphasia and other neurogenic language disorders*. San Diego: Singular.

SHEELA STUART
George Washington University

APHASIA
DYSPHASIA
LANGUAGE DISORDERS

WESTERN EUROPE, SPECIAL EDUCATION IN

Current special education practices in Europe differ from country to country and from region to region in any particular country. These practices have been strongly influenced by the affluence of particular European nations and their social welfare outlook. While Spain and Portugal are concerned about their handicapped children and youth, the funds and services available to them are far less than in Scandinavia.

The nature of special education funding and services also varies from country to country, depending on political structures and traditions. The degree of political-educational centralization plays an important role. In France, national authority is likely to be more strongly felt in the education of the handicapped than in West Germany, where the federal government has little or no authority in public schools, and where financial support and the provision of services for special education are likely to vary from one region to another. Generally, the most comprehensive financial support for services to the handicapped, at all ages, has been in Scandinavia.

Curriculum

Special education curriculum in Western Europe has not been as narrowly academic as in the United States. Traditionally, Western European special education has been more responsive to the extra-academic aspects of special education. The graphic arts, music, and social and vocational experiences are more often woven into the handicapped child's daily activities. Thus, music therapy for handicapped students has received widespread support (Pratt, 1983), and the educational usefulness of toy libraries has been widely recognized (deVincentis, 1984). Theater programs for children with mental retardation, motor disabilities, and cerebral palsy have received acclaim (Cohen, 1985). Excursions and travel are considered important educational experiences. The quality of relationships between teachers and pupils is strongly emphasized.

Europeans may be becoming more Americanized in their special education outlooks in that a more instructionally directed focus appears to be emerging. American influences are also revealed in European movements toward noncategorical types of special education, often in the face of previously accepted, and often complicated, categorical models (as in the Netherlands). European attention to integration of special education with general education has also been influenced by American practices, albeit in European terms (Organization for Economic Cooperation and Development, 1985a, 1985b). Even though Europeans have led the way in assisting the transition of handicapped youths into the world of work, American efforts in this area have influenced their practices considerably.

Early Intervention

The most pervasive effective interventions with Western European handicapped children, prior to their enrollment in formal educational programs, are medically related. Most European nations provide mandatory health screening and reporting for young children, as well as free medical services. In Austria, a multidisciplinary team headed by a social pediatrician steps in as soon as a child has a problem. Indeed, as soon as a child is officially identified as being handicapped, the child' parents begin receiving a disability pension. In France, early intervention begins with the compulsory screening of all infants at birth and again at 2 years. Interdisciplinary teams operate out of "early medico-social activity centers to provide therapies, education, and support in home and natural environments" (Zucman, 1985). However, day care of a more educational nature also can be observed. In Switzerland, a handicapped child's involvement with itinerant educational services begins at an early age (even at birth) and continues, when needed, until the child's integration into school (Pahud & Besson, 1985).

Preschool

Preschool special education had its beginnings in Germany, where Froebel was the first educator to formalize it on a public basis. Current preschool special education in Western Europe varies from nation to nation. For example, different nations have different beginning ages for compulsory education, so that even the definition of preschool education varies. Also, the Europeans have traditionally favored parents as the main educators of their children, particularly when young. The social welfare underpinnings of such states as Sweden have been very supportive of parents who remain at home with their young, offering them paid leave from employment. Countries such as Italy have made remarkable advances in integrating preschoolers into regular education programs.

Least Restrictive Environment and Mainstreaming

Modern-day principles of least restrictive environment and mainstreaming originated with the Bill of Rights for the mentally retarded and the principle of normalization in Scandinavia. Both concepts strongly influenced much of Western Europe. Thus the notion of integrating handicapped students into the main body of education was well on its way, even without American influences. Indeed, reforms in this respect were begun in Norway in 1920 (Booth, 1982). Nevertheless, the United States can take credit for institutionalizing the ideas of least restrictive environment and mainstreaming, and for offering models for the Europeans to adopt. The degree to which the principles of least restrictive environment have prevailed has differed from country to country.

In Denmark, special education is an integral part of regular education within a sophisticated range of educational services. In fact, administrative integration of services for the handicapped with those for the nonhandicapped was passed into law on January 1, 1979, on the premise that handicapped individuals should receive services in the same way as the nonhandicapped (Juul, 1980). Italy's Law 517/1977 has gone far beyond general recommendations for implementation of least restrictive environments to providing procedural plans for implementing the education of handicapped students within regular classrooms (Strain, 1985). On the other hand, in West Germany, where responsibility for the education of the handicapped was traditionally assumed by religious and voluntary organizations, terminology for such education was originally couched in the language of segregation. Public school teachers were unfamiliar with the education of children with special needs, and it was difficult for the teachers to prepare to work with the handicapped. This meant some hesitancy in certain European nations with respect to mainstreaming; however, mainstreaming has moved forward at an steady pace overall.

Transition

European efforts in transition education have been in the vanguard in many respects (Booth, 1982; Organization for Economic Cooperation Development, 1981, 1985a, 1985b), with significant efforts being made to help handicapped youths and young adults to move into the world of work. The Netherlands has been noteworthy for providing sheltered workshops for more involved handicapped youths and adults while supervising more able ones who are actively employed in the open market. Again, the social welfare outlook in nations such as the Netherlands, which even purchases paintings from artists unable to sell their works, conditions Western European attitudes toward the handicapped. In France, the Union Nationale des Association de Parents d'Enfants Inadaptes, which operates hun-dreds of schools for moderately to severely handicapped children and youths, has a strong vocational emphasis in its curriculum. It also has operated the Centres d'Aide pour Travail to aid in the employment of the handicapped. In Austria an organization called Jugend am Werk (Youth at Work), which originated with the idea of providing shelter and work to disadvantaged youths, went on to provide vocational training centers, sheltered workshops, and residential centers for the handicapped. Unfortunately, the employment picture in most European countries has been dismal over the past decade, with high unemployment rates for nonhandicapped workers. Opportunities for the handicapped to work in the normal marketplace have been significantly reduced as a consequence.

The Educateur Movement

Educateurs are special types of teacher/child-care workers who are competent to work with maladapted young people, including handicapped youths. They are trained in non-academic subjects such as sports, acting, arts and crafts, and other leisure-time activities. They teach vocational subjects, supervise vocational placements, work with families, schools, and communities, and act as advocates for their student clients. The educateur profession is well established in France, with numerous colleges providing rigorous training. The educateur movement has spread across much of Western Europe. It has also influenced Canadian services. In the United States, Project Re-Ed was a variant of the educateur model. In European nations, there have been adaptations according to national and local needs. Similar professions have emerged under different names with somewhat different identities and functions. In West Germany the educateurs are called erziehers; in the Netherlands they are identified as orthopedagogues; and in Scandinavia they are milieu therapists.

Therapeutic Communities

The Europeans have also been noted for their creation of therapeutic communities. Professionals and lay people critical of traditional government and professional roles in serving the handicapped and the ill have been instrumental in fostering these.

In Great Britain, psychiatrists Laing and Cooper created a therapeutic home at Kingsley Hall, London. They viewed mentally ill individuals as victims of home and society, and saw hospitals as degrading and dehumanizing them (1971). Laing's views of the causes of mental illness have altered over the years. His perceptions that mental hospitals dehumanize and often harm their residents, and that relationships between professionals and their clients on a day-to-day personal basis may be the best way to help the latter, have been increasingly shared by others.

In France the movement toward therapeutic communities following World War II began in earnest with the work of Jean Vanier (Wolfensberger, 1973) in the movement called l'Arche (place of refuge). Vanier built a small community in Trosly-Breuil, France, where mentally handicapped and nonhandicapped adults could live and work together as families. Vanier's work has inspired the creation of other similar facilities across France and elsewhere.

Most important in the therapeutic community movement has been the anthroposophic movement. This was inaugurated at the turn of the twentieth century by Rudolf Steiner, an Austrian philosopher and educator. The inspirations of the anthroposophic movement led to the creation of the Waldorf method and Waldorf schools. The Waldorf method, while originally intended for normal children, was found also to be applicable to handicapped children. Anthroposophic education is developmental in orientation, and multifaceted. It emphasizes art, bodily movement, music, community involvement, and work. Anthroposophic schools have sought to integrate therapy with education and to engage in therapies that find their expression in art, drama, role playing, etc. Anthroposophic schools serving the handicapped are now numerous in Great Britain and on the continent. Originally oriented toward the mentally retarded and multiply handicapped, they have recently expanded to serve the emotionally disturbed as well.

Particularly noteworthy within the anthroposophic movement has been the Camphill movement. This was begun in the early 1940s by Karl Konig, an Austrian psychiatrist who came to Scotland to escape Nazi persecution. Inspired by anthroposophic philosophy, which views an individual's inner personality as remaining whole and intact despite the nature and degree of that individual's handicaps, Konig created a special village in the vicinity of Aberdeen, Scotland, in which mentally retarded villagers and normal coworkers could live and worked together. The original Camphill movement has spread considerably since that time, both in Europe and the United States. Some settlements serve children, while others serve adults. The orientation of the Camphill settlements, which are self-contained communities, is contrary to modern-day notions of least restrictive environment. Nevertheless, they offer a remarkable combination of care and opportunity for self-fulfillment to many handicapped individuals.

Minority Handicapped

Changed immigration policies and intensive industrialization during the postwar period saw an influx of millions of immigrants or "guest workers" from Africa, Asia, and less affluent European nations into Western Europe. Today, there are second and third generations of these minorities in most Western European nations. With some exceptions, there has been difficulty in integrating them. Decreases in employment opportunities in Western Europe have meant increased hardships and alienation for many; e.g., Turks in Germany, Arabs in France, Indians and Pakistanis in Great Britain. The children of such families constitute a large proportion of underprivileged and disadvantaged students in Western Europe. Elevated levels of handicaps and school failure are the consequence. At the same time, such students, because of their alienated status, are less likely to benefit from benign European attitudes toward the handicapped. It should be observed that the Dutch have been particularly accepting of such minority populations.

Professional Preparation

There is considerable variation in the professional preparation of special education teachers in Europe. In some countries, there appear to be few special requirements. In others, licensure or certification requirements are demanding. In certain countries, there are likely to be differences from one region to another. Germany has traditionally been interested in experimenting with different training models. In England and Wales, more systematic training was instituted as a consequence of the Warnock Report. Switzerland has a number of different teacher institutes, each of which has a special orientation to the cantons that they serve. The Institut des Science de l'Education, at Geneva, associated with the name of Piaget, has been known for its research into the cognitive processes of handicapped students; it is a national training resource. Switzerland's Zentralstelle fur Heilpadagogik coordinates the efforts of its various teacher training centers in respect to special education. In several countries, specialization in special education is entirely on the graduate level. Some countries, e.g., Scotland, require that candidates for special education training have at least one year of teaching in regular education. In France, theoretical studies and practicum requirements are distinguished from each other.

Voluntary Agencies

As in the United States, voluntary organizations have a significant place with respect to assisting handicapped students. They run preschool centers, schools, sheltered workshops, group homes, and hospitals. They even provide professional training. In West Germany the largest of these is the Catholic Caritas. There is also Lebenshilfe, the National Association of Parents and Friends of the Mentally Handicapped, which operates day school nurseries, sheltered workshops, and hostels. In Switzerland, an umbrella organization called Pro Infirmis coordinates the work of other organizations serving the handicapped. It provides a comprehensive educational program as well, publishes books and brochures, and offers consultations for children and adults. In Austria, the Save the Children Society assists children with special needs in homes and rehabilitation centers. It also offers help in times of crisis. In Great Britain, voluntary agencies work closely with public authorities. In Scandinavia, the Norwegian Red Cross has created special schools and vocational rehabilitation centers; after making them viable, it turns them over to the government.

Auxiliary Services

Widespread, comprehensive, and effective support services for handicapped students are likely to be obtained in most of the nations of Western Europe. For one thing, these nations have broad-based national health insurance systems combining private and public institutions into an easily accessible network of services (Massie, 1985). Many of the medical and ancillary medical services that handicapped children require are obtainable through such government-supported services.

REFERENCES

Booth, T. (1982). *Special need in education.* Stratford, England: Open University Educational Enterprises.

Cohen, H. U. (1985). "Var Teater": A Swedish model of children's theatre for participants with disabilities. *Children's Theatre Review, 34.*

deVincentis, S. (1984, April). *Swedish play intervention for handicapped children.* Paper presented at the annual convention of the Council for Exceptional Children. Washington, DC.

Juul, K. D. (1979). European approaches and innovations in serving the handicapped. *Exceptional Children, 44,* 322–330.

Juul, K. D. (1980). Special education in Western Europe and Scandinavia. In L. Mann & D. A. Sabatino (Eds.), *The fourth review of special education.* New York: Grune & Stratton.

Juul, K. D. (1984, April). *Toy libraries for the handicapped.* Paper presented at the annual convention of the Council for Exceptional Children, Washington, DC.

Juul, K. D., & Linton, T. E. (1978). European approaches to the treatment of behavior disordered children. *Behavior Disorders, 3,* 232–249.

Kugel, F. B., & Wolfensberger, W. (Eds.). (1968). *Changing patterns of residential services for the mentally retarded.* Washington, DC: President's Committee on Mental Retardation.

Linton, T. E. (1971). The educateur model: A theoretical monograph. *Journal of Special Education, 5,* 155–190.

Massie, R. K. (1985). The constant shadow: Reflections on the life of a chronically ill child. In N. Hobbes & J. M. Perrin (Eds.), *Issues in the care of children with chronic illness.* San Francisco: Jossey-Bass.

Organization for Economic Cooperation and Development. (1981). *Integration in the school.* Washington, DC: Author.

Organization for Economic Cooperation and Development. (1985a). *Integration of the handicapped in secondary schools: Five case studies. The Education of the handicapped adolescent: II.* Washington, DC: Author.

Organization for Economic Cooperation and Development. (1985b). *Handicapped youth at work: Personal experiences of school-leavers: The education of the handicapped adolescent: III.* Paris: Centre for Educational Research and Innovation.

Oyer, H. J. (1976). *Communication for the hearing handicapped. An international perspective.* Baltimore, MD: University Park Press.

Pahud, D., & Besson, F. (1985, Summer). Special education in Switzerland: Historical reflections and current applications. *Journal of the Division of Early Childhood, 9,* 222–29.

Pratt, R. R. (Ed.). (1983). *The International Symposium on Music in Medicine, Education, and Therapy for the Handicapped.* Lanham, MD: University Press of America.

Strain, P. (1985). A response to preschool handicapped in Italy: A research based developmental model. *Journal of the Division for Early Childhood, 29,* 269–271.

Tarnapol, L., & Tarnapol, M. (1976). *Reading disabilities: An international perspective.* Baltimore, MD: University Park Press.

Taylor, E. J. (1980). *Rehabilitation and world peace.* New York: International Society for Rehabilitation of the Disabled.

Taylor, W. W., & Taylor, I. W. (1960). *Special education of physically handicapped children in Western Europe.* New York: International Society for the Welfare of Cripples.

Wolfensberger, W. (1964). General observations on European countries. *Mental Retardation, 2,* 331–337.

Wolfensberger, W. (1973). *A selective overview of the work of Jean Vanier and the movement of L'Arche.* Toronto, Canada: National Institute of Mental Retardation.

Zucman, E. (1985). Early childhood programs for the handicapped in France. *Journal of the Division for Early Childhood, 9,* 237–245.

DON BRASWELL
Research Foundation,
City University of New York

EASTERN EUROPE, SPECIAL EDUCATION IN
FRANCE, SPECIAL EDUCATION IN
UNITED KINGDOM, SPECIAL EDUCATION IN

WHELAN, RICHARD J. (1931–   )

Born in Emmett, Kansas, Richard J. Whelan received his BA (cum laude) from Washburn University in 1955 with majors in history, political science, psychology and education. By 1957, he completed all requirements for a MA in history, with concentrations in American, European, and Far Eastern history at the University of Kansas. In 1966, he received the EdD from the University of Kansas with concentrations in special education (emotional and behavior disorders), educational psychology and research. He is currently licensed as a social studies and psychology teacher as well as a teacher of students with emotional and behavior disorders. He also holds licenses as a special edu-

Richard J. Whelan

cation supervisor/coordinator, director of special education and school psychologist. The Supreme Court of the State of Kansas has certified him as a mediator and an approved trainer of mediators. He also serves as a special education administrative hearing officer and hearing officer trainer for the Kansas State Board of Education. In addition, he is a special education hearing officer for the Bureau of Indian Affairs. During the Korean War, he served as an Instructor of Electronics, Computers and Power Control Systems at the U.S. Army Radar and Guided Missile School.

Whelan's earliest professional experiences were at the Southard School of the Menninger Clinic where he served as a recreational therapist, child care worker, teacher and Director of Education. At the University of Kansas and University of Kansas Medical Center, he has held academic appointments in psychiatry, pediatrics, and special education. His administrative posts have included chairperson of the Department of Special Education, dean of a Graduate Division, dean of the School of Education, and Director of Education for the University Affiliated Program at the Medical Center. Since 1968, he has held the chair for the Ralph L. Smith Distinguished Professor of Child Development. From 1972 to 1974, he served as director of the Division of Personnel Preparation in the Bureau of Education for the Handicapped (now Office of Special Education and Rehabilitation Services) in the Department of Health, Education, and Welfare.

Whelan has held numerous board memberships and serves as a consultant to psychiatric hospitals, universities, government agencies, schools, and other education related organizations. During his career, Whelan has served on seven publication boards, and has held offices in state and national professional organizations. He was chairperson of the Evaluation Training Consortium, a nationwide

evaluation training project funded by the U.S. Office of Education. He was a founder and officer of the Kansas Federation of the Council for Exceptional Children. He is a member of Phi Kappa Phi, and has been recognized by Leaders in Education, Who's Who in America, and Outstanding Educators of America. He has received several service awards including the Award for Leadership in Behavior Disorders from the Midwest Symposium Organization.

Whelan has contributed over 100 publications, including *Emotional and Behavioral Disorders: A 25 Year Focus* (1998) and *Educating Students with Mild Disabilities: Strategies and Methods* (1998). His professional preparation included extensive experiences in psychoanalysis, psychoeducational and applied behavior analysis theories, and interventions. He emphasizes experimental research designs and precise measurement in his own research, as well as in the classes he teaches for graduate students. More importantly, he believes that the best teachers of professionals are the children they serve: "They will let you know if you are doing it correctly." Whelan has put this belief into practice while teaching and while directing a psychoeducational clinic for children with disabilities and their families at the University of Kansas Medical Center.

REFERENCES

Whelan, R. J. (Ed.). (1998). *Emotional and behavioral disorders: A 25 year focus*. Denver: Love.

Meyen, E. L., Vergason, G. A., & Whelan, R. J. (Eds.). (1998). *Educating students with mild disabilities: Strategies and methods*. Denver: Love.

STAFF

OFFICE OF SPECIAL EDUCATION

WHOLE WORD TEACHING

The term whole word teaching has been used as the label for two different approaches to beginning reading instruction. Mathews (1966) in *Teaching to Read: Historically Considered* describes the first approach as a "words-to-letters" method that was introduced into reading instruction in Germany in the eighteenth century and later brought to the United States.

The development of the words-to-letters method was motivated by dissatisfaction with the ABC method, the prevailing method of reading instruction since the invention of the Greek alphabet. Critics of the ABC method did not disagree with its underlying philosophy that mastery of the alphabet and syllables (combinations of vowels and consonants such as *ba, bē, bu*) were prerequisite skills for learning to read. However, they took issue with the procedures used to teach those skills, namely, years of drill, which they described as senseless, tortuous, desperately dull work. The method that eventually evolved presented beginning readers with whole words in their total form followed by an analysis of the sounds and letters. This was an analytic approach to teaching the alphabet, whereas the ABC method was a synthetic approach under which students were taught to combine syllables into words only after having mastered their pronunciation as isolated units.

Mathews (1966) refers to the second approach that has been called whole word teaching as a "words-to-reading" method. This method, commonly called the "look-and-say" method, also had its roots in Germany and may have been used by some teachers in the United States as early as the 1830s. Horace Mann, a strong advocate of the method is often credited with having brought about its widespread use (Betts, 1946). However, according to Mathews (1966), it was Francis Parker, the first widely known practitioner of the look-and-say method, who played a far more significant role in its initiation. Under his leadership as superintendent of schools in Quincy, Massachusetts (1875–1878), and later as principal of Cooke County Normal School, Illinois (1883–1899), students were taught to read 150 to 200 words in the context of sentences and stories before being introduced to the sounds of letters. The teaching of names of letters was delayed for at least 2 years so that they would not be confused with the sounds of letters. While Parker's schools were widely acclaimed, it is doubtful that the look-and-say method would have gained the foothold it did had he not become closely associated with John Dewey, head of the departments of philosophy, psychology, and pedagogy at the University of Chicago.

When Parker was appointed director of the School of Education at the university in 1900, the two joined forces. Although Dewey was not interested in developing a methodology for teaching children to read, he thoroughly agreed with Parker's educational philosophy and adopted the look-and-say method strongly advocated by Parker. In this way, the look-and-say method came to occupy a prominent place in a new system of education (advocated by Dewey) to which the adjective progressive was applied (Mathews, 1966). As the influence of the progressive education movement grew, so did the use of the look-and-say approach to reading. During the first two decades of the twentieth century, it became firmly entrenched in elementary reading programs and remained so until the mid-1950s, when Rudolf Flesch (1955) captured the growing public alarm over what was happening in the nation's elementary schools in his book *Why Johnny Can't Read*. Flesch challenged the prevailing practice in beginning reading instruction that emphasized a look-and-say approach. He advocated a return to a phonic approach using existing research as support for his position.

Flesch's book led to a great deal of public debate, which in turn spawned numerous research efforts to identify the best method(s) for beginning reading instruction. Among these were 27 U.S. Office of Education grade 1 studies and a study funded by the Carnegie Corporation of New York (Chall, 1967).

REFERENCES

Betts, E. A. (1946). *Foundations of reading instruction*. New York: American Book.

Chall, J. (1967). *Learning to read: The great debate*. New York: McGraw-Hill.

Flesch, R. (1955). *Why Johnny can't read and what you can do about it*. New York: Harper & Brothers.

Mathews, M. M. (1966). *Teaching to read: Historically considered*. Chicago: University of Chicago Press.

MARIANNE PRICE
Montgomery County
Intermediate Unit,
Norristown, Pennsylvania

PHONOLOGY
READING DISORDERS
READING REMEDIATION

WIDE RANGE ACHIEVEMENT TEST—THIRD EDITION (WRAT-3)

The Wide Range Achievement Test—Third Edition (WRAT-3; Wilkinson, 1993) and the Wide Range Achievement Test—Revised (WRAT-R) are both instruments used to measure skills in the area of spelling, arithmetic and reading. The revised 1993 WRAT-3 has returned to its original format with two alternate test forms (Blue and Tan). Both forms provide information in three areas: 1) Reading—recognizing and naming letters and pronouncing words; 2) Spelling—writing name, writing letters and words to dictation; and 3) Arithmetic—counting, reading number symbols, solving oral problems, and performing written computations. The three subtests may be administered in any order. Each form can be given to individuals between the ages of 5 to 75 and can take between 15 to 30 minutes to administer depending on the skill level. The Blue or the Tan form can be used separately or both forms may be administered together (Combined Form) to measure the respective academic skills and convert the resulting raw scores to absolute scores, standard scores, grade scores and percentiles. The WRAT-3 was designed to take out the comprehension factor. This enables the examiner to use the results obtained from this measure and compare it to a measure of intelligence such as the Wechsler scales in order to determine the areas of difficulty for an individual.

Criticism of the WRAT and WRAT-R instruments have

mentioned the absence of reliability in presentation and quality as well as validity information provided in the test manuals, and the lack of nationally representative norms (Merwin, 1978; Salvia & Ysseldyke, 1985; Sattler, 1982; Thorndike, 1978). In addition, the authors have been faulted by not reporting tables showing how the standardization sample compared with the targeted population proportions (Jastak & Wilkinson, 1984). This criticism remains in the WRAT-3 as well.

The WRAT-R supports the notion that there is no difference between White and non-White groups for reading, spelling, and mathematics for Level 1. A slight difference in the area of mathematics was noted on Level 2, which resulted in an increase of time from 10 minutes to 15 minutes on the WRAT-3. Coefficient alpha was used to determine internal consistency for each test over the 23 age groups. The median test coefficient alphas ranged from 0.85 to 0.95 over the nine WRAT-3 subtests. For the three Combined tests, the coefficient alpha scores ranged from 0.92 to 0.95. The stability of third edition was measured by the test-retest method resulting in coefficient scores ranging from 0.91 to 0.98. Correlations between the WRAT-3 and other achievement measures remain low. The authors state that this is due to the different formats of the instruments, with most achievement tests presented as multiple choice unlike the WRAT-3. There does, however, seem to be a high correlation between the WRAT-R and the new edition.

The highlights of the WRAT-R and the WRAT-3 are the ease of administration and scoring by teachers and psychologists. The WRAT-3 is a valuable tool used to determine academic abilities and to identify those in need of special education services.

REFERENCES

Jastak, S., & Wilkinson, G. S. (1984). *Wide Range Achievement Test—Revised administration Manual*. Wilmington, DE: Jastak.

Merwin, J. (1978). Review of the Wide Range Achievement Test. In O. K. Buros (Ed.), *The seventh mental measurements yearbook* (pp. 66–67). Highland Park, NJ: Gryphon.

Salvia, J., & Ysseldyke, J. E. (1985). *Assessment in special and remedial education* (3rd ed.). Boston: Houghton Mifflin.

Sattler, J. M. (1982). *Assessment of children's intelligence and special abilities* (2nd ed.). Boston: Houghton Mifflin.

Thorndike, R. L. (1978). Review of the Wide Range Achievement Test. In O. K. Buros (Ed.), *The seventh mental measurements yearbook* (pp. 66–67). Highland Park, NJ: Gryphon.

Wilkinson, G. S. (1993). *Wide Range Achievement Test—Third edition administration manual*. Wilmington, DE: Wide Range, Inc.

LISA FASNACHT HILL
*California School of
Professional Psychology*

ACHIEVEMENT TESTS

WIDE RANGE ASSESSMENT OF MEMORY AND LEARNING (WRAML)

The Wide Range Assessment of Memory and Learning (WRAML; Sheslow & Adams, 1990) is a test to assess one's ability to learn and to memorize different types of information for children between 5 and 17 years of age. The WRAML is an individually-administered test used to clarify memory deficits in children with a learning disability and/or who have suffered some type of head trauma. The WRAML is comprised of three index scales yielding a Verbal Memory Index, a Visual Memory Index, and a Learning Index, each consisting of three subtests. The nine total subtests yield a General Memory Index. It can be administered by a trained clinician with experience in administration of testing under the direct supervision of a psychologist.

The Verbal Memory Index Scale measures the learner's ability to utilize language as it relates to enhance or detract in remembering. The Visual Memory Index serves to compare rote memory demands as it relates to memory, and the Learning Scale is used by the evaluator to assess the performance over trials. The WRAML also utilizes several delayed subtests in the area of Verbal Learning, Visual Learning, Sound Symbol, and Story Memory procedures. This group of tasks requires only 1 to 2 minutes each and can provide the examiner with important information regarding the learner's capacity to remember. The total administration time of the WRAML ranges from 45 minutes to one hour if all the Delayed Recall tasks are given.

A scaled score and standard score can be obtained from all of the indices. Scaled scores and standard scores allow an age-based comparison of performance. In addition, four delayed recalled subtests can be administered to determine the level of recall performance in the categories of "Bright Average," "Average," "Low Average," "Borderline," or "Atypical," compared to others of the same age. The Story Memory Recognition subtest can yield similar scores as well. In order to accommodate time constraints, the short version of the WRAML is comprised of four subtests: Picture Memory, Design Memory, Verbal Learning, and Story Memory. The correlations between the Screening Form and the complete WRAML standard form are .846 (ages 8 and younger) and .86 (ages 9 and older). The Screening version can be completed in only 10 to 15 minutes.

The WRAML is not an intelligence test, nor is it designed to measure all aspects of memory. Specifically, this instrument lacks the ability to assess the function of long-term memory. Instead, the test provides useful information with the Delayed Recall subtests by assessing immediate recall and then measuring the learner's ability to recall that information after approximately 20 to 40 minutes have elapsed.

The manual provides technical information for the instrument indicating internal consistency reliability values (coefficient alpha) ranging from 0.78 to 0.90 for each of the subtests and from 0.90 to 0.96 for the memory indices. The test-retest statistics resulted in a stability coefficient of 0.84 for General Memory, 0.82 for Verbal Memory, 0.61 for Visual Memory and 0.81 for Learning Memory. The test-retest reliability was evaluated over an average of 108 days with a normative sample of 87 subjects. Validity studies indicate that the correlation between the WRAML and the McCarthy Scales of Children's Ability has shown the WRAML General Memory Index correlated 0.72 while only a 0.10 correlation was evidenced between the WRAML Learning Index and the McCarthy. The WRAML was also correlated with the Wide Range Achievement Test—Revised (WRAT-R) and the Wechsler Memory Scale—Revised (WMS-R), both studies demonstrating low correlations.

Because the WRAML does not utilize one theory, but instead uses various theories, the test does not seem to be a consideration of the developmental aspects of memory, such as the idea that children do not systematically use active encoding strategies until about the age of 8 or 9 years and that children older than 10 gradually refine their use of strategies, making them both more effective and more flexible (Kail & Hagen, 1982). In addition, the concept that children will vary in the degree to which they benefit from multiple trials as a function of developmental status are not addressed by the authors (Boyd, 1988). Nonetheless, The Wide Range Achievement Assessment of Memory and Learning is thought to be the most efficient method of memory assessment for children between the ages of 5 to 17, even with the limitations.

REFERENCES

Boyd, T. A. (1988). Clinical assessment of memory in children: A developmental framework for practice. In M. G. Tramontana & S. R. Hooper (Eds), *Assessment issues in child neuropsychology* (pp. 177–204). New York: Plenum.

Kail, R., & Hagen, J. W. (1982). Memory in childhood. In B. Wolman, G. Stricker, S. Ellman, P. Keith-Siegel, & D. Palermo (Eds.), *Handbook of developmental psychology* (pp. 350–366). Englewood Cliffs, NJ: Prentice Hall.

Sheslow, D., & Adams, W. (1990). *Wide Range Assessment of Memory and administration manual.* Wilmington, DE: Jastak Assessment Systems.

LISA FASNACHT HILL
*California School of
Professional Psychology*

WIEACKER SYNDROME

Wieacker syndrome, also known as apraxia, involves the inability to execute familiar voluntary movements. A child with Wieacker syndrome is physically able to perform motor acts and has a desire to perform the acts, but is unable to perform the movements upon request (Merck, 1987). When motor movement does occur in a child with this syndrome, the movement is often uncontrolled, unintentional, inappropriate, and clumsy.

Selective apraxias do exist. For example, a child with constructional apraxia is unable to draw, whereas a child with oculomotor apraxia is unable to move his or her eyes (Thoene, 1992).

Apraxia results from a lesion in the neural pathways of the brain associated with the memory of learned patterns (Merck, 1987). The lesion may be due to a stroke, head injury, dementia, congenital malformation of the central nervous system, or metabolic or structural disease (Merck, 1987; Thoene, 1992).

Physical and occupational therapy is recommended to help a child with apraxia to relearn voluntary movements. If apraxia is a symptom of another disorder, treatment of the primary disorder is required (Thoene, 1992).

REFERENCES

Merck manual of diagnosis and therapy. (1987). (15th ed.). Rahway, N.J: Merck & Co.

Thoene, J. G. (Ed.). (1992). *Physician's guide to rare diseases.* Montvale, NJ: Dowden.

JOAN MAYFIELD
*Baylor Pediatric Specialty
Services*

PATRICIA LOWE
Texas A & M University

WILBUR, HERVEY BACKUS (1820–1883)

Hervey Backus Wilbur, physician and educator, established the first school for mentally retarded children in the United States when he took a group of retarded children into his home in Barre, Massachusetts, in 1848. With the published accounts of the educational work of Edouard Seguin to guide him, Wilbur fashioned out of his own experience a system of teaching that was successful to a degree not previously thought possible.

In 1851, the New York State legislature established an experimental residential school for mentally retarded children, the second state school for the mentally retarded in the United States, with Wilbur as superintendent. Residential schools were opened in a number of other states during the next few years, many of them patterned after the New York School. This school, over which Wilbur presided until his death, is today the Syracuse Developmental Center.

Wilbur was a founder and the first vice president (with Edouard Seguin as president) of the Association of Medical Officers of American Institutions for Idiotic and Feeble-Minded Persons, now the American Association on Mental Deficiency. He produced numerous pamphlets and articles dealing with the care and treatment of mentally retarded persons.

REFERENCES

Godding, W. W. (1883). In memoriam: Hervey Backus Wilbur. *Journal of Nervous & Mental Diseases, 10*, 658–662.

Scheerenberger, R. D. (1983). *A history of mental retardation.* Baltimore, MD: Brookes

PAUL IRVINE
Katonah, New York

AAMD ADAPTIVE BEHAVIOR SCALES

WILD BOY OF AVEYRON

The Wild Boy of Aveyron—or Victor, as he later came to be known—first was noticed by a group of peasants who witnessed him fleeing through the woods of south central France. He was spotted on subsequent occasions digging up turnips and potatoes or seeking acorns. He was captured in the forest of Aveyron, France, by three hunters in July 1799. It was determined that the boy was about 11 or 12 years of age, was unable to speak, and had been living a wild existence. He was taken to the Institution of Deaf Mutes in Paris and was assigned to the care of Jean Itard.

Itard, a young French physician, believed that this wild creature was physiologically normal and that his intellectual deficiencies were due to a lack of "appropriate sensory experiences in a socialized environment" (Scheerenberger, 1983). Itard was convinced that with an adequate training program, Victor would show great intellectual development and could be transformed from a savage to a civilized being. Because Victor's intellectual deficiencies were not seen as physiologically based, but were attributed to isolation and social and educational neglect, this was viewed as an opportunity to substantiate the effectiveness of educational methods being developed at the time (Maloney & Ward, 1979).

Over the next 5 years, Itard worked intensively with Victor and established a sequence of educational activities designed to teach him speech, self-care, and manners, and to develop his intellectual functions and emotional faculties. Itard employed socialization techniques and sensory training methods much like those he had used with deaf children (Robinson & Robinson, 1965).

Victor's progress was sometimes frustratingly slow, despite Itard's affection, effort, and ingenuity. Still, the doctor made tremendous gains in his 5 years of work with the boy, later documenting this in great detail (Kirk & Gallagher, 1979). Victor accomplished a great deal: he was able to recognize objects, identify letters of the alphabet, and comprehend the meaning of many words (Maloney & Ward, 1979). However, he never learned to speak, and Itard felt his program of instruction had failed. The physician decided to terminate the program after 5 years of intensive work with Victor.

Itard's experiences with the Wild Boy of Aveyron are particularly notable since his work was the first documented, systematic attempt to teach a handicapped person. Although his attempts to make the boy "normal" failed, Itard did make significant gains, and showed that even a severely handicapped individual could make great improvements with training.

REFERENCES

Kirk, S. A., & Gallagher, J. J. (1979). *Educating exceptional children* (3rd ed.). Boston: Houghton Mifflin.

Maloney, M. P., & Ward, M. P. (1979). *Mental retardation and modern society.* New York: Oxford University Press.

Robinson, H. B., & Robinson, N. M. (1965). *The mentally retarded child.* New York: McGraw-Hill.

Scheerenberger, R. C. (1983). *A history of mental retardation.* Baltimore, MD: Brookes.

KATHLEEN RODDEN-NORD
GERALD TINDAL
University of Oregon

**HISTORY OF SPECIAL EDUCATION
ITARD, JEAN MARC**

WILL, MADELEINE C. (1945–   )

Madeleine C. Will obtained her BA (1967) from Smith College and her MA (1969) at the University of Toronto, Canada. As assistant secretary for special education and rehabilitative services in the US Department of Education from 1983 to 1989, Will held the highest ranking federal position for the advocacy of individuals with disabilities. During her tenure, she was responsible for the programs in the department's Office of Special Education, the Rehabilitation Services Administration, and the National Institute for Handicapped Research—the three units comprising the Office of Special Education and Rehabilitative Services. She supervised education department programs serving 4.5 million disabled children and 936,000 adults with disabilities. Committed to the belief that federal programs must not be administered on the basis of concepts that underestimate the potential contribution of disabled citizens, Will was responsible for the initiation of transition and supported work models that strive to direct those

Madeleine C. Will

with disabilities toward independent living and meaningful employment.

Will has written extensively on the topic of special education, its successes, failures, and recommendations for improvements (Will, 1984, 1986, 1988). She is a strong advocate of a more cohesive, less fragmented system: what she terms a *partnership* between special education and regular education to improve service delivery to all students. For students with learning problems in regular classrooms, she proposes increased time for instruction, support systems for teachers, principal-controlled programs and resources at the building level, and new instructional approaches.

Will has advocated for individuals with disabilities in numerous ways, including her service as chair of the Government Affairs Committee of the Montgomery County Association for Retarded Citizens (1979) and member of the Government Affairs Committee of the National Association for Retarded Citizens. Additionally, from 1974 to 1976, she assisted in the development and operation of a program integrating preschoolers with handicaps into two nursery schools in Montgomery County, Maryland.

REFERENCES

Will, M. C. (1984). Let us pause and reflect—but not too long. *Exceptional Children, 51*(1), 11–16.

Will, M. C. (1986). Educating children with learning problems: A shared responsibility. *Exceptional Children, 52*(5), 411–415.

Will, M. C. (1988). Educating students with learning problems and the changing role of the school psychologist. *School Psychology Review, 17*(3), 476–478.

TAMARA J. MARTIN
*The University of Texas of the
Permian Basin*

OFFICE OF SPECIAL EDUCATION
NATIONAL ASSOCIATION OF RETARDED CITIZENS

WILLIAM'S SYNDROME

See INFANTILE HYPERCALCEMIA.

WILLOWBROOK CASE

The Willowbrook case, or *New York State Association for Retarded Children* v. *Carey*, was litigation tried by Judge Orrin Judd in which the conditions in the Willowbrook State School in New York State were challenged. Specific charges included widespread physical abuse, overcrowded conditions and understaffing, inhumane and destructive conditions, extended solitary confinement, and lack of therapeutic care. Brought on behalf of more than 5000 residents of the Willowbrook State School, this class-action suit is recognized as a landmark in protection from harm litigation.

During a series of Willowbrook trials, witnesses appeared and provided court testimony documenting the inhumane conditions and the physical, mental, and emotional deterioration of residents. On April 21, 1975, the New York Civil Liberties Union, the Legal Aid Society, the Mental Health Law Project, and the U.S. Department of Justice announced that the parties to the Willowbrook litigation had agreed on a consent judgment that would resolve the suit. This consent decree, which was approved on May 5, 1975, established standards in 23 areas to secure the constitutional rights of the Willowbrook residents to protection from harm.

This consent decree, which was to be implemented within 13 months or less, identified duty ratios of direct-care staff to residents of one to four during waking hours for most residents, and required an overall ratio of one clinical staff member for every three residents. The decree prohibited seclusion, corporal punishment, degradation, medical experimentation, and routine use of restraints. It established the primary goal of Willowbrook as the preparation of residents for development and life in the community, and it mandated individual plans for the residents' education, therapy, care, and development.

Additionally, the decree required (1) 6 hours of programmed activity each weekday; (2) nutritionally adequate diets; (3) dental services; (4) 2 hours of daily recreational activities; (5) adaptive equipment as needed; (6) adequate clothing; (7) continually available physicians; (8) contracted services with an accredited hospital; (9) an immunization program; (10) compensation for voluntary labor in accordance with minimum wage laws; and (11) correction of health and safety hazards.

Another set of requirements to be implemented, but not subject to the 13-month timetable, included reduction in the number of Willowbrook beds, establishment of 200 new community placements, increased funding to Willowbrook, creation of a review panel to oversee implementation of standards of the consent decree, initiation of a consumer advisory board composed of parents and relatives of residents, community leaders, residents, and former residents, and creation of a professional advisory board.

This Willowbrook case promoted improvements in the lives of the Willowbrook residents, focused public attention on the conditions of institutionalized individuals, and, as with other landmark cases, affected many similar cases.

DOUGLAS FUCHS
LYNN S. FUCHS
Vanderbilt University

DEINSTITUTIONALIZATION
HUMANISTIC SPECIAL EDUCATION
MENTAL RETARDATION

WILSON'S DISEASE

See KAYSER-FLEISCHER RING

WISC-III

See WECHSLER INTELLIGENCE SCALE FOR CHILDREN—III.

WITMER, LIGHTNER (1867–1956)

Lightner Witmer established the world's first psychological clinic, at the University of Pennsylvania in 1896, an event that marked the beginning not only of clinical psychology but also of the diagnostic approach to teaching. Previously director of the psychological laboratory at the University of Pennsylvania, where he succeeded James McKeen Cattell, Witmer moved psychology from the theoretical concerns of the laboratory to the study of learning and behavior problems of children in the classroom. Proposing a merging of the clinical method in psychology and the diagnostic method in teaching, Witmer developed an interdisciplinary approach to education; his clinic provided training for psychologists, teachers, social workers, and physicians. He formed special classes that served as training grounds for teachers from across the nation and as models for many of the special classes that were established in the early part of the twentieth century. Anticipating special education's strong influence on mainstream

Lightner Wilmer

education, Witmer suggested that learning-disabled children would show the way for the education of all children.

REFERENCES

Watson, R. I. (1956). Lightner Witmer: 1867–1956. *American Journal of Psychology, 69,* 680.

Witmer, L. (1911). *The special class for backward children.* Philadelphia: Psychological Clinic.

PAUL IRVINE
Katonah, New York

WOLF-HIRSCHHORNE SYNDROME

Wolf-Hirschhorne syndrome, also known as Wolf Syndrome or 4p-Syndrome, is a genetic disorder resulting from a defect in chromosome 4. The incidence rate of Wolf-Hirschhorne syndrome is 1 out of 50,000 births (Thoene, 1992). The syndrome occurs more often in females than males by a ratio of 2:1. Approximately one-third of the children who are born with the syndrome die in the first two years of life as a result of either cardiac failure and bronchopneumonia (O'Brien & Yule, 1995).

Primary features of the disorder include low birth weight, deficit or low muscle tone, physical and mental retardation, and a very small head. Prominent facial characteristics are also found in this syndrome, such as cleft lip, cleft palate, downturned mouth, small jaw, low-set ears, high forehead, and beak-like nose. Squinting of the eyes is another common feature. Heart and kidney problems and seizures occur in approximately 50% of the children with this disorder. In some cases, reconstructive surgery is needed to address facial abnormalities.

In schools, special education may be needed to address learning disabilities. Due to delayed psychomotor development and speech/communication abilities, physical therapy, occupational therapy, and speech services will be needed (O'Brien & Yule, 1995). Vocational services may be helpful. Genetic counseling may also be beneficial (Thoene, 1992).

REFERENCES

O'Brien, G., & Yule, W. (Eds.). (1995). *Behavioural phenotypes.* London: Mac Keith Press.

Thoene, J. G. (Ed.). (1992). *Physician's guide to rare diseases.* Montvale, NJ: Dowden.

JOAN MAYFIELD
*Baylor Pediatric Specialty
Services*

PATRICIA A. LOWE
Texas A & M University

WOLFENSBERGER, WOLF P. J. (1934–)

Born and raised in Germany in the period just before and during World War II, Wolf P. J. Wolfensberger studied in the United States. He earned a BA in philosophy from the now-defunct Siena College of Memphis, Tennessee. He subsequently pursued graduate training in psychology and education at St. Louis University, during which time he became a naturalized US citizen (1956), and received his MA in psychology in 1957. Wolfensberger continued his studies of psychology and special education, earning his PhD in these fields in 1962 from George Peabody College for Teachers (now Peabody College, Vanderbilt University).

Wolfensberger was mentored by two widely known psychologists while an intern: Walter Klopfer, the famous personality psychologist, at the Norfolk (Nebraska) State Hospital; and Jack Tizard, while Wolfensberger was a postdoctoral research fellow in mental retardation at Maudsley Hospital (the University of London teaching hospital) in England. Following the latter experience, Wolfensberger became a mental retardation research scientist at the Nebraska Psychiatric Institute (1964–1971), where he eventually rose to the rank of associate professor of medical psychology in the departments of psychiatry and pediatrics. For two years (1971–1973), he was a visiting scholar at the Canadian National Institute on Mental Retardation, with a joint faculty appointment at York University. From 1973 to 1992, Wolfensberger served as a professor in the Division of Special Education and Rehabilitation at Syracuse University, and from 1992 to the present, he has been a research professor in the School of Education there. At the same time, he has been the director of the Syracuse University Training Institute for Human Ser-

vice Planning, Leadership and Change Agentry (Wolfensberger, pers. comm., June 9, 1998).

A prolific writer and researcher, Wolfensberger has devoted nearly his entire career to social advocacy for better life conditions for and high quality services to people with handicaps. He has been one of the major proponents, arguably *the* major proponent, of the principle of normalization, in 1983 designing Social Role Valorization, focusing on the relation between social roles and consequences, as the successor to this concept. His instruments (PASS and PASSING) for evaluating services in terms of normalization and Social Role Valorization criteria have been used worldwide. Additionally, Wolfensberger is the originator of the Citizen Advocacy scheme, which promotes one-to-one advocacy for people with handicaps and is used throughout the English-speaking world. Many other advocacy-related schemes have borrowed this concept (Wolfensberger, pers. comm., June 9, 1998).

In 1991, Wolfensberger's work in the area of normalization was recognized by a Delphi panel of experts as the most influential work in the field of mental retardation in the US during a 50-year period. He continues the work he began in the 1970s, conducting training workshops for human services personnel and the families of individuals with handicaps, and serves as an advocate in 11 different countries. Wolfensberger has also spoken and written against the growing legitimization of "deathmaking" of all sorts of unwanted and devalued people (Wolfensberger, 1994).

REFERENCES

Kugel, R., & Wolfensberger, W. (Eds). (1968). *Changing patterns in residential services for the mentally retarded.* Washington, DC: President's Committee on Mental Retardation.

Wolfensberger, W. (1972). *The principle of normalization in human services.* Toronto, Canada: National Institute on Mental Retardation.

Wolfensberger, W. (1980). Research, empiricism, and the principle of normalization. In R. J. Flynn & K. E. Witsch (Eds.), *Normalization, social integration, and community services*, Baltimore, MD: University Park Press.

Wolfensberger, W. (1994). A personal interpretation of the mental retardation scene in light of the "Signs of the Times", *Mental Retardation, 32*, 19–33.

Wolfensberger, W., & Zauha, H. (Eds.). (1973). *Citizen advocacy and protective services for the impaired and handicapped.* Toronto, Canada: National Institute on Mental Retardation.

CECIL R. REYNOLDS
Texas A & M University
First edition

TAMARA J. MARTIN
*The University of Texas of the
Permian Basin*
Second edition

NORMALIZATION

WOOD, M. MARGARET (1931–   )

M. Margaret (Peggy) Wood began in special education as an NDEA fellow at the University of Georgia where, following the awarding of her BA in elementary education in 1953 from Goucher College, she earned her MEd (special education) in 1960. Wood immediately followed the MEd with an EdD, awarded with distinction in 1963 from the University of Georgia with a major in special education and a minor in psychology. Wood then did postdoctoral study at the Hillcrest Residential Treatment Center in Washington, DC. From 1964 to 1969, Wood was director of the teacher preparation program for teachers of emotionally disturbed students in the division for exceptional children at the University of Georgia. It was during this time that her view of therapeutic approaches to children in the schools matured and she began to work in earnest toward developing a psychoeducational approach to these children's problems. This approach has become known widely as developmental therapy.

In 1970 Wood received funding for the establishment of the Rutland Center for Severely Emotionally Disturbed Children; she directed the center until 1974. Developmental therapy, as practiced at the Rutland Center under Wood's direction, became a model approach to the provision of special education services to emotionally disturbed children in the public schools. More than 250 developmental therapy centers have been established in schools worldwide, though nearly all are in North and South America. Wood has continued her active interest in developmental therapy but has focused on research and dissemination ac-

tivities since 1974, when she became project director of a federally sponsored model in-service training program. Wood was promoted to the rank of professor in the division for exceptional children at the University of Georgia in 1977, a position she still holds.

Wood has more than 50 scholarly publications to her credit, most dealing with some aspect of developmental therapy, and has authored or edited six books (Wood, 1975, 1982; Williams & Wood, 1977). Wood is best known as the originator of developmental therapy, a major innovation in public school delivery of special education services to severely emotionally disturbed children. Wood has a significant reputation as a mentor and many well-known professionals have studied with her and practiced developmental therapy at the Rutland Center.

REFERENCES

Williams, G. H., & Wood, M. M. (1977). *Developmental art therapy*. Baltimore, MD: University Park Press.

Wood, M. M. (Ed.). (1975). *Developmental therapy*. Baltimore, MD: University Park Press.

Wood, M. M. (1982). Developmental therapy: A model for therapeutic intervention in the schools. In C. R. Reynolds & T. B. Gutkin (Eds.), *The handbook of school psychology*. New York: Wiley.

CECIL R. REYNOLDS
Texas A & M University

DEVELOPMENTAL THERAPY

M. Margaret Wood

WOODCOCK DIAGNOSTIC READING BATTERY

The *Woodcock Diagnostic Reading Battery* (WDRB; Woodcock, 1997) is a set of carefully engineered (Woodcock, 1992) tests for clinical measurement of reading achievement and important abilities related to reading. Test development, item calibration, scaling, cluster composition, and interpretation were accomplished through the Rasch single-parameter logistic test model (Rasch, 1960; Wright & Stone, 1979), and stepwise multiple regression analysis. Continuous-year norming, based on a nationally representative sample of 6,026 individuals ranging in age from 4 to 95 years, produced highly accurate normative data—10 points at each grade level and 12 points at each age level for school-aged individuals.

The WDRB is comprised of six tests from the WJ-R Tests of Cognitive Ability (Woodcock & Johnson, 1989) and four tests from the WJ-R Tests of Achievement (Woodcock & Johnson, 1989). The tests were combined into one format to be "more useful to those who are reading specialists and researchers" (Rudman, in press). That is, one short battery of tests includes (1) tests of basic reading and reading comprehension skills, (2) important reading-related tests (phonological awareness and oral comprehension), and (3) reading aptitude tests.

The reading tests include Letter-Word Identification, Passage Comprehension, Word Attack, and Reading Vocabulary. The phonological awareness tests include Incomplete Words and Sound Blending. The oral comprehension tests are Oral Vocabulary and Listening Comprehension.

Four tests comprise the Reading Aptitude cluster: Memory for Sentences, Visual Matching, Sound Blending, and Oral Vocabulary. These tests are based on tasks that are statistically and logically associated with proficiency in reading, but are uncontaminated with reading content. The median correlation between the WDRB Reading Aptitude cluster and Broad Reading achievement clusters is .78.

The Reading Aptitude cluster in this battery is particularly notable in that it makes a valid aptitude measure available to a wide array of specialists who might otherwise not be trained to administer an intellectual ability test. Because the aptitude tests were conormed with the achievement tests, actual discrepancy norms are available. Use of conormed tests is the most accurate and valid method for determining the presence and severity of an aptitude/achievement discrepancy (McGrew, 1994). This is because the discrepancy norm calculation procedure fully accounts for regression to the mean (McGrew et al., 1991). (Practitioners who use separately normed instruments for aptitude/achievement discrepancy analysis do not possess actual data for both the predictor and criterion variables from the same sample of subjects.)

A reading performance model, included in the examiner's manual, helps examiners interpret the reading-related abilities. An individual's phonological awareness exerts a major influence on his or her decoding or basic reading skills. His or her oral comprehension exerts a major influence on reading comprehension. When these related tests are administered in conjunction with the reading achievement tests, examiners can obtain a better picture of why an individual has a reading problem.

Administration time is approximately 50 to 60 minutes for all 10 tests. A wide range of scores are available, notably age and grade equivalents, standard scores, percentile ranks, and instructional zones. Rudman (in press) seemed particularly impressed by the associated *Scoring and Interpretive Program for the Woodcock Diagnostic Reading Battery* (Schrank & Woodcock, 1978). He said "The narrative reports are remarkably smooth and do not read as most computer narratives normally do" (p. 8).

The reliability and validity characteristics of the WDRB are very good and meet basic technical requirements for both individual placement and programming decisions. Repeated-measures reliability (for individuals retested one to seventeen months after initial testing) is extremely high (McArdle and Woodcock, in press), especially for the learned abilities, such as Letter-Word Identification (.92)

and Passage Comprehension (.82). The median test stability over this wide range of time for all 10 tests is .81. Rudman (in press) described this as "a surprising picture of stability of traits." Concurrent validity evidence is established through moderate to strong correlations between the WDRB and measures of cognitive abilities, achievement, and language proficiency, including the Peabody Individual Achievement Test (Dunn & Markwardt, 1970), the Wechsler Intelligence Scale for Children—Revised (Wechsler, 1974), the Stanford-Binet Intelligence Scale—Fourth Edition (Thorndike, Hagen, & Sattler, 1986), the Kaufman Intelligence Battery for Children (Kaufman & Kaufman, 1983), the Kaufman Tests of Educational Achievement (Kaufman & Kaufman, 1985), the Basic Achievement Skills Individual Screener (Psychological Corporation, 1983), the Wide Range Achievement Tests—Revised (Jastak & Wilkinson, 1984), and the Mini-Battery of Achievement (Woodcock, McGrew, & Werder, 1994). Construct validity evidence is presented via a pattern of increasing scores with age.

REFERENCES

Dunn, L. M., & Markwardt, F. C. (1970). *Peabody Individual Achievement Test*. Circle Pines, MN: American Guidance Service.

Jastak, S. R., & Wilkinson, G. S. (1984). *Wide Range Achievement Test—Revised*. Wilmington, DE: Jastak.

Kaufman, A. S., & Kaufman, N. L. (1983). *Kaufman Assessment Battery for Children*. Circle Pines, MN: American Guidance Service.

Kaufman, A. S., & Kaufman, N. L. (1985). *Kaufman Tests of Educational Achievement*. Circle Pines, MN: American Guidance Service.

McArdle, J., & Woodcock, R. W. (in press). Modeling developmental components of change from time-lagged test-retest data. *Applied Psychological Measurement*.

McGrew, K. S. (1994). *Clinical interpretation of the Woodcock-Johnson Tests of Cognitive Ability—Revised*. Boston: Allyn & Bacon.

McGrew, K. S., Werder, J. K., & Woodcock, R. W. (1991). *WJ-R Technical Manual*. Itasca, IL: Riverside.

Psychological Corporation. (1983). *Basic Achievement Skills Individual Screener*. San Antonio: Author.

Rasch, G. (1960). *Probabilistic models for some intelligence and attainment tests*. Copenhagen, Denmark: Danish Institute for Educational Research.

Rudman, H. C. (in press). Review of the Woodcock Diagnostic Reading Battery. *The fourteenth mental measurements yearbook*. Lincoln, NB: University of Nebraska Press.

Schrank, F. A., & Woodcock, R. W. (1998). *Scoring and interpretive program for the Woodcock Diagnostic Reading Battery*. Itasca, IL: Riverside.

Thorndike, R. L., Hagen, E. P., & Sattler, J. M. (1986). *Stanford-Binet Intelligence Scale—Fourth Edition*. Itasca: Riverside.

Wechsler, D. (1974). *Wechsler Intelligence Scale for Children—Revised*. San Antonio: Psychological Corporation.

Woodcock, R. W. (1992, April). *Rasch technology and test engineering*. Invited presentation to the American Educational Research Association annual conference, San Francisco.

Woodcock, R. W. (1997). *Woodcock Diagnostic Reading Battery*. Itasca, IL: Riverside.

Woodcock, R. W., & Johnson, M. B. (1989). *Woodcock-Johnson—Revised Tests of Achievement*. Itasca, IL: Riverside.

Woodcock, R. W., & Johnson, M. B. (1989). *Woodcock-Johnson—Revised Tests of Cognitive Ability*. Itasca, IL: Riverside.

Woodcock, R. W., McGrew, K. S., & Werder, J. K. (1994). *Mini-Battery of Achievement*. Itasca, IL: Riverside.

Wright, B. D., & Stone, M. H. (1979). *Best test design*. Chicago: MESA Press.

FREDRICK A. SCHRANK
*The Riverside Publishing
Company*

WOODCOCK-JOHNSON PSYCHOEDUCATIONAL BATTERY—REVISED

The Woodcock-Johnson Psychoeducational Battery—Revised (WJ-R) contains a variety of tests that measure cognitive and academic achievement abilities and is, therefore, applicable in educational, clinical, and research settings. The WJ-R has two major components: The Tests of Cognitive Abilities (WJ-R COG; Woodcock & Johnson, 1989b) and the Tests of Achievement (WJ-R ACH; Woodcock & Johnson, 1989a). Each component is further divided into a Standard and Supplementary Battery. These batteries yield several Cluster Standard Scores as well as age and grade equivalents and percentiles. The components are designed so that the clinician may select only the tests required to provide additional information regarding particular abilities or skills in question. The test may be administered to children and adults between the ages of 2 and 90. In general, administration of the WJ-R can range from 40 to 180 minutes.

Derived from the Horn-Cattell intelligence model, the WJ-R COG is comprised of 21 subtests that yield seven factors including Long-Term Retrieval, Short-Term Memory, Processing Speed, Auditory Processing, Visual Processing, Comprehension-Knowledge, and Fluid Reasoning. In addition, the WJ-R COG generates predictions about an individual's achievement abilities based on reading, mathematics, written language, knowledge, and oral language. The WJ-R ACH includes nine standard subtests and five supplemental subtests. The following ten cluster scores are derived from this component: Broad Reading, Basic Reading Skills, Reading Comprehension, Broad Mathematics, Basic Mathematics Skills, Mathematics Reasoning, Basic Written Language, Basic Writing Skills, Written Expression, and Skills. Further detail regarding each cluster is provided in the WJ-R manuals.

The examiner's manual offers information regarding technical aspects such as norming, reliability, and validity. The tests were normed using a national sample of 6,359 subjects between the ages of 2 and 95. In a separate norming sample, college and university students were used. With regard to reliability, coefficients were not reported for timed tests, such as Visual Matching, Cross Out, and Writing Fluency. The Spearman-Brown split-half statistical procedure indicated that, on the cognitive subtests, median reliability coefficients range from .72 (Visual Closure) to .94 (Concept Formation). On the achievement subtests, median reliability coefficients range from .75 (Writing Fluency) to .94 (Letter-Word Identification). Content, criterion-related, and concurrent validity were established. For the WJ-R COG, content validity was established with the aid of the Horn-Cattell model of intelligence, while being established by outside experts and experienced teachers for the WJ-R ACH. Concurrent validity was reported with such tests as the Kaufman Assessment Battery for Children (.74), the Stanford-Binet Composite (.77), and the Wechsler Intelligence Scale for Children–Revised (.75).

The WJ-R is a comprehensive tool used to assess cognitive and academic achievement skills. Both components were based on the same norming sample, allowing direct comparisons to be made between the scores (Woodcock, 1997). Although it was developed using a strong theoretical basis, some problems exist. Sattler (1992) indicates that no factor analysis studies have supported using the cluster scores. In addition, because the WJ-R COG subtests are used to measure academic achievement, the Full-Scale cluster may underestimate the cognitive skills of children with language delays. Cummings (1982) noted that the Full-Scale cluster classifications fluctuate according to age or grade.

REFERENCES

Cummings, J. A. (1982). Interpreting functioning levels: Woodcock-Johnson Psychoeducational Battery. *Psychological Reports, 50,* 1167–1171.

Sattler, J. M. (1992). *Assessment of children: Revised and updated third edition*. San Diego: Sattler.

Woodcock, R. W. (1997). The Woodcock-Johnson Tests of Cognitive Abilities—Revised. In D. P. Flanagan, J. L. Genshaft, & P. L. Harrison (Eds.), *Contemporary intellectual assessment: Theories, tests, and issues*. New York: Guilford.

Woodcock, R. W., & Johnson, M. B. (1989a). *The Woodcock-Johnson Tests of Achievement—Revised*. Chicago: Riverside.

Woodcock, R. W., & Johnson, M. B. (1989b). *The Woodcock-Johnson Tests of Cognitive Abilities—Revised*. Chicago: Riverside.

DARIELLE GREENBERG
*California School of
Professional Psychology*

ACHIEVEMENT TESTS
CRITERION REFERENCED TESTS

WOODCOCK LANGUAGE PROFICIENCY BATTERY—REVISED

The *Woodcock Language Proficiency Battery—Revised* (Woodcock, 1991; Woodcock & Muñoz-Sandoval, 1995; WLPB-R) is designed to provide an overview of a subject's language skills in English (or Spanish), to diagnose language abilities, to identify students for English as a second language instruction, and to plan broad instructional goals for developing language competencies. The instrument is appropriate for individuals aged 2 to over 90 years of age. For interpretive purposes, each WLPB-R provides cluster scores for Broad Language Ability (English or Spanish), Oral Language Ability, Reading Ability, and Written Language Ability. When the entire battery is used, the WLPB-R provides a procedure for evaluating the strengths and weaknesses among an individual's oral language, reading, and written language abilities. When both the English and Spanish forms are administered, examiners can obtain information about language dominance and relative proficiency in each language.

The WLPB-R oral language tests measure linguistic competency, semantic expression, expressive vocabulary, and verbal comprehension/reasoning. The WLPB-R reading tests measure the ability to identify sight vocabulary, to apply structural analysis skills, and comprehend single-word stimuli and short passages. The written language tests assess a broad range of writing tasks. These include tasks measuring the ability to produce simple sentences with ease, writing increasingly complex sentences to meet varied demands, and other tasks measuring punctuation, capitalization, spelling, word usage, and the ability to detect and correct errors in spelling, punctuation, capitalization, and word usage in written passages.

Administration time varies depending on the purposes of the assessment and the number of tests administered (20 minutes to over one hour). A wide variety of interpretive scores are available, including age and grade equivalents, instructional ranges, standard scores, and percentile ranks.

The English form was standardized on more than 6,300 individuals ranging in age from 2 to over 90. Lehmann (1995), who reviewed the WLPB-R primarily from a psychometric perspective, commented favorably on the development of continuous (gathered throughout the school year), rather than interpolated, norms. The Spanish form was standardized on more than 2,000 native Spanish-speaking subjects. The Spanish form uses equated US norms for interpretive purposes.

Internal consistency reliability coefficients and stan-dard errors of measurement (SEMs) were calculated for all tests and clusters and are reported in the *WLBP-R Examiner's Manual*. Reliabilities are generally in the high .80s and low .90s for the individual tests, and in the mid .90s for the clusters. Test-retest reliability, interrater reliability, and alternate forms reliability statistics are also reported. All provide evidence that scores from the WLPB-R are reliable. Poteat (1995) said that "the profusion of reliability data varies but generally the WLPB-R appears to have satisfactory to excellent reliability (p. 416)."

The manual also presents evidence of concurrent validity as established through moderate to strong correlations between the WLPB-R and other measures of cognitive abilities, achievement, and language proficiency. Poteat (1995) said that "it is difficult to summarize these very diverse data very succinctly, but the WLPB-R is positively correlated to measures of language development and ability" (p. 416). Intercorrelations among WLPB-R tests are also presented in the manual, providing adequate evidence of construct validity. In addition, a study by Schrank, Fletcher, and Alvarado (1996) provides evidence that the WLPB-R tests are good measures of cognitive-academic language proficiency (CALP; Cummins, 1984). The study by Schrank et al. (1996) also showed that the WLPB-R correlated highly with language performance in the classroom. This additional validity evidence was recommended in the review by Poteat (1995).

REFERENCES

Cummins, J. (1984). *Bilingualism and special education: Issues in assessment and pedagogy*. Austin, TX: Pro-Ed.

Lehmann, I. J. (1995). Review of the Woodcock Language Proficiency Battery—Revised. *The twelfth mental measurements yearbook* (pp. 1118–1120) Lincoln, NB: University of Nebraska Press.

Poteat, G. M. (1995). Review of the Woodcock Language Proficiency Battery—Revised. *The twelfth mental measurements yearbook* (pp. 1120–1121). Lincoln, NB: University of Nebraska Press.

Schrank, F. A., Fletcher, T. V., & Alvarado, C. G. (1996). Comparative validity of three English oral language proficiency tests. *Bilingual Research Journal, 20*(1), 55–68.

Woodcock, R. W. (1991). *Woodcock Language Proficiency Battery—Revised, English Form*. Itasca, IL: Riverside.

Woodcock, R. W., & Muñoz-Sandoval, A. (1995). *Woodcock Language Proficiency Battery—Revised, Spanish Form*. Itasca, IL: Riverside.

FREDRICK A. SCHRANK
The Riverside Publishing Company

NONDISCRIMINATORY ASSESSMENT
WOODCOCK-JOHNSON PSYCHOEDUCATIONAL TEST BATTERY

WOODCOCK READING MASTERY TESTS—REVISED

Available in two forms, the Woodcock Reading Mastery Tests—Revised (WRMT-R; Woodcock, 1987) is an individually-administered test designed to assess a variety of reading abilities of individuals between the ages of 4 and 75. The WRMT-R is useful in various settings, such as instructional placement, individual program planning, and progress evaluation (Cohen & Cohen, 1994). The test consists of six subtests, including Visual-Auditory Learning, Letter Identification, Word Identification, Word Attack, Word Comprehension, and Passage Comprehension. Visual-Auditory Learning involves learning several unfamiliar visual symbols representing words. Letter Identification assesses an individual's ability to identify by name or sound the letters of the alphabet. Word Identification requires the test taker to read words ranging in difficulty. Word Attack evaluates the ability to pronounce nonsense words using phonic skills. Word Comprehension is comprised of antonyms, synonyms, and analogies. Finally, Passage Comprehension is designed to evaluate reading comprehension skills. From these subtests, five cluster scores are obtained: Readiness, Basic Skills, Reading Comprehension, Total Reading-Full Scale, and Total Reading-Short Scale. Percentile ranks, grade and age equivalent scores, instructional ranges, and strengths and weaknesses can also be obtained. Depending on the form used, administration time ranges from 30 to 60 minutes.

The WRMT-R was recently renormed, and is now referred to as the Woodcock Reading Mastery Test—Revised/Normative Update (WRMT-R/NU; Woodcock, 1997) The examiner's manual for the WRMT-R/NU offers information regarding technical aspects such as norming, reliability, and validity. The WRMT-R/NU was normed using approximately 3,700 subjects; however, new norms were not collected for subjects in grades 13–16 or ages 23 and older. Subjects were randomly selected using a stratified sampling method based on variables such as geographic region, community size, sex, and so on from 1994 US Census data. Split-half reliability coefficients of the original WRMT-R ranged from .34 to .98, and ranged from .87 to .89 in the WRMT-R Normative Update. Content and concurrent validity were described. However, the authors do not substantiate the content validity of the WRMT-R, although they report using "outside experts" and experienced teachers. Concurrent validity was established with comparisons to such tests as Iowa Tests of Basic Skills, Peabody Individual Achievement Test—Revised, KeyMath—Revised, and Kaufman Test of Educational Achievement.

In comparing the original WRMT-R norms with those from the 1997 update, it appears that there is little change in the level of performance of students who are average to above average for their grade or age (Woodcock, 1997). However, the performance of students who are below average appears to have declined. The result of these changes is that where student performance has improved, the WRMT-R/NU standard scores and percentiles will be lower than on the original norms, and conversely, where performance has declined, WRMT-R/NU standard scores and percentiles will be higher (Woodcock, 1997).

The WRMT-R has been revised several times. An atheoretical development of this test allows for the test to be applied to many clinical and remedial settings. However, several problems with this scale exist. Cooter (1989) reported that the WRMT-R assesses reading "in fragments rather than holistically." In addition, reliability and validity data is limited. The authors report data on WRMT-R split-half reliability and establish validity in a questionable fashion (Compton, 1990). In addition, the reliability of WRMT-R individual subtests for Grade 11 and above do not appear to be consistent with the reported norms of other age groups (Cohen & Cohen, 1994).

REFERENCES

Cohen, S. H., & Cohen, J. (1994). Review of the Woodcock Reading Mastery Tests—Revised. In D. J. Keyser & R. C. Sweetland (Eds.), *Test critiques: Volume X.* Austin: Pro-Ed.

Compton, C. (1990). *A guide to 85 tests for special education.* Belmont: Fearon/Janus.

Cooter, R. (1989). Review of the Woodcock Reading Mastery Tests—Revised. In J. C. Conoley & J. J. Kramer (Eds.), *The tenth mental measurements yearbook.* Lincoln: University of Nebraska Press.

Woodcock, R. W. (1987). *Woodcock Reading Mastery Tests—Revised.* Circle Pines, MN: American Guidance Service.

Woodcock, R. W. (1997). *Woodcock Reading Mastery Tests—Revised/Normative Update.* Circle Pines, MN: American Guidance Service.

DARIELLE GREENBERG
California School of Professional Psychology

WOODCOCK-JOHNSON PSYCHOEDUCATIONAL BATTERY

WOODS SCHOOLS

The Woods Schools, located in Langhorne, Pennsylvania, was established in 1913 to provide educational and training programs for students with development delays, retardation, brain damage, and learning disabilities. The school is primarily a residential facility that features group home life in small cottages with an intensive staff ratio that provides for direct care and services to meet the individual needs of students. The school provides for day and residential students on a coed basis.

The school programs offer a wide range of educational experiences to students who are severely handicapped and who require therapeutic services. Vocational training is provided. Students are trained in a wide range of vocational exploration experiences that establish appropriate work habits, basic working skills, and prevocational experiences that lead to job training. Remedial services, tutorial instruction, and therapeutic services are designed to meet the individual needs of students as they progress through the programs.

REFERENCE

Sargent, J. K. (1982). *The directory for exceptional children* (9th ed.). Boston: Porter Sargent.

PAUL C. RICHARDSON
Elwyn Institutes

VOCATIONAL TRAINING

WORD BLINDNESS

Congenital word blindness, word blindness, dyslexia, developmental dyslexia, specific dyslexia, developmental alexia, visual aphasia, and strephosymbolia are all terms that have on some occasions been used interchangeably in the special education literature (Evans, 1982; Orton, 1937; Wallin, 1968) to indicate a child's inability to learn to read. Developmental dyslexia was defined by Critchley (1964) as a specific difficulty in learning to read, often of genetic origin, which existed in spite of good general intelligence, and without emotional problems, brain damage, or impairments of vision or hearing. Ford (1973) defined congenital word blindness or dyslexia as the inability of a child to learn the meaning of graphic symbols.

Although literature is available from as early as the 1800s (Kussmaul, 1877), there is no clear agreed on cause for this problem. Causes that have been hypothesized ranged from maternal and natal factors, ophthalmological factors, cerebral dominance issues, and minor neurological impairments, to genetic issues (Critchley, 1964). Clemesha (1915) attributed word blindness to a congenital defect or deficiency in the brain or to some pathological process. Heitmuller (1918) felt that developmental alexia or word blindness was a developmental defect of the visual memory center for the graphic symbols of language. Orton (1937) postulated that dyslexic symptoms were the result of mixed dominance, which he called motor integrating abilities. His theory attributed reading reversals to the possibility that the mirrored counterparts of words located in the dominant hemisphere were stored in the subdominant hemisphere; therefore, children without a clearly established dominant hemisphere would have confusion with learning to read words. He also believed that this difficulty in establishing dominance was inherited. DeHirsch (Hallahan & Cruickshank, 1973) postulated a central nervous system dysfunction or developmental lag as the cause of word blindness. She believed "that both delayed cerebral dominance and language disorders may reflect a maturational dysfunction" (p. 106).

Although there continues to be a lack of consensus on which terminology to use, as well as on the meaning of the terms chosen, the literature is clearly divided between the medical (those professionals who are looking for a cause) and the educational (those professionals who are more interested in determining a means to remediate the problem). The medically oriented group is more likely to see word blindness or dyslexia as an inability to learn to read owing to a central nervous system dysfunction or brain damage, while the educationally oriented group is more likely to describe this group as children who are having trouble learning to read. There are other distinctions between the medical and educational professions. Educators are more concerned with the developmental sequence of reading skills; the medical community is concerned with disabilities in language and speech, motor development, and perception. Educators differentiate between reading problems of children and adults, and make a distinction between maturational lag and a central nervous system dysfunction. Educators do not see one easy way of remediating but base remediation on intensive diagnostic information related to the specific skills that individual children are missing, the child's best modality for learning, the appropriate materials, etc. Educators are less likely to recommend individual treatment, but work within the entire school population to improve reading instruction for all children (Lerner, 1971). One final distinction between the two groups of professionals is that the medically oriented research has been conducted most often by physicians in Europe, while the educational research has been done by educators, psychologists, and reading specialists in the United States. DeHirsch, a language pathology theorist and psychiatrist (Hallahan & Cruickshank, 1973), has done extensive research in the area of dyslexia and has been greatly responsible for the integration of research from both of these groups.

Specific behavioral characteristics that may be present in children who have been diagnosed as word blind include a general clumsiness or spatial disorientation, minor sensory disorders, difficulty in eye control, defects in body image, confusion of right and left, faulty estimates of spatial and temporal categories, difficulty in interpreting the meaning of facial expressions, difficulty in arithmetic skills, difficulty with processing of complex linguistic verbalizations, difficulty with formulation, a tendency for cluttering, disorganized verbal output, hyperactivity, and difficulty with figure-group concepts (Critchley, in Franklin, 1962; DeHirsch, 1952).

Heller (1963) described screening criteria for detecting word blindness in school-aged children. These criteria include normal intelligence, normal vision and hearing, marked reduction in reading and spelling ability, descrepancy between reading and other abilities, inability to read by the sight method, ability to learn to read by auditory repetition, and evidence of dissociation of visual word-image from acoustic word-image. Remediation techniques traditionally have emphasized the phonetic approach (Hinshelwood, 1917; Holt, 1962; Miles, 1962; Orton, 1937), with training occurring in individualized sessions. A more individualized eclectic approach was hypothesized by Naidoo (1972) and DeHirsch (Hallahan & Cruickshank, 1973), with emphasis on evaluating each student's strengths and weaknesses and devising an individualized program based on the results. Specific remediation techniques have been well developed by Wagner (1976).

The Word Blind Centre for Dyslexic Children was established in 1962 in London, England, by the Invalid Children's Aid Association (ICAA; Naidoo, 1972). It was in operation from 1962 to 1970; its goals were both research and the treatment of dyslexic children. The ICAA has been responsible, since 1963, for the publication of the *Word Blind Bulletin*. In the United States, the National Advisory Committee on Dyslexia and Related Reading Disorders was created by the Secretary of Health, Education and Welfare (HEW) in 1968. Its purpose was to investigate, clarify, and resolve the controversial issues surrounding dyslexia. The committee determined that the term dyslexia served no useful educational purpose. It recommended the creation of an Office of Reading Disorders within HEW to improve reading instruction for all children who were experiencing difficulty in reading (*Report to the Secretary of the Department of Health, Education and Welfare*, 1969).

REFERENCES

Clemesha, J. C. (1915). Congenital word blindness or inability to learn to read. *Journal of Ophthalmology Oto-Laryngoloy, 9*(1), 1–6.

Critchley, M. (1962). In A. W. Franklin (Ed.), *Word-blindness or specific developmental dyslexia*. Proceedings of a conference called by the Invalid Children's Aid Association. London: Pitman.

Critchley, M. (1964). *Developmental dyslexia,* London: Heinemann Medical.

DeHirsch, K. (1952). Specific dyslexia or strephosymbolia. *Folia Phoniatrica, 4,* 231–248.

DeHirsch, K. (1973). In D. P. Hallahan & W. M. Cruickshank (Eds.), *Psychoeducational foundations of learning disabilities*. Englewood Cliffs, NJ: Prentice-Hall.

Evans, M. M. (1982). *Dyslexia: An annotated bibliography. Contemporary problems of childhood #5.* Westport, CT: Greenwood.

Fisher, J. H. (1905). Case of congenital word-blindness (inability to learn to read). *Ophthalmic Review, 20,* 315–318.

Ford, F. R. (1973). Developmental word blindness and mirror writing. In *Diseases of the nervous system in infancy, childhood, and adolescence* (6th ed.). Springfield, IL: Thomas.

Franklin, A. W. (Ed.). (1962). *Word-blindness or specific developmental dyslexia*. Proceedings of a conference called by the Invalid Children's Aid Association. London: Pitman.

Hallahan, D. P., & Cruickshank, W. M. (1973). *Psychoeducational foundations of learning disabilities*. Englewood Cliffs, NJ: Prentice-Hall.

Heitmuller, G. H. (1918). Cases of developmental alexia or congenital word blindness. *Washington Medical Annual, 17,* 124–129.

Heller, T. M. (1963). Word-blindness—A survey of the literature and a report of twenty-eight cases. *Pediatrics, 31*(4), 669–691.

Hinshelwood, J. (1917). *Congenital word-blindness*. London: H. K. Lewis.

Holt, L. M. (1962). In A. W. Franklin (Ed.), *Word-blindness or specific developmental dyslexia*. Proceedings of a conference called by the Invalid Children's Aid Association. London: Pitman.

Kussmaul, A. (1877). Word-deafness—Word blindness. In A. H. Buck & H. von Ziemssen (Eds.), *Diseases of the nervous system, and disturbances of speech. Vol. 14 of Cyclopaedia of the Practice of Medicine*. New York: Wood.

Lerner, J. W. (1971). *Children with learning disabilities* (2nd ed.). Boston: Houghton Mifflin.

Miles, T. R. (1962). In A. W. Franklin (Ed.), *Word-blindness or specific developmental dyslexia*. Proceedings of a conference called by the Invalid Children's Aid Association. London: Pitman.

Naidoo, S. (1972). *Specific dyslexia: The research report of the ICAA Word Blind Centre of Dyslexic Children*. London: Pitman.

Orton, S. T. (1937). *Reading, writing, and speech problems in children*. New York: Norton.

Orton, S. T. (1966). *Word-blindness in school children and other papers on strephosymbolia (specific language disability—dyslexia) 1925–1946*. Pomfret, CT: Orton Society.

Report to the Secretary of the Department of Health, Education, and Welfare. (1969, August). Washington, DC: National Advisory Committee on Dyslexia and Related Disorders.

Wagner, R. F. (1976). *Helping the word blind: effective intervention techniques for overcoming reading problems in older students*. West Hyzck, NY: Center for Applied Research in Education.

Wallin, J. E. W. (1968). Congenital word blindness (dyslexia) in children. *Journal of Education, 151*(1), 36–51.

SUSANNE BLOUGH ABBOTT
Stanford, Connecticut

DSYLEXIA
READING DISORDERS
READING REMEDIATION

WORD BLINDNESS

See CONGENITAL WORD BLINDNESS, HISTORY OF.

WORDS IN COLOR

Words in Color is a one-to-one sound-symbol approach to teaching reading that was devised in 1957 by Caleb Gattegno. Gattegno, a scientist, approached the problems of reading as he did the problems of mathematics and physics. He introduced the concept of temporal sequence into reading methodology (Gattegno, 1970) and proposed that our language is coded into a series of sounds that, when uttered in sequence, produce wholes that we call words. The timing of the sounds in sequence is essential learning for correct pronunciation (Aukerman, 1971). Words in Color is based on the premise that reading is a process of decoding printed symbols and translating them into sounds and words. Color is used in the initial stage of reading to help the learner make an association between the symbol and the sound.

In the Words in Color program, there are 21 charts of letter sounds, letters in combination, and word families. Included on these charts are the 47 distinct sounds of American English in 280 different instances of letters and letter combinations. In beginning reading instruction, the child looks at the colored charts of words, then writes the same letters or words in black and white and reads what he or she has written. The names of the letters are not used, only the sounds and colors. In Words in Color the vowels are taught as sound-symbol shapes. The learner's attention is focused on the shape of the letter and how it relates in shape to the other vowels.

Gattegno introduced his Words in Color program as a novel approach to teaching reading. He asserted that, "illiteracy can be wiped out at a far smaller cost than any wild dreamer has ever dreamed. [He is] prepared to do the computation if asked" (Gattegno, 1970). Results of research studies on the Words in Color program are mixed (Aukerman, 1971). Some studies have shown positive results (DeLacy, 1973) but Gattegno is far from reaching his goal of wiping out illiteracy with the Words in Color program.

REFERENCES

Aukerman, R. C. (1971). *Approaches to beginning reading*. New York: Wiley.

DeLacy, E. (1973). Clinical reading cases—Some speculations concerning sequence in colour and look-and-say. *Slow Learning Child, 20*(3), 160–163.

Gattegno, C. (1969). *Towards a visual culture*. New York: Outerbridge Dienstfrey.

Gattegno, C. (1970). The problem of reading is solved. *Harvard Educational Review, 40*(2), 283–286.

NANCY J. KAUFMAN
University of Wisconsin at Stevens Point

READING DISORDERS
READING REMEDIATION

WORKFARE

Workfare is a term that was coined in the 1980s to describe welfare reform efforts that require able-bodied AFDC parents to work in public service projects in exchange for monthly benefits. These unpaid jobs were typically at the city or county level and involved entry-level positions in clerical, human services, or park maintenance work. The majority of the participants were single females with children over the age of 6.

In 1981 the Reagan administration proposed a mandatory national workfare program, but Congress, reluctant to endorse such sweeping legislation in the absence of empirical evidence, instead passed the 1981 Omnibus Budget Reconciliation Act. This 1981 legislation encouraged, but did not require, the states to implement workfare programs as part of their welfare reform initiatives. By 1985, 37 states were experimenting with some type of workfare (*Wall Street Journal*, August, 5, 1985). In most cases, workfare was but one small component in a broader employment effort that might include career planning, vocational training, high school equivalency courses, job placement services, child-care vouchers, transportation assistance, and on-the-job training with subsidies to employers. The states were allowed to use Federal Work Incentive Program funds in these reform initiatives.

As the states began to generate their own welfare reform models compatible with local philosophies and resources, it became clear that there were widely different approaches being tried across the country. This diversity provided social researchers with an unprecedented natural laboratory in which to study different systems. The most thorough research on workfare was conducted by the Manpower Demonstration Research Corporation (MDRC) of New York City. In 1982, with financial help from the Ford Foundation, this nonprofit research group began a 4-year comparative study of welfare reform in 11 different states. The following generalizations and quotations were taken from MDRC's report on the first three study sites (February, 1986): San Diego, California; Baltimore, Maryland; and two counties in Arkansas:

1. The studied states are increasing the employment of welfare recipients and, in some cases, reducing the costs of welfare. "Moreover, for the first time, there is reliable evidence that several different approaches—including a form of workfare—are cost-effective to operate."

2. The states place more emphasis on job search activities than on workfare activities and workfare "has

not turned out to be either as punitive as its critics feared or as praiseworthy as its advocates claimed."

3. The findings indicate that the public service jobs are generally valued by both the participants and their supervisors, and are not considered "make work" activities.

4. In most cases, the participants already possess the necessary entry-level skills before they begin their jobs, so the workfare experience does not contribute to new vocational skills development.

5. Supervisors report that participants' productivity and attendance are as good as that of most other paid employees.

6. The majority of the participants agree that the work requirement is fair. Many feel positive about the work they do, and feel that they are making a contribution.

Undoubtedly, the most widely reported success story in work welfare reform comes from the state of Massachusetts, where 20,000 welfare recipients were placed in jobs in the past 2 years (*U.S. News & World Report*, October 28, 1985). This program, which was voluntary and did not have the punitive quality often associated with workfare, reported that 86% of its first-year beneficiaries were still off welfare after 12 months. This represented savings to the state of over $60 million. This was not a controlled experiment so it is not clear how much of Massachusetts' success was due to other variables such as general economic recovery.

In California another approach, which has the overwhelming support of both conservatives and liberals, is being tried. This approach will make participation mandatory with "strict provisions for cutting off payments to those who do not participate, and a large-scale effort to make sure that those who do will get adequate training and job-placement services" (*Time*, October 7, 1985).

In conclusion, workfare is being tried in numerous settings and has wide emotional appeal because of its logical connection with such concerns as the federal deficit and the poverty cycle of AFDC families. However, a final accounting of workfare and related strategies will not be available for a number of years so it would seem prudent for policy makers to heed the advice of Manpower Demonstration Research Corporation (1986) when it says, no one model—including workfare—is at this point recommended for national replication.

REFERENCES

Gueron, J. (1986). *Work initiatives for welfare recipients: Lessons from a multi-state experiment.* New York: Manpower Demonstration Research.

States refocus welfare, with eye on "real" jobs. (1985, October 28). *U.S. News & World Report.*

Work for welfare. (1985, October 7). *Time.*

Work-not-welfare effort encounters the deficit. (1985, July 19). *Wall Street Journal.*

JOHN D. SEE
University of Wisconsin at Stout

**REHABILITATION
SOCIOECONOMIC STATUS**

WORLD FEDERATION OF THE DEAF (WFD)

The World Federation of the Deaf (WFD) was founded in 1951. It consists of 83 members representing the languages of English, French, and Italian. Its central office is in Rome, Italy. The WFD is a collection of associations of the deaf from various countries. These national or international organizations encompass societies and bodies acting for the deaf, health, social, and educational groups related to the aims of the federation, professionals involved with deafness or performing special assignments for the federation, and parents and friends of the deaf. Through social rehabilitation of deaf individuals, the WFD is a leader in the fight against deafness.

Among its services, the federation makes available social legislation concerning the deaf as well as statistical data. It also serves as consultant to the World Health Organization and UNESCO. The WFD sustains a library and bestows awards for merit and special achievement in education and social rehabilitation of the deaf. The federation holds commissions in the areas of communication, arts and culture, pedagogy, psychology, medicine, audiology, social and vocational rehabilitation, and spiritual care. The federation publishes a journal triannually entitled *Voices of Silence*, in addition to the *Proceedings of International Congresses and Meetings* and a dictionary.

MARY LEON PEERY
Texas A & M University

WORLD HEALTH ORGANIZATION

WORLD HEALTH ORGANIZATION (WHO)

The World Health Organization (WHO) is a specialized agency of the United Nations with primary responsibility for international health matters and public health. Created in 1948, it comprises of delegates representing member states and is attended by representatives of intergovernmental organizations and nongovernmental organizations in official relationships with WHO. Assemblies are held annually, usually in Geneva.

The official functions of WHO are varied; they include (1) directing and coordinating authority on international health work; (2) assisting governments in strengthening health services; (3) furnishing technical assistance and emergency aid; (4) stimulating and advancing work to eradicate or control epidemic, endemic, and other diseases; (5) promoting improved nutrition, housing, sanitation, recreation, economic and working conditions, and other aspects of environmental hygiene; (6) encouraging cooperation among scientific and professional groups that contribute to the advancement of health; (7) promoting material and child health and welfare, and fostering the ability to live harmoniously in a changing total environment; (8) fostering activities in the field of mental health; (9) working for improved standards of teaching and training in health, medical, and related professions; (10) studying and reporting on administrative and social techniques affecting public health and medical care from preventive and curative perspectives; and (11) assisting in developing informed public opinion on health matters.

Several WHO activities relate directly to diagnostic and classificatory issues in special education. First, WHO produces key writings concerning the use of health statistics and undertakes psychiatric epidemiology devoted to comparative research on mental disorders. Second, WHO compiles the International Classification of Diseases (ICD), a statistical classification of diseases; complications of pregnancy, childbirth, and the puerperium; congenital abnormalities; accidents, poisonings, and violence; and symptoms and ill-defined conditions. The ICD has been adapted for use as a nomenclature of diseases, with mental disorders constituting one major category. Subsumed in this category are classifications along with operational definitions of handicapping conditions.

Several other systems are tied to the ICD, including the *Diagnostic and Statistical Manual (DSM)* as well as the *Grossman Manuals on Terminology and Classification* of the American Association on Mental Deficiency. Third, the Mental Health Unit of WHO has implemented an intensive program to acquire systematic data on variables in diagnostic practice and use of diagnostic mental disorder terms. This has resulted in a multiaxial scheme for the classification of childhood mental disorders, with three main axes: clinical psychiatric syndromes, individual intellectual levels of functioning regardless of etiology, and associated physical, organic, and psychosocial factors in etiology.

DOUGLAS FUCHS
LYNN S. FUCHS
Vanderbilt University

WORLD FEDERATION OF THE DEAF

WORLD REHABILITATION FUND

The World Rehabilitation Fund, also known as the International Exchange of Experts and Information in Rehabilitation (IEEIR), seeks to identify, "import," disseminate, and promote the use of innovative rehabilitation and special education knowledge from other countries. Information about unique programs, practices, and research, as well as the policies of other nations, is sought for dissemination to professionals in the United States.

The IEEIR program is substantially supported by the Office of Special Education and Rehabilitation Services (OSERS) of the U.S. Department of Education. It is an outgrowth of the National Institute of Handicapped Research (NIHR, an OSERS division) mandate to facilitate the use of selected ideas and practices generated in other countries. Selection of knowledge or problem areas to guide the program staff are set jointly by OSERS, NIHR, and IEEIR staffs.

The IEEIR engages in the awarding of fellowships, the publication of monographs, and the dissemination of information. The fellowship program enables qualified U.S. experts to study and report on either special education or rehabilitation developments in other lands. This group includes rehabilitation and special education faculty, researchers, and administrators. Other specialists such as rehabilitation engineers, physicians, psychologists, independent living leaders, and consumer advocates also participate.

Overseas experts with substantial qualifications germane to the priorities set for the United States are identified and commissioned to prepare monographs for publication by the IEEIR program. Five monographs a year are commissioned.

To facilitate dissemination efforts, fellows commit themselves to reporting their observations and recommendations to their peers in relevant journals and at professional meetings. Since one of the criteria for selecting fellows is the degree to which they are centers of influence within their fields, IEEIR expects that they will influence not only students and researchers, but also practitioners and administrators. The communication skills and past record of a fellow are key considerations in awarding fellowships.

In addition to the reports they submit, fellows are expected to report their experiences and observations to professional meetings and other interested groups. Publication in professional journals is also encouraged. Both U.S. fellows and foreign monograph authors may be invited to present their findings at conferences designed for U.S. specialists to keep them abreast of innovations and new ideas.

The World Rehabilitation Fund headquarters is located at 400 East 34th Street, New York, NY 10016. Information on specific programs and monographs available may be requested from this office.

DIANE E. WOODS
World Rehabilitation Fund

WORLD HEALTH ORGANIZATON

WPPSI—REVISED

See WECHSLER PRESCHOOL AND PRIMARY SCALE OF INTELLI-GENCE—REVISED.

WRAT-III

See WIDE-RANGE ACHIEVEMENT TEST—THIRD EDITION.

WRITING AS EXPRESSIVE LANGUAGE

Since written expression is the most complex and the last form of language to be achieved, it can best be explained from a perspective that considers the influence of linguistic and cognitive abilities as well as the uniqueness of this expressive mode. The interrelatedness of language skills has been conceptualized by Myklebust (1965) in terms of a hierarchical construct that suggests that listening, speaking, reading, and writing develop in a progression that is ascendable and reciprocal. Implicit to this theory is the premise that competency at each rung of the language ladder is prerequisite to success at the next. Credibility for this paradigm has been provided by many researchers, including Loban (1976), who longitudinally followed a group of students from kindergarten through twelfth grade and found a positive relationship of achievement among the language arts. Children who were judged to be good listeners and speakers in kindergarten were the same students who later excelled in reading and writing, retaining their status as superior language users throughout their school careers. Conversely, children who did not begin their schooling with oral language competence continued to be evaluated as below average in all language skills.

The concept that achievement in written forms is influenced by development in preceding forms has been easier to verify than the nature of the reciprocity that occurs among the linguistic functions. Wolf and Dickinson (1985) described the development of oral and written language systems as being profoundly interactive in that growth in each mode results in cognitive processing changes that exert influence in a cyclical manner. For example, these researchers noted that early phonological and metalinguistic development in oral language affects the acquisition of reading skills; in turn, achievement in the reading form influences perspectives of listening, speaking, and writing. Wolf and Dickinson further explained that written expres-sion with its emphasis on refining alters one's cognitive orientation to speaking and reading. Thus it appears that written expression can be thought of as a shaper or enhancer of other linguistic forms.

Another complicating factor to understanding the relationship among language processes concerns the consideration that changes occur as development unfolds. Kroll (1981) has proposed a developmental model for examining the relationship between speaking and writing. This model describes four principal associations between these two expressive forms: the first phase is termed separate and involves the preparation for writing (the learning of technical skills required to produce the written symbols for speech); the second phrase involves consolidation of oral and written language (the understanding that writing is similar to talk written down); the third phase focuses on differentiation of oral and written language (awareness that talking is more casually conversational than the formality of writing); and the fourth stage addresses the systematic integration of speaking and writing (the knowledge that a wide range of different forms can be used in both speaking and writing depending on the context, audience, and purpose of the communication). Although Kroll admitted that this model presents an oversimplification of the interaction that occurs, it is nonetheless helpful for explaining broad outlines of development.

For the handicapped population, the acquisition of written expression is typically problematic. Difficulties that inhibit achievement in this skill can occur in each or all of the preceding forms; a child who has oral language deficits and/or reading problems will, in all likelihood, have deficiencies in written expression also. However, instruction in writing should not be postponed until competency in the other modes has been achieved. It is much more viable to simultaneously teach all language skills in a holistic manner that will encourage growth through reciprocity.

Phelps-Gunn and Phelps-Terasaki (1982) have described written expression from a multidimensional framework that considers the dynamics involved in effective writing. They have developed a Total Writing Process Model for identifying and remediating deficits. This model addresses problems with form, content, and structure; pragmatic abilities for audience and mode; and proofreading. This instructional plan appears to be extremely comprehensive and may prove to be an effective method for remediating writing deficits.

REFERENCES

Kroll, B. M. (1981). Developmental relationships between speaking and writing. In B. M. Kroll & R. J. Vann (Eds.), *Exploring speaking-writing relationships: Connections and contrasts* (pp. 32–54). Urbana, IL: National Counsel of Teachers of English.

Loban, W. (1976). *Language development: Kindergarten through grade twelve*. Urbana, IL: National Counsel of Teachers of English.

Myklebust, H. R. (1965). *Development and disorders of written language* (Vol. 1). New York: Grune & Stratton.

Phelps-Gunn, T., & Phelps-Terasaki, D. (1982). *Written language instruction*. Rockville, MD: Aspen.

Wolf, M., & Dickinson, D. (1985). From oral to written language: Transition in school years. In J. B. Gleason (Ed.), *The development of language* (pp. 227–276). Columbus, OH: Merrill.

PEGGY L. ANDERSON
University of New Orleans

WRITING ASSESSMENT
WRITTEN LANGUAGE OF THE HANDICAPPED
WRITING REMEDIATION

WRITING ASSESSMENT

Competence in writing requires the mastery and automation of a vast array of skills. To ensure that these skills develop in an efficient and efficacious manner, it is generally believed that assessment should be included as an integral part of handicapped students' writing programs. This belief is primarily based on the assumption that information from the assessment process should make it possible for teachers to more readily determine a student's writing strengths and weaknesses, individualize instruction, monitor writing performance, and evaluate the effectiveness of the composition program.

The assessment of handicapped students' writing should focus on both the written product and the process of writing (Graham, 1982). There are a host of procedures for evaluating the various attributes embodied in the written product; the most popular of these will be reviewed at length. Relatively few techniques, however, are available for examining the process by which students compose. The most common procedures include: (1) observing and, in some instances, timing the various activities and behaviors that the student engages in during the act of writing; (2) interviewing students about their approach to writing and questioning them about their reasons for particular composing behaviors; and (3) asking students to verbally report what they are thinking while they write. Regrettably, the reliability and validity of these procedures have not been adequately established and the results from such assessments may, as many critics have suggested, yield a distorted picture of the writing process (Humes, 1983).

Both formal and informal assessment procedures have been used to examine the relative merits and/or shortcomings of handicapped students' writing. The most frequently used standardized test is the Test of Written Language (TOWL). According to the authors (Hammill & Larsen, 1983), this instrument "can be used to ascertain the general adequacy of a product written by a student and to determine specific proficiency in word usage, punctuation and capitalization (style), spelling, handwriting, vocabulary, and sentence production" (p. 5). The TOWL consists of six subtests. Scores for three of these subtests (vocabulary, thematic maturity, and handwriting) are derived from a spontaneous sample of writing. The remaining word usage, spelling, and style subtests employ a contrived format; e.g., a student's proficiency in word usage is determined by a sentence completion activity. Although the TOWL appears to have a sound theoretical basis and to be reasonably valid and reliable, there is some question as to the value of the vocabulary and thematic maturity scores (Williams, 1985).

A second standardized test that has been used with handicapped students is the Picture Story Language Test (PSLT) (Myklebust, 1965). The PSLT has been used as a writing achievement test, a diagnostic instrument, and a research tool for studying the development and disorders of written language. In using this test, a student writes a story in response to a picture and the resulting composition is scored in terms of productivity (number of words, sentences, and words per sentence), correctness (word usage, word endings, and punctuation), and meaning (actual content conveyed). Although the PSLT has been widely used with handicapped students, serious questions regarding the validity and reliability of the instrument have been raised (Anastasiow, 1972).

Informal assessment procedures have been used to assess a variety of factors ranging from story quality to writing mechanics. Not surprisingly, the quality of students' writing has proven to be the most difficult factor to define and measure. Probably the oldest measure of writing quality is the holistic method. With this method, an examiner makes a single overall judgment on the quality of a student's writing (Mishler & Hogan, 1982). Each paper is read at a fairly rapid pace and the examiner attempts to weigh the various factors (e.g., content, organization, grammar, etc.) in roughly equal proportions. The examiner's overall impression is quantified on a Likert-type scale, ranging from poor to high quality. To increase accuracy and reliability, most holistic scoring systems include representative examples of specific scores.

A more complex procedure for determining the quality of a student's writing is the analytic method. With this method, the student's paper is analyzed and scored on the basis of several different factors such as ideation, grammar, and spelling (Moran, 1982). The scores for each of these factors are then averaged to produce a single grand score. Although the analytic method may provide more useful information for instructional purposes, it is much more time-consuming than the holistic method.

A relatively recent development in the measurement of writing quality is the primary trait scoring method. With this procedure, different scoring systems are developed for different writing tasks. For a task such as writing a short story, the examiner would decide ahead of time what traits should be evaluated and what type of responses will be considered appropriate and inappropriate for each trait. For example, for a short story one of the primary traits might be the introduction and development of the protagonist (Graham & Harris, 1986). Consequently, stories that adequately present and develop the leading character would receive credit for this trait.

It must be pointed out that measures of writing quality can be influenced by a variety of factors (Graham, 1982). One prominent source of variability involves the writer. Students often evidence considerable variation in their writing quality from one assignment to the next. Writing performance also can be influenced by the popularity of the proctor, the intended audience, teacher directions, and so on. An additional source of variability resides in the examiner. There is considerable evidence that grades assigned to student's papers tend to be unreliable. Fortunately, the consistency with which examiners score writing quality can be improved if the following guidelines and recommendations are followed: (1) examiners should receive considerable practice and training in using the intended scoring procedure; (2) the writing task should be highly structured and the assigned topic should be interesting; (3) identifying factors such as name, grade, and date should be removed from each paper; and (4) papers should not be graded for lengthy periods of time or in noisy or distracting environments.

A number of procedures have been used to evaluate the various elements embodied in the written products. Writing fluency has typically been assessed by examining total number of words written, average sentence length, and number of words written per minute. Vocabulary diversity has been measured by counting the occurrence of particular vocabulary items such as adjectives or adverbs and by computing the corrected type/token ratio (number of different words divided by the square root of twice the number of words in the sample) or the index of diversification (average number of words that appear between each occurrence of the most frequently used word in a composition). Proficiency with the mechanics of writing is generally determined by tabulating the occurrence of a particular behavior (e.g., spelling errors), while syntactic maturity is often defined in terms of the average length of T-units (main clause plus any attached or embedded subordinate clauses).

It is important to note that students' knowledge of their writing performance can be a powerful motivator and have a potent effect on learning. Nevertheless, the value of circling every misspelled word, writing "AWK" above every clumsy wording, or red-marking each deviation from standard English is questionable. Intensive evaluation may have little or no effect on writing improvement and may, in fact, make students more aware of their limitations and less willing to write (Burton & Arnold, 1963). Feedback on

the positive aspects of a student's composition, in contrast, can have a facilitative effect on writing performance (Beaven, 1977). It also is desirable to dramatize a student's success through the use of charts, graphs, verbal praise, and so on.

REFERENCES

Anastasiow, N. (1972). Review of the Picture Story Language Test. In O. K. Buros (Ed.), *Seventh mental measurement yearbook*. Highland Park, NJ: Gryphon.

Beaven, M. (1977). Individualized goal setting, self-evaluation, and peer evaluation. In C. Cooper & L. Odell (Eds.), *Evaluating writing: Describing, measuring, judging*. Urbana, IL: National Council of Teachers of English.

Burton, D., & Arnold, L. (1963). *The effects of frequency of writing and intensity of teacher evaluation upon high school students' performance in written composition*. (Research Report No. 1523). Tallahassee, FL: USOE Cooperative.

Graham, S. (1982). Composition research and practice: A unified approach. *Focus on Exceptional Children, 14,* 1–16.

Graham, S., & Harris, K. (1986). *Improving learning disabled students' compositions via story grammars: A component analysis of self-control strategy training*. Paper presented at the American Educational Research Association, San Francisco.

Hammill, D., & Larsen, S. (1983). *Test of written language*. Austin, TX: Pro-Ed.

Humes, A. (1983). Research on the composing process. *Review of Educational Research, 53,* 201–216.

Mishler, C., & Hogan, T. (1982). Holistic scoring of essays: Remedy for evaluating the third R. *Diagnostique, 8,* 4–16.

Moran, M. (1982). Analytic evaluation of formal written language skills as a diagnostic procedure. *Diagnostique, 8,* 17–31.

Myklebust, H. (1965). *Development and disorders of written language*. New York: Grune & Stratton.

Williams, R. (1985). Review of test of written language. In J. V. Mitchell (Ed.), *Ninth mental measurement yearbook*. Lincoln: University of Nebraska Press.

STEVE GRAHAM
University of Maryland

WRITTEN LANGUAGE OF THE HANDICAPPED
WRITING REMEDIATION

WRITING DISORDERS

While research on writing disorders in context is limited, the sources of difficulty emerge when they are considered within a framework or model of writing. Writing is a complex cognitive activity (Hayes & Flower, 1980) that requires writers to coordinate and regulate the use of task-specific strategies during three overlapping and recursive writing stages (i.e., prewriting, drafting, and revising).

During prewriting, task-specific strategies focus on planning and organizing. Writers generate and select writing topics, decide on a purpose for writing, identify the audience, generate and gather ideas about the topic, and organize the ideas into a network or structural plan (e.g., text structure such as story narrative, compare/contrast, sequence). During drafting, task-specific strategies involve the activation of the structural plan, translation of ideas into printed sentences, fleshing out of placeholders in the plan with details, and signaling of relationships among the elements of the plan. During monitoring and revising, task-specific strategies pertain to evaluation and analysis. The writer reads the draft to see whether the objectives concerning audience, topic, purpose, and structure have been achieved, and applies correction strategies to portions of the text that fail to meet expectations.

Though these task-specific strategies are necessary, they are not sufficient for skilled writing. A second domain involves the execution of these strategies. Metacognitive knowledge is the executive or self-control mechanism that helps writers activate and orchestrate activities in each of the writing stages. Metacognitive knowledge includes the ability to self-instruct or direct oneself in the writing stages, to monitor strategy use, and to modify or correct strategy use on the basis of outcomes. Without metacognitive knowledge, writers fail to access writing strategies and monitor their use even when the strategies are in their behavioral repertoire.

A third domain includes the mechanical skills that make writing a fluent process. This domain involves writers' knowledge of rules related to spelling (orthographic knowledge), writing conventions (punctuation, capitalization), and language (syntactic knowledge). These skills are of primary importance to writers in the stage of final revision in light of the importance of legibility to the audience. In addition, for the successful strategic employment of these skills, writers must not only acquire mechanical skills, they must acquire the task-specific strategies and metacognitive knowledge governing their use. For example, writers who lack task-specific strategies may not know how to rehearse or study spelling words to improve recall, whereas writers who lack metacognitive knowledge may learn to accurately spell words for the weekly spelling test, but fail to accurately spell or monitor their spelling of the same words in written compositions. Skillful writers not only acquire the mechanical means to produce text, they acquire the cognitive tools that help them know when and how to use those means, how to monitor their use, and how to correct errors when they occur.

According to this model of writing, writing disorders may result from one of several causes (Walmsley, 1983). First, writing disorders may emanate from a lack of understanding of task-specific strategies. For example, disabled writers with task-specific strategy deficits in the use of specific organizational structures may have trouble em-

ploying a relevant text structure that can guide them in planning, organizing, drafting, and monitoring their ideas. Second, writing disabilities may result from deficiencies in metacognitive knowledge. Such writers may have learned strategies but fail to activate them in the appropriate situations. Third, impairments in related cognitive processes may affect writing performance. Specifically, inadequate or delayed development in listening, speaking, or reading may affect writing performance since these processes share a common language base and rely on similar strategic processes involving the communication and comprehension of ideas. Finally, the failure to acquire specific rule-governed principles in spelling, grammar, and writing conventions can detrimentally affect the mechanics of writing, writing fluency, and overall comprehensibility.

More is known about the specific disabilities of students in the domain of writing mechanics than is known about disabilities in the use of task-specific strategies or metacognitive knowledge. Several studies confirm that disabled learners commit more punctuation and capitalization errors than nondisabled learners (Myklebust, 1973; Poplin et al., 1980; Poteet, 1978). These deficiencies have been observed in terms of students' ability to rewrite sentences containing punctuation and capitalization errors and to generate error-free compositions. Even greater performance differences between disabled and nondisabled students have been found on measures of spelling accuracy (Myklebust, 1973; Poplin et al., 1980; Poteet, 1978). Furthermore, disabled learners have deficiencies in their ability to apply task-specific strategies involving the study of spelling words (Foster & Torgesen, 1983) and in their application of metacognitive knowledge to detect and correct spelling errors (Deshler, 1978). However, several studies suggest that strategy and metacognitive deficits may be ameliorated with training. For example, research suggests that spelling deficits can be partly overcome by the teaching of task-specific strategies involving procedures for studying spelling words (Graham & Freeman, 1985; Nulman & Gerber, 1984), and for spelling novel words by analogy to known words (Englert, Hiebert, & Stewart, 1985). Likewise, metacognitive deficiencies involving the monitoring, detection, and correction of spelling errors or mechanical errors may be remediated with self-instructional training that directs students to re-read and correct errors (Schumaker et al., 1982).

Mechanical aspects involving syntactic skills also have been studied, but the results are more equivocal. On tasks that require students to produce the correct syntactic form (e.g., subject-verb agreement, plurals) in incomplete sentences, disabled writers perform significantly lower than nondisabled writers (Poplin et al., 1980). On the other hand, on measures of syntactic complexity based on the average length of sentences and clauses produced by students, several studies have reported no qualitative differences in the presence of certain syntactic structures or the complexity of sentences (Moran, 1981; Nodine, Barenbaum, & Newcomer, 1985; Poteet, 1978). At the same time, several studies have found quantitative differences in students' written productions: disabled writers produced significantly fewer sentences and fewer total words (Myklebust, 1973; Nodine et al., 1985; Poteet, 1978). Thus performance seems to be delimited less by students' syntactic inadequacies than by difficulties in knowing how to generate ideas and how to sustain thoughts about a topic.

Though mechanical skills are important, they are not the barrier to proficient writing once thought (Walmsley, 1983). The teaching of mechanical skills does not necessarily improve the quality of compositions, and young writers do not need to master the mechanics of writing before being introduced to writing. Instead, writers' knowledge of task-specific strategies in the actual composing process may be a more critical determinant of writing success. Of particular importance in the domain of composing strategies is students' awareness of text structures. Text structures are specific organizational schemes internalized by writers that describe the elements that should be included and how they should be ordered. There are different text structures for different writing purposes. For example, stories usually consist of five major elements: a setting (i.e., main character, time, place), a problem confronting the main character, the main character's response to the problem, the outcome of the response, and the story's conclusion. Similarly, expository materials contain structures such as compare/contrast, problem/solution, and chronological sequence. Knowledge of these structures influences the ability of writers to successfully plan, generate, organize, compose, and monitor their ideas.

Nodine et al. (1985) conducted one of the few studies examining children's use of a story structure in written compositions. A group of learning-disabled, reading-disabled, and normally achieving students were asked to write a story about three related pictures. The results suggested that learning-disabled (LD) students differed from both reading-disabled and normally achieving students in their ability to produce a tale that was storylike. Almost half of the LD students failed to generate a story that met story structure expectations. Furthermore, LD students were less aware of potential confusions caused by unrelated or inexplicable events in their compositions. Similar deficits in structural awareness have been reported in studies examining students' knowledge of expository text structures (Wong & Wilson, 1984).

The domain important to both the successful use of task-specific strategies and mechanical skills in composing is metacognitive knowledge. Metacognitive knowledge includes the abilities to self-instruct, self-monitor, self-correct, and self-regulate the writing process. Several studies suggest that disabled learners have serious deficiencies in their ability to activate previously learned strategies and to self-instruct or self-monitor during text production and comprehension (Bos & Filip, 1984; Wong, 1985). That these problems are attributable to metacognitive knowledge is suggested by two studies that indicate that the training of self-control processes improves composing and organizational abilities. Wong and Sawatsky (1984), for example, taught learning-disabled students to elaborate on or finish an initial sentence stem (e.g., The tall man helped the woman) by employing a five-step self-control procedure that helped students determine the writing purpose, draft a response, and monitor their writing. Following training, the sentence elaborations of students significantly improved. Similarly, Wong and Wilson (1984) trained learning-disabled students to organize scrambled passages by applying a five-step self-instructional procedure. The ease with which students were trained suggested that the learning-disabled children may have had some rudimentary idea about passage organization, but it was either incompletely developed or not spontaneously activated by the students. Since students readily benefited from self-control training, the results suggested that metacognitive strategies were similarly inactive or incomplete.

In summary, the literature suggests that several deficiencies may impede students' writing performance. Deficiencies in spelling, grammar, and writing conventions have been reported—though these may not be the barriers to writing success as much as students' lack of task-specific strategies and metacognitive knowledge. Research is still needed to determine the impact of other elements of the writing process (e.g., audience, prior knowledge) on performance in each of the writing stages. However, it is certain that writing competence will be associated not only with the acquisition of efficient strategies pertaining to the use of each element, but with the metacognitive knowledge that helps the writer know when and how to use the element in planning, drafting, monitoring, and revising compositions.

REFERENCES

Bos, C. S., & Filip, D. (1984). Comprehension monitoring in learning disabled and average students. *Journal of Learning Disabilities, 17,* 229–233.

Deshler, D. D. (1978). *Psychoeducational aspects of learning-disabled adolescents.* In L. M. Mann, L. Goodman, & T. L. Wiederholt (Eds.), *Teaching the learning-disabled adolescent.* Boston: Houghton Mifflin.

Englert, C. S., Hiebert, E. H., & Stewart, S. R. (1985). Spelling unfamiliar words by an analogy strategy. *Journal of Special Education, 19,* 291–306.

Englert, C. S., & Thomas, C. C. (in press). Sensitivity to text structure in reading and writing: A comparison of learning disabled and nonhandicapped students. *Learning Disability Quarterly.*

Hayes, J. R., & Flower, L. S. (1980). Writing as problem solving. *Visible Language, 14,* 388–399.

Foster, K., & Torgesen, J. K. (1983). The effects of directed study on the spelling performance of two subgroups of learning disabled students. *Learning Disability Quarterly, 6,* 252–257.

Graham, S., & Freeman, S. (1985). Strategy training and teacher- vs. student-controlled study conditions: Effects on LD students' spelling performance. *Learning Disability Quarterly, 8,* 267–274.

Moran, M. R. (1981). Performance of learning disabled and low achieving secondary students on formal features of a paragraph-writing task. *Learning Disability Quarterly, 4,* 271–280.

Myklebust, H. R. (1973). *Development and disorders of written language. Vol. 2. Studies of normal and exceptional children.* NY: Grune & Stratton.

Nodine, B. F., Barenbaum, E., & Newcomer, P. (1985). Story composition by learning disabled, reading disabled, and normal children. *Learning Disability Quarterly, 8,* 167–179.

Nulman, J. A. H., & Gerber, M. M. (1984). Improving spelling performance by imitating a child's errors. *Journal of Learning Disabilities, 17,* 328–333.

Poplin, M. S., Gray, R., Larsen, S., Banikoski, A., & Mehring, T. (1980). A comparison of components of written expression abilities in learning disabled and non-learning disabled students at three grade levels. *Learning Disability Quarterly, 3,* 46–53.

Poteet, J. A. (1978). *Characteristics of written expression of learning disabled and non-learning disabled elementary school students.* Muncie, IN: Ball State University. (ERIC Document Reproduction Service No. ED 1590830)

Schumaker, J. B., Deshler, D. D., Alley, G. R., Warner, M. M., Clark, F. L., & Nolan, S. (1982). Error monitoring: A learning strategy for improving adolescent academic performance. In M. W. Cruickshank & J. W. Lerner (Eds.), *Coming of age: Vol. 3. The best of ACLD.* Syracuse, NY: Syracuse University Press.

Walmsley, S. A. (1983). Writing disability. In P. Mosenthal, L. Tamor, & S. A. Walmsley (Eds.), *Research on writing: Principles and methods.* New York: Longman.

Wong, B. Y. L. (1985). Metacognition and learning disabilities. In D. L. Forrest-Pressley, G. E. MacKinnon, & T. G. Waller (Eds.), *Metacognition, cognition and human performance: Vol. 2. Instructional Practices* (pp. 137–180). New York: Academic.

Wong, B. Y. L., & Sawatsky, D. (1984). Sentence elaboration and retention of good, average and poor readers. *Learning Disability Quarterly, 7,* 229–236.

Wong, B. Y. L., & Wilson, (1984). Investigating awareness of and teaching passage organization in learning disabled children. *Journal of Learning Disabilities, 17,* 477–482.

CAROL SUE ENGLERT
Michigan State University

WRITING ASSESSMENT
WRITING REMEDIATION
WRITTEN LANGUAGE OF THE HANDICAPPED

WRITING REMEDIATION

The writing difficulties exhibited by many handicapped students necessitate the development and use of instructional procedures aimed at improving writing competence, particularly in terms of handicapped students' functional writing skills. The remediation of handicapped students' writing difficulties, however, has not received much attention in either the research literature or in school settings. Leinhardt, Zigmond, and Cooley (1980) found, for example, that handicapped students may spend less than 10 minutes a day generating written language. Although there are many possible reasons why writing remediation appears to receive a limited amount of time and emphasis in handicapped students' instructional programs, teacher attitudes and backgrounds may be the key factors in determining the quantity and quality of writing instruction for these students. According to Graham (1982), many teachers do not enjoy writing and are not prepared to teach composition. Furthermore, many special education teachers may feel that writing is not a critical skill for their students and may choose to spend their instructional time teaching what they consider to be more important skills (e.g., reading and arithmetic).

For the most part, writing instruction for handicapped students has drawn heavily on techniques used with normally achieving youngsters. One commonly recommended instructional procedure has been to use a phase approach. This approach emphasizes the various stages of the composition process (prewriting, writing, and revising) and is designed to develop security in the use of these stages. In a phase approach described by Silverman et al. (1981), the teacher first structures the writing process with prewriting activities that involve thinking, experiencing, discussing, and interacting. The student and the teacher then develop a series of questions that are used to guide the writing process. During the revising stage, the teacher critiques the student's writing and they jointly revise the student's paper. Although empirical support for this particular model or other phase approaches is limited, this writing procedure does stress the development of two important skills: thinking as a preliminary facet of composing and revision of the initial draft of the written product. In addition, a phase approach to writing may be especially suitable for handicapped students since it helps reduce cognitive strain by taking a large complex problem such as writing and breaking it down into smaller sub-problems.

Another traditional approach that has been used to teach specific writing skills to handicapped students is modeling. With this approach, students may be asked to imitate a specific type of sentence pattern, a well-known style of writing, a certain type of paragraph, and so on. There are two basic approaches to modeling. One approach stresses strategy explanation and model illustration; the other emphasizes problem solving. With the former, a student may be asked to mimic a specific type of paragraph (e.g., topic sentence located at the start of the paragraph) following an examination and analysis of several examples that are representative of the style to be emulated. The latter can be illustrated by examining a procedure developed by Schiff (1978). With this procedure, examples of a particular type of paragraph are selected. Sentences for each paragraph are then written on a separate strip of paper and their order randomized. Students rearrange the sentences in each paragraph and compare their arrangements with the original model. At present, it is impossible to draw any definitive conclusions on the relative effectiveness of these procedures, as there is virtually no research that examines them.

A great deal of attention has been directed at teaching handicapped students information about language and writing with the aim of promoting the correct use of structure, form, and language. One of the most consistently held beliefs in the history of writing instruction is that the teaching of grammar and usage is critical to the development of writing competence. Formal grammar, however, is difficult to master and knowledge of grammatical concepts does not appear to be necessary for the skillful use of written language (Blount, 1973). This is not meant to imply that teachers should not attend to handicapped students' use of structure or form in their writing or that these skills cannot be improved. Rather, improvement of usage and form "may be more effectively achieved through direct practice of desirable forms when the need arises" (Graham, 1982, p. 6).

An interesting alternative to traditional writing approaches is the use of procedures that seek to minimize or circumvent handicapped students' poor writing skills. The most commonly used alternative is dictation. Traditionally, dictation has involved having a student furnish the content or ideas orally while the teacher or a peer structures the form the material takes on paper. The conventional dictation process can be adapted by using a tape recorder as an aid to organizing content; i.e., ideas are taped and later written and edited by the student. In some instances, dictation is employed as a temporary aid and its use diminishes as the student becomes more adept at the mechanics of writing. Dictation may represent a viable alternative for students with adequate oral language skills who have been unable, after years of intensive instruction, to automate and integrate basic writing skills.

A recent alternative to traditional writing instruction approaches is the cognitive-behavior modification (CBM) procedure. Typically CBM training involves teaching students to regulate task-specific and metacognitive strategies through processes such as self-instruction, self-assessment, and self-reinforcement (Harris, 1982). For example, Harris and Graham (1985) reported a CBM composition training procedure that significantly increased learning-disabled students' use of verbs, adverbs, and adjectives and resulted in higher story quality ratings. Further, generalization and maintenance probes taken up to 14 weeks after training yielded positive results. The CBM training regimen in this study included skills training (instruction on specific task-appropriate strategies), meta-

cognitive training (instruction in the self-regulation of those strategies), and instruction concerning the significance of such activities. In a second study, Graham and Harris (1986) found that CBM procedures also could be used to improve the overall structure of learning-disabled students' compositions through the use of a story grammar strategy. Training procedures were similar to those in the first study; however, strategy training consisted of instruction in story grammar elements: setting, goal(s), action(s), emotional responses, and ending.

Educators also have attempted to improve handicapped students' writing skills by further refining or developing their reading, oral language, and thinking skills. Since reading, writing, thinking, and language skills are interrelated, it is assumed that intensive and generalized instruction in an area such as oral language, for example, will have an indirect and positive effect on a student's writing ability (Groff, 1978). Although these skills may be interrelated, they do not necessarily function in an interactive and supportive way. Generalized instruction in an area such as reading or oral language appears to be of limited value in the immediate improvement of a student's writing (Graham, 1982).

A recent development in the teaching of writing to the handicapped has been the advent of the computer, particularly the word processor. The word processor, with its various capabilities for storing and editing texts, has the potential to both strengthen and significantly change the nature of writing instruction. The word processor and other technological advances should not, however, be viewed as a cure-all for handicapped students' writing problems. MacArthur and Graham (1986), for instance, found no major differences between handwritten stories and those composed on a word processor, even though the learning-disabled students in their study had considerable experience using the computer.

Additional instructional recommendations for teaching writing to the handicapped have been summarized by Graham (1982). These include (1) providing students with plenty of opportunities to write and exposing them to a variety of practical and imaginative assignments; (2) having writing assignments, whenever possible, serve a real purpose and be directed at an authentic audience; (3) having a pleasant and encouraging composition program; and (4) de-emphasizing writing errors.

REFERENCES

Blount, N. (1973). Research on teaching literature, language, and composition. In R. Travers (Ed.), *Second handbook of research on teaching*. Chicago; Rand McNally.

Graham, S. (1982). Composition research and practice: A unified approach. *Focus on Exceptional Children, 14*, 1–16.

Graham, S., & Harris, K. (1986). *Improving learning disabled students' compositions via story grammars: A component analysis* of self-control strategy training. Paper presented at the American Educational Research Association, San Francisco.

Groff, P. (1978). Children's oral language and their written composition. Elementary School Journal, 78, 181–191.

Harris, K. (1982). Cognitive behavior modification: Application with exceptional students. Focus on Exceptional Children, 15, 1–16.

Harris, K., & Graham, S. (1985). Improving learning disabled students' composition skills: Self-control strategy training. Learning Disability Quarterly, 8, 27–36.

Leinhardt, G., Zigmond, N., & Cooley, W. (1980). Reading instruction and its effects. Paper presented at the American Educational Research Association, Boston.

MacArthur, C., & Graham, S. (1986). LD students' writing under three conditions: Word processing, dictation, and handwriting. Paper presented at the American Educational Research Association, San Francisco.

Schiff, P. (1978). Problem solving and the composition model: Reorganization, manipulation, analysis. Research in the Teaching of English, 12, 203–210.

Silverman, R., Zigmond, N., Zimmerman, J., & Vallecorsa, A. (1981). Improving written expression in learning disabled students. Topics in Language Disorders, 1, 91–99.

STEVE GRAHAM
KAREN R. HARRIS
University of Maryland

WRITING ASSESSMENT
WRITING DISORDERS
WRITTEN LANGUAGE OF THE HANDICAPPED

WRITTEN LANGUAGE OF HANDICAPPED

In addition to other academic problems, it is generally agreed that handicapped students have difficulty using the medium of written language to express their ideas and thoughts (Graham, 1982). It would be difficult at present, however, to substantiate this belief since the written language problems of the handicapped have received little attention from either researchers or the educational community in general. While there are many possible reasons why there has been a notable lack of interest in this important language skill, two factors merit special attention. First, it is likely that handicapped students' writing problems have not received much emphasis because most special educators lack specific training in this particular area and feel that writing is not a critical skill for their students. Second, the difficulties inherent in measuring written language have proven to be formidable obstacles to researchers interested in describing the writing characteristics of the handicapped. Adequate procedures for measuring a complex phenomena such as composition quality, for instance, do not exist.

The information that is available on the written language of the handicapped has primarily centered on two disabilities: learning disabilities and hearing impairments. Even though some students with visual impairments and/or physical disabilities may require special writing programs and technological adaptations (Napier, 1973), no information is available on the writing characteristics of these students. Furthermore, the definitive source on the writing problems of students with emotional/behavioral difficulties, mental retardation, and speech and language disorders is a single large-scale study conducted by Myklebust (1973).

Even in areas where a more solid research base exists, knowledge of students' writing characteristics is extremely limited. For example, considerable information has been gathered on the length, syntactic complexity, vocabulary diversity, etc., of learning-disabled students' compositions. Most of our knowledge concerning these factors, however, is restricted to elementary-age students and a fairly narrow range of writing tasks (primarily creative writing assignments). Our understanding of how handicapped students' writing skills develop is, at best, spotty. Virtually no attention has been directed at determining how they plan and revise their compositions, and the effects of different audiences on their writing performance is unknown.

Although it is generally agreed that written language development may be influenced by a variety of factors (Bereiter, 1980), surprisingly little research has been conducted with handicapped students to determine the relationship between their writing performance and various genetic and environmental variables. If research conducted with normal students can be used as a benchmark, then handicapped students' writing performance may be related to and, in some instances, influenced by the following: general language development, intelligence, maturity, reading achievement, sex, socioeconomic status, personality characteristics, school locale, and specific cognitive abilities such as short- and long-term memory (Graham, 1982).

It is also important to point out that although some similarities may exist, students with different disabilities often have different writing characteristics and ultimately different instructional needs. As a result, the remainder of this article will provide a brief survey of the writing characteristics of each disability area in which empirical evidence is available.

An examination of the available literature reveals that students who are labeled mentally retarded have severe writing difficulties that tend to persist over time. From elementary to high school, they score significantly lower than normal students on a variety of written language tasks. Retarded students make consistently more grammatical and spelling errors and their written compositions evidence less vocabulary diversity (Sedlack & Cartwright, 1972). If a study by Myklebust (1973) is representative, it also appears that creative stories composed by mentally retarded students are written on a more concrete level than those written by their normal counterparts. The severity of retarded students' writing difficulties is further reflected in the finding that these students have more problems with writing than they do with speaking, listening, or reading (Durrell & Sullivan, 1958). Unfortunately, most retarded students evidence only modest growth in writing skills, which may reach its peak at the time of adolescence (Myklebust, 1973).

It is difficult to draw any definitive conclusions on the writing characteristics of students with emotional/behavioral problems because only one study was located that examined this question. Myklebust (1973) investigated the story writing characteristics of school-identified emotionally disturbed children and youths. In comparison with normal peers, these students scored lower on written measures of fluency, correctness, and meaning. Their greatest proficiency was in the area of syntax. It is interesting to note that they made impressive gains in several skill areas over time. Not surprisingly, the writing of the emotionally disturbed was superior to that of the mentally retarded, but inferior to the writing of students with reading disabilities.

Myklebust (1973) also examined the writing performance of students with articulation disorders. These students wrote extremely short stories comprised of only two to six sentences. While their stories tended to be less abstract than those written by normal students, the written syntax of the older students with articulation disorders was within the normal range. In comparison with other handicapped students, their writing performance was superior to that of students classified as emotionally disturbed and mentally retarded.

Studies examining the writing performance of students with hearing impairments have primarily been restricted to examining sentence structure, vocabulary diversity, spelling and grammatical errors, and productivity. In comparison with normal students, sentences composed by the hearing impaired tend to be less complex, with more errors and less diversity in vocabulary usage (Powers & Wilgus, 1983; Yoshinaga-Itano & Snyder, 1985). Wilbur and Nolen (in press) have indicated that stories written by the deaf often lack creativity, cohesiveness, and complexity in terms of temporal sequence. They further point out that the material written by these students is generally stilted and vocabulary choice is restricted to a small number of words. Although hearing-impaired students' poor performance on measures of written language is, in part, due to their hearing loss and resulting language deficits, instructional variables also appear to be a contributing factor.

Learning-disabled students typically have a great deal of difficulty expressing themselves in writing. In terms of overall quality and content, their writing has consistently been found to be inferior to that of average students.

Graham and Harris (1986), for example, compared the stories of sixth-grade learning-disabled and average students using holistic ratings of quality. With the holistic method, raters make a single overall judgment about the quality of the writing sample based on a variety of factors, including content, imagination, structure, word choice, and writing conventions. Mean scores for the learning-disabled and average groups, on a scale ranging from 1 to 8, were 2.2 and 4.5, respectively.

In addition, Poplin et al. (1980) compared learning-disabled and normal students in grades three through eight on the thematic maturity subtest of the Test of Written Language. This subtest reportedly measures whether the student's story has been written in a logical manner that efficiently conveys meaning. The differences between the learning-disabled and normal students on the thematic maturity subtest increased with age. There were no significant differences between third to fourth graders, but at fifth through eighth grades, average students outperformed the learning disabled.

Other investigators have studied the structure and completeness of stories written by the learning disabled. MacArthur and Graham (1986) used an analytical scale based on the common elements contained in most short stories. Most of the stories written by learning-disabled students included main and supporting characters, action, and an ending, but few included explicit goals, starter events, or emotional reactions. Nodine, Barenbaum, and Newcomer (1985), on the other hand, had 11-year-old learning-disabled, reading-disabled, and normal students write narratives in response to a sequence of pictures. The students' compositions were classified as stories, storylike, descriptive, or expressive. To be judged as a story, a composition had to include a setting, conflict, and resolution. Complete stories were written by 71% of the normal students, 47% of the reading disabled, and only 30% of the learning disabled. Nearly half of the learning-disabled students (48%) wrote compositions with no story line.

Research has also shown that learning-disabled students write stories and essays that are shorter than those of their normally achieving peers. For instance, Nodine et al. (1985) reported that learning-disabled students' stories were on the average 54 words in length, while normal children wrote stories with approximately 104 words. Limited fluency may be related to lower overall quality and content. MacArthur and Graham (1986) found significant correlations between length and story structure and a measure of overall quality.

An additional difficulty exhibited by most learning-disabled students involves the mechanics of writing. On both standardized tests and informal measures of contextual writing, these students demonstrate considerable difficulty in spelling words correctly or using proper punctuation and capitalization (Moran, 1981). Spelling problems appear to be particularly pronounced among learning-disabled students.

Although it is generally assumed that learning-disabled students have difficulty with written grammar and vocabulary, research has yielded conflicting results concerning this issue. Morris and Crump (1982), for example, reported that learning-disabled students' written vocabulary is less varied than that of normal students. In contrast, Deno, Marston, & Mirkin (1982) found no differences between normal students and the learning disabled on several vocabulary measures. In terms of grammatical or syntactical difficulties, several studies have found no differences in the syntactical maturity of learning-disabled and normal students' compositions (Nodine et al., 1985). Learning-disabled students, however, tend to make more grammatical errors than their normal peers (Moran, 1981).

Finally, only one study was located that examined both the product and process of writing. MacArthur and Graham (1986) videotaped learning-disabled students as they composed stories using three different methods: handwriting, dictation, and word processing. Results from the study revealed that dictated stories were over three times as long as stories produced under the other conditions and that they were rated significantly higher on overall quality. Regardless of the mode of writing, students engaged in almost no planning prior to writing their stories. Furthermore, students made a few revisions (on average, about 24 per 100 words), but most revisions (57%) involved surface changes such as changing the spelling of a word. Only 10% of all revisions affected the meaning of what the student wrote. Further research on the writing process of learning-disabled and other handicapped students is needed to understand how these students write so that teachers can help them learn to write more effectively.

REFERENCES

Bereiter, C. (1980). Development in writing. In L. Gregg & E. Steinberg (Eds.), *Cognitive processes in writing*. Hillsdale, NJ: Erlbaum.

Deno, S., Marston, D., & Mirkin, P. (1982). Valid measurement procedures for continuous evaluation of written expression. *Exceptional Children, 48,* 368–371.

Durrell, D., & Sullivan, H. (1958). *Language achievement of mentally retarded children* (USOE Cooperative Research Report No. 014). Boston: Boston University.

Graham, S. (1982). Composition research and practice: A unified approach. *Focus on Exceptional Children, 14,* 1–16.

Graham, S., & Harris, K. (1986). *Improving learning disabled students' compositions via story grammars: A component analysis of self-control strategy training*. Paper presented at the American Educational Research Association, San Francisco.

MacArthur, C., & Graham, S. (1986). *LD students' writing under three conditions: Word processing, dictation, and handwriting*. Paper presented at the American Educational Research Association, San Francisco.

Moran, M. (1981). Performance of learning disabled and low achieving secondary students on formal features of a paragraph-writing task. *Learning Disability Quarterly, 4,* 271–280.

Morris, N., & Crump, D. (1982). Syntactic and vocabulary development in the written language of learning disabled and non-learning disabled students at four age levels. *Learning Disability Quarterly, 5,* 163–172.

Myklebust, H. (1973). *Development and disorders of written language: Studies of normal and exceptional children*. New York: Grune & Stratton.

Napier, G. (1973). A writing study relative to braille contractions to be mastered by primary level children. *Education of the Visually Handicapped, 5,* 74–78.

Nodine, B., Barenbaum, E., & Newcomer, P. (1985). Story composition by learning disabled, reading disabled, and normal children. *Learning Disability Quarterly, 8,* 167–179.

Poplin, M., Gray, R., Larsen, S., Banikowski, A., & Mehring, T. (1980). A comparison of components of written expression abilities in learning disabled and non-learning disabled students at three grade levels. *Learning Disability Quarterly, 3,* 46–53.

Powers, A., & Wilgus, S. (1983). Linguistic complexity of the written language of hearing-impaired children. *Volta Review, 85,* 201–210.

Sedlack, R., & Cartwright, G. (1972). Written language abilities of EMR and nonretarded children with the same mental age. *American Journal of Mental Deficiency, 77,* 95–99.

Wilbur, S., & Nolen, S. (in press). Reading and writing. In *Gallaudet encyclopedia of deaf people and deafness*. New York: McGraw-Hill.

Yoshinaga-Itano, C., & Snyder, L. (1985). Form and meaning in the written language of hearing-impaired children. *Volta Review, 87,* 75–90.

STEVE GRAHAM
CHARLES A. MACARTHUR
University of Maryland

DYSGRAPHIA
HANDWRITING
WRITING DISORDERS

WYATT *v.* STICKNEY

The case of *Wyatt* v. *Stickney* established constitutionally minimum standards of care; in the last two decades, *Wyatt* has been credited with establishing the legal precedent for a constitutional right to treatment for involuntarily committed mentally ill patients. Directly addressing Alabama's state institutions for the mentally ill and mentally retarded, this case represented a landmark federal judicial intervention in the mental institutions of a sovereign state, and signaled dozens of *Wyatt*-type "right to treatment" lawsuits in nearly every part of the country.

As a result of the unrefuted "atrocities" documented in

Wyatt (1972), the "shocking" and "inhumane" conditions in New York's Willowbrook State School for the Mentally Retarded (1973), and 25 other suits involving the U.S. Justice Department (1979), congressional legislation for financial assistance and a "Bill of Rights" for institutionalized persons were enacted.

Only six decisions based on the Wyatt case have ever been published in the law reports (1971–1981), although it is cited in over 200 judicial decisions and is the subject of numerous law reviews and other professional journal articles.

Ricky Wyatt was one of about 5000 mental patients at Bryce State Hospital, Tuscaloosa, the same hospital established in 1861 through the urging of the advocate Dorothea Dix. Stonewall B. Stickney was a psychiatrist and the chief administrative officer of Alabama's Mental Health Board. The case was filed initially by 99 of 100 dismissed staff members plus Ricky Wyatt's aunt and other guardians on October 23, 1970. The plaintiff employees alleged that this reduction in staff would deprive patients at Bryce of necessary treatment and sued for reinstatement. Stickney had released over 100 of the 1600 employees at Bryce owing to reduced state cigarette tax revenues allocated to the department, while redirecting the limited funds to community mental health services. Stickney believed in preventing institutionalization.

The employee plaintiffs withdrew their reinstatement claim prior to Judge Frank M. Johnson's initial reported decision on March 12, 1971. The court found that more than 1500 geriatric patients and about 1000 mentally retarded patients were involuntarily committed at Bryce for reasons other than being mentally ill, and were receiving custodial care but not treatment.

Judge Johnson ordered the development and implementation of adequate treatment standards and a report within 6 months; he requested the U.S. departments of Justice and Health, Education, and Welfare, as "friends of the court," to assist in evaluating the treatment programs and standards. On August 12, 1971, the court allowed the request. All involuntary patients from Partlow State School and Hospital in Tuscaloosa, housing nearly 2500 mental retardates with segregated facilities for blacks, and Searcy Hospital in Mount Vernon, a formerly all-black hospital for the mentally ill, were to be included in the class suit. Defendants filed the court-directed report on September 23, 1971, and Judge Johnson ruled on December 10, 1971, allowing the state 6 months to correct three basic deficiencies. He called for "a humane psychological and physical environment, . . . qualified staff in numbers sufficient to administer adequate treatment, and . . . individualized treatment plans." Following additional testimony, briefs, and standards proposed by "the foremost authorities on mental health in the United States," the parties agreed to standards that mandated a "constitutionally acceptable minimum treatment program" for the mentally ill at Bryce and Searcy as ordered by the court on April 13, 1972.

Judge Johnson also ruled, in a supplemental order issued the same day, that unrebutted evidence of the "hazardous and deplorable inadequacies in the institution's operations at Partlow was more shocking than at Bryce or Searcy." He said that "The result of almost 50 years of legislative neglect has been catastrophic; atrocities occur daily"; Judge Johnson published these findings (1972):

> A few of the atrocious incidents cited at the hearing in this case include the following: (a) a resident was scalded to death by hydrant water; (b) a resident was restrained in a strait jacket for 9 years in order to prevent hand and finger sucking; (c) a resident was inappropriately confined in seclusion for a period of years, and (d) a resident died from the insertion by another resident of a running water hose into his rectum. Each of these incidents could have been avoided had adequate staff and facilities been available.

Judge Johnson ordered the defendants to (1) implement the standards for adequate habilitation for the retarded at Partlow; (2) establish a human rights committee; (3) employ a new administrator; (4) submit a progress report to the court within 6 months; and (5) pay attorneys' fees and costs to the plaintiffs.

The defendants appealed both decisions to the Fifth Circuit Court of Appeals in May 1972. The review court, on November 8, 1974, upheld the constitutional right to treatment concept and ruled that the federal judicially determined standards did not violate the state's legislative rights.

Although subsequent implementation and compliance with the court's orders continue to produce controversies, numerous motions, briefs, hearings, and additional opinions have been issued. However, no legal changes have occurred in *Wyatt* as of the last published order of the court on March 25, 1981.

REFERENCE

Civil rights of the institutionalized. Report of the Committee on Judiciary United States Senate on S.10 together with minority and additional views. (1979). Washington, DC: U.S. Government Printing Office.

LOUIS SCHWARTZ
Florida State University

HISTORY OF SPECIAL EDUCATION
LEGAL REGULATIONS OF SPECIAL EDUCATION
PHILOSOPHY OF EDUCATION FOR THE HANDICAPPED

X

X-LINKED DOMINANT INHERITANCE

The consequences of the presence of a recessive gene on one X chromosome are well known. X-linked dominant inheritance, however, follows a different pattern. First, males and females can show the trait equally, and, if a pathologic gene is concerned, patients of both sexes are affected. Second, if a male carrier of the dominant trait "A" marries an homozygous recessive female "aa," all his daughters will exhibit the trait "A" (they are heterozygous "Aa," having received one X from the "aa" mother and the paternal X with "A"), and all his sons will show the trait "a" (they have received the X chromosome from their mothers and the recessive "a" behaves like a dominant). This mode of transmission, from father to daughter, is in fact so characteristic that, when it is observed, the presence of an X-dominant gene is almost demonstrated. Only a few rare diseases are known to be X-linked dominants. X-linked dominant inherited diseases, though rare, result in a variety of handicapping conditions. Not all genetic disorders need result in handicaps, however. Proper care during pregnancy and throughout life can avoid many natural consequences of genetic disorders.

L. KOULISCHER
Institut de Morphologie
Pathologique

ETIOLOGY
X-LINKED RECESSIVE INHERITANCE

X-LINKED RECESSIVE INHERITANCE

It is well known that the same gene may present different forms, called alleles. All alleles are located at a fixed place of a chromosome, the locus. In any person, only two alleles are present, one at each locus of the same chromosome pair. One of the two alleles originates from the father, the other from the mother. Alleles can be either dominant (usually represented by a capital letter: "A"), or recessive (represented by a small letter: "a"). As indicated by its name, the dominant form prevails over the recessive one. This means that the carrier of "Aa" (heterozygote) will show the character "A," the recessive "a" being masked. To express itself, "a" must be in the homozygote state "aa." This happens when two "Aa" heterozygotes marry: 25% of all their children will be "aa."

This general rule does not apply to the sex chromosomes. In the XX female, only one X is active in any cell, the other one being inactivated (Lyon, 1961). In a heterozygote female "Aa," the gene "A" will express itself in half of the cells, and "a" in the other half. Most often, the fact that the normal allele is active in half of the cells is enough to determine normal characteristics. For instance, if a woman is a carrier of the recessive mutation responsible for blindness for the red color (daltonism), half of the cells of her retina will be blind for red, but the others not and this will be sufficient to give almost normal color vision. The male has an XY sex chromosome set: only one X, transmitted by the mother, is present. The Y chromosome is very small and has only a few genes.

Any boy has a 50% chance to inherit one of the two maternal Xs. If he receives the X with a normal dominant allele, there will be no problem. If he receives an X with a recessive abnormal allele from an heterozygous mother, all his cells (not half of them, as in his mother) will be affected. The gene "a" alone, although recessive, behaves like a dominant (e.g., in the case of daltonism, he will be blind to the red). In short, an X-linked recessive gene is transmitted by the mother to half of her sons. If the gene determines a disease, half of the male progeny will be affected, the mother herself being apparently normal. Moreover, half of her daughters will be "normal carriers" and thus will be at risk of having half of their sons affected. When an affected male marries, all his children will be normal. The boys receive their X chromosome from the normal mother and the girls are heterozygous (the problem concerns their future children). Only the exceptional and seldom reported marriage of a heterozygous woman "Aa" with an affected man "a" can produce affected "aa" homozygous females.

The striking fact in this sort of X-linked recessive pedigree is that only males are affected (black squares). Inversely, when a family is found with only males presenting a disease, the transmission of an X-linked recessive gene is likely. According to McKusick (1983), there are at present 115 confirmed and 128 possible X-linked genes. It is not possible to cite them all in this entry. The most commonly known recessives are those associated with hemophilia, agammaglobulenemia and other immunological diseases, eye diseases including colorblindness, ocular albinism, and some forms of cataract, a few deafness syndromes, Lesch-Nyhan syndrome (mental retardation, spastic cerebral palsy, choreoathetosis, uric acid urinary stones, and self-destructive biting of fingers and lips), muscular dystrophy, myopathy, and testicular feminization.

Mental deficiency and X-linked recessive genes deserve special comment. It is well known that more boys than girls show mental retardation. This suggests an excess of X-linked recessive diseases. Often, mental retardation is associated with other symptoms to form a syndrome (e.g., Lesch-Nyhan syndrome). A newly discovered disease is mental retardation, macroorchidism, and elongated face associated with the presence of a fragile site on the X-chromosome, known as the Xq28 fragile site, observed in 1 out of 2000 male births. Fryns (1984) has published a review of 83 families ascertained through 83 index patients. He summarizes the problems raised by this particular chromosome anomaly: in one-third of the families, pedigree data were consistent with X-linked recessive inheritance in the other two-thirds, the presenting symptom was familial mental retardation with a mentally retarded mother, or mental subnormality with hyperkinetic behavior. Even the transmission through a normal asymptomatic X-fragile male carrier seemed likely in four families. Although more data are still necessary, at present the fragile Xq28 syndrome appears to be an important cause of X-linked mental retardation, with the advantage that carriers can be detected by means of relatively simply cytogenetic techniques.

From a preventive point of view, it is important first to diagnose correctly any X-linked disease with mental retardation, and to detect the normal heterozygote mothers at risk. This is not always possible, but it is a new area of research and it is hoped, with the help of biochemistry and molecular DNA analysis, to prevent in the near future the birth of affected males.

REFERENCES

Fryns, J.-P. (1984). The fragile X syndrome. A study of 83 families. *Clin. Genet., 26,* 497–528.

Lyon, M. F. (1961). Gene action in the X-chromosome of the mouse. (Mus musculus). *Nature, 190,* 372–373.

L. KOULISCHER
*Institut de Morphologie
Pathologique*

CONGENITAL DISORDERS
GENETIC COUNSELING

X-RAYS AND HANDICAPPING CONDITIONS

Irradiation of the developing fetus during the early stages of development as a consequence of maternal X-rays is now clearly recognized as a potential cause of later physical and cognitive abnormalities. There may be dramatic effects associated with irradiation that are clearly recognized at birth. There may be other, more subtle effects appearing at later ages such as reduced head size. Pioneer studies on the subject were done by Zappert (1926), Murphy (1929), and Goldstein (1930; Berg, 1968).

Clinical X-rays are a major source of the radiation absorbed by the human body during any particular year. It has been estimated that people on the average absorb less than 4 rads a year and that half of this is from medical X-rays, e.g., upper gastrointestinal series, abdominal X-rays, and dental and chest X-rays. This does not include treatment for cancer during which ranges somewhere between 30–250 rads have been observed (Batshaw & Perrett, 1981).

Though the potential dangers to the fetus from X-ray radiation were recognized before World War II, the dangers of radiation were most dramatically brought into focus by the events of that war. It was found that there was a direct relationship between the distance of a pregnant woman from the point of impact of the atomic bombs at Hiroshima and Nagasaki and the degree of damage suffered by her unborn child. Women who survived the bomb explosion but were within a half-mile of it were found to have miscarriages, while there was an extremely high incidence of microcephalic children born to those who were 1¼ miles away (Wood, Johnson, & Omiri, 1967). Still farther away, there was no clear evidence of cognitive or physical damage to the children that were later born, but some 20 years later, as adults, they had a high incidence of leukemia (Miller, 1968).

One major study of pregnant women who were receiving cobalt treatments for cancer discovered that 20 out of 75 of the infants born to them had definitive central nervous system abnormalities. Sixteen of these were microcephalic (Cooper & Cooper, 1966). The corroboration of these findings in later studies has resulted in caution and forbearance on the part of physicians with respect to the use of X-rays with pregnant women. Normally, women should not have abdominal X-rays more than 2 weeks after the last period. X-rays during the first trimester are discouraged on any but the most necessary grounds. X-rays as diagnostic tests, such as those once carried out to establish fetal size, have been replaced with less invasive procedures like ultrasound. Indeed, there has been recent evidence suggesting that some of the more subtle kinds of handicaps, e.g., those associated with learning disabilities, may be the consequence of X-ray use.

On the positive side it should be observed that X-rays have played a role in assisting in the assessment of handicapped individuals. Thus X-rays of the bone structures of hands and wrists have provided estimates of carpal ossification in cases where delayed maturation has been suspected. X-rays also are essential for the diagnosis of various physical problems and deformities, e.g., dislocations, fractures, internal injuries, and congenital defects. Recently, computerized axial tomography (CAT) has revolutionized medical diagnosis. While X-rays by themselves can show only the length and width of a bodily organ, the CAT scan can also reveal depth. Significant contributions to our understanding of learning disorders have been made by CAT scans (Mann & Sabatino, 1985).

REFERENCES

Batshaw, M. L., & Perrett, Y. M. (1981). *Children with handicaps*. Baltimore, MD: Brookes.

Berg, J. M. (1968). Aetiological aspects of mental subnormality: Pathological factors. In A. M. Clarke & A. D. B. Clarke (Eds.), *Mental deficiency*. New York: Free Press.

Cooper, G., & Cooper, J. B. (1966). Radiation hazards to mother and fetus. *Clinical Obstetrics & Gynecology, 9,* 11.

Mann, L., & Sabatino, D. A. (1985). *Foundations of cognitive processes in remedial and special education*. Rockville, MD: Aspen.

Miller, R. W. (1968). Effects of ionizing radiation from the atomic bomb on Japanese children. *Pediatrics, 72,* 1483.

Wood, J. W., Johnson, K. G., & Omiri, Y. (1973). In utero exposure to the Hiroshima atomic bomb. An evaluation of head size and mental retardation: Twenty years after. *Pediatrics, 39,* 385.

LESTER MANN
Hunter College

CAT SCAN
NEURAL EFFICIENCY ANALYZER

X-RAY SCANNING TECHNIQUES

The history of X-ray scanning techniques of the brain is eloquently outlined in the text by Oldendorf (1980). Up until the advent of CAT (computed axial tomography) scanning in 1973, the image of the brain could only be grossly inferred by either bony abnormalities of the skull as seen on routine skull X-rays or by a technique (pneumoencephalography) in which air was introduced into the brain ventricles (either directly or via spinal puncture). The resultant shadowy contrast between ventricle, brain, and bone would permit some visualization of major cerebral landmarks sufficient to detect some types of gross structural pathology (e.g., hydrocephalus, tumor). However, the technique of pneumoencephalography had significant morbidity risks and was invasive. The pneumoencephalogram has been replaced by CAT scanning.

An historical predecessor of CAT scanning was the radioactive isotope scan (based on differences in rate of absorption of radioactive particles in normal and abnormal brain tissue), which began clinical use in 1947 and continued until the advent and clinical implementation of CAT scanning. The CAT and other neuroimaging techniques

have essentially replaced the radioactive isotope scan. This is also the case with routine cerebral arteriography, which used to be the only way to visualize blood vessels of the neck and head; it has been replaced in large part by digital subtraction angiography (DSA). The DSA is an X-ray scanning technique that uses a computer program to "subtract" background tissue in the X-ray image that is not of the same density as blood vessels. Comparisons of these techniques, sample figures, and a more complete discussion of their diagnostic usefulness are presented in Bigler (1988).

Positron emission tomography (PET) is a new technique that permits the mapping of brain metabolism by using radioactive-labeled glucose or oxygen. Based on different metabolic rates, an image of the major cerebral structures can be obtained with specific indication of which brain areas were using the most glucose or oxygen (e.g., the brain area most involved in a particular task while PET scanning was being done).

REFERENCES

Bigler, E. D. (1988). *Diagnostic clinical neuropsychology* (2nd ed.). Austin: University of Texas Press.

Oldendorf, W. H. (1980). *The quest for an image of brain*. New York: Raven.

ERIN D. BIGLER
Austin Neurological Clinic
University of Texas

CAT SCAN
NUCLEAR MAGNETIC RESONANCE
X-RAY, ASSOCIATED WITH LEARNING DISORDERS

XYY SYNDROME

Polysomy Y or XYY syndrome is a sex chromosome variation characterized by an extra Y chromosome in males. That is, rather than having two sex chromosomes of the normal male (46, XY), those with the XYY genotype have an extra male sex chromosome (47, XYY). There are no dysmorphic factors associated with this syndrome other than most males with it are tall (i.e., height is typically above the ninetieth percentile by age six and older). There are also no chronic health disorders associated with the syndrome, but XYY males were found to have a higher rate of broken bones and infections than normal peers (Stewart, 1982). Fertility appears to be normal (Cohen & Durnham, 1985). The incidence of XYY syndrome is 1 in 700 to 1 in 1000 live male births (Cohen & Durnham, 1985). Many XYY males are never identified because they are generally indistinguishable from the general male population.

There have been misconceptions in the past regarding

the behavioral and developmental sequelae of XYY syndrome. Research with biased samples indicated that XYY males were typically violent criminals and mentally retarded (e.g., Jacobs et al., 1965). More recent and well-controlled studies have indicated that only 1 of every 950 is institutionalized. While this is higher than the general population, it is much less than suggested earlier (Jarvik, Klodin, & Matsuyama, 1973).

Research has identified the following developmental and behavioral problems when comparing school-age XYY males with normal peers and siblings: (1) IQ scores are slightly lower than normal but there is no increased risk for mental retardation; (2) fine-motor coordination and language development tend to be mildly decreased; (3) reading difficulties and a wide spectrum of learning disorders are more often present; (4) aggressive behavior does not have a higher frequency of occurrence rate; (5) behavioral problems related to general immaturity, impulsivity, and low frustration tolerance are more often present (Robinson, Lubs, & Bergsma, 1985; Stewart, 1982).

Cohen and Durnham (1985) have provided a comprehensive review of school management of children with XYY syndrome as well as other sex chromosome variations. It is suggested that children with suspected XYY syndrome be referred to school health personnel. Once identified, psychoeducational assessment is typically needed to identify possible learning and behavioral disorders. Anticipatory guidance concerning the risks of XYY syndrome is especially needed in view of the typical misconceptions cited earlier. Cohen and Durnham have listed the following resources for school personnel and parents for gaining further information about sex chromosome variations:

March of Dimes Birth Defects Foundation
1275 Mamaroneck Avenue
White Plains, NY 10605

Metropolitan Turner's Syndrome Association
P.O. Box 407C
Convent Station, NH 07961

National Center for Education in Maternal and Child Health
3520 Prospect Street NW
Washington, DC 20027

National Health Information Clearing House
Box 1133
Washington, DC 20013

National Information Center for Handicapped Children
1201 16th Street, NW
Washington, DC 20036

REFERENCES

Cohen, F. L., & Durnham, J. D. (1985). Sex chromosome variations in school-aged children. *Journal of School Health, 55,* 99–102.

Jacobs, P. A., Brunton, M., Mellville, M. M., Brittain, R. P., & McClemont, W. F. (1965). Aggressive behavior, mental subnormality, and the XYY male. *Nature, 208,* 1351–1352.

Jarvik, L. F., Klodin, V., & Matsuyama, S. S. (1973). Human aggression and the extra Y chromosome. *American Psychologist, 28,* 674–682.

Robinson, A., Lubs, H. A., & Bergsma, D. (1985). *Sex chromosome aneuploidy: Prospective studies on children.* New York: Liss.

Stewart, D. A. (1982). *Children with sex chromosome aneuploidy: Follow-up studies.* New York: Liss.

JOSEPH D. PERRY
Kent State University

CHROMOSOMAL ABNORMALITIES
GENETIC COUNSELING

Y

YALE, CAROLINE A. (1848–1933)

Caroline A. Yale, teacher and principal at Clarke School for the Deaf in Northampton, Massachusetts, from 1870 to 1922, was a leading figure in the development of educational services for the deaf in the United States. She developed a system for teaching speech to the deaf and was a founder, with Alexander Graham Bell and others, of the American Association to Promote the Teaching of Speech to the Deaf. At Clarke School, she organized a teacher-education department that was responsible for the training of large numbers of student teachers. Through her teacher-training activities and numerous publications, Yale was a major contributor to the acceptance of instruction in speech as an essential element in the education of deaf children.

REFERENCES

Taylor, H. (1933). Caroline Ardelia Yale. *The Volta Review, 35,* 415–417.

Yale, C. A. (1931). *Years of building.* New York: Longmans, Green.

PAUL IRVINE
Katonah, New York

DEAF EDUCATION

YEAR-ROUND SCHOOLS

The concept and use of year-round schools for special and general education has developed, in part, as a result of changing expectations and roles of public education in the community (Hanna, 1972). The traditional answer to the question of school responsibility was simple: transmit the heritage, or at least that part of it considered to be important to the educated person. The traditional school said, in effect, fit children and youths into the fixed curriculum of academic subjects. If they do not care, or in the case of many exceptional students, cannot cope with it, that is unfortunate. In the cases of many exceptional students, traditional education models forced them out or openly expelled them if attendance laws permitted. In other cases, students were tracked into vocational education or home economics. More progressive educators organized schools around a child-centered orientation in order to more effectively stimulate student interest, provide for the exploration and expression of those interests, and, therefore, assist in desirable personality growth (Olsen & Clark, 1977).

A system embracing year-round schooling is able to affirm the central values of the earlier concepts while providing programming in light of the school's basic responsibility to help improve the quality of living in the local community or region. The traditional school curriculum is still almost standard practice (Ysseldyke & Algozzine, 1983). The approach involved in year-round schools, however, provides curriculum flexibly structured about the enduring life concerns of humans everywhere. These concerns, with their attendant problems, are those of earning a living, communicating ideas and feelings, enjoying recreation, and finding some measure of self-identity.

REFERENCES

Hanna, P. (1972, May). What thwarts the community education curriculum? *Community Education Journal* (pp. 27–30).

Olsen, E. G., & Clark, P. A. (1977). *Life-centering education.* Midland, MI: Pendell.

Ysseldyke, J., & Algozzine, B. (1983). *Introduction to special education.* Boston: Houghton Mifflin.

CRAIG D. SMITH
Georgia College

LICENSING AND CERTIFICATION OF SCHOOLS
SUMMER SCHOOL FOR HANDICAPPED

YPSILANTI PERRY PRESCHOOL PROJECT

The Perry Preschool Project, which operated from 1962 to 1967, was a program to help poor black children in Ypsilanti, Michigan, overcome the apparent effects of their disadvantaged environment. The project evolved from the recognition that a disproportionate number of low-income or minority children with no specific organic etiology were labeled mentally retarded. David Weikart and his associates who initiated the project sought to provide an equal educational opportunity at the preschool level for under-privileged children. Schweinhart and Weikart (1986) believe that effective programs for preschool children can compensate for socioeconomic factors that correlate with school performance. By providing preschool programs, Weikart's goal was to increase the probability of children succeeding in elementary and secondary school as well as the probability of their gaining employment.

Enrolled in the project for 2 years were 3- and 4- year old children (except for four-year-olds enrolled during the project's first year). The school year lasted for 7½ months; classes ran for 2½ hours each morning, 5 days a week. Teachers also made home visits once a week for 1½ hours to work with each parent and child. The preschool was staffed with four classroom teachers with graduate degrees and extensive in-service training at a ratio of five students for every teacher (Schweinhart & Weikart, 1986; Thurman & Widerstrom, 1985).

The Perry Preschool Project used a Piagetian-based curriculum consisting of a set of cognitive/developmental objectives (Thurman & Widerstrom, 1985; Weikart, 1974). Emphasis in the curriculum was on children developing the ability to reason and to understand their relation to the environment. Activities were designed so that learning to think and to solve problems took place through direct experiences. Development of cognitive abilities was viewed as more important and useful at the preschool level than direct instruction of academic skills. Consequently, pre-academic and academic skills (i.e., reading and math concepts) were not emphasized in the curriculum. Rote memory and drill activities typically used in academic skills instruction were not part of the instructional format. Instead, an open format of instruction was used to allow teachers to devise activities that they believed would help individual children through the stages of cognitive development. Ispa and Matz (1978) contend that "because each child works at activities that are developmentally appropriate, he or she has the opportunity to grow and experience success without infringing on the needs of other children for a faster (or slower) pace or for an activity that is more personally interesting" (p. 171).

Activities were both teacher and child initiated. Children enrolled in the project were able to select and engage in their own activities (Thurman & Widerstrom, 1985). Planning time was provided to children to devise their activities for the work time period. During work time, they executed their activities with the assistance of their teachers and peers. Snack time and small group activity time followed the work period. Outdoor activities emphasizing gross motor skills were also provided.

Extensive longitudinal research on the effects of early intervention has been generated from the Perry Preschool Project. Researchers from the project monitored five sets or "waves" of children from the time of enrollment until age 19. In the south side of Ypsilanti, where the preschool was located, project staff surveyed neighborhoods to identify preschool-aged children. A variety of socioeconomic and ability measures were taken on the children and their families, including parents' education, level of employment of the head of household, ratio of rooms in the home to persons in the household, and IQ levels of the preschool-aged children (Schweinhart, Berrueta-Clement, Barnett, Epstein, & Weikart, 1985). Neighborhood 3 and 4 year olds were then randomly assigned to the preschool group and the nonpreschool group.

The outcome variables measured in the longitudinal study were divided into three domains: scholastic success, socioeconomic success, and social responsibility (Schweinhart et al., 1985). In terms of scholastic success, at age 19 individuals enrolled in the preschool were more likely to have graduated from high school, receive college or vocational training, and perform better on measures of functional competence. In addition, fewer of them were subsequently labeled mentally retarded and they spent a lower percentage of their school years in special education programs. On measures of social responsibility, fewer of the preschool group were ever arrested or detained by police and fewer of the females had teenage pregnancies. In terms of economic success, nearly twice as many individuals from the preschool group were employed and half as many were receiving welfare (Schweinhart et al., 1985).

A benefit-cost analysis of the project indicated that the Perry Preschool Project paid dividends in the long run. The return on investment was estimated to be three and a half times greater than the cost of the 2 years of preschool. The results of the analysis showed that the benefit of the project was in the areas of increased earnings and reduced educational costs for those who had been enrolled in the program (Schweinhart et al., 1985).

REFERENCES

Ipsa, J., & Matz, R. D. (1978). Integrating handicapped preschool children within a cognitively oriented program. In M. J. Guralnick (Ed.), *Early intervention and the integration of handicapped and nonhandicapped children*. Baltimore, MD: University Park Press.

Schweinhart, L. J., Berrueta-Clement, J. R., Barnett, W. S., Epstein, A. S., & Weikart, D. P. (1985). The promise of early childhood education. *Phi Delta Kappan, 67,* 548–553.

Schweinhart, L. J., & Weikart, D. P. (1986). What do we know so far? A review of the Head Start Synthesis Project. *Young Children, 41,* 50–55.

Thurman, K. S., & Widerstrom, A. E. (1985). *Young children with special needs: A developmental and ecological approach.* Boston: Allyn & Bacon.

Weikart, D. P. (1974). Curriculum for early childhood special education. *Focus on Exceptional Children, 6,* 1–8.

LAWRENCE J. O'SHEA
University of Florida

EARLY IDENTIFICATION OF HANDICAPPED CHILDREN
SOCIOECONOMIC IMPACT OF DISABILITIES
SOCIOECONOMIC STATUS

YSSELDYKE, JAMES EDWARD (1944–)

James Edward Ysseldyke, noted educator, psychologist, and researcher, was born in Grand Rapids, Michigan, in 1944. He received his BA (1966) in psychology and biology from Western Michigan University and both his MA (1968) and PhD (1971) in school psychology from the University of Illinois, where he studied with T. Ernest Newland. He is currently professor of educational psychology at the University of Minnesota, teaching primarily in school psychology and also in special education, and since 1991, he has been director of the National Center on Educational Outcomes at the university. Ysseldyke is the former director of the University of Minnesota Institute for Research in Learning Disabilities.

Much of Ysseldyke's work has been concentrated in the area of special education assessment. He and his colleagues have investigated the relationship of psychometric properties of tests, particularly reliability and validity, to the decision-making process in multidisciplinary team meetings (Poland, Thurlow, Ysseldyke, & Mirkin, 1982). Ysseldyke's work in this area has indicated that, in many instances, decisions on eligibility for special education and programming are made prior to the official team meeting, with test data having little or no effect on the process. Similarly, he has found little correlation between the results of a child's standardized tests and the child's subsequent classroom placement (Ysseldyke, Algozzine, Richey, & Graden, 1982). These findings have encouraged additional detailed research on the issue.

Ysseldyke has recently noted the exclusion of students with disabilities in significant numbers from state and national data collection programs, thus precluding the evaluation of these students in terms of educational outcomes (Vanderwook, McGrew, & Ysseldyke, 1998). He has also coauthored, with Bob Algozzine, a book with instructional approaches for teachers of special needs students, *Special Education: A Practical Approach for Teachers* (1995). Ysseldyke is perhaps best known to students of special education, however, for his highly successful text coauthored with John Salvia, *Assessment in Special and Remedial Education* (1985).

REFERENCES

Poland, S. F., Thurlow, M. L., Ysseldyke, J. E., & Mirkin, P. K. (1982). Current psychoeducational assessment and decision-making practices as reported by directors of special education. *Journal of School Psychology, 20,* 171–179.

Salvia, J., & Ysseldyke, J. E. (1985). *Assessment in special remedial education.* Boston: Houghton Mifflin.

Vanderwood, M., McGrew, K. S., & Ysseldyke, J. E. (1998). Why we can't say much about students with disabilities during education reform. *Exceptional Children, 64*(3), 359–370.

Ysseldyke, J. E., & Algozzine, B. (1995). *Special education: A practical approach for teachers* (3rd ed.). Boston: Houghton Mifflin.

Ysseldyke, J. E., Algozzine, B., Richey, L., & Graden, J. (1982). Declaring students eligible for learning disability services: Why bother with the data? *Learning Disability Quarterly, 5,* 37–44.

E. VALERIE HEWITT
Texas A & M University
First edition

TAMARA J. MARTIN
*The University of Texas of the
Permian Basin*
Second edition

**COUNCIL FOR EXCEPTIONAL CHILDREN
INSTITUTES FOR RESEARCH IN LEARNING DISABILITIES**

James Edward Ysseldyke

YUNIS-VARON SYNDROME

Yunis-Varon Syndrome is a rare genetic disorder caused by an autosomal recessive gene. Children with Yunis-Varon Syndrome have skeletal ectodermal tissue (e.g., nails and teeth), and cardiorespiratory defects. Skeletal defects include complete or partial absence of the shoulder blades, digital abnormalities (i.e., absence or underdeveloped thumbs, big toes, and fingertips), and abnormal growth of the bones of the cranium (i.e., the skull). These children have abnormally large hearts and respiratory difficulties, along with feeding problems, which can be life-threatening, especially in infancy (National Organization for Rare Disorders [NORD], 1997). In fact, neonatal death is a significant feature of Yunis-Varon Syndrome (Lapeer & Fransman, 1992).

Other physical features of this disorder include abnormal or unusual facial characteristics. Children with this syndrome have sparse or no eyebrows and eyelashes, thin lips, and excessively small jaws. These children are also short in stature due to pre- and postnatal growth retardation (NORD, 1997).

Twelve cases of the syndrome have been reported in the literature, which suggests a rare disorder and/or a high mortality rate associated with the disorder. Children who have survived the infancy period have been reported to have additional problems, including bilateral hearing loss, spinal defects, and impacted teeth (Lapeer & Fransman, 1992). Special education support services, such as speech services, may be helpful, especially if a hearing loss is evident.

REFERENCES

Lapeer, G. L., & Fransman, S. L. (1992). Hypodontia, impacted teeth, spinal defects, and cardiomegaly in previously diagnosed case of the Yunis-Varon syndrome. *Oral Surgery, Oral Medicine, and Oral Pathology, 73*(4), 456–60.

National Organization for Rare Disorders (NORD). (1997). Yunis-Varon syndrome. New Fairfield, CT: Author.

PATRICIA A. LOWE
Texas A & M University

JOAN W. MAYFIELD
*Baylor Pediatric Specialty
Services*

Z

ZEAMAN, DAVID (1921–1984)

After receiving his PhD from Columbia University in experimental psychology in 1948, David Zeaman embarked on a lifelong career developing and elaborating on an attention theory of retardate discriminative learning. In the early 1950s, he conducted pilot studies specializing in animal learning with his wife, Betty House, at the Mansfield State Training School in Connecticut. They thought that the techniques developed for studying animal behavior could be adapted for retarded children with low ability to speak or understand language. That early work proved promising, leading to funding by the National Institute of Mental Health for a project that lasted 20 years. The Mansfield State School administrative provided space for a permanent laboratory that is still in existence.

The initial target behavior for Zeaman and House's research was a discriminative learning task disguised as a candy-finding game. Early results convinced them that the deficiency they observed in retarded subjects was due to attentional deficits rather than slow learning. They developed a mathematical attention model with the basic assumption that discriminative learning requires a learning chain of two responses: attending to the relevant dimension and approaching the correct cue of that dimension.

Their approach to retardation was to look for changes in parameter values of the model related to intelligence. The parameter that was most affected by level of intelligence turned out to be the initial probability of attending to the colors and forms that were the relevant dimensions of the tasks. Later work related this finding to three factors: (1) breadth and adjustability of breadth of attention—subjects of higher intelligence can attend to more dimensions at once and can narrow attention when necessary; (2) dimensionality of the stimulus—subjects of low intelligence are likely to attend to stimuli holistically rather than analytically; and (3) fixed as well as variable components of attention such that strong dimensional preferences interfere with learning—salience of position cues in retardates slows learning about colors, forms, sizes, and other aspects of stimuli. A history of research and theory development from the first publication of the model in 1963 to 1979 can be found in Ellis's *Handbook of Mental Deficiency* (1963).

Zeaman served as editor of the *Psychological Bulletin* and as associate editor of *Intelligence*. He received many awards and honors from organizations such as the American Psychological Association and the National Institute of Mental Health.

REFERENCE

Zeaman, D., & House, B. J. (1963). The role of attention in retardate discrimination learning. In N. R. Ellis (Ed.), *Handbook of mental deficiency: Psychological theory and research*. New York: McGraw-Hill.

STAFF

HOUSE, BETTY
ZEAMAN HOUSE RESEARCH

ZEAMAN-HOUSE RESEARCH

David Zeaman and Betty House, along with other researchers located primarily at the University of Connecticut and the Mansfield Training School, have contributed substantial research on attention theory to the literature on mental retardation. Though more than 100 years of psychological and educational research on attention has concluded that the process is multifactorial (Alabiso, 1972), the Zeaman-House, and later Fisher-Zeaman, focus on selective attention has provided several learning theories useful in understanding and teaching mentally retarded persons.

Using a series of simple visual discrimination tasks, Zeaman and House found that plotting of individual, rather than averaged, group responses produced learning curves that differed significantly from traditional learning curves. The former curves stayed around the chance (50%) correct level, then jumped quickly to 100% accuracy. Prior to plotting individual data with backward learning curves, the expectation would have been for a gradual, incremental curve from chance to the 100% correct level. This discontinuity caused these researchers to postulate two processes, one controlling the length of the first part of the curve, and one determining the rapid jump to correct problem solution. Mentally retarded learners in the 2- to 4-year mental age range performed more poorly on these tasks than children of normal intelligence at comparable mental ages. Also, Zeaman and House determined that, among mentally retarded subjects, IQ was a more accurate predictor of better discrimination, independent of mental age (Robinson & Robinson, 1976).

The two-stage or two-phase discrimination learning process proposed by Zeaman and House (1963) suggests an early attention phase during which the plotted learning curve is essentially horizontal, indicating chance-level responses. During this phase, the subject has not discovered the relevant stimuli of an object and is randomly attending to various stimulus dimensions. The second phase of the discrimination process involves attention to relevant stimulus dimensions, leading to rapid improvement in learning (Mercer & Snell, 1977).

Because mentally retarded subjects produced chance-level curves of longer initial duration (yet also demonstrated steeply sloped curves comparable to subjects with higher mental ages), Zeaman and House argued that the inefficient learning of mentally retarded persons was, at its core, a function of their attention. This finding was important because it suggested that the actual learning potential of mentally retarded persons was not defective, and that interventions could be devised to improve attention and discrimination. The differences observed between slower learning mentally retarded persons and faster or normal learners were based more on the time it took to learn to attend to relevant stimuli than to select the relevant cue itself (Zeaman & House, 1963). The work by Zeaman and House in the area of attention and discrimination learning led to studies of other relevant variables such as transfer of training, stimulus factors (e.g., size, position, color, shape), novelty and oddity learning, and the effects of reward characteristics.

Later, their attention theory was expanded to include examinations of the relationship of retention to attention and learning. Ten years after publication of the earlier work, Fisher and Zeaman (1973) noted that although the attention deficits that affect learning in mentally retarded persons are amenable to manipulation and improvement, the retention limitations attributable to the reduced cognitive capacity of such subjects may not be so flexible. Both the earlier and more recent work by Zeaman, House, and their colleagues have generated considerable productive research by others. These latter focuses, many of which suggest implications for education and training of mentally retarded learners, include work on the number of stimulus dimensions employed, reward and incentive conditions, and transfer and oddity learning.

REFERENCES

Alabiso, F. (1972). Inhibitory functions of attention in reducing hyperactive behavior. *American Journal of Mental Deficiency, 77,* 259–282.

Fisher, M. A., & Zeaman, D. (1973). An attention-retention theory of retardate discrimination learning. In N. R. Ellis (Ed.), *The international review of research in mental retardation* (Vol. 6). New York: Academic.

Mercer, C. D., & Snell, M. E. (1977). *Learning theory research in mental retardation: Implications for teaching.* Columbus, OH: Merrill.

Robinson, N. M., & Robinson, H. B. (1976). *The mentally retarded child: A psychological approach.* New York: McGraw-Hill.

Zeaman, D., & House, B. J. (1963). The role of attention in retardate discrimination learning. In N. R. Ellis (Ed.), *Handbook of mental deficiency.* New York: McGraw-Hill.

JOHN D. WILSON
Elwyn Institutes

HOUSE, BETTY
ZEAMAN, DAVID

ZERO INFERENCE

Zero inference is a term that refers to the instructional needs of individuals with severe handicaps (Brown, Nietupski, & Hamre-Nietupski, 1976). Typically, teachers of nonhandicapped students teach a series of core skills using a variety of materials (e.g., counting using wooden cubes). It is assumed that these students will then learn strategies, roles, and concepts necessary to the use of such core skills in other natural settings. It cannot be inferred that severely handicapped students can be taught critical skills in an artificial (i.e., nonnatural) setting using artificial materials and be expected to perform the same skills in more natural settings.

Because of the nature of their mental, physical, or emotional problems, severely handicapped students often need educational, social, psychological, or medical services that are beyond those offered in classes for nonhandicapped students. Educational needs are notable in that some students with severe handicaps may have severe language or perceptual-cognitive deficits. They may fail to attend to even pronounced social stimuli and may lack even the most rudimentary forms of verbal control (U.S. Office of Education, 1975). Severely handicapped students may have the need for intensive instruction in areas including social behavior, communication skills, personal care, mobility and ambulation skills, academic and cognitive behaviors, and vocational skills (Wehman, Renzaglia, & Bates, 1985). Many of the skills required for adaptive performance in postschool environments will need to be taught to severely handicapped students because of the nature of their performance and cognitive deficits. Such instruction is referred to as the zero-degree inference strategy.

Characteristics of the zero-degree inference strategy of instruction include the belief that no inferences can be made about training a student to perform at a skill level that he or she will be able to use in postschool settings. In order for severely handicapped students to generalize skills taught in more natural (i.e., nonschool) settings, strategies must be used to ensure that generalization will occur (Stokes & Baer, 1977). Training across multiple settings, materials, and trainers may be included in instruction of students with severe handicaps. General case programming (Horner, Sprague, & Wilcox, 1982), in which common characteristics of several materials or settings are assessed in an effort to teach students a strategy that can be used in a variety of postschool settings, may be used. Additionally, techniques of systematic instruction, including data-based instruction and assessment of student progress, are necessary to ensure the acquisition of usable skills on the part of severely handicapped learners (Lynch, McGuigan, & Shoemaker, 1977).

Employing training techniques including generalization or general case strategies and systematic instruction will ensure the acquisition of skills that can be used by severely handicapped students in all necessary environments. Teachers who make zero inferences regarding student performance will be more likely to see success in student performance across situations requiring similar skills.

REFERENCES

Brown, L., Nietupski, J., & Hamre-Nietupski, S. (1976). Criterion of ultimate functioning. In M. A. Thomas (Ed.), *Hey, don't forget about me!* Reston, VA: Council for Exceptional Children.

Horner, R. H., Sprague, J., & Wilcox, B. (1982). General case programming for community activities. In B. Wilcox & G. T. Bellamy (Eds.), *Design for high school programs for severely handicapped students* (pp. 61–68). Baltimore, MD: Brookes.

Lynch, V., McGuigan, C., & Shoemaker, S. (1977). Systematic instruction: Defining the good teacher. In N. Haring (Ed.), *An inservice program for personnel serving the severely handicapped.* Seattle: Experimental Education Unit, University of Washington.

Stokes, T. F., & Baer, D. M. (1977). An implicit technology of generalization. *Journal of Applied Behavior Analysis, 10,* 349–367.

U.S. Office of Education. (1975). *Estimated number of handicapped children in the United States, 1974–75.* Washington, DC: Bureau of Education for the Handicapped.

Wehman, P., Renzaglia, A., & Bates, P. (1985). *Functional living skills for moderately and severely handicapped individuals.* Austin, TX: Pro-Ed.

CORNELIA LIVELY
University of Illinois

SELF-CONTAINED CLASS
SELF-HELP TRAINING
TRANSFER OF LEARNING
TRANSFER OF TRAINING

ZERO-REJECT

The term *zero-reject* identifies a policy of providing to all children with handicapping conditions a free, appropriate, and publicly supported education. The constitutional foundation of zero-reject is the Fourteenth Amendment, which guarantees that no state may deny any person within its "jurisdiction the equal protection of the laws." The courts have interpreted this to mean that no government may deny public services to a person because of his or her unalterable characteristics (e.g., sex, race, age, or handicap). Advocates of children with handicaps claimed that these children have the same rights to education as children who are not handicapped. If a state treats children with handicaps differently (e.g., by denying them the opportunity to attend school or by inappropriately assigning them to a special education program), then it is denying them "equal protection of the laws" on the basis of their unalterable characteristics.

In 1975 Congress noted that over one million children with disabilities in the United States were being denied an appropriate public education, and passed PL 94-142, the Education of All Handicapped Children Act, which specified that no child with a handicapping condition (aged 3 to 21) could be excluded from school by recipients of federal funds for the education of children with handicaps. Zero-reject, the mandate to include all children in public schools and to provide an appropriate education for them, represented a new responsibility for public school systems at the time. The policy of zero-reject has remained strong throughout the revisions to PL 94-142, which include the 1990 passage of the Individuals with Disabilities Act (IDEA), and the 1997 Amendments to the IDEA.

The law promotes the zero-reject policy by requiring the schools to provide an education that would be meaningful to the child when he or she leaves school, particularly in facilitating the movement of qualified individuals with disabilities into mainstream employment. State education agencies have the responsibility of ensuring the policy of zero-reject, but the rule applies to the state, each school district, private schools, and state-operated programs such as schools for students with visual or hearing impairments.

Judicial interpretation of the zero-reject rule has included the order that students whose behavior is caused by their disability may not be expelled or suspended. The courts have also ordered, under the zero-reject policy, that students with contagious diseases may not be excluded from public education with other students unless there is a high risk that other students will be infected (Turnbull, Turnbull, Shank, & Leal, 1995).

REFERENCE

Turnbull, A. P., Turnbull, H. R., Shank, M., & Leal, D. (1995). *Exceptional lives: Special education in today's schools.* Englewood Cliffs, NJ: Prentice Hall.

CAROLE REITER GOTHELF
Hunter College
First edition

DONNA WALLACE
*The University of Texas of the
Permian Basin*
Second edition

EDUCATION FOR ALL HANDICAPPED CHILDREN ACT
OF 1975
PUBLIC SCHOOL'S ROLE IN SPECIAL EDUCATION

tal retardation (Vol. 1, pp. 267–281). Baltimore: University Park Press.

ELAINE FLETCHER-JANZEN
University of Northern Colorado

ZIGLER, EDWARD (1930–   )

Edward Zigler received his BA in history from the University of Missouri at Kansas City in 1954 and his PhD in psychology from the University of Texas, Austin in 1958. He is currently Sterling Professor of Psychology at Yale University, Director of the Bush Center in Child Development and Social Policy, and head of the psychology section of the Child Study Center.

Named by President Carter to chair the fifteenth anniversary Head Start Committee in 1980, Zigler was a member of the National Planning and Steering Committee for Head Start and was appointed to Head Start's first National Research Council. He was also the first director of the Office of Child Development and Chief of the U.S. Children's Bureau.

The essence of Zigler's work has been the systemic evaluation of experiential, motivational, personality factors in the behavior of mentally retarded persons, and the demonstration of how these factors (delineated by experimental results) affect retarded children's performance. He also proposed a classification system for mental retardation along two axes: one, individuals would be ordered by IQ and on the other, by organic, familial, and/or undifferentiated etiologies. Zigler believes that beyond any doubt, many of the reported differences between retarded and non-retarded persons of the same MA are a result of motivational and emotional differences that reflect variations in experiential histories (Blatt & Morris, 1984).

Zigler has authored and co-authored over 300 publications in the field including: *Familial Mental Retardation: A continuing dilemma* (1967), and, with D. Balla, *The Social Policy Implications of a Research Program on the Effects of Institutionalization on Retarded Persons* (1977).

Recipient of many awards and honors, Zigler's current research interests are cognitive and social-emotional development in children (particularly those with mental retardation), motivational determinants of children's performance, and the applicability of developmental theory to the area of psychopathology.

REFERENCES

Blatt, B., & Morris, R. J. (1984). Perspectives in Special Education Personal Orientations, Glenview, Illinois: Scott, Foresman.

Zigler, E. (1967). Familiar mental retardation: A continuing dilemma. *Science, 155,* 292–298.

Zigler, E., & Balla, D. (1977). The social policy implications of a research program on the effects of institutionalization on retarded persons. In P. Mittler (Ed.), *Research to practice in men-*

HEAD START

ZONE OF PROXIMAL DEVELOPMENT

The concept of the zone of proximal development was outlined by the Soviet psychologist L. S. Vygotsky in several papers published in the years immediately preceding his death in 1934. This concept was a critical component of Vygotsky's more developed perspectives on the role of social interaction in cognitive development and offered the theoretical foundations for alternative approaches to the assessment of cognitive development. As part of Vygotsky's general theoretical framework, the concept has influenced the development of important traditions of theory, research, and practice within the Soviet Union, in particular, the theory of "activity" as it has been developed by Vygotsky's students and colleagues. In the past decade, as the work of Vygotsky et al. has become more widely known and more fully understood in the West, the concept of the zone of proximal development has stimulated theory and research on cognitive development (Rogoff & Wertsch, 1984; Wertsch, 1985a, 1985b) and its assessment (Brown & French, 1979; Lidz, 1988, Minick, 1988).

Four postulates were central to Vygotsky's theory and research:

1. The agent of complex cognitive processes such as thinking or remembering is not always an individual. It is often a dyad or larger group whose common activity is organized and mediated by speech. According to Vygotsky, cognitive functions are often intermental rather than intramental.

2. The development of certain cognitive processes in the individual is the product of his or her mastery and internalization of means of organizing and mediating cognitive activities that are first encountered in social interaction or intermental functioning.

3. These means of organizing and mediating complex cognitive activities represent one aspect of the historical development of human social and cultural systems.

4. These socially and historically developed means of mediating cognitive activity are transferred from one generation to the next through the child's interaction with adults and more capable peers in cooperative activity.

The concept of the zone of proximal development is a natural extension of these postulates. Vygotsky argued that two different measures of the individual's cognitive development are possible at any point in ontogenesis. First, focusing on the individual's activity when he or she is working alone, one can assess what Vygotsky called mature cognitive processes. In his view, these processes reflect the individual's mastery of modes of organizing and mediating cognitive activity that are first encountered in social interaction. It is this aspect of the individual's cognitive development that is tapped by traditional methodologies of experimentation and assessment. Second, Vygotsky argued that by analyzing the activity of the individual when assistance is provided by someone more skilled in a particular task or by someone at a more advanced level of cognitive development, it is possible to assess cognitive processes that are maturing. By focusing on the level at which the individual performs when acting in collaboration, one can gain insight into the individual's current development state and the next or proximal stage that will emerge in his or her development given adequate experience with appropriate social interaction or collaboration.

Vygotsky defined the zone of proximal development as the difference between the child's actual level of development as defined by his or her independent activity and the level of performance that he or she achieves in collaboration with an adult or more competent peer (Vygotsky, 1978, pp. 85–86). Strictly speaking, the upper range of the zone of proximal development is not a characteristic of the child. It is created in the interaction between the child and those who provide the child with assistance. The level at which the child is able to participate in cooperative cognitive activity is determined simultaneously by the adult's interest and skills in facilitating the child's participation and by the knowledge, skills, and interests that allow the child to participate in intermental activity and benefit from this experience.

Reflecting his lifelong interest in developmental disabilities and delays, Vygotsky felt that one important application of the concept of the zone of proximal development would be in assessing cognitive development in abnormal populations and designing techniques to facilitate that development. In his view, the application of the concept in assessment practice would permit a qualitative assessment of the child's strengths and weaknesses and help identify the kinds of assistance needed to move the child to more advanced levels of cognitive functioning (Minick, 1988). These ideas are currently being developed and applied in the West by Brown and Campione (Brown & French, 1979; Campione, Brown, Ferrara, & Bryant, 1984) and are compatible with work being done by Feuerstein and others in developing dynamic assessment techniques (Feuerstein, 1979; Lidz, 1988).

REFERENCES

Brown, A. L., & French, L. A. (1979). The zone of potential development: Implications for intelligence testing in the year 2000. *Intelligence, 3,* 255–273.

Campione, J. C., Brown, A. L., Ferrara, R. A., & Bryant, N. R. (1984). The zone of proximal development: implications for individual differences and learning. In B. Rogoff & J. V. Wertsch (Eds.), *Children's learning in the "zone of proximal development"* (pp. 77–92). San Francisco: Jossey-Bass.

Feuerstein, R. (1979). *The dynamic assessment of retarded performers: The learning potential assessment device, theory, instruments, and techniques.* Baltimore, MD: University Park Press.

Leont'ev, A. N. (1978). *Activity, consciousness, and personality* (M. J. Hall, Trans.). Englewood Cliffs, NJ: Prentice-Hall. (Original work published 1975).

Lidz, C. S. (Ed.). (1988). *Foundations of dynamic assessment.* New York: Guilford.

Minick, N. (1988). The zone of proximal development and dynamic assessment. In C. S. Lidz (Ed.), *Foundations of dynamic assessment.* New York: Guilford.

Rogoff, B., & Wertsch, J. V. (Eds.). (1984). *Children's learning in the "zone of proximal development."* San Francisco: Jossey-Bass.

Vygotsky, L. S. (1978). *Mind in society.* Cambridge, MA: Harvard University Press.

Wertsch, J. V. (1985a). *Vygotsky and the social formation of mind.* Cambridge, MA: Harvard University Press.

Wertsch, J. V. (Ed.). (1985b). *Culture, communication, and cognition: Vygotskian perspectives.* New York: Cambridge University Press.

NORRIS MINICK
Center for Psychosocial Studies,
The Spencer Foundation

ACTIVITY, THEORY OF
VYGOTSKY, L. S.

ZONING: FAMILY CARE HOME

A family care home, sometimes referred to as a community residential facility, is a home intentionally located in residential neighborhoods and designed for handicapped adults as a permanent residence or a transitional training residence.

General zoning guidelines have been established by each state in conjunction with federal guidelines; however, specific procedures are developed by the individual municipality. The general statutes of North Carolina (1982) state:

A family care home shall be deemed a residential use of property for zoning purposes and shall be a permissible use in all residential districts of all political subdivisions. No political subdivision may require that a family care home, its owner, or operator obtain, because of the use, a conditional use permit, special use permit, special exception or variance from any such zoning ordinance or plan; provided, however, that a political subdivision may prohibit a family care home from being located within a one-half mile radius of an existing family care home. (Article 3, 168-22, p. 178)

An example of specific procedures developed for family care homes is given for Durham City, North Carolina. In this city, family care homes are permitted in all residential and residential apartment districts but are subject to certain limitations. These limitations include: (1) no more than five persons served residing in such a home; (2) no more than one employee other than the primary family residing in and operating the home shall be employed on the premises; (3) a minimum of 100 square feet shall be provided in the way of bedroom area for each person served, except where two or more occupy a given bedroom, a minimum of 80 square feet shall be provided for each person; (4) all such homes shall be licensed by the state of North Carolina Department of Human Resources, and no person failing to secure such a license or allowing such a license to lapse shall operate a home; (5) a family care home shall be operated in a manner compatible with the surrounding residential land use and shall not create a public nuisance; (6) no traffic shall be generated by such a home in greater volumes than would normally be expected in a residential neighborhood, and any need for parking generated by the conduct of such a home, over and above that normally generated by a residential use in the neighborhood, shall be met off the street and other than in a required front yard; and (7) any house and lot on which such a family care home is hereafter initiated shall be in compliance with the housing code, the building code, and the zoning ordinance of Durham.

Cecelia Steppe-Jones
*North Carolina Central
University*

COMMUNITY PLACEMENT
COMMUNITY RESIDENTIAL PROGRAMS
DEINSTITUTIONALIZATION

Z SCORES, IN DETERMINATION OF DISCREPANCIES

Since the passage of PL 94-142 (Education for all Handicapped Children Act of 1975) several measurement discrepancy models have been recommended in the measurement and special education literature for defining a child as learning disabled (Berk, 1984; Boodoo, 1985; Reynolds et al., 1984; Willson & Reynolds, 1985). These models are all used to estimate the difference between a child's aptitude and achievement, and to determine whether such a

difference constitutes a severe discrepancy. The models recommended for use involve the use of standard scores. Under each model, a true discrepancy between a subject's aptitude and achievement is estimated using the subject's standard score on the respective aptitude and achievement test. Many of the standardized aptitude and achievement measures used for individualized testing are normed using the standard score scale with a mean ($\bar{X}$) of 100 and a standard deviation (S) of 15.

An alternative scale that simplifies the statistical formulas used in the discrepancy models for assessing a severe discrepancy is the Z score scale (Hopkins & Stanley, 1981). This scale has a mean of 0 and a standard deviation of 1 and has the advantage of representing the scores directly in standard deviation units. The following illustrates its use with the Simple Difference Model. Under this model, a difference is defined as [Aptitude (X)–Achievement (Y)] with the standard deviation of this difference, S_D, given by

$$S_D = \left(S_X{}^2 + S_Y{}^2 - 2r_{XY}S_XS_Y\right)^{1/2}$$

where r_{XY} is the correlation between X and Y. The standard error of estimate of a difference, SE, is given by

$$SE = \left[S_X{}^2(1 - r_{XX'}) + S_Y{}^2(1 - r_{YY'})\right]^{1/2}$$

where $r_{XX'}$, $r_{YY'}$, are the reliabilities of X and Y respectively.

Using the Z score scale, each of the aptitude and achievement scores is converted to the corresponding Z score using

$$Z_X = \frac{X - \bar{X}}{S_X}$$

and

$$Z_Y = \frac{Y - \bar{Y}}{S_Y}$$

Then, a simple difference is ($Z_X - Z_Y$). The standard deviation of this difference is

$$S_D = \left(2 - 2r_{XY}\right)^{1/2}$$

where r_{XY} is the correlation between X and Y, and the standard error of estimate is given by

$$SE = \left(2 - r_{XX'} - r_{YY'}\right)^{1/2}$$

REFERENCES

Berk, R. A. (1984). *Screening and diagnosis of children with learning disabilities*. Springfield, IL: Thomas.

Boodoo, G. M. (1985). A multivariate perspective for aptitude-achievement discrepancy in learning disability assessment. *Journal of Special Education, 18*, 489–449.

Hopkins, K. D., & Stanley, J. C. (1981). *Educational and psychological measurement and evaluation* (6th ed.). Englewood Cliffs, NJ: Prentice-Hall.

Reynolds, C. R., Berk, R. A., Boodoo, G. M., Cox, J., Gutkin, T. B., Mann, L., Page, E. B., & Willson, V. L. (1984). *Critical measurement issues in learning disabilities.* Report of the USDE, SEP Work Group on Measurement Issues in the Assessment of Learning Disabilities.

Willson, V. L., & Reynolds, C. R. (1985). Another look at evaluating aptitude-achievement discrepancies in the diagnosis of learning disabilities. *Journal of Special Education, 18,* 477–488.

GWYNETH M. BOODOO
Texas A & M University

DISCREPANCY FROM GRADE
LEARNING DISABILITIES, SEVERE DISCREPANCY
   ANALYSIS IN
SEVERE DISCREPANCY ANALYSIS

ZYGOSITY

Zygosity is twinning that may result in monozygotic (MZ) or identical twins and dizygotic (DZ) or fraternal twins. The cause of MZ twinning remains unknown while the cause of DZ twinning is largely the result of multiple ovulation (Groothuis, 1985). Placentation helps to explain zygosity of twins, where dichorionic placentas take place in all DZ pairs and in about 30% of MZ twins. Monochorionic placentas occur only with MZ twins (Siegel & Siegel, 1982). A twin birth occurs in approximately 1 in 80 pregnancies. For women who already have given birth to twins, the incidence of having a second set rises to 1 in 20. The incidence of MZ twins is 3.5 per 1000 live births independent of race and maternal age. With maternal age DZ twinning increases. It is slightly more frequent in blacks and most unusual in Orientals (Groothuis, 1985; Siegel & Siegel, 1982).

Twinning is of relevance to special education personnel because there are increased risks for medical, psychological, developmental, and educational problems. Twin pregnancies have been associated with higher rates of such symptoms as nausea and vomiting. The greatly increased mortality of twins at birth (i.e., 15%) has been attributed to the high prematurity rate (i.e., 60%) in terms of both gestation time and birth weight. Twins also experience a higher rate of such perinatal problems as entangling of cords, prolapsed cords, hypoxia anemia, respiratory distress syndrome, and jaundice. These risks are generally higher for MZ twins and the second born of both MZ and DZ twins (Young et al., 1985). Twins also experience congenital anomalies such as heart disease, cleft lip, and cleft palate about twice as frequently as children of single births.

There is a general consensus that twins experience higher rates of developmental and behavioral problems than the general population. Like the medical difficulties, these risks are generally more severe for MZ and second-born twins. During the preschool years, problems are focused in such areas as verbal and motor development, discipline, sharing, toilet training, separation, and individual needs. Many of the problems continue for school-aged twins with classroom assignments, school avoidance, peer relations, and academic performance as special concerns. During adolescence, the identity crisis could be exacerbated for twins who have not resolved separation and individuation issues earlier. Regarding school-related abilities, the degree of impairment has been found to be dependent on birth problems and illness as antecedents (Matheny, Dolan, & Wilson, 1976). Moreover, Matheny et al. reported that twins in comparison with the general population have higher rates of learning disabilities and social immaturity. Siegel and Siegel (1982) point out that IQ deficits are questionable, especially when antecedent and environmental factors are controlled.

Typical recommendations for management and guidance follow: (1) encourage parents to avoid emphasizing similarities; (2) separate twins at school as soon as possible but delay if problems are encountered; (3) establish individual expectations for school performance; (4) give psychoeducation assessment to twins with early medical problems. Parents are referred to the National Mother of Twins Club for information and resources.

REFERENCES

Groothuis, J. R. (1985). Twins and twin families. A practical guide to outpatient management. *Clinics in Perinatology, 12,* 459–474.

Matheny, A. P., Dolan, A. B., & Wilson, R. S. (1976). Twins with academic learning problems: Antecedent characteristics. *American Journal of Orthopsychiatry, 46,* 464–469.

Siegel, S. J., & Siegel, M. M. (1982). Practical aspects of pediatric management of families with twins. *Pediatrics in Review, 4,* 8–12.

Young, B. K., Suidan, J., Antoine, C., Silverman, F., Lustig, I., & Wasserman, J. (1985). Differences in twins: The importance of birth order. *American Journal of Obstetrics and Gynecology, 151,* 915–921.

JOSEPH D. PERRY
Kent State University

SIBLINGS
TWINS

AUTHOR INDEX

AAHPER, 34
Aangeenbrug, M. H., 1444
Aaron, I. E., 572, 1343
Abbeduto, L., 1454
Abbot, R. D., 1565
Abbott, S. B., 1129, 1216, 1217, 1432, 1591, 1923
Abel, E. L., 748
Abelson, M. A., 977
Abend, A., 1582
Abend, A. C., 211
Abercrombie, M., 1885
Abeson, A., 306, 394
Abikoff, H., 448
Abikoff, M., 171
Ablon, J., 633
Abmayr, S. B., 1718
Abraham, S., 1112
Abrams, J. C., 1526
Abramson, L. Y., 55, 1064
Abramson, M., 47, 941, 1236, 1688
Abramson, P. A., 141, 349, 465, 699, 959
Abroms, K. I., 15–16
ABT Associates, 598
Abudarham, S., 251
Abu-Saad, H., 399
Abuzzahab, F., 1156
Achenbach, T. M., 69, 169, 358, 684, 1134, 1353, 1460
Acker, N., 510
Ackerman, A., 1616
Ackerman, D. L., 849
Ackerman, P., 1426
Ackerman, P. L., 1032
Ackerman, P. R., 1738
Ackerman, P. T., 917, 1067
Acredolo, L., 411
Acredolo, L. T., 411
Adams, C., 1707
Adams, F. M., 1305
Adams, G. L., 599
Adams, H. M., 1232
Adams, J., 752
Adams, K. M., 1124
Adams, L., 985, 1767
Adams, M., 1660
Adams, N., 920
Adams, P. J., 823
Adams, R. B., 571
Adams, R. C., 1370, 1707
Adams, R. D., 31, 1528
Adams, R. M., 1335
Adams, W., 1912
Adams, W. R., 1190
Adamson, L. B., 1270
Adelman, H. S., 1068, 1085
Adelson, B., 18
Adelson, E., 1156
Adenigba, S. A., 59, 1680

Adesso, V. J., 352
Adevai, G., 676
Adey, K. L., 289
Adinolfi, M., 109
Adkins, P. G., 497
Adler, A., 41, 265, 1213
Adronico, M. P., 755
Affleck, G., 839
Agard, J. A., 832
Ager, J. W., 750
Ageton, A. R., 75
Agner, J., 1238
Agras, S., 201, 1473
Agras, W. S., 240, 409
Aguirre-Roy, A. R., 472
Ahlgren, E., 542
Ahmandi, R., 915
Aicardi, J., 1548
Aiken, L. R., 148, 1790
Ainsa, T., 613, 664
Ainsworth, M. D.S., 1623
Aitkin, M., 1328
Akil, H., 689
Akmajian, A., 1821
Aksenova, L. I., 1575
Alabiso, F., 1947
Alajouanine, T., 362
Albee, G., 260
Albert, M. L., 104
Albert, N. L., 1451
Alberto, P. A., 131, 214, 559, 607, 781, 782, 951, 1220, 1472, 1618, 1619, 1808, 1820
Alborz, A., 1268
Alcanters, P. R., 1738
Alcohol, Drug Abuse, and Mental Health Administration, 1348
Alcorn, J., 336
Alden, J., 1844
Alegria, J., 540
Alexander Graham Bell Association for the Deaf, 77
Alexander, C., 175
Alexander, K., 299, 1103
Alexander, K. L., 267
Alexander, L., 50
Alexander, M. D., 735
Alexander, P., 1769
Alexander, P. A., 18, 1236, 1490, 1491, 1493, 1501
Alford, C. A., 1572
Alfred, E. D., 168
Algert, N. E., 517
Algozzine, B., 43, 78, 190, 235, 248, 517, 584, 650, 655, 883, 958, 983, 1195, 1210, 1265, 1306, 1417,

1468, 1514, 1524, 1606, 1633, 1639, 1691, 1746, 1943, 1945
Alkin, M. C., 715
Allan, C. L., 1589
Allen, A. J., 1283
Allen, D., 43, 1292
Allen, D. A., 636, 839, 1178, 1823,
Allen, D. W., 1187
Allen, J. T., 792
Allen, K. D., 258
Allen, M., 510
Allen, N., 1355, 1824
Allen, T. E., 85, 329, 869, 1720
Allen, V. L., 1857
Alley, G., 162, 1067, 1738
Alley, G. R., 81–82, 958
Alley, J., 1229
Allington, R. L., 1296
Almanza, E., 1436
Almeida, M. C., 69
Almond, M., 739, 821, 850, 861, 868, 881, 908, 1014, 1017, 1084, 1240, 1248, 1455, 1467
Almond, P., 1553
Alonso, L., 1693
Alpers, B. J., 288
Alter, M., 832, 1313
Altman, K., 1374
Altrocchi, J., 461
Alvarado, C. G., 1921
Alvarez, W. F., 1188
Alves, W. M., 1836
Alvino, J. J., 821
Alvis, G. R., 872, 1545
AMA Drug Evaluations, 1807
Amabile, T. M., 993
Aman, M. G., 1718
Amari, A., 1415
Ambrosini, P. J., 593
Ameli, N. O., 872
American Academy of Family Physicians, 1758
American Academy of Pediatrics, 1334, 1336, 1452
American Association for the Advancement of Science, 86
American Association of Collegiate Registrars and Admissions Officers, 733
American Association of Health, Physical Education and Recreation, 1369

American Association of Mental Deficiency, 626
American Association on Mental Retardation, 1171
American Council on Education, 102
American Counseling Association, 703
American Diabetes Association, 584
American Educational Research Association, 88, 980
American Foundation for the Blind, 620
American Liver Foundation, 792
American Medical Association, 107
American National Standards Institute, 180, 181
American Occupational Therapy Association, 1284
American Orthopsychiatric Association, 92, 1302
American Printing House for the Blind, 93
American Psychiatric Association, 20, 54, 68, 75, 112, 124, 126, 166, 235, 280, 303, 365, 367, 448, 564, 587, 628, 657, 674, 676, 684, 686, 688, 695, 716, 895, 1134, 1155, 1172, 1191, 1283, 1348, 1352, 1385, 1463, 1595, 1628, 1715, 1717, 1727, 1746, 1802, 1804, 1815
American Psychological Association, 250, 703, 1269
American School Counselors Association, 703
American Society of Clinical Hypnosis-Education and Research Foundation, 916
American Speech-Language-Hearing Association, 37, 82, 187, 254
Americans with Disabilities Act of 1990, 97
Ames, C., 1497
Ames, L. B., 103, 815, 816, 1067, 1627
Amidon, E. J., 1878
Amir, S., 689
Amit, Z., 689
Ammons, C. H., 1340, 1456
Ammons, D. C., 1707
Ammons, P. W., 1318

Ammons, R. B., 399, 1457
Amonette, L., 592
Ampola, M. G., 1178
Anarnow, J., 924
Anastas, J. W., 1635
Anastasi, A., 22, 32, 107, 135, 150, 300, 435, 481, 577, 970, 1275, 1307, 1522, 1711
Anastasi, A. A., 502
Anastasiow, N., 1929
Anastasiow, N. J., 108, 794
Anastopolous, A. D., 171, 775
Anderson, A. C., 1061, 1062
Anderson, A. E., 114
Anderson, C., 804
Anderson, D. R., 612
Anderson, E., 65, 1155
Anderson, F., 1156
Anderson, G. M., 193
Anderson, J. E., 832
Anderson, K., 1094, 1135, 1161, 1257, 1557, 1564, 1772, 1847, 1852
Anderson, K. N., 1557
Anderson, L., 1142
Anderson, L. M., 1760
Anderson, L. T., 1098
Anderson, M. A., 1782
Anderson, M. L., 108
Anderson, P. L., 1928
Anderson, R., 1441
Anderson, R. C., 1296, 1489, 1490, 1499
Anderson, R. M., 927
Anderson, R. P., 917
Anderson, S., 286
Anderson, S. R., 194
Anderson, T. H., 1490
Andreasen, N. C., 1728
Andrews, J., 316
Andrulonis, P., 38
Andrulonis, P. A., 1361
Angel, R., 1181
Angle, C. R., 1730
Angoff, W. H., 1077
Angst, J., 266
Aninger, M., 933
Anisfeld, M., 574
Anisman, H., 106
Anker, J., 615
Anker, S., 950
Annegers, J. F., 1834
Annett, M., 854, 875, 1092, 1093
Annis, L. F., 1388
Annuals of the Deaf, 1156
Ansara, A. S., 1656
Ansel, B., 82

Apasche, J., 69
Apgar, V., 128, 886
Apolloni, T., 1662
Aponte, J. F., 643
Apostolos, M. K., 159
Appelbaum, M. I., 1382
Appelboom-Fondu, J., 1463
Applebaum, A. S., 755
Appleby, J. A., 1815
Applefield, 1280
Applefield, J. M., 50, 68, 265
Applefield, P., 778
Applefield, P. F., 39, 1388
Applegate, B., 171
Apsche, J., 1473
Apt, R., 423
Arajarvi, T., 1230
Aram, D., 564
Aram, D. M., 345, 363
Aramburo, D., 1264, 1356
Arbitman-Smith, R., 503
Arc of the United States,
    The, 140
Archer, R. P., 280, 1198
Ardila, A., 652
Ardilla, A., 1675
Ardizzone, J., 56
Arena, A. M., 27
Arick, J. R., 940
Ariel, R., 1124
Arieti, S., 480
Arizona Deaf-Blind Pro-
    gram, 538
Arky, R., 38
Armitage, T. R., 148
Arms, V. M., 442
Armstrong, B. B., 220
Armstrong, D. F., 318
Armstrong, F. D., 708
Armstrong, M., 201
Armstrong, P. M., 1612
Armstrong, R. G., 185
Armstrong, S. W., 1145
Arnold, B. R., 1181
Arnold, C. R., 1780
Arnold, L., 1930
Arnold, L. E., 258
Arnow, B., 409
Aronfreed, J., 1287
Aronson, A., 1894
Arredondo, G. A., 1182
Arredondo, K. R., 1117,
    1120, 1562
Arredondo, P., 881
Arricale, B., 216, 633,
    1310
Arrigo, H. R., 1472
Arrington, R. E., 1806
Arter, J. A., 72, 138, 589,
    1452, 1769
Arthritis Foundation, 151
Artiles, A., 1356
Artiles, A. J., 250, 513, 514,
    1271
Artuso, D. A., 611
Arvedson, J. C., 639
Asarnow, J., 1151
Asbury, C. A., 1310
Ascione, F. R., 229, 1231
Asesoría General de Edu-
    cación Especial, 472
Asghar, K., 751
Ash, M., 444

Ash, M. J., 359, 603, 1204,
    1391
Ashburn, E. A., 956
Ashburn, S. S., 1416
Ashcroft, S., 1155
Ashen, M. J., 1707
Asher, J. J., 1109
Asher, S. R., 1662
Ashlock, R. B., 24
Ashworth, M. R., 13
Asmus, J. M., 780
Asp, C., 1877
Asperger, H., 369
Associate Consultants, 1442
Association for Children
    with Learning Disabili-
    ties, 1069
Association of Persons with
    Severe Handicaps, 929
Asthma and Allergy Foun-
    dation of America, 162
Astin, A. W., 1086
Astuto, T. A., 1890
Atim, S., 61, 1683
Atkeson, B. M., 616
Atkins, L., 1857
Atkins, M., 1676
Atkinson, J., 950
Atkinson, J. W., 31, 1352
Atkinson, L., 1595
Atkinson, R. C., 1039
Atler, M., 516
Attanucci, J. S., 266
Atwater, M., 1259
Atwell, C. W., 1715
Auden, W. H., 124
Audette, B., 1691
Audette, D., 1433
August, J. A., 560
Aukerman, R. C., 954, 1925
Ault, M. H., 782
Aumend, S. A., 46
Ausburn, F. B., 1089
Ausburn, L. J., 1089
Austin, G. A., 416
Austin, J. D., 902
Austin, J. S., 559
Austin, W. G., 125, 364,
    1461
Australian Education
    Council, 190
Ausubel, D. P., 50, 443
Auxter, D., 34, 1372
Avant, A. H., 1030
Avery, D. L., 194
Avery, G., 289
Avery, M. E., 1349
Avezaat, C. J., 264
Aviezer, Y., 1349
Avioli, L. V., 33
Avni, E. F., 1853
Axelrod, F. B., 730
Axelrod, S., 69, 1473
Axline, V., 1393
Axtell, L., 1100
Ayer, F. C., 42
Ayers, A. J., 202–203, 837
Ayllon, T., 202, 688, 1720,
    1807
Aylward, G. P., 437
Ayres, A., 1347
Ayres, A. J., 721, 1345, 1453,
    1528, 1622,

Ayres, L. P., 1545
Azrin, N. H., 562, 696, 1156,
    1400, 1473, 1612, 1808,
    1850
Azuma, H., 511

Babbie, E. R., 625
Baca, L., 591, 1109, 1356
Baca, L. M., 1436
Bach, R., 688
Bachara, G. H., 547
Bachman, J. G., 76
Bachman, L. F., 1506
Bachor, D., 316
Bachor, D. G., 315
Backer, T., 49
Backiel, M., 163
Backman, J., 1111
Baddeley, A. D., 1165
Badderley, M., 1259
Badian, N. A., 634
Baehner, R. L., 1100
Baer, D., 788
Baer, D. M., 3, 207, 249, 803,
    1282, 1287, 1544, 1719,
    1820, 1948
Baer, J. S., 925
Bagby, G., 1837
Baghurst, P., 1062
Bagnato, S. J., 1251, 1420,
    1422
Bahling, E., 1732
Bahr, J., 878
Baiby, R., 864
Bailey, D., 781, 1399
Bailey, D. B., 949
Bailey, D. B., Jr., 510, 524,
    781, 951, 1220
Bailey, E., 648
Bailey, J. D., 1857
Bailey, J. S., 1337
Bailey, R., 248, 850, 1760,
    1895, 1905
Bailey-Dempsey, C. A., 1594
Bailey-Richardson, B., 1041
Baillargeon, R., 31, 158
Baillie, E., 159
Baine, D., 144
Bajan, J. W., 1425
Bajema, C. J., 1018
Bakan, P., 1093
Baker, B., 159, 1770
Baker, B. L., 544, 1894
Baker, C., 80
Baker, D. B., 1223
Baker, E., 227
Baker, E. H., 1774
Baker, H., 1595
Baker, J., 1766
Baker, J. M., 928
Baker, K., 537
Baker, L., 54, 1179, 1317
Baker, M., 80
Baker, S., 537
Bakere, C. A., 1265
Bakker, D., 571
Bakker, D. J., 284, 855
Baldwin, A. Y., 507
Baldwin, J. A., 698
Baldwin, V., 1441
Baldy, M., 130, 920
Balester, R. J., 1637
Balise, R., 1304

Ball, J., 1094, 1852
Ball, P. M., 1374
Balla, D. A., 35, 1880, 1881
Balla, D., 19, 503, 1380,
    1950
Ballaban-Gil, K., 556
Ballard, J., 306
Ballard, K. D., 1263
Ballard, T. A., 256
Ballard-Campbell, M., 977
Ballard-Rosa, 1427
Balling, J. D., 575
Balow, B., 260, 1134, 1345,
    1454, 1557, 1639
Baltaxe, C., 1293
Bambara, L., 783
Bambara, L. M., 1738
Banbury, M. M., 1823
Bandler, R., 1258
Bandura, A., 69, 207–208,
    223, 236, 237, 240, 395,
    580, 675, 1117, 1168,
    1280, 1497, 1508, 1663
Bang, M-Y., 429
Banks, C. A., 511
Banks, J., 511
Banks, J. A., 497, 1355
Banks, S. R., 1251
Bankson, N., 152
Bankson, N. W., 1784
Bannatyne, A., 773, 780,
    1528
Bannatyne, A. D., 208–209
Barabas, G., 1098, 1155
Barbaro, F., 1069, 1086
Barbe, W., 823, 861
Barbe, W. B., 818, 822
Barbizet, J., 1164
Barbour, A. B., 1161
Barbour, D. E., 792
Barbrack, C. S., 716
Barcus, M., 428, 1735
Bard, B., 374
Barden, T. P., 709
Bardo, M. T., 352
Bardon, J., 1597
Bardon, J. I., 209, 247
Barenbaum, E., 1932, 1936
Barglow, P., 648
Baringer, J. R., 687
Barker, L. H., 1789
Barker, R., 194
Barker, R. G., 1508
Barkley, R., 1717
Barkley, R. A., 38, 166, 169,
    170, 630, 743
Barkus, C., 1603
Barlow, D., 1220
Barlow, D. H., 222, 328, 717,
    1221, 1536, 1647
Barlow, I. H., 22
Barltrop, D., 1061
Barnard, C. P., 19, 46, 356,
    360
Barnes, K. E., 1423
Barnes, S. E., 555
Barnett, A., 1259
Barnett, D. W., 651, 1420,
    1474
Barnett, L. A., 1782
Barnett, S. W., 1406
Barnett, W. S., 1944
Barnhart, C. L., 1113

Barnwell, D. A., 510
Baroff, G. A., 788
Baron, E. B., 603
Baron, I., 1590
Baron, J., 416
Baron, M., 1804
Baron, M. A., 1050
Baron, R. A., 68
Bar-On, R., 968
Barona, A., 250, 1669
Baroody, A. J., 1785
Barowsky, E. I., 109, 370,
    674, 730, 1313
Barr, A. S., 42
Barr, H. M., 748, 848
Barr, M. L., 384
Barr, R. D., 1129
Barraga, N., 664, 1057,
    1594
Barraga, N. C., 210, 787,
    1122, 1322, 1884, 1885
Barrera, R. D., 1537
Barrett, C., 1263
Barrett, C. L., 1366
Barrett, E. K., 285
Barrett, M. C., 46
Barron, A. P., 1775
Barron, F., 819
Barron, S., 748
Barsch, R., 1347
Barsch, R. H., 212, 1217,
    1341, 1343, 1345, 1452,
    1552, 1816
Barsh, E. T., 764
Barsh, R., 1320
Bartel, N. R., 39, 316, 490
Barteneiff, I., 531
Barth, R. P., 374
Bartlett, C. J., 773
Bartlett, C. S., 1158
Bartlett, J. A., 879
Bartley, S., 1885
Barton, C. J., 229
Barton, L. E., 213, 214, 237,
    326, 559, 1732
Bartosik, V., 106
Bartro, J. J., 382
Baser, C. A., 415
Bash, M. A. S., 313, 1800
Bashford, A., 986
Baskin, E. J., 1666
Bass, L., 194
Bass, M. S., 1636
Basser, L. S., 362
Bassis, M. S., 1671
Bassuk, E. L., 849, 1106,
    1361, 1714, 1801
Bateman, B., 52, 215, 881,
    1497
Bateman, B. D., 1754, 1795
Bates, E., 976
Bates, H. G., 32
Bates, J. E., 1774
Bates, P., 67, 427, 785, 1661,
    1799, 1827, 1948
Bath, H., 1374
Bat-Haee, M. A., 1550
Batshaw, M. L., 165, 166,
    311, 637, 706, 709, 747,
    766, 869, 926, 1363, 1940
Batshaw, R. L., 265
Battegay, R., 955

Battison, R., 756
Battle, C., 1871
Baucom, L. D., 1440
Bauer, A. M., 117, 164, 732, 1602, 1723, 1781
Bauer, J. N., 1073
Bauer, R. H., 413
Bauerschmidt, E., 1349
Bauerschmidt, E. R., 264, 1144, 1415
Bauerschmidt, M., 1349
Baum, D. D., 876, 905
Bauman, J. F., 213
Bauman, K. E., 1616
Bauman, M., 130
Baumeister, A., 201, 1618
Baumeister, A. A., 217, 773, 1714
Baumgart, D., 1323, 1766
Baumrind, D., 647
Baurie, P., 507
Bauters, M., 1676
Bauwens, J., 1766
Bawkin, H., 688
Bawkin, R. M., 688
Bayer, C. A., 1850
Bayley, N., 217, 573
Bayroff, A. G., 136
Beale, I. L., 854, 1092, 1558
Beales, J. G., 151
Bean, F. D., 714
Bean, M. F., 277
Bean, T. W., 925
Bear, R. M., 880
Bearn, A. G., 926
Beattie v. State Board of Education of Wisconsin, 1560
Beattie, G. W., 798
Beattie, J., 1859
Beattie, J. R., 478, 491, 617, 913, 1103, 1435, 1639, 1654, 1722, 1724
Beattie, S., 1195
Beauchamp, G. R., 527, 597, 914, 1546, 1547, 1780
Beauchamp, T. L., 703
Beaudoin, A. R., 1780
Beaumont, J., 343
Beaumont, J. G., 1705
Beaven, M., 1930
Beaver, D. P., 1707
Bechtel, D. R., 1400
Bechterev, V. M., 219
Beck, A. T., 55, 240, 1730
Beck, G. R., 624
Beck, I. L., 1488
Beck, M., 1293
Beck, M. D., 1785
Becker, H. S., 1047
Becker, W. C., 131, 144, 219, 1318, 1415, 1780
Beckers, C., 453
Bedell, B. T., 968
Beech, H. R., 1283
Beer, M., 1299
Beers, C., 360
Beers, C. W., 220
Beery, K. D., 1887
Beery, K. E., 220, 721
Beery, R., 819
Beeson, P. M., 424
Begali, V., 1828, 1833

Begley, S., 1062
Behan, P., 1092
Behan, P., 80
Behan, P., 854
Behnke, M., 646
Behrman, R., 1019, 1306, 1814
Behrman, R. E., 166, 295, 319, 593, 1703
Beilin, H., 411, 1377
Beirne-Smith, M., 1429
Beiser, H. R., 399
Bejar, I. I., 24
Belcerek, M., 1394
Belch, P. J., 884
Belfer, M. L., 708
Belkin, G. S., 1505
Belknap, J. K., 76
Bell, A. G., 242
Bell, D. B., 118
Bell, J., 766
Bell, R., 469
Bell, R. Q., 612, 647, 1084, 1319, 1589
Bell, S., 409
Bell, T. H., 242–243
Bellack, L., 1797
Bellamy, G., 321
Bellamy, G. T., 1205, 1822, 1824
Bellamy, W. E., Jr., 910
Bellanca, J., 150
Bellinger, D., 1061
Bellinger, D. C., 168, 1062
Bellodi, L., 382
Bell-Ruppert, N., 603
Bellugi, U., 95, 537, 1136, 1647
Bellvue Hospital Center, 243
Belmont, I., 1148
Belmont, J. M., 416
Belmont, L., 187, 266
Bemis, K. M., 113
Bemis, S. E., 136
Bempechat, J., 1497
Benady, S., 730
Benbow, C. P., 1725
Benda, C. E., 13
Bender, B., 1856
Bender, L., 185, 244–245, 364, 367, 764, 913, 1389
Bender, L. A., 1552
Bender, R., 1296
Benderly, B. L., 1296
Bendro, L. K., 1779
Beneke, A. Y., 162
Benjamin, L. T., Jr., 401
Bennett, A. T., 498, 510
Bennett, C. I., 660, 1088
Bennett, E. L., 648, 989
Bennett, F. C., 1429
Bennett, G. K., 136, 481
Bennett, J., 1019
Bennett, J. W., 15
Bennett, K. J., 448
Bennett, P., 295
Bennett, R., 956
Bennett, R. E., 922, 1082, 1298, 1364, 1443, 1514, 1515, 1521
Bennett, T., 118, 665
Bennett, V. C., 246–247
Bennion, K., 1190

Ben-Porath, Y. S., 1196
Bensberg, G. J., 842
Bensky, J., 1758
Benson, B. A., 1730
Benson, D. F., 361, 652, 1506
Benson, D. R., 1601
Bentler, P. M., 75, 1327
Benton, A. L., 104, 345, 570, 815, 913
Benton, A. L. M., 115
Benton, D., 1161
Bentz, J. L., 1337
Bentzen, F. A., 285, 611
Berbaum, M. L., 266
Berdine, W. H., 215, 522, 901, 927
Bereiter, C., 144, 247, 598, 691, 1935
Bereiter, G., 674
Berenson, C., 1479
Berent, S., 1155
Berg, B., 615, 616
Berg, B. O., 1853
Berg, I., 1595
Berg, J. M., 483, 626, 1940
Berg, R. A., 118, 286, 555, 596, 665, 677, 740
Berg, W. K., 780
Bergan, J., 1326
Bergan, J. R., 3, 170, 222, 223, 459, 1327, 1764, 1840
Berger, B. J., 610
Berger, K., 1296
Berger, M., 1317
Berger, P., 1828
Berger, R., 1510
Bergerud, D., 1119
Bergeson, T., 644
Bergholz, K., 114
Bergin, V., 887
Bergman, P., 912
Bergmann, K., 1164
Bergsma, D., 950, 1274, 1942
Beritic, T., 1061
Berk, 294
Berk, L. E., 1664
Berk, R. A., 488, 1268, 1952
Berkell, D. E., 427
Berkow, R., 384, 636, 1364
Berkowitz, 1553
Berkowitz, G., 162, 199, 466, 1108, 1665, 1668, 1869
Berkowitz, R. I., 1385
Berkson, G., 1714
Berlin, C., 334
Berlin, C. M., 1334
Berlinger, D. C., 1761
Berlyne, D., 174
Berman, A., 547
Berman, G., 685
Bermúdez, A., 507
Bernard, H. W., 906
Bernbaum, J. C., 709
Berndt, T. J., 267, 576
Berney, B. L., 1061
Berney, M., 1757
Bernfeld, G. A., 925
Bernheimer, L., 1776
Bernheimer, L. P., 1036
Bernier, J., 587
Berniger, V., 611

Bernikis, E. A., 613
Berninger, V. W., 1565
Bernstein, B., 673
Bernstein, D. K., 1053
Bernstein, H. K., 359
Bernstein, M., 963
Bernstein, N. R., 1143
Bernthal, J., 152
Berring, R. C., 742
Berrueta-Clement, J. R., 1944
Berry, H. K., 1362
Berry, K., 508
Berry, M. F., 347
Bersoff, D., 17, 700, 1268, 1325
Bersoff, D. N., 457, 609, 631, 700, 735, 896, 1519, 1892
Bertschi, J. D., 1419
Besag, F. M., 1274
Bess, F. H., 184
Besson, F., 1906
Best, G. A., 1313
Betkouski, M., 1758
Bettelheim, B., 193, 248, 367, 646, 745, 1300
Bettison, S., 189
Betts, E. A., 952, 1911
Beukelman, D., 82
Bevins, S. A., 828
Beyerstein, B. L., 1259
Bhat, V. K., 1904
Bhatara, V., 258
Biaggio, M. K., 579
Bialer, I., 248
Bickel, H., 453
Bickel, W. E., 609, 1514, 1591
Bickerstaff, E. R., 12
Biddle, B. J., 671
Biederman, J., 168, 171, 1717
Bieliauskas, V. J., 904
Biemiller, A., 1162
Biernath, K., 1402
Biernath, K. R., 1402
Biesanz, K. Z., 471
Biesanz, M. H., 471
Biesanz, R., 471
Bigelow, K. M., 195
Bigge, J., 318, 867, 1301
Bigge, J. L., 529, 1642
Bigi, L., 399
Bigler, E. D., 174, 261, 331, 549, 826, 1277, 1474, 1555, 1728, 1787, 1836, 1941
Bijou, S. W., 249–250, 782, 1287
Biklen, D., 856
Biklen, D. P., 725
Bilenker, R., 1155
Billman, J., 1776
Bimbela, A., 195
Binder, C., 195, 1413
Binder, G. A., 331
Binder, L. M., 1836
Bindler, R., 1094, 1852
Bindra, D., 1806
Binet, A., 11, 255
Bingol, N., 750
Bini, L., 676

Birbaumer, N., 1602
Birch, D. R., 1879
Birch, H., 887
Birch, H. G., 13, 187, 262–263, 625, 683, 710, 988, 1148, 1774
Birch, J., 1470, 1582, 1722
Birch, J. W., 263–264, 326, 486, 590, 662, 664, 805, 1001, 1306, 1344, 1348, 1365, 1557, 1630
Birrell, J., 918
Bish, C. E., 822
Bishop, C. H., 1190
Bishop, D. V. M., 363, 1093
Bishop, K. D., 1612
Bishop, M., 982, 1114
Bisighini, R., 325, 358, 454, 720
Biskin, B. H., 136
Bitgood, S. C., 1374
Bitter, J. A., 1893
Bittle, R. G., 766
Bittner, E., 579
Bjerrum, J., 1166
Blaauw, G., 912
Blacher, J., 838, 1185
Blacher-Dixon, J., 824
Black, A., 1285
Black, D., 732
Black, F. W., 1163, 1177
Black, H., 1143, 1268
Black, J. L., 1304
Black, P., 1844
Black, P. D., 166
Black, R. S., 428
Black, S., 1143
Black's medical dictionary, 1572
Blackhurst, A. E., 215, 522, 901, 927
Blackman, L. S., 18
Blackman, M., 556
Blackman, S., 419
Blackwood, R. O., 1154
Blair, T. R., 1502, 1525
Blake, J., 266
Blake, K. A., 215
Blakely, E., 194
Blakeslee, D., 1796
Blakeslee, T., 782
Blakiston's Gould medical dictionary, 115, 311, 636, 697
Blakiston's pocket medical dictionary, 1099
Blanchard, E. B., 258
Blaney, C., 1796
Blankenship, C. S., 1145
Blanton, B., 139
Blanton, G. H., 534
Blanton, R. L., 186
Blasch, B. B., 621
Blaschke, C., 1567
Blass, E. M., 446
Blaszczynski, A., 201
Blatner, H. A., 1451
Blatt, B., 269, 526, 905, 1950
Blattner, K. C., 1152
Blau, A. F., 325
Bleck, E. E., 347, 869, 1226
Bleck, E. G., 179

Bledsoe, C. W., 1203
Bless, G., 1738, 1742
Blessed, G., 1164
Blessing, K. R., 43, 1315
Blesz, D., 928
Blisk, D., 615
Bliss, C. K., 274
Bliss, L., 1292
Bliss, L. S., 1506
Bloch, V., 693, 1163
Block, E. E., 628
Block, J. R., 954
Block, J. H., 1142
Block, N., 1249
Block, N. J., 989
Block, S. R., 1642
Blom, G. E., 408, 1509, 1637
Blond, J., 1806
Bloodstein, O., 1697
Bloom, B., 1659
Bloom, B. S., 275, 520, 523,
  811, 821, 827, 1065, 1142,
  1419, 1755
Bloom, F., 1306
Bloom, F. E., 31, 551, 689,
  826
Bloom, L., 1456
Bloom, M. R., 1666
Bloomfield, L., 1113
Blosser, J., 1841
Blosser, J. L., 1829
Blount, N., 1934
Blount, R. L., 302
Bluestone, C. D., 1308
Blum, A., 1398
Blum, K., 674, 698, 851,
  1106
Blum, K. B., 1466, 1818
Blum, R., 1159
Bluma, S., 1399
Blume, H. W., 1464
Blume, R. A., 906
Blumenthal, A. L., 1455
Blythe, B. J., 374
Bobak, I., 1557
Bobak, I. M., 1144
Bobath, B., 951
Bobath, K., 276, 951, 1257
Bober, H., 302
Boberg, E., 404
Bobic, J., 246
Bochner, S., 189
Bock, R. D., 1328
Boder, E., 276, 1085
Boehm, A., 1422
Bogdan, R., 856
Bogen, J. E., 1625
Bogen, J. H., 874
Bogen, T. E., 872
Boggs, E. M., 566
Bohr, V., 1166
Boies, S. J., 173
Bolen, L. M., 1150
Boles, S. M., 1205, 1824
Bolick, N., 394
Bolinsky, K., 933
Boll, T., 1155
Boll, T. J., 853, 1158
Bollinger, M., 504
Bolmeier, E. C., 299
Bologna, N. B., 579
Bolter, J. F., 1844
Bolton, B., 245

Bolton, F. E., 1390
Bolton, L. W., 75, 352
Bond, G. L., 1503, 1527
Bond, I. K., 717
Bond, V., 1385
Bondi, J., 468
Bonet, J. P., 279–280
Bonstrom, 1418
Bontke, C. F., 1834
Bonwick, M., 1572
Boocock, S. S., 1671
Boodoo, G. M., 338, 658, 802,
  1709, 1952
Booker, H. E., 119
Boomer, L., 734
Boon, R., 879
Boone, D. R., 424, 853
Boone, R., 1824
Booth, T., 1862, 1907
Boothby, P., 823
Bootzin, R., 259, 1456
Bootzin, R. R., 1807
Borchardt, F. L., 439
Borden, K. A., 527, 593
Bordier, J., 1396
Bordier, N., 1395
Borkowski, J. G., 418, 681,
  925, 1153
Borland, J. H., 507
Borlée-Grimée, I., 451
Bormans, J., 1714
Borstein, P. H., 1616
Borteryu, J. P., 749
Bortner, M., 887
Bos, C. S., 940, 1932
Bosch, J., 855
Boschee, F., 1050
Boshe, B., 1067
Bosker, R. J., 1591
Bosman, A. J., 1405
Boss, M., 1727
Bossert, S. T., 1593
Bostock, R., 1274
Bosworth, K., 629
Botel, M., 1498
Bottel, H., 1411
Bottomley, P. A., 1278
Bouchard, T. J., Jr., 1249
Bouchard, T., 1774
Boudah, D. J., 928, 1766
Bootzin, R., 259, 1456
Boué, A., 452
Boué, J., 452
Boulware, B. J., 213
Bourbeau, P. E., 1735
Bourdot, M., 1878
Boustany, R. M., 288
Bouvet, D., 542
Bowen, H. R., 47
Bowen, M., 364
Bower, B. D., 555, 1853
Bower, E. M., 280–281, 683
Bower, G. H., 343, 382, 693,
  1163
Bower, T. G. R., 371, 411
Bowers, W. A., 246
Bowlby, J., 46, 126, 575, 646,
  728, 1623
Bowman, B. T., 497
Boyan, C., 321, 377
Boyd, H. F., 1009
Boyd, T. A., 1913
Boyer, M. G., 1839

Boykin, R. A., 1616
Boyle, M. H., 167, 448, 683
Braaten, S., 458
Bracht, G. H., 137
Bracken, B., 1902
Bracken, B. A., 281, 774,
  1420, 1864
Bradburn, N. M., 1479
Braddick, F., 950
Braddick, O., 950
Braddock, D., 544
Braden, J. P., 19, 1902
Bradfield, R. H., 1757
Bradford, T. S., 696
Bradley, C., 364
Bradley, C. L., 404
Bradley, K. L., 170
Bradley, L. J., 519
Bradley, R. H., 266, 312,
  711, 1423
Bradley, S., 1230
Bradley, S. J., 280
Bradley, V. J., 842
Brady, M., 158, 442
Brady, M. P., 805, 1103
Brady, S., 229
Braff, A. M., 46
Bragg, B., 1208
Bragg, W. A., 1265
Brahm, R. M., 760
Braidwood, T., 282
Braille, L., 283–284
Brain Injury Association,
  290, 1835
Brainerd, C. J., 30, 158
Braithwaite, R., 349
Braithwaite, R. L., 510
Bran, A. W., Jr., 709
Branca, R. A., 533
Brand, J. S., 534, 787, 1228,
  1693, 1884
Brandstater, M. E., 1834
Brandt, R., 275
Brann, A., Jr., 154
Brann, A. W., 264
Brannigan, G. G., 246
Brannigan, M. J., 246
Bransfield, S., 421
Bransford, J. D., 1179
Brantlinger, E., 1396
Braswell, D., 318, 769, 1516,
  1586, 1906
Braswell, L., 171, 221
Bratteseni, K., 1337
Braud, L., 258
Braud, W. G., 258
Braun, C., 670
Braun, H. I., 1783
Brauntlinger, E. A., 1641
Brawell, D., 1146
Brawner, J., 1297
Bray, G. A., 1279
Brazelton, T. B., 292–293,
  1252
Brazier, M. A. B., 741
Brazil, N., 883
Brebner, J., 1776
Bredosian, 84
Breen, M., 220
Breese, G. R., 1098
Bregman, J. D., 767
Breier, A., 260
Bremer, D. L., 951

Brengelman, S., 1604
Brennan, E. L., 1427
Brennan, R. L., 803
Brennan, W., 1861
Brenner, A., 760
Breslin, M., 1042
Bresnan, M. J., 1227
Bretherton, I., 576, 1272
Breunig, N., 1604
Brewster, A., 106
Bricker, D., 648, 788, 1860
Bricker, W. A., 1879
Bridgman, L. D., 293–294
Brigance, A. H., 294
Briggs, L. J., 194
Briggs, T., 951
Brigham, T. A., 1616
Brim, O. G., Jr., 645
Brinker, R. P., 111
Brinkerhoff, L., 610
Brislin, R., 1354
Bristol, M., 194
Bristol, M. M., 464
British Medical Journal,
  1458
Britton, G. E., 1489
Britton, W. H., 1001, 1389
Broadbent, D. E., 341, 594
Broadbooks, D. Y., 562, 595,
  1031–1033, 1723
Broadbooks, D., 217, 651
Broca, P., 342, 1261
Broca, P. P., 295–296
Brockhaus, U., 414
Brodal, A., 826
Brodin, J., 295
Brodsky, C., 279
Brodsky, L., 639
Brody, G. H., 1231
Brodzinsky, D. M., 46, 68
Brolin, D., 434
Brolin, D. E., 321, 529, 1429
Bromley, K., 1406
Bronfenbrenner, U., 297
Bronson, W. C., 576, 1662
Brook, R. H., 784
Brooke, G. A. G., 701
Brooke, V., 428
Brooks, G. W., 1818
Brooks, J., 949
Brooks, M. J., 496
Brooks, R., 954, 1351, 1528
Brooks-Gunn, J., 949, 1610
Brookshire, R. H., 718
Brophy, J., 395, 1337
Brophy, J. E., 640, 1760
Brouillette, R. T., 1775
Brouwer, W. H., 1838
Browder, D. M., 1732
Brown, A., 413
Brown, A. C., 417
Brown, A. L., 297–298, 1153,
  1179, 1950
Brown, A. M., 1093
Brown, B. F., 615
Brown, D., 1597
Brown, D. T., 476, 1597
Brown, F., 520
Brown, F. M., 1472
Brown, G., 1836
Brown, G. I., 905
Brown, J., 1428
Brown, J. A. C., 687, 1224

Brown, J. E., 165, 823
Brown, J. L., 709
Brown, J. S., 24, 223
Brown, J. W., 906
Brown, L., 67, 298, 426, 431,
  520, 523, 538, 785, 788,
  801, 1203, 1323, 1754,
  1790, 1859, 1948
Brown, M. B., 909
Brown, M. G., 1817
Brown, P. A., 1665
Brown, R., 587
Brown, R. T., 38, 39, 120,
  260, 269, 299, 385, 445,
  487, 501, 526, 593, 623,
  645, 647, 652, 680, 684,
  704, 707, 725, 728, 743,
  745, 747, 752, 760, 766,
  792, 878, 963, 973, 987,
  988, 1023, 1025, 1128,
  1199, 1280, 1286, 1362,
  1385, 1544, 1548, 1747,
  1796, 1808
Brown, S., 484, 1321, 1727
Brown, S. A., 448
Brown, T. L., 284
Brown, T. R., 119
Brown, V., 1001
Brown, W. T., 766
Brown, Z. W., 689
Brown-Cheatham, M., 492
Browne, E., 1231
Brownell, H. H., 604, 1559
Brownell, K. D., 717
Brubaker, R. G., 124, 245,
  280, 627, 682, 1178, 1350,
  1386, 1610, 1797
Bruce, C. O., 111, 373, 1206,
  1623, 1707
Bruce, D. A., 345, 1834
Bruce, T., 1207
Bruch, H., 113
Bruder, M. B., 648, 1335,
  1824
Bruhns, B., 61, 1682
Bruininks, R. H., 300, 1275
Bruininks, R. J., 35
Bruininks, R. K., 1586
Bruininks, V. L., 857, 906
Brulle, A., 17
Brulle, A. R., 116, 464, 1111,
  1804, 1805, 1807
Brumback, R. A., 556
Brumbaugh, R. S., 1390
Brumberg, J. J., 112
Brummer, J. J., 1869
Brunder, E., 1795
Bruner, E. C., 1068, 1143
Bruner, J., 301, 976
Bruner, J. S., 416, 445, 695
Bruning, R. H., 50
Brunner, M., 547
Brunner, R. L., 1362
Brusca-Vega, R., 1436
Brutting, L. K., 1518, 1730
Bruun, R. D., 1804
Bryan, J., 958
Bryan, J. H., 1658
Bryan, L. H., 1658
Bryan, T., 634, 958, 1455
Bryan, T. H., 897, 1068
Bryan, T. S., 611
Bryant, B. R., 837, 1790

Bryant, D. C., 1707
Bryant, D. M., 4, 988, 989
Bryant, L. E., 1462, 1804
Bryant, N. R., 1951
Bryen, D., 83
Bryen, D. N., 1292
Brynska, A., 1624
Bryson, S. E., 192, 1230
Buchanan, M. L., 1534
Bucher, B., 1400
Buchsbaum, K., 70
Buchwach, L., 45
Buck, C. S., 159
Buck, J. N., 904
Bucy, J. E., 1792
Buda, F. B., 1226, 1675
Budd, K. S., 1464, 1804
Budden, S. S., 1548
Budoff, M., 1087, 1147, 1245, 1246, 1339, 1474
Buffery, A. W. H., 873
Buka, S. L., 784
Buktenica, N. A., 1887
Bulgarelli, O. A., 472
Bullard, C., 18, 443
Bullard, C. L., 184, 334, 1697
Bullard, H., 1398
Bulleit, T. N., 267
Bullis, G., 816
Bullock, L., 518
Bunch, G. O., 316
Bundesamt für Statistik, 1739
Bundesministerium, 813
Bunin, G. R., 292
Buonanno, F. S., 1278
Burak, J. A., 768
Bureau of Justice Statistics, 470
Bureau of Labor Statistics, 1893
Burello, J. M., 1767
Burello, L. C., 42, 43, 53, 1767
Burg, C., 638
Burgard, D., 1279
Burgdorf, R. L., 97
Burger, A. L., 18
Burgess, C. A., 725
Burgess, D. M., 748
Burke, C., 1200
Burke, P., 1440
Burke, P. J., 1316, 1441, 1471
Burke, P. M., 420
Burke, T., 314, 795, 1229, 1285, 1512
Burke, T. R., 33, 110, 1369
Burks, J., 1774
Burland, S., 1135
Bürli, A., 1741
Burlingame, A. W., 902
Burlingham, D., 273
Burnett, C. K., 1589
Burns, R. C., 1041
Burns, S., 503
Burns, W. J., 1252
Buros, O. K., 273, 307, 308, 1423, 1794
Burr, R., 1400
Burr, R. L., 1868
Burrello, D., 1090

Burrello, L. C., 1733
Burroughs, M., 824
Burrow, W. H., 1657
Burrows, D., 467
Burstein, N., 1355
Bursuck, W., 316
Bursuk, L. A., 138
Burt, C., 10, 308–309, 500, 1390
Burton, C., 1216
Burton, D., 1930
Burton, R. R., 223
Burton, S. B., 902
Burton, T. A., 1315
Busch, J. C., 1724
Busch-Rossnagel, N., 499
Bush, J. P., 615
Bushnell, I. W. R., 951
Buss, A. H., 1774
Busse, J., 1565
Busse, R., 146
Butcher, J. N., 1196
Butler, J. C., 279
Butler, K. G., 25, 604, 1050, 1054, 1056, 1411
Butler, S. R., 420
Butterfield, E. C., 416, 1392
Butters, N., 104
Butterworth, T., 562
Button, J., 858, 1192, 1518, 1865
Buysse, V., 510
Byrd, D., 200
Byrne, D., 68
Bzoch, K. R., 1506

Cabello, B., 1355
Caccamise, F., 1658
Caddy, G. R., 75
Cadoret, R. J., 1674
Caetano, A. P., 273
Cagauan, C. A., 1879
Cahill, M., 38
Cain, A. C., 912
Cain, E., 1594
Cairns, N., 663
Caladarci, T., 1760
Calculator, S., 84
Caldwell, B., 1669
Caldwell, B. M., 266, 311–312
Caldwell, B. W., 1421
Caldwell, J., 1775
Caldwell, M. L., 788
Caldwell, R. R., 159
Calfee, R., 174
California Department of Education, 1604
Callahan, C., 556
Callahan, K., 1639
Callahan, W. P., 553
Calore, D., 533
Calvert, D. R., 541
Camara, K. A., 616
Camara, W., 1711
Cameron, J., 993
Cameron, J. R., 1775
Cameron, M., 1775
Camfield, C. S., 118
Camp, B. W., 312–313, 408, 1800
Camp, L. T., 1419
Campbell, A., 1017, 1284

Campbell, A. G. M., 205
Campbell, A. J., 1751
Campbell, A. L., 872
Campbell, D., 1388
Campbell, D. M., 350
Campbell, D. P., 1723
Campbell, D. T., 466, 1534, 1713
Campbell, F. A., 4, 7, 711, 989
Campbell, F. J., 313
Campbell, J., 353
Campbell, J. Y., 554
Campbell, L., 869
Campbell, M., 193, 366, 369, 630
Campbell, M. F., 695
Campbell, P., 1373
Campbell, P. H., 1257
Campbell, R. F., 1864
Campbell, R. J., 636
Campbell, R. V., 195
Campbell, W., 399
Campione, J., 413
Campione, J. C., 1153, 1179, 1951
Campling, J., 1863
Campos, J. J., 1774
Camras, L. A., 399
Canadian Charter of Rights and Freedoms, 316
Canby, J., 1049
Candee, B. L., 1154
Candland, D. K., 746
Canivez, G. L., 773
Canning, C., 625
Canter, A., 510
Canter, L., 1267
Canter, M., 1267
Cantor, L., 395
Cantor, M., 395
Cantor-Graae, E., 1200
Cantrell, M. L., 319
Cantrell, R. P., 318–319
Cantwell, D., 1717
Capanelli, P., 612
Capildeo, R., 1314
Caplan, D., 129
Caplan, F., 1393
Caplan, G., 223, 461, 484
Caplan, P., 1635
Caplan, P. J., 1639
Caplan, T., 1393
Caple, F. S., 511
Cappelen, J., 1837
Cappelleri, J. C., 216
Capps, C. F., 1891
Capute, A., 1687
Capute, A. J., 347
Caputo, J., 1758
Carbino, R., 764
Carbo, M., 1089
Cardinal, D. N., 725
Carey, K. T., 2, 1625
Carey, R. G., 1400
Carey, S., 362
Carey, W. B., 1774
Caribbean Association for the Mentally Retarded or Developmental Disabilities, 323
Carjuzza, J., 1356
Carlberg, C., 844

Carlson, B., 796
Carlson, C., 1598
Carlson, C. F., 560
Carlson, C. L., 171, 167
Carlson, C. S., 1780
Carlson, E. A., 168
Carlson, F., 37
Carlson, G., 1717
Carlson, G. A., 171
Carlson, J. R., 1158
Carlson, L., 773
Carlson, M., 1403
Carlson, S. A., 590
Carlton, P. L., 848
Carman, R. A., 1190
Carmel, S. J., 756
Carmichael Olson, H., 748
Carnine, D., 194, 598, 1145, 1453
Carnine, D. W., 324, 599, 1552
Carpenter, B., 336
Carpenter, C. D., 294
Carpenter, D. G., 1429
Carpenter, J., 583
Carpenter, M., 433
Carpenter, M. B., 1474
Carpignano, J., 1301
Carr, A., 1400
Carr, C. J., 330
Carr, D., 1296
Carr, E., 1613
Carr, E. G., 1538, 1621
Carr, R. A., 111
Carr, T., 1751
Carrison, M. P., 1129
Carroll, J. B., 588, 964, 1096, 1249
Carroll, M. E., 1824
Carroll-Johnson, R. M., 320
Carrow, E., 325
Carrow-Woolfolk, E., 1050, 1053, 1055, 1290, 1292, 1332
Carson, G., 594
Carstens, A. A., 836
Carta, J. J., 708
Carter, C., 74, 493, 851, 909, 1714, 1814
Carter, C. O., 452
Carter, K. R., 1382
Cartwright, C., 857, 866, 1048, 1068, 1495, 1502, 1542, 1771
Cartwright, C. A., 26, 270, 327, 738, 876, 885, 901, 903, 934, 1218, 1288, 1630, 1659, 1816, 1883, 1884
Cartwright, C. P., 1659
Cartwright, D., 1542
Cartwright, G., 1048, 1935
Cartwright, G. P., 45, 270, 325–326, 327, 440, 738, 876, 885, 901, 903, 934, 1218, 1288, 1630, 1816, 1883, 1884
Cartwright, P., 857, 866, 1068, 1495, 1502, 1541, 1542, 1771
Cartwright, P. G., 26
Caruso, D., 968

Carver, R., 538, 1621
Cascino, G. D., 1278
Case, R., 522
Case, R. S., 412
Casey, A., 1417
Casey, P. H., 637
Cashmore, J., 511
Caskey, C. T., 1098
Caspari, I., 1905
Casper, J. K., 1894
Cassidy, J., 1738
Cassidy, S. B., 1409
Castaneda, A., 375
Casteel, J. D., 1869
Castellucci, V. F., 848
Casterline, D. C., 95, 1136
Castillo, G., 472
Castle, J., 1060
Castle, T. C., 829, 830, 831, 1331, 1333, 1399
Castonguay, L., 409
Cataldo, C., 1135, 1161
Cataldo, M. F., 562
Caterino, L. C., 250
Cattanach, A., 1391
Cattell, N. R., 1820
Cattell, R. B., 136, 494, 502, 727, 964, 1029, 1096, 1352, 1849, 1875
Cavalier, A. R., 1311
Cavallaro, C. C., 1427
Cavalli-Sforza, L. L., 877
Cavanaugh, J. C., 418
Cave, C., 1862
Cavenaugh, P. J., 446
Cawley, J. F., 148, 332, 786, 1144, 1146, 1525, 1657
Ceci, S., 1408
Ceci, S. J., 200, 1552
Cegelka, P. T., 482, 1540
Cegelka, W. G., 843
Celaya, C. Y., 1352, 1569
Center for Applied Special Technology, 333
Center for Field Research and School Services, 1113
Centers for Disease Control, 624, 629, 1061
Central Government of Peru, 1357
Centro Ann Sullivan, 1359
Cepeda, M., 118, 120
Cerletti, U., 676
Cermack, L. A., 345
Cerreto, M. C., 876
Certo, N., 1203, 1754
Céspedes, V. H., 472
Cessna, K., 1767
Cevey, B., 1602
Chace, M., 1216
Chadwick, O., 872, 1836
Chaffin, J. D., 1542
Chai, H., 80
Chaing, B., 1338
Chalfant, J., 492, 1212, 1885
Chalfant, J. C., 337, 350–351, 747, 1067, 1071, 1072, 1076, 1148, 1151, 1440, 1593, 1793
Chalkley, 1290
Chall, J., 1114, 1911
Chall, J. S., 351, 588, 1115
Chalmers, J. B., 70

Chamberlain, H. D., 1093
Chamberlin, P., 250
Chamot, A. U., 25, 604, 1110
Chan, K. S., 1218
Chan, S., 510, 643
Chan, S. Q., 497
Chandler, H. N., 683, 1195
Chandler, M. J., 645, 710, 1382
Chandra, P. S., 361
Chandra, R., 420
Chao, D., 1458
Chapey, R., 129, 296
Chapin, M., 177
Chapman, A. H., 1859
Chapman, C., 1050
Chapman, C. A., 331
Chapman, C. F., 1389
Chapman, J. W., 1262
Chard, R. L., 318, 1100
Charema, J., 62, 1683
Charles, B., 472
Charles, C. M., 395
Charlier, B., 540
Charnas, L. R., 1120
Charney, D. S., 260
Chase, J., 1156
Chase, J. A., 103
Chasen, B., 1295
Chatelanat, G., 187
Chatman, S. P., 1793
Chaudhry, M. R., 118
Cheek, E. H., 1503
Cheek, M. C., 1503
Chelune, G. J., 285
Cheney, C., 626
Cheng, L., 1604
Cherkes-Julkowski, M., 1145
Cherney, L. R., 1050, 1054
Cherniss, C., 907, 1584
Chernoff, G. F., 750
Cherrington, C., 82, 1200
Cherry, R., 183, 185, 334
Chesapeake Institute, 1629
Chess, S., 355–356, 683, 710, 1389, 1774
Chethik, M., 1232
Chevalier, R. L., 1398
Chi, M. T. H., 18
Children's Book Council, 1500
Children's Defense Fund, 374, 643
Children's Hope Foundation, 1334
Childress, J. F., 703
Childs, K. E., 782
Chimedza, R., 58, 59, 1679, 1681
Chinn, K. M., 183, 184, 334
Chinn, P. C., 250, 887
Chisholm, A. H., 1833
Chisolm, J. J., Jr., 1061
Cho, S., 792
Chomsky, A. N., 383
Chomsky, C., 1533
Chomsky, N., 1820
Chow, M. P., 165
Christ, B. A., 1766
Christ, M., 166
Christensen, C. C., 1119
Christenson, S., 1417, 1514

Christian, W. P., 194
Christiansen, B., 1727
Christiansen, J., 485, 1143
Christiansen, J. L., 485, 1143
Christie, D. J., 258
Christie, P., 1677
Christodoulou, G. N., 1859
Christophersen, E. R., 1415
Christophersen, R., 1374
Chubon, R. A., 1637
Churchill, J. A., 13
Chusid, J. G., 384, 677, 837
Chyczij, M. A., 594
Cicchetti, D., 711
Cicchetti, D. V., 35, 1880, 1881
Cichon, R. J., 1757
Cicirelli, V. G., 866
Ciottone, R., 511
Cipriano, R., 1285
Clark, B., 21, 479, 824
Clark, C. R., 1333
Clark, E., 1828
Clark, F., 162
Clark, G. M., 321
Clark, G. R., 847
Clark, H. B., 1338
Clark, H. T., 18
Clark, J., 606, 1423
Clark, J. H., 286, 973, 1080
Clark, M. D., 1064
Clark, P. A., 1943
Clark, R. G., 384
Clarke, A., 469
Clarke, A. D. B., 647, 745, 1025, 1194
Clarke, A. M., 647, 745, 1025, 1194
Clarke, B. R., 495
Clarke, D. B., 469
Clarke, E., 1841
Clarke, L., 1722
Clarke, M., 385, 1042
Clarke, S., 782
Clarren, S. K., 748, 1411
Clausen, J., 396
Clawson, A., 185
Clayton, R. R., 75
Cleary, T. A., 501, 1270
Cleckley, H., 1674
Cleckly, H. M., 124
Cleland, C. C., 397–398, 1699
Cleland, C. S., 1503
Clements, D. D., 179
Clements, S. D., 226, 917, 1067, 1148, 1348
Clemesha, J. C., 1923
Cleminshaw, H. K., 616
Clerc, L., 398
Cleveland, D. W., 1643
Clifford, G. J., 1115
Clift, J. C., 1187
Clinchy, E., 1129
Clingempeel, W. G., 616
Clinkenbeard, P., 1849
Clinton, L., 819, 823
Clippard, D. S., 1835
Close, D. W., 840
Cloud, N., 1355, 1605
Clowers, M. R., 791
Cloyd, I., 870

Coates, T. J., 224, 1758
Cobb, J. A., 68
Cobb, R. B., 1891
Cobble, N. D., 1834
Coben, S. S., 1210
Cocchi, R., 998, 1000
Coceani, F., 741
Coelen, C., 533
Coelho, C. A., 1050, 1054
Coffey, O. D., 470
Coggins, T., 1292
Cohen, D. J., 468, 1728
Cohen, F. L., 1941
Cohen, H. H., 1398
Cohen, H. U., 1906
Cohen, J. H., 1002
Cohen, J., 772, 1675, 1922
Cohen, L., 175
Cohen, L. G., 1785
Cohen, M., 341, 507, 855, 1440
Cohen, M. J., 774
Cohen, M. L., 742
Cohen, M. M., 387
Cohen, M. M., Jr., 681
Cohen, N. J., 262
Cohen, R., 1303
Cohen, R. A., 173
Cohen, S., 76, 352, 851, 1543, 1830, 1860
Cohen, S. A., 640
Cohen, S. H., 1922
Cohn, E. R., 1878
Cohn, R., 27, 634
Colango, N., 818
Colarusso, R. P., 1213
Colavita, F. J., 1152
Colby, A., 1209
Colby, K. M., 336
Colcough, G. L., 381
Cole, C. L., 1049, 1615, 1616, 1656, 1718, 1719
Cole, E., 1112
Cole, H. P., 434
Cole, J., 175, 1604
Cole, J. C., 32
Cole, K., 605
Cole, K. N., 1050
Cole, S. S., 1638
Cole, T. M., 1638
Coleman, C. L., 159
Coleman, J., 1468
Coleman, J. C., 525, 910
Coleman, J. S., 901
Coleman, M., 193
Coleman, T., 1293
Colenbrander, A., 270, 1122, 1322
College Entrance Exam Board, 50
Collie, W. R., 637
Collins, C., 1677
Collins, E., 1274
Collins, J. K., 279
Collins, R., 938
Collins, R. L., 1093
Colman, G., 1616
Colombo, J., 648
Colorado Evaluative Report, 360
Colt, G. H., 705
Colter, N., 676
Colton, R. H., 1894

Colvin, G., 1734
Combined Disabilities of Jamaica, 323
Combs, A. W., 906
Combs, G. E., 161
Comer, J. P., 512
Comings, B. G., 468
Comings, D. E., 468
Comision Nacional de Accion en Favor de la Infancia, 1183
Commission on Reading, 1759
Committee of Enquiry into the Education of Handicapped Children and Young People, 189
Committee on Classification of Feeble-minded, 742
Committee on Education and Labor, 1759
Committee on Nutrition American Academy of Pediatrics, 728
Committee to Review the Standards for Educational and Psychological Testing, 1710
Committee to Revise the Standards, 457, 1011
Compas, B. E., 1068
Compton, C., 157, 587, 1330, 1922
COMRISE, 349, 609
Conderman, G., 1672, 1673, 1839
Condon, J. L., 747, 752
Cone, J., 1222
Cone, J. D., 221, 1823
Cone, T. E., 330, 1068, 1073
Conel, J. L., 573
Conen, P. E., 1851
Conference of Educational Administrators of Schools and Programs for the Deaf, 85
Conger, J. C., 1661
Conger, R. E., 68
Congress, E. P., 1824
Conley, R. R., 382
Conlon, C. J., 747
Connally, J., 625
Connell, P. H., 605
Connell, P. J., 325
Conner, D. F., 169
Conner, F. P., 884, 958
Conners, C. K., 38, 454, 630, 743, 760, 1023
Conners, G., 1726
Conner-Warren, R. L., 1645
Connery, A. R., 510
Connolly, A., 1145
Connolly, A. J., 1038, 1331
Connor, F. P., 165, 1314
Connors, C. K., 612
Connors, E. T., 1103
Conoley, C. W., 170, 225, 460
Conoley, J. C., 170, 225, 307, 308, 460, 589, 798, 1794, 1840
Conrad, 536
Conrad, R., 186, 343, 541, 1812

Conroy, J. W., 842
Conroy, M., 805
Consortium on Inclusive Schooling Practices, 1593
Conte, J. M., 602
Conti, D. J., 399
Contreras, J., 648
Convention of Executives of American Schools for the Deaf, 1296
Conway, B. E., 963
Conway, B. L., 288
Conway, R. N. F., 189
Cook, A. M., 159
Cook, D., 864
Cook, J., 175
Cook, L., 1766
Cook, R., 1622
Cook, R. E., 643
Cook, S. A., 907
Cook, T., 1389
Cook, T. D., 466
Cook, T. V., 1594
Cooke, T. P., 1662
Cooley, D., 423, 1306
Cooley, S., 1074
Cooley, W., 1933
Coolidge, J., 1595
Coombs, M. L., 1662
Cooper, C. S., 1318
Cooper, G., 1940
Cooper, J., 1388
Cooper, J. B., 1940
Cooper, J. O., 782, 1220, 1411
Cooper, J. R., 31, 551, 689
Cooper, L. J., 780
Cooper, M., 760, 1666
Cooper, P. J., 304
Cooperman, P., 1469
Coopersmith, S., 1610
Cooter, R., 1922
Cooter, R. B., 798
Copeland, E. D., 167
Copeland, R., 1145
Copeland, W. C., 1395
Coplan, R. L., 1337
Corballis, M. C., 854, 1092, 1558, 1706
Corbett, J., 1549
Corbett, J. A., 118, 119
Cordoni, B., 1086
Coren, S., 1093
Corey, G., 844, 1505
Corey, L., 878
Corey, M. S., 844
Corkhill, A., 50
Corkin, S., 262, 1164
Corn, A., 1122
Cornell Medical Center, 792
Cornett, O., 1813
Cornett, R. O., 494
Cornett-Ruiz, S., 1716
Cornfield, J., 803
Corno, L., 138
Corns, R., 299
Cornwell, A. C., 13, 625
Corr, C. A., 664
Correa, V. I., 1764
Correa, V. I., 272, 510, 538, 763, 1210, 1356, 1372, 1509, 1536, 1581, 1764

Correctional Education Association, 469
Corrigan, D. C., 1692
Cortes, J., 279
Cortner, R. H., 612
Cosden, M., 1617
Coss, R. G., 798
Cossairt, A., 414, 1061
Costello, A. J., 399, 1807
Costello, E. J., 169
Costin, L. B., 1668
Cote, L. S., 1479
Cotler, S. R., 29
Cotman, C. W., 551, 826
Cotton, K., 610
Cotton, S., 511
Coulombe, P., 482
Coulter, A., 1306
Council for Exceptional Children, 272, 427, 566, 929, 1355
Council for Learning Disabilities, 929
Council of Administrators of Special Education, 1442
Couturier, K. D., 67
Covan, F. L., 244
Covey, D. G., 590
Covill-Servo, J., 628
Covington, M. V., 819
Cowan, W. M., 573
Cowell, C. A., 1857
Cowley, J., 1308
Cox, A., 1400
Cox, A. E., 1868
Cox, C. M., 810, 822
Cox, M., 614
Cox, P. W., 443, 682
Cox, R., 615
Cox, W. M., 751
Coxe, J. M., 1422
Coyle, J. T., 1813
Crabbe, A., 789
Crabbe, A. B., 789
Crabbe, J. C., 76, 353
Craft, A., 1636
Craft, M., 745, 1636
Craig, A., 404
Craig, E., 542
Craig, G. J., 266
Craig, R. T., 544
Craighead, W. E., 132
Craik, F. I. M., 1163
Crain, C., 531
Crain, L. S., 885
Crain, S., 84
Cramer, S., 725
Cramer, V., 725
Crandall, V. J., 32
Crandell, C. C., 449
Crane, G., 1361
Cratty, B., 1347
Cratty, B. J., 476–477, 1343, 1344
Cravioto, J., 709, 1137
Crawford, 1760
Crawford, D., 546, 1084
Crawford, J., 494, 1129
Crawley, M., 763
Creaghead, N. A., 25, 604, 1051, 1054, 1056
Creak, M., 198, 367
Crealock, C., 316

Creasy, R. K., 1349
Creedman, T. S., 471
Creedon, C. F., 1617
Creer, P. P., 79
Creer, T. L., 79
Crelly, C., 425, 1050, 1053
CRESAS Researchers, 770
Cressey, J., 1195
Cresson, O., 788
Crick, N. R., 69
Crimmins, D., 782
Cripps, C., 1554
Cripps, M. H., 1042
Crisalle, S. R., 1482
Crisco, J. J., 292
Crissey, M. S., 487
Critchley, M., 186, 1495, 1923
Critelli, J., 1390
Crivelli, C., 998, 1000
Crnic, K. A., 933, 1643
Crocker, H. C., 1423
Crockett, D. J., 873
Croft, K., 411
Croft, P. B., 104
Cromwell, R. L., 248
Cronbach, L. J., 155, 489, 577, 715, 802, 1081, 1276, 1442, 1627, 1711
Croneberg, C. G., 95, 1136
Crook, W. G., 80
Crosson, B. A., 1837
Crouch, R. T., 643
Crouchman, M., 1837
Croughan, J., 1352
Crow, F., 1314
Crow, T. J., 366
Crowe, R. R., 1674
Crowel, R. L., 1648
Crowley, K., 413
Crowner, T. T., 1634
Cruickshank, B. M., 168
Cruickshank, D., 395
Cruickshank, W., 721, 1066, 1315, 1346
Cruickshank, W. E., 285
Cruickshank, W. M., 139, 185, 278, 284, 493, 611, 669, 861, 1148, 1217, 1341, 1344, 1697, 1923
Crump, D., 1937
Cruse, R. P., 468
Cruz, D., 1181, 1472
Cruz, R. S., 250
Crystal, D., 542, 1113, 1821
Csapo, M., 59, 1680
Csikszentmihalyi, M., 993
CTB/McGraw-Hill, 22
Cuconan-Lahr, R., 98
Cuijpers, P., 249
Culatta, B., 25, 604, 1051, 1056
Culbertson, J. L., 1555
Cullen, P. M., 615
Cullinan, D., 234, 620
Culliton, B. J., 1464
Culpert, T. P., 258
Cummins, J., 25, 251, 253, 604, 1268, 1355, 1604, 1921
Cummings, J. A., 22, 1656, 1920
Cummings, J. L., 652

Cummins, R., 725
Cundick, B. P., 1201
Cuneo, K., 1352
Cunningham, C. E., 743
Cunningham, G. K., 22
Cunningham, J., 1636
Cunningham, K., 510
Cunningham, R., 1107
Curcio, J. L., 97
Curfs, L. M. G., 767
Curlee, R. F., 403
Current Science, 1385
Currie, S., 1458
Currin, F. M., 1534
Curson, A., 273
Curtis, L. T., 485
Curtis, M., 1515
Curtis, M. J., 463, 1764
Curtis, W. J., 517
Curtiss, S., 588, 809, 810
Cushenbery, D., 823
Cushing, P. J., 562
Cushna, B., 1423
Cuskey, W. R., 151
Cutherbertson, E. B., 1190
Cutler, S. J., 1100
Cutrona, M. P., 1453
Cutsforth, T. D., 1874
Cutts, N. E., 1598
Cuvo, A. J., 1176
Cyclopedia of Education, 71
Cyr, J. J., 1595
Czaczkes, J. W., 591

D'Alonzo, B., 1541
D'Amato, R. C., 258, 1260, 1598, 1841
D'Ambrosio, B., 1771
D'Ippolito, C., 1510
D'Ippolito, M., 610
Dadouche, J., 1095
Dahl, H., 633
Dahl, P. R., 1815
Dahlquist, L. M., 278
Dahlstrom, L. E., 1196
Dahlstrom, W. G., 1196
Dailey, J. L., 1835
Dalby, J. T., 46, 570
Dalby, M. A., 119
Dalby, P. R., 1835
Dale, E., 351
Dale, P. S., 372, 1050
Daley, S., 1776
Dalley, S., 154
Daly, D. A., 403
Daly, E. J., III, 1220
Daly, P. M., 658
Damasio, A. R., 560, 1449
Damasio, H., 1449
Damberg, P. R., 681
Damico, J. S., 250, 253
Damon, W., 1391, 1610
Dana, R. H., 245
Danaher, B. G., 1415
Danaher, J., 1423, 1425
Dane, E., 111
Danford, D., 1385
Danforth, J. S., 455
Daniels, M., 1647
Daniels, W. G., 659
Danielson, L. C., 1073
Danish, M., 593
Danseco, E. R., 498

Dansereau, D. F., 1491
Dao, M., 498
Darch, C., 1337, 1338
Dardig, J. C., 1754
Darley, F., 129
Darley, S. A., 200
Darling, R. B., 497
Darlington, R., 504, 866
Darlington, R. B., 1224, 1268
Darwin, C., 968
Das, J. P., 405, 504
Das, J. P., 1625
Dassy, C., 320
Davanloo, H., 1462
Davern, N., 1204
Daves, W. E., 1344
David, K. S., 564
Davidson, E. S., 1282
Davidson, J. E., 957
Davidson, J. R. T., 1278
Davidson, P. S., 496
Davidson, R. J., 336
Davies, C. O., 1333
Davies, M., 1199
Davies, R. R., 1462
Davila, R. R., 169
Davis, A., 1324
Davis, A. B., 764
Davis, B. L., 564
Davis, C. J., 1350
Davis, E. E., 884
Davis, G., 129, 507
Davis, H., 449, 1310
Davis, H. P., 261
Davis, H. T., 1299
Davis, J., 1135, 1161
Davis, J. E., 859, 866
Davis, K. B., 1318
Davis, M., 1274
Davis, P. K., 1176
Davis, R., 1191
Davis, R. A., 224
Davis, R. D., 260
Davis, S., 45
Davis, S. V., 1098
Davis, W. E., 1160, 1671
Davison, A., 1488
Davison, G. C., 239, 1168, 1673
Davison, L. A., 853, 1522
Davison, M. L., 1209
Davison, W., 873
Davydov, V. V., 1798
Dawes, R. M., 1570
Dawson, G., 336, 985
Dax, G., 342
Day, H. D., 1718
Day, K. A., 1775
Day, L., 708
Day, M., 510
Day, R. L., 730
Day, S. R., 470
De Jong, T. H., 264
De L'Epée, A. C. M., 546
De Leon, J., 1109, 1604
De Lorenzo, M. E. G. E., 548
De Pry, R. L., 780, 781, 1220, 1734
de Quiros, J. B., 1622
de Roiste, A., 951
de Valenzuela, J. S., 591
de Villiers, J. G., 574

de Villiers, P. A., 574
de Vincentis, S., 1906
De Vriendt, S., 673, 1136, 1812
De Wals, P., 451
Dean, R. S., 12
Dean, R. S., 77, 340, 342, 344, 382, 415, 594, 693, 702, 819, 855, 873, 874, 1092, 1093, 1163, 1256, 1261, 1598
Deasy-Spinetta, P. M., 354
Deaton, A. V., 1840
Deaver, G. G., 348
Deborah P. v. Turlington, 543
DeCecco, J. P., 444
Decharms, R., 177
Decroly, O., 543
DeFries, J. C., 707, 1774
Degangi, G. A., 1257
Deglin, J., 1564, 1772
DeGraff, A. H., 29
DeHirsch, K., 1923
Deighton, L. C., 1001, 1002
Deinard, A., 1774
Dejnozka, E. L., 1002
DeJong, R. N., 104, 910
Delacato, C. H., 545, 1260, 1552
DeLacy, E., 1925
Delaney, H. D., 1039
Delaney, J. J., 453
Delaney, M., 1297
Delange, F., 453
Delawyer, D. D., 1823
Delclos, V. R., 503
DeLemos, M., 191
Delgado, B. M., 643, 644
Delgado, R. A., 1850
Delicardie, E., 709
Dellabella, P., 1792
DeMaso, D. R., 92
Dembo, M. H., 1318
Demchak, M., 626
Demchak, M. A., 1323
Demers, L. A., 1069
Demers, R. A., 1821
Demos, G. D., 833
DeMott, R. M., 1658
DeMyer, M. K., 1278
DeMyer, W. E., 1278
Denemark, G., 1692
Denenberg, V. H., 645
Denham, S. A., 69
Denhoff, E., 167, 347, 1155
Deniston, T., 1824
Denkla, M. B., 331
Dennis, A. B., 305
Dennis, H. F., 1103
Dennis, M., 872
Dennis, R. E., 499
Dennis, W., 745
Denny, R. K., 395
Deno, E., 43, 326, 1090, 1470, 1542, 1764
Deno, E. N., 553, 805
Deno, S., 958, 1937
Deno, S. L., 111, 520, 521, 523, 716, 827, 844, 958, 1348, 1489, 1640

De-Nour, A. K., 591
Denovac, M., 246
Densmore, A. E., 25, 604, 1050, 1054
Denton, D., 541, 1524
Deoliveira, I. J., 476
Department of Education, 935
Department of Education, Queensland, 189
Department of Employment, Education, Training and Youth Affairs, 189
Department of National Education, 1678
DePauw, K. P., 1707
DePompei, R., 1829, 1841
Deppe, P. R., 885
DeQuiros, J. B., 1067
Derrick, T., 1423, 1425
Derry, S. J., 50
Derryberry, D., 1774
Des Lauriers, A. M., 560
DeSanctis, S., 367
Deshler, D., 162, 1067, 1074, 1738
Deshler, D. D., 928, 958, 1190, 1766, 1931
Desmond, M. M., 1572
Despert, J. L., 561
DeStefano, L., 135, 238, 273, 300, 1876
Desy-Spinetta, P., 663
Determan, K. D., 681
Detre, K. C., 153
Detre, T., 666
Detre, T. P., 674
Detterman, D. K., 818, 963, 967
Dettmer, P., 1764, 1766
Detweiler, J. B., 968
Deuchar, M., 1136
Deuel, R. K., 1506
Deutsch, G., 1091, 1706
Deutsch, J. A., 31
Deutscher Bildungsrat, 814
Devaney, J., 1621
Devaney, K., 956
Devany, C. W., 1835
Devault, S., 1230
Dever, R. B., 1697, 1821
Devine, V. T., 612
Devin-Sheehan, L., 1857
Devito, J. A., 1272
Devlieger, P., 58, 1679
Devlin, M., 114
DeWeerd, J., 859, 1425
Dewey, D., 564
Dewey, J., 1389
DeWitt, L. D., 1278
Dewitt, R. A., 258
Deykin, E., 130
Dezolt, D. M., 239
di Cecco, J., 511
Di Scala, C.,
Diamond, J., 1385
Diamond, L., 1263
Diamond, M. C., 648, 989
Diamond, S., 393
Diana v. Board of Education, 1481
Dias, K., 1548

Diaz-Mitorna, F., 879
DiCarlo, L., 1297
Dice, T. L., 316
Dickerson, A. E., 1617
Dickerson, M. O., 1668
Dickey, S. E., 1367
Dickinson, D., 1928
Dickman, S., 1155
Dicks-Mireaux, M. J., 13
Dickson, W., 863
Dickson, W. P., 399, 511
Dickstein, E. B., 1382
DiCuio, R. F., 1150
Dieter, J. N. I., 951
Dietrich, K. N., 1062
DiGangi, S. A., 546
Dignan, K., 1665
Digneo, E. H., 1113
DiLalla, D. L., 194
Diller, L., 285, 415
Dillman, D., 1479
DiLorenzo, T. M., 1613
DiMattia, P., 1433
Dimond, S., 343
Dineen, J. P., 1338
Dingle, A. D., 39
Dinitz, S., 1324
Dinkmeyer, D., 563, 755, 1318
Dinkmeyer, D., Jr., 563
Dinner, D., 1458
Dinnsen, D., 1367
DiPasalegne, R. W., 145
DiPietro, E. K., 194
Direccion General de Educacion Especial, 1183
Direct instruction management handbook, 611
Directorate of School Education, Victoria, 189
Directory of living aids for the disabled person, 36
Dishion, T. J., 710
Dishner, E. K., 1503
Distefano, J. J., 754
Division for the Visually Handicapped, Council for Exceptional Children, 270
Dix, D. L., 619
Dixon, M., 171
Dixon, M. L., 420
Dixon, S. D., 293
Dodd, B., 1554
Dodds, K., 118
Dodge, K. A., 69, 448
Dodgeon, B. J., 1704
Dodrill, C. B., 118, 665, 666, 1360
Dodson-Burk, B., 1676
Doe v. Withers, 1103
Doershuk, C. F., 527
Doherty, D., 1129
Dolan, A. B., 1953
Dolan, N. K., 174
Dolch, E. W., 621
Dole, J. A., 823
Doleys, D. M., 688, 695
Doll, E. A., 300, 621–622
Doll, E. E., 1881
Dollard, J., 1280
Doman, G., 622
Domek, D., 728
Dominguez, L., 1354

Donahue, M., 958, 1456
Donald, C. A., 784
Donaldson, G., 494
Donati, A., 1000
Donder, D., 1553
Donders, J., 1834
Done, D. J., 366
Donnelly, A. C., 216
Donovan, W., A., 575
Dooley, A. R., 244
Doraiswamy, P., 1387
Dore, T., 114
Dorfman, A., 1211
Dorfman, S., 1614
Doris, J., 655, 1188, 1320, 1396
Dorland's illustrated medical dictionary, 115
Dorn, F. J., 1259
Dorn, S., 628
Dornbush, M. P., 635, 977, 1804, 1813,
Dorr, D., 224
Dorsch, A., 70
Dorsey, M. F., 1472
Doubleday, C., 1780
Douds, A., 1591
Douglas, D. R., 1666
Douglas, R. G., Jr., 880
Douglas, V., 1258
Douglas, V. I., 167, 408, 612
Dowdy, C., 1297
Dowling, S., 152, 1366
Down, J. L., 624
Downey, R. S., 902
Downing, J., 954
Dox, I., 329
Doyle, D., 1828
Doyle, K. E., 819
Doyle, M. B., 1315
Drabman, R. S., 1615, 1617
Drake, G. P., 633
Drane, J. F., 703
Draper, N. R., 1224
Dreelin, E., 39
Dreifuss, F. E., 16, 912, 1869
Dreikurs, R., 755, 1318, 1393
Drescher, C., 250
Drew, C. I., 1660
Drew, C. J., 67, 788, 1534, 1643, 1659
Dreyer, Z., 278
Droegemueller, W., 356
Drotar, D., 1835
Drotar, P., 728
Drummond, N. W., 188
Drydyk, J., 764
Dseposito, F., 792
Duane, D., 1728
DuBoff, B., 539
DuBose, R. F., 949
Dubow, S., 982
Dubowitz, L. M. S., 1416
Dubowitz, V., 1416
Ducanis, A. J., 1219
Duchan, J. F., 1050, 1056, 1410
Dudley-Marling, C. C., 897
Duff, R. S., 205
Duffelmeyer, F. A., 1488
Duffy, F. H., 826
Duffy, J. R., 1215

Dufrense, D., 1374
Dugdale, R. L., 1018
Duh, J., 1751
DuHamel, T., 80
Duke-Elder, S., 914, 1780
Duke-Elder, S. A., 1883
Dulaney, C. L., 681
Dulberg, L., 1635
Dumont, R., 1729
Duncan, D., 357
Duncan, O. D., 1326
Dunham, C. S., 1518, 1730
Dunham, J. R., 1518
Dunivant, N., 1083
Dunkin, M. J., 671, 1187
Dunlap, G., 194, 782, 783, 961
Dunlap, K., 1401
Dunn, J., 267, 1774
Dunn, K., 1089
Dunn, L., 1047, 1331, 1332
Dunn, L. M., 632–633, 927, 929, 1107, 1186, 1331, 1332, 1611, 1688, 1919
Dunn, R., 1089
Dunson, R. M., III, 170
Dunst, C. J., 218, 511, 1442
Duorak, R., 1190
DuPaul, G. J., 169, 170, 455
Dupois, M. M., 1498
Durand, B. A., 165
Durand, V. M., 782, 1538
Durbin, B., 1822
Durham, P., 1839
Durham, R. H., 846
Durieux-Smith, A., 291
Durkin, D., 913
Durnham, J. D., 1941
Durrell, D., 1936
Dussault, J. H., 482
Duszynski, K., 627
Dutton, W. H., 148
Duvinant, N., 546
Dweck, C. S., 176, 1064, 1497, 1730
Dworkin, B., 1602
Dworkin, G., 989, 1249
Dwyer, D. C., 1593
Dwyer, K. P., 1598
Dyck, D. G., 177
Dyck, N., 1764, 1766
Dyck, P. J., 846
Dyer, K., 961
Dykens, E., 767
Dykens, E. M., 1409
Dykes, M. K., 276, 867, 868, 1159, 1227, 1301, 1373
Dykman, R. A., 917, 1067
Dykstra, L. A., 31, 623, 674, 1163, 1801

Eachus, H. T., 1807
Eagle, E., 1229
Eagney, P., 756
Earle, R. A., 1500
Earls, F., 1775
Easton, D. F., 1774
Easton, J., 1668
Eaves, R. C., 910, 911, 921, 983, 1115, 1368
Ebaugh, F. G., 167
Ebbesen, E. B., 456

Ebel, R., 1079, 1190
Ebel, R. L., 715
Ebersole, J. B., 1348
Ebersole, M., 1348
Eberwein, H., 814
Ebner, A., 1458
Eccles, J. C., 340, 689, 1706
Echenrode, J., 216
Echevarria, J., 505, 506
Economic Commission for Latin America and the Caribbean, 471
Edelbrock, C., 399
Edelbrock, C. S., 168, 169, 1134
Edelfelt, R., 956
Edelfelt, R. A., 1759
Edelstein, S., 764
Eden, J., 85, 329, 1721
Edgar, E., 584, 1425, 1732
Edgell, D., 740
Edgerton, M., 1589
Edgerton, R. B., 504, 656, 1652
Edmiaston, R. K., 650
Edmondson, R., 510
Edmonson, B., 1636
Edmonton, A., 879
Edna, T. H., 1837
Edran, A., 505
Education of the Handicapped, 1521
Edwards, A. L., 1534
Edwards, C. G., 291
Edwards, G., 168
Edwards, G. L., 194
Edwards, J. H., 1851
Edwards, M. O., 478
Edwards, N., 128
Edwards, P., 285, 1839
Eells, 951
Eells, J. M., 212, 402, 1889
Efron, M., 539
Egan, M. W., 1660
Egbert, R. L., 672
Egel, A. I., 428
Egel, A. L., 194
Egeland, B., 1774
Eggen, P. D., 50
Eggermont, J., 558
Ehlers, W. H., 566
Ehly, S. W., 1858
Ehrenberg, M., 1138
Ehrlich, J., 1571
Ehrlich, R. M., 918
Ehrlich, V. Z., 1419
Ehrlichman, H., 798
Eichel, V. J., 273
Eichler, A., 728
Eidenberg, E., 679
Eighteenth Annual Report to Congress on the Implementation of the IDEA, 360
Eignor, D. R., 1329
Eikeseth, S., 1118
Eisen, A. R., 1595
Eisen, M., 784, 1610
Eisenberg, H. M., 345, 1836
Eisenberg, L., 92, 263, 367, 912
Eisenberg, M. G., 876
Eisenberg, N., 1665

Eisenberger, R., 993
Eisenhart, M., 531
Eisenson, 347
Eisenson, J., 636, 638, 672–673, 719, 1006, 1291, 1343
Eisner, E. W., 715
Eisner, G., 329
Eklof, M., 663
Ekman, P., 1272
Ekwall, E. E., 402
Elardo, P., 1666
El-Ashawal, A. E., 1187
Elbert, M., 1367
Elder, J. O., 1422
Elder, P., 84
Elderton, E. M., 748
Eldredge, K. L., 409
Eleas, M. J., 1659
Eliason, M., 168, 1230
Elkin, V., 377
Elkind, D., 145
Elkins, J., 329
Elkisch, P., 912
Ellerstein, N. S., 216
Ellingham, T., 272
Ellingson, R., 1674
Elliot, C. D., 595
Elliot, C., 684
Elliot, J., 1754
Elliot, R., 629
Elliot, S., 1081
Elliot, S. M., 1665
Elliot, S. N., 146, 450, 643, 654, 939, 1667, 1848
Elliot, T. A., 555
Elliott, J. D. S., 75
Elliott, R. T., 1314
Elliott, S., 1068
Elliott, S. N., 24, 1167, 1400, 1401, 1455, 1473, 1508, 1599
Ellis, C. R., 517
Ellis, E., 1524
Ellis, H., 1524
Ellis, J. M., 979
Ellis, J. R., 1002
Ellis, K. L., 405
Ellis, N. R., 681
Ellis, R. S., 1732
Ellis, W. K., 1736
Ellison, R. L., 819, 965
Ellwood, J., 540, 1404, 1414
Elmore, R., 1760
Elmquist, E., 621
Elska, V., 1395
Elson, A., 1232
Emanuelsson, I., 1586
Embretson, S. E., 1328
Emde, R. N., 645
Eme, R., 1635
Emerick, L. L., 1050
Emory, K., 951
Empey, L. T., 1021
Emslie, G. J., 556
Endicott, J., 1352, 1675
Endres, M., 823
Engel, A. M., 42
Engel, G., 259
Engel, S., 885
Engelhard, G., 1712
Engelman, S., 144, 247
Engelmann, S., 194, 598,

324, 674, 884, 1068, 1143, 1795
Englemann, S. E., 690–691
Engler, L., 1406
Englert, C. S., 515, 640, 961, 1438, 1539, 1930
English now minority tongue, 316
Enos, S. L., 764
Ensminger, A. H., 1128
Ensminger, M. E., 1128
Enson, A., 1487
Entwistle, D. R., 267
Enz, B. J., 1225
Epilepsy school alert, 698
Eplle, W. A., 1541
Eppright, T. D., 448
Epps, S., 1471
Epstein, H. T., 289
Epstein, J. H., 1388
Epstein, M. H., 234, 640, 1067
Epstein, R., 594
Eranko, O., 330
Erdos, P. L., 1479
Erenberg, G., 468
ERIC, 903
ERIC, Clearinghouse on Handicapped and Gifted Children, 440
Erickson, E. H., 1462
Erickson, M. L., 1021
Erickson, M. T., 1073, 1385
Erickson, R., 260, 1128
Erickson, R. L., 1697–1700
Erikson, E., 645
Erikson, E. H., 412, 580
Erikson, L., 303
Erin, J. N., 1665
Erkman, B., 1851
Erler, S. F., 183, 184, 334
Ernhart, C. B., 750, 1062
Ernst, C., 266
Ernst, M., 1098
Eron, L. D., 70
Errera, J., 414, 1061
Erting, C., 542
Ertl, J., 702, 1256
Erzegovesi, S., 382
Escalona, S., 912
Escoll, P., 674
Eshleman, J. W., 1411
Eso, K. L., 1164, 1841
Espin, C. A., 420, 531, 847, 1601
Esquivel, G. B., 250
Esten, R. A., 1611, 1688
Esterreicher, C. A., 604
Estrabrook, A. H., 1018
Esveldt-Dawson, K., 1613
Etches, P., 1714
Etemad, J. G., 1230
Etzel, B. C, 1444
Eufemia, R. L., 695
Eustis, D. H., 715
Evans, H. E., 162
Evans, I. M., 1406, 1613
Evans, J. R., 702, 1256
Evans, L., 494, 1812
Evans, M., 1164
Evans, M. M., 1923
Evans, R. B., 489, 908, 1012, 1555

Evans, R. W., 193
Evans, S. S., 468
Evans, S. W., 169
Evans, W. H., 468
Eveleth, P. B., 574
Everett, B. A., 411
Everitt, B. S., 726
Evers, U., 414
Everson, J., 1735
Evertson, C., 1761
Evertson, C. M., 1760
Ewbank, W. A., 495
Ewije, P., 295
Ewing, N. J., 1195
Ewing-Cobbs, L., 1835, 1845
Exceptional Children, 1438
Exner, J. E., 1352, 1569
Eyler, F. D., 646
Eysenck, H. J., 722, 963, 1773

Fabre, T., 598
Fact Sheet: Neurofibromatosis, 311
Fadiman, A., 511
Fafard, M., 1317
Fafunwa, A. B., 1265
Fagan, E. R., 961
Fagan, T., 1597
Fagen, S. A., 70, 1611
Fairburn, C. J., 304
Faison, M. W., 613
Falbo, T., 266
Falik, L., 1435
Fallen, N., 1425
Fallen, N. H., 1816
Falstein, E. J., 1594
Falvey, M. A., 1612
Falwell, K., 878
Falwell, K. D., 963, 1098
Family Educational Rights and Privacy Act of 1974, 733
Fanning, P., 1272
Fantie, B., 282
Faraone, S. V., 168
Farber, B., 1643, 1660
Farber, S. L., 1249
Fargo, C., 1879
Fargo, G. A., 1879
Farling, W. H., 1238
Farmer, J. E., 1834, 1846
Farmer, J. L., 1272
Farmer, L., 679
Farmer, R. H., 1730
Farmer, S. S., 25, 424, 564, 604, 1050, 1052, 1053, 1055, 1270, 1272, 1410, 1559
Farquhar, J., 60, 1681
Farr, R., 22
Farrell, E. E., 740
Farrell, P., 1862
Farthing, M. C., 1135, 1137, 1279
Faterson, H., 1876
Favell, J. E., 1374
Faw, G. D., 1612
Fay v. South Colonie Central School District, 734
Fay, G., 1835
Fay, W. H., 652, 1293
Faye, E. E., 270, 1122

Fayve, E. E., 1883
FCLD guide for parents of children with learning disabilities, 422
Feagans, L., 654
Federal Ministry of Education, Nigeria, 1263
Federal Ministry of Information and Culture, 1265
Federal Register, 489, 700, 939, 1066, 1076, 1292, 1737, 1829, 1839
Feely, M. G., 1112, 1773
Feigley, D. A., 848
Feigl, J. E., 1883
Fein, D., 192, 193, 854, 1092
Feinberg, B. F., 38, 80, 168, 743, 760, 1023, 1067
Feingold, H., 760
Feingold, M., 732
Feinmesser, M., 885
Feinstein, C., 192
Feistritzer, C. E., 349
Feld, J. D., 224
Feld, J. K., 1327
Feld, S., 819
Feldhusen, J. F., 693, 744, 810, 820, 821, 822, 823, 825
Feldman, D., 555
Feldman, D. H., 1782
Feldman, H. A., 1166
Feldman, M. N., 165
Feldman, R. S., 1857
Feldman, S., 1546
Félix-Holt, M., 507
Felman, D., 299
Fenichel, C., 744–745
Fennell, E., 1590
Fennema, E., 1635
Fenrick, N. J., 175
Fenske, E. C., 194
Fenton, K., 940
Ferguson, C., 976
Ferguson, D. L., 1323
Ferinden, W., 688
Ferinden, W. E., 1528
Fernald, G., 1552
Fernald, G. M., 746, 1225, 1527, 1867
Fernald, W. E., 746
Fernandez, A. T., 1604
Fernandez, P., 1389
Ferrara, R. A., 1179, 1951
Ferrari, M., 1282, 1849
Ferrell, K., 272, 1509
Ferretti, R. P., 1311
Ferris, L. M., 1788
Ferster, C., 366
Festinger, L., 444
Feuerstein, P., 1776
Feuerstein, R., 504, 1087, 1529, 1951
Fewell, D., 1222
Fewell, R., 538, 949
Fewell, R. R., 753
Fey, M. E., 1055
Fiedler, C. R., 459
Field, D., 19
Field, K., 245
Field, S., 1734, 1823
Field, T., 40, 1776
Fields, H., 1389

Figiel, G. S., 1387
Figueroa, M., 323
Figueroa, R. A., 250
Filip, D., 1932
Filips, D., 178, 1509
Filips, D. A., 1716
Filler, J. W., 1087
Filly, R. A., 1144, 1349
Filskov, S. B., 677
Fimian, M. J., 1315
Finch, A. J., 924, 925
Finch, S. M., 1450
Fine, M., 544
Fine, M. J., 225, 499, 1318
Fink, A. H., 614, 1639
Fink, M., 665
Finkelstein, N. W., 650
Finlayson, M. A. J., 634
Finn, J. D., 515, 608, 1635
Finn, S. E., 1198
Finnegan, M., 537
Finnerty, K., 258
Finnie, N., 1257
Finnis, E., 289
First, P. F., 97
Fiscella, J., 1782
Fischer, C. T., 905
Fischer, J., 171
Fish, B., 367
Fish, J., 1861
Fisher, 1760
Fisher, G. L., 353
Fisher, L., 1729
Fisher, M. A., 1948
Fisher, R., 1180
Fisher, W. W., 1415
Fishman, M. A., 1360
Fisk, J. L., 284, 1085
Fister, S., 1119
Fitz-Gerald, D., 1636
Fitzgerald, E., 758
Fitzgerald, G. G., 1489
Fitz-Gerald, M., 1636
Fitzgibbons, D., 754
Fitzhardinge, P. M., 154
Fitzpatrick, K., 1761
Flach, A., 304
Flagler, S. F., 909
Flagler, S. L., 74, 492, 851, 950, 1037, 1155, 1274, 1291, 1714, 1814
Flakierska, P. N., 1597
Flanagan, D. M., 656
Flanagan, D. P., 498
Flanagan, J. C., 1448
Flanders, N. A., 1878
Flanigin, H., 336
Flaugher, R. L., 1268
Flavell, E. R., 411
Flavell, J., 409, 412, 1384
Flavell, J. H., 399, 445, 580, 1153, 1435
Flax, N., 1720
Fleenor, J. W., 1628
Fleischner, J., 145, 199
Fleischner, J. E., 958
Fleisher, L., 1297
Fleming, A., 1707
Fleming, D. T., 878
Flesch, R., 1113, 1911
Fletcher, D., 655
Fletcher, J. M., 571, 1835
Fletcher, P., 1821

Fletcher, T., 1183
Fletcher, T. V., 1921
Fletcher-Janzen, D., 755
Fletcher-Janzen, E., 15, 104, 107, 108, 205, 210, 212, 215, 216, 243, 244, 245, 257, 261, 306, 307, 355, 359, 397, 448, 476, 533, 535, 538, 544, 546, 553, 556, 565, 569, 580, 587, 598, 600, 603, 628, 656, 722, 881, 899, 941, 1007, 1041, 1209, 1234, 1335, 1389, 1654, 1950
Flexibrod, J. J., 1618
Fliess, J., 1675
Flint, H., 80
Flod, N. E., 163
Flor, H., 1602
Flores, J., 499
Flower, L. A., 1930
Flynn, J. M., 277, 1639
Flynn, J. R., 966, 1193, 1900
Flynn, W. L., 112, 303, 627, 645
Foa, E. B., 1283
Focus on IDEA, 941
Fodor's great American vacations for travelers with disabilities, 1847
Fogel, A., 194
Foley, C. L., 213
Folstein, S., 698
Folstein, S. E., 192
Fones, D. M., 1757
Forbes, M. A., 547
Ford, A., 431, 1637
Ford, B. A., 1355
Ford, D. Y., 508
Ford, F. R., 1923
Ford, L., 250, 1032, 1604
Ford, L. A., 644
Ford, M. E., 1665
Ford, P., 645, 680, 708
Forehand, R., 1618, 1714
Forehand, R. L., 616
Foreman, N., 1575
Foreman, P., 190
Forer, L. K., 266
Forest, D. W., 795
Forman, S. G., 225
Forness, S., 235, 1219, 1538, 1582, 1729, 1769, 1886, 1887
Forness, S. R., 41, 80, 330, 392, 691, 761–762, 804, 1023, 1068, 1190, 1430
Forrest v. Ambach, 762
Forssman, H., 1043
Forster, F., 118
Forsythe, A., 118
Fortier, L., 1320
Foss, D. J., 1455
Foster, G., 1452
Foster, G. E., 667
Foster, K., 1931
Foster, M., 1317
Foster, P. H., 764
Foulds, R., 83
Fowler, J. W., 177
Fowler, M., 1274
Fowler, M. G., 220
Fowler, R. C., 780

Fowler, S. A., 511
Fox, A. E., 1418
Fox, C. J., 1438
Fox, C. L., 1196
Fox, J., 1676
Fox, L., 194
Fox, L. H., 28, 590, 1225, 1713
Fox, M., 1775
Fox, N., 949
Fox, R. M., 1612
Fox, S. L., 46
Fox, W., 130
Fox, W. L., 1542
Foxx, R. M., 561, 696, 765–766, 1311, 1374, 1537
Fracasso, M., 499
Fraiberg, L., 769
Fraiberg, S., 270, 272, 1390
Fraiberg, S. H., 769
Frame, C., 70
Frame, C. L., 69
Frampton, M. E., 1716
Francescani, C., 56
Francomano, C. A., 706
Frank, B., 958
Frank, C., 732
Frank, D., 1403
Frank, H. F., 1211
Frank, J., 571, 1346
Frank, T. A., 179, 181, 182, 183, 291, 643, 1620
Frankel, D., 1155
Frankel, F., 562
Frankie, G., 1282
Frankiewicz, R., 50
Franklin, A. W., 1923
Franklin, M., 1355
Frankowski, R. F., 1834
Fransman, S. L., 1946
Franz, M. L., 163
Franzblau, S. H., 259, 260
Franzen, M. D., 1571
Franzen, R., 717
Franzini, L. R., 239, 456
Fraser, B. A., 1301
Fraser, J., 381
Frasier, M., 507
Frasier, M. F., 1810
Frasier, M. M., 477–479, 812, 1305
Frazita, R., 1145
Fredericks, H. D., 1214, 1441
Frederiksen, C. B., 1618
Frederiksen, L. W., 1618
Fredrickson, D. S., 911
Freedman, A. M., 686
Freedman, J., 863
Freeman, A., 1115
Freeman, A. W., 1721
Freeman, B., 199
Freeman, C. W., 1318
Freeman, H., 1398, 1442, 1454
Freeman, J., 155, 920
Freeman, J. M., 118, 289, 708, 1853
Freeman, R. D., 272, 1883
Freeman, S., 1129, 1701, 1931
Freeman, W., 1464
French, D. C., 1665

French, E. L., 776–777
French, J. H., 1085
French, J. L., 582, 729, 777, 1226, 1262, 1485, 1600, 1899
French, L. A., 1950
French, N. H., 1667
French, N. K., 1318
French, R., 1372
Freud, A., 580, 778
Freud, S., 55, 479, 646, 778, 968, 1392, 1508
Freudenberger, H. J., 1758
Frey-Mason, P., 786
Freys, H., 1157
Frick, P. J., 166, 171
Friedlander, B. Z., 1392
Friedman, A. G., 527
Friedman, D. L., 88, 374, 741, 1245
Friedman, E., 110
Friedman, H. S., 421
Friedman, R., 1231
Friedman, S., 468
Friedman, S. B., 151
Friedrich, W. N., 1643
Friel, J., 571
Friend, M., 316, 1190, 1766
Fries, C. C., 1113
Friesen, W. V., 1272
Frisina, R., 535
Fristoe, M., 829, 830, 831
Froehlinger, V., 1582
Froham, A., 1401
Fromkin, 810
Frost, G. J., 918
Frost, I., 676
Frostig, M., 492, 579, 779, 780, 1341, 1343, 1344, 1347, 1454, 1528, 1552, 1887
Fry, D., 542
Fryns, J. P., 766, 767, 1940
Fuchigami, R., 1879
Fuchs, D., 327, 492, 521, 827, 928, 958, 1348, 1489, 1887, 1915, 1926
Fuchs, E. F., 136
Fuchs, L., 928
Fuchs, L. S., 111, 492, 520, 521, 523, 827, 958, 1084, 1339, 1348, 1489, 1566, 1887, 1915, 1926,
Fueyo, V., 1604
Fujiki, M., 1656
Fujita, T., 675
Fullard, W., 1775
Fuller, C. G., 1581
Fuller, C. W., 1698
Fuller, D., 336
Fuller, D. L., 1666
Fuller, G. B., 246, 521, 1459, 1666, 1769
Fullwood, H., 1042
Fulton, J. F., 1465
Fundudis, T., 1230
Furakawa, C. T., 80
Furey, E. M., 885
Furness, S. A., 743
Furstenberg, F. F., 615
Fyans, L. J., 803
Fyfe, B., 350

Gaar, B. L., 843
Gable, R. A., 1654
Gaddes, W., 1067
Gaddes, W. H., 12, 284, 340, 570, 633, 635, 721, 873, 1161, 1506, 1675
Gade, A., 1166
Gadow, K., 612
Gadow, K. D., 630
Gaffney, R., 982, 1103, 1114, 1404, 1414, 1523, 1567, 1646
Gage, N. L., 667, 1760
Gagné, F., 693
Gagne, G., 821
Gagne, N. E., 1088
Gagne, R. M., 194, 443, 1331
Gahl, W. A., 1120
Gaillard, F., 118
Gaither, G. A., 195
Galaburda, A. M., 361, 826
Galanter, M., 244
Galantz, F., 533
Galarza, A., 250, 644, 1604
Galasso, V. G., 822
Galfo, A., 719
Galfo, A. J., 1534
Galizio, M., 75, 1726
Galjaard, H., 385
Gall, E. D., 1716
Gallagher, J., 951, 1320, 1687
Gallagher, J. J., 330, 664, 793–794, 820–822, 901, 903, 1312, 1429, 1611, 1764, 1914
Gallagher, J. M., 1377
Gallagher, M. C., 1761
Gallagher, R. J., 949, 951
Gallaudet College, 1640
Gallaudet, E. M., 794
Gallaudet, T. H., 794
Gallegos, D., 887, 1188
Gallimore, R., 511, 887
Galloway, D., 1263, 1863
Galloway, H. F., 277
Galton, F., 265, 795, 810
Galvin, G. A., 1667
Galvin, M., 623
Gamel, N., 1274
Ganchrow, J. R., 446
Gandara, P., 1084
Gandelamn, R., 646
Gandor, M. J., 1774
Gandy, A., 1117, 1562
Gange, J. J., 1782
Gannon, G., 1617
Gant, N. F., 106, 748
Gantzer, S., 1415
Ganz, S. B., 730
Garber, H., 1193
García, E., 507
Garcia, H. S., 252
Garcia, J., 222, 446
García, J. H., 507
Garcia, L. T., 703
Garcia, S. B., 1218, 1354, 1604
Gardill, M. C., 464
Gardner, A., 225, 499
Gardner, E., 289
Gardner, E. F., 1712
Gardner, E. G., 22

Gardner, G. E., 1303
Gardner, H., 507, 964, 968, 1408, 1849
Gardner, L., 914, 918
Gardner, L. I., 728
Gardner, S., 130, 920
Gardner, S. L., 1418
Gardner, W. I., 490, 1616, 1719
Garfinkel, P. E., 114, 303
Gargiulo, M., 754
Gargiulo, R. M., 1643
Gargoulas, A., 1859
Garner, D. M., 114, 303
Garner, R., 1491
Garnett, K., 145, 199, 958, 1055, 1069, 1086, 1259, 1304, 1316, 1341
Garret, J. E., 883
Garretson, M. D., 1812
Garrett, C. J., 114
Garrett, E., 796
Garrett, M. S., 797
Garrison, K. M., 615
Garrison, S. O., 797
Garrod, A. E., 256
Garside, R. F., 1775
Garson, C., 408
Garstecki, D. C., 183, 184, 334
Gartner, A., 928, 1315, 1823
Garvey, W. P., 1595
Garza, R., 1181
Gaskell, S. L., 1143
Gast, D. L., 1443, 1536
Gastaut, H., 1459
Gates, R. D., 570
Gathercole, S. E., 1165
Gattegno, C., 1925
Gatti, F., 279
Gaub, M., 167
Gaudin, J. M., 1318
Gaultieri, T., 193
Gautier, M., 482
Gautur, M., 625
Gawler, J., 1853
Gay, B. B., Jr., 1652
Gay, G., 1357
Gazzaniga, M., 1745
Gazzaniga, M. D., 343
Gazzaniga, M. S., 874, 1627, 1706
Gearheart, B., 1607
Gearheart, B. R., 42, 348, 482, 483, 485, 663, 747, 800, 1307, 1429, 1589
Gearheart, C., 1607
Gearheart, C. J., 800
Geen, R. G., 1782
Geer, S., 982
Geffin, C., 1539
Gehring, T., 470
Gelbard, H. A., 288
Gelfano, D. M., 1282
Gelfer, M. P., 424
Geller, K., 1033
Gelles, R. J., 1671
Gelman, R., 31, 158, 409, 1379
Gelzheiser, L. M., 958
Gemma, A., 602
Gench, B. E., 1370
Gendlin, E. T., 923

General Services Administration, 329
Genshaft, J., 1350
Genshaft, J. L., 1487
Geogoric, A. F., 1089
George, M. M., 1873
George, S., 1774
George, W. R., 811–812
Gerald, P., 1186
Gerald, P. S., 389
Gerber, M. M., 928, 1620, 1665, 1931
Gerber, P., 1069
Gerber, P. J., 1823
Germain, R., 836
German, D., 638
German, D. F., 760
German, D. J., 1791
Germann, G., 1766
Germanos-Koutsounadis, V., 190
Gerra, L. L., 1614
Gerry, M. H., 471
Gershaw, N. J., 1143
Gerstein, J., 314
Gersten, R., 219, 250, 505, 598, 1440, 1604
Gersten, R. M., 610, 1538
Gerstmann, J., 815
Gerton, M. I., 916
Gerwirtz, J. L., 1280
Geschwind, N., 80, 336, 343, 826, 854, 874, 1092, 1506
Gesell, A., 565, 578, 815, 816
Gesell, A. L., 745, 815
Geshwind, N., 361
Gest, D. L., 1691
Getman, G., 578, 1341, 1346, 1888
Getman, G. N., 721, 816–817, 1493, 1887
Gettinger, M., 643, 1649, 1760
Getzels, J. W., 481
Giacobini, E., 382
Giangreco, M. F., 499
Gibbons, A. S., 440
Gibbs, H., 940
Gibbs, J., 1209
Gibbs, J. T., 498
Gibbs, R. M., 1252
Gibson, D., 1211
Gibson, E. J., 1497, 1552
Gibson, J. J., 338
Gibson, P. H., 1164
Gierut, J., 1367
Gil, D., 216, 356
Gilbert, B. O., 1879
Gilbert, E. C., 1782
Gilbert, H. R., 426
Gilbert, T., 907
Gildea, J. H., 320
Gill, D. H., 644
Gillam, R. B., 1050, 1054
Gillberg, C., 13, 72, 192, 405, 469, 502, 560, 731, 807, 829, 1003, 1011, 1019, 1093, 1138, 1554, 1597
Gillberg, C. I., 560
Giller, H., 1580
Gillespie, B. S., 815
Gillespie, C., 816

Gillespie, P. H., 1639
Gillifan, S. C., 1060
Gilligan, C., 1209
Gillingham, A., 825, 1225, 1304, 1527, 1552, 1867
Gillman, J., 1859
Gilman, A., 106
Gilman, A. G., 106
Gilman, C. B., 1833
Gilmartin, K. J., 1448
Gilmor, R. L., 1278
Gilroy, J., 1100
Gilroy, M., 305
Gilstrap, L. C. III, 748
Gingland, D., 796
Ginott, H., 1393
Ginott, H. G., 1318
Ginsberg, G., 1802
Ginsberg, H., 30
Ginsburg, H., 158
Ginsburg, H. P., 1785
Ginther, D., 1042, 1335
Ginther, J. L., 495
Gintis, H., 508
Giolas, T., 1405
Giovannoni, J., 1454
Giroux, N., 283
Gist, J. W., 1807
Gittelman, R., 171, 1596
Gittelman-Klein, R., 1569
Givens, T. S., 1528
Givens-Olge, L., 1766
Gladding, S. T., 531
Gladic, V. A., 1877
Glaros, A. G., 302
Glaser, G. H., 555, 666, 741
Glaser, R., 18, 488, 1328
Glasner, P. J., 1232
Glass, A., 420
Glass, G. V., 3, 73, 435, 488, 667, 952, 1528
Glass, R., 485
Glass, R. M., 1143
Glasser, A., 1569
Glasser, W., 603, 1505
Glaze, D. G., 1548
Gleason, C., 226
Gleason, J., 976
Gleason, J. J., 375, 416, 818, 1359, 1815
Gleason, W. P., 657
Gleitman, L. R., 1457
Glennen, S., 423
Glennen, S. L., 82, 187, 274, 678
Gleser, G. C., 125, 489, 802
Gleuck, E., 1021
Glidewell, O. J., 1101
Gliedman, J., 39
Glitter, L. L., 1206
Glover, J. A., 50
Glueck, E., 279
Glueck, S., 1021
Glutting, J., 1087
Goble, J. L., 270, 1289
Goda, S., 1292
Goddard, H. H., 503, 827–828, 1018, 1881
Goertzel, M. G., 811
Goertzel, V., 811
Goetestan, K. G., 303
Goetz, E. T., 177
Goetz, L., 539

Goffin, G., 507
Goffman, E., 1716
Goh, D. S., 521
Golbus, M. S., 1144, 1349
Gold, A. P., 1853
Gold, M., 819, 828
Gold, M. C., 1754
Gold, M. W., 1175, 1816
Gold, V., 45, 1143
Gold, Y., 1757
Goldberg, H. K., 1526
Goldberg, I., 458
Goldberg, I. I., 52
Goldberg, J., 1441
Goldberg, M. A., 555, 741
Goldblatt, R., 974
Golden, C., 336
Golden, C. J., 286, 565, 828–829, 1029, 1124, 1125
Golden, G., 1156
Golden, G. S., 261, 1804
Golden, S., 154
Goldenberg, D., 1424
Goldenberg, H., 732
Goldenberg, I., 732
Goldensohn, E. S., 555, 741
Goldenson, R. M., 728, 1518
Goldfarb, R. B., 1188
Goldfarb, W., 368
Goldin-Meadow, S., 1136
Goldman, D., 676
Goldman, M., 1727
Goldman, P., 1844
Goldman, R., 829, 830, 831, 1819
Goldman, S. J., 563
Goldman, S. L., 968
Goldman-Eisler, F., 83
Goldsen, E., 1416
Goldsmith, B. Z., 1028
Goldsmith, H. H., 1774
Goldson, E., 1120
Goldstein, A., 689
Goldstein, A. P., 70, 845, 1143
Goldstein, D., 951
Goldstein, F. C., 1834
Goldstein, G., 1439, 1831, 1840
Goldstein, H., 1486
Goldstein, K., 1885, 1888
Goldstein, K. M., 419
Goldstein, L., 175
Goldstein, M. A., 831
Goldstein, S., 13
Goldstein, S. G., 677
Goldwein, J., 292
Goleman, D., 968
Golin, A. D., 1219
Gollnitz, G., 1510
Golter, G., 49
Golter, M., 49
Gomes, A., 1272
Gomez, A., 1292
Gomez, M. R., 1460, 1853
Gonzales, R., 207, 560, 1025, 1765
González Trejos, F., 472
González, A., 507
González, C., 507
Gonzalez, D., 250, 1604
González, V., 444, 507, 1436
González-Vega, C., 472

Goocher, B. E., 658
Good, T., 1337
Good, T. L., 1760
Goodall, P., 428, 1824
Goodenough, D. R., 443, 682, 1876
Goodenough, F. L., 831–832, 1806
Goodenough, U., 257
Goodenough-Trepagnier, C., 84
Good-Hamilton, R., 902
Goodlad, J. I., 1499
Goodlin, R. C., 920
Goodlund, L., 1231
Goodman, H., 832, 1673
Goodman, J., 132, 399, 408, 924
Goodman, J. D., 1169
Goodman, K. S., 1200, 1491
Goodman, L., 137, 326, 329, 434, 589, 640, 843, 1195, 1206, 1342, 1343, 1345, 1607
Goodman, L. S., 106
Goodman, R., 469, 1291
Goodman, R. M., 483
Goodman, S., 374
Goodman, Y. M., 1200, 1491
Goodnow, J. J., 416, 511
Goodrich, G. L., 1045
Goodstein, H. A., 1657
Goodwin, D. L., 224
Goodwin, D. M., 653
Goodwin, M. W., 1208
Goosens, C., 84
Gordon, B. N., 1230
Gordon, D. E., 609
Gordon, E. M., 1775
Gordon, E. W., 533
Gordon, H. W., 343, 874
Gordon, J., 1701
Gordon, M., 168
Gordon, N., 1388
Gordon, R., 194, 285, 755
Gordon, S., 1143, 1636
Gordon, T., 755, 1317, 1318
Gordon, W. A., 415
Gore, S., 930
Gorin, S., 1598
Gorlin, R., 469, 1291
Gorlin, R. J., 483
Gorman, M., 1821
Gorrell, J., 1298
Gorski, P. A., 886
Gortmaker, S. L., 391
Gothelf, C. R., 165, 205, 482, 742, 1474, 1618, 1642, 1860, 1949
Gott, P. S., 872
Gottesman, I. I., 560, 1774
Gottfredson, L. S., 965
Gottlieb, B., 175
Gottlieb, B. W., 516
Gottlieb, G., 646
Gottlieb, J., 175, 516, 832, 1048, 1474, 1673
Gottling, S. H., 407
Gottman, J. M., 3, 576, 1661, 1662
Gottschalk, L. O., 125
Gough, H. G., 1352
Gough, P. B., 1751

Gould, S. J., 1018
Gounaris, C., 382
Gourgey, C., 1661
Gouze, K. R., 69
Gove, S., 381
Gover, F. J., 1310
Gowan, J. C., 832–833
Goyette, C. H., 38, 612
Grabowski, J. G., 1879
Grace, N. C., 1415
Gracon, S., 382
Graden, J., 958, 1417, 1945
Grados, M. A., 1283
Graham, E. M., 880
Graham, F. K., 1627
Graham, J. R., 156, 1196, 1439
Graham, M. A., 988
Graham, P., 697, 1774
Graham, S., 860, 1700, 1780, 1929, 1931, 1933–1935
Graham-Keegan, L., 1905
Grala, R., 1591
Granato, S., 533
Grande, C. G., 547
Grandon, G. M., 267, 1194
Granich, B., 1324
Granick, S., 421
Granon, M., 675
Grant, C. A., 1187
Grant, S. H., 1550
Graves, A., 506
Gravitz, M. A., 916
Gray, C. T., 1494
Gray, H., 1674
Gray, J., 1169
Gray, J. W., 382, 693, 702, 1163, 1256
Gray, M. A., 905
Gray, P. A., Jr., 1143
Gray, W. S., 1494
Graziani, L., 913
Graziani, L. J., 1120
Grebenc, R., 1824
Greeley, D. M., 730
Green, A., 216
Green, G., 194
Green, J. G., 1747
Green, L., 192
Green, M. F., 399
Green, O. C., 1775
Greenan, J. P., 1890
Greenbaum, P. E., 1629
Greenberg, D., 1880, 1881, 1920, 1922
Greenberg, D. R., 278
Greenberg, L. M., 1791
Greenberg, M. L., 1883
Greenberg, M. T., 411, 1643
Greenberg, R., 1776
Greenburg, S. F., 1758
Greene, G., 1825
Greene, J. F., 1456
Greene, R. L., 1196
Greenfield, N. S., 677
Greenspan, S., 531, 1011
Greenspan, S. I., 399
Greenwald, D. F., 1729
Greenwood, C. R., 1420, 1662
Greer, B. B., 1315
Greer, T., 163

Gregory, I., 1236
Gregory, R. J., 1828
Gregory, R. L., 1345
Gregory, T. B., 1186
Greist, J. H., 849
Grek, A. J., 1278
Grenier, D., 283
Gresham, F., 235, 953, 1068, 1529
Gresham, F. M., 1127, 1441, 1445, 1665
Gresham, G. M., 857
Gresham, P. M., 1650
Gress, J., 1727
Gress, J. R., 1824
Gridley, B. E., 773
Griesbach, G., 572
Grieve, B., 538
Griffin, H. C., 1823
Griffin, T., 1757
Griffith, H. W., 879
Griffiths, M. D., 1391
Grigg, E. E., 316
Grigorenko, E. L., 1849
Grimes, G. H., 602
Grimm, L. C., 455, 1167, 1208
Grimm, L. G., 1673
Grinder, J., 1258
Grise, P., 1195
Groce, N., 511
Groff, P. J., 1934
Groht, M. A., 839–840
Gronlund, N. E., 1662
Groothuis, J. R., 1953
Grosenick, J. K., 840
Grosjean, F., 96
Gross, 1087
Gross, B., 1468
Gross, M., 1270
Gross, R., 1468
Grossi, J., 824
Grossman, A. S., 1143
Grossman, F. K., 1643
Grossman, H., 841, 1067
Grossman, H. G., 1171
Grossman, H. J., 1, 2, 179, 429, 502, 533, 568, 657, 731, 1141, 1175, 1428, 1746
Grossman, P., 1317
Grossman, R. G., 104, 115, 345
Grossman, S. H., 841
Grosvenor, T., 1495
Groth-Marnat, G., 627, 1797
Grotpeter, J. K., 68
Group for the Advancement of Psychiatry, 685
Grouws, D. A., 1760
Grover, J. W., 269
Groze, V., 1405
Gruba, J., 782
Gruber, K., 870
Grumbach, M. M., 574
Grumet, L., 1433, 1633
Grunewald, K., 1638
Grunwell, P., 1367
Grusec, J. E., 1281
Gruskin, A., 1398
Gruzelier, J. H., 336
Guarino, R. L., 1433
Guberina, P., 541, 1877
Guenther, J. E., 1692

Guerney, B. G., 1317
Gueron, J., 1926
Guerra, N. G., 69, 70
Guess, D., 67, 520, 788, 1175
Guevremont, D. C., 171
Guey, J., 119
Guidubaldi, J., 614, 616
Guilford, J. P., 136, 466, 479, 481, 817, 845–846, 1352, 1724, 1774, 1876
Guillemard, L., 250
Guillen, D. B., 107, 207, 209, 219, 247
Guindon, J., 658
Guinet, L., 146, 610
Guinn, B., 278
Guitar, B., 1725
Guitierrez, S., 1427
Gulliksen, H., 1522
Gullison, M. E., 1318
Gumaer, J., 1392
Gumerman, S., 153, 494, 560, 753, 925
Gump, P. V., 654
Gumpel, T., 995
Gunnison, J., 1530, 1627
Gunter, P. L., 395
Gupta, D., 258
Gupta, R., 1552
Guralnick, M. J., 533, 987
Gurland, J. E., 1883
Gurney, B., 755
Guskey, L., 1143
Guskin, S. L., 39, 1048
Gussow, J. D., 710, 988
Gustaffson, J. E., 1096
Gustason, G., 1297
Gustavson, J. L., 1124
Guthrie, D., 1582
Guthrie, R., 453, 731, 927
Gutjahr, P., 292
Gutkin, T. B., 450, 463, 476, 654, 773, 939, 1078, 1167, 1417, 1440, 1508, 1598, 1764, 1793
Gutterman, J. E., 1350
Gutting, J. M., 644
Guttman, E., 362
Guy, R. F., 46
Guyda, H., 482
Guyot, G. W., 754
Guyton, A. C., 633
Gysbers, N. C., 434
Gyurke, J. S., 773

Haaf, R. B., 275
Haak, R. A., 1829, 1838
Haavik, S. F., 1641
Hacaen, H., 341, 362, 874
Haddad, C., 1549
Haddad, H. M., 1857
Haensly, P. A., 744, 922, 1040
Hafner, L., 1731
Hagberg, B., 1548
Hage, C., 540
Hagell, A., 1580
Hagen, C., 1839
Hagen, E., 1077
Hagen, E. P., 577, 834, 1276, 1522, 1711, 1919
Hagen, J. W., 174, 1913
Hagen, K. M., 1417

Hagerman, R., 767
Hagerty, G. J., 29, 141, 664, 771, 1239, 1864
Hagerty, S. J., 89
Haggard, H. W., 749
Haggerty, R., 1159
Hagin, R. A., 1792
Hahn, M. E., 69
Hahn, P., 1595
Haimowitz, B., 1511
Haines, J., 815
Haines, T., 816
Haka-Ikse, K., 1042
Hakes, D. T., 1456
Hakstian, A. R., 136
Haladyna, T. M., 488
Haldane, D., 314
Haldin, W., 1393
Haley, J., 1317
Halgren, M., 1346
Hall, C. R., 923
Hall, D. L., 1757
Hall, F. H., 849–850
Hall, G. S., 850
Hall, H., 429
Hall, J., 774
Hall, M., 1491
Hall, M. C., 1805
Hall, P. K., 564
Hall, R. J., 1775
Hall, R. V., 1805
Hall, S., 1524
Hall, V. C., 1765
Hall, W. M., 322, 323
Hallahan, D., 780, 983, 1066, 1068, 1155, 1346, 1886, 1888
Hallahan, D. P., 27, 72, 139, 174, 329, 413, 475, 490, 553, 612, 633, 662, 669, 721, 747, 843, 850–851, 883, 958, 1026, 1067, 1217, 1251, 1275, 1306, 1445, 1552, 1766, 1923
Hallenbeck, M. J., 1510
Haller, D. L., 1197
Haller, M. H., 713
Hallgren, B., 1066
Halliday, A. M., 676
Halliday, M., 976
Halliday, M. A. K., 604, 1054
Halliday, W., 288
Halmstad, R. E., 484, 486, 524, 601
Halpin, G., 905
Halstead, W. C., 852, 853, 1521
Halverson, C. F., 638, 697
Halvorson, P. S., 112, 303
Hamann, J., 1355
Hamayan, E. V., 250
Hambleton, R., 488
Hambleton, R. K., 32, 1329
Hamblin, R. L., 194
Hamerlynck, L. A., 764
Hamerton, J. L., 1851
Hamill, D., 952
Hamilton, L. W., 848
Hammeke, T. A., 1124
Hammerberg, K. W., 1550
Hammersen, G., 453
Hammill, D., 562, 589, 853–854, 1342, 1343,

1345, 1346, 1771, 1886, 1889, 1929
Hammill, D. D., 19, 72, 139, 316, 436, 437, 490, 667, 758, 917, 922, 1001, 1002, 1068, 1113, 1213, 1435, 1452, 1473, 1542, 1785, 1786
Hammittee, D. J., 1766
Hammond, E. J., 796
Hammond, M. A., 638
Hammond, R. L., 715
Hammons, P. F., 1598
Hampe, E., 1366
Hampson, R. B., 764
Hamre-Nietupski, S., 427, 785, 1637, 1859, 1948
Han, K., 1197
Hancock, A. C., 200
Hancock, B. L., 1668
Handen, B. L., 1438, 1539
Handleman, J. S., 194
Handley, D. M., 269
Hanes, M., 108
Hanes, M. L., 108
Haney, W., 1195
Hanft, B., 581
Haniff, M. H., 325
Hankinson, J., 912
Hanks, S., 1550
Hanley, J. M., 403
Hanline, M. F., 951
Hanna, G. S., 136
Hanna, P., 1943
Hannigan, J. H., 748
Hansen, J. B., 1792
Hansen, J. C., 1723
Hansen, M. J., 497
Hanson, D. R., 560
Hanson, F. M., 1315
Hanson, H., 1174, 1661, 1799
Hanson, M. J., 511, 643, 951, 1319, 1776
Hanson, M. R., 1101
Hanzel, E. P., 1096
Harada, M., 193
Harbin, G., 1423, 1425
Harbin, G. L., 566
Harder, D. W., 1729
Hardin, L., 1890
Harding, J. K., 780
Hardman, M., 1825
Hardman, M. L., 67, 1643, 1659, 1660
Hardoff, D., 1143
Hardy, M., 316
Hare, B. A., 1443
Hare, R. D., 1674
Hare, V. C., 1491
Harel, S., 108
Hargan, L., 1299
Hargrave, L. J., 1602
Hargrove, L. J., 659,
Harines, J. K., 763
Haring, H., 1860
Haring, K. A., 1823
Haring, N., 226, 1315
Haring, N. G., 591, 731, 861–862, 864, 941, 1413, 1450, 1879
Haring, N. R., 901

Haring, T., 941
Haring, T. G., 1537, 1617
Harkey, J., 1155
Harley, J., 1155
Harley, J. P., 38, 743
Harley, R. K., 85, 283, 329, 1720
Harling, P. R., 763
Harlow, H., 647
Harm, D. L., 163
Harman, D. R., 25, 604, 1050, 1054
Harman, H. H., 727
Harmin, M., 1870
Harmon, R. J., 645
Harnish, R. M., 1821
Harousseau, H., 749
Harper, C. R., 556
Harper, H. A., 256
Harper, J., 44, 429, 532, 933, 1275, 1664, 1669, 1671, 1672, 1737, 1738, 1816
Harr, G. A., 853, 854, 873, 1091, 1522, 1558
Harrell, K. L., 1430
Harrell, L. G., 928
Harriman, P. L., 33
Harrington, D., 1835
Harrington, F., 1868
Harrington, F. T., 393, 1137, 1320, 1401, 1731
Harrington, R., 1423
Harrington, R. G., 3, 300, 566
Harris, A., 221, 640, 1636
Harris, A. J., 212, 606, 1494, 1504, 1526, 1889
Harris, C. V., 751
Harris, D., 678
Harris, D. B., 627
Harris, E. S., 370
Harris, F. R., 1288
Harris, H., 256
Harris, I., 605
Harris, I. D., 266
Harris, J. D., 1665
Harris, J. J., 508
Harris, J. R., 647
Harris, K., 1701, 1930, 1934, 1936
Harris, K. C., 663, 1306, 1436
Harris, K. R., 1934
Harris, L. G., 1050
Harris, L. J., 1092, 1558, 1635
Harris, M., 456
Harris, R., 507
Harris, R. E., 1198
Harris, S., 194
Harris, T. L., 1525, 1526
Harris, V. W., 1337
Harrison, D. W., 80
Harrison, H., 1673
Harrison, M. R., 1144, 1349
Harrison, P. L., 2, 34, 36, 651, 815, 816, 970, 1134, 1150, 1880
Harrison, R. H., 832
Harrison, R. V., 535
Harrow, A. J., 1214, 1755
Harrow, M., 666

Harry, B., 253, 497, 510, 511, 515, 517, 882, 1355, 1823
Harryman, E., 636
Harshman, H., 1636
Hart, B., 648, 992
Hart, B. M., 1415
Hart, D., 1610
Hart, E. L., 171
Hart, J., 1217
Hart, K. J., 303
Hart, M., 1538
Hart, V., 1819
Harter, S., 1610
Hartig, M., 456
Hartl, D. L., 877
Hartlage, L., 244
Hartlage, L. C., 118, 164, 286, 330, 336, 345, 432, 572, 583, 634, 641, 665, 912, 1095, 1116, 1123, 1148, 1250, 1528, 1555, 1706, 1869
Hartlage, P. L., 641, 665, 776, 836, 912, 1034, 1149, 1386, 1528, 1555,
Hartlage, R. L., 118
Hartlage, L. C., 336
Hartman, A. C., 1659
Hartman, D. E., 414
Hartmann, J. R., 318, 1100
Hartshorne, T., 97, 733, 734, 941
Hartsough, C. S., 168
Hartup, W. W., 372
Hartwick, P., 1829
Harvard, J. G., 80
Harvey, P., 1229
Hasazi, J. E., 1552
Hasazi, S. B., 1822
Hasazi, S. E., 1552
Hashimoto, T., 193
Haskell, S. H., 285, 1720
Haslam, R. A., 1703
Haslam, R. H., 46
Haslam, R. M. A., 1644
Hass, G., 468
Hassler, D. M., 961
Hassold, T. J., 389
Hastings, J., 1142, 1718
Hastings, J. T., 520, 523
Hastins, J. T., 827
Hatchette, R., 702, 1256
Hater, M. A., 495
Hatfield, E. M., 1322
Hatfield, F. N., 1124
Hathaway, S. R., 1196, 1352
Hathorn, N., 1374
Hatt, D., 151
Hattrup, D., 136
Hauck, M., 192
Hauck, P. A., 185
Haughton, V. M., 331
Haugsgjerd, H., 1117
Hauser, W. A., 1837
Hausotter, A., 812
Hautamäki, J., 758
Haüy, V., 862–863
Havighurst, R. J., 863
Havinghurst, R. J., 44
Hawaii Department of Health, 360
Hawk, B., 1230

Hawkins, K. K., 520, 523
Hawkins, L., 1297
Hawkins, R. P., 520, 523, 1214
Hawkins, V. J., 495
Hawkins-Shepard, C., 1524
Hawn, P., 701
Hay, R., 1844
Hayden, A., 1425
Hayden, A. H., 584, 624, 731, 859, 864
Hayden, T. L., 675, 1230
Hayes, J. R., 1930
Hayes, M. C., 1531
Hayes, S., 1220
Hayes, S. C., 221, 717, 1616, 1647
Haynes, N. M., 512
Haynes, S. N., 222, 240, 399
Haynes, W. O., 1050, 1052, 1053, 1055, 1411, 1784
Hays, P. A., 409
Haywood, H. C., 503, 760, 864–865, 866, 953, 1087, 1529
Hazzard, A., 175
Heal, L., 1203
Heal, L. W., 1736
Healy, A., 347
Healy, J. M., 913
Hearnshaw, L. S., 309
Hearsey, K., 1601
Heathfield, K. W. G., 104
Hebb, D. O., 989
Hebben, N., 1062
Heber, R., 1193
Heber, R. F., 35, 868, 921
Hebert, F., 408
Hebert, M., 587
Hecaen, H., 104, 1449
Hecht, F., 766
Hechtman, L. R., 171
Heckhausen, H., 1782
Hecklman, R. G., 1259
Heckmatt, J., 118
Hedberg, N. L., 25, 604, 1051, 1054, 1412
Hedge, M., 296
Hedges, W. D., 906
Hegarty, J. R., 1723
Hegarty, S., 1862
Hegde, M., 129, 1905
Hegde, M. N., 424, 548, 1050, 1053, 1559
Hegerty, J., 382
Hegge, T., 869
Heggestad, T., 303
Hegrenes, J. R., 1595
Hegvik, R. L., 1775
Hehner, B., 274
Heid, M. K., 1725
Heider, F., 177
Heidrick, W. P., 920
Heijbel, J., 302
Heilman, K. M., 1474
Heimburger, R. F., 852
Heinicke, S., 869–870
Heinonen, O. P., 421
Heintz, E. I., 470
Heinzen, J., 465
Heipertz, W., 701
Heise, H., 1100
Helfer, R. E., 356

Helge, D., 1633
Helge, D. I., 1573
Heller, H. H., 1438
Heller, H. W., 620, 1190
Heller, K., 609, 1141
Heller, K. A., 1271, 1514
Heller, T., 369
Heller, T. M., 1924
Heller, W., 666
Helm, S., 151
Helton, G. B., 1160
Helzer, J. E., 1352
Hemond, M. K., 1086
Hendeles, L., 80
Henderson, D., 508
Henderson, F. M., 283
Henderson, H., 911
Henderson, J., 350
Henderson, K., 99
Hendin, H., 76
Hendrick, D. L., 1625
Hendrick, I. G., 929
Hendricks, B., 1716
Hendrie, H. C., 1278
Heninger, G. R., 260
Henke, J., 1335
Henker, B., 624, 1154
Hennings, S. S., 589
Henningson, P. N., 170
Henning-Stout, M., 492
Hennis, R., 720
Henroid, L., 1285
Henry, D., 931
Henry, G. W., 525
Henry, J., 194
Hensinger, R. N., 1301
Henson, H. W., 1086
Hensyl, W. R., 384, 636, 837
Hepler, R., 1428
Herbert, M., 425, 1033, 1050, 1053
Hering, W. M., 1759
Herjanic, B., 399
Herman, D. O., 273
Herman, J. L., 20
Hermans, H. J. M. A., 31
Hernandez, A., 887
Hernández, L., 507
Herndon, K., 792
Hernley, R., 1707
Heron, T. E., 457, 461, 663, 782, 1220, 1306
Herr, B., 504
Herr, S. S., 52
Herrick, S. M., 1314
Herring, J., 1094
Herrnstein, R., 973
Herrnstein, R. J., 711, 989
Herron, S. R., 1786
Herschel, M., 571
Hersen, M., 222, 240, 328, 1221, 1439, 1536
Hersen, N., 1647
Hersh, R., 1414
Hersov, L., 1580, 1806
Hersov, L. A., 1595
Hertz, T. W., 1084
Hertzig, M., 1774
Herzog, D. B., 304
Hes, R., 264
Hesdorffer, D. C., 1837
Heshusius, L., 897
Hess, R., 880–881

Hess, R. D., 511, 616, 989
Hesse, P. P., 675
Hesselman, S., 675
Hetherington, E. M., 13, 371, 614, 1282
Hetmuller, G. H., 1923
Heubach, K. M., 213
Heubert, J. P., 300
Heubner, R. A., 260
Heuchert, C. M., 1108
Heumann, J. H., 932
Heusler, A. F., 665
Heuvel, K. V., 1374
Heward, H. L., 1738
Heward, L., 1057
Heward, W., 856
Heward, W. L., 270, 491, 782, 913, 1122, 1220, 1338, 1807
Hewett, F. M., 41, 330, 392, 611, 691, 881
Hewett, L. E., 179
Hewitt, E. V., 78, 202, 217, 219, 249, 263, 292, 318, 324, 325, 350, 769, 779, 816, 832, 840, 863, 1095, 1102, 1121, 1207, 1212, 1251, 1413, 1478, 1480, 1513, 1519, 1556, 1568, 1581–1583, 1589, 1619, 1855, 1872, 1945
Hewitt, F. M., 804
Hewitt, L. E., 1056, 1410
Heyward, W., 1321
Hick, W., 1487
Hickman, J. A., 149, 450, 662, 736, 841, 939, 1392, 1528, 1572, 1625
Hicks, R. E., 1558
Hiebert, E. H., 1296, 1489, 1490, 1931
Hiemenz, J. R., 336, 342
Hier, D., 1857
Hieronymus, A. N., 22
Higbee, K. L., 1201
Higgenbotham, D. J., 84
Higgens, A. T., 174
Higgins, C. S., 88
Hildebrand, V., 467
Hildeschmidt, A., 814
Hilgard, E. R., 916
Hilgard, J. R., 916
Hill, B., 1586
Hill, B. K., 35, 431, 1541
Hill, D., 665, 1674
Hill, E., 272
Hill, E. W., 1676
Hill, I. D., 1807
Hill, J., 427, 1871
Hill, J. M., 69
Hill, L. F., 1911, 1912
Hill, M., 431
Hill, M. M., 1676
Hill, R., 1356
Hillgard, E. R., 382, 693, 1163
Hilliam, J., 1263
Hilliard, A. G., 973
Hilliard, J., 1399
Hillyard, S. A., 199
Hilton, A., 838, 1540, 1613
Hiltonsmith, R. W., 1785
Himell, K., 878

Hinde, R. A., 1774
Hinshaw, S., 1154
Hinshaw, S. P., 239
Hinshelwood, J., 454, 1493, 1924
Hinsie, L., E., 636
Hinzman, A. R., 403
Hipp, T., 1398
Hirsch, J. F., 292
Hirsch, N., 1385
Hirsch, N. D. M., 810
Hirschauer, J., 1836
Hirshoren, A., 1315
Hite, H., 955
Hittinger, D. H., 1090
Hittinger, D. J., 1103, 1192
Ho, K-C., 331
Ho, M., 118, 665
Hoadley, S. L., 707, 1548
Hoaken, P. C. S., 1042
Hobbes, N., 571
Hobbs, N., 391, 591, 658, 843, 896, 905, 984, 1107, 1157, 1426, 1445, 1446, 1765
Hobbs, N. L., 654, 1047
Hobbs, S. A., 1311
Hobel, C. J., 1349
Hobson v. Hansen, 1481
Hochheimer, W., 1216
Hockenberry, C. M., 471
Hocutt, A. M., 929, 1629
Hodapp, R. M., 767
Hodapp, R. M., 768, 1172
Hodges, D., 931
Hodges, H. M., 1671
Hodges, L., 1072
Hodges, R. E., 1525, 1526
Hodges, W., 760
Hodgins, A. S., 1317
Hoeffel, E., 819
Hoemann, H., 1293
Hoen, R., 146, 611
Hofer, M. A., 574
Hofer, P. T., 735
Höfer, R., 453
Hoff, H. E., Jr., 1045
Hoffer, A., 1161
Hoffer, T., 901
Hoffman, J., 293
Hoffman, M. B., 504
Hoffman, M. L., 372, 603
Hofman, W. H. A., 1591
Hofstadter, L., 826
Hogan, A. E., 1423
Hogan, T., 1929
Hogan, T. P., 22
Hogue, D., 17
Hohman, R. J., 1154
Hoim, V. A., 1409
Hoko, J. A., 1444
Holaday, D., 128
Holcomb, C., 467
Holcomb, E., 91
Holden, E. W., 682, 686
Holdsworth, J., 1586
Holdsworth, L., 118
Holland, A., 788
Holland, J. G., 1101
Holland, M. J., 1427
Holland, M. L., 1422
Holland, P. W., 1783
Holland, R. P., 1088

Hollandsworth, J. G., Jr., 68
Hollenbeck, G. P., 773
Hollinger, C. S., 1716
Hollingworth, L. A. S., 898–899
Hollingworth, L. S., 822
Hollins, E., 1355
Holmes, C. S., 690
Holmes, C. T., 836, 1545
Holmes, D. L., 194
Holmes, E. W., 1098
Holmes, F. B., 1366
Holmes, J. E., 12
Holmes, L. B., 1796
Holmes, T., 357
Holowach, J., 1457
Holowinsky, I. C., 548
Holowinsky, I., 1360
Holowinsky, I. Z., 219, 383, 396, 783, 1305, 1394, 1704
Holt, F. D., 1041
Holt, L. M., 1924
Holt, P. L., 151
Holt, W., 899
Holton, B., 139
Holton, J. B., 792
Holtzman, W., 609, 1141
Holtzman, W. H., 1269, 1514
Holtzman, W. H., Jr., 899–890
Holtzman, W. H., Sr., 900
Holvoet, J., 520
Holz, A. W., 496
Holz, W. C., 1473
Holzemer, W. L., 399
Homme, L., 1415
Honzik, M., 949
Honzik, M. P., 1178
Hood, C. M., 1883
Hood, S. B., 403
Hook, E. B., 1851
Hooper, S. R., 1125
Hoover, H. D., 22
Hoover, J. H., 1259
Hoover, T., 382
Hopkins, J. R., 1021
Hopkins, K. D., 1517, 1672, 1710, 1952
Hopper, P., 433
Hops, H., 1662
Horev, Z., 1398
Horn, J. L., 494, 773, 964, 1029, 1096, 1849
Horn, L. J., 1834
Horn, M., 318
Horne, D., 1347, 1452, 1528, 1552, 1887
Horner, R., 783, 1734
Horner, R. D., 1205, 1315, 1440
Horner, R. H., 801, 1205, 1220, 1616, 1734, 1949
Hornsby, L. G., 755
Horowitz, E. C., 1382
Horowitz, F. D., 1423
Horrobin, J. M., 731
Horton, A. M., 1530
Horton, N. G., 1879
Horton, S. V., 1119
Horwitz, S. J., 13
Hosford, P., 1879
Hoskins, B., 604
Hostetter, C., 1828

Hough, J. B., 1878
Hounsfield, G. N., 331
Hourcade, J. J., 1766
House, A. E., 1875
House, B. J., 625, 904, 1947, 1948
Housenblas, H. A., 923
Houston, A., 118
Houston, J. E., 568
Hovne, R., 730
Howard, M. R., 1055, 1411
Howard, R. G., 1093
Howe, C., 43
Howe, C. E., 43
Howe, S. G., 904–905
Howell, H., 823
Howell, K. W., 517, 520, 522, 591, 1315
Howell, M., 645, 680, 708
Howey, K., 956
Howlin, P., 194
Howsam, R. B., 1692
Hoyson, M., 194
Hoyt, W. F., 1546
Hresko, W. P., 1405, 922, 1785, 1786
Hsieh, C., 130
Hsu, T., 304
Hu, S., 980
Hua, M. S., 874
Huang, G. G., 510
Huang, L. N., 498
Huang, T-J., 1550
Huba, G. J., 75
Hubbell, R., 866
Hubel, D. H., 558
Huber, A., 1385
Hubert, N. C., 1774
Huberty, C., 607
Huckins, W. C., 906
Hudd, S. S., 1823
Hudgins, B. B., 174
Hudson, C., 1828
Hudson, F., 1766
Hudson, G. R., 1870
Hudson, J. I., 923
Huesmann, L. R., 70
Huey, E. B., 82
Huford, D. P., 1786
Hughes, C., 1271
Hughes, C. A., 68, 1190, 1617
Hughes, D., 25, 604
Hughes, H. M., 1386
Hughes, J. N., 131, 132, 170, 228, 407, 459, 461, 844, 1238, 1417, 1466
Hughes, J. R., 1067
Hughes, K. E., 588, 589, 797, 798
Hughes, S., 250
Huitt, W., 1804
Hulek, A., 1394
Hulit, L. M., 1055, 1411
Hull, F. M., 403
Hulme, P., 1359
Hulse, A., 918
Humes, A., 1929
Humes, M., 854, 1092
Hummel, D. L., 735
Hummel-Schulgar, A. O., 925
Humphrey, E. S., 907–908

Humphrey, J. H., 249, 1510
Humphrey, J. N., 249
Humphrey, N., 443
Humphreys, L. G., 501, 965, 1268, 1747
Hungerford, R. H., 908
Hunt, A., 1853
Hunt, C. E., 1775
Hunt, D. E., 1088
Hunt, E., 494, 965
Hunt, F. M., 490, 1405
Hunt, G. M., 258
Hunt, G., 13
Hunt, J., 1298
Hunt, J. M., 908–909, 989, 1381
Hunt, N., 1391
Hunt, S., 1228
Hunter, A. R., 269, 1199, 1796
Hunter, J. E., 501
Hunter, R., 501
Huntze, S. L., 840
Hurley, A. D., 1641
Hurley, D., 34
Hurley, O., 1426
Hurzt, R., 470
Husain, M., 1387
Husek, T. R., 488
Hutchens, T., 914
Hutchings, B., 1674
Hutchins, M., 1582
Hutchins, M. P., 655
Hutchinson, D., 1819
Hutchinson, H. C., 717, 1674
Hutchinson, N., 316
Hutchinson, N. L., 316, 322, 1152, 1552
Hutchinson, T. A., 1628
Hutt, C., 655
Huttenlocher, J., 912
Huttenlocher, P. R., 912
Huynen, K. B., 195
Hwang, Y. G., 1666
Hyde, J. S., 1635
Hyerstay, B., 1128
Hyerstay, B., 260
Hyman, J. B., 699
Hynd, C. R., 594
Hynd, G., 341, 482
Hynd, G. W., 285, 571, 594, 855, 1706
Hytten, F. E., 1388
Hyun, J. K., 511

Ianna, S. O., 612
Ianna, S., 1068
Iannaccone, C. J., 1666
Iano, R. P., 329, 1380
Ibunnah, A. C., 1265
Idol, L., 1764, 1766
Idol-Maestas, L., 532, 805
Ihunnah, A. C., 1264
Ileana, D., 1403
Ilg, F., 103
Ilg, F. L., 578, 815, 816, 1627
Ilg, V., 816
Illback, R. J., 1299, 1443
Illingworth, R., 909, 1037
Ima, K., 1604
Immune Deficiency Foundation, 1431

Impara, J. C., 2, 307, 308, 589, 1794
In re Forrest, 762
Individuals with Disabilities Act of 1997, 940
Individuals with Disabilities Education Act Amendments of 1997, 930
Inglis, J., 336
Ingraham, F. D., 912
Ingram, C. P., 1657
Ingram, D., 1113, 1367
Ingram, M. J., 1758
Ingstad, B., 58, 59, 1679, 1680
Inhelder, B., 503, 575, 578, 1029, 1380, 1885
Inkpen, T., 1433, 1633
Intagliata, J., 429, 763
Intagliata, T., 431
International Child Neurology Association, 977
International League Against Epilepsy, 1458
International Reading Association, 979
Interstate Migrant Education Council, 1188
Ipsa, J., 1944
Ira, V., 211
Irby, B., 506, 507
Ireland, W. W., 745
Ireton, H., 1422
Ireys, H. T., 391
Irvine, P., 41, 108, 148, 220, 242, 255, 262, 269, 279, 282, 283, 293, 295, 308, 313, 332, 398, 543, 561, 619, 621, 624, 703, 715, 740, 744, 746, 776, 778, 794, 796, 797, 811, 815, 827, 831, 839, 845, 849, 850, 862, 869, 889, 896, 898, 899, 904, 907, 908, 995, 1000, 1009, 1023, 1035, 1036, 1043, 1044, 1045, 1128, 1177, 1206, 1237, 1304, 1322, 1347, 1359, 1384, 1386, 1399, 1568, 1571, 1575, 1607, 1644, 1653, 1705, 1717, 1721, 1781, 1895, 1898, 1913, 1916
Irvine, P. J., 1943
Irwin, R. B., 995
Isaacs, A. F., 1418
Isaksen, S. G., 1305
Ishii, S., 511
Ismail, B., 1200
Israel, A. C., 688, 1385
Itabashi, H. H., 104
Itard, J. M. G., 1000
Itard, J. M., 960
Ito, R. H., 1069
Ivarie, J., 17
Iwamura, G., 1546
Iwata, B. A., 1220, 1614, 1616
Izard, C., 1580
Izzo, M. V., 1824

Jaben, T. H., 467
Jacklin, C. N., 267, 372, 1635

Jackson, A., 1410
Jackson, D. J., 778
Jackson, G. B., 836, 1545
Jackson, H., 58, 1679
Jackson, J. H., 340, 342, 1261
Jackson, L. A., 299
Jackson, L. A. Jr., 259, 466, 863, 1128, 1214, 1388, 1454, 1603, 1751,
Jackson, L. B., 67
Jackson, N. E., 1418, 1565
Jackson, P. W., 481
Jackson, T. W., 170
Jacobs, F., 392
Jacobs, F. H., 876, 1373
Jacobs, J. H., 1636
Jacobs, L., 510, 1405
Jacobs, P. A., 389, 1942
Jacobsen, C. F., 1465
Jacobsen, E., 1864
Jacobson, D. S., 616
Jacobson, E., 1216
Jacobson, J. W., 725, 1172, 1541
Jacobson, L., 670, 1047, 1474, 1765
Jacobson, S., 1453, 1528
Jacob-Timm, S., 97, 733, 941
Jacoby, J., 414
Jacques-Dalcroze, E., 1510
Jaffa, A. S., 218
Jaffe v. Redmond, 1434
Jaffe, K. M., 1835
Jaffe, S., 593
Jagger, J., 1813
Jago, A. G., 1538
Jago, J. L., 1538
Jahnukainen, M., 757
Jahoda, M. G., 385
Jakielski, K. J., 564
Jakobiec, F. A., 914
Jakobsen, R., 129
James, J., 1318
James, J. A., 1836
James, L., 128
James, M. A., 494
James, R. J., 258
James, W. H., 109, 421
Jamieson, B., 194
Jan, J. E., 272, 1883
Jangira, N. K., 937
Janicki, M. R., 1541
Janke, W., 414
Jansen, M. A., 876
Jansovec, N., 957
Janzen, H. L., 220
Jardan, R., 901
Jarecki, G. H., 674
Jarman, R. F., 1625
Jarrico, S., 276
Jarvik, L. F., 1942
Jarvis, D. J., 1018
Jarvis, D., 713, 817, 963, 1487, 1687
Jasper, H. H., 677
Jastak, J. F., 249
Jastak, S., 1912
Jastak, S. R., 1919
Jastrzembska, Z., 1156
Jay, S., 151, 684, 685
Jay, S. M., 151
Jayaram, V., 303

Jeavons, P. M., 1853
Jefferson, J. W., 849
Jeffrey, P., 664
Jeffries, J. S., 258
Jegede, O., 1265
Jeggo, P., 809
Jellinek, E. M., 749
Jencks, C., 1448
Jenkins, J. B., 256
Jenkins, J. J., 638, 718
Jenkins, J. R., 72, 138, 521, 589, 716, 857, 1299, 1454, 1531, 1769
Jenkins, R. L., 179
Jenkinson, J. L., 494
Jennett, B., 1835
Jenni, C. B., 1597
Jennings, K., 1373
Jens, K. G., 524, 951
Jensema, C., 538
Jensen, A., 887, 1272, 1875
Jensen, A. R., 501, 818, 963, 973, 989, 995, 1007, 1081, 1249, 1268, 1487, 1670, 1748
Jensen, M. D., 1144
Jensen, P. S., 1390
Jensen, R., 1735
Jensen, R. N., 1187
Jenson, W. R., 1841
Jereb, R., 1259
Jersild, A. T., 1366
Jessell, T., 12, 109, 165, 665, 676
Jessop, D. J., 690, 784
Jimenez, R., 1604
Jiménez-Pabón, E., 638
Jirsa, J. E., 1031
Jacobvitz, D., 168
Joanette, Y., 604, 1559
Joha, D., 1715
John K. v. Board of Education for School District 65, Cook County, 735
Johns, J. L., 621
Johnsen, S. J., 1790
Johnson, A., 507
Johnson, A. M., 1594
Johnson, C., 304, 1722
Johnson, D., 300, 401, 492, 1008, 1403, 1452
Johnson, D. D., 212, 402, 951, 1658, 1889
Johnson, D. J., 18, 571, 634, 635, 1507, 1553
Johnson, D. L., 1310
Johnson, D. W., 857, 1069
Johnson, E. M., 439
Johnson, E. R., 1659
Johnson, G. O., 1008–1009, 1657
Johnson, H., 229
Johnson, J., 194, 483, 1785
Johnson, J. J., 702, 1256
Johnson, K. G., 1940
Johnson, K. L., 456
Johnson, K. M., 687
Johnson, L. J., 1024, 1418, 1766
Johnson, M., 311, 374, 520, 523, 955, 1337
Johnson, M. B., 1918, 1920
Johnson, M. L., 1725

Johnson, M. S., 952, 1527
Johnson, N., 524, 951
Johnson, P. H., 177
Johnson, R., 1069
Johnson, R. A., 1422
Johnson, R. T., 687, 857, 1166
Johnson, S. H., 1416
Johnson, W. R., 1636
Johnston, J. T., 1807
Johnston, L. D., 76
Johnston, M. C., 1009
Johnston, W. P., 109
Johnstone, B., 1582
Johnstone, E. R., 1009–1010
Jolle, I., 904
Jolly, D. E., 554
Jolly, H., 1731
Jolly, N., 1721
Jones, B., 1217
Jones, C. D., 1232
Jones, E., 208, 280, 370, 545, 579, 632, 690, 861, 880, 1008, 1036
Jones, G., 620, 1203, 1885
Jones, G. R., 602
Jones, H. B., 1591
Jones, H. G., 1077
Jones, I. S., 914
Jones, K., 683
Jones, K. L., 748, 752, 766, 1603, 1624, 1657, 1658, 1772, 1851
Jones, M., 1799
Jones, M. C., 447
Jones, M. H., 1301
Jones, M. I., 1374
Jones, M. L., 1374
Jones, N., 725
Jones, P. R., 92, 659, 662, 739, 927, 1242, 1244, 1251, 1252, 1450
Jones, R., 469, 1048
Jones, R. K., 855
Jones, R. L., 175, 1010–1011, 1219, 1474, 1716
Jones, R. R., 68, 228
Jones, R. S., 395
Jones, S., 1089
Jones, S. A., 17, 85, 91, 210, 663, 719, 1071, 1246, 1469, 1516
Jones, S. C., 683
Jones, W., 1068
Jordan, B. T., 1011
Jordan, J. B., 859
Jordan, L. S., 564
Jordon, M. K., 1362
Jordan, T. E., 911
Joreskog, K. G., 1327
Jorgenson, L., 278
Jorm, A. F., 650
Joschko, M., 774
Jose, R. T., 1883
Jose, R., 1057, 1289, 1290
Joseph P. Kennedy, Jr., Foundation, 1285
Josey, W., 878
Journal of Applied Behavior Analysis, 1012
Journal of Communication Disorders, 1014

Journal of Fluency Disorders, 1014
Journal of Psychological Assessment, 1016
Journal of Special Education, 1017
Journal of School Psychology, 1016
Journal of Visual Impairment and Blindness, 1017
Joy, D. C., 65
Joy, S., 192
Joyce, C., 1830
Joyce, D., 83
Judd, C. H., 1494
Junell, J. S., 1870
Junginger, J., 1616
Justice, B., 20, 357
Justice, R., 20, 357
Juul, K. D., 1907
JWK International, 1771

Kaback, M. M., 106
Kaban, B. T., 266
Kadushin, A., 46
Kaduson, H. G., 258
Kaemmer, B., 1196
Kagan, J., 645, 710, 924, 925, 949, 1066, 1670
Kagan, S., 887
Kahanovitz, N., 730
Kail, R., 1913
Kajander, R. L., 258
Kalat, J. W., 200, 260, 261, 261, 847, 1212, 1516
Kalichman, S. C., 1429
Kalinowsky, L., 1464
Kaltenbach, P., 258
Kalyanpur, M., 510, 512
Kameenui, E, J., 1734
Kamii, C., 1145
Kamin, L., 1270
Kamphaus, B., 1134
Kamphaus, K. W., 342
Kamphaus, R. W., 1117
Kamphaus, R. W., 26, 40, 126, 157, 169, 178, 230, 232, 336, 358, 1519, 1555, 1729, 1756, 1788, 1806, 1892, 1897
Kamps, K. G., 496
Kanadanian, M., 259, 260
Kandel, D., 75, 76
Kandel, D. B., 353
Kandel, E., 12, 165, 665, 676
Kandel, E. R., 261, 362, 848
Kandel, S., 109
Kane, E., 1346, 1888
Kane, E. R., 1887
Kane, G., 1415
Kane, H., 980
Kane, M. S., 1591
Kanengiser, A., 866
Kanfer, F. H., 399, 455, 1168
Kang, H., 1361
Kaniel, S., 602
Kaniklides, C., 1094
Kann, R., 1259, 1533
Kann, U., 58, 1679
Kanner, L., 192, 198, 365, 367, 482, 560, 912, 1023, 1178, 1229
Kanter, A., 982, 1115

Kanter, S., 534
Kantowitz, B. H., 953
Kanuk, L., 1479
Kapche, R., 221
Kapel, D. E., 1002
Kaplan, D., 381
Kaplan, E., 1788, 1831, 1840
Kaplan, H., 1696
Kaplan, H. I., 686, 1123, 1235
Kaplan, J., 221
Kaplan, J. S., 522, 591
Kaplan, S. I., 674
Kapotes, C., 163
Kapperman, G., 1289
Karacostas, D. D., 353
Karagon, N., 1231
Karambelas, J., 495
Karan, O. C., 1518, 1616
Karcz, S., 1268
Karcz, S. A., 469, 547, 659, 1020, 1021
Karen, L., 1864
Karlsen, B., 22, 1712
Karlsson, J. A., 690
Karmel, P., 189
Karmes, M., 1426
Karnes, M. B., 602, 859, 1024, 1315, 1418
Karp, E., 1148
Karp, S. A., 1876
Karpman, I. J., 769
Kashani, J. H., 448
Kashigawi, K., 511
Kasik, M. M., 33, 401, 903, 1541, 1542, 1611, 1688
Kaskowitz, D., 1804
Kasparyan, A., 626
Kastner, T. A., 544
Kates, B., 188, 274
Katsiyannis, A., 518, 1385, 1839
Katz, D. I., 1833
Katz, E., 432
Katz, E. R., 292, 354
Katz, J., 1258
Katz, K., 200
Katz, L., 510
Katz, M., 638
Katz, S., 1441
Katzman, R., 1291
Katzung, B. G., 1818
Katzung, B. G., 31, 674, 698, 1466
Kauchack, D., 436
Kauchak, D. P., 50
Kauffman, J., 1155, 1346, 1886
Kauffman, J. M., 27, 72, 329, 413, 475, 490, 553, 662, 671, 747, 843, 883, 905, 1025–1026, 1067, 1175, 1199, 1249, 1275, 1306, 1365, 1552, 1659, 1747
Kauffman, S. H., 148
Kaufman, A., 581
Kaufman, A. S., 436, 501, 612, 772, 773, 970, 970, 973, 994, 1026–1027, 1028–1033, 1078, 1149, 1331, 1332, 1408, 1439,

1454, 1627, 1729, 1789, 1793, 1873, 1874, 1919, 1899, 1901, 1903
Kaufman, D. M., 687, 1224
Kaufman, J. C., 772, 968, 993, 1027, 1408, 1849
Kaufman, J., 780, 938
Kaufman, J. J., 832
Kaufman, J. M., 273, 928, 1445
Kaufman, M., 145
Kaufman, M. J., 940
Kaufman, N., 1627
Kaufman, N. J., 897, 1142, 1452, 1658, 1925
Kaufman, N. L., 973, 1026, 1027–1028, 1029–1033, 1150, 1331, 1332, 1408, 1530, 1627, 1919
Kaufman, N. S., 994
Kaufman, P. M., 1835
Kaufman, S. H., 1041
Kavale, K., 139, 743, 844, 1134, 1219, 1452, 1538, 1769, 1886, 1887
Kavale, K. A., 73, 80, 630, 667, 715, 1023, 1068, 1670, 1729
Kavanaugh, R. D., 1282
Kavesh, L., 648
Kawamura, H., 1546
Kawi, A., 1324
Kay, J., 1586
Kayser, H., 254
Kazdin, A., 236
Kazdin, A. E., 3, 70, 116, 240, 448, 464, 1221, 1616, 1648, 1656, 1667, 1719, 1807, 1848
Keane, P., 1661
Keane, S. P., 70
Kearney, C. A., 1595
Kearney, D. S., 40
Kearns, K., 1648
Kearns, K. P., 296
Keat, D. B., 476
Keating, D. P., 1713
Keating, T., 219
Keck, P. E., 923
Keen, J. H., 151
Keesbury, F., 869
Keesbury, F. E., 780
Kehle, T. J., 1841
Keilitz, I., 483, 546, 1083
Keith, R. W., 185, 334
Keith, T. Z., 901, 1029, 1150
Kelker, K., 1824
Kelleher, D. K., 1122
Keller, H., 1128
Keller, H. A., 1035
Keller, M., 54
Keller, M. R., 1873
Keller, S. E., 879
Kellerman, J., 354
Kelley, C. R., 1495
Kelley, M. L., 464
Kellow, J. T., 431
Kelly, C., 490
Kelly, D., 130, 1464
Kelly, E. L., 645
Kelly, E. W., 1595
Kelly, J. B., 614
Kelly, J. A., 1429

Kelly, K. L., 171
Kelly, L. J., 484
Kelly, M. L., 171
Kelly, R., 616
Kelly, T. E., 637
Kelty, M. F., 1538
Kemp, K., 1119
Kemp, P. B., 1024
Kemp, S., 1253
Kempe, C. H., 20, 216, 356
Kemper, S., 1489
Kemper, T. L., 826
Kempton, W., 1636
Kendall, B. S., 1627
Kendall, C. R., 418
Kendall, P. C., 221, 924, 1662
Kendall, R. M., 1227
Kendler, H. H., 1153
Kendler, T. S., 1153
Kendrick, C., 1774
Kendrick, S. A., 501
Kennedy, K., 1489
Kennedy, K. M., 1111
Kennedy, M. M., 1442
Kennedy, W. A., 1595
Kenny, A. P., 1228
Kenny, E., 1035
Kenny, F. M., 482
Kenowitz, L., 1732
Kent, C., 1668
Kent, L., 1086
Kent, R., 1696
Keogh, B., 1190, 1421, 1773
Keogh, B. H., 1036
Keough, B. K., 754, 958, 1036, 1084, 1453, 1552, 1775
Keough, B., 1656
Kephart, N., 1341, 1346, 1509, 1722
Kephart, N. C., 578, 1036, 1342, 1344, 1348, 1473, 1528, 1552, 1887
Kerlin, I. N., 1036–1037
Kerlinger, F. N., 1477
Kern, L., 782
Kern, L. H., 1641
Kerns, K. A., 1164, 1841
Kerr, A., 1549
Kerr, D. L., 1335
Kerr, M. M., 464
Kerrigan, D. C., 1687
Kerrin, R. G., 725
Kershaw, J. D., 1723
Kerwin, M. E., 1385
Kesler, J. W., 1460
Kessen, W., 371
Kessler, C., 1637
Kessler, J. W., 1722
Kessler, R. C., 353
Kessler, R., 75
Ketenberger, K. E., 242
Ketron, J. L., 963
Ketzenberger, K., 85, 703
Ketzenberger, K. E., 78, 86, 87, 91, 93, 94, 96, 111, 161, 244, 318, 493, 553, 657, 895, 1132, 1433, 1815
Key, E., 360
Khatena, J., 833, 923, 1040
Khoury, K., 482
Kiang, L., 1775

Kicklighter, R. H., 35, 1040–1041
Kidd, A., 110
Kidd, K. K., 468
Kierkegaard, S., 124
Kiernan, C., 429, 901
Kiernan, J., 1323
Kilbey, M. M., 751
Kilgore, S., 901
Killam, P. E., 258
Killen, C. C., 1766
Killian, G. A., 1252
Kiloh, L. G., 676
Kiluk, D., 615
Kim, M., 1859
Kim, Y., 610
Kimble, G. A., 236
Kimbler, D. L., 1566
Kimm, C. H., 1612
Kimura, D., 341, 594, 874
Kincaid, D., 783
Kindlon, D. J., 1227
King, C., 1501
King, D. S., 80
King, F. S., 1067
King, J., 950
King, J. D., 838
King, M. N., 1131
King, O. M., 319
King-Stoops, J., 491
Kinney, A., 409
Kinsbourne, M., 343, 1344, 1558, 1640
Kinshore, A., 361
Kipping, P., 1111, 1501
Kiraly, J., 248
Kirby, D. F., 478, 480, 1380, 1419
Kirby, J. R., 406, 1625
Kircaali-Iftar, G., 1854
Kirchner, C., 1509
Kirejczyk, K., 1394
Kirk, R. E., 1406
Kirk, S., 747, 794, 869, 922, 1067, 1068, 1687, 1885
Kirk, S. A., 178, 329, 338, 377, 664, 1041–1042, 1066, 1152, 1310, 1343, 1429, 1452, 1528, 1594, 1611, 1716, 1764, 901, 903, 1875, 1914
Kirk, U., 1255
Kirk, W., 869, 922, 1067, 1068
Kirk, W. D., 1066, 1343, 1452, 1528, 1875
Kirkland, M., 1335
Kirp, D., 394, 1396
Kirton, E., 510
Kisanji, J., 58, 1679
Kisker, G. W., 921
Kissman, K., 1319
Kistner, J. A., 178
Kitano, M. K., 478, 480, 508, 1377, 1419
Kitchell, M. M., 912
Kitchener, K., 703
Kitsner, J. A., 1064
Kitson, L., 1089
Kitzenberger, K. E., 383
Kivitz, M. S., 847
Klare, G. R., 1488

Klass, D. W., 1458
Klaus, D. J., 488
Kleckner, J., 851
Kleffner, F. R., 362
Klein, A. H., 482
Klein, A. E., 1277
Klein, D. B., 10
Klein, H., 350
Klein, M. D., 643
Klein, N. K., 1380
Klein, P., 1143
Klein, R. G., 448, 455, 1623
Klein, R. D., 1616
Kleinberg, S., 591
Kleinberg, S. B., 13
Klevstrand, M., 1118, 1550
Klima, E., 1136, 1647
Klima, E. S., 95
Kline, F., 531
Kline, P., 964
Klinger, E., 922
Klinger, J. H., 470
Kliot, D., 269
Klodin, V., 1942
Klopfer, W. G., 1797
Kloza, E. M., 109
Klukas, N., 1616
KMK, 813
Knackendoffel, E. A., 1766
Knapczyk, D. R., 918
Knapp, M. L., 1272
Knapp, P. K., 370
Knapp, S., 1434
Knappett, K., 1637
Kneedler, R. D., 612, 662, 903, 1306
Kneif, L. M., 494
Knell, S. M., 55
Kneller, G. F., 480
Knight, H. M., 1043
Knight, R., 511
Knights, R., 571
Knobloch, H., 645, 816, 1066
Knoblock, P., 738, 1321, 1594
Knoff, H. M., 475, 1116, 1763, 1657
Knopf, I. J., 1309
Knopf, K. F., 220
Knoster, T., 1732
Knoster, T. P., 783
Knowles, F., 495
Kobayashi, I., 675
Kobayashi, K., 345
Koch, H. L., 266
Koch, J. H., 1429
Koch, K., 625, 926, 1211
Koch, M., 1231
Koch, R., 625, 926, 1211, 1429
Kocoshis, P. R., 420
Koegel, L. K., 194
Koegel, P., 1652
Koegel, R. L., 194, 428, 961, 1441
Koelling, R. A., 446
Koenig, C. H., 1413
Koenigsberger, R., 130
Koestler, F. A., 89
Koetting, J. R., 1879
Koff, R. H., 1757
Koffka, K., 957
Kogan, K. L., 40

Kogan, N., 418, 480, 1066
Kohl, J. W., 42
Kohlberg, L., 497, 580, 1209
Kohlenberg, R. J., 688
Kohler, W., 957
Kohn, B., 872
Kohn, M., 1671
Kohut, H., 895
Kokaska, C., 434
Kokaska, C. J., 321, 833, 1430
Kokkinidis, L., 106
Kolata, G., 1226, 1554
Kolata, G. B., 344, 875
Kolb, B., 284, 1389, 1528, 1728
Kolb, L., 1802
Kolen, M. J., 1783
Koller, H., 638
Kolodny, E. H., 1019
Kolvin, I., 367, 1230, 1775
Kong, S. L., 1268
König, M. P., 453
Konlande, J. E., 1128
Konold, T. R., 773
Koopmans-Van Beinum, F. J., 396
Koorland, M. A., 547
Koplewicz, H. S., 455
Koplewicz, M. S., 1596
Kopp, C. B., 13, 456, 705
Koppitz, E. M.
Koppitz, E. M., 185, 245, 860, 1044, 1130, 1351
Korinck, L., 235
Korinek, L., 883
Korkman, M., 1253, 1845
Korn, S., 1389, 1774
Korn, S. J., 279
Kornarski, E. A., 418
Kosc, L., 633
Kosiak, M., 1314
Kotelchuck, M., 728
Kotin, L., 457, 631
Kottke, F. J., 1314
Kottler, S. B., 1207
Koulischer, L., 451, 1851, 1939
Kounin, J. S., 654
Kovach, J. A., 609
Kovaleski, J., 783
Kovalinsky, T., 1454
Kowalski, A. P., 392
Kozal, J., 1759
Kozleski, E. B., 275
Kozloff, M., 985
Kozloff, M. A., 192, 194, 732, 985
Kozulin, A., 1435
Kraepelin, E., 1044
Krager, J. M., 169
Krakow, J. B., 456
Kramer, I. I., 1360
Kramer, J. J., 302, 308, 798, 1672
Kramer, U., 414
Krantz, P. J., 194
Krantz, R. C., 330
Kranz, P., 507
Krashen, S. D., 343, 1110
Krasnegor, N., 1278
Kratchowill, T. R., 1665

Krathwohl, D. R., 1065, 1755
Kratochvil, D. W., 610
Kratochwill, T. R., 3, 170, 328, 559, 643, 1109, 1231, 1365, 1436, 1647, 1840
Kraus, J. F., 1835
Kraus, S., 429
Krauss, D., 1561
Krebs, D. L., 456
Krech, D., 648, 989
Krechevsky, M., 1408
Kregel, J., 431
Kreiner, D. S., 418
Kreisher, C., 421
Krener, P. K., 708
Kresheck, J., 636
Kress, R. A., 952
Kretschmer, E., 278, 1773
Kretschmer, R., 1414
Kretschmer, R. F., 541
Kreutler, P. A., 1137
Kreutzer, J. S., 1835
Krieg, W. J. S., 336
Krill, A. E., 1546
Kringlen, E., 1283
Krishnan, K., 1387
Krishnan, K. R. R., 1278
Krishnan, V. H. R., 1549
Krismann, C., 564
Kristensen, K., 59, 1680
Kristoff, B., 194
Kroger, A., 701
Krogh, S. L., 1207
Kroll, B. M., 1928
Kronick, D., 1816
Kronig, W., 1742
Krounin, J., 395
Krouse, J. P., 561, 630, 688, 695, 716, 1199
Kruesi, M. J. P., 448
Krug, D., 1553
Kruger, L. A., 1298
Kruger, L. J., 906, 907, 1444, 1468, 1695
Krugman, M., 1303
Krupski, A., 612
Kretschmer, R. E., 536
Kuan, L. A., 516
Kubitz, R. L., 920
Kubler-Ross, E., 664, 738, 1317
Kuczaj, S., 325
Kuder, S. J., 611, 1270
Kugel, R. B., 526, 842
Kuhlmann, F., 1045
Kuhn, D., 575
Kuhn, J. P., 1652
Kujanek, G., 414
Kukic, M. B., 832
Kukla, A., 32
Kulik, C. C., 28
Kulik, J. A., 28
Kumar, C., 295
Kumar, G., 1730
Kun, L. E., 292
Kundert, D. K., 838
Kupersmidt, J. B., 1188
Kupietz, S. S., 675
Kuprian, W., 701
Kurado, Y., 193
Kurdek, L. A., 615
Kurtz, B. E., 925

Kush, J. C., 773
Kushner, M. I., 250
Kussmaul, A., 1923
Kutas, M., 199
Kuusela, J., 758
Kwiatkaowski, J., 564

L'Abate, L., 485
La Du, B. N., 256
La Mantina, J., 1314
La Voie, A. L., 682
Laaksonen, R. K., 1714
Laban, R., 1216
Labbe, E. E., 1231
Laberge, C., 482
LaBerge, D., 1493, 1533
Labov, W., 674
Labuda, M. C., 1283
Lackaye, T. D., 1085, 1533, 1881
Lackner, J. R., 1292
Lacks, P., 245
Laconia, State School, 544
Lacy, G., 820
Ladd, F. T., 80
Ladson-Billings, G., 1357
Lafferman, J. A., 760
Lago-Delello, E., 1629
LaGreca, A. M., 1875
LaGrow, S. J., 1715
Lahey, B. B., 166, 168, 239
Lahey, M., 1454
Lahm, E. A., 438, 441
Lake, R., 602
Laker, M., 414
Lakin, C., 544
Lakin, K. C., 201, 430
Lamb, C. S., 112, 303, 381, 652, 878
Lamb, P., 429, 823
Lambert, N., 2, 35
Lambert, N. M., 94, 161, 168, 657, 1058, 1455, 1652, 1776
Lamin, J., 1639
Lamm, O., 594
Lampe, J. B., 793
Lancaster, N. P., 676
Landau, B., 1455
Landau, S., 612
Landau, S. I., 1796
Landau, W. M., 362
Landesman-Dwyer, S., 750
Landreth, G. L., 1393
Landrum, T. J., 518
Lane, H., 96, 280, 745, 960, 1812
Lane, S., 1329
Lane, V. W., 1050, 1053, 1055, 1271, 1272, 1412
Langan, J., 1447
Langdell, J. I., 1178
Langer, J., 574
Langereis, M. C., 1405
Langevin, M., 404
Langford, C. A., 805
Langford, K., 1259
Langford, W. S., 730
Langley, M. B., 787
Langone, J., 428, 566, 955
Langstaff, A. L., 1693
Lankford, F. G., 24
Lankton, S., 1259

Lanning-Ventura, S., 1581, 1738
Lansdell, H., 336, 494
Lansdown, R., 664
Lansing, M., 194
Lansman, M., 494
LaNunziata, L. J., 201, 720, 1473, 1805
Lapeer, G. L., 1946
LaPointe, L., 129
LaPorte, D. J., 278
LaPorte, M. A., 1356
Lapouse, R., 1366
Lara-Alecio, R., 506
Larkin, D., 1891
Larocca, F., 998, 999
Laroche, S., 693, 1163
Larrivee, B., 1068, 1620
Larry P. v. Riles, 1481
Larsen, L. A., 67
Larsen, N. S., 213
Larsen, S., 1343, 1346, 1672, 1886, 1929
Larsen, S. C., 72, 667, 903, 1452, 1858
Larsin, L., 566
Larson, E., 229
Larson, G. E., 415
Larson, J. A., 1038
Larson, K., 1297
Larson, O. W., 1188
Larson, S. A., 430, 544
Larson, V. L., 25, 604, 1050, 1054, 1056
Larzerson, A., 826
Lash, J., 1128
Lash, J. P., 538
Laskoeski, M. A., 200
Last, A., 1723
Latané, B., 1674
Latham, E. E., 1227
Latham, G. P., 1213
Lathey, J. W., 162
Lathom, W., 1229
Latkin, K. C., 431
Laufer, M. W., 167
Laurent, J., 1432, 1635
Laurie, T. E., 45
Lauritzen, P., 1318
LaVeck, F., 638
LaVeck, G. D., 638
LaVor, M. L., 306
Lavos, G., 1297
Law of the People's Republic of China on the Protection of Disabled Persons, 379
Law, M., 1257
Lawlis, G. F., 612
Lawrence, B., 1373
Lawrence, E. A., 418
Lawrence, G. A., 85, 329, 1720
Lawrence, J. K., 1086
Lawrence, K. M., 13
Lawton, S., 701
Laybourne, P., 1231
Lazar, I., 504, 866
Lazar, P., 452
Lazarus, A., 399, 823
Lazarus, A. A., 476
Lazarus, M., 434
Leach, D. J., 174
League, R., 1506

Leal, D., 1734, 1949
Learman, L., 1859
Learner, J., 401, 1541, 1542
Learner, J. W., 475
Learning Disabilities Association, 1071
Leavitt, F., 382, 623, 698, 851, 1466, 1801
Leavitt, L. A., 575
LeBaron, S., 291, 354, 354, 690, 1157, 1159
LeBlanc, J. F., 495
LeBlanc, J. M., 1444
LeBlanc, R., 1614
Leboyer, F., 269
Lechner, H., 414
Lechtenberg, R., 687, 846, 1225
Leckliter, I. N., 773
Leckman, J. F., 468, 767
Leckman, J., 767
Leconte, P., 1891
Lee, B. C., 1853
Lee, C. L., 869
Lee, E. M. C., 193
Lee, L. J., 1668
Lee, L. L., 1277
Lee, M-L., 731
Leen, T., 953
Leeper, L. H., 1215
Lees, A. J., 467
Lees, J. M., 38
Lefco, H., 1510
Lefever, D. W., 579
Lefkowitz, M. M., 70, 684
Leguire, L. E., 951
Lehman, I. J., 1274, 1276, 1712, 1921
Lehman, L. C., 882
Lehmann, J. P., 1824
Lehr, E., 345, 1178, 1834
Lehtinen, L., 1095, 1350, 1722, 1885
Lehtinen, L. E., 27, 167, 1341, 1344
Lehtinen, L. U., 1148
Leibold, S. R., 80
Leigh, D., 1845
Leigh, J. E., 897
Leiman, A. L., 826
Leinhardt, G., 1933
Leitch, I., 1388
Leiter, R. G., 1096
Lejeune, J., 482, 625
Leland, H., 2, 329
Lelio, D. F., 448
Lemanek, K. L., 1650
LeMaster, B., 756
LeMay, M., 331
Lemert, E., 984
Lemeshaw, S., 74, 909, 950, 1037, 1274, 1291, 1714
Lemke, E. A., 702, 1258
Lemoine, P., 749
Lenk, L. L., 1210
Lenke, R. R., 1363
Lenkowsky, B., 249
Lenkowsky, R., 249
Lenkowsky, R. S., 248, 591, 662, 663, 876, 900, 903
Lenneberg, E., 374
Lenneberg, E. H., 362, 809

Lennon, M. L., 922, 1364, 1477, 1521
Lennon, R. T., 1307
Lennox, C., 1700
Lennox, M. A., 1457
Lennox, W. G., 118, 1457
Lennox-Buchtal, M., 740
Lentz, F. E., 1732
Lenz, B. K., 81
Leon, E., 1188
Leonard, H., 384
Leonard, H. L., 1283
Leonard, J. L., 772
Leonard, J. V., 792
Leonard, L. B., 1113
Leonard, M. F., 1042
Leone, P. E., 546
Leong, C. K., 341
Leont'ev, A. N., 1798
Lerea, L., 1230
Lerner, B., 1268
Lerner, J., 164, 248, 565, 721, 787, 1346, 1350, 1399, 1424, 1659, 1731, 1888
Lerner, J. V., 307, 1774
Lerner, J. W., 492, 1074, 1097–1098, 1217, 1607, 1816, 1867, 1887, 1923
Lerner, R. M., 279, 645, 1774, 1775
Lerner, T., 1722
LeRoy, B., 1668
Leske, M., 1156
Lesser, I. M., 399
Lester, B. M., 293
Letarte, J., 482
Lettieri, D. J., 75
Leu, D. J. Jr., 1201
Leu, P. W., 258
Leucht, C. A., 409
Leung, E. K., 510
Leung, P., 163
Leutner, D., 244
Levenstein, D., 1361
Leventhal, T., 1595
Levin, H., 1552
Levin, H. A., 115
Levin, H. S., 104, 345, 1834, 1835
Levin, J. R., 1039, 1088, 1201
Levine, A., 1671
Levine, D. D., 730
Levine, D. U., 1635
Levine, E., 982, 1567
Levine, G., 684
Levine, H. G., 503
Levine, J., 1390
Levine, M. D., 954, 1351, 1528
LeVine, R. A., 267
Levinson, B., 110
Levinson, E. M., 1891
Levinson, F., 1346
Levinson, H., 571
Levita, E., 337
Leviton, L., 168
Leviton, L. C., 466
Levy, B., 1115
Levy, D. M., 1302
Levy, H., 336, 1363

Levy, J., 341, 875, 1093, 1625, 1706
Levy, L., 832
Levy, P., 1486
Levy, S. A., 438, 441
Lewak, R., 1196
Lewandowski, D., 1439
Lewinsohn, P. M., 55, 677
Lewis, A., 201
Lewis, D., 531
Lewis, G. F., 1024, 1419
Lewis, H. C., 194
Lewis, I., 6
Lewis, J., 1394, 1747
Lewis, J. E., 35, 36, 502
Lewis, J. F., 507
Lewis, L., 938
Lewis, M., 372, 949, 949, 1102, 1610
Lewis, M. H., 623, 1730
Lewis, M. L., 1875
Lewis, N. D. C., 279
Lewis, R., 603
Lewis, R. B., 1067, 1068, 1527, 1785, 1790
Lewis, T. J., 781
Lewis, V., 193
Leyva, C., 322
Lezak, M. D., 77, 285, 345, 633, 1164, 1507, 1788, 1828, 1833
Lhermitte, F., 362
Li, A. K. F., 1268
Liberman, R. P., 399
Libet, J., 201, 1472
Licht, B. G., 169, 178, 1064
Lichtenberger, E. O., 294, 774, 801, 1009, 1087, 1125, 1149, 1252, 1290, 1307, 1330, 1331, 1332, 1386, 1625, 1628, 1712, 1811, 1881, 1026, 1029, 1030, 1791, 1794, 1899, 1901, 1902, 1904
Lichtenberger, L., 502, 973
Lichtenstein, R., 1422
Lichtman, M., 788
Liddell, S., 95
Lidz, C. S., 1087, 1420, 1950
Lieberman, M., 1209
Liebert, R. M., 1282
Lieb-Lundell, C., 1551
Liebowitz, M. R., 260
Lifson, S., 1190
Light, J., 84
Light, R. J., 698
Lightel, J., 616
Lightfoot, S. L., 1762
Liker, J., 1408
Lilly, M. S., 330, 532, 805, 883, 928, 1468, 1474, 1542
Lily, R. S., 156
Lin, P., 378
Linakis, J. G., 1061, 1062
Linan-Thompson, S., 510
Lindamood, C. H., 1111
Lindamood, P. C., 1111
Lindamood, P. D., 1111
Lindborg, S., 510
Lindemann, J. E., 876
Linden, J. D., 149
Linden, K. W., 149
Linder, T. W., 1051, 1421

Lindholm, B. W., 266
Lindow, J. A., 1594
Lindquist, E. F., 22
Lindqvist, B., 302
Lindsey, C. N., 80
Lindsley, D. F., 12
Lindsley, O. R., 195, 655, 1111–1112, 1413, 1454
Lindstroem, M., 1597
Lindstrom, J. P., 1597
Lines, P. M., 435
Linfoot, K., 188
Linfoot, K. W., 189
Ling, D., 495, 541, 1112
Lingle, J., 382
Lingoes, J. C, 1198
Link, M. P., 318
Linksz, A., 423
Linnemeyer, S. A., 1024, 1418
Linner, B., 1638
Linshaw, M. A., 1400
Linton, T. E., 658
Lipinski, D. P., 1616
Lipka, D. D., 870, 915, 919, 1166, 1477, 1703, 1744, 1811
Lippke, B. A., 1367
Lippman, L., 52, 458
Lipschutz, J., 1419
Lipsitt, L. P., 1435
Lipsky, D. K., 928, 1823
Lipson, M. Y., 1493
Liptak, G. S., 708, 1703
Lipton, E. L., 1720
Liscio, M. A., 422
List, L. K., 1867
Litow, L., 395
Litrownik, A. J., 456, 1616
Litt, I. F., 151
Little, B. B., 748
Little, J. W., 956
Litton, F. W., 482, 483
Lively, C., 426, 785, 1204, 1257, 1301, 1322, 1948
Livingston, R., 787, 1546, 1646
Livingston, R. B., 1829, 1838
Livingston, S., 740, 1360, 1458
Livingston-Dunn, C., 1207
Lloyd, J., 1026
Lloyd, J. W., 27, 72, 174, 475, 747, 1552
Lloyd, L., 1049
Lloyd, L. L., 1422
Lloyd, S., 805
Lo, W. H., 1283
Loban, W., 1050, 1054, 1928
Lobovitz, G., 1604
Locke, E. A., 1213
Lockhard, J. S., 799
Lockhart, R. S., 1163
Lockwood, A. L., 1870
Loeb, D. G., 1859
Loeb, H. W., 1178
Loeb, T. B., 112
Loeber, R., 124, 171
Loeffler, C. A., 469
Loevinger, J., 580
Logan, D. R., 67, 1643, 1659
Logan, P., 1259
Logan, W. J., 118

Logemann, J. A., 639
Lohman, D. F., 1486
Lombana, J. H., 249
Lombardino, L., 1373
Lombroso, C., 810
Loney, J., 612, 1717
Long, C. J., 284, 285, 872, 1360, 1545, 1844, 1846
Long, H. J., 484
Long, J. W., 405
Long, K. A., 683
Long, N., 1594
Long, N. J., 70, 486, 905, 1216, 1611
Long, S. H., 1791
Lonnerholm, T., 1094
Loose, F. F., 80
Lopata, C., 1120
Loper, A., 1068
Lopez, E. C., 299
Lora v. Board of Education of City of New York, 1482
Lorance, T., 258
Lorch, E. P., 612
Lord, C., 192, 194, 1348
Lord, F. M., 1268, 1328
Lord, J., 544
Lord-Maes, J., 1845
Lorenz, K., 68, 646
Lorenz, L., 1259
Lovass, O., 1293
Lovaas, O. I., 194, 201, 237, 985, 1118, 1550, 1613
Love, E., 1636
Love, H., 860
Love, R., 382
Love, V. L., 167
Loveland, K. A., 652, 1049
Loveland, N., 118
Lovely, D. F., 159
Lovett, D. L., 1823
Lovitt, T. C., 1118–1119, 1145, 1615, 1817
Low, K., 1773
Low, P. A., 1652
Lowdermilk, D., 1557
Lowe Syndrome Association, 1121
Lowe, L. A., 359
Lowe, P., 166
Lowe, P., 501
Lowe, P., 503
Lowe, P., 1913
Lowe, P. A., 97, 733, 940, 1602, 1624, 1828, 1833, 1850, 1916, 1945
Lowe, S. S., 334
Lowenfeld, B., 270, 1121–1122
Lowrey, G. H., 68
Lowrey, L. G., 1302
Lubart, T. I., 993
Lubic, L. G., 345
Lubicky, J. P., 1550
Lubin, B., 1569
Lubs, H. A., 766, 1042, 1942
Lubs, M., 33
Luby, E., 879
Lucas, V. H., 1659
Lucca-Irizarry, C., 511
Lucci, D., 854, 1092
Luce, S. C., 194
Luchsinger, R., 1858

Ludlow, B. L., 350
Ludwig, A. M., 1472
Lueders, H., 1459
Luerssen, T. G., 1834
Luiselli, J. K., 1099
Lukas, J., 878
Lumpkin, M. C., 1489
Lunberg, I., 1700
Lund, K., 1452
Lund, K. A., 667
Lund, N. J., 1050
Lupart, J., 316
Lupi, M. H., 175, 856, 1098, 1409, 1643, 1644, 1702, 1757
Lupin, M. N., 258
Luprowski, A. E., 275, 311, 777, 793, 832, 1024, 1565, 1567, 1713
Luria, A. R., 18, 285, 635, 783, 917, 1029, 1124, 1152, 1625, 1896
Lusthaus, C. S., 940
Lusthaus, E. W., 940
Luterman, D., 738
Lutey, C., 773, 1875
Luthans, F., 864
Luthe, W., 1216
Lutz, C., 1135, 1161
Lutz, R. J., 321, 1430
Lutzker, J. R., 195, 1641
Lykken, D. T., 1674
Lyle, 326
Lyman, R. D., 111
Lynch, E. W., 497, 510, 643, 1068, 1427, 1823
Lynch, J. I., 1292
Lynch, P., 431, 1822
Lynch, P. S., 1824
Lynch, V., 1949
Lynch, W. J., 1398
Lynn, L. Jr., 1396
Lyon, G., 1765, 1819
Lyon, G. R., 1085, 1278
Lyon, M. A., 688
Lyon, M. F., 1939
Lyon, P. E., 73, 201, 483, 1090, 1138, 1248
Lyon, S., 1765, 1819
Lyons, M., 1805
Lyons, M. J., 345
Lysen, V. C., 1306
Lytwyn, P., 360

Maag, J. W., 170, 517, 1621, 1672
MacAnally, P. L., 1480
MacArthur, C., 860, 1700, 1934, 1935
Maccoby, E. E., 267, 372, 580, 647, 1635
MacDonald, B. J., 159
MacDonald, C., 56, 106
MacDonald, J., 17, 128, 173, 221, 328, 399, 650, 1320, 1785
MacDonald, J. T., 169
MacDonald, K., 648
Mace, F. C., 1897
Mace, F. C., 780
Macfarlane, 1338
MacGinitie, R. K., 797, 798
MacGinitie, W. H., 797, 798

Machover, K., 627
Mack, D. E., 923
MacKay, A. W., 316
MacKenzie, D. E., 1592
MacKenzie-Keating, S. E., 1400
Mackie, R. P., 42
MacKinnon, D. W., 479
MacKinnon, R., 1803
Mackinzie, D. E., 1762
Maclean, C., 745
Maclean, R., 650
MacLean, W. E. Jr., 1730
MacLusky, N. J., 344
MacMahon, B., 1094
MacMillan, D., 516, 1048, 1582
MacMillan, D. C., 657
MacMillan, D. L., 175, 235, 929, 1127, 1171, 1185, 1315, 1405, 1441, 1445, 1670, 1747, 1765, 1823
MacMurray, B., 291
Macnair, A. L., 120
Macnicol, J., 1661
MacPhee, D., 6
MacPherson, E. M., 1154
Macy, A. S., 1127–1128
Madan, A., 861
Madaus, G. F., 520, 523, 827, 1195
Maddison, P., 1862
Maddox, T., 2, 437, 586, 837, 436, 437, 1330, 1367, 1506, 1570, 1784, 1790–1792
Madsen, C. H., 1780
Maer, F., 336
Magalini, S., 33, 115, 846, 1224, 1554
Mager, R. F., 227
Maggs, A., 598, 1538
Maggs, R. K., 598
Magnum, C. T., 422
Magnuson, J. V., 593
Magrab, P. R., 1336, 1422
Magy, M. A., 456
Mahanna-Boden, S., 829, 830, 831, 1331, 1333, 1399
Mahapatra, M., 1209
Maher, C., 956
Maher, C. A., 716, 906, 907, 1298, 1442, 1468, 1522, 1659, 1695, 1857
Maher, C. J., 479
Maher, M. C., 775
Maheshwari, M. C., 1360
Mahler, M., 365, 895
Mahler, M. S., 912, 1129–1130, 1623
Mahlios, M. C., 754
Mahoney, A., 1676
Mahoney, M. J., 70, 240
Mahoney, N. D., 1879
Main, M., 575
Main, T. F., 1799
Mainieri Hidalgo, A., 472
Maisto, S., 1726
Maisto, S. A., 75
Major, S., 1509
Major, S. M., 1084
Majouski, L. V., 262

Maker, C. J., 508, 695, 1130–1131
Maker, J., 824
Makhortova, G. H., 1578
Malcuit, G., 200
Maldonado-Colon, E., 1603
Malé, A., 542
Maletsky, B. M., 717
Malkin, D. H., 1218, 1355, 1604
Malkmus, D., 1839
Maller, S. J., 1865
Malone, S., 1666
Maloney, M. P., 1569, 1914
Malouf, D., 860
Malseed, R., 1128
Maltby, G. P., 1264
Mamula, R. A., 430
Mancoll, E. L., 288
Mandell, C. J., 45, 1143, 1422
Mangold, P. N., 1641
Mangold, S., 282
Mangold, S. S., 1641
Mangrum, C. T., 1086
Mani, M. N. G., 937
Maniscalco, G., 1859
Maniscalco, G. O., 617
Mank, D., 49
Mankinen, M., 1148
Mann, D. C., 302, 553
Mann, D. L., 391
Mann, L., 10, 53, 375, 414, 417, 418, 780, 867, 952, 983, 1088, 1100, 1510, 1524, 1528, 1607, 1868, 1941
Manni, J. L., 1873
Manning, D., 468
Manning, N., 1799
Manning, W., 1725
Mannino, F. C., 463, 1850
Mansueto, C. S., 676
Mapolelo, D., 1679
Marascuilo, L. A., 339
Marcel, T., 342, 874
March of Dimes Birth Defects Foundation, 1137, 1644, 1852
Marchand-Martella, W. E., 1338
Marcheschi, M., 925
Marco, G. L., 1783
Marcontel, M., 1335
Mardell-Czudnowski, C., 1426, 1625
Mardiros, M., 511
Marfo, K., 472
Margarf, J., 624
Margo, K. L., 878
Margulies, R., 353
Marholin, D., 1361, 1828
Mariga, L., 61, 1682
Marinopoulou, A., 1859
Marion, M., 1616
Marion, R., 510
Marion, R. J., 79, 163
Mark, D., 1735
Mark, D. M., 1205
Mark, F. D., 175
Markiewicz, B., 848
Markowitz, J., 609
Markowitz, M., 120

Marks, I. M., 1366
Marks, P. A., 1198
Markus, G. B., 266
Markwardt, F. C., 1330, 1919
Marland, S., 822
Marland, S. P., Jr., 1138
Marlowe, M., 414, 1061
Marnell, M., 409
Marolla, F. A., 266
Marozas, D. S., 1885, 1887
Marozas, P. S., 882
Marquardt, T. P., 564
Marriott, E. B., 728, 1199
Marro, T. D., 42
Marsch, A. J., 1864
Marsh, G. E., 42, 655, 1405, 1542, 1607, 1673
Marsh, G. E., II, 174
Marshalek, B., 1486
Marshall, E. D., 278
Marshall, G. M., 470
Marshall, H. H., 1339
Marshall, J., 1154
Marshall, J. F., 345
Marshall, R. M., 1158
Marston, D., 1640, 1937
Martella, R. C., 1338
Martens, B. K., 35, 1848
Martens, B., 112, 117, 131, 654, 804
Martens, B. K., 1220
Martens, P., 1201
Martier, S., 750
Martin, D., 702, 1256
Martin, D. A., 206
Martin, D. C., 748, 848
Martin, E. W., 459, 929
Martin, F., 118
Martin, G. L., 562, 607
Martin, J., 1203, 1734, 1823
Martin, J. A., 647
Martin, J. C., 750
Martin, J. P., 766
Martin, L., 319
Martin, R., 394, 463, 941, 1320
Martin, R. P., 1775
Martin, S. L., 1188
Martin, T. C., 469
Martin, T. J., 77, 81, 88, 89, 90, 93, 160, 197, 202, 207, 210, 212, 242, 263, 275, 280, 290, 292, 297, 298, 301, 311, 324, 350, 351, 355, 383, 545, 548, 560, 581, 622, 632, 656, 672, 722, 744, 753, 765, 769, 777, 793, 800, 816, 832, 840, 841, 845, 863, 864, 880, 899, 900, 977, 1007, 1008, 1010, 1012, 1013, 1016, 1017, 1024, 1025, 1036, 1040, 1071, 1095, 1111, 1118, 1130, 1177, 1185, 1207, 1210, 1212, 1234, 1236, 1238, 1241, 1243, 1245, 1246, 1251, 1262, 1305, 1323, 1360, 1364, 1413, 1429, 1478, 1480, 1513, 1519, 1533, 1555, 1556, 1562, 1565, 1568, 1579, 1581, 1582,

1583, 1589, 1619, 1620, 1654, 1704, 1713, 1753, 1856, 1857, 1895, 1914, 1917, 1945
Martindale, C., 1341
Martinez, I., 512
Martin-Reynolds, J., 175
Marton, P., 408
Martorella, P. H., 443
Martson, D., 521
Maruyama, G., 266
Marvell, T., 719
Marvin, R. S., 411
Marwitz, J. H., 1835
Mascovitch, M., 343
Mash, E. J., 221
Masi, G., 925
Masi, B. B., 1065, 1755
Masland, R., 1345
Masland, R. L., 13, 1148
Maslow, P., 579, 780
Mason, B. J., 1570
Mason, H., 701
Mason, P., 1402
Mason, S. A., 1539
Massagli, T. L., 1704
Masse, P., 693
Massie, R. K., 1909
Masten, A. S., 1405
Masters, L. F., 977
Masterson, J. F., 895
Mastroianni, L., 319
Mastropieri, 27
Mastropieri, M. A., 71, 803, 884, 1039, 1201, 1551
Mastyukova, E. M., 1362
Masutto, C., 572
Matarazzo, J. D., 150, 584, 773
Mateer, C. A., 1164, 1841
Matfield, J., 1657
Matheny, A. P., 345, 1953
Matheny, A. P., Jr., 1774
Mathews, G. J., 1002
Mathews, M. M., 1911
Matson, D. M., 912
Matson, J. L., 1099, 1613
Matsuyama, S. S., 1942
Mattaini, M. A., 194
Mattes, J. A., 80
Mattes, J., 120
Mattes, L. J., 1050
Matthews, C. G., 38, 743
Matthews, G., 1155
Matthews, J. R., 401
Matthews, K. M., 836, 1545
Matthews, M. M., 82
Matthews, M., 650
Matthews, W., 1155
Mattick, P., 1637
Mattie T. v. Holladay, 1147, 1481
Mattis, S., 1085
Mattson, P. D., 139
Mattson, S. N., 748
Matuszek, P. A., 1160
Matz, R. D., 1944
Maurer, R. G., 560, 1165
Maurer, S., 427
Maurice, C., 194
Max, J. E., 1844
Maxwell, A., 1314

Maxwell, J. P., 940
Maxwell, K., 989
May, D. C., 882, 1346, 1424, 1637, 1885, 1887, 1888
May, R., 124
Mayanagi, Y., 1464
Mayberry, R., 374
Mayer, G. R., 201, 232, 562, 607, 720, 1472, 1536, 1545, 1805, 1820
Mayer, J. D., 968
Mayer, R., 497
Mayer, R. E., 50
Mayes, B., 145
Mayes, P. A., 256
Mayeux, R., 362
Mayfield, J., 1624, 1835, 1850, 1913, 1916
Mayfield, J. W., 1602, 1652, 1945
Mayo Clinic, 677
Mayo, L., 1359
Mayo Physician Group, 1094
Mayron, L., 80
Maziade, M., 1775
Mazurkiewicz, A. J., 954
Mba, P. O., 1188
McAfee, J. K., 31, 41, 392, 788, 902
McAfee, J. G., 1050
McAllister, J., 1835
McAllister, J. R., 644
McAllister, V. L., 912
McAnally, P., 1501
McAnarney, E. R., 151
McArdle, J., 1919
McArthur, D., 1564
McBurnett, K., 168
McCabe, E. R. B., 1362
McCabe, L. L., 1362
McCall, B., 289
McCall, R. B., 949, 1282
McCallister, C., 1418
McCall-Perez, F., 1452
McCall-Perez, F. C., 667
McCallum, R. S., 774, 1864
McCammon, C., 1756
McCandless, B., 279, 375
McCane, M. R., 470
McCann, W., 299
McCarthy, D., 995, 1149, 1149, 1420
McCarthy, E., 1890, 1891
McCarthy, E. F., 1735, 1753, 1821
McCarthy, J., 922, 1068, 1528
McCarthy, J. J., 1217
McCarthy, M. M., 836, 1195
McCarthy, P., 1735
McCartney, K., 1249
McCauley, C., 1591
McCauley, R., 1791
McClannahan, L. E., 194
McClearn, G. E., 647, 705
McClellan, E., 438, 439, 440, 442, 1566, 1770
McClelland, D. C., 31, 1352
McClennen, S. E., 1625
McCloskey, G., 307, 886, 1096
McClung, H., 1859
McClung, M., 435

McCoin, J. M., 431
McCollum, S., 215
McConaghy, N., 201
McConnell, F. E., 184
McConnell, S., 1659
McCorkle, L. S., 928
McCormick, C. B., 424, 1050, 1054
McCormick, L., 678, 941, 962, 1819
McCormick, S., 823
McCoughvin, W. B., 1736
McCoy, K. M., 1414
McCracken, R. A., 1491
McCreary, B. D., 483
McCullough, L., 1766
McDade, H. L., 325
McDaniel, E. A., 17
McDavis, R. J., 881
McDermott, P., 213
McDermott, P. A., 1087, 1455
McDevitt, S. C., 1775
McDill, E. L., 1436
McDonald, J. E., 560
McDonald, J. R., 495
McDonald, L., 607, 1400
McDonald, R. S., 802
McDonnel, R. C., 821
McDonnell, J., 426, 1825
McDonnell, J. J., 802, 1824
McDougle, C. J., 987
McDowell, R. L., 44, 1317, 1738
McEachin, J., 986
McEachlin, J. J., 194
McElroy, S. L., 923
McEntire, E., 1297
McEvoy, G. K., 382, 698, 849, 1106, 1163
McEvoy, R. E., 652, 1049
McEwen, B. S., 1250
McFall, R. M., 1616
McGaugh, J. L., 551, 826
McGaw, B., 667
McGhee, P. E., 575
McGillivray, L., 25, 604
McGimsey, J. F., 1376
McGinnis, M. A., 1150, 1507
McGlone, J., 873
McGonigle, J. J., 1616
McGothlin, M., 851
McGothlin, W., 851
McGovern, J., 1425
McGrath, D., 439
McGreer, E. G., 689
McGreer, P. L., 689
McGreevy, P., 1411
McGrew, K. S., 1919, 1945
McGue, M., 1249
McGuffin, P., 705
McGuigan, C., 1949
McGuinness, D., 1635
McGunn, C., 1668
McGurk, H., 266
McInerney, M., 1518
McIntire, M. S., 1730
McIntyre, R. M., 1824
McIntyre, T., 517
McIntyre, T. C., 1554
McKay, D., 409
McKay, F. W., 1101
McKay, G., 755, 1318

McKay, M., 1272
McKay, R. J., 166
McKee, G., 1346, 1888
McKee, G. W., 1887
McKenry, L., 1564, 1772
McKenzie, B., 1282
McKeon, K. J., 1225
McKeown, M. G., 1488
McKinley, J. C., 1196, 1352
McKinley, N., 25, 604, 1050, 1054, 1056
McKinney, J. D., 929, 958, 1085, 1195, 1382, 1629, 1766
McKinnon, A. J., 248
McKusick, V., 452
McKusick, V. A., 706, 877, 1562
McLarty, J. R., 1785
McLaughlin, D. H., 1448
Mclaughlin, J., 531
McLaughlin, M., 510, 1355, 1824
McLaughlin, P. J., 955, 1602
McLaughlin, S., 1055, 1411
McLaughlin, T., 1701
McLaughlin, T. F., 1611
McLean, M., 1317
McLellan, D. S., 12
McLellan, M. J., 436
McLeod, J., 316, 659
McLeod, T. M., 1145
McLeskey, J., 931
McLoone, B. B., 1039
Mcloughlin, C. S., 616
McLoughlin, J., 120
McLoughlin, J. A., 78, 80, 1066, 1542, 1785, 1790
McMahon, J., 1732
McMenemy, R. A., 1525, 1526
McMorrow, M. J., 1537
McMurray, M. B., 170
McNaughton, S., 188, 274
McNeil, A., 414
McNeil, T. F., 1200
McNeill, B., 1864
McNutt, G., 897, 1190
McQuain, S., 1433
McQueen, D., 534
McQueen, D. V., 683
McRae, D., 190
McReynolds, L., 1648
McSweeney, M., 339
McSwigan, J. D., 76
McTate, G. A., 374
Meacham, M. L., 223
Meadow, E., 1297
Meadow, K., 537
Meadow-Orlans, K., 1208
Mearig, J. S., 1227
Mech, E. V., 46
Medaus, G., 1142
Medeiros-Landurand, P., 250
Medenis, R., 527
Medical College of Wisconsin Physicians & Clinics, 1558
Medina, V., 250
Mednick, S. A., 1674
Medoff, M., 373
Medway, F., 1037

Medway, F. J., 225, 463, 835, 1764, 1857
Meehl, P. E., 1076
Meeker, M., 1419
Meeker, M. N., 507
Meeker, R., 507
Meerman, R., 114, 305
Megan, E. L., 1218
Mehegan, C. C., 912
Mehrens, W. A., 563, 1274, 1276
Mehta, V., 934
Meichenbaum, D., 236, 395, 1135, 1151, 1154, 1162, 1616, 1666
Meichenbaum, D. H., 408, 924
Meichenbaum, D. N., 132
Meier, M. J., 853
Meier, N. C., 136
Meijer, A., 675, 730
Meir, J. H., 949
Meisel, C. J., 1582
Meisels, S. J., 1422
Meisgeier, C., 1666
Melamed, B. G., 302
Melendez, F. J., 1214
Melichar, J. F., 36
Mellard, D., 1074
Meller, R. E., 1774
Mellits, D., 184
Melloni, B. J., 329
Melloni's illustrated medical dictionary, 1165, 1224
Mellor, C. M., 283, 679
Meltzer, S., 482
Meltzoff, A., 1282
Melvin, B., 1119, 1415
Mendeville, B., 764
Mendez Barrantes, Z., 472
Menendez, F. J., 626
Menkes, J. H., 16, 264
Menlove, F. L., 1281
Mennemeier, M., 1537
Menninger, K. A., 1641
Mental Disability Law Reporter, 1148
Menuet, J. C., 749
Menyuk, P., 1113, 1291
Merbler, J. B., 1202
Mercer, A. R., 490, 884, 1659, 1672, 1867
Mercer, C., 27, 72
Mercer, C. D., 454, 490, 605, 650, 655, 884, 1177, 1602, 1654, 1672, 1722, 1867, 1948
Mercer, D. D., 1659
Mercer, J., 505, 1047, 1747
Mercer, J. R., 35, 36, 160 507, 1270, 1394, 1437
Mercer, S. R., 1602
Merck manual of diagnosis and therapy, 1913
Merenstein, G. B., 1416
Merino, B., 250
Merkel, S. P., 1765
Merlo, M., 836
Merrell, K. W., 1422, 1659
Merrett, J. D., 109
Merrifield, B., 168
Merrill, A. W., 1276
Merrill, M. A., 1177–1178

Merritt, D. D., 25, 604, 1051, 1056
Merritt, J. F., 877
Merwin, J., 1912
Merwin, J. C., 22
Meryash, D. L., 389
Merz, J. M., 1659
Meshcheryakov, A. N., 1799
Mesibov, G., 192
Mesibov, G. B., 192, 1601
Mesibov, R., 986
Messer, S. B., 68, 925
Messick, S., 609, 1141, 1269, 1514
Mesulam, M., 1177, 1465
Metfessel, N. S., 715
Metz, M. H., 1129
Meucke, L., 1279
Mewhort, D. J. K., 1751
Meyen, E. L., 927, 1542, 1910
Meyer, A., 360
Meyer, J. S., 1100
Meyer, L. H., 1613
Meyer, R. G., 1674
Meyerhoff, J. L., 1813
Meyers, A. W., 132
Meyers, C. E., 175, 1185–1186
Meyers, J., 463, 490, 1191
Meyers, L., 159
Meyers, R. E., 823
Michael, W. B., 258, 715
Michaud, L. J., 1835
Michaux, D., 1458
Michels, R., 1803
Michelson, P. E., 913
Michigan Department of Education, 360
Mick, E., 168
Middaugh, L. D., 752
Middlestadt, 1337
Middleton, G., 1904
Midence, K., 391
Miescher, A., 244
Might, J., 198, 985
Mignot, E., 1237
Mikkelsen, E. J., 593
Mikulecky, L., 1510
Milazzo, T. C., 43
Miles, S. E., 1433
Miles, T. R., 1924
Milholland, J. R., 1432
Milich, R., 169, 171, 612
Milkman, H. B., 751
Millbul, J., 1143
Miller, A., 319
Miller, B., 431, 432
Miller, B. S., 273
Miller, C. D., 1824
Miller, D., 464
Miller, F. B., 708
Miller, G. A., 1163
Miller, I., 1701
Miller, J. D., 76
Miller, J. F., 1292
Miller, J. G., 1209
Miller, J. H., 215, 786, 1144, 1823
Miller, K. L., 1693, 1730
Miller, L., 25, 860, 1050, 1054, 1056
Miller, L. C., 1366

Miller, L. J., 1097
Miller, L. S., 455
Miller, M. D., 1031
Miller, M. S., 823
Miller, N., 251, 266, 1643
Miller, N. E., 257, 1280
Miller, P. H., 399
Miller, R., 504, 1734, 1823
Miller, R. W., 1101, 1940
Miller, S., 1391, 1591, 1693
Miller, S. D., 1297
Miller, S. L., 483
Miller, S. P., 1177
Miller, S. R., 321, 847, 1870
Miller, T. L., 394, 721, 882, 884, 1065, 1581, 1611, 1746
Miller, W., 1730
Miller, W. H., 273
Millichap, J. G., 120
Millman, H. L., 684
Millman, J., 1190
Millon, C., 1191
Millon, T., 260, 895, 1191
Mills v. Board of Education of District of Columbia, 1192–1193, 1481
Mills, M. A., 165
Milner, B., 77, 262, 341, 1558
Milosky, L. A., 1270
Miltenberger, R. G., 780
Milunsky, A., 1429
Mims, A., 1132
Mims, S. K., 1228
Minami, J., 511
Minear, W. L., 347
Miner, M. E., 1835
Mingo, J., 43
Minick, N., 1797, 1895, 1896, 1950
Minifie, F. D., 425
Ministerio de Educacion, 1184
Ministry of Education of the Central Government of Peru, 1357
Ministry of Education, Taiwan 1752
Ministry of Education, Culture, and Sport, Israel, 996
Ministry of Education, Western Australia, 189
Ministry of Education, Youth Affairs, and Culture, Barbados, 323
Ministry of Welfare, India, 934
Minner, S., 701
Minnis, H., 295
Minskoff, E., 667, 1452
Minskoff, E. H., 1659, 1666
Minskoff, J. G., 1452
Minto, H., 316
Mintz, J., 399
Minuchin, S., 361, 1317
Mira, M. P., 1835
Miran, J., 59, 1680
Miranda, A. H., 498
Mirenda, P., 83
Mirkin, P., 1627, 1640, 1937

Mirkin, P. K., 111, 521, 716, 1452, 1528
Mirsky, A. F., 16, 612
Mischel, W., 456
Mishler, C., 1929
Misra, A., 934
Missiuna, C., 564
Mitchell, D. R., 1262
Mitchell, J. E., 303
Mitchell, J. V., 780
Mitchell, J. V., Jr., 307, 1794
Mitchell, R. G., 1714
Mitchell, R. S., 193
Mitchell-Heggs, N., 1464
Mithaug, D. E., 428, 1754
Mitiguy, J. S., 1836
Mittleman, B. B., 1283
Mittler, P., 1400, 1594
Miyazaki, M., 193
Mkaali, C. B., 63, 1684
Moallen, A., 770
Moallen, M., 770
Moberg, A., 1094
Mock, K. R., 534
Modell, W., 73, 405, 1202
Modgil, C., 964
Modgil, S., 964
Moe, C., 141
Moe, G. L., 1667
Moely, B. E., 773
Moen, R. E., 819
Moersch, M., 1321
Moffett, J., 1889
Mohlman, G., 1760
Mohr, G. J., 1302
Molloy, M., 1094
Molyneaux, D., 1050, 1053, 1055, 1271, 1272, 1410
Monaco, F., 453
Monat, R. K., 1640
Money, J., 20, 1042, 1857
Monk, M. A., 1368
Montagu, A., 680, 749
Montague, M., 1629
Montanelli, D. S., 1293
Montemayor, R., 1610
Montessori, M., 1206
Montgomery, L. M., 86, 401, 739, 1563
Montour, K., 1645
Moodie, A., 611
Moodie, A. G., 145
Moody, B., 960
Moon, C., 414
Moon, M. S., 1214
Moon, S., 428, 1735
Moore v. District of Columbia, 945
Moore, C. A., 443, 682
Moore, D., 1745
Moore, E. J., 434
Moore, G. B., 1566, 1771
Moore, J. A., 764
Moore, K. L., 385, 707, 1796
Moore, M., 1426
Moore, M. K., 1282
Moore, R. Y., 289
Moore, S., 272
Moores, D., 1049, 1567
Moores, D. F., 539, 758, 960, 1207–1208
Mora, G., 1230
Moran, M., 1929, 1936

Moran, M. R., 1932
Morehead, D. M., 1113
Moreland, R. I., 266
Moreno, J. L., 1451, 1669, 1672
Morey, R., 679
Morgan, C., 923
Morgan, D. G., 1879
Morgan, D. I., 483
Morgan, D. J., 470
Morgan, M., 1427
Morgan, M. A., 880
Morgan, W. P., 454, 1493
Mori, A. A., 977
Morkovin, B., 541
Mornex, R., 914
Morningstar, M. E., 1823
Morris, D., 1272
Morris, H. L., 1050
Morris, J. N., 697
Morris, J. V., 1231
Morris, N., 1937
Morris, R. D., 320
Morris, R. J., 1060, 1365, 1594, 1950
Morris, Y. P., 1060
Morrissey, A., 938
Morrissey, P., 1196
Morrow, G. R., 1390
Morrow, L. W., 430, 431, 1154, 1428
Morrow, S. A., 430, 431, 1154, 1428
Morrow-Tlucak, M., 750
Morse, A., 272
Morse, C., 114
Morse, W., 658, 1594
Morse, W. C., 56, 278, 484, 486, 905, 1209–1210, 1216
Morsink, C. V., 1143, 1210–1211, 1764
Mosby's GenRx, 596
Mosby's medical and nursing dictionary, 115, 687, 846, 1225, 1554
Moser, H. W., 1548
Moses, J. A., 1124
Moses, N., 1379
Moshe, S., 556
Moshman, D., 575
Moskowitz, D. S., 754
Mosley, A. M., 599
Moss, D., 562
Moss, E., 1419
Moss, H. A., 645, 949
Moss, J. W., 1212
Mosseler, D. G., 411
Mott, T., 148
Motta, R. W., 970
Motulsky, A. G., 386, 705
Mountjoy, P. T., 696
Mowder, B. A., 650
Mowrer, O. H., 447, 1168
Moyer, J. R., 1754
Moyer, K. E., 69
Moyer, S. B., 1533
Moylan, J. J., 688
Moyle, D., 1731
Moyle, L., 1731
Moynahan, E. I., 1853
Moynihan, L., 1157
Moynihan, P., 561

Mpofu, E., 58, 62, 1679, 1683
Mrazek, P. B., 20
Mueller, A. B., 1098
Mueller, C. M., 1064
Mueller, R. M., 1789
Muenz, T. A., 32, 398, 434, 435, 521
Mukhopadhyay, S., 1565
Mulcahey, M. J., 1314, 1704
Mulhern, J., 520, 523
Mulhern, R. K., 292
Mulick, J. A., 725, 1172
Mulins, J. B., 856
Mullen, J. K., 1780
Muller, G. E., 693
Muller, H. J., 713
Mulligan, M., 520
Mullin, J. B., 154
Muma, J. R., 1055, 1411, 1821
Mundschenk, N. A., 195
Mundy, P., 1272
Munoz, A. M., 222
Munoz-Sandoval, A., 1921
Munson, D., 1286
Munson, Grace E., 1226
Munson, S. M., 1251
Mupedziswa, R., 1679
Mupedziswa, R., 58
Murakawa, K., 193
Murdock, B. B., Jr., 186
Murdock, J. Y., 725
Murphy, A., 625
Murphy, A. T., 1643
Murphy, D. A., 169, 546, 1431
Murphy, G., 1622
Murphy, J., 777
Murphy, K. R., 135, 169, 1790
Murphy, L., 572
Murphy, L. L., 307, 308, 1794
Murphy, M., 413
Murphy, P., 1769
Murphy, P. K., 18
Murphy, R. R., 70
Murphy, S., 666
Murray, C., 711, 989
Murray, C. A., 1083
Murray, D. J., 186
Murray, H. A., 31, 1797
Murray, J., 524, 1646
Murray, N. M. F., 467
Murray, W., 1770
Muscular Dystrophy Association, 1227
Musselwhite, C. R., 37, 788
Mussen, P. H., 371
Myers, C. A., 747
Myers, C. E., 34
Myers, F. L., 403, 404
Myers, M. G., 448
Myers, P., 952, 1771, 1886, 1889
Myers, P. E., 1559
Myers, P. I., 19, 139, 758, 917, 1113
Myers, R. E., 479
Myers, S. L., 1835
Mykelbust, H., 401, 492, 606, 638, 1067, 1293, 1929, 1935

Myklebust, H. R.
Myklebust, H. R., 18, 571, 1148, 634, 635, 1234, 1452, 1507, 1553, 1928, 1931
Myles, B., 1385
Myquel, M., 675
Myrick, R., 1393

Nachtman, W., 1145
Nada, N., 1859
Nadler, H. L., 387
Nafpakitis, M., 562
Naftolin, F., 344
Nagel, D. A., 179
Nagle, R., 869
Nagle, R. J., 1421, 1775
Naglieri, J. A., 170, 405, 627, 977, 1030, 1150
Nagylaki, T., 1093
Nahmias, A., 878
Naib, Z., 878
Naicker, S., 1677
Naicker, S. M., 1678
Naidoo, S., 1924
Naidu, S., 1548
Nakamura, Y., 1546
Nall, M., 78, 80, 1067
Namias, A. J., 1808
Namir, L., 1646
Nanda, H., 802
Napier, G., 1935
Nardella, M. T., 1409
Naremore, R. C., 25, 604, 1050, 1054, 1697
Naron, N. K., 1435
Nash, C. E., 1235–1236
Nash, R. J., 1692
Nash, R. T., 422, 468, 1132, 1219, 1447, 1759, 1795
Nash, W. R., 1236, 1418
Nass, R., 560
Nastasi, B. K., 614, 616
Nathan, J., 1711
Nathanson, D. S., 1060
Nation, J. E., 363
Nation, P., 910
National Advisory Committee for the Handicapped, 1540
National Advisory Committee on Hyperkinesis and Food Additives, 760
National Association for Gifted Children, 1237
National Association for Sickle Cell Disease, 1644
National Association for the Deaf, 1237
National Association of School Psychologists, 1238
National Association of Social Workers, 703
National Association of State Boards of Education, 1239
National Association of State Directors of Special Education, 97, 737, 942, 1239, 1517
National Center for Education Statistics, 733

National Center for Law and the Handicapped, 141
National Center on Educational Outcomes, 1240
National Clearinghouse for Alcohol and Drug Information, 629
National Coalition of Advocates for Students, 1298
National Commission on Excellence in Education, 1115, 1468
National Council for Accreditation of Teacher Education, 1241
National Council of Churches, 392
National Easter Seal Society, 1242
National Education Association, 1242
National Education Policy Investigation, 1677
National Endowment for the Humanities, 1243
National Foundation for Infantile Paralysis, 1138
National Information Center for Children and Youth with Disabilities, 270, 643, 1245, 1628, 1828
National Information Center for Children and Youth with Handicaps, 643
National Information Center for Handicapped Children and Youth, 1245, 1320
National Institute of Mental Health, 556, 1245
National Institute of Neurological Disorders and Stroke, 1257
National Institute on Alcohol Abuse and Alcoholism, 751
National Institutes of Health, 741, 1360
National Joint Committee on Learning Disabilities, 1246
National Organization for Rare Disorders, 1602, 1603, 1652, 1946
National Recreation and Park Association, 1512
National Technical Institute for the Deaf, 1250
Natriello, G., 1436
Naugle, R. I., 1834
Naumberg, M., 153
Naville, S., 1509
Naylor, A. A., 13
NCERT, 935
Neal, M. C., 320
Neale, J. M., 1168, 1673
Neason, S., 1409
Ng, A. M., 1021
Nguyen, V. A., 1721
Niccum, N., 594
Nicholls, G. H., 541
Nicholls, J. G., 1497
Nichols, K., 1595

Neef, N. A., 1220
Neff, W. S., 1430
Neigut, D., 420
Neill, A. S., 905
Neill, S. R. St. J., 1272
Neilson, S., 303
Neisser, U., 199, 963, 1408
Neisser, W., 1625
Neisworth, J. T., 490, 567, 753, 1251, 1405, 1420, 1422, 1747
Nelson, C., 803
Nelson, C. M., 464, 470, 546, 1020
Nelson, D., 585
Nelson, G. E., 1198
Nelson, K. B., 1360
Nelson, L. B., 1289, 1780
Nelson, N. M., 269
Nelson, N. W., 25, 425, 604, 1050, 1052, 1053, 1055, 1410
Nelson, R. O., 221, 1617, 1647
Nelson, W. E., 13, 319, 593
Neman, R., 1345
Ness, J. E., 621, 954
Nesse, R. M., 260
Nesselroade, J., 1774
NetHealth, 556
Netick, A., 1066
Neubert, D. A., 1824
Neuenfeldt, J., 1879
Neufeld, G. R., 544
Neuman, P. A., 303
Neumann, K. N., 1388
Nevin, A., 1764, 1766
Nevin, N. C., 109
New Mexico State Department of Education, 1335
New York University Health System, 1562
Newall, A., 417
Newberger, D. A., 905
Newberger, E. H., 216
Newcomb, M., 112
Newcomer, P., 667, 1786, 1932, 1936
Newcomer, P. L., 586, 922, 1450
Newell, J. D., 703
Newhouse, J. H., 1278
Newland, T. E., 273, 819, 1264
Newlin, D. B., 336
Newman, B. M., 352
Newman, N., 430
Newman, P. A., 112
Newman, P. R., 352
Newman, R., 1594
Newman, R. G., 484, 486, 905, 1216
Newman, S. A., 206
Newsbriefs, 1066
Newsom, C. D., 1621
Neziroglu, F., 409
Nezirogly, F. A., 1283

Needham, R., 1092, 1558
Needle, R., 1757
Needleman, H. L., 168, 646, 1061, 1061, 1429
Needles, M., 1760

Nichols, R. C., 713, 817, 963, 1018, 1487, 1687
Nicholson, J. I., 213
Nicol, A. R., 1775
Nicolosi, L., 636
Nielsen, L. B., 1227
Nielson, A. B., 1130
Nielson, J. M., 1148
Nieman, H., 415
Nientimp, E. G., 1049
Nietupski, J., 427, 785, 962, 1553, 1859, 1948
Nigeria Federal Ministry of Information, 66
NIH, 39
Nihira, K., 2
Nihira, K., 34
Nijhof, G., 1715
Nineteenth Annual Report to Congress on the Implementation of the Individuals with Disabilities Education Act, 565
Nippold, M. A., 1270
Nirje, B., 67, 1275
Nisbet, J., 431
Nissani, H., 576
Nitko, A. J., 156, 488, 1328
Niva, W. L., 1301
Nix, G., 540
Nixon, J. A., 1051
Njuki, E. P., 60, 1681
Nleya, P., 1679
Noachter, S., 1458
Nochimson, G., 1094
Nodine, B., 1936
Nodine, B. F., 1932
Noel, M. M., 1382, 1471–1472
Nolan, C., 1155
Nolen, S., 1936
Noller, R. B., 478
Non Oral Communication: A Training Guide for the Child Without Speech, 37
Noonan, M. J., 67
Noore, N., 664
Nora, J. J., 319
Nordoff, P., 1229
Nores, L., 950
Norman, A. P., 13
Norman, C. A., 1639
Norman, D. A., 1163
North, B., 1834
Northcott, W., 982, 1406
Northern Territory Board of Studies, 189
Northern, J. L., 80
Northwest Territories, Department of Education, Culture and Employment, 317
Norvell, M., 46
Noshpitz, J. D., 371
Novak, J. D., 50
Novak, M. A., 40
Novell, I., 464
Nowaka, A. J., 553
NSW Department of School Education, 189
Nulman, J. A. H., 1931
Nunn, A. J., 80
Nunn, R. G., 1156, 1850

Nunnally, J., 1081
Nunnally, J. C., Jr., 156
Nurick, E. L., 1277
Nuss, S. M., 1774
Nussbaum, N. L., 1304
Nussbaum, R. L., 1121
Nuttall, E. V., 250, 1747
Nutter, N., 1692
Nyanungo, K. R., 62, 1683
Nye, C., 630
Nyhan, W. L., 1098, 1178
Nystrom, L. A., 639

O'Brien, G., 1916
O'Brien, K., 1195
O'Brien, S., 1415
O'Bryan, A., 1736
O'Connell, C. Y., 522
O'Connell, J. C., 510
O'Connell-Mason, C., 522
O'Conner, K., 1393
O'Conner, K. P., 676
O'Conner, P. A., 1675
O'Dell, C., 556
O'Dell, S. L., 1879
O'Donnell, C. R., 1730
O'Donnell, J. G., 529
O'Donnell, J. P., 612
O'Donnell, L. G., 1348
O'Donnell, P. A., 1343
O'Hanlon, J. F., 244
O'Leary, D., 1155
O'Leary, K. D., 717, 1618
O'Malley, J. M., 25, 604
O'Malley, P. M., 76
O'Neill, C. T., 1735
O'Neill, J., 278, 801, 1414,
   1612, 1616
O'Neill, R. E., 780, 781,
   1220, 1734
O'Neill, S. O., 612
O'Quinn, A. N., 565, 567,
   709, 1808
O'Shea, L., 1333
O'Shea, L. J., 467, 691,
   1867, 1943
Oakander, S., 37
Oakland, T., 36, 58, 62, 980,
   1016, 1268, 1304, 1432,
   1597, 1635, 1636, 1679,
   1680, 1683, 1749
Oates, R. K., 216
Oats, R. G., 1417
Obiakor, F. E., 1263, 1355,
   1610
Obrzut, J. E., 285, 571,
   1706, 1835, 1845
Obrzut, J. W., 594
Ochoa, H. S., 250, 252
Ochoa, S. H., 250, 644, 1603
Ockwood, L., 962
Oddy, M., 1838
Oden, M. H., 1781
Oden, S. C., 1662
Odle, S. J., 927
Odom, P. B., 186
Odom, S. L., 857, 1659
Oehlkers, W. J., 1527
Oetter, P., 221, 1051
Oetzel, R., 1635
Office for Civil Rights, 514
Office for Medical Applica-
   tions of Research, 80

Office of Civil Rights, 98,
   393, 608
Office of Juvenile Justice
   and Delinquency Preven-
   tion (OJJDP), 546
Office of Special Education
   and Rehabilitation, 1373
Office of Special Education,
   628
Offord, D. R., 167, 448, 683
Ogbu, J. U., 518
Ogbue, R. M., 1267
Ogelsby, K., 821, 822
Ogle, P. A., 1319, 1643
Ogletree, E. J., 145
Ogletree, G. S., 145
Ogonda, G., 59, 1680
Ohi, M., 675
Ohmori, A. K., 1409
Ohta, M., 1003
Ojemann, L. M., 1360
Okafor, M. C., 1265
Okagaki, L., 1408
Okifuji, A., 1406
Oldendorf, W. H., 331, 1941
Oliver, A. I., 468
Oliver, J. E., 698
Oliver, M., 1568
Ollendick, T., 685, 698
Ollendick, T. H., 303, 1616
Olley, G., 40
Olsen, E. G., 1943
Olsen, J., 763
Olsen, K. R., 1196
Olsen, T. F., 1231
Olshansky, S., 838
Olson, J., 1208
Olson, J. R., 104
Olson, M. R., 283
Olson, R., 684
Olson, W. C., 1806
Oluigbo, F. C., 1265
Olweus, D., 69
Omanson, R. C., 1488
Omiri, Y., 1940
Omizo, M. M., 258, 1723
Omori, H., 1084
Ondell, J. T., 1890
189th General Assembly of
   the United Presbyterian
   Church, 392
Onen, N., 60, 1681
Oppenheim, A. N., 1479
Opper, S., 30, 158
Orelove, F., 1286
Orelove, F. P., 1765
Orem, R. C., 1207
Organization for Economic
   Cooperation and Develop-
   ment, 1906
Orgiazzi, J. J., 914
Orlansky, M., 1321
Orlansky, M. D., 270, 491,
   856, 913, 1057, 1122, 1738
Ormrod, J. E., 1382
Ornby, R., 80
Orne, M., 1390
Ornstein, A. C., 601, 1635
Orozco, S., 1181
Ort, S. I., 767
*Ortho: Interdisciplinary
   approaches to mental
   health,* 1303

Ortiz, A., 250
Ortiz, A. A., 252, 1110, 1355,
   1604
Ortíz, V., 507
Orton, G. L., 1366
Orton, J. L., 1527
Orton, S. T., 71, 340, 635,
   825, 854, 1093, 1303–
   1304, 1493, 1551, 1867,
   1923
Orton-Gillingham Practi-
   tioners and Educators,
   571
Orvaschel, H., 399
Orwid, H. L., 1297
Osborn, A. F., 477, 478, 789,
   1305, 1669
Osborn, F., 714
Osborn, R. W., 1640
Osborne, A. G., 1433
Osborne, J. G., 1415
Osborne, S. S., 1766
Oseroff, A., 938
Osgood, C. E., 447, 1305
Osguthorpe, R. T., 1858
Osherson, D., 1455
Oshima, K., 1546
Osofsky, J. D., 950
Osterling, J., 985
Oswald, D. P., 517
Otis, A. S., 1307
Otto, P. L., 1409
Otto, W., 1525, 1526
Ovando, C. J., 1109
Over, R., 1282
Overcast, B., 1561
Overcast, T. D., 450, 457,
   700
Owen, M. J., 705
Owens, R. E., 1051, 1053,
   1055, 1411
Owings, S., 1835
Oxendine, J. B., 1214
Oxorn, H., 264, 1349
Ozolins, D. A., 917

Pacheco, A., 511
Pachman, J. S., 1615
Packard, D., 1622
Padden, C. A., 756
Padi, M. H., 1398
Padilla, C., 1195
Padron, M., 498, 510
Padula, J. B., 1883
Padula, W. V., 1883
Paez, D., 496, 499
Page, E. B., 267, 1193
Page, G. T., 903
Page, T. J., 1220
Page-El, E., 1067
Paget, C., 581
Paget, K. D., 375, 1087,
   1421, 1422, 1439, 1775
Pahud, D., 1906
Pahz, J. A., 1296
Pahz, S. P., 1296
Paine, C., 1569
Paine, S., 1338
Paine, S. C., 1204
Painter, T. S., 386
Painting, D. H., 1350
Paivio, A., 343, 923
Pajak, E. F., 1450

Pakin, D. T., 877
Palermo, D., 375
Palermo, M., 1774
Palfai, T. P., 968
Palfreman, J., 725
Palincsar, A. S., 417, 1180
Palkovitz, H. P., 345
Palladino, P., 925
Pallas, A. M., 1436
Palloway, E. A., 786
Palmer, D. J., 176, 177,
   1179, 1188
Palmer, D. L., 804, 887,
   1691
Palmer, J. M., 425
Palmer, R. S., 333
Pambookian, H. S., 783
Pampiglione, G., 1853
Pancsofar, E., 1271
Pancsofar, E. L., 1222, 1250,
   1251, 1310, 1319, 1374
Paneth, N., 155
Pang, D., 1834
Pankaskie, S., 803
Pankratz, L. D., 584
Pannbacker, M., 1904
Pany, D., 521
Paolucci-Whitcomb, P., 1764,
   1766
Pape, K. E., 154
Papenfuss, H. L., 920
Papert, S., 439, 440
Pappo, M., 556
Parette, H. P., 1158
Parish, P., 1128
Park, E., 1857
Parke, R. D., 13, 69, 371,
   1282
Parker, E. B., 1231
Parker, K., 773
Parker, K. A., 1569
Parker, R. S., 1837
Parkhurst, H., 1322
Parkin, J. M., 918
Parkinson, C., 336
Parks, B. T., 1621
Parks, L. D., 392
Parliament of South Africa,
   1678
Parmalee, R., 1268
Parmar, R. S., 1145
Parmelee, A. H., 13
Parnes, S. J., 477, 478, 480
Paroz, J., 1542
Parrish, L. H., 517, 804
Parry, P., 408
Parry, W., 130, 920
Parson, L. R., 1338
Parsons, H., 863
Parsons, J. L., 1236
Parsons, P. J., 848
Parsons, R. D., 463
Parsonson, B. S., 3
Parten, M. B., 1391, 1806
Pasamanick, B., 645, 816,
   1066, 1323–1324
Pascual-Leone, J., 412, 1269
Pasick, P., 56
Passarge, E., 888
Passow, H., 506
Passow, H. A., 659
Pataki, C., 171
Patch, V. D., 1818

Patel, A. N., 345
Paterson, A., 544
Paterson, A. S., 1516
Paterson, M., 1112
Patrick, J. L., 35
Patterson, C. J., 456
Patterson, D. G., 970
Patterson, D. R., 193
Patterson, G. B., 228
Patterson, G. R., 68, 710,
   1318
Patterson, R., 80
Patton, J., 394
Patton, J. M., 349, 510
Patton, J. R., 117, 175, 786,
   901, 1429
Patton, R. G., 728
Paul, J., 1524
Paul, P., 982, 1414, 1567,
   1646
Paul, P. V., 1480
Paul, R., 1050, 1052, 1053,
   1055, 1411
Paul, S. M., 807
Pauli, L. L., 1360
Pauls, D. L., 468
Paulson, D. R., 248, 321,
   628, 1106, 1240, 1891
Pausewang Gelfer, M., 1697
Pavicevic, L., 246
Paviour, R., 292
Pavlidis, G. T., 1492
Pavlov, I. P., 162, 445
Payne, J., 394
Payne, J. C., 548, 1559
Payne, J. S., 45, 117, 175,
   786, 901, 1429
Payne, R. A., 175, 786, 901
Payne, R. W., 1077
Paz, T. H., 264
Peace Corps, 1333
Peach, F., 189
Peak, P. K., 1786
Peak, R., 414
Pearl, D., 571
Pearl, R., 958
Pearon, P. D., 1489
Pearson, C., 1232
Pearson, H. W., 75
Pearson, K., 748, 795
Pearson, L., 924
Pearson, M. E., 1277, 1625
Pearson, N. A., 437, 579
Pearson, P. D., 1761, 1889
Peck, A., 1595
Peck, C. A., 1766
Peck, E. B., 1279
Peck, V. A., 681, 925
Peckham, P. D., 223
Peckham, V. C., 318
Pedhazur, E., 1224
Pedlar, A., 544
Peery, M. L., 160, 207, 978,
   1016, 1118, 1243, 1248,
   1406, 1562, 1579, 1926
Pehrsson, R. S., 952
Peiper, A., 1516
Pekelharing, H., 1715
Pelham, W., 171
Pelham, W. E., 169
Pelland, M., 1776
Pelletier, J. G., 1137
Pendarvis, E., 824

Pendergrass, T. W., 318, 1100
Pendley, J. S., 278
Penfield, D. A., 294
Penfield, W., 341, 874
Pennington, B., 175
Pennington, B. F., 1364
Pennypacker, H. S., 1413
Penry, J. K., 1869
People First of California, 1339
Peoples, A., 1622
Pepe, H. J., 1001
Peplau, L., 863
Percy, A. K., 1548
Pereire, J. R., 1347–1348
Peresleni, L. I., 1360
Peresuh, M., 59, 62, 1680, 1683
Perez, J., 732
Perfetti, C. A., 1501
Périer, O., 449, 535, 539, 540, 558, 959, 1877
Perkins School for the Blind, 1350
Perkins, S., 316
Perkins, W., 1696
Perlman, A. L., 639
Perlman, M., 730
Perlo, V., 1857
Perret, Y. M., 165, 166, 265, 311, 637, 869, 926, 1940
Perrin, J. M., 391, 591
Perrin, J., 1157
Perry, A., 1549
Perry, E. K., 382, 1164
Perry, J. D., 616, 1042, 1178, 1397, 1801, 1856, 1941, 1953
Perry, M. L., 87
Perry, R. H., 1164
Perry, S., 1557
Perryman, P., 546
Perske, R., 1827
Peshawaria, R., 936
Peske, M., 382
Pestalozzi, J. H., 1359
Peters, D., 154
Peters, J. E., 917
Peters, K. G., 167
Peters, M. L., 1554
Peters, R. D., 925, 1374
Peters, R. G., 77
Petersen, A. C., 1635
Petersen, N. S., 1783
Petersen, T. K., 175
Peters-Martin, P., 1774
Peterson, D. R., 238, 1134
Peterson, J., 921
Peterson, L., 1834, 1846
Peterson, M., 1891
Peterson, M. J., 1152
Peterson, N. L., 1320
Peterson, P. L., 177, 671
Peterson, R. F., 782
Peterson, R. L., 327, 1633
Peterson's guide to colleges with programs for learning disabled students, 422
Petrauskas, R. J., 571
Petrosko, J., 80, 1067
Pevzner, M. S., 1360
Pfeiffer, S. I., 977, 1261

Pfiffner, L. J., 168
Pflaum, S., 958
Pflaum, S. W., 897
Pflugrad, D., 1616
Pfohl, W., 940
Phachaka, L., 61, 1682
Phares, E. J., 401
Phelps, A. L., 1430
Phelps, L., 751, 867, 1487
Phelps, L. A., 321
Phelps, N., 940
Phelps-Gunn, T., 1928
Phelps-Terasaki, D., 1928
Phibbs, R. H., 155
Phifer, S. J., 1051
Philbrick, L. A., 194
Phillips, B., 1600
Phillips, B. N., 1364, 1563
Phillips, D., 1361
Phillips, E. L., 1450
Phillips, J. L., 239
Phillips, J. S., 456, 1168
Phillips, L., 1213
Phillips, R. D., 1393
Phillips, V., 1766
Pholoho, K., 61, 1682
Physician's desk reference, 405
Piacentini, J. C., 239
Piaget, J., 372, 409, 444, 574, 578, 580, 1029, 1066, 1208, 1377, 1384, 1459, 1509, 1885
Piao, Y., 378
Piazza, C. C., 1550
Pickar, J., 1590
Pickett, A. L., 1316
Picton, T., 291
Pierce, C. M., 1302
Pierce, R. M., 1591
Piercy, M., 183
Piers, E. V., 1386, 1610
Piersel, W., 646
Piersel, W. C., 224, 1231, 1647
Pierson, W. E., 80
Pieterse, M., 189
Pijl, S. J., 1253
Pikulski, J. J., 1525
Pillitteri, A., 1557
Pilzecker, A., 693
Pincus, J. H., 13, 261, 1344
Pindzola, R. H., 1050
Pine, D. S., 1199
Pinel, P., 1386–1387
Pines, A., 1758
Pintner, R., 970
Piontrowski, D., 174
Pipes, P. L., 1279
Pipho, C., 435, 1195
Pires, S., 429
Pirozzolo, F. J., 570, 1345, 1751
Pisarchick, S. E., 624, 926, 1107, 1186, 1211, 1313, 1344
Pitrowski, C., 246
Plahn, M. R., 279
Plaisted, J. R., 1124
Plake, B., 1440
Plake, B. S., 2, 308
Planning Institute of Jamaica, 323

Plante, E., 424, 1276
Plapinger, D. S., 1621
Plata, M., 1218
Plato, 1390
Platt, J. J., 408, 1666
Platt, M. M., 443
Plaud, J. J., 195
Plaue, E., 1614
Pleck, J., 1635
Pless, I. B., 151, 391
Pleydell-Pearce, C. W., 420
Plomin, R., 168, 267, 647, 705, 1774
Plue, W. V., 843
Pocklington, K., 1862
Podell, D. M., 1670
Podemski, R. S., 42
Podhajski, B., 1292
Poggio, J., 1074
Poland, S. F., 1945
Polansky, N. A., 1318
Polatajko, H., 564
Poli, P., 925
Polifka, J. C., 940
Pollack, D., 541, 535
Pollard, A., 429
Pollatsek, A., 572, 1751
Pollitt, E., 709, 728
Polloway, E. A., 175, 796, 901
Polsgrove, L., 561
Polvinale, R. A., 1641
Pomeroy, J. C., 1042
Pomeroy, J., 1512
Pond, D. A., 118
Ponterotto, J. G., 882, 1598
Poole, D. L., 1594
Poorman, C., 1553
Poostay, E. J., 572, 1343
Pope, B., 106, 116, 920
Pope, B. M., 130, 154, 385
Pope, H. G., 923
Popham, W. J., 227, 488, 715
Pople, M. T., 1488
Poplin, M., 1936
Poplin, M. S., 897, 903, 1218, 1931
Poploukas, A., 1859
Popper, C. W., 120, 1717
Porac, C., 1093
Porcella, J. E., 295, 314, 423, 469, 1019, 1306
Porch, B., 1399
Porter, I. H., 808
Porter, K. L., 1112
Porter, R., 824
Posner, M. I., 173, 1487
Possi, M. K., 63, 1684
Post, C. H., 1083
Poteat, G. M., 563, 1712, 1921
Poteet, J. A., 659, 983, 1602, 1931
Potter, H., 367
Potter, H. W., 364, 1171
Potts, L., 1411
Potts, N. L. S., 1278
Poulson, C. L., 1536
Powell, J., 222, 1806
Powell, M. P., 250, 1605
Powell, T. H., 1319, 1643
Power, D. J., 1293, 1821

Power, J., 1129
Powers, A., 1936
Powers, J. L., 216
Powers, M., 985
Powers, M. D., 1648
Pradelli, J., 1135
Prasse, D. P., 609, 762
Prather, E. M., 1625
Pratt, R. R., 1906
Preator, A. A., 644
Preator, K., 1534
Preddy, D., 958
Predebon, J., 1261
Prehem, H. J., 482, 620, 1415–1416
Prehm, H. J., 1540
Preiser, W. F. E., 655
Premack, D., 238, 1288, 1401, 1414
Prescott, G. A., 22
President's Commission for the Study of Ethical Problems in Medicine and Biomedical and Behavioral Research, 206, 806
President's Committee on Mental Retardation, 567, 1428, 1429, 1652
President's Panel on Mental Retardation, 1315
Pressley, M., 424, 1039, 1050, 1054
Pribram, K. H., 1124
Price, A. W., 470
Price, A. L., 1335
Price, B. J., 42, 174, 655, 1405, 1542, 1673
Price, G. G., 511
Price, J. H., 554
Price, M., 758, 1113, 1910
Price, R. A., 468
Price-Williams, D., 887
Prichett, E. M., 1145
Pride, C., 1479
Prieto, A. G., 1221
Prifitera, A., 773, 1902
Primmer, H., 846
Prince, V. T., 1833
Pringle, M. L. K., 698
Prinz, E. A., 95
Prinz, P. M., 95, 96, 134, 975, 1113
Prior, M., 725
Pritchard, C., 1595
Pritchard, J. A., 106
Prizant, B. M., 193
Professional guide to diseases, 1572
Proger, B., 1510
Programs for the handicapped, 1225
Project Action, 1847
Proos, L., 1403
Proposed federal regulations for the Individuals with Disabilities Education Act, 945
Prothero, J. C., 566
Prout, H. T., 476
Prouty, R., 430, 432
Provus, M., 1299
Provus, M. M., 716
Pruce, I., 1360

Pruitt, A. W., 120, 1869
Prupis, S., 1675
Prutting, C., 976
Prutting, C. A., 325
Pryor, C. B., 1668
Pryzwansky, W. W., 1764
Przytulski, K., 1135, 1161
Psychological Corporation, 1919
Ptacek, J., 453
Puck, M., 1856
Pucket-Cliatt, M. J., 467
Puente, A., 1711
Puente, A. E., 244, 1091, 1701
Puente, K. L., 1091
Pueschel, S., 625
Pueschel, S. M., 385, 1061, 1061, 1062, 1211
Pugach, M. C., 1766
Pugh, B. L., 759
Pugh, G., 1292
Pugh, K. R., 1278
Pugliese, R., 553
Puig, N., 151
Pulkkinen, L., 923
Pullis, M., 1380
Pullis, M. E., 1775
Pumroy, D. K., 395
Purisch, A., 1124
Pustrom, E., 1232
Pyer, J., 34, 1370
Pykett, I. L., 1278
Pym, H. A., 933
Pysh, M. V., 1072

Quance, W., 316
Quandt, I. J., 1382
Quarrington, B., 1595
Quay, H. C., 33, 238, 364, 1066, 1134, 1451, 1478–1479, 1594, 1747
Quereshi, M. Y., 1432
Quigley, S., 982, 1414, 1501, 1567, 1646
Quigley, S P., 541, 536, 1293, 1480, 1821
Quinn, P. O., 638
Quirk, D. A., 717
Quirk, J. P., 19
Quirk, M., 511

Rabe, E. F., 1148
Rabinovitch, M. S., 341
Rabinowicz, B. H., 343
Racine, Y. A., 448
Radcliffe, J., 292
Radin, N., 819
Radman, M., 809
Radzikhovskii, L. A., 1798
Rae-Grant, Q., 684
Ragan, P. E., 547
Ragusa, D. M., 168
Rahbar, M. H., 1639
Rahe, R., 357
Raimondi, A. J., 1836
Rainer, T. D., 1804
Raison, S. B., 522
Rajan, P., 342, 874
Rajaratnam, N., 802
Rakic, P., 289
Rakow, S., 507
Ramage, J. C., 223

Ramey, C. T., 4, 5, 648, 650, 711, 711, 989
Ramey, S. L., 648, 711, 989
Ramirez, B., 471
Ramirez, S. Z., 1230
Ramos, O., 1548
Ramsay, R., 295
Ramsey, R., 517
Ramussen, G., 276
Rand, Y., 504
Randal, J., 159
Randall, T., 1138
Randolf, S. M., 576
Randolph, J. L., 1668
Randolph, M., 876
Rank, B., 365
Rank, O., 269
Rao, S. M., 302
Rao, S. S., 512
Rapaport, H. G., 80
Rapaport, J. L., 638
Rapin, I., 13, 362, 558, 636, 1085
Rapoff, M., 152
Rapoff, M. A., 1374
Rapoport, J. L., 593
Rapoport, R. N., 1799
Rapp, D. L., 1828, 1833
Rappaport, Z. H., 1464
Rapport, M. D., 169, 171
Rasch, G., 1918
Rashid, N., 1098
Rasmussen, P., 1093
Rasmussen, T., 341, 874, 1558
Ratcliff, K. S., 1352
Rathjen, D. P., 1665
Raths, L. E., 1870
Rattan, A. L., 594
Rattan, A. I., 1093
Rattan, G., 340, 344, 873
Ratzeburg, E. H., 285
Ratzeburg, F. H., 611
Raven, J. C., 1627
Rawls, D. J., 80
Rawls, J. R., 80
Ray, B. M., 857
Ray, O. S., 1466
Ray, R. S., 68
Ray, S., 1486
Rayder, N. F., 905
Rayner, K., 1492
Rayner, R., 236, 238, 447
Rayo, D., 118
Razeghi, J. A., 45
Read, P., 1580
Readance, J. E., 925, 1503
Reaney, J. B., 258
Reardon, S. M., 170
Reber, A., 881
Records, R. E., 597
Redden, K., 394
Redden, M. R., 211
Reding, G. R., 302
Redl, F., 484, 1108, 1513–1514
Reed, C. F., 675
Reed, D., 258
Reed, E. W., 731, 1042, 1856
Reed, H., 260
Reed, H. B. C., 1330
Reed, J. C., 1148
Reed, S. C., 731

Reed, V. A., 1052, 1053
Reeder, S. J., 319
Rees, E., 18
Rees, N., 976
Rees, N. S., 185, 335
Reese, H. W., 373, 1435
Reetz, L. J., 1259
Reeve, P. T., 1766
Reeve, R. A., 297
Reeve, R. E., 174
Regan, C., 1061
Reger, R., 1542, 1716
Reich, M., 1636
Reich, W., 1216
Reichert, A., 118
Reichler, R. J., 193
Reid, D. D., 697
Reid, D. H., 1175, 1612
Reid, D. K., 922, 951, 1377, 1405, 1785
Reid, G., 1495, 1502
Reid, H. P., 1084
Reid, J., 602
Reid, J. B., 68, 228, 710
Reid, J. C., 448
Reid, J. G., 1374
Reid, M. K., 925
Reid, R., 170
Reid, W. J., 1594
Reilley, R. R., 916, 1505
Reinert, H. R., 56, 1293
Reinherz, H., 1635
Reis, E., 18
Reis, J., 1635
Reis, S. M., 1533
Reiser, D., 365
Reisman, F., 1146, 1525
Reisman, F. K., 144, 146, 495, 590, 765, 1519, 1628
Reiss, S., 1730
Reitan, R. M., 837, 852, 853, 1521, 1831, 1840
Rende, R., 168
Renfield, M., 638
Rennebohm, R. M., 151
Rennie, K. M., 322
Renzaglia, A., 67, 427, 655, 785, 1204, 1214, 1582, 1827, 1948
Renzaglia, A. M., 1223
Renzulli, J., 824
Renzulli, J. S., 21, 507, 693, 694, 818, 821, 1419, 1532–1533
Report to the Secretary of the Department of Health, Education, and Welfare, 1924
Repp, A. C., 116, 561, 1415, 1715, 1806
Repucci, N. D., 616
Reschly, D., 17, 700, 1326, 1892
Reschley, D. J., 35, 330, 514, 592, 608, 610, 773, 1047, 1139, 1218, 1325, 1711, 1748
Rescorla, R. A., 446
Research and Training Center in Rehabilitation and Childhood Trauma, 1828, 1834
Resnick, L. B., 221

Rest, J. R., 1209
Rett, A., 1548
Rett Syndrome Diagnostic Criteria Work Group, 1548
Rettig, E., 259, 260
Rettig, P., 381
Reutzel, D. R., 213
Revusky, S. H., 446
Reynolds, B. J., 175
Reynolds, C., 717, 1134
Reynolds, C. R., 13, 37, 40, 72, 74, 87, 91, 92, 104, 109, 125, 126, 143, 149, 157, 166, 169, 174, 178, 207, 209, 230, 246, 261, 276, 286, 299, 336, 342, 375, 405, 437, 441, 450, 458, 476, 481, 493, 500, 503, 543, 557, 584, 592, 634, 641, 654, 661, 665, 684, 700, 710, 729, 733, 764, 773, 783, 829, 833, 848, 855, 860, 868, 875, 896, 910, 939, 940, 941, 952, 954, 973, 1003, 1011, 1012, 1014, 1015, 1026, 1027, 1041, 1053, 1068, 1074, 1075, 1076, 1092, 1117, 1118, 1127, 1130, 1138, 1167, 1185, 1210, 1213, 1218, 1236, 1241, 1260, 1261, 1268, 1274, 1300, 1323, 1339, 1341, 1345, 1350, 1353, 1364, 1368, 1376, 1423, 1440, 1451, 1508, 1519, 1528, 1555–1556, 1590, 1593, 1598, 1622, 1627, 1634, 1645, 1657, 1669, 1686, 1710, 1747, 1748, 1756, 1782, 1787, 1793, 1828, 1833, 1850, 1874, 1903, 1917, 1918, 1952
Reynolds, M., 805, 1090, 1470, 1692
Reynolds, M. C., 326, 486, 590, 662, 664, 928, 1001, 1306, 1365, 1556–1557, 1630, 1764
Reynolds, W. M., 1730, 1904
Rhine, W. R., 760
Rhoades, K., 1830
Rhodes, L. E., 431, 1736
Rhodes, L. K., 897
Rhodes, R. L., 396, 496, 652, 653, 1050, 1697
Rhodes, W. C., 378, 984
Rhodes, W. L., 395
Rholes, W. S., 1063
Ricca, J., 1089
Riccio, C. A., 774
Ricciuti, J. R., 29, 48, 328, 433, 679
Rice, A., 1453
Rice, J. P., 818
Rice, T. K., 862, 1013, 1014, 1017, 1174
Rich, C. R., 1374
Rich, H., 1293
Richards, R. A., 1785
Richardson, A., 1465
Richardson, C., 382

Richardson, G. A., 708
Richardson, G. T., 1086
Richardson, P. C., 90, 681, 1007, 1150, 1329, 1922
Richardson, S. A., 503, 638
Richardson, S. O., 825
Richek, M. A., 1867
Richert, E. S., 821, 822
Richey, L., 1945
Richman, L. C., 912, 1230
Richman, P. A., 1726
Richmond, B. O., 35, 124, 158, 375, 1041, 1555, 1779, 1782
Richmond, G., 302, 1444
Richmond, J. B., 784
Richtenberg, R., 602
Richter, C. P., 1516
Rickard, K. M., 616
Rickli, F., 542
Ricks, D. M., 1293
Ricks, N. L., 612
Riddle, M. A., 1283
Riding, R. J., 420
Ridler, M. A., 483
Riessman, F., 601
Rieth, H. J., 640
Rigler, D., 354, 357
Rikhye, C. H., 243, 482, 981, 1003, 1104
Riklan, M., 337
Riley, C. M., 730
Riley, E. P., 748
Riley, R. W., 300
Rimland, B., 192, 415, 725, 1309, 1562–1563
Rimm, S., 507
Rimm, S. B., 507
Rincover, A., 194, 428, 1441, 1621
Rinders, J. E., 731
Rindfleisch, N., 823
Ring, E. N., 1659
Ringler, L. H., 213
Ripich, D. N., 25, 604, 1051, 1054, 1056
Risley, T., 201
Risley, T. R., 3, 648, 803, 992, 1338, 1415
Risner, G. P., 213
Risner, M. E., 352
Risser, A., 740
Ritter, K., 412
Ritvo, E., 368
Rivara, F. P., 1835
Rivera, B., 250
Rivera, B. D., 1604
Rivera, E., 258
Rivera, O., 181
Rizzo, A. A., 905
Rizzo, J. V., 903, 905
Roach, E. G., 1473
Robbins, M., 484
Robbins, M. P., 1528
Robbins, W. J., 302
Robbis, C., 1229
Robert, J. M., 452
Roberts, A. R., 470
Roberts, F. C., 439
Roberts, G., 1564
Roberts, G. H., 24
Roberts, J. A. F., 256
Roberts, L., 341, 874

Roberts, N. M., 923
Roberts, T., 239
Robertson, A. D., 336
Robertson, G. J., 578, 717, 1275, 1522
Robertson, M., 467
Robertson, P., 250
Robertson, S. J., 1615
Robertson-Courtney, P., 253
Robin, A. L., 305
Robin, D. A., 564
Robins, L. N., 1169, 1352, 1674
Robinson, A., 1942
Robinson, B., 519
Robinson, B. D., 448
Robinson, E. J., 399
Robinson, E. P., 1490
Robinson, F., 1512
Robinson, H., 609, 1186
Robinson, H. B., 911, 926, 1211, 1313, 1405, 1418, 1545, 1565, 1697, 1914, 1948
Robinson, H. M., 1495
Robinson, N., 609, 1186
Robinson, N. M., 911, 926, 1211, 1313, 1405, 1545, 1565, 1697, 1914, 1948
Robinson, S. L., 1259
Robinson, S. M., 1766
Robinson, W. P., 399
Robles-Pina, R., 250, 1604
Robson, J. R. K., 1128
Rocco, S., 576
Rockwell, J., 719
Rodden-Nord, K., 72, 1469, 1639, 1914
Rodgers, S., 1553
Rodriguez, F., 660, 1218
Rodriguez, J., 498
Rodwell, V. W., 256
Roe, A., 695
Roebuck, J., 75
Roedell, W. C., 1418, 1565
Roeper Review, 1567
Roesen, H. M., 1060
Roesner, R. J., 449
Roessing, L. J., 787
Roessler, R. T., 1893
Roethlisberger, F., 863
Rogan, P., 1204
Roger, H. B., 1568
Roger, J., 119
Roger, R. A., 1868
Rogers, B. G., 1331
Rogers, C., 1465
Rogers, E. S., 1462
Rogers, G. L., 951
Rogers, H. J., 32
Rogers, J. A., 1131
Rogers, K., 508
Rogers, M. R., 1009, 1598
Rogers, R. S., 1637
Rogers, S. B., 531
Rogers, S. J., 985
Rogers, S. L., 194
Roghmann, K. J., 391
Rohindekar, S. R., 934
Roid, G., 507
Roid, G. H., 488, 773, 1097
Roit, M. L., 940

Roleff, T. L., 544
Rolfes, S., 1135, 1161
Romanczyk, R. G., 1220
Romney, D. M., 258
Romski, M., 84
Romski, M. A., 1270
Rondal, J. A., 1049, 1052
Roninson, A., 1856
Ronning, R. R., 50
Roome, J. R., 258
Rooney, K. J., 174
Roos, P., 1315, 1568–1569, 1661
Roos, P. R., 51
Roos, S., 763
Rorschach, H., 1352
Roscoe, B., 216
Rose, J. S., 835
Rose, M. C., 1201
Rose, R., 923
Rose, S., 1480, 1501
Rose, T. L., 620, 1297
Roselli, M., 1675
Rosen, J. A., 118
Rosen, L., 838
Rosen, M., 847
Rosen, M. F., 628
Rosen, M. G., 154, 265
Rosenbaum, M. S., 1617
Rosenbek, J., 129
Rosenberg, A., 151
Rosenberg, B. G., 266
Rosenberg, H., 1891
Rosenberg, J. B., 638, 697
Rosenberg, L., 1042
Rosenberg, R. L., 1612
Rosenberg, R. N., 288, 311
Rosenberg, S., 374, 1456
Rosenbloom, A. L., 690
Rosenbloom, L., 363
Rosenfeld, C. R., 748
Rosenfeld, M., 1597
Rosenfield, S., 585, 733
Rosenhan, D., 1128
Rosenhan, D. L., 717
Rosenshine, B., 598, 640, 939
Rosenshine, B. V., 17
Rosenthal, A. C., 1298
Rosenthal, B. L., 336, 342
Rosenthal, B. P., 578, 1882
Rosenthal, D., 371, 511
Rosenthal, R., 670, 1047, 1474, 1765
Rosenthal, S. R., 701
Rosenzweig, M. R., 648, 826, 989
Rosett, H. L., 747
Rosman, B., 1317
Ross, A. O., 240, 612, 1497
Ross, B. M., 186
Ross, B. W., 1704
Ross, C. M., 774
Ross, D., 1280
Ross, D. B., 559
Ross, D. H., 59, 1680
Ross, D. M., 38, 526, 624, 743, 760
Ross, E. M., 1670
Ross, L. K., 1846
Ross, L. M., 878
Ross, P., 838
Ross, S. A., 38, 526, 624, 743, 760, 1280

Rossi, A. O., 1640
Rossi, P., 1442
Rossol, M., 1582
Roswell, F. G., 351, 588
Roswell-Chall Diagnostic Reading Test of Word Analysis Skills, Revised and Extended; Manual of Instructions, 1571
Roszkowski, M., 1729
Roth, K. S., 793
Roth, R. H., 31, 551, 689
Roth, W., 39
Rothbart, M. K., 266, 1774
Rothenberg, D., 1737
Rothenberg, M. A., 1389
Rothlisberg, B. A., 1841
Rothman, D. J., 524
Rothner, A. D., 468
Rotter, J. B., 32, 1116
Rouke, B. P., 284, 570, 634, 774, 1085, 1085
Rouse, M. W., 164
Rousseau, J. J., 1571–1572
Routtenberg, A., 1546
Rovet, J. F., 918
Rowan, B., 1593
Rowe, M. B., 961
Rowe, R. D., 319
Rowland, C. M., 1534
Rowland, L. P., 1226
Ruben, D. H., 696
Ruben, R. J., 450, 558
Rubenstein, M., 1774
Rubin, D. B., 670
Rubin, D. P., 1444
Rubin, I., 1155
Rubin, J. A., 154
Rubin, K., 1306
Rubin, K. H., 1337
Rubin, L., 955
Rubin, R., 1639
Rubin, R. A., 1134
Rubin, S. E., 1893
Rucher, C. N., 939
Ruconich, S., 283
Ruddle, F. H., 1042
Rude, R. T., 1527
Rudel, R., 284
Rudel, R. G., 1728, 1844
Rudman, H. C., 22, 1918
Rudolph, A. J., 1572
Rudolph, A. M., 1603, 1851
Rudrud, E. H., 1616
Rueda, R., 505, 512, 1218, 1437
Ruff, R. M., 415
Rugel, R. P., 774
Rugh, J. D., 302
Ruhl, K., 517, 961
Ruhl, K. L., 68, 658, 1153, 1617
Ruhland, D., 819
Ruiz, C. M., 300
Ruiz, R., 249
Rumsey, J., 1278
Rupert, J., 495
Rupley, W. H., 1502, 1525
Rusch, F., 1203
Rusch, F. R., 428, 1176, 1271, 1736, 1828
Rushakoff, G., 1373
Rushton, J. P., 456

Rusk, P., 701
Russ, S. W., 1570
Russell, N. K., 1838
Russell, R., 1261, 1512
Russell, W. K., 1821
Russell, W. R., 1844
Russo, A. A., 1789
Russo, C. J., 1433
Russo, D. C., 562, 1441
Russo, J. M., 475, 747, 976, 1249, 1589
Rutherford, R., 803
Rutherford, R. B., 470, 546, 546, 1020, 1221, 1621
Rutherford, R. B., Jr., 226, 470, 1221, 1621
Rutherford, W. H., 1837
Ruttenberg, B., 199
Rutter, M., 192, 192, 194, 284, 345, 367, 571, 647, 697, 698, 728, 872, 1230, 1293, 1579–1580, 1723, 1774, 1836, 1844
RXLIST, 583
Ryan, A. S., 510
Ryan, J. B., 164
Ryan, K. A., 1187
Ryan, L. G., 939
Ryan-Arredondo, K., 1060, 1182, 1897
Ryckman, M., 279
Rye, J., 402
Rymer, R., 810
Rynders, J. E., 175

Saari, L. M., 1213
Sabatino, A., 121, 1708
Sabatino, D., 300
Sabatino, D. A., 9, 52, 185, 225, 226, 232, 234, 417, 418, 517, 798, 983, 1001, 1088, 1375, 1377, 1449, 1542, 1581, 1611, 1738, 1941
Sabortine, S. J., 857
Sachs, J., 374
Sacken, D., 1561
Sacker, A., 366
Sacks, E. S., 385
Sacksteder, S., 320
Saddock, B. J., 686
Sadker, D., 1639
Sadker, M., 1639
Sadler, W. A. Jr., 898
Sadock, D. J., 1123, 1235
Saenz, A., 501, 503
Saever, M. D., 902
Safer, D., 938
Safer, D. J., 169, 901
Safford, P., 1425
Safford, P. L., 1380
Sage, D., 1090
Sage, D. D., 42, 53, 1733
Saigh, P. A., 1680
Sailor, P., 1724
Sailor, W., 788, 928, 1175
St. James-Roberts, I., 872
St. Louis, K. O., 403
St. Louis, K. W., 37, 788
Sajwaj, T., 201, 1472
Saklofske, D., 1902
Salant, E. G., 154
Salasin, S. E., 1299

Salbenblatt, J., 1856
Saleeby, D., 1758
Salend, S. J., 511, 547, 1539, 1589
Salerno, E., 1772
Sales, B., 30, 720
Sales, B. D., 450, 457, 700, 1561
Saletu, B., 915
Salfield, D. J., 1231
Salimi, L., 114
Sallustro, F., 1715
Salovey, P., 968
Salsido, R. M., 511
Saltz, P., 571
Saltzman, R. L., 879
Salvia, J., 22, 520, 589, 606, 721, 938, 1068, 1074, 1077, 1425, 1432, 1439, 1455, 1582, 1747, 1886, 1912, 1945
Salvioli, G., 1135
Salzberg, C. L., 1536
Sambo, E. W., 65
Sameroff, A. J., 446, 645, 710
Sampson, L. J., 563, 1298, 1486, 1729
Sampson, P. D., 748
Samuda, R. J., 1268
Samuels, S. J., 1259, 1493, 1533
Sanche, R., 633
Sanche, R. P., 316
Sandberg, B., 1422
Sandel, A., 336, 1418
Sander, A., 812
Sander, E., 152
Sanders, D., 1114
Sanderson, H. W., 763
Sanderson, P. E., 689
Sandifer, P. H., 288
Sandoval, J., 250, 612, 773, 1326, 1747, 1902
Sanford, A., 1068
Sankey, R. J., 80
Sano, M., 1464
Sanok, R. L., 1231
Sansom, D., 1549
Santmyer, K., 114
Santos de Barona, M., 250
Santos, S. L., 1218
Santrock, J. W., 445
Sanz, M. T., 626, 1214
Sapir, S. G., 1583
Sarason, S., 1396
Sarason, S. A., 1320
Sarason, S. B., 57, 655, 907, 1583–1584
Saren, D., 1823
Sargent, J. K., 582
Sarlo-McGarvey, 1549
Saslow, G., 399
Sassi, E., 730
Sasso, G. M., 195
Sataloff, J., 1308, 1309
Satterwhite, B., 151
Sattler, J., 1325
Sattler, J. M., 156, 922, 970, 994, 1134, 1218, 1268, 1439, 1584–1585, 1711, 1873, 1874, 1880, 1912, 1919, 1920

Sattler, R. O., 1210
Satz, P., 594, 854, 1092, 1093
Saunders, C., 901
Sautter, S. W., 289, 570, 914, 917, 918
Savage, R. C., 1832, 1833
Savard, W. G., 610
Saville-Troike, M., 1593
Sawery, J. M., 1313
Sawicki, R. F., 31, 382, 623, 674, 676, 698, 849, 851, 1106, 1162, 1176, 1361, 1463, 1466, 1714, 1801, 1818
Sawrey, J., 926, 1186
Sawrey, J. M., 959
Sawyer, D. J., 571
Sayers, D., 1604
Sayers, M., 75
Sbordone, R. J., 1846
Scalfani, A., 918
Scanlan, J. M., 675
Scanlon, C. A., 940
Scanlon, D. M., 1454
Scannell, D., 1692
Scardamalia, M., 247
Scarpati, S., 510
Scarr, S., 1249
Schaaf, J. M., 699
Schacht, R., 510
Schachter, J., 381
Schachter, S., 1674
Schackenberg, H. L., 1444
Schacker, T., 878
Schacter, S., 266
Schaefer, A., 1595
Schaefer, A. B., 527, 1043, 1398
Schaefer, C., 1393
Schaefer, C. E., 684
Schaefer, E. S., 1589
Schaefer, R. T., 496
Schaeffer, R. M., 1612
Schafer, A., 583
Schaffer, B., 194
Schain, R. J., 1360
Schaller, J. G., 151
Schallert, D., 444
Schalock, R. L., 429, 656
Schanzer, S. S., 1510
Schaumann, B., 1313
Schechter, D. E., 46
Scheer, J., 511
Scheerenberger, R. C., 392, 430, 482
Scheerer, M., 1885, 1888
Scheffelin, M., 492
Scheffelin, M. A., 337, 1148, 1442, 1793
Schein, J. D., 756
Scheiner, L., 1731
Scheiver, S. W., 508
Schell, A., 168
Schell-Frank, D., 1404
Schelsinger, H. S., 541
Scheman, J. D., 799
Schenk, S. J., 1196
Scherer, K., 1136
Schery, T., 442
Scheuneman, J. D., 1268
Scheutz, G., 962
Schiefelbusch, R. L., 1292, 1589–1590

Schiever, S. W., 1131
Schifani, J. W., 927
Schiff, G., 1776
Schiff, P., 1934
Schiffman, G. B., 1526
Schiffrin, D., 604
Schilit, J., 788
Schilling, R. F., 374
Schinke, S. P., 374
Schlachman, S., 1614
Schlack, H. G., 555
Schlanger, B. S., 1292
Schleien, S., 1323, 1707
Schleifer, M., 839
Schleifer, S. J., 879
Schlesinger, I., 1646
Schlien, S., 796
Schlindler, P. J., 57
Schlinger, H. D., 194
Schloper, E., 986
Schloss, P., 321, 1338
Schloss, P. J., 489, 620, 738,
    847, 1186, 1283, 1591,
    1870
Schlowinski, E., 1782
Schmauk, F. J., 1674
Schmeck, H. M., 1250
Schmelzer, R. V., 595, 801,
    1571
Schmid, R., 655, 1639
Schmidek, M., 25, 604
Schmidt, C. R., 1581, 1611
Schmidt, F. L., 501, 1078
Schmitt, C. S., 155
Schmitt, J. F., 1784
Schmitt, N., 136
Schmitt, S., 1847
Schmuck, R. A., 223, 461
Schnachenberg, H., 961
Schnacker, L. E., 780
Schneider, M. R., 1666
Schneider, W. J., 559
Schnell, I., 814
Schoenfeldt, L. F., 1447
Schofield, S., 562
Scholom, A., 1776
Scholtz, C. L., 13
Scholwinski, E., 375
Schomer, D. L., 1464
Schonfeld, I. S., 1199
Schooler, C., 267
Schoonover, S. C., 849, 1106,
    1363, 1714, 1801
Schopler, E., 192, 194, 199,
    366, 367, 560, 1013, 1230,
    1601, 1756
Schrader, B., 902
Schram, A., 1060
Schrank, F. A., 1586 1918,
    1919, 1921
Schreenberger, R. C., 1914
Schreibman, L., 195
Schroeder, C. S., 1230
Schroeder, S. R., 648,
    1098
Schroeder, W., 1716
Schroeder, W. L., 47
Schroth, G., 1693
Schuckit, M. A., 76
Schuell, H., 129
Schuler, A., 1419
Schulman, E. D., 1659
Schulsinger, F., 1674

Schulte, A. C., 1766
Schulte, K., 541
Schultz, E., 1723
Schultz, J. H., 1216
Schulz, J., 1322
Schulz, J. B., 1512
Schulze-Delrieu, K. S., 639
Schumacher, E., 1232
Schumaker, J. B., 928, 958,
    1190, 1766, 1931
Schumm, J. S., 928
Schumon, S. J., 1701
Schutz, R. E., 136, 1432
Schutz, R. P., 428
Schwann, J. B., 1665
Schwartz, A. A., 725
Schwartz, G. E., 336
Schwartz, G., 49
Schwartz, J., 12, 109, 165,
    665, 676
Schwartz, J. F., 709
Schwartz, J. H., 261
Schwartz, L., 938, 1481,
    1937
Schwartz, L. L., 1337
Schwartz, N. H., 589
Schwartz, R., 1203
Schwarz, J. I., 145
Schweinhart, L., 1427
Schweinhart, L. J., 990,
    1944
Schwejda, P., 442
Schwirian, P. M., 1643
Schwitzer, A. M., 114
Sciback, J. W., 1175, 1612
Science News, 1796
Sciorra, L. J., 732
Scobee, J., 694, 957, 1236,
    1811
Scoloveno, M., 1557
Scott, E. P., 272, 1883
Scott, G., 1423
Scott, J. P., 645
Scott, J. A., 1296, 1489, 1490
Scott, R. N., 159
Scott, T. M., 781
Scouten, E., 541
Scribner, A. P., 251
Scribner, S., 1408
Scriven, M., 715
Scruggs, T. E., 27, 71, 803,
    884, 1039, 1190, 1201,
    1551
Seamon, J. G., 343
Sean, S., 1656
Searfoss, L. W., 1225
Searl, S., 838
Sears, D., 863
Sears, R. R., 1623
Seashore, C. E., 136
Seashore, H. G., 136
Sechenov, I., 1516
Sechrest, L., 1570
Secord, W. A., 424, 1050,
    1052
Secretaria de Educacion
    Publica, 1184
Sederer, H. B., 751
Sedlack, J. R., 1935
Sedlak, D. M., 24, 657, 1814,
    1895
Sedlak, R., 490, 1338
Sedlak, R. A., 24, 332, 657,

702, 901, 923, 1088, 1202,
    1307, 1308, 1309, 1545,
    1611, 1760, 1768, 1769,
    1894
See, J. D., 1893, 1925
Seeman, W., 1197
Seese, L. M., 448
Sefer, J. W., 638
Segalowitz, S. J., 1091, 1474
Segars, J., 1804
Segawa, M., 1728
Seguin, E., 742, 1607–1608
Seidel, J. F., 708
Seiden, L. S., 31, 623, 674,
    1163, 1801
Seidenberg, M., 1155
Seitz, V., 373, 1345
Sekino, H., 1465
Select Committee on Chil-
    dren, Youth, and Families,
    1425
Seligman, M., 497, 1128,
    1317
Seligman, M. E. P., 55, 446,
    717, 1064, 1730
Selikowitz, M., 1161
Selling, L. S., 525
Sells, C. J., 1429
Selmar, J. W., 1367
Seltzer, C., 496
Seltzer, G. B., 544, 568,
    1894
Seltzer, M. M., 544, 1894
Selye, H., 1600
Semaan, L., 1263
Semel, E., 639, 1067
Semel, E. M., 1292
Semmel, M. I., 928, 977,
    1619–1620
Semper, T., 278
Semrud-Clikeman, M., 170
Senault, B., 623
Senf, G. M., 1620
Sengupta, R. P., 912
Senna, J. J., 483
Serafetinides, E. A., 1460
Sergeant, J. A., 925
Sern_iclaes, W., 558
Serow, R. C., 1195
Servis, M., 432
Sessoms, H., 314
SEST Project, 43
Sevcik, R., 84
Sexon, S. B., 593
Shackelford, J., 566
Shadden, B. B., 1050, 1054
Shadish, W. R., 466
Shafer, S. Q., 1675
Shaffer, D., 593, 872, 1199,
    1675, 1807, 1836
Shaffer, D. R., 267
Shaffer, H. L., 1308
Shaffer, J., 627
Shafran, S. D., 879
Shah, M. R., 448
Shahinpoor, M., 1566
Shallice, T., 1163
Shames, G. H., 424, 1052
Shanahan, T., 1738
Shandelmier, S., 701, 1820
Shaner, A., 399, 988, 1726
Shank, M., 1734, 1949
Shanker, S., 301

Shanley, D. A., 257, 522,
    1390, 1878
Shannon, C., 1758
Shannon, D., 130
Shannon, M., 1564, 1772
Shantz, C. U. 1379
Shapiro, A. K., 1804, 1813
Shapiro, D. A., 1785
Shapiro, E., 24
Shapiro, E. S., 146, 239, 521,
    1599, 1616, 1804
Shapiro, G. G., 79
Shapiro, S. T., 562
Shapiro, S., 112
Shapiro, T., 560
Share, D. L., 650
Sharpley, C. F., 258
Sharpton, W. R., 725
Shasby, G., 279
Shattuck, R., 745, 1025
Shatz, M., 399
Shaughnessy, M., 878
Shaughnessy, M. F., 602
Shavelson, R. J., 803
Shaver, K., 538
Shaw, C., 1388
Shaw, D. L., 1259
Shaw, J. C., 676
Shaw, J. M., 467
Shaw, K. N., 1213
Shaw, M. C., 185
Shaw, R. E., 638
Shaw, S. R., 1031
Shaw, W. J., 1334
Shaya, T., 1113
Shayne, M., 1157
Shaywitz, B. A., 1278, 1728
Shaywitz, S. E., 1278, 1728
Shea, T. M., 395, 486, 1216,
    1472, 1805, 1879
Sheanan, D. B. III, 1152
Shearer, A., 526
Shearer, D., 1426
Shearer, M., 1399, 1426
Shearer, M. S., 1816
Shebilske, W., 1803
Sheehan, R., 949, 951,
    1421
Sheehy, G., 507
Sheffelin, M. A., 496
Shekim, L., 548
Sheldon, W., 1773
Sheldon, W. H., 278
Shellenberger, S., 1261
Shelton, I. S., 1050
Shelton, M. N., 905
Shepard, J. J., 958
Shepard, L., 1074
Shepard, L. A., 488, 1268
Shepard, R. N., 923
Shepard, T. A., 275
Shepard, T. H., 452
Sheperd, G., 560
Shepherd, M. J., 1082
Sher, J. P., 1573
Sheras, P., 1388
Sherbenou, R. J., 1790
Sherer, K., 1135, 1161
Sherick, R. B., 1667
Sheridan, S. D., 534
Sheridan, S. M., 170, 1228,
    1840
Sherman, J., 1635

Sherman, J. A., 1282
Sherman, J. L., 885
Sherman, M., 560
Sherrill, C., 34, 1369
Sherrington, C., 1885
Sherry, L., 1297
Sherwen, L., 1557
Sherwin, R., 1637
Sherwood, J. J., 907
Sherwood, J. M., 467
Sheslow, D., 1912
Shevin, M., 1823
Shields, S. A., 200
Shiflett, S. C., 879
Shifman, M. A., 1087
Shigley, H., 986
Shimberg, B., 1597
Shimizu, N., 1003
Shindell, P. E., 1636
Shinn, M., 78
Shinn, M. R., 1766
Shinnar, S., 556, 1361
Shipitsina, L. M., 1575
Shipley, K. G., 1050
Shipman, V. C., 989
Shirkey, E. A., 1698, 1725
Shirley, H. F., 1228
Shively, J. E., 496
Shmatko, N. D., 1578
Shneidman, E. S., 1130
Shockley, W., 713
Shoemaker, S., 1949
Sholomskas, D., 399
Shonkoff, J. P., 954, 1351,
    1528
Shontz, F. C., 39
Shor, N. F., 288
Shore, M. F., 463
Shore, R., 648
Short, P., 603
Shortridge, J., 1639
Shown, D. G., 65
Shriberg, L., 564
Shriberg, L. D., 1368
Shriver, M. D., 258, 646
Shrout, P. E., 1838
Shrybman, J. A., 1737
Shtulman, J., 1895
Shukla, P. D., 934
Shulamn, E., 643
Shulman, B. B., 1050, 1052,
    1053, 1055, 1411
Shumaker, J., 162
Shure, M. B., 69, 408, 1666
Shureen, A., 644
Shurka, E., 1441
Shuster, C. S., 1416
Shute, N., 1333
Shuy, R. W., 1114
Shwedel, A. M., 1024
Shweder, R. A., 1209
Sibbald, R. G., 879
Sibbison, J. B., 1062
Sicard, A., 960
Sichula, B., 59, 1680
Sidgwick, H., 703
Sidis, W. J., 1645
Sidman, M., 3, 788, 1534
Sidman, R. L., 289
Sieber, J. E., 1782
SIECUS, 1639
Siegal, A., 547
Siegal, L. J., 483, 587

Siegal, L. S., 1700
Siegel, E., 1754
Siegel, E. V., 1216
Siegel, L. J., 371, 688, 696, 1335
Siegel, M. M., 1953
Siegel, S., 446
Siegel, S. J., 1953
Siegelman, E., 925
Siegenthaler, L., 1542
Siegfried, L., 599
Siegle, S. E., 354
Siegler, R. S., 412
Siepp, J. M., 165
Siesky, A. E., 615
Sigelman, C. K., 399
Sigman, M., 1135
Sikkema, K. J., 1429
Sikora, D. M., 1621
Silberberg, D., 1554
Silberberg, M. C., 912
Silberberg, N. E., 912
Silbergeld, E. K., 760
Silberman, R. K., 270, 272, 282, 1057, 1122, 1288, 1289, 1290, 1322, 1350
Silbert, J., 324, 599, 1145, 1453
Silberzahn, M., 1622
Silikovitz, R. G., 350
Siller, J., 175
Silliman, E. R., 193, 725, 1050
Sills, J. A., 80
Sills, M., 1595
Silver, H., 356
Silver, L. B., 675
Silver, L., 1066
Silverberg, E., 1101
Silverman, C. R., 1252
Silverman, F., 274, 356
Silverman, F. H., 37, 424
Silverman, H., 188
Silverman, I. W., 168
Silverman, K., 1112
Silverman, L. K., 1418
Silverman, R., 45, 521, 590, 1933
Silverman, S. R., 449, 541, 1309
Silverman, W. A., 1547
Silverman, W. K., 1595
Silverstein, A. B., 773, 1880
Silverstein, L., 269
Simeon, J. G., 1388
Simmel, E. C., 69
Simmons, A. A., 1293
Simmons, J., 1293
Simmons, J. O., 201
Simmons, J. Q., 562
Simmons, R. G., 1610
Simmons-Martin, A., 541
Simner, M. L., 220
Simon, M., 822
Simon, S., 1869
Simon, S. B., 1870
Simon, S. G., 17
Simon, S. J., 688, 1615
Simon, T., 11
Simon, Z., 1509
Simonsen, L., 1544
Simonton, D. K., 993
Simpson, A. E., 1774

Simpson, E. L., 905
Simpson, G. A., 1315
Simpson, J. L., 390
Simpson, R. L., 1870
Simpson, S., 1348
Sims-Tucker, B., 538
Sinclair, R., 615
Sindelar, P. T., 56, 378, 619, 620, 803, 844, 938, 1356, 1542
Sines, J., 1565
Sing, K., 1591
Singer, B. D., 1640
Singer, C., 467
Singer, J. E., 1674
Singer, J. L., 535
Singer, L. M., 46
Singer, N., 1566
Singh, J., 1297
Singh, N. N., 448, 517, 1099, 1297, 1374, 1629
Singh, S., 1398
Single, E., 75
Sipay, E. R., 1494, 1504, 1526
Siperstein, G. N., 656, 1441, 1447, 1600
Siro, A., 1774
Sirvis, B., 318, 592, 663, 867, 1301
Skaggs, S., 278
Skarbrevik, K., 1587
Skaric, I., 541, 1877
Skarvold, J., 860
Skeels, H. M., 487, 1653–1654
Skeffington, A., 578
Skidmore-Roth, L., 1564, 1772
Skinner, B. F., 116, 223, 236, 237, 532, 1286, 1401, 1414, 1444, 1508, 1654–1655, 1656
Skinner, C. H., 1259
Skinner, S., 1512
Skodak, M., 487
Skolnick, M. L., 1878
Skrtic, T., 928
Skudlarski, P., 1278
Skuse, D., 647, 1025
Skuy, M., 1775
Slaby, D., 1662
Slaby, R. G., 69, 70
Slade, K., 1259
Slager, U. T., 288
Slater, A. M., 1552
Slater, P. L., 1164
Slesnick, T., 1566
Slick, M. H., 1511
Slimmers, E., 760
Slingerland, B. H., 1304, 1656
Sloan, J. L., 198, 236, 237, 367
Sloane, H., 464
Sloman, L., 1230
Sluyter, D., 968
Small, A. M., 630
Smart, J. F., 1180
Smead, V. S., 589
Smeltzer, D. J., 1235
Smeraldi, E., 382
Smith, A., 872

Smith, A. N., 1327
Smith, B., 5, 118
Smith, B. J., 471
Smith, B. M., 490
Smith, C. B., 1510
Smith, C. D., 242, 434, 605, 1606, 1943
Smith, C. R., 327, 402, 454, 1089, 1342, 1633
Smith, D., 469, 1016, 1824
Smith, D. A., 319
Smith, D. C., 1380
Smith, D. D., 620, 657, 1145, 1815
Smith, D. E. P., 1297
Smith, D. J., 1580
Smith, D. W., 386, 748, 750, 1409
Smith, F., 382, 1491, 1493
Smith, F. J., 336
Smith, G., 1727
Smith, G. F., 483, 626
Smith, H., 1224
Smith, J., 658, 1195
Smith, J. D., 504, 1019
Smith, J. E., 45
Smith, K., 1069
Smith, L. H., Jr., 1362
Smith, M. A., 494, 884, 885, 1291, 1295
Smith, M. J., 510
Smith, M. L., 667
Smith, N. B., 1525
Smith, O. S., 1373
Smith, R., 1280
Smith, R. J., 212, 402, 951, 1889
Smith, R. M., 401, 567, 1251, 1405
Smith, R. R., 1438
Smith, R. S., 504, 1774
Smith, S. L., 1510
Smith, T., 194, 266, 510, 986, 1118, 1550
Smith, T. E., 1673
Smith, T. E. C., 42, 174, 1405, 1542
Smith, W. D., 1211
Smith-Bell, M., 1434
Smith-Davis, J., 660, 960, 1105, 1471, 1694
Smithsonian Institute National Air and Space Museum, 1228
Smits-Engelman, B. C. M., 635
Smoorenburg, G. F., 1405
Snell, D., 1775
Snell, L. M., 748
Snell, M., 201
Snell, M. A., 1642
Snell, M. E., 116, 179, 520, 523, 530, 633, 788, 1204, 1223, 1618, 1716, 1948
Snow, C., 976
Snow, D., 188
Snow, M. E., 267
Snow, R., 1486
Snow., R. E., 138
Snyder, D., 854, 1092
Snyder, L., 1936
Snyder, M. C., 1738
Snyder, S. H., 261, 1813

Snyder, W. E., 42
Sobsey, D., 1765
Soddy, K., 921
Soder, A. L., 1367
Sokol, R. J., 747, 748, 750
Solan, H., 578
Solar, R. A., 958
Soli, S. D., 612
Soll, C. D., 1864
Sollee, N. D., 1227
Soloman, R., 360
Solomons, G., 167, 527, 583, 1398, 1595
Soltz, V., 755, 1318, 1393
Somer, H. V. K., 1714
Sommer, B. A., 1194
Sommer, R., 1194
Sommer-Border, K., 1867
Sommers-Flanagan, J., 448
Sommers-Flanagan, R., 448
Sonies, B. C., 639
Sonnenmeier, R. M., 1056, 1410
Sontag, E., 1316, 1441
Sontag, J. C., 510
Soodlak, L. C., 1670
Sorbom, D., 1327
Sorenson, R. J., 141
Sorochan, W. D., 918
Sorosky, A. D., 1850
Sorotzkin, B., 695
Soulayrol, R., 119
Sours, J., 399
Sours, J. A., 1169
Southeastern Community College v. Davis, 30
Southeastern Regional Coalition for Personnel Preparation to Work with Severely/Profoundly Handicapped, 1440
Southwick, D. A., 38
Southworth, L. E., 1868
Southworth, L., 1400
Sovner, R., 1641
Sowers, J., 1828
Spache, G. D., 1494
Spaeth, G. L., 1780
Spain, B., 13, 1155
Spangler, R. S., 1581
Spanier, G. B., 615
Spaniol, L., 1758
Sparks, D., 1758
Sparks, R. L., 1304
Sparling, J., 6
Sparrow, S., 594
Sparrow, S. S., 35, 1880, 1881
Spaw, L., 442
Speaks, C., 594
Spear, N. E., 848
Spearman, C., 10, 494, 817, 963, 1849
Spearman, C. E., 1687–1688
Spears, R. W., 1232
Special Education Consultative Committee, 189
Special Education Law of 4358, 996
Speece, D. L., 1382
Speed, J., 405
Speer, B. S., 633, 796, 917, 1161, 1258, 1506

Speer, S. K., 1666
Speery, J. B., 1068
Speery, R. W., 341, 874
Spekman, N. J., 1382
Speltz, M. L., 857
Spence, K., 1414
Spence, W., 1732
Spenciner, L. J., 1785
Sperling, K., 385
Sperry, R. W., 343, 1091, 1701–1702, 1706
Spiegler, M. D., 720
Spielberger, C. D., 125
Spiers, P. A., 1124, 1464
Spinetta, J., 357
Spinetta, J. J., 354, 663
Spisto, M. A., 775
Spitz, H., 1704–1705
Spitz, H. H., 989, 1381
Spitz, R., 1403
Spitz, R. A., 558, 1705
Spitzer, A., 130
Spitzer, A. R., 1415
Spitzer, R., 1675
Spitzer, R. L., 1352
Spivak, G., 69, 408, 1666
Spooner, F., 1311
Sprafkin, R. P., 1143
Sprague, J., 801, 1949
Sprague, R. L., 169, 623, 630, 1068
Sprakin, J. N., 1282
Spreat, S., 1729
Spreen, O., 740, 1292, 1675
Spriestersbach, D. C., 1050
Springer, S. P., 1091, 1706
Spunt, A. L., 527
Squire, L., 104
Squire, L. R., 261, 262, 676, 1164
Squires, D., 1804
Squires, J., 360
Srinath, S., 361
Srinivasan, T. N., 303
Sroufe, L. A., 630
Staas, W. E., 1314
Stafferi, J., 279
Stager, S., 1610
Stahl, R. J., 1869
Stainback, S., 928
Stainback, W., 928
Stake, R. E., 715
Staley, A., 612
Stallings, J. A., 26, 1760, 1804
Stanbury, J. B., 911
Stancin, T., 1835
Standards for services for developmentally disabled individuals, 842
Stanford Diagnostic Mathematics Test–Fourth Edition, 1712
Stanford, E., 701
Stanford, G., 1304
Stang, C., 1564, 1772
Stang, R., 1751
Stang, J., 1280
Stankov, L., 494
Stanley, J. C., 28, 694, 1534, 1672, 1710, 1713, 1725, 1952
Stanley, L. S., 1394

Stanovich, K. E., 174
Stanton, H. C., 546, 857, 1083, 1492
Stapleton, S., 591
Starfield, B., 784
Stark, J., 555
Stark, R., 184
Stark, R. I., 155
Starks, J., 250
Stary, J., 915
State Report about the Situation of Children in Russian Federation-1996, 1577
Stauffer, R. G., 212, 1526, 1889
Stavrou, E., 777
Steadward, R. D., 1708
Stedman, D. J., 1438
Stedman, J. M., 612
Steele, B., 356
Steele-Clapp, L., 1639
Steelman, L. C., 267
Steen, D., 1745
Steer, R. A., 1730
Steffin, S. A., 466
Stein, D. K., 200
Stein, J., 1512
Stein, M., 324, 599, 1145
Stein, M. B., 1792
Stein, R., 510
Stein, R. C., 1823
Stein, R. E., 690
Stein, R. E. K., 784
Steiner, C., 1228
Steiner, H. G., 496
Steiner, J. E., 446
Steiner, R., 117
Steinert, R. R., 676
Steinhauer, P. D., 684, 685
Steininger, M., 703
Steinkomp, M., 1213
Steketee, G. S., 1283
Stellern, J., 414
Stenzler, Y., 1582
Stephens, B., 1381
Stephens, J. T., 607, 1560, 1561, 1730, 1819, 1859
Stephens, T. M., 1659
Stephenson, W., 1477
Steppe-Jones, C., 1, 24, 346, 374, 393, 544, 1573, 1687, 1722, 1724, 1733, 1951
Sterling, D., 1138
Sterling, P., 1138
Stermer, D., 1385
Stern, G., 861
Stern, R. C., 527
Stern, W., 969, 1717
Sternat, J., 962
Sternbach, R. A., 677
Sternberg, L., 1871
Sternberg, R. J., 887, 957, 963, 968, 993, 993, 1030, 1408, 1849
Sternberg, S., 1487
Sternlicht, M., 248
Stettner-Eaton, B., 359
Steuer, F. B., 1280
Stevens, A., 1603
Stevens, D., 1611
Stevens, D. J., 70
Stevens, D. M., 221

Stevens, G., 1722
Stevens, G. D., 600, 1344, 1348, 1755, 1885
Stevens, L., 1066
Stevens, L. J., 30, 158, 661, 1296, 1488
Stevens, M., 1829
Stevens, R., 939
Stevens-Dominguez, M., 1051
Stevenson, D. K., 1120
Stevenson, R. J., 164, 339, 384, 597, 636, 653, 791, 837, 871
Stevenson-Hinde, J., 1774
Steward, D. A., 1042
Stewart, D. A., 1941
Stewart, D. G., 448
Stewart, E. E., 1783
Stewart, K. J., 773
Stewart, M., 1570
Stewart, S. R., 1931
Stice, G. F., 1352
Stick, S. L., 1277
Sticker, M. B., 1850
Stickle, T., 1570
Stiefel, D. J., 554
Stiles, K., 1061
Still, G. F., 167
Stillman, B., 825, 1225, 1304, 1867
Stillman, B. W., 1527, 1552
Stinnett, R. D., 1414
Stinnett, T. A., 3, 1785
Stipek, D., 26
Stoewe, J. K., 448
Stoff, D., 1676
Stoffel, D., 1770
Stoiba, K., 1760
Stokes, R., 1112
Stokes, R. C., 81, 242, 622, 672, 753, 841, 1040, 1620, 1686
Stokes, T., 464
Stokes, T. F., 803, 1820, 1948
Stokoe, W. C., 95, 1136
Stolberg, A. L., 615
Stolov, W. C., 791
Stone, B. J., 773
Stone, C. A., 224, 1327
Stone, M. H., 1918
Stoner, G., 171
Stoops-King, J., 1188
Stores, G., 118
Storm-Mathisen, A., 448
Storms, L., 468
Stotoke, W. C., 537
Stough, C., 1776
Stough, L. M., 471, 472
Stout, J. T., 1098
Stovall, K. W., 1555
Stover, S. L., 1844
Stowe, M., 1079
Stowe, M. L., 177
Strain, P., 1907
Strain, P. S., 175, 194, 1659, 1662
Strand, E. A., 1647
Strang, J. D., 284, 634
Stratford, B., 626
Stratton, M. C., 1828
Straub, R. L., 1163

Strauss, A., 1346, 1348, 1885
Strauss, A. A., 27, 71, 167, 1148, 1341, 1344, 1721, 1722, 1887
Strauss, C. C., 166
Strauss, D., 544
Strayer, F. F., 1419
Strayrook, N., 1760
Strecker, E., 167
Streissguth, A. P., 748, 848
Strelau, J., 710, 1774
Strichart, S., 1086
Strichart, S. S., 422
Strickberger, M. W., 877
Striffler, N., 581
Stringer, E. M., 766
Stringer, L. A., 1591
Stringer, S. A., 1875
Strom, D. A., 12
Strom, P., 507
Strom, R., 507
Strom, S., 507
Strong, M. A., 96
Strosnider, R., 1335
Stroufe, L. A., 168
Strubb, R. L., 1177
Stuart, R. B., 239, 464
Stuart, S., 82 129, 187 296, 423, 548, 1905
Stubblefield, H. W., 47
Stubbs, S., 59, 61, 1584, 1680, 1682
Stuckey, K., 1603
Stuckey, R. A., 621
Stuckless, E. R., 1297
Stufflebeam, D. L., 715
Stump, C. S., 1119
Sturgis, R., 702, 1256
Sturm, L., 728
Subkoviak, M. J., 488
Suci, G. J., 1305
Sudman, S., 1479
Sue, D., 882
Sue, D. W., 881
Suess, W. M., 80
Sugai, G., 781, 782, 1220, 1734
Sugar, O., 872
Sullivan Associates, 1731
Sullivan, H., 1936
Sullivan, H. J., 1444
Sullivan, H. S., 1216
Sullivan, K. A., 351, 800, 904, 967
Sullivan, M. F., 258
Sullivan, P. D., 17
Sullivan, P. M., 1486
Sullivan, R. M., 1486
Sulloway, F. J., 267
Sulzbacher, S. I., 1409
Sulzer-Azaroff, B., 201, 232, 562, 607, 720, 1438, 1473, 1536, 1545, 1805, 1820
Sunshine, P., 1120
Suntup, M., 1253
Suntup, S., 1033, 1038
Suomi, S., 647
Suran, B. G., 903, 905
Suresh, T. R., 303
Susser, P. L., 1433
Sutaria, S., 162
Sutherland, G. R., 766

Sutin, J., 1475
Sutkin, L. C., 876
Sutter, E. G., 743, 760, 1023
Sutton, L. N., 292
Sutton, P. A., 1297
Sutton-Smith, B., 266
Suzuki, L. A., 1865
Svendsen, M., 1594
Svendsen, R., 1757
Swaiman, K. F., 109
Swales, T. P., 708
Swallow, H., 1186
Swaminathan, H., 32
Swann, W., 1862
Swanson, H. L., 1293, 1666
Swanson, H. S., 1348
Swanson, L., 420
Swanson, M., 686
Swanson, P. D., 1360
Swartz, E., 1050
Swartz, J. E., 1699
Swartz, M. N., 1166
Swash, M., 13, 104
Swassing, R. H., 818
Swassing, R. H., 820, 823
Swedo, J. J., 253, 1605
Swedo, S. E., 384, 557, 1283
Sweet, M., 1891
Sweet, R., 381
Sweet, R. D., 1804
Sweeting, C. V. M., 250
Sweetland, R. D., 495
Sweitzer, M., 1318
Swenson, C. H., 627
Swenson, R., 956
Swerdlik, M. E., 611, 969, 994, 1307, 1451, 1792, 1874
Swift, C., 325
Swisher, L. P., 1293
Switzky, H. N., 953, 1529
Symons, F. J., 1615
Synder, S. H., 689
Syndulko, K., 1674
Szabo, M., 961
Szanton, V. J., 80
Szanton, W. C., 80
Szasz, T. S., 1168
Szatmari, P., 167
Szekeres, S., 605, 1054
Szelag, E., 1404
Szliwowski, H. B., 361, 1457, 1714, 1853
Szurek, S., 367
Szurek, S. A., 1230, 1594
Szymanski, E. M., 1822
Szymanski, L. S., 1730

Taba, H., 1380
Taber, C. W., 13
Taeusch, H. W., 1349
Taggart, G. L., 1051
Tait, P. E., 1637, 1870
Talamo, Y., 876
Talbutt, L. C., 735
Tallal, P., 183
Tallent, M. K., 21, 28, 49
Tallmadge, G. K., 1274
Tamminga, C. A., 382
Tamplin, A. M., 1774
Tan, S-Y., 409
Tanaka, T., 675

Tannenbaum, A. J., 694, 822, 1310
Tannenbaum, P., 1305
Tanner, J. M., 574
Tanner, L. N., 395
Tannhauser, M. T., 285
Tannhauser, R., 611
Tanyzer, H. J., 954
Tarver, S. G., 612
Tashman, C. M., 421, 595, 697, 870, 1147
Tasman, W., 1546, 1547
Tatum, V., 1542
Taulbee, E. S., 1797
Tavormina, J. B., 764
Tawney, I. W., 1220
Tawney, J. W., 350, 1443, 1536, 1691, 1754, 1773
Tayama, M., 193
Taybi, H., 319
Taylor, A., 655
Taylor, C. W., 819, 965, 1419
Taylor, D. L., 1143
Taylor, E., 1717
Taylor, E. H., 1169
Taylor, F., 881
Taylor, F. D., 611, 691
Taylor, G., 1835
Taylor, H., 285
Taylor, H. G., 571, 1844
Taylor, I. A., 479
Taylor, J. A., 125, 375
Taylor, J. C., 1220
Taylor, K. H., 1813
Taylor, L., 511, 1085
Taylor, L. J., 49
Taylor, R. L., 156, 503, 1785, 1785
Taylor, S. W., 764
Taylor, W. L., 402
Tchicaloff, M., 118
Teasdale, G., 1835
Teasdale, J. D., 55, 1064
Teberg, A. J., 13
Teele, D. W., 80
Teelucksingh, E. A., 1240
Telch, C. F., 409
Telesensory Systems, 1289
Telford, C., 926, 1186
Telford, C. W., 959, 1313
Tell, L., 885
Tellegen, A. M., 1196
Telzrow, C., 651
Telzrow, C. F., 33, 73, 115, 286, 288, 311, 405, 572, 634, 636, 637, 687, 697, 698, 846, 1091, 1094, 1096, 1128, 1160, 1165, 1202, 1224, 1226, 1257, 1530, 1554, 1675
Telzrow, R., 638
Temkin, N. R., 1360
Tempey, F. W., 1398
Templeman, T. P., 533
Templer, D., 1462
Templin, M. C., 1293
Tenney, A. M., 279
Terdal, L. G., 221
Terestman, N., 1776
Terman, L. M., 810, 821, 969, 1177, 1495, 1781, 1781
Terminie, T. J., 1598

Terrell, T. D., 1110
Tervoort, B. T., 542
Tesauro, G., 953
Tesiny, E. P., 684
Teska, J. A., 1315
Teslow, C. J., 521
Tesolowski, D. G., 1891
Tessier, A., 643
Teuber, H. L., 262, 284, 362, 1148, 1844
Teunissen, J., 855
Thal, D. J., 1050
Tharp, R. G., 511, 1436, 1764
Thatcher, R. W., 1278
The Psychological Corporation, 136, 1900
Thedinger, B., 1188
Thelen, E., 573, 1715
Thepphavongsa, P., 1585
Thielman, V., 540
Thoene, J., 1429
Thoene, J. G., 1603, 1624, 1658, 1851, 1913, 1916
Thoma, S. J., 1209
Thomas, A., 356, 683, 710, 1404, 1774
Thomas, C., 627
Thomas, C. C., 1210, 1764
Thomas, C. L., 77, 1144
Thomas, D., 1639
Thomas, D. R., 1879
Thomas, E., 467
Thomas, E. A., 1570
Thomas, R., 260
Thomas, S., 1037
Thomas, T., 821, 822
Thomason, J., 475
Thomlinson, S., 1863
Thompson, B., 658
Thompson, D. G., 1870
Thompson, D. L., 590, 1225
Thompson, G., 1155, 1836
Thompson, J., 872
Thompson, J. S., 706, 807
Thompson, K., 1859
Thompson, L., 168
Thompson, M. W., 706, 807
Thompson, R. G., 690
Thompson, R. J., 565, 567, 709, 1808
Thompson, S., 836, 1663
Thompson, S. K., 1063, 1208
Thompson, T., 725
Thomson, W. A. R., 115, 687, 911, 1128, 1165, 1224
Thoresen, C. E., 1758
Thorn, I., 118
Thorn, L., 956
Thornburg, H. D., 289
Thorndike, A. E. L., 1286
Thorndike, E. L., 17, 236, 238, 1401, 1494, 1801
Thorndike, R. L., 577, 834, 1077, 1276, 1522, 1711, 1912, 1919
Thorn-Gray, B. E., 1641
Thornton, C. A., 1145
Thornton, C. E., 1636
Thornton, R., 1597
Thorp, E. K., 512
Thorpe, H., 1133, 1338
Thorpe, H. W., 1867
Thorpe, M. E., 111

Throckmorton, M. C., 1231
Thuline, H., 423
Thurlow, M., 958, 1470
Thurlow, M. L., 190, 377, 1945
Thurman, K. S., 1399, 1944
Thurman, S. K., 1441
Thurston, L. P., 1764, 1766
Thurstone, L., 1432
Thurstone, L. L., 135, 817, 964
Thurstone, T., 1432
Tibbits, D. F., 1055
Tibbles, J. A., 681
Tiegerman-Farber, E., 1053, 1055
Tienari, P., 711
Tierney, R. J., 1503
Tierno, M. J., 395
Tilker, H. A., 239
Tilly, W. D. III, 783
Tilson, G. P., 1824
Times of India, 934
Timmermans, S. R., 277, 589
Tindal, D., 1471
Tindal, G., 72, 215, 521, 579, 1348, 1470, 1639, 1766, 1914
Tinker, M. A., 1493, 1503
Tirosh, E., 1049
Tjossem, T., 1425
Tjossem, T. D., 859
Tobias, S., 162
Tobin, A. R., 1625
Todaro, J., 409
Todd, N. M., 1420
Todd, W. R., 330
Toffler, A., 1770
Tokizane, T., 1546
Tolfa-Veit, D., 1039
Tollefson, N. A., 1782
Tombari, M. L., 222, 224, 225, 459
Tombaugh, T. N., 1374
Tomblin, J. B., 1050
Tomeh, M. O., 1808
Tomkins, F., 1445
Tomlinson, B. E., 1164
Tomlinson, J. R., 510
Tomlinson-Keasey, C., 573
Tompkins, F., 910, 948, 950, 1202
Tompkins, W. J., 159
Tong, S., 1062
Tongier, J., 566
Tonkovich, J. L., 548
Tonsager, M. E., 1198
Toohey, M. A., 1145
Toole, J. F., 345
Toomey, J., 985
Toon, C. J., 1370
Torbett, D. S., 1637
Torff, B., 993, 1408, 1849
Torgersen, A. M., 1774
Torgeson, J., 1084
Torgesen, J. K., 612, 1067, 1111, 1435, 1790, 1931
Torkelson, G. M., 864
Torrance, E. P., 124, 479, 479, 507, 695, 812, 823, 833, 1419, 1669, 1809, 1810, 1811

Torrance, J. P., 812
Torres, C., 1258
Torres, D., 507
Torres, J. L., 409, 444, 603
Torrey, E. F., 193, 647
Torrey, G., 1385
Torrey, G. K., 1672
Torrey, J., 912
Toth, S. L., 711
Touchette, P., 1828
Touchette, P. E., 195
Tough, J., 25, 604
Touliatos, J., 266
Touretzky, D., 953
Townsend, M. A. R., 70
Townsend, W. A., 252
Tracy, M. I., 984
Tracy, M. L., 378, 395
Tracy, M. W., 378
Tracy, W., 702, 1256
Traill, R. D., 1187
Training School Bulletin, 1009
Tramer, M., 1230
Tran, X. C., 510
Trancone, J., 200
Traub, N., 1304
Traweek, D., 611
Tredgold, R. F., 921
Treffinger, D. J., 1305
Treffry, D., 562
Treherne, D., 316
Trenholm, S., 1272
Trent, S., 1356
Trent, S. C., 250, 513, 514, 1269
Treuper, J., 1230
Trevarthen, C., 341, 1706
Trevino, F., 1643
Trevisan, M. S., 1786
Trice, A. D., 695
Trickett, D. K., 784
Trief, E., 272
Trieschmann, A. E., 1779
Trifiletti, J. J., 650
Trimble, M. R., 118, 119, 467
Tripp, A., 1374
Trippe, M. J., 1303
Trivette, C. M., 511
Trivette, P. S., 909
Trotter, R., 1193
Troupin, A. S., 1360
Troutman, A. C., 131, 214, 559, 607, 781, 782, 1220, 1472, 1618, 1619, 1808, 1820
Truan, M. B., 283
Truch, S., 1111
Trueba, H., 507, 510
Trueba, H. T., 882
Trueman, D., 1596
Trujillo, T., 499
Tseng, M. S., 695
Tucker, B. F., 1835
Tucker, D. M., 336
Tucker, G. J., 13, 261, 666, 1344
Tucker, J., 1066
Tucker, J. A., 250, 751
Tucker, P. J., 1315
Tuft, L., 79
Tuikka, R. A., 1714

Tukey, J. W., 803
Tukianen, K., 154
Tulbert, B., 1356
Tulving, E., 1164, 1214
Tunali, B., 652, 1049
Tungaraza, F. D., 58, 1679
Tunley, R., 1759
Tuokko, H., 740
Tupper, D., 740
Turco, T. L., 1457, 1667, 1848
Turiel, E., 580, 1209
Turk, K., 910, 1032
Turkewitz, G., 13
Turnbull, A., 626, 772, 1322, 1734
Turnbull, A. P., 510, 827, 1512, 1734, 1823, 1855, 1949
Turnbull, H., 626
Turnbull, H. R., 510, 772, 827, 942, 1823, 1856
Turnbull, H. R., III, 1734
Turnbull, J. R., III, 459
Turnbull, R., 1734
Turner, G., 1274
Turner, P. E., 1879
Turner, R. L., 1441
Turney, C., 1187
Turnure, J. E., 174
Turpin, R., 482, 625
Tursman, C., 1725
Turvey, C., 968
Tuunainen, K., 1587
Tweddle, E. G., 1775
Tyler, J. L., 843
Tyler, J. S., 1835
Tyler, L. E., 969
Tyler, R. W., 715
Tymitz, B. L., 827
Tymitz-Wolf, B., 1723
Tyrer, P., 1746
Tyson, M. E., 1311
Tzeng, O. C., 1305

U.S. Bureau of the Census, 496, 643
U.S. Congress, 772
U.S. Department of Education, 514, 518, 609, 632, 664, 931, 1156, 1470, 1521, 1628, 1690, 1692, 1694, 1825
U.S. Department of Education National Center for Education Statistics, 628
U.S. Department of Education, Office for Civil Rights, 211
U.S. Department of Education, Office of Educational Research and Improvement, 507
U.S. Department of Health and Human Services, 1727
U.S. Department of Housing and Urban Development, 29, 141
U.S. Department of Labor, Employment, and Training Administration, 136, 595

U.S. Department of Justice, 1020, 1021, 1847, 470
U.S. Government Accounting Office, 1188
U.S. Government, 30
U.S. Juvenile Justice and Delinquency Prevention Office, 1021
U.S. News & World Report, 1926
U.S. Office of Education, 251, 1223, 1514, 1633, 1948
U.S. Office of Special Education, 413
Uchida, I. A., 319
Udang, L., 1186
Udesen, H., 1166
Uganda Ministry of Education, 63, 1684
Uhl, W. L., 1494
Uiterwijk, M. M., 244
Ulett, G. A., 665
Ulleland, C. N., 748
Ullian, D., 1635
Ullman, S., 163
Ullmann, R., 630
Ullrich, H. D., 1279
Ulrey, G., 1623
Ulrich, R. F., 612
Umansky, W., 1816
UNESCO, 65, 143, 471, 536, 542, 935, 1358
Unger, K. V., 1591
UNICEF, 59, 1679
Uniform Federal Accessibility Standards (UFAS), 211
United Cerebal Palsy, 347, 1860
United Nations, 981, 1636
United States Catholic Conference, 392
United States Employment Services, 801
United States Senate, 1147
United Way, 1895
Unrich, L. E., 584
Uphouse, L., 261
Urbain, E. S., 1662
Urion, D. K., 495
Uschold, K., 1716
USES General Aptitude Test Battery, 801
Usha, M. N., 934
Utley, B., 539
Utley, C. A., 1355
Uzgiris, I. C., 1381
Uzgirus, T. C., 1298

Vadasy, P., 538
Vaglum, P., 448
Valcante, G., 961, 1262, 1302, 1660
Valencia, R. R., 1865
Valenstein, E., 1474
Valenta, L., 1736
Valett, R. E., 1868
Valk, J., 721
Vallarta, J. M., 118
Vallecorsa, A., 590, 1564, 1772
Vallett, R. E., 1528

Valletutti, P. J., 1644, 1703, 1758
Van Acker, R., 1550
Van Camp, C. M., 1220
Van Court, M., 714
Van Daal, V. H., 1701
Van der Leij, A., 1701
van Dijk, J., 538, 1870–1871
Van Doorninck, W. J., 408
Van Galen, G. P., 635
Van Handel, D., 688
Van Horn, P., 510
Van Lingen, G., 437
Van Noorden, 597
Van Olphen, A. F., 1405
Van Osdol, W. R., 592
Van Reusen, A. K., 940
van Rijswijk, K., 1575
Van Riper, C., 153, 404, 1697–1700, 1871–1872
Van Tasell, D., 594
Van Tassel-Baska, J., 744
Van Uden, A., 541
Van Veggel, L. M., 244
Vance, B., 246
Vance, H. R., 1218, 1659
Vance, H. B., 1187, 1581
Vance, V. L., 43
VandeCreek, L., 1434
Vandell, D. L., 267
Vandereycken, W., 114, 305
Vanderheiden, G., 678, 1373, 1770
Vanderheiden, G. C., 159
Vanderwood, M., 1945
Vane, T. R., 970
VanHoesen, G. W., 1449
VanLehn, K., 24
Vanta, K. S., 638, 652, 718, 852, 1006
Van-Tassel, J. L., 820
Vantassel-Baska, J., 1419
VanZomeren, A. H., 1838
Vargas, J. S., 116
Varni, J. W., 151, 258, 1336
Varrone, S., 453
Vasa, S. F., 170, 1672
Vaughan, M., 1283
Vaughan, R. W., 1072
Vaughan, T. D., 42
Vaughan, V., 295, 1306
Vaughan, V. C., 166
Vaughn, B., 1774
Vaughn, B. E., 648
Vaughn, B. J., 1220
Vaughn, S., 928, 1701
Vaughn, V., 1019
Vaughn, V. C., 319, 593, 1703
Vedder, R., 1230
Velicer, W. F., 1774
Vellutino, F. R., 1341, 1455
Venkatagiri, H. S., 1700
Venn, J., 867, 868, 1301
Venn, J. J., 1330
Vennum, M. K., 584
Ventura, J., 399
Ventura, P., 1135
Vergason, G. A., 484, 1910
Verity, C. M., 872
Vernon, E., 394
Vernon, M., 538
Vernon, P. A., 975

Vernon-Levett, P., 1834
Veroff, J., 819
Verstegen, D. A., 459
VHGI, 792
Viazey, J. M., 655
Victor, B., 593
Victor, M., 31, 1528
Vida, L., 823
Viglione, D. J., 1569
Vignolo, L. A., 78
Vila, J., 1283
Villa, R., 928
Villarreal, B., 472
Vinçotte-Mols, M., 451
Vinton, L., 518
Virkkunen, M., 918
Vitelli, R., 974
Vitello, B., 1676
Vocational Transition, 1822
Vockell, E., 1259
Vockell, E. L., 1637
Voeller, K., 1590
Voeltz, L. M., 175
Vogel, F., 386, 705
Vogel, S., 1086
Volenski, L. T., 1321, 1723
Volkmar, F. R., 193
Volkmor, C. B., 1693
Vollmer, T. R., 1220
Volpe, B. T., 1745
Volpe, J., 130
von Békésy, G., 449
Von Bonin, G., 336
Von Doorninck, W. J., 1362
Von Misch, A., 1231
von Recklinghausen, F., 1895
Voress, J. K., 759, 985, 1014, 1015, 1017, 1508, 1524
Vorhees, C. V., 752
Vosters, R. P. L., 385
Voyat, G. E., 1145
Vrensen, G., 558
Vrono, M., 367
Vuchinich, R. E., 751
Vuurman, E. F., 244
Vygotsky, L. S., 443, 783, 1087, 1152, 1798, 1895–1896, 1950

Wachs, T. D., 1774
Wachtel, P., 1168
Wacker, D. P., 780
Wada, J. A., 341, 874
Waddington, C. H., 646
Waddington, J. L., 1200
Wade, M. G., 1816
Wade, S. L., 1835
Wagner, A. R., 446
Wagner, B. J., 1889
Wagner, B. M., 1730
Wagner, E. E., 860
Wagner, N. N., 1637
Wagner, R., 809
Wagner, R. F., 1924
Wagner, R. K., 1408
Wagner, W. W., 194
Wahlen, E., 418, 1088, 1883
Wahler, R. G., 653
Wahman, T., 1286
Walberg, H. J., 671, 901, 928, 1557, 1761
Wald, A., 258

Wald, B. A., 431
Wald, G., 423
Waldenstrom, E., 1093
Walder, L. D., 70
Waldron, S., 152
Waldrop, M. F., 638, 697, 1199
Walk, A., 367
Walker, B. J., 590
Walker, C. E., 401
Walker, D. K., 392, 784, 876, 1373
Walker, G., 1292
Walker, G. E., 1335
Walker, H. M., 1420, 1662, 1897
Walker, J. E., 395, 1473, 1805
Walker, J. G., 1611
Walker, R., 279, 1306
Walker, S., 472
Walker, W. A., 420
Walkup, J. T., 1283
Wall Street Journal, 1925
Wallace, D., 140, 1014, 1041, 1102, 1121, 1174, 1237, 1246, 1599, 1949
Wallace, G., 436, 1066, 1542, 1659, 1672
Wallace, G. L., 746
Wallach, G. P., 25, 604, 1050, 1054, 1056, 1411
Wallach, M. A., 480, 481
Wallenberg, R., 1575
Waller, H., 1546
Wallerstein, J. S., 614
Wallin, J. E. W., 1897–1898, 1923
Wallis, R. R., 1569
Wallon, H., 1461
Walmsley, S. A., 1931
Walsch, G., 165
Walsch, R., 558
Walsh, B. T., 114
Walsh, F. B., 1546
Walsh, J., 1104
Walsh, M., 1509
Walsh, W. B., 969
Walstead, L., 1373
Walter, G. G., 1297
Walters, J. K., 69
Walters, R. H., 1280
Walther, B., 292
Walton, J. N., 104, 288
Walz, L., 1766
Wandel, C., 1306
Wang, M. C., 221, 928, 1557
Wang, Z. M., 980
Wanless, R., 1320
Wannamaker, O. D., 117
Wanschura, P. B., 1153
Wapner, S., 511
Ward, B., 1230
Ward, J. D., 1833
Ward, K. D., 470
Ward, M., 270, 857, 1048, 1068, 1350, 1495, 1502, 1541, 1542, 1734, 1771, 1823
Ward, M. E., 26, 458, 600, 679, 738, 885, 934, 1218, 1630, 1659, 1754, 1816

Ward, M. J., 876, 901, 903, 1883, 1884
Ward, M. P., 1914
Ward, V. S., 28, 695, 851
Ware, J. E., 784
Ware, L. P., 512
Warfield, G., 1275
Warkany, J., 451
Warner, M., 162
Warner, M. M., 958
Warren, B., 1229
Warren, D., 538
Warren, D. H., 272
Warren, D. R., 1382
Warren, G. T., 1524
Warren, M. P., 574
Warren, R. D., 1544
Warren, S. A., 502, 503, 533, 730, 759, 859, 866, 1170, 1448
Warren, S. F., 1055, 1654
Warrenburg, S., 336
Warzak, W. J., 1835
Wasco, J., 1836
Washin, B., 547
Washington, E., 381
Wass, H., 664, 906
Wasserman, J., 1711
Watanabe, H., 1409
Waterhouse, D., 854
Waterhouse, L., 192, 193, 1092
Waternik, J., 1230
Waters, D. B., 685
Waters, E., 576
Waters, L., 194
Watkins, M., 902
Watson v. Cambridge, Mass., 1560
Watson, D. P., 902
Watson, G., 1637
Watson, H., 320
Watson, J., 236, 238, 1274
Watson, J. B., 446, 1898
Watson, L., 194
Watson, M., 767
Watson, R. I., 332
Watson, T., 110, 699
Watson, T. S., 294
Watteyne, L., 425, 1050, 1053
Watts, J. W., 1465
Wayman, K. I., 643
Weatherman, R. F., 35, 1586
Weaver, F. L., 1196
Webb, E. J., 223
Webb, G., 1878
Webb, N. M., 803
Weber, A., 1230
Weber, C. K., 213
Webster, A., 540, 1404, 1414
Webster, D. B., 450, 558
Webster, E., 1320
Webster, J. G., 159
Webster, L., 725
Webster, L. M., 1060, 1385
Webster, M., 450, 558
Webster, R., 273
Webster, R. E., 1117
Webster's New Collegiate Dictionary, 897
Webster-Stratton, C., 1879

Wechsler, D., 596, 773, 994, 1332, 1793, 1900, 1902, 1903, 1919
Wechsler, H. A., 517
Wedding, D., 1123, 1235, 1387, 1705, 1745, 1756
Weed, W., 594
Weekly, R., 423
Weener, P., 1769
Weerdenburg, G., 220
Wehman, P., 67, 427, 431, 655, 785, 1323, 1602, 1707, 1736, 1827, 1948
Wehmeyer, M., 1734, 1823
Wehrly, B., 496
Weiderholt, J. L., 1001, 1002
Weikart, D., 1427
Weikart, D. P., 990, 1944
Weiler, P., 1759
Weimer, L., 80
Weinberg, R. A., 1249
Weinberg, S. L., 1791
Weinberg, W. A., 556
Weinberger, M., 80
Weiner, B., 32, 177, 1497, 1782
Weiner, F., 1226, 1644
Weiner, F. F., 96, 1699
Weiner, I. B., 1569, 1570, 1730
Weiner, L., 747
Weingarten, C., 1557
Weinstein, L., 1446
Weinstein, R. S., 1337
Weintraub, F. J., 306
Weintraub, M., 824, 949
Weintraub, S., 1177
Weisbrod, J. A., 1216
Weisbrott, I., 128
Weisgerber, R. A., 1444, 1815
Weishahn, M. W., 485, 663, 800, 1307
Weiskopf, P. A., 1757
Weismer, S. E., 1791
Weisner, T., 1036
Weiss, B., 54
Weiss, D., 403
Weiss, G., 171
Weiss, K. L., 1208
Weiss, L. G., 773
Weiss, P., 821, 822
Weissbluth, M., 1775
Weissman, M. M., 399
Weisz, J. R., 1209
Weitzman, R. A., 136
Welbourne, A., 1641
Welch, K., 414, 1061
Welch, L., 924
Welch, M. W., 1807
Welks, D., 1830
Well, A. D., 612
Weller, C., 425, 1050, 1053
Weller, G. M., 638, 697
Weller, R. O., 13
Wellman, H. M., 412, 1153
Wells, S. P., 269, 565, 1341
Welsch, C., 1350
Welsh, G. S., 1196, 1198, 1903
Wenck, L. S., 258
Wenz-Gross, M., 1600
Wepman, J., 1454
Wepman, J. J., 852

Wepman, J. M., 1904
Werder, J. K., 1919
Wergeland, H., 675
Werner, E. E., 504, 1774
Werner, H., 1346, 1885, 1887
Werner, H., 27, 71, 1905
Werner, S. C., 914
Wernicke, C., 1148
Werry, J., 1293, 1594
Werry, J. S., 168, 364, 593, 624, 630, 1478
Werth, L. H., 56
Wertheimer, M., 185, 957
Wertsch, J. V., 784, 1798, 1896
Wertsch, J., 640
Wertz, R., 129
Weschler, D., 1899
Wesman, A., 501
Wesman, A. G., 136
Wesolowski, M. D., 695, 1400, 1612
Wesson, C., 958
Wesson, M. D., 220
West, E. S., 330
West, J. R., 748
West, R., 533
West, R. R., 1641
West, W. L., 1284
Westaway, M., 1775
Westbrook, D. C., 918
Westby, C. E., 25, 221, 604, 1051, 1054, 1410
Westling, D., 1090
Westing, D. L., 502, 731, 1429, 1440, 1723
Wetherby, A. M., 194
Wetzburger, C., 361
Whalen, L., 1154
Whalen, C. K., 611, 624, 1805
Whalen, W. T., 267
Whaley, L. F., 257, 265, 319
Whaley, S., 1135
Wheeler, J., 878, 1202
Wheeler, L. J., 174, 1309, 1405, 1511
Whelan, R. J., 1909–1910
Whelan, T, 1598
Whetnall, E., 542
Whimby, A., 898
Whishaw, I. Q., 1389, 1528, 1728
Whitaker, H. A., 872
White, B., 110
White, B. F., 433
White, B. L., 266, 573
White, D., 285
White, J., 914
White, J. H., 755
White, K. R., 136
White, M. A., 327, 1633
White, O. R., 591, 1413
White, W., 975
White, W. J., 1069
Whitehouse, F. A., 1219
Whiteman, P., 911
Whitman, S., 1431, 1834
Whitman, T. L., 1175, 1612
Whitmore, J., 824
Whitmore, J. R., 28, 1131, 1310, 1418

Whitmore, K., 118
Whitney, E., 1135, 1161
Whitstock, R. H., 621
Whitt, J. K., 591
Whittaker, J. K., 1779
Whitten, C. F., 1644
Whitten, T. M., 1440
Whittlesey, J. R. B., 579
Whitworth, J. M., 764
Who's Who of American Women, Ninth Edition, 769
Whyte, S. R., 58, 1679
Wickelgren, W. A., 186
Wicks-Nelson, R., 688, 1385
Widerstrom, A. E., 1944
Widerstrom, H. A., 1399
Widiger, T. A., 280
Wiederholt, J. L., 437, 589, 837, 1342, 1343, 1542
Wiegers, A. M., 767
Wielkiewicz, R. M., 773
Wiemann, Y. L., 1835
Wiener, J., 456
Wienke, W. D., 350
Wierzbicki, M., 556
Wiesel, T. N., 558
Wigdorowicsz-Makowerowa, N., 302
Wigg, N. R., 345
Wiggins, D. M., 1388
Wiggins, J. S., 1076
Wiig, E., 639, 1292
Wiig, E. H., 424, 1052, 1056, 1067
Wikler, L., 1319
Wilansky, C., 1732
Wilber, R. B., 1293
Wilberger, J. E., 1837
Wilbur, H. B., 1913–1914
Wilbur, R. B., 95, 494
Wilbur, S., 1936
Wilcox, B., 1822, 1824, 1949
Wilcox, B., 321, 801
Wilcox, L. E., 924
Wilcox, M., 976
Wilcox, M. R., 657
Wilder, B. J., 796
Wildman, R. W., 688
Wilen, D. K., 250
Wilens, T. E., 1717
Wilensky, A. J., 1360
Wiles, K., 468
Wilgus, S., 1936
Wilkening, G. N., 16, 68, 104, 565, 1124, 1449, 1806, 1838, 1869
Wilkerson, I. A. G., 1490
Wilkins, L., 1857
Wilkins, R., 675
Wilkinson, C. Y., 253, 1355, 1605, 1749
Wilkinson, G. S., 1911, 1919
Wilkinson, I. A. G., 1296, 1489
Wilkinson, L. C., 1050
Wilkinson, V. A., 151
Wilkus, R. J., 666
Will, M., 1735, 1821
Will, M. C., 1914–1915
Willer, B., 429, 763, 843
William, J. P., 958
William, M. L., 169

Williams, C. E., 273
Williams, C. L., 1198
Williams, D. I., 1807
Williams, G. E., 1415
Williams, J., 1216
Williams, J. A., 802
Williams, J. D., 1038
Williams, J. W., 20
Williams, K., 354
Williams, M. C., 319
Williams, R., 50, 1929
Williams, R. H., 1077
Williams, R. L., 1268
Williams, R. T., 1785
Williams, R. W., 353
Williams, S., 1135
Williams, S. R., 1137
Williams, W., 1754
Williams, W. M., 1408
Williamson, D. A., 1231
Williamson, F., 611
Williamson, G. G., 165
Willig, A. C., 253, 1605
Willis, D. J., 682, 684, 685, 686
Willis, G., 482
Willis, J. O., 1729
Willis, S. M., 557
Willoughby, C., 564
Wills, U., 1595
Willson, V. L., 431, 435, 488, 606, 726, 1076, 1077, 1223, 1274, 1340, 1517, 1783, 1793
Wilson, A. A., 1211
Wilson, B., 1564, 1772
Wilson, B. J., 559
Wilson, C. F., 1757
Wilson, C. P., 1417
Wilson, G. T., 239, 240, 717
Wilson, J. D., 51, 165, 474, 581, 640, 654, 779, 1641, 1947
Wilson, K. S., 267
Wilson, L. R., 1068, 1073
Wilson, M., 1107, 1155
Wilson, M. E., 36, 325
Wilson, P. G., 1612
Wilson, R. S., 1774, 1953
Wilson, R. M., 1503
Wilson, S., 498, 510
Wilson, S. R., 1448
Wilson, V., 1231
Wilson, V. L., 3, 1151, 1952
Wilton, K., 1262
Winborne, D. G., 576
Windle, M., 1775
Windmiller, M., 35, 1776
Windsor, J., 1055
Wineman, D., 1513
Wing, J., 364
Wing, L., 193, 1293
Wingard, J. A., 75
Winikur, D. W., 1873
Winneke, G., 414
Winograd, P. N., 177
Winschel, J. F., 418
Winslade, W. J., 1434
Winterbottom, M. R., 1213
Winters, W. G., 1668
Winton, A. S. W., 1297, 1374
Wise, L. L., 1448
Wise, M. S., 1235

Wise, S. L., 136
Wiseman, D., 314
Wiseman, D. E., 1454
Wish, J., 1636
Wishner, J., 516
Wisland, M. V., 42, 156
Witelson, S. F., 336, 341, 344, 875
Withers, P. S., 1143
Witkin, H. A., 443, 682, 753, 1066, 1674, 1876
Witmer, L., 401, 1916
Witryol, S. I., 1289
Witt, J., 804, 1068
Witt, J. C., 35, 450, 653, 654, 939, 1081, 1167, 1508, 1667, 1824, 1848
Witt-Engerstrom, I., 1548
Wittig, M. A., 1635
Wittrock, M. C., 26, 1491
Witty, P., 21
Witty, P. A., 822
Wixson, K. K., 590, 1493
Wixson, K. L., 1201
Wlefel, E. R., 703
Wolanczyk, T., 1624
Wolchik, S. A., 1621
Wolcott, G. F., 1833
Wolery, M., 524, 781, 949, 1220
Wolf, B., 467
Wolf, H. S., 1360
Wolf, L. C., 624
Wolf, M., 1928
Wolf, M. M., 3, 803, 1288, 1667, 1848
Wolf, S. M., 118
Wolfe, D. A, 1318
Wolfe, V. V., 1823
Wolfensberger, W., 190, 430, 544, 738, 842, 959, 1175, 1275, 1540, 1908
Wolfensberger, W. P. J., 1917
Wolford, B. I., 470
Wolford, B. J., 1020
Wolfson, D., 1831, 1840
Wolfson, L., 613
Woll, B., 1861
Wollersheim, J., 175
Wollman, J., 1771
Wolman, B. B., 370, 1302
Wolpe, J., 128, 238, 240
Wolraich, M., 1703
Woltmann, A., 1393
Wong, B., 316, 1068, 1084
Wong, B. Y. L., 454, 1152, 1226, 1382, 1435, 1552, 1931
Wong, D., 1094, 1257, 1564, 1772, 1852
Wong, D. L., 257, 265, 319
Wong, K., 1265
Wong-Fillmore, L. W., 1111
Wood, B. S., 1272
Wood, C. T., 1274
Wood, F. H., 201, 56
Wood, F. J., 470
Wood, I. K., 448
Wood, J., 1286
Wood, J. W., 928, 1940
Wood, M., 580, 1051, 1426
Wood, M. M., 580, 859, 1918

Wood, R. H., 1563
Wood, R. L., 1831
Wood, T. A., 1202
Woodard, C. V., 699
Woodcock, R. W., 35, 830, 831, 1333, 1586, 1918, 1920–1922
Wooden, H. Z., 474
Woodhill, E., 1817
Woodman, R. W., 907, 977
Woodrow, H., 1529
Woods, B. T., 362
Woods, D., 1718
Woods, D. E., 1927
Woodward, J., 250, 505
Woodward, M., 1381
Woodworth, R. S., 332, 1345
Wooley, O. W., 113, 304
Wooley, S. C., 113, 304
Woolfolk, A. E., 56, 162
Worchel, F. F., 1352, 1392, 1564, 1802
Worchel, S., 1803
Word, T. J., 665
Work for Welfare, 1926
Work Program for Disabled Persons During the 9th Five-Year National Development Plan, 380
Workman, E. A., 1160
World Health Organization, 600, 1223, 1755
Worley, M., 1399
Worrall, N., 773
Worthen, B. R., 1724
Worthington-Roberts, B. S., 1409
Wortis, J., 909, 1561
Wray, B. B., 151
Wright, B., 600
Wright, B. D., 1918
Wright, C. R., 1009
Wright, E., 1835
Wright, E. B., 566, 681, 889, 1170, 1341, 1764
Wright, F. S., 109, 361
Wright, G., 170
Wright, G. N., 1893
Wright, H. L., 1231
Wright, L., 151, 162, 507, 527, 583 1043, 1334, 1335, 1398, 1442, 1595
Wright, P., 250
Wright, P. W., 1217
Wright, S., 1326
Wright, W. S., 42
Wrightsman, L., 1751
Wulach, J. S., 1570
Wunderlich, R. C., 612
Wuori, D. F., 1158
Wyatt v. Stickney, 842
Wyche, K. F., 143
Wylie, R. C., 1610
Wylie, R. J., 1433
Wyngaarden, J. B., 911
Wynne, M. E., 623
Wysocki, A. C., 278
Wysocki, B. A., 278

Yaffe, S. J., 593
Yalant, S. P., 163
Yale, C. A., 1943
Yamamoto, S., 511

Yannet, H., 1037
Yansen. E., 643
Yantis, P. A., 425
Yantis, S., 494
Yarrow, L. J., 372, 1623
Yaryura-Tobias, J. A., 409, 1283
Yates, J., 250
Yates, J. R., 253, 1110, 1357, 1604
Yawkey, R., 1436
Yawkey, T. D., 1509
Yeates, K. O., 6, 1835, 1845
Yell, M. L., 930
Yeo, F., 1593
Yerkes, R. M., 149
Yiannakis, A., 266
Yin, R. K., 1566, 1771
Ylvisker, M., 605, 1054, 1829, 1835
Yoakum, C. S., 149
Yoder, D. E., 1292
York, R., 1316, 1441
Yoshida, R., 940
Yoshida, R. K., 306, 457, 631, 907, 1132, 1185, 1694
Yoshida, T., 1354
Yoshimoto, T., 193
Yoshinaga-Itano, C., 1936

Young, B. K., 1953
Young, G. A., 162
Young, J., 1567
Young, J. G., 1728
Young, J. L., 1101
Young, J. W., 1031
Young, K. R., 1338
Young, R. D., 1610
Young, R. G., 497
Young, R. M., 416
Young, S., 1639
Youngblood, G. S., 842
Ysseldyke, 1068
Ysseldyke, J., 43, 958, 1066, 1077, 1425, 1468, 1514, 1528, 1627, 1633, 1754, 1886, 1943
Ysseldyke, J. E., 22, 78, 138, 190, 248, 377, 520, 521, 584, 589, 640, 721, 883, 977, 983, 1068, 1074, 1240, 1306, 1417, 1432, 1439, 1451, 1524, 1582, 1606, 1669, 1746, 1912, 1945
Yudkin, J., 1128
Yudof, M., 1396
Yule, W., 571, 698, 1595, 1916

Yussen, S. R., 445
Yusuf, H., 1098

Zaba, J. N., 547
Zabel, M. K., 581
Zabel, R. H., 327, 1633
Zachau-Christiansen, B., 1670
Zaffran, R. T., 818
Zaga, B., 541, 1877
Zaidel, E., 872, 1706
Zais, R. S., 522
Zajonc, R. B., 266
Zalenski, S., 194
Zane, T., 1201, 1438, 1444, 1464, 1533
Zanna, M., 1388
Zappia, I. A., 508
Zaremba, S., 382
Zarfas, D. E., 624
Zarski, J. A., 1780
Zausmer, E., 625
Zdunich, L., 1732
Zeaman, D., 625, 904, 1947, 1948
Zeff, S. B., 905
Zegiob, L., 1616
Zehrbach, R., 1426
Zehrback, R. R., 1423

Zeichner, K. M., 1354
Zeiger, H. E., 1844
Zeiss, A. R., 456
Zeithofer, J., 915
Zelman, J., 1068
Zeltzer, L. K., 354, 690, 1157, 1159
Zeltzer, P. M., 291, 354
Zemlin, R., 1696
Zener, K., 446
Zentall, S., 1582
Zentall, S. S., 166, 655
Zercher, C., 1427
Zetlin, A., 34, 498, 510
Ziai, M., 1601
Ziarnik, J. P., 1616
Zich, J., 456
Ziegler, D., 47
Ziegler, E. F., 117
Zigler, C., 612
Zigler, E., 19, 503, 710, 767, 768, 866, 1171, 1209, 1288, 1345, 1380, 1950
Zigler, E. F., 533, 784
Zigmond, N., 45, 521, 590, 928, 1639, 1766, 1933
Zilboorg, G., 525
Zill, N., 683, 1107
Zimet, G. D., 258

Zimmerman, D. W., 1077
Zimmerman, H., 1037
Zimmerman, P. D., 366
Zimmerman, R. A., 1834
Zimmerman, W., 1774
Zimmerman, W. S., 136, 1352
Zimpher, N. L., 956
Zinchenko, V. P., 1798
Zindi, F., 62, 1683
Zins, J. E., 1300, 1515
Zipperlan, H. R., 117
Zirkel, P. A., 299, 725
Zohn, C. J., 1616
Zola-Morgan, S., 262
Zondlo, F. C., 675
Zook, K. B., 50
Zorinsky, E., 1759
Zucker, S., 1039
Zucker, S. H., 1221, 1414
Zuckerman, W., 1295
Zucman, E., 1906
Zumberg, C., 1216
Zumberg, M., 1216
Zurif, E. J., 594
Zych, K. A., 805, 806, 807, 808, 1024, 1060

SUBJECT INDEX

AAAS *See* American Association for the Advancement of Science

AAMD Classification Systems, 1

AAMR Adaptive Behavior Scales-Residential and Community: Second Edition (ABS-RC-S:2), 2

AAMR Adaptive Behavior Scales-School: Second Edition (ABS-S:2), 2

ABAB Design, 3

Abecedarian Project, 4

Ability Training, 9

Abnormalities, Neurophysiological, 12

ABPP, *See* American Board of Professional Psychology

Abroms, Kippy I. (1942–), 15

Absence of Speech, *See* Speech, Absence of

Absence Seizures, 16

Absenteeism/Attendance of Handicapped Children, 17

Abstraction, Capacity for, 17

Abstract Thinking, Impairment in, 18

Abused Children, 19

Academically Talented Children, 21

Academic Assessment, 22

Academic Language, 25

Academic Skills, 26

Academic Therapy, 27

Academic Therapy Publications (ATP), 27

Acalculia, 27

Acceleration of Gifted Children, 28

Accessibility of Buildings, 29

Accessibility of Programs, 29

Accommodation, 30

Acetylcholine, 31

Achievement Need, 31

Achievement Tests, 32

Achondroplasia, 33

Acid Maltase Deficiency, *See* Rare Diseases

Acting Out, 33

Adapted Physical Education, 33

Adaptive Behavior, 34

Adaptive Behavior Inventory for Children (ABIC), 36

Adaptive Behavior Scale, *See* Vineland Adaptive Behavior Scales

Adaptive Devices, 36

Adaptive PE, *See* Adapted Physical Education

Adderall, 37

Additive-free Diets, 38

Adjustment of the Handicapped, 39

Adler, Alfred (1870–1937), 41

Administration of Special Education, 41

Adolescence and Special Problems of the Handicapped, 44

Adoptees, 46

Adult Basic Education (ABE), 47

Adult Programs for the Disabled, 48

Advanced Placement Program, 49

Advance Organizers, 50

Adventitious Disabilities, 51

Advocacy for Children with Disabilities, 51

Advocacy Groups, Citizen, 52

Advocacy Organizations, 53

Affective Disorders, 54

Affective Education, 56

Africa: East and Southern, Special Education in, 58

Africa, Special Education in, 65

Age-Appropriate Curriculum, 67

Age at Onset, 68

Aggression, 68

Agraphia, 71

Aicardi Syndrome (Callosal Dysgenesis), 72

Aides to Psycholinguistic Teaching, 72

AIDS, *See* Pediatric Acquired Immune Deficiency Syndrome

Akineton, 73

Al-Anon, 73

Alateen, 74

Albinism, 74

Albright's Hereditary Osteodystrophy (Pseudohypoparathyroidism), 74

Alcohol and Drug Abuse Patterns, 75

Alexander Graham Bell Association for the Deaf, 77

Alexia, 77

Algozzine, Bob (1946–), 78

Allergic Disorders, 78

Alley, Gordon R. (1934–), 81

Alphabetic Method, 82

Alternative Communication Methods in Special Education, 82

Amaroutic Familial Idiocy, *See* Tay-Sachs Syndrome

Amblyopia, 85

American Academy for Cerebral Palsy and Developmental Medicine (AACPDM), 85

American Annals of the Deaf, 85

American Association for the Advancement of Science (AAAS), 86

American Association for the Severely Handicapped, *See* TASH

American Association of Colleges for Teacher Education (AACTE), 86

American Association of Marriage and Family Therapists (AAMFT), 86

American Association on Mental Retardation (AAMR), 87

American Board of Professional Neuropsychology, (ABPN), 87

American Board of Professional Psychology (ABPP), 87

American Cancer Society (ACS), 88

American Educational Research Association (AERA), 88

American Foundation for the Blind (AFB), 89

American Guidance Service, 90

American Institute–The Training School at Vineland, 90

American Journal of Mental Retardation (AJMR), 90

American Journal of Occupational Therapy (AJOT), 91

American Journal of Orthopsychiatry (AJO), 91

American Journal of Psychiatry, 91

American Occupational Therapy Foundation, 91

American Orthopsychiatric Association (ORTHO), 92

American Physical Therapy Association, 92

American Printing House for the Blind (APH), 93

American Psychiatric Association (APA), 93

American Psychological Association, 94

American Psychologist, 94

American Sign Language, 95

American Society for Deaf Children (ASDC), 96

American Speech-Language-Hearing Association (ASHA), 96

Americans with Disabilities Act (ADA), 97

Ames, Louise Bates (1908–1996), 103

Amnesia, 104

Amniocentesis, 106

Amphetamine Psychosis, 106

AMSLAN, *See* American Sign Language

Anastasi, Anne (1908–), 107

Anastasiow, Nicholas J. (1924–), 108

Anderson, Meta L. (1878–1942), 108

Anencephaly, 109

Angelman Syndrome, 109

Animals for the Handicapped, 110

Annals of Dyslexia, 111

Annual Directory of Educational Facilities for the Learning Disabled, *See* Biennial Directory of Educational Facilities for the Learning Disabled

Annual Goals, 111

Anomalies, Physical, *See* Physical Anomalies

Anorexia Nervosa, 112

Anosmia, 115

Anoxia116

Antecedent Teaching, 116

Anthroposophic Movement, 117

Anticonvulsants, 118

Antihistamines, 120

Antisocial Behavior, 121

Antisocial Personality, 124

Anxiety, 124

Anxiety Disorders, 125

Apgar Rating Scale, 128

Aphasia, 129

Aphasia, Developmental, *See* Childhood Aphasia; Language Disorders

Apnea, 130

Applied Behavior Analysis, 131

Applied Psycholinguistics, 134

Apraxia, *See* Developmental Apraxia

Aptitude Testing, 135

Aptitude–Treatment Interaction, 137

ARC, The, 140

Architectural Barriers, 140

Architecture and the Handicapped, 141

Archives of Clinical Neuropsychology (ACN), 143

Argentina, Special Education Services for Young Children in, 143

Arithmetic Instruction, 144

Arithmetic Remediation, 146

Armitage, Thomas Rhodes (1824–1890), 148

Armstrong *vs.* Kline (1979), 149

Army Group Examinations, 149

Arthritis, Juvenile, 151

Articulation Disorders, 152

Art Therapy, 153

Asphyxia, 154

Assessment, Curriculum Based, *See* Curriculum Based Assessment

Assessment, Educational, 155

Assimilation, 158

Assistive Devices, 158

Association for Childhood Education International (ACEI), 160

Association for Children and Adults with Learning Disabilities (ACLD), *See* Learning Disabilities Association

Association for Persons with Severe Handicaps, The (TASH), *See* TASH

Association for Special Education Technology (ASET), *See* Center for Applied Technology (CAST)

Association for the Advancement of Behavior Therapy (AABT), 160

Association for the Gifted, The, 161

Association of Black Psychologists, 161

Associative Learning, 162

Asthma, 162

Astigmatism, 164

Asymmetrical Tonic Neck Reflex (ATNR), 164

Atarax, 164

Ataxia, 165

Athetosis, 165

Attention-Deficit Hyperactivity Disorder (ADHD), 166

Attention Span, 173

Attitudes of Handicapped Students with Disabilities, 174

Attitudes Toward the Handicapped, 175

Attributional Retraining, 176

Attributions, 177

Atypical Child Syndrome, 178

Audiogram, 179

Audiology, 181

Audiometry, 181

Auditory Abnormalities, 182

Auditory Discrimination, 183

Auditory Perception, 183

Auditory Processing, 184

Auditory-Visual Integration, 185

Augmentative Communication Systems, 187

Australia, Special Education in, 188

Autism, 192

Autism Society of America (ASA), 197

Autism Treatment Options (ATO), 198

Autistic Behavior, 198

Automaticity, 199

Automutism, See Elective Mutism

Autonomic Reactivity, 200

Aversive Control, 201

Aversive Stimulus, 201

Aveyron, Wild Boy of, See Wild Boy of Aveyron

Ayllon, Teodoro (1929–), 202

Ayres, A. Jean (1920–1988), 202

Babinski Reflex, 205

Baby Doe, 205–207

Backward Readers, 207

Baer, Donald M. (1931–), 207

Bandura, Albert (1925–), 207

Bannatyne, Alexander D. (1925–), 208

Bardon, Jack 1. (1925–1993), 209,

Barraga, Natalie C. (1915–), 210

Barrier-Free Education, 210

Barriers, Architectural, See Architectural Barriers

Barsch, Ray H. (1917–), 212

BASC, See Behavior Assessment System for Children

Basal Readers, 212

Baseline Data, 213

Base Rate, 214

Basic Skill Training, 215

Bateman, Barbara (1933–), 215

Battered Child Syndrome, 216

Baumeister, Alfred A. (1934–), 217

Bayley Scales of Infant Development-Second Edition (BSID-II), 217

Bechterev (Bekhtiarev), Vladimir M. (1857–1927), 219

Becker, Wesley C. (1928–), 219

Beers, Clifford W. (1876–1943), 220

Beery-Buktenica Development Test of Visual-Motor Integration (VMI), 220

Behavioral Assessment, 221

Behavioral Consultation, 223

Behavioral Deficit, 225

Behavioral Disorders, 226

Behavioral Objectives, 226

Behavioral Observation, 228

Behavioral Support, See Support, Behavioral

Behavior Analysis, See Applied Behavior Analysis

Behavior Assessment Scale for Children (BASC), 230

Behavior Charting, 232

Behavior, Destructive, See Destructive Behavior

Behavior Disorders, 232

Behaviorism, 236

Behavior Modeling, 237

Behavior Modification, 237

Behavior Problem Checklist, Revised (RBPC), 238

Behavior Therapy, 239

Behavior Therapy, 242

Bell, Alexander Graham (1847–1922), 242

Bell, Terrel H. (1921–1996), 242

Bellevue Psychiatric Hospital, 243

Benadryl, 244

Bender, Lauretta (1897–1987), 244

Bender Gestalt, 245

Bennett, Virginia C. (1916–), 246

Benzedrine, 247

Bereiter, Carl (1930–), 247

Bettelheim, Bruno (1903–1990), 248

Bialer, Irving (1919–), 248

Bibliotherapy, 248

Bielscholwsky Syndrome, See Juvenile Cerebromacular Degeneration

Biennial Directory of Educational Facilities for the Learning Disabled, 249

Bijou, Sidney W. (1908–), 249

Bilingual Assessment and Special Education, 250

Bilingual Special Education, 252

Bilingual Speech Language Pathology, 254

Bill of Rights for the Disabled, 255

Binet, Alfred (1857–1911), 255

Biochemical Irregularities, 256

Biofeedback, 257

Biogenic Models, 259

Biological Basis of Emotional Disorders, 260

Biological Basis of Learning and Memory, 261

Biological Factors and Social Class, See Social Class and Biological Factors

Birch, Herbert G. (1918–1973), 262

Birch, Jack W. (1915–1998), 263

Birth Injuries, 264

Birth Order, 265

Birth Trauma, 269

Blatt, Burton (1927–1985), 269

Blind, 270

Blind Infants, 272

Blindisms, 272

Blind Learning Aptitude Test (BLAT), 273

Blissymbols, 274

Bloom, Benjamin S. (1913–), 275

Bobath Method, 276

Boder Test of Reading-Spelling Patterns, 276

Body Image, 277

Body Types, 278

Bonet, Juan P. (1579–1629), 279

Borderline Personality Disorder, 280

Bower, Eli M. (1917–1991), 280

Bracken Basic Concept Scale-Revised (BBCS-R), 281

Braidwood, Thomas (1715–1806), 282

Braille, 282

Braille, Louis (1809–1852), 283

Brain Damage/Injury, 284

Brain Disorders (Degenerative Motor Dysfunction), 288

Brain Growth Periodization, 289

Brain Injury Association, 290

Brain Organization, See Neurological Organization

Brain Stem Audiometry, 291

Brain Tumors, 291

Brazelton, Thomas B. (1918–), 292

Bridgeman, Laura Dewey (1829–1899), 293

Brigance Diagnostic Inventories, 294

Brittle Bone Disease (Osteogenesis Imperfecta), 295

Broca, Pierre Paul (1824–1880), 295

Broca's Aphasia, 296

Bronfenbrenner, Uri (1917–), 297

Brown, Ann L. (1943–), 297

Brown, Lou (1939–), 298

Brown, Robert T. (1940–), 299

Brown v. Board of Education, 299

Bruininks-Oseretsky Test of Motor Proficiency, 300

Bruner, Jerome (1915–), 301

Bruxism and the Handicapped Student, 302

Buckley Amendment, See Family Educational Rights and Privacy Act (FERPA)

Bulimia Nervosa, 303

Bureau of Education for the Handicapped (BEH), 306

Bureau of Indian Affairs: Office of Indian Education Programs, 306

Burks' Behavior Rating Scales (BBRS), 307

Buros, Oscar K. (1905–1978), 307

Buros Mental Measurements Yearbook, 308

Burt, Sir Cyril (1833–1971), 308

Café au Lait Spots, 311

Caldwell, Bettye M. (1924–), 311

Camp, Bonnie W. (1931–), 312

Campbell, Sir Francis Joseph (1832–1914), 313

Camphill Community Movement, 314

Camping for the Handicapped, 314

Canada, Special Education in, 315

Cancer, Childhood, 318

Cantrell, Robert P. (1938–), 318

Cardiac Disorders, 319

Career Education for the Handicapped, 321

Caribbean, Special Education in, 322

Carnine, Douglas W. (1947–), 324

Carrow Elicited Language Inventory (CELI), 325

Cartwright, G. Phillip (1937–), 325

Cascade Model of Special Education Services, 326

Case History, 328

Catalog of Federal Domestic Assistance, 328

Cataracts, 329

Categorical Education, 329

Catecholamines, 330

Cat Scan, 331

Cattell, James McKeen (1860–1944), 332

Cawley's Project Math, 332

Center for Applied Special Technology (CAST), 333

Centile Scores, See Percentile Scores

Central Auditory Dysfunction, 334

Central Nervous System, 336

Central Processing Dysfunctions in Children, 337

Central Tendency, 338

Cerebellar Disorders, 339

Cerebral Dominance, 340

Cerebral Function, Lateralization of, 342

Cerebral Infarction, 344

Cerebral Lesion, Chronic, 345

Cerebral Palsy (CP), 346

Certification/Licensure Issues, 349

Chalfant, James C. (1932–), 350

Chall, Jeanne S. (1921–), 351

Character Disorder, See Personality Disorder

Chemically Dependent Youths, 352

Chemotherapy, 354

Chess, Stella (1914–), 355

Child Abuse, 356

Child Anxiety Scale (CAS), 358

Child Behavior Checklist/4–18 (CBCL), 358

Child Development, 359

Child Find, 359

Child Guidance Clinic, 360

Childhood Aphasia, 361

Childhood Neurosis, See Psychoneurotic Disorders

Childhood Psychosis, 364

Childhood Schizophrenia, 367

Child Psychiatry, 370

Child Psychology, 371

Children of a Lesser God, 373

Children of the Handicapped, 374

Children's Defense Fund, 374

Children's Early Education Developmental Inventory, See Battelle Developmental Inventory

Children's Manifest Anxiety Scale (CMAS), 375

Child Service Demonstration Centers (CSDC), 375

Child Variance Project, 378
China, Special Education in, 378
Chlamydia Trachomatis Infections, 381
Chlorpromazine, 382
Cholinesterase, 382
Chomsky, Avram Noam (1928–), 383
Chorea, 384
Chorionic Villus Sampling (CVS), 385
Chromosomes, Human, Anomalies and Cytogenic Abnormalities, 385
Chronic Illness in Children, 391
Church Work with the Handicapped, 392
Citizen Advocacy Group, See Advocacy Group, Citizen
Civil Rights of the Handicapped, 393
Class-Action Suits, 393
Classroom Management, 394
Clausen, Johs (1913–), 396
Cleft Lip/Palate, 396
Cleland, Charles C. (1924–), 397
Clerc, Laurent (1785–1869), 398
Clinical Evaluation of Language Fundamentals (CELF–3), 398
Clinical Interview, 399
Clinical Psychology, 401
Clinical Teaching, 401
Cloze Technique, 402
Cluttering, 403
Cockayne Syndrome (CS), 405
Cogentin, 405
Cognitive Assessment System (CAS), 405
Cognitive Behavior Therapy, 407
Cognitive Development, 409
Cognitive Impairment and Metal Pollutants, 414
Cognitive Retraining, 415
Cognitive Strategies, 416
Cognitive Styles, 418
Colitis, 420
Collaboration, See Inclusion
Collaborative Perinatal Project, 421
College Programs for Disabled College Students, 422
Color Blindness, 423
Communication Aids, Electronic, See Electronic Communication Aids
Communication Boards, 423
Communication Disorders, 424
Communication Methods in Special Education, Alternative, See Alternative Communication Methods in Special Education

Communication Specialist, 426
Community-Based Instruction, 426
Community-Based Job Training for Students with Autism and Developmental Disabilities, 427
Community-Based Services, 429
Community Placement, 430
Community Residential Programs, 431
Compazine, 432
Compensatory Education, 433
Competency Education, 434
Competency Test, 434
Competency Testing for Teachers, 435
Comprehensive Receptive and Expressive Vocabulary Test (CREVT), 436
Comprehensive Test of Nonverbal Intelligence (CTONI), 437
Compulsory Attendance (and Students with Disabilities), 437
Computer-Assisted Instruction, 438
Computerized Axial Tomography, See Cat Scan
Computer Literacy, 439
Computer-Managed Instruction, 440
Computers and Education, an International Journal, 441
Computers in Human Behavior, 441
Computer Use with Students with Disabilities, 442
Concept Formation, 443
Concept of Activity, See Theory of Activity; Vygotsky, L.S.
Concrete Operations, 444
Conditioning, 445
Conduct Disorder, 448
Conductive Hearing Loss, 449
Confidentiality of Information, 450
Congenital Disorders, 451
Congenital Word Blindness, History of, 454
Conners' Parent-Rating Scales-Revised, Conners' Teacher-Rating Scales-Revised, Conners'-Wells' Adolescent Self-Report Scale, 454
Conscience, Lack of in Handicapped, 455
Consent, Informed, 457
Consent Agreement, See Consent Decree
Consent Decree, 458
Constitutional Law (in Special Education), 458
Consultation, 459

Consultation, Inclusion and, See Inclusion
Consultation, Mental Health, 461
Contingency Contracting, 464
Continuing Education for the Handicapped, 465
Continuum of Special Education Services, See Inclusion
Contract Procurement, 465
Control Groups, 466
Convergent and Divergent Thinking, 466
Convulsions, Febrile, See Febrile Convulsions
Convulsive Disorders, See Seizure Disorders
Cooperative Teaching, See Inclusion
Coprolalia, 467
Copropraxia, See Coprolalia
Core School, 468
Cornelia De Lange Syndrome, 469
Correctional Education, 469
Correctional Special Education, 470
Costa Rica, Special Education in, 471
Co-Teaching, See Inclusion
Council for Children with Behavioral Disorders, 473
Council for Exceptional Children, 474
Council for Learning Disabilities, 475
Council of Administrators of Special Education (CASE), 475
Counseling the Handicapped, 475
Cratty, Bryant J. (1929–), 476
Creative Problem Solving (CPS), 477
Creative Problem Solving Institute (CPSI), 478
Creative Studies Program, 478
Creativity, 479
Creativity Tests, 481
Cretinism, 482
Cri Du Chat Syndrome (Cat Cry Syndrome), 482
Crime and the Handicapped, 483
Crisis Intervention, 484
Crisis Teacher, 486
Crissey, Marie Skodak (1910–), 487
Criterion-Referenced Testing, 488
Cronbach, Lee J. (1916–), 489
Cross Categorical Programming, 489
Cross-Cultural Adaptability Inventory, 490
Cross Cultural Special Education, 491

Cross Modality Training, 492
Cross Syndrome, See Rare Diseases
Cross-McKusic-Breen Syndrome, See Rare Diseases
Crouzon's Syndrome (Craniofacial Dysostosis) (CS), 492
Cruickshank, William M. (1915–1992), 493
Cryptophasia, 493
Crystallized v. Fluid Intelligence, 494
Cued Speech, 494
Cuisenaire Rods, 495
Cultural Attitudes Towards Special Education, 496
Cultural Bias in Testing, 500
Cultural Deprivation, See Early Experience and Critical Periods; See Socioeconomic Status
Culture Fair Test, 502
Cultural-Familial Retardation, 502
Culturally/Linguistically Diverse Issues in Early Childhood, See Early Childhood, Culturally/Linguistically Diverse Issues in
Culturally/Linguistically Diverse Students and Learning Disabilities, 505
Culturally/Linguistically Diverse Gifted Students, 506
Culturally and Linguistically Diverse Students in Special Education, Families of, 510
Culturally/Linguistically Diverse Students, Representation of, 513
Cultural Perspectives on Behavioral Disorders, 517
Cumulative Deficit Hypothesis
Curriculum, 520
Curriculum, Age Appropriate, See Age Appropriate Curriculum
Curriculum-Based Assessment (CBA), 521
Curriculum for Students with Mild Disabilities in Special Education, 522
Curriculum for Students with Severe Disabilities, 523
Curriculum in Early Childhood Intervention, 524
Custodial Care of the Handicapped, 524
Cylert, 526
Cystic Fibrosis, 527
Cystic Fibrosis Foundation, 527
Cytomegalovirus, 528

Daily Living Skills, 529
Dance Therapy, 531
Dandy-Walker Syndrome (DWS), 531
Data-Based Instruction, 532
Day-Care Centers, 533
Daydreaming, 534
Deaf, 535
Deaf, Interpreters for, See Interpreters for the Deaf
Deaf-Blind, 538
Deaf Education, 539
Deborah P. v. Turlington, 543
Decroly, Ovide (1871–1932), 543
Defective Speech, See Speech
Deinstitutionalization, 544
Delacato, Carl H. (1923–), 545
Delayed Language, See Language Delays
De Leon, Pedro, See Ponce De Leon, Pedro De
de l'Epee, Abbe Charles Michel (1712–1789), 546
Delinquency, Handicapping Conditions and, 546
De Lorenzo, Maria E. G. E. (1927–), 548
Dementia, 548
Demography of Special Education, 549
Dendrites, 551
Deno, Evelyn N. (1911–), 553
Dentistry and the Handicapped Child, 553
Depakene, 555
Depression, 556
Deprivation, See Neglect; Post Institutionalized Child
Deprivation, Bioneural Results of, 558
Desensitization, 559
Des Lauriers, Austin M. (1917–), 560
Des Lauriers-Carlson Hypothesis, 560
Despert, Juliette L. (1892–1982), 561
Destructive Behaviors, 561
Detroit Tests of Learning Aptitude-Fourth Edition (DTLA–4), 562
Developing Understanding of Self and Others-Revised (DUSO-R), 563
Developmental Aphasia, See Childhood Aphasia; Language Disorders
Developmental Apraxia, 564
Developmental Delay, 565
Developmental Disabilities, 566
Developmental Disabilities Assistance and Bill of Rights Act, 569
Developmental Disabilities Legal Resource Center, See Protection and Advo-

cacy System-Developmentally Disabled (P&A)

Developmental Dyslexia, 570

Developmental Milestones, 573

Developmental Norms, 577

Developmental Optometry, 578

Developmental Psychology, 579

Developmental Test of Visual Perception: Second Edition (DTVP–2), 579

Developmental Therapy, 580

Devereux Foundation, The, 581

Deviation IQ, 582

Dexedrine, 583

Diabetes, 583

Diagnosis in Special Education, 584

Diagnostic Achievement Battery-Second Edition (DAB–2), 586

Diagnostic and Statistical Manual of Mental Disorders (DSM-IV), 587

Diagnostic Assessments of Reading with Trial Teaching Strategies (DARTTS), 588

Diagnostic Prescriptive Teaching, 589

Diagnostic Teaching, 590

Dialysis and Special Education, 591

Diana v. State Board of Education, 592

Diazepam, 593

Dichotic Listening, 594

Dictionary of Occupational Titles, 595

Differential Abilities Scale, 595

DiGeorge Syndrome, See Velocranial Facial Syndrome

Dilantin, 596

Diplegia, 597

Diplopia, 597

Direct Instruction, 598

Disability, 600

Disability Culture

Disadvantaged Child, 601

Discipline, 603

Discourse, 604

Discrepancy Analysis, See Learning Disabilities, Severe Discrepancy Analysis in

Discrepancy from Grade, 605

Discriminant Analysis, 606

Discrimination Learning, 607

Disproportionality, 608

Distar, 610

Distractibility, 611

Division of International Special Education & Services (DISES), 614

Divorce and Special Education, 614

Dix, Dorothea L. (1802–1887), 619

Doctoral Training in Special Education, 619

Dog Guides for the Blind, 620

Dolch Word List, 621

Doll, Edgar A. (1889–1968), 621

Doman, Glenn (1919–), 622

Dopamine, 623

Double-Blind Design, 623

Down, J. (John) Langdon (1828–1896), 624

Down's Syndrome, 624

Draw-a-Person Test, 627

Dropout, 628

Drug Abuse, 628

Drugs, See Specific Drugs

Drug Therapy, 630

Due Process, 631

Dunn, Lloyd M. (1917–), 632

DUSO, See Developing Understanding of Self and Others

Dwarfism, 633

Dyscalculia, 633

Dyscopia, See Apraxia

Dysfluency, See Stuttering

Dysgraphia, 635

Dyskinesia, 636

Dyslexia, See Developmental Dyslexia

Dyslogic Syndrome, 636

Dysmetria, 637

Dysmorphic Features, 637

Dysnomia, 638

Dysphagia, 639

Dysphonia, See Voice Disorders

Dyspedagogia, 640

Dysphasia, See Language Disorders

Dyspraxia, See Apraxia

Dystonia Musculorum Deformans (DMD), 641

Eagle-Barrett Syndrome, See Rare Diseases

Ear and Hearing, 643

Early Childhood, Culturally and Linguistically Diverse Issues in, 643

Early Experience and Critical Periods, 645

Early Identification of Handicapped Children, 650

Early Infantile Autism, See Autism

Early Screening Profiles (ESP), 651

Eating Disorders, 652

Echolalia, 652

Echopraxia, 653

Ecological Assessment, 653

Ecological Education for the Handicapped, 654

Edgerton, Robert B. (1931–), 656

Educability, 656

Educable Mentally Retarded (EMR), 657

Educateur, 658

Educational and Psychological Measurement, 658

Educational Diagnostician, 659

Educationally Disadvantaged, 659

Educational Products Information Exchange (EPIE), 660

Educational Resources Information Center (ERIC), 661

Educational Testing Service (ETS), 661

Education and Training in Mental Retardation and Developmental Disabilities, 662

Education and Treatment of Children (ETC), 662

Education for All Handicapped Children Act of 1975 (PL 94-142), See Individuals with Disabilities Education Act (IDEA)

Education for "Other Health Impaired" Children, 662

Education for the Handicapped Law Report (EHLR), 663

Education for the Terminally Ill, 663

Education of the Blind/Visually Handicapped, 664

Education Week, 665

EEG Abnormalities, 665

EEOC, See Equal Employment Opportunity Commission

Effectiveness of Special Education, 667

Egbert, Robert L. (1923–), 672

Eisenson, Jon (1907–), 672

Elaborated v. Restricted Verbal Codes, 673

Elavil, 674

Elective Mutism, 674

Electroconvulsive Therapy (ECT), 676

Electroencephalograph, 677

Electromechanical Switches, 678

Electronic Communication Aids, 678

Electronic Travel Aids, 679

Elementary and Secondary Education Act (ESEA), 679

Elephant Man, The, 680

Ellis, Norman R. (1924–), 681

Elwyn Institutes, 681

Embedded Figures Test (EFT), 682

Emotional Disorders, 682

Emotional Lability, 686

Encephalitis, 687

Encopresis, 688

Endorphins, 689

Endocrine Disturbances, 690

Engelmann, Siegfried E. (1931–), 690

Engineered Classroom, 691

English as a Second Language (ESL) and Special Education, See Second Language Learners

Engrams, 693

Enrichment, 693

Enrichment Triad Model, 694

Enuresis, 695

Epicanthic Fold, 697

Epidemiology, 697

Epilepsy, See Seizure Disorders

Epilepsy Foundation of America (EFA), 698

Epinephrine, 698

Equal Educational Opportunity, 699

Equal Employment Opportunity Commission (EEOC), 700

Equal Protection, 700

Equine Therapy, 701

Errorless Learning, 702

Ertl Index, 702

Esquirol, Jean E. (1722–1840), 703

Ethics, 703

Etiology, 704

Eugenics, 713

Eustis, Dorothy Harrison (1886–1946), 715

Evaluation, 715

Exceptional Children (EC), 716

Exhibitionism, 716

Expectancy Age, 717

Expressive Dysphasia, 718

Expressive Language Disorders, See Language Disorders

Expressive Vocabulary Test (EVT), 719

Extended School Year for the Handicapped, 719

Extinction, 720

Eye-Hand Coordination, 721

Eysenck, Hans J. (1916–), 722

Facilitated Communication, 725

Factor Analysis, 726

Failure to Thrive, 728

False Positive and False Negative, 729

Familial Dysautonomia, 730

Familial Retardation, 730

Families of Culturally/Linguistically Diverse Students in Special Education, See Culturally/Linguistically Diverse Students, Families of

Family Counseling, 732

Family Educational Rights and Privacy Act (FERPA), 733

Family Policy Compliance Office (FPCO), 738

Family Response to a Child with Disabilities, 738

Family Service America (FSA), 739

Family Therapy, 739

Farrell, Elizabeth E. (1870–1932), 740

Fears, See Phobias and Fears

Febre-Languepin Syndrome, See Rare Diseases

Febrile Convulsions, 740

Federal Interagency Coordinating Council (FICC), 741

Federal Register (FR), 741

Feeble-Minded, 742

Feingold Diet, 743

Feldhusen, John F. (1926–), 744

Fenichel, Carl (1905–1975), 744

Feral Children, 745

Fernald, Grace Maxwell (1879–1950), 746

Fernald, Walter E. (1859–1924), 746

Fernald Method, 747

Fetal Alcohol Syndrome (FAS), 747

Fetal Face Syndrome, See Rare Diseases

Fetal Hydantoin Syndrome, 752

Fewell, Rebecca R. (1936–), 753

Field Dependence-Independence, 753

Filial Therapy, Special Education and, 755

Fingerspelling, 756

Finland, Special Education in, 757

Fitzgerald Key, 758

Focus on Autism and Other Developmental Disabilities, 759

Folling Disease, See Phenylketonuria, 759

Follow Through, 759

Food Additives, 760

Forness, Steven R. (1939–), 761

Forrest v. Ambach, 762

Foster Homes for the Handicapped, 763

Foundation for Children with Learning Disabilities (FCLD), 764

Fountain Valley Teacher Support System in Mathematics, 765

Fourteenth Amendment Rights, See Equal Protection,

Foxx, Richard M. (1944–), 765

Fragile X Syndrome, 766

Fraiberg, Selma Horowitz (1918–1981), 769
France, Special Education in, 769
Franceschetti-Klein Syndrome, See Rare Diseases
Free Appropriate Public Education, 771
Freedom from Distractibility, 772
Freeman Sheldon Syndrome, 776
French, Edward Livingston (1916–1969), 776
French, Joseph L. (1928–), 777
Freud, Anna (1895–1982), 778
Freud, Sigmund (1856–1939), 778
Friedreich's Ataxia (FA), 779
Frostig, Marianne (1906–1985), 779
Frostig Remedial Program, 780
Functional Analysis, 780
Functional Assessment, 781
Functional Centers Hypothesis, 783
Functional Domains, 784
Functional Instruction, 785
Functional Skills Training, 786
Functional Vision, 787
Functional Vocabulary, 788
Future Problem Solving Program (FPSP), 789

Gait Disturbances, 791
Galactosemia, 792
Gallagher, James J. (1926–), 793
Gallaudet, Edward M. (1837–1917), 794
Gallaudet, Thomas Hopkins (1787–1851), 794
Gallaudet College, 794
Galton, Francis (1822–1911), 795
Games for the Handicapped, 795
Gamma-Aminobutyric Acid (GABA), 796
Gargoylism, See Hurler's Syndrome
Garrett, Emma (1846–1893), 796
Garrett, Mary Smith (1839–1925), 797
Garrison, S. Olin (1853–1900), 797
Gates-MacGinitie Reading Tests (GMRT), Third Edition, 797
Gates-MacGinitie Reading Tests (GMRT), Fourth Edition (In Press), 798
Gaze Aversion, 798
Gearheart, Bill R. (1918–), 800
General Aptitude Test Battery (GATB), 801

General Case Programming, 801
Generalizability Theory, 802
Generalization, 803
Generic Special Education, 804
Genetic Counseling, 805
Genetic Factors in Behavior, 806
Genetic Transmissions, 807
Genetic Variations, 808
Genie, 809
Genius, 810
George, William Reuben (1866–1936), 811
Georgia Studies of Creative Behavior, 812
Germany, Special Education in, 812
Gerstmann Syndrome, 815
Gesell, Arnold Lucius (1880–1961), 815
Gesell Developmental Schedules, 815
Gesell School Readiness Test, 816
Getman, Gerald N. (1913–1990), 816
g Factor Theory, 817
Gifted, Counseling the, 818
Gifted and Talented, Underachievement in the, 819
Gifted and Talented Children, 820
Gifted Child Quarterly, 821
Gifted Children, 821
Gifted Children and Reading, 823
Gifted Education Resource Institute, 823
Gifted Handicapped, 824
Gifted International, 825
Giftedness, Cultural and Linguistic Diversity in, See Culturally/Linguistically Diverse Gifted Students
Gillingham-Stillman: Alphabetic Approach, 825
Glaucoma, See Visually Impaired
Glial Cells, 826
Goals, Annual, See Annual Goals
Goals, Use of, 827
Goddard, Henry H. (1866–1957) 827
Gold, Marc (1931–1982), 828
Golden, Charles J. (1949–), 828
Goldenhar Syndrome (GS), 829
Goldman-Fristoe Test of Articulation (GFTA), 829
Goldman-Fristoe-Woodcock Auditory Skills Test Battery (G-F-W Battery), 830
Goldman-Fristoe-Woodcock Test of Auditory Discrimination (G-F-W), 831
Goldstein, Max A. (1870–1941), 831

Goodenough, Florence Laura (1886–1959), 831
Gottlieb, Jay (1942–), 832
Gowan, John C. (1912–1986), 832
Grade Equivalents (GEs), 833
Grade Retention, 835
Grand Mal Seizures, See Seizure Disorders
Granulomatous Disease, Chronic, 836
Graphesthesia, 837
Gray Oral Reading Tests–Third Edition (GORT–3), 837
Grieving Process, 838
Groht, Mildred A. (1890–1971), 839
Grosenick, Judith K. (1942–), 840
Grossman, Herbert (1934–), 841
Group Homes, 841
Grouping of Children–Implications for Special Education, 843
Group Therapy, 844
Guadalupe v. Tempe Elementary School District, See Diana vs. State Board of Education
Guggenbuhl, Johann J. (1816–1863), 845
Guilford, J.P. (1897–1987), 845
Guillain-Barre Syndrome, 846

Habilitation of the Handicapped, 847
Habituation, 847
Halderman s. Pennhurst State School and Hospital (1977), 848
Haldol, 849
Hall, Frank H. (1843–1911), 849
Hall, G. Stanley (1844–1924), 850
Hallahan, Daniel P. (1944–), 850
Hallermann-Streiff Syndrome (Oculo-Mandibulo-Facial Syndrome) (HSS), 851
Hallucinogens, 851
Halstead Aphasia Test, 852
Halstead-Reitan Neuropsychological Test Battery, 853
Hammill, Donald (1934–), 853
Handedness and Exceptionality, 854
Handicapism, 856
Handicapped, Definition of, 856
Handicapped Children, Social Mainstreaming of, 857
Handicapped Children's Early Education Assistance Act (Public Law 90-538), 858

Handicapped Children's Early Education Program (HCEEP), 859
Handicapping Conditions, High Incidence, See High Incidence Handicaps
Handicaps, Low Incidence, See Low Incidence Handicaps
Hand Test, 860
Handwriting, 860
Happy Puppet Syndrome, See Angelman Syndrome
Hard of Hearing, See Deaf
Haring, Norris G. (1923–), 861
Harvard Educational Review, 862
Hauy, Valentin (1745–1822), 862
Havighurst, Robert J. (1900–1991), 863
Hawthorne Effect, 863
Hayden, Alice Hazel (1909–1994), 864
Haywood, H. Carl (1931–), 864
Head Injury, See Traumatic Brain Injury
Head Start, 866
Health Impairments, 867
Health Maintenance, Invasive Procedures for, 867
Health Maintenance Procedures, 868
Hearing Impaired, See Deaf
Heber, Rick F. (1932–), 868
Heelcord Operation, 869
Hegge, Kirk, Kirk Approach, 869
Heinicke, Samuel (1727–1790), 869
Helen Keller International, 870
Hemiballismus, 870
Hemiparesis, 871
Hemiplegia, 871
Hemispherectomy, 872
Hemispheric Asymmetry, Sex Differences in, 873
Hemispheric Functions, 873
Hemophilia and Special Education, 876
Heredity, 877
Herpes Simplex I and II, 878
Hess, Robert D. (1920–1993), 880
Heterophoria, See Strabismus, Effect on Learning
Hewett, Frank M. (1927–), 881
Higher Education, Minority Students with Disabilities and, 881
High-Incidence Handicaps, 882
High Interest-Low Vocabulary, 884
High Risk, 884
High-Risk Registry, 885

Hiskey-Nebraska Test of Learning Aptitude (HNTLA), 886
Hispanic Students with Disabilities, 887
Hirschsprung's Disease, 888
History of Special Education, 889
Histrionic Personality Disorder, 895
Hobbs, Nicholas (1915–1983), 896
Hobson v. Hansen, 896
Holistic Approach and Learning Disabilities, 897
Holand, Special Education in, See Netherlands, Special Education in
Hollingworth, Leta A. S. (1886–1939), 898
Holt, Winifred (1870–1945), 899
Holtzman, Wayne H., Jr. (1948–), 899
Holtzman, Wayne H., Sr. (1923-), 900
Homebound Instruction, 900
Homework, 901
Horseback Riding for the Handicapped, See Equine Therapy
Horticultural Therapy, 902
Hospitalization and Special Education, 903
Hospital Schools, 903
House, Betty J. (1923–), 904
House-Tree-Person (HTP), 904
Howe, Samuel Gridley (1801–1876), 904
Humanism and Special Education, 905
Human Resource Development (HRD), 906
Humphrey, Elliott S. (1888–1981), 907
Hungerford, Richard H. (1903–1974), 908
Hunt, Joseph McVicker (1906–1991), 908
Hunter's Syndrome (Mucopoly Saccharidosis II), 909
Huntington's Chorea (HC), 910
Hurler's Syndrome, 910
Hydrocephalus, 911
Hyperactivity, See Attention-Deficit/Hyperactivity Disorder
Hypercalcemia, See Infantile Hypercalcemia
Hyperkinesis, 912
Hyperlexia, 912
Hyperopia, 913
Hypertelorism, 914
Hyperthyroidism, 914
Hypertonia, 915
Hypnosis, 916
Hypoactivity, 917
Hypoglycemia, 917
Hypothyroidism, 918
Hypotonia, 919

Hypoxia, 920
Hysterical Personality, See Histrionic Personality Disorder

Idiot, 921
Idiot Savant, 921
IEP, See Individualized Education Plan
Illinois Test of Psycholinguistic Abilities (ITPA), 922
Imagery, 922
Impersistence, See Perseveration
Impulse Control, 923
Impulsivity-Reflectivity, 925
Inborn Errors of Metabolism, 926
Incidence, 927
Inclusion, 928
Inclusion and Co-Teaching, See Teaching: Inclusion and Co-Teaching
Incorrigibility, See Conduct Disorder
Independent Living, 933
India, Special Education in, 934
Individualization of Instruction, 938
Individualized Education Plan (IEP), 939
Individual Variability, See Test Scatter
Individuals with Disabilities Education Act (IDEA), PL 105-17, 940
Infant Assessment, 948
Infantile Autism, See Autism
Infantile Hypercalcemia, 950
Infant Stimulation, 950
Informal Reading Inventory (IRI), 951
Information Processing, 952
Informed Consent, See Consent, Informed
Initial Teaching Alphabet (i/t/a), 954
Insatiable Child Syndrome, 954
In-Service Training for Special Education Teachers, 955
Insight (in the Gifted), 957
Institutes for Research on Learning Disabilities, 958
Institutionalization, 959
Institution Nationale des Sourds-Muets, 959
Instructional Media/Materials Center, 960
Instructional Pacing, 961
Instructional Technology for the Handicapped, 961
Integrated Therapy, 962
Intellectual Deficiency, See Mental Retardation; Intelligence
Intelligence, 963

Intelligence: A Multidisciplinary Journal, 967
Intelligence, Emotional, 968
Intelligence, Practical, See Practical Intelligence
Intelligence Quotient, 969
Intelligence Testing, 970
Intelligent Testing, 973
Interactive Language Development, 975
Interdisciplinary Teams, 976
International Child Neurology Association (ICNA), 977
International Classification of Diseases (ICD), 978
International Dyslexia Association, 978
International Journal of Clinical Neuropsychology (IJCN), See Archives of Clinical Neuropsychology
International Reading Association (IRA), 979
International Test Use in Special Education, 980
International Year of Disabled Persons, 1981, 981
Interpreters for the Deaf, 982
Intervention, 983
Intervention in School and Clinic, 985
Interventions for Autism, 985
Intervention Programs, Early, 987
Intervention Programs for At-Risk Children, 988
Investment Theory of Creativity, 993
IQ, 994
Irwin, Robert Benjamin (1883–1951), 995
Israel, Special Education in, 995
Italy, Special Education in, 998
Itard, Jean M. G. (1775–1838), 1000
Itinerant Services, 1001
Itinerant Teacher, 1001

Jactatio Captis (JC), 1003
Japan, Special Education in, 1003
Jargon Aphasia, 1006
Jensen, Arthur R. (1923–), 1007
J.E.V.S., 1007
Johnson, Doris (1932–), 1008
Johnson, G. Orville (1915–), 1008
Johnston Informal Reading Inventory, 1009
Johnstone, Edward Ransom (1870–1946), 1009
Joint Technical Standards for Educational and Psychological Tests, See Standards for Educational and Psychological Testing

Jones, Reginald L. (1931–), 1010
Jordan Left-Right Reversal Test, 1011
Joubert Syndrome (JS), 1011
Journal for Education of the Gifted (JED), 1012
Journal of Abnormal Child Psychology, 1012
Journal of Applied Behavior Analysis (JABA), 1012
Journal of Autism and Developmental Disorders, 1013
Journal of Clinical Child Psychology, 1013
Journal of Communication Disorders, 1013
Journal of Consulting and Clinical Psychology, 1014
Journal of Emotional and Behavioral Disorders, 1014
Journal of Fluency Disorders, 1014
Journal of Forensic Neuropsychology, (JFN), 1015
Journal of Intellectual Disability Research, 1015
Journal of Learning Disabilities (JLD), 1015
Journal of Mental Deficiency Research, See Journal of Intellectual Disability Research
Journal of Positive Behavior Interventions, 1015
Journal of Psychoeducational Assessment, 1016
Journal of School Psychology (JSP), 1016
Journal of Special Education, 1017
Journal of Speech and Hearing Disorders, 1017
Journal of the American Association for the Severely Handicapped, See TASH
Journal of Visual Impairment and Blindness (JVIB), 1017
Journals in Education of Individuals with Disabilities and Special Education, See Specific Journal
Jukes and the Kallikaks, 1018
Juvenile Arthritis, See Arthritis, Juvenile
Juvenile Cerebromacular Degeneration, 1019
Juvenile Court System and Individuals with Disabilities, 1020
Juvenile Delinquency, 1021

Kaiser-Permanente Diet, 1023
Kanner, Leo (1894–1981), 1023
Karnes, Merle (1916–), 1024

Karyotype, 1024–1025
Kasper Hauser Children, 1025
Kauffman, James M. (1940–), 1025
Kaufman, Alan S. (1944–), 1026
Kaufman, Nadeen L. (1945–), 1027
Kaufman Adolescent and Adult Intelligence Test (KAIT), 1029
Kaufman Assessment Battery for Children (KABC), 1030
Kaufman Brief Intelligence Test (K-BIT), 1031
Kaufman Functional Academic Skills Test (K-FAST), 1031
Kaufman Short Neurological Procedure (K-SNAP), 1032
Kaufman Survey of Early Academic and Language Skills (K-Seals), 1033
Kaufman Test of Educational Achievement/Normative Update (KTEA/NU), 1033
Kayser-Fleischer Ring, 1034
Kearnes Sayre Syndrome, 1034
Keller, Helen A. (1880–1957), 1035
Kenny, Sister Elizabeth (1886–1952), 1035
Keogh, Barbara H. (1925–), 1036
Kephart, Newell C. (1911–1973), 1036
Kerlin, Isaac Newton (1834–1893), 1036
Kernicterus, 1037
Keymath-Revised: A Diagnostic Inventory of Essential Mathematics, 1038
Keyword Method, 1039
Khatena, Joe (1925–), 1040
Kicklighter, Richard H. (1931–), 1040
Kinetic-Family-Drawing (KED), 1041
Kirk, Samuel A. (1904–1996), 1041
Klinefelter's Syndrome, 1042
Knight, Henry M. (1827–1880), 1043
Koppitz, Elizabeth M. (1919–1983), 1044
Kraepelin, Emil (1856–1926), 1044
Kuhlmann, Frederick (1876–1941), 1045
Kurzweil Reading Machine, 1045

Labeling, 1047
Laminar Heterotopia, 1049
Language, Absence of, 1049
Language Assessment, 1050

Language Deficiencies and Deficits
Language Delays, 1052
Language Disorders, 1053
Language Disorders, Expressive, See Language Disorders
Language Therapy, 1055
Large-Print Books, 1057
Larry P., 1058
Laterality, See Cerebral Dominance
Laurence-Moon Syndrome, 1060
Lead Poisoning, 1060
League School, 1063
Lenz's Syndrome, See Rare Diseases
Learned Helplessness, 1063
Learner Taxonomies, 1065
Learning Disabilities, 1066
Learning Disabilities and Culturally/Linguistically Diverse Students, See Culturally/Linguistically Diverse Students and Learning Disabilities
Learning Disabilities Association (LDA), 1071
Learning Disabilities, Problems in Definition of, 1071
Learning Disabilities, Severe Discrepancy Analysis in, 1075
Learning Disabilities and Juvenile Delinquency, 1083
Learning Disabilities Marker Variables Project, 1084
Learning Disability Quarterly, 1084
Learning Disability Subtypes, 1085
Learning-Disabled College Students, 1086
Learning Potential, 1087
Learning Potential Assessment Device (LPAD), 1087
Learning Strategies, 1088
Learning Styles, 1088
Least Restrictive Environment (LRE), 1090
Left Brain, Right Brain, 1091
Left-Handedness, 1091
Left-Handedness, Pathological, 1093
Legal Regulations of Special Education, See Special Education, Legal Regulation of
Legg-Calve-Perthes Disease, 1094
Lehtinen, Laura E. (1908–), 1095
Leisure-Time Activities, 1095
Leiter International Performance Scale-Revised (Leiter-R), 1096

Lennox-Gaustaut Syndrome, *See* Seizure Disorders

Lenz Microphthalmia Syndrome, *See* Rare Diseases

Leopard Syndrome, *See* Rare Diseases

Lerner, Janet Weiss (1926–), 1097

Lesch-Nyhan Syndrome, 1098

Lesions, 1099

Leukemic Child, 1100

Lewis, Michael (1937–), 1102

Lexington School for the Deaf, 1103

Liability of Teachers in Special Education, 1103

Libraries for the Blind and Physically Handicapped, 1104

Library Services for the Handicapped, 1105

Librium, 1106

Licensing and Certification of Schools, Centers and Facilities, 1106

Life Expectancy and the Handicapped, 1107

Life Space Interviewing, 1108

Lightner Witmer Award, 1109

Limited English Proficiency and Special Education, 1109

Lincoln Oseretesky Test, *See* Bruininks-Oseretsky Test of Motor Proficiency

Lindamood Phoneme Sequencing Program for Reading, Spelling, and Speech (LiPS), 1111

Lindsley, Ogden R. (1922–), 1111

Ling Method, 1112

Linguistic Deviance, 1113

Linguistic Readers, 1113

Lipreading/Speechreading, 1114

Literacy, 1115

Lithane, 1116

Lithium, *See* Lithane, Lithonate, *See* Lithane

Locus of Control, 1116

Louis-Bar Syndrome, 1117

Lovaas, O. Ivar (1927–), 1118

Lovitt, Thomas C. (1930–), 1118

Low Birth Weight Infants, 1119

Lowe Syndrome, 1120

Lowenfeld, Berthold (1901–1994), 1121

Low-Incidence Handicaps, *See* Specific Syndrome or Disorder

Low Vision, 1122

Loxitane, 1123

LSD, 1123

Luria, Alexander R. (1902–1977), 1124

Luria-Nebraska Neuropsychological Battery, 1124

Luria-Nebraska Neuropsychological Battery: Children's Revision, 1125

MA, *See* Mental Age

Macmillan, Donald L. (1940–), 1127

Macroglossia, *See* Rare Diseases

Macy, Anne Sullivan (1866–1936), 1127

Magical Model, 1128

Magnesium, 1128

Magnet Schools, 1129

Mahler, Margaret Schoenberger (1897–1985), 1129

Make-A-Picture Story (MAPS) Test, 1130

Maker, C. June (1948–), 1130

Mainstreaming, 1132

Maintenance, 1132

Maladaptive Behavior, 1134

Male Turner's Syndrome, *See* Noonan's Syndrome

Malnutrition, 1135

Mandibulofacial Dystosis, *See* Rare Diseases

Mannosidosis, *See* Rare Diseases

Manual Communication, 1136

Marasmus, 1137

March of Dimes, 1137

Marfan Syndrome, 1138

Marland Report, 1138

Marshall *v.* Georgia, 1139

Mastery Learning and Special Education, 1142

Masturbation, Compulsive, 1143

Maternal Serum Alpha-Fetoprotein (AFP) Screening, 1144

Mathematics, Learning Disabilities in, 1144

Mathematics, Remedial, 1146

Mathias Amendment, 1147

Mattie T. *v.* Holladay 1147

Maturational Lag, *See* Developmental Delay

MBD Syndrome, 1148

McCarthy, Dorothea (1906–1974), 1149

McCarthy Scales of Children's Abilities (MSCA), 1149

McCune-Albright Syndrome, *See* Rare Diseases

McGinnis Method, 1150

Measurement, 1151

Mediation, 1151

Mediational Deficiency, 1152

Mediation Essay, 1153

Medical Concerns of Handicapped Children, 1155

Medical History, 1157

Medically Fragile Student, 1159

Medical Management, 1159

Medical Model, Defense of, 1160

Medication, *See* Specific Medication

Medium Chain Acyl-Coenzyme A Dehydrogenase Deficiency (MCAD), *See* Rare Diseases

Megavitamin Therapy, 1161

Meichenbaum, Donald (1940–), 1162

Mellaril, 1162

Memory Disorders, 1163

Meningitis, 1165

Meningomyelocele, 1166

Mental Age, 1167

Mental Deficiency, *See* Mental Retardation

Mental Illness, 1167

Mentally Retarded, Educable, *See* Mental Retardation

Mental Retardation, 1170

Mental Retardation: A Journal of Policy, Practices, and Perspectives, 1174

Mental Retardation, Severe, 1174

Mental Status Exams, 1176

Mercer, Cecil D. (1943–) 1177

Mercer, Jane R., *See* System of Multicultural Pluralistic Assessment

Merrill, Maude Amanda (1888–1985), 1177

Merrill-Palmer Scale, 1178

Metabolic Disorders, 1178

Metacognition, 1179

Mexican American Culture and Disability, 1180

Mexico, Special Education in, 1182

Meyers, C. Edward (1912–), 1185

Microcephaly, 1186

Microtraining, 1186

Middle East, Special Education in the, 1187

Migrant Handicapped, 1188

Mildly Handicapped, Test-Taking Skills and the, 1190

Millon Clinical Multiaxial Inventory-III (MCMI-III), 1191

Mills *v.* Board of Education of the District of Columbia (1972), 1192

Milwaukee Project, 1193

Minimal Brain Dysfunction, *See* MBD Syndrome

Minimum Competency Testing, 1195

Minnesota Multiphasic Personality Inventory–2 (MMPI–2), 1196

Minnesota Multiphasic Personality Inventory-

Adolescent (MMPI-A), *See* Minnesota Multiphasic Personality Inventory (MMPI–2)

Minor Physical Anomalies, 1199

Miscue Analysis, 1200

Mixed Connective Tissue Disease, *See* Rare Diseases

Mnemonics, 1201

Moban, 1202

Mobile Education Units, 1202

Mobility Instruction, 1202

Mobility Trainers, 1203

Model Programs for Severely and Profoundly Disabled Individuals, 1204

Monographs of the Society for Research in Child Development, 1206

Montessori, Maria (1870–1952), 1206

Montessori Method, 1206

Moores, Donald F. (1935–), 1207

Moral Reasoning, 1208

Morse, William C. (1915–), 1209

Morsink, Catherine V. (1937–), 1210

Mosaicism, 1211

Moss, James W. (1926–), 1212

Motivation, 1212

Motor-Free Visual Perception Test–Revised (MVPT-R), 1213

Motor Learning, 1214

Motor Speech Disorders, 1215

Movement Therapy, 1216

Movigenics, 1217

Multicultural Special Education, 1217

Multidisciplinary Team (MDT), 1219

Multi-Element Design, 1220

Multiple Baseline Design, 1221

Multiple Handicapping Conditions, 1222

Multiple Regression, 1223

Multiple Sclerosis (MS), 1224

Multisensory Instruction, 1225

Munson, Grace E. (1883–1980), 1226

Muscular Dystrophy (MD), 1226

Muscular Dystrophy Association (MDA), 1227

Muscular Imbalance1227

Museums and Individuals with Disabilities, 1228

Music Therapy, 1229

Mutism, 1229

Mutism, Elective, *See* Elective Mutism; Communication Disorders

Myklebust, Helmer R. (1910–), 1234

Myopia, *See* Visual Impairment

Narcolepsy, 1235

Nash, Charles E. (1875–1953), 1235

Nash, William R. (1943–), 1236

National Advisory Committee on Handicapped Children and Youth, 1236

National Association for Gifted Children (NAGC), 1237

National Association for Retarded Citizens, *See* ARC, The

National Association for the Deaf (NAD), 1237

National Association of School Psychologists (NASP), 1238

National Association of State Boards of Education (NASBE), 1239

National Association of State Directors of Special Education (NASDSE), 1239

National Center, Educational Media and Materials for the Handicapped, 1240

National Center on Educational Outcomes (NCEO), 1240

National Council for Accreditation of Teacher Education (NCATE), 1241

National Easter Seal Society, 1242

National Education Association (NEA), 1242

National Endowment for the Humanities (NEH), 1243

National Federation of the Blind (NFB), 1244

National Head Injury Foundation (NHIF), *See* Brain Injury Association

National Information Center for Children and Youth with Disabilities (NICHCY), 1245

National Institutes of Mental Health, 1245

National Institute of Neurological Disorders and Stroke, 1246

National Joint Committee on Learning Disabilities (NJCLD), 1246

National Learning Disabilities Assistance Program, 1246

National Merit Scholarship Corporation, 1247

National Organization for Rare Disorders (NORD), 1247

National Rehabilitation Association (NRA), 1247

National Society for Autistic Children (NSAC), 1248

National Society for Children and Adults with Autism, 1248

National Society for Crippled Children and Adults, *See* National Easter Seal Society

National Society for the Prevention of Blindness (NSPB), 1248

National Technical Institute for the Deaf (NTID), 1248

Nature Versus Nurture, 1249

Navane, 1250

NCATE, *See* National Council for Accreditation of Teacher Education

Negative Punishment, 1250

Negative Reinforcement, 1251

Neisworth, John T. (1937–), 1251

Neonatal Behavioral Assessment Scale (NBAS), 1252

NEPSY: A Developmental Neuropsychological Assessment, 1253

Netherlands, Special Education in the, 1253

Neural Efficiency Analyzer (NEA), 1256

Neurodevelopmental Therapy (NDT), 1257

Neurofibromatosis, 1257

Neurolinguistic Programming (NLP), 1258

Neurological Impress Method, 1259

Neurological Organization, 1260

Neuropsychology, 1260

Newland, T. Ernest (1903–1992), 1262

New York State Association for Retarded Children *v.* Cary, *See* Willowbrook Case

New Zealand, Special Education in, 1262

Nigeria, Special Education in, 1264

NIMH, *See* National Institute of Mental Health

NIND, *See* National Institute of Neurological and Communicative Disorders and Stroke

NMR, *See* Nuclear Magnetic Resonance

Noncompliant Children, 1266

Nondiscriminatory Assessment, 1268

Nonliteral Language, 1270

Nonsheltered Employment, 1271

Nonverbal Language, 1272

Noonan's Syndrome (Male Turner's Syndrome), 1274

Normal Curve Equivalent (NCE), 1274

Normalization, 1275

Norm-Referenced Testing, 1275

Northwestern Syntax Screening Test, 1277

Nuclear Magnetic Resonance (NMR) or Magnetic Resonance Imaging (MRI), 1277

Nutritional Disorders, *See* Malnutrition; Eating Disorders; Pica

Obesity, 1279

Objective Personality Tests, *See* Personality Test, Objective

Observational Learning, 1280

Obsessive Compulsive Disorders, 1283

Occulocerebral-Hypopigmentation Syndrome, *See* Rare Diseases

Occupational Therapy, 1284

Office of Rare Diseases, National Institute of Health, 1285

Office of Special Education and Rehabilitative Services (OSERS), 1285

Olympics, Special, 1285

On-Line Databases for Special Education, *See* Appendix

Operant Conditioning, 1286

Opthalmologist, 1288

Optacon, 1289

Optometrist (OD), 1290

Oral and Written Language Scales (OWLS), 1290

Oral Facial Digital Syndrome (OFDS), 1291

Oral Language of the Handicapped, 1291

Oral Reading, 1294

Oral *vs.* Manual Communication, 1295

Ordinal Scales of Psychological Development, 1298

Organizational Change, 1298

Orphan Diseases, *See* Low-Incidence Handicaps; Office of Rare Diseases; National Organization of Rare Diseases (NORD)

Orthogenic School, 1300

Orthopedically Handicapped, 1301

Orthopsychiatry, 1302

Orthopsychiatry Movement, 1302

Orton, Samuel T. (1879–1948), 1303

Orton Dyslexia Society, *See* International Dyslexia Association

Orton-Gillingham Method, 1304

Osborn, Alexander Faickney (1888–1966), 1305

Osgood, Charles E. (1916–1991), 1305

Osteoporosis, 1306

Other Health Impaired, 1306

Otitis Media, 1307

Otolaryngologist, 1308

Otology, 1308

Otosclerosis, 1309

Overachievement and Special Education, 1309

Overachievement and the Gifted, 1310

Overcorrection, 1310

Palmar Crease, 1313

Paraplegia, 1313

Paraprofessionals, 1315

Parental Counseling, 1316

Parent Education, 1318

Parenting Skills, 1319

Parents of the Handicapped, 1320

Parkhurst, Helen (1887–1973), 1322

Partially Sighted, 1322

Partial Participation, 1322

Pasamanick, Benjamin (1914–1996), 1323

Pase *v.* Hannon, 1325

Path Analysis, 1326

Path-Referenced Assessment, 1327

Patterning, 1329

PDR, *See* Physicians' Desk Reference

Peabody Developmental Motor Scales (PDMS), 1330

Peabody Individual Achievement Test–Revised/Normative Update (PIAT-R), 1330

Peabody Language Development Kits—Revised (PLDK-R), 1331

Peabody Picture Vocabulary Test—Third Edition (PPVT-III), 1332

Peabody Rebus Reading Program, 1333

Peace Corps, Special Education in, 1333

Pediatrician, 1334

Pediatric Acquired Immune Deficiency Syndrome (AIDS), 1334

Pediatric Psychologist, 1335

Pedro De Ponce, *See* Ponce De Leon, Pedro De

Peer Relationships, 1337

Peer Tutoring, 1337

Pennsylvania Association for Retarded Citizens *v.* Pennsylvania (1972), 1338

People First, 1339

Percentile Scores, 1340

Perceptual and Motor Skills, 1340

Perceptual Constancy, 1341

Perceptual Deficit Hypothesis, 1341

Perceptual Development, Lag in, 1342

Perceptual Distortions, 1344

Perceptual-Motor Difficulties, 1344

Perceptual Span, 1345

Perceptual Training, 1346

Pereire, Jacob R. (1715–1780), 1347

Performance Instability, 1348

Perinatal Factors in Handicapping Conditions, 1348

Perkins-Binet Tests of Intelligence for the Blind, 1350

Perkins School for the Blind, 1350

Perseveration, 1350

Personality Assessment, 1352

Personality Inventory for Children (PIC), 1353

Personality Test, Objective, 1354

Personnel Preparation for Working with Diverse Individuals, 1354

Personnel Training in Special Education, *See* Special Education, Teacher Training in

Peru, Special Education in, 1357

Pestalozzi, Johann Heinrich (1746–1827), 1359

Pets in Special Education, 1360

Pevzner, Maria Semenovna (1901–1986), 1360

Phenobarbital, 1360

Phenothiazines, 1361

Phenylketonuria (PKU), 1362

Phillips, Beeman N. (1927–), 1364

Philosophy of Education for the Handicapped, 1364

Phobias and Fears, 1365

Phonology, 1366

Photo Articulation Test-Third Edition (PAT–3), 1367

Physical Anomalies, 1368

Physical Education for Students with Disabilities, 1369

Physically Handicapped, 1372

Physical Restraint, 1374

Physical Therapy, 1375

Physicians' Desk Reference (PDR), 1376

Physiotherapy, 1377

Piagetian Approach to Special Education, 1377

Piaget, Jean (1896–1980), 1384

PIC, *See* Personality Inventory for Children

Pica, 1385

Pierre-Robin Syndrome, 1386

Piers-Harris Children's Self-Concept Scale, 1386

Pinel, Philippe (1745–1826), 1386

Pituitary Gland, 1387

PKU, *See* Phenylketonuria

Placebos, 1388

Placenta, 1388

Plantar Reflex, 1389

Plasticity, 1389

Plato and the Gifted, 1390

Play, 1391

Playtest, 1392

Play Therapy, 1392

Pluralism, Cultural, 1394

Poikiloderma Congenitale, *See* Rare Diseases

Poland, Special Education in, 1394

Politics and Special Education, 1395

Polydipsia, 1398

Pompe's Disease, *See* Rare Diseases

Ponce De Leon, Pedro De (1520–1584), 1399

Popliteal Pterygium Syndrome, *See* Rare Diseases

Porch Index of Communicative Abilities (PICA), 1399

Portage Project, 1399

Positive Practice, 1400

Positive Reinforcement, 1401

Post-Institutionalized Child Project, 1402

Post-Institutionalized Children, 1402

Postlingual Deafness, 1404

Poverty, Relationship to Special Education, 1405

Power and Research in Special Education, 1406

Practical Intelligence, 1408

Prader-Willi Syndrome (PWS), 1409

Pragmatics and Pragmatic Communication Disorders, 1410

Precision Teaching, 1411

Prehm, Herbert J. (1937–1986), 1413

Prelingual Deafness, 1414

Premack Principle, 1414

Prematurity/Preterm, 1415

Prereferral Intervention, 1417

Preschool-Age Gifted Children, 1418

Preschool Assessment, 1420

Preschool Screening, 1422

Preschool Special Education, 1424

President's Committee on Mental Retardation (PCMR), 1428

Prevention, Primary, 1428

Prevocational Skills, 1430

Primary Immunodeficiency Disorders, 1431

Primary Mental Abilities Test (PMA), 1432

Private Schools and Special Education, 1433

Privileged Communication, 1434

Problem Solving, Creative, See Creative Problem Solving

Procedural Safeguards, See Due Process

Process Training, See Ability Training

Production Deficiency, 1435

Pro-Ed, Incorporated, 1436

Professional Competencies for Working with Culturally and Linguistically Diverse Students, 1436

Professional School Psychology, 1436

Professional Standards for Special Educators, 1438

Profile Analysis, 1439

Profile Variability, 1440

Profoundly Handicapped, Competencies of Teachers of, 1441

Profoundly Retarded, See Mental Retardation

Program Evaluation, 1442

Programmed Instruction, 1444

Projective Techniques, See Personality Assessment

Project on Classification of Exceptional Children, 1445

Project Re-ED, 1446

Project Success (PS), 1447

Project Talent, 1447

Prosopagnosia, 1449

Prosthetic Devices, 1449

Protection and Advocacy System–Developmentally Disabled (P&A), 1450

Prune Belly Syndrome, See Rare Diseases

Psychoanalysis and Special Education, 1450

Psychodrama, 1451

Psychoeducational Methods, 1452

Psychogenic Models, 1454

Psycholinguistics, 1455

Psychological Abstracts (PA), 1456

Psychological Clinics, 1456

Psychological Corporation, 1457

Psychological Reports, 1457

Psychology in the Schools, 1457

Psychometrics, See Measurement

Psychomotor Seizures, 1458

Psychomotricity, 1459

Psychoneurotic Disorders, 1460

Psychopathy, See Sociopathy

Psychosis, Amphetamine, See Amphetamine Psychosis

Psychosocial Adjustment, 1462

Psychosomatic Disorders, 1463

Psychosurgery, 1464

Psychotherapy with the Individuals with Disabilities, 1465

Psychotropic Drugs, 1466

Psyc Scan, 1467

Public Law 94-142, See Individuals with Disabilities Act (IDEA).

Public Law 95-561, 1467

Public Schools and Special Education, 1468

Puerto Rico, Special Education in, 1471

Punishment, 1472

Punishment, Positive, 1473

Purdue Perceptual-Motor Survey (PPMS), 1473

Putamen, 1474

Pygmalion Effect, 1474

Q-Sort, 1477

Quadriplegia, 1477

Quay, Herbert C. (1927–), 1478

Quay-Peterson Revised Problem Behavior Checklist

Questionnaires in Special Education, 1479

Quigley, Stephen P. (1927–), 1480

Racial Bias in Testing, See Cultural Bias in Testing

Racial Discrimination in Special Education, 1481

Rare Diseases, 1482

RASE, See Remedial and Special Education

Ratio IQ, 1485

Raven's Matrices, 1486

Ray Adaptation of the Ray Wechsler Intelligence Scale for Children Revised, 1486

Reaction Time, 1487

Readability and Readability Formulas, 1488

Readability Formulas, 1489

Reading, 1490

Reading and Eye Movements, 1492

Reading Disorders, 1493

Reading in the Content Areas, 1498

Reading Milestones (Second Edition), 1501

Reading Remediation, 1501

Reality Therapy, 1505

Receptive-Expressive Emergent Language Test—Second Edition (REEL–2), 1506

Receptive Language Disorders, 1506

Reciprocal Determinism, 1508

Reclaiming Children and Youth: Journal of Emotional and Behavioral Problems, 1508

Recording for the Blind (RFB), 1509

Recreation, Therapeutic, 1509

Recreational Reading for the Handicapped, 1510

Recreational Therapy, 1511

Recreation for the Handicapped, 1512

Redl, Fritz (1902–1988), 1513

Referral Process, 1514

Reflex, 1516

Regional Media Centers for the Deaf, 1516

Regional Resource Centers (RRCs), 1516

Regression (Statistical), 1517

Regular Class Placement, See Mainstreaming; Inclusion

Rehabilitation, 1518

Rehabilitation Act of 1973, 1518

Rehabilitation Act of 1973, Section 504 of, 1519

Rehabilitation Literature, 1519

Reisman, Fredricka Kauffman (1930–), 1520

Reitan-Indiana Neuropsychological Test Battery for Children (RINTBC), 1520

Related Services, 1521

Reliability, 1522

Religious Education for the Handicapped, 1523

Remedial and Special Education (RASE), 1524

Remedial Intruction, 1524

Remedial Reading, 1525

Remediation, Deficit-Centered Models of, 1528

Remediation, Strength Models of, See Remediation, Deficit-Centered Models of

Renzulli, Joseph S. (1936–), 1532

Repeated Reading, 1533

Research in Special Education, 1533

Residential Facilities, 1540

Resource Room, 1541

Resource Teacher, 1542

Respite Care, 1543

Response Generalization, 1544

Restraint, See Physical Restraint

Retardation, See Cultural-Familial Retardation; Mental Retardation

Retention in Grade, 1545

Reticular Activating System, 1545

Retinitis Pigmentosa (RP), 1546

Retrolental Fibroplasia (RLF), 1547

Rett Syndrome (RS), 1548

Reversals in Reading and Writing, 1551

Reverse Mainstreaming, 1552

Revised Children's Manifest Anxiety Scale (RCMAS), See Children's Manifest Anxiety Scale

Revisualization, 1553

Reye's Syndrome, 1554

Reynolds, Cecil R. (1952–), 1555

Reynolds, Maynard C. (1922–), 1556

Rh Factor Incompatibility, 1557

Right-Handedness, 1558

Right Hemisphere Syndrome (Linguistic, Extralinguistic and Nonlinguistic), 1559

Right to Education, 1560

Right to Treatment, 1561

Riley-Day Syndrome, 1562

Rimland, Bernard (1928–), 1562

Risk Management in Special Education, 1563

Ritalin, 1564

Roberts Apperception Test for Children (RATC), 1564

Robinow's Dwarfism, See Rare Diseases

Robinow's Syndrome, See Rare Diseases

Robinson, Halbert B. (1925–1981) and Robinson, Nancy M. (1930–), 1565

Robotics, 1566

Robotics in Special Education, 1566

Rochester Method, 1567

Roeper Review, 1567

Roger, Harriet B. (1834–1919), 1568

Roos, Philip (1930–), 1568

Rorschach, 1569

Rorschach Inkblot Test, 1569

Ross Information Processing Assessments-Second Edition (RIPA–2), 1570

Roswell-Chall Diagnostic Reading Test of Word Analysis Skills, Revised and Extended, 1571

Rothmund-Thompson Syndrome, See Rare Diseases

Rousseau, Jean J. (1712–1778), 1571

Rubella, 1572

Rubinstein-Taybi Syndrome, See Rare Diseases

Rural Special Education, 1573

Rush, Benjamin (1745–1813), 1575

Russell-Silver Syndrome, See Rare Diseases

Russia, Special Education in, 1575

Rutter, Michael (1933–), 1579

Sabatino, David A. (1938–), 1581

Safety Issues in Special Education, 1581

Salvia, John (1941–), 1582

Sapir, Selma Gustin (1916–), 1583

Sarason, Seymour B. (1919–), 1583

Sattler, Jerome M. (1931–), 1584

Save the Children Fund and Children with Disabilities, 1585

Scales of Independent Behavior-Revised (SIB-R), 1586

Scales of Ordinal Dominance, See Ordinal Scales of Psychological Development

Scandinavia, Special Education in, 1586

Scapegoating, 1588

Schaeffer, Earl S. (1926–), 1589

Schiefelbusch, Richard L. (1918–), 1589

Schizencephaly, 1590

Schizophrenia, See Childhood Schizophrenia

School Attendance of Handicapped, 1591

School Effectiveness, 1591

School Failure, 1593

School Phobia (School Refusal), 1594

School Psychology, 1597

School Psychology Digest, See School Psychology Review

School Psychology Review, 1599

School Records, See (FERPA) Family Education & Privacy Rights Act

School Refusal, See School Phobia

School Stress, 1600

Schopler, Eric (1927–), 1601

Schwartz-Jampel Syndrome, See Rare Diseases

Scoliosis, 1601

Scope and Sequence, 1602

Scott Craniodigital Syndrome with Mental Retardation, 1602

Scouting and the Handicapped, 1603

Seckel Syndrome, 1603

Second Language Learners in Special Education, 1603

Secondary Special Education, 1606

Section 504 of the 1973 Rehabilitation Act, *See* Rehabilitation Act of 1973

Seeing Eye Dogs, *See* Animals for the Handicapped; Dog Guides for the Blind

Seguin, Edouard (1812–1880), 1607

Seizure Disorders, 1608

Self-Care Skills, *See* Self Help Skills; Daily Living Skills

Self-Concept, 1610

Self-Contained Class, 1611

Self-Control Curriculum, 1611

Self-Fulling Prophecy, *See* Pygmalion Effect

Self-Help Training, 1612

Self-Injurious Behavior, 1613

Self-Management, 1615

Self-Monitoring, 1616

Self-Selection of Reinforcement, 1617

Self-Stimulation, 1618

Semmel, Melvyn I. (1931–), 1619

Senf, Gerald M. (1942–), 1620

Sensorineural Hearing Loss, 1620

Sensory Extinction, 1621

Sensory Integrative Therapy, 1622

Sensory Motor Integration, *See* Sensory Integrative Therapy

Separation Anxiety and Children with Disabilities, 1623

Septo-Optic Dysplasia, 1624

Sequenced Inventory of Communication Development, Revised (SICD-R), 1625

Sequential and Simultaneous Cognitive Processing, 1625

Sequential Assessment of Mathematics Inventories: Standardized Inventory (SAMI)

Seriously Emotionally Disturbed, 1628

Service Delivery Models, 1630

Severe Discrepancy Analysis (SDA), 1634

Sex Differences in Learning Abilities, 1635

Sex Education of the Handicapped, 1636

Sex Information and Education Council of the United States (SIECUS), 1639

Sex Ratios in Special Education, 1639

Sexual Disturbances in Handicapped Children, 1640

Sheltered Workshops, 1642

Siblings of the Handicapped, 1643

Sicard, Abbe Roche Ambroise Cucurron (1742–1822), 1644

Sickle-Cell Disease, 1644

Sidis, William James (1898–1944), 1645

Sidis Fallacy, *See* Sidis, William James

Sight-Saving Classes, 1646

Sign Language, 1646

Simultaneous Cognitive Processing, *See* Sequential and Simultaneous Cognitive Processing

Single-Subject Research Design, 1647

Singleton-Merton Syndrome, 1652

Six-Hour Retarded Child, 1652

Skeels, Harold M. (1901–1970), 1653

Skill Training, 1654

Skinner, Burrhus Fredrick (1904–1990), 1654

Skinner's Functional Learning Model, 1656

Slingerland Screening Tests, 1656

Slosson Intelligence Test (SIT), 1657

Slow Learner, 1657

Smith-Lemli-Opitz Syndrome, 1657

Snellen Chart, 1658

Social Behavior of the Handicapped, 1659

Social Competence, *See* Adaptive Behavior

Social Darwinism, 1660

Social Integration of Handicapped in School, *See* Inclusion; Mainstreaming

Social Isolation, 1661

Social Learning Theory, 1663

Social Maturity, *See* Adaptive Behavior

Social Security, 1664

Social Skills and the Handicapped

Social Skills/Competence Training, 1665

Social Validation, 1667

Social Work, 1668

Sociodrama, 1669

Socioeconomic Impact of Disabilities, 1669

Socioeconomic Status (SES), 1671

Sociogram, 1672

Sociometric Techniques with the Handicapped, 1672

Sociopathy/Antisocial Personality Disorder, 1673

Soft (Neurological) Signs, 1675

SOMPA, *See* System of Multicultural Pluralistic Assessment

Sonicguide, 1676

South Africa, Special Education in, 1677

South America, Special Education in, *See* Argentina, Special Education in; Mexico, Special Education in; Peru, Special Education in

Southern and Eastern Africa, Special Education in, 1679

Soviet Education, 1686

Soviet Union and Eastern Europe, Special Education in, *See* Russia, Special Education in

Spache Diagnostic Reading Scale, *See* Diagnostic Reading Scale

Span of Apprehension, *See* Perceptual Span

Spasticity, 1687

Spearman, C.E. (1863–1945), 1687

Special Class, 1688

Special Education, Effectiveness of, *See* Effectiveness of Special Education, 1688

Special Education, Federal Impact on, 1688

Special Education, Generic, *See* Generic Special Education

Special Education, History of, *See* History of Special Education

Special Education, Humanistic, *See* Humanistic Special Education

Special Education, Philosophers' Opinions about, *See* Philosophy of Education for the Handicapped

Special Education, Professional Standards for, *See* Professional Standards for Special Educators

Special Education, Racial Discrimination in, *See* Racial Discrimination in Special Education

Special Education, Supervision in, *See* Supervision in Special Education

Special Education, Teacher Training in, 1691

Special Education, Telecommunication Systems in, *See* Telecommunication Systems in Special Education

Special Education and Politics, *See* Politics and Special Education

Special Education Instructional Materials Centers (SEIMCs), 1693

Special Education in the United Kingdom, *See* United Kingdom, Special Education in the

Special Education Programs (SEP), 1694

Specialnet, 1694

Special Olympics, *See* Olympics, Special

Special Services in the Schools (SSS), 1695

Specific Learning Disabilities, *See* Learning Disabilities

Speech, 1696

Speech, Absence of, 1697

Speech and Language Handicaps, *See* Communication Disorders; Language Disorders

Speech-Language Pathologist, 1698

Speech-Language Services, 1699

Speech Synthesizer, 1699

Speech Therapy, 1700

Spelling Disabilities, 1700

Sperry, Roger W. (1913–1994), 1701

Spielmeyer-Vogt Disease, *See* Juvenile Cerebromacular Degeneration

Spina Bifida, 1702

Spinal Cord Injury, 1703

Spinocerebellar Degeneration, *See* Friedreich's Ataxia

Spitz, Herman (1925–), 1704

Spitz, Rene Arpad (1887–1974), 1705

Splinter Skill, *See* Idiot Savant

Split-Brain Research, 1705

Sports for the Handicapped, 1707

Staff Development, 1708

Standard Deviation, 1709

Standards for Educational and Psychological Testing (SEPT), 1710

Stanford-Binet Intelligence Scale: Fourth Edition, 1711

Stanford Diagnostic Mathematics Test—Fourth Edition (SDMT4), 1712

Stanford Diagnostic Reading Test—Third (SDRT4), 1712

Stanley, Julian C. (1918–), 1713

Steinart's Disease (Myotonic Dystrophy), 1714

Stelazine, 1714

Stereotypic Behaviors, 1714

Stereotypism, 1716

Stern, William (1871–1938), 1717

Stigmatization, *See* Labeling

Stimulant Drugs, 1717

Stimulus Deprivation, 1718

Stimulus Satiation, 1719

Strabismus, Effect on Learning of, 1720

Strauss, Alfred A. (1897–1957), 1721

Strauss Syndrome, 1722

Strength Models of Remediation, *See* Remediation, Deficit-Centered Models of

Strephosymbolia, 1722

Stress and the Handicapped Student, 1723

Strong Interest Inventory, 1723

Structure of Intellect, 1724

Study of Mathematically Precocious Youth (SMPY), 1724

Stuttering, 1725

Substance Abuse, 1726

Substantia Nigra, 1728

Subtest Scatter, 1729

Suicide, 1730

Sullivan, Anne, *See* Macy, Ann Sullivan

Sullivan Programmed Reading, 1731

Summer School for the Handicapped, 1732

Supervision in Special Education, 1733

Support, Behavioral, 1734

Supported Employment, 1735

Surrogate Parents, 1737

Survival Skills, 1738

Sweden, Special Education in, *See* Scandinavia, Special Education in

Switzerland, Special Education in, 1738

Sydenham's Chorea, 1744

Synapses, 1745

Syntactic Deficiencies, *See* Childhood Aphasia; Language Disorder, Expressive; Language Disorders

Systems of Classification, 1746

System of Multicultural Pluralistic Assessment (SOMPA), 1747

Tachistoscope, 1751

Taiwan, Special Education in, 1751

Talented Children, *See* Specific Talent, e.g., Academically Talented Children

Talking Books, 1753

TASH, 1753

Task Analysis, 1753

TAT, *See* Thematic Apperception Test

Taxonomies, 1754

Tay-Sachs Syndrome, 1756

TEACCH, 1756

Teacher Burnout, 1757

Teacher Centers (TC), 1759

Teacher Education and Special Education, 1760

Teacher Effectiveness, 1760

Teacher Expectancies, 1763

Teaching and Consultation, 1764

Teaching Exceptional Children (TEC), 1765

Teaching: Inclusion and Co-Teaching, 1766

Teaching Strategies, 1768

Techniques: A Journal for Remedial Education and Counseling, 1769
Technology for the Disabled, 1770
TECSE, See Early Childhood Special Education, Topics in
Tegretol, 1772
Telecommunication Devices for the Deaf (TDDs; TTYs), 1773
Telecommunications Systems in Special Education, 1773
Temperament, 1773
Temper Outburst, 1779
Teratogen, 1780
Terman, Lewis M. (1877–1956), 1781
Terman's Studies of the Gifted, 1781
Test Anxiety, 1782
Test Equating, 1783
Test for Auditory Comprehension of Language—Third Edition (TACL–3), 1784
Test of Adolescent and Adult Language—Third Edition (TOAL–3), 1784
Test of Early Mathematical Ability-Second Edition (TEMA–2), 1785
Test of Early Reading Ability, Second Edition (TERA–2), 1785
Test of Early Written Language, Second Edition (TEWL–2), 1786
Test of Language Development—Primary: Third Edition, 1786
Test of Memory and Learning (TOMAL), 1787
Test of Nonverbal Intelligence—Third Edition (TONI–3), 1790
Test of Phonological Awareness (TOPA), 1790
Test of Word Finding (TWF), 1791
Test of Variables of Attention (TOVA), 1791
Test of Written Language—Third Edition (TOWL–3), 1792
Test Scatter, 1793
Tests in Print, 1794
Tests, See Specific Test; Measurement
Test-Teach-Test Paradigm (TTT-P), 1795
Thalidomide, 1796
Their World, 1797
Thematic Apperception Test (TAT), 1797
Theory of Activity, 1797
Therapeutic Community, 1799
Therapeutic Recreation, See Recreation, Therapeutic
Think Aloud, 1800

Thinking Centers, See Creative Studies Program
Thorazine, 1801
Thorndike, Edward L. (1847–1949), 1801
Thought Disorders, 1802
Tics, 1804
Time on Task, 1804
Time-Out, 1805
Time Sampling, 1805
Tinnitus
Tofranil, 1806
Token Economics, 1807
TONI, See Test of Nonverbal Intelligence, 1808
Tonic Neck Reflex, Asymmetrical, See Asymmetrical Tonic Neck Reflex, 1808
Topics in Early Childhood Special Education, 1808
Topics in Language Disorders, 1808
TORCH Complex, 1808
Torrance, Ellis Paul (1914–), 1809
Torrance Center for Creative Studies, 1810
Torrance Tests of Creative Thinking, 1811
Torsional Dystonia, 1811
Total Communication, 1812
Tourette Syndrome, 1813
Tourette Syndrome Association, 1813
Toxoplasmosis, 1814
Toy Lending Libraries, 1814
Trace Minerals, 1815
Trainable Mentally Retarded, 1815
Training for Employment in Traditional Settings, 1815
Training in the Home, 1816
Training Schools, 1817
Tranquilizers, 1818
Transdisciplinary Model, 1819
Transenvironmental Programming
Transfer of Training, 1819
Transformational Generative Grammar, 1820
Transition, 1821
Transition Planning for Culturally and Linguistically Diverse Students, 1822
Transportation of Handicapped Students, 1827
Traumatic Brain Injury
Traumatic Brain Injury and School Re-entry, 1828
Traumatic Brain Injury and Special Education Services, 1833
Traumatic Brain Injury in Children, 1844
Travel Aids, Electronic, See Electronic Travel Aids
Travel Aids for Individuals with Disabilities, 1847
Treacher-Collins Syndrome, See Rare Diseases

Treatment Acceptability, 1848
Triarchic Theory of Intelligence, 1849
Trichotillomania, 1850
Trichorhinophalangeal Syndrome, 1850
Trisomy 18, 1851
Trisomy 21, 1852
Tuberculosis, See Chronic Illness in Children
Tuberous Sclerosis, 1853
Turkey, Special Education in, 1854
Turnbull, Ann P. (1937–), 1855
Turnbull, H. Rutherford (1937–), 1856
Turner's Syndrome, 1856
Tutoring, 1857
Twins, 1858

Ulcers and Handicapped Children, 1859
Ultimate Instruction for the Severe and Profoundly Retarded, 1859
United Cerebral Palsy (UCP), 1860
United Kingdom, Special Education in the, 1861
United States Office of Education, 1864
Universal Nonverbal Intelligence Test, 1864
University Affiliated Facilities (UAF), 1865

VAKT, 1867
Valett Developmental Survey of Basic Learning Abilities, 1868
Valium, 1869
Valproic Acid, 1869
Values Clarification, 1869
Van Dijk, Jan (1937–), 1870
Van Riper, Charles (1905–1991), 1871
Velo-cardio-facial Syndrome (Shprintzen Syndrome), 1872
Velopharyngeal Inadequacy (VPI), 1872
Verbal Deficiency, 1873
Verbalisms, 1874
Verbal-Performance IQ Discrepancies, 1874
Verbal Scale IQ, 1876
Verbo-Tonal Method (VTM), 1877
Versabraille, 1878
Videofluoroscopy, 1878
Videotaping in Special Education, 1878
Vineland Adaptive Behavior Scales (VABS), 1880
Vineland Social-Emotional Early Childhood Scales, 1881
Vineland Training School, 1881
Vision Training, 1882
Visual Acuity, 1883

Visual Efficiency, 1884
Visual Impairment, 1885
Visual-Motor and Visual-Perceptual Problems, 1885
Visual-Motor Integration, 1887
Visual Perception and Discrimination, 1887
Visual Training, See Vision Training
Visuomotor Complex, 1888
Vocabulary Development, 1889
Vocational Education, 1890
Vocational Education Act of 1963, 1891
Vocational Evaluation, 1891
Vocational Rehabilitation Act of 1973, 1892
Vocational Rehabilitation Counseling, 1893
Vocational Training of Handicapped, See Vocational Education
Vocational Village, 1894
Voice Disorders (Dysphonia), 1894
Volta Review, The, 1895
Voluntary Agencies, 1895
Von Recklinghausen, Friedrich (1833–1910), 1895
Vygotsky, Lev S. (1896–1934), 1895

WAIS-III, See Wechsler Adult Intelligence Scale–Third Edition
Walker Problem Behavior Identification Checklist (WBPIC), 1897
Wallin, John Edward (J.E.) Wallace (1876–1969), 1897
Watson, John B. (1878–1958), 1898
Wechsler, David (1896–1981), 1899
Wechsler Adult Intelligence Scale–Third Edition (WAIS-III), 1899
Wechsler Intelligence Scale for Children—Revised (WISC-III), 1901
Wechsler Preschool and Primary Scale of Intelligence—Revised (WPPSI-R), 1902
Welsh Figure Preference Test, 1903
Wepman's Auditory Discrimination Test, Second Edition, 1904
Werner, Heinz (1890–1964), 1905
Wernicke's Aphasia, 1905
Western Europe, Special Education in, 1906
Whelan, Richard J. (1931–), 1909
Whole Word Teaching, 1910

Wide Range Achievement Test–Third Edition (WRAT–3), 1911
Wide Range Assessment of Memory and Learning (WRAML), 1912
Wieacker Syndrome, 1913
Wilbur, Hervey Backus (1820–1883), 1913
Wild Boy of Aveyron, 1914
Will, Madeleine C. (1945–), 1914
William's Syndrome, See Infantile Hypercalcemia
Willowbrook Case, 1915
Wilson's Disease, See Kayser-Fleischer Ring
WISC-III, See Wechsler Intelligence Scale for Children–Third Edition
Witmer, Lightner (1867–1956), 1916
Wolf-Hirschhorne Syndrome, 1916
Wolfensberger, Wolf P. J. (1934–), 1917
Wood, M. Margaret (1931–), 1918
Woodcock Diagnostic Reading Battery (WDRB), 1918
Woodcock-Johnson Psychoeducational Battery—Revised (WJ-R), 1920
Woodcock Language Proficiency Battery-Revised (WLPB-R), 1921
Woodcock Reading Mastery Test-Revised (WRMT-R), 1922
Woods Schools, 1922
Word Blindness, 1923
Words in Color, 1925
Workfare, 1925
World Federation of the Deaf (WFD), 1926
World Health Organization (WHO), 1926
World Rehabilitation Fund, 1927
WPPSI-Revised, See Wechsler Preschool and Primary Scale of Intelligence–Revised
WRAT-III, See Wide-Range Achievement Test–Third Edition
Writing as Expressive Language, 1928
Writing Assessment, 1929
Writing Disorders, 1930
Writing Remediation, 1930
Written Language of Handicapped, 1935
Wyatt v. Stickney, 1937

X-Linked Dominant Inheritance, 1939
X-Linked Recessive Inheritance, 1939
X-Rays and Handicapping Conditions, 1940

X-Ray Scanning Techniques, 1941

XYY Syndrome, 1941

Yale, Caroline A. (1848–1933), 1943

Year-Round Schools, 1943

Ypsilanti Perry Preschool Project, 1943

Ysseldyke, James Edward (1944–), 1945

Yunis-Varon Syndrome, 1945

Zeaman, David (1921–1984), 1947

Zeaman-House Research, 1947

Zero Inference, 1948

Zero-Reject, 1949

Zigler, Edward (1930–), 1950

Zone of Proximal Development, 1950

Zoning: Family Care Home, 1951

Z Scores, in Determination of Discrepancies, 1952

Zygosity, 1953